The
CHALLENGE
of
DEMOCRACY

Government in America

THIRD EDITION

The
CHALLENGE
of
DEMOCRACY

Government in America

THIRD EDITION

Kenneth Janda
Northwestern University

Jeffrey M. Berry
Tufts University

Jerry Goldman
Northwestern University

Houghton Mifflin Company   **Boston**   **Toronto**
Dallas   Geneva, Illinois   Palo Alto   Princeton, New Jersey

Sponsoring Editor: Margaret H. Seawell
Senior Project Editor: Susan Piland
Electronic Production Specialist: Jeff Zabin
Design Coordinator: Martha Drury
Cover and Interior Designer: Sandra Gonzalez
Senior Production Coordinator: Renée Le Verrier
Manufacturing Coordinator: Priscilla Bailey
Marketing Manager: Karen Natale

Printed in the U.S.A.

Library of Congress Catalog Card Number: 91-71985

ISBN: 0-395-47287-3

BCDEFGHIJ-D-95432

Illustration Credits

Illustrations by Illustrious, Inc.
Cover photograph by Renée Fraser
Frontispiece: Robert Rathe/Stock Boston
Preface photo: Paul Conklin

Chapter 1: **Page 2 (Opener):** Robert Llewellyn; **5:** Insight Magazine/Jon A. Rembold; **6:** By permission of the Houghton Library, Harvard University; **8:** Dallas & John Heaton/Stock Boston; **9:** Wide World Photos; **12–13:** Printed by permission of the Estate of Norman Rockwell. Copyright © 1943 Estate of Norman Rockwell; **16:** © 1990 Chicago Tribune Company, all rights reserved, used with permission; **18:** © Filip Horvat/SABA; **27:** © 1990 Chicago Tribune Company, all rights reserved, used with permission.
Chapter 2: **Page 32 (Opener):** © Joe Sohm/Chromosohm/Uniphoto; **35:** © Mario Villafuerte/Picture Group; **36:** © Baldev/Sygma; **38:** © Spratt/The Image Works; **43:** © Bob Daemmrich/The Image Works; **45:** © J. Sohm/The Image Works; **48:** Terry Ashe/Time Magazine; **49:** Paul Conklin; **52:** © Brian Lanker; **54:** Wide World Photos.

Copyright page continues on A-95.

To our wives
Ann Janda
Lori Berry
Susan Kennedy

BRIEF CONTENTS

BOXED FEATURES

FEATURES

CONTENTS

PREFACE

It's remarkable to us how much change can take place in a few short years. Since the publication of the Second Edition of *The Challenge of Democracy*, the Cold War ended, the United States and its allies fought and won a lopsided war against Iraq, a recession took hold here at home, the savings and loan industry collapsed, and conservatives seemed to take firm control of the Supreme Court.

Yet in the past few years there has also been much that is all too familiar to observers of American politics. Questions and controversy revolving around such long-standing issues as education, drugs, race, budget deficits, and poverty continue to command attention.

Underlying all political issues are two enduring foundations of American politics: the clash among the values of freedom, order, and equality, and the tensions between pluralist and majoritarian visions of democracy. A knowledge of these conflicts enables us to recognize and think critically about the difficult choices we face as citizens and voters.

Thematic Framework

To give students a framework for understanding contemporary problems in a fast-changing world, *The Challenge of Democracy* analyzes these two kinds of conflict—among freedom, order, and equality, and between majoritarian and pluralist democracies. As in our previous editions, we develop our two themes in the opening chapters and return to them throughout the text as a means of organizing our explication of various institutions, processes, and policies.

In Chapter 1, we introduce the first part of the framework, outlining how American politics often reflects conflicts between the values of freedom and order, and between the values of freedom and equality. These conflicts have been powerful forces throughout American history and continue to explain political consensus and controversy today.

For instance, in Chapter 3 we argue that the Constitution was designed to promote order and virtually ignored issues of political and social equality. Equality was later served, however, by several amendments to the Constitution. In Chapter 15, "Order and Civil Liberties," and Chapter 16, "Equality and Civil Rights," we demonstrate how many of this nation's most controversial issues represent conflicts among individuals or groups who hold differing views on the values of freedom, order, and equality. Views on issues such as abortion are not just isolated opinions; they also reflect choices about the philosophy citizens want government to follow. Yet choosing among these values is difficult, sometimes excruciatingly so.

The second theme, outlined initially in Chapter 2, asks students to consider two competing models of government. One way that government can make decisions is by means of majoritarian principles—that is, by taking the actions desired by a majority of citizens. For instance, in Chapter 20, "Global Policy," we discuss the role of public opinion in influencing foreign policy. A contrasting model of government, pluralism, is built around the interaction of decision makers in government with groups concerned about issues that affect them. Pluralism is a focus of Chapter 17, "Policymaking," which discusses issue networks in the nation's capital.

These models are not mere abstractions; we use them to illustrate the dynamics of the American political system. In Chapter 9, "Nominations, Campaigns, and Elections," and Chapter 12, "The Presidency," we discuss the problem of divided government. In recent years, Americans have elected Republican presidents and at the same time returned Democrats to Congress in large numbers; in fact, Democrats have typically controlled both the House and the Senate. Although many Americans would prefer that elections act as fairly direct instruments of majoritarian democracy, our political system seems to be arranged in a way that makes that difficult.

Throughout the book we stress that students must make their own choices among the competing values and models of government. Although the three of us hold strong opinions about which choices are best, we do not believe it is our role to tell students our answers to the broad questions we pose. Instead, we want our readers to learn firsthand that a democracy requires difficult choices. That is why we titled our book *The Challenge of Democracy*.

Features of the Third Edition

This new edition mirrors the change and continuity in American politics. Although we have maintained the basic structure of the book and all the popular features of our approach, we have done some elaborating and reorganizing to give more attention to certain subjects.

A great deal of material throughout the text has been updated and revised. For instance, there is a new discussion of drug policy in Chapter 19, "Domestic Policy." Chapter 20, "Global Policy," has been thoroughly revised. And Chapters 15, "Order and Civil Liberties," and 16, "Equality and Civil Rights," are now set off in a separate part to provide a more flexible organization that better suits individual needs.

The greatest changes in this edition, however, are manifested in Chapters 8, 9, and 17. Although each retains material from the Second Edition, they also add a great deal of new information.

Where previously we had a single chapter on political parties, campaigns, and elections, to do justice to this broad and fascinating aspect of American politics we now devote two chapters to these topics. Chapter 8, "Political Parties," focuses on the historical development of American political parties. Chapter 9, "Nominations, Campaigns, and Elections," gives our book expanded coverage of the election process, including information on modern campaign strategy and technology.

Chapter 17, "Policymaking," is also new to this edition. The first half of this chapter offers students a framework for understanding the policymaking process, which helps to tie the earlier chapters on political institutions with the chapters on various policy areas that follow. The second half of the chapter includes coverage of how actors operating outside the government may affect policy choices, drawn largely from the "Washington Community" chapter in previous editions.

As in previous editions, each chapter begins with a vignette that draws students into the substance of the material that chapter examines and suggests one of the themes of the book. For example, we begin Chapter 15, "Order and Civil Liberties," by discussing the debate over the exhibition of Robert Mapplethorpe's photographs at Cincinnati's Contemporary Arts Center. Were the efforts of city officials to ban these photographs, which they considered obscene, an appropriate attempt to maintain order or an infringement on freedom of expression?

We believe that students can better evaluate how our political system works when they compare it with politics in other countries. Once again, each chapter has at least one boxed feature called "Compared with What?" which treats its topic in a comparative perspective. How much importance do citizens in other parts of the world place on freedom, order, and equality? How do other multicultural societies deal with the question of affirmative action? Are Americans more or less supportive of redistributing wealth than are citizens of other countries?

We also make frequent use of other boxed features throughout the text. They allow us to explore some topics in more detail or discuss matters that don't fit easily into the regular flow of text. Examples include an inside look at how CBS news reporter Lesley Stahl tried to expose the Reagan administration's manipulation of the media, a historical account of Martin Luther King, Jr.'s "I Have a Dream" speech, and a case history of how breast cancer is becoming a political issue.

Each chapter concludes with a brief summary, a list of key terms, and a short list of recommended readings. At the end of the book, we have included the Declaration of Independence, an annotated copy of the Constitution, *Federalist* Nos. 10 and 51, a glossary of key terms, and some other valuable appendices.

The Teaching Package

When we began writing *The Challenge of Democracy*, we viewed the book as part of a tightly integrated set of instructional materials. We have worked closely with some very talented political scientists and with educational specialists at Houghton Mifflin to produce what we think is a superior set of ancillary materials to help both students and instructors.

The primary purpose of the *Instructor's Resource Manual*, written by the authors (and ably updated by Earl Huff of California Polytechnic State University, San Luis Obispo), is to provide teachers with material that relates directly to the thematic framework and organization of the book. It includes learning objectives, chapter synopses, detailed lecture outlines, and suggested classroom and individual activities. The *Test Item Bank*, prepared by Nicholas Strinkowski of Eastern Oregon State College, provides over 1,500 test items—identification, multiple-choice, and essay. The *Study Guide*, written by Melissa Butler of Wabash College, contains an overview of each chapter, exercises on reading tables and graphs, topics for student research, and mutiple-choice questions for practice. The chapter-length *State and Local Supplement*, written by Dennis L. Dresang of the University of Wisconsin—Madison, provides coverage of the structure and functions of state and local governments; it will be shrink-wrapped with the text upon request. The transparency package, containing forty full-color overhead transparencies, is available to adopters of the book. Adopters may also receive videotapes from Houghton Mifflin's Videotape Program in American Government, written and produced by Ralph Baker and Joseph Losco of Ball State University. A corresponding *Video Guide* contains summaries and scripts of each tape, definitions of key terms, multiple-choice questions, and ideas for class activities.

Software ancillaries available to adopters include *LectureBank*, an inventory of ideas for lecture topics, and *Microtest*, a test generation program containing all the items in the printed *Test Item Bank*. Other software ancillaries are designed to improve students' understanding: *MicroGuide*, a computerized study guide, and *IDEAlog*, an interactive exercise introducing students to the value-conflicts theme in the book. For instructors who want to introduce students to data analysis, a disk and workbook called *Crosstabs* allows students to do research using survey data on the 1988 presidential election and data on voting in Congress, updated after the 1990 election. The *Crosstabs* materials were prepared in collaboration with Philip Schrodt of the University of Kansas. The *Supreme Court Tutorial*, a Hypercard tour of the Supreme Court and its history, includes information on key decisions, biographical material, and photos of all the justices.

We invite your questions, suggestions, and criticisms. You may contact us at our respective institutions, or, if you have access to an electronic mail service, such as BITNET or INTERNET, you may contact us through the following e-mail address: *cod@nwu.edu*.

Acknowledgments

Over the course of writing this edition and its predecessors, we've compiled enough unpaid debts to qualify as a savings and loan. We especially want to thank Phil Galanter, Gary Greenberg, and William Parod, Aca-

The authors (left to right): Ken Janda, Jeff Berry, Jerry Goldman

demic Computing, Northwestern University; Robert Baumgartner, Sally Roberts, and Michele Strange of Northwestern University Library; Phyllis Siegel, Program in American Culture; Dennis Hartman, Andersen Consulting; Ronald Inglehart, the University of Michigan; Richard Johnson and Leslie Bailey of the Northwestern Language Laboratory; Philip Schrodt, the University of Kansas; Peter S. Ginsberg, Esq.; Alexander Stephens; Tom Smith, National Opinion Research Center; and Ken Thomson, Lincoln Filene Center for Citizenship and Public Affairs at Tufts.

Our colleagues at Northwestern and Tufts are a constant source of citations, advice, and constructive criticism. Special thanks to T. H. Breen, Jonathan Casper, R. Barry Farrell, Herbert Jacob, Jane Mansbridge, Jock McLane, Carl Smith, and Garry Wills (Northwestern); and Richard Eichenberg, Don Klein, and Kent Portney (Tufts). Our research assistants were indispensable: at Northwestern, Scott Barclay, David Iannelli, Sharon Kollmorgen, James McCoy, and David Wrobel; and at Tufts, Mike Denning, Maria Figueroa, and Tracy Turner.

We owe special thanks to Ted and Cora Ginsberg, whose research endowment helped launch several small investigations by our students that eventually found their way into this edition.

With this edition we were again lucky enough to have Melissa Butler work with us. Professor Butler is the author of Chapter 20, "Global Policy." She is also the author of the excellent Study Guide that accompanies the text.

We have been fortunate to obtain the help of many outstanding political scientists across the country who provided us with critical reviews of our work as it has progressed through three separate editions. We found their comments enormously helpful, and we thank them for taking valuable time away from their own teaching and research to write their detailed reports. More specifically, our thanks go to

David Ahern, University of Dayton
James Anderson, Texas A & M University
Theodore Arrington, University of North Carolina, Charlotte
Denise Baer, Northeastern University
Linda L. M. Bennett, Wittenberg University
Stephen Earl Bennett, University of Cincinnati
Thad Beyle, University of North Carolina, Chapel Hill
Michael Binford, Georgia State University
Bonnie Browne, Texas A & M University
J. Vincent Buck, California State University, Fullerton
Gregory A. Caldeira, University of Iowa
Robert Casier, Santa Barbara City College
James Chalmers, Wayne State University
John Chubb, Stanford University
Allan Cigler, University of Kansas
Stanley Clark, California State University, Bakersfield
Ronald Claunch, Stephen F. Austin State University
Gary Copeland, University of Oklahoma
Cornelius P. Cotter, University of Wisconsin, Milwaukee
Victor D'Lugin, University of Florida
Art English, University of Arkansas
Henry Fearnley, College of Marin
Elizabeth Flores, Del Mar College
Patricia S. Florestano, University of Maryland
Steve Frank, St. Cloud State University
Mitchel Gerber, Hofstra University
Dorith Grant-Wisdom, Howard University
Kenneth Hayes, University of Maine
Ronald Hedlund, University of Wisconsin, Milwaukee
Roberta Herzberg, Indiana University
Peter Howse, American River College
Scott Keeter, Virginia Commonwealth University
Sarah W. Keidan, Oakland Community College (Mich.)
Beat Kernen, Southwest Missouri State University
Vance Krites, Indiana University of Pennsylvania
Clyde Kuhn, California State University, Sacramento
Wayne McIntosh, University of Maryland
Michael Maggiotto, University of South Carolina
Edward S. Malecki, California State University, Los Angeles
Steve J. Mazurana, University of Northern Colorado
Jim Morrow, Tulsa Junior College
William Mugleston, Mountain View College
David A. Nordquest, Pennsylvania State University, Erie

Bruce Odom, Trinity Valley Community College
Bruce Oppenheimer, University of Houston
Richard Pacelle, Indiana University
Robert Pecorella, St. John's University
James Perkins, San Antonio College
Denny E. Pilant, Southwest Missouri State University
Curtis Reithel, University of Wisconsin, La Crosse
Susan Rouder, City College of San Francisco
Gilbert K. St. Clair, University of New Mexico
Barbara Salmore, Drew University
William A. Schultze, San Diego State University
Thomas Sevener, Santa Rosa Junior College
Kenneth S. Sherrill, Hunter College
Sanford R. Silverburg, Catawba College
Mark Silverstein, Boston University
Candy Stevens Smith, Texarkana College
Charles Sohner, El Camino College
Robert J. Spitzer, State University of New York, Cortland
Dale Story, University of Texas, Arlington
Nicholas Strinkowski, Eastern Oregon State College
Neal Tate, University of North Texas
Gary D. Wekkin, University of Central Arkansas
Jonathan West, University of Miami
John Winkle, University of Mississippi
Clifford Wirth, University of New Hampshire
Alan Wyner, University of California, Santa Barbara
Ann Wynia, North Hennepin Community College
Jerry L. Yeric, University of North Texas

Finally, we want to thank the many people at Houghton Mifflin who helped make this book a reality. Jean Woy, now editor in chief in charge of social science and education, signed us to do the book when she was sponsoring editor for political science, and she and our project editor, Lance Wickens, suffered through the traumas of the First Edition. Greg Tobin took over as sponsoring editor for the Second Edition and contributed greatly to its form and content. In the wake of Greg's promotion to editor in chief, Margaret Seawell, our sponsoring editor for this edition, had to jump onto a moving ship but did an exemplary job of handling vexing problems along the way. We are especially indebted to our project editor, Susan Piland. This book has benefited enormously from her knowledge of politics and publishing and from her persistence in pinning down authors to writing schedules. With due regard for equality of treatment, Susan curtailed our freedom and imposed order on our efforts.

Overall, we could not have worked with a more capable and conscientious staff. Houghton Mifflin is an author's house, where gifted professionals give extraordinary attention to a manuscript as it moves through the editing and production process. This kind of care is an increasingly rare commodity in the publishing world.

K.J., J.B., J.G.

PART

ONE

Dilemmas of
Democracy

1 FREEDOM, ORDER, OR EQUALITY?

WHICH IS BETTER: TO LIVE under a government that allows individuals complete freedom to do whatever they please or under one that enforces strict law and order? Which is better: to allow businesses and private clubs to choose their customers and members or to pass laws that require them to admit and serve everyone, regardless of race or sex?

For many people, none of these alternatives is satisfactory. All of them pose difficult dilemmas of choice. These dilemmas are tied to opposing philosophies that place different values on freedom, order, and equality.

This book explains American government and politics in light of these dilemmas. It does more than explain the workings of our government; it encourages you to think about what government should—and should not—do. And it judges the American government against democratic ideals, encouraging you to think about how government should make its decisions. As its title implies, *The Challenge of Democracy* argues that good government often involves tough choices.

College students frequently say that American government and politics are hard to understand. In fact, many people voice the same complaint. Seventy percent of a national sample interviewed after the 1988 presidential election agreed with the statement "Politics and government seem so complicated that a person like me can't understand what's going on."[1] With this book, we hope to improve your understanding of "what's going on" by analyzing and evaluating the *norms*, or values, that people use to judge political events. Our purpose is not to preach what people ought to favor in making policy decisions; it is to teach what values are at stake.

Teaching without preaching is not easy; no one can exclude personal values completely from political analysis. But our approach minimizes this problem by concentrating on the dilemmas that confront governments when they are forced to choose between policies that threaten equally cherished values. An example: Americans value both the U.S. flag and the Bill of Rights to the U.S. Constitution. In a split decision, the Supreme Court ruled in 1989 that burning the flag as a form of protest is a valid expression of "freedom of speech" and is thus protected under the First Amendment in the Bill of Rights. Dissenting justices argued that the people and their representatives should be entitled to safeguard the nation's symbol. Should the government act to uphold the Constitution or to protect the flag?

Every government policy reflects a choice between conflicting values. We want you to understand this idea, to understand that all government policies reinforce certain values (norms) at the expense of others. We want you to interpret policy issues (for example, should flag burning go unpunished?) with an understanding of the fundamental values in question (freedom of expression versus order and protection of national symbols) and the broader political overtones (liberal or conservative politics).

By looking beyond specifics to underlying normative principles, you should be able to make more sense out of politics. Our framework for analysis does not encompass all the complexities of American government, but it should help your knowledge grow by improving your digestion of political information. We begin by considering the basic purposes of government. In short, why do we need it?

No Women Allowed

The Virginia Military Institute, founded in 1839, has historically limited its enrollment to male cadets and is fighting to continue to do so. However, a number of federal laws and Supreme Court decisions mandating coeducation in most colleges may make that a losing battle. According to those decisions, private schools that have always been single-sex (like Smith College, a women's school in Massachusetts) may remain single-sex. But VMI is a public institution and may someday have to follow the example of the Mississippi University for Women, which was ordered by the Supreme Court to admit men into its nursing program.

The Purposes of Government

Most people do not like being told what to do. Fewer still like being coerced into acting a certain way. Yet every day, millions of American motorists dutifully drive on the right-hand side of the street and obediently stop at red lights. Every year, millions of U.S. citizens struggle to complete their income tax forms before midnight, April 15. In both of these examples, the coercive power of government is at work. If people do not like being coerced, why do they submit to it? In other words, why do we have government?

Government can be defined as the legitimate use of force—including imprisonment and execution—within territorial boundaries to control human behavior. All governments require citizens to surrender some freedom in the process of being governed. Although some governments minimize their infringement on personal freedom, no government has as a goal the maximization of personal freedom. Governments exist to control; *to govern* means "to control." Why do people surrender their freedom to this control? To obtain the benefits of government. Throughout history, government seems to have served two major purposes: maintaining order (preserving life and protecting property) and providing public goods. More recently, some governments have pursued a third purpose: promoting equality.

Maintaining Order

Maintaining order is the oldest objective of government. **Order** in this context is rich with meaning. Let's start with "law and order." Maintaining order in this sense means establishing the rule of law to preserve life and to protect property. To the seventeenth-century philosopher Thomas Hobbes (1588–1679), preserving life was the most important function of government. In his classic philosophical treatise, *Leviathan* (1651), Hobbes described life without government as life in a "state of nature." Without rules, people would live like predators, stealing and killing for personal benefit. In Hobbes's classic phrase, life in a state of nature would be "solitary, poor, nasty, brutish, and short." He believed that a single ruler, or *sovereign*, must possess unquestioned authority to guarantee the safety of the weak against the attacks of the strong. Hobbes characterized his all-powerful government as Leviathan, a biblical sea monster. He believed that complete obedience to Leviathan's strict laws was a small price to pay for the security of living in a civil society.

Most of us can only imagine what a state of nature would be like. We might think of the "Wild West" in the days before a good guy with a white hat rode into town and established law and order. But in some parts of the world today, people actually live in a state of lawlessness. For more than a decade, the Lebanese had a central government that was not strong enough to control warring religious factions. Films of the street fighting in the strife-torn city of Beirut, often shown on television news, suggested what a state of nature might be like. Throughout history, authoritarian rulers used people's fears of civil disorder to justify their governments. Not surprisingly, the ruling group itself—whether monarch, aristocracy, or political party—became known as the "established order."

Leviathan, Hobbes's All-Powerful Sovereign

This engraving is from the 1651 edition of Leviathan, *by Thomas Hobbes. It shows Hobbes's sovereign brandishing a sword in one hand and the scepter of justice in the other. He watches over an orderly town, made peaceful by his absolute authority. But note that the sovereign's body is composed of tiny images of his subjects. He exists only through them. Hobbes explains that such governmental power can be created only if men "confer all their power and strength upon one man, or upon one assembly of men, that may reduce all their wills, by plurality of voices, unto one will."*

In his focus on life in the cruel state of nature, Hobbes saw government primarily as a means for survival. Other theorists, taking survival for granted, believed that government protected order by preserving private property (goods and land owned by individuals). Foremost among them was John Locke (1632–1704), an English philosopher. In *Two Treatises on Government* (1690), he wrote that the protection of life, liberty, and property was the basic objective of government. His thinking strongly influenced the Declaration of Independence. The declaration's famous phrase that identifies "Life, Liberty, and the pursuit of Happiness" as "unalienable Rights" of citizens under government reflects that influence.

Not everyone believes that the protection of private property is a valid objective of government. The German philosopher Karl Marx (1818–1883) rejected the private ownership of property that is used in the production of goods or services. Marx's ideas form the basis of **communism,** a complex theory that gives ownership of all land and productive facilities to the people—in effect, to the government. In line with communist theory, the 1977 Constitution of the Soviet Union sets forth the following principles of government ownership:

> State property, i.e., the common property of the Soviet people, is the principal form of socialist property.
> The land, its minerals, waters, and forests are the exclusive property of the state. The state owns the basic means of production in industry, construction, and agriculture; means of transport and communication; the banks; the property of state-run trade organizations and public utilities, and other state-run undertakings; most urban housing; and other property necessary for state purposes.[2]

As the Soviet Union began to move away from communism, proposals to amend the 1977 constitution to permit the private ownership of land caused an uproar when introduced in the Soviet parliament in 1990. President Mikhail Gorbachev even sought a national referendum on legalizing the private ownership of land! Outside communist societies, the extent to which government must protect property or can take it away is a political issue that forms the basis of much ideological debate across the world.

Providing Public Goods

After governments have established basic order, they can pursue other ends. Using their coercive powers, they can tax citizens to raise funds to spend on **public goods,** benefits and services that are available to everyone—such as education, sanitation, and parks. Public goods benefit all citizens but are not likely to be produced by the voluntary acts of individuals. The government of ancient Rome, for example, built aqueducts to carry fresh water from the mountains to the city. Road building was another public good provided by the Roman government—which also used the roads to move its legions and to protect the established order.

Government action to provide public goods can be controversial. During President James Monroe's administration (1817–1825), many people thought that building the Cumberland Road (between Cumberland, Maryland, and Wheeling, West Virginia) was not a proper function of the

A Concrete Example of a Public Good
Governments use tax money to undertake projects that benefit citizens generally but are not likely to be undertaken by any group of individuals. The Hoover Dam on the Colorado River created the Lake Mead Reservoir, which provides water, offers recreation, and helps control floods—benefiting millions of residents in the Southwest.

national government, the Romans notwithstanding. Over time, the scope of government functions in the United States has expanded. During President Dwight Eisenhower's administration in the 1950s, the national government outdid the Romans' noble road building. Despite his basic conservatism, Eisenhower launched the massive Interstate Highway System at a cost of $27 billion (in 1950s' dollars). Yet some government enterprises that have been common in other countries—running railroads, operating coal mines, generating electric power—are politically controversial or even unacceptable in the United States. People disagree on how far the government ought to go in using its power to tax in providing public goods and services and how much should be handled by private business for profit.

Promoting Equality

The promotion of equality has not always been a major objective of government. It has gained prominence only in this century, in the aftermath of industrialization and urbanization. Confronted by the contrast

Rosa Parks: She Sat for Equality

Rosa Parks had just finished a day's work as a seamstress and was sitting in the front of a bus in Montgomery, Alabama, going home. A white man claimed her seat, which he could do according to the law in December 1955. When she refused to move and was arrested, angry blacks, led by Dr. Martin Luther King, Jr., began a boycott of the Montgomery bus company.

of poverty amid plenty, some political leaders in European nations pioneered extensive government programs to improve life for the lower classes. Under the emerging concept of the **welfare state,** government's role expanded to provide individuals with medical care, education, and a guaranteed income, "from the cradle to the grave." Sweden, Britain, and other nations adopted welfare programs aimed at reducing social inequalities. This relatively new purpose of government has been by far the most controversial. Taxation for public goods (building roads and schools, for example) is often opposed because of its cost alone. Taxation for government programs to promote economic and social equality is opposed more strongly on principle.

The key issue here is the government's role in redistributing income—taking from the wealthy to give to the poor. Charity (voluntary giving to the poor) has a strong basis in Western religious traditions; using the power of the state to support the poor does not. (In Charles Dickens's nineteenth-century novels, the power of the state was used to imprison the poor, not to support them.) Using the state to redistribute income was originally a radical idea, set forth by Marx as the ultimate principle of developed communism: "from each according to his ability, to each according to his needs."[3] This extreme has never operated in any government, not even in communist states. But over time, taking from the rich to help the needy has become a legitimate function of most governments.

That legitimacy is not without controversy, however. Especially since the Great Depression of the 1930s, the government's role in redistributing income to promote economic equality has been a major source of policy debate in the United States. Food stamps and Aid to Families with Dependent Children (AFDC) are typical examples of government programs that tend to redistribute income—and generate controversy.

Government can also promote social equality through policies that do not redistribute income. For example, it can regulate social behavior to enforce equality—as it did when the Supreme Court ruled in 1987 that Rotary Clubs must admit women members. Policies that regulate social behavior, like those that redistribute income, inevitably clash with the value of personal freedom.

A Conceptual Framework for Analyzing Government

Citizens have very different views on how vigorously they want government to maintain order, provide public goods, and promote equality. Of the three objectives, providing for public goods usually is less controversial than maintaining order or promoting equality. After all, government spending for highways, schools, and parks carries benefits for nearly every citizen. Moreover, these services merely cost money. The cost of maintaining order and promoting equality is greater than money; it usually means a trade-off of basic values.

To understand government and the political process, you must be able to recognize these trade-offs and identify the basic values they entail. Just as people sit back from a wide-screen motion picture to gain perspective, to understand American government you need to take a broad view, a much broader view than that offered by examining specific political events. You need to employ political concepts.

A *concept* is a generalized idea of a class of items or thoughts. It groups various events, objects, or qualities under a common classification or label. The conceptual framework that guides this book consists of five concepts that figure prominently in political analysis. We regard these five concepts as especially important to a broad understanding of American politics, and we use them repeatedly throughout the book. This framework will help you evaluate political happenings long after you have read this text.

The five concepts that we emphasize deal with the fundamental issues of *what* government tries to do and *how* it decides to do it. The concepts that relate to what government tries to do are *order, freedom,* and *equality.* All governments by definition value order; maintaining order is part of the meaning of government. Most governments at least claim to preserve individual freedom while they maintain order, although they vary widely in the extent to which they succeed. Very few governments even profess to guarantee equality, and governments differ greatly in policies that pit equality against freedom. Our conceptual framework should help you evaluate the extent to which the United States pursues all three values through its government.

How government chooses the proper mix of order, freedom, and equality in its policymaking has to do with the *process* of choice rather than the outcome. We evaluate the American governmental process using two models of democratic government: the *majoritarian* and the *pluralist.* Most governments profess to be democracies. Whether they are or not depends on their (and our) meaning of the term. Even countries that Americans agree are democracies—for example, the United States and Britain—differ substantially in the type of democracy they practice. We use our conceptual models of democratic government both to classify the type of democracy practiced in the United States and to evaluate the government's success in fulfilling that model.

These five concepts can be organized into two groups.

- Concepts that identify the *values* pursued by government:
  Freedom
  Order
  Equality
- Concepts that describe *models* of democratic government:
  Majoritarian democracy
  Pluralist democracy

The rest of this chapter examines freedom, order, and equality as conflicting values pursued by government. Chapter 2 discusses majoritarian democracy and pluralist democracy as alternative institutional models for implementing democratic government.

The Concepts of Freedom, Order, and Equality

These three terms—*freedom, order,* and *equality*—have different connotations in American politics. Both *freedom* and *equality* are positive terms that politicians have learned to use to their own advantage. Consequently, *freedom* and *equality* mean different things to different people at different times—depending on the political context in which they are used. *Order,* on the other hand, has negative connotations for many people, for it symbolizes government intrusion in private lives. Except during periods of social strife, few politicians in western democracies call openly for more order. Because all governments infringe on freedom, we examine that concept first.

Freedom

Freedom can be used in two major senses: *freedom to* and *freedom from.* Franklin Delano Roosevelt used the word in both senses in a speech he made shortly after the Unites States entered World War II. He described four freedoms—freedom of religion, freedom of speech, freedom from fear, and freedom from want. The noted illustrator Norman Rockwell gave Americans a vision of these freedoms in a classic set of paintings published in the *Saturday Evening Post* (see Feature 1.1).

FEATURE 1.1   *The Four Freedoms*

Norman Rockwell became famous in the 1940s for the humorous, homespun covers he painted for the *Saturday Evening Post,* a weekly magazine. Inspired by an address to Congress in which President Roosevelt outlined his goals for world civilization, Rockwell painted "The Four Freedoms," which were reproduced in the *Saturday Evening Post.* Their immense popularity led the government to print posters of the illustrations for the Treasury Department's war

Freedom of Speech

Freedom of Worship

Freedom to is the absence of constraints on behavior. In this sense, freedom is synonymous with *liberty.* Two of Rockwell's paintings—*Freedom of Worship* and *Freedom of Speech*—exemplify this type of freedom.

Freedom from underlies the message of the other paintings, *Freedom from Fear* and *Freedom from Want.* Here *freedom* suggests immunity from fear and want. In the modern political context, **freedom from** often symbolizes the fight against exploitation and oppression. The cry "Freedom Now!" of the civil rights movement in the 1960s conveyed this meaning. If you recognize that freedom in this sense means immunity from discrimination, you can see that it comes close to the concept of equality.[4] We avoid using *freedom* to mean "freedom from"; for this sense of the word, we simply use *equality.*

bond drive. The Office of War Information also reproduced "The Four Freedoms" and circulated the posters in schools, clubhouses, railroad stations, post offices, and other public buildings. Officials even had copies dropped into the European front to remind soldiers of the liberties for which they were fighting. It is said that no other paintings in the world have ever been reproduced or circulated in such vast numbers as "The Four Freedoms."

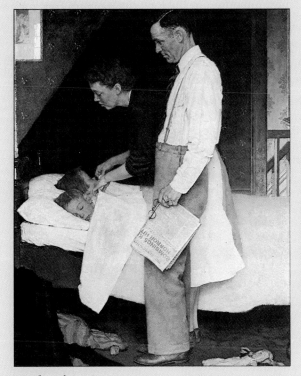

Freedom from Fear

Freedom from Want

Order

When order is viewed in the narrow sense of preserving life and protecting property, most citizens would concede the importance of maintaining order and thereby grant the need for government. For example, "domestic tranquility" (order) is cited in the preamble to the Constitution. However, when order is viewed in the broader sense of preserving the social order, people are more likely to argue that maintaining order is not a legitimate function of government (see Compared with What? 1.1). *Social order* refers to established patterns of authority in society and to traditional modes of behavior. It is the accepted way of doing things. The prevailing social order prescribes behavior in many different areas: how students should dress in school (neatly, no purple hair) and behave to-

COMPARED WITH WHAT? 1.1

The Importance of Order as a Political Value

Compared with citizens in other nations, Americans simply do not think maintaining order is very important. Surveys in the United States and twelve European countries asked respondents to select which of the following four national goals was the "most important in the long run":

- Maintaining order in the nation
- Giving the people more say in important government decisions
- Fighting rising prices
- Protecting freedom of speech

Just 29 percent of those surveyed in the United States chose "maintaining order." Only respondents in Belgium, who were more concerned about "fighting rising prices" than were people in any other nation, attached less importance to maintaining order. Compared with citizens in most other Western countries, Americans seem to want less government control of social behavior.

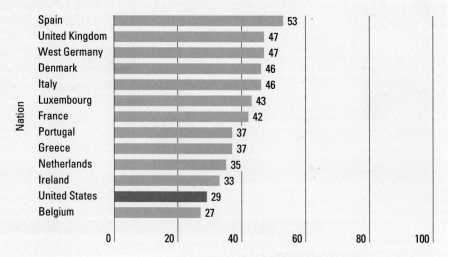

Percentage choosing "maintaining order"
as most important goal

Source: Jacques-René Rabier, Helene Riffault, and Ronald Inglehart, *Euro-Barometer 24: Entry of Spain and Portugal, October, 1985* (Ann Arbor, Mich.: Inter-University Consortium for Political and Social Research, Study 8513, 1986), p. 12. Conducted by Faits et Opinions, Paris. The original collector of the data, ICPSR, and the relevant funding agency bear no responsibility for uses of this collection or for interpretations or inferences based upon such uses.

ward their teachers (respectfully); under what conditions people should have sexual relations (married, different sexes); what the press should not publish (sexually explicit photographs); and what the proper attitude toward religion and country should be (reverential). It is important to remember that social order can change. Today, perfectly respectable men and women wear bathing suits that would have caused a scandal at the turn of the century.

A government can protect the established order under its **police power**—its authority to safeguard citizens' safety, health, welfare, and morals. The extent to which government should use this authority is a topic of ongoing debate in the United States and is constantly being redefined by our courts. In the 1980s, many states employed their police powers to legislate against smoking in public places. In 1990 a Fort Lauderdale jury convicted a record store owner of obscenity for selling a 2 Live Crew album that made explicit references to sexual violence. There are those who fear the evolution of a *police state*—government that uses its power to regulate nearly all aspects of behavior. For example, South Africa passed laws governing intermarriage between blacks and whites and prescribing where married people of mixed race could live. It is no accident that the chief law enforcement officer in South Africa is the minister of law and order.

Most governments are inherently conservative; they tend to resist social change. But some governments have as a primary objective the restructuring of the social order. Social change is most dramatic when a government is overthrown through force and replaced by a revolutionary government. Governments can work at changing social patterns more gradually through the legal process. Our use of the term *order* in this book includes all three aspects of the term: preserving life, protecting property, and maintaining traditional patterns of social relationships.

Equality

Like *freedom* and *order*, *equality* is used in different senses, to support different causes.

Political equality in elections is easy to define: Each citizen has one and only one vote. This basic concept is central to democratic theory—a subject explored at length in Chapter 2. But when some people advocate political equality, they mean more than "one person, one vote." These people contend that an urban ghetto dweller and the chairman of the board of General Motors are not politically equal despite the fact that each has one vote. Through occupation or wealth, some citizens are more able than others to influence political decisions. For example, wealthy citizens can exert influence by advertising in the mass media or by contacting friends in high places. Lacking great wealth and political connections, most citizens do not have this kind of influence. Thus, some analysts argue that equality in wealth, education, and status—that is, **social equality**—is necessary for true political equality. There are two routes to achieving social equality: providing equal opportunities and ensuring equal outcomes.

Equality of opportunity means that each person has the same chance to succeed in life. This idea is deeply ingrained in American culture. The Constitution prohibits titles of nobility, owning property is not a requirement for holding public office, and public schools and libraries are

Welcome Home, Soldier
During World War II, the men went away to fight while the women stayed home. Today, as a result of the drive for sexual equality, many women are soldiers, too. And many men found themselves in interesting role reversals when their loved ones were called to duty during the Persian Gulf crisis.

free to all. To many people, the concept of social equality is satisfied just by offering opportunities for people to advance themselves. It is not essential that people end up being equal after using those opportunities.

For others, true social equality means nothing less than **equality of outcome.**[5] They believe that society must see to it that people *are* equal. It is not enough for governments to provide people with equal opportunities; they must also design policies to redistribute wealth and status so that economic and social equality are actually achieved. In education, equality of outcome has led to federal laws that require comparable funding for men's and women's college sports. In business, equality of outcome has led to affirmative action programs to increase minority hiring and to the active recruitment of women, blacks, and Hispanics to fill jobs. Equality of outcome here also has produced federal laws that require employers to pay men and women equally for equal work.

Some link equality of outcome with the concept of governmental **rights**—the idea that every citizen is entitled to certain benefits of government, that government should guarantee its citizens adequate (if not equal) housing, employment, medical care, and income as a matter of right. If citizens are entitled to government benefits as a matter of right, then government efforts to promote equality of outcome become legitimized.

Clearly, the concept of equality of outcome is very different from that of equality of opportunity, and it requires a much greater degree of government activity. It is also the concept of equality that clashes most directly with the concept of freedom. By taking from one to give to another—which is necessary for the redistribution of income and status—the government clearly creates winners and losers. The winners may believe that justice has been served by the redistribution. The losers often feel strongly that their freedom to enjoy their income and status has suffered.

Two Dilemmas of Government

The two major dilemmas facing American government in the 1990s stem from the oldest and the newest objectives of government. The oldest is maintaining order; the newest, promoting equality. Both order and equality are important social values, but government cannot pursue either without sacrificing a third important value: individual freedom. The clash between freedom and order forms the *original* dilemma of government; the clash between freedom and equality, the *modern* dilemma of government. Although the dilemmas are very different, each involves trading off some amount of freedom for another value.

The Original Dilemma: Freedom Versus Order

The conflict between freedom and order originates in the very meaning of government as the legitimate use of force to control human behavior. How much freedom must a citizen surrender to government? This dilemma has occupied philosophers for hundreds of years. In the eighteenth century, French philosopher Jean Jacques Rousseau (1712–1778) wrote that the problem of devising a proper government "is to find a form of association which will defend and protect with the whole common force the person and goods of each associate, and in which each, while uniting himself with all, may still obey himself alone, and remain free as before."[6]

The original purpose of government was to protect life and property, to make citizens safe from violence. How well is the American government doing today in providing law and order to its citizens? More than 40 percent of the respondents in a 1989 national survey said that they were afraid to walk alone at night within a mile of their homes.[7] In our cities, their fears seem justified. Three out of ten people in urban areas reported in 1988 that they, or a member of their family, had been touched by a crime within the past year.[8] Visitors to New York are well advised to keep out of Central Park, in particular, after dark. Simply put, Americans do not trust their urban governments to protect them from crime when they go out alone at night.

When the old communist governments still ruled in Eastern Europe, the climate of fear in urban America stood in stark contrast with the pervasive sense of personal safety in such cities as Moscow, Warsaw, and

Prague. Then it was common to see old and young strolling along late at night on the streets and in the parks of these communist cities. The old communist regimes gave their police great powers to control guns, monitor citizens' movements, and arrest and imprison suspicious people —which enabled them to do a better job of maintaining order. Communist governments deliberately chose order over freedom. It is perhaps not surprising that some Russians who emigrated to the United States found life here too threatening and returned to the security of the Soviet Union. After living for eight years in New York City, Rebecca Katsap (age sixty-seven) returned to Odessa in 1987, saying, "I was afraid to go out in the street after four in the afternoon."[9] But with the collapse of order under communism, things have changed in the Soviet Union. In fact, the leaders of the abortive coup against Gorbachev in August 1991 said that two of their goals were to "restore law and order" and "declare a war without mercy in the criminal world."[10]

The crisis over Acquired Immune Deficiency Syndrome (AIDS) adds a new twist to the dilemma of freedom versus order. Some health officials believe that AIDS, for which there is presently no known cure, is the greatest threat in the medical history of the United States. The U.S. Public Health Service estimated that about 1 million Americans were infected with the AIDS virus by mid-1990, when 139,765 cases of the disease had been reported to the Centers for Disease Control, and 85,430 people had died. The Health Service also estimated that 390,000 to 480,000 people will develop AIDS by 1994.[11]

To combat the spread of the disease in the military, the Department of Defense began testing all applicants for the AIDS virus. Other government agencies have begun testing current employees. And some officials now are calling for widespread mandatory testing within the private sector as well. These programs are strongly opposed by those who believe

Freedom as a Weapon in the Velvet Revolution

Armed with banners proclaiming "Svobodu"—"freedom," in Czech—students in Prague confront police in November 1989. The confrontation was no contest. Within weeks, the nonviolent "Velvet Revolution" in Czechoslovakia forced the communist government out of power, ending more than four decades of authoritarian rule. Free elections were held in 1990.

they violate individual freedom. Those who are more afraid of AIDS than an infringement on individual rights support aggressive government action to combat the disease.

The value conflict between freedom and order represents the original dilemma of government. In the abstract, people value both freedom and order; but in real life, the two values inherently conflict. Any policy that works toward one of these values by definition takes away from the other. The balance of freedom and order is an issue in major matters (whether or not to allow capital punishment) and in minor ones (how to deal with urban teenagers who spray-paint subway cars; whether to allow art galleries to display sexually explicit photographs). And in a democracy, policy choices hinge on how much citizens value freedom and how much they value order.

The Modern Dilemma: Freedom Versus Equality

Popular opinion has it that freedom and equality go hand in hand. In reality, these two values usually clash when governments enact policies to promote social equality. Because social equality is a relatively recent government objective, deciding between policies that promote equality at the expense of freedom, and vice versa, is the modern dilemma of politics. Consider these examples:

- During the 1960s, Congress (through the Equal Pay Act) required employers to pay women and men the same rate for equal work. This means that some employers are forced to pay women more than they would if hiring were based on a free market.

- During the 1970s, the courts ordered the busing of schoolchildren to achieve equal proportions of blacks and whites in public schools. This action was motivated by concern for educational equality, but it also impaired freedom of choice.

- During the 1980s, some states passed legislation that went beyond the idea of equal pay for equal work to the more radical notion of *pay equity*—equal pay for *comparable* work. Women had to be paid at a rate equal to men's—even if they had different jobs—providing the women's jobs were of "comparable worth." For example, if the skills and responsibilities of a female nurse were found comparable to those of a male sanitation engineer in the same hospital, the woman's salary and the man's salary would have to be the same (see Feature 1.2).

- In the 1990s, Congress prohibited discrimination in employment, public services, and public accommodations on the basis of a person's physical or mental disability. Under the 1990 Americans with Disabilities Act, businesses with 25 or more employees could not pass over an otherwise qualified handicapped person in employment or promotion, and new buses and trains had to be made accessible to them.

These examples illustrate the problem of using government power to promote equality. The clash between freedom and order is obvious, but that between freedom and equality is more subtle. Often it goes unnoticed by the American people, who think of freedom and equality as complementary rather than conflicting values. When forced to choose

FEATURE 1.2   *Promoting Equality by Assessing Comparable Worth*

Women's advocates contend that men tend to be paid more than women in part because sex discrimination exists in job classifications and pay rates. They back the idea of pay equity for jobs of comparable worth. If the idea becomes national law, it will involve the government more deeply in promoting social equality. The following excerpt describes one way employers (and government) might determine the comparable worth of two different jobs traditionally held by different sexes.

Should a nurse, usually a woman, be paid as much as a sanitation engineer, often a man? Questions about providing equal pay for jobs of equal value are being raised as interest grows in the relatively new doctrine called "comparable worth." And attempting to answer them is spawning a new career path, mainly in management consulting firms.

Anton Armbruster, an associate of William M. Mercer-Meidinger, an employee benefit and compensation consulting firm, has come up with the following example of how management consultants are providing answers. He uses a point system based on four factors—know-how, problem-solving requirements, accountability and working conditions.

The nurse probably needs more know-how and more problem-solving ability, but total accountability is about the same because both are important to community health. Working conditions for the engineer, often outdoors in bad weather, are obviously more difficult than those for the typical nurse, so the engineer is credited with a higher number of points in that category.

	Nurse	Sanitary Engineer
Know-how	150	60
Problem solving	75	40
Accountability	175	165
Working conditions	50	185
Total	450	450

In the 1980s, more than twenty states began to make pay equity adjustments for government workers. The state of Washington embarked on the biggest program of pay equity for its employees and succeeded in narrowing the gap between average wages of men and women from 20 percent to 5 percent. But the program led to a decrease in male employment in government jobs, as private industry lured away workers in male-dominated jobs whose wages have fallen. The Washington program is up for re-evaluation in 1992.

Sources: Elizabeth M. Fowler, "Comparing the Value of Jobs," *New York Times*, 23 January, 1985. Copyright © 1985 by The New York Times Company. Reprinted by permission. Peter T. Kilbourn, "Wage Gap Between Sexes Is Cut in Test, but at a Price," *New York Times*, 31 May 1990, p. 1.

between the two, however, Americans tend to choose freedom over equality more often than do people in other countries (see Compared with What? 1.2). The emphasis on equality over freedom has been especially strong in the Soviet Union, which traditionally guaranteed its citizens medical care, inexpensive housing, and other social services under communism. Although the quality of these benefits was not much by Western standards, Soviet citizens experienced a sense of equality in sharing their deprivations. A Communist party official admitted that this ingrained attitude hindered economic development, saying, "The ideal of social justice here is that everybody should have nothing, not that entrepreneurs should prosper and spread the wealth."[12]

The conflicts among freedom, order, and equality explain a great deal of the political conflict in the United States. These conflicts also underlie the ideologies that people use to structure their understanding of politics.

Ideology and the Scope of Government

People hold different opinions about the merits of government policies. Sometimes their views are based on self-interest. For example, senior citizens vociferously oppose increasing their contributions to Medicare, the government program that defrays medical costs for the elderly, preferring to have all citizens pay for their coverage. Policies also are judged according to individual values and beliefs. Some people hold an assortment of values and beliefs that produce contradictory opinions on government policies. Others organize their opinions into a **political ideology**—a consistent set of values and beliefs about the proper purpose and scope of government.

Political writers often describe the ideologies of politicians and voters as "liberal" or "conservative." In popular usage, liberals favor an active, broad role for government in society; conservatives, a passive, narrow role. For example, liberals favored the Social Security Act of 1935 because they wanted the government to help the elderly. Conservatives opposed the act because it committed the federal government to a costly new program. Although relatively few citizens today would advocate scrapping social security, they often divide sharply on ideological grounds over the desirability of other government programs. By carefully analyzing their political ideologies, we can explain their support of and opposition to seemingly diverse government policies.

How far should government go to maintain order, provide public goods, and promote equality? In the United States (as in every other nation), citizens, scholars, and politicians have different answers to this question. We can analyze their positions by referring to philosophies about the proper scope of government—the range of its permissible activities. Imagine a continuum. At one end is the belief that government should do everything; at the other, the belief that government should not exist. These extreme ideologies—from most government to least government—and those that fall between them are shown in Figure 1.1.

Totalitarianism

Totalitarianism is a belief that government should have unlimited power. A totalitarian government controls all sectors of society: business, labor, education, religion, sports, the arts. A true totalitarian favors

The Importance of Freedom and Equality as Political Values

Compared with citizens' views of freedom and equality in eleven other nations, Americans value freedom more than others do. Respondents in each country were asked which of the following statements came closer to their own opinion:

- "I find that both freedom and equality are important. But if I were to make up my mind for one or the other, I would consider personal freedom more important, that is, everyone can live in freedom and develop without hindrance."

- "Certainly both freedom and equality are important. But if I were to make up my mind for one of the two, I would consider equality more important, that is, that nobody is underprivileged and that social class differences are not so strong."

Americans chose freedom by a ratio of nearly 3 to 1, followed closely by the British. No other nations showed such a strong preference for freedom, and citizens in three countries favored equality instead. When we look at this finding together with Americans' disdain for order (see Compared with What? 1.1), the importance of freedom as a political concept in the United States is very clear.

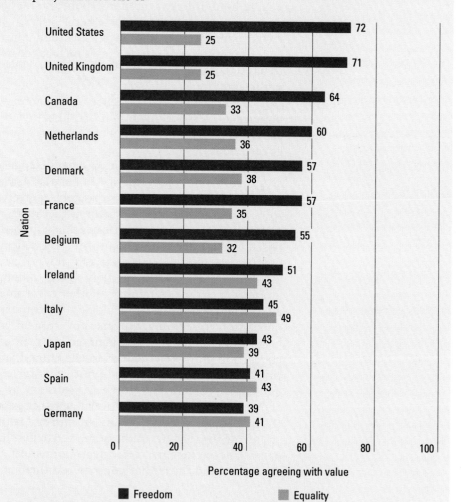

Percentage agreeing with value

■ Freedom   ■ Equality

Source: *World Values Survey, 1981–1982.* The tabulation was provided by Professor Ronald F. Inglehart.

FIGURE 1.1 *Ideology and the Scope of Government*

We can classify political ideologies according to the scope of action that people are willing to give government in dealing with social and economic problems. In this chart, the three lines map out various philosophical positions along an underlying continuum ranging from "most" to "least" government. Notice that conventional politics in the United States spans only a narrow portion of the theoretical possibilities for government action.

In popular usage, liberals favor a greater scope of government; conservatives, a narrower scope. But over time, this traditional distinction has eroded and now oversimplifies the differences between liberals and conservatives. See Figure 1.2 on page 28 for a more discriminating classification of liberals and conservatives.

MOST
GOVERNMENT

LEAST
GOVERNMENT

POLITICAL THEORIES		
Totalitarianism	Libertarianism	Anarchism

ECONOMIC THEORIES		
Socialism	Capitalism	Laissez Faire

POPULAR POLITICAL LABELS IN AMERICA	
Liberal	Conservative

a network of laws, rules, and regulations that guides every aspect of individual behavior. The object is to produce a perfect society serving some master plan for "the common good." Totalitarianism has reached its terrifying potential only in literature and films (for example, George Orwell's *1984*), but several real societies have come perilously close to "perfection." One thinks of Germany under Hitler and the Soviet Union under Stalin. Not many people openly profess totalitarianism today, but the concept is useful because it anchors one side of our continuum.

Socialism

Whereas *totalitarianism* refers to government in general, *socialism* pertains to government's role in the economy. Like communism, socialism is an economic system based on Marxist theory. Under **socialism** (and communism), the scope of government extends to ownership or control of the basic industries that produce goods and services. These include communications, mining, heavy industry, transportation, and power. Although socialism favors a strong role for government in regulating private industry and directing the economy, it allows more room than communism does for private ownership of productive capacity.

Many Americans equate socialism with the communism practiced in the old closed societies of the Soviet Union and Eastern Europe. But there is a difference. Although communism in theory was supposed to result in a "withering away" of the state, communist governments in practice tended toward totalitarianism, controlling both political and social life through a dominant party organization. Some socialist governments, however, practice **democratic socialism.** They guarantee civil liberties (such as freedom of speech and freedom of religion) and allow their citizens to determine the extent of government activity through free elections and competitive political parties. Outside the United States, socialism is not an inherently bad thing. In fact, the governments of Britain, Sweden, Germany, and France—among other democracies—have at times since World War II been avowedly "socialist." More recently, the former communist regimes of Eastern Europe have abandoned the controlling role of government in their economies in favor of elements of capitalism.

Capitalism

Capitalism also relates to the government's role in the economy. In contrast to both socialism and communism, **capitalism** supports *free enterprise*—private businesses operating without government regulations. Some theorists, most notably economist Milton Friedman, argue that free enterprise is necessary for free politics.[13] This argument, that the economic system of capitalism is essential to democracy, contradicts the tenets of democratic socialism. Whether or not it is valid depends in part on our understanding of democracy—a subject discussed in Chapter 2.

The United States is decidedly a capitalist country, more so than Britain or most other Western nations. Despite the U.S. government's enormous budget, it owns or operates relatively few public enterprises. For example, railroads, airlines, and television stations are privately owned in the United States; these businesses are frequently owned by the government in other countries. But our government *does* extend its authority into the economic sphere, regulating private businesses and directing the overall economy. American liberals and conservatives both embrace capitalism, but they differ on the nature and amount of government intervention in the economy.

Libertarianism

Libertarianism opposes all government action except that which is necessary to protect life and property. Libertarians grudgingly recognize the necessity of government but believe that it should be as limited as possible. For example, libertarians grant the need for traffic laws to ensure safe and efficient automobile travel. But they oppose laws that set a minimum drinking age as a restriction on individual actions. Libertarians believe that social programs that provide food, clothing, and shelter are outside the proper scope of government. Helping the needy, they insist, should be a matter of individual choice. Libertarians also oppose government ownership of basic industries; in fact, they oppose any government intervention in the economy. This kind of economic policy is called **laissez faire**—a French phrase that means "let (people) do (as they please)."

Libertarians are very vocal advocates of "hands-off" government—in both social and economic spheres. Whereas those who favor a broad scope of government action shun the description "socialist," libertarians make no secret of their identity. The Libertarian party has run candidates in every presidential election from 1972 through 1988. Not one of these candidates, however, has won more than a million votes.

Don't confuse *libertarians* with *liberals*. The words are similar, but their meanings are very different. *Libertarianism* draws on *liberty* as its root and means "absence of governmental constraint." In American political usage, *liberalism* evolved from the root word *liberal*. Over time, liberal has come to mean something closer to "generous" and "tolerant," in the sense that liberals are willing to support government spending on social programs as well as to respect different lifestyles. (Critics might simply say that liberals are "indulgent.")

Anarchism

Anarchism stands opposite totalitarianism on the political continuum. Anarchists oppose all government, in any form. As a political philosophy, anarchism values freedom above all else. Because all government involves some restriction on personal freedom (for example, forcing people to drive on one side of the road), a pure anarchist would even object to traffic laws. Like totalitarianism, anarchism is not a popular philosophy, but it does have adherents on the political fringes.

In July 1989, more than 1,500 anarchists from around the world convened in San Francisco. The conference featured more than 100 workshops on history, philosophy, culture, sexuality, and the environment. But the older organizers who wanted to discuss history and debate philosophy were countered by "punk anarchists" with shaved heads marked by fluorescent streaks who knew more about Sid Vicious and Johnny Rotten than about the philosophy of anarchism. Like their last convention in Chicago in 1986, this one erupted in rioting that broke store windows in nearby Berkeley—underscoring the anarchists' rejection of order.[14] For our purposes, anarchism serves to anchor the right side of the government continuum and to indicate that libertarians are not as extreme in opposing government as is theoretically possible.

Liberals and Conservatives—The Narrow Middle

As shown in Figure 1.1, practical politics in the United States ranges over only the central portion of the continuum. The extreme positions—totalitarianism and anarchism—are rarely argued in public debate. And in this era of distrust of "big government," few American politicians would openly advocate socialism—although one did in 1990 and won election to Congress. (This was the exception that proved the rule; see Chapter 8.) On the other hand, more than fifty people ran for Congress in 1990 as candidates of the Libertarian party. Although none won, American libertarians are sufficiently vocal to be heard in the debate over the role of government.

Still, most of that debate is limited to a narrow range of political thought. On one side are people commonly called *liberals*; on the other, *conservatives*. In popular usage, liberals favor more government, conservatives less. This distinction is very clear when the issue is government spending to provide public goods. Liberals favor generous government support for education, wildlife protection, public transportation, and a whole range of social programs. Conservatives want smaller government budgets and fewer government programs. They support free enterprise, arguing against government job programs, regulation of business, and legislation of working conditions and wage rates.

But in other areas, liberal and conservative ideologies are less consistent. In theory, liberals favor government activism, yet they oppose government regulation of abortions. In theory, conservatives oppose government activism, yet they support government control over the publication of sexually explicit material. What's going on? Are American political attitudes hopelessly contradictory, or is something missing in our analysis of these ideologies today? Actually, something *is* missing. To understand the liberal and conservative stances on political issues, we have to look not only at the scope of government action but also at the purpose of government action. That is, to understand a political ideology, it is necessary to understand how it incorporates the values of freedom, order, and equality.

American Political Ideologies and the Purpose of Government

Much of American politics revolves around the two dilemmas just described: freedom versus order and freedom versus equality. These two dilemmas do not account for all political conflict, but they help us gain insight into the workings of politics and organize the seemingly chaotic world of political events, actors, and issues.

Liberals Versus Conservatives: The New Differences

Liberals and conservatives are different, but their differences no longer hinge on the narrow question of the government's role in providing public goods. Liberals still favor more government and conservatives less, but this is no longer the critical difference between them. Today that difference stems from their attitudes toward the purpose of government. Conservatives support the original purpose of government, maintaining social order. They are willing to use the coercive power of the state to force citizens to be orderly. They favor firm police action, swift and severe punishment for criminals, and more laws regulating behavior. Conservatives do not stop with defining, preventing, and punishing crime, however. They want to preserve traditional patterns of social relations—the domestic role of women and the importance of religion in school and family life, for example.

Liberals are less likely than conservatives to use government power to maintain order. In general, liberals are more tolerant of alternative lifestyles—for example, homosexual behavior. Liberals do not shy away from using government coercion, but they use it for a different purpose—to promote equality. They support laws ensuring that homosexuals receive equal treatment in employment, housing, and education; that

A Kiss Is but a Kiss

A city worker stares at a controversial poster on an elevated train station in Chicago. Part of a national AIDS awareness campaign, this advertisement was intended to show that AIDS is not transmitted through kissing. Public officials and clergy who tried to ban the ad found that they could not because it was neither untruthful nor obscene; it simply conveyed unconventional images of a conventional act.

require busing schoolchildren to achieve racial equality; that force private businesses to hire and promote women and members of minority groups; that require public carriers to provide equal access to the handicapped; that order cities and states to reapportion election districts so that minority voters can elect minority candidates to public office.

Conservatives do not oppose equality, but they do not value it to the extent of using the government's power to enforce equality. For liberals, the use of that power to guarantee equality is both valid and necessary.

A Two-Dimensional Classification of Ideologies

To classify liberal and conservative ideologies more accurately, we have to incorporate freedom, order, and equality in the classification. We do this using the model in Figure 1.2. It depicts the conflicting values along two separate dimensions, each anchored in maximum freedom at the lower left. One dimension extends horizontally from maximum freedom on the left to maximum order on the right. The other extends vertically from maximum freedom at the bottom to maximum equality at the

FIGURE 1.2   *Ideologies: A Two-Dimensional Framework*

The four ideological types below are defined by the values they favor in resolving the two major dilemmas of government: How much freedom should be sacrificed in pursuit of order and equality? Test yourself by thinking about the values that are most important to you. Which box in the figure best represents your combination of values?

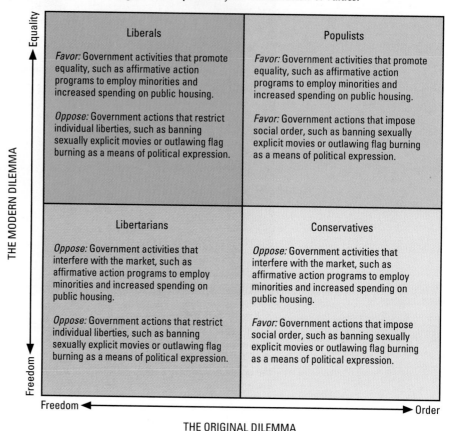

top. Each box represents a different ideological type: libertarians, liberals, conservatives, and populists.*

Libertarians value freedom more than order or equality. (We will use this term for people who have libertarian tendencies but who may not accept the whole philosophy.) In practical terms, libertarians want minimal government intervention in both the economic and the social spheres. For example, they oppose food stamp programs and laws against abortion.

Liberals value freedom more than order, but not more than equality. Liberals oppose laws against abortion but support food stamp programs. **Conservatives** value freedom more than equality but would restrict free-

* The ideological groupings we describe here conform to the classification in William S. Maddox and Stuart A. Lilie, *Beyond Liberal and Conservative: Reassessing the Political Spectrum* (Washington, D.C.: Cato Institute, 1984), p. 5. However, our formulation—in terms of the values of freedom, order, and equality—is quite different.

dom to preserve social order. Conservatives oppose food stamp programs but favor laws against abortion.

Finally, we have the ideological type positioned at the upper right in Figure 1.2. This group values *both* equality and order more than freedom. Its members support both food stamp programs and laws against abortion. We will call this new group **populists.** The term *populist* derives from a rural reform movement that was active in the United States in the late 1800s. Populists thought of government as an instrument to promote the advancement of common people against moneyed or vested interests. They used their voting power both to regulate business and to enforce their moral judgments on minorities whose political and social values differed from the majority's.[15] Today the term aptly describes those who favor government action both to reduce inequalities and to ensure social order.

By analyzing political ideologies on two dimensions rather than one, we can explain why people seem to be liberal on one issue (favoring a broader scope of government action) and conservative on another (favoring less government action). The answer hinges on the action's *purpose:* which value does it promote, order or equality? According to our typology, only libertarians and populists are consistent in their attitudes toward the scope of government activity, whatever its purpose. Libertarians value freedom so highly that they oppose most government efforts to enforce either order or equality. Populists are inclined to trade off freedom for both order and equality. Liberals and conservatives, on the other hand, favor or oppose government activity depending on its purpose. As you will learn in Chapter 5, large groups of Americans fall into each of the four ideological categories. Because Americans choose four different resolutions to the original and modern dilemmas of government, the simple labels *liberal* and *conservative* no longer describe contemporary political ideologies as well as they did in the 1930s, 1940s, and 1950s.

Summary

The challenge of democracy is making difficult choices—choices that inevitably bring important values into conflict. *The Challenge of Democracy* outlines a normative framework for analyzing the policy choices that arise in the pursuit of the purposes of government.

The three major purposes of government are maintaining order, providing public goods, and promoting equality. In pursuing these objectives, every government infringes on individual freedom. But the degree of that infringement depends on the government's (and by extension, its citizens') commitment to order and equality. What we have, then, are two dilemmas. The first—the original dilemma—centers on the conflict between freedom and order. The second—the modern dilemma—focuses on the conflict between freedom and equality.

Some people have political ideologies that help them resolve the conflicts that arise in political decision making. These ideologies outline the scope and purpose of government. At opposite extremes of the continuum are totalitarianism, which supports government intervention in every aspect of society, and anarchism, which rejects government entirely. An important step back from totalitarianism is socialism. Democratic socialism favors government ownership of basic industries but preserves civil liberties. Capitalism, another economic system, promotes free enterprise. A significant step short of anarchism is libertarianism, which allows government to protect life and property but little else.

In the United States, the terms *liberal* and *conservative* are used to describe a narrow range toward the center of the political continuum. This usage is probably accurate when the scope of government action is being discussed. That is, liberals support a broader role for government than do conservatives. But when both the scope and the purpose of government are considered, a different, sharper distinction emerges. Conservatives may want less government, but not at the price of maintaining order. In other words, they are willing to use the coercive power of government to impose social order. Liberals, too, are willing to use the coercive powers of government, but for a different purpose—promoting equality.

It is easier to understand the differences between liberals and conservatives and their views on the scope of government if the values of freedom, order, and equality are incorporated into this description of political ideologies. Libertarians choose freedom over both order and equality. Populists are willing to sacrifice freedom for both order and equality. Liberals value freedom and equality more than order. Conservatives value freedom and order more than equality.

The concepts of government objectives, values, and political ideologies appear repeatedly as we determine who favors what government action and why. So far, we have said little about how government should make its decisions. In Chapter 2, we complete our normative framework for evaluating American politics by examining the nature of democratic theory. There we introduce two key concepts for analyzing how democratic governments make decisions.

KEY TERMS

government	political ideology
order	totalitarianism
communism	socialism
public goods	democratic socialism
welfare state	capitalism
freedom to	libertarianism
freedom from	laissez faire
police power	anarchism
political equality	libertarians
social equality	liberals
equality of opportunity	conservatives
equality of outcome	populists
rights	

SELECTED READINGS

Bowie, Norman E. (ed.). *Equal Opportunity.* Boulder, Col.: Westview, 1988. A series of essays on the theory of equal opportunity and its practice and social impact on education, employment, and political participation.

Ebenstein, William, and Edwin Fogelman. *Today's Isms: Communism, Fascism, Capitalism, Socialism.* 9th ed. Englewood Cliffs, N.J.: Prentice-Hall, 1985. This standard source describes the history of each of the four major "isms" and relates each to developments in contemporary politics. It is concise, informative, and readable.

Institute for Cultural Conservatism. *Cultural Conservatism: Toward a New National Agenda.* Washington, D.C.: Free Congress Research and Education Foundation, 1987. This book assumes that traditional values are necessary for individual fulfillment and that society and government must play an active role in upholding traditional culture.

King, Desmond S. *The New Right: Politics, Markets and Citizenship.* Chicago, Ill.: Dorsey Press, 1987. King uses the concepts of freedom, order, and equality to analyze ideological tendencies in Margaret Thatcher's government in Britain and in Reagan's government here. He uses *liberalism* in the European sense, to mean "limiting" state intervention in the economy. In fact, contrary to American practice, this is the way most of the world uses the term.

Maddox, William S., and Stuart A. Lilie. *Beyond Liberal and Conservative: Reassessing the Political Spectrum.* Washington, D.C.: Cato Institute, 1984. Not satisfied with the conventional labels *liberal* and *conservative*, Maddox and Lilie have devised a typology of ideologies based on two dimensions: expansion of personal freedom and government intervention in economic affairs. It is similar to our framework but less theoretical.

Medcalf, Linda J., and Kenneth M. Dolbeare. *Neopolitics: American Political Ideas in the 1980s.* Philadelphia: Temple University Press, 1985. This slim volume reviews the history of ideological labels in American politics. It explains the changing meanings of various labels and updates their usage in contemporary politics. It also describes more recent ideologies, among them the "New Right."

Skogan, Wesley G. *Disorder and Decline: Crime and the Spiral of Decay in American Neighborhoods.* New York: The Free Press, 1990. This study of neighborhood crime and disorder in six cities explores the nature of disorder and the limits to the state's police powers in dealing with urban decline.

Verba, Sidney, et al. *Elites and the Idea of Equality: A Comparison of Japan, Sweden, and the United States.* Cambridge, Mass.: Harvard University Press, 1987. The authors surveyed leaders in each country representing established organizations, challenging groups, and mediating institutions to determine their views on equality and to learn how economics and politics affect the distribution of income in the modern welfare state.

Westen, Peter. *Speaking of Equality: An Analysis of the Rhetorical Force of "Equality" in Moral and Legal Discourse.* Princeton, N.J.: Princeton University Press, 1990. This philosophical treatise is not easy to read, but it has an especially useful chapter on "equal opportunity," which Westen says does not mean the "same" opportunity.

2 MAJORITARIAN OR PLURALIST DEMOCRACY?

The Theory of Democratic Government

The Meaning and Symbolism of Democracy • The Procedural View of Democracy • A Complication: Direct Versus Indirect Democracy • The Substantive View of Democracy • Procedural Democracy Versus Substantive Democracy

Institutional Models of Democracy

The Majoritarian Model of Democracy • An Alternative Model: Pluralist Democracy • The Majoritarian Model Versus the Pluralist Model • An Undemocratic Model: Elite Theory • Elite Theory Versus Pluralist Theory

Democracies Around the World

Testing for Democratic Government • American Democracy: More Pluralist than Majoritarian

RAM CHUN'S FAMILY ESCAPED Cambodia to search for a better life in the United States. They settled in Stockton, California, where many Cambodian families had come to start their pursuit of the American dream. Ram Chun, who was eight, attended the Cleveland Elementary School. On January 17, 1989, she was playing during recess when Patrick Purdy opened fire with his AK-47 and shot her to death.

Purdy's two-minute rampage with his semiautomatic rifle killed four other children besides Ram Chun. Twenty-nine students and a teacher were injured, too. "He was just standing there with a gun making wide sweeps," said one teacher. When he had finished firing over a hundred rounds, Purdy took out a pistol and shot himself to death. Purdy was a drifter with an extensive criminal record, but there is no clear motive for his rampage. What is clear is that he was very interested in things military. The day of his murder spree he was wearing fatigues and a flak jacket; in his hotel room were more than a hundred plastic toy figures of soldiers, tanks, and weapons.[1]

Although AK-47s and other semiautomatic rifles are military assault weapons, it is perfectly legal for civilians to own them. (Machine guns that fire continuously as long as the trigger is depressed are automatic weapons; semiautomatics require that the trigger be pulled each time to shoot, but they can fire in succession very rapidly.) Purdy purchased his AK-47 for $349.95 at a gun store in Sandy, Oregon. He did have to fill out a federal form declaring that he wasn't a convicted criminal, mentally ill, a drug addict, or under indictment, but this is a meaningless step, since there is no restraint on lying. Under current law the government has no authority to check on the truthfulness of gun purchasers.[2]

The Stockton massacre prompted some members of Congress to push for a ban on semiautomatic weapons like the AK-47. The National Rifle Association (NRA) vehemently disagreed, claiming that such a ban was an infringement on the constitutional right of the people to "bear arms." The 2.6-million-member NRA is a powerful group because those who belong to the organization are so vocal in communicating their impassioned views to their representatives and senators. The group has been very successful in defeating gun control measures when they've been proposed in the Congress. Indeed, in 1986 the organization was successful in getting Congress to pass a law weakening a very modest gun control bill that was passed in 1968 in the wake of the assassinations of Robert Kennedy and Martin Luther King, Jr.

The NRA's ability to thwart gun control efforts is particularly interesting in light of the American people's opinion on the subject. Seventy percent of the public favors stricter gun control laws. Seventy-two percent favors a ban on assault rifles.[3] The Senate managed to include (by a one-vote margin) a ban on nine types of assault rifles in its 1990 anti-crime bill, but the House refused to go along. The provision on semiautomatics was stripped from the final version of the legislation by a House-Senate conference committee.[4]

Over the years the Congress has regularly backed the interests of this particular minority opposed to gun control over the preferences of the majority, which favors gun control. Is it democratic for policymakers to favor an intense minority at the expense of a less committed majority?

Go Ahead, Make My Day
The National Rifle Association is a powerful organization because of a fervent constituency; its vocal and active members clearly love their guns. This woman is examining one vendor's wares in the exhibition hall of an NRA convention.

In Chapter 1, we discussed three basic values that underlie what government should do. In this chapter, we examine *how* government should decide what to do. In particular, we set forth criteria for judging whether or not a government's decision-making process is democratic.

The Theory of Democratic Government

The origins of democratic theory lie in ancient Greek political thought. Greek philosophers classified governments according to the number of citizens involved in the process. Imagine a continuum running from rule by one person, through rule by a few, to rule by many.

At one extreme is an **autocracy**, in which one individual has the power to make all important decisions. The concentration of power in the hands of one person (usually a king) was a more common form of government in earlier historical periods, although some argue that Hitler ruled Germany autocratically.

Oligarchy puts government power in the hands of "the few." At one time, it was common for the nobility or the major landowners to rule as an aristocracy. Today, military leaders are often the rulers in countries governed by an oligarchy.

Freedom, the Universal Language
These demonstrators in Beijing hoped to embarrass the authoritarian Chinese government during a state visit by Soviet leader Mikhail Gorbachev. Their message was, if freedom could come to the Soviet Union, why not to China?

At the other extreme of the continuum is **democracy,** which means "authority in, or rule by, the people."[5] Most scholars believe that the United States, Britain, France, and other countries in Western Europe are genuine democracies. Dissenters contend that these countries appear to be democracies because they hold free elections, but that they actually are run by wealthy business elites for their own benefit. Nevertheless, most people today agree that governments *should* be democratic—whatever that means.

The Meaning and Symbolism of Democracy

Americans have a simple answer to the question "Who should govern?" It is "The people." Unfortunately, this answer is too simple. It fails to define who "the people" are. Should we include young children? Recent immigrants? Illegal aliens? This answer also fails to tell us how the people should do the governing. Should they be assembled in a stadium? Vote by mail? Choose others to govern for them? We need to take a closer look at what *government by the people* really means.

The word *democracy* originated in Greek writings around the fifth century B.C. *Demos* referred to the common people, the masses; *Kratos* meant "power." The ancient Greeks were afraid of democracy—rule by the people. That fear is evident in the term *demagogue.* We use the term today to refer to a politician who appeals to and often deceives the masses by manipulating their emotions and prejudices.

Many centuries after the Greeks first defined *democracy*, the idea still carried the connotation of mob rule. When George Washington was president, opponents of a new political party disparagingly called it a "democratic" party. No one would do that in politics today. In fact, the term has become so popular that the names of more than 20 percent of the world's political parties contain some variation of *democracy*.[6]

In the United States, democracy has become the apple pie and motherhood of political discourse. Like *justice* and *decency, democracy* is used reverently by politicians of all persuasions. Even totalitarian regimes use it. North Korea calls itself the Democratic People's Republic of Korea, even though by our standards it is one of the most undemocratic places on the face of the earth. Like other complex concepts, democracy means different things to different people.

There are two major schools of thought about what constitutes democracy. The first believes democracy is a form of government. It emphasizes the *procedures* that enable the people to govern—meeting to discuss issues, voting in elections, running for public office. The second sees democracy in the *substance* of government policies, in freedom of religion and providing for human needs. The *procedural* approach focuses on *how* decisions are made; the *substantive* approach is concerned with *what* government does.[7]

The Procedural View of Democracy

Procedural democratic theory sets forth principles that describe how government should make decisions. These principles address three distinct questions:

1. *Who* should participate in decision making?
2. *How much* should each participant's vote count?
3. *How many* votes are needed to reach a decision?

According to procedural democratic theory, all adults should participate in government decision making. This means everyone within the boundaries of the political community should be allowed to participate in its decision making. If some people, such as recent immigrants, are prohibited from participating, they are excluded for practical or political reasons. The theory of democracy itself does not exclude any adults from participation. We refer to this principle as **universal participation.**

How much should each participant's vote count? According to procedural theory, all votes should be counted *equally.* This is the principle of **political equality.**

Notice that universal participation and political equality are two distinct principles. It is not enough for everyone to participate in a decision; all votes must carry equal weight. President Abraham Lincoln reportedly once took a vote among his cabinet members and found that all of them opposed his own position on the issue. He summarized the vote and the decision like this: "Seven noes, one aye—the ayes have it."[8] Everyone participated, but Lincoln's vote counted more than all the others combined. (No one ever said that presidents have to run their Cabinets democratically.)

Finally, how many votes are needed to reach a decision? Procedural theory prescribes that a group should decide to do what the *majority* of its participants (50 percent plus one person more) wants to do. This principle is called **majority rule.** (If participants divide over more than two alternatives and none receives a simple majority, the principle usually defaults to *plurality rule,* in which the group should do what most participants want.)

A Complication: Direct Versus Indirect Democracy

These three principles—universal participation, political equality, and majority rule—are widely recognized as necessary for democratic decision making. In small, simple societies, these principles can be met in a **direct democracy,** in which all members of the group meet to make decisions, while observing political equality and majority rule. The origins of direct democracy go back to the Greek city-state, where the important decisions of government were made by its adult citizens meeting in an assembly. The people ruled for themselves rather than having a small number of notables rule on their behalf. (In Athens the "people" who were permitted to go to the assemblies excluded women, slaves, and

Hands Up for Secession

At this town meeting in Block Island, a small island off the Rhode Island coast, citizens debated whether to secede from Rhode Island and join Connecticut instead. Some residents were upset over a proposed state regulation limiting moped use on the island. The movement for secession failed; Block Island remains part of Rhode Island.

those whose families had not lived there for generations. Still, the Greek city-state represented a dramatic transformation in the theory of government.)[9]

Something close to direct democracy is practiced in some New England villages, where citizens gather in town meetings to make community decisions. Citizens in Derry, New Hampshire, governed themselves in annual town meetings for 158 years. Usually held the second Tuesday in March, the Derry town meeting was an all-day affair that began with the election of officers, then proceeded to decisions on road repairs, building maintenance, and other town issues.

In large, complex societies, however, the people cannot assemble in one place to participate directly in government. In Derry, as the population increased, the town meeting was no longer a viable form of government. There was no place to assemble even a fraction of the 25,000 townspeople. In 1985, Derry bowed to growth and switched to a different form of government, an elected town council headed by a mayor.[10] The town still follows democratic principles in voting for members of the town council, but the council decides village policies in place of the people.

Derry changed from direct to indirect democracy, or what is commonly called **representative democracy**. Its citizens now participate in government by electing public officials to make government decisions for them. Their elected officials are expected to represent the voters' views and interests—that is, to serve as the agents of the citizenry and to act for them.

Philosopher Jean Jacques Rousseau contended that true democracy is impossible unless all citizens gather together to make their own decisions and to supervise their government. Rousseau said that decisions of government should embody the general will and "will cannot be represented."[11] Other theorists, among them the nineteenth-century English philosopher John Stuart Mill (1806–1873), accept the necessity of indirect democracy; they believe representative government is the best *possible* form of government.[12]

A number of contemporary political theorists believe that we have come to rely too much on representative democracy and are now facing a weakening of citizenship, of the sense of obligation to participate in civic life.[13] Even if representative democracy is inevitable on a national scale, people can still be directly involved in local government (see Feature 2.1).

Within the context of representative democracy, we adhere to the principles of universal participation, political equality, and majority rule to guarantee that elections are democratic. But what happens after the election? The elected representatives might not make the same decisions the people would have made if they had gathered for the same purpose. To cope with this possibility in representative government, procedural theory gives us a fourth decision-making principle: **responsiveness.** Elected representatives should respond to public opinion. This does not mean that legislators simply cast their ballots on the basis of whether the people back home want alternative A or alternative B. Issues are not usually so straightforward. Rather, responsiveness means following the

FEATURE 2.1   *St. Paul, Minnesota: Where the Grassroots Rule*

The steady decline in the percentage of Americans who vote has created a great deal of concern about the health of our democracy. In general, citizens don't seem to care much about becoming involved in government. They feel alienated from the political process because they don't believe their participation makes much of a difference.

In one American city, however, there is little alienation, a lot of confidence, and a lot of meaningful citizen participation in government. One reason why the government in St. Paul, Minnesota, has gained the respect of its citizens is that the city relies on a form of direct democracy. St. Paul is officially divided into seventeen neighborhoods, each governed by a district council. The district councils are made up of residents who volunteer to serve, and a council's meetings are open to every adult who lives in the neighborhood. The city provides a small amount of financial support so each district council can rent office space and hire at least one professional staffer to do community organizing.

But money isn't the most important thing the city gives the district councils; the city also gives them the *authority* to govern their neighborhoods. The greatest of the powers turned over to the neighborhoods is zoning. Through zoning permits and variances, a district council can regulate business development and control the physical appearance of a neighborhood. Residents are thereby given the means to make crucial decisions at a very local level, decisions that might otherwise be made by a faceless bureaucrat downtown in city hall.

When St. Paul residents were asked a standard political science survey question about confidence in government, the results were revealing. Compared with other respondents, the citizens of St. Paul were much more likely to say they trusted their local government to do what's right. Of those who participate in district council meetings or activities, an astounding 86 percent said they trusted the government of St. Paul.

---

general contours of public opinion as complex pieces of legislation are formulated.

Adding responsiveness to deal with the case of indirect democracy, we now have four principles of procedural democracy:

- Universal participation
- Political equality
- Majority rule
- Government responsiveness to public opinion

The Substantive View of Democracy

According to procedural theory, the principle of responsiveness is absolute. The government should do what the majority wants, regardless of what it is. At first this seems a reasonable way to protect the rights of citizens in a representative democracy. But think for a minute. Chris-

The district councils in St. Paul encourage residents to take responsibility for the well-being of their neighborhoods. Instead of simply blaming elected officials for not representing them well, citizens can represent themselves by participating directly in the policymaking process. Residents know that if they want to have a say in government, they can go down the street and join their neighbors in deliberating what is best for their community.

Question: How much of the time do you think you can trust the government in St. Paul [in your city] to do what is right — just about always, most of the time, or only some of the time?

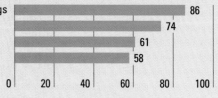

Participants in St. Paul district council meetings ████████ 86
All St. Paul residents ███████ 74
Residents of ten other cities* ██████ 61
National sample** ██████ 58

0   20   40   60   80   100

Percentage responding "always"
or "most of the time"

Source: Excerpted from Jeffrey M. Berry, Kent E. Portney, and Ken Thomson, *The Case for Participatory Democracy.* The Brookings Institution. Forthcoming.

*This figure comes from a survey of residents of ten medium-sized American cities. Respondents were asked about their confidence in their own local government.

**This figure comes from the 1987 General Social Survey (taken around the same time as the St. Paul and ten-city surveys). Respondents were asked about their confidence in their own local government.

tians account for more than 90 percent of the U.S. population. Suppose that the Christian majority backs a constitutional amendment to require Bible reading in public schools, that the amendment is passed by Congress, and that it is ratified by the states. From a strict procedural view, the action would be democratic. But what about freedom of religion? What about the rights of minorities? To limit the government's responsiveness to public opinion, we must look outside procedural democratic theory to substantive democratic theory.

Substantive democratic theory focuses on the substance of government policies, not on the procedures followed in making those policies. It argues that in a democratic government, certain principles must be embodied in government policies. Substantive theorists would reject a law that requires Bible reading in schools because it would violate a substantive principle, the freedom of religion.

In defining the principles that underlie democratic government—and the policies of that government—most substantive theorists agree on a basic criterion: Government policies should guarantee civil liberties (for example, freedom of religion and freedom of expression) and civil rights (for example, protection against discrimination in employment and housing). According to this standard, the claim that the United States is a democracy rests on its record in ensuring its citizens these liberties and rights. (We look at how good this record is in Chapters 15 and 16.)

Agreement among substantive theorists breaks down when discussion moves from civil rights to *social* rights (adequate health care, quality education, decent housing) and *economic* rights (private property, steady employment). They disagree most sharply on whether a government must promote social equality to qualify as a democracy. For example, must a state guarantee unemployment benefits and adequate public housing to be called democratic? Some insist that policies that promote social equality are essential to democratic government.[14] Others reject expanding the requirements of substantative democracy beyond those policies that safeguard civil liberties—guaranteed freedoms of action —and civil rights—social treatment to which citizens are entitled. The core of our substantive principles of democracy are, of course, embedded in the Bill of Rights and other amendments to the Constitution.

The political ideology of a theorist tends to explain his or her position on what democracy really requires in substantive policies. Conservative theorists have a narrow view of the scope of democratic government and a narrow view of the social and economic rights guaranteed by that government. Liberal theorists believe that a democratic government should guarantee its citizens a much broader spectrum of social and economic rights. In later chapters, we review important social and economic policies that our government has actually followed over time. Keep in mind, however, that what the government *has* done is not necessarily a good guide to what a democratic government *should* do.

Procedural Democracy Versus Substantive Democracy

There is a problem with the substantive view of democracy. It does not provide clear, precise criteria that allow us to determine whether a government is or is not democratic. It is, in fact, open to unending arguments over which government policies are truly democratic in the substantive sense. Theorists are free to promote their pet values—separation of church and state, guaranteed employment, equal rights for women, whatever—under the guise of substantive democracy.

There is also a problem with the procedural viewpoint. Although it presents specific criteria for democratic government, those criteria can produce undesirable social policies that prey on minorities. This clashes with **minority rights**—the idea that citizens are entitled to certain things that cannot be denied by majority decisions. There are many different opinions on what those "certain things" are, but freedom of religion is definitely one of them. One way to protect minority rights is to limit the principle of majority rule—requiring a two-thirds majority or some other extraordinary majority when decisions must be made on certain subjects—or to put the issue in the Constitution, beyond the reach of majority rule.

Standing Room Only

This overcrowded classroom in the Edgewood district of San Antonio, Texas, illustrates the conflict between procedural and substantive democracy. State law left some school districts without a sufficient tax base to fund their schools adequately. After many years of conflict, the Texas supreme court finally ruled that a failure to provide equal resources for schools denies students in poor districts like Edgewood their constitutional right to an equal education.

The issue of prayer in school is a good example of the limits on majority rule. No matter how large, majorities in Congress cannot pass a law to allow organized prayer in public schools because the Supreme Court has determined that the Constitution forbids this kind of law. The Constitution could be changed so that it no longer protects religious minorities, but amendment is a cumbersome process that involves extraordinary majorities. When limits like these are put on the principle of majority rule, the minority often rules instead.

Clearly, procedural and substantive democracy are not always compatible. In choosing one over the other, we are also choosing to focus on either procedures or policies. As authors of this text, we favor a compromise between the two. On the whole we favor the procedural conception of democracy because it more closely approaches the classical definition of *democracy*—"government by the people." And procedural democracy is founded on clear, well-established rules for decision making. But the theory has a serious drawback: It allows a democratic government to enact policies that can violate the substantive principles of democracy. Thus it is best that pure procedural democracy be diluted so that minority rights guaranteeing civil liberties and civil rights are part of the structure of government. If this compromise seems familiar, it is: this is the approach used in the course of American history to balance legitimate minority and majority interests.

In the real world of politics, drawing the appropriate line between which issues should be subject to procedural democracy and which should fall under the coverage of substantive democracy is not always easy. People frequently disagree over this division. But if we realize that democratic government and desirable policies are not necessarily synonymous, then we should be able to live with a political system that sets standards for the decision-making process if not the decisions themselves.

Institutional Models of Democracy

A small group of people can agree to make democratic decisions directly by using the principles of universal participation, political equality, and majority rule. But even the smallest nations have too many citizens to practice direct democracy. If nations want democracy, they must achieve it through some form of representative government, electing officials to make government decisions. Even then, democratic government is not guaranteed. Governments must have a means for determining what the people want, as well as some means for translating those wants into decisions. In other words, democratic government requires *institutional mechanisms*—established procedures and organizations—to translate public opinion into government policy, to be responsive. Elections, political parties, legislatures, and interest groups (which we discuss in later chapters) are all examples of such institutional mechanisms in politics.

Some democratic theorists favor institutions that tie government decisions closely to the desires of the majority of citizens. If most citizens want laws against the sale of pornography, then the government should outlaw pornography. If citizens want more money spent on defense and less on social welfare (or vice versa), the government should act accordingly. For these theorists, the essence of democratic government is majority rule and responsiveness.

Other theorists place less importance on the principles of majority rule and responsiveness. They do not believe in relying heavily on mass opinion; instead, they favor institutions that allow groups of citizens to defend their interests in government decisions.

Both schools hold a procedural view of democracy but differ in how they interpret *government by the people*. We can summarize these theoretical positions using two alternative models of democracy. As a model, each is a hypothetical plan, a blueprint, for achieving democratic government through institutional mechanisms. The *majoritarian model* values participation by the people in general; the *pluralist model* values participation by the people in groups.

The Majoritarian Model of Democracy

The **majoritarian model of democracy** relies on the classical, textbook theory of democracy. It interprets *government by the people* as government by the *majority* of the people. The majoritarian model tries to ap-

Surf's Up, Dudes: Vote for Big Green

California voters have a long and rich history of using initiatives to write state law. In 1990, they voted on Proposition 128 (also known as "Big Green"), a far-reaching initiative that would have put some very strict environmental standards into place. Voters rejected Big Green by a 2–1 margin.

proximate the people's role in a direct democracy within the limitations of representative government. To force the government to respond to public opinion, the majoritarian model depends on several mechanisms that allow the people to participate directly in the political system.

The popular election of government officials is the primary mechanism for democratic government in the majoritarian model. Citizens are expected to control their representatives' behavior by choosing wisely in the first place and by re-electing or defeating public officials according to their performance. Elections fulfill the first three principles of procedural democratic theory: universal participation, political equality, and majority rule. And the prospect of re-election and the threat of defeat at the polls are expected to motivate public officials to be responsive.

Usually we think of elections only as mechanisms for choosing between candidates for public office. Majoritarian theorists also see them as a means for deciding government policies. An election on a policy issue is called a **referendum.** When a policy question is put on the ballot by the action of citizens circulating petitions and gathering a required minimum number of signatures, it is called an **initiative**. Twenty-one of the states allow their legislatures to put referenda before the voters as well as give citizens the right to place initiatives on the ballot. Five other states make provision for one or the other mechanism.[15]

Statewide referenda have been used to decide a wide variety of important questions, many of which have national implications. In 1978 the voters of California passed Proposition 13, an initiative that cut people's property taxes by half.[16] The vote on Proposition 13 is widely regarded as the beginning of the "tax revolt" in this country. In 1990, California voters decided on Proposition 111, which mandated an increase in the gasoline tax to allow greater spending on highways and mass transit. When Proposition 111 was approved, many felt it was a sign that the antitax feeling had ebbed a little and that voters were willing to tolerate tax increases for specific, demonstrable needs.[17]

In the United States there are no provisions for referenda at the national level, though some countries do allow policy questions to be put before the public. In Italy national referenda were used to make both divorce and abortion legal in that heavily Catholic country. In a 1990 election in Italy, voters cast ballots on a referendum that would have banned hunting. Although a majority of those who voted favored the ban, it was not enacted because turnout fell below the 50 percent required by Italian law.[18]

Americans are strongly in favor of a system of national referenda. A recent survey showed that 76 percent of the public felt that voters should have a say on some national issues. Only 18 percent felt that we should leave all policy decisions to our elected representatives.[19] The most fervent advocates of majoritarian democracy would like to see modern technology used to maximize the government's responsiveness to the majority. Some have proposed incorporating public opinion polls, first used regularly in the 1930s, into government decision making. More recently, some have suggested that computers could be used in the referendum process. For instance, citizens could vote on an issue by inserting plastic identification cards into computer terminals installed in all homes.[20] People disagree on the merits of "video voting," but it certainly is technically possible.

The majoritarian model contends that citizens can control their government if they have adequate mechanisms for popular participation. It also assumes that citizens are knowledgeable about government and politics, that they want to participate in the political process, and that they make rational decisions in voting for their elected representatives.

If these factors are truly necessary to the functioning of majoritarian democracy, then the majoritarian model in the United States is in trouble. Only 22 percent of a national sample of voters said that they "followed what's going on" in government "most of the time." More (40 percent) said that they followed politics "only now and then" or "hardly at all."[21] Further, as discussed in Chapter 7, voter turnout in presidential elections has fallen to just half of the eligible electorate. And those who do vote often choose candidates more from habit (along party lines) than from a close examination of the candidates' positions on the issues.

An Alternative Model: Pluralist Democracy

For years, political scientists struggled valiantly to reconcile the majoritarian model of democracy with polls that showed a widespread ignorance of politics among the American people. If most voters do not know enough to make rational political judgments, why pretend that they should govern at all? In short, why argue for democracy?

In the 1950s, an alternative interpretation of democracy evolved, one tailored to the limited knowledge and participation of the *real* electorate, not the perfection of the ideal one. It was based on the concept of *pluralism*—that modern society consists of innumerable groups of people who share economic, religious, ethnic, or cultural interests. Often people with similar interests organize formal groups: the Future Farmers of America, the Junior Chamber of Commerce, and the Knights of Columbus, for example. Many of these social groups have little contact with government, but occasionally they find themselves backing or opposing government policy. When an organized group seeks to influence government policy, it is called an **interest group.** Many interest groups regularly spend a great deal of time and money trying to influence government policy (see Chapter 10). Among them are the AFL-CIO, the American Hospital Association, the Associated Milk Producers, the National Education Association (NEA), the National Association of Manufacturers, the National Organization for Women (NOW), and, of course, the NRA.

The **pluralist model of democracy** interprets *government by the people* to mean government by people operating through competing interest groups. According to this model, democracy exists when many (plural) organizations operate separately from the government, press their interests on the government, and even challenge the government.[22] Compared with majoritarian thinking, pluralist theory shifts the focus of democratic government from the mass electorate to organized groups. It changes the criterion for democratic government from responsiveness to mass public opinion to responsiveness to organized groups of citizens.

The two major mechanisms in a pluralist democracy are interest groups and a decentralized structure of government that provides ready access to public officials and that is open to hearing the groups' arguments for or against government policies. In a centralized structure, decisions are made at one point, the top of the hierarchy. The few decision makers at the top are too busy to hear the claims of competing interest groups or to consider those claims in making their decisions. But a decentralized, complex government structure offers the access and openness necessary for pluralist democracy. The ideal is a system that divides government authority among numerous institutions with overlapping authority. Under such a system, competing interest groups have alternative points of access to present and argue their claims.

Our Constitution approaches the pluralist ideal in the way it divides authority among the branches of government. When the National Association for the Advancement of Colored People (NAACP) could not get Congress to outlaw segregated schools in the South, it turned to the federal court system, which did what Congress would not. According to the pluralist democracy ideal, if all opposing interests are allowed to organize, and if the system can be kept open so that all substantial claims have an opportunity to be heard, then the diverse needs of a pluralist society will be served when an issue is decided.

Although many scholars have contributed to the model, pluralist democracy is most closely identified with political scientist Robert Dahl. According to Dahl, the fundamental axiom of pluralist democracy is that "instead of a single center of sovereign power there must be multiple centers of power, none of which is or can be wholly sovereign."[23] Some

Why They Are Called Lobbyists

At the national level, interest groups are usually represented by highly paid lobbyists. These people are called lobbyists because they often gather in the lobby outside congressional meeting rooms, positioned to contact senators and representatives coming and going. Here, lobbyists are waiting to help members of the House Ways and Means Committee understand the importance of their pet tax loopholes.

watchwords of pluralist democracy, therefore, are *divided authority, decentralization,* and *open access.*

The Majoritarian Model Versus the Pluralist Model

In majoritarian democracy, the mass public—not interest groups—controls government actions. The citizenry must be knowledgeable about government and willing to participate in the electoral process. Majoritarian democracy relies on electoral mechanisms that harness the power of the majority to make decisions. Conclusive elections and a centralized structure of government are mechanisms that aid majority rule.

Pluralism does not demand much knowledge from citizens in general. It requires specialized knowledge only from groups of citizens, in particular their leaders. Unlike majoritarian democracy, pluralist democracy seeks to limit majority action so that interest groups can be heard. It relies on strong interest groups and a decentralized government structure—mechanisms that interfere with majority rule, thereby protecting minority interests. We could even say that pluralism allows minorities to rule.

An Undemocratic Model: Elite Theory

If pluralist democracy allows minorities to rule, how does it differ from **elite theory**—the view that a small group of people (a minority) makes most important government decisions? According to elite theory, important government decisions are made by an identifiable and stable

The Power Elite?

This picture symbolizes the underlying notion of elite theory—that government is driven by wealth. In truth, wealthy people usually have more influence in government than do people of ordinary means. Critics of elite theory point out that it is difficult to demonstrate that an identifiable ruling elite usually sticks together and gets its way in government policy.

minority that shares certain characteristics, usually vast wealth and business connections.*

Elite theory contends that these few individuals wield power in America because they control its key financial, communications, industrial, and governmental institutions. Their power derives from the vast wealth of America's largest corporations and the perceived importance of the continuing success of those corporations to the growth of the economy. An inner circle composed of top corporate leaders provides not only effective advocates for individual companies and for the interests of capitalism in general but also supplies people for top government jobs—from which they can further promote their interests.[24]

According to elite theory, the United States is not a democracy but an oligarchy. Although the voters appear to control government through elections, elite theorists argue that the powerful few in society manage to define the issues and to constrain the possible outcomes of government decisions to suit their own interests. Clearly, elite theory describes a government that operates in an undemocratic fashion.

* The classic book on elite theory in American politics is C. Wright Mills, *The Power Elite* (New York: Oxford University Press, 1956). Actually, elite theory argues that elite rule is inevitable in *every* government, indeed in every large organization. See Thomas R. Dye, *Who's Running America? The Bush Era*, 5th ed. (Englewood Cliffs, N.J.: Prentice-Hall, 1990), especially pp. 2–6, for a summary of elite theory.

Elite theory appeals to many people, especially those who believe that wealth dominates politics. The theory also provides plausible explanations for specific political decisions. For example, government spending for new military weapons systems—including enormous overruns in estimated costs—often seems to be controlled by agreements between the military and giant defense contractors.[25] Even President Dwight Eisenhower, himself a former five-star general, warned of the influence of the "military-industrial complex" on government policy.

Elite theory breaks down, however, when an attempt is made to use it to explain a broader range of political decisions. Dahl suggests that convincing research on the ruling elite model must meet three tests:

1. The hypothetical ruling elite must be a well-defined group.

2. A fair sample of cases involving key political decisions must exist. In those decisions, the preferences of the hypothetical ruling elite must be shown to run counter to the preferences of any other likely group. . . .

3. In such cases, the preferences of the elite must regularly prevail.[26]

Some researchers have attempted the first test, defining the ruling group. One study identified 7,314 "elite positions" in the corporate, public interest, and governmental sectors of society.[27] Although this number represents only a tiny fraction of the nation's population, 7,314 rulers somehow seems many more than "the few."

The second test, identifying a number of government decisions that pit the special interests of the ruling elite against the interests of others, has not been performed in serious research at the national level. This means the third test, determining whether or not elite interests regularly prevail in such decisions, also has not been met. Careful studies of decision making in American cities, which should be even more susceptible to elite rule than the nation as a whole, have shown that different groups win on different issues.[28] This also seems to be true in some cases at the national level. For instance, the giant oil, chemical, and steel industries do not always triumph over environmental groups on the issue of air pollution. And what was once the nation's largest corporation, AT&T, was forced to break up its telephone monopoly in suits brought by much smaller communications companies.

The available evidence of government decisions on many different topics does not generally support elite theory—at least in the sense that an identifiable ruling elite usually gets its way on government policy. Not surprisingly, elite theorists reject this logic. They argue that studies of decision making on individual issues does not adequately test the influence of the power elite. Rather, they contend that much of the elite's power comes from its ability to keep things off the political agenda. That is, it is powerful because it manages to maintain its privileged position by keeping people from questioning fundamental assumptions about American capitalism.[29]

Consequently, elite theory is not dead; it is still forcefully argued by radical critics of American politics.[30] Although we don't feel that the scholarly evidence supports elite theory, we do recognize that contemporary American pluralism favors some segments of society over others. The poor are chronically unorganized and are not well represented by interest groups. On the other hand, business is very well represented in the political system. As many interest group scholars who reject the elitist theory have documented, business is better represented than any other sector of the public.[31] Thus one can endorse pluralist democracy as a more accurate description of American politics than elitism without believing all groups are equally well represented in the political system.

Elite Theory Versus Pluralist Theory

The key difference between elite and pluralist theory lies in the durability of the ruling minority. Unlike elite theory, pluralist theory does not define government conflict in terms of a minority versus *the* majority; instead, it sees many minorities vying with one another in different policy areas. In the management of national forests, for example, many interest groups—logging companies, recreational campers, environmentalists—have joined the political competition. They press their various interests on government through group representatives who are well informed about the issues as they affect group members (see Feature 2.2). According to elite theory, the financial resources of big logging companies ought to win out over the arguments of campers and environmentalists, but this does not always happen.

The pluralist model holds that this type of competition among minority interests also takes place in other policy arenas, such as transportation, agriculture, public utilities, and urban housing. Although some groups with "better connections" in government may win more often in individual arenas, no identifiable elite wins consistently across a broad range of issues. The pluralist model, then, rejects the primary implication of elite theory: that a single group dominates government decisions.

Instead, pluralist democracy makes a virtue of the struggle among minority interests. It argues for government that accommodates this struggle and channels the result into government action. According to pluralist democracy, the public is best served if the government structure provides access for different groups to press their claims in competition with one another. Notice that pluralist democracy does not insist that all groups have equal influence on government decisions. In the political struggle, wealthy, well-organized groups have an inherent advantage over poorer, inadequately organized groups. In fact, unorganized segments of the population may not even get their concerns placed on the agenda for government consideration, which means that what government does not discuss (its *non*decisions) may be as significant as what it does discuss and decide. This is a critical weakness of pluralism, and critics relentlessly attack this theory because it seems to justify great disparities in levels of political organization and resources among different segments of society. Pluralists contend that as long as all groups are able to participate vigorously in the decision-making process, the process is democratic.

Obviously, pluralist democracy differs from the classic, ideal conception based on universal participation, political equality, and majority

FEATURE 2.2   *Hoo Governs?*

Northern spotted owls are threatened with extinction. Unfortunately, so are the jobs of many people who make their living cutting and hauling logs in the forests the spotted owls inhabit. As a result, the national government must decide a complicated issue: whether to save the spotted owl or as many as twenty-eight thousand timber-related jobs in the Pacific Northwest.

The case of the spotted owl illustrates a basic dynamic of American pluralism—the decision does not pit a minority against the majority but, rather, two minorities against each other. On the one hand, environmental interest groups believe it is vitally important to save the owls. On the other, loggers want to continue to harvest the forests where the owls live. There is no majority opinion to guide the government's response; in general, Americans are oblivious to the issue. Except for environmental activists and loggers, most Americans just don't give a hoot about what happens to the spotted owl.

The opposing sides hold equally impassioned views. Those in the timber industry are infuriated by the environmentalists' push to preserve the owls. Timber jobs pay $8 to $13 an hour, and there are few other job possibilities in the small towns of

the Northwest. Loggers fear losing their jobs and their way of life. A popular bumper sticker in the area reads: "I like spotted owls . . . fried." A spokesman for communities whose economic viability depends on logging in the owls' forests accuses the "radical environmental movement" of trying "to remove man from the public lands."

rule. But the pluralist reliance on access is compatible with contemporary thinking that democratic government should be open to groups that seek redress of grievances. The pluralist concept also fits the facts about the limited political knowledge of most American citizens. Clearly, pluralist democracy is worthy of being embraced as a rival model to majoritarianism, the traditional model of procedural democracy.

Democracies Around the World

We have proposed two models of democratic government. The majoritarian model conforms to classical democratic theory for a representative government. According to this model, democracy should be a form of government that features responsiveness to majority opinion. According to the pluralist model, a government is democratic if it allows minority interests to organize and press their claims freely on government.

No government actually achieves the high degree of responsiveness demanded by the majoritarian model. It is also true that no government offers complete and equal access to the claims of all competing groups, as required by an optimally democratic pluralist model. Still, some na-

Environmentalists counter that citizens have an obligation to preserve wildlife for all generations to come. They acknowledge that restrictions on logging might initially create economic hardships for Northwest communities but insist that new industries and new jobs can be created. They suggest, for example, curbing the export of whole logs to Japan, forcing those logs to be milled here. A representative of the Wilderness Society says, "Good environmentalism is, for the most part, good economics."

In the summer of 1990, after analyzing available scientific evidence, the Fish and Wildlife Service declared the northern spotted owl a "threatened species." This determination, according to the Endangered Species Act of 1973, requires the government to take action to preserve the habitat of the six thousand owls that remain.

Concerned about an adverse economic impact on Washington, Oregon, and California, the Bush administration resisted implementing the 50 percent cut in logging the Fish and Wildlife Service said was necessary to save the owl. As is often the case with pluralist politics, the government wanted to find a compromise that would please all sides. But when the administration did propose a compromise plan that would have reduced logging by 20 percent, both loggers and environmentalists denounced it. Neither side believed they could afford to make those concessions.

Subsequently, in response to a law suit filed by environmental groups, a federal district judge in Seattle ordered the Fish and Wildlife Service to issue a plan to protect the endangered owl. The agency designated 11.6 million acres as a critical habitat for the spotted owl, an action that seemed to favor environmentalists more than loggers. The plan is not final, however, and more wrangling over the spotted owl is sure to follow.

Sources: Timothy Egan, "10,000 Are Expected to Lose Jobs to Spotted Owl," *New York Times*, 4 April, 1990; Dianne Dumanoski, "Whose Forests? Owl vs. Timber Battle Approaches its Climax," *Boston Globe*, 19 June 1990, p. 1; Timothy Egan, "U.S. Declares Owl to Be Threatened by Heavy Logging," *New York Times*, 23 June 1990, p. A1; and Timothy Egan, "Softening Stand on Spotted Owl, Administration Delays Protection," *New York Times*, 27 June 1990, p. A1; Timothy Egan, "Bush Plan Would Reduce Logging in Northwest," *New York Times*, 22 September 1990, p. 8; and Rudy Abramson, "Curbs Sought on 11.6m Acres to Protect Owls," *Boston Globe*, 27 April 1991, p. 1.

tions approach these ideals closely enough to be considered practicing democracies.

Testing for Democratic Government

How can it be determined which countries qualify as practicing democracies? A government's degree of responsiveness or access cannot be measured directly, so indirect tests of democracy must be used. One test is to look for traits normally associated with democratic government—whether defined from a procedural or from a substantive viewpoint. One scholar, for example, established five criteria for a democracy:[32]

1. *Most adults can participate in the electoral process.* (Embodies the principle of universal participation)

2. *Citizens' votes are secret and are not coerced.* (Embodies the principle of political equality)

3. *Leaders are chosen in free elections, contested by at least two viable political parties.* (Embodies the principle of majority rule)

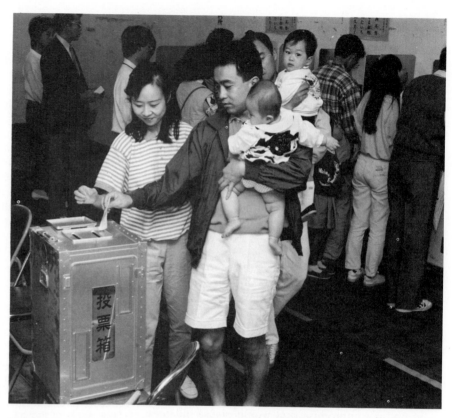

Voting: An American Export That Does Well in Japan
Japan became a democracy during the years immediately following World War II. However, its constitution was not written or adopted in the most democratic of manners. American occupation forces, led by General Douglas MacArthur, outlined the contents of the Japanese constitution and required its enactment.

4. *The government bases its legitimacy on representing the desires of its citizens.* (Embodies the principle of responsiveness)
5. *Citizens, leaders, and party officials enjoy basic freedoms of speech, press, assembly, religion, and organization.* (Substantive policies that create conditions for the practice of the other criteria)

Because the United States fits all these criteria to a fairly high degree, it qualifies as a democracy. How about the other nations of the world? Applying standards similar to these to all nations with a population over 3 million, one writer identified just eighteen nations in addition to the United States as democracies.[33] Like the United States, the following nations have government traditions of widespread participation, political equality, and free elections to choose representatives who pay close attention to public opinion.

Australia	Denmark	Ireland
Austria	Finland	Israel
Belgium	France	Italy
Canada	Germany (West Germany)	Japan

Netherlands   Norway   Switzerland

New Zealand   Sweden   United Kingdom

Given that more than ninety nations have populations greater than 3 million, nineteen democracies—only about 20 percent of the world's nations—do not seem like very many. By any reckoning, democratic government is relatively rare across the world. Yet the list seems destined to grow. The Soviet Union and the East bloc countries have taken significant steps (in varying degrees) toward becoming real democracies. (President George Bush said the attempted coup against Soviet president Mikhail Gorbachev in August 1991 failed because "you can't put freedom and democracy back into a box and keep it contained.") Since the studies cited here require that countries demonstrate a tradition of fulfilling these criteria, it is much too early to conclude that the Soviet bloc will emerge as a stable set of democracies. Nevertheless, the trend in world politics is toward democratization rather than away.

Four of the five preceding criteria apply to government procedures rather than to the substance of government policy. But all of these criteria apply equally to the majoritarian and pluralist models of democracy. Although the United States clearly qualifies as a democracy according to these criteria, they cannot be used to judge whether it is closer to a majoritarian or to a pluralist democracy.

American Democracy: More Pluralist than Majoritarian

It is not idle speculation to ask what kind of democracy is practiced in the United States. The answer to this question can help us understand why our government can be called *democratic* despite a low level of citizen participation in politics and despite government actions that run contrary to public opinion. The answer may also help us understand why many Americans are not satisfied with the democratic form of government here. As shown in Compared with What? 2.1, only 59 percent of a national sample reported that they were satisfied with the way democracy works in the United States.

Throughout the rest of this book, we probe more deeply to determine how well the United States fits the two alternative models of democracy, majoritarian and pluralist. If our answer is not already apparent, it soon will be. We argue that the political system in the United States rates relatively low according to the majoritarian model of democracy, but that it fulfills the pluralist model very well. It should not be surprising, then, that 80 percent of the wealthiest group of respondents in a national survey were satisfied with the way democracy works in the United States compared with only 43 percent of the poorest group (see Figure 2.1). An advocate of majoritarian democracy once wrote, "The flaw in the pluralist heaven is that the heavenly chorus sings with a strong upper-class accent."[34]

This evaluation of the pluralist nature of American democracy may not mean much to you now. But you will learn that the pluralist model makes the United States look far more democratic than does the majoritarian model. Eventually, it will be up to *you* to decide the answers to

COMPARED WITH WHAT?   2.1

Satisfaction with Democracy, by Nation

Compared with citizens in twelve other Western countries, Americans are only moderately satisfied with their form of democratic government. When asked in 1985 whether they were "satisfied with the way democracy works" in their country, respondents in five other nations reported higher levels of satisfaction than the 59 percent who were satisfied with "the way democracy is working" in the United States. Of the seven nations whose respondents were less satisfied, three (Spain, Greece, and Portugal) do not have democratic traditions. Spain and Portugal suffered under decades of dictatorship until the late 1970s, and Greece has had a spotty record of free elections since World War II.

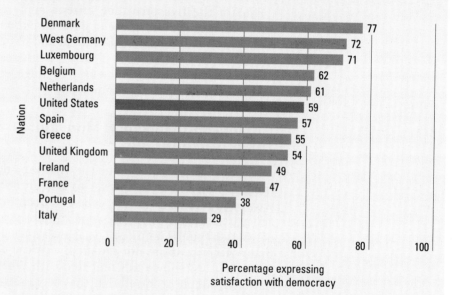

Percentage expressing
satisfaction with democracy

Sources: Data for the United States are from *The Gallup Poll, Public Opinion 1985* (Wilmington, Del.: Scholarly Resources, 1986), p. 32; data for the other nations are from Jacques-René Rabier, Helene Riffault, and Ronald Inglehart, *Euro-Barometer 24: Entry of Spain and Portugal, October, 1985* (Ann Arbor, Mich.: Inter-University Consortium for Political and Social Research, Study 8513, 1986), pp. 10–11.

these three questions: Is the pluralist model really an adequate expression of democracy, or is it a perversion of classical ideals designed to portray America as democratic when it really is not? Does the majoritarian model result in a "better" type of democracy? If so, is it possible to devise new mechanisms of government to produce a desirable mix of majority rule and minority rights? These questions should play in the back of your mind as you read more about the workings of American government in meeting the challenge of democracy.

FIGURE 2.1 *Satisfaction with Democracy in the United States, by Income*

As shown in Compared with What? 2.1, Americans surveyed in 1985 were only moderately satisfied with "the way democracy is working" in the United States when compared
with citizens in other Western nations. But satisfaction in the United States was closely
linked to income. Nearly twice the percentage of the wealthiest respondents were satisfied
with the workings of democracy compared with the poorest respondents. There were only
slight differences in satisfaction among the vast majority of people in the three middle
categories. (Source: The Gallup Poll, Public Opinion 1985 [Wilmington, Del.: Scholarly
Resources, 1986], p. 32.)

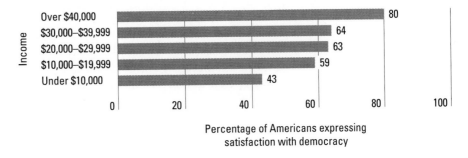

Percentage of Americans expressing
satisfaction with democracy

Summary

There are not many democracies in the world. In fact, scholars agree that
only about nineteen of the world's larger countries are democratic. Is the
United States a democracy? Most scholars believe that it is. But what
kind of democracy is it? The answer depends on the definition of *democracy.* Some believe democracy is procedural in nature; they define *democracy* as a form of government in which the people govern through
certain institutional mechanisms. Others hold to substantive theory,
claiming a government is democratic if its policies promote civil liberties and rights.

In this book, we use the procedural conception of democracy, distinguishing between direct and indirect (representative) democracy. In a direct democracy, all citizens gather to govern themselves according to the
principles of universal participation, political equality, and majority rule.
In an indirect democracy, the citizens elect representatives to govern for
them. If a representative government is elected mostly in accordance
with the three principles just listed and is also usually responsive to public opinion, then it qualifies as a democracy.

Procedural democratic theory has produced rival institutional models
of democratic government. The classical majoritarian model assumes
that people are knowledgeable about government, that they want to participate in the political process, and that they carefully and rationally
choose among candidates. But surveys of public opinion and behavior,
and voter turnouts, show that this is not the case for most Americans.
The pluralist model of democracy was devised to accommodate these
findings. It argues that democracy in a complex society requires only
that government allow private interests to organize and to press their

competing claims openly in the political arena. It differs from elite theory by arguing that different minorities win on different issues. Pluralist democracy works better in a decentralized, organizationally complex government structure than in a centralized, hierarchical one.

In Chapter 1, we talked about three political values—freedom, order, and equality. Here, we've described two models of democracy—majoritarian and pluralist. These five concepts are critical to an understanding of American government. The values discussed in the last chapter underlie the two questions with which the text began:

- Which is better: to live under a government that allows individuals complete freedom to do whatever they please or under one that enforces strict law and order?
- Which is better: to allow businesses and private clubs to choose their customers and members or to pass laws that require them to admit and serve everyone, regardless of race or sex?

The models of democracy described here lead to another:

- Which is better: a government that is highly responsive to public opinion on all matters or one that responds deliberately to organized groups that argue their cases effectively?

If by the end of this book you understand the issues involved in answering these questions, you will have learned a great deal about American government.

KEY TERMS

autocracy
oligarchy
democracy
procedural democratic theory
universal participation
political equality
majority rule
direct democracy
representative democracy
responsiveness

substantive democratic theory
minority rights
majoritarian model of democracy
referendum
initiative
interest group
pluralist model of democracy
elite theory

SELECTED READINGS

Barber, Benjamin R. *Strong Democracy: Participatory Politics for a New Age.* Berkeley, Calif.: University of California Press, 1984. Barber favors a "strong democracy," a government that features a high degree of participation by individuals, much as a direct democracy does. He suggests specific institutional reforms to stimulate civic discussion and popular participation in government.

Cronin, Thomas E. *Direct Democracy.* Cambridge, Mass.: Harvard University Press, 1989. Cronin thoroughly examines the experience of the states with referenda and initiatives, and concludes that they have been used in a sensible, moderate manner.

Dahl, Robert A. *Democracy and Its Critics.* New Haven: Yale University Press, 1989. The nation's leading expert on pluralist theory examines the basic foundations of democracy. Dahl defends democracy against a variety of criticisms that have focused on its shortcomings.

Green, Philip. *Retrieving Democracy: In Search of Civic Equality.* Totowa, N.J.: Rowman and Allanheld, 1985. Green contends that representative government is "pseudodemocracy" because government is not under the direct control of the people. He argues for "egalitarian democracy," a society of truly equal citizens, and urges fundamental economic reforms to produce a redistribution of wealth, which would facilitate direct democracy.

Mansbridge, Jane. *Beyond Adversary Democracy.* New York: Basic Books, 1982. Mansbridge contrasts "adversary democracy," the kind of open contest that occurs among groups in a large nation, with "unitary democracy," a cooperative form of decision making based on common rather than opposing interests. She illustrates unitary democracy with two case studies of decision making: one in a New England village, the other in an urban crisis center.

Spitz, Elaine. *Majority Rule.* Chatham, N.J.: Chatham House, 1984. Spitz reviews the various meanings of *majority* and *rule* and the place of majority rule in democratic theory, then goes beyond the narrow definition of *majority rule* as a method of deciding between policies. She argues that majoritarianism should be viewed as a "social practice" among people who want to hold their society together when making decisions.

PART

TWO

Foundations of American Government

THE
DECLARATION OF INDEPENDENCE
THE
CONSTITUTION
OF THE
UNITED STATES OF AMERICA
AND THE
BILL OF RIGHTS

3 THE CONSTITUTION

THE MIDNIGHT BURGLARS made a mistake. It led to their capture in the early hours of June 17, 1972, and triggered a constitutional struggle that eventually involved the president of the United States, the Congress, and the Supreme Court. The burglars' mistake seems small: They left a piece of tape over the lock they had tripped to enter the Watergate office and apartment complex in Washington, D.C. But a security guard discovered their tampering and called the police, who surprised the burglars in the offices of the Democratic National Committee at 2:30 A.M. They arrested five men—four Cuban exiles and a former CIA agent.

The arrests took place a month before the 1972 Democratic National Convention. Investigative reporting by Carl Bernstein and Bob Woodward of the *Washington Post*, and a simultaneous criminal investigation by assistant United States attorney Earl J. Silbert and his staff, uncovered a link between the Watergate burglary and the forthcoming election.[1] The burglars were carrying the telephone number of another former CIA agent, now working in the White House. At a news conference on June 22, President Richard Nixon said, "The White House has had no involvement whatsoever in this particular incident."[2]

At its convention in July, the Democratic party nominated Senator George McGovern of South Dakota to oppose Nixon in the presidential election. McGovern tried to make the break-in at the Democratic headquarters a campaign issue, but the voters either didn't understand or didn't care. In November 1972, Richard Nixon was re-elected president of the United States, winning forty-nine of fifty states in one of the largest electoral landslides in American history.

The events that followed are described in Feature 3.1. Here it need only be noted that the Watergate affair posed one of the most serious challenges to the constitutional order of modern American government. The incident ultimately developed into a struggle over the rule of law between the presidency on the one hand and Congress and the courts on the other. President Nixon attempted to use the powers of his office to hide his tampering with the electoral process. In the end, the cover-up was thwarted by the Constitution and by leaders who believed in the Constitution. The constitutional principle of separation of powers among the executive, legislative, and judicial branches prevented the president from controlling the Watergate investigation. The principle of checks and balances allowed Congress to threaten Nixon with impeachment and removal from office. The belief that Nixon had violated the Constitution finally prompted members of his own party to support impeachment.

Nixon resigned the presidency after little more than a year and a half into his second term. In some countries, such an irregular change in government leadership provides an opportunity for a palace coup, an armed revolution, or a military dictatorship. But here, significantly, there was no political violence after Nixon's resignation; in fact, none was expected. Constitutional order in the United States had been put to a test, and it passed with high honors.

This chapter poses some questions about the Constitution. How did it evolve? What form did it take? How is it altered? What values does it

Senators Investigate a President

The Select Committee on Presidential Campaign Activities, shown here, was created by the Senate in 1973 to investigate events surrounding Watergate. Its chairman was Democrat Sam Ervin (seated at the center); its ranking minority member was Republican Howard Baker (to Ervin's right). Baker was prominent during another congressional investigation into possible abuses of executive power, but not as a senator. He was President Ronald Reagan's chief of staff during the Iran-Contra hearings in 1987.

reflect? And which model of democracy—majoritarian or pluralist—does it fit best?

The Revolutionary Roots of the Constitution

The Constitution itself is just 4,300 words. But those 4,300 words define the basic structure of our national government. It is a comprehensive document that divides the government into three branches and describes the powers of those branches, their relationships, and the interaction between government and governed. The Constitution makes itself the supreme law of the land and binds every government official to support it.

Most Americans revere the Constitution as political "scripture." To charge that a political action is unconstitutional is like claiming that it is unholy. And so the Constitution has taken on a symbolism that has strengthened its authority as the basis of American government. Their strong belief in the Constitution has led many politicians to abandon party for principle when constitutional issues are in question. The power and symbolic value of the Constitution were proved once again in the Watergate affair.

The U.S. Constitution, written in 1787 for an agricultural society huddled along the coast of a wild new land, now guides the political life of a massive urban society in the nuclear age. The stability of the Constitution—and of the political system it created—is all the more remarkable because the Constitution itself was rooted in revolution. In fact, the U.S. Constitution (along with its immediate predecessor, the Articles of

FEATURE 3.1   *Watergate*

The frightening details of the Watergate story did not unfold until after President Nixon's re-election in November 1972. Two months later, in January 1973, seven men went to trial for the break-in itself. They included the five burglars and two men closely connected with the president: E. Howard Hunt (a former CIA agent and White House consultant) and G. Gordon Liddy (counsel to the Committee for the Re-election of the President, or CREEP). The burglars entered guilty pleas. Hunt and Liddy were convicted by a jury. In a letter to the sentencing judge, one of the burglars charged that they had been pressured to plead guilty, that perjury had been committed at the trial, and that others were involved in the break-in. The Senate launched its own investigation of the matter. It set up the Select Committee on Presidential Campaign Activities, chaired by a self-styled constitutional authority, Democratic Senator Sam Ervin from North Carolina.

The testimony before the Ervin committee was shocking. The deputy director of Nixon's re-election committee, Jeb Magruder, confessed to perjury and implicated John Mitchell, Nixon's campaign manager and former attorney general, in planning the burglary. Special Counsel to the President John Dean said that the president had been a party to a cover-up of the crime for eight months. And there were more disclosures of other political burglaries and of forged State Department cables that were intended to embarrass a possible Democratic candidate, Senator Edward M. Kennedy of Massachusetts.

A stunned nation watching the televised proceedings learned that the president had secretly tape-recorded all of his conversations in the White House. The Ervin committee asked for the tapes. Nixon refused to produce them, citing the separation of powers between the legislative and executive branches and claiming "executive privilege" to withhold information from Congress.

In the midst of all this, Nixon's vice president, Spiro T. Agnew, resigned while under investigation for income tax evasion. The Twenty-fifth Amendment to the Constitution (1967) gave the president the power to choose a new vice president with the consent of Congress. Nixon nominated Gerald Ford, then the Republican leader in the House of Representatives. On December 6, 1973, Ford became the first appointed vice president in the nation's history.

Meanwhile, Nixon was fighting subpoenas demanding the White House tapes. Ordered by a federal court to deliver specific tapes, Nixon proposed a compromise. He would release written summaries of the taped conversations. Archibald Cox, the special prosecutor of the attorney general's office, refused the compromise. Nixon retaliated with the "Saturday Night massacre," in which Attorney General Elliot L. Richardson and his deputy resigned, Cox was fired, and the special prosecutor's office was abolished.

The ensuing furor forced Nixon to appoint another special prosecutor, Leon Jaworski, who eventually brought indictments against Nixon's closest aides. Nixon himself was named as an unindicted co-conspirator. Both the special prosecutor and the defendants wanted the White House tapes, but Nixon continued to resist. Finally, on July 24, 1974, the Supreme Court ruled that the president had to hand over the tapes. At almost the same time, the House Judiciary Committee voted to recommend to

Confederation) was the first of several national constitutions that stemmed from revolution. Three others—the French constitution of 1791, the Mexican constitution of 1917, and the Russian constitution of 1918—were also products of revolutionary movements.

The noted historian Samuel Eliot Morison observed that "the American Revolution was not fought to *obtain* freedom, but to *preserve* the liberties that Americans already had as colonials."[3] The U.S. Constitution was designed to prevent anarchy by forging a union of states. To understand the values embedded in the Constitution, we must understand its historical roots. They lie in colonial America, in the revolt against the full House that Nixon be impeached for, or charged with, three offenses: impeding and obstructing the investigation of the Watergate break-in, abuse of power and repeated violation of the constitutional rights of citizens, and defiance of House subpoenas.

The Judiciary Committee vote was decisive but far from unanimous. On August 5, however, the committee and the country finally learned the contents of the tapes released under the Supreme Court order. They revealed that Nixon had been aware of a cover-up on June 23, 1972, just six days after the break-in. He had also issued an order to the FBI, saying, "Don't go any further in this case, period!"* Now even the eleven Republican members of the House Judiciary Committee, who had opposed the first vote to impeach, were ready to vote against Nixon.

Faced with the collapse of his support and likely impeachment by the full House, Nixon resigned the presidency on August 9, 1974. Vice President Gerald Ford became the first unelected president of the United States. A month later, acting within his constitutional powers, Ford pardoned private citizen Richard Nixon for all federal crimes that he had committed or may have committed. When questioned by Congress about the circumstances surrounding the pardon, President Ford said, "There was no deal, period." Others were not so fortunate. Three members of the Nixon cabinet (two attorneys general and a secretary of commerce) were convicted and sentenced for their crimes in the Watergate affair. Nixon's White House chief of staff, H. R. Haldeman, and his domestic affairs adviser, John Ehrlichman, were convicted of conspiracy, obstruction of justice, and per-

jury. Other officials were tried, and most were convicted, on related charges.**

Watergate Postscript

John Dean is an investment banker in Los Angeles.

John Ehrlichman writes spy novels in Santa Fe. In 1987, he appeared in a television commercial endorsing a brand of ice cream; negative feedback from viewers caused the commercial to be removed from the air.

H. R. Haldeman works as a venture capitalist in Santa Barbara; a recent project is the construction of a $110 million office complex in Moscow. He no longer wears a crewcut, his trademark during the Watergate years.

E. Howard Hunt is a novelist. He has also been trying to find investors for a musical he's written about Claus von Bulow, the Newport millionaire convicted and later acquitted of trying to kill his wife.

G. Gordon Liddy owns a security firm and is a twice-a-week talk-show host on a radio station in Glendale, California. He has acted in several movies and television shows, including *Street Asylum* and *Miami Vice*. In 1990, he became a spokesman in print advertisements for a wine company.

Jeb Magruder is the pastor of a Presbyterian church in Lexington, Kentucky, and has also served as the head of a commission on ethics and values in Columbus, Ohio.

* *The Encyclopedia of American Facts and Dates* (New York: Crowell, 1979), p. 946.

** Richard B. Morris, ed., *Encyclopedia of American History* (New York: Harper & Row, 1976), p. 544.

British rule, and in the failure of the Articles of Confederation that governed the new nation after the Revolution.

Freedom in Colonial America

Although they were British subjects, the American colonists in the eighteenth century enjoyed a degree of freedom denied most people in the world. They were able to inherit property, to attend church (but perhaps not *any* church), to enter a trade or profession with few of the restrictions imposed by Europe's feudal past.

The Founders' Nation

At the treaty negotiations that ended the Revolution, this detailed map, first drawn in 1755, was used to establish the boundaries of the United States. This was the country for which the founders fashioned a constitution in 1787. The remarkable document they created, written to govern a small society spread along the coast of a largely uncharted land, is equally powerful and authoritative today, in a society of far greater size and complexity.

By 1763, Britain and the colonies had reached a compromise between imperial control and colonial self-government. America's foreign affairs and overseas trade were controlled by the king and Parliament, the British legislature; the rest was left to home rule. But the cost of administering the colonies was substantial. The colonists needed protection from the French and their Indian allies during the Seven Years' War (1756–1763), which was an expensive undertaking. Because Americans benefited the most, contended their English countrymen, Americans should bear that cost.

The Road to Revolution

The British believed that taxing the colonies was the obvious way to meet administrative costs; the colonists did not agree. Like most people, they did not want to be taxed. And they especially did not want to be taxed by a distant government in which they had no representation. During that period, a series of direct taxes was imposed on the colonies by the Crown. In each instance, public opposition was widespread and immediate.

A group of citizens—merchants, lawyers, prosperous tradesmen—created an intercolonial association, the Sons of Liberty. This group destroyed taxed items and forced official distributors to resign. In October 1765, Charleston, South Carolina, residents celebrated the forced resignation of the colony's stamp distributor by displaying a British flag with the word *liberty* across it. (They were horrified a few months later when local slaves paraded through the streets calling for "Liberty!"[4])

Women also participated in the resistance to the hated taxes. They joined in symbolic displays of patriotism. Young townswomen, calling themselves the Daughters of Liberty, met in public to spin homespun cloth and encourage the elimination of British cloth from colonial markets. They consumed American food and drank local herbal tea as symbols of their opposition.[5]

On the night of December 16, 1773, colonists reacted to a British duty on tea by giving the Boston Tea Party. A mob boarded three ships and

A Uniquely American Protest

Americans protested the Tea Act (1773) by holding the Boston Tea Party (see background, left) and by employing a unique form of punishment—tarring and feathering. An early treatise on the subject offered the following instructions: "First, strip a person naked, then heat the tar until it is thin, and pour upon the naked flesh, or rub it over with a tar brush. After which, sprinkle decently upon the tar, whilst it is yet warm, as many feathers as will stick to it."

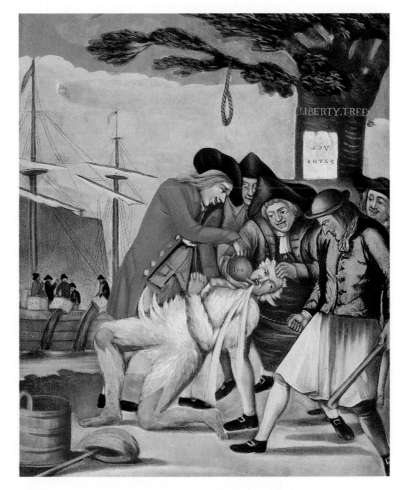

emptied 342 chests of that valuable substance into Boston Harbor. This act of defiance and destruction could not be ignored. "The die is now cast," wrote George III. "The Colonies must either submit or triumph."[6] In an attempt to reassert British control over its recalcitrant colonists, Parliament passed the Coercive (or Intolerable) Acts (1774). One of the acts imposed a blockade on Boston until the tea was paid for; another gave royal governors the power to quarter British soldiers in private homes. Now the taxation issue was secondary; more important was the conflict between British demands for order and American demands for liberty. The Virginia and Massachusetts assemblies summoned a **continental congress,** an assembly that would speak and act for the people of all the colonies.

The First Continental Congress met in Philadelphia in September 1774. All the colonies except Georgia sent representatives. The objective of the assembly was to restore harmony between Great Britain and the American colonies. In an effort at unity, all colonies were given the same voting power—one vote each. A leader, called the "president," was elected. (The terms *president* and *congress* in American government trace their origins to the First Continental Congress.) In October 1774, the delegates adopted a statement of rights and principles, many of which later found their way into the Declaration of Independence and the Constitution. For example, the congress claimed a right "to life, liberty, and property" and a right "peaceably to assemble, consider of their grievances, and petition the king." Then the congress adjourned, planning to reconvene in May 1775.

Revolutionary Action

By early 1775, however, a movement that the colonists themselves were calling a revolution had already begun. The colonists in Massachusetts were fighting the British at Concord and Lexington. Delegates to the Second Continental Congress, meeting in May, faced a dilemma: Should they prepare for war? Or should they try to reconcile with Britain? As conditions deteriorated, the Second Continental Congress remained in session, to serve as the government of the colony-states.

On June 7, 1776, the Virginia delegation called on the Continental Congress to resolve "that these United Colonies are, and of right ought to be, free and Independent States, that they are absolved from all allegiance to the British Crown, and that all political connection between them and the State of Great Britain is, and ought to be, totally dissolved." The congress debated but did not immediately adopt the resolution. A committee of five men was appointed to prepare a proclamation expressing the colonies' reasons for declaring independence.

The Declaration of Independence

Thomas Jefferson, a young farmer and lawyer from Virginia, was a member of the committee. Because of his "peculiar felicity of expression," he prepared the draft of the proclamation. The document Jefferson drafted—the **Declaration of Independence**—was substantially unchanged by the committee and the congress. It remains a cherished statement of

Voting for Independence

The Second Continental Congress voted for independence on July 2, 1776. John Adams of Massachusetts viewed the day "as the most memorable epocha [significant event] in the history of America." In this painting by John Trumbull, the drafting committee presents the Declaration of Independence to the patriots who would later sign it. The committee, grouped in front of the desk, consisted of (from left to right): Adams, Roger Sherman (Conn.), Robert Livingston (N.Y.), Thomas Jefferson (Va.), and Benjamin Franklin (Pa.).

our heritage, expressing simply, clearly, and rationally the arguments in support of separation from Great Britain.

The principles underlying the declaration were rooted in the writings of the English philosopher John Locke and expressed many times by speakers in congress and in the colonial assemblies. Locke argued that people have God-given, or natural, rights that are inalienable—that is, they cannot be taken away by any government. In addition, Locke believed that all legitimate political authority exists to preserve these natural rights, and this authority is based on the consent of those who are governed. The idea of consent is derived from **social contract theory,** which states that the people agree to set up rulers for certain purposes and that they have the right to resist or remove rulers who persist in acting against those purposes.[7]

Jefferson used similar arguments in the Declaration of Independence. Although he was not an orator, Jefferson was a brilliant wordsmith. His "impassioned simplicity of statement" reverberates to this day with democratic faith:

> We hold these truths to be self-evident, that all men are created equal, that they are endowed by their Creator with certain unalienable Rights, that among these are Life, Liberty and the pursuit of Happiness.

The First Continental Congress had declared in 1774 that the colonists were entitled to "life, liberty, and property." Jefferson reformulated the objectives of government as "Life, Liberty, and the pursuit of Happiness." And he continued:

> That to secure these rights, Governments are instituted among Men, deriving their just powers from the consent of the governed. That whenever any Form of Government becomes destructive of these ends, it is the Right of the People to alter or to abolish it, and to institute new Government, laying its foundation on such Principles and organizing its Powers in such form, as to them shall seem most likely to effect their Safety and Happiness.

COMPARED WITH WHAT?   3.1

Exporting the American Revolution

For more than forty years, Czechoslovakia lay in the grip of the Soviet Union. But over the course of a few weeks at the end of 1989, a revolution rooted in the demand for freedom brought Czechoslovakia to independence. Here is how it began:

PRAGUE, Nov. 27—Soon after the strike began today, Zdenek Janicek, a brewery worker, rose on a platform in grimy overalls and began to speak.

"We hold these truths to be self-evident," he said, "that all men are created equal, that they are endowed by their creator with certain unalienable rights, that among these rights are life, liberty, and the pursuit of happiness."

For the nearly 1,500 workers who gather to listen to him, today was a day of declaring independence from the stifling Communist leadership that has ruled Czechoslovakia for 40 years. Like millions of workers throughout the nation, workers here walked off their jobs at noon today in a two-hour general strike demanding greater democracy and an end to the Communist Party's monopoly on power.

"Americans understood these rights more than 200 years ago," Mr. Janicek said after reciting part of the Declaration of Independence to his co-workers. "We are only now learning to believe that we are entitled to the same rights."

Source: "Millions of Czechoslovaks Increase Pressure on Party with 2-Hour General Strike," *New York Times*, 28 November 1989, p. 1. Copyright © 1989 by The New York Times Company. Reprinted by permission.

He went on to list the many deliberate acts of the king that were working against the legitimate ends of government. Finally, he declared that the colonies were "Free and Independent States," with no political connection to Great Britain.

The major premise of the Declaration of Independence is that the people have a right to revolt when they determine that their government is denying them their legitimate rights. The long list of the king's actions was evidence of that denial. And so the people had the right to rebel, to form a new government. (See Compared with What? 3.1.)

On July 2, 1776, the Second Continental Congress finally voted for independence. The vote was by state, and the motion carried 11 to 0. (Rhode Island was not present, and the New York delegation, lacking instructions, did not cast its "yea" vote until July 15.) Two days later, the Declaration of Independence was approved with very few changes. Jefferson's original draft had indicted the king for allowing the slave trade to continue. But representatives from Georgia and South Carolina insisted that this phrase be deleted before they would vote for approval. Other representatives removed language they thought would arouse the colonists. But, in the end, Jefferson's compelling words were left almost exactly as he had written them.

The vote for independence came on July 2; the Declaration of Independence was adopted, but not signed, on July 4. By August, fifty-five revolutionaries had signed it, pledging "our Lives, our Fortunes and our sacred Honor" in support of rebellion from the world's most powerful nation.

This was no empty pledge: An act of rebellion was treason. If they had lost the revolutionary war, the signers would have faced a gruesome fate. The punishment for treason was hanging, drawing, and quartering—the victim is first hanged until half-dead from strangulation, then disemboweled, and finally cut into four quarters while still alive. We celebrate the Fourth of July with fireworks and flag waving, parades and picnics. We sometimes forget that the Revolution was a matter of life and death.

The War of Independence lasted far longer than anyone expected. It began in a moment of confusion, when a shot rang out while British soldiers approached the town of Lexington on the way to Concord, Massachusetts, on April 19, 1775. It ended with Lord Cornwallis's surrender of his six-thousand-man army at Yorktown, Virginia, on October 19, 1781. It was a costly war: There were more dead and wounded in relation to the population than in any other conflict except the Civil War.[8]

With hindsight, of course, we can see that the British were engaged in an arduous and, perhaps, hopeless conflict. America was simply too vast to subdue without instituting complete military rule there. Britain also had to transport men and supplies over the enormous distance of the Atlantic Ocean. Finally, although the Americans had neither paid troops nor professional soldiers, they were fighting for a cause—the defense of their liberty. The British never understood the power of this fighting faith.

From Revolution to Confederation

By declaring their independence from England, the colonies were leaving themselves without any real central government. So the revolutionaries proclaimed the creation of a *republic.* Strictly speaking, a **republic** is a government without a monarch, but the term had come to mean a government rooted in the consent of the governed, in which power is exercised by representatives who are responsible to the governed. A republic need not be a democracy, and this was fine with the founders; at that time *democracy* was associated with mob rule and instability (see Chapter 2). The revolutionaries were less concerned with who would control their new government than with limiting the powers of that government. They had revolted in the name of liberty, and now they wanted a government with sharply defined powers. To make sure they got one, they meant to define its structure and powers in writing.

The Articles of Confederation

Barely a week after the Declaration of Independence was signed, the Second Continental Congress received a committee report on "Articles of Confederation and Perpetual Union." A **confederation** is a loose association of independent states that agree to cooperate on specified matters. In a confederation, the states retain their **sovereignty,** which means that each has supreme power within its borders. The central government is weak; it can only coordinate, not control, the actions of its sovereign states. Consequently, the individual states are strong.

The congress debated the **Articles of Confederation,** the compact among the thirteen original states that established a government of the United States, for more than a year. The Articles were adopted by the Continental Congress on November 15, 1777. They took effect on March 1, 1781, following approval by all thirteen states. For more than three years, then, Americans fought a revolution without an effective government. Raising money, troops, and supplies for the war daunted and exhausted the leadership.

The Articles jealously guarded state sovereignty; their provisions clearly reflected the delegates' fears that a strong central government would be substituted for British rule. Article II, for example, stated:

> Each State retains its sovereignty, freedom, and independence, and every Power, Jurisdiction and right, which is not by this confederation expressly delegated to the United States, in Congress assembled.

Under the Articles, each state, regardless of its size, had one vote in the congress. Votes on financing the war against Britain and other important issues required the consent of at least nine of the thirteen states. The common danger—the war—forced the young republic to function under the Articles, but this first try at a government was inadequate to the task. The delegates had succeeded in crafting a national government that was largely powerless.

The Articles failed for at least four reasons: First, they did not give the national government the power to tax. As a result, the congress had to plead for funds with which to conduct the continuing war with Great Britain and to carry on the affairs of the new nation. Second, except for the appointment of a presiding officer of the congress (the president), the Articles made no provision for an independent leadership position to direct the government. This omission was planned—the colonists feared the re-establishment of a monarchy—but it left the nation without a leader. Third, the Articles did not allow the national government to regulate interstate and foreign commerce. (When John Adams proposed that the confederation enter into a commercial treaty with Britain after the war, he was asked, "Would you like one treaty or thirteen, Mr. Adams?"[9]) Finally, the Articles themselves could not be amended without the unanimous agreement of the congress and the assent of all the state legislatures; thus, each state had the power to veto any changes in the confederation.

The goal of the delegates who drew up the Articles of Confederation was to retain power in the states. This was consistent with republicanism, which viewed the remote power of a national government as a danger to liberty. In this sense alone, the Articles were a grand success. They completely hobbled the infant government.

Disorder Under the Confederation

Once the Revolution ended and independence was a reality, it became clear that the national government had neither the economic nor the military power to function. Americans, freed from wartime austerity, rushed to purchase goods from abroad. The national government's efforts

Farmers' Protest Stirs Rebellion
Shays' Rebellion (1786–1787) became a symbol for the urgent need to maintain order. Here, farmers led by Daniel Shays close the courthouse to prevent farm foreclosures by creditors. The uprising demonstrated the military weakness of the confederation: The national government could not muster funds to fight the insurgents.

to restrict foreign imports were blocked by exporting states, which feared retaliation from their foreign customers. Debt mounted and, for many, bankruptcy followed.

The problem was particularly severe in Massachusetts, where high interest rates and high state taxes were forcing farmers into bankruptcy. In 1786, Daniel Shays, a revolutionary war veteran, marched on a western Massachusetts courthouse with fifteen hundred supporters armed with barrel staves and pitchforks. They wanted to close the courthouse to prevent the foreclosure of farms by creditors. Later they attacked an arsenal. This revolt against the established order was called **Shays' Rebellion;** it continued into 1787.

Massachusetts appealed to the confederation for help. Horrified by the threat of domestic upheaval, the congress approved a $530,000 requisition for the establishment of a national army. But the plan failed: Every state except Virginia rejected the request for money. Finally the governor of Massachusetts called out the militia and restored order.[10]

The rebellion demonstrated the impotence of the confederation and the urgent need to suppress insurrection and maintain domestic order. It was proof to skeptics that Americans could not govern themselves.

From Confederation to Constitution

Order, the original purpose of government, was breaking down under the Articles of Confederation. The "league of friendship" envisioned in the Articles was not enough to hold the nation together in peacetime.

Some states had taken halting steps toward a change in government. In 1785, Massachusetts asked the congress to revise the Articles of Confederation, but the congress took no action. In 1786, Virginia invited the states to attend a convention at Annapolis to explore revisions aimed at improving commercial regulation. The meeting was both a failure and a success. Although only five states sent delegates to Annapolis, the delegates seized the opportunity to call for another meeting, with a far broader mission, in Philadelphia the next year. That convention would be charged with "devis[ing] such further provisions as shall appear . . . necessary to render the constitution of the Federal Government adequate to the exigencies of the Union." The congress later agreed to the convention but limited its mission to "the sole and express purpose of revising the Articles of Confederation."

Shays' Rebellion lent a sense of urgency to the task before the Philadelphia convention. Congress's inability to confront the rebellion was evidence that a stronger national government was necessary to preserve order and property—to protect the states from internal as well as external dangers. "While the Declaration was directed against an excess of authority," remarked Supreme Court Justice Robert H. Jackson some 150 years later, "the Constitution [that followed the Articles of Confederation] was directed against anarchy."[11]

Twelve of the thirteen states named a total of seventy-four delegates to convene in Philadelphia in May 1787. (Rhode Island, derisively renamed "Rogue Island" by a Boston newspaper, was the one exception. The state legislature sulkily rejected participation because it feared a strong national government.) Fifty-five delegates eventually showed up at the State House in Philadelphia, but no more than thirty were present at any one time during that sweltering spring and summer (see Feature 3.2). Although well versed in ideas, they subscribed to the view that "experience must be our guide. Reason may mislead us." The delegates' goal was to fashion a government that would maintain order and preserve liberty.

The Constitutional Convention—at the time, it was called the *Federal Convention*—officially opened on May 25, when representatives of seven states were present to make a quorum. Remember that a year earlier, at Annapolis, five states had called for the convention to draft a new, stronger charter for the national government. The spirit of the Annapolis meeting seems to have pervaded the Constitutional Convention, even though the delegates were authorized only to "revise" the Articles of

FEATURE 3.2   *Behind the Scenes in 1787*

When the framers of the Constitution convened . . . on May 25, 1787, to try to keep the American Union from falling to pieces, Philadelphia was the foremost city of America.

It was a place of urban culture and accomplishment. Its streets were crowded with people of diverse national origins. Sailors from many countries mixed with leather-clad frontiersmen and with Shawnee and Delaware Indians from the forest.

But the city also reflected the hard life that most Americans lived then. More than half the population existed on the edge of poverty. Prostitution and disease were widespread. Many streets were open sewers. Flies and mosquitoes added their torment to the oppressive heat of that summer, the worst in nearly 40 years. . . .

Court records revealed much child and spouse abuse. Drunkenness was pervasive. Servants of the wealthy, including those of George Washington, spent their evenings in the taverns of a rough waterfront district called Helltown.

Independence Hall, then called the Pennsylvania State House, had seen better days: Its steeple had become shaky and had to be taken down. Across Walnut Street was a four-story stone prison. Prisoners called out for alms and cursed passers-by who failed to oblige.

When George Washington arrived in Philadelphia, he perceived a radical, divisive atmosphere that reflected the country's mood at a time when dissolution of the Union seemed likely and foreign powers waited to pounce. That perception is said to have contributed to a decision to keep the Constitutional Convention's proceedings secret. . . .

There was no press coverage. The public did not learn anything about what had gone on until after the convention adjourned on Sept. 17. Two days later, the *Pennsylvania Packet* published the Constitution, devoting its entire issue to the text. Newspapers everywhere followed suit. No political story had commanded so much space until then.

Sometimes, extraordinary measures were taken to maintain the secrecy. It seemed impossible to keep Benjamin Franklin quiet, wrote Catherine Drinker Bowen in *Miracle at Philadelphia,* a respected history of the convention. As a result, she reported, "a discreet member" of the convention attended Franklin's convivial dinners to head off the conversation whenever he appeared ready to divulge a secret.

The delegates stayed at private homes and spent many of their evenings talking and plotting strategy at the City Tavern, the Black Horse, the George and the Indian Queen. They drank a lot: The bill for one dinner party of 12 included sixty bottles of wine.

That may be one reason why so many delegates, as historians have noted, were so corpulent. Few stood more than about 5 feet 8 inches tall, but many weighed about 200 pounds or more. The most striking exception was Washington. Every inch the general at 6 feet 2 inches, with wide shoulders and narrow hips, he towered above the convention both literally and figuratively.

The framers were not demi-gods. But many historians believe that their like will not be seen again in one place. Highly educated, they typically were fluent in Latin and Greek. Products of the Enlightenment, they relied on classical Liberalism for the Constitution's philosophical underpinnings.

They were also veterans of the political intrigues of their states and as such were highly practical politicians who knew how to maneuver.

Still, if it were not for Washington, some historians believe, the convention would never have succeeded. His character and authority kept the convention from flying apart.

One facet of his authority is revealed in an anecdote reported by Mrs. Bowen. Gouverneur Morris, a Pennsylvania delegate who drafted the Constitution's final version, accepted a bet proposed by Alexander Hamilton. To win it, Morris had to greet Washington with a slap on the back. That was just not done. "Well, General!" Morris said, and laid his hand on Washington's shoulder. The general said nothing, but Morris later said that Washington's imperious look made him wish . . . that he could sink through the floor.

James Madison, Father of the Constitution

Although he dismissed the accolade, Madison deserved it more than anyone else. Like most fathers, he exercised a powerful influence in debates (and was on the losing side of more than half of them).

Confederation. Within the first week of debate, Edmund Randolph of Virginia had presented a long list of changes, suggested by fellow Virginian James Madison, that would replace the weak confederation of states with a powerful national government. The delegates unanimously agreed to debate Randolph's proposal, which was called the *Virginia Plan.* Almost immediately, then, they rejected the idea of amending the Articles of Confederation, working instead to create an entirely new constitution.

The Virginia Plan

The **Virginia Plan** served as the basis of the convention's deliberations for the rest of the summer. It made several important proposals for a strong central government:

- That the powers of the government be divided among three separate branches: a **legislative branch,** for making laws; an **executive branch,** for enforcing laws; and a **judicial branch,** for interpreting laws.

- That the legislature consist of two houses. The first would be chosen by the people; the second by the members of the first house from among persons nominated by the state legislatures.

- That representation in the legislature be in proportion to taxes paid to the national government, or in proportion to the free population of each state.

- That an executive of unspecified size be selected by the legislature and serve for a single term.

- That the national judiciary include one or more supreme courts and other lower courts, with judges appointed for life by the legislature.

- That the executive and a number of national judges serve as a council of revision, to approve or veto (disapprove) legislative acts. Their veto could be overridden, however, by a vote of both houses of the legislature.

- That the range of powers of all three branches be far greater than that assigned the national government by the Articles of Confederation and include the power of the legislature to override state laws.

By proposing a powerful national legislature that could override state laws, the Virginia Plan clearly advocated a new form of government. It was a mixed structure, with more authority over the states and new authority over the people.

Madison was a monumental force in the ensuing debate on the proposals. He kept records of the proceedings that reveal his frequent and brilliant participation and give us insight into his thinking about freedom, order, and equality.

For example, his proposal that senators serve a nine-year term reveals his thinking about equality. Madison foresaw an increase "of those who will labor under all the hardships of life, and secretly sigh for a more equal distribution of its blessings. These may in time outnumber those who are placed above the feelings of indigence."[12] Power, then, could flow into the hands of the numerous poor. The stability of the Senate, however, with its long elective term of nine years and election by the state legislatures, would provide a barrier against the "sighs of the poor" for more equality. Although most of the delegates shared Madison's apprehension of equality, the nine-year term was voted down.

The constitution that emerged from the convention bore only partial resemblance to the document Madison wanted to create. Of the seventy-one specific proposals that Madison endorsed, he ended up on the losing side on forty of them.[13] And the parts of the Virginia Plan that were ultimately adopted in the Constitution were not adopted without challenge. Conflict revolved primarily around the basis of representation in the legislature, the method of choosing legislators, and the structure of the executive branch.

The New Jersey Plan

When it appeared that much of the Virginia Plan would be carried by the large states, the smaller states united in opposition. William Paterson of New Jersey introduced an alternative set of nine resolutions, written to preserve the spirit of the Articles of Confederation by amending rather than replacing them. His **New Jersey Plan** included the following proposals:

- That a single-chamber legislature have the power to raise revenue and regulate commerce.
- That the states have equal representation in the legislature and choose the members of that body.
- That a multiperson executive be elected by the legislature, with powers similar to those listed in the Virginia Plan but without the right to veto legislation.
- That a supreme judiciary be created with a very limited jurisdiction. (There was no provision for a system of national courts.)
- That the acts of the legislature be binding on the states; that is, be regarded as the "supreme law of the respective states," with force used to compel obedience.

The New Jersey Plan was defeated in the first major convention vote, 7–3. However, the small states had enough support to force a compromise on the issue of representation in the legislature. Table 3.1 compares the New Jersey Plan with the Virginia Plan.

The Great Compromise

The Virginia Plan provided for a two-chamber legislature, with representation in both chambers based on population. The idea of having two chambers was never seriously challenged, but the idea of representation according to population stirred up heated and prolonged debate. The smaller states demanded equal representation for all states, but another

TABLE 3.1   *Major Differences Between the Virginia Plan and the New Jersey Plan*

Characteristic	Virginia Plan	New Jersey Plan
Legislature	Two chambers	One chamber
Legislative power	Derived from the people	Derived from the states
Executive	Unspecified size	More than one person
Decision rule	Majority	Extraordinary majority
State laws	Legislature can override	Compel obedience
Executive removal	By Congress	By a majority of the states
Courts	National judiciary	No provision
Ratification	By the people	By the states

vote rejected that concept for the House of Representatives. The debate continued. Finally, the Connecticut delegation moved that each state have an equal vote in the Senate. Still another poll showed that the delegations were equally divided on this proposal.

A committee was created to resolve the deadlock. It consisted of one delegate from each state, chosen by secret ballot. The committee worked through the Independence Day recess, then reported the **Great Compromise** (sometimes called the *Connecticut Compromise*): The House of Representatives would initially consist of fifty-six members, apportioned *according to the population of each state.* Revenue-raising acts would originate in the House. Most important, *the states would be represented equally in the Senate*, with two senators each. Senators would be selected by their state legislatures, not directly by the people.

The delegates accepted the Great Compromise. The smaller states got their equal representation; the larger states, their proportional representation. The small states might dominate the Senate and the large states might control the House, but because all legislation had to be approved by both chambers, neither group would be able to dominate the other.

Compromise on the Presidency

Contention replaced compromise when the delegates turned to the executive branch. They did agree on a one-person executive—a president—but they disagreed on how the executive would be selected and what the term of office would be. The delegates distrusted the people's judgment and the public passions they might arouse. Consequently, the delegates rejected the idea of popular election. At the same time, representatives of the smaller states feared that election by the legislature would allow the larger states to control the executive.

Once again, a committee with one member from each participating state was chosen to effect a compromise. That committee fashioned the cumbersome presidential election system that we know today as the **electoral college.** The college consists of a group of electors who are chosen for the sole purpose of selecting the president and vice president. Each state legislature would choose a number of electors equal to the number of representatives it had in Congress. Each elector would then vote for two people. The person with the most votes would become president, provided that that person had a majority of the votes; the person with the next greatest number of votes would become vice president. (This procedure was changed in 1804 by the Twelfth Amendment, which mandates separate votes for each office.) If no candidate won a majority, then the House of Representatives would choose a president, *with each state having one vote.*

The electoral college compromise removed the fear of a popular vote for president. At the same time, it satisfied the small states. If the electoral college failed to produce a president—which the delegates expected would happen—then an election by the House would give every state the same voice in the selection process.

Finally, the delegates agreed that the president's term of office should be four years and that the president should be eligible for re-election.

The delegates also realized that removing a president from office would be a very serious political matter. For that reason, they involved the other two branches of government in the process. The House alone was empowered to charge a president with "Treason, Bribery, or other high Crimes and Misdemeanors," by a majority vote. The Senate was given the sole power to try the president on the House's charges. It could convict, and thus remove, a president only by a two-thirds vote (an extraordinary majority). And the chief justice of the United States was required to preside over the Senate trial.

The Final Product

Once the delegates resolved their major disagreements, they dispatched the remaining issues relatively quickly. A committee was then appointed to organize and write up the results of the proceedings. Twenty-three resolutions had been debated and approved by the convention; these were reorganized under seven articles in the draft constitution. The Preamble, which was the last section to be drafted, begins with a phrase that would have been impossible to write when the convention opened. This single sentence contains four elements that form the foundation of the American political tradition.[14]

- *It creates a people:* "We the People of the United States" was a dramatic departure from a loose confederation of states.
- *It explains the reason for the Constitution:* "in Order to form a more perfect Union" was an indirect way of saying that the first effort, under the Articles of Confederation, had been inadequate.
- *It articulates goals:* "establish Justice, insure domestic Tranquility, provide for the common defence, promote the general Welfare, and secure the Blessings of Liberty to ourselves and our Posterity"; in other words, the government exists to promote order and freedom.
- *It fashions a government:* "do ordain and establish this Constitution for the United States of America."

FEATURE 3.3   *The Intellectual Origins of the Constitution*

The creation of the U.S. Constitution was a remarkable achievement by a young nation. However, only one of its four basic political principles was "made in America." The other three were inspired by ideas that first grew on foreign soil.

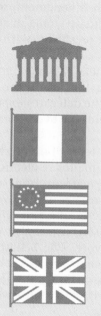

- *Republicanism.* In this form of government, power resides in the people and is exercised by their elected representatives; government is the common business of the citizens, conducted for the common good. The idea of republicanism may be traced to the Greek philosopher Aristotle (384–322 B.C.), who advocated a "mixed" constitution that contained principles of democratic and oligarchic government.
- *Federalism.* The powers of government are shared by a central body and territorial units. Citizens in a federal government are subject to two different bodies of law. Federalism is a distinctly American idea, created by the Constitutional Convention of 1787.
- *Separation of powers.* The responsibilities of government are divided among separate branches. This idea was formulated in a fragmentary way by John Locke and others, but its fullest exposition came from French philosopher Charles-Louis de Secondat Montesquieu (1689–1755).
- *Checks and balances.* The branches of government scrutinize and restrain each other. This idea was first advanced by two Englishmen, the statesman Henry St. John Bolingbroke (1678–1751) and the jurist William Blackstone (1723–1780).

The Basic Principles

In creating the Constitution, the founders relied on four political principles that together established a revolutionary new political order. These principles were republicanism, federalism, separation of powers, and checks and balances. (See Feature 3.3 for a discussion of the philosophical origins of these principles.)

Republicanism. **Republicanism** is a form of government in which power resides in the people and is exercised by their elected representatives. The framers were determined to avoid aristocracy (rule by a hereditary class), monarchy (rule by one), and direct democracy (rule by the people). A republic was both new and daring: No people had ever been governed by a republic on so vast a scale.

The framers themselves were far from sure that their government could be sustained. They had no model of republican government to follow; moreover, at the time, republican government was thought to be suitable only for small territories, where the interest of the public would be obvious and where government would be within the reach of every citizen. After the convention had ended, Benjamin Franklin was asked what sort of government the new nation would have. "A republic," he replied, "if you can keep it."

Federalism. **Federalism** is the division of power between a central government and regional units. It stands between two competing government schemes. On the one side is **unitary government**, in which all power is vested in a central government. On the other side stands confederation, a loose union with powerful states. In a confederation, the states surrender some power to a central government but retain the rest. The Articles of Confederation embodied a division of power between loosely knit states and a weak central government. The Constitution also embodied a division of power, but conferred substantial powers on a national government at the expense of the states.

According to the Constitution, the powers vested in the national and state governments are derived from the people, who remain the ultimate sovereign. National and state governments can exercise their powers over persons and property within their own spheres of authority. But, at the same time, the people can restrain both national and state governments to preserve their liberty through participating in the electoral process or amending their governing charters.

The Constitution lists the powers of the national government and the powers denied to the states. All other powers remain with the states. Generally, the states are required to give up only the powers necessary to create an effective national government; the national government is limited to the powers specified in the Constitution. In spite of these specific lists, the Constitution does not clearly describe the spheres of authority within which these powers can be exercised. As we discuss in Chapter 4, limits on the exercise of power by the national government and the states have evolved as a result of political and military conflict; moreover, these limits have changed continually.

Separation of powers. **Separation of powers** is the assignment of the lawmaking, law-enforcing, and law-interpreting functions to independent legislative, executive, and judicial branches of government. Nationally, the lawmaking power resides in Congress, the law-enforcing power resides in the presidency, and the law-interpreting power resides in the courts. Service in one branch prohibits simultaneous service in the others. Separation of powers safeguards liberty by ensuring that all government power does not fall into the hands of a single person or group of people. But the framers' concern with protecting the liberty of the people did not extend to the election process. The Constitution constrained majority rule by limiting the direct influence of the people on that process (see Figure 3.1).

In theory, separation of powers means that one branch cannot exercise the powers of the other branches. In practice, however, the separation is far from complete. One scholar has suggested that what we have instead is "separate institutions *sharing* powers."[15]

Checks and balances. The constitutional system of **checks and balances** is a means of giving each branch of government some scrutiny of and control over the other branches. The framers reasoned that these checks and balances would prevent one branch from ignoring or overpowering the others.

FIGURE 3.1 *The Constitution and the Electoral Process*

*The framers were afraid of majority rule, and that fear is reflected in the electoral proc-
ess described in the Constitution. The people, speaking through the voters, had direct
input only in the choice of their representatives in the House. The president and senators
were elected indirectly, through the electoral college and state legislatures. (The direct
election of senators did not become law until 1913, when the Seventeenth Amendment
was ratified.) Judicial appointments are, and always have been, far removed from representative links to the people. Judges are nominated by the president and approved by the
Senate.*

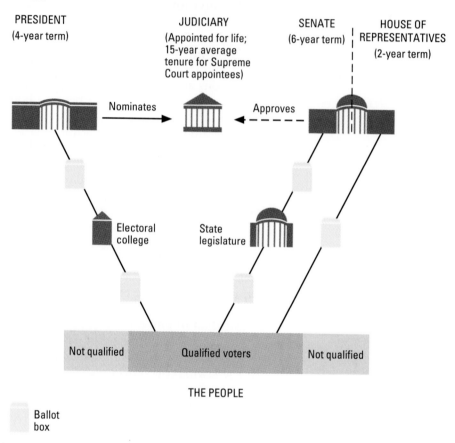

Separation of powers and checks and balances are two distinct principles, but both are necessary to ensure that one branch does not dominate
the government. Separation of powers divides government responsibilities among the legislative, executive, and judicial branches; checks and
balances prevent the exclusive exercise of those powers by any one of the
three branches. For example, only the Congress can enact laws. But the
president (through the power of the veto) can cancel them, and the courts
(by finding a law in violation of the Constitution) can nullify them. And
the process goes on. In a "check on a check," the Congress can override
a president's veto by an extraordinary (two-thirds) majority in each
chamber; and it is empowered to propose amendments to the Constitution, counteracting the courts' power to find a national law invalid. Fig-

FIGURE 3.2 *Separation of Powers and Checks and Balances*

Separation of powers is the assignment of lawmaking, law-enforcing, and law-interpreting functions to the legislative, executive, and judicial branches. This is illustrated by the diagonal grid in the figure. Checks and balances give each branch some power over the other branches. For example, the executive branch possesses some legislative power, and the legislative branch possesses some executive power. These checks and balances are illustrated within the columns and outside the diagonal grid.

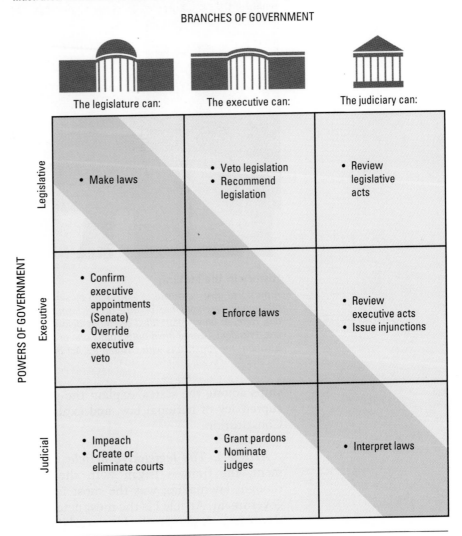

BRANCHES OF GOVERNMENT

	The legislature can:	The executive can:	The judiciary can:
Legislative	• Make laws	• Veto legislation • Recommend legislation	• Review legislative acts
Executive	• Confirm executive appointments (Senate) • Override executive veto	• Enforce laws	• Review executive acts • Issue injunctions
Judicial	• Impeach • Create or eliminate courts	• Grant pardons • Nominate judges	• Interpret laws

POWERS OF GOVERNMENT

ure 3.2 depicts the relationship between separation of powers and checks and balances.

The Articles of the Constitution

In addition to the Preamble, the Constitution includes seven articles. The first three establish the internal operation and powers of the separate branches of government. The remaining four define the relation-

History in the Making

A president gives approval to legislation by signing a bill into law. Since the 1960s, the bill-signing ceremony has become an art form, garnering much attention from the media. Here, in an emotion-filled ceremony before 2,000 disabled visitors and their families, President George Bush autographs one of the most important statutes of his administration, the Americans with Disabilities Act of 1990, . . .

ships among the states, explain the process of amendment, declare the supremacy of national law, and explain the procedure for ratifying the Constitution.

Article I: The legislative article. In structuring their new government, the framers began with the legislative branch because they thought lawmaking was the most important function of a republican government. Article I is the most detailed and therefore the longest of all the articles. It defines the **bicameral** (two-chamber) character of the Congress and describes the internal operating procedures of the House of Representatives and the Senate. Section 8 of Article I expresses the principle of **enumerated powers,** which means that Congress can exercise only the powers that the Constitution assigns to it. Eighteen powers are enumerated; the first seventeen are specific powers. For example, the third clause of Section 8 gives Congress the power to regulate interstate commerce. (One of the chief problems with the Articles of Confederation was the lack of a means to cope with trade wars between states. The solution was to vest control of interstate commerce in the national government.)

History for the Taking

. . . and presents a ceremonial pen to the Reverend Harold Wilke, who, because he has no arms, accepted it with his left foot. Ceremonial pens serve as mementos of the task of lawmaking and tokens of appreciation for those who aided in the process.

The last clause in Section 8, known as the **necessary and proper clause** (or the **elastic clause**), gives Congress the means to execute the enumerated powers (see the Appendix). This clause is the basis of Congress's **implied powers**—those powers that Congress must have in order to execute its enumerated powers. The power to levy and collect taxes (Clause 1) and the power to coin money and regulate its value (Clause 5), when joined with the necessary and proper clause (Clause 18), *imply* that Congress has the power to charter a bank. Otherwise, the national government would have no means of managing the funds it collects through its power to tax. Implied powers clearly expand the enumerated powers conferred on Congress by the Constitution.

Article II: The executive article. Article II sets the president's term of office, the procedure for electing a president through the electoral college, the qualifications for becoming president, and the president's duties and powers. The last include acting as commander in chief of the military; making treaties (which must be ratified by a two-thirds vote of the Senate); and appointing government officers, diplomats, and judges (again, with the advice and consent of the Senate).

The president also has legislative powers—part of the constitutional system of checks and balances. For example, the Constitution requires that the president periodically inform the Congress of the "State of the Union" and of the policies and programs that the executive branch intends to advocate in the forthcoming year. Today this is done annually, in the president's State of the Union address. Under special circumstances, the president can also convene or adjourn Congress.

The duty to "take Care that the Laws be faithfully executed" in Section 3 has provided presidents with a reservoir of power. President Nixon tried to use this power when he refused to turn over the Watergate tapes despite a judicial subpoena in a criminal trial. He claimed executive privilege, an extension of the executive power implied in Article II. But the Supreme Court struck down his claim, arguing that it violated the separation of powers, that the decision to release or withhold information *in a criminal trial* is a judicial, not an executive, function.

Article III: The judicial article.   The third article was purposely vague. The Constitution established the Supreme Court as the highest court in the land. But beyond that, the framers were unable to agree on the need for, the size of, or the composition of a national judiciary, or on the procedures it should follow. They left these issues to the Congress, which resolved them by creating a system of national courts separate from the states.

Short of impeachment, federal judges serve for life. They are appointed to indefinite terms on "good Behavior," and their salaries cannot be lowered while they hold office. These stipulations reinforce the separation of powers; they see to it that judges are independent of the other branches, that they do not have to fear retribution in their exercise of judicial power.

The judicial branch can be checked by Congress through its power to create (and eliminate) lower federal courts. Congress can also restrict the power of the lower courts to decide cases. And, as we have noted, the president appoints—with the advice and consent of the Senate—the justices of the Supreme Court and the judges of the lower federal courts.

Article III does not explicitly give the courts the power of **judicial review,** the authority to invalidate congressional or presidential actions. That power has been inferred from the logic, structure, and theory of the Constitution.

The remaining articles.   The remaining four articles of the Constitution cover a lot of ground. Article IV requires that the citizens, judicial acts, and criminal warrants of each state be honored in all other states. This is a provision that promotes equality; it keeps the states from treating outsiders differently from their own citizens. For example, an Illinois court awards Goldman damages against Janda for $10,000. Janda moves to Alaska to avoid payment. Rather than force Goldman to bring a new suit against Janda, the court in Alaska (Judge Berry presiding), under the full faith and credit clause of Article IV, honors the Illinois judgment and enforces it as its own. In other words, states will command respect for each other's judgments. The origin of this clause can be traced to the Articles of Confederation.

Article IV also allows the addition of new states and stipulates that the national government will protect the states against invasion and domestic violence.

Article V specifies the methods for amending (changing) the Constitution. We will have more to say about this shortly.

An important component of Article VI is the **supremacy clause,** which asserts that, when they conflict, the Constitution, national laws, and treaties take precedence over state and local laws. This stipulation is vital to the operation of federalism. In keeping with the supremacy clause, Article VI also requires that all national and state officials, elected or appointed, take an oath to support the Constitution. The article also mandates that religion cannot be a qualification for holding government office.

Finally, Article VII describes the ratification process, stipulating that approval by conventions in nine states was necessary for the "Establishment" of the Constitution.

The Framers' Motives

Some argue that the Constitution is essentially a conservative document written by wealthy men to advance their own interests. One distinguished historian writing in the early 1900s, Charles A. Beard, maintained that the delegates had much to gain from a strong national government.[16] Many held government securities that were practically worthless under the Articles of Confederation. A strong national government would protect their property and pay off the nation's debts. Beard claimed that the Constitution was crafted to protect the economic interests of this small group of creditors.

Beard's argument provoked a generation of historians to examine the existing financial records of the convention delegates. Their scholarship has largely discredited his once-popular view.[17] For example, it turns out that seven of the delegates who left the convention or refused to sign the Constitution held public securities worth more than twice the holdings of the thirty-nine delegates who did sign. Moreover, the most influential delegates owned no securities. And only a small number of the delegates appeared to benefit economically from the new government.[18]

What did motivate the framers? Surely economic issues were important, but they were not the major issues. The single most important factor leading to the Constitutional Convention was the inability of the national or state governments to maintain order under the loose structure of the Articles of Confederation. Certainly order involved the protection of property, but the framers had a broader view of property than their portfolios of government securities. They wanted to protect their homes, their families, and their means of livelihood from impending anarchy.

Although they disagreed bitterly on structure, mechanics, and detail, the framers agreed on the most vital issues. For example, three of the most crucial parts of the Constitution—the power to tax, the necessary and proper clause, and the supremacy clause—were approved unanimously without debate; experience had taught the delegates that a strong national government was essential if the United States was going to survive. The motivation to create order was so strong, the framers were willing to draft clauses that protected the most undemocratic of all institutions—slavery.

The Slavery Issue

The institution of slavery was well ingrained in American life at the time of the Constitutional Convention, and slavery helped shape the Constitution, although the term is not mentioned anywhere in it. (According to the first annual census of population in 1790, nearly 18 percent—697,000—of the population lived in slavery). It is doubtful, in fact, that there would have been a Constitution if the delegates had had to resolve the slavery issue, for the southern states would have opposed a constitution that prohibited slavery. Opponents of slavery were in the minority and were willing to tolerate its continuation in the interest of forging a union, perhaps believing that the issue could await another day.

The question of representation in the House of Representatives brought the slavery issue close to the surface of debate leading to the Great Compromise. Representation according to population was an element of the accord. But who counted in the "population"? States with large slave populations wanted all persons, slave and free, counted equally; states with few slaves wanted only free persons counted. The delegates agreed unanimously that in apportioning representatives in the House and in assessing direct taxes, the population of each state was to be determined by adding "the whole Number of free Persons" and "three

DOONESBURY   Garry Trudeau

Doonesbury "Equality and the Constitution"

All Were Not Created Equal

This 1845 photograph of Isaac Jefferson, who had been one of Thomas Jefferson's slaves at Monticello, reminds us that the framers of the Constitution did not extend freedom and equality to all. Slavery was a widely accepted social norm in the eighteenth century.

fifths of all other Persons" (Article I, Section 2). The phrase "all other Persons" is, of course, a substitute for slaves.

The three-fifths formula had been employed by the 1783 congress under the Articles of Confederation to allocate financial assessments among the states. The rule reflected the view that slaves were less efficient producers of wealth than free people, not that slaves were three-fifths human and two-fifths personal property.[19]

The three-fifths clause gave states with large slave populations (the South) greater representation in Congress than states with small slave populations (the North). This overrepresentation translated into greater influence in presidential selection, since electoral votes were determined by the size of each state's congressional delegation. The three-fifths clause also undertaxed states with large slave populations.

Another issue centered around the slave trade. Several southern delegates were uncompromising in their defense of the slave trade, while some delegates favored prohibition. The delegates compromised, agreeing that the slave trade could not be ended before twenty years had elapsed (Article I, Section 9).

Finally, the delegates agreed, without serious challenge, that fugitive slaves be returned to their masters (Article IV, Section 2).

In addressing these points, the framers in essence condoned slavery. Clearly, slavery existed in stark opposition to the idea that "All men are created equal," and though many slaveholders, including Jefferson and Madison, agonized over it, few made serious efforts to free their own slaves. Most Americans seemed indifferent to slavery and felt no embarrassment at the apparent contradiction between the Declaration and slavery.

Nonetheless, the eradication of slavery proceeded gradually in the states. Opposition to slavery on moral or religious grounds explains some of this shift. Economic forces—such as the change to less labor-intensive agricultural production—were a contributing factor, too. By 1787, Connecticut, Massachusetts, New Jersey, New York, Pennsylvania, Rhode Island, and Vermont abolished slavery or provided for gradual emancipation. No southern state adopted similar laws, although several enacted laws easing the ability of masters to free their slaves. This slow but perceptible shift on the slavery issue in many states masked a volcanic force capable of destroying the Constitutional Convention and the Union.

Selling the Constitution

On September 17, 1787, nearly four months after the Constitutional Convention opened, the delegates convened for the last time, to sign the final version of their handiwork. Because several delegates were unwilling to sign the document, the last paragraph was craftily worded to give the impression of unanimity: "Done in Convention by the Unanimous Consent of the *States* present."

Before it could take effect, the Constitution had to be ratified by a minimum of nine state conventions. The support of key states was crucial. In Pennsylvania, the legislature was slow to convene a ratifying convention. Pro-Constitution forces became so frustrated at this dawdling that they broke into a local boardinghouse and hauled two errant legislators through the streets to the state house so the assembly could schedule the convention.

The proponents of the new charter, who wanted a strong national government, called themselves *Federalists*. The opponents of the Constitution were quickly dubbed *Antifederalists*. They claimed, however, that *they* were true federalists because they wanted to protect the states from the tyranny of a strong national government. Elbridge Gerry, a vocal Antifederalist, called his opponents "rats" (because they favored ratification) and maintained that he was an "antirat."[20] Such is the Alice in Wonderland character of political discourse. Whatever they were called, the viewpoints of the two groups formed the bases of the first American political parties.

The Federalist Papers

The press of the day became a battlefield of words, filled with extravagant praise or vituperative condemnation of the proposed Constitution. Beginning in October 1787, an exceptional series of eighty-five newspaper articles defending the Constitution appeared under the title *The Fed-*

eralist: A Commentary on the Constitution of the United States. The essays were reprinted extensively during the ratification battle. They bore the pen name "Publius" (for the legendary Roman emperor and defender of the Republic, Publius Valerius, who was later known as Publicola). The essays were written primarily by James Madison and Alexander Hamilton, with some assistance from John Jay. Rationally and quietly, Publius argued in favor of ratification. *The Federalist* (also called the *Federalist Papers*) remains the best single commentary we have on the meaning of the Constitution and the political theory it embodies.

The Antifederalists, not to be outdone, offered their own intellectual basis for rejecting the Constitution. In several essays, the most influential authored under the pseudonyms "Brutus" and "Federal Farmer," the Antifederalists attacked the centralization of power in a strong national government, claiming it would obliterate the states, violate the social contract of the Declaration of Independence, and destroy liberty in the process. They defended the status quo, maintaining that the Articles of Confederation established true federal principles.[21]

Of all the *Federalist Papers,* the most magnificent and most frequently cited is "Federalist No. 10," which was written by James Madison (see the Appendix). He argued that the proposed constitution was designed "to break and control the violence of faction": "By a faction, I understand a number of citizens, whether amounting to a majority or minority of the whole, who are united and actuated by some common impulse of passion, or of interest, adverse to the rights of other citizens, or to the permanent and aggregate interests of the community."

Of course, Madison was discussing what we described in Chapter 2 as *pluralism.* What Madison called *factions* today are interest groups or even political parties. According to Madison, "The most common and durable source of factions has been the various and unequal distribution of property." Madison was concerned not with reducing inequalities of wealth (which he took for granted) but with controlling the seemingly inevitable conflict stemming from them. The Constitution, he argued, was "well-constructed" for this purpose.

Through the mechanism of *representation,* wrote Madison, the Constitution would prevent the tyranny of the majority (mob rule). Government would not be controlled directly by the people, but would be governed indirectly, by their elected representatives. And those representatives would have the intelligence and the understanding to serve the larger interests of the nation. Moreover, the federal system would require that majorities form first within each state, then organize for effective action at the national level. This and the vastness of the country would make it unlikely that a majority would form "to invade the rights of other citizens."

The purpose of "Federalist No. 10" was to demonstrate that the proposed government was not likely to be ruled by any faction. Contrary to conventional wisdom, Madison argued, the key to controlling the evils of faction is to have a large republic—the larger, the better. The more diverse the society, the less likely it is that an unjust majority can form. Madison certainly had no intention of creating a majoritarian democracy; his view of popular government was much more consistent with the model of pluralist democracy discussed in Chapter 2.

Madison pressed his argument from a different angle in "Federalist No. 51" (see the Appendix). Asserting that "ambition must be made to counteract ambition," he argued that the separation of powers and checks and balances would control tyranny from any source. If power is distributed equally across the three branches, then each branch has the capacity to counteract the other. In Madison's words, "usurpations are guarded against by a division of the government into distinct and separate departments." Because legislative power tends to predominate in republican governments, legislative authority is divided between the Senate and the House of Representatives, with different methods of selection and terms of office. Additional protection comes through federalism, which divides power "between two distinct governments"—national and state—and subdivides "the portion allotted to each . . . among distinct and separate departments."

The Antifederalists wanted additional separation of powers and additional checks and balances, which, they maintained, would eliminate the threat of tyranny entirely. The Federalists believed that this would make decisive national action virtually impossible. But to ensure ratification, they agreed to a compromise.

A Concession: The Bill of Rights

Despite the eloquence of the *Federalist Papers,* many prominent citizens, including Thomas Jefferson, were unhappy that the Constitution did not list basic civil liberties—the individual freedoms guaranteed to citizens. The omission of a bill of rights was the chief obstacle to the adoption of the Constitution by the states. (In fact, seven of the eleven state constitutions that were written in the first five years of independence already included such a list.) The colonists had just rebelled against the British government to preserve their basic freedoms; why didn't the proposed Constitution spell out those freedoms?

The answer was rooted in logic, not politics. Because the national government was limited to those powers that were granted to it and because no power was granted to abridge the people's liberties, then a list of guaranteed freedoms was not necessary. Hamilton, in "Federalist No. 84," went even further, arguing that the addition of a bill of rights would be dangerous. To deny the exercise of a nonexistent power might lead to the exercise of a power that is not specifically denied. Because it is not possible to list all prohibited powers, wrote Hamilton, any attempt to provide a partial list would make the remaining areas vulnerable to government abuse.

But logic was no match for fear. Many states agreed to ratify the Constitution only after Washington suggested that a list of guarantees be added through the amendment process. Well over a hundred amendments were proposed by the states. These were eventually narrowed down to twelve, which were approved by Congress and sent to the states. Ten of them became part of the Constitution in 1791, after securing the

T A B L E 3.2 *The Bill of Rights*

The first ten amendments to the Constitution are known as the Bill of Rights. *The following is a list of those amendments grouped conceptually. For the actual order and wording of the Bill of Rights, see the Appendix.*

Guarantees	Amendment
Guarantees for Participation in the Political Process	
No government abridgement of speech or press; no government abridgement of peaceable assembly; no government abridgement of petitioning government for redress.	1
Guarantees Respecting Personal Beliefs	
No government establishment of religion; no government prohibition of free religious exercise.	1
Guarantees of Personal Privacy	
Owners' consent necessary to quarter troops in private homes in peacetime; quartering during war must be lawful.	3
Government cannot engage in unreasonable searches and seizures; warrants to search and seize require probable cause.	4
No compulsion to testify against oneself in criminal cases.	5
Guarantees Against Government Overreaching	
Serious crimes require a grand jury indictment; no repeated prosecution for the same offense; no loss of life, liberty, or property without due process; no government taking of property for public use without just compensation.	5
Criminal defendants will have a speedy public trial by impartial local jury; defendants informed of accusation; defendants confront witnesses against them; defendants use judicial process to obtain favorable witnesses; defendants have legal assistance for their defense.	6
Civil lawsuits can be tried by juries if controversy exceeds $20; in jury trials, fact-finding is a jury function.	7
No excessive bail; no excessive fines; no cruel and unusual punishment	8
Other Guarantees	
No government trespass on unspecified fundamental rights.	9
The states or the people reserve the powers not delegated to the national government or denied to the states.	10
The people have the right to bear arms.	2

approval of the required three-fourths of the states. Collectively, these ten amendments are known as the **Bill of Rights.** They restrain the national government from tampering with fundamental rights and civil liberties and emphasize the limited character of national power (see Table 3.2).

Ratification

The Constitution officially took effect with its ratification by the ninth state, New Hampshire, on June 21, 1788. However, the success of the new government was not assured until August 1788, when the Constitution was ratified by the key states of Virginia and New York after lengthy debate.

The reflection and deliberation that attended the creation and ratification of the Constitution signaled to the world that a new government could be launched peacefully. The French observer Alexis de Tocqueville (1805–1859) later wrote:

> That which is new in the history of societies is to see a great people, warned by its lawgivers that the wheels of government are stopping, turn its attention on itself without haste or fear, sound the depth of the ill, and then wait for two years to find the remedy at leisure, and then finally, when the remedy has been indicated, submit to it voluntarily without its costing humanity a single tear or drop of blood.[22]

Constitutional Change

The founders realized that the Constitution would have to be changed from time to time. To this end, they specified a formal amendment process in Article V—a process that was used almost immediately to add the Bill of Rights. With the passage of time, the Constitution also has been altered through judicial interpretation and changes in political practice.

The Formal Amendment Process

There are two stages in the amendment process, **proposal** and **ratification;** both are necessary for an amendment to become part of the Constitution. The Constitution provides two alternative methods for completing each stage (see Figure 3.3). Amendments can be proposed (1) by a two-thirds vote of the House of Representatives and of the Senate, or (2) by a national convention, summoned by Congress at the request of two-thirds of the state legislatures. All constitutional amendments to date have been proposed by the first method; the second has never been used.

A proposed amendment can be ratified (1) by a vote of the legislatures of three-fourths of the states, or (2) by a vote of constitutional conventions held in three-fourths of the states. Congress chooses the method of ratification. It has used the state convention method only once, for the Twenty-first Amendment, which repealed the Eighteenth (Prohibition).

Notice that the amendment process requires the exercise of **extraordinary majorities.** The framers purposely made it difficult to propose and ratify amendments (although nowhere near as difficult as the amendment process under the Articles of Confederation). They wanted only the most significant issues to lead to constitutional change. Notice, too, that the president plays no formal role in the process. His approval is not required to amend the Constitution, although his political influence affects the success or failure of any amendment effort.

Calling a national convention to propose an amendment has never been tried. Certainly the method raises several thorny questions. For example, the Constitution doesn't address the number of delegates who should attend, the method by which they should be chosen, or the rules

FIGURE 3.3 *Amending the Constitution*

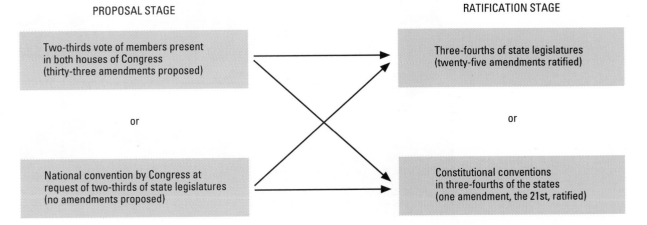

There are two stages in amending the Constitution: proposal and ratification. Congress has no control over the proposal stage, but it prescribes the ratification method. Once it has ratified an amendment, a state cannot retract its action. A state's rejection of an amendment does not bar future reconsideration, however.

PROPOSAL STAGE

RATIFICATION STAGE

Two-thirds vote of members present in both houses of Congress (thirty-three amendments proposed)

or

National convention by Congress at request of two-thirds of state legislatures (no amendments proposed)

Three-fourths of state legislatures (twenty-five amendments ratified)

or

Constitutional conventions in three-fourths of the states (one amendment, the 21st, ratified)

for debating and voting on a proposed amendment. Confusion surrounding the convention process tends to deter resort to it, securing the amendment process in congressional hands.[23]

The major issue is the limits, if any, on the business of the convention. Remember that the convention in Philadelphia in 1787 was charged with revising the Articles of Confederation, yet it drafted an entirely new charter. Would a national convention, called to consider a particular amendment, be within its bounds to rewrite the Constitution? No one really knows.

A recent movement to convene a constitutional convention to write an amendment that would require a balanced budget was well under way when it faltered and appeared to reverse its course. From 1974 to 1988, thirty-two of the required thirty-four states voted to issue a convention call on the budget issue. Then, in 1988, the Alabama legislature rescinded its 1976 vote in favor of a convention. The legislators were motivated by the fear that a convention would become a Pandora's box, loosing a whirlwind of political change and fundamentally altering the national government. Alabama's action raised additional thorny issues: May a state withdraw its call for a convention? And, how long does a state's call for a convention stay in effect? In the absence of authoritative answers and political support, a constitutional convention now appears doubtful.

Congress moved quickly but unsuccessfully in 1990 to propose a constitutional amendment against flag burning. The amendment sprint followed a Supreme Court decision striking down a law passed by Congress making it a crime to burn or deface the flag. (The Court invalidated a similar state law in 1989.) The Court invoked the Constitution's free-speech guarantee when it invalidated the law.

Roll Out the Barrels

The Eighteenth Amendment, which was ratified by the states in 1919, banned the manufacture, sale, or transportation of alcoholic beverages. The amendment was spurred by moral and social reform groups, like the Women's Christian Temperance Union, founded by Evanston, Illinois, resident Frances Willard in 1874. The amendment proved to be an utter failure. People continued to drink, but their alcohol came from illegal sources.

Congress proposed the following amendment to trump the Court's decision:

> The Congress and the States shall have power to prohibit the physical desecration of the flag of the United States.

The public gave strong support to the proposal: 68 percent of the public backed the amendment.[24] But majority sentiment does not necessarily translate to government action. After winning passage in the Senate, the proposed amendment failed, 254–177 (34 votes shy of the required two-thirds approval) in the House of Representatives.

Most of the Constitution's twenty-six amendments were adopted to help keep it abreast of changes in political thinking. The first ten amendments (the Bill of Rights) were the price of ratification, but they have been important to our current system of government. The last sixteen amendments fall into three main categories: They make *public policy*; they correct deficiencies in *government structure*; or they promote *equality* (see Table 3.3). One attempt to make public policy through a constitutional amendment was disastrous. The Eighteenth Amendment (1919) prohibited the manufacture or sale of intoxicating beverages. Prohibition lasted for fourteen years and was an utter failure. Gangsters began bootlegging liquor; people died from drinking homemade booze; and millions regularly broke the law by drinking anyway. Congress had to propose another amendment in 1933 to repeal the Eighteenth. The states

T A B L E 3.3 *Constitutional Amendments: 11 through 26*

No.	Proposed	Ratified	Intent	Subject
11	1794	1795	G	Prohibits an individual from suing a state in a federal court without the state's consent.
12	1803	1804	G	Requires the electoral college to vote separately for president and vice president.
13	1865	1865	E	Prohibits slavery.
14	1866	1868	E	Gives citizenship to all persons born or naturalized in the United States (former slaves); prevents states from depriving any "person of life, liberty, or property, without due process of law."
15	1869	1870	E	Guarantees that citizens' right to vote cannot be denied "on account of race, color, or previous condition of servitude."
16	1909	1913	E	Gives Congress power to collect an income tax.
17	1912	1913	E	Provides for popular election of senators, who were formerly elected by state legislatures.
18	1917	1919	P	Prohibits making and selling intoxicating liquors.
19	1919	1920	E	Gives women the right to vote.
20	1932	1933	G	Changes the presidential inauguration from March 4 to January 20 and sets January 3 for the opening date of Congress.
21	1933	1933	P	Repeals the Eighteenth Amendment.
22	1947	1951	G	Limits a president to two terms.
23	1960	1961	E	Gives citizens of Washington, D.C., the right to vote for president.
24	1962	1964	E	Prohibits charging citizens a poll tax to vote.
25	1965	1967	G	Provides for succession in event of death, removal from office, incapacity, or resignation of the president or vice president.
26	1971	1971	E	Lowers the voting age to eighteen.

P   Amendments legislating public policy.
G   Amendments correcting perceived deficiencies in government structure.
E   Amendments advancing equality.

ratified this amendment, the Twenty-first, in less than ten months, less time than it took to ratify the Fourteenth Amendment, guaranteeing citizenship, due process, and equal protection.

Since 1787, about ten thousand constitutional amendments have been introduced; only a fraction have passed through the proposal stage. Once an amendment has been voted by the Congress, however, the chances of ratification are very high. Only seven amendments submitted to the states have failed to be ratified. Two such failures occurred in the 1980s. The first was the Equal Rights Amendment (see Chapter 16). The second, which called for full congressional representation for Washington, D.C., mustered approval in just sixteen states, twenty-two states short of the required three-fourths.

Interpretation by the Courts

In 1803, in its decision in *Marbury* v. *Madison*, the Supreme Court declared that the courts have the power to nullify government acts when they conflict with the Constitution. (We elaborate on the power of *judicial review* in Chapter 14.) The exercise of judicial review forces the courts to interpret the Constitution. In a way, this makes a lot of sense. The judiciary is the law-interpreting branch of the government; the Constitution is the supreme law of the land, fair game then for judicial interpretation. But in interpreting the Constitution, the courts cannot help but give new meaning to its provisions. This is why judicial interpretation is a principal form of constitutional change.

What guidelines should judges use in interpreting the Constitution? For one thing, they must realize that our language—particularly the usage and meaning of many words—has changed over the last two hundred years. They must be careful to think about what the words meant at the time the Constitution was written. Some insist they also must consider the original intent of the framers—not an easy task. Of course, there are records of the Constitutional Convention and the debates surrounding ratification. But there are also many questions about the completeness and accuracy of those records, even Madison's detailed notes. And, at times, the framers chose to be general or vague in writing the document. In part, this may reflect their lack of agreement on or universal understanding of certain provisions in the Constitution. Other scholars and judges maintain that the search for original meaning is hopeless and that contemporary notions of constitutional provisions must hold sway. Critics say that this approach comes perilously close to amending the Constitution as the judges see fit, transforming the law interpreters into the lawmakers.

Political Practice

The Constitution remains silent on many issues. For example, it says nothing about political parties or the president's Cabinet, yet both parties and cabinets have exercised considerable influence in American politics. Some constitutional provisions have fallen out of use. The electors in the electoral college, for example, were supposed to exercise their own judgment in voting for president and vice president. Today the electors function simply as a rubber stamp, reflecting the outcome of election contests in their states.

Political practice has altered the distribution of power without changes in the Constitution. The framers intended Congress to be the strongest branch of government. But the president has come to overshadow Congress. Presidents like Abraham Lincoln and Franklin Roosevelt used their powers imaginatively to respond to national crises. And their actions served as springboards for future presidents to further enlarge the powers of the office.

The framers could scarcely imagine an urbanized nation of 250 million people stretching across a land mass some 3,000 miles wide. They could never in their wildest nightmares have foreseen the destructiveness of nuclear war or envisioned the influence this would have on the power to declare war. The Constitution gives that power to Congress, to consider and debate this momentous step. But with nuclear annihilation perhaps only minutes away, the legislative power to declare war must give way to the president's power to wage war as the nation's commander in chief. Strict adherence to the Constitution here could destroy the nation's ability to protect itself.

An Evaluation of the Constitution

The U.S. Constitution is one of the world's most praised political documents. It is the oldest written national constitution and one of the most widely copied, sometimes word for word. It is also one of the shortest, containing about 4,300 words, not counting the amendments. In fact, the twenty-six amendments (about 3,500 words) are nearly as long as the Constitution itself. The brevity of the Constitution may be one of its greatest strengths. As we noted earlier, the framers simply laid out a structural framework for government; they did not describe relationships and powers in detail. For example, the Constitution gives Congress the power to regulate "Commerce . . . among the several States," but does not define *interstate commerce*. This kind of general wording allows interpretation in keeping with contemporary political, social, and technological developments. Air travel, for instance, was unknown in 1787, but it now falls easily within Congress's power to regulate interstate commerce.

The generality of the U.S. Constitution stands in stark contrast to the specificity of most state constitutions. The constitution of California, for example, provides that "fruit and nut-bearing trees under the age of four years from the time of planting in orchard form and grapevines under the age of three years from the time of planting in vineyard form . . . shall be exempt from taxation" (Article XIII, Section 12). Because they are so specific, most state constitutions are much longer than the U.S. Constitution.

Freedom, Order, and Equality in the Constitution

The revolutionaries' first try at government was embodied in the Articles of Confederation. The result was a weak national government that leaned too much toward freedom at the expense of order. Deciding that the confederation was beyond correcting, the revolutionaries chose a new form of government—a *federal* government—that was strong enough to maintain order but not so strong that it could dominate the states or infringe on individual freedoms. In short, the Constitution provided a judicious balance between order and freedom. It paid virtually no attention to equality.

Consider social equality. The Constitution never mentioned slavery—a controversial issue even then. In fact, as we discussed earlier, the

FIGURE 3.4   *"We the People" Evaluate the Constitution*

Two hundred years after the Constitutional Convention, a survey of Americans evaluated the success of the goals articulated in the Preamble to the Constitution. According to the results, the Constitution has done a good job of forging one nation from separate states and securing an orderly and free society. Though equality was not an explicit goal in the Preamble, the Constitution's success in treating all people equally received a relatively poor grade. (Source: New York Times, 26 May 1987, p. 10. Copyright © 1987 by the New York Times Company. Reprinted by permission.)

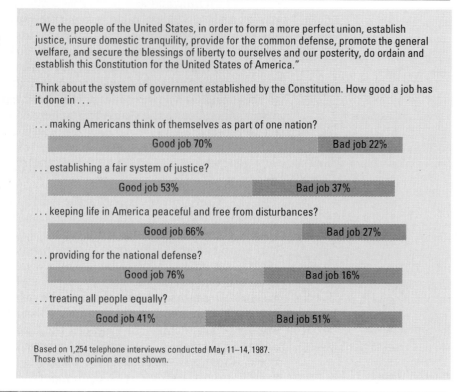

"We the people of the United States, in order to form a more perfect union, establish justice, insure domestic tranquility, provide for the common defense, promote the general welfare, and secure the blessings of liberty to ourselves and our posterity, do ordain and establish this Constitution for the United States of America."

Think about the system of government established by the Constitution. How good a job has it done in . . .

. . . making Americans think of themselves as part of one nation?

Good job 70%   Bad job 22%

. . . establishing a fair system of justice?

Good job 53%   Bad job 37%

. . . keeping life in America peaceful and free from disturbances?

Good job 66%   Bad job 27%

. . . providing for the national defense?

Good job 76%   Bad job 16%

. . . treating all people equally?

Good job 41%   Bad job 51%

Based on 1,254 telephone interviews conducted May 11–14, 1987. Those with no opinion are not shown.

Constitution implicitly condones slavery in the wording of several articles. Not until the ratification of the Thirteenth Amendment in 1865 was slavery prohibited.

The Constitution was designed long before social equality was ever even thought of as an objective of government. In fact, in "Federalist No. 10," Madison held that protection of the "diversities in the faculties of men from which the rights of property originate" is "the first object of government." Over a century later, the Constitution was changed to incorporate a key device for the promotion of social equality—the income tax. The Sixteenth Amendment (1913) gave Congress the power to collect an income tax; it was proposed and ratified to replace a law that had been declared unconstitutional in an 1895 court case. The idea of **progressive taxation** (in which the tax rate increases with income) had long been closely linked to the income tax, and the Sixteenth Amendment gave it a constitutional basis.[25] Progressive taxation later helped promote social equality through the redistribution of income. That is, higher-income people are taxed at higher rates to help fund social programs that benefit low-income people. Social equality itself has never been, and is not now, a prime *constitutional* value. The Constitution has been much more effective in securing order and freedom. A recent poll of Americans reinforces this evaluation (see Figure 3.4).

The Constitution also did not take a stand on political equality. It left voting qualifications to the states, specifying only that people who could vote for "the most numerous Branch of the State Legislature" could also vote for representatives to Congress (Article I, Section 2). In most states at that time, only tax-paying or property-owning white males could vote. With few exceptions, blacks and women were universally excluded from voting. These inequalities have been rectified by several amendments (see Table 3.3).

The Constitution did not guarantee blacks citizenship until the Fourteenth Amendment was ratified (1868) and did not give them the right to vote until the Fifteenth Amendment (1870). Women were not guaranteed the right to vote until the Nineteenth Amendment (1920). Finally, the *poll tax* (a tax that people had to pay in order to vote and that tended to disenfranchise blacks) was not eliminated until the Twenty-fourth Amendment (1964). Two other amendments expanded the Constitution's grant of political equality. The Twenty-third Amendment (1961) allowed citizens of Washington, D.C., who are not considered residents of any state, to vote for president. The Twenty-sixth Amendment (1971) extended voting rights to all citizens who are at least eighteen years old.

The Constitution and Models of Democracy

Think back to our discussion of the models of democracy in Chapter 2. Which model does the Constitution fit: the pluralist or majoritarian? Actually, it is hard to imagine a government framework better suited to the pluralist model of democracy than the Constitution of the United States. It is also hard to imagine a document more at odds with the majoritarian model. Consider Madison's claim, in "Federalist No. 10," that government inevitably involves conflicting factions. This concept fits perfectly with the idea of competing groups in pluralist theory (see Chapter 2). Think about his description in "Federalist No. 51" of the Constitution's ability to guard against the concentration of power in the majority through its separation of powers and checks and balances. This concept—avoiding a single center of government power that might fall under majority control—also fits perfectly with pluralist democracy.

The delegates to the Constitutional Convention intended to create a republic, a government based on majority consent; they did not intend to create a democracy, which rests on majority rule. They succeeded admirably in creating that republic. Along the way, they also produced a government that grew into a democracy . . . but a particular type of democracy. The framers neither wanted nor got a democracy that fit the majoritarian model. They perhaps wanted and certainly did get a government that conforms to the pluralist model.

Summary

The U.S. Constitution is more than a historic document, an antique curiosity. Although over two hundred years old, it still governs the politics of a mighty modern nation. It still has the power to force from office a president who won re-election by a landslide and the power to see the country through government crises.

The Constitution was the end product of a revolutionary movement aimed at preserving existing liberties. That movement began with the Declaration of Independence, a proclamation that everyone is entitled to certain rights (among them, life, liberty, and the pursuit of happiness) and that government exists for the good of its citizens. When government denies those rights, the people have the right to rebel.

War with Britain was only part of the process of independence. Some form of government was needed to replace the British monarchy. The Americans chose a republic and defined the structure of that republic in the Articles of Confederation. The Articles, however, were a failure. Although they guaranteed the states their coveted independence, they left the central government too weak to deal with disorder and insurrection.

The Constitution was the second attempt at limited government. It replaced a loose union of powerful states with a strong national government, incorporating four political principles: republicanism, federalism, separation of powers, and checks and balances. Republicanism is a form of government in which power resides in the people and is exercised by their elected representatives. Federalism is a division of power between the national government and the states. The federalism of the Constitution conferred substantial powers on the national government at the expense of the states. Separation of powers is a further division of the power of the national government into legislative (lawmaking), executive (law-enforcing), and judiciary (law-interpreting) branches. Finally, the Constitution established a system of checks and balances, giving each branch some scrutiny of and control over the others.

The document written, work began on ratification. A major stumbling block was the failure of the Constitution to list the individual liberties the Americans had fought to protect. With the promise of a bill of rights, the Constitution was ratified. These ten amendments guaranteed participation in the political process, respect for personal beliefs, and personal privacy. They also embodied guarantees against government overreaching in criminal prosecutions. Over the years the Constitution has evolved through the formal amendment process, through the exercise of judicial review, and through political practice.

The Constitution was designed to strike a balance between order and freedom. It was not designed to promote equality; in fact, it had to be amended to redress inequality. The framers did not set out to create a democracy. There was little faith in government by the people two centuries ago. Nevertheless, they produced a democratic form of government. That government, with its separation of powers and checks and balances, is remarkably well suited to the pluralist model of democracy. Simple majority rule, which lies at the heart of the majoritarian model, was precisely what the framers wanted to avoid.

The framers also wanted a government that would balance the powers of the national government and the states. The exact balance was a touchy issue, skirted by the delegates at the Constitutional Convention. Some seventy years later, a civil war was fought over that balance of power. That war and countless political battles before and after it have demonstrated that the national government dominates the state governments in our political system. In the next chapter, we look at how a loose confederation of states has evolved into a "more perfect Union."

KEY TERMS

Continental Congress
Declaration of
    Independence
social contract theory
republic
confederation
sovereignty
Articles of
    Confederation
Shays' Rebellion
Virginia Plan
legislative branch
executive branch
judicial branch
New Jersey Plan
Great Compromise
electoral college
republicanism

federalism
unitary government
separation of powers
checks and balances
bicameral
enumerated powers
necessary and proper
    clause
elastic clause
implied powers
judicial review
supremacy clause
Bill of Rights
proposal
ratification
extraordinary majorities
progressive taxation

SELECTED READINGS

Beard, Charles A. *Economic Interpretation of the Constitution of the United States.* New York: Macmillan, 1913. Beard argues that the framers' economic self-interest was the motivating force behind the Constitution.

Becker, Carl. *The Declaration of Independence: A Study in the History of Political Ideas.* New York: Knopf, 1942. A classic study of the theory and politics of the Declaration of Independence.

Bowen, Catherine Drinker. *Miracle at Philadelphia.* Boston: Atlantic–Little, Brown, 1966. An absorbing, well-written account of the events surrounding the Constitutional Convention.

Kammen, Michael. *A Machine That Would Go of Itself: The Constitution in American Culture.* New York: Knopf, 1986. A remarkable examination of the Constitution's cultural impact. The author argues that Americans' reverence for the Constitution is inconsistent with their ignorance of its content and meaning.

Kurland, Philip B., and Ralph Lerner (eds.) *The Founders' Constitution* (5 vols.) Chicago: University of Chicago Press, 1987. A thorough collection of primary documents designed to explain the Constitution; it is organized around the structure of the Constitution from Preamble through Amendment XII.

McDonald, Forrest. *Novus Ordo Seclorum: The Intellectual Origins of the Constitution.* Lawrence, Kan.: University Press of Kansas, 1985. An authoritative examination of the intellectual ferment surrounding the birth of the U.S. Constitution.

Rakove, Jack N. *The Beginnings of National Politics: An Interpretive History of the Continental Congress.* New York: Knopf, 1979. A history of the Continental Congress and the difficulties of governing under the Articles of Confederation.

Storing, Herbert J. *What the Anti-Federalists Were For.* Chicago: University of Chicago Press, 1981. An analysis of the arguments against the Constitution.

Wills, Garry. *Explaining America: The Federalist.* Garden City, N.Y.: Doubleday, 1981. This arresting work analyzes the intellectual background of the framers.

Wood, Gordon S. *The Creation of the American Republic, 1776–1787.* Chapel Hill, N.C.: University of North Carolina Press, 1969. A penetrating study of political thought in the early period of the new republic.

4 FEDERALISM

STEVE OLIGMUELLER, AGE nineteen, Highmore High School class of 1986, had returned home to South Dakota for the summer. At night, he would get together with old friends and swap stories about freshman year at college. They would meet at The Stable, a local bar, to sit, talk, listen to music, and have a couple of beers. In the spring of 1987, South Dakota was one of four states that still allowed people under twenty-one to drink beer. Soon, however, the cost of letting nineteen-year-olds drink beer would go up drastically—not just for Steve and his friends, but for all the taxpayers of South Dakota. The state stood to lose nearly $10 million in federal highway funds unless it raised its minimum drinking age to twenty-one.

Just three years earlier, twenty-nine states and the District of Columbia allowed people under twenty-one to purchase and consume some forms of alcoholic beverages. In 1984, however, an action taken in Washington, D.C., marked the beginning of the end of legalized drinking for those under twenty-one. What happened? Did Congress establish a national minimum drinking age? No, at least not directly. Congress simply added a provision to a highway bill. Under that provision, states would lose 5 percent of their federal highway funds in 1986 and 10 percent in 1987 if they allowed the purchase or consumption of alcohol by those under twenty-one. States themselves would have to change their own laws or risk losing federal funds. This was a roundabout method to achieve a national objective. If the national government wanted to set twenty-one as a national drinking age, why not act directly and pass legislation to do so?

The simplest answer has to do with the federal system of government. The Constitution divided power between the national and state governments. With only one sobering exception (Prohibition and the Eighteenth Amendment), regulating liquor sales and setting minimum drinking ages had always been the responsibilities of state governments. But over the years, the national government has found ways to extend its influence into areas well beyond those originally defined in the Constitution.

How did the national government become concerned about the drinking age? Mothers Against Drunk Driving (MADD) and other interest groups had fought hard to increase public awareness of the dangers of driving drunk, and they argued that a uniform drinking age of twenty-one would reduce highway fatalities. The National Transportation Safety Board estimated that 1,250 lives could be saved each year by raising the drinking age. But campaigning for change on a state-by-state basis would be slow and might even be dangerous. As long as some states allowed teenagers to drink, young people would be able to drive across state lines in order to drink legally. The borders between states would become "blood borders," strewn with the victims of teenage drinking and driving.

Supporters of the legislation believed that the national government's responsibility to maintain order justified intervention. The lives and safety of people were at stake. Opponents of the plan argued that it constituted age discrimination and infringed on states' rights. They claimed the act was an unwarranted extension of national power, that it limited the freedom of the states and of their citizens.

Wall of Shame

The group Mothers Against Drunk Driving (MADD) campaigns hard to get drunk drivers off the road. It supports national legislation and also takes aim at state legislatures, urging tougher sanctions for driving under the influence. Here, relatives of victims of drunk drivers examine MADD's "victim board," displayed on the west steps of the U.S. Capitol to mark MADD's tenth anniversary.

Despite this opposition, the bill passed handily and went to President Reagan for signing. Reagan had campaigned on a pledge to reduce the size and scope of the national government, and he strongly opposed replacing state standards with national ones. Where would he come out on this issue, which pitted order against freedom and national standards against state standards? Early on, he opposed the bill; later, he changed his position. At the signing ceremony, he said, "This problem is bigger than the individual states. It's a grave national problem and it touches all our lives. With the problem so clear cut and the proven solution at hand we have no misgiving about this judicious use of federal power. I'm convinced that it will help persuade state legislators to act in the national interest."[1]

Several states took the matter to court, hoping to have the provision declared unconstitutional under the Tenth and the Twenty-first Amendments. In June 1987, the Supreme Court reached its decision in *South Dakota* v. *Dole*.[2] The justices conceded that direct congressional control of the drinking age in the states would be unconstitutional. Nevertheless, there was no constitutional barrier to the *indirect* achievement of such objectives. The 7–2 majority argued that far from being an infringement on states' rights, the law was a "relatively mild encouragement to the states to enact higher minimum drinking ages than they otherwise would choose." After all, Chief Justice William Rehnquist wrote, the goal of reducing drunk driving was "directly related to one of the main purposes for which highway funds are expended: safe interstate travel."

Rehnquist's words show how much the role of the national government has changed since the Constitution was adopted. In the early part of the last century, chief executives routinely vetoed bills authorizing roads, canals, and other interstate improvements. They believed these kinds of projects exceeded the constitutional authority of the national government. Eventually, the national government used its authority over interstate commerce to justify a role in building roads. Witness the 46,000-mile interstate highway system. In 1991, the national government contributed more than $15 billion to cost-sharing projects with the states for road research, planning, and construction.[3]

The Highway Act of 1984 shows how national and state governments can interact. Congress did not challenge the constitutional power of the states to regulate the minimum drinking age (under the Twenty-first Amendment), but it used its own powers to tax and spend to encourage the states to implement a national standard (see Article I, Section 8, clause 1). Lawmakers in Washington believed that few states would pass up highway funds to retain power, and they were right.

An important element of federalism was at work here: the respective sovereignty of national and state governments. (Sovereignty is the quality of being supreme in power or authority.) Congress acknowledged the sovereignty of the states by not legislating a national drinking age. And the states were willing to barter their sovereignty in exchange for needed revenues. As long as this remains true, there are few areas where national power cannot reach.

Sovereignty also affects political leadership. A governor may not be the political equal of a president, but a governor and a president represent different sovereignties. Consequently, presidents rarely command governors; they negotiate, even plead.

In this chapter, we examine American federalism in theory and in practice. Is the division of power between nation and states a matter of constitutional principle or practical politics? How does the balance of power between nation and states relate to the conflicts between freedom and order, and between freedom and equality? Does federalism reflect the pluralist or the majoritarian model of democracy?

Theories of Federalism

The delegates who met in Philadelphia in 1787 were supposed to repair weaknesses in the Articles of Confederation. Instead, they tackled the problem of making one nation out of thirteen independent states by doing something much more radical. They wrote a new constitution and invented a new political form—federal government—which combined features of a confederacy with features of unitary government (see Chapter 3). Under this principle of **federalism,** two or more governments would exercise power and authority over the same people and the same territory. (Table 4.1 provides instances of federalism in the Constitution.) For example, the governments of the United States and Pennsylvania would share certain powers (the power to tax, for instance), while other

TABLE 4.1 *Examples of Federalism in the U.S. Constitution*

These examples illustrate some ways in which the Constitution provides guarantees to and limits on the states.

Guarantees to the States	Limits on the States
1. General	
Powers not delegated to the U.S. by the Constitution, or prohibited by it to the states, are reserved to the states (Amend. X)	States cannot enter into treaties, alliances, or confederations (Art. I, Sec. 10)
No division or consolidation of states without state legislative consent (Art. IV, Sec. 2)	No separate coinage (Art. I, Sec. 10)
	Constitution, all laws and treaties made under it, to be the supreme law of the land, binding every state (Art. VI)
2. Military	
Power to maintain and appoint militia officers (Art. I, Sec. 8; Amend. II)	No maintenance of standing military forces in peacetime without congressional consent (Art. I, Sec. 10)
3. Commerce, Money, and Taxation	
Equal apportionment of direct federal taxes (Art. I, Sec. 2, 9)	No levying of duties on vessels of other states (Art. I, Sec. 10)
No preferential treatment for ports of one state (Art. I, Sec. 9)	No legal tender other than gold or silver (Art. I, Sec. 10)
4. Justice	
Federal criminal trials to be held in state where crime was committed (Art. III, Sec. 2)	No bills of attainder or ex post facto laws (Art. I, Sec. 10)
Extradition for crimes (Art. IV, Sec. 2)	No denial of life, liberty, or property without due process of law (Amend. XIV)
5. Representation: Congress	
Members of House of Representatives chosen by voters (Art. I, Sec. 2)	Representatives must be 25 years old and U.S. citizens for seven years (Art. I, Sec. 2)
At time of elections, senators and representatives must be inhabitants of the states from which they are elected (Art. I, Sec. 2, 3)	Senators must be 30 years old and U.S. citizens for nine years (Art. I, Sec. 4)
	Congress may make or alter regulations as to the times, places, and manner of holding elections for senators and representatives (Art. I, Sec. 4)
Representation: President	
To be selected by the electors of the several states, with each allotted a number of electors equal to the total number of senators and representatives (Art. II, Sec. 1)	Congress may determine the time of choosing electors and a uniform day on which they shall cast their votes (Art. II, Sec. 1)
Each state shall have one vote if the presidential election is decided in the House of Representatives (Art. II, Sec. 1)	
6. Amendments to the Constitution	
Amendments must be ratified by three-fourths of the states (Art. V)	
Amendments can be proposed by two-thirds of the states (Art. V)	
7. Voting	
	Cannot be denied or abridged on grounds of race, color, or previous condition of servitude (Amend. XV, Sec. 1)
	Cannot be denied or abridged on account of sex (Amend. XIX, Sec. 1)
8. Foreign Affairs	
Treaties must be ratified by two-thirds of the Senate (Art. II, Sec. 2)	Treaties binding on states are the supreme law of the land (Art. VI)

Local Cops, National Cops

Local, state, and national governments share certain powers, such as law enforcement. Houston police officers enforce local criminal laws in a continuing campaign against illegal drugs (left). A SWAT team from the Federal Bureau of Investigation, the principal investigative arm of the national government, arrives to quiet a riot at a federal penitentiary in Atlanta (right).

powers would belong exclusively to one or the other. As James Madison wrote in "Federalist No. 10," "The federal Constitution forms a happy combination . . . the great and aggregate interests being referred to the national, and the local and particular to state governments." So the power to coin money belongs to the national government; the power to grant divorces remains a state prerogative. By contrast, authority over the state militia may sometimes belong to the national government and sometimes to the state government. The history of American federalism reveals that it has not always been easy to draw a line between what is "great and aggregate" and what is "local and particular."*

Nevertheless, federalism offered a solution to the problem of diversity in America. It also provided a new political model. A leading scholar of federalism estimates that today 40 percent of the world's population lives under a formal federal constitution, while another 30 percent lives in polities that apply federal principles or practices without formal constitutional acknowledgment.[4] Although federalism offers an approach that unifies diverse people into nations, it also retains the elements that can lead to national disunity. Canada and the Soviet Union are examples of federal systems now coping with the possible dissolution of their constituent parts (see Compared with What? 4.1).

Representations of American Federalism

The history of American federalism is full of attempts to capture its true meaning in an adjective or metaphor. By one recent reckoning,

---

* The everyday phrase Americans use to refer to their central government—*federal government*—muddies the waters even more. Technically speaking, we have a *federal system of government* that includes both national and state governments. To avoid confusion from here on, we use the term *national government* rather than *federal government* when we are talking about the central government.

COMPARED WITH WHAT?   4.1

Canadian Break-up and Soviet Split?

Federalism tolerates the centrifugal forces that can sunder a nation (such as language, culture, religion) and provides the centripetal forces that bind it (such as the powers to tax and spend, raise armies, and control a national economy). But federalism is no guarantee that the forces of unity will always overcome the forces of disunity. In fact, the seeds of conflict may be sewn into the federal form of government. Consider two current examples.

Canada is a federation composed of ten provinces. But the Canadian province of Quebec is different. Eighty percent of its population is French-speaking; almost half speak little or no English. (The vast majority of Canadians outside Quebec speak only English.) Quebec has its own holidays, music videos, even its own literature. By law, all signs must be in French. English is barely tolerated.

For decades, Canadians have struggled with the dual challenge of assimilating and differentiating Quebec. When Canada drafted a new constitution in 1982, Quebec refused to sign it. Quebecers conditioned their union with the other provinces on a constitutional amendment that would recognize Quebec as a "distinct society" within the country. The amendment, known as the Meech Lake Accord, had to be approved by all ten provinces. The accord failed when two provinces—Newfoundland and Manitoba—refused to ratify the Quebec agreement by the June 1990 deadline. The dissenting provinces complained that Quebec would become "more equal" than the other provinces through the constitutional protection and promotion of its distinct society.

Quebec officials now hope for a substantial change in the federal arrangement. If Quebec has its way, the central government in Ottawa would be reduced to overseeing matters of defense, customs, and common currency. Even foreign policy and the post office would be shared by Quebec and federal officials.

Will Quebec secede? Will Canada tolerate secession? The answers are not yet clear.

The Union of Soviet Socialist Republics is a federation of fifteen republics. In 1991, after five years of openness and political and social reform under

Quebec Demonstration, 1990

the leadership of President Mikhail Gorbachev, Soviet voters had a chance to express a *"Da"* or a *"Nyet"* on a complex issue: "Do you consider it necessary to preserve the Union of Soviet Socialist Republics as a renewed federation of equal sovereign republics in which the rights and freedoms of the people of any nationality will be fully guaranteed?"

More than 80 percent of the nation's 178 million eligible voters took part; 78 percent of those who voted sided with continued union. But the threat of a splintered nation remains. Eight republics refused to participate in the referendum on the ground that they have already resolved to exercise greater independence from Moscow. And the Baltic republics (Estonia, Latvia, and Lithuania) had previously vowed to separate from the federation, so the referendum there was viewed as irrelevant.

Disunion remains a threat in the Soviet Union as continued economic distress produces more shortages, lines, impoverishment, and disorder.

Will one or more republics secede? Will the central government tolerate secession? The answers are not yet clear.

Federalism in a diverse nation requires a delicate balance to sustain national cohesion and protect legitimate regional differences. Relaxing the cohesive forces may encourage splintering. Yet attempts to extinguish regional differences may prompt revolution. Only time will tell whether Canada and the Soviet Union will resolve their internal differences peacefully or aggressively.

scholars have generated nearly five hundred ways to describe federalism.[5] Let us concentrate on two such representations: dual federalism and cooperative federalism.

Dual Federalism

The expression **dual federalism** sums up a theory about the proper relationship between the national government and the states. This theory has four essential parts. First, the national government rules by enumerated powers only. Second, the national government has a limited set of constitutional purposes. Third, each government unit—nation and state—is sovereign within its sphere. And fourth, the relationship between nation and states is best characterized by tension rather than cooperation.[6]

Dual federalism portrays the states as powerful components of the federal system—in some ways, the equals of the national government. Under dual federalism, the functions and responsibilities of the national and state governments are theoretically different and practically separate from each other. Dual federalism sees the Constitution as a compact among sovereign states. Of primary importance in dual federalism are **states' rights,** a concept that reserves to the states all rights not specifically conferred on the national government by the Constitution. Claims of states' rights often come from opponents of a national government policy. Their argument is that the people have not delegated the power to make such policy, and thus the power remains in the states or the people. According to the theory of dual federalism, a rigid wall separates nation and states. After all, if the states created the nation, by implication, they can set limits on the activities of the national government. Proponents of states' rights believe that the powers of the national government should be interpreted very narrowly. They insist that, despite the elastic clause, which gives Congress the implied powers needed to execute its enumerated powers (see Chapter 3), the activities of Congress should be confined to the enumerated powers only. And they support their view by quoting the Tenth Amendment: "The powers not delegated to the United States by the Constitution, nor prohibited by it to the States, are reserved to the states respectively, or to the people."

Political scientists use a metaphor to describe dual federalism. They call it *layer-cake federalism*. The powers and functions of national and state governments are separate—as separate as the layers of a cake (see Figure 4.1). Each government is supreme in its own "layer," its own sphere of action; the two layers are distinct; and the dimensions of each layer are fixed by the Constitution.

This concept of federalism has found its way into Supreme Court opinions, particularly in the late nineteenth and early twentieth centuries. For example, in *Hammer* v. *Dagenhart* (1918), which declared a national child labor law unconstitutional, Justice William R. Day wrote that "the powers not expressly delegated to the national government are reserved" to the states and to the people.[7] In his wording, Day revised the Constitution slightly and changed the intent of the framers: The Tenth Amendment does not use the word *expressly*. The framers purposely left it out

FIGURE 4.1 *Metaphors for Federalism*

The two views of federalism can be represented graphically.

Dual Federalism:
The Layer-Cake Metaphor

Citizens cutting into the political system will find clear differences between state and national powers, functions, and responsibilities.

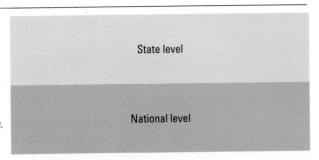

State level

National level

Cooperative Federalism:
The Marble-Cake Metaphor

Citizens cutting into the political system at any point will find national and state powers, functions, and responsibilities mixed and mingled.

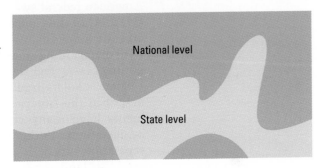

National level

State level

of the amendment because they believed they could not possibly specify every power that might be needed in the future to run the government. As discussed in Chapter 3, those powers not specifically mentioned, but necessary for the implementation of the enumerated powers, are called the **implied powers.**

Dual federalism—the theory that underlies the layer-cake metaphor—has been challenged on historical and other grounds. Some critics argue that if the national government is really a creation of the states, it is a creation of only thirteen states—those that ratified the Constitution. The other thirty-seven states were admitted after the national government came into being and were created by that government out of land it had acquired. Another challenge has to do with the ratification process. Remember, the original thirteen states ratified the Constitution in special conventions, not in state legislatures. Ratification, then, was an act of the *people,* not the *states.* Moreover, the Preamble to the Constitution begins "We the people of the United States . . . ," not "We the States . . . ." The question of just where the people fit into the federal system is not handled very well by dual federalism.

Cooperative Federalism

Cooperative federalism, a phrase coined in the 1930s, embraces a different theory of the relationship between national and state governments. It acknowledges the increasing overlap in state and national functions and rejects the idea of separate spheres, or layers, for the states and the national government. Cooperative federalism includes three elements. First, national and state agencies typically undertake governmental functions jointly, rather than exclusively. Second, nation and states routinely share power. And, third, power is not concentrated at any government level, or in any agency; this fragmentation of responsibilities gives people and groups access to many centers of influence.

Unlike dual federalism, cooperative federalism blurs the distinction between national and state powers. The bakery metaphor used to describe this kind of federalism is a *marble cake.* The national and state governments do not act in separate spheres; they are intermingled in vertical and diagonal strands and swirls. Their functions are mixed in the American federal system. Critical to cooperative federalism is an expansive view of the Constitution's supremacy clause (Article VI), which specifically subordinates state law to national law and charges every judge with disregarding state laws that are inconsistent with the Constitution, national laws, and treaties.

Some scholars argue that the layer-cake metaphor has never accurately described the American political structure.[8] National and state governments have many common objectives and have often cooperated to achieve them. In the nineteenth century, for example, cooperation—not separation—made it possible to develop transportation systems and to establish land-grant colleges. The layer cake might be a good model of what dual federalists *think* the relationship between national and state governments should be, but it does not square with the facts of American history.

A critical difference between the theories of dual and cooperative federalism is the way they interpret two sections of the Constitution that set out the terms of the relationship between the national and state governments. Article I, Section 8 lists the enumerated powers of the Congress, then concludes with the **elastic clause,** which gives Congress the power to "make all Laws which shall be necessary and proper for carrying into Execution the foregoing Powers." The Tenth Amendment, as we have seen, reserves to the states or the people "powers" not given to the national government or denied to the states by the Constitution. Dual federalism postulates an inflexible elastic clause and a capacious Tenth Amendment. Cooperative federalism postulates suppleness in the elastic clause and confines the Tenth Amendment to a self-evident, obvious truth.

In their efforts to limit the scope of the national government, conservatives have given much credence to the layer-cake metaphor. In contrast, liberals, believing that one of the functions of the national government is to bring about equality, have argued that the marble-cake metaphor is more accurate. These are not the only metaphors used to describe federalism, however.

- Ronald Reagan saw federalism as a *masonry wall*: "The founding fathers saw the federal system constructed as something like a masonry wall. The states are the bricks and the national government is the mortar. For the structure to stand plumb, there must be a proper mix of bricks and mortar."[9]

- *Flypaper federalism* describes the growth of federal restraints on state and city recipients. State and local government welcome money from the national government but "before you are through, you are in the middle of all sorts of side effects. There are more and more things you get stuck to."[10]
- *Fruitcake federalism* (a term discussed later in this chapter) sees intergovernmental relations as "bogged down, congealed, suffocated, sodden and shapeless."[11]
- Finally, one scholar uses the image of an *upside-down cake* to describe the inversion of power in the current system of federalism. According to this metaphor, national government officials appear to have enormous power and can insist on conformity with all sorts of conditions as prerequisites for state and local governments. But program administration rests almost totally with state and local governments. National officials are virtually powerless to see that a program is successfully administered and that national objectives are accomplished. Hence, upside-down cake federalism![12]

Instructive or amusing as these metaphors may be, they cannot completely describe federalism in the United States. Federalism isn't something written or implied in the Constitution; the Constitution is only the starting point in the debate. The real meaning of American federalism must be found in its implementation.

The Dynamics of Federalism: Legal Sanctions and Financial Incentives

Although the Constitution defines a kind of federalism, the actual balance of power between nation and states has always been more a matter of politics than of formal theory. A discussion of federalism, then, must do more than simply list the powers the Constitution assigns the levels of government. The balance of power has shifted substantially since President Madison agonized over the proper role the national government should play in funding roads. Today, that government has assumed functions never dreamed of in the nineteenth century.

Why has power shifted so dramatically from the states to the national government? The answer lies in historical circumstances, not debates over constitutional theory. For example, the greatest test of states' rights came when several southern states attempted to secede from the union. The threat of secession challenged the supremacy of the national government, a supremacy that northern armies established militarily in the nation's greatest bloodbath, the Civil War. But the Civil War by no means settled all the questions about relations between governments in the United States. Many more remained to be answered, and new issues kept cropping up.

Some changes in the balance of power were the product of constitutional amendments. Several amendments have had an enormous impact, either direct or indirect, on the shape of the federal system. For example, the due process and equal protection clauses of the Fourteenth Amendment (1868) limited states' rights, as did the income tax mandated by the Sixteenth Amendment (1913) and the Seventeenth Amendment's provision for the direct election of senators (1913).*

Most of the national government's power has come to it through legislation, judicial interpretation, and political coercion. Al Capone, the notorious Chicago gangster of the Prohibition era, once observed, "You can get much further with a kind word and a gun than you can with a kind word alone." The national government has used force of arms only once against the states (in the Civil War). But the states, like Capone's associates, understand the ultimate threat of coercion.

The national government has relied primarily on two distinct approaches to expand its power. Some are incentives to win state cooperation; others are sanctions (that is, mechanisms of social or economic control) designed to "pinch" in an effort to secure cooperation. Here we look at these tools of political change.

Legislation and the Elastic Clause

The elastic clause of the Constitution gives Congress the power to make all laws that are "necessary and proper" to carry out its responsibilities. By using this power in combination with its enumerated powers, Congress has been able to increase the scope of the national government tremendously over the last two centuries. Change has often come in times of crisis and national emergency—the Civil War, the Great Depression, the world wars. The role of the national government has grown as it has responded to needs and demands that state and local governments were unwilling or unable to meet.

Legislation is one of the prods the national government has used to achieve goals at the state level, to force the states to comply. The Voting Rights Act of 1965 is a good example. Section 2 of Article I of the Constitution gives the states the power to set voter qualifications. But the Fifteenth Amendment (1870) provides that no person should be denied the right to vote "on account of race, color, or previous condition of servitude." Before the Voting Rights Act, states could not specifically deny blacks the right to vote, but they could require that voters pass literacy tests or pay poll taxes, requirements that virtually disenfranchised blacks in many states. The Voting Rights Act was designed to correct this political inequality (see Chapter 16).

The act gives officials of the national government the power to decide whether individuals are qualified to vote and requires that qualified individuals be allowed to vote in all elections—including primaries and national, state, and local elections. If there seem to be widespread denials of voting rights, the act authorizes the appointment of national voting examiners, who will examine and register voters for *all* elections. By replacing state election officials, the act intrudes well inside the political sovereignty of the states. The constitutional authority for the act rests on the second section of the Fifteenth Amendment, which

---

* The Fourteenth Amendment was itself a product of the Civil War.

gives Congress the power to enforce the amendment through "appropriate legislation."

Judicial Interpretation

The Voting Rights Act was not a unanimous hit. Its critics adopted the language of dual federalism and insisted that the Constitution gives the states the power to determine voter qualifications. Its supporters claimed that the Fifteenth Amendment guarantee of voting rights takes precedence over states' rights and gives the national government new responsibilities. In this instance, the states tried to defend their freedom to set voter qualifications against the national government's effort to promote political equality.

The conflict was ultimately resolved by the Supreme Court, the arbiter of the federal system. The Court settles disputes over the powers of the national and state governments by deciding whether actions of the national or state governments are constitutional (see Chapter 14). In the nineteenth and early twentieth centuries, the Supreme Court often decided in favor of the states; however, since 1937, it has almost always supported the national government in contests involving the balance of power between nation and states.

The growth of national power has been accomplished through a variety of routes. One is the Supreme Court's interpretation of the Constitution's **commerce clause.** The third clause of Article I, Section 8 states that "Congress shall have the power . . . to regulate Commerce . . . among the several States. . . ." In early Court decisions Chief Justice John Marshall (1801–1835) interpreted the word *commerce* broadly to include virtually every form of commercial activity. The clause's grant of commerce power regulation to the national government substantially withdrew that power from the states. Later decisions by the Court attempted to restrict the national commerce power, but events such as the Great Depression necessitated an enlargement of it. One scholar went so far as to charge that the justices have toyed with the commerce clause, treating it like a shuttlecock to be volleyed by changing majorities.[13] For today, the only limit on the exercise of the commerce power is Congress itself. A future Supreme Court majority may offer yet another view.

During Chief Justice Earl Warren's tenure (1953–1969), the Court used the Fourteenth Amendment to extend various provisions of the Bill of Rights to the states, shifting power from the states to the national government. Court decisions seriously reduced the states' freedom to decide what constitutes due process of law within their jurisdictions. For example, in the landmark *Miranda* decision, the Court ordered that citizens apprehended by the police must be informed of their constitutional rights and that the arresting officer must preserve those rights.[14] Through the Supreme Court, the national government set minimum standards for due process in criminal cases, standards that the states would have to meet. These standards provide equality before the law for individuals who are suspected of crimes, but critics argue that they hamper state officials in trying to maintain order.

A series of decisions concerning reapportionment—resetting the boundaries of electoral districts—also eroded the power of the states in the early 1960s.[15] Until that time, states had set the boundaries of voting districts, but some had failed to adjust those boundaries to reflect changes in population. As a result, in certain areas, small numbers of rural voters were able to elect as many representatives as were large numbers of urban voters. In deciding cases involving reapportionment, the Court set down a new standard of one person, one vote and forced the states to apply this principle in redrawing their districts and apportioning their legislatures.

In the due process and reapportionment cases, the Supreme Court protected individual rights, in the process championing political equality. But remember, the Supreme Court is part of the national government. When it defends the rights of an individual against a state, it also substitutes a national standard for the state standard governing that relationship.

Grants-in-Aid

In the last three decades, Washington's use of financial incentives has rivaled its use of legislation and judicial interpretation as a means of shaping relationships between national and state governments. Since the 1960s, state and local governments have looked to Washington for money more and more often. In 1960, the national government provided 15 percent of the funds spent by state and local governments; by 1980, it was providing 23 percent of those funds. This was the high-water mark in national government revenue for state and local government functions. The principal method the national government uses to make money available to the states is through grants-in-aid.

A **grant-in-aid** is money paid by one level of government to another, to be spent for a specific purpose. Most grants-in-aid come with standards or requirements prescribed by Congress. Many are awarded on a matching basis; that is, recipients must make some contribution of their own, which is then matched by the national government. Grants-in-aid take two general forms: categorical grants and block grants.

Categorical grants are targeted for specific purposes, and restrictions on their use often leave the recipient government relatively little discretion. Recepients today include state governments, local governments, and public and private nonprofit organizations. There are two kinds of categorical grants: formula grants and project grants. **Formula grants,** as their name implies, are distributed according to a particular formula, which specifies who is eligible for the grant and how much each eligible applicant will receive. The formulas used to distribute grant money vary from one grant to another. They may weigh such factors as state per capita income, number of school-age children, urban population, and number of families below the poverty line. In 1989, 155 of the 478 categorical grants offered by the national government were formula grants, a 13 percent increase in two years. The remaining 323 grants were **project grants**—grants awarded on the basis of competitive applications.[16] New grants have focused on AIDS, homelessness, and substance abuse.

TABLE 4.2 *Block and Categorical Grants*

The national government distributed a total of fourteen block grants in 1989; all of them are listed here. These grants cover broad areas and give substantial discretion to recipients. The bottom half of the list contains a few examples of categorical grants, which are only for specific, narrowly defined activities and offer little discretion to recipients. Most aid to state and local governments comes in the form of categorical grants.

Block Grants—1989	Recipient
Urban mass transit	Local government
Community development (two grants)	State and local governments
Elementary, secondary, and vocational education	State government
Job training for disadvantaged adults and youth	State government
Social services	State government
Community services	State government
Mental health for the homeless	State government
Preventive health and health services	State government
Community youth activity	State government
Alcohol, drug abuse, and mental health services	State government
Maternal and child health services	State government
Low-income home energy assistance	State government
Criminal justice	State government

Examples of Categorical Grants	Recipient
Handicapped infants and toddlers	State government
Robert C. Byrd Honors Scholarships	State government
Vocational education: consumer and homemaking education	State government
Library literacy	State and local governments
School construction assistance in case of disasters	Local government
Weatherization assistance for low-income persons	State government
Hunter safety program	State government
Hurricane preparedness	State government

In contrast to categorical grants, **block grants** are awarded for broad, general purposes. They allow recipients considerable freedom in deciding how to allocate money to individual programs. While a categorical grant might be given to promote a very specific activity—say, ethnic heritage studies—a block grant could be offered for elementary, secondary, and vocational education. The state or local government receiving the block grant would then choose the specific educational programs to fund with it. The recipient might use some of the money to support ethnic heritage studies and some to fund consumer education programs. Or the recipient might choose to put all of the money into consumer education programs and spend nothing on ethnic heritage studies. Table 4.2 lists all fourteen block grants and some of the categorical grants made in 1989.

Grants-in-aid are a method of redistributing income. Money is collected by the national government from citizens of all fifty states, then allocated to other citizens, supposedly for worthwhile social purposes. Many grants have worked to remove gross inequalities among states and their citizens. But the formulas used to redistribute this income are not impartial; they are themselves highly political and often subject to debate in Congress.

Whatever its form, grant money comes with strings attached. Many of the strings are there to ensure that the money is used for the purpose for which it was given; other regulations are designed to evaluate how well the grant is working. To this end, the national government may stipulate that recipients follow certain procedures. For example, a recipient may be required to adopt particular accounting procedures or set up special agencies to guarantee that the funds are administered properly.

The national government may also attach other restrictions to the money it grants. Often, these restrictions are designed to achieve some broad national goal, a goal that is not always closely related to the specific purpose of the grant. For example, as noted earlier, the Highway Act of 1984 reduced the amount of money available to states that allowed those under age twenty-one to purchase and consume alcoholic beverages. Other grants prohibit discrimination in the activities funded through them. States have been more than willing to accept these limitations. By March 1988, for example, every state in the nation had approved legislation setting twenty-one as the minimum drinking age. The lure of financial aid has proved to be a powerful incentive for states to relinquish the freedom to set their own standards and to accept those set by the national government.

The Developing Concept of Federalism

A student of federalism once remarked that "each generation faced with new problems has had to work out its own version of federalism." Succeeding generations have used judicial and congressional power in varying degrees to shift the balance of power back and forth between national and state governments.

McCulloch v. Maryland

Early in the nineteenth century, the nationalist interpretation of federalism triumphed over states' rights. In 1819, under Chief Justice John Marshall, the Supreme Court expanded the role of the national government in its decision in *McCulloch* v. *Maryland*.[17] The Court was asked to rule whether Congress had the power to establish a national bank and, if so, whether states had the power to tax that bank. In a unanimous opinion written by Marshall, the Court conceded that Congress had only the powers that the Constitution conferred, and it nowhere mentioned banks. However, Article I granted to Congress the authority to enact all laws "necessary and proper" to the execution of Congress's enumerated powers. Marshall gave a broad interpretation to this elastic clause: "Let the end be legitimate, let it be within the scope of the constitution, and all means which are appropriate, which are plainly adapted to that end, which are not prohibited, but consistent with the letter and spirit of the constitution, are constitutional."

The Court clearly agreed that Congress had the power to charter a bank. But did the states—in this case, Maryland—have the power to tax the bank? Arguing that "the power to tax is the power to destroy," Marshall insisted that states could not tax the national government because the powers of the national government came not from the states but from the people. Marshall here was embracing cooperative federalism, which sees a direct relationship between the people and the national government, with no need for the states to act as intermediaries. To assume that states had the power to tax the national government would be to give them supremacy over the national government. In that case, Marshall wrote, "the declaration that the constitution, and the laws made in pursuance thereof, shall be the supreme law of the land is empty and unmeaning declamation." The framers of the Constitution did not intend to create a meaningless document, he reasoned. Therefore, they must have meant to give the national government all the powers necessary to carry out its assigned functions, even if those powers are only implied.

States' Rights and Dual Federalism

Roger B. Taney became chief justice in 1836, and during his tenure (1836-1864), the balance of power began to shift back toward the states. The Taney Court recognized firm limits on the powers of the national government. As Taney saw it, the Constitution spoke "not only in the same words but with the same meaning and intent with which it spoke when it came from the framers." In the infamous *Dred Scott* decision (1857), for example, the Court decided that Congress had no power to prohibit slavery in the territories.[18]

Many people assume that the Civil War was fought over slavery. It was not. The real issue was the character of the federal union, of federalism itself. At the time of the Civil War, regional variations between northern and southern states were considerable. The southern economy was based on labor-intensive agriculture, very different from the mechanized manufacturing that was developing in the North. As a result, southerners wanted cheap manufactured goods and cheap plantation labor. This led them to support both low tariffs on imported goods and slavery. Northerners, to protect their own economy, wanted high tariffs. When they sought national legislation that threatened southern interests, southerners demanded states' rights. They even introduced the theory of **nullification**—the idea that a state could declare a particular action of the national government null and void. The Civil War rendered the idea of nullification null and void, but it did not settle the balance between national and state power.

In the decades after the Civil War, the Supreme Court continued to place limits on national power, particularly when the national government attempted to regulate industry. Early in the nineteenth century, the Court decided that the national government had supreme power to regulate interstate commerce.[19] Later on, however, the Court rejected the idea that this power could be used to justify policies not directly related to the smooth functioning of interstate commerce—policies such as set-

Made in the U.S.A.
A young factory worker in the early part of this century. The Supreme Court decided in 1918 that Congress had no power to limit child labor. According to the Court, that power belonged to the states, which resisted imposing limits for fear such legislation would drive businesses to other (less restrictive) states.

ting a national minimum wage or abolishing child labor. In the late nineteenth and early twentieth centuries, the justices were influenced by laissez-faire economic theory, a hands-off approach to business. Time and again the Court ruled that congressional legislation that limited the activities of corporations was unconstitutional because it invaded the domain of the states.

In 1918, for example, when Congress tried to use its power to regulate interstate commerce as the basis for legislation regulating child labor, the Court declared the law unconstitutional. The national government argued that a national child labor law was necessary because individual states would not enact such laws; to do so would increase the cost of labor in the state, making it less attractive to industry. The Court recognized this argument but was not persuaded, ruling that national legislation regulating child labor ran counter to both the commerce clause (of Article I, Section 8) and the Tenth Amendment. As Justice Day wrote in *Hammer* v. *Dagenhart:*

> The commerce clause was not intended to give Congress a general authority to equalize conditions [of competition between the states]. If Congress can thus regulate matters intrusted to local authority . . . all freedom of commerce will be at an end, and the power of the states over local matters may be eliminated, and thus our system of government practically destroyed.

The New Deal and Its Consequences

It took the Great Depression to place dual federalism in repose. The problems of the Depression proved too extensive for either state governments or private businesses to handle. So the national government assumed a heavy share of responsibility for providing relief and directing efforts toward economic recovery. Under the New Deal, President Franklin D. Roosevelt's response to the Depression, Congress enacted various emergency relief programs to restore economic activity and help the unemployed (see Chapter 19). Many of these measures required the cooperation of national and state governments. For example, the national government offered funds to stimulate state relief efforts. To receive these funds, however, states were usually required to provide administrative supervision or to contribute some money of their own. Relief efforts were removed from the hands of local bodies and centralized. Through the regulations it attached to funds, the national government extended its power and control over the states.[20]

At first, the Supreme Court's view of the Depression was different from that of the other branches of the national government. The justices believed the Depression was an accumulation of local problems, not a national problem demanding national action. In the Court's opinion, the whole structure of federalism was threatened when collections of local troubles were treated as one national problem. Justice Owen Roberts, in the decision in *United States* v. *Butler* (1936), wrote: "It does not help that local conditions throughout the nation have created a situation of national concern; for this is but to say that whenever there is a widespread similarity of local conditions, Congress may ignore constitutional limitations on its own powers and usurp those reserved to the states."[21] In this decision and others, the Court struck down several pieces of regulatory legislation, including the National Industrial Recovery Act, which would have regulated wages, working hours, and business competition.

In 1937, though, with no change in personnel, the Court began to alter its course. It upheld the Social Security Act and the National Labor Relations Act—both New Deal measures. Perhaps the Court had studied the 1936 election returns (Roosevelt had been re-elected in a landslide, and the Democrats commanded a substantial majority in Congress) and was responding to the country's endorsement of the use of national policies to address national problems. In any event, the Court gave up its effort to set a rigid boundary between national and state power. Only a few years earlier, the Supreme Court had based its thinking about federalism on the Tenth Amendment; but in 1941, Chief Justice Harlan Fiske Stone referred to the Tenth Amendment as "a truism that all is retained that has not been surrendered."[22] In short, the Court agreed that the layer cake was stale and unpalatable. From then on, the division of power in the federal system became less relevant, and the relationship between governments became increasingly important.

Some call the New Deal era "revolutionary." There is no doubt that the period was critical in reshaping federalism in the United States. The national and state governments had cooperated before, but the extent of nation-state interaction during Franklin Roosevelt's administration clearly made the marble cake the more accurate metaphor for American federalism. In addition, the size of the national government and its budget increased tremendously. But perhaps the most significant change was in the way Americans thought about both their problems and the role of the national government in solving them. Difficulties that at one time had been seen as personal or local problems were now national problems, requiring national solutions. The *general welfare,* broadly defined, became a legitimate concern of the national government.

In other respects, however, the New Deal was not very revolutionary. Congress, for example, did not claim that any new powers were needed to deal with the nation's economic problems; it simply used the constitutional powers it had to suit the circumstances. And with one brief exception from the late 1930s on, the Supreme Court upheld Congress's power on virtually every issue.

Desegregation and the War on Poverty

During the 1950s and 1960s, the national government assumed the task of promoting social equality by combating racism and poverty (see Chapters 16 and 19). Both of these problems had seemed impossible to solve at the state level.

Matters of race relations had generally been left to the states, which more or less ignored them despite the constitutional amendments passed after the Civil War. Moreover, when the Supreme Court adopted the separate-but-equal doctrine in 1896,* states were free to do as much—or as little—as they pleased about racial inequality.[23]

In 1954, however, in *Brown* v. *Board of Education,* the Supreme Court decided that racially separate but objectively equal public schools were inherently *unequal.*[24] This put the national government in the position of ordering the desegregation of public schools. As the civil rights movement focused increasing attention on the problems of discrimination, Congress passed two important pieces of legislation: the Civil Rights Act of 1964 and the Voting Rights Act of 1965. Through these acts, the national government used its legislative sanction to outlaw racial discrimination in employment, in public accommodations, and in voter qualifications. The acts themselves sharply limited states' rights where the effect of those rights had been to deny equality.

In the 1960s, President Lyndon Johnson's War on Poverty generated an enormous amount of social legislation and a massive increase in the scope of the national government. In an attempt to provide equality of opportunity and improve the quality of life throughout the United States, the national government used money inducements to introduce a number of new programs, including vastly increased aid to higher education, aid to elementary and secondary schools, school breakfasts and lunches, food stamps, and a huge array of economic development, public service, and employment-training projects. To administer these programs, government bureaucracies were enlarged, on both national and state levels. In fact, during the 1960s and 1970s, state bureaucracies grew even faster than the national bureaucracy.

Johnson's recipe for marble-cake federalism included some new ingredients. Before 1960, nearly all intergovernmental assistance (that is, aid from one level of government to another) had gone from the national

---

* In *Plessy* v. *Ferguson* (1896), the Supreme Court upheld state-imposed racial segregation, ruling that separate facilities for blacks and whites could be maintained as long as they were "equal" (see Chapter 16).

Reach Out and Touch Someone

The levels of government in the federal system are now intertwined. Here, in an intergovernmental conference call, New York senators Daniel Patrick Moynihan and Alfonse D'Amato discuss funding projects with the governor of New York and the mayor of New York City.

government to state governments. But the War on Poverty often gave aid directly to local governments or even to community groups.

As the role of the national government grew larger and was more generally accepted, the focus of the debate over federalism changed. National, state, and local governments were no longer separate, distinct layers; they interacted. But how? The search for answers to this question placed **intergovernmental relations** at center stage. Since the 1960s, the various levels of American government have become highly interdependent. The study of intergovernmental relations looks at that interdependence and the connections among personnel and policies at different levels of government. It also examines the ways that national, state, and local governments influence one another.

The political dynamics of intergovernmental relations since the 1960s suggested a new metaphor for federalism: **picket fence federalism** (see Figure 4.2). Here, the fence rails are the levels of government—national, state, and local—and the fence slats are the interests of lobbies and groups, both inside and outside of government, and the functions of government. The communities of interest (or functions) represented by each slat make contact at each of the three levels of government. They are able to share information, develop common standards, and exert pressure on each level of government. Government officials themselves may move along the interest slats to influence officials on other rails. On a typical trip to Washington, for instance, the head of a state department of education might have a morning meeting with members of the state's congressional delegation to make them aware of the state's educational needs and priorities, then go to lunch with lobbyists from the National

Education Association (NEA) before testifying in front of a congressional committee on education and meeting with officials from the U.S. Department of Education. Our tired official might return to the office the next day to find an education chief from a neighboring state on the phone, hoping to find out how the visit went.

Since the 1960s, the national government has provided money for all sorts of local programs—rat control, jellyfish control, crime control, bike path construction, urban gardening, rural fire protection, solid waste disposal, home insulation, library services (see Figure 4.3). Far from being unresponsive, Congress has become hyperresponsive. And its willingness to spend national funds has increased the importance of existing interest groups and led to the creation of new ones. The result is not just pluralist democracy, but *hyperpluralism*—every conceivable interest has its group. Many smaller (and weaker) state groups have united nationally to lobby for national solutions (via national money) to their problems. A number of state and local governments have seen a need to lobby for their own interests, perhaps in self-defense.

The growth of government programs, the hyperresponsiveness of Congress, and the pressure of interest groups have created a federal system that critics describe as "overloaded and out of control." In keeping with the bakery metaphors often used to describe federalism, one writer suggested that layer-cake federalism and marble-cake federalism have given way to "fruitcake" federalism—a federalism that is formless and indestructible and offers lots of sweets for everyone.[25]

When the Advisory Commission on Intergovernmental Relations (ACIR), a group created by Congress to monitor the federal system, reviewed the operation of that system in 1980, it concluded that fruitcake

FIGURE 4.2 *Picket Fence Federalism*

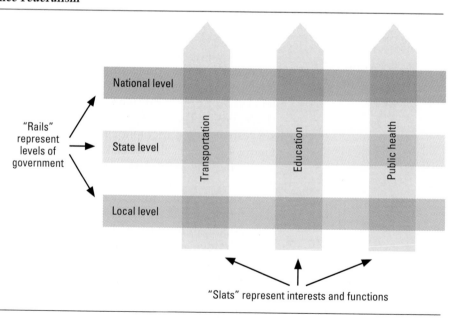

The picket fence model shows how functions cross government lines and also connect the officials who work at different levels of government.

"Rails" represent levels of government

National level

State level

Local level

Transportation

Education

Public health

"Slats" represent interests and functions

FIGURE **4.3** *The Growth and Decline of Categorical Grants and Grants-in-Aid, 1946–1989*

Numbers of categorical grants and amounts of grants-in-aid increased sharply during the War on Poverty. Although the Carter and Reagan years saw substantial cuts in programs funded by the national government, by the late 1980s new programs to meet new needs were again being funded. Nevertheless, from 1978 to 1988 grant money to state and local governments decreased in real value by 14 percent. (Sources: Advisory Commission on Intergovernmental Relations [ACIR], The Federal Role in the Federal System: The Dynamics of Growth [Washington, D.C., 1980], pp. 120–121; ACIR, Significant Features of Fiscal Federalism [Washington, D.C., 1983], p. 120; ACIR, A Catalogue of Federal Grant-in-Aid Programs to State and Local Governments, Grants Funded FY 1987 [Washington, D.C., 1987], p. 1; and Budget of the United States Government, FY 1991, Historical Table 12.1, p. A-321.)

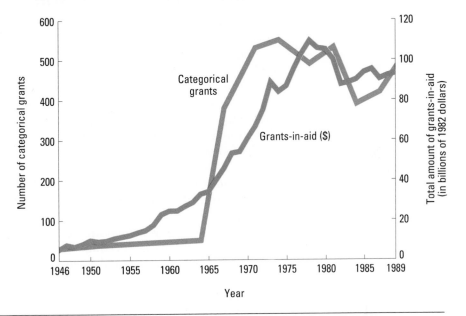

federalism was dysfunctional; it just did not work. Over the last two decades, the commission said, the system of intergovernmental relations had become "more pervasive, more intrusive, more unmanageable, more ineffective, more costly and more unaccountable."[26]

A New, Newer, Newest Federalism

Every president since Richard Nixon has expressed disenchantment with the unmanageability of the federal system. Every president since Nixon has pledged to cut the size of the bureaucracy and return power to the states. Yet reform has been difficult to implement. At the national level, a growing body of rules and regulations often places new responsibilities on state and local government without providing adequate resources to carry out the national mandate. The national government can and does operate at a deficit and can print money to make up the difference between revenues and expenditures. However, all the states (except Vermont) are bound by law to balance their budgets. If spend they must, the states face only two choices: reduce overall spending or raise revenues.

There are limits in exercising these options. Voters will tolerate spending cuts as long as their favorite programs remain intact, and they will tolerate increases in taxes as long as increases are minimal or others pay a greater share. But when budget cutting affects programs with wide appeal and when taxes rise significantly, politicians head for cover and voters look with increasing disfavor on incumbents.

Nixon's New Federalism: Revenue Sharing

When Nixon came to office in 1969, he pledged to change a national government he characterized as "overly centralized, overbureaucratized . . . unresponsive as well as inefficient." He dubbed his solution to the problem "New Federalism" and claimed it would channel "power, funds and authority . . . to those governments closest to the people." He expected New Federalism to help restore control of the nation's destiny "by returning a greater share of control to state and local authorities."[27] New Federalism was nothing more than dual federalism in modern dress.

The centerpiece of Nixon's New Federalism was *revenue sharing,* in which the national government would turn tax revenues over to the states and localities to spend as they pleased. The plan had two parts: general revenue sharing and special revenue sharing. **General revenue sharing** provided new money to be used as state and local governments saw fit, with very few strings attached. Initially, Congress was quite willing to fund the general revenue sharing program. Because it was a new program, no one was required to give up anything for it. And, when general revenue sharing began in 1972, many states and cities were in the middle of financial crises. The program was very popular with the governments it helped, but over the years members of Congress became less enamored of it. They did not have the same control over revenue sharing funds that they had over the more traditional categorical grants. And lawmakers could not take credit for these widely dispersed funds; they preferred the good will derived from narrowly focused grants to their districts. As a result, Congress did not allow the funding for general revenue sharing to grow as categorical grant funds had. In 1986, general revenue sharing was phased out completely.

The second part of Nixon's New Federalism, **special revenue sharing,** was a plan to consolidate existing categorical grant programs. Money available under several categorical programs in a particular area (for example, health services) would be combined into one large block grant. But Congress was reluctant to lose the political credit and control it had under the existing grant system. In addition, the dynamics of intergovernmental relations worked against the consolidation of programs: Interest groups lobbied hard to keep their pet projects from being consolidated. All of this combined to slow the progress of special revenue sharing during the Nixon years.

Nixon's New Federalism, then, was not very successful in stemming the flow of power from the states to the national government. The dollar

FIGURE 4.4 *The National Government's Contribution Fades*

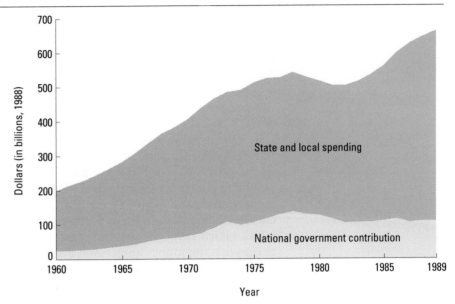

In the 1970s, the national government contributed 25 percent of state and local government spending. By the end of the 1980s, the national government's contribution declined to about 17 percent. As the national government's spending declined, state and local government spending accelerated, especially for Medicaid, welfare, prisons, and education. (Source: "80's Leave States and Cities in Need," New York Times, 30 December 1990, Sec. 1, p. 1. Copyright © 1990 by The New York Times Company. Reprinted by permission.)

amounts of aid continued to grow, and the programs funded continued to increase in number and kind. The national government gave more aid to the states, and that aid carried more and more strings.

The perception that the federal system was bloated and out of control began to take hold. In 1976, Jimmy Carter campaigned for president as an outsider who promised to reduce the size and cost of the national government. And he did have some success. As Figure 4.4 shows, after 1978, national government aid to states and localities actually did begin to drop.

New Federalism Under Reagan and Bush

Ronald Reagan took office in 1981 promising a "new New Federalism" that would "restore a proper constitutional relationship between the federal, state and local governments." He criticized the contemporary version of federalism, charging that "the federal system had been bent out of shape." The national government had become the senior partner in intergovernmental relations, treating "elected state and local officials as if they were nothing more than administrative agents for federal authority."

Reagan's commitment to reduce taxes as well as government spending meant he could not offer the incentive of new funding to make his New Federalism palatable. He did resurrect an element of Nixon's New Federalism, however, in the use of block grants. In the first year of the Reagan administration, Congress agreed to combine seventy-seven categorical grants into nine block grants. To build support for the plan, Reagan emphasized the freedom state officials would have in using their block grant money. He pointed out that the elimination of restrictive categorical programs would reduce administrative burdens, and, as a result, state and local programs could be run at lower cost. State officials were enthusiastic about the prospect of having greater control over grant funds; they were less enthusiastic when they realized that the amounts they received would be cut by approximately 25 percent. The share of state and local bills footed by the national government began to fall (see Figure 4.4). In 1978, the national government footed 25 percent of state and local budgets. By 1989, the national government provided 17 percent of the costs.

In 1982, Reagan proposed a more thorough overhaul of the federal system. This time he offered a *program swap,* in which some forty-four programs previously funded or administered by the national government would be put under state control. At the same time, the national government would take over responsibility for Medicaid, a program of health care for the poor. Initially, Washington would turn back to the states revenues raised through various federal excise and energy taxes, providing them with the money they needed to run the new programs. Eventually, however, the states would be expected to pick up the costs themselves or eliminate the programs.

Reagan's proposed exchange of programs aroused intense opposition. He could not build a winning coalition in support of the plan, and, as a result, his most ambitious effort to remake American federalism failed. Furthermore, after his initial success in 1981, the momentum behind Reagan's efforts to reduce the proliferation of categorical grant programs also slowed considerably. In fact, as Figure 4.3 shows, the number of categorical grants is again on the increase. Many grant programs have been added to respond to new problems and national priorities—for example, halting the spread of AIDS and fighting drug abuse (see Chapter 19). But Figure 4.3 also reveals that the *value* of grants-in-aid (expressed in constant dollars) has declined from its peak in 1978.

If the Reagan administration did not achieve a wholesale reorganization of the federal system, it did prompt a re-evaluation of the role of the national government in that system. For example, in the years before Reagan took office, the national government had been used to foster greater economic equality through the redistribution of wealth. The national government played a large part in setting eligibility requirements and benefit levels for food stamps, Aid to Families with Dependent Children (AFDC), and other programs that help the poor. Liberals preferred to use this centralized power to set minimum standards because the national government was willing to do more for the poor than many individual states would have chosen to do had they been left completely to their own devices. But when conservatives, who did not share this commitment to equality, came to power in Washington, these very aid programs proved most vulnerable. Many of Reagan's budget reductions came about by raising eligibility requirements and cutting available benefits of programs designed to assist those living in poverty. As a result, "in the final analysis, Reagan's cuts in federal aid . . . fell disproportionately on one segment of the population: the poor."[28]

President Bush has reaffirmed Reagan's New Federalism and reasserted Reagan's policy of assuring that proposed policies and legislation give maximum discretion to state and local governments.[29] In his 1991 State

Bart Says, "Pay Up, Dudes!"
Californians urge their state legislators to provide more support for California's school system. In 1980, the national government shouldered more than 11 percent of public education costs. By 1991, that contribution had declined to approximately 8 percent. Because a 1 percent reduction in school aid equals nearly $3 billion, state governments are really feeling the pinch.

of the Union address, Bush proposed to consolidate $15 billion into a single grant for turnover to the states. He supported the turnover approach because it allows the national government to reduce its overhead; it allows the states to manage programs more flexibly and more efficiently; and it reinforces the idea that states can serve as laboratories for policy innovation (see page 137). But those laboratories can cause regulatory havoc when states employ different standards. The upshot may be a veritable tower of Babel (see Feature 4.1).

Some Consequences of New Federalism

New Federalism has changed dramatically since 1960. Through 1978, there was nearly steady growth in aid to states and local communities, either in the form of grants or in direct payments for the poor (Medicaid and welfare). But during the last decade, the picture changed again. A period of decline began in 1978 and bottomed out in 1982. Aid has increased only slightly since then. Further, the components of aid for states and cities have changed substantially compared to earlier periods. Payments for the poor now take an increasing share of the national government's contribution to the states (see Chapter 19). "Medicaid is becoming the Pac-Man of state government, eating up every dollar," remarked one official.[30] And that trend is likely to continue.

The national government is no longer a benefactor, bestowing generosity on worthy state and local units. Yet spending pressures on state and

FEATURE 4.1   *Food Fight!*

Federalism embraces many governments, each possessing elements of sovereignty. This structure inevitably leads to regulatory proliferation and variation from state to state. When does national uniformity take priority over state regulation? Consider food labeling. In 1990, the national government proposed to increase the amount of label information available to consumers on nutrition, serving sizes, cholesterol content, and recommended daily intake. Would the new regulations nullify the labeling laws in twenty states, health warnings on cancer-causing chemicals in California, and maple syrup grading requirements in Vermont?

Consumer advocates maintained that the states should be free to set stricter standards than the national government. Business groups protested. If some states imposed stricter food labeling standards than other states or the national government, then food processors would have to adjust their packaging to meet the requirements of each state, or more likely, to comply with the strictest state standard. Although this last step would have satisfied all states, some food processors fear sales losses when the public knows all the ingredients.

A remedy for the proliferation of rules spawned by federalism is *pre-emption,* the invalidation of state laws by superior national laws. Congress and the courts decide whether state laws may survive a new national regulatory scheme. Pre-emption has jumped dramatically in the last twenty years: From 1970 to 1988, Congress enacted 186 laws that pre-empted the states.

Initially, pre-emption was a device championed by liberals. During the New Deal, it was used to promote economic and labor regulations. In subsequent years, pre-emption benefited many other items on the liberal agenda, such as national guarantees for fair housing and voting rights, and national guidelines for water quality and asbestos removal.

Recently, however, conservatives have championed the use of pre-emption to protect businesses from state regulations. For example, pre-emption conditions accompanied banking deregulation in the Reagan administration and alcoholic beverage labeling in the Bush administration. The food labeling issue is one example of the extent to which conservatives may now endorse the need for strong national government. As a food industry official observed, "I would rather deal with one federal gorilla than fifty state monkeys."

The food industry captured its federal gorilla in late 1990, when President Bush signed the Nutritional Labeling and Education Act. The act broadly pre-empted state nutritional labeling requirements. However, the law not only required more nutritional information on labels, it also prohibited manufacturers from making health claims unless they are proved scientifically according to the standards of the national government's watchdog agency, the Food and Drug Administration.

local governments are enormous. For example, the public demands better schools, harsher sentences for criminals (and more prisons to hold them), more and better day care for the elderly and the poor. The sober reality of national budget deficits erases hope of increased aid. For the first time in decades, many state and local governments are raising taxes or adopting new ones to pay for public services that were once the shared responsibility of cooperative federalism.

Other Governments in the Federal System

We have concentrated in this chapter on the roles the national and state governments play in shaping the federal system. Although the Constitution explicitly recognizes just national and state governments, the American federal system has spawned a multitude of local governments as well. In a recent count, the number exceeded eighty-three thousand![31]

The Kinds of Local Governments

Americans are citizens of both nation and state but they also come under the jurisdiction of various local government units. These units include **municipal governments,** the governments of cities and towns. Municipalities, in turn, are located in (or may contain or share boundaries with) counties, which are administered by **county governments.** In addition, most Americans also live in a **school district,** which is responsible for administering local elementary and secondary educational programs. They also may be served by one or more **special districts,** government units created to perform particular functions, often when those func-

Her Honor, the Mayor. Hizzoner, the Mayor.

A mayor is the elected chief executive and ceremonial officer of a city. In some modest-sized cities, mayors serve part-time. Many big-city mayors rise to national prominence, though no mayor has yet made the leap from city hall to the White House. These mayors are (clockwise, from top left): Linda Shaw of Lakewood, Colorado; Xavier Suarez of Miami, Florida; Kurt Schmoke of Baltimore, Maryland; and Robert J. McKenna of Newport, Rhode Island.

tions are best performed across jurisdictional boundaries. Examples of special districts include the Port Authority of New York, the Chicago Sanitation District, and the Southeast Pennsylvania Transit Authority.

These local governments are created by state governments either in their constitutions or through legislation. This means their organization, powers, responsibilities, and effectiveness vary considerably from state to state. About forty states provide their cities with various forms of **home rule**—the right to enact and enforce legislation in certain administrative areas. By allowing a measure of self-government, home rule gives cities greater freedom of action than they would otherwise have. In contrast, county governments, which are the main units of local government in rural areas, tend to have relatively little legislative power or none at all. Instead, county governments generally serve as administrative units, performing the specific duties assigned to them under state law.

The functions of national, state, city, and county governments and of school and special districts often overlap. In practice, it is now virtually impossible to distinguish among them by using Madison's criteria of great and aggregate interests and local and particular interests. Consider, for example, the case of the rural health officer, or "sanitarian":

> The sanitarian is appointed by the state under merit standards established by the federal government. His base salary comes jointly from state and federal funds, the county provides him with an office and office emenities and pays a portion of his expenses, and the largest city in the county also contributes to his salary by virtue of his appointment as a city plumbing inspector. It is impossible from moment to moment to tell under which governmental hat the sanitarian operates. His work of inspecting the purity of food is carried out under federal standards; but he is enforcing state laws when inspecting commodities that have not been in interstate commerce; and somewhat perversely he also acts under state authority when inspecting milk coming into the county from producing areas across the state border. He is a federal official when impounding impure drugs shipped from a neighboring state; a federal-state officer when distributing typhoid immunization serum; a state officer when enforcing standards of industrial hygiene; a state-local officer when inspecting the city's water supply; and [to complete the circle] a local officer when insisting that the city butchers adopt more hygienic methods of handling their garbage. But he cannot and does not think of himself as acting in these separate capacities. All business in the county that concerns health and sanitation he considers his business.[32]

If a health officer cannot manage to separate national, state, city, and county functions, how can the ordinary citizen be expected to make sense of this maze of governments? And does the ordinary citizen really benefit from all these governments?

So Many Governments: Advantages and Disadvantages

In theory, at least, one benefit of localizing government is that it brings government closer to the people; it gives them an opportunity to participate in the political process, to have a direct impact on policy. Localized government conjures up visions of informed citizens deciding their own political fate in small communities—the New England town meeting repeated across the nation. From this perspective, overlapping governments appear compatible with a majoritarian view of democracy.

The reality is somewhat different, however. Studies have shown that people are much more likely to vote in national elections than local elections. Voter turnout in local contests tends to be very low, even though the impact of individual votes is much greater. Furthermore, the fragmentation of powers, functions, and responsibilities among national, state, and local governments makes government as a whole seem very complicated and hence less comprehensible and accessible to ordinary people. In addition, citizens who are busy with the daily matter of making a living have only limited time to devote to public affairs, and involvement in politics can be very time consuming. All these factors tend to keep individual citizens out of politics and to make government more responsive to organized groups, which have the resources—time, money, and know-how—to influence policymaking (see Chapter 10). Instead of bringing government closer to the people and reinforcing majoritarian democracy, then, the system's enormous complexity tends to encourage pluralism.

One possible benefit of having many governments is that they enable the country to experiment with new policies on a small scale. New programs or solutions to problems can be tested in one city or state or in a few cities or states. Successful programs can then be adopted by other cities or states or by the nation as a whole. For this reason, states are sometimes called the "laboratories of democracy." For example, when President Reagan asked for a constitutional amendment requiring a balanced national budget—that is, one in which expenditures cannot be greater than income—he had a precedent. Many states have a constitutional provision like this.

The large number of governments also makes it possible for government to respond to the diversity of conditions that prevails in different parts of the country. States and cities differ enormously in population, size, economic resources, climate, and other characteristics—all the diverse elements that French political philosopher Montesquieu argued needed to be taken into account in formulating laws for a society. Smaller political units are better able to respond to particular local conditions and can generally do so quickly. On the other hand, smaller units may not be able to muster the economic resources to meet challenges.

Of course, the United States remains one nation no matter how many local governments there are. The question of how much diversity the nation should tolerate in the way different states treat their citizens is important. As Feature 4.2 shows, public opinion is split on this issue. Also important is the question of whether the national government (and, indirectly, the citizens of other states) should be called on to foot the bill for the problems that diversity produces. (Yet some evidence shows that the American public is largely ambivalent about most issues relating to the power of the national government. Polling evidence from 1932 through 1988 indicates that Americans increasingly feel such issues are remote to their lives.[33])

FEATURE 4.2   *Who Should Make the Rules? Federalism and Public Opinion*

Where do American citizens stand on the question of the distribution of power between national and state governments? What areas do they believe require uniform national standards? A CBS/*New York Times* poll taken in May 1987 put questions like these to 1,254 people and found some deep divisions on the issues.

Only a few respondents (5 percent) believed that the states have too much power; most (47 percent) thought the balance between states and nation is about right; a sizable minority (39 percent) claimed that the national government has too much power.

When it came down to deciding whether national or state standards are better, here's how opinion divided (respondents with no opinion are not shown):

Should there be one national policy set by the federal government or should the fifty states make their own rules . . .

	Federal	State
. . . in controlling pollution?	49%	46%
. . . in setting penalties for murder?	62	34
. . . on the issue of registration and voting?	64	31
. . . in selecting textbooks in public schools?	35	61
. . . in setting minimum wages?	51	45
. . . in establishing safety standards in factories?	65	31
. . . in setting highway speed limits?	42	56

Ironically, this evidence says that Americans want the national government to assume greater responsibility for such things as penalties for murder, registration and voting, and safety standards, matters traditionally within the states' domain. Yet most Americans hold to the view that the national government already has either enough or too much power.

Source: William K. Stevens, "Pagentry and the Ideals of 200 Years," *New York Times*, 26 May 1987, pp. A1 and A20. Copyright © 1987 by The New York Times Company. Reprinted by permission.

Differences among states have led the national government to play a role in regional development. Throughout American history, the national government has used its funds to equalize disparities in wealth and development among states. The development of the Sunbelt (the southern and southwestern regions of the country), for example, has been, and continues to be, helped considerably by national policies and programs: Tennessee Valley Authority (TVA) electrification and western irrigation projects were funded by the national government; the South, in particular, was helped enormously by national funding formulas designed to aid poorer areas of the country; and California has benefited from national largesse in the form of huge defense contracts. Overall, the

Sunbelt states have received more money from the government than they have paid in taxes.

Contemporary Federalism and the Dilemmas of Democracy

When President Reagan came to the White House, conservatives were delighted. They were surely relieved (and hardly surprised) when President Bush advocated similar views. Conservatives believed a preference for layer-cake federalism would mean the dismantling of the liberal welfare state and the end of the national government's efforts to promote social and political equality at the expense of freedom. They argued that different states had different problems and resources, and asserted that by returning control to state governments, it would be possible to give more play to diversity. States would be free to experiment with alternatives for meeting their problems. States would compete with one another. And people would be free to choose the state government they preferred by simply "voting with their feet"—moving to another state.

In addition, conservative proponents of New Federalism argued that the national government was too remote, too tied to special interests, not responsive to the public at large. The national government overregulated and tried to promote too much uniformity. Moreover, they added, the size and complexity of the federal system led to waste and inefficiency. States, on the other hand, were closer to the people and better able to respond to specific local needs. If state governments were revitalized, individuals might believe that they could have a greater impact on decision making. The quality of political participation would improve. Furthermore, conservatives believed that shifting power to the states would help them achieve other parts of their political agenda. States, they thought, would work harder to keep taxes down; they would not be willing to spend a lot of money on social welfare programs; and they would be less likely to pass stiff laws regulating businesses. Reagan's New Federalism would bring back the days of laissez faire, when states found it difficult to regulate businesses for fear that industries might move to less restrictive states. Rivalry between states could become a "competition in laxity."

What conservatives hoped for, liberals feared. They remembered that the states' rights model allowed political and social inequalities, that it supported racism. Blacks and city dwellers were often left virtually unrepresented by white state legislators who disproportionately served rural interests. Liberals believed the states were unwilling or unable to protect the rights or provide for the needs of their citizens, whether those citizens were consumers seeking protection from business interests, defendants requiring guarantees of due process of law, or poor people seeking a minimum standard of living.

To what extent were conservative hopes and liberal fears realized as federalism developed in the 1980s? And how did the development of federalism during this period relate to the dilemmas of democracy?

Federalism and the Values of Freedom, Order, and Equality

Neither the conservatives' hopes nor the liberals' fears were fully realized under the New, Newer, or Newest Federalism, nor has the array of recent conservative presidents always embraced the states' rights position. Federalism of the Bush-Reagan variety has mainly been used as a tool for cutting the national budget by offering less money to the states. Contrary to the expectations of conservatives and liberals alike, however, states themselves proved willing to approve tax increases to pay for social services and education. In an era when Washington was less willing to enforce antitrust legislation, civil rights laws, or affirmative action plans, state governments were more likely to do so. At a time when a conservative national government put little emphasis on the value of equality, state governments did more to embrace it.

Conservatives had thought that the value of freedom would be enhanced if more matters were left to the states. Traditionally, state governments had been relatively small, lacking the wherewithal to limit large corporate interests, for example. But over the past two decades, state governments have changed. Their legislatures have become more professional. They meet regularly, for longer periods of time. They maintain larger permanent staffs. Governors have shown themselves willing to support major programs to enhance the skills of the work force, to promote research and development, and to subsidize new industries.

Nevada Sintax

Las Vegas, Nevada, is a gambler's heaven and a tax collector's dream. All states, with the exception of Nevada, raise revenue primarily through property, sales, and income taxes. But Nevada also collects revenue by taxing its casinos on the basis of their total receipts and the number of machines and games they employ. When you place a bet in Las Vegas, rest assured the state always wins.

State governments have become "big governments" themselves. They are better able to tackle problems, and they are not afraid to use their power to promote equality.

To the surprise of liberals, who had originally looked to the national government to protect individuals by setting reasonable minimum standards for product safety, welfare payments, and employee benefits, states are now willing to set higher standards than the national government. As states take a more active role in setting these standards, they highlight another challenge for our democracy—the need to maintain order by protecting the lives of citizens.

In summary, the relationship among the federal system, political ideology, and the values of freedom, order, and equality is no longer as simple as it appeared two decades ago. Then, liberals could look to the national government and marble-cake federalism to help secure equality. Conservatives could wish for a return to small government, states' rights, and layer-cake federalism. In the 1980s, conservatives gave lip service to the ideals of New Federalism but were often reluctant to give up the national power that helped them achieve their vision of order. After all, if they returned power to the states, they might well do more to promote equality than freedom. As one prominent conservative put it, "The Great Society may be over in Washington, but it has just begun in the states."[34]

Federalism and Pluralism

As discussed in Chapter 2, the system of government in America today supports the pluralist model of democracy. Federalism is an important part of that system. How has it contributed to American pluralism? Do each of the competing views of federalism support pluralism?

Our federal system of government was designed to allay citizens' fears that they might be ruled by majorities of citizens who were residents of distant regions and with whom they did not necessarily agree or share interests. By recognizing the legitimacy of the states as political divisions, the federal system also recognized the importance of diversity. The existence and cultivation of diverse interests are hallmarks of pluralism.

Each of the two competing theories of federalism supports pluralism but in somewhat different ways. Dual federalism, which has evolved into New Federalism, wants to decentralize government, to shift power to the states. It recognizes the importance of local rather than national standards and applauds the diversity of those standards. This variety allows people, if not a voice in policymaking, at least the choice of policy under which to live. These factors tend to support pluralist democracy.

In contrast, cooperative federalism is perfectly willing to override local standards for a national standard in the interests of promoting equality. Yet this view of federalism, particularly in its picket fence version, also supports pluralist democracy. It is highly responsive to all manner of group pressures, including pressure at one level from groups unsuccessful at other levels. By blurring the lines of national and state responsibility, this kind of federalism encourages petitioners to try their luck at whichever level of government offers the best chance of success.

Summary

The government framework outlined in the Constitution was the product of political compromise, an acknowledgment of the states' fear of a powerful central government. The division of powers sketched in the Constitution was supposed to turn over "great and aggregate" matters to the national government, leaving "local and particular" concerns to the states. Exactly what was great and aggregate and what was local and particular was not fully explained.

Federalism comes in many varieties. Two stand out because they capture valuable differences between the original and modern vision of a federal government. Dual, or layer-cake, federalism wants to retain power in the states and to keep the levels of government separate. Cooperative, or marble-cake, federalism emphasizes the power of the national government and sees national and state government working together to solve national problems. In its own way, each view supports the pluralist model of democracy.

Over the years, the national government has used both its enumerated and its implied powers to become involved in virtually every area of human activity. The tools of political change include direct legislation, judicial decisions, and financial rewards in the form of grants.

As its influence grew, so did the government itself. At the same time, intergovernmental relations became more complex. New Federalists, generally conservative, suggested cutting back the size of the national government, reducing federal spending, and turning programs over to the states as a solution to the problem of unwieldy government. Liberals worried that New Federalists, in their haste to decentralize and cut back, would turn over important responsibilities to states that were unwilling or unable to assume them. Government, rather than being too responsive, would become unresponsive. But neither conservative hopes nor liberal fears were fully realized in the 1980s. The states proved both willing and able to tackle some major problems. More than this, they were willing to fund many programs that promoted equality.

The debate over federalism will continue in the 1990s and beyond. Cooperative federalism will surely be replaced by another theory of intergovernmental relations, and the ghost of dual federalism may still return. One truth emerges from this overview of federalism: the balance of power between the national and state governments will be settled by political means, not by theory.

KEY TERMS

federalism
dual federalism
states' rights
implied powers
cooperative federalism
elastic clause
commerce clause
grant-in-aid

categorical grant
formula grant
project grant
block grant
nullification
intergovernmental
  relations
picket fence federalism

general revenue sharing
special revenue sharing
municipal government
county government

school district
special district
home rule

SELECTED READINGS

Berger, Raoul. *Federalism: The Founder's Design.* Norman, Okla.: University of Oklahoma Press, 1987. Berger, a constitutional historian, argues that the states preceded the nation and that the states and the national government were to have mutually exclusive spheres of sovereignty.

Dye, Thomas R. *American Federalism: Competition Among Governments.* Lexington, Mass.: Lexington Books, 1990. Presents a theory of competitive federalism that encourages rivalry among states and local governments to offer citizens the best array of public services at the lowest cost.

Gittell, Marilyn, ed. *State Politics and the New Federalism.* New York: Longmans, 1986. A collection of works on intergovernmental relations that emphasizes the role of the states.

Hall, Kermit L., ed. *Federalism: A Nation of States.* New York: Garland, 1987. A collection of the most important historical and political science scholarship on federalism.

Nathan, Richard P., and Fred C. Doolittle. *Reagan and the States.* Princeton, N.J.: Princeton University Press, 1987. An overview and set of case studies of fiscal federalism as a part of Reagan's New Federalism.

O'Toole, Laurence J., ed. *American Intergovernmental Relations.* Washington, D.C.: Congressional Quarterly Press, 1985. This collection of readings includes classics on the subject as well as analyses of intergovernmental relations in the Reagan administration.

Reagan, Michael, and John Sanzone. *The New Federalism.* New York: Oxford University Press, 1981. A classic analysis of fiscal federalism with heavy emphasis on grants.

Walker, David B. *Toward a Functioning Federalism.* Cambridge, Mass.: Winthrop, 1981. Analyzes the overloaded system of intergovernmental relations and offers alternatives to it.

PART

THREE

Linking People
with Government

5 PUBLIC OPINION AND POLITICAL SOCIALIZATION

FRIDAYS ARE DIFFERENT in Saudi Arabia. After prayers, criminals are paraded in the streets, then punished publicly. Murderers are beheaded, adulterers are flogged, and thieves have their hands chopped off. The Saudi government wants its citizens to get the message: Crime will not be tolerated. Moreover, what constitutes a crime in Saudi Arabia may not be a crime in the United States. Members of the U.S. armed forces sent there in 1990 during the Persian Gulf crisis learned this as their mail from home was opened to keep out alcohol and sexually oriented magazines, both of which are illegal. It is also illegal for a woman to drive a car there. Saudi Arabia, which claims the lowest crime rate in the world, is a country that greatly values order.

In contrast, the United States has one of the highest crime rates in the world. Its homicide rate, for example, is three to ten times that of most other Western countries. Although no one is proud of this record, our government would never consider beheading, flogging, or dismembering as a means of lowering the crime rate. First, the Eighth Amendment to the Constitution forbids "cruel and unusual punishment." Second, the public would not tolerate this kind of punishment.

However, the public definitely is not squeamish about the death penalty (capital punishment), at least for certain crimes. The Gallup organization has polled the nation on this issue for fifty years. Except in 1966, most respondents have consistently supported the death penalty for murder.[1] In fact, public support for capital punishment has increased dramatically since the late 1960s. In 1988, 79 percent of all respondents were in favor of the death penalty for murder, while only 16 percent opposed it. Substantial segments of the public also were in favor of the death penalty for attempting to assassinate the president (63 percent), rape (51 percent), and hijacking an airplane (49 percent).

Government has been defined as the legitimate use of force to control human behavior. We can learn much about the role of public opinion in politics by reviewing the government's use of force. Through most of American history, the execution of people who threaten the social order has been a legal practice of government. In colonial times, capital punishment was imposed not just for murder but for antisocial behavior—for denying the "true" God, cursing one's parents, adultery, witchcraft, or being a rebellious child.[2] In the late 1700s, some writers, editors, and clergy argued for abolishing the death sentence. The campaign intensified in the 1840s, and a few states responded by eliminating capital punishment. With the pressures of the Civil War and its aftermath, interest in the cause waned until 1890, when New York State adopted a new technique, electrocution, as the instrument of death. By 1917, twelve states had passed laws against capital punishment. But the outbreak of World War I fed the public's suspicion of foreigners and fear of radicals, leading to renewed support for the death penalty. Reacting to this shift in public opinion, four states restored it.

The security needs of World War II and postwar fears of Soviet communism fueled continued support for capital punishment. After the Red Scare subsided in the late 1950s, public opposition to the death penalty increased. But public opinion was neither strong enough nor stable enough to force state legislatures to outlaw the death penalty. In keeping

Women Should Be Heard and Not Seen

The culture of a nation shapes public attitudes and opinions. In Saudi Arabia, women completely cover their heads and bodies when out in public in strict accordance with Islamic principles. The Saudi culture also prohibits women from engaging in many activities (like driving automobiles) typically enjoyed by women in the United States.

with the pluralist model of democracy, abolition efforts shifted from the legislative arena to the courts.

One of the major arguments the abolitionists used was that the death penalty is cruel and unusual punishment, and therefore unconstitutional. Certainly the public in the 1780s did not think capital punishment was either cruel or unusual. But two hundred years later, opponents contended that execution by the state had become cruel and unusual by contemporary standards. Their argument had some effect on public opinion; in 1966, a plurality of respondents opposed the death penalty for the first (and only) time since the Gallup surveys began.

The states responded to this shift in public opinion by reducing the number of executions each year until, in 1968, they were stopped completely in anticipation of a Supreme Court decision. By then, however, public opinion had again reversed itself in favor of capital punishment. Still, in 1972, the Court ruled in a 5–4 vote that the death penalty as imposed by existing state laws was unconstitutional.[3] The Court's decision was not well received in many states, and thirty-five state legislatures passed new laws to get around its ruling. Meanwhile, the nation's homicide rate increased. Public approval of the death penalty jumped almost 10 points and began climbing higher.

In 1976, the Supreme Court changed its position and upheld three new state laws that provided for consideration of the defendant and the offense before imposing the death sentence.[4] The Court also rejected the argument that punishment by death itself violates the Constitution while noting that public opinion favored the death penalty. Now endorsed by the courts, as well as the public, the death penalty was again

The Death Chamber

This uncomfortable apparatus is the electric chair in a Louisiana state prison. It dramatizes the ultimate power that government has to control behavior. Capital crimes may draw capital punishment.

available to the states. Through the end of the 1970s, though, few states applied the penalty: Only three criminals were executed. Eventually, however, the states began to heed the clamor, executing about twenty criminals a year by the mid-1980s.

Does the death penalty deter people from committing murder? Two-thirds of the public think it does.[5] What do people think is the most humane method of execution? Opinion polls tell us that most people favor lethal injection (62 percent) over electrocution (18 percent). The gas chamber has more support (9 percent) than the old-fashioned firing squad (3 percent). But hanging (1 percent) is generally unpopular, and no respondents regard beheading as humane.

The history of public thinking on the death penalty reveals several characteristics of public opinion:

1. *The public's attitudes toward a given government policy can vary over time, often dramatically.* Opinions about capital punishment tend to fluctuate with threats to the social order. The public is more likely to favor capital punishment in times of war and fear of foreign subversion and when crime rates are high.

2. *Public opinion places boundaries on allowable types of public policy.* Chopping off a hand is not acceptable to the public (and surely to courts interpreting the Constitution) as a punishment for theft in the United States, but electrocuting a murderer in private (not in public) is all right.

3. *Citizens are willing to register opinions on matters outside their expertise.* People clearly believe execution by lethal injection is more humane than electrocution, asphyxiation in the gas chamber, or hanging. How can the public know enough about execution to make these judgments?

4. *Governments tend to react to public opinion.* State laws for and against capital punishment have reflected swings in the public mood. Moreover, the Supreme Court's decision in 1972 against capital punishment came when public opinion on the death penalty was sharply divided; the Court's approval of capital punishment in 1976 coincided with a rise in public approval of the death penalty.

5. *The government sometimes does not do what the people want.* Although public opinion overwhelmingly favors the death penalty for murder, few states actually punish murderers with execution. The United States averaged over twenty thousand homicides annually in the 1980s but executed fewer than twenty murderers a year.

The last two conclusions bear on our discussion of the majoritarian and pluralist models of democracy in Chapter 2. Here we probe more deeply into the nature, shape, depth, and formation of public opinion in a democratic government. What is the place of public opinion in a democracy? How do people acquire their opinions? What are the major lines of division in public opinion? How do individuals' ideology and knowledge affect their opinions? What is the relationship between public opinion and ideological type?

Public Opinion and the Models of Democracy

The majoritarian and pluralist models of democracy differ greatly in their assumptions about the role of public opinion in democratic government. According to the classic majoritarian model, the government should do what a majority of the public wants. In contrast, pluralists argue that the public as a whole seldom demonstrates clear, consistent opinions on the day-to-day issues of government. At the same time, pluralists recognize that subgroups within the public do express opinions on specific matters—often and vigorously. The pluralist model requires that government institutions allow the free expression of opinions by these "minority publics." Democracy is at work when the opinions of many different publics clash openly and fairly over government policy.

Thanks to opinion polling, we can better understand the conflict between these two institutional models of democracy. *Polling* involves interviewing a sample of citizens to estimate public opinion as a whole (see Feature 5.1). **Public opinion** is simply the collected attitudes of citizens on a given issue or question. Opinion polling is such a common part of contemporary life that we often forget it is a modern invention, dating only from the 1930s (see Figure 5.1). In fact, survey methodology did not develop into a powerful research tool until the advent of computers in the 1950s.

Before polling became an accepted part of the American scene, politicians, journalists, and everyone else could argue about what "the people" wanted, but no one really knew. Observers of America before the 1930s had to guess at national opinion by analyzing newspaper stories, politicians' speeches, voting returns, and travelers' diaries. When no one really knows what the people want, it is impossible for the national government to be responsive to public opinion. As we discussed in Chapter 3,

FEATURE 5.1   *Sampling a Few, Predicting to Everyone*

How can a pollster tell what the nation thinks by talking to only a few hundred people? The answer lies in the statistical theory of *sampling*. Briefly, the theory holds that a sample of individuals selected by chance from any population is "representative" of that population. This means that the traits of individuals in the sample—their attitudes, beliefs, sociological characteristics, and physical features—reflect the traits of the whole population. Sampling theory does not say that a sample exactly matches the population, only that it reflects the population with some predictable degree of accuracy.

Three factors determine the accuracy of a sample. The most important is the way the sample is selected. For maximum accuracy, the individuals in the sample must be chosen randomly. *Randomly* does not mean "at whim"; it means that every individual in the population has the same chance of being selected.

For a population as large and widespread as that of the United States, direct random sampling of individuals by name is practically impossible. Instead, pollsters first divide the country into geographic regions. Then they randomly choose areas and sample individuals who live within those areas. This departure from strict random sampling does decrease the accuracy of polls, but only by a relatively small amount. Today, most polls conducted by the mass media are done by telephone, with computers randomly dialing numbers within predetermined telephone areas. (Random dialing ensures that even people with unlisted numbers are called.)

The second factor that affects the accuracy of sampling is the size of the sample. The larger the sample, the more accurately it represents the population. For example, a sample of four hundred individuals predicts accurately to a population within 6 percentage points (plus or minus), 95 percent of the time. A sample of six hundred is accurate within 5 percentage points. (Surprisingly, when the population is very large compared with the sample—which is usually the case in opinion polling—the size of the population has essentially no effect on the sampling accuracy. So a sample of,

say, six hundred individuals selected within a city, a state, or even the nation reflects the traits of its population with equal accuracy, within 5 percentage points. Why this is so is better discussed in a course on statistics.)

The final factor that affects the accuracy of sampling is the amount of variation in the population. If there were no variation in a population, every sample would reflect the population's characteristics with perfect accuracy. But the greater the variation within the population, the greater the chance that one random sample will be different from another.

The Gallup Poll and most other national opinion polls usually survey about 1,500 individuals and are accurate within 3 percentage points, 95 percent of the time. As shown in Figure 5.1, the predictions of the Gallup Poll for fourteen presidential elections since 1936 have deviated from the voting results only an average of 2.1 percentage points. Even this small margin of error can mean an incorrect prediction in a close election. But for the purpose of estimating public opinion on political issues, a sampling error of 3 percentage points is acceptable.

Poll results can be wrong because of problems that have nothing to do with sampling theory. In particular, question wording can bias the results. For example, in surveys during the 1980s concerning aid to the Nicaraguan contras fighting the Sandinista government, questions that mentioned President Reagan's name produced almost 5 percentage points more support for increased aid.[*] Survey questions are also likely to get superficial responses from busy respondents who say anything, quickly, to get rid of a pesky interviewer. Recently, some newspaper columnists have even urged readers to lie to pollsters outside voting booths, to confound election-night television predictions. But despite its potential for abuse or distortion, modern polling has told us a great deal about public opinion in America.

---

[*] Brad Lockerbie and Stephen A. Borrelli, "Question Wording and Public Support for Contra Aid, 1983–1986," *Public Opinion Quarterly* 54 (Summer 1990), p. 200.

FIGURE 5.1 *Gallup Poll Accuracy*

One of the nation's oldest polls was started by George Gallup in the 1930s. The accuracy of the Gallup Poll in predicting presidential elections over nearly fifty years is charted below. Although not always on the mark, its predictions have been fairly close to election results. The poll was most notably wrong in 1948, when it predicted that Thomas Dewey, the Republican candidate, would defeat the Democratic incumbent, Harry Truman, underestimating Truman's vote by 5.4 percentage points. In the 1988 election, the Gallup Poll estimated that George Bush would obtain 56 percent of the vote, and he actually obtained 53.9 percent, which happened to equal the average accuracy of the Gallup Poll over the years.
(Source: Gallup Report, December 1988, p. 44. Used by permission of The Gallup Poll.)

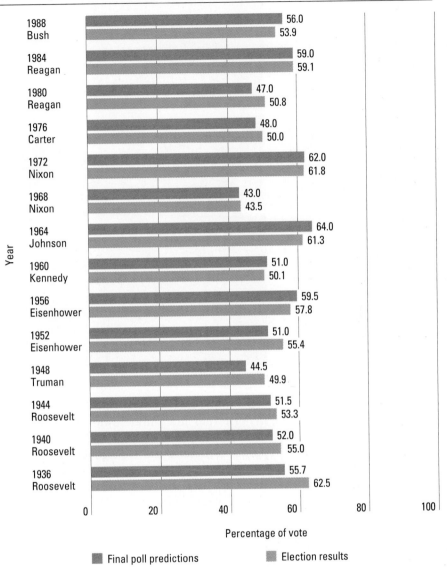

the founders wanted to build public opinion into our government structure by allowing the direct election of representatives to the House and apportioning representation there according to population. Attitudes and actions in the House of Representatives, the framers thought, would reflect public opinion, especially on the crucial issues of taxes and government spending.

In practice, bills passed by a majority of elected representatives do not necessarily reflect the opinions of a majority of citizens. This would not have bothered the framers because they never intended to create a full democracy, a government completely responsive to majority opinion. Although they wanted to provide for some input of public opinion, they had little faith in the ability of the masses to make public policy.

Stop the Presses! Oops, Too Late . . .

As the 1948 election drew near, few people gave President Harry Truman a chance to defeat his Republican opponent, Thomas E. Dewey. Polling was still new, and virtually all the early polls showed Dewey far ahead. Most organizations simply stopped polling weeks before the election. The Chicago Daily Tribune *believed the polls and proclaimed Dewey's victory before the votes were counted. Here, the victorious Truman triumphantly displays the most embarrassing headline in American politics. Later it was revealed that the few polls taken closer to election day showed Truman catching up to Dewey, which demonstrates that polls estimate the vote only at the time they are taken.*

Sampling methods and opinion polling have altered the debate over the majoritarian and pluralist models of democracy. Now that we know how often government policy runs against majority opinion, it becomes harder to defend the U.S. government as democratic under the majoritarian model. Even at a time when Americans overwhelmingly favored the death penalty for murderers, the Supreme Court decided that existing state laws applying capital punishment were unconstitutional. Even after the Court approved new state laws as constitutional, relatively few murderers were actually executed. Consider, too, the case of prayer in public schools. The Supreme Court has ruled that no state or local government can require the reading of the Lord's Prayer or Bible verses in public schools. Yet surveys continually show that a clear majority of Americans (about 60 percent) do not agree with that ruling.[6] Because government policy sometimes runs against settled majority opinion, the majoritarian model is easily attacked.

Each of the two models of democracy makes certain assumptions about public opinion. The majoritarian model assumes that a majority of people hold clear, consistent opinions on government policy. The pluralist model insists that public opinion is often divided, and opinion polls certainly give credence to that claim. What are the bases of these divisions? What principles, if any, do people use to organize their beliefs and attitudes about politics? Exactly how do individuals form their political opinions? We look for answers to these questions in this chapter. In later chapters, we assess the effect of public opinion on government policies.

The results should help you make up your own mind about the viability of the majoritarian and pluralist models in a functioning democracy.

The Distribution of Public Opinion

A government that tries to respond to public opinion soon learns that people seldom think alike. To understand, then to act on, the public's many attitudes and beliefs, governments must pay attention to the way public opinion distributes among the choices on an issue. In particular, government must analyze the *shape* and the *stability* of the distribution.

Shape of the Distribution

The results of public opinion polls are often displayed on charts like those in Figure 5.2. The response categories run along the baseline. The height of the columns indicates the percentage of those polled who gave each response. The *shape* of the opinion distribution is the pattern, or physical form, of all the responses when counted and plotted. The figure depicts three idealized patterns of distribution—normal, skewed, and bimodal—superimposed on three actual survey items.[7]

Figure 5.2a shows how respondents to a national survey in 1990 placed themselves along a liberal-conservative continuum. The most frequent response, called the *mode*, was "moderate." Progressively fewer people classified themselves in each category toward the liberal and conservative extremes. The shape of the graph resembles what statistical theory calls a **normal distribution**—a symmetrical, bell-shaped distribution around a single mode. Opinions that are *normally distributed* tend to support moderate government policies. At the same time, they allow government policies that range to either side of the center position, shifting from liberal to conservative and back again, as long as they do not stray too far from the moderate center.

Figure 5.2b plots the percentages of those who agreed or disagreed with the statement "The private business system in the United States works better than any other system yet devised for industrial countries."[8] The shape of this graph is very different from the symmetrical distribution of ideological attitudes. In this graph, the mode (containing the vast majority who agree with the statement) lies off to one side, leaving a "tail" (the few who disagree) on the other. This kind of asymmetrical distribution is called a **skewed distribution.** The amount of skew depends on the ratio between the proportion of respondents in the mode of the distribution and those in the tail.

In a skewed distribution, the opinions of the majority cluster around a point on one side of the issue. A skewed distribution indicates less diversity of opinion than does a normal distribution. The skewed distribution in Figure 5.2b tells us that most Americans are happy with capitalism as an economic system. Obviously, then, a candidate would have little hope of winning an election by denouncing free enterprise. In fact, when consensus on an issue is this strong, those with minority opinions risk social ostracism and even persecution if they persist in voicing their opin-

FIGURE 5.2   *Three Distributions of Opinion*

We've superimposed three hypothetical patterns of distribution—normal, skewed, and bimodal—on three actual distributions of responses to survey questions. Although the actual responses do not match the shapes exactly, they match closely enough so that we can describe the distribution of (a) ideological attitudes as approximately normal, (b) belief in capitalism as skewed, and (c) opinions on firing a communist teacher as bimodal. (Sources: (a) 1990 General Social Survey. The total sample size was 1,372. Only 4 percent of the sample chose "don't know" or didn't answer the question. (b) 1981 Survey by Civic Service, Inc., reported in Public Opinion 5 [October–November 1982]:21. (c) 1990 General Social Survey. Data for both (a) and (c) were kindly provided by Tom W. Smith, Director of the GSS at the National Opinion Research Center.)

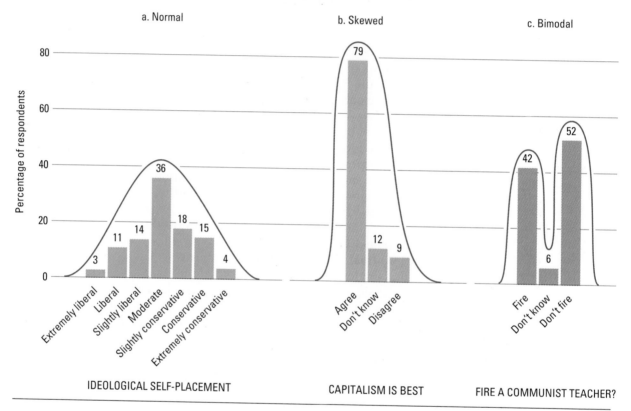

a. Normal   IDEOLOGICAL SELF-PLACEMENT

b. Skewed   CAPITALISM IS BEST

c. Bimodal   FIRE A COMMUNIST TEACHER?

ions. If the public does not feel intensely about an issue, however, politicians can sometimes discount a skewed distribution of public opinion. This is what's happened with the death penalty. Although most people favor capital punishment, it is not a burning issue for them. This means politicians can discount public opinion on the issue without serious consequences.

Figure 5.2c plots the percentages of respondents who favored or opposed firing a college teacher who was an admitted communist. These responses fall into a **bimodal distribution:** Respondents chose two categories almost equally as the most frequent responses. Americans divide almost evenly over allowing an admitted communist (an opponent of capitalism) to teach in a college. Nearly half the American population would fire the teacher; somewhat more would allow the individual to continue teaching. Because they split the electorate in nearly equal parts,

Polling Booth

No, this person is not voting in an election. He is conducting a survey for the Gallup Poll, the nation's best-known public opinion survey organization. To cut down on research costs, many polls are now done by telephone, and responses are entered directly into a computer to speed analysis. This methodology allows national surveys to be launched and completed literally overnight.

bimodal distributions of opinion carry the greatest potential for political conflict, especially if both sides feel strongly about the issue.

Stability of the Distribution

A **stable distribution** shows little change over time. Public opinion on important issues can change, but it is sometimes difficult to distinguish a true change in opinion from a difference in the way a question is worded. When different questions on the same issue produce similar distributions of opinion, the underlying attitudes are stable. When the same question (or virtually the same question) produces significantly different responses over time, the surveys are more likely to be signaling an actual shift in public opinion.

Consider Americans' attitudes toward capitalism. In the 1981 survey plotted in Figure 5.2b, 79 percent of the respondents chose capitalism over any alternative economic system. Forty years earlier, in 1941, respondents had been asked whether they "would be better off if the concern you worked for were taken over and operated by the federal government." The responses at that time were also heavily skewed: 81 percent said that they preferred "business management." The nation's support for capitalism is very stable; it has barely changed over four decades.[9]

People's placement of themselves on the liberal-conservative continuum is another distribution that has remained surprisingly stable from the 1960s to the 1990s (see Figure 5.3a). Even in 1964, when liberal Lyndon Johnson won a landslide victory over conservative Barry Goldwater in the presidential election, more voters described themselves as conservative than liberal. Indeed, this has been the public's ideological self-classification in every presidential election year since 1964.[10] Despite all the talk about the nation becoming conservative in recent years,

FIGURE 5.3 *Stability and Change in Public Opinion*

Public opinion remains stable over time on some issues and changes dramatically on others. Part (a) indicates great stability in respondents' ideological self-classifications in separate surveys in 1964 and 1990. Opinions at both times were approximately normally distributed around "moderate," the modal category. (The 1964 distribution is slightly more compact because that survey had only five response categories.) Part (b) shows how much public opinion on school integration has changed over four decades. (Sources: (a) Data for 1964 are from Lloyd A. Free and Hadley Cantril, The Political Beliefs of Americans. *Copyright © 1967 by Rutgers, The State University. Reprinted by permission of Rutgers University Press. Data for 1990 were kindly provided by Tom W. Smith, Director of the General Social Survey at the National Opinion Research Center; (b) Surveys conducted by the National Opinion Research Center; reported in and recalculated from Tom W. Smith and Paul B. Sheatsley, "American Attitudes Toward Race Relations,"* Public Opinion *7 [October–November 1984]:15. Reprinted with permission of the American Enterprise Institute for Public Policy Research, Washington, D.C.)*

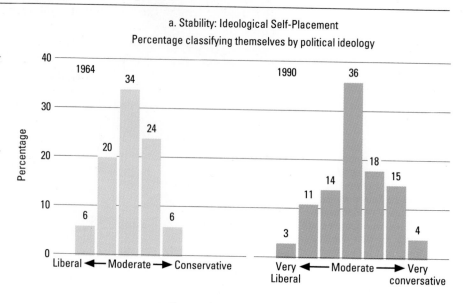

a. Stability: Ideological Self-Placement
Percentage classifying themselves by political ideology

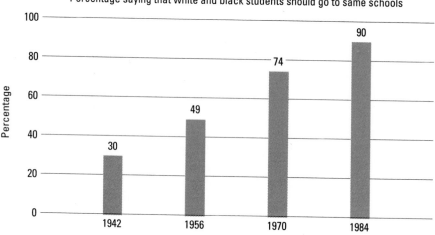

b. Change: Opinions on School Integration
Percentage saying that white and black students should go to same schools

the fact is that most people did not describe themselves as liberal *at any time* during the last three decades. People have shifted about 5 percentage points toward the right since 1964, but more considered themselves conservative, rather than liberal, to begin with.

Public opinion in America *is* capable of massive change over time, however. Moreover, change can occur on issues that were once highly controversial. A good example of a dramatic change in American public opinion is race relations, specifically integrated schools. A national survey in 1942 asked whether "white and Negro students should go to the same schools or separate schools."[11] Only 30 percent of white respondents said that the students should attend schools together. When virtually the same question (substituting *black* for Negro) was asked in 1984, 90 percent of the white respondents endorsed integrated schools (see Figure 5.3b).

Scholars writing on this trend in racial attitudes have commented on "(1) its massive magnitude, moving from a solid pro-segregation majority to an overwhelming pro-integration consensus; (2) its long duration, continuing over four decades; and (3) its steady, relentless pace."[12] But they note that white Americans have not become "color-blind." Despite their endorsement of integrated schools, only 23 percent of the whites surveyed in 1984 were in favor of busing to achieve racial balance. And whites were more willing to bus their children to a school with a few blacks than to one that was mostly black.[13] So white opinion changed dramatically with regard to the *principle* of desegregated schools, but whites seemed divided on how that principle should be implemented. Trying to explain this contradiction and the way in which political opinions in general are formed, political scientists cite the process of political socialization, the influence of cultural factors, and the interplay of ideology and knowledge. In the next several sections, we examine how these elements combine to create and affect public opinion.

Political Socialization

Public opinion is grounded in political values. People acquire their values through **political socialization,** a complex process through which individuals become aware of politics, learn political facts, and form political values. Think for a moment about your political socialization. What is your earliest memory of a president? When did you first learn about political parties? If you identify with a party, how did you decide to do so? If you don't, why don't you? Who was the first liberal you ever met? The first conservative? How did you first learn about the hydrogen bomb? About the Soviet Union?

Obviously, the paths to political awareness, knowledge, and values differ among individuals, but most people are exposed to the same influences, or *agents of socialization,* especially in childhood through young adulthood. These influences are family, school, community, peers, and—of course—television.

The Agents of Early Socialization

Like psychologists, scholars of political socialization place great emphasis on early learning. Both groups point to two operating principles that characterize early learning:[14]

- The *primacy principle.* What is learned first is learned best.
- The *structuring principle.* What is learned first structures later learning.

Because most people learn first from their family, the family tends to be a very important agent of early socialization. The extent of family influence—and of the influence of other socializing agents—depends on the extent of our *exposure, communication,* and *receptivity* to them.[15]

Family.   In most cases, exposure, communication, and receptivity are highest in family-child relationships, although parental influence has declined with the rise of single-parent families. Especially in two-parent homes, children learn a wide range of values—social, moral, religious, economic, and political—that help shape their opinions. It is not surprising, then, that most people link their earliest memories of politics with their families. Moreover, when parents are interested in politics, they influence their children to become more politically interested and informed.[16]

One of the most politically important things that many children learn from their parents is party identification. Party identification is learned in much the same way as religion. Children (very young children, anyway) imitate their parents. When parents share the same religion, children almost always are raised in that faith. When parents are of different religions, children are more likely to follow one or the other than to adopt a third. Similarly, parental influence on party identification is greater when both parents strongly identify with the same party.[17] Overall, about half of young American voters identify with the political party of their parents. Moreover, those who change their partisanship over time are more likely to move from being partisan to independent or independent to partisan than to convert from one party to the other.[18]

Two crucial differences between party identification and religion may explain why youngsters are socialized into a religion much more surely and strongly than into a political party. The first is that most parents care a great deal more about their religion than about their politics. So they are more deliberate about exposing their children to religion. The second is that religious institutions themselves recognize the value of socialization; they offer Sunday schools and other activities that are high

American Government 101

These teenagers in a mock government workshop at the Texas legislature in Austin are learning about the legislative process. They are also being socialized into politics, acquiring attitudes toward government that will affect their political behavior throughout their lives.

FEATURE 5.2 *The Goodyear Blimp over Washington*

Elementary schools provide the first contact with American government for many children. Sometimes, youngsters fail to get the message right away. How many of you pledged allegiance to an "invisible" rather than an "indivisible" nation? In the excerpt below, playwright Arthur Miller relates his own misunderstanding of the Pledge of Allegiance.

ROXBURY, Conn. I no longer remember how many years it took for me to realize I was making a mistake in the Pledge of Allegiance. With high passion, I stood beside my seat in my Harlem grammar school and repeated the Pledge to the Flag, which always drooped next to the teacher's desk. My feelings were doubtless warmed by my having two uncles who had been in the Great War, one in the Navy, the other as a mule driver in the Army who brought ammunition up to the front in France.

Dirigibles were much in the news in the early 20's, and the Navy, as far as I was able to make out, owned them. Thus, the patriotic connection, which was helped along by the fact that nobody I had ever heard speaking English had ever used the word Indivisible. Or Divisible either, for that matter.

None of which inhibited me from rapping out the Pledge each and every morning: ". . . One Nation in a Dirigible, with Liberty and Justice for All." I could actually see in my mind's eye hordes of faces looking down at Earth through the windows of the Navy's airships. The whole United States was up there, all for one and one for all—and the whole gang in that Dirigible. One day, maybe I could get to ride in it, too, for I was deeply patriotic, and the height of Americanism, as I then understood it, was to ride in a Dirigible.

Source: Arthur Miller, "School Prayer: A Political Dirigible," *New York Times*, 12 March 1984. Copyright © 1984 by The New York Times Company. Reprinted by permission.

on exposure, communication, and receptivity—reinforcing parental guidance. American political parties, on the other hand, sponsor few activities to win the hearts of little Democrats and Republicans, which leaves children open to counterinfluences in the school and community.*

School. According to some researchers, schools have an influence on political learning that is equal to or greater than that of parents.[19] Here, however, we have to distinguish between primary and secondary schools on the one hand and institutions of higher education on the other. Primary schools introduce children to authority figures outside the family—the teacher, the principal, the police officer. This is one way these schools prepare children to accept the social order. They also teach the nation's slogans and symbols—the Pledge of Allegiance, the national anthem, national heroes and holidays. And they stress the norms of group behavior and democratic decision making (respecting the opinions of others, voting for class officers). In the process, they are teaching youngsters about the value of political equality.

Children do not always understand the meaning of the patriotic rituals and behaviors they learn in primary school (see Feature 5.2). In fact, much of this early learning—in the United States and elsewhere—is more indoctrination than education. By the end of the eighth grade, how-

* In its heyday, by contrast, the Communist party of the Soviet Union actively promoted the party image through the Young Pioneers, a group resembling a combined Boy Scout and Girl Scout organization.

FIGURE 5.4   *Children's Images of Government*

This graph shows how the political understanding of primary school students moves from people to institutions. Students in different grades were given a series of pictures and were asked to pick the two that best depicted our government. In the second and third grades, most chose pictures of Presidents Washington and Kennedy. By the eighth grade, Congress and voting were selected much more frequently than the presidents. (Source: David Easton and Jack Dennis, Children in the Political System *[Chicago: University of Chicago Press, 1969]. Copyright © 1969. Reprinted with permission of the publisher, The University of Chicago Press.)*

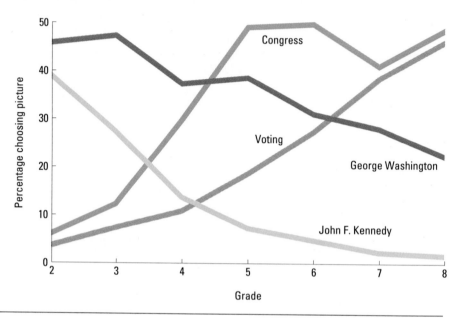

ever, children begin to distinguish between government leaders and institutions. They become more aware of collective institutions, of Congress and elections, than they were earlier, when they tended to focus on the president and other single figures of government authority (see Figure 5.4).[20] In sum, most children emerge from elementary school with a sense of nationalism and an idealized notion of American government.[21]

Although newer curriculums in many secondary schools emphasize citizens' rights in addition to their responsibilities, high schools continue to build "good citizens." Field trips to the state legislature or the city council impress students with the majesty and power of government institutions. Secondary schools also offer more explicit political content in their curricula, including courses in recent U.S. history, civics, and American government. Better teachers challenge students to think critically about American government and politics; others concentrate on teaching civic responsibilities. The end product is a greater awareness of the political process and the people involved in that process (see Figure 5.5).

Despite teachers' efforts to build children's trust in the political process, outside events can erode that trust when children grow up. Surveys of adults showed substantial drops in trust in the national government during the Watergate affair (1972–1974) and when American embassy personnel were held hostage in Iran in 1980. Ronald Reagan's presidency reversed that slide, and by 1986 surveys showed that Americans trusted their government as much as or more than citizens of some other Western nations. But more recent surveys during George Bush's administration revealed another erosion of trust in government, though that level of trust rose immediately after the conclusion of the war in the Persian Gulf.[22]

Political learning at the college level can be very like that in high school or very different. The degree of difference is apt to increase if professors (or the texts they use) encourage their students to question authority. Questioning dominant political values does not necessarily mean rejecting them. For example, this text encourages you to recognize that freedom and equality—two idealized values in our culture—often conflict. It also invites you to think of democracy in terms of competing institutional models, one of which challenges the idealized notion of de-

FIGURE 5.5 *Knowledge of Political Leaders, by Age Groups*

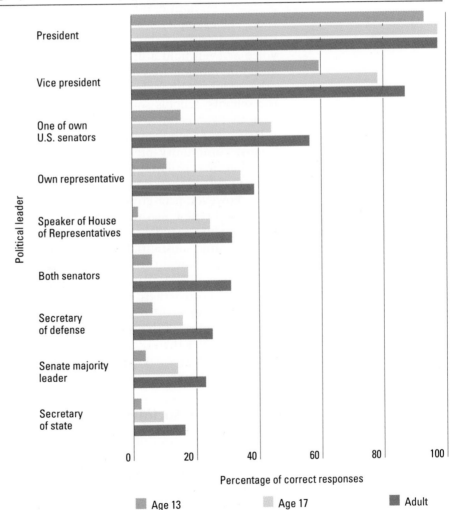

Do people actually learn anything about politics during high school? They seem to, according to a study that asked children at ages 13 and 17 and young adults to write down the last names of people who held the public offices listed below. (Respondents were not penalized for spelling errors.) The percentage of correct responses increased for each age group, but the greatest increases occurred during the high school years, between ages 13 and 17. (Source: Fred I. Greenstein, "What the President Means to Americans," in Choosing the President, *ed. James D. Barber, p. 125. New York: The American Assembly, 1974. Used by permission.)*

mocracy. These alternative perspectives are meant to teach you about American political values, not to subvert those values. College courses that are intended to stimulate critical thinking have the potential to introduce to or develop in some students political ideas that are radically different from those they bring to class. And this is something most high school courses do not do. Still, specialists in socialization contend that taking particular courses in college has little effect on attitude change, which comes from dealing with new role conflicts in the context of sustained interactions with classmates.[23]

Community and peers.   Your community and your peers are different but generally overlapping groups. Your *community* is the people of all ages with whom you come in contact because they live or work near you. Your *peers* are friends, classmates, and coworkers. Usually, they are your age and live within your community.

The makeup of the community has a lot to do with how political opinions are formed. *Homogeneous communities*—those with members similar in ethnicity, race, religion, or occupational status—can exert strong pressures on both children and adults to conform to the dominant attitude. For example, if all your neighbors talk up the candidates of one party and criticize the candidates of the other, it makes it difficult to voice or even hold a dissenting opinion.[24] Communities of one ethnic group or religion may also hold negative attitudes about members of other groups. Although community socialization is usually reinforced in the schools, schools sometimes teach ideas (one example is sex education) that run counter to community values.

Peer groups are sometimes used by children and adults as a defense against community pressures. Adolescent peer groups are particularly useful against parental pressures. In adolescence, children rely on their peers to defend their dress and lifestyle, not their politics. At the college level, however, peer group influence on politics can grow substantially, often fed by new learning that clashes with parental beliefs. A classic study of female students at Bennington College in the 1930s found that many became substantially more liberal than their affluent conservative parents. A follow-up study twenty-five years later showed that most retained their liberal attitudes, in part because their spouses and friends (peers) supported their views.[25] Later evidence shows that the "baby boomers" who went to college during the late 1960s and became the affluent "yuppies" of the 1980s (perhaps your parents) became more liberal on social issues than their high school classmates who did not go to college and land good-paying jobs. However, yuppies were about as conservative as nonyuppies on economic matters.[26]

Continuing Socialization

Political socialization continues throughout life. As parental and school influences wane, peer groups (neighbors, coworkers, club members) assume a greater importance in promoting political awareness and in developing political opinions.[27] Because adults usually learn about political events from the mass media—newspapers, magazines, television, and radio—the media themselves emerge as socialization agents. The role of television is especially important: Nearly three-quarters of adult Americans report regularly watching news on television.[28] (The mass media are so important in the political socialization of both children and adults that we devote a whole chapter—Chapter 6—to a discussion of their role.)

Regardless of how people learn about politics, as they grow older, they gain perspective on government. They are apt to measure new candidates (and new ideas) against the old ones they remember. Their values also change, reflecting their own self-interest. As voters age, for example, they begin to see more merit in government spending for social security than they did when they were younger. Finally, political learning comes simply through exposure and familiarity. One example is the simple act of voting, which people do with increasing regularity as they grow older.

Social Groups and Political Values

No two people are influenced by precisely the same socialization agents in precisely the same way. Each individual experiences a unique process of political socialization and forms a unique set of political values. Still, people with similar backgrounds do share learning experiences; this means they tend to develop similar political opinions. In this section, we examine the ties between people's social backgrounds and their political values. In the process, we look at two questions that appeared in a survey taken in 1990:[29]

1. Would you allow an admitted communist to teach in a college?
2. Do you think that the government should reduce income differences between rich and poor?

Other questions might not produce identical results but would probably show the same general tendencies.

We introduced the first question, about allowing a communist to teach, in Figure 5.2. This question is politically relevant because of the original dilemma of government, the conflict between freedom and order. Those who answered "no" to the question were willing to deny freedom of speech to a teacher who threatens the existing economic and political order. They apparently valued order over individual freedom. The second question, about the government reducing income differences, deals with the modern dilemma of government, the conflict between freedom and equality. Those who answered "yes" think that government should promote economic equality, even if that means taxing the rich more heavily (reducing their freedom to use their money as they want). These respondents apparently valued equality over freedom.

Overall, the responses to each of these questions were divided approximately equally. For the entire national sample, slightly more than half the respondents (52 percent) opposed firing a communist teacher. And more than half (also 52 percent) of all respondents thought the government should reduce income differences. However, sharp differences in attitudes on both issues emerged when respondents were grouped by socioeconomic factors—education, income, region, origin, race, and religion. These differences are shown in Figure 5.6 as positive and negative

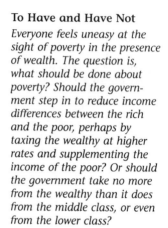

To Have and Have Not
Everyone feels uneasy at the sight of poverty in the presence of wealth. The question is, what should be done about poverty? Should the government step in to reduce income differences between the rich and the poor, perhaps by taxing the wealthy at higher rates and supplementing the income of the poor? Or should the government take no more from the wealthy than it does from the middle class, or even from the lower class?

deviations in percentage points from the national averages on the two questions. (To learn what the national average is on income distribution in other countries, see Compared with What? 5.1.) Bars that extend to the right identify groups that are more likely than most Americans to sacrifice freedom for a given value of government, either equality or order. Below we examine these opinion patterns more closely for each socioeconomic group.

Education

Education increases citizens' awareness and understanding of political issues. Higher education also underscores the value of free speech in a democratic society, increasing our tolerance for those who dissent. This result is clearly shown in Figure 5.6a, where those with more education are more willing to let an admitted communist teach. (That is, respondents with no high school education would tend to fire the teacher, while those with college education would oppose dismissal.) When confronted with issues that involve a choice between personal freedom and social order, college-educated respondents tend to choose freedom.

With regard to the role of government in reducing income inequality, Figure 5.6b shows that more education produces opinions that favor freedom, this time over equality. The higher their level of education, the less respondents supported the redistribution of income. You may think that better-educated people should be humanitarian, that they should support government programs to help the poor. However, educated people tend to be wealthier people, who would be more heavily taxed to help the poor. Thus in this case at least, the effect of education on public opinion is overridden by the effect of income.

FIGURE 5.6 *Group Deviations from National Opinion on Two Questions*

Two questions—one on the dilemma of freedom versus order and the other on the dilemma of freedom versus equality—were asked of a national sample in 1990. Public opinion for the nation as a whole was sharply divided on each question. These two graphs show how respondents in several social groups deviated from overall public opinion. The longer the bars next to each group, the more its respondents deviated from the expression of opinion for the entire sample. Bars that extend to the left show group opinions that deviate toward freedom. Bars that extend to the right show deviations away from freedom, toward order (part a) or equality (part b). (Source: National Opinion Research Center, 1990 General Social Survey. These data were kindly furnished by Tom W. Smith, study director. Used by permission.)

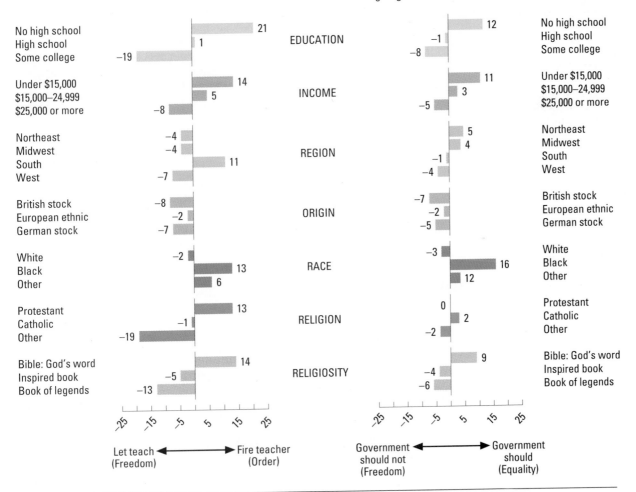

a. I should like to ask you some questions about a man who admits he is a communist. Suppose he is teaching in a college? Should he be fired or not?

b. Should the government in Washington D.C. reduce income differences between the rich and the poor, perhaps by raising taxes of wealthy families or by giving income assistance to the poor?

Income

In many countries, differences in social class—based on social background and occupational status—divide people in their politics.[30] In the United States, we have avoided the uglier aspects of class conflict, but

COMPARED WITH WHAT? 5.1

Opinions on Income Redistribution

Compared with citizens in other Western nations, Americans are much less likely to support government programs that redistribute wealth. Respondents interviewed in 1987 in nine nations were asked whether they agreed or disagreed with the statement "It is the responsibility of the government to reduce the difference in income between people with high incomes and those with low incomes." Only in the U.S. are citizens overwhelmingly opposed to redistribution of wealth as an objective of government.

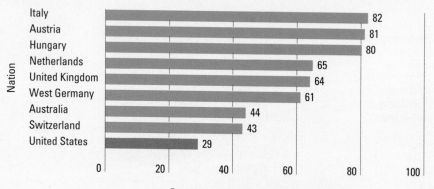

Source: "Public Opinion Report," *The American Enterprise* (March–April 1990), p. 113. Copyright 1990, *The American Enterprise*. Distributed by Special Features/Syndication Sales. Reprinted with permission from The New York Times Syndication Sales Corp.

here wealth sometimes substitutes for class. As shown in Figure 5.6, wealth is consistently related to opinions that limit the government's role in promoting order and equality. Those with higher incomes are more likely to allow a communist to teach and more likely to oppose the redistribution of income. We find that wealth and education, then, have a similar impact on opinion here: In both cases, the groups with more education and higher income opt for freedom. But education has a stronger effect on opinions about order than about equality.[31]

Region

Early in our country's history, regional differences were politically important—important enough to spark a civil war between the North and South. For nearly a hundred years after the Civil War, regional differences continued to affect politics. The moneyed Northeast was thought to control the purse strings of capitalism. The Midwest was long regarded as the stronghold of "isolationism" in foreign affairs. The South was virtually a one-party region, almost completely Democratic. And the rustic West pioneered its own mixture of progressive politics.

In the past, cultural differences among regions were fed by differences in wealth. In recent decades, however, the movement of people and wealth away from the Northeast and Midwest to the Sunbelt states in the South and Southwest has equalized the per capita income of the regions (see Figure 5.7). One product of this equalization is that the "Solid South" is no longer solid for the Democratic party. In fact, the South has become inclined toward voting for Republican candidates for president over the last two decades.

There are differences in public opinion among the four major regions of the United States, but not much. Figure 5.6 shows that people in the

FIGURE **5.7**   *Per Capita Income Across Regions, 1900–1987*

At the beginning of the century, vast differences in wealth could be found among the nation's regions. The wealthiest people were located in the Northeast and on the West Coast; the poorest were in the Southeast. Over time, regional differences in income have narrowed dramatically. The graph below shows per capita income as a percentage of the national average for eight different regions from 1900 to 1987. As per capita incomes have converged, the regions have lost a basis for political differences. However, note that regional differences increased in the 1980s, especially favoring New England. Some attribute this upswing to the flow of investment income to eastern financial institutions, a result of the economic policies of the Reagan administration (see Chapter 18). (Source: Data for 1900 to 1985 come from Public Opinion *[January–February, 1988], p. 25; data for 1987 were adapted from Kevin Phillips,* The Politics of Rich and Poor *[New York: Random House, 1990], p. 187.)*

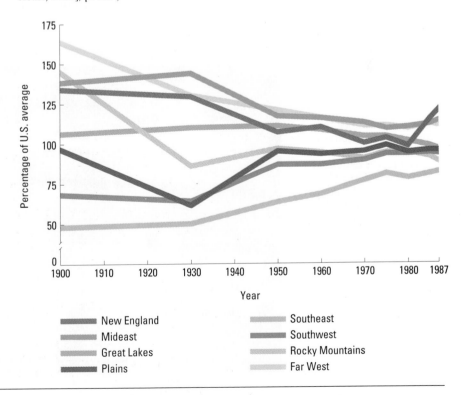

West are somewhat more likely to oppose government efforts to equalize income than are people in the Northeast. Regional differences are greater on the question of social order, particularly between the West, where respondents are more likely to support freedom of speech, and the South, where they are more likely to stop a communist from teaching. Despite these differences, regional effects on public opinion toward these issues are weaker than the effects of most other socioeconomic factors.

The "Old" Ethnicity: European Origin

At the turn of the century, the major ethnic groups in America were immigrants from Ireland, Italy, Germany, Poland, and other European countries, who came to the United States in waves during the late 1800s and early 1900s. These immigrants entered a nation that had been founded by British settlers over a hundred years earlier. They found themselves in a strange land, usually without money and unable to speak the language. Moreover, their religious backgrounds—mainly Catholic and Jewish—differed from the predominant Protestantism of the earlier settlers. Local politicians saw these newcomers, who were concentrated in urban areas in the Northeast and Midwest, as a new source of votes and soon mobilized them into politics. Holding jobs of lower status, these urban ethnics became part of the great coalition of Democratic voters that President Franklin Roosevelt forged in the 1930s. And for years after, studies of public opinion and voting behavior found consistent differences between their political preferences and those of the native Anglo-Saxons.[32]

More recent studies of public opinion show these differences are disappearing. Figure 5.6 analyzes public opinion for three groups of white eth-

Sure 'n' I'm Irish Today!
St. Patrick's Day brings out the Irish in everyone, and politicians of every nationality and ethnic group build their popular support while celebrating the day. But not everyone has to pretend they're descended from the Emerald Isle; Mayor Richard M. Daley of Chicago, pressing the flesh along this parade route, is Irish 365 days a year.

nics, who accounted for about half of the sample interviewed. Respondents who claimed English, Scottish, or Welsh ancestry ("British stock") and German, Austrian, or Swiss ancestry ("German stock") each comprise about 15 percent of the sample. "European ethnics" (primarily Catholics and Jews from Ireland, Italy, and Eastern Europe) comprise about 20 percent. The differences in opinions among these groups are not large. Americans of British stock—mostly "WASPs" (White Anglo-Saxon Protestants)—and German Americans are only slightly more opposed to government action on both issues of order and equality than are European ethnics, who are no longer very different from other white Americans in language, education, or occupation.[33] But if this **"old"** **ethnicity**—European origin—is disappearing, a **"new"** ethnicity—race—is taking its place.

The "New" Ethnicity: Race

For many years after the Civil War, the issue of race in American politics was defined as "how the South should treat the Negro." The debate between North and South over this issue became a conflict of civil rights and states' rights—a conflict in which blacks were primarily objects, not participants. But with the rise of black consciousness and the grassroots civil rights demonstrations led by Dr. Martin Luther King, Jr., and others in the late 1950s and 1960s, blacks emerged as a political force. Through a series of civil rights laws backed by President Lyndon Johnson and northern Democrats in Congress, blacks secured genuine voting rights in the South and exercised those rights more vigorously in the North. Although they made up only about 12 percent of the total population, blacks comprised sizable voting blocs in southern states and in urban areas in northern states. Like the European ethnics before them, American blacks were being courted for their votes; suddenly their opinions were politically important.

Blacks presently constitute the largest racial minority in American politics but not the only significant one. Another 5 percent of the population are Asians, American Indians (Native Americans), and other non-whites. People of Spanish origin—Hispanics—are also commonly but inaccurately regarded as a racial group. According to the 1990 census, Hispanics make up about 9 percent of the nation's population; but they comprise up to 26 percent of the population in California and Texas, and 38 percent in New Mexico.[34] Although they are politically strong in some communities, Hispanics have lagged behind blacks in mobilizing across the nation. However, Hispanics are being wooed by non-Hispanic candidates and are beginning to run more of their own candidates.

Blacks and members of other racial minorities display similar political attitudes. The reasons are twofold.[35] First, racial minorities (excepting second-generation Asians) tend to have low **socioeconomic status** (a combination of education, occupational status, and income). Second, all have been targets of racial prejudice and discrimination. Figure 5.6b clearly shows the effects of race on the freedom-equality issue. Blacks and other minority members (mostly Hispanics) strongly favor government action to equalize incomes and to promote order.

Religion

Since the last major wave of European immigration in the 1930s and 1940s, the religious makeup of the United States has remained fairly stable. Almost 65 percent of those surveyed in 1990 were Protestant, about 25 percent identified themselves as Catholic, only 2 percent were Jewish, and about 10 percent denied any religious affiliation or chose some other.[36] For many years, analysts had found strong and consistent differences in the opinions of Protestants, Catholics, and Jews. Protestants were more conservative than Catholics, and Catholics tended to be more conservative than Jews.

Some differences remained in 1990, especially on the government's role in the question of freedom versus order (the communist teacher). Protestants, who constitute the religious majority in America, tend toward order, especially in comparison with the "other" religious grouping. Even greater differences emerge when respondents are classified by their "religiosity." The 1990 survey asked respondents about their attitudes toward the Bible. A third of the sample responded that it should be taken literally as the actual word of God. Another 50 percent regarded it as an inspired book, but not to be taken literally. About 15 percent viewed it as an ancient book of fables, legends, history and moral precepts recorded by humans.

As Figure 5.6 indicates, those who believed that the Bible is the word of God favored more government action in promoting both order and equality than those with more pragmatic interpretations. The minority who do not think the Bible is inspired are more inclined to freedom, especially over order. This way of classifying respondents reveals that political opinions in the U.S. can differ sharply according to religious beliefs.

From Values to Ideology

So far we have studied differences in groups' opinions on two survey questions. Although responses to these questions reflect value choices between freedom and order and between freedom and equality, we have not yet interpreted group opinions in the context of *political ideology* (the set of values and beliefs people hold about the purpose and scope of government). Political scientists generally agree that ideology enters into public opinion on specific issues; there is much less consensus on the extent to which people think in ideological terms.[37] They also agree that the public's ideological thinking cannot be categorized adequately in conventional liberal-conservative terms.

The Degree of Ideological Thinking in Public Opinion

In an early but important study, respondents were asked about the parties and candidates in the 1956 election.[38] Only about 12 percent of the sample volunteered responses that contained ideological terms (such as *liberal, conservative,* and *capitalism).* Most of the respondents (42 percent) evaluated the parties and candidates in terms of "benefits to groups" (farmers, workers, or businesspeople, for example). Others (24 percent) spoke more generally about "the nature of the times" (for example, inflation, unemployment, and the threat of war). Finally, a good portion of the sample (22 percent) displayed no classifiable issue content in their responses. Other studies have found that the vast majority of the electorate are confused by ideological terms. Consider this response from a resident of the San Francisco Bay Area in 1972 to the question "What do the terms *liberal* and *conservative* mean to you?"

> Oh conservative. Liberal and conservative. Liberal and conservative. I haven't given it much thought. I wouldn't know. I don't know what those would mean! Liberal . . . liberal . . . liberal. And conservative. Well, if a person is liberal with their money they squander their money? Does it fall in that same category? If you're conservative you don't squander so much, you save a little, huh?[39]

A woman in Utica, New York, chosen for a separate in-depth study of how people think about politics, replied when asked if she had an idea about the meaning of liberal and conservative, "No. I read it. I read it in the paper. I read the editorials sometimes and sometimes it's just a little over my head. And I'd like to know more, but then I'll say why bother."[40]

Subsequent research found somewhat greater ideological awareness within the electorate, especially during the 1964 presidential contest between Lyndon Johnson, a Democrat and ardent liberal, and Barry Goldwater, a Republican and arch-conservative.[41] But more recent research has questioned whether American voters have really changed in their ideological thinking.[42] The tendency to respond to questions by using ideological terms is strongly related to education, which helps people understand political issues and relate them to one another. Personal experiences in the socialization process can also lead people to think ideologically. For example, children raised in strong union households may be taught to distrust private enterprise and to value collective action through the government.

True ideologues hold a consistent set of values and beliefs about the purpose and scope of government, and they tend to evaluate candidates in ideological terms.[43] There are people who respond to questions in ways that *seem* ideological but aren't, because the people do not understand the underlying principles. For example, most respondents dutifully comply when they are asked to place themselves somewhere on a liberal-conservative continuum. The result, as shown in Figure 5.2, is an approximately normal distribution centering on "moderate," the modal category. But many people settle on "moderate" when they do not clearly understand the alternatives because it's a safe choice. An earlier study in 1988 gave respondents another choice: the statement "I haven't thought much about it"—which allowed them to avoid placing themselves on the liberal-conservative continuum. In this study, 26 percent of the respondents admitted that they had not thought much about liberalism or conservatism.[44] The extent of ideological thinking in America, then, is considerably less than it might seem from responses to questions that ask people to describe themselves as liberals or conservatives.[45]

The Quality of Ideological Thinking in Public Opinion

It is also not clear what people's ideological self-placement means in the 1990s. Originally, the liberal-conservative continuum represented a single dimension: attitudes toward the scope of government activity. Liberals were in favor of more government action to provide public goods, and conservatives were in favor of less. This simple distinction is not as useful today. Many people who call themselves "liberals" no longer favor government activism in general, and many self-styled "conservatives" no longer oppose it in principle.

In Chapter 1, we proposed an alternative ideological classification based on the relationships among the values of freedom, order, and equality. We described liberals as people who believe that government should promote equality, even if some freedom is lost in the process, but who oppose surrendering freedom to government-imposed order. Conservatives do not oppose equality in and of itself, but put a higher value on freedom than equality when the two conflict. Yet conservatives are not above restricting freedom when threatened with the loss of order. So both groups value freedom, but one is more willing to trade freedom for equality, and the other is more inclined to trade freedom for order.

If you have trouble thinking about these tradeoffs on a single dimension, you are perfectly normal. The liberal-conservative continuum presented to survey respondents takes a two-dimensional concept and squeezes it into a one-dimensional format.[46] As a result, many people have difficulty deciding whether they are liberal or conservative, and others confidently choose the same point on the continuum for entirely different reasons. People describe themselves as *liberal* or *conservative* because of the symbolic value of the terms as much as for what they know about ideology.[47]

Studies of the public's ideological thinking find that two themes run through people's minds when they are asked to describe liberals and conservatives. One associates liberals with change and conservatives with traditional values. This theme corresponds to the distinction between liberals and conservatives on the exercise of freedom and the maintenance of order.[48]

The other theme has to do with equality. The conflict between freedom and equality was at the heart of President Roosevelt's New Deal economic policies (social security, minimum wage legislation, farm price supports) in the 1930s. These policies expanded the interventionist role of the national government. And government intervention in the economy served to distinguish liberals from conservatives for decades afterward.[49] Attitudes toward government interventionism still underlie contemporary opinions of domestic economic policies.[50] Liberals support intervention to promote their ideas of economic equality; conservatives favor less government intervention and more individual freedom in economic activities.

FIGURE 5.8 *Respondents Classified by Ideological Tendencies*

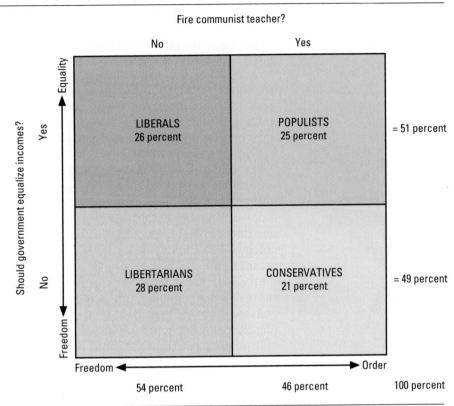

Choices between freedom and order and between freedom and equality were represented by two survey questions that asked respondents whether a communist should teach in college and whether the government should equalize income differences. People's responses to the questions showed no correlation, demonstrating that these value choices cannot be explained by a simple liberal-conservative continuum. Instead, their responses conform to four different ideological types. (Source: National Opinion Research Center, 1990 General Social Survey. These data were kindly furnished by Tom W. Smith, study director.)

Ideological Types in the United States

Our ideological typology in Chapter 1 incorporates these two themes (see Figure 1.2). It classifies people as *liberals* if they favor freedom over order and equality over freedom. *Conservatives* favor the reverse set of values. *Libertarians* favor freedom over both equality and order—the opposite of *populists*. We can classify respondents according to their ideological *tendencies*, cross-tabulating their answers to the two questions about order and equality. As shown in Figure 5.8, people's responses to the questions about firing a communist teacher and redistributing income are virtually unrelated, which indicates that people do not decide about government activity according to a one-dimensional ideological standard.

Figure 5.8 can also be used to classify the sample according to the two dimensions in our ideological typology. There is substantial room for error in using only two issues to classify people in an ideological framework. Moreover, the responses on each issue were forced into two categories for simplicity in presentation, and a "yes" response by some people is weaker than the same response by others. Still, if the typology is worthwhile, the results should be meaningful, and they are.

The respondents in the 1990 sample depicted in Figure 5.8 divide almost evenly in their ideological tendencies among the four categories of the typology. (But remember that these categories—like letter grades *A*, *B*, *C*, and *D*—are more rigid in the typology than in the respondents. Many would cluster toward the center of the figure, if their attitudes were measured more sensitively.) Surprisingly, the libertarian response pattern accounts for the largest portion of the sample.[51] Although pure conservatives are the smallest group, they still account for almost one-quarter of the public. These results are similar to findings for earlier years by other researchers who conducted more exhaustive analyses involving more survey questions. Using the same basic typology, these scholars classified substantial portions of their respondents in each ideological category in 1980.[52]

Respondents who readily locate themselves on a single dimension running from liberal to conservative later often contradict their self-placement when answering questions that trade off freedom for either order or equality.[53] Obviously, most Americans' opinions do not fit a one-dimensional liberal-conservative continuum. A two-dimensional typology—like the one in Figure 5.8—allows us to analyze responses more meaningfully.[54] Most Americans do not express opinions that are consistently liberal or conservative. In fact, most Americans hold combinations of opinions about the scope of government action that are either conservative or libertarian. However, there are important differences in ideological tendencies among socioeconomic groups.

Populists are prominent among minorities and others with little education and low income, groups that tend to look favorably on the benefits of government in general. *Libertarians* are concentrated among respondents with more education and with higher income, who live in the West. These groups tend to be suspicious of government interference in their lives. *Conservatives* are found mainly in the South, and *liberals* are concentrated in the Northeast.

This more refined analysis of political ideology explains why even some Americans who pay close attention to politics find it difficult to locate themselves on the liberal-conservative continuum. Their problem is that they are liberal on some issues and conservative on others. Forced to choose along just one dimension, they choose the middle category, "moderate." However, our analysis also indicates that many respondents who classify themselves as liberals and conservatives do conform to our typology. There is value, then, in the liberal-conservative distinction, as long as we understand its limitations.

The Process of Forming Political Opinions

So far we have learned that people acquire their values through the socialization process and that different social groups develop different sets of political values. We also have learned that some people, but only a minority, think about politics ideologically, holding a consistent set of political attitudes and beliefs. However, we have not really discussed how people form opinions on any particular issue. In particular, how do those who are not ideologues—in other words, most citizens—form political opinions? Four factors—self-interest, political information, opinion schemes, and political leadership—play a part in the process.

From the California Assembly to the U.S. Congress

Democrat Maxine Waters was elected to the House of Representatives in 1990, succeeding Augustus Hawkins, who retired after serving Los Angeles for fourteen terms. Representative Waters is expected to be a forceful advocate of women's rights and social programs, reflecting the interests of her low-income, largely black and Hispanic district.

Self-Interest

The **self-interest principle** states that people choose what benefits them personally.[55] This principle plays an obvious role in the way opinions are formed on government economic policies. Taxpayers tend to prefer low taxes to high taxes; farmers tend to favor candidates who promise them more support than those who promise them less. The self-interest principle also operates, but less clearly, for some government policies outside of economics. Members of minority groups tend to see more personal advantage in government policies that promote social equality than do members of majority groups; teenage males are more likely to oppose compulsory military service than are older people of either sex. Group leaders often "cue" group members, telling them what they should be for or against.[56]

For many government policies, however, the self-interest principle plays little or no role, because the policies directly affect relatively few citizens. Outlawing prostitution is one example; legalized abortion is another. When such moral issues are involved in government policy, people form opinions based on their underlying values.[57]

When moral issues are not in question and when they do not benefit directly from a policy, many people have trouble relating to the policy and forming an opinion. This tends to be true of the whole subject of foreign policy, which few people interpret in terms of personal benefits. Here, many people have no opinion, or their opinions are not firmly held and are apt to change quite easily, given almost any new information.

Political Information

In the United States today, education is compulsory (usually to age sixteen), and the literacy rate is relatively high. The country boasts an unparalleled network of colleges and universities entered by one-third of all high school graduates. American citizens can obtain information from a variety of daily and weekly news publications. They can keep abreast of national and international affairs through nightly television news, which brings live coverage of world events via satellite from virtually anywhere in the world. Yet the average American displays an astonishing lack of political knowledge.

Citizens' knowledge of politics just after an election is low enough to question the basis of their vote. After the 1988 election, for example, only 28 percent of a national sample could correctly identify even one of their candidates for the House of Representatives, and only 40 percent correctly named either of their candidates for the Senate.[58] In June 1990, the Supreme Court made news by overturning an act of Congress that outlawed flag burning as a protected means of expression. Despite the great publicity given the decision, 31 percent of a national sample incorrectly thought the court had supported the anti–flag burning law, while 17 percent admitted that they did not know. Only 52 percent of the public knew (guessed?) what the Court had decided on this highly charged issue.[59]

But Americans do not let political ignorance stop them from expressing their opinions. They readily offer opinions on issues ranging from capital punishment to nuclear power to the government's handling of the economy. If opinions are based on little information, they change easily when new information becomes available. The result is a high degree of instability in public opinion poll results, depending on the way questions are worded and current events that bear on the issue.

Researchers use the term **political sophistication** to mean having a broad range of opinions, based on factual information, that are consistent and organized conceptually.[60] One study of political sophistication counted the number of specific political issues, actors, and events that 143 respondents brought up in hour-long interviews on political alienation. The average number of political references was 27. The highest number was 94, and the lowest was one—just a single reference to a political subject in an hour-long interview on politics! What did people talk about during all that time? The researcher said that they talked about themselves: "Asked whether they are satisfied about the way things have been going in this country, they responded only about their job, family, friends, and other aspects of their own life."[61]

The author of this study classified the American public into three broad groups of political sophistication. The least sophisticated (about 20 percent of the electorate) pay little attention to public affairs and seldom participate in politics. Most adults (about 75 percent) are only moderately sophisticated. "They half-attentively monitor the flow of political news, but they run for the most part on a psychological automatic pilot." Only a small portion of the electorate (about 5 percent) is politically sophisticated, sharing the knowledge and conceptualization of professional politicians, journalists, and political analysts. As expected, education is strongly related to political sophistication, but so is participation in groups and parents' interest in politics. The author likens the development of political sophistication to a "spiral process . . . a gradual process in which interest breeds knowledge, which, in turn, breeds further interest and knowledge over time."[62] Political events and the actions of political leaders can contribute to that spiraling process.

We should note that researchers have not found any meaningful relationship between political sophistication and self-placement on the liberal-conservative scale. That is, people with equal knowledge about public affairs and with similar levels of conceptualization are as likely to think of themselves as liberals as conservatives.[63] Equal levels of political understanding, then, may produce very different political views as a result of individuals' unique patterns of political socialization.

Opinion Schemas

We have learned that only a minority of the population, about one person in five, can be classified as ideologues. These people regularly think about politics in ideological terms and come to new political issues with a set of political beliefs and values that helps them form opinions on these issues. But even people who do not approach politics with full-blown ideologies interpret political issues in terms of some preexisting mental structure.

Psychologists refer to the packet of pre-existing beliefs that people apply to specific issues as an **opinion schema**—a network of organized knowledge and beliefs that guides the processing of information on a particular subject.[64] Figure 5.9 shows an opinion schema about George Bush that might be held by a Republican conservative. It is only a partial schema, but it suggests the wide range of attitudes and beliefs that affect thinking about political leaders and their policies. Our opinion schemas change as we acquire new information. A conservative acting on the opinion schema in Figure 5.9 probably would have reacted more strongly to Bush's abandonment of his 1988 campaign pledge of "no new taxes" than a liberal Democrat.

The schema concept gives us a sharper tool for analyzing public opinion than the blunter concept of ideology. Opinion schemas can pertain to any political figure and to any subject—race, economics, or international relations, for example.[65] For instance, one study found that African-Americans' views on the importance of race in determining one's chances in life could be analyzed according to five distinct schemas.[66]

Still, the more encompassing concept of ideology is hard to escape. Researchers have found that people tend to organize their personal schemas

FIGURE 5.9   *Hypothetical Opinion Schema About George Bush*

People express opinions on issues, persons, or events according to pre-existing attitudes and beliefs that they associate with the question being asked. Psychologists sometimes refer to this network of attitudes and beliefs, and their relationships, as an opinion schema. Below is a hypothetical opinion schema that might be associated with George Bush in the mind of a Republican conservative who voted for Bush in 1988.

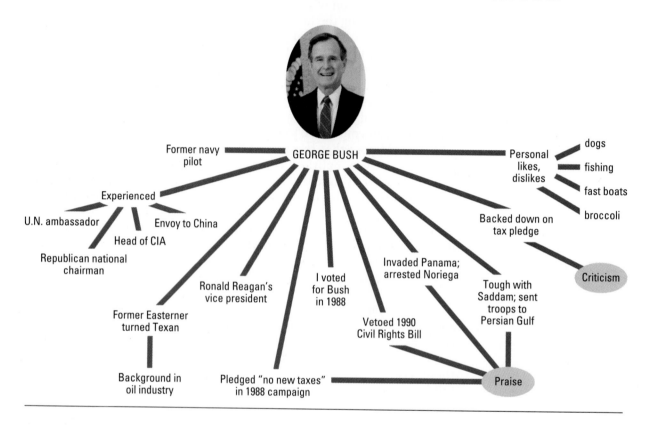

within a hierarchy of opinion that parallels broader ideological categories. A liberal's opinion schema about Bush may not differ from a conservative's in the facts it contains, but it differs considerably in its evaluation of those facts.[67] In the liberal's schema, for example, anger might replace the conservative's praise for Bush's decision to invade Panama in 1989. The main value of schemas for understanding how opinions are formed is that they remind us that opinion questions trigger many different images, connections, and values in the mind of each respondent. Given the complexity of factors in individual opinion schemas, it is surprising that researchers find as many strong correlations as they do among individuals' social backgrounds, general values, and specific opinions.

Some scholars argue that most citizens, in their attempt to make sense out of politics, pay less attention to the policies pursued by government than to their leaders' "style" in approaching political problems—whether they are seen as tough, compassionate, honest, or hard-working.[68] When a leader acts in the manner preferred by style-oriented citizens, they view his or her policy favorably. In this way citizens can relate the complexities of politics to their own personal experiences. If many citizens view politics according to governing style, the role of political leadership becomes a more important determinant of public opinion than the leader's actual policies.

Political Leadership

Public opinion on specific issues is stimulated by political leaders, journalists, and policy experts. Because of their office and the media attention it receives, presidents are uniquely positioned to shape popular attitudes. Consider the issue of nuclear disarmament and Ronald Reagan. In late 1987, President Reagan and Mikhail Gorbachev signed a treaty banning intermediate-range nuclear forces (INF) from Europe and the Soviet Union. Soon afterward, a national survey found that 82 percent of the sample approved the treaty while 18 percent opposed it. As might be expected, those hard-liners who viewed the Soviet Union as highly threatening were least enthusiastic about the INF treaty. Respondents were then asked to agree or disagree with this statement: "President Reagan is well known for his anticommunism, so if he thinks this is a good deal, it must be." Analysis of the responses showed that those hard-liners who agreed with the statement were nearly twice as likely to approve the treaty as those who were unmoved by his involvement. The researcher concluded that "a highly conciliatory move by a president known for long-standing opposition to just such an action" can override expected sources of opposition among the public.[69] The implication is that another president, such as Jimmy Carter or even Gerald Ford, could not have won over the hard-liners.

The role of political leaders in affecting public opinion has been enhanced enormously with the development of the broadcast media, especially television.[70] The majoritarian model of democracy assumes that government officials respond to public opinion, but there is substantial evidence that the causal sequence is reversed: that public opinion responds instead to the actions of government officials.[71] If this is true, how much potential is there for public opinion to be manipulated by political leaders through the mass media? We examine the manipulative potential of the mass media in the next chapter.

Summary

Public opinion does not rule in America. On most issues, it merely sets general boundaries for government policy. The shape of the distribution of opinion (normal, skewed, or bimodal) indicates how sharply the public is divided. Bimodal distributions harbor the greatest potential for political conflict. The stability of a distribution over time indicates how settled people are in their opinions. Because most Americans' ideological opinions are normally distributed around the "moderate" category and have been so for decades, government policies can vary from left to right over time without provoking severe political conflict.

People form their values through the process of political socialization. The most important socialization agents in childhood and young adulthood are family, school, community, and peers. Members of the same social group tend to experience similar socialization processes and thus to adopt similar values. People in different social groups, who hold different values, often express vastly different opinions. Differences in education, race, and religion tend to produce sharper divisions of opinion today on questions of order and equality than do differences in income, region, and ethnicity.

Although most people do not think about politics in ideological terms, when asked to do so by pollsters, they readily classify themselves along a liberal-conservative continuum. Many respondents choose the middle category, "moderate," the safe choice. Others classify themselves as liberals or conservatives for vague or contradictory reasons. Our two-dimensional framework for analyzing ideology according to the values of order and equality produces four ideological types: liberals, conservatives, libertarians, and populists.

Responses to the survey questions we used to establish our ideological typology divide the American electorate almost equally into these four ideological tendencies. The quarter of the public that gave liberal responses, opposing government action to impose order but not equality, was opposed by nearly as large a portion who gave the opposite conservative responses. Similarly, the group of populists, who wanted government to impose both order and equality, was opposed by a slightly larger group of libertarians, who wanted government to do neither.

In addition to ideological orientation, many other factors enter the process of forming political opinions. When individuals stand to benefit or suffer from proposed government policies, they usually base their opinions on self-interest. When citizens lack information on which to base their opinions, they usually respond anyway, which leads to substantial fluctuations in poll results, depending on how questions are worded and intervening events. The various factors that impinge on the process of forming political opinions can be mapped out within an opinion schema, a network of beliefs and attitudes about a particular topic. The schema imagery helps us visualize the complex process of forming opinions. This process, however, is not completely idiosyncratic: People tend to organize their schemas according to broader ideological thinking. In the absence of information, respondents are particularly susceptible to cues of support or opposition from political leaders, communicated through the mass media.

Which model of democracy, the majoritarian or the pluralist, is correct in its assumptions about public opinion? Sometimes the public shows clear and settled opinions on government policy, conforming to the majoritarian model. However, often public opinion is firmly grounded not in knowledge but in ideological bias. Moreover, powerful groups often divide on what they want government to do. This lack of consensus leaves politicians with a great deal of latitude in enacting specific policies, a finding that conforms to the pluralist model. Of course, politicians' actions are under close scrutiny by journalists reporting in the mass media. We turn to the impact of this scrutiny and the mass media on politics in Chapter 6.

KEY TERMS

public opinion
normal distribution
skewed distribution
bimodal distribution
stable distribution
political socialization

"old" ethnicity
"new" ethnicity
socioeconomic status
self-interest principle
political sophistication
opinion schema

SELECTED READINGS

Asher, Herbert. *Polling and the Public: What Every Citizen Should Know.* Washington, D.C.: Congressional Quarterly Press, 1988. A concise text on polling methodology that gives special attention to election polls.

Crespi, Irving. *Public Opinion, Polls, and Democracy.* Boulder, Col.: Westview Press, 1989. Focuses on polling methodology but also discusses at some length the use of polls by the news media.

Ichilov, Orit. *Political Socialization, Citizenship Education, and Democracy.* New York: Teachers College Press, 1990. A collection of studies on how people acquire political attitudes, with special attention to childhood processes and with examples drawn from other cultures.

Maddox, William S., and Stuart A. Lilie. *Beyond Liberal and Conservative: Reassessing the Political Spectrum.* Washington, D.C.: Cato Institute, 1984. Uses an ideological typology similar to the one in this chapter to analyze surveys in presidential elections from 1952 through 1980.

Margolis, Michael, and Gary A. Mauser (eds.). *Manipulating Public Opinion: Essays on Public Opinion as a Dependent Variable.* Pacific Grove, Calif.: Brooks/Cole, 1989. Studies the abilities of political elites to manage public opinion in election campaigns, in shaping public policies, and in political socialization.

Neuman, W. Russell. *The Paradox of Mass Politics: Knowledge and Opinion in the American Electorate.* Cambridge, Mass.: Harvard University Press, 1986. Analyzes major voting surveys from 1948 to 1980, assessing citizens' political interest, knowledge, and level of conceptualization.

Niemi, Richard G., John Mueller, and Tom W. Smith. *Trends in Public Opinion: A Compendium of Survey Data.* New York: Greenwood Press, 1989. This handy volume collects some fifty years of polling data, with heavy concentration on annual data from the General Social Surveys, begun in 1972. The survey data are organized into fifteen chapters, each preceded by a useful descriptive essay.

Sanders, Arthur. *Making Sense of Politics.* Ames, Iowa: Iowa State University Press, 1990. Sanders interviewed twenty-six citizens from Ithaca, New York, at length about their thoughts on politics. In contrast to the short responses gathered from many people in opinion polls, this study reports at length on the thinking that average citizens devote to politics. It concludes that more people try to make sense of politics by focusing on the style of decision making than on the content of government policies.

Yeric, Jerry L., and John R. Todd. *Public Opinion: The Visible Politics,* 2d ed. Itasca, Ill.: F. E. Peacock, 1989. A basic textbook on public opinion, especially good on the development of individual opinions. It also contains useful case studies of public opinion as it developed on six national issues.

6 THE MASS MEDIA

WHEN THE AIR ATTACK ON Baghdad began the evening of January 16, 1991, President Bush watched it on television. At 6:35 P.M., he and the rest of the world saw the night sky over the Iraqi capital erupt in lethal fireworks. Like so many other Americans, the president switched between the live reports broadcast initially by ABC and the Cable News Network (CNN).[1] Soon, however, only CNN provided live coverage of the bombing, because it had Iraq's permission to run a special phone line for its exclusive use. Such preferential treatment enabled CNN to score a stunning coup in broadcast journalism.

Even before the war, Saddam Hussein was well aware of CNN, which was received in Baghdad and in most of the other major capitals of the world. The station, which started in 1980 to broadcast news twenty-four hours a day, had by 1990 turned the world into a global village, beaming news to 120 stations. When insomniac King Fahd of Saudi Arabia can't sleep, he watches CNN. When the United States invaded Panama in 1989, CNN cameras were summoned to the Kremlin in the middle of the night so that Mikhail Gorbachev's press aide could condemn the invasion. Gorbachev counted on the instantaneous transmission of the condemnation to Washington; the official protest came later. In Washington, President Bush often watches CNN—while others watch him. Bush ended a press conference on the Gulf crisis by stating that he was about to call Turkish President Turgut Ozal. When the phone rang in Istanbul, Ozal himself picked up the phone; he had been watching CNN and expected Bush's call.[2]

Saddam Hussein had paid close attention to CNN's reports on congressional opposition to Bush's policy prior to January 16. In front of television cameras, the Senate Foreign Relations Committee asked Secretary of State James Baker to answer probing questions about President Bush's strategic thinking. Assuming that Saddam would be watching, Baker was reluctant to answer. In our democracy, it is proper for Congress to question presidential foreign policy, but it is also sensible to withhold information from your foreign opponents. That is difficult to do in an open society, especially when the news media broadcast freely to the global village. In the Senate hearings, Senator Richard Lugar said, "In order to be credible, Baker needs to have a united country behind him."[3] Saddam could plainly see that the United States was not united behind the president's policy.

Ironically, the preferential treatment accorded to CNN probably contributed to Iraq's quick defeat. The live coverage of the bombing convinced the public that the U.S. raid was limited to strategic targets. By allowing CNN to televise the raid, Saddam unwittingly eliminated the bombing of Baghdad as a basis of antiwar protest. Indeed, the appearance of a clean, high-tech war quickly crystallized American opinion in support of U.S. troops in the Gulf and Bush's handling of the war. Although the press protested vigorously against the severe restrictions imposed on reporters covering the war, the public largely sided with the military and against the media.[4]

Some people believe that the freewheeling television coverage of the horrors of the Vietnam War contributed to antiwar sentiment. Acting on that belief, the military sharply controlled reporters and reporting in the

Tell Uncle Saddam

Attempting to portray himself as a kindly gentleman with the welfare of his guests at heart, Iraqi president Saddam Hussein smiles at a tense young hostage whose eyes are on members of Saddam's elite guards. Hussein videotaped his staged visit with British men, women, and children held captive somewhere in Iraq during the first month of the 1990 Persian Gulf crisis. He released the tape to the Cable News Network for broadcast to the world. CNN thought it was great video and took less than 30 seconds to decide to broadcast it, unedited and uncut.

invasions of Grenada in 1983 and Panama in 1989—with satisfactory military results and little public outcry. In dealing with reporters in the much larger Persian Gulf conflict, the military continued its post-Vietnam policy of press restrictions. To get around these restrictions, some journalists began traveling with Saudi and Egyptian forces to cover the war. Other journalists tried to operate on their own and were captured by Iraqi forces (but eventually released).

When the ground war began on February 23, the Pentagon further restricted news coverage, even suspending regular press briefings. However, the ground campaign was such a success that the military repealed its blackout to get out the good news. If the fighting had been fierce, the public would have been told less and told later. Many journalists claim that our government infringed on freedom of the press in the last three international conflicts. Is this a cause for public concern, or does free press coverage of foreign conflict unduly hamper the military conduct of war and the pursuit of order?

Freedom of the press is essential to democratic government, but the news media both assist and complicate the governmental process. What is the nature of the mass media in America? Who uses the media, and what do they learn? Do the media promote or frustrate democratic ideals? Does freedom of the press conflict with the values of order or equality? In this chapter, we describe the origin and growth of the media, assess their objectivity, and examine their impact on politics.

People, Government, and Communications

"We never *talk* anymore" is a common lament among people who are living together but not getting along very well. In politics, too, citizens and their government need to communicate in order to get along well. **Communication** is the process of transmitting information from one individual or group to another. **Mass communication** is the process by which individuals or groups transmit information to large, heterogeneous, and widely dispersed audiences. The term **mass media** refers to the technical devices employed in mass communication. The mass media are commonly divided into two types:

1. **Print media** communicate information through the publication of written words and pictures. Prime examples of print media are daily newspapers and popular magazines. Because books seldom have very large circulations relative to the population, they are not typically classified as a mass medium.

2. **Broadcast media** communicate information electronically through sounds or sights. Prime examples of broadcast media are radio and television. Although the telephone also transmits sounds, it is usually used for more targeted communications and so is not typically included within the mass media.

In the United States, the mass media are in business to make money, which they do mainly by selling advertising through their major function, entertainment. We are more interested in the five specific functions the mass media serve for the political system: *reporting* the news, *interpreting* the news, *influencing* citizens' opinions, *setting the agenda* for government action, and *socializing* citizens about politics.

Our special focus is on the role of the mass media in promoting communication from a government to its citizens *and* from citizens to their government. In totalitarian governments, information flows more freely in one direction (from government to people) than in the other. In democratic governments, information must flow freely in both directions; a democratic government can be responsive to public opinion only if its citizens can make their opinions known. Moreover, the electorate can hold government officials accountable for their actions only if voters know what their government has done, is doing, and plans to do. Because the mass media provide the major channels for this two-way flow of information, they have the dual capability of reflecting and shaping our political views.

Mass media are not the only means of communication between citizens and government. As we discussed in Chapter 5, various agents of socialization (especially schools) function as "linkage mechanisms" that promote such communication. In the next four chapters, we discuss other major mechanisms for communication: voting, political parties, campaigning in elections, and interest groups. Certain linkage mechanisms communicate better in one direction than in the other. Primary and secondary schools, for example, commonly instruct young citizens about government rules and symbols, whereas voting sends messages from citizens to government. Parties, campaigns, and interest groups foster communications in both directions. The mass media, however, are the only linkage mechanisms that *specialize* in communication.

Although this chapter concentrates on political uses of the four most prominent mass media—newspapers, magazines, radio, and television—you should understand that political content can also be transmitted through other mass media, such as recordings and motion pictures. Rock acts like Peter Gabriel and U2 often express political ideas in their music.

And motion pictures often convey particularly intense political messages. In the 1976 film *All the President's Men*, Dustin Hoffman and Robert Redford played Carl Bernstein and Bob Woodward, the two *Washington Post* reporters who doggedly exposed the Watergate scandal in a series of articles that led to President Richard Nixon's resignation in 1974. This motion picture dramatized a seamy side of political life that contrasted sharply with an idealized view of the presidency. In his series of "Rambo" films, Sylvester Stallone played a paramilitary superhero who solved difficult international problems through combat. In contrast, the award-winning *Born on the Fourth of July* starred Tom Cruise in the real-life story of Ron Kovic, who enlisted in the marines and was severely wounded in Vietnam. Paralyzed from the waist down, he underwent painful rehabilitation and turned into an antiwar activist. This film presents a very different view of fighting.

The Development of the Mass Media in the United States

Although the record and film industries sometimes convey political messages, they are primarily entertainment. Our focus is on mass media in the news industry—on print and broadcast journalism. The development of the news media in the United States has been shaped by the growth of the country, technological inventions, and political attitudes toward the scope of government—as well as the need to entertain.

Newspapers

When the revolutionary war broke out in 1775, thirty-seven newspapers (all weeklies) were being published in the colonies.[5] Most of them favored the colonists' side against the British, and they played an important part in promoting the Revolution. However, these weekly papers cannot be regarded as instruments of mass communication. Their circulations were small (usually a thousand copies or so), and they were expensive. Type had to be set by hand, the presses printed quite slowly, transportation was costly, and there were few advertisers to defray the costs of publication. Still, politicians of the day quickly saw the value of the press and started papers that expressed their own views. During George Washington's administration, for example, the Federalists published the *Gazette of the U.S.*; the Antifederalists published the *National Gazette*.

The first newspapers were therefore political organs, financed by parties and advocating party causes. Newspapers did not move toward independent ownership and large circulations until the 1830s, with the publication of two successful dailies (the *New York Sun* and the *New York Herald*) that sold for just a penny. Various inventions spurred the growth of the news industry. The telegraph (invented in 1837) eventually replaced the use of carrier pigeons for transmitting news and allowed the simultaneous publication of news stories by papers across the country. The rotary press (1847) soon enabled publishers to print much more quickly and cheaply.

According to the 1880 census, 971 daily newspapers and 8,633 weekly newspapers and periodicals were then published in the United States. Most larger cities had a number of newspapers—New York had 29 pa-

The Origin of Yellow Journalism

The term yellow journalism *means sleazy, sensational reporting. It derives from the "Yellow Kid," a popular cartoon character in the* New York World, *one of the first newspapers to use color for cartoons and comic strips in the late 1800s. The* World *also boosted its circulation by emphasizing entertainment over straight news and by crusading for political causes, some of which were manufactured.*

TRAINING FOR THE FOOTBALL CHAMPIONSHIP GAME IN HOGAN'S ALLEY.

pers; Philadelphia, 24; San Francisco, 21; and Chicago, 18. Competition for readers grew fierce among the big-city dailies. Toward the latter part of the nineteenth century, imaginative publishers sought to win readers by entertaining them with photographs, comic strips, sports sections, advice to the lovelorn, and stories of sex and crime. The sensational reporting of that period came to be called **yellow journalism**—after the "Yellow Kid," a comic-strip character featured in the *New York World*, published by Joseph Pulitzer (the same man who established the Pulitzer prizes for distinguished journalism).[6] Contests calculated to sell papers were also popular with publishers. Some promotional schemes had lasting political consequences. Pulitzer raised funds to put the Statue of Liberty on its pedestal after Congress turned down a request for $100,000. Each person who donated to the cause had his or her name printed in the *New York World*'s list of donors. And William Randolph Hearst, publisher of the rival *New York Journal*, helped get the nation into a war with Spain. When the U.S. battleship *Maine* blew up mysteriously in Havana harbor on February 15, 1898, Hearst proclaimed it the work of enemy agents, charging his readers to "Remember the Maine!"

By the 1960s, intense competition among big-city dailies had nearly disappeared. New York, which had 29 papers in 1880, had only 3 by 1969. This pattern was repeated in every large city; most were left with 1 to 3 major papers. The net result is that the number of newspapers per person has dropped about 30 percent since 1950.[7]

The daily paper with the largest circulation at the start of the 1990s (almost 2 million copies) is the *Wall Street Journal*, which appeals to a

Uh, the News Is on the Front
The U.S. invasion of Iraq on January 16, 1991, was headlined the next morning in papers across the nation. At a diner in Rock Falls, Illinois, these men are absorbed with their reading. (Presumably they read the stories on the front page before turning to the sports on the back.)

national audience because of its extensive coverage of business news and its close analysis of political news. The *New York Times*, which many journalists consider the best newspaper in the country, sells about a million copies, placing it fourth in national circulation. In comparison, *The National Enquirer*, which carries stories about people who return from the dead or marry aliens from outer space, sells 4.3 million copies. Neither the *Times* nor the *Wall Street Journal* carries any comic strips, which no doubt limits their mass appeal. They also print more political news and news analyses than most readers want to confront.

Magazines

Magazines differ from newspapers primarily in the nature of their coverage, the frequency of their publication, and the quality of their production. In contrast to the broad coverage of daily papers, many magazines focus on narrow topics such as sports. Even news-oriented magazines cover the news in a more specialized manner than newspapers. Magazines are often used as forums for opinion, not strictly for news. However, magazines dealing with public affairs have had relatively small circulations and select readerships, making them questionable as mass media. The earliest public affairs magazines, such as *Nation, McClure's,* and *Harper's*, were published in the mid-1800s. These magazines were often politically influential—especially in framing arguments against slavery and later in publishing exposés of political corruption and business exploitation by such writers as Lincoln Steffens and Ida Tarbell. These writers, derisively called **muckrakers** (a term derived from a special rake used to collect manure), practiced an early form of investigative reporting that involved detailing basic unsavory facts about government and business. Because their writings were lengthy critiques of the existing political and economic order, muckrakers found a more hospitable outlet in magazines of opinion than in newspapers with large circulations. Yet magazines that have limited readerships can wield political power. Magazines may influence **attentive policy elites**—leaders who follow news in specific areas—and thus influence mass opinion indirectly through a **two-step flow of communication.** As scholars originally viewed the two-step flow, it conformed ideally to the pluralist model of democracy. Magazines informed a few policy elites (for instance, union or industry leaders) about relevant developments or political thought; these leaders in turn informed their more numerous followers, mobilizing them to apply pressure on government. Today, according to a revised interpretation of the two-step flow, policy elites are more likely to influence public opinion (not necessarily their "followers") and other policy elites by airing their views in the media.

Three weekly news magazines—*Time* (founded in 1923), *Newsweek* (1933), and *U.S. News & World Report* (1933)—have enjoyed large circulations (2.5 million to 4.5 million copies in 1990). The audiences of these magazines, however, are not as large as the 17 million readers of *TV Guide*, or the 16 million readers of *Reader's Digest*.[8] In contrast to these mainstream "capitalist" publications, a newer "alternative" press is more critical of the prevailing power structure. Such periodicals as *Mother Jones* and the *Utne Reader* have spearheaded various investiga-

FIGURE 6.1   *Audiences of Selected Media Sources*

Television, newspapers, and magazines differ sharply in their appeal to mass audiences as news sources. The difference shows clearly when the figures for the average number of homes that are tuned nightly to one of the three major network news programs are compared with the circulation figures for the three top news magazines, the eight top newspapers, and the two largest opinion magazines. Clearly, television news enters many more homes than does news from the other media. All three news magazines (which are published weekly) have more readers than any daily newspaper, and opinion magazines reach only a small fraction of the usual television news audiences. (Sources: Average television news audiences from the New York Times, *29 November 1990, p. B4, and from* Nielsen Homevideo Index, *"Daily Cumulative Analysis," July 1990; magazine circulations are from* Standard Periodical Directory, *1990; newspaper circulations are from* Editor & Publisher, *3 November 1990, p. 14.)*

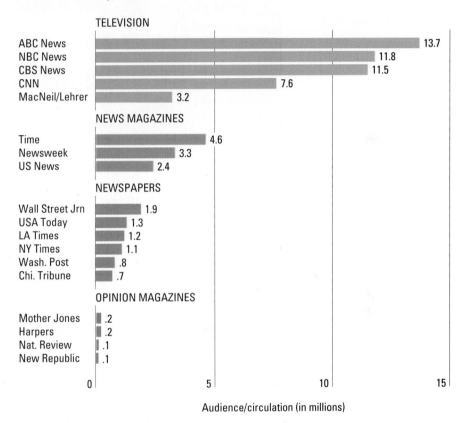

Audience/circulation (in millions)

tions into the Iran-Contra affair and the connection between President Bush and General Manuel Noriega when Bush was head of the CIA, for instance.[9] As shown in Figure 6.1, some of these publications are read more widely than mainstream opinion magazines like the *National Review* and the *New Republic*.

Radio

Regularly scheduled and continuous radio broadcasting began in 1920 on stations KDKA in Pittsburgh and WWJ in Detroit. Both stations claim to be the first commercial station, and both broadcast returns of the 1920

Listening to the President on Radio

Before television, friends often gathered around a radio to hear the president make an important address. In 1941, American soldiers, friends, and visiting relatives gathered in the Army YMCA on Governors Island in New York to hear President Franklin Roosevelt warn of the approaching war. Of course, the message had a special meaning for this group. Still, see how intently they are listening to what the president is saying. Maybe we should consider using radio instead of television for critically important speeches.

election of President Warren G. Harding. The first radio network, the National Broadcasting Company (NBC), was formed in 1926. The Columbia Broadcasting System (CBS) was created in 1927, followed by the American Broadcasting System (ABC) and the Mutual Broadcasting System. By linking thousands of local stations, the four major networks transformed radio into a national medium. Millions of Americans were able to hear President Franklin D. Roosevelt deliver his first "fireside chat" in 1933. However, the first coast-to-coast broadcast did not occur until 1937, when listeners were shocked by an eyewitness report of the explosion of the dirigible *Hindenburg* in New Jersey.

Because the public could sense reporters' personalities over radio in a way they could not in print, broadcast journalists quickly became national celebrities. Edward R. Murrow, one of the most famous radio news personalities, broadcast news of the merger of Germany and Austria by shortwave from Vienna in 1938 and later gave stirring reports of German air raids on London during World War II.

Television

Experiments with television began in France in the early 1900s. By 1937, seventeen experimental television stations were operating in the United States. By 1940, twenty-three television stations were operating on a more regular basis, and—repeating the feat of radio twenty years earlier—two stations broadcast the returns of a presidential election, Roosevelt's 1940 re-election.[10] The onset of World War II paralyzed the development of television technology, but following the war growth in the medium exploded. By 1950, ninety-eight stations were covering the major population centers of the country, although only 9 percent of American households had television receivers.

Watching the President on Television

Television revolutionized presidential politics by allowing millions of voters to look closely at the candidates' faces and to judge their personalities in the process. This close-up of John Kennedy during a debate with Richard Nixon in the 1960 campaign showed Kennedy to good advantage. Close-ups of Nixon, on the other hand, made him look as though he needed a shave. Kennedy won one of the closest elections in history; it's possible that his good looks on television made the difference.

The first commercial color broadcast came in 1951, as did the first coast-to-coast broadcast—President Harry Truman's address to delegates at the Japanese Peace Treaty Conference in San Francisco. That same year, Democratic Senator Estes Kefauver of Tennessee called for public television coverage of his committee's investigation into organized crime. For weeks, people with television sets invited their neighbors to watch underworld crime figures answering questions before the camera. And Kefauver became one of the first politicians to benefit from television coverage. Previously unknown and representing a small state, he nevertheless won many of the 1952 Democratic presidential primaries. His performance led to his nomination as the Democrats' vice presidential candidate in 1956.

The number of television stations increased to over five hundred in 1960, and 87 percent of households had television receivers. By 1990, the United States had more than one thousand commercial and three hundred public television stations, and virtually every household (98 percent) had receivers. Now, television claims by far the largest news audiences of the mass media (see Figure 6.1). From television's beginning, most stations were linked into networks founded by three of the four major radio networks. (Only the Mutual Broadcasting System did not make the transition into television.) Many of the early "anchormen" on network news programs (among them, Walter Cronkite) came to the medium with years of experience as radio broadcast journalists. Now that the news audience could actually see the broadcasters as well as hear them, news personalities became even greater celebrities. When he retired from anchoring the "CBS Evening News" in 1981, Walter Cronkite was one of the most trusted persons in America.

Just as the appearance of the newscaster became important for television viewers, so did the appearance of the news itself. Television's great advantage over radio—that it *showed* people and events—both contributed to the impact of television news coverage and to some extent determined the news that television chose to cover. However, television is not alone among the mass media in focusing on news that appeals to its audience's emotions. The 1890s newspapers that engaged in yellow journalism also played on emotions. In fact, private ownership of the mass media ensures that news is selected for its audience appeal.

Private Ownership of the Media

In the United States, private ownership of the media is an accepted fact. Indeed, most Americans would regard government ownership of the media as an unacceptable threat to freedom that would interfere with the "marketplace of ideas" and result in one-way communication, from government to citizens. When the government controls the news flow, the people may have little chance to learn what the government is doing or to pressure it to behave differently. Certainly that was true in the Soviet Union prior to President Gorbachev. Under his presidency, the government allowed political criticism before restricting it again in early 1991.[11] It was the independent foreign media that mobilized the democratic forces that defeated the August coup later that year. China offers another illustration of how government control of the media can be relaxed, permitting televised coverage of protests for democracy in Bejing's Tiananmen Square during the summer of 1989, and then harshly reimposing censorship overnight to smother the democracy movement. Private ownership of the media offers a more stable, continuing forum for government criticism.

The Consequences of Private Ownership

The print media (both newspapers and magazines) are privately owned in the Western democratic countries, but the broadcast media often are not. Before the 1980s, the government owned and operated the major broadcast media in most of these countries. Now in Western Europe government radio and television stations compete with private stations.[12] In the United States, except for about 300 public television stations (out of about 1,400) and 300 public radio stations (out of about 5,000), the electronic media are privately owned. Private ownership of both print and broadcast media gives the news industry in America more political freedom than any other in the world, but it also makes the media more dependent on advertising revenues to cover their costs and make a profit. Because advertising rates are tied to audience size, the news operations of mass media in America must appeal to the audiences they serve.

The news function of the mass media in the United States cannot be separated from their entertainment function. Entertainment increases audiences, which increases advertising revenues. Of the four hours or so that the average American spends watching television every day, only about ninety minutes are devoted to news or documentaries; the remainder goes to entertainment, movies, or sports.[13] More than 60 million

This Is Your Captain Speaking

The pilot of a TWA plane hijacked in 1985 is muffled as he tries to speak with television reporters on the runway of Beirut's airport. ABC television news broadcast this brief interview, which helped to dramatize international terrorism. In the end, the hijackers got what they wanted: the release of hundreds of Shi'ite prisoners held by Israel.

newspapers circulate daily among the population, but more than 60 percent of their content is devoted to advertising.[14] Only a portion of the remaining newspaper space is devoted to news of any sort, and only a fraction of that news—excluding stories about fires, robberies, murder trials, and the like—can be classified as "political."

You might think that a story's political significance, educational value, or broad social importance determines whether it is covered in the media. The sad truth is that most potential news stories are not judged by such grand criteria. The primary criterion of a story's **newsworthiness** is usually its audience appeal, as judged by its *high impact* on readers or listeners; its *sensationalist* aspect (as exemplified by violence, conflict, disaster, or scandal); its treatment of *familiar* people or life situations; its *close-to-home* character; and its *timeliness*.[15]

Reliance on audience appeal has led the news industry to calculate its audience very carefully. The print media can easily determine the size of their circulations through sales figures, but the broadcast media must estimate their audiences through various sampling techniques. Because both print and broadcast media might be tempted to inflate their estimated audiences (to tell advertisers that they reach more people than they actually do), a separate industry has developed to rate audience size impartially. The rating reports have resulted in a "ratings game," in which the media try to increase ratings by adjusting the delivery or content of their news. Some local television stations favor "happy talk" on their news broadcasts—witty on-the-air exchanges among announcers, reporters, sportscasters, and meteorologists. Other stations use the "eyewitness" approach, showing a preponderance of film with human interest, humorous, or violent content. Many stations combine the two, often pleasing viewers, but perhaps not informing them properly (see Figure 6.2). Even the three mighty television networks have departed from their traditionally high journalistic standards, following their acquisition in the 1980s by other conglomerate corporations: Capital Cities acquired ABC, General Electric bought NBC, and Loews controlled CBS.

From 1980 to 1990, ABC, CBS, and NBC suffered severe losses in their prime-time audiences, dropping from nearly 90 to only 63 percent of all television viewers.[16] Increasingly, viewers have been watching cable stations or videotapes instead of network programs. Audience declines brought declining profits and cutbacks in network news budgets. As their parent corporations demanded that news programs "pay their way," the networks succumbed to **infotainment**—mixing journalism with theater. In one notable instance of *simulation journalism,* ABC's "World News Tonight" in 1989 used actors to "recreate" the passing of a brief-

---

F I G U R E   6.2   *Local Television: No News Is Good News*

To document the suspicion that local television contains little political information, Robert Entman analyzed the content of the local television news broadcast in 1986 over two full weeks on two television stations in Raleigh-Durham, North Carolina. He found that reporting on local policy issues averaged under two minutes per half-hour program. That amounts to about 250 words. The stations devoted more time to weather and twice as much time to sports. "Happy talk," previews of forthcoming programs, and credits accounted for the largest segment of the half-hour program. The total coverage of all substantive policy or political matters averaged about seven minutes per broadcast. (Source: Robert M. Entman, Democracy without Citizens *[New York: Oxford University Press, 1989], p. 111. Copyright © 1989 by Robert M. Entman. Reprinted by permission of Oxford University Press, Inc. The stations were WRAL and WTVD in Raleigh-Durham, North Carolina.)*

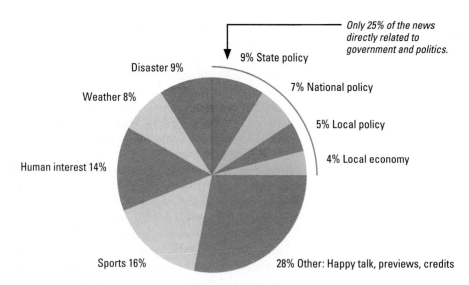

AVERAGE TIME DEVOTED TO NINE NEWS CATEGORIES

case between an American diplomat and a Soviet agent. Following an uproar in journalistic circles, ABC apologized for deceiving its viewers with the phony news clip.

The Concentration of Private Ownership

Media owners can make more money either by increasing their audiences or by acquiring additional publications or stations. There is a decided trend toward concentrated ownership of the media, enhancing the possibility that a few major owners could control the news flow to promote their own political interests—much as political parties influenced the content of early newspapers. In fact, the number of *independent* newspapers has declined as more papers have been acquired by newspaper chains (two or more newspapers in different cities under the same ownership). Most of the more than 150 newspaper chains are small, owning fewer than ten papers.[17] Some, however, are very large. The Gannett chain, which owns *USA Today* with the second largest circulation in the nation, also owns over eighty newspapers in thirty-six states. Only about four hundred dailies are still independent, and many of these papers are too small and unprofitable to invite acquisition.

At first glance, ownership concentration in the television industry does not seem to be a problem. Although there are only three major networks, the networks usually do not own their affiliates. About half of all the communities in the United States are served by ten or more stations.[18] This figure suggests that the electronic media offer enough diversity of views to balance ownership concentration. Like newspapers, however, television stations in different cities are sometimes owned by the same group. In 1990, for example, the Capital Cities/ABC group owned outright eight television stations—in New York, Los Angeles, Chicago, Philadelphia, San Francisco, Houston, Fresno, and Raleigh-Durham—serving 24 percent of the television market.[19]

Ownership concentration can also occur across the media. Sometimes the same corporation owns a television station, a radio station, and a newspaper in the same area. For example, the Gannett Company, mentioned earlier as the largest newspaper chain, also operates ten television, nine FM, and seven AM broadcasting stations. Some people fear the concentration of media under a single owner, and government has addressed those fears by regulating media ownership, as well as other aspects of media operation (see Feature 6.1).

Government Regulation of the Media

Although most of the mass media in the United States are privately owned, they do not operate free of government regulation. The broadcast media, however, operate under more regulations than the print media, due initially to technical concerns in broadcasting. In general, government regulation of the mass media falls into three categories: technical, ownership, and content.[20]

FEATURE 6.1　　*Cross-Ownership = Cross-Censorship?*

Is there good reason to fear the growing cross-media media ownership by a few giant corporations? Those who extol the benefits of ownership deregulation contend that competition in the information marketplace will guarantee that the public gets a diversity of information sources. Critics argue that the information may be controlled by the governing corporation, whether or not it is owned by Americans or foreigners. Consider these examples.

Robert Hilliard, professor of mass communications at Boston's Emerson College, was invited by the *Boston Herald* in 1987 to review two new television programs, "Married . . . with Children" and "The Tracey Ullman Show," that launched the debut of the Fox Network. He initially refused because the network's creator, Rupert Murdoch, owned both the newspaper and the local Fox television channel. But Hilliard agreed to be one of the outside experts when told by the *Herald*'s editors that they wanted an honest review. He did not like the programs, even calling "Married . . . with Children" one of the "worst sitcoms" he had even seen. None of his prepared remarks, nor those of any non-*Herald* employee who screened the programs, were published by the newspaper, which headlined a review by its regular critic, "Fox Network offers new, lively variety."

Peter Karl, an investigative reporter for Chicago's NBC affiliate, WMAQ-TV, prepared a story for the "Today" show in 1989 about the faulty nuts and bolts used in important construction projects such as bridges, airplane engines, nuclear missile silos, and in the NASA space program. Karl also cited the General Electric Corporation, which builds airplane engines, as a user of shoddy nuts and bolts. The story was broadcast on November 30, 1989, but it was edited to delete all references to General Electric, which happens to own the NBC Network.

When Matsushita Electric bought MCA in 1990, its president, Akio Tanii, held a news conference. He sought to quell American fears about Japanese censorship of motion pictures made by MCA's Universal Studios by announcing that he would keep MCA's American chairman in his position. Then a reporter asked whether the new company would "be willing to produce a movie about the wartime role of the late Emperor Hirohito." Mr. Tanii seemed agitated and said, "I could never imagine such a case, so I cannot answer such a question." Would Matsushita permit the making of movies that criticized Japanese society or economic practices? Again he said, "I never dreamed of hearing such a question."

Sources: Paul Starobin, "Murdoch v. Murdoch," *Congressional Quarterly Weekly Report*, 3 June 1989, p. 1316; James Warren, "'Today' Edited GE from News Story," *Chicago Tribune*, 2 December 1989, p. 3; and David E. Sanger, "Politics and Multinational Movies," *New York Times*, 27 November 1990, p. C5.

Technical and Ownership Regulations

The broadcast media confront certain technical limitations in transmission not faced by the print media. In the early days of radio, stations that operated on similar frequencies in the same area often jammed each other's signals, and no one could broadcast clearly. At the broadcasters' insistence, Congress passed the Federal Radio Act (1927), which declared that the public owned the airwaves and that private broadcasters could use them only by obtaining a license from the Federal Radio Commission. So, government regulation of broadcasting was not forced on the industry by socialist politicians; it was requested by capitalist owners to impose order on the use of the airwaves (thereby restricting others' freedom to enter broadcasting).

The Federal Communications Act (1934) forms the basis for current regulation of the broadcasting industry. It created the **Federal Communi-**

cations Commission (FCC), consisting of seven members (no more than four from the same political party) chosen by the president for terms of seven years. The commissioners serve overlapping terms—beginning and ending in different years—and can be removed from office only through impeachment and conviction. Consequently, the FCC is considered an *independent regulatory commission:* It is insulated from political control by either the president or Congress. (We discuss independent regulatory commissions in Chapter 13.) Today, the FCC is charged with regulating interstate and foreign communication by radio, television, telephone, telegraph, cable, and satellite.

The FCC also regulates the ownership structure of the electronic media. When radio began broadcasting to millions of citizens, the FCC became concerned about the concentration of too much power in the hands of single owners. In 1943, the FCC ordered the National Broadcasting Company to sell one of its two radio networks, leading to the creation of the American Broadcasting Company. Also during the 1940s, the FCC prohibited any company from owning more than one AM, one FM, or one television station in a single community.[21]

In the early 1950s, the FCC ruled that a single company could own no more than seven AM, seven FM, and seven television stations across the nation. By 1984, as the number of television stations quadrupled and the number of radio stations tripled, a majority of FCC commissioners (President Reagan's appointees) opted to relax regulations by increasing the ownership rule from seven to twelve of each type of broadcast media. Now there is pressure from three sources for removing all congressional restrictions on media ownership.

One source of this pressure is technological; the growth of cable television has weakened the need to parcel out frequencies for television broadcasts. With more than half of all homes wired for cable television, cable firms have become powerhouses in the television industry.[22] One firm is connected to more than 20 percent of the nation's cable subscribers, and traditional media companies are increasing their cross-ownership by acquiring cable stations. In 1989, the merger of Time Inc. and Warner Communications not only linked together these firms' publishing activities (magazines, books), and their film and record industries, but also their extensive cable interests (HBO, Cinemax, Warner Cable).

Congress was uneasy about the Time-Warner merger, which created the world's largest media-and-entertainment company, but it consented due to the second source of pressure: the desire to combat foreign ownership of U.S. media. Not only had Japan's Sony Corporation purchased CBS records in 1988 and Columbia Pictures in 1989, but Australia's Rupert Murdoch owned 20th Century-Fox, the Fox Television Network, *TV Guide,* and several television stations and newspapers. In 1990, Sony's Japanese rival, Matsushita, acquired MCA (Universal Pictures) in the biggest buyout yet of any American company. Threatened from the outside, Congress is re-examining FCC restrictions on media ownership inside the country.

The third source of pressure to relax restrictions on media ownership lies in the argument that there is already enough diversity among media news sources to provide citizens with enough diversity in the content of political ideas.

Regulation of Content

The First Amendment to the Constitution prohibits Congress from abridging the freedom of the press. Over time, the *press* has come to mean *all* the mass media. As might be expected, the press—particularly the print media—has interpreted "freedom of the press" in the broadest possible way, citing the Constitution for its right to print or broadcast anything it wants to print or broadcast. Over the past two hundred years, the courts have decided numerous cases that define how far freedom of the press extends under the law. The most important of these cases, which are often quite complex, are discussed in Chapter 15. Usually the courts have struck down government attempts to restrain the press from publishing or broadcasting the information, events, or opinions that it finds newsworthy. One notable exception concerns strategic information during wartime; the courts have supported censorship in the publishing or broadcasting of such information as the sailing schedules of troop ships or the movements of troops in battle. Otherwise, the courts have recognized a strong constitutional case against press censorship. This stand has given the United States some of the freest, most vigorous news media in the world.

Because the broadcast media are licensed to use the public airwaves, they are subject to some regulation of the content of their news coverage that is not applied to the print media. The basis for the FCC's regulation of content lies in its charge to ensure that radio (and, later, television) stations would "serve the public interest, convenience, and necessity." For over fifty years, broadcasters operated under three constraints rooted in the 1934 Federal Communications Act. Two of these constraints are still in effect; one has been revoked. In its **equal opportunities rule,** the FCC required that a broadcast station that gives or sells time to a candidate for any public office must make an equal amount of time under the same conditions available to all other candidates for that office. The **reasonable access rule** required that stations make their facilities available for the expression of conflicting views or issues from all responsible elements in the community. Finally, the **fairness doctrine** obligated broadcasters to discuss public issues and to provide fair coverage to each side of those issues.

These regulations seem unobjectionable to most people, but they have been at the heart of a controversy about the deregulation of the broadcast media. Note that *none* of these regulations is imposed on the print media, which has no responsibility to give equal treatment to political candidates, to give fair coverage to all sides of an issue, or to express conflicting views from all responsible elements of the community. In fact, one aspect of a free press is its ability to champion causes that it favors (such as erecting the Statue of Liberty or starting a war with Spain) without having to argue the case for the other side. The broadcast media have traditionally been treated differently, because they were licensed by the

FCC to operate as semimonopolies.[23] With the rise of one-newspaper cities and towns, however, there is now more competition among television stations than among newspapers in virtually every market area. Critics who advocate dropping FCC content regulations argue that the broadcast media should be just as free as the print media to decide which candidates they endorse and which issues they support.

Under Reagan, the FCC itself moved toward this view of unfettered freedom for broadcasters by repealing the fairness doctrine in 1987 on the grounds that it chilled freedom of speech. One media analyst noted that the FCC acted in the belief that competition in the supply of news from broadcasters, cable, radio, newspapers, and magazines would provide a vibrant marketplace of ideas. However, he feared that the FCC overestimated the public's demand for high-quality news and public affairs broadcasting. Without that demand, the media are unlikely to compete to supply the news coverage needed to sustain a genuine marketplace.[24]

Reporting and Following the News

"News," for most journalists, is an important event that has happened within the past twenty-four hours. A presidential news conference or an explosion in the Capitol qualifies as news. And a national political convention certainly qualifies as news, although it may not justify the thousands of media representatives at the 1992 party conventions. Who decides what is important? The media, of course. In this section, we discuss how the media cover political affairs, what they choose to report (which then becomes "news"), and who follows the news and what they remember and learn.

Covering National Politics

All the major news media seek to cover political events through first-hand reports from journalists on the scene. Because so many significant political events occur in the nation's capital, Washington has by far the largest press corps of any city in the world—almost 6,000 accredited reporters: 2,500 from newspapers, 1,025 from magazines, and 2,400 from radio and television.[25] Only a small portion of these reporters are assigned to cover the presidency, and there are only about seventy-five "regular" journalists in the White House press corps.[26] Since 1902, when President Theodore Roosevelt provided a special room in the White House for reporters, the press has had special access to the presidency. As late as the Truman administration, reporters enjoyed informal personal relationships with the president. Today, the media's relationship with the president is mediated primarily through the Office of the Press Secretary.

To meet their daily deadlines, White House correspondents rely heavily on information they receive in the press room in the west wing of the White House. Information for their stories routinely comes in one of three forms, each carefully crafted by the White House in an attempt to

Feeding Time in the Press Room

President Bush's press secretary, Marlin Fitzwater, gives the daily news briefing to the White House press corps. Both print and broadcast journalists depend on getting the White House's views on the news to frame their reporting for the day.

control the news output. The most frequent form is the *news release*—a prepared text distributed to reporters in the hope that it will be used verbatim. A *news briefing*, traditionally held daily at 11:30, enables reporters to question the press secretary about news releases and allows television correspondents time to prepare their stories and videos for the evening newscast. A *news conference* involves questioning high-level officials in the executive branch—including the president on occasion. News conferences appear to be freewheeling, but precise answers to anticipated questions tend to be carefully rehearsed. Still, President Reagan encountered difficulty in news conferences and avoided them more than most presidents. In fact, he held an average of one every other month, compared with about two per month for President Bush.

Occasionally, news conferences are given *on background*, meaning that the information can be quoted but the source must not be identified specifically. A vague reference—"a senior official says"—is all right. (When he was secretary of state, Henry Kissinger himself was often the "senior official" reporting on foreign policy developments.) Information disclosed *off the record* cannot even be printed. Journalists who violate these well-known rules risk losing their welcome at the White House. In a sense, the press corps is captive to the White House, which feeds reporters information they need to meet deadlines and frames stories so they are covered on the evening news.[27] Beginning in the Carter White House, press secretaries have obliged photographers with "photo opportunities," a few minutes to take pictures or videos, often with a visiting dignitary or a winning sports team. The photographers can keep their editors supplied with visuals, while the press secretary ensures that the coverage is favorable by controlling the environment.

Most reporters in the Washington press corps are accredited to sit in the House and Senate press galleries, but only about four hundred cover

Congress exclusively.[28] Most of the news about Congress comes from innumerable press releases issued by its 535 members and from an unending supply of congressional reports. A journalist, then, can report on Congress without inhabiting its press galleries.

Not so long ago, individual congressional committees allowed radio and television coverage of their proceedings only on special occasions—as Senator Kefauver did during his committee's investigation of organized crime, and as the Senate select committee did during the Watergate investigation. Congress banned microphones and cameras from its chambers until 1979, when the House permitted live coverage, while insisting on controlling the shots being televised. Nevertheless, televised broadcasts of the House were surprisingly successful, thanks to C-SPAN (the Cable Satellite Public Affairs Network), which is linked to 90 percent of the cable systems across the country and has a cultlike following among hundreds of thousands of regular viewers.[29] To share in the television exposure, the Senate began television coverage in 1986. C-SPAN coverage of Congress has become very important to professionals in government and politics in Washington—perhaps more so than to its devoted, but limited, viewers across the country. Even members of the Washington press corps watch C-SPAN.

In addition to these recognized news channels, selected reporters occasionally benefit from *leaks* of information released by officials who are guaranteed anonymity. Officials may leak news to interfere with others' political plans or to float ideas ("trial balloons") past the public and other political leaders to gauge their reactions. At times, one carefully placed leak can turn into a gusher of media coverage through the practice of *pack journalism*—the tendency of journalists to adopt similar viewpoints toward the news simply because they hang around together, exchanging information and defining the day's news. Often a story hounded by the pack does not offer enough substance to sustain pursuit, and the chase is abandoned as quickly as it was begun.

Presenting the News

Media executives, news editors, and prominent reporters function as **gatekeepers** in directing the news flow: They decide which events to report and how to handle the elements in those stories. Only a few individuals—no more than twenty-five on the average newspaper or news weekly and fifty on each of the major television networks—qualify as gatekeepers, defining the news for public consumption.[30] They are usually very selective in choosing what goes through the gate.

It is impossible for the media to communicate *everything* about public affairs. There is neither space in newspapers or magazines nor time on television or radio to do so. Time limitations impose especially severe constraints on television news broadcasting. Each half-hour network news program devotes only about twenty minutes to the news (the rest of the time is taken up by commercials). The average story lasts about one minute, and few stories run longer than two minutes. The typical script for an entire television news broadcast would fill less than two columns of one page of the *New York Times*.[31]

A parade of unconnected one-minute news stories, flashing across the television screen every night, would boggle the eyes and minds of the viewers. To make the news understandable and to hold viewers' attention, television editors and producers carefully choose their lead story and group stories together by theme. The stories themselves concentrate on individuals, because individuals have personalities; political institutions do not—except for the president in the presidency. A careful content analysis of a year's network news coverage of the president, Congress, and the Supreme Court showed the average television news program devoting seven and a half minutes to the president compared with one minute for Congress and only a half a minute for the court.[32] When television covers Congress, moreover, it tries to personify the institution by focusing on prominent quotable leaders, such as the speaker of the House or the Senate majority leader. Such personification for the purpose of gaining audience acceptability tends to distort the character of an institution.

During elections, personification encourages **horse race journalism,** in which media coverage becomes a matter of "who's ahead?" Studies of television news coverage of the 1988 presidential election found that only about 20 percent of the air time during the primary campaigns and 29 percent during the general election campaign dealt with policy issues; the rest went to the horse race—"who's ahead in the polls, who's raising the most money, who's got TV ads and who's getting endorsed."[33] Consequently, elections are presented as contests between individuals rather than as confrontations between parties and platforms.

Campaigning for office is a type of political news that lends itself to media coverage, especially if the candidates create a **media event**—a situation that is too "newsworthy" to pass up. One tried-and-true method is to conduct a walking campaign. Newspapers and television can take pictures of the candidate on the highway and conduct interviews with local folks who just talked to the political hiker. (See Chapter 9 for further discussion of media in political campaigns.) Television is particularly partial to events that have *film value* (visual impact). Organized protests and fires, for example, "show well" on television, so television tends to cover them. Violent conflict of any kind, especially unfolding dramas that involve weapons, rate especially high in visual impact.

Where the Public Gets Its News

Until the early 1960s, most people reported getting more of their news from newspapers than from any other source. As shown in Figure 6.3, television nudged out newspapers as the public's major source of news in the early 1960s. At the end of the 1980s, about two-thirds of the public cited television as their news source, compared with less than one-half who named newspapers and less than one-fifth who relied on radio. Not only is television the public's most important source of news, but television news is also rated as more trustworthy than newspaper news—by a margin of nearly 2 to 1 (see Figure 6.4).

However, these frequently cited data may overstate both people's reliance on television for news and their trust in the medium. In a series of

FIGURE 6.3   *Changes in the Public's Sources of News*

For more than a quarter of a century, the Roper Organization has put this question to a national sample: "I'd like to ask you where you usually get most of your news about what's going on in the world today—from the newspapers or radio or television or magazines or talking to people or where?" Until the early 1960s, newspapers were cited as the main source of news for people in the Roper sample. Then television replaced newspapers, and the gap between the two has grown rather steadily. Radio has declined dramatically as a source of news, but magazines have retained most of their audience over the last decade. (Source: Harold W. Stanley and Richard G. Niemi, eds., Vital Statistics on American Politics, *2d ed. [Washington, D.C.: Congressional Quarterly Press, 1989], p. 69. Used by permission. The percentages do not total 100 because people were allowed to cite more than one news source.)*

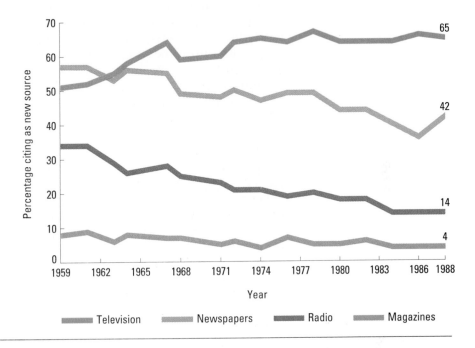

national surveys, nearly 75 percent of the respondents vowed they regularly watched news on television, yet only 52 percent testified that they actually watched "yesterday."[34] In another study, people again identified television as their most common news source, but they named newspapers more frequently as the source of specific news stories.[35] Finally, a study of believability and the press found that respondents were more likely to trust the major national newspapers and news magazines than local television, and that news anchor persons were more trusted than the television networks they represented.[36] So television may not be as dominant a news medium as it might seem, and we should inquire into the public's specific sources of news.

One major study of the American news media, based on nearly 5,000 interviews over four months in 1990, found that 84 percent of the public said that they had read or heard the news yesterday through print or broadcast media: newspaper, television, or radio. However, only a bare majority (51 percent) used a national rather than a local news source.[37]

The study further divided those who regularly used national news sources into four categories (see Figure 6.5). The small group of *news sophisticates* read specialized opinion magazines and listened to news programs on national public radio or public television. The much larger group of *other serious news consumers* read a weekly news magazine, a major metropolitan daily newspaper, or watched Sunday morning interview shows or CNN. A slightly larger group of *moderate consumers* read or watched news, but not from a national source. The smallest group, the *nonusers*, did not regularly read or watch any news.

As one would expect, level of education is strongly related to these categories of news attentiveness, and nearly half the news sophisticates are college graduates. Figure 6.5 shows that age is also related to attentiveness, with nearly half of the news sophisticates age fifty or older and nearly half of the nonusers under thirty. Among other factors, race bears no relationship to news attentiveness (nonwhites are equally likely as whites to be news sophisticates),[38] but sex has a decided effect, with news sophisticates more likely to be male (56 percent) and nonusers to be female (60 percent). Researchers have attributed this finding and oth-

FIGURE 6.4 *Credibility of the News Media*

In the same survey that asked people about their sources of news, the Roper Organization asked, "If you got conflicting or different reports of the same news story from radio, television, the magazines and the newspapers, which of the four versions would you be most inclined to believe?" Here, the gap between television and newspapers is even greater—and it, too, has been growing. By the 1980s, more people saw television as a more credible news source than all the other media combined. (Source: Harold W. Stanley and Richard G. Niemi, eds., Vital Statistics on American Politics, *2d ed. [Washington, D.C.: Congressional Quarterly Press, 1989], p. 69. Used by permission.)*

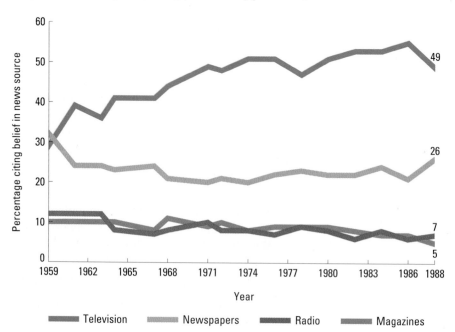

FIGURE 6.5   *Typology of News Consumers*

In a major study of the American media, the Times Mirror Center classified respondents according to the types of news sources they used regularly. News sophisticates regularly followed news programs on National Public Radio, or public television's "MacNeil/Lehrer Newshour" or read opinion magazines like The Atlantic, Harpers, or The New Yorker. Serious consumers did not follow these sources but did read a news magazine or a major metropolitan daily newspaper, the Wall Street Journal, or USA Today, or watched Sunday morning interview shows or CNN. Moderate consumers read some other daily paper or watched or listened to news regularly. Nonusers followed no news source on a regular basis.

Surveys conducted from 1941 to 1975 showed that Americans under 30 years old followed news stories, such as Watergate and Vietnam, about as closely as their elders and knew almost as much about public affairs. But since then, they have been much less attentive, even to major developments. The opening of the Berlin Wall, ending the division between East and West Germany, was followed very closely by only 42 percent of those under 30 compared with 58 percent of those over 50.

Leaders in the world of government, business, and higher education stand at the extreme end of news consumption. Virtually none of these leaders fail to follow the news, and from 40 to 60 percent report spending from one to two hours per day reading, listening, or watching the news. In fact, from one-third to one-half say that they spend from two to five hours per day following the news.. (Source: Used by permission of The Times Mirror Center for The People & The Press, Washington, D.C. Reports dated November 1989 and June 28, 1990.)

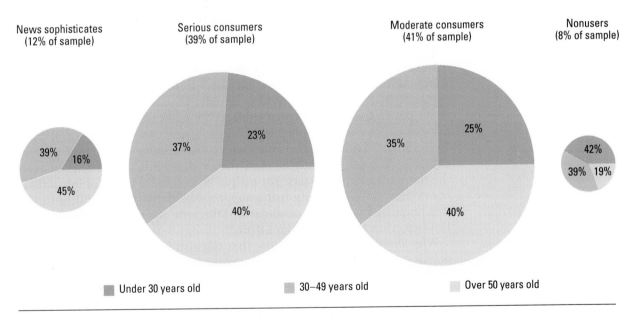

News sophisticates (12% of sample)

Serious consumers (39% of sample)

Moderate consumers (41% of sample)

Nonusers (8% of sample)

Under 30 years old   30–49 years old   Over 50 years old

ers on women's low interest in politics to what is taught at home and in school, saying that "changes in girls' early learning experiences" must occur before such gender differences evaporate.[39]

What People Remember and Know

If 84 percent of the public read or heard the news the previous day, and if nearly 75 percent say they regularly watch the news on television, how much political information do they absorb? By all accounts, not much.

In the first two months of 1990, respondents in two national surveys identified the political changes taking place in Eastern Europe as the most important news event. In February 1990, Vaclav Havel, the new president of Czechoslovakia, visited the United States and addressed the U.S. Congress. In March, a national survey asked, "Do you happen to know who Vaclav Havel is?" and only 14 percent could identify him. The same survey asked, "Do you happen to know who Marla Maples is?" and 37 percent correctly identified her as New York multi-millionaire Donald Trump's current girlfriend.[40]

When tested for their political knowledge, those who are more attentive to news answer more questions correctly than those who are less attentive—as expected. Given the enormous improvements in television technology and the increasing reliance of the public on high-tech television news coverage, we might also expect that the public today knows more than it did twenty years ago.[41] Unfortunately, that is not so. Similar surveys in 1967 and in 1987 asked respondents to name their state governor, representative in the House, and head of the local school district. Only 9 percent failed to name a single official in 1967 compared with 17 percent in 1987. The author of this study attributed the lower performance today to greater reliance on television for news.[42]

Several studies have found that increased exposure to television news has a numbing effect on a person's capacity to discriminate among news messages. A comparison between viewers' and readers' abilities to explain the reasons for their Senate voting choices in 1974 found that reading more newspapers produced more reasons for voting choices but watching more television news did not.[43] In fact, the researchers found evidence that watching television actually tended to *inhibit* knowledge about politics. A later study of subjects' abilities to distinguish between the campaign issues of presidential candidates Gerald Ford and Jimmy Carter in 1976 found that regular television viewers saw no more difference between the candidates than those who neither watched nor read the news on a regular basis. For people with similar levels of education, heavy television watching had a suppressing effect on the ability to see differences between the candidates. Different researchers studying the 1984 election found a similar effect.[44]

Why should this be? We know that television tends to squeeze public policy issues into one-minute or, at most, two-minute fragments, which makes it difficult to explain candidates' positions. Television also tends to cast abstract issues in personal terms to enhance the visual image that the medium conveys.[45] Thus, viewers may become more adept at visually identifying the candidates and knowing their personal habits than at knowing their positions on issues (see Feature 6.2). Finally, the television networks, whose content is regulated by the FCC, are concerned about being fair and equal in covering the candidates, which may result in equalizing candidates' positions as well. Newspapers, which are not regulated, enjoy more latitude in choosing which candidates they cover and how they cover them. Whatever the explanation, the technological wonders of television seem to have contributed little to citizens' knowledge of public affairs. Indeed, electronic journalism may work against the citizen knowledge that democratic government requires.

FEATURE 6.2   *The Medium Is the Message*

Television reporter Lesley Stahl feared she had gone too far. She risked being shunned by the Reagan White House and even losing her job. Still, she felt her story was important. Convinced that Reagan and his advisers had been using television to create an image of his presidency that did not match his policies, she put together a tough report for airing on the "CBS Evening News" to puncture his public relations balloon.

In a story that lasted nearly six minutes—very long for television—Stahl's voice told her audience:

The orchestration of television coverage absorbs the White House. Their goal? To emphasize the president's greatest asset, which, his aides say, is his personality. They provide pictures of him looking like a leader. Confident, with his Marlboro Man walk. A good family man. They also aim to erase the negatives. Mr. Reagan tries to counter the memory of an unpopular issue with a carefully chosen backdrop that actually contradicts the president's policy. Look at the handicapped Olympics, or the opening ceremony of an old-age home. No hint that he tried to cut the budgets for the disabled and for federally subsidized housing for the elderly. . . .

As she spoke, viewers saw four years of Reagan videos. There was Reagan among flag-waving supporters. Reagan talking to farmers. Reagan at a picnic with middle Americans. Reagan at the handicapped Olympics, at a senior citizens center, at a gathering of veterans. More flags. More balloons. Reagan smiling at children . . . and so on.

Soon after her story ran on October 4, 1984, the telephone rang in her press room. As expected, the call came from one of the president's assistants, who said, "Great piece. We loved it." She couldn't believe her ears, replying, "How can you say you loved it—it was tough!"

The Reagan assistant explained, "We're in the middle of a campaign, and you gave us four and a half minutes of great pictures of Ronald Reagan, and that's all the American people see. . . . They don't listen to you if you're contradicting great pictures. They don't hear what you are saying if the pictures are saying something different."

Lesley Stahl thought that her viewers would be *listening* to her instead of watching the president, but the White House advisers knew better the limitations of the television audience. The entertainment quality—the message—of the news shows came in its pictures. By emphasizing the pictures, the White House advisers managed to get television news shows to do their bidding, whether the journalists realized it or not.

Source: This vignette draws heavily on Martin Schram, "The Great American Video Game," in Doris A. Graber, *Media Power in Politics*, 2d ed. (Washington, D.C.: Congressional Quarterly Press, 1990), pp. 184–192. That article was reprinted and abridged from Martin Schram, *The Great American Video Game* (New York: William Morrow, 1987.) Copyright 1987 by William Morrow and Company, Inc. Used by permission of William Morrow and Company, Inc./Publishers, New York.

There is also evidence that suggests those people who rely on television coverage of politics are more confused and cynical than those who do not.[46] This problem may be even more acute where foreign affairs are concerned, since most of the public has relatively little interest in foreign affairs, but the networks tend to "overreport" them.[47] The public witnesses conflict, criticism, and controversy in countries they know little about. Not knowing what to think or whom to believe, the public responds "by becoming more cynical, more negative, and more critical of leadership and institutions."[48]

The Political Effects of the Media

Virtually all citizens must rely on the mass media for their political news. Although television news programs claim far larger audiences than news magazines and newspapers, many people may watch television news programs for their entertainment value without learning much about public affairs. In this section, we probe the media's effects on public opinion, the political agenda, and political socialization.

Influencing Public Opinion

Americans overwhelmingly believe that the media exert a strong influence on their political institutions, and almost nine out of ten Americans believe that the media strongly influence public opinion (see Compared with What? 6.1). However, it is not easy to determine the extent of media influence on public opinion. Because very few of us learn about political events except as they are reported through the media, it is arguable that the media create public opinion simply by reporting events. Consider the dismantling of the Berlin Wall in 1989. Surely the pictures of joyous Berliners defying that symbol of oppression affected American public opinion about the reunification of Germany.

Broader studies of opinion change have found systematic, and in some cases dramatic, effects of television news. One study repeatedly polled the public on eighty issues in foreign and domestic affairs. In nearly half these items, public opinion changed over time by about 6 percentage points. The researchers compared these changes with policy positions taken by ten different sources of information: commentators on television network news, the president, members of the president's party, members of the opposition party, and members of interest groups, for instance. The study found the news commentators to have the most dramatic effect—a single commentary could be linked to more than 4 percentage points of opinion change.[49] As examples, the researchers cited Howard K. Smith's support of Nixon's Vietnam policies in 1969, John Chancellor's stand on the importance of fighting unemployment rather than inflation in 1976, and various 1981 commentaries that argued that Reagan's tax cuts would benefit the wealthy.[50]

Setting the Political Agenda

Despite the media's potential for influencing public opinion, most scholars believe that their greatest impact on politics is found in their power to set the agenda. An *agenda* is a list of things to do or consider; a **political agenda** is a list of issues that need government attention. Those who set the political agenda define what issues should be discussed and debated by government decision makers. Like the tree that falls in the forest without anyone hearing it, an issue that does not get on the political agenda will not have anyone in government working on its behalf.

The mass media in the United States have traditionally played an important role in defining the political agenda. As noted earlier, newspaper publisher William Randolph Hearst helped put war with Spain on the political agenda in 1898. The muckrakers' magazine articles helped put political and business reforms on the political agenda in the early 1900s. Radio helped put opposition to the Nazis' rise to power on the political

COMPARED WITH WHAT? 6.1

Opinions on the Media

Americans are more likely to perceive the media as politically powerful than are citizens in four other Western democracies. This finding comes from sample surveys taken in Great Britain, France, West Germany, Spain, and the United States during the spring of 1987. Respondents in each country were asked, "Would you say that the influence exerted by the media on [name of institution] is very large, somewhat large, or not large at all?" The combined percentages of "very large" and "somewhat large" responses form the bars of the accompanying graph. Although most citizens in each country perceive the media as having a large influence on public opinion, only Americans think the media also influence the major branches of government.

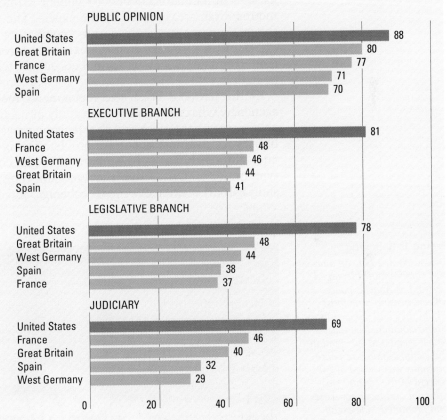

Percentage citing media's influence on institution

Source: Laurence Parisot, "Attitudes About the Media: A Five-Country Comparison," *Public Opinion* 10 (January–February 1988):60. Reprinted by permission.

agenda in the late 1930s. Television, which reaches daily into virtually every home, has an even greater potential for setting the political agenda. A careful study designed to isolate and examine television's effects on public opinion concluded, "By attending to some problems and ignoring others, television news shapes the American public's political priorities."[51] Furthermore, "the more removed the viewer is from the world of public affairs, the stronger the agenda-setting power of television news."[52]

Today's newspapers also heighten the public's concern about particular social issues. Crime is a good example. Certain types of crime—particularly murder—are especially attractive to the media, which therefore tend to distort the incidence of crime by their reporting. A study of newspaper coverage of crime in nine cities found more attention given to violent crimes (murder, rape, and assault) than was justified by official police statistics. In addition, the study found that newspapers in recent years have given increased attention to political crimes—such as assassinations or kidnapings—and to violent crimes committed outside the metropolitan areas served by the papers. The author concluded that, although newspapers helped put "combating crime" on the political agenda, they also distorted the extent and even the nature of the problem, confusing local policymakers about what should, or could, be done.[53]

At the national level, the major news media help set the political agenda by what they report. One study of media coverage in newspapers, news magazines, and network television news found that what the public sees as "the most important problem facing this country today" correlates differently with the amount of media coverage, depending on the type of event. *Crises* like the Vietnam War, racial unrest, and energy shortages drew extensive media coverage, and each additional news mag-

Seeing Is Believing

On March 3, 1991, an amateur cameraman videotaped several Los Angeles police officers beating a motorist whom they had stopped for a traffic violation. The tape, which seemed to substantiate the victim's charge of police brutality, was viewed by 80 percent of the country via national and local newscasts and prompted widespread scrutiny of the behavior of law officers across the country.

How the President Gets His News

During the Persian Gulf crisis, the president often watched television to keep abreast of developments. Here, he is joined by other White House officials, including Chief of Staff John Sununu (right) and National Security Adviser Brent Scowcroft (foreground), to get the latest report from the government in Baghdad.

azine story per month generated almost one percentage point increase in the public citing the event as an important problem. But public opinion was even more responsive to media coverage of recurring *problems* like inflation and unemployment. Although these events received less extensive coverage, each magazine story tended to increase public concern by almost three percentage points.[54] What's more, evidence shows that television networks, at least, tend to give greater coverage to bad economic news than to good news.[55] The media's ability to influence public opinion by defining "the news" makes politicians eager to influence media coverage.

The political impact of the mass media is not limited to public opinion. One prominent media scholar contends that "elites define media influence as affecting the opinions of other elites."[56] Clearly, political leaders believe that the media are influential, and they act accordingly. Top government leaders closely follow the news reported in the major national news sources, and the president receives a daily digest of news from many sources. Just as the president tries to learn what the media think is happening in government and politics, other political elites try to keep abreast of developments by following news in the media. Moreover, even journalists work hard at following the news in other media sources.

In a curious sense, the mass media have become a network for communicating among attentive elites, all trying to influence one another or to assess others' weaknesses and strengths. Suppose the White House is under pressure on some policy matter and is asked for a spokesperson to appear for fifteen minutes of intensive questioning on the "MacNeil/Leher Newshour." The White House complies not so much to influence opinions among the relatively few "news sophisticates" in the public as to influence the thinking of other elites who faithfully follow the program. Criticisms of the president's policies, especially when made by members of his own party, embolden others to be critical in their comments to other media. In this way, opposition spreads and may eventually be reflected in public opinion.[57]

Socialization

We discussed the major agents of political socialization in Chapter 5, but, for reasons of emphasis and space, we did not include the mass media among them. The mass media act as very important agents of political socialization. Young people who rarely follow the news by choice nevertheless acquire political values through the entertainment function of the broadcast media. Years ago, children learned from radio programs; now they learn from television: The average American child has watched about 19,000 hours of television by the end of high school.[58] What children learned from radio, however, was very different from what they are learning now. In the "golden days of radio," youngsters listening to the popular radio drama "The Shadow" heard repeatedly that "crime does not pay . . . the *Shadow* knows!" Action programs—such as "The FBI in Peace and War" and "Gangbusters!"—taught children that the major law enforcement agencies inevitably caught criminals and put them behind bars. In program after program—"Dragnet," "Junior G-Men," "Crime Fighters"—the message never varied: Criminals are bad; the police are good; criminals get caught and are severely punished for their crimes.

Needless to say, television today does not portray the criminal justice system in the same way, even in police dramas. Consider programs like "Cop Rock" and "Gabriel's Fire," which have portrayed police and prison guards as killers. These programs are not unique in their messages about institutional corruption. Other series, such as "Law and Order" and "Against the Law," also operate within a tainted criminal justice system.[59] Although no one knows for sure, the effect of years of television messages about distrust of law enforcement, disrespect for the criminal justice system, cynicism and materialism, and violence on impressionable youngsters may be severe. Whatever the effects, it would be difficult to argue that television's entertainment programs help prepare law-abiding citizens.

Some scholars argue that the most important effect of the mass media, particularly television, is to further the "hegemony," or dominance, of the existing culture under an existing ideology or order. According to the hegemony model, social control occurs not through institutions of force (police, military, and prisons) but through social institutions, like the media, that cause people to accept "the way things are."[60] By displaying the lifestyles of the rich and famous, for example, the media induce the public to accept the unlimited accumulation of private wealth. Similarly, citizens are socialized to value the "American way," to be patriotic, to back their country "right or wrong."

So the media play contradictory roles in the socialization process. On one hand, they promote popular support for government by joining in the celebration of national holidays, heroes' birthdays, political anniversaries, and civic accomplishments. On the other hand, the media erode public confidence by publicizing citizens' grievances, airing investigative reports of agency malfeasance, and giving front-page and prime-time coverage to political critics, protestors, and even terrorists and assassins. Some critics contend that the media give too much coverage to government opponents, especially to those who engage in unconventional opposition (see Chapter 7). However, strikes, sit-ins, violent confrontations, and hijackings draw large audiences and thus are very newsworthy by the mass media's standards.

Evaluating the Media in Government

We have described how the media developed, their current status, how they report the news to their audiences. Are the media fair or biased in reporting the news? What contributions do the media make to democratic government? What effects do they have on freedom, order, and equality?

Is Reporting Biased?

News professes to reflect reality, yet critics of modern journalism contend that this reality is colored by the way it is filtered through the ideological biases of the owners and editors (the gatekeepers) and of the reporters themselves.

The argument that news is politically biased has two sides. On one hand, news reporters are criticized for tilting their stories in a liberal direction, promoting social equality and undercutting social order. On the other hand, wealthy and conservative media owners are suspected of preserving inequalities and reinforcing the existing order by serving a relentless round of entertainment that numbs the public's capacity for critical analysis.

Although the picture is far from clear, available evidence seems to confirm the charge of liberal bias among reporters in the major news media. Studies of the voting behavior of hundreds of reporters and broadcasters show that they voted overwhelmingly for Democratic candidates in presidential elections from 1964 through 1980.[61] Moreover, a 1989 survey of 1,200 news and editorial staffers on 72 papers found that 62 percent of the journalists described themselves as liberal/Democrat, versus 22 percent conservative/Republican.[62]

A study of the media coverage of the campaigns for the 1988 presidential nomination in both parties concluded that Democratic candidates got better treatment than Republican candidates on the television news networks.[63] Of course, the judgment of whether news is negative or positive is inherently subjective. A film clip showing George Bush answering questions about his role in the Iran-Contra affair would certainly be negative, counting as "bad press." But a story about a neutral topic could also be bad press if the reporter put a negative "spin" on it. For example, a reporter could put spin on a story about a local candidate's stand in support of public education by noting that the candidate's children went to a private school.

Although most journalists classify themselves as liberal, more of them describe the newspapers for which they worked as conservative (pro-Reagan and pro-business) than liberal (42 percent to 28 percent).[64] To some extent, working journalists are at odds with their own editors, who tend to be more conservative. The editors, in their function as gatekeepers, tend to tone down the liberal biases of their reporters by editing their stories or not placing them well in the medium. In fact, newspapers are far more likely to endorse Republican than Democratic presidential candidates. In a survey of editorial endorsements of 772 newspapers in 1988, half the papers were uncommitted between the Republican candidate Bush and the Democrat candidate Dukakis, but those who chose sides favored Bush nearly three to one.[65]

If media owners and their editors are indeed conservative supporters of the status quo, we would expect them to support officeholders over challengers in elections. However, the campaign news that emerges from both print and broadcast media tends in the other direction. One researcher who found evidence of liberal bias in the 1984 presidential campaign had also studied the 1980 campaign, when Reagan was the challenger and Jimmy Carter the incumbent president.[66] In that campaign, the media covered Carter more negatively than his conservative challenger. Taking both election years into consideration, the researcher concluded that there is virtually no *continuing* ideological or partisan bias on the evening television news. Instead, what was seen as ideological or partisan bias in 1980 and 1984 was actually a bias against presidential *incumbents* and *front-runners* for the presidency.[67]

According to this reasoning, if journalists have any pronounced bias, it is against politicians. When an incumbent runs for re-election, journalists may feel a special responsibility to counteract his or her advantage by putting the opposite partisan spin on the news.[68] Thus, whether the media coverage of campaigns is seen as pro-Democratic (and therefore liberal) or pro-Republican (and therefore conservative) depends on which party is in office at the time.

Of course, bias in reporting is not limited to campaigning for elections, and different media may reflect different biases. A study of stories on nuclear energy carried in the media over a period of ten years found that stories in the *New York Times* were well balanced between pronuclear and antinuclear sources. In contrast, the major newsmagazines and television tended to favor antinuclear sources and to slant their stories against nuclear energy.[69] Some researchers also found that, prior to the outbreak of war in the Persian Gulf, media coverage of the crisis reported more public criticism of Bush's policy than the public disclosed in opinion surveys.[70]

Contributions to Democracy

As noted earlier, the communication flow in a democracy must move in two directions: from government to citizens and from citizens to government. In fact, because the media are privately owned, political communication in the United States seldom goes directly from government to citizens without passing *through* the media. This is an important point because, as just discussed, news reporters tend to be highly critical of politicians; they instinctively search for inaccuracies in fact and weaknesses in argument. Some observers have characterized the news media and the government as adversaries—each mistrusting the other, locked in competition for popular favor. To the extent that this is true, the media serve both the majoritarian and the pluralist models of democracy well by improving the quality of information transmitted to people about their government.

The mass media transmit information from citizens to government by reporting citizens' reactions to political events and government actions. The press has traditionally reflected public opinion (and often created it) by defining the news and suggesting courses of government action. But the media's role in reflecting public opinion has become much more refined in the information age. Before the widespread use of sample surveys, collections of newspaper stories from across the country were analyzed to assess public opinion on political affairs.[71] After commercial polls (such as the Gallup and Roper polls) were established in the 1930s, newspapers began to report more reliable readings of public opinion. By the 1960s, the media (both national and local) began to conduct their own surveys. In the 1970s, survey research groups became formal divisions of some news organizations. Occasionally, print and electronic media joined forces to conduct major national surveys.

The media now have the tools to do a better job of reporting mass opinion than ever before, and they use those tools extensively, doing "precision journalism" with sophisticated data collection and analysis techniques. The well-respected *New York Times*/CBS News Poll conducts surveys that are aired first on the "CBS Evening News," then analyzed at length in the *Times*. During the 1988 election campaign, the *Times* conducted 31 separate polls, most jointly with CBS News, which formed the basis of 35 articles and were cited in another 135 articles on the campaign.[72] The *Wall Street Journal* and NBC News are also allies in opinion polling, as are the *Washington Post* and ABC News. In fact, 40 percent of the daily newspapers are directly involved in polling.[73]

Citizens and journalists alike complain that heavy reliance on polls during election campaigns causes the media to emphasize the horse race and slight the discussion of issues.[74] But the media use their polling expertise for other purposes, such as gauging support for going to war against Iraq and for balancing the budget. Although polls sometimes create opinions just by asking questions, their net effect has been to generate more accurate knowledge of public opinion and to report that knowledge back to the public. Although widespread knowledge of public opinion does not guarantee government responsiveness to popular demands, such knowledge is required if government is to function according to the majoritarian model of democracy.

Effects on Freedom, Order, and Equality

The media in the United States have played an important role in advancing equality, especially racial equality. Throughout the civil rights movement of the 1950s and 1960s, the media gave national coverage to

F E A T U R E   6.3   *Today's News: Sex and Scandal*

In 1990, books about President John F. Kennedy and Dr. Martin Luther King, Jr., were published accusing them of womanizing. In Kennedy's case, the evidence is abundant—reputed liaisons with Marilyn Monroe, accounts of women procured for him by the Secret Service, and an established relationship with Judith Exner, a girlfriend of a Mafia boss. In King's case, the documentation is contested but credible. In both cases, it is significant that reporters covering these men sat on their inside knowledge and suspicions.

Thirty years ago, the media limited coverage of political candidates and officeholders to their public acts. Today, the media accept no limits to coverage of politicians' private lives, and exposing marital infidelity is standard journalism. In 1988, reporters from the *Miami Herald* staked out Gary Hart's home in Washington, D.C., to get the goods on his relationship with model Donna Rice. The front-page story helped drive the frontrunner Hart from the race for the Democratic nomination for president. Later the same year, Henry Cisneros, the mayor of San Antonio, left office over stories about his affair with a woman staff member. In 1990, Jon Grunseth, the Republican candidate for governor in Minnesota, dropped out of the race just before the election due to reports of his lengthy extramarital relationship.

If the media acted properly in exposing these affairs, did it fail the public by not telling on Kennedy and King? Publicizing Kennedy's sexual appetite surely would have cost him his victory over Richard Nixon in the razor-thin election of 1960, and reports of King's indiscretions would certainly have impaired his leadership of the civil rights movement. Would the nation have been better off

without these unfaithful husbands? Might Hart, Cisneros, or Grunseth also have made outstanding government leaders?

Reporters pursue these stories of sex and scandal because they increase media audiences, raise company profits, and help make journalistic careers. The media cloak their private motives with public values: First, reporters defend their investigations into private lives as justifiable assessments of the candidate's "character." Since anything may influence character, there is no limit to what reporters feel entitled to investigate.

Second, the media raise the shield of "freedom of the press" against *all* attempts to limit their coverage of "news." Consider Madonna's music video, "Justify My Love," which celebrated "voyeurism, masturbation, group sex, soft-core sadomasochism and bisexuality." Even MTV refused to air it, saying, "This one is just not for us." ABC's "Nightline" rode to the rescue, showing the steamy video in its entirety to a nationwide audience while soberly treating it as an issue in freedom of expression. The news-starved public responded by giving the program its highest rating of 1990.

Not many businesses can camouflage their private interests—making money—under the guise of public interest. Now that the media are learning to exploit this position, look for more sizzling infotainment.

Sources: C. David Heymann, *A Woman Named Jackie* (New York: New American Library, 1990). Ralph David Abernathy, *And the Walls Came Tumbling Down* (New York: Harper and Row, 1989). Joan Beck, "Sex, Hype and Videotape Drown Out Voices of Reason," *Chicago Tribune*, 6 December 1990, p. 21.

conflict in the South, as black children tried to attend white schools or civil rights workers were beaten and even killed in the effort to register black voters. Partly because of the media coverage, civil rights moved up on the political agenda, and coalitions were formed in Congress to pass new laws promoting racial equality. Women's rights have also been advanced through the media, which focused attention on the National Organization for Women (NOW) and other groups working for sexual equality. In general, the mass media offer spokespersons for any disadvantaged group an opportunity to state their case before a national audience and to work for a place on the political agenda.

Although the media are willing to mobilize government action to infringe on personal freedom for equality's sake, they resist government's attempts to infringe on freedom of the press to promote order. The media, far more than the public, believe freedom of the press is sacrosanct. For example, 98 percent of 2,703 journalists surveyed by the *Los Angeles Times* opposed allowing a government official to prevent the publication of a story seen as inaccurate, compared with only 50 percent of the public. Whereas the public felt that certain types of news should never be published—"exit polls saying who will win an election, secret documents dealing with national security issues, the names of CIA spies, photographs that invade people's privacy"—journalists are more reluctant to draw the line anywhere (see Feature 6.3).[75] Although reporters covering the Persian Gulf crisis chafed at restrictions imposed by the military, a survey during the war found that 57 percent of the public thought that the military "should exert more control" over reporting.[76]

To protect their freedom, the media operate as an interest group in a pluralist democracy. They have an interest in reporting whatever they wish, whenever they wish, which certainly erodes government's efforts to maintain order. Three examples illustrate this point.

- The media's sensational coverage of airline hijacking fits a general pattern of coverage given to all sorts of terrorist activities. By publicizing terrorism, the media give terrorists exactly what they want, making it more difficult to reduce terrorist threats to order.
- The portrayal of brutal killings and rapes on television, often under the guise of entertainment, has produced "copycat" crimes, those admittedly committed "as seen on TV."
- The national publicity given to deaths from adulterated drugs (for instance, Tylenol capsules laced with cyanide) has prompted similar tampering with other products.

Freedom of the press is a noble value and one that has been important to our democratic government. But we should not ignore the fact that we sometimes pay a price for pursuing it without qualification.

Summary

The mass media transmit information to large, heterogeneous, and widely dispersed audiences through print and broadcasts. The main function of the mass media is entertainment, but the media also perform the political functions of reporting news, interpreting news, influencing citizens' opinions, setting the political agenda, and socializing citizens about politics.

The mass media in the United States are privately owned and in business to make money, which they do mainly by selling space or air time to advertisers. Both print and electronic media determine which events are newsworthy, a determination made on the basis of audience appeal. The rise of mass-circulation newspapers in the 1830s produced a politically independent press in the United States. In their aggressive competition for readers, those newspapers often engaged in sensational reporting, a charge sometimes leveled at today's media.

The broadcast media operate under technical, ownership, and content regulations set by the government, which tend to promote the equal treatment of political contests on radio and television more than in newspapers and news magazines.

The major media maintain staffs of professional journalists in major cities across the world. Washington, D.C., has the largest press corps in the world, but only a portion of those correspondents concentrate on the presidency. Because Congress is a more decentralized institution, it is covered in a more decentralized manner. All professional journalists recognize rules for citing sources that guide their reporting. What actually gets reported in the media depends on the media's gatekeepers, the publishers and editors.

Although more people today get more news from television than newspapers, newspapers usually do a more thorough job of informing the public about politics. Despite heavy exposure to news in the print and electronic media, the ability of most people to retain much political information is shockingly low—and less than it was in the mid-1960s. It appears that the problem is not with the media's inability to supply quality news coverage, but the the lack of demand for it by the public. The role of the news media may be more important for affecting interactions among attentive policy elites than in influencing public opinion.

The media's elite, including reporters from the major television networks, tend to be more liberal than the public, as judged by the journalists' tendency to vote for Democratic candidates and by their own self-descriptions. However, if the media systematically demonstrate pronounced bias in their news reporting, it tends to work against incumbents and frontrunners, regardless of their party, rather than for liberal Democrats.

From the standpoint of majoritarian democracy, one of the most important effects of the media is to facilitate communication from the people to the government through the reporting of public opinion polls. The media zealously defend the freedom of the press, even to the point of encouraging disorder through criticism of the government and the granting of extensive publicity to violent protests, terrorist acts, and other threats to order.

KEY TERMS

communication
mass communication
mass media
print media
broadcast media
yellow journalism
muckrakers
attentive policy elites
two-step flow of
    communication
newsworthiness

infotainment
Federal Communications Commission (FCC)
equal opportunities rule
reasonable access rule
fairness doctrine
gatekeepers
horse race journalism
media event
political agenda

SELECTED READINGS

Bozell, L. Brent, II, and Brent H. Baker, eds. *And That's the Way It Isn't*. Alexandria, Va.: Media Research Center, 1990. Prepared by a conservative research group, this study documents the liberal bias of the media. Contrast this book with that by Kellner, below.

Entman, Robert. *Democracy without Citizens: Media and the Decay of American Politics*. New York: Oxford University Press, 1989. A penetrating study of the "supply" side of news reporting and the "demand" side of news consumption. Entman concludes that the media do not do a better job of reporting news because the public does not demand it.

Graber, Doris A. *Mass Media and American Politics.* 3d ed. Washington, D.C.: Congressional Quarterly Press, 1989. Emphasizes the political coverage and impact of the mass media.

Graber, Doris A. *Media Power and Politics.* 2d ed. Washington, D.C.: Congressional Quarterly Press, 1990. A collection of seminal essays on political journalism and empirical studies of media effects.

Graber, Doris A. *Processing the News: How People Tame the Information Tide.* New York: Longman, 1988. Reports results of a yearlong panel study of how twenty-one individuals followed the news in local newspapers and through local and national television.

Iyengar, Shanto, and Donald R. Kinder. *News That Matters: Television and American Opinion.* Chicago: University of Chicago Press, 1987. Reports fourteen experiments with townspeople in New Haven and Ann Arbor designed to assess the effects of television news on opinion.

Kellner, Douglas. *Television and the Crisis of Democracy.* Boulder, Col.: Westview Press, 1990. A critical, leftist account of the role mass media play in controlling the limits of political discussion by extending the hegemony of the dominant culture. Serves as a counterpoint to the book by Bozell and Baker, above.

Lavrakas, Paul J., and Jack K. Holley, eds. *Polling and Presidential Election Coverage.* Newbury Park, Calif.: Sage Publications, 1991. Studies of the media's use of public opinion surveys in covering the 1988 presidential election.

Serfaty, Simon, ed. *The Media and Foreign Policy.* New York: St. Martin's Press, 1990. A collection of short accounts, mostly anecdotal, by insiders who were in a position to observe the relationship of the media to the White House during foreign policy crises.

Wanniski, Jude, ed. *1990 Media Guide: A Critical Review of the Media's Recent Coverage of the World Political Economy.* Morristown, N.J.: Polyconomics, 1990. A handbook of the year's major stories and an assessment of the media coverage. This critical source evaluates the alternative press as well as the mainstream media.

7 PARTICIPATION AND VOTING

SHOUTS OF "NO BLOOD FOR OIL! No war for Bush!" rang out from the Senate gallery. The eleven demonstrators who briefly interrupted Democratic Senator Sam Nunn's speech during the historic debate over war in the Persian Gulf were quickly removed by police officers.[1] Ironically, Nunn was speaking against the rush to use force, but neither his speech nor the protesters' shouts altered the outcome. The next day, on January 12, 1991, the Senate voted 52–47 to authorize the use of force to implement the United Nations resolution requiring Iraq to withdraw its troops from Kuwait. The House concurred in the joint resolution by a vote of 250–183. Within five days, the United States was at war with Iraq.

Unlike the antiwar movement of the 1960s, antiwar protesters in the 1990s were in disarray. From the beginning, vocal opposition to war over Kuwait came from some staunch conservatives, such as columnist Patrick Buchanan, who argued that the nation had no compelling interest in a conflict with Iraq.[2] These critics kept uneasy company with some former Vietnam antiwar protesters, but old partners in the Vietnam peace coalition were badly split over actions in the Persian Gulf.[3] In fact, Democratic Representative Stephen Solarz from New York, who introduced the congressional resolution that backed Bush's use of force, had been active in the protest movement against the Vietnam War.

The congressional vote served to refine the antiwar coalition. Most right-wing critics, including Patrick Buchanan, quickly lined up behind the president. This left a left-wing flavor to the antiwar movement, evoking images of the Vietnam-era protests. New cries against "dying for U.S. oil profits" joined with the old slogan "Hell no, we won't go!" On the first Saturday after the war began, an antiwar rally in Washington, D.C., drew an estimated 75,000 people; another rally a week later drew 150,000.[4] Although these rallies represented a wide spectrum of America, polls taken the night war began showed about 80 percent of the public supported Bush's actions.[5] As in the Vietnam era, antiwar protests were prominent on college campuses across the nation, but student opinion was more divided this time. At one rally, police had to separate antiwar demonstrators from about 100 counterdemonstrators, mostly from the College Republican National Committee, who waved U.S. flags and chanted "U.S.A!"[6] On many campuses, students demonstrated their support of the war by displaying flags or yellow ribbons.

Before the war with Iraq, many observers felt that today's college students were politically apathetic. Certainly they have not reflected the broad student activism of the 1960s, and it is not clear whether the war will have a lasting effect on their political involvement. Had anything happened during the 1970s and 1980s to change the political behavior of American youth? Or are we witnessing widespread political apathy among Americans of all ages? Are Americans today less active politically? How do they compare with citizens of other countries? And how much and what kind of participation are necessary to sustain the pluralist and majoritarian models of democracy?

In this chapter, we try to answer these and other important questions about popular participation in government. Although most people think of political participation primarily in terms of voting, there are other forms of political participation, which are sometimes more effective than voting. We begin by looking at the role of participation in democratic

No Blood for Oil . . . No Tolerance for Tyranny
The outset of military action in the Persian Gulf provoked antiwar demonstrations on campuses, but, unlike their predecessors during the Vietnam War, protesters did not draw broad support from American citizens. On some campuses more students participated in rallies that supported the military effort than rallies that opposed it.

government, distinguishing between conventional and unconventional participation. Then we evaluate the nature and extent of both types of participation in American politics. Next, we study the expansion of voting rights and voting as the major mechanism for mass participation in politics. Finally, we examine the extent to which the various forms of political participation serve the values of freedom, equality, and order, and the majoritarian and pluralist models of democracy.

Democracy and Political Participation

"Government ought to be run by the people." That is the democratic ideal in a nutshell. But how much and what kind of citizen participation are necessary for democratic government? Neither political theorists nor politicians, neither idealists nor realists, can agree on an answer. Champions of direct democracy believe that if citizens do not participate *directly* in government affairs, making government decisions among themselves, they should give up all pretense of democracy. More practical observers contend that people can govern indirectly through their elected representatives. And they maintain that choosing leaders through **elections**—formal procedures for voting—is the only workable approach to democracy in a large, complex nation.

We talked about the distinction between direct and indirect democracy in Chapter 2. In a direct democracy, citizens meet and make decisions themselves. In an indirect democracy, citizens participate in government by electing representatives to make decisions for them. Voting is central to the majoritarian model of government, but it is not the only means of political participation. In fact, the pluralist model of democracy relies less on voting and more on other forms of participation.

Elections are a necessary condition of democracy, but they do not guarantee democratic government. Even prior to *glasnost*, the Soviet Union regularly held elections in which more than 90 percent of the electorate turned out to vote, but the Soviet Union certainly did not function as a democracy. Both the majoritarian and pluralist models of democracy rely on voting to varying degrees, but both models expect citizens to take part in other forms of political behavior as well. For example, they expect citizens to discuss politics, to form interest groups, to contact public officials, to campaign for political parties, to run for office, and even to protest government decisions.

We define **political participation** as "those actions of private citizens by which they seek to influence or to support government and politics."[7] This definition embraces both conventional and unconventional forms of political participation. In plain language, *conventional* behavior is behavior that is acceptable to the dominant culture in a given situation. Wearing a swimsuit at the beach is conventional; wearing one at a formal dance is not. Plastering campaign posters on public buildings is conventional; writing political slogans on walls is not.

At times, it is difficult to decide whether a particular political act is conventional or unconventional. We find the following distinction useful in analyzing political participation:

- **Conventional participation** is relatively routine behavior that uses the institutional channels of representative government, especially campaigning for candidates and voting in elections.
- **Unconventional participation** is relatively uncommon behavior that challenges or defies government channels or the dominant culture (and thus is personally stressful to participants and their opponents).

Voting and writing letters to public officials are examples of conventional political participation; staging sit-down strikes in public buildings and chanting slogans outside officials' windows are examples of unconventional participation. Demonstrations can be conventional (supporting Operation Desert Storm in the Persian Gulf) or unconventional (beating drums outside the White House to protest the war). Some forms of unconventional participation are used by powerless groups to gain political benefits while still working within the system.[8]

There is no question that voting and other methods of conventional participation are important to democratic government. So, however, are unconventional forms of participation. We will discuss both kinds of political participation in the United States, beginning with unconventional forms and working toward the most visible form of conventional participation—voting in elections.

Unconventional Participation

On Sunday, March 7, 1965, a group of about six hundred people attempted to march fifty miles from Selma, Alabama, to the state capital at Montgomery. The marchers were demonstrating in favor of voting rights for blacks. (At the time, Selma had fewer than five hundred registered black voters, out of fifteen thousand who were eligible.)[9] Alabama Governor George Wallace declared the march illegal and sent state troopers to stop it. The two groups met at the Edmund Pettus Bridge over the

Bridge Over Troubled Waters

On March 7, 1965, civil rights marchers were beaten by Alabama state troopers and local law enforcement officers. Twenty-five years later, on March 4, 1990, an aging group of civil rights workers marched without incident to commemorate Bloody Sunday. Some things do change.

Alabama River at the edge of Selma. The marchers were beaten and trampled by state troopers and deputy sheriffs—some on horseback—using clubs, bullwhips, and tear gas. The day became known as "Bloody Sunday."

The march from Selma was a form of unconventional political participation. Marching fifty miles in a political protest is certainly not common; moreover, the march challenged existing institutions, which prevented blacks from voting. From the beginning, the marchers knew they were putting themselves in a dangerous situation, that they certainly would be taunted by whites along the way and could be physically hurt as well. But they had been prevented from participating conventionally—voting in elections—for many decades, and they chose this unconventional way of dramatizing their cause.

The march ended in violence because Governor Wallace would not allow even this peaceful mode of unconventional expression. Unlike some of the demonstrations against the Vietnam War somewhat later, this civil rights march posed no threat of violence. The brutal response to the marchers helped the rest of the nation realize the seriousness of the civil rights problem in the South. Unconventional participation is stressful and occasionally violent, but it is sometimes worth the risk.

Support for Unconventional Participation

Unconventional political participation has a long history in the United States. The Boston Tea Party in 1773, in which American colonists dumped three cargoes of British tea into Boston Harbor, was only the first in a long line of violent protests against British rule that eventually led to revolution. Yet, we know less about unconventional political participation than about conventional participation. The reasons are twofold: First, data on conventional means are easier to collect and so are more frequently studied. Second, political scientists are biased toward "institutionalized," or conventional, politics. In fact, some basic works on political participation explicitly exclude any behavior that is "outside the system."[10] One major study of unconventional political action asked people whether they had engaged in or approved of ten types of political participation outside of voting.[11] As shown in Figure 7.1, of the ten activities, only signing petitions was clearly regarded as conventional, in the sense that the behavior is nearly universally approved and widely practiced.

There was a question about the conventionality of two other forms of behavior. Nearly a quarter of the respondents disapproved of lawful demonstrations, and only one out of ten had ever participated in a lawful demonstration. What is and is not "lawful" is hard to determine, however. The marchers in Selma, although peaceful, violated Governor Wallace's decree, which itself may have violated their rights. If we measure conventionality in terms of the number of people who disapprove of an action and the number who actually practice it, then it might be argued

FIGURE 7.1   *What Americans Think of as Unconventional Political Behavior*

A survey of Americans asked whether they approved or disapproved of ten different forms of participation outside of the electoral process. The respondents disapproved of most of the ten forms, often overwhelmingly, although signing petitions was rarely disapproved of—and also widely done. But even attending lawful demonstrations (a right guaranteed in the Constitution) was disapproved of by 24 percent of the respondents and rarely practiced. Boycotting products was more objectionable but more widely practiced. Attending demonstrations and boycotting products are only marginally conventional. The other seven forms are clearly unconventional. (Source: Samuel H. Barnes and Max Kaase, eds., Political Action: Mass Participation in Five Western Democracies [Beverly Hills, Calif.: Sage, 1979], p. 545.)

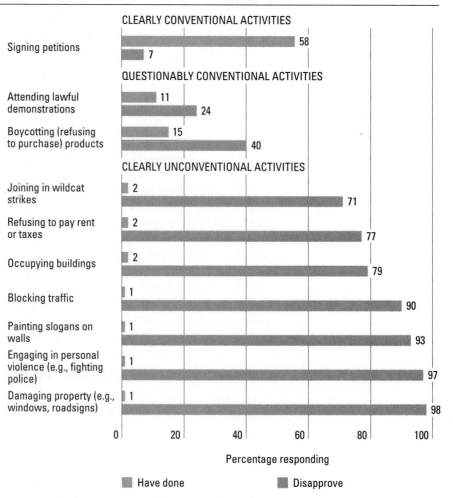

Antiwar Protest, 1968

In August 1968, thousands of youthful antiwar protestors gathered in Chicago, where the Democrats were holding their national convention. Protests against the war had already forced President Lyndon Johnson not to seek re-election. Mayor Richard Daley vowed that the protesters would not disturb the impending nomination of Hubert Humphrey, Johnson's vice president. Daley's police kept the youths from demonstrating at the convention, but the resulting violence did not help Humphrey, who lost to Richard Nixon in an extremely close election.

that all demonstrations border on the unconventional. The same reasoning could be applied to boycotting products—for example, refusing to buy lettuce or grapes picked by nonunion farm workers. Lawful demonstrations and boycotts are problem cases in deciding what is and is not conventional political participation.

The other political activities listed in Figure 7.1 are clearly unconventional. In fact, when political activities interfere with daily living (blocking traffic) or involve the destruction of property (painting slogans on walls, breaking windows) or physical violence, disapproval is nearly universal. Americans do not approve of unconventional political behavior. When protesters demonstrating against the Vietnam War disrupted the 1968 Democratic National Convention in Chicago, they were clubbed off the streets by the city's police. Although it saw graphic videotape of the confrontations and heard reporters' criticisms of police behavior, the viewing public condemned the demonstrators, not the police.

The Effectiveness of Unconventional Participation

Protests against war in the Persian Gulf did not prevent President Bush from ordering an attack against Iraq in 1991. Does unconventional participation ever work, especially when it provokes violence? Yes. Antiwar protesters discouraged President Lyndon Johnson from seeking re-election in 1968, and they heightened public concern over U.S. participation in the Vietnam War. American college students who disrupted campuses in the late 1960s and early 1970s helped end the military draft in

1973, and, although this was not a stated goal, sped up the passage of the Twenty-sixth Amendment, which lowered the voting age to eighteen.

The unconventional activities of the civil rights workers also had notable success. Dr. Martin Luther King, Jr., led the 1955 Montgomery bus boycott (prompted by Rosa Parks's refusal to surrender her seat to a white man) that sparked the civil rights movement. He used **direct action,** assembling crowds to confront businesses and local governments, to demand equal treatment in public accommodations and government. The civil rights movement used over a thousand such newsworthy demonstrations nationwide—387 in 1965 alone.[12] And, like the march in Selma, many of these protests provoked violent confrontations between whites and blacks.

Denied opportunities for conventional political participation, members of the civil rights movement used unconventional politics to pressure Congress to pass a series of civil rights laws in 1957, 1960, 1964, and 1968—each one in some way extending federal protection against discrimination by reason of race, color, religion, or national origin. (The 1964 act also prohibited discrimination in employment on the basis of sex.)

In addition, the Voting Rights Act of 1965 put state electoral procedures under federal supervision, increasing the registration of black voters and the rate of black voter turnout—especially in the South, where much of the violence occurred. Black protest activity (both violent and nonviolent) has also been credited with increased welfare support for blacks in the South.[13] The civil rights movement shows that social change can occur, even when it is violently opposed at first. Twenty-five years after law enforcement officers beat civil rights marchers in Selma, some of the same marchers walked peacefully to commemorate Bloody Sunday, with a few police there to ensure they would not be disturbed.

Although direct political action and the politics of confrontation can work, it takes a special kind of commitment to use them. Studies show that direct action appeals most to those who both (1) *distrust* the political system, and (2) have a strong sense of political *efficacy*—the feeling that they can do something to affect political decisions.[14] Whether or not this combination of attitudes produces behavior that challenges the system depends on the extent of organized group activity.[15] The civil rights movement involved many organized groups: King's Southern Christian Leadership Conference (SCLC); the Congress of Racial Equality (CORE), headed by James Farmer; and the Student Non-Violent Coordinating Committee (SNCC), led by Stokely Carmichael—to mention a few.

The decision to behave unconventionally also depends on the extent to which individuals develop a *group consciousness*—identification with the group and an awareness of its position in society, its objectives, and its intended course of action.[16] These factors were present among blacks and young people in the mid-1960s and are strongly present today among blacks and to a lesser degree among women. Indeed, some researchers contend that black consciousness has heightened distrust of the political system and the sense of individual efficacy, producing more participation of different types by poor blacks than by poor whites.[17] The National Organization for Women (NOW) and other women's groups have also heightened women's consciousness, which may have contributed to their increased participation in politics, in both conventional and unconventional ways.

Unconventional Participation in America

Although most Americans may disapprove of some forms of participation to protest government policies, our citizens are about as likely to take direct action in politics as those in European democracies. Surveys in 1981 of citizens in Britain, Germany, and France, found that Americans claim to "have done" as much or *more* in the way of unconventional behavior, such as participating in lawful demonstrations, joining in boycotts, participating in unlawful strikes, occupying buildings, damaging property, and even engaging in personal violence.[18] Contrary to the popular view that Americans are apathetic about politics, a recent study suggests that they are more likely to engage in political protests of various sorts than citizens in other democratic countries.[19]

Is there something wrong with our political system if citizens resort to unconventional—and widely disapproved—methods of political participation? To answer this question, we must first learn how much Americans use conventional methods of participation.

Conventional Participation

A practical test of the democratic nature of any government is whether citizens can affect its policies by acting through its institutions—meeting with public officials, supporting candidates, voting in elections. If people must operate outside government institutions in order to influence policymaking—as civil rights workers had to do in the South—then the system is not democratic. Citizens should not have to risk life and property to participate in politics, and they should not have to take direct action to force their views to be heard in government. The objective of democratic institutions is to make political participation *conventional*—to allow ordinary citizens to engage in relatively routine, nonthreatening behavior to cause government to heed their opinions, interests, and needs.

It is not unusual in a democracy for a group to gather at a statehouse or city hall to dramatize its position on an issue—say, a tax increase. This kind of demonstration is a form of conventional participation. The group is not powerless, and its members are not risking their personal safety by demonstrating. But violence can erupt between opposing groups demonstrating in a political setting, for instance, between antiabortion and prochoice groups. Circumstances, then, often determine whether organized protest is or is not conventional. In general, the less the threat to participants, the more conventional the protest.

Several types of participation are conventional except in extreme circumstances. (For example, voting is ordinarily a conventional act, but it would not have been conventional for a black to vote in Selma in the early 1960s.) The most visible form of conventional participation is voting to choose candidates. However, we must not rush to study voting too quickly; it leads us away from less prominent but equally important forms of conventional political participation. In fact, these other forms of participation are in many ways more important than voting, especially in the United States, where voter turnout is much lower than that in most other democratic nations.

There are two major categories of conventional political behaviors: actions that show *support* for government policies and those that try to change or *influence* policies.

Supportive Behavior

Supportive behaviors are actions that express allegiance to country and government. When we recite the Pledge of Allegiance or fly the American flag on holidays, we are showing support for the country and, by implication, its political system. These kinds of ceremonial activities usually require little effort, knowledge, or personal courage; that is, they demand little initiative on the part of the citizen. The simple act of turning out to vote is in itself a show of support for the political system. Other supportive behaviors—for example, serving as an election judge in a nonpartisan election or organizing a holiday parade—demand greater initiative.

At times, their perception of patriotism moves people across the line from conventional to unconventional behavior. In their eagerness to support the American system, they break up a meeting or disrupt a rally of a group they believe is radical or somehow "un-American." Radical groups may threaten the political system with wrenching change, but superpatriots pose their own threat. Their misguided excess of allegiance denies nonviolent means of dissent to others.[20]

Influencing Behavior

Influencing behaviors are used to modify or even reverse government policy to serve political interests. Some forms of influencing behavior seek particular benefits from government; other forms have broad policy objectives.

Particular benefits.   Some citizens try to influence government to obtain benefits for themselves, their immediate families, or close friends. Two examples of influence attempts that do not require much initiative are voting to elect a relative to local office and voting against an increase in school taxes when one's own children have already left school. Serving one's own self-interest through the voting process is certainly acceptable to democratic theory. Each individual has only one vote, and no single voter can wangle particular benefits from government through voting unless a majority of voters agree.

Political actions that require considerable knowledge and initiative are another story, however. Individuals or small groups who influence government officials to advance their self-interests—for instance, to obtain a lucrative government contract—may benefit without others knowing about it. Those who quietly obtain particular benefits from government pose a serious challenge to a democracy. Pluralist theory holds that groups ought to be able to make government respond to their special problems and needs. On the other hand, majoritarian theory holds that government should not do what a majority does not want it to do. A majority of citizens might very well not want the government to do what any particular person or group seeks—if it is costly to other citizens.

What might individual citizens or groups ask of their government, and how might they go about asking? Few people realize that using the court system is a form of political participation, a way for citizens to press their rights in a democratic society. Although most people use the courts to serve their particular interests, some also use them, as we discuss shortly, to meet broad objectives. Going to court demands high personal initiative.[21] It also demands a knowledge of the law and the financial resources to afford a lawyer.

Some citizens ask for special services from their local government. Such requests may range from contacting the city forestry department to remove a dead tree in front of a house to calling the county animal control center to deal with a vicious dog in the neighborhood. Studies of such "contacting" behavior as a form of political participation find that it tends not to be related to other forms of political activity but is related to socioeconomic status: People of higher socioeconomic status are more likely to contact public officials.[22]

Americans demand much more of local government than of national government. Although many people value self-reliance and individualism in national politics, most people expect local government to solve a wide range of social problems. A study of residents of Kansas City, Missouri, found that more than 90 percent thought it was the city's responsibility to provide services in thirteen areas, including maintaining parks, setting standards for new home construction, demolishing vacant and unsafe buildings, ensuring that property owners clean up trash and weeds, and providing bus service. The researcher noted that "it is difficult to imagine a set of federal government activities about which there would necessarily be any more consensus—defense, environmental controls, and other areas."[23] Citizens can also mobilize against a project. The 1980s saw emergence of the "Not-in-My-Back-Yard," or *NIMBY*, phenomenon, as citizens pressured local officials to stop undesirable projects from being located near their homes.

Finally, contributing money to a candidate's campaign is another form of influencing behavior. Here, too, the objective can be particular or broad benefits, although sometimes it can be difficult to determine which. An example: Charles H. Keating, a wealthy banker, had raised and contributed more than $1.3 million to the campaign committees and political causes of five U.S. Senators: Democrat John Glenn from Ohio, Democrat Alan Cranston from California, Democrat Dennis DeConcini from Arizona, Republican John McCain from Arizona, and Democrat Donald W. Riegle, Jr., from Michigan. They became known as the "Keating Five" when the Senate Ethics Committee considered charges that they tried to deflect government regulation of Keating's Lincoln Savings and Loan Association, which failed in 1989. Although the Keating Five met twice with federal regulators in April 1987, the senators contended that they acted only to help a constituent deal with a complex government bureaucracy. After more than a year of investigation, the Ethics Committee found only that all of the five senators were guilty of poor

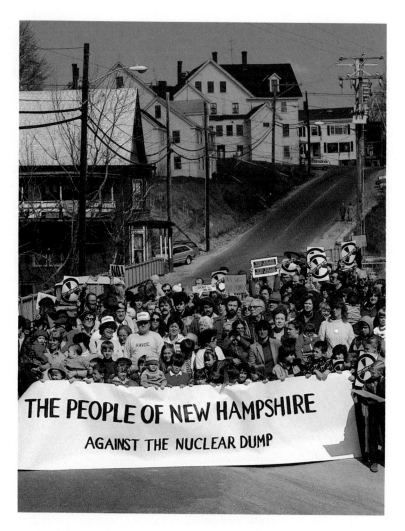

Not In Our Town

Perhaps not everyone in New Hampshire is pictured here, but these protesters made their point. A cross-section of Hillsboro, New Hampshire, residents marched to protest a proposed nuclear waste disposal site in their town. Politicians usually listen closely when a diverse group of citizens is concerned enough to protest a specific government action. These citizens won: The dump site did not come to Hillsboro.

judgment and one (Senator Cranston) may have acted improperly, pending further investigation.[24]

Several points emerge from this review of "particularized" forms of political participation. First, approaching government to serve one's particular interests is consistent with democratic theory, because it encourages input from an active citizenry. Second, particularized contact may be a form of participation unto itself, not necessarily related to other forms of participation, such as voting. Third, such participation tends to be used more by citizens who are advantaged in terms of knowledge and resources. Fourth, particularized participation may serve private interests to the detriment of the majority.

Broad policy objectives. We come now to what many scholars have in mind when they talk about political participation: activities that influence the selection of government personnel and policies. Here, too, we find behaviors that require little initiative (such as voting) and high initiative (attending political meetings, persuading others how to vote).

Even when voting is used to influence government policies, it remains a low-initiative activity. Such "policy voting" differs from voting to show support or to gain special benefits by its broader impact on the community or the society. Obviously, this distinction is not sharp: Citizens vote for a number of reasons that mix allegiance, particularized benefits, and policy concerns. In addition to policy voting, many other low-initiative forms of conventional participation—wearing a campaign button, watching a party convention on television, posting a bumper sticker—are also connected with elections. In the next section, we focus on elections as a mechanism for participation. For now, we simply note that voting to influence policy is usually a low-initiative activity. As we discuss later, it actually requires more initiative to *register* to vote in the United States than to cast a vote on election day.

Other types of participation to affect broad policies require high initiative. Running for office requires the most (see Chapter 9). Some high-initiative activities, such as attending party meetings and working in campaigns, are associated with the electoral process; others, such as attending legislative hearings and writing letters to Congress, are not. These nonelectoral activities are a form of contacting, but their objective is to obtain government benefits for some group of people—farmers, the unemployed, children, oil producers. In fact, studies of citizen contacts in the United States show that about two-thirds deal with broad social issues and only one-third are for private gain.[25]

As noted earlier, the courts can be used for both personal benefit and broad policy objectives. **Class-action suits** are brought by a person or

A Line of Argument

Tension may fill the air when citizens turn out in large numbers at local political meetings, and speaking out in such meetings requires high personal initiative. Knowledge of the issues involved helps, too. Citizens at this public transportation hearing in Austin, Texas, have come prepared to state their views. Looks like a long evening ahead.

group on behalf of other people in similar circumstances. Lawyers for the National Association for the Advancement of Colored People pioneered this form of litigation in the famous school desegregation case *Brown* v. *Board of Education* (1954).[26] They succeeded in getting the Supreme Court to outlaw segregation in public schools, not just for Linda Brown, who brought suit in Topeka, Kansas, but for all others "similarly situated"—that is, for all other black students who want to attend white schools. Usually this form of participation is beyond the means of individual citizens, but it has proved to be effective for organized groups, especially those who have been unable to gain their objectives through Congress or the president.

Individual citizens can also try to influence policies at the national level by direct participation in the legislative process. One way is to attend congressional hearings, which are public events occasionally held in various parts of the country. Especially since the end of World War II, the federal government has sought to increase citizen involvement in creating regulations and laws by making information on government activities available to interested parties. For example, government agencies are required to publish notices of regulations in the *Federal Register* (a list, published daily, of all proposed and approved regulations) and to make documents available to citizens on request.

Conventional Participation in America

You may know someone who has taken part in a congressional or administrative hearing; the odds are better, though, that you do not. This

Mongolians Trot Toward Democracy

In the summer of 1990, Mongolia held its first multiparty elections. Approximately 92 percent of the nation's 735,000 registered voters, scattered throughout the vast rural land, cast their ballots, often inserting them into portable boxes borne on horses. Where there's a will, there's a way.

is a form of high-initiative behavior. Relatively few people—only those with high stakes in the outcome of a decision—are willing to participate this way. How often do Americans contact government officials and engage in other forms of conventional political participation, compared with citizens in other countries?

The most common political behavior reported in a study of five countries was voting to choose candidates (see Compared with What? 7.1). Americans are *less* likely to vote than citizens in the other four countries. On the other hand, Americans are as likely (or substantially more likely) to engage in all of the other forms of conventional political participation—just as they are as likely or more likely to take part in unconventional behaviors. Americans, then, are more apt to engage in nearly all forms of unconventional *and* conventional political participation, *except* voting.

The researchers noted this paradox and wrote: "If, for example, we concentrate our attention on national elections we will find that the United States is the least participatory of our five nations." But looking at the other indicators, they found that "political apathy, by a wide margin, is lowest in the United States. Interestingly, the high levels of overall involvement reflect a rather balanced contribution of both . . . conventional and unconventional politics."[27] Clearly, low voter turnout in the United States constitutes something of a puzzle. We will work at that puzzle, but first we focus on elections and electoral systems.

Participating Through Voting

The heart of democratic government lies in the electoral process. Whether a country holds elections and, if so, what kind constitute the critical differences between democratic and nondemocratic government. Elections are important to democracy for their potential to institutionalize mass participation in government according to the three normative principles for procedural democracy discussed in Chapter 2. Electoral rules specify (1) *who* is allowed to vote, (2) *how much* each person's vote counts, and (3) *how many* votes are needed to win.

Again, elections are formal procedures for making group decisions. **Voting** is the act that individuals perform when they choose among alternatives in an election. **Suffrage** and the **franchise** both mean "the right to vote." By formalizing political participation through rules for suffrage and counting ballots, electoral systems allow large numbers of people, who individually have little political power, to wield great power. Electoral systems decide collectively who governs and, in some instances, what government should do.

The simple fact of holding elections is less important than the specific rules and circumstances that govern voting. According to democratic theory, everyone should be able to vote. In practice, however, no nation grants universal suffrage. All countries have age requirements for voting, and all disqualify some inhabitants on various grounds: lack of citizenship, a criminal record, mental incompetence, and so forth. What is the record of enfranchisement in the United States?

COMPARED WITH WHAT? 7.1

Conventional Political Participation

A study of five nations found that Americans are more likely than citizens in other countries to engage in various forms of conventional political behavior—except voting. These findings clearly contradict the idea that Americans are politically apathetic.

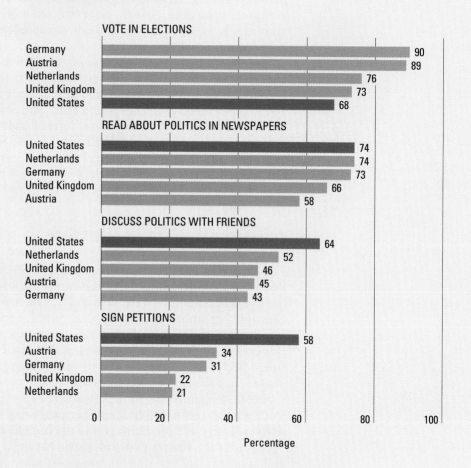

VOTE IN ELECTIONS

Country	
Germany	90
Austria	89
Netherlands	76
United Kingdom	73
United States	68

READ ABOUT POLITICS IN NEWSPAPERS

Country	
United States	74
Netherlands	74
Germany	73
United Kingdom	66
Austria	58

DISCUSS POLITICS WITH FRIENDS

Country	
United States	64
Netherlands	52
United Kingdom	46
Austria	45
Germany	43

SIGN PETITIONS

Country	
United States	58
Austria	34
Germany	31
United Kingdom	22
Netherlands	21

Percentage

Expansion of Suffrage

The United States was the first country to provide for general elections of representatives through "mass" suffrage, but the franchise was far from universal. When our Constitution was framed, the idea of full adult suffrage was too radical to be considered seriously, much less adopted. Instead, the framers left the issue of enfranchisement to the states, stipulating only that individuals who could vote for "the most numerous

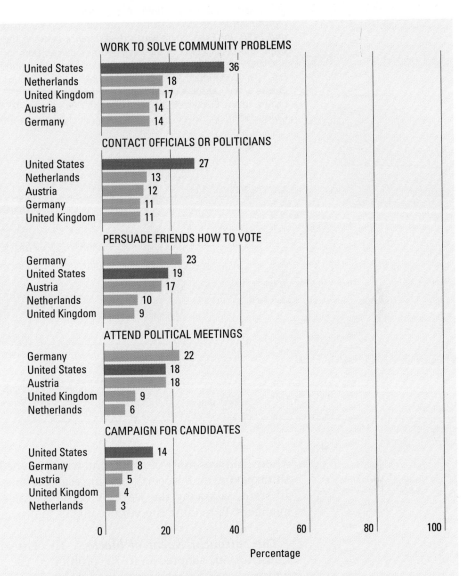

WORK TO SOLVE COMMUNITY PROBLEMS

United States	36
Netherlands	18
United Kingdom	17
Austria	14
Germany	14

CONTACT OFFICIALS OR POLITICIANS

United States	27
Netherlands	13
Austria	12
Germany	11
United Kingdom	11

PERSUADE FRIENDS HOW TO VOTE

Germany	23
United States	19
Austria	17
Netherlands	10
United Kingdom	9

ATTEND POLITICAL MEETINGS

Germany	22
United States	18
Austria	18
United Kingdom	9
Netherlands	6

CAMPAIGN FOR CANDIDATES

United States	14
Germany	8
Austria	5
United Kingdom	4
Netherlands	3

Percentage

Source: Samuel H. Barnes and Max Kaase, eds., *Political Action: Mass Participation in Five Western Democracies* (Beverly Hills, Calif.: Sage, 1979), pp. 541–542.

Branch of the State Legislature" could also vote for their representatives to the U.S. Congress (Article I, Section 2).

Initially, most states established taxpaying or property-holding requirements for voting, limiting political equality. Virginia, for example, required ownership of 25 acres of settled land or 500 acres of unsettled land. The original thirteen states began to lift these kinds of requirements after 1800. Expansion of the franchise accelerated after 1815, with the admission of new "western" states (Indiana, Illinois, Alabama),

FIGURE 7.2   *Voter Registration in the South, 1960, 1980, and 1988*

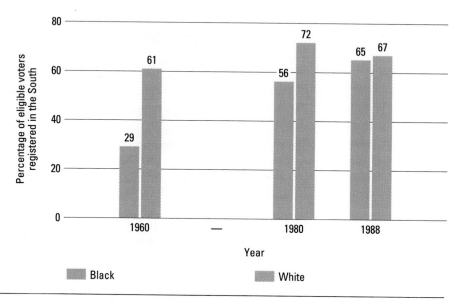

As a result of the Voting Rights Act of 1965 and other federal actions, black voter registration in the eleven states of the old Confederacy nearly doubled between 1960 and 1980. By 1988, there was little difference between the voting registration rates of white and black voters in the deep South. (Sources: Data for 1960 and 1980 are from the Bureau of the Census, Statistical Abstract of the United States, 1982–1983 *[Washington, D.C.: U.S. Government Printing Office, 1983], p. 488; data for 1988 are computed from the Bureau of the Census,* Current Population Reports, Series P-20, No. 440, Voting and Registration in the Election of November 1988 *[Washington, D.C.: U.S. Government Printing Office, 1989], pp. 36–40.)*

where land was more plentiful and widely owned. By the 1850s, virtually all taxpaying and property-holding requirements had been eliminated in all states, allowing the working class to vote—at least its white male members. Extending the vote to blacks and women took more time.

The enfranchisement of blacks.   The Fifteenth Amendment to the Constitution, adopted in 1870, prohibited the states from denying the right to vote "on account of race, color, or previous condition of servitude." However, the southern states of the old Confederacy worked around the amendment by re-establishing restrictive requirements (poll taxes, literacy tests) that worked against blacks. Some southern states also cut blacks out of politics through a cunning circumvention of the amendment. The amendment said nothing about voting rights in private organizations, so blacks were denied the right to vote in the "private" Democratic *primary* elections held to choose the party's candidates for the general election. Because the Democratic party came to dominate politics in the South, the "white primary" effectively disenfranchised blacks despite the Fifteenth Amendment. Finally, in many areas of the South, the threat of violence kept blacks from the polls.

The extension of full voting rights to blacks came in two phases, separated by twenty years. In 1944, the Supreme Court decided in *Smith* v.

Allwright that laws preventing blacks from voting in primary elections were unconstitutional, holding that party primaries are part of the continuous process of electing public officials.[28] The Voting Rights Act of 1965, which followed Selma's Bloody Sunday by less than five months, suspended discriminatory voting tests against blacks. The act also authorized federal registrars to register voters in seven southern states, where fewer than half of the voting-age population had registered to vote in the 1964 election. For good measure, in 1966 the Supreme Court ruled in *Harper* v. *Virginia State Board of Elections* that state poll taxes are unconstitutional.[29] Although long in coming, these actions by the national government to enforce political equality within the states dramatically increased the registration of southern blacks (see Figure 7.2).

The enfranchisement of women.

The enfranchisement of women in the United States is a less sordid story, but nothing to be proud of. Women had to fight long and hard to win the right to vote. Until 1869, women could not vote anywhere—in the United States or in the world.[30] Women began to organize to obtain suffrage in the mid-1800s. Known then as *suffragettes,* these early feminists initially had a limited impact on politics. Their first victory did not come until 1869, when Wyoming, while still a territory, granted women the right to vote. No state followed suit until 1893, when Colorado enfranchised women.

In the meantime, the suffragettes became more active. In 1884, they formed the Equal Rights party and nominated Belva A. Lockwood, a lawyer who could not herself vote, as the first woman candidate for president.[31] Between 1896 and 1918, twelve other states gave women the vote. Most of these states were in the West, where pioneer women often departed from traditional women's roles. Nationally, the women's suffrage movement intensified, often resorting to unconventional political be-

The Fights for Women's Suffrage . . . and Against It

Young people and minorities are not the only groups who have resorted to unconventional means of political participation. In the late 1800s and early 1900s, women marched and demonstrated for equal voting rights, sometimes encountering strong opposition. Their gatherings were occasionally disrupted by men—and other women— who opposed extending the right to vote to women.

haviors (marches, demonstrations), which occasionally invited violent attacks from men and even other women. In June 1919, Congress finally passed the Nineteenth Amendment to the Constitution, which prohibits states from denying the right to vote "on account of sex." The amendment was ratified in August 1920, in time for the November election.

Evaluating the expansion of suffrage in America. The last major expansion of suffrage in the United States took place in 1971, when the Twenty-sixth Amendment to the Constitution lowered the voting age to eighteen. For most of its history, then, the United States has been far from the democratic ideal of universal suffrage. Voting rights were initially restricted to white male taxpayers or property owners, and wealth requirements lasted until the 1850s. Through demonstrations and a constitutional amendment, women won the franchise just seventy years ago. Through civil war, constitutional amendments, court actions, massive demonstrations, and congressional action, blacks finally achieved full voting rights only twenty-five years ago. Our record has more than a few blemishes.

But compared with other countries, the United States looks pretty democratic.[32] Women did not gain the vote on equal terms with men until 1921 in Norway; 1922 in the Netherlands; 1944 in France; 1946 in Italy, Japan, and Venezuela; 1948 in Belgium; and not until 1971 in Switzerland. It is difficult to compare the enfranchisement of minority racial groups because most other democratic nations do not have this kind of racial division. We should, however, note that the indigenous Maori population in New Zealand won suffrage in 1867, but the aborigines in Australia were not fully enfranchised until 1961. And, of course, in notoriously undemocratic South Africa, blacks have no voting rights at all—even though they outnumber whites by more than four to one. With regard to voting age, nineteen of twenty-seven countries that allow free elections also have a minimum voting age of eighteen (none has a lower age), and eight have higher age requirements.

When it is judged against the rest of the world, then, the United States—which launched mass participation in government through elections—has as good a record of providing for political equality in voting rights as other democracies, and a better record than many.

Voting on Policies

Disenfranchised groups have struggled to gain voting rights because of the political power that comes with suffrage. Belief in the ability of ordinary citizens to make political decisions and to control government through the power of the ballot box was strongest in the United States during the Progressive Era, which began around 1900 and lasted until about 1925. **Progressivism** was a philosophy of political reform that trusted the goodness and wisdom of individual citizens and distrusted "special interests" (railroads, corporations) and political institutions (traditional political parties, legislatures).

The leaders of the progressive movement were prominent politicians (former president Theodore Roosevelt, Senator Robert La Follette of Wisconsin) and eminent scholars (historian Frederick Jackson Turner, philosopher John Dewey). Not content to vote for candidates chosen by party leaders, the Progressives championed the **direct primary**—a preliminary election, run by the state government, in which the voters choose the party's candidates for the general election. Wanting a mechanism to remove elected candidates from office, the Progressives backed the **recall**—a special election initiated by petition signed by a specified number of voters. Although about twenty states provide for recall elections, this device is rarely used. Only a handful of statewide elected officials have actually been unelected through recall.[33]

Progressives also relied on the voting power of the masses to propose and pass laws, thus approximating direct democracy—citizen participation in policymaking. They developed two voting mechanisms for policymaking that are still in use:

- A **referendum** is a direct vote by the people either on a proposed law or on an amendment to the state constitution. The issues subject to vote are known as **propositions.** About twenty-five states permit popular referenda on laws, and all but Delaware require a referendum on constitutional amendments. Most referenda are placed on the ballot by legislatures, not voters.

- The **initiative** is a procedure by which voters can propose an issue to be decided by the legislature or by the people in a referendum. The procedure involves gathering a specified number of signatures from registered voters (usually 5 to 10 percent of the total in the state), then submitting the petition to a designated state agency. About twenty states currently provide for some form of voter initiative.

The westward spread of these democratic mechanisms across the nation is shown in Figure 7.3. One scholar estimates that there have been more than 17,000 referenda since 1898 and over 2,300 between 1968 and 1978 alone.[34] There were almost 250 state issues on the ballots in each general election during the 1980s, although relatively few (usually less than 50) got there by the initiative.[35] In the 1990 election, however, citizens placed at least 67 initiatives on state ballots, the largest number since 1932.[36]

At times, the initiatives that citizens propose and approve are strongly opposed by politicians. A prominent example is Proposition 13, a proposal submitted to California voters in 1978. The law was designed to cut property taxes and drastically reduce government expenditures. Proposition 13 was opposed by most of the state's political, business, educational, communications, and labor leaders, and was heavily attacked in the media. But the voters passed it by a landslide margin, 65 percent to 35 percent. Another example is the electorate voting in 1990 to limit the tenure of elected officials in Oklahoma, Colorado, and California. A referendum can also work to the advantage of politicians, freeing them from taking sides on a hot issue. In 1990, voters in Arizona rejected a state holiday to honor Dr. Martin Luther King, Jr., and prochoice forces won on ballot initiatives regarding abortion in Oregon and Nevada.[37]

What conclusion can we draw about the Progressives' legacy of mechanisms for direct participation in government? One scholar who studied the use of the initiative and referendum paints an unimpressive picture.

FIGURE 7.3 *Westward Ho!*

This map shows quite clearly the westward expansion of the initiative, referendum, and recall mechanisms that were intended to place government power directly in the hands of the people. Advocates of "direct legislation" sought to bypass entrenched powers in state legislatures. They were dismissed as radicals and cranks by established groups and parties in the East, but they gained the support of farmers and miners in the Midwest and West. In most of these states, these progressive forces usually aligned with Democrats in the legislatures to enact their proposals, often against Republican opposition. (Source: Thomas E. Cronin, Direct Democracy: The Politics of Initiative, Referendum, and Recall *[Cambridge, Mass.: Harvard University Press, 1989], p. 47. Used by permission.)*

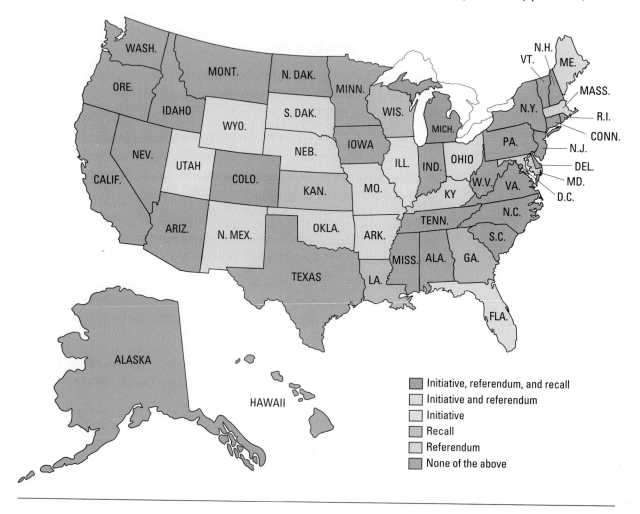

He notes that an expensive "industry" developed in the 1980s that makes money circulating petitions, then managing the large sums of money needed to run a campaign to approve (or defeat) a referendum.[38] In 1990, various industries conducted a $10 million campaign to defeat "Big Green," a sweeping environmental initiative that would have imposed restrictions on offshore drilling, pesticide use, and air pollutants.[39] The money required to mount a statewide campaign has increased the involvement of special interest groups in referendum politics. Moreover, most voters confess they do not know enough about most ballot propositions to vote intelligently on them. The 1990 election in California contained seventeen initiatives and constitutional amendments that were described in a ballot pamphlet more than 200 pages long.[40] Although another major study concluded that direct democracy devices "worked better at the state and local levels than most people realize," the study also proposed fourteen safeguards "to ensure that they serve the larger and longer-term public interest" at the state and local levels.[41] Noting that the United States was one of the few democracies that do not permit a national referendum, the study nevertheless opposed adopting the initiative and referendum at the national level.[42]

It is clear that citizens can exercise great power over government policy through the mechanisms of the initiative and referendum. What is not clear is whether these forms of direct democracy improve on the policies made by representatives elected for that purpose.

Voting for Candidates

We have saved for last the most visible form of political participation: voting to choose candidates for public office. Voting for candidates serves democratic government in two ways. First, it allows citizens to choose the candidates they think will best serve their interests. If citizens choose candidates "like themselves" in personal traits or party affiliation, elected officials should tend to be like-minded on political issues. (Of course, if public officials really thought like most of the voters, they would automatically reflect the majority's views when making public policy. Then the majority would not have to worry about monitoring the behavior of public officials and directing their policymaking.)

Second, voting allows the people to re-elect the officials they guessed right about and to kick out those they guessed wrong about. This is a very different function from the first. It makes public officials *accountable* for their behavior through the reward-and-punishment mechanism of elections. It assumes that officeholders are motivated to respond to public opinion by the threat of electoral defeat. It also assumes that the voters (1) know what politicians are doing while they are in office, and (2) participate actively in the electoral process. We look at the factors that underlie voting choice in Chapter 9. Here, we examine Americans' reliance on the electoral process.

In national politics, voters seem content to elect just two executive officers—the president and vice president—and to trust the president to appoint a cabinet to round out his administration. But at the state and local levels, voters insist on selecting all kinds of officials. Every state elects a governor (and forty-two of them elect a lieutenant governor, too). Forty-three elect an attorney general; thirty-eight, a treasurer and a secretary of state; twenty-five, an auditor. The list goes on, down through the superintendent of education, secretary of agriculture, controller, board of education, and public utilities commissioners.[43] Elected county officials commonly include a sheriff, a treasurer, a clerk, a superintendent of schools, and a judge (often several). Even at the local level, all but about

600 of 15,300 school boards across the nation are elected.[44] Instead of trusting state and local chief executives to appoint lesser administrators (as we do for more important offices at the national level), we expect voters to choose intelligently among scores of candidates they meet for the first time on a complex ballot in the polling booth (see Feature 7.1).

In the American version of democracy, there seems to be no limit to voters' ability to make informed choices among candidates and thus to control government through voting. The reasoning seems to be that elections are good; therefore, more elections are better, and the most elections are best. By this thinking, the United States clearly has the best and most democratic government in the world because it is the undisputed champion at holding elections. The author of a study that compared elections in the United States with elections in twenty-six other democracies concluded:

> No country can approach the United States in the frequency and variety of elections, and thus in the amount of electoral participation to which its citizens have a right. No other country elects its lower house as often as every two years, or its president as frequently as every four years. No other country popularly elects its state governors *and* town mayors; no other has as wide a variety of nonrepresentative offices (judges, sheriffs, attorneys general, city treasurers, and so on) subject to election. . . . The average American is entitled to do far more electing—probably by a factor of three or four—than the citizen of any other democracy.[45]

However, we learn from Compared with What? 7.2 that the United States ranks at the bottom of twenty-seven countries in voter turnout! How do we square low voter turnout with Americans' devotion to elections as an instrument of democratic government? To complicate matters further, how do we square low voter turnout with the findings we talked about earlier, which establish the United States as the leader among five Western democratic nations in both conventional and unconventional political participation? Americans seem to participate at high levels in everything except elections.

Explaining Political Participation

As you have seen, political participation can be unconventional or conventional, can require little or much initiative, and can serve to support the government or influence its decisions. Researchers have found that people who take part in some form of political behavior often do not take part in others. For example, the same citizens who contact public officials to obtain special benefits may not vote regularly, participate in campaigns, or even contact officials about broader social issues. In fact, "particularized contacting" stands by itself as a form of participation. Because this sort of participation serves individual rather than public interests, it is not even considered *political* behavior by some people.

This section examines some factors that affect the more obvious forms of political participation, with particular emphasis on voting. Our first task is to determine how much variation there is in patterns of participation within the United States over time.

FEATURE 7.1   *If It Moves in Office, Elect it*

No other country requires its voters to make so many ballot decisions in a general election. Here is just a portion of the official ballot confronting voters in the city of Evanston at the 1990 election in Cook County, Illinois. It listed 23 different types of offices, from which voters were asked to choose 46 separate candidates from 104 lines of names. In addition, voters were presented with the names of 51 lesser judges and asked to decide, yes or no, whether "each judge shall be retained in his present position." For good measure, the ballot also contained two countywide referenda and two city referenda. Most ballots in other states are comparably complex. If citizens feel unable to vote intelligently when facing such a ballot, they can hardly be blamed.

OFFICIAL BALLOT
GENERAL ELECTION
COOK COUNTY, ILLINOIS
TUESDAY, NOVEMBER 6, 1990

FOR UNITED STATES SENATOR — VOTE FOR ONE
- REPUBLICAN — LYNN MARTIN — 35 →
- DEMOCRATIC — PAUL SIMON — 36 →

FOR GOVERNOR AND LIEUTENANT GOVERNOR — VOTE FOR ONE GROUP
- REPUBLICAN — GOVERNOR JIM EDGAR — LIEUTENANT GOVERNOR and BOB KUSTRA — 38 →
- DEMOCRATIC — GOVERNOR NEIL F. HARTIGAN — LIEUTENANT GOVERNOR and JAMES B. BURNS — 39 →
- ILLINOIS SOLIDARITY — GOVERNOR JESSIE FIELDS — LIEUTENANT GOVERNOR and MARISELLIS BROWN — 40 →

FOR ATTORNEY GENERAL — VOTE FOR ONE
- REPUBLICAN — JIM RYAN — 42 →
- DEMOCRATIC — ROLAND W. BURRIS — 43 →

FOR SECRETARY OF STATE — VOTE FOR ONE
- REPUBLICAN — GEORGE H. RYAN — 45 →
- DEMOCRATIC — JERRY COSENTINO — 46 →

FOR COMPTROLLER — VOTE FOR ONE
- REPUBLICAN — SUE SUTER — 48 →
- DEMOCRATIC — DAWN CLARK NETSCH — 49 →

FOR TREASURER — VOTE FOR ONE
- REPUBLICAN — GREG BAISE — 51 →
- DEMOCRATIC — PATRICK QUINN — 52 →

FOR TRUSTEES OF THE UNIVERSITY OF ILLINOIS — VOTE FOR THREE
- ← 27 — REPUBLICAN — SUSAN LOVING GRAVENHORST
- ← 28 — REPUBLICAN — RALPH CRANE HAHN
- ← 29 — REPUBLICAN — JOHN G. HUFTALIN
- ← 30 — DEMOCRATIC — GLORIA JACKSON BACON
- ← 31 — DEMOCRATIC — TOM LAMONT
- ← 32 — DEMOCRATIC — JOE LUCCO
- ← 33 — ILLINOIS SOLIDARITY — MARTIN C. ORTEGA

FOR REPRESENTATIVE IN CONGRESS NINTH CONGRESSIONAL DISTRICT — VOTE FOR ONE
- REPUBLICAN — HERBERT SOHN — 60 →
- DEMOCRATIC — SIDNEY R. YATES — 61 →

FOR STATE SENATOR SECOND LEGISLATIVE DISTRICT — VOTE FOR ONE
- ← 53 — REPUBLICAN — BURLEIGH A. NETZKY
- ← 54 — DEMOCRATIC — ARTHUR L. BERMAN

FOR REPRESENTATIVE IN THE GENERAL ASSEMBLY FOURTH REPRESENTATIVE DISTRICT — VOTE FOR ONE
- ← 64 — REPUBLICAN — JOAN W. BARR
- ← 65 — DEMOCRATIC — JANICE D. (JAN) SCHAKOWSKY

FOR COMMISSIONER OF THE METROPOLITAN WATER RECLAMATION DISTRICT (FULL 6 YEAR TERM) — VOTE FOR THREE
- ← 70 — REPUBLICAN — KATHLEEN S. MICHAEL
- ← 71 — REPUBLICAN — TERESA A. VALDES
- ← 72 — REPUBLICAN — ESEQUIEL "ZEKE" IRACHETA
- ← 73 — DEMOCRATIC — THOMAS S. FULLER
- ← 74 — DEMOCRATIC — FRANK EDWARD GARDNER
- ← 75 — DEMOCRATIC — KATHLEEN THERESE MEANY

FOR STATE'S ATTORNEY OF COOK COUNTY (UNEXPIRED 2 YEAR TERM) — VOTE FOR ONE
- REPUBLICAN — JOHN M. "JACK" O'MALLEY — 79 →
- DEMOCRATIC — CECIL A. PARTEE — 80 →
- HAROLD WASHINGTON — JANICE H. ROBINSON — 81 →

FOR COUNTY CLERK OF COOK COUNTY — VOTE FOR ONE
- REPUBLICAN — SAMUEL "SAM" PANAYOTOVICH — 85 →
- DEMOCRATIC — DAVID D. ORR — 86 →
- HAROLD WASHINGTON — HELDIA R. RICHARDSON — 87 →

FOR TREASURER OF COOK COUNTY — VOTE FOR ONE
- REPUBLICAN — THOMAS D. EILERS — 91 →
- DEMOCRATIC — EDWARD J. ROSEWELL — 92 →
- HAROLD WASHINGTON — CHARLES W. ALEXANDER — 93 →

FOR SHERIFF OF COOK COUNTY — VOTE FOR ONE
- REPUBLICAN — JAMES E. O'GRADY — 100 →
- DEMOCRATIC — MICHAEL F. SHEAHAN — 101 →
- ILLINOIS SOLIDARITY — WILLIAM M. PIECUCH, SR. — 102 →
- HAROLD WASHINGTON — TOMMY BREWER — 103 →

FOR SUPERINTENDENT OF EDUCATION SERVICE REGION — VOTE FOR ONE
- ← 82 — REPUBLICAN — WILLIAM C. "BILL" MICELI
- ← 83 — DEMOCRATIC — RICHARD J. MARTWICK
- ← 84 — HAROLD WASHINGTON — DOROTHY C. HOGAN

FOR ASSESSOR OF COOK COUNTY — VOTE FOR ONE
- ← 88 — REPUBLICAN — RONALD BEAN
- ← 89 — DEMOCRATIC — THOMAS C. HYNES
- ← 90 — HAROLD WASHINGTON — DONALD PAMON

FOR COMMISSIONER OF THE BOARD OF APPEALS OF COOK COUNTY — VOTE FOR TWO
- ← 94 — REPUBLICAN — CHARLES A. WILSON
- ← 95 — REPUBLICAN — GILBERT M. VEGA
- ← 96 — DEMOCRATIC — WILSON FROST
- ← 97 — DEMOCRATIC — JOSEPH BERRIOS
- ← 98 — HAROLD WASHINGTON — WILL LAWRENCE
- ← 99 — HAROLD WASHINGTON — KENNETH G. HOPKINS

FOR PRESIDENT OF THE COOK COUNTY BOARD — VOTE FOR ONE
- REPUBLICAN — ALDO A. DeANGELIS — 105 →
- DEMOCRATIC — RICHARD J. PHELAN — 106 →
- HAROLD WASHINGTON — BARBARA J. NORMAN — 107 →

FOR COUNTY COMMISSIONER OF COOK COUNTY — VOTE FOR SEVEN
- REPUBLICAN — CARL R. HANSEN — 111 →
- REPUBLICAN — MARY M. McDONALD — 112 →
- REPUBLICAN — ALLAN C. CARR — 113 →
- REPUBLICAN — RICHARD A. SIEBEL — 114 →
- REPUBLICAN — ALDO A. DeANGELIS — 115 →
- REPUBLICAN — ANGELO "SKIP" SAVIANO — 116 →
- REPUBLICAN — HERBERT T. SCHUMANN, JR. — 117 →
- DEMOCRATIC — SHEILA H. SCHULTZ — 118 →
- DEMOCRATIC — THOMAS M. O'DONNELL — 119 →
- DEMOCRATIC — PATRICIA KANE McLAUGHLIN — 120 →
- DEMOCRATIC — RICHARD J. PHELAN — 121 →
- DEMOCRATIC — ERVIN F. KOZICKI — 122 →
- DEMOCRATIC — EDWARD C. REINFRANCK — 123 →
- DEMOCRATIC — PAT CAPUZZI — 124 →

FOR JUDGE OF THE SUPREME COURT FIRST JUDICIAL DISTRICT (To fill the vacancy of the Hon. Seymour Simon) — VOTE FOR ONE
- ← 143 — REPUBLICAN — ROBERT CHAPMAN BUCKLEY
- ← 144 — DEMOCRATIC — CHARLES E. FREEMAN

FOR JUDGE OF THE SUPREME COURT FIRST JUDICIAL DISTRICT (To fill the vacancy of the Hon. Daniel P. Ward) — VOTE FOR ONE
- ← 146 — REPUBLICAN — ROBERT V. BOHARIC
- ← 147 — DEMOCRATIC — MICHAEL A. BILANDIC

FOR JUDGE OF THE APPELLATE COURT FIRST JUDICIAL DISTRICT (To fill the vacancy of the Hon. R. Eugene Pincham) — VOTE FOR ONE
- ← 149 — REPUBLICAN — MICHAEL P. TOOMIN
- ← 150 — DEMOCRATIC — JOSEPH GORDON

FOR JUDGE OF THE APPELLATE COURT FIRST JUDICIAL DISTRICT (To fill the vacancy of the Hon. William R. Quinlan) — VOTE FOR ONE
- ← 152 — REPUBLICAN — JAMES J. HEYDA
- ← 153 — DEMOCRATIC — THOMAS R. RAKOWSKI

FOR JUDGE OF THE APPELLATE COURT FIRST JUDICIAL DISTRICT (To fill the vacancy of the Hon. John J. Stamos) — VOTE FOR ONE
- ← 155 — REPUBLICAN — JOHN A. WASILEWSKI
- ← 156 — DEMOCRATIC — EDWARD J. EGAN

FOR JUDGE OF THE APPELLATE COURT FIRST JUDICIAL DISTRICT (To fill the vacancy of the Hon. John J. Sullivan) — VOTE FOR ONE
- REPUBLICAN — WARREN L. SWANSON — 157 →
- DEMOCRATIC — JILL KATHLEEN McNULTY — 158 →

FOR JUDGE OF THE APPELLATE COURT FIRST JUDICIAL DISTRICT (To fill the vacancy of the Hon. William S. White) — VOTE FOR ONE
- REPUBLICAN — LESTER A. BONAGURO — 161 →
- DEMOCRATIC — JOHN P. TULLY — 162 →

FOR JUDGE OF THE CIRCUIT COURT COOK COUNTY JUDICIAL CIRCUIT (To fill the vacancy of the Hon. Arthur J. Cieslik) — VOTE FOR ONE
- REPUBLICAN — THOMAS E. NOWINSKI — 165 →
- DEMOCRATIC — MARGARET STANTON McBRIDE — 166 →

FOR JUDGE OF THE CIRCUIT COURT COOK COUNTY JUDICIAL CIRCUIT (To fill the vacancy of the Hon. Richard J. Fitzgerald) — VOTE FOR ONE
- REPUBLICAN — GORDON S. MASH — 169 →
- DEMOCRATIC — THEMIS KARNEZIS — 170 →

FOR JUDGE OF THE CIRCUIT COURT COOK COUNTY JUDICIAL CIRCUIT (To fill the vacancy of the Hon. Jacques F. Heilingoetter) — VOTE FOR ONE
- REPUBLICAN — STEPHEN Y. BRODHAY — 173 →
- DEMOCRATIC — RICHARD J. ELROD — 174 →

FOR JUDGE OF THE CIRCUIT COURT COOK COUNTY JUDICIAL CIRCUIT (To fill the vacancy of the Hon. Frank B. Petrone) — VOTE FOR ONE
- REPUBLICAN — PAUL J. NEALIS — 177 →
- DEMOCRATIC — PHILIP L. BRONSTEIN — 178 →

FOR JUDGE OF THE CIRCUIT COURT COOK COUNTY JUDICIAL CIRCUIT (To fill the vacancy of the Hon. Richard L. Samuels) — VOTE FOR ONE
- ← 159 — REPUBLICAN — JOHN K. MADDEN
- ← 160 — DEMOCRATIC — THOMAS P. DURKIN

FOR JUDGE OF THE CIRCUIT COURT COOK COUNTY JUDICIAL CIRCUIT (To fill the vacancy of the Hon. Adam W. Stillo) — VOTE FOR ONE
- ← 163 — REPUBLICAN — MICHAEL BUCKLEY BOLAN
- ← 164 — DEMOCRATIC — JAMES PATRICK FLANNERY

FOR JUDGE OF THE CIRCUIT COURT COOK COUNTY JUDICIAL CIRCUIT OUTSIDE THE CITY OF CHICAGO (To fill the vacancy of the Hon. George M. Marovich) — VOTE FOR ONE
- ← 167 — REPUBLICAN — BERNARD CAREY
- ← 168 — DEMOCRATIC — AHMED A. PATEL

FOR JUDGE OF THE CIRCUIT COURT COOK COUNTY JUDICIAL CIRCUIT OUTSIDE THE CITY OF CHICAGO (To fill the vacancy of the Hon. Dean M. Trafelet) — VOTE FOR ONE
- ← 171 — REPUBLICAN — LORETTA C. DOUGLAS
- ← 172 — DEMOCRATIC — ROBERT A. STEVENSON

COMPARED WITH WHAT? 7.2

Voter Turnout in Democratic Nations

Americans participate as much as or more than citizens of other nations in all forms of political behavior—except voting. Voter turnout in American presidential elections ranks at the bottom of voting rates for twenty-seven countries with competitive elections. As discussed in the text, the facts are correct, but the comparison is not as damning as it appears.

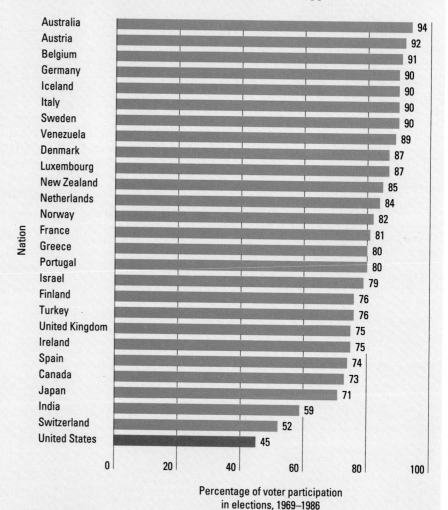

Percentage of voter participation
in elections, 1969–1986

Source: Congressional Research Service, "Voter Participation Statistics from Recent Elections in Selected Countries" (Report to Congressman Mario Biaggi, 18 November 1987).

Patterns of Participation over Time

Have Americans become more politically apathetic in the 1980s than they were in the 1960s? The answer lies in Figure 7.4, which plots several measures of participation from 1952 through 1988. The graph shows a mixed pattern of participation over the thirty-six years. Participation was *stable* across time in the percentage of citizens who worked for candidates (3 to 6 percent), who attended party meetings (6 to 9 percent), and who persuaded people how to vote during presidential election years (29 to 35 percent). Interest in campaigns even *increased* across time by 8 to 10 percentage points. Participation *decreased* over time when measured as voter turnout in presidential elections (dropping from 63 to 50 percent). The plot has thickened. Not only is voter turnout low in the United States compared with that in other countries, but turnout has declined over time. Moreover, while voting has decreased, other forms of

FIGURE 7.4 *Electoral Participation in the United States over Time*

Participation patterns over three decades show that Americans participated about as much or more in election campaigns in the 1980s as in the 1950s on every indicator except voting. The turnout rate dropped more than ten percentage points from 1952 to 1988. The drop in turnout compared with the other indicators also runs counter to the rise in educational level, constituting a puzzle that is discussed in the text. (Source: Warren E. Miller, Arthur H. Miller, and Edward J. Schneider, American National Election Studies Data Sourcebook, 1952–1978 *[Cambridge, Mass.: Harvard University Press, 1980]. Used by permission of Harvard University Press. Data after 1978 come from the National Election Studies distributed by the Inter-University Consortium for Political and Social Research.)*

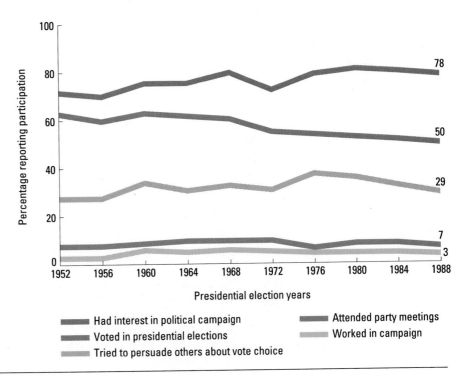

participation have increased. What is going on? Who votes? Who doesn't? Why? And does it really matter?

The Standard Socioeconomic Explanation

Researchers have found that socioeconomic status is a good indicator of most types of conventional political participation. People with more education, higher incomes, and white-collar or professional occupations tend to be more aware of the impact of politics on their lives, to know what can be done to influence government actions, and to have the necessary resources (time, money) to take action. So they are more likely to participate in politics than are people of lower socioeconomic status. This relationship between socioeconomic status and conventional political involvement is called the **standard socioeconomic model** of participation.[46]

Unconventional political behavior is less clearly related to socioeconomic status. Studies of unconventional participation in other countries have found that protest behavior is related to low socioeconomic status and especially to youth.[47] However, scattered studies of unconventional participation in the United States have found that protesters (especially blacks) are often higher in socioeconomic status than those who do not join in protests.[48]

Obviously, socioeconomic status does not account for all the differences in the ways people choose to participate in politics, even for conventional participation. Another important variable is age. As just noted, young people are more likely to take part in political protests, but they are less likely to participate in conventional politics. Voting rates tend to increase as people grow older until about age sixty-five, when physical infirmities begin to lower rates again.[49]

Two other variables—race and sex—have been related to participation in the past, but as times have changed, so have those relationships. Blacks, who had very low participation rates in the 1950s, now participate at rates comparable to whites, when differences in socioeconomic status are taken into account.[50] Women also exhibited low participation rates in the past, but sex differences in political participation have virtually disappeared.[51] (The one exception is in attempting to persuade others how to vote, which women are less likely to do than men.)[52] Recent research on the social context of voting behavior has shown that married men and women are more likely to vote than those of either sex living without spouses.[53]

Of all the social and economic variables, education is the strongest single factor in explaining most types of conventional political participation. The striking relationship between level of formal education and various types of conventional political behaviors is shown in Figure 7.5. This strong link between education and electoral participation raises questions about low voter turnout in the United States both over time and relative to other democracies. The fact is that the proportion of individuals with college degrees is greater in the United States than in other countries. Moreover, that proportion has been increasing steadily. Why, then, is voter turnout in elections so low? And why is it dropping over time?

Low Voter Turnout in America

Voting is a low-initiative form of participation that can satisfy all three motives for political participation—showing allegiance to the nation, obtaining particularized benefits, and influencing broad policy. Yet voter turnout in the United States has steadily dropped since 1960, while other forms of participation have increased. And, although Americans participate as much or more than citizens of other countries in conventional and unconventional political behaviors, they rank well below citizens of other countries in voter turnout. How do we explain the decline in voting within the United States over time and the low voter turnout in this country?

The decline in voting over time. The graph of voter turnout (Figure 7.6) shows that the sharpest drop (5 percentage points) occurred between the 1968 and 1972 elections. It was during this period (in 1971, actually) that Congress proposed and the states ratified the Twenty-sixth Amendment to the Constitution, which expanded the electorate by lowering the voting age from twenty-one to eighteen. Because people under twenty-one are much less likely to vote, they actually reduced the overall national turnout rate (the percentage of those eligible to vote who actually vote). Some observers estimate that the enfranchisement of eighteen-

FIGURE 7.5 *Effects of Education on Political Participation in 1988*

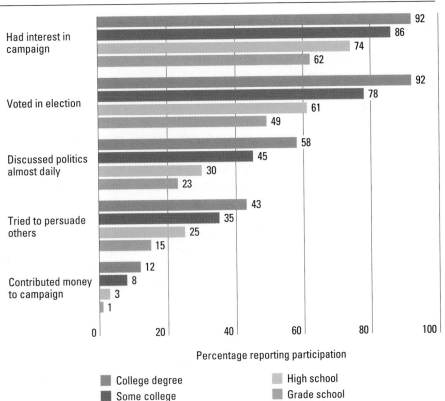

Education has a powerful effect on political participation in the United States. These data for a 1988 sample show that level of education is directly related to five different forms of conventional political participation. (Source: This analysis was based on the 1988 National Election Study distributed by the Inter-University Consortium for Political and Social Research.)

Percentage reporting participation

■ College degree   ▨ High school
■ Some college   ▨ Grade school

FIGURE 7.6   *The Decline of Voting Turnout: An Unsolved Puzzle*

Level of education is one of the strongest predictors of a person's likelihood of voting in the United States, and the percentage of citizens over 25 years of age with a high school education or more has grown steadily since the end of World War II. Nevertheless, the overall rate of voting turnout has gone down almost steadily in presidential elections since 1960. This phenomenon is recognized as an unsolved puzzle in American voting behavior. (Sources: "Percentage voting" data come from Michael Nelson, ed., Congressional Quarterly's Guide to the Presidency [Washington, D.C.: Congressional Quarterly Inc., 1989], p. 170; "percentage with four years of high school" data are for persons 25 years and older and come from the Bureau of the Census, Statistical Abstract of the United States, 1990 [Washington, D.C.: U.S. Government Printing Office, 1990], p. 133.)

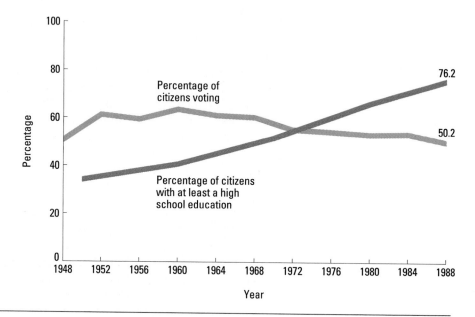

year-olds accounts for about 1 or 2 percentage points in the total decline in turnout since 1952, but that still leaves more than ten percentage points to be explained.[54]

Researchers have not been very successful in solving the puzzle of the decline in voting turnout since 1968.[55] Some scholars attribute most of the decline to changes in voters' attitudes toward politics. One major factor is the growing belief that government is not responsive to citizens and that voting doesn't do any good. Another is a change in attitude toward political parties, along with a decline in the sense of party identification.[56] According to these psychological explanations, voting turnout in the United States is not likely to increase until the government does something to restore people's faith in the effectiveness of voting—with or without political parties. According to the age explanation, turnout in the United States is destined to remain a percentage point or two below its highs in the 1960s because of the lower voting rate of citizens under twenty-one.

U.S. turnout versus turnout in other countries.   Given the high level of education in the United States and our greater than usual participation in other forms of political activity, voter turnout is much lower than might be expected compared with that in other countries. Scholars cite two factors to explain the low percentage of voters in the United States. First, there are differences in voting laws and administrative machinery.[57] In a few countries, voting is compulsory, and, obviously, turnout is extremely high. But there are other ways to encourage voting—declaring election days to be public holidays, providing a two-day voting period, making it easy to cast absentee ballots. The United States does none of these things. Moreover, nearly every other democratic country places the burden of registration on the government rather than on the individual voter.

This is very important. Voting in the United States is a two-stage process, and the first stage—going to the proper officials to register—requires more initiative than the second stage—going to the polling booth to cast a ballot. In most American states, the registration process is separated from the voting process by both time (usually weeks in advance of the election) and geography (often at the county courthouse, not the polling place). Moreover, registration procedures are often obscure and require calling around to find out what to do. Furthermore, people who move (and roughly one-third of the U.S. population moves between presidential elections) must reregister. In short, although voting requires little initiative, registration usually requires high initiative. If we compute voter turnout on the basis of those who are registered to vote, then about 87 percent of Americans vote—a figure that moves the United States to the middle (but not the top) of all democratic nations.[58]

The second factor usually cited to explain low turnout in American elections is the lack of political parties that mobilize the vote of particular social groups, especially lower-class and less-educated people. American parties do make an effort to get out the vote, but neither party is as closely linked to specific groups as parties are in many other countries, where certain parties work hand in hand with ethnic, occupational, or religious groups. Research shows that strong party-group links can significantly increase turnout.[59]

To these explanations for low voter turnout in the United States—the burden of registration and the lack of strong party-group links—we add another. Although the act of voting requires low initiative, the process of learning about the scores of candidates on the ballot in American elections requires a great deal of initiative. Some people undoubtedly fail to vote simply because they feel inadequate to the task of deciding among candidates for the many offices on the ballot in U.S. elections.

Teachers, newspaper columnists, and public affairs groups tend to worry a great deal about low voter turnout in the United States, suggesting that it signifies some sort of political sickness—or at least that it gives us a bad mark for democracy. Some others who study elections closely seem less concerned.[60] Voter turnout is only one indicator of political participation, and Americans tend to do better according to most other indicators. Moreover, one scholar argues:

> Turnout rates do not indicate the amount of electing—the frequency of occasion, the range of offices and decisions, the "value" of the vote—to which a country's citizens are entitled. . . . Thus, although the turnout rate in the

United States is below that of most other democracies, American citizens do not necessarily do less voting than other citizens; most probably, they do more.[61]

Despite these words of assurance, the nagging thought remains that turnout ought to be higher, so various organizations mount "get-out-the-vote" campaigns before elections (see Feature 7.2). Civic leaders often back these campaigns because they value voting for its contribution to political order.

Participation and Freedom, Equality, and Order

As we have seen, Americans do participate in government in a variety of ways and to a reasonable extent, compared with citizens of other countries. What is the relationship of political participation to the values of freedom, equality, and order?

Participation and Freedom

From the standpoint of normative theory, the relationship between participation and freedom is clear. Individuals should be free to participate in government and politics the way they want and as much as they want. And they should be free *not* to participate as well. Ideally, all barriers to participation (such as restrictive voting registration and limitations on campaign expenditures) should be abolished—as should any schemes for compulsory voting. According to the normative perspective, we should not worry about low voter turnout because citizens should have the freedom not to vote as well as to vote.

In theory, freedom to participate also means that individuals should be able to use their wealth, connections, knowledge, organizational power (including sheer numbers in organized protests), or any other resource to influence government decisions, provided they do so legitimately. Of all these resources, the individual vote may be the weakest—and the least important—means of exerting political influence. Obviously, then, freedom as a value in political participation favors those with the resources to advance their own political self-interest.

Participation and Equality

The relationship between participation and equality is also clear. Each citizen's ability to influence government should be equal to that of every other citizen, so that differences in personal resources do not work against the poor or otherwise disadvantaged. Elections, then, serve the ideal of equality better than any other means of political participation. Formal rules for counting ballots—in particular, one person, one vote—negate differences in resources among individuals.

At the same time, groups of people who have few individual resources can combine their votes to wield political power. This power was exercised in the late nineteenth and early twentieth century by various Euro-

FEATURE 7.2   *Madonna Raps for Democracy*

In one of the more bizarre get-out-the-vote campaigns, Madonna aired a music video on MTV before the 1990 election that was intended to encourage voting by young viewers of voting age.

Madonna

Wrapped in the flag, rapping to the beat of her hit recording "Vogue," Madonna modified the lyrics and exhorted her fans to "Vote!" Undulating in red lingerie and combat boots, she also proclaimed, "Dr. King, Malcolm X; freedom of speech is as good as sex." Her contribution to good government was part of a broader campaign by the recording industry to mobilize young voters to participate in the political process and perhaps to oppose obscenity charges against musical groups. How well did the campaign work nationwide? Voting turnout is always lower in congressional elections than presidential elections; only 18.6 percent of the eligible electorate aged 18–20 had voted in 1986, the previous nonpresidential election. Alas, in the 1990 congressional elections the turnout was even lower: Only 14 percent of the same age group voted. More significantly, the record shows that Madonna herself failed to vote.

Sources: Bureau of the Census, *Statistical Abstract of the United States, 1990* (Washington, D.C.: U.S. Government Printing Office, 1990), p. 262; 1990 figure computed from the 1990 National Election Study distributed by the Inter-University Consortium for Political and Social Research; and "Johnny B. Goody-Goody," *Newsweek*, 25 February 1991, pp. 59–60.

pean ethnic groups whose votes won them entry into the sociopolitical system and allowed them to share in its benefits (see Chapter 5). More recently, blacks, Hispanics, homosexuals, and the handicapped have used their voting power to gain political recognition. However, minorities often have had to use unconventional forms of participation to win the right to vote. As two major scholars of political participation put it, "Protest is the great equalizer, the political action that weights intensity as well as sheer numbers."[62]

Participation and Order

The relationship between participation and order is complicated. Some types of participation (pledging allegiance, voting) promote order and so are encouraged by those who value order; other types promote disorder and so are discouraged. Even giving women the right to vote was resisted by many citizens (men and women alike) for fear of upsetting the social order, of altering the traditional roles of men and women.

Both conventional and unconventional participation can lead to the ouster of government officials, but the *regime*—the political system itself—is threatened more by unconventional participation. To maintain

America's Largest Civil Rights Demonstration

On August 28, 1963, more than 200,000 blacks and whites participated in a march on Washington, D.C., to rally for jobs and freedom. Martin Luther King, Jr., one of the march's leaders, delivered his electrifying "I Have a Dream" speech from the steps of the Lincoln Memorial. The demonstrators pressed for legislation ensuring full civil rights for blacks, and their leaders were welcomed at the White House by President John F. Kennedy.

order, the government has a stake in converting unconventional participation to conventional participation whenever possible. We can easily imagine this tactic being used by authoritarian governments, but it is used by democratic governments as well.

Think about the student unrest on college campuses during the Vietnam War. In private and public colleges alike, thousands of students stopped traffic, occupied buildings, destroyed property, struck classes, disrupted lectures, staged guerrilla theater, and behaved in other unconventional ways while protesting the war, racism, capitalism, their college presidents, the president of the United States, the military establishment, and all other institutions. (We are not exaggerating here. For example, students did all these things at Northwestern University in Evanston, Illinois, after four students were killed by National Guardsmen in a demonstration at Kent State University in Ohio on May 4, 1970.)

Confronted by civil strife and disorder in the nation's institutions of higher learning, Congress took action. On March 23, 1971, it passed and sent to the states the proposed Twenty-sixth Amendment, lowering the voting age to eighteen. Three-quarters of the state legislatures had to ratify the amendment before it became part of the Constitution. Astonishingly, thirty-eight states (the required number) complied by July 1, establishing a new record for speedy ratification, cutting the old record nearly in half.[63] (Ironically, voting rights were about the only thing that students were not demanding.)

Testimony by members of Congress before the Judiciary Committee stated that the eighteen-year-old vote was needed to "harness the energy of young people and direct it into useful and constructive channels," to keep students from becoming "more militant" and engaging "in destructive activities of a dangerous nature."[64] As one observer argued, the right to vote was not extended to eighteen-year-olds because young people demanded it, but because "public officials believed suffrage expansion to be a means of institutionalizing youths' participation in politics, which would, in turn, curb disorder."[65]

Participation and the Models of Democracy

Ostensibly, elections are institutional mechanisms that implement democracy by allowing citizens to choose among candidates or issues. But elections also serve several other important purposes:[66]

- *Elections socialize political activity.* They transform what might otherwise consist of sporadic citizen-initiated acts into a routine public function. That is, the opportunity to vote for change encourages citizens to refrain from demonstrating in the streets. This helps preserve government stability by containing and channeling away potentially disruptive or dangerous forms of mass political activity.

- *Elections institutionalize access to political power.* They allow ordinary citizens to run for political office or to play an important role in selecting political leaders. Working to elect a candidate encourages the campaign worker to identify problems or propose solutions to the new official.

- *Elections bolster the state's power and authority.* The opportunity to participate in elections helps convince citizens that the government is responsive to their needs and wants, which increases its legitimacy.

Participation and Majoritarianism

Although the majoritarian model assumes that government responsiveness to popular demands comes through mass participation in politics, majoritarianism does not view participation broadly. It favors conventional, institutionalized behavior of a narrow form—primarily, voting in elections. Because majoritarianism relies on counting votes to determine what the majority wants, it is strongly biased toward political equality of citizens in political participation. Favoring collective decisions formalized through elections, majoritarianism offers little opportunity for motivated, resourceful individuals to exercise private influence over government actions.

Majoritarianism also reduces individual freedom in another way. By focusing on voting as the major means of mass participation, it narrows the scope of conventional political behavior. In this way, the mechanisms for participation in the majoritarian model restrict freedom by defining what political action is "orderly" and acceptable. By favoring equality and order in political participation, majoritarianism goes hand in hand with the ideological orientation of populism (see Chapter 1).

Participation and Pluralism

Resourceful citizens who want the government's help with problems find a haven in the pluralist model of democracy. A decentralized and organizationally complex form of government allows many points of access and is well suited to various forms of conventional participation aside from voting. For example, wealthy people and well-funded groups can afford to hire lobbyists to press their interests in Congress. In one view of pluralist democracy, citizens are free to ply and wheedle public officials to further selfish visions of the public good. From another viewpoint, pluralism offers citizens the opportunity to be treated as individuals when dealing with the government, to influence policymaking in special circumstances, and to fulfill (insofar as is possible in representative government) their social potential through participation in community affairs.

Summary

To have "government by the people," the people must participate in politics. Conventional forms of participation—contacting officials and voting in elections—come most quickly to mind. However, citizens can also participate in politics in unconventional ways—staging sit-down strikes in public buildings, blocking traffic, and so on. Most citizens disapprove of most forms of unconventional political behavior. Yet, unconventional tactics have won blacks and women important political and legal rights, including the right to vote.

People are motivated to participate in politics for various reasons: to show support for their country, to obtain particularized benefits for themselves or their friends, or to influence broad public policy. Their political actions may demand very little political knowledge or personal initiative, or a great deal of both.

The press often paints an unflattering picture of political participation in America. Clearly, the proportion of the electorate that votes in general elections in the United States is dropping and is far below that in other nations. When compared with other nations on a broad range of conventional and unconventional political behavior, however, the United States tends to show as much or more citizen participation in politics. Voter turnout in the United States suffers by comparison with that in other nations, because of differences in voter registration here and elsewhere. We also lack institutions (especially strong political parties) that increase voter registration and help bring those of lower socioeconomic status to the polls.

The tendency to participate in politics is strongly related to socioeconomic status. Education, one component of socioeconomic status, is the single strongest predictor of conventional political participation in the United States. Because of the strong effect of socioeconomic status on political participation, the political system is potentially biased toward the interests of higher-status people. Pluralist democracy, which provides many avenues for resourceful citizens to influence government decisions, tends to increase this potential bias.

Majoritarian democracy, which relies heavily on elections and the concept of one person, one vote, offers citizens without great personal resources the opportunity to control government decisions through elections. However, elections also serve to legitimize government simply by involving the masses in government through voting. Whether or not the vote means anything depends on the nature of the voters' choices in elections. The range of choice is a function of the nation's political parties, the topic of the next chapter.

KEY TERMS

election
political participation
conventional
   participation
unconventional
   participation
direct action
supportive behavior
influencing behavior
class-action suit
voting

suffrage
franchise
progressivism
direct primary
recall
referendum
proposition
initiative
standard socioeconomic
   model

SELECTED READINGS

Cloward, Richard, and Frances Fox Piven. *Why Americans Don't Vote.* New York: Pantheon, 1988. An in-depth analysis of voting and registration regulations that exclude citizens from voting.

Conway, M. Margaret. *Political Participation in the United States,* 2d ed. Washington, D.C.: Congressional Quarterly Press, 1990. An excellent review of survey data on conventional political participation.

Cronin, Thomas E. *Direct Democracy: The Politics of Initiative, Referendum, and Recall.* Cambridge, Mass.: Harvard University Press, 1989. A sweeping study of three mechanisms of direct democracy; the data come from a national survey of citizens commissioned specifically for this study.

Dalton, Russell J. *Citizen Politics in Western Democracies.* Chatham, N.J.: Chatham House, 1988. Studies public opinion and behavior in the United States, Britain, Germany, and France. Two chapters compare conventional citizen action and protest politics in these countries.

Gant, Michael M., and Norman R. Luttbeg. *American Electoral Behavior: 1952–1988.* Itasca, Ill.: F. E. Peacock, 1991. Chapter 3 provides a concise, up-to-date analysis of trends in political participation in the United States.

Ginsberg, Benjamin. *Politics by Other Means: The Declining Importance of Elections in America.* New York: Basic Books, 1990. Contends that a deadlock has occurred in the electoral arena and that po-litical struggles have been waged outside of elections.

Jennings, M. Kent, Jan W. van Deth, et al. *Continuities in Political Action: A Longitudinal Study of Political Orientations in Three Western Democracies.* New York: Walter de Gruyter, 1990. The three democracies are the United States, West Germany, and the Netherlands. This study also compares political participation across time, drawing on panel studies in the 1970s and the 1980s.

LeMay, Michael C. *The Struggle for Influence: The Impact of Minority Groups on Politics and Public Policy in the United States.* Lanham, Md.: University Press of America, 1985. The subtitle describes it well; the book discusses women and religious groups as well as virtually all racial and European ethnic groups.

Marone, James A. *The Democratic Wish: Popular Participation and the Limits of American Government.* New York: Basic Books, 1990. A reflective study arguing that in their search for more direct democracy, Americans have built up a weaker but more bureaucratic and intrusive government.

Sharp, Elaine B. *Citizen Demand-Making in the Urban Context.* University, Ala.: University of Alabama Press, 1986. The author interviewed thousands of residents of Kansas City, Missouri, about their contacts with local government.

Teixeira, Ruy A. *Why Americans Don't Vote: Turnout Decline in the United States, 1960–1984.* New York: Greenwood Press, 1987. A quantitative study of the demographic and political factors that explain voter turnout.

Verba, Sidney, and Norman H. Nie. *Participation in America: Political Democracy and Social Equality.* New York: Harper & Row, 1972. An analysis of data from surveys of citizens and political leaders; one of the classic studies of political participation.

Zimmerman, Joseph F. *Participatory Democracy: Populism Revived.* New York: Praeger, 1986. A comprehensive review of the town meeting and the mechanisms (referendum, initiative, recall) that approximate direct democracy.

8 POLITICAL PARTIES

HE WAS THE EXCEPTION that proved the rule. Bernard Sanders, the self-styled socialist from Vermont, was the only candidate elected to the U.S. House of Representatives in 1990 who was neither a Democrat nor a Republican. Moreover, he was the only one out of 535 members of the House and Senate serving in the 101st Congress who did not belong to one of those two parties. Furthermore, when he entered the House in 1991, he was the only member elected in *thirty-eight years* who did not join one of the two party groupings in the House. Bernard Sanders, the lonely socialist, proved the rule that party politics in the United States is two-party politics. And the two parties are the Democrats and the Republicans.

Since the end of World War II, fewer than ten members have served in either chamber who did not join either the Democratic or Republican parties. In the Senate, there were three: Wayne Morse (Independent-Oregon) serving in the 1950s, James Buckley (Conservative-New York) in the 1970s, and Harry F. Byrd (Independent-Virginia) in the 1970s and early 1980s. Preceding Sanders in the much larger House, there were only four: Vito Macantonio (Labor-New York) and Merlin Hull (Progressive-Wisconsin) in the 1940s, Henry Frazier Reams (Independent-Ohio) in the 1950s, and Joe Moakley (Independent-Massachusetts) in the early 1970s. Moakley, however, was invited into the Democratic Caucus (the House party organization) when he promised to run as a Democrat in future elections.[1] Even including Moakley, out of approximately 10,000 individual elections to the House and Senate since 1946, fewer than one-tenth of 1 percent were won by the candidate of a minor party who then represented that party in the chamber.

Sanders described himself as a socialist with a small *s*, but he had been one of three presidential electors representing the Socialist Workers' party in 1980. Nevertheless, he always ran for office as an independent, and he was elected mayor of Burlington, Vermont's largest city, five times from 1981 through 1989. In his House campaign, he announced "disgust with Republican-Democratic corporate-dominated politics" and drew support for his fight against "the establishment."[2] After his election, Sanders said that he hoped to participate in the Democratic Party Caucus. However, he was denied admission because he refused to join the party. As a Democrat, Sanders would have been able to vote in leadership elections, accrue seniority, and eventually serve as a committee chair under Democratic control of the House. After Representative Moakley joined the Democrats, he advanced under the two-party system to chair the House Rules Committee. Of Sanders, Moakley simply said that he "will not be allowed in the Democratic Caucus because he is not a Democrat."[3]

The Democratic and Republican parties have dominated national and state politics in the United States for more than 125 years. Their domination is more complete than that of any other pair of parties in any other democratic government. Indeed, very few democracies even have a two-party system (Britain and New Zealand being the most notable exceptions; see Compared with What? 8.1)—although all have some form of multiparty politics. Most people take our two-party system for granted, not realizing that it is perhaps the most unique aspect of American government. Why do we have political parties? What functions do

Party of One

In 1990, independent candidate Bernard Sanders ran against a Republican incumbent and a Democratic challenger for Vermont's sole seat in the House of Representatives. Sanders, a self-described socialist and former mayor of Burlington, won 56 percent of the vote on an antiparty, anti-establishment campaign. Not only did he defeat the candidates of both major parties, he became the first truly independent candidate elected to the House since Henry Frazier Reams in 1952.

they perform? How did we become a nation of Democrats and Republicans? Do these parties truly differ in their platforms and behavior? Are parties really necessary for democratic government, or do they just interfere in the relationship between citizens and government? In this chapter, we answer these questions with an examination of political parties, perhaps the most misunderstood element in American politics.

Political Parties and Their Functions

According to democratic theory, the primary means by which citizens control their government is voting in free elections. Most Americans agree that voting is important: Of those surveyed after a recent presidential campaign, 86 percent felt that elections made the government "pay attention to what the people think."[4] However, Americans are not nearly as supportive of the role played by political parties in elections. An overwhelming majority (73 percent) surveyed in 1980 believed that "the best way to vote is to pick a candidate regardless of party label." A clear majority (56 percent) thought that "parties do more to confuse the issues than to provide a clear choice on issues." In fact, 49 percent took the extreme position: "It would be better if in all elections, we put no party labels on the ballot."[5]

On the other hand, Americans are quick to condemn as "undemocratic" countries that do not hold elections contested by political parties. In truth, Americans have a love-hate relationship with political parties. They believe that parties are necessary for democratic government; at the same time, they think parties are somehow "obstructionist" and not to be trusted. This distrust is particularly strong among younger voters. To better appreciate the role of political parties in democratic government, we must understand exactly what parties are and what they do.

COMPARED WITH WHAT?   8.1

Only Two to Tangle

Compared with other countries, the two-party system in the United States is very unusual indeed. First of all, most democracies have multiparty systems, in which four or five parties win enough seats in the legislature to contest for governmental power. Even those countries classified as having two-party systems, such as the United Kingdom and New Zealand, really have some minor parties that regularly gain seats and thus complicate governmental politics. The purity of the U.S. pattern shows clearly in these graphs of party strength over time in the U.S. House compared with the British House of Commons and the New Zealand House of Representatives.*

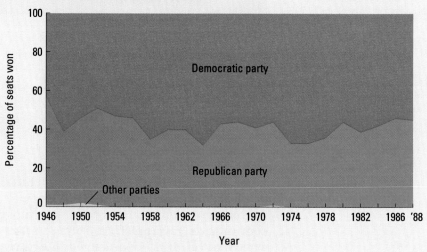

* In the New Zealand graph, data for the New Zealand Democratic party, formed in 1985 to succeed the Social Credit party, have been included as part of the Social Credit party segment.

Definitions

A **political party** is an organization that sponsors candidates for political office *under the organization's name.* The italicized part of this definition is important. True political parties **nominate** candidates for election to public office by designating individuals as official candidates of the party. This function distinguishes the Democratic and Republican

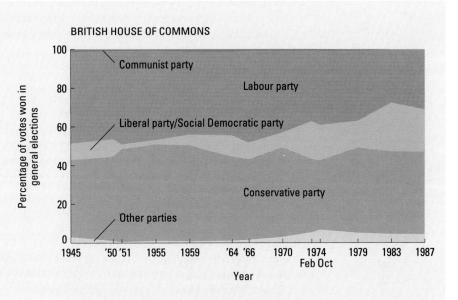

BRITISH HOUSE OF COMMONS

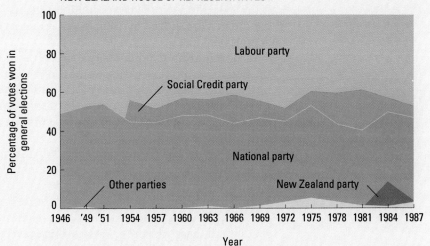

NEW ZEALAND HOUSE OF REPRESENTATIVES

Source: Dick Leonard, *World Atlas of Elections* (London: The Economist Publications, 1986), pp. 102 and 130. Used by permission.

parties from interest groups. The AFL-CIO and the National Association of Manufacturers are interest groups. They often support candidates in various ways, but they do not nominate them to run as their avowed representatives. If they do, the interest groups become transformed into political parties. In short, it is the giving and accepting of a political label by organization and candidate that defines an organization as a party.

Most democratic theorists agree that a modern nation-state could not practice democracy without at least two political parties that regularly contest elections. (All nineteen countries rated democracies in Chapter 2 have at least two competing parties.) In fact, the link between democracy and political parties is so close that many people define democratic government in terms of competitive party politics.

Party Functions

Parties contribute to democratic government through the functions they perform for the **political system**—the set of interrelated institutions that links people with government. Four of the most important party functions are nominating candidates for election to public office, structuring the voting choice in elections, proposing alternative government programs, and coordinating the actions of government officials.

Nominating candidates.   Political parties contribute to democratic government simply by nominating candidates for election to public office. In the absence of parties, voters would be confronted with a bewildering array of self-nominated candidates, each seeking a narrow victory over others on the basis of personal friendships, celebrity status, or name. Parties can provide a form of quality control for their nominees through the process of *peer review*. Party insiders, the nominees' peers, usually know potential candidates much better than the average voter does, and candidates are judged by their peers for acceptability as the party's representatives.

In nominating candidates, parties often do more than pass judgment on potential office seekers; sometimes they go so far as to recruit talented individuals to become party candidates. In this way, parties help not only to ensure a minimum level of quality among candidates who run for office but also to raise the quality of those candidates.

Structuring the voting choice.   Political parties also help democratic government by structuring the voting choice—reducing the number of candidates on the ballot to those who have a realistic chance of winning. Established parties—those that have contested elections in the past—acquire a following of loyal voters who guarantee the party's candidates a predictable base of votes. Parties that have won sizable portions of the vote in past elections are likely to win comparable portions of the vote in future ones by mobilizing their electorate. This has the effect of discouraging nonparty candidates from running for office and new parties from forming. Consequently, the realistic choice is between candidates offered by the major parties. This choice focuses the election on the contest between parties and on candidates with established records, which reduces the amount of new information that voters need in order to make a rational decision.

Proposing alternative government programs.   Parties also help voters choose candidates by proposing alternative programs of government action—general policies that party candidates will pursue if they win control of government. Even if voters know nothing about the qualities of the parties' candidates, they can vote rationally for candidates of the party that stands closest to the policies they favor. The specific policies advocated in an election campaign vary from candidate to candidate and from election to election. However, the types of policies advocated by candidates of one party tend to differ from those proposed by candidates of other parties. Although there are exceptions, candidates of the same party tend to favor policies that fit their party's underlying political philosophy, or ideology. In many countries, party labels—such as "conservative" and "socialist"—reflect their political stance.

Although the Democrats and Republicans have issue-neutral names, many minor parties in the United States have used their names to advertise their policies: the Prohibition party, the Farmer-Labor party, and the Socialist party, for example. The neutrality of their names suggests that the two major parties are also undifferentiated in their policies. This is not true. They regularly adopt very different policies in their platforms, a fact discussed at length later.

Coordinating the actions of government officials. Finally, party organizations help coordinate the actions of public officials. A government based on the separation of powers, like that of the United States, divides responsibilities for making public policy. The president and the leaders of the House and Senate are not required to cooperate with one another. Political party organizations are the major means for bridging the separation of powers, of producing coordinated policies that can govern the country effectively. Individuals of the same party in the presidency, the House, and the Senate are likely to share political principles and thus to cooperate in making policy.

A History of U.S. Party Politics

The two major U.S. parties are among the oldest in the world. In fact, the Democratic party, founded in 1828 but with roots reaching back into the late 1700s, has a strong claim to being the oldest party in existence. Its closest rival is the British Conservative party, formed in 1832, two decades before the Republican party was organized, in 1854. Both the Democratic and Republican parties have been supported by several generations of citizens and are part of American history. They have become *institutionalized* in our political process.

The Preparty Period

Today we think of party activities as normal, even essential, to American politics. It was not always so. The Constitution makes no mention of political parties, and none existed when the Constitution was written in 1787. Instead, it was common to refer to groups pursuing some common political interest as *factions*. Although factions were seen as inevitable in politics, they were also considered dangerous. One argument for adopting the Constitution—proposed in "Federalist No. 10" (see Chapter 3 and the Appendix)—was that its federal system would prevent factional influences from controlling the government.

Factions existed even under British rule. In colonial assemblies, supporters of the governor (and thus of the Crown) were known as *Tories* or *Loyalists*, and their opponents were called *Whigs* or *Patriots*. After independence, the arguments over whether or not to adopt the Constitution produced a different alignment of factions. Those who backed the Constitution were loosely known as "federalists"; their opponents, as "antifederalists." At this stage, the groups could not be called parties because they did not sponsor candidates for election.

Elections then were vastly different from elections today. The Constitution provided for the president and vice president to be chosen by an **electoral college**—a body of electors who meet in the capitals of their respective states to cast their ballots. Initially, these electors (one for each senator and representative in Congress) were chosen by the state legislatures, not the voters. Presidential "elections" in the early years of the nation, then, actually were decided by a handful of political leaders. (See Chapter 9 for a discussion of the electoral college in modern presidential politics.) Often they met in small, secret groups, called **caucuses,** to discuss candidates for public office. And often these caucuses were held among like-minded members of state legislatures and Congress. This was the setting for George Washington's election as the first president in 1789.

We can classify Washington as a federalist because he supported the Constitution, but he was not a factional leader and actually opposed factional politics. His immense prestige coupled with his political neutrality left Washington unopposed for the office of president, and he was elected unanimously by the electoral college. During Washington's administration, however, the political cleavage sharpened between those who favored a stronger national government and those who wanted a less powerful, more decentralized national government.

The first group, led by Alexander Hamilton, proclaimed themselves *Federalists*. The second group, led by Thomas Jefferson, called themselves *Republicans*. (Although they used the same name, they were not Republicans as we know them today.) The Jeffersonians chose the name *Republicans* to distinguish themselves from the "aristocratic" tendencies of Hamilton's Federalists. The Federalists countered by calling the Republicans the *Democratic Republicans*, attempting to link Jefferson's party to the disorder (and beheadings) spawned by the "radical democrats" in France during the French Revolution of 1789.

The First Party System: Federalists and Democratic Republicans

Washington was re-elected president unanimously in 1792, but his vice president, John Adams, was opposed by a candidate backed by the Democratic Republicans. This brief skirmish foreshadowed the nation's first major-party struggle over the presidency. Disheartened by the political split in his administration, Washington spoke out against "the baneful effects" of parties in his farewell address in 1796. Nonetheless, the party concept was already firmly entrenched in the political system (see Figure 8.1).

F I G U R E 8.1 *Two-Party Systems in American History*

Over time, the American party system has undergone a series of wrenching transformations. Since 1856, the Democrats and the Republicans have alternated irregularly in power, each party enjoying a long period of dominance.

1789	*Washington unanimously elected president*			PREPARTY PERIOD	
1792	*Washington unanimously reelected*				
1796	Federalist *Adams*		Democratic Republican		
1800	—		*Jefferson*	FIRST PARTY SYSTEM	
1804	—		*Jefferson*		
1808	—		*Madison*		
1812	—		*Madison*		
1816	—		*Monroe*		
1820			*Monroe*	"ERA OF GOOD FEELING"	
1824			*J.Q. Adams*		
1828			Democratic *Jackson*	National Republican	
1832			*Jackson*	Whig	
1836	SECOND PARTY SYSTEM		*Van Buren*	—	
1840				*Harrison*	
1844			*Polk*	—	
1848			—	*Taylor*	
1852			*Pierce*	—	
1856			*Buchanan*		Republican
1860	Constitutional Union	Southern Democrat	—		*Lincoln*
1864			—		*Lincoln*
1868			—		*Grant*
1872			—		*Grant*
1876	THIRD PARTY SYSTEM		—		*Hayes*
1880			—		*Garfield*
1884			*Cleveland*		—
1888	Rough Balance		—		*Harrison*
1892			*Cleveland*		—
1896			—	Populist	*McKinley*
1900			—		*McKinley*
1904			—		*T. Roosevelt*
1908			—		*Taft*
1912	Republican Dominance		*Wilson*	Progressive	—
1916			*Wilson*		—
1920			—		*Harding*
1924			—		*Coolidge*
1928			—		*Hoover*
1932			*F.D. Roosevelt*		—
1936			*F.D. Roosevelt*		—
1940			*F.D. Roosevelt*		—
1944			*F.D. Roosevelt*		—
1948	Democratic Dominance		*Truman*	States' Rights	—
1952			—		*Eisenhower*
1956			—		*Eisenhower*
1960			*Kennedy*		—
1964			*Johnson*		—
1968			—	American Independent	*Nixon*
1972			—		*Nixon*
1976			*Carter*		—
1980			—	Independent	*Reagan*
1984			—		*Reagan*
1988			—		*Bush*

In the election of 1796, the Federalists supported Vice President John Adams to succeed Washington as president. The Democratic Republicans backed Thomas Jefferson for president but could not agree on a vice presidential candidate. In the electoral college, Adams won 71 votes to Jefferson's 68, and both ran ahead of other candidates. At that time, the Constitution provided that the presidency went to the candidate who won the most votes in the electoral college and the vice presidency went to the runner-up. So Adams, a Federalist, had to accept Jefferson, a Democratic Republican, as his vice president. Obviously, the Constitution did not anticipate a presidential contest between candidates from opposing political parties.

The party function of nominating candidates emerged more clearly in the election of 1800. Both parties caucused in Congress to nominate candidates for president and vice president.[6] The result was the first true party contest for the presidency. The Federalists nominated John Adams and Charles Pinckney; the Democratic Republicans, Thomas Jefferson and Aaron Burr. This time, the Democratic Republican candidates won. However, the new party organization worked too well. The Democratic Republican electors unanimously cast all their votes for both Jefferson and Burr. Unfortunately, the presidency had to go to the candidate with the most votes, and the top two candidates were tied.

Despite the fact that Jefferson was the party's presidential candidate and Burr its vice presidential candidate, the House of Representatives was empowered by the Constitution to choose one of them as president. After seven days and thirty-six ballots, the House decided in favor of Jefferson.

The Twelfth Amendment, ratified in 1804, prevented a repeat of the troublesome election outcomes of 1796 and 1800. It required the electoral college to vote separately for president and vice president, implicitly recognizing that presidential elections would be contested by party candidates nominated for the separate offices but running on the same ballot.

The election of 1800 marked the beginning of the end for the Federalists, who lost the next four elections. By 1820, the Federalists were no more. The Democratic Republican candidate, James Monroe, was re-elected in the first presidential contest without party competition since Washington's time. (Monroe received all but one electoral vote, which was reportedly cast against him so that Washington would remain the only president ever elected unanimously.) Ironically, the lack of partisan competition under Monroe, dubbed the "Era of Good Feelings," also signaled the beginning of the end for his party, the Democratic Republicans.

Lacking competition from another party, the Democratic Republicans neglected their function of nominating candidates. The party continued to hold a congressional caucus to nominate candidates for president, but attendance dropped off. Although a caucus was held in 1824, its nominee was challenged by three other Democratic Republicans, including John Quincy Adams and Andrew Jackson, who proved to be the most popular candidates among the voters in the ensuing election.

Prior to 1824, the parties' role in structuring the popular vote was relatively unimportant because relatively few people were entitled to vote.

But the states began to drop restrictive requirements for voting after 1800, and voting rights for white males expanded even faster after 1815 (see Chapter 7). With the expansion of suffrage, more states began allowing voters to choose presidential electors. The 1824 election was the first in which presidential electors were selected through popular vote in most states. Still, the role of political parties in structuring the popular vote had not yet developed fully.

Although Jackson won a plurality of both the popular vote and the electoral vote in 1824, he did not win the necessary majority vote in the electoral college. The House of Representatives was again required to decide the winner. It chose the second-place John Quincy Adams (from the established state of Massachusetts) over the voters' choice, Jackson (from the frontier state of Tennessee). The factionalism among the leaders of the Democratic Republican party became so intense that the party split in two.

The Second Party System: Democrats and Whigs

The Jacksonian faction of the Democratic Republican party represented the common people in the expanding South and West, and its members took pride in calling themselves, simply, *Democrats*. Jackson ran again for the presidency as a Democrat in 1828, a milestone that marked the beginning of today's Democratic party. That election was also the first "mass" election in U.S. history. Although many presidential electors had been chosen by popular vote in 1824, the total votes cast in that election numbered fewer than 370,000. By 1828, relaxed requirements for voting (and the use of popular elections to select presidential electors in more states) had increased the vote by more than 300 percent, to over 1.1 million.

As the electorate expanded, the parties changed. No longer could a few party members in Congress rely on close connections among relatively few political leaders in the state legislatures to control the votes cast in the electoral college. Parties now needed to campaign for votes cast by hundreds of thousands of citizens. Recognizing this new dimension of politics, parties responded with a new method for nominating presidential candidates.

Instead of selecting candidates in a closed caucus of party representatives in Congress, the parties devised the **national convention.** At these gatherings, delegates from state parties across the nation would choose candidates for president and vice president and adopt a statement of policies called a **party platform.** The first national convention was called in 1831 by the Anti-Masonic party, which was the first "third" party in American history to challenge the two major parties for the presidency. The Democrats adopted the convention idea in 1832 to nominate Jackson for a second term; so did their new opponents that year, the National Republicans.

The label *National Republicans* was applied to John Quincy Adams's faction of the former Democratic Republican party. However, the National Republicans did not become today's Republican party. Adams's followers called themselves *National Republicans* to signify their old Federalist preference for a strong national government, but the symbolism did not appeal to the voters, and the National Republicans lost to Jackson in 1832.

Elected to another term, Jackson began to assert the power of the nation over the states (acting more like a National Republican than a Democrat). His policies drew new opponents, who started calling him "King Andrew." A coalition made up of former National Republicans, Anti-Masons, and Jackson-haters formed the Whig party in 1834.[7] The name harked back to the English Whigs, who opposed the powers of the British throne; the implication was that Jackson was governing like a king. For the next thirty years, Democrats and Whigs alternated in the presidency. However, the issues of slavery and sectionalism eventually destroyed the Whigs. Although the party had won the White House in 1848 and had taken 44 percent of the vote in 1852, the Whigs were unable to field a presidential candidate in the 1856 election.

The Present Party System: Democrats and Republicans

In the early 1850s, antislavery forces (including Whigs, Free Soilers, and antislavery Democrats) began to organize. At meetings in Jackson, Michigan, and Ripon, Wisconsin, they recommended the formation of a new party, the Republican party, to oppose the extension of slavery into the Kansas and Nebraska territories. It is this party, founded in 1854, that continues as today's Republican party.

The Republican party contested its first presidential election in 1856. Although it was an entirely new party, it took 33 percent of the vote. Moreover, its candidate (John Fremont) carried eleven states—all in the North. Then, in 1860, the Republicans nominated Abraham Lincoln. The Democrats were deeply divided over the slavery issue and actually split into two parties. The northern wing kept the *Democratic party* label and nominated Stephen Douglas. The *Southern Democrats* ran John Breckinridge. A fourth party, the *Constitutional Union* party, nominated John Bell. Regional voting was obvious in the election of 1860. Lincoln took 40 percent of the popular vote and carried every northern state. Breckinridge won every southern state. But all three of Lincoln's opponents together still did not win enough electoral votes to deny him the presidency.

The election of 1860 is considered the first of three critical elections during the present party system.[8] A **critical election** produces a sharp change in the existing patterns of party loyalties among groups of voters. Moreover, this change in voting patterns, which is called an **electoral realignment,** does not end with the election. Instead, the altered party loyalties last through several subsequent elections.[9] The election of 1860 divided the country between the northern states, which mainly voted Republican, and the southern states, which were overwhelmingly Democratic. The victory of the North over the South in the Civil War cemented Democratic loyalties in the South, particularly following the withdrawal of federal troops after the 1876 election.

For forty years, from 1880 to 1920, no Republican presidential candidate won even one of the eleven states of the Confederacy. The South's solid Democratic record earned it the nickname the "Solid South." The

Republicans did not puncture the Solid South until 1920, when Warren G. Harding carried Tennessee. Republicans also won five southern states in 1928, when the Democrats ran the first Catholic candidate, Al Smith. Republican presidential candidates won no more southern states until 1952, when Dwight Eisenhower broke the pattern of Democratic dominance in the South—ninety years after that pattern had been set by the Civil War.

Eras of Party Dominance Since the Civil War

The critical election of 1860 established the Democratic and Republican parties as the major parties in our two-party system. In a **two-party system**, most voters are so loyal to one or the other of the major parties that candidates from a third party—which means any minor party—have little chance of winning office. When third-party candidates do win (and, as Bernard Sanders proved, occasionally they do), they are most likely to win offices at the local or state level. Since the present two-party system was established, relatively few minor-party candidates have won election to the U.S. House, very few have won election to the Senate, and *none* has won the presidency.

Although voters in most states have been divided in their loyalties between the Republicans and the Democrats, they have not always been equally divided. In some states, counties, and communities, voters favor the Republicans, while voters in other areas prefer the Democrats. When one party in a two-party system *regularly* enjoys support from most of the voters, it is called the **majority party**; the other is called the **minority party**. Over the lifetime of the present two-party system, there have been three different periods of balance between the two major parties.

A rough balance: 1860–1894. From 1860 through 1894, the Grand Old Party (or GOP, as the Republican party is sometimes called) won eight of ten presidential elections, which would seem to qualify it as the majority party. However, some of its success in presidential elections came from running Civil War heroes and from the North's domination of southern politics. Seats won in the House of Representatives are a better guide to the breadth of national support. An analysis shows that the Republicans and Democrats won the same number of congressional elections, each controlling the chamber for nine sessions between 1860 and 1894.

A Republican majority: 1896–1930. A second critical election, in 1896, transformed the Republican party into a true majority party. Grover Cleveland, a Democrat, was in the White House, and the country was in a severe economic depression. The Republicans nominated William McKinley, governor of Ohio and a conservative, who stood for a high tariff against foreign goods and sound money tied to the value of gold. Rather than tour the country seeking votes, McKinley ran a dignified campaign from his Ohio home.

The Democrats, already in trouble because of the depression, nominated the fiery William Jennings Bryan. In stark contrast to McKinley, Bryan advocated the free and unlimited coinage of silver—which meant

William Jennings Bryan: When Candidates Were Orators

Today, televised images of a candidate waving his hands and shouting to an audience would look silly. But candidates once had to resort to such tactics to be effective with large crowds. One of the most commanding orators around the turn of the century was William Jennings Bryan (1860–1925), whose stirring speeches extolling the virtues of the free coinage of silver were music to the ears of thousands of westerners and southern farmers.

cheap money and easy payment of debts through inflation. Bryan was also nominated by the young Populist party, an agrarian protest party that had proposed the free-silver platform that Bryan adopted. (The book *The Wonderful Wizard of Oz*, which you probably know as a movie, was actually a Populist political fable; see Feature 8.1.)[10] Conservatives, especially businesspeople, were aghast at the Democrats' radical turn, and voters in the heavily populated Northeast and Midwest surged toward the Republican party—many of them permanently.[11] McKinley carried every northern state east of the Mississippi (see Figure 8.2). The Republicans also won the House and continued to control it for the next six elections.

The election of 1896 helped solidify the Republican majority in industrial America and forged a link between the Republican party and business. In the subsequent electoral realignment, the Republicans emerged as a true majority party. The GOP dominated national politics—controlling the presidency, the Senate, and the House—almost continuously from 1896 until the Wall Street crash of 1929, which burst big business's bubble and launched the Great Depression.*

A Democratic majority: 1932 to the present.   The Republicans' majority status ended in the critical election of 1932 between incumbent president Herbert Hoover and the Democratic challenger, Franklin Delano Roosevelt. Roosevelt promised new solutions to unemployment and the economic crisis of the Depression. His campaign appealed to labor, middle-class liberals, and new European ethnic voters. Along with Democratic voters in the Solid South, urban workers in the North, Catholics,

---

* The sole exception came in 1912, when Teddy Roosevelt's Progressive party split from the Republicans, allowing Democrat Woodrow Wilson to win the presidency and giving the Democrats control of Congress.

F E A T U R E 8.1   *The Wizard of Oz: A Political Fable*

Most Americans are familiar with *The Wizard of Oz* through the children's books or the 1939 motion picture, but few realize that the story was written as a political fable to promote the Populist movement around the turn of the century. Next time you see or read it, try interpreting the Tin Woodsman as the industrial worker, the Scarecrow as the struggling farmer, and the Wizard as the president, who is powerful only as long as he succeeds in deceiving the people. (Sorry, but in the book Dorothy's ruby slippers were only silver shoes.)

The Wonderful Wizard of Oz was written by Lyman Frank Baum in 1900, during the collapse of the Populist movement. Through the Populist party, Midwestern farmers, in alliance with some urban workers, had challenged the banks, railroads, and other economic interests that squeezed farmers through low prices, high freight rates, and continued indebtedness.

The Populists advocated government ownership of railroads, telephone, and telegraph industries. They also wanted silver coinage. Their power grew during the 1893 depression, the worst in U.S. history until then, as farm prices sank to new lows and unemployment was widespread. . . .

In the 1894 congressional elections, the Populist party got almost 40 percent of the vote. It looked forward to winning the presidency, and the silver standard, in 1896. But in that election, which revolved around the issue of gold versus silver, Populist Democrat William Jennings Bryan lost to Republican William McKinley by 95 electoral votes. Bryan, a congressman from Nebraska and a gifted orator, ran again in 1900, but the Populist strength was gone.

Baum viewed these events in both rural South Dakota—where he edited a local weekly— and urban Chicago—where he wrote *Oz*. He mourned the destruction of the fragile alliance between the Midwestern farmers (the Scarecrow) and the urban industrial workers (the Tin Woodsman). Along with Bryan (the Cowardly Lion with a roar but little else), they had been taken down the yellow brick road (the gold standard) that led nowhere. Each journeyed to Emerald City seeking favors from the Wizard of Oz (the President). Dorothy, the symbol of Everyman, went along with them, innocent enough to see the truth before the others.

Along the way they meet the Wicked Witch of the East who, Baum tells us, had kept the little Munchkin people "in bondage for many years, making them slave for her night and day." She also had put a spell on the Tin Woodsman, once an independent and hardworking man, so that each time he swung his axe, it chopped off a different part of his body. Lacking another trade, he "worked harder than ever," becoming like a machine, incapable of love, yearning for a heart. Another witch, the Wicked Witch of the West, clearly symbolizes the large industrial corporations.

. . . The small group heads toward Emerald City where the Wizard rules from behind a papier-mâché facade. Oz, by the way, is the abbreviation for ounce, the standard measure for gold.

Like all good politicians, the Wizard can be all things to all people. Dorothy sees him as an enormous head. The Scarecrow sees a gossamer fairy. The Woodsman sees an awful beast, the Cowardly Lion "a ball of fire so fierce and glowing he could scarcely bear to gaze upon it."

Later, however, when they confront the Wizard directly, they see he is nothing more than "a little man, with a bald head and a wrinkled face."

"I have been making believe," the Wizard confesses. "I'm just a common man." But the Scarecrow adds, "You're more than that . . . you're a humbug."

"It was a great mistake my ever letting you into the Throne Room," admits the Wizard, a former ventriloquist and circus balloonist from Omaha.

This was Baum's ultimate Populist message. The powers-that-be survive by deception. Only people's ignorance allows the powerful to manipulate and control them. Dorothy returns to Kansas with the magical help of her Silver Shoes (the silver issue), but when she gets to Kansas she realizes her shoes "had fallen off in her flight through the air, and were lost forever in the desert." Still, she is safe at home with Aunt Em and Uncle Henry, simple farmers.

Source: Peter Dreier, *Today Journal*, 14 February 1986, p. 11. Copyright © Pacific News Service. Reprinted by permission.

FIGURE 8.2   *The Critical Election of 1896*

In the presidential election of 1896, voters in the populous and industrial East and Midwest elected Republican William McKinley (who was probusiness) over Democrat William Jennings Bryan (advocate of the rural West and South). The Republicans emerged as the majority party in national elections following this election.

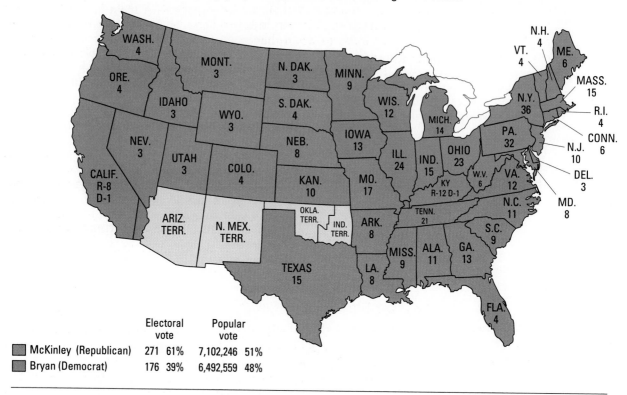

	Electoral vote		Popular vote	
McKinley (Republican)	271	61%	7,102,246	51%
Bryan (Democrat)	176	39%	6,492,559	48%

Jews, and white ethnic minorities formed the "Roosevelt coalition." (The relatively few blacks who voted at that time tended to remain loyal to the Republicans—the "party of Lincoln.")

Roosevelt was swept into office in a landslide, carrying huge majorities into the House and Senate to enact his liberal activist programs. The electoral realignment prompted by the election of 1932 made the Democrats the majority party. Not only was Roosevelt re-elected in 1936, 1940, and 1944, but Democrats held control of both houses of Congress from 1933 through 1980—interrupted by only two years of Republican control in 1953 and 1954, during the Eisenhower administration. Moreover, at the state level, the Democrats have held about 60 percent or more of the total legislative seats and have controlled about two-thirds or more of the chambers through the 1990 election.

In presidential elections, however, the Democrats have not fared so well since Roosevelt. In fact, they have won only four elections (Truman, Kennedy, Johnson, and Carter), compared with the Republicans, who have won seven times (Eisenhower twice, Nixon twice, Reagan twice, and Bush once). In Reagan's stunning election in 1980, Republicans wrested control of the Senate from the Democrats for the first time since 1954 but lost it after the 1986 election.

There are strong signs that the coalition of Democratic voters forged by Roosevelt in the 1930s has already cracked. Certainly the South is no longer solid for the Democrats. Since 1952, in fact, it has voted more consistently for Republican presidential candidates than for Democrats. The party system in the United States does not seem to be undergoing another realignment; rather, we seem to be in a period of **electoral de-alignment,** in which party loyalties have become less important in the decisions of voters when they cast their ballots. We examine the influence of party loyalty on voting in the next chapter, after we study the operation of our two-party sytem.

The American Two-Party System

Our review of party history has focused on the major parties competing for presidential office. But we should not ignore the special contributions of certain minor parties, among them the Anti-Masonic party, the Populists, and the Progressives of 1912. In this section, we study the fortunes of minor, or third, parties in American politics. We also look at the reasons why we have just two major parties, explain how federalism helps the parties survive, and describe voters' loyalties toward the major parties today.

Minor Parties in America

Minor parties have always figured in party politics in America. In recent years, the Libertarian party, which has run candidates for president in every election since 1972, has emerged as the most active and fastest-growing minor party, claiming organizations in all fifty states.[12] The Libertarian party expounds libertarian ideology, stressing freedom over order and equality.

There are several different types of minor parties:[13]

- **Bolter parties** are formed from factions that have split off from one of the major parties. Six times in thirty presidential elections since the Civil War, disgruntled leaders have "bolted the ticket" and challenged their former parties. Bolter parties have occasionally won significant proportions of the vote. However, with the exception of Teddy Roosevelt's Progressive party in 1912 and the possible exception of George Wallace's American Independent party in 1968, bolter parties have not affected the outcome of presidential elections.

- **Farmer-labor parties** represent farmers and urban workers who believe that they, the working class, are not getting their share of society's wealth. The People's party, founded in 1892 and nicknamed the "Populist party," was a prime example of a farmer-labor party. The Populists won 8.5 percent of the vote in 1892 and also became the first third party since 1860 to win any electoral votes. Flush with success, it endorsed William Jennings Bryan, the Democratic candidate, in 1896. When he lost, the party quickly faded. Many Populist ideas were revived by farm and labor groups in the Progressive party in 1924, which nominated Robert La Follette for the presidency. Although the party won 16.6 percent of the popular vote, it carried only La Follette's home state of Wisconsin. The party died in 1925, although populist ideals—most notably a commitment to order and equality over freedom—still play a part in today's political system (see Chapter 7). To illustrate how political labels get mixed up in politics, ex–Ku Klux Klansman David E. Duke—who opposes social equality—ran for president under the Populist party banner in 1988, receiving fewer than 50,000 votes out of more than 91,000,000 cast. His antiblack platform fits more under the next category of minor parties.

- **Parties of ideological protest** go further than farmer-labor parties in criticizing the established system. These parties reject prevailing doctrines and propose radically different principles, often favoring more government activism. The Socialist party has been the most successful party of ideological protest. However, at its high point in 1912, it garnered only 6 percent of the vote, and Socialist candidates for president have never won a single state. In recent years, the sound of ideological protest has been heard more from rightist parties, arguing for the radical disengagement of government from society. Ron Paul, the Libertarian candidate in 1988, received more votes than all the leftist candidates put together, but that was still less than 1 percent of the total votes cast.

- **Single-issue parties** are formed to promote one principle, not a general philosophy of government. The Anti-Masonic parties of the 1820s and 1830s, for example, opposed Masonic lodges and other secret societies. The Free Soil party of the 1840s and 1850s worked to abolish slavery. The Prohibition party, the most durable example of a single-issue party, opposed the consumption of alcoholic beverages. Prohibition candidates consistently won from 1 to 2 percent of the vote in nine presidential elections between 1884 and 1916, and the party has run candidates in every presidential election since.

Third parties, then, have been formed primarily to express discontent with the choices offered by the major parties and to work for their own objectives within the electoral system.[14] How have they fared? As *vote getters*, minor parties have not performed well, with two exceptions. First, bolter parties have twice won more than 10 percent of the vote; no other type has ever won as much. Second, the Republican party originated in 1854 as a single-issue third party opposed to slavery in new territories; in its first election, in 1856, the party came in second, displacing the Whigs. (Undoubtedly, the Republican exception to the rule has inspired the formation of other hopeful third parties.)

As *policy advocates*, minor parties have a slightly better record. At times, they have had a real effect on the policies adopted by the major parties. Women's suffrage, the graduated income tax, and the direct election of senators all originated in third parties.[15] Of course, third parties may fail to win more votes because their policies lack popular support. This was a lesson the Democrats learned in 1896, when they adopted the Populists' free-silver plank in their own platform. Both candidate and platform went down to a defeat that stained the Democratic party for decades.

Most important, minor parties function as *safety valves*. They allow those who are unhappy with the status quo to present their policies within the system, to contribute to the political dialogue. If minor parties indicate discontent, what should we make of the numerous minor parties—including the Libertarian, Workers', and Prohibition parties—in the 1988 election? Not much. Despite the presence of minor parties, the two major parties collected over 99 percent of the vote. The number of third parties that contest elections is much less important than the total number of votes they receive.

Why a Two-Party System?

The history of party politics in the United States is essentially the story of two parties alternating control of the government. With relatively few exceptions, elections for national office and for most state and local offices are conducted within the two-party system. This pattern is unusual in democratic countries, where multiparty systems are more common. Why does the United States have only two major parties? The two most convincing answers to this question stem from the electoral system in the United States and the process of political socialization here.

In the typical U.S. election, one office is contested by two or more candidates and is won by the single candidate who collects the most votes. When these two principles of (1) *single winners* chosen by (2) a *simple plurality* of votes are used to elect the members of a legislature, the system is known as **majority representation**. Think about the way the states choose representatives to Congress. If a state is entitled to ten representatives, the state is divided into ten congressional districts, and one representative is elected by a majority of voters in each district. Majority representation of voters through single-member districts is also employed in most state legislatures. Alternatively, a legislature might be chosen through a system of **proportional representation**, which awards legislative seats to a party in proportion to the vote it won in elections. Under this system, the state might have a single statewide election for all ten seats, with each party presenting a list of ten candidates. Voters could vote for the entire party list they preferred, and candidates would be elected from the top of each list, according to the proportion of votes won by the party.

Although this form of election may seem strange, it is used in many democratic countries. Proportional representation tends to produce (or to perpetuate) several parties, each of which has enough voting strength nationwide to elect some minimum number of candidates on its party list. In contrast, our system of single winners by simple plurality vote forces groups in society to work within one of the only two parties with any realistic chance of winning an election. Therefore, the system tends to produce only two parties. Moreover, the two major parties in a state benefit from laws that automatically list candidates on the ballot if their party won some minimum percentage of the vote in the previous election. These laws discourage minor parties, which must petition before every election for a place on the ballot.[16]

The rules of our electoral system may explain why only two parties tend to form in specific election districts. But why do the *same* two parties (Democratic and Republican) operate within each state? The contest for the presidency is the key to this question. The presidential election can be won only by the single candidate who wins a majority of electoral votes across the entire nation. Presidential candidates must win votes under the same label in each state so that they can pool their states' electoral votes to win in the electoral college. The presidency is a big enough prize to produce uncomfortable coalitions of voters (southern white Protestants allied with northern Jews and blacks in the Democratic party, for example) just to win the electoral vote and the presidential election.

The American electoral system may force party politics into a two-party mold, but why must the same parties *reappear* from election to election? In fact, they do not. The earliest two-party system pitted the Federalists against the Democratic Republicans. A later two-party system involved the Democrats and the Whigs. Over 130 years ago, the Republicans replaced the Whigs in what is our present two-party system. But, with modern issues so different from the issues then, why do the Democrats and Republicans persist? This is where *political socialization* comes into play. These two parties persist simply because they *have* persisted. After more than 100 years of political socialization, the two parties today have such a head start in structuring the vote that they discourage challenges from new parties. Of course, third parties still try to crack the two-party system from time to time, but most have had little success.

The Federal Basis of the Party System

Studying the history of American parties by focusing on contests for the presidency is convenient and informative. It also oversimplifies party politics to the point of distortion. By concentrating only on presidential elections, we tend to ignore electoral patterns in the states, where elections often buck national trends. In a party's darkest defeats for the presidency, it can still claim many victories for state offices. These victories outside the arena of presidential politics give each party a base of support that keeps its machinery oiled and running for the next contest.

The Republican victory in the 1984 presidential election helps illustrate how the states serve as a refuge for parties defeated for the presidency. Ronald Reagan swept forty-nine states in 1984—winning in every state but Minnesota, the home of his opponent, Walter Mondale. Even in the wake of Reagan's stunning victory, however, the Democrats kept control of the House of Representatives. They wound up with thirty-four state governorships to the Republicans' sixteen (unchanged from before the election) and 65 percent of the state legislatures. They controlled the governorship, the upper house, and the lower house in eighteen states compared to only four states for the Republicans.[17]

Reagan's victory in 1980, his 1984 landslide, and Bush's convincing win in 1988 may suggest that the Democrats are doomed to extinction in presidential politics. Perhaps in an earlier time, when the existing parties were not so well institutionalized, that would have been so. However, the Democratic party not only remains alive but thrives within most

Wild about Wilder

In November 1989, Democrat L. Douglas Wilder was elected governor of Virginia by a margin of less than one-half of 1 percent of the vote. He is the nation's first elected black governor. Wilder's victory demonstrates the federal structure of the party system: One party may win executive office at the national level, while another party wins executive offices at the state level. Currently, approximately 60 percent of the nation's governors are Democrats.

states in our federal system. The separation of state politics from national trends affords each party a chance to lick its wounds after a presidential election debacle and return to campaign optimistically in the next election.

Party Identification in America

The concept of **party identification** is one of the most important in political science. It refers to the voter's sense of psychological attachment to a party, which is not the same thing as voting for the party in any given election. Scholars measure party identification simply by asking, "Do you usually think of yourself as a Republican, a Democrat, an independent, or what?"[18] Voting is a behavior; identification is a state of mind. For example, millions of southerners voted for Eisenhower for president in 1952 and 1956 although they still considered themselves Democrats. Across the nation, more people identify with one of the two major parties than reject a party attachment.

The proportions of self-identified Republicans, Democrats, and independents (no party attachment) in the electorate since 1952 are shown in Figure 8.3. Three significant points stand out.

- The proportion of Republicans and Democrats combined far exceeds the proportion of independents in every year.

FIGURE 8.3 *Distribution of Party Identification, 1952–1990*

In every presidential election since 1952, voters across the nation have been asked, "Generally speaking, do you usually think of yourself as a Republican, a Democrat, an independent, or what?" Most voters readily admit to thinking of themselves as either Republicans or Democrats, but the proportion of those who think of themselves as independents has increased over time. The Democrats' status as the majority party has also lessened over time. Nevertheless, most Americans today still identify with one of the two major parties, and there are still more Democrats than Republicans. (Sources: Warren E. Miller, Arthur H. Miller, and Edward J. Schneider, American National Election Studies Data Sourcebook, 1952–1978 [Cambridge, Mass.: Harvard University Press, 1980, 1981]. Supplemented by data from the 1980 and 1984 National Election Studies conducted at the Center for Political Studies, University of Michigan, and distributed by the Inter-University Consortium for Political and Social Research. Data for 1988 and 1990 come from the General Social Survey, provided by Dr. Tom W. Smith, National Opinion Research Center.)

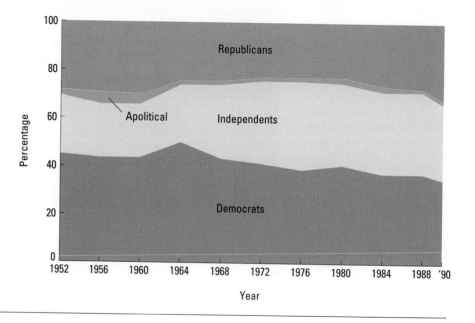

- The proportion of Democrats consistently exceeds that of Republicans.
- The proportion of Democrats has shrunk somewhat over time, to the benefit of both Republicans and independents.

Although a sense of party identification predisposes citizens to vote for their favorite party, other factors may cause voters to choose the opposition candidate. If they vote against their party often enough, they may rethink their party identification and eventually switch. Apparently, this rethinking has gone on in the minds of many southern Democrats over time. In 1952, about 70 percent of white southerners thought of themselves as Democrats, and fewer than 20 percent thought of themselves as Republicans. By 1988, white southerners were only 37 percent Democratic, 25 percent Republican, and 38 percent independent. Much of the nationwide growth in the proportion of Republicans and independents

(and the parallel drop in the number of Democrats) stems from party switches among white southerners.

Who are the self-identified Democrats and Republicans in the electorate? Figure 8.4 shows party identification by social groups in 1988. The effects of socioeconomic factors are clear. People who have lower incomes, less education, less prestigious occupations, and who live in union households tend to think of themselves as Democrats more than Republicans. But the cultural factors of religion and race produce even sharper differences between the parties. Jews are strongly Democratic compared with other religious groups. Members of minority groups (especially blacks) are also overwhelmingly Democratic. Differences between the sexes have opened a "gender gap" in American politics: Women tend to be more Democratic than men.

The influence of region on party identification has altered over time. The South is now only slightly more Democratic than the other regions, while the West has become predominantly Republican. Despite the erosion of Democratic support in the South, we still see elements of Roosevelt's old Democratic coalition in the socioeconomic groups. Perhaps the major change in that coalition has been the replacement of white European ethnic groups by blacks, attracted by the Democrats' backing of civil rights legislation in the 1960s.

Studies show that about half the citizens in the United States adopt their parents' party. But it often takes time for party identification to develop. The youngest group of voters is most likely to be independent, but they also identified more with Republicans during the Reagan years. The oldest group shows the most partisan commitments. Also, the youngest and oldest age groups are most evenly divided between the parties. Some analysts believe this division of party identification among the young will continue as they age, contributing to further erosion of the Democratic majority and perhaps greater electoral dealignment.

Still, citizens find their political niche, and they tend to stay there.[19] The widespread enduring sense of party loyalty among American voters tends to structure the vote even before the election is held, even before the candidates are chosen. In Chapter 9 we examine the extent to which party identification determines voting choice. But first, we look to see if there are any significant differences between the Democratic and Republican parties.

Party Ideology and Organization

George Wallace, a disgruntled Democrat who ran for president on the American Independent party ticket, complained that "there isn't a dime's worth of difference" between the Democrats and Republicans. Humorist Will Rogers said, "I am not a member of any organized political party—I am a Democrat." Wallace's comment was made in disgust; Rogers's in jest. Wallace was wrong; Rogers was close to being right. Here we try to dispel the myth that the parties do not differ significantly on issues and explain how they are organized to coordinate the activities of party candidates and officials in government.

FIGURE 8.4   *Party Identification by Social Groups*

Respondents to a 1988 survey were divided into nine different social groups—by income, education, occupation, union membership, religion, race, sex, region, and age—and analyzed according to their self-descriptions as Democrats, independents, or Republicans. Region was found to have the least effect on party identification; religion and race had the greatest effects. (Source: 1988 General Social Survey; tabulations provided by Dr. Tom W. Smith, National Opinion Research Center. Used by permission.)

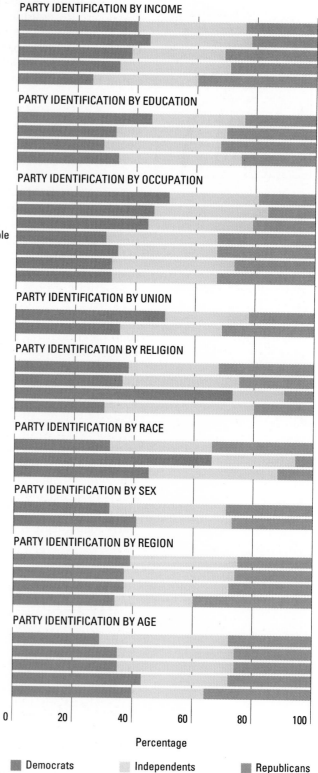

Differences in Party Ideology

George Wallace notwithstanding, there *is* more than a dime's worth of difference between the two parties. In fact, the difference amounts to many billions of dollars, the cost of the different government programs supported by each party. Democrats are more disposed to government spending to advance social welfare (and hence to promote equality) than are Republicans. And social welfare programs cost money, a lot of money. (You will see how much money in Chapters 18 and 19.) Republicans, on the other hand, are not adverse to spending billions of dollars for the projects they consider important, among them, national defense. Ronald Reagan portrayed the Democrats as big spenders, but the defense buildup during just his first administration cost the country over $1 trillion—more precisely, $1,007,900,000,000.[20] And Reagan's Strategic Defense Initiative (the "Star Wars" space defense), which Bush has backed, cost many billions more, even by conservative estimates. These differences in spending patterns reflect some real philosophical differences between the parties.

Voter and activists.   One way to examine these differences is to compare party identifiers (those who identify themselves as Democrats or Republicans) among the voters with those who are active in the party at election time. As shown in the middle portion of Figure 8.5, 25 percent of those who identified themselves as Democrats in 1988 described themselves as conservatives, compared with more than 40 percent of those who identified themselves as Republicans. As we discussed in Chapter 5, many ordinary voters do not think about politics in ideological terms, but party activists often do. The ideological gap between the parties looms even larger when we focus on the party activists on the left- and right-hand sides of the figure. Only 4 percent of the delegates to the 1988 Democratic convention considered themselves conservatives, compared with 60 percent of the delegates to the Republican convention.

Platforms: Freedom, order, and equality.   Surveys of voters' ideological orientations may reflect differences in personal self-image rather than actual differences in party ideology. For another test of party philosophies, we can look to the platforms adopted in party conventions. Although many people feel that party platforms don't matter very much, several scholars using different approaches have demonstrated that winning parties tend to carry out much of their platforms when in office.[21] One study matched the parties' platform statements from 1948 to 1985 against subsequent fund allocations in the federal budget and found that spending priorities were quite closely linked to platform emphases of the winning party, especially if the party also controlled the presidency.[22]

Party platforms also matter a great deal to delegates at conventions. The wording of a platform plank often means the difference between victory and defeat for factions within the party. Delegates fight not only over ideas but also over words and even punctuation in a plank. Platforms, then, give a good indication of policy preferences among party activists. A study of activists in both parties during the 1980s, for example, indicated that the "Reagan revolution" polarized their attitudes, increas-

FIGURE 8.5 *Ideologies of Party Identifiers and Delegates in 1988*

Contrary to what many people think, the Democratic and Republican parties differ sub-
stantially in their ideological centers of gravity. When citizens were asked to classify
themselves on an ideological scale, more Republican than Democratic identifiers de-
scribed themselves as conservative. When delegates to the parties' national conventions
were asked to classify themselves, even greater ideological differences appeared. (Sources:
Michael Oreskes, "Delegates Conservative, Poll Shows," New York Times, 14 August 1988,
p. 14; and E. J. Dionne, Jr., "Democrats Are Hoping to End the Lean Years," New York Times,
17 July 1988, p. 10.)

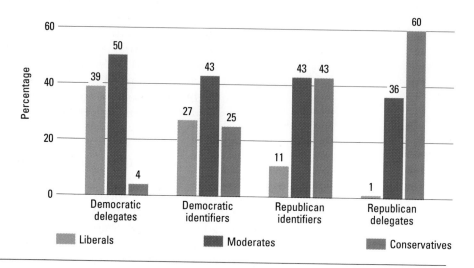

ing the conservatism of Republicans and causing Democrats to react
more liberally on defense spending, abortion, and affirmative action.[23]

The platforms adopted by the Democratic and Republican conventions
in 1988 were strikingly different in style and substance. The Democrats,
who met first, produced an unusually short document (fewer than 4,500
words), about one-tenth as long as their 1984 platform. It stressed broad
themes rather than specific policies. The platform led with this principle: "We believe that all Americans have a fundamental right to economic justice"—a phrase usually interpreted as a commitment to reducing economic inequality. The party also pledged

> equal access to education . . . equal access to government services, employ-
> ment, housing, business, business enterprise and education to every citizen
> regardless of race, sex, national origin, religion, age, handicapping condition or
> sexual orientation . . . the adoption of the equal rights amendment to the Con-
> stitution . . . equal access of women and minorities to elective office and party
> endorsement.

Accusing the Democrats of hiding behind a vague platform, the Republicans adopted a detailed document of 50,000 words and 150 pages. But
the Republicans had a theme, too—*freedom*:

> *Freedom works.* This is not slogaaneering, but a verifiable fact. . . . Our plat-
> form reflects on every page our continuing faith in the creative power of hu-
> man freedom. . . . Defending and expanding freedom is our first priority.

The Democrats supported "an indexed minimum wage that can help lift and keep families out of poverty"; the Republicans, on the other hand, opposed increases in the minimum wage as "inflationary—and job-destroying."

The Democrats said the national, state, and local governments "exist to help us solve our problems instead of adding to them"; the Republicans said "government empowers people to solve their own problems and to have more choices in their lives."

Although the Republicans opposed the use of government to promote equality, they were willing to use government to promote social order. The Democrats supported free choice on the abortion issue; the Republicans favored a constitutional amendment to outlaw abortion. The Democrats were silent on the death penalty; the Republicans urged the reinstatement of the death penalty for certain federal crimes.

These statements of values clearly separate the two parties on the values of freedom, order, and equality that underlie the dilemmas of government discussed in Chapter 1. According to the typology presented there, the Republicans' 1988 platform places their party in the conservative category, while the Democrats' platform puts their party squarely into the liberal category.

Different but similar. The Democrats and the Republicans have very different ideological orientations. Yet many observers claim that the parties are really quite similar in ideology, especially when compared with other countries' parties. They are similar in that both support capitalism; that is, both reject government ownership of the means of production (see Chapter 1). A study of Democratic and Republican positions on four economic issues—ownership of the means of production, role in economic planning, redistribution of wealth, and providing for social welfare—found that Republicans consistently oppose increased government activity. Comparing these findings with data on party positions in thirteen other democracies, the researchers found about as much difference between the American parties as is usual within two-party systems. However, both American parties tend to be more conservative on economic matters than parties in other two-party systems. In most multiparty systems, the presence of strong socialist and antisocialist parties ensures a much greater range of ideological choice than we find in our system, despite genuine differences between the Democrats and Republicans.[24]

National Party Organization

Most political observers would agree with Will Rogers's description of the Democrats as an unorganized political party. This used to be true of the Republicans, too, but this has changed over the last decade—at least at the national level. Bear in mind the distinction between levels of party structure. American parties parallel our federal system: They have separate national and state organizations (and virtually separate local organizations, in many cases).

At the national level, each major party has four main organizational components:

- *National convention.* Every four years, each party assembles thousands of delegates from the states and other entities (such as Puerto Rico and Guam) in a *national convention* for the purpose of nominating a candidate for president. This presidential nominating convention is also the supreme governing body of the party. It determines party policy through the platform, formulates rules to govern party operations, and designates a national committee, which is empowered to govern the party until the next convention.

- *National committee.* The **national committee** of each party is composed of party officials representing the states and territories and including the chairpersons of their party organizations. In 1989, the Republican National Committee (RNC) had 162 members, consisting of the national committeeman, national committeewoman, and the chairperson from each state and from the District of Columbia, Guam, Puerto Rico, and the Virgin Islands. The Democratic National Committee (DNC) had 403 members, including in addition to the national committee members and party chairs, other members apportioned to the states and representing auxiliary organizations.[25] The chairperson of each national committee is chosen by the party's presidential nominee, then duly elected by the committee. If the nominee loses the election, the national committee usually replaces the nominee's chairperson.

- *Congressional party conferences.* At the beginning of each session of Congress, the Republicans and Democrats in each chamber hold separate **party conferences** (the House Democrats call theirs a "caucus") to select their party leaders and to decide committee assignments. (As noted in the chapter opening, Bernard Sanders, the lone independent in

Leading Man

Ronald Brown, the first African-American to head a major political party, became the Democratic National Committee chairman in February 1989, after managing Jesse Jackson's presidential campaign in 1988. As chair, Brown has declared he will be a neutral player in the presidential nomination process.

1991, was excluded from the House Democratic Caucus.) These party conferences, held on occasion to deal with congressional matters, have no structural relationship to each other and no relationship to the national committee. Each party conference is autonomous and concerned only with the party's legislative activities within each chamber.

- *Congressional campaign committees.* Democrats and Republicans in the House and Senate also maintain separate **congressional campaign committees,** each of which raises its own funds to support its candidates in congressional elections. The fact that these are separate organizations tells us that the national party structure is loose; the national committee seldom gets involved with the election of any individual member of Congress. Moreover, even the congressional campaign organizations merely supplement the funds that senators and representatives raise on their own to win re-election.

It is tempting to think of the national party chairperson sitting at the top of a hierarchical party organization that not only controls its members in Congress but runs through the state committees to the local level. Few ideas could be more wrong.[26] There is virtually no national committee control of congressional activity and very little national direction of and even less national control over state and local campaigns. In fact, the RNC and DNC do not really direct or control presidential campaigns. Individual candidates hire their own campaign staffs to contest the party primaries to win delegates who will support them for nomination at the party conventions. The successful party nominees then keep their winning staffs to contest the general election. The main role of a national committee is to cooperate with its candidate's personal campaign staff, in the hope of winning the election.

In this light, the national committees appear to be relatively useless organizations. For many years, their role was essentially limited to planning for the next party convention. The committee would select the site, issue the call to state parties to attend, plan the program, and so on. In the 1970s, however, the roles of the DNC and RNC began to expand—but in different ways.

In response to street rioting during the 1968 Democratic convention, the Democrats created a special commission to introduce party reforms. The McGovern-Fraser Commission attempted to open the party to greater participation by women, minority members, and young voters and to weaken local party leaders' control over the process of selecting delegates. The commission formulated guidelines for the selection of delegates to the 1972 Democratic convention. Included in these guidelines was the requirement that state parties take "affirmative action"—that is, do something to see to it that women, blacks, and young people were included among their delegates "in reasonable relationship to the group's presence in the population of the state."[27] Many state parties rebelled at the imposition of quotas by sex, race, and age. But the DNC threatened to deny seating to any state delegation at the 1972 convention that did not comply with the guidelines.

Never before had a national party committee imposed these kinds of rules on a state party organization, but it worked. Even the powerful Illinois delegation, led by Chicago mayor Richard Daley, was denied seating at the convention for violating the guidelines. And overall, women, blacks, and young voters gained dramatically in representation at the 1972 Democratic convention. Although the party has since reduced its emphasis on quotas, the gains by women and blacks have held up fairly well. The representation of young people, however, has declined substantially. Many "regular" Democrats feared that the political activists who took over their 1972 convention would cripple the party organization, but most of the challengers were socialized into the party within a decade and became more compromising and supportive of the need for organization to combat developments within the Republican party.[28]

While the Democrats were busy with *procedural* reforms, the Republicans were making *organizational* reforms.[29] The RNC did little to open up its delegate selection process; Republicans were not inclined to impose quotas on state parties through their national committee. Instead, the RNC strengthened its fund-raising, research, and service roles. Republicans acquired their own building and their own computer, and in 1976 they hired the first full-time chairperson of either national party. (Until then, the chairperson worked part-time and usually had some other career.) As RNC chairman, William Brock expanded the party's staff, launched new publications, started seminars, conducted election analyses, advised candidates, and did most of the things that national party committees had done routinely in other countries for years.

The vast difference between the Democratic and Republican approaches to reforming the national committees shows in the funds raised by the DNC and RNC during election campaigns. Since Brock's tenure as chairman of the RNC, the Republicans have raised three to four times the money raised by the Democrats. In 1990, for example, the Republicans' national, senatorial, and congressional committees spent $159 million compared with $40 million for the comparable Democratic committees.[30] Although Republicans have traditionally raised more campaign funds than Democrats, they no longer rely on a relatively few wealthy contributors. In fact, the Republicans received the larger portion of their funds from smaller contributors (of less than $100), mainly through direct-mail solicitation. In short, the RNC has recently been raising far more money than the DNC from many more citizens, in a long-term commitment to improving its organizational services. Evidence of its efforts has appeared at the level of state party organizations.

State and Local Party Organizations

At one time, both major parties were firmly anchored in strong state and local party organizations. Big-city party organizations, such as the Democrats' Tammany Hall in New York City and the Cook County Central Committee in Chicago, were prototypes of the party machine. The **party machine** was a centralized organization that dominated local politics by controlling elections—sometimes by illegal means, often by providing jobs and social services to urban workers in return for their votes. The patronage and social service functions of party machines were undercut as government expanded its role in providing unemployment compensation, aid to families with dependent children, and other social services. As a result, most local party organizations lost their ability to deliver votes and thus to determine the outcome of elections. However, machines are still strong in certain areas. In Nassau County, New York, for example, suburban Republicans have shown that they can run a machine as well as urban Democrats.[31]

The state organizations of both parties vary widely in strength, but Republican state organizations tend to be stronger than Democratic organizations. The Republicans are likely to have larger budgets and staffs and tend to recruit candidates for more offices. Republicans also differ from Democrats in the help that the national organization gives to state organizations. A survey of forty Republican and thirty Democratic state chairpersons revealed that 70 percent of the Republican organizations received financial aid from the national organization compared with only 7 percent of the Democratic organizations.[32] In 1990, for example, the RNC transferred more than twice as much money to various state Republican committees, $3.7 million compared with $1.6 million for the Democrats.[33] Republicans at the state level also received more candidate training, poll data and research, and campaign instruction from the national organization. The only service that the DNC supplied more often than the RNC was "rule enforcement"—reflecting the national party's enforcement of guidelines for selecting convention delegates.[34] Otherwise, the dominant pattern in both parties was for the national organization *not* to intervene in state activities unless asked, and then only to supply services. However, the national-state-county linkages are not as weak as some believe; they do not seem to be getting any weaker; and they may actually be growing stronger.[35]

Decentralized but Growing Stronger

If strong party organization means that control is vested in the national headquarters, then both the Democrats and Republicans are, in Will Rogers's phrase, unorganized political parties. Far from exercising centralized power from Washington, American political parties are among the *most* decentralized parties in the world.[36] Not even the president can count on loyalty from the members or even officers of his party. Consider the embarrassment to President Bush on October 5, 1990, when—after months of tense negotiation—his carefully crafted budget package to deal with the exploding deficit was rejected by the House. The Republican president actually drew less support from Republican legislators than from Democrats. Indeed, the second-ranking Republican leader in the House, Newt Gingrich of Georgia, even led the revolt against the budget package—although as the "whip" his job was to mobilize party support! Despite his mutinous behavior, Gingrich was easily re-elected as party whip in 1991.

The absence of centralized power has always been the most distinguishing characteristic of American political parties. Only a few years ago, scholars wrote that these weak parties were in further decline.[37] But there is evidence that our political parties today are enjoying a period of resurgence. As shown in Figure 8.6, fewer voters fail to see any differences between the parties in election years now than during the previous three decades, and more votes in Congress are being decided along party lines. Despite the Newt Gingrich party mutiny, a specialist in congressional politics concluded, "When compared to its predecessors of the last half-century, the current majority party leadership is more involved and more decisive in organizing the party and the chamber, setting the policy agenda, shaping legislation, and determining legislative outcomes."[38] However, the American parties have traditionally been so weak that these positive trends have not altered their basic character. American political parties are still so organizationally diffuse and decentralized that they raise questions about how well they link voters to government.

The Model of Responsible Party Government

According to the majoritarian model of democracy, parties are essential to making the government responsive to public opinion. In fact, the ideal role of parties in majoritarian democracy has been formalized in the four principles of **responsible party government**:[39]

1. Parties should present clear and coherent programs to voters.
2. Voters should choose candidates according to the party programs.
3. The winning party should carry out its program once in office.
4. Voters should hold the governing party responsible at the next election for executing its program.

How well are these principles being met in American politics? You've learned that the Democratic and Republican platforms are different and that they are much more ideologically consistent than many people be-

FIGURE 8.6 *Evidence of Party Resurgence*

These graphs provide two different types of evidence for the resurgence of political parties since the 1970s. Figure 8.6a shows the percentage of registered voters who say that they see "no difference" between the Democrats and Republicans when asked which party "will do a better job" either in keeping the country prosperous or in keeping it out of war. Note that this percentage has declined substantially since the 1970s and was lower in 1988 than in any time since the 1950s. Figure 8.6b plots the percentage of "party unity" votes taken in the House and the Senate in even years. A party unity vote pits a majority of Democrats against a majority of Republicans on issues before the chamber. It shows that the amount of party voting in Congress has risen almost steadily since its low point around 1970 and that the parties divide in their voting patterns about as much or more as they did in the 1950s. (Sources: Data for Figure 8.6a come from The Gallup Poll Monthly (September 1990), p. 32. Data for Figure 8.6b come from Harold W. Stanley and Richard G. Niemi, Vital Statistics on American Politics, 2d ed. [Washington, D.C.: Congressional Quarterly Press, 1990], p. 192.)

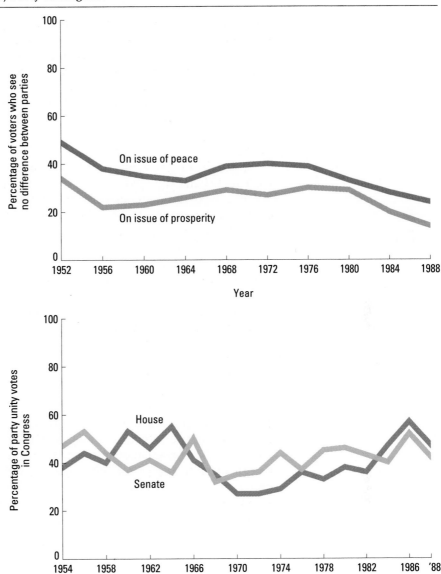

lieve. So the first principle is being met fairly well. So is the third principle: once parties gain power, they usually do what they say they would do. From the standpoint of democratic theory, the real question lies in principles 2 and 4: Do voters really pay attention to party platforms and policies when they cast their ballots? If so, do voters hold the governing party responsible at the next election for delivering, or failing to deliver, on its pledges? To answer these questions, we must consider in greater detail the parties' role in nominating candidates and in structuring the voters' choice in elections. At the conclusion of Chapter 9, we will return to evaluating the role of political parties in democratic government.

Summary

Political parties perform four important functions in a political system: nominating candidates, structuring the voting choice, proposing alternative government programs, and coordinating the activities of government officials. Political parties have been performing these functions longer in the United States than in any other country. The Democratic party, founded in 1828, is the world's oldest political party. When the Republican party emerged as a major party after the 1856 election, it joined the Democrats to produce our present two-party system—the oldest party system in the world.

America's two-party system has experienced three critical elections, each of which realigned the electorate for years and affected the party balance in government. The election of 1860 established the Republicans as the major party in the North and the Democrats as the dominant party in the South. Nationally, the two parties were roughly balanced in Congress until the critical election of 1896. This election strengthened the link between the Republican party and business interests in the heavily populated Northeast and Midwest and produced a surge in voter support that made the Republicans the majority party nationally for more than three decades. The Great Depression produced conditions for the critical election of 1932, which transformed the Democrats into the majority party, giving them almost uninterrupted control of Congress since then.

Minor parties have not enjoyed much electoral success in America, although they have contributed ideas to the Democratic and Republican platforms. The two-party system is perpetuated in the United States because of the nature of our electoral system and the political socialization process, which results in most Americans identifying with either the Democratic or the Republican party. The federal system of government has also helped the Democrats and Republicans survive major national defeats by sustaining them with electoral victories at the state level. The pattern of party identification has been changing in recent years: As more people are becoming independents and Republicans, the number of Democratic identifiers is dropping. Nonetheless, the proportion of Democrats consistently exceeds that of Republicans, and both far outnumber the independents.

Party identifiers, party activists, and party platforms show consistent differences in ideological orientations between the two major parties. Democratic identifiers and activists are more likely to describe themselves as liberal; Republican identifiers and activists tend to be conservative. The 1988 Democratic party platform also showed a more liberal orientation by stressing equality over freedom; the Republican platform was more conservative, concentrating on freedom but also emphasizing the importance of restoring social order. Organizationally, the Republicans have recently become the stronger party at both national and state levels, and both parties are showing signs of resurgence. Nevertheless, both parties are very decentralized compared with parties in other countries.

As demanded by the model of responsible party government, American parties do tend to enact their platform positions into government policy if elected to power. But we must see whether citizens pay much attention to parties and policies when casting their vote. If not, parties do not fulfill the majoritarian model of democratic theory.

KEY TERMS

political party	party of ideological
nominate	protest
political system	single-issue party
electoral college	majority representation
caucus	proportional
national convention	representation
party platform	party identification
critical election	national committee
electoral realignment	party conference
two-party system	congressional campaign
majority party	committee
minority party	party machine
electoral dealignment	responsible party
bolter party	government
farmer-labor party	

SELECTED READINGS

Advisory Commission on Intergovernmental Relations. *The Transformation of American Politics: Implications for Federalism.* Washington, D.C.: Report A-106, August 1986. A general study of American political parties, especially useful for its data on state party organizations.

Frantzich, Stephen E. *Political Parties in the Technological Age.* New York: Longman, 1989. This text on political parties discusses the impact of technological change on parties and evaluates proposals for party reform.

Goldman, Ralph M. *The National Party Chairmen and Committees: Factionalism at the Top.* Armonk, N.Y.: M.E. Sharpe, 1990. A sweeping historical survey from the origins of both parties to the 1960s.

Jewell, Malcolm E., and David M. Olson. *Political Parties and Elections in American States.* 3d ed. Chicago: The Dorsey Press, 1988. Compares the political party and electoral systems in the fifty states drawing on generalizations backed by empirical research and years of experience.

Maisel, L. Sandy, ed. *The Parties Respond: Changes in the American Party System.* Boulder, Col.: Westview Press, 1990. Essays on state party organization, parties in the electoral arena, the relationship between parties and voters, and parties in government.

Rosenstone, Steven J., Roy L. Behr, and Edward H. Lazarus. *Third Parties in America: Citizen Response to Major Party Failure.* Princeton, N.J.: Princeton University Press, 1984. The authors not only provide an excellent review of the history of third-party movements in American politics, but they also analyze the factors that lead third-party voters and candidates to abandon the two major parties. They conclude that third-party efforts improve the performance of the party system.

Sabato, Larry J. *The Party's Just Begun: Shaping Political Parties for America's Future.* Glenview, Ill.: Scott, Foresman, 1988. The book's premise is that citizens' partisan loyalty can be regenerated and that the parties can be strengthened organizationally—indeed, that they are stronger at the national level than ever before in modern times.

Schattschneider, E. E. *Party Government.* New York: Holt, 1942. A clear and powerful argument for the central role of political parties in a democracy according to the model of responsible party government; a classic book in political science.

Shafer, Byron E. *Bifurcated Politics: Evolution and Reform in the National Party Convention.* Cambridge, Mass.: Harvard University Press, 1988. Argues that the national conventions lost the function to nominate candidates in the 1950s and now are used to launch a campaign and to politic for other causes. Thanks to television, conventions are now bifurcated: one version is show to viewers, and the other is experienced by delegates.

Sorauf, Frank J. *Money in American Elections.* Glenview, Ill.: Scott, Foresman, 1988. Surveys receipts and expenditures in presidential and congressional campaigns, including financing by individuals, political action committees, parties, and government.

9 NOMINATIONS, CAMPAIGNS, AND ELECTIONS

"WEEKEND PASSES" WAS THE most controversial television advertisement in the 1988 presidential campaign. In a thirty-second spot, the screen displayed side-by-side images of Vice President George Bush and Governor Michael Dukakis while the narrator said, "Bush and Dukakis on crime." Shown a picture of Bush, viewers were told, "Bush supports the death penalty for first-degree murderers." Shown Dukakis, they heard, "Dukakis not only opposes the death penalty, he allowed first-degree murderers to have weekend passes from prison."

A scowling mug shot of a black convict then flashed on the screen: "One was Willie Horton, who murdered a boy in a robbery, stabbing him nineteen times." Another picture showed Horton with a policeman as the narrator said, "Despite a life sentence, Horton received ten weekend passes from prison. Horton fled, kidnaped a young couple, stabbing the man and repeatedly raping his girlfriend." Meanwhile, the words *kidnaping, stabbing,* and *raping* appeared on the screen. The ad ended with a photo of Dukakis as the narrator intoned solemnly, "Weekend prison passes. Dukakis on crime."[1]

This commercial, which appeared nationally on cable television for twenty-eight days before the election, attracted a storm of criticism from Democrats.[2] A month after the election, when virtually all the top managers of both campaigns convened at Harvard University to dissect the 1988 presidential campaign, they spent a good deal of time discussing this single ad.[3] In addition to the charge of racism, Democrats said the commercial was blatantly unfair. Most states had programs to furlough prisoners, and released convicts, like Willie Horton, had committed murders before. In fact, it happened once in California while Ronald Reagan was governor, and also in the federal furlough program while Reagan was president and Bush vice president.[4] Nevertheless, the hard-hitting ad helped mold voter opinion that Dukakis was soft on criminals.[5]

Interestingly, the controversial ad was not produced by Bush's campaign organization or by the Republican party. It was created and run by the National Security Political Action Committee, which mailed literature under the heading "Americans for Bush." Although the National Security PAC employed an advertising firm that had long-standing ties with the Republican party, it claimed to operate as an independent group within the Federal Election Campaign Act, under which it reported spending over $7 million for Bush's election.[6] (Earlier in the campaign, in fact, officials from both party organizations had asked such outside groups to stop raising money to spend in their own campaign activities.[7] These independent groups not only dried up sources of funds but sometimes interfered with party campaign plans.) Although officials in the Bush campaign disavowed the Horton commercial, Bush's campaign manager, Lee Atwater, once said, "By the time we're finished they're going to wonder whether Willie Horton is Dukakis's running mate."[8]

The Willie Horton commercial illustrates several points about contemporary campaigns for election in the United States. First, election campaigns, particularly for the presidency, are largely conducted through the mass media, especially television. Second, political parties have little control over election campaigns, which are typically conducted by organizations built around the candidates. Third, campaigns for major offices

Many are still at large.

Turnstile Justice?

The notorious "Willie Horton" television advertisement, which accused Michael Dukakis of being soft on crime, was produced by an organization not affiliated with the Bush campaign. However, Bush's campaign did run a graphic ad that conveyed the same message—Democrats go easy on criminals—by showing convicts leaving prison through a revolving door.

consume a great deal of money. Fourth, today's campaigns are marked by negative advertising. Finally, advertising is widely believed to affect the outcome of elections for major offices.[9]

But are campaigns really important in deciding elections, especially for the presidency? Allan Lichtman and Ken DeCell, two scholars who have studied all the presidential elections since 1860, think otherwise:

> Nothing either party has said or done during the fall campaign has ever changed its prospects at the polls. Debates, television appearances, fund-raising, advertising, news coverage and campaign strategies—the usual grist for the punditry mills—count for virtually nothing on Election Day. The only issues that matter are the ones for which the results are already in.[10]

Lichtman and DeCell contend that presidential elections are primarily referenda on the performance (and luck) of the incumbent administration during the last four years. They isolate thirteen factors, or "keys," that, they say, determine the outcome of every presidential election—regardless of the candidates' campaigns.

At the end of this chapter, we examine their thirteen keys to the presidency as predictors of the 1992 presidential election. But first we consider how election campaigns have changed over time, how candidates get nominated in the United States, what factors are important in election campaigns, and why voters choose one candidate over another. We also address these important questions: What roles do political parties play today in campaigns and nominations? Do election campaigns function more to inform or to discourage voters? How important is money in conducting a winning election campaign? What is the role of party identification, issues, and candidate attributes in influencing voters' choices and thus election outcomes? How do campaigns, elections, and parties fit into the majoritarian and pluralist models of democracy?

Evolution of Campaigning

Voting in free elections to choose leaders is the primary way that citizens control government. As discussed in Chapter 8, political parties help structure the voting choice by reducing the number of candidates on the ballot to those who have a realistic chance of winning or who offer distinctive policies. An **election campaign** is an organized effort to persuade voters to choose one candidate over others competing for the same office. An effective campaign requires sufficient resources to identify and acquire information about voters' interests, to develop a strategy and matching tactics for appealing to these interests, to deliver the candidate's message to the voters, and to get them to cast their ballots.[11]

Historically, political parties have played a central role in all phases of the election campaign. Time was when the state and local party organizations "felt the pulse" of their rank-and-file members to learn what was important to voters. They chose the candidates and then lined up their public officials to support the candidates and to ensure large crowds at campaign rallies. They also prepared buttons, banners, and newspaper advertisements that touted their candidates, proudly named under the prominent label of the party. Finally, candidates relied heavily on the local precinct and county party organization to canvass voters before elections, to mention their names, to extol their virtues, and—most important—to make sure they voted, and voted correctly.

Today, candidates seldom rely much on political parties to do what they did even in the 1950s, just forty years ago. How do candidates learn about voters' interests today? By contracting for public opinion polls, not by asking the party. How do candidates plan their campaign strategy and tactics now? By hiring political consultants to devise clever "soundbites" (brief, catchy phrases) that catch voters' attention, not by consulting party headquarters. How do candidates deliver their messages to voters? By conducting a media campaign, not by counting on party leaders to canvass the neighborhoods.

Increasingly, election campaigns have evolved from being party-centered to being candidate-centered.[12] This is not to say that political parties no longer have a role to play in campaigns, for they do. As noted in Chapter 8, the Democrats, since 1972, have exercised more control over the delegate selection process than they did earlier. Since 1976, the Republicans have greatly expanded their national organization and fund-raising capacity. But the parties' roles have been substantially altered from that of production to support. Whereas parties virtually conducted or produced election campaigns in the past, now they exist mainly to support campaigns by ensuring democratic procedures or by providing services or funds to party candidates. Although candidates often avoid publicizing their party affiliation, we will see that the party label is usually a candidate's most important attribute at election time.

Perhaps the most important change in electoral campaigning is that candidates don't campaign just to get elected anymore. It is now necessary to campaign for *nomination* as well. Chapter 8 stated that nominating candidates to run for office under the party label is one of the main functions of political parties. That function was once controlled by the

Political Ventriloquist

Peggy Noonan, one of Ronald Reagan's most creative and celebrated speechwriters, also applied her talents to George Bush's campaign for the presidency. When Bush praised the "thousand points of light" that make up America's spirit of volunteerism, he was speaking Noonan's words.

party organizations. In the nineteenth century, for example, parties commonly rotated congressional seats among candidates from different counties. Thus, Abraham Lincoln served only one term in the House before the party transferred the nomination to someone else.[13] For most important offices today, however, candidates are no longer nominated *by* the party organization but *within* the party. That is, party leaders seldom choose candidates themselves; they organize and supervise the election process by which party *voters* choose the candidates. Because almost all individuals who aspire to be a party candidate for a major office must first win an election to gain the party's nomination, those who would campaign for election must first campaign for the nomination.

Nominations

The most important feature of the nomination process in American party politics is that it usually involves an election by party voters. National party leaders do not choose the party's nominee for president or even the party's candidates for House and Senate seats. Virtually no other political parties in the world nominate candidates to the national legislature through party elections.[14] In more than half the world's parties, legislative candidates are chosen by local party leaders—and in most of those cases, even these choices must be approved by the national organization. In fact, in more than one-third of the world's parties, the national organization itself selects the party candidates for the national legislature (see Compared with What? 9.1).[15]

COMPARED WITH WHAT?   9.1

Choosing Legislative Candidates

In the United States, we believe that the nomination of party candidates through primary elections is the normal way to select candidates. Compared with the practice in other countries, however, it is not "normal" at all. Most competitive political parties in Western democracies exercise far more control over who is allowed to represent the party in elections. As shown in this graph, the most common method of selection, used by thirty-two parties in nine European countries, is to have a group of party activists interview the candidates and then select among them in committees or conventions. A few parties allow all enrolled party members to hear the candidates and then vote on them in party meetings, but more parties exercise even greater control, having national executive committees choose the candidates. This is evidence of how weak our parties are compared with those elsewhere.

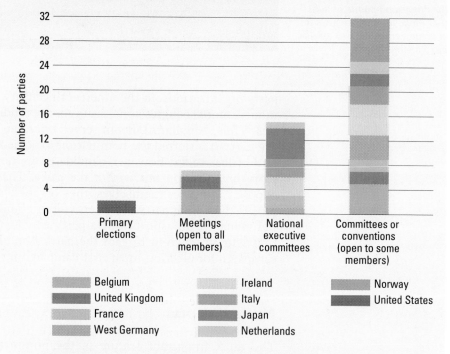

Source: Data are tabulated from Table 11.1 in Michael Gallagher, "Conclusion," in Michael Gallagher and Michael Marsh, eds., *Candidate Selection in Comparative Perspective: The Secret Garden of Politics* (London: Sage Publications, 1988), p. 237. Some parties use a combination of methods and are thus counted twice in the tabulation.

Democrats and Republicans nominate their candidates for national and statewide offices somewhat differently across the country because each state is entitled to make its own laws governing the nomination process. (This is significant in itself, for political parties in most other countries are largely free of laws stating how they must select their candidates.) Their nomination practices can be summarized according to the types of party elections and by the level of office sought.

For Congress and State Offices

In the United States, most aspiring candidates for major offices are nominated through a **primary election,** a preliminary election conducted within the party to select candidates who will run for office in a subsequent election. In thirty-seven states, primary elections alone are used to nominate candidates for all state and national offices, and primaries figure in the nomination process in important ways in all other states.[16] The nomination process, then, is highly decentralized, resting on the decisions of thousands, perhaps millions, of the party rank and file who participate in primary elections.

In both parties, only about half of the regular party voters (about one-quarter of the voting-age population) vote in a given primary, although the proportion varies greatly by state and contest.[17] Early research on primary elections concluded that Republicans who voted in their primaries were more conservative than those who did not, while Democratic primary voters were more liberal than other Democrats. This finding led to the belief that primary voters nominated candidates who were more ideologically extreme than preferred by the party as a whole. But not all party identifiers vote in general elections either. Recent research, which matches primary voters against those who missed the primary but voted in the general election, reports little evidence that primary voters are unrepresentative of the ideological orientations of other party voters.[18]

There are different types of primary elections for state and congressional offices, depending on the state in which they are held. The most common type (used by about forty states) is the **closed primary,** in which voters must declare their party affiliation before they are given the primary ballot, which lists the party's potential nominees. A handful of states use the **open primary,** in which voters need not declare a party affiliation but must choose one party's ballot to take into the polling booth. In a **blanket primary,** currently used in only two or three states, voters receive a ballot listing both parties' potential nominees and can participate in nominating candidates for all offices.

Most scholars believe that closed primaries strengthen party organization while blanket primaries weaken it. But the differences among types of primaries are much less important than the fact that the parties hold elections to choose their candidates. Placing the nomination of party candidates in the hands of voters rather than party leaders is a key factor in the decentralization of power in American parties. The decentralized nature of American parties is clearly illustrated in campaigns for the party nomination for president.

For President

Party candidates for president are nominated by delegates attending national conventions held the summer before the presidential election in

November. At one time, the nomination was decided right at the convention, sometimes after repeated balloting over several candidates who divided the vote and kept anyone from getting the majority needed to nominate. In 1920, for example, the Republican convention was deadlocked over two leading candidates after nine ballots. Party leaders then met in a "smoke-filled room" and compromised on Warren G. Harding, who won on the tenth. Harding was not among the leading candidates and had won only one primary (in his native Ohio). Four years later, the Democrats met for seventeen days and held a record 103 ballots before nominating John Davis to run (unsuccessfully) against Calvin Coolidge. The last time that either party needed more than one ballot to nominate its presidential candidate was in 1952, when the Democrats took three ballots to nominate Adlai E. Stevenson. Although the Republicans took only one ballot that year to nominate Dwight Eisenhower, his nomination was contested by Senator Robert Taft, and Eisenhower won his nomination on the floor of the convention.

According to a leading scholar of convention politics, 1952 was the last year that each party "realized the construction of a nominating majority inside the convention hall."[19] The Democratic convention in 1960 and the Republican convention in 1964 also made genuine choices, but otherwise the nomination function has left the convention arena. Since 1968, both parties' nominating conventions have simply ratified the results of the complex process for selecting the convention delegates (see Feature 9.1).

Selecting convention delegates. There is no national legislation specifying how state parties must select delegates to their national conventions. Instead, state legislatures have enacted a bewildering variety of procedures that often differ for Democrats and Republicans in the same state. The most important distinction in delegate selection is between the presidential primary and the local caucus.

A **presidential primary** is a special primary used to select delegates to attend the party's national nominating convention. In *presidential preference primaries* (used in about thirty states in 1988), party supporters vote directly for the person they favor as their party's nominee for president, and delegates are won accordingly through a variety of formulas. In *delegate selection primaries* (used in only about five states in 1988), party voters directly elect convention delegates, who may or may not have declared for a presidential candidate.

The **local caucus** method of delegate selection has several stages. It begins with a *caucus*, a local meeting of party supporters to choose delegates to attend a subsequent meeting, usually at the county level. Most delegates selected in the local caucus openly back one of the presidential candidates. The county meetings, in turn, select delegates to a higher level. The process culminates in a state *convention*, which actually selects the delegates to the national convention. About twenty states used the caucus process in 1988 (a few states combined caucuses with primaries), and caucuses were employed more by Democrats than Republicans.

Primary elections (which were stimulated by the Progressive movement discussed in Chapter 7) were first used to select delegates to nomi-

FIGURE 9.1 *Growth of Primaries for Delegate Selection*

Using primary elections to select delegates to national conventions to nominate the party's presidential candidate was championed by the progressive forces early in this century. By 1916, nearly half the states employed primaries to select more than half the delegates to both party conventions. As progressivism waned in the 1930s, however, so did presidential primaries. They regained popularity during the reform movement of the 1970s, which sought to broaden participation in the nominating process. In 1988, approximately 80 percent of the delegates to both party conventions were chosen through primaries, and this figure should not change much for 1992. (Source: Harold W. Stanley and Richard G. Niemi, Vital Statistics on American Politics, 2d ed. [Washington, D.C.: CQ Press, 1990], p. 134. Used by permission.)

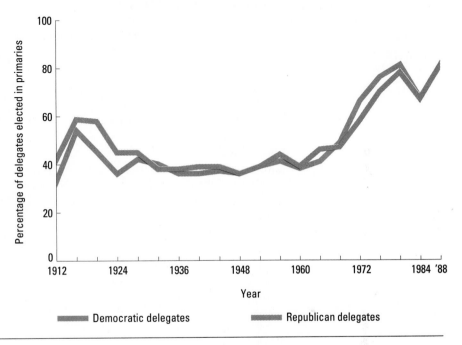

nating conventions in 1912. Figure 9.1 shows the growth of presidential primaries over time and the increase in convention delegates selected through primaries. Now parties in nearly forty states rely on presidential primaries, which generate over 80 percent of the delegates.

Campaigning for the nomination. The process of nominating party candidates for president in the United States is a complex, drawn-out affair that has no parallel in party politics in any other nation. Would-be presidents announce their candidacies and begin campaigning many months before the first convention delegates are selected. The selection process in 1988 began in early February with the Iowa caucuses, closely followed by the New Hampshire primary. By historical accident, these two small states have become the first tests of candidates' popularity with party voters. Accordingly, each basks in the media spotlight once every four years. The Iowa and New Hampshire legislatures are now committed to leading off the delegate selection process, ensuring their states' share of national publicity and their bid for political history.

FEATURE 9.1   *Changes in the Presidential Nomination Process*

When President Lyndon Johnson abruptly announced in late March 1968 that he would not run for re-election, the door was opened for his vice president, Hubert Humphrey. Humphrey felt it was too late to campaign in primaries against other candidates already in the race; nevertheless, he commanded enough support among party leaders to win the Democratic nomination. The stormy protests outside the party's convention against the "inside politics" of his nomination led to major changes in the way both parties have nominated their presidential candidates since 1968.

Presidential Nominating Process

Before 1968	*Since 1968*
Party-Dominated	Candidate-Dominated
The nomination decision is largely in the hands of party leaders. Candidates win by enlisting the support of state and local party machines.	Campaigns are independent of party establishments. Endorsements by party leaders have little effect on nomination choice.
Few Primaries	Many Primaries
Most delegates are selected by state party establishments, with little or no public participation. Some primaries are held, but their results do not necessarily determine the nominee. Primaries are used to indicate candidate's "electability."	Most delegates are selected by popular primaries and caucuses. Nominations are determined largely by voters' decisions at these contests.
Short Campaigns	Long Campaigns
Candidates usually begin their public campaign early in the election year.	Candidates begin laying groundwork for campaigns three or four years before the election. Candidates who are not well organized at least 18 months before the election may have little chance of winning.

The Iowa caucuses and the New Hampshire primary have served different functions in the presidential nominating process.[20] The contest in Iowa tended to winnow out candidates who were rejected by the party faithful. The New Hampshire primary, held one week after the Iowa caucuses, tested the Iowa front-runners' appeal to ordinary party voters, which foreshadowed their likely strength in the general election. Because voting takes little effort, more citizens vote than attend caucuses, which can last for hours. In 1988, only about 11 percent of the voting-age population participated in the Iowa caucuses, whereas 37 percent voted in the New Hampshire primary. The role of the Iowa caucuses in future presidential elections remains to be seen. During the 1976, 1980, 1984, and 1988 elections, several candidates in the party out of power began their run for the presidency more than a year in advance of the Iowa con-

Before 1968

Easy Money

Candidates frequently raise large amounts of money quickly by tapping a handful of wealthy contributors. No federal limits on spending by candidates.

Limited Media Coverage

Campaigns are followed by print journalists and, in later years, by television. But press coverage of campaigns is not intensive and generally does not play a major role in influencing the process.

Late Decisions

Events early in the campaign year, such as the New Hampshire primary, are not decisive. States that pick delegates late in the year, such as California, frequently are important in selecting the nominee. Many states enter the convention without making final decisions about candidates.

Open Conventions

National party conventions sometimes begin with the nomination still undecided. The outcome is determined by maneuvering and negotiations among party factions, often stretching over multiple ballots.

Since 1968

Difficult Fund Raising

Campaign contributions are limited to $1,000 per person, so candidates must work endlessly to raise money from thousands of small contributors. PAC contributions are important in primaries. Campaign spending is limited by law, both nationally and for individual states.

Media-Focused

Campaigns are covered intensively by the media, particularly television. Media treatment of candidates plays a crucial role in determining the nominee.

"Front-loaded"

Early events, such as the Iowa caucuses and New Hampshire primary, are important. The nomination may be decided even before many major states vote. Early victories attract great media attention, which gives winners free publicity and greater fund-raiser ability.

Closed Conventions

The nominee is determined before the convention, which does little more than ratify the decision made in primaries and caucuses. Convention activities focus on creating a favorable media image of the candidate for the general election campaign.

Source: Michael Nelson, ed., *Congressional Quarterly's Guide to the Presidency* (Washington, D.C.: Congressional Quarterly Inc., 1989), p. 201. Used by permission.

test. But the first Democratic challenger to George Bush in 1992, former senator Paul Tsongas of Massachusetts, did not announce his candidacy until April 1991, leaving less time to prepare for Iowa.

By winning the New Hampshire primary in 1988, both George Bush and Michael Dukakis overcame their third-place finishes in Iowa. By going on to win their party's nominations in 1988, Bush and Dukakis also added to the developing legend of the New Hampshire primary. Since 1952, no candidate has won the presidency without first winning that primary. In thirteen of the sixteen nominating contests in both parties since 1960, the candidate who won New Hampshire also won the party nomination. This remarkable record means that every four years, candidates will spend weeks of their life and millions of dollars trudging through snow, contesting for votes in a tiny northeastern state.

More than 35 million citizens voted in both parties' presidential primaries in 1988, and another million participated in party caucuses. Requiring prospective presidential candidates to campaign before many millions of party voters in primaries and hundreds of thousands of party activists in caucus states has several consequences:

- The uncertainty of the nomination process attracts a half-dozen or so plausible candidates, especially when the party does not have a president seeking re-election. For example, seven Democrats and six Republicans took part in the process in 1988.

- Candidates usually cannot win the nomination unless they are favored by most party identifiers. There have been only two exceptions to this rule since 1936, when poll data first became available: Adlai E. Stevenson in 1952 and George McGovern in 1972.[21] Both were Democrats; both lost impressively in the general election.

- Candidates who win the nomination do it mainly on their own and owe little or nothing to the national party organization, which usually does not promote a candidate. In fact, Jimmy Carter won the nomination in 1976 against a field of nationally prominent Democrats, even though he was a party outsider with few strong connections in the national party leadership.

Campaigns

As Barbara Salmore and Stephen Salmore have observed, election campaigns have been studied more through anecdotes than through systematic analysis.[22] These authors developed a framework of analysis that emphasizes the political context of the campaign, the financial resources available for conducting the campaign, and the strategies and tactics that underlie the dissemination of information about the candidate.

Political Context

The two most important structural factors that face each candidate planning a campaign are the office the candidate is seeking and whether he or she is the **incumbent**, the current officeholder running for re-election, or the **challenger**, who seeks to replace the incumbent. Alternatively, the candidate can be running in an **open election**, which lacks an incumbent due to resignation or death. Incumbents usually enjoy great advantages over challengers, especially in elections to Congress. As explained in Chapter 11, incumbents in the House of Representatives are almost impossible to defeat in elections, winning over 95 percent of the time. However, incumbent senators are somewhat more vulnerable. An incumbent president is also difficult to defeat, but not impossible—as Jimmy Carter learned in 1980.

Every candidate organizing a campaign must also examine the characteristics of the electorate in the territory that votes for the office. These include its physical size, its voting population, and its sociological make-

Political Campaigning: The Inside Story

Actually, it's not all that exciting. Conducting a successful campaign usually involves a careful statistical analysis of voting trends and various social and economic characteristics of the electorate. The sign in Republican strategist Karl Rove's office in Austin, Texas, says a lot: These days, computers may be everything.

up. In general, the larger, more populous, and more diverse the electorate, the more complicated and costly the campaign. Obviously, running for president means conducting a huge, complicated, and expensive campaign. After receiving the nominations at their party conventions, George Bush and Michael Dukakis visited thirty and thirty-two states, respectively, on campaign stops, spending more than two days in most of them.[23]

Despite comments in the news about the decreased influence of party affiliation in voting behavior, the political tendency of the electorate is a very important factor in the context of a campaign. Not only is it easier for a candidate to get elected when his or her party matches the electorate's preference, but it is easier to raise the funds needed to conduct a winning campaign. Challengers for Congress, for example, get far less money from organized groups than incumbents and must rely more on their personal funds and on raising funds from individuals.[24] So candidates of the minority party not only have to overcome a voting bias, they must also overcome a funding bias. Finally, significant political issues—such as economic recession, personal scandals, and war—can not only affect a campaign but dominate it and even negate positive factors like incumbency and normal inclinations of the electorate. For example, the Watergate affair overshadowed the 1974 congressional elections, resulting in the loss of thirty-six seats of Republican representatives seeking re-election, mostly in Republican districts, regardless of the quality of their campaigns.

Financing

Speaking about election campaigns, former House Speaker Thomas ("Tip") O'Neill once said, "As it is now, there are four parts to any campaign. The candidate, the issues of the candidate, the campaign organization, and the money to run the campaign with. Without money you can forget the other three."[25] Money is needed to pay for office space, staff salaries, telephone bills, postage, travel expenses, campaign literature, and, of course, advertising in the mass media. In addition to money, Salmore and Salmore cite the campaign organization and the candidate as resources.[26] However, enough money will buy the best campaign managers, equipment, transportation, research, and consultants—making the quality of the organization only a function of money. Although the equation is not quite as strong, when ample campaign funds are available, so are good candidates. So from a cynical but practical viewpoint, campaign resources boil down to campaign funds.

It is difficult to generalize about raising funds for political campaigns. Campaign financing is now heavily regulated by national and state governments, and regulations vary according to the level of the office—national, state, or local. Even at the national level, there are major differences in financing laws for presidential and congressional elections.

Regulating campaign financing. Strict campaign financing laws are relatively new to American politics. Early laws to limit campaign contributions and to control campaign spending were flawed in one way or another, and none clearly provided for administration and enforcement. In 1971, during the period of party reform, Congress passed the *Federal Election Campaign Act* (FECA), which imposed stringent new rules for full reporting of campaign contributions and expenditures. The weakness of the old legislation soon became apparent. In 1968, before the FECA was passed, House and Senate candidates reported spending $8.5 million for their campaigns. With the FECA in force, the same number of candidates confessed to spending $88.9 million in 1972.[27]

The FECA has been amended several times since 1971, but the amendments have for the most part strengthened the law. For example, the original law legalized political action committees, but a 1974 amendment limited the amounts that they could contribute to election campaigns. (Political action committees are discussed in Chapter 10.) The 1974 amendment also created the **Federal Election Commission (FEC)** to implement the law. The FEC now enforces limits on financial contributions to national campaigns and requires full disclosure of campaign spending. The FEC also administers the public financing of presidential campaigns, which began with the 1976 election.

Financing presidential campaigns. Presidential campaigns have always been expensive, and at times the methods of raising funds to support them were open to question. In the presidential election of 1972, the last election before the FEC took over the funding of presidential campaigns and the regulating of campaign expenditures, President Richard Nixon's campaign committee spent over $65 million, some of it obtained illegally (for which campaign officials went to jail). In 1974, a new campaign finance law made public funds available to presidential primary and general election candidates under certain conditions.

Candidates for the nomination for president can qualify for federal funding by raising $5,000 (in private contributions no greater than $250 each) in each of twenty states. The FEC then matches these contributions up to one-half of the spending limit. Originally, under the 1974 law, the FEC limited spending in presidential primary elections to $10 million. But cost-of-living provisions had raised the limit in the 1988 primaries to $23.05 million (plus $4.6 million for fund-raising activities). The amount will be increased again in 1992 to match increases in the cost of living.

The presidential nominees of the Democratic and Republican parties receive twice the primary election limit in public funds for the general election campaign ($46.1 million in 1988) provided that they spend only the public funds. Every major candidate since 1976 has accepted public funding, holding the costs of presidential campaigns well below Nixon's record expenditures in 1972.

Public funds are given directly to each candidate's campaign committee, not to the national committee of either party. But the FEC also limits what the national committees can spend on behalf of the nominees. In 1988, that limit was $8.3 million. And the FEC limits the amount individuals ($1,000) and organizations ($5,000) can contribute to candidates per election. They are not limited, however, in the amount of *expenses* they can incur to promote candidates of their choice.* That's how the National Security Political Action Committee was allowed to spend more than $7 million producing and running the Willie Horton commercial and otherwise promoting Bush's candidacy.

Public funding has had several effects on campaign financing. Obviously, it has limited campaign costs. Also, it has helped equalize the amounts spent by major candidates in general elections. And it has strengthened the trend toward "personalized" campaigns since federal funds are given to the presidential candidate of each party, not to the party organization that the candidate represents. Finally, public funding has forced candidates to spend a great deal of time seeking thousand-dollar contributions—a limit that has not changed since 1974, despite the inflation that has more than doubled the FEC's spending limits. In the 1980s, however, both parties began to exploit a loophole in the law that allowed them to raise virtually unlimited funds from individuals and organizations—provided it was spent for the entire ticket on party mailings, voter registration, and get-out-the-vote campaigns. The Democratic

---

* The distinction between contributions and expenses hinges on whether funds are spent as part of a coordinated campaign (a contribution) or spent independently of the candidate's campaign (an expense). The 1974 amendment to the FECA established limits on both campaign contributions and independent expenditures by interested citizens. In *Buckley* v. *Valeo* (1976), the Supreme Court struck down the limits on citizens' expenditures as an infringement on the freedom of speech, protected under the First Amendment.

Buddy, Can You Spare a Buck?

In 1991, the Federal Election Commission, which provides public funds to major presidential candidates, prepared and distributed this advertisement. Not enough taxpayers were checking off the box on income tax forms that routes a dollar of their taxes to the campaign fund. The FEC had hoped to persuade more taxpayers to contribute to the fund, but the resulting response was not overwhelming.

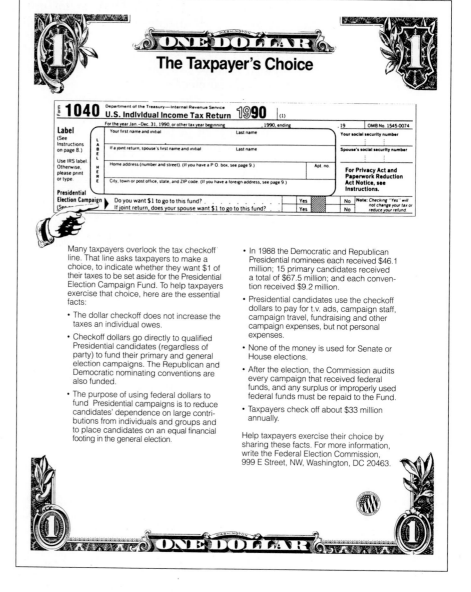

The Taxpayer's Choice

Many taxpayers overlook the tax checkoff line. That line asks taxpayers to make a choice, to indicate whether they want $1 of their taxes to be set aside for the Presidential Election Campaign Fund. To help taxpayers exercise that choice, here are the essential facts:

• The dollar checkoff does not increase the taxes an individual owes.

• Checkoff dollars go directly to qualified Presidential candidates (regardless of party) to fund their primary and general election campaigns. The Republican and Democratic nominating conventions are also funded.

• The purpose of using federal dollars to fund Presidential campaigns is to reduce candidates' dependence on large contributions from individuals and groups and to place candidates on an equal financial footing in the general election.

• In 1988 the Democratic and Republican Presidential nominees each received $46.1 million; 15 primary candidates received a total of $67.5 million; and each convention received $9.2 million.

• Presidential candidates use the checkoff dollars to pay for t.v. ads, campaign staff, campaign travel, fundraising and other campaign expenses, but not personal expenses.

• None of the money is used for Senate or House elections.

• After the election, the Commission audits every campaign that received federal funds, and any surplus or improperly used federal funds must be repaid to the Fund.

• Taxpayers check off about $33 million annually.

Help taxpayers exercise their choice by sharing these facts. For more information, write the Federal Election Commission, 999 E Street, NW, Washington, DC 20463.

National Committee raised about $20 million in so-called "soft money" this way and its Republican counterpart about $30 million, which they channeled to state and local party committees for registration drives and other activities that were not exclusively devoted to their presidential candidates but helped them nonetheless.[28] The net effect of these "coordinated campaigns" was to increase the organization role of both the national and state parties in the campaigns.

You might think that a party's presidential campaign would be closely coordinated with the campaigns of the party's candidates for Congress. But remember that campaign funds go to the presidential candidate, not the party, and that the national party organization does not run the presidential campaign. Presidential candidates may join congressional candidates in public appearances for mutual benefit, but presidential campaigns are usually isolated—financially and otherwise—from congressional campaigns.

Strategies and Tactics

In a military campaign, *strategy* refers to the scheme for winning the war, while *tactics* refers to the conduct of localized hostilities.[29] In an election campaign, *strategy* refers to the overall approach used to persuade citizens to vote for the candidate, and *tactics* to the content of the messages and the way they are delivered. Salmore and Salmore identify three basic strategies, which campaigns may blend in different mixes: (1) a *party-centered* strategy, which relies heavily on voters' partisan identification as well as on the party's organization to provide the resources necessary to wage the campaign; (2) an *issue-oriented* strategy, which seeks support from groups that feel strongly about various policies; and (3) an *image-oriented* strategy, which depends on the candidate's perceived personal qualities, such as experience, leadership ability, integrity, independence, trustworthiness, and the like.[30]

The campaign strategy must be tailored to the political context of the election. Obviously, a party-centered strategy is inappropriate when campaigning for the nomination, for opponents all have the same party affiliation. Research suggests that a party-centered strategy is more suited to voters with less political information than those with more.[31] How

The Blanton Bunch

With his family in tow, Republican candidate Ted Blanton sets forth to campaign against a long-time Democratic incumbent in North Carolina's Eighth Congressional District. During their first match-up in 1988, the incumbent, W. G. "Bill" Hefner, defeated Blanton by only a slim margin. But in 1990, Hefner was more prepared to counter Blanton's homespun approach, spending more time campaigning in rural areas. This time the incumbent defeated the challenger by a wider margin, taking 55 percent of the vote.

does the candidate learn what the electorate knows and thinks about politics, and how can he or she use this information? Candidates today usually turn to pollsters and political consultants, of whom there are hundreds.[32] Well-funded candidates can purchase a "polling package" that includes the following:

- a *benchmark poll* that provides "campaign information about the voting preferences and issue concerns of various groups in the electorate and a detailed reading of the images voters have of the candidates in the race"
- *focus groups,* consisting of ten to twenty people "chosen to represent particular target groups the campaign wants to reinforce or persuade . . . led in their discussion by persons trained in small-group dynamics," giving texture and depth to poll results
- a *trend poll* "to determine the success of the campaigns in altering candidate images and voting preferences"
- *tracking polls* that begin in early October "conducting short nightly interviews with a small number of respondents, keyed to the variables that have assumed importance"[33]

Using information from such sources, professional campaign managers can settle on a strategy that mixes party, issues, and images in its messages. In major campaigns, these messages are disseminated to voters via the mass media through news coverage and advertising.[34]

Making the news.   Campaigns value news coverage by the media for two reasons: the coverage is free, and it seems objective to the audience. If news stories do nothing more than report the candidate's name, that is important (see Feature 9.2). The first task is to attract reporters to cover candidates' news conferences and campaign activities, which is helped by anticipating the reporters' deadlines and needs. Holding a conference early on a slow news day (like Sunday) improves the chance for coverage on the evening news.[35] It also helps to provide opportunities for good pictures and to link the statement to ongoing news stories. Getting free news coverage is yet another advantage that incumbents enjoy over challengers, for incumbents can command attention simply by announcing political decisions—even if they had little to do with them. Members of Congress are so good at this that House members may have made news organizations their "unwitting adjuncts."[36]

Campaigns can be more or less effective in transmitting their messages via the news media. Effective tactics recognize the limitations of both the audience and the media. The typical voter is not deeply interested in politics and has trouble keeping track of multiple themes supported with details. By the same token, neither is television ready to air lengthy statements from candidates. A study of all weekday evening newscasts from Labor Day to Election Day in 1968 found that the average statement from a candidate ran 42.3 seconds; over the same period in 1988, the average candidate utterance was reduced to a soundbite of only 9.8 seconds![37] The same study found that the time the networks devoted to "visuals" of the candidates unaccompanied by their words increased by

FEATURE 9.2 *Oh,* That *Charles Johnson!*

In the state of Washington, Chief Justice Keith M. Callow, a widely respected judge, was voted out of office in 1990 by voters who cast more ballots for Charles W. Johnson, a lawyer who specialized in representing "the little guy" in assault, drunken driving, and other criminal cases and who did not campaign. Chief Justice Callow did not campaign either, but Johnson had something else going for him: name recognition. Only 20 percent of the voters bothered to vote in the judicial election, and interviews of those voters after the election indicate that most thought they were voting for another Johnson. There were three other prominent Charles Johnsons in the area: one was a Tacoma television anchor, another a former sergeant-at-arms of the state senate, and the third a superior court judge—who reported that voters thought *he* was the Charles Johnson on the ballot. About half the voters thought they could recall something positive about candidate Johnson, but they could not remember what it was. Neither side had hired consultants, but a Seattle-based consultant thought that the election would be good for his business: "The low voter awareness and the kind of

Former Chief Justice Keith M. Callow

name confusion that happened here probably spell good news for political consulting firms."

The confusion over Charles Johnson was not a fluke. In a race for a seat on the Texas Supreme Court in 1990, lawyer and retired Air Force officer Gene Kelly defeated district court judge Robert Cornyn. Cornyn had been endorsed by the bar association and virtually every newspaper and had spent $350,000 on his campaign, compared with the $4,000 spent by Kelly. Apparently, however, having the same name as a famous dancer gave Kelly the edge.

Even in more prominent races, many voters may not know the candidates. Nearly one-third of the voters interviewed after the 1988 presidential election could not identify Governor Michael Dukakis's running mate (Senator Lloyd Bentsen).

Candidate Charles W. Johnson

Sources: Robb London, "For Want of Recognition, Chief Justice Is Ousted," *New York Times*, 28 September 1990, p. B9; Robb London, "What Is in a Familiar Name Could Well Be a Judgeship," *New York Times*, 19 October 1990, p. B10; and Michael Oreskes, "Study Finds 'Astonishing' Indifference to Elections," *New York Times*, 6 May 1990, sec. 1, p. 16.

more than 300 percent between 1968 and 1988. Not surprisingly, a series of detailed proposals announced by the Dukakis campaign to protect middle-income families from increased costs of higher education were ignored by television, while the simple messages of the Bush campaign ("No new taxes"; "My opponent is soft on crime") came through clearly on the medium.[38]

Given the media's preoccupation with horse race journalism (see Chapter 6), it is not surprising that television news contains little information about the issues in the campaign. In fact, a study of television news and television advertising in the last weeks of the 1984 campaign found that "voters got the overwhelming majority of their campaign information from political ads, rather than from television coverage."[39]

Paid advertising. The first objective of paid advertising is name recognition. The next is to promote the candidate by extolling his or her virtues. Finally, campaign advertising can have a negative objective, attacking the opponent to promote the candidate. But name recognition is the most important. Studies show that many voters cannot recall the names of their U.S. senators or representative, but they can recognize their names on a list—as on the ballot. Researchers attribute the high re-election rate for members of Congress mainly to high levels of name recognition (see Chapter 11).

At one time, candidates for national office relied heavily on newspaper advertising in their campaigns; today, they overwhelmingly use the electronic media. A study of campaign spending in the 1986 primary and general elections calculated that candidates running for the House spent almost 20 percent of their campaign expenditures on television and radio, versus only 6 percent for print advertisements. Candidates for the Senate spent almost 40 percent for the electronic media, versus less than 1 percent for print media.[40] This emphasis on electronic media, particularly on television, has raised concern about the promotion of candidates by developing a "videostyle" for them that helps win elections but is irrelevant to performance in office.

In cultivating a candidate's videostyle, both consultant and candidate arrive at a campaign theme by anticipating audience reactions. Then the consultant coaches the candidate on how to deliver the theme quickly and effectively in a thirty-second commercial. A scholar who analyzed television use by six candidates in three Senate campaigns found that audiences do not usually spend time dissecting the message in a television spot; instead, they form impressions of the mood, which the producer creates using "background music, the sharpness of the visual images, and the persuasiveness of the verbal content."[41]

Consultants and candidates do not focus on issues in developing a videostyle because their audience does not react well to issue-oriented discussions. One scholar who recorded scores of speeches by the major candidates seeking nomination in 1980 observed that audiences generally applauded less enthusiastically when candidates mentioned specific policies than when they made other appeals.[42] That year, Ronald Reagan regularly drew cheers from his audiences for references to "godless totali-

Running in Office

Democratic senator Paul Wellstone of Minnesota, a former professor of political science at Carleton College, conducted an imaginative television campaign in 1990. As an underdog running against an incumbent, Wellstone was shown racing from place to place, speaking rapidly—comically illustrating the contrast between his bare-bones campaign and his opponent's well-funded operation. In Washington, the new senator still tries to get in his daily three-mile run.

tarians" in the Soviet Union and "welfare cheats" at home. (Not surprisingly, he stressed these themes in office after his election.)

The trend in recent years, however, has been away from promoting candidates through slick ads to attacking them in slick ads. The Willie Horton ad in 1988 was a prime example of negative advertising, but the practice was widely used in 1990 as well. A national survey in the heat of the campaign found that half the respondents reported seeing negative ads that attacked, and 40 percent said that they were more prevalent than a decade ago.[43] Although negative campaigns may turn some people away from politics, they often work. Liberal Democrat Joan Kelly Horn relied on attack ads in her campaign against incumbent Republican Jack Buechner in a conservative suburb of St. Louis, where he seemed comfortably entrenched. Challenger Horn, herself a political consultant, used an ad showing Buechner saying that service in Congress was "a public trust, not a public trough," which then cut to a scene of hogs snorting dollar bills in the mud "while an announcer recited Buechner's financial benefit from honoraria, overseas travel, the congressional pay raise and a cable TV stock deal."[44] Horn won the election.

Elections

By national law, all seats in the House of Representatives and one-third of the seats in the Senate are filled in a **general election** held on the first Tuesday after the first Monday in November in even-numbered years. Every state takes advantage of the national election to fill some of nearly 500,000 state and local offices across the country, which makes the election even more "general."[45] When the president is chosen every fourth year, the election year is identified as a *presidential election.* The intervening years are known as *congressional, midterm,* or *off-year elections.*

Presidential Elections

Unlike elections for almost all other offices in the United States, the office of president does not go automatically to the candidate who wins the most votes. Instead, elections for president are decided by a two-stage procedure specified in the Constitution that requires the president to be chosen by a group (college) of electors representing the states.

The electoral college.   Voters choose the president only indirectly; they actually vote for a little-known slate of electors (their names are usually not even on the ballot) pledged to one of the candidates. Occasionally, electors break their pledges when they cast their written ballots at their state capitols in December. This even happened in 1988, when Margaret Leach, chosen as a Democratic elector in West Virginia, abandoned Dukakis and voted for his running mate, Senator Lloyd Bentsen.[46] But usually the electors are faithful, especially when their votes are needed to determine the winner. The more important issue surrounding the electoral college is the match between the outcome of the popular vote and the outcome of the electoral vote. Whether a candidate wins a state by five or five hundred thousand votes, he or she wins *all* that state's electoral votes.*

In the electoral college, each state is accorded one vote for each of its senators (100 votes total) and representatives (435 votes total), adding up to 535 votes. In addition, the Twenty-third Amendment to the Constitution awarded three electoral votes to the District of Columbia, even though it elects no voting members of Congress. So the total number of electoral votes is 538, and a majority of 270 electoral votes are needed to win the presidency.**

These electoral votes are apportioned among the states according to their representation in Congress, which depends, in turn, on their popu-

---

* The one exception is in Maine, where two of the state's electoral votes are awarded by congressional district. The presidential candidate who carries each district wins a single electoral vote.

** If no candidate receives a majority when the electoral college votes, the election is thrown into the House of Representatives. The House votes by state, with each state casting one vote for a single presidential candidate. The top three finishers in the general election are the candidates in the House election. A presidential election has gone to the House only twice in American history, the first time in 1800 and the second in 1824. Both cases occurred before a stable two-party system had developed.

FIGURE 9.2 *Distribution of Electoral Votes in 1992*

The 1990 census produced some major changes in congressional reapportionment with implications for presidential elections. Remember that each state has as many electoral votes as its combined representation in the Senate (always two) and in the House (which depends on population). As shown on the map, states in the South and West gained population and thus picked up seats in the House of Representatives, mainly at the expense of the Northeast. Thus, California, with two senators and fifty-two representatives, now has fifty-four electoral votes—or more than 10 percent of the total of 538. (Washington, D.C., has three electoral votes—equal to the smallest state—although it has no representation in Congress.) (Source: Congressional Quarterly Weekly Report, 23 March 1991, p. 765.)

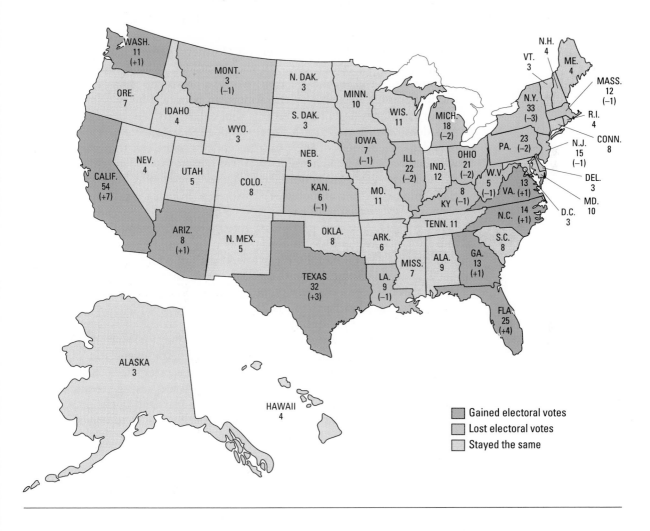

lation. Because of population changes recorded by the 1990 census, there are important changes in the distribution of electoral votes among the states between the 1988 and 1992 presidential elections (see Figure 9.2). California, the largest state in 1980, grew even more in 1990 and now claims fifty-four electoral votes for its fifty-two representatives and two senators. The greatest population growth occurred in the so-called Sunbelt states: For example, Florida and Texas picked up additional representatives at the expense of Frostbelt states like New York, Pennsylvania, Illinois, Michigan, and Ohio.

The most troubling aspect of the electoral college is the possibility that despite winning a plurality or even a majority of popular votes, a candidate could lose the election in the electoral college. This could happen if one candidate wins some states by a very large amount, while the other candidate wins some states by a slim margin. Indeed, it *has* happened in three elections, most recently in 1888, when Grover Cleveland received 48.6 percent of the popular vote to Benjamin Harrison's 47.9 percent. Cleveland nevertheless trailed Harrison in the electoral college, 168 to 233, and Harrison was elected president.

Abolish the electoral college? Reformers argue that it is simply wrong to have a system that allows a candidate who receives the most popular votes to lose the election. Would a president-elect be regarded as the legitimate "winner" by the American people if he or she received a minority of popular votes? Reforms that call for the direct election of the president would institute a purely majoritarian means of choosing the president. Defenders of the electoral college point out that this system, warts and all, has been a stable one. It might be riskier to replace it with a new arrangement that could alter our party system or the way presidential campaigns are conducted. Tradition has in fact prevailed, and recent proposals for fundamental reform have not come close to adoption.

For the last one hundred years, fortunately, the candidate winning a plurality of the popular vote has also won a majority of the electoral vote. In fact, the electoral college operates to magnify the victory margin (see Figure 9.3). Some scholars argue that this increases the legitimacy of the president-elect. For instance, John F. Kennedy defeated Richard Nixon by less than 1 percent of the vote in 1960, but he won 56 percent of the electoral vote, strengthening his claim on the presidency. In any event, the indirect method of electing the president has acted in practice like a direct method of popular election, with the exception that presidential candidates must plan their campaign strategy to win states, not just votes. Given population shifts and statewide voting trends, Democratic party strategists face a special problem in winning the presidency, for Republicans appear to control a majority of votes in the electoral college (see Figure 9.4).

Congressional Elections

The candidates for the presidency are listed at the top of the ballot in a presidential election, followed by candidates for other national, state, and local offices. A voter is said to vote a **straight ticket** when he or she chooses only one party's candidates for all the offices. A voter who switches parties when choosing candidates for different offices is said to vote a **split ticket.** About half the voters admit to splitting their tickets between the parties for state and local offices, and the proportion of voters who chose a presidential candidate from one party and a congressional candidate from the other has increased from about 13 percent in

FIGURE 9.3 *Popular Vote and the Electoral Vote*

Elections for president are decided by the electoral vote, not the popular vote. Although it is possible that a candidate could win a plurality of the popular vote but not the majority of the electoral vote needed to be elected president, this has not happened since 1888. More commonly, candidates who win a plurality of the popular vote win an even larger majority of the electoral vote, as shown here. Even when Richard Nixon won only 43 percent of the vote in 1968 against Hubert Humphrey, the Democratic candidate, and George Wallace of the American Independent party, he took 56 percent of the electoral vote. The effect is to magnify the victory and increase the legitimacy of the president-elect. (Source: Harold W. Stanley and Richard G. Niemi, Vital Statistics on American Politics, *2d ed. [Washington, D.C.: CQ Press, 1990], pp. 104–106.)*

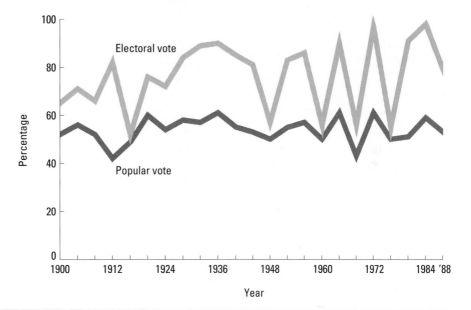

1952 to 25 percent in 1988.[47] The most common pattern in recent years has been to choose a Republican for president but to re-elect Democratic incumbents in the House and Senate. The net effect has been to produce divided government, in which Republicans control the presidency and Democrats the Congress (see Chapter 12).

If Republicans have a lock on the presidency through the electoral college, Democrats seem to have a lock on congressional elections. Not only have they won a majority of House elections every year since 1955, they have controlled the Senate for all but six years during that period. Republicans complain that they have been denied their fair share of votes through inequitable districts drawn by Democrat-dominated state legislatures. For example, the Republicans contested 349 House seats in 1990 and won 47 percent of the vote, but they won only 37 percent of the seats. Since 1954, Republicans have won a lower percentage of seats than votes (on average, 6.8 percent) in *every* House election. Despite the Republicans' complaint, election specialists point out that this is the inevitable consequence of **first-past-the-post** elections—a British term for elections conducted in single-member districts that award victory to the candidate with the most votes. In all such elections around the world,

FIGURE 9.4 *Politics of the Electoral Vote, 1960–1988*

Republican candidates won five of the eight presidential elections between 1960 and 1988. This in itself does not seem very daunting, but look at the voting history of the states during that period. Thirty states voted Republican at least six times in those elections. These predominantly Republican states hold 291 of the electoral votes in 1992—and only 270 are needed to elect the president. By comparison, only five states (plus the District of Columbia) voted at least six times for Democratic candidates during the same period, and these predominantly Democratic states have only 38 electoral votes. Even if the Democratic candidate in 1992 held all the Democratic states and took all of the competitive states, the candidate would have to win at least some Republican states to win the election. (Source: Michael Nelson, ed., Congressional Quarterly's Guide to the Presidency [Washington, D.C.: Congressional Quarterly Press, 1989], pp. 1423–1427.)

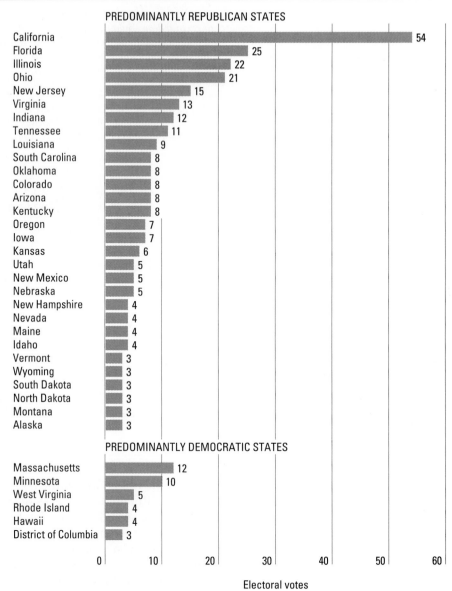

parties that win the most votes tend to win proportionately more seats. The same process operates in the electoral college, which, as discussed, produces a larger majority in the electoral vote over the fifty states than the candidate won nationwide.*

* If you have trouble understanding this phenomenon, think of a basketball team that scores, on average, 51 percent of the total points scored in all games it plays during the season. Such a team usually wins more than half its games, for it wins systematically and tends to win the close ones.

Sweeping Indictment

The 1990 congressional elections drew a series of protests against incumbent candidates, as expressed in this sign of the times. Although 95 percent of incumbents were re-elected (close to the usual rate in recent years), other evidence pointed to anti-incumbent sentiment. According to the Congressional Quarterly Weekly Report, *the typical incumbent facing major party opposition won 63.5 percent of the vote in 1990, down from 68.2 percent in 1988.*

DON'T GET MAD .... GET EVEN!

RE-ELECT NOBODY!

ALL INCUMBENTS OUT!

Nevertheless, the fact is that, historically, voters have favored Democratic candidates for both the House and the Senate, even when electing Republican candidates for president. Some analysts see special significance in that voting pattern. They credit citizens for consciously voting to produce divided government, with a Republican executive pushing one way and a Democratic legislature the other.[48] If so, voters behave quite rationally in making their ballot choices. It remains to be seen whether the evidence of voting choice in general elections can support such a rational interpretation of electoral behavior.

Explaining Voting Choice

Why do people choose one candidate over another? That is not easy to determine, but there are ways to approach the question. Individual voting choices can be analyzed as products of *long-term* and *short-term* forces. Long-term forces operate over a series of elections, predisposing voters to choose certain types of candidates. Short-term forces are associated with particular elections; they arise from a combination of the candidates and the issues of the time. *Party identification* is by far the most important long-term force affecting U.S. elections. The most important short-term forces are *candidate attributes* and their *policy positions.*

Party Identification

Most research on voting in presidential elections stems from a series of studies that originated at the University of Michigan. Comparable surveys have been conducted for every presidential election and most congressional elections since 1952. When respondents to the 1988 survey were asked at what point they had decided how to vote for president, nearly half (49 percent) said that they "knew all along" or had decided before the conventions.[49] This figure is somewhat higher than average. In other presidential elections since 1952, about 40 percent of the voters reported making up their minds before the candidates squared off in the general election campaign. And voters who make an early voting decision generally vote according to their party identification.

Despite frequent comments in the media about the decline of partisanship in voting behavior, party identification had a substantial effect on the presidential vote in 1988 (see Figure 9.5). Avowed Democrats voted 84 percent for Dukakis, while Republicans voted 92 percent for Bush. Fifty-three percent of the independents who voted also voted for Bush. This is a common pattern in presidential elections. The winner holds nearly all of the voters who identify with his party. The loser also holds most of his identifiers, but some percentage defects to the winner, a product of the short-term forces—the candidates' attributes and the issues—surrounding the election. The winner usually gets most of the independents, who split disproportionately for him, also because of short-term forces.

Because there are more Democrats than Republicans, the Democrats should benefit. Why, then, have Republican candidates won seven out of ten presidential elections since 1952? For one thing, Democrats do not turn out to vote as consistently as Republicans. For another, Democrats defect more easily from their party. Defections are sparked by the candidates' attributes and the issues, which have favored Republican presidential candidates since 1952. Compared with party, it is much harder to identify the effects of attributes and issues on the voting choice.

Candidates' Attributes

Candidates' attributes are especially important to voters who lack good information about a candidate's past behavior and policy stands—which means most of us. Without this kind of information, voters search for clues about the candidates to try to predict their behavior in office.[50] Some fall back on their firsthand knowledge of religion, gender, and race in making political judgments. Such stereotypic thinking accounts for patterns of opposition and support met by a Catholic candidate for president (John Kennedy), a woman candidate for vice president

FIGURE 9.5 *Effect of Party Identification on the Vote, 1988*

The 1988 presidential election showed that party identification still plays a key role in voting behavior. This chart displays the results of a postelection survey that asked people what party they identified with and how they voted for president. Note that party identification affects the decision to vote as well as voting choice. Respondents who regarded themselves as independents were least likely to vote in the election, and those who did split almost evenly between the candidates. However, 75 percent of the Republicans not only voted but voted for George Bush. Similarly, 59 percent of the Democrats voted for Dukakis, but 11 percent defected from their party and voted for Bush. If one were to compute the effects of party identification only for those who voted, 92 percent of the Republicans who voted cast their ballot for Bush, while 84 percent of the Democrats who voted chose Dukakis. (Source: 1988 National Election Survey, made available through the Inter-University Consortium for Political and Social Research. Used by permission.)

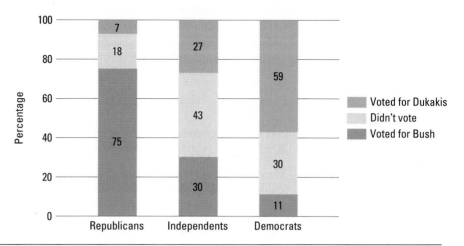

(Geraldine Ferraro), and a black contender for a presidential nomination (Jesse Jackson).

Apart from candidates' sociological attributes, voters say that candidates' personal qualifications are very important to them. Two election surveys in 1988 asked, "What must the winner of the election have within himself, and bring to the job, in order to be a good president?" In both surveys, about 55 percent of the voters cited character traits, with the overwhelming majority of those emphasizing "trustworthiness." About 40 percent believed that competence traits, spread across "leadership," "knowledge," and "experience," were very important. Only about a third linked issue positions to being a good president, and about half of those mentioned "concern for needs of all the people" or some kind of fairness.[51]

Nevertheless, when the same survey asked for factors "most important to you in terms of deciding who to support for president," respondents listed issue positions and competence first (about 40 percent for each)—substantially above personal traits (about 15 percent) and party identification (6 percent).[52] Moreover, when voters were asked just before the election, "What is the most important reason for choosing (Bush/Dukakis) over his opponent?" party identification emerged next to experience at the top of the list (16 percent each), followed by trustworthiness, dislike of the other candidate, and continuation of Reagan's policies (all tied at 11 percent)—trailed by a variety of concerns, only some of which were issues.[53] So voters may say a candidate's party is not important in their election decisions, but they often behave otherwise.

Issues and Policies

Choosing among candidates according to personal attributes might be understandable, but it is not rational voting according to democratic theory. According to that theory, citizens should vote according to the candidates' past performance and proposed policies. By any objective standard, the candidates clearly differed on their policies in the presidential election of 1988. Michael Dukakis, trying to recapture the presidency for the Democrats, stressed the government's responsibility to provide "good jobs for good wages." George Bush, seeking to retain the office for the Republicans, charged that his opponent was a spendthrift liberal who would surely raise taxes and release criminals.

How well did the electorate understand the candidates' issue positions, and how much learning occurred during the presidential campaign? In a unique study, Bruce Buchanan tested a national sample on the candidates' issue positions in September and again just before the election.[54] Figure 9.6 shows the results for the nine issues that received extensive media coverage or were featured in paid advertisements. Respondents were asked to attribute each issue position to a candidate, and they were scored "right" for a correct placement. Because respondents had more correct answers on all issues in the second survey than the first, the figure shows that some learning occurred during the campaign. It also showed that Bush, who focused on fewer issues, did a better job of educating voters in his campaign than Dukakis, whose media campaign was said to be in "disarray."[55] An impressive 78 percent of the voters knew that Bush was in favor of capital punishment (also favored by a majority of the voters). Dukakis did best in convincing voters that he was against the Midgetman missile, which may have suggested to them that he was soft on defense as well as on crime. But barely one-half of the voters knew where he stood on most of his key issues.

Voters who choose between candidates on the basis of their policies are voting "on the issues," which fits the idealized conception of democratic theory. However, issues, candidate attributes, and party identification *all* figure in the voting decision. Although it is difficult to sort out their relative influence, their effects can be estimated using multivariate statistical models. Some scholars contend that issues played a more important role in the voting decision in the 1980s than in the 1950s.[56] Unfortunately for democratic theory, most studies of presidential elections show that issues are less important than either party identification or the candidate's image when people cast their ballots. Only in 1972, when voters perceived George McGovern as too liberal for their tastes, did issue voting exceed party identification in importance.[57] Even that year, issues were less important than the candidate's image. According to polls

FIGURE 9.6 *Does Learning Occur During a Campaign?*

Ideally, election campaigns should educate voters about the candidates' positions on issues. However, given the emphasis on soundbites and image manipulation in the media, one wonders how much voters actually learn about the candidates' positions during a campaign. A recent study tested respondents' knowledge of candidates' positions on important issues in early September and then again just before the election and provides some evidence that voters do learn something. In both surveys, respondents were presented with a series of issue positions and asked to link them to the two candidates. The graph below reports results only for the nine issues that received extensive media coverage, showing the percentage of respondents who connected the positions correctly in each survey. A majority of the public knew about Bush's positions on capital punishment and taxes even before the general election campaign got under way, and his campaign was quite successful in developing a high level of awareness of his support for capital punishment in particular. Moreover, some learning occurred on every issue. (Source: Bruce Buchanan, Electing a President: The Markle Commission Reseach on Campaign '88. *Austin: University of Texas Press. © 1991. These data came from Table 5.7 in excerpts from the book published by the University of Texas Press, p. 93. Reprinted by permission.)*

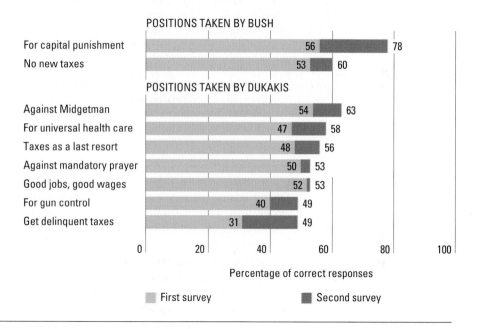

taken at the time, voters saw McGovern as weak and uncertain, Nixon as strong and (ironically) highly principled.[58]

Although there has been some decline in party voting since the 1950s, there is a closer alignment now between voters' positions on the issues and their party identification. For example, Democratic party identifiers—who are more likely than Republican identifiers to describe themselves as liberal—are now even more likely than Republican identifiers to favor government spending for social welfare and abortions. The more closely party identification is aligned with ideological orientation, the more sense it makes to vote by party. In the absence of detailed information about candidates' positions on the issues, party labels are a handy indicator of those positions.[59]

Campaign Effects

If party identification is both the most important factor in the voting decision and also resistant to short-term changes, there are definite limits to the effects of an election campaign on the outcome of elections.[60] In a close election, however, just changing a few votes means the difference between victory and defeat, so a campaign can be decisive even if it has little overall effect. Not surprisingly, campaigns are most effective when one side has weapons that other side lacks. One major limitation to the capacity of image makers and campaign consultants to control elections, however, is that they regularly offset one another by working on opposite sides in an election. In the 1990 elections, for example, the magazine *Campaigns & Elections* prepared a "scorecard" for 137 of America's leading consultants who worked on at least two campaigns for any federal or major state offices. In all, these consultants were involved in 759 campaigns, winning 456 and losing 303—for a batting average of 60 percent.[61] That sounds fine, except that, according to chance, about half their clients in two-candidate races are likely to win without expert assistance. Moreover, specialists in the new campaign technology argue that

> no one has even a vague idea of what percentage of the vote a consultant or a piece of new campaign technology can or does add to a candidate under any given circumstances. Campaign observers rarely even have a precise idea of what event or series of events produced the election result. Campaigning remains complex, unpredictable, and very unscientific, and one may expect and be grateful that it always will be.[62]

Another school of thought holds that campaigns for the presidency and other major offices are overridden by salient political issues, especially economic conditions such as unemployment and inflation. Numerous scholars have developed models of voting behavior in presidential and congressional elections based primarily on the voters' past or future views of economic conditions.[63] Additional factors outside the control of campaign managers, such as war and incumbency, also have powerful effects on voting behavior and can be incorporated into rather successful models for forecasting presidential elections in advance of the campaign.[64]

As we learned at the beginning of this chapter, two scholars, Allan Lichtman and Ken DeCell, have concluded that campaigns have no material effect on presidential elections. They contend that presidential elections are decided by turning any six of thirteen keys that are determined well in advance of election day (see Feature 9.3). Moreover, these keys are largely in the hands of the incumbent party. Short of nominating a national hero (such as General Norman Schwarzkopf) or a charismatic leader, the party out of power can do nothing to affect the election results. According to Lichtman and DeCell, even if the Willie Horton commercial had never been aired, Michael Dukakis would have lost in 1988 because only three keys had been turned in his favor.

We leave you to fit these keys to the 1992 presidential election. In the process, you can reflect on the effect of the election campaign on the election outcome.

F E A T U R E   9.3   *The Thirteen Keys to the Presidency*

In their provocative book, Allan J. Lichtman and Ken DeCell contend that presidential elections depend on the performance of the previous administration and on certain political conditions that are established well in advance of the election campaign. They identify thirteen keys, or conditions, that have been critical to the outcome of every presidential election since 1860. When five or fewer keys were false, the incumbent party won the election. When six or more were false, the incumbent party lost. The list below shows which keys are likely to be false or true for the 1992 presidential election. Note that four keys are assumed to be false already, and only one economic key and the Democratic nominee remain undecided (*??*). According to this theory, Bush is probably guaranteed re-election unless the economy is in recession (Key 5) and the Democrats nominate a charismatic leader or national hero (Key 13).

The Thirteen Keys to the Presidency

The keys to the presidency are stated as conditions that favor the re-election of the incumbent party. When five or fewer statements are false, the incumbent party wins. When six or more are false, the challenging party wins.

Key 1: Party mandate   After the midterm elections, the incumbent party holds more seats in the U.S. House of Representatives than it did after the previous midterm elections. *False*

Key 2: Contest   There is no serious contest for the incumbent-party nomination. *True*

Key 3: Incumbency   The incumbent-party candidate is the sitting president. *True*

Key 4: Third party   There is no significant third-party or independent campaign. *True*

Key 5: Short-term economy   The economy is not in recession during the election campaign. *??*

Key 6: Long-term economy   Real per-capita economic growth during the term equals or exceeds mean growth during the previous two terms. *False*

Key 7: Policy change   The incumbent administration effects major changes in national policy. *False*

Key 8: Social unrest   There is no sustained social unrest during the term. *True*

Key 9: Scandal   The incumbent administration is untainted by major scandal. *True*

Key 10: Foreign/military failure   The incumbent administration suffers no major failure in foreign or military affairs. *True*

Key 11: Foreign/military success   The incumbent administration achieves a major success in foreign or military affairs. *True*

Key 12: Incumbent charisma   The incumbent-party candidate is charismatic or a national hero. *False*

Key 13: Challenger charisma   The challenging-party candidate is not charismatic or a national hero. *??*

Source: Allan J. Lichtman and Ken DeCell, *The Thirteen Keys to the Presidency* (Lanham, Md.: Madison Books, 1990), p. 7. Copyright © 1990 by Madison Books. Reprinted by permission of the publisher and the author.

Campaigns, Elections, and Parties

Election campaigns in contemporary American politics tend to be highly personalized, centered on the candidates and conducted outside the control of party organizations. The increased use of electronic media, especially television, has encouraged candidates to personalize their campaign messages, while the decline of party identification has decreased the power of party-related appeals. Although the party affiliation of the candidates and the party identification of the voters work together to explain a good deal of electoral behavior, party organizations are not central to elections in America. This fact has implications for democratic government.

Parties and the Majoritarian Model

According to the majoritarian model of democracy, parties are essential in linking people with their government by making government responsive to public opinion. Chapter 8 closed by outlining the model of responsible party government in a majoritarian democracy. This model holds that parties should present clear and coherent programs to voters, that voters should choose candidates according to the party programs, that the winning party should carry out its programs once in office, and that voters should hold the governing party responsible at the next election for executing its program. As noted in Chapter 8, the Republican and Democratic parties do follow the model to the extent that they do formulate different platforms and do tend to pursue their announced policies when in office. The stumbling blocks to this model of responsible party government lie more with the linkage of candidates to voters through campaigns and elections.

You have not read much about the role of the party platform in nominating candidates, in conducting campaigns, or in explaining vote choice. In nominating presidential candidates, it is true that basic party principles (as captured in the party platform) do interact with the presidential primary process, and the candidate who wins enough convention delegates through the primaries will surely be comfortable with any platform that his or her delegates adopt. But individual contests for House and Senate nominations are rarely fought over the party platform. And in general, thoughts about the party platforms are virtually absent from campaigning and from voters' minds when casting their ballots.

The fact of the matter is that voters do *not* choose between candidates according to party programs, and they do not hold the governing party responsible at the next election for executing its program. In large part, it has been impossible for them to hold the governing party responsible, because there is no "governing party" when the president is of one party and Congress is controlled by the other, which has occurred most of the time since the end of the Second World War (and in ten of twelve congresses since 1969). As long as voters seem destined to elect Republican presidents and Democratic congresses, there is little hope for the majoritarian model of party government.

Parties and the Pluralist Model

The way parties in the United States operate is more in keeping with the pluralist model of democracy than the majoritarian model. Our parties are not the basic mechanism through which citizens control their government; instead, they function as two giant interest groups. The parties' interests are in electing and re-electing party candidates to enjoy the benefits of public office. Except in extreme cases, the parties care little about the issues or ideologies favored by candidates for Congress and statewide offices. One exception that proves the rule is the Republican party's rejection of David E. Duke, the former Ku Klux Klan leader who in 1990 emerged as the party's nominee for senator in Louisiana but, in a highly unusual move, was disowned by national party leaders and lost the election. Otherwise, the parties are grateful for victories by almost any candidate. In turn, individual candidates operate like entrepreneurs, running their own campaigns as they like without party interference.

Some scholars believe that stronger parties would contribute more to democratic government, even if they could not meet all the requirements of the responsible party model. Although our parties perform valuable functions in structuring the vote along partisan lines and in proposing alternative government policies, stronger parties might be able to play a more important role in coordinating government policies after elections. At present, the decentralized nature of the nominating process and campaigning for election offers many opportunities for organized groups outside the party to identify and back candidates who favor their interests when elected to government. This is in keeping with pluralist theory, although it is certain to frustrate majority interests on occasion.

Summary

Campaigning for elections has evolved from a party-centered to a candidate-centered process. The successful candidate for public office usually must campaign first to win the party nomination, then to win the general election. A major factor in the decentralization of American parties is their reliance on primary elections to nominate candidates. Democratic and Republican nominations for president are no longer actually decided in the party's national conventions but are determined in advance of the convention through the complex process of selecting delegates pledged to those seeking the nomination. Although candidates cannot win the nomination unless they have broad support within the party, the winners can legitimately say that they captured the nomination through their own efforts and that they owe little to the party organization.

Candidates usually retain the staffs that got them the nomination to help them win the general election. The dynamics of campaign financing also force candidates to rely mainly on their own resources or—in the case of presidential elections—on public funds. Party organizations contribute relatively little toward campaign expenses, and candidates must raise most of the money themselves. Money is essential in conducting a modern campaign for a major office. Funds are needed to conduct polls that disclose the voters' interests and to advertise the candidate's name, qualifications, and issue positions through the media. Free news coverage is sought whenever possible, but most candidates must rely on paid advertising to get across their messages. Ironically, voters also get most of their campaign information from advertisements. There has been a trend in recent years toward negative advertising, which seems to work, although it contributes to voters' distaste for politics.

Presidential elections are structured by the need to win a majority of votes in the electoral college. Although it is possible for a candidate to win a majority of the popular vote but lose in the electoral college, that has not happened in over one hundred years. The electoral college operates to magnify the victory margin of the winning candidate. Since World War II, Republicans seem to have a lock on the presidency, while Democrats appear to have a lock on Congress, certainly on the House of Representatives.

Voting choice can be analyzed in terms of party identification, candidates' attributes, and policy positions. Party identification is still the most important long-term factor in shaping the voting decision, but few candidates rely on party in their campaigns. Most candidates today run personalized campaigns that stress their attributes or their policies. There is evidence that presidential campaigns do increase people's knowledge about issues, but there is some disagreement about how important campaigns are in affecting election outcomes.

The way that nominations, campaigns, and elections are conducted in America makes it difficult for parties to fulfill the ideals of responsible party government that fit the majoritarian model of democracy. In particular, there is a problem in linking parties to voters through campaigns and elections. American parties are better suited to the pluralist model of democracy, which sees them as major interest groups competing with lesser groups to further their own interests. At least political parties aspire to the noble goal of representing the needs and wants of most of the people. As we see in the next chapter, interest groups do not even pretend as much.

KEY TERMS

election campaign	challenger
primary election	open election
closed primary	Federal Election
open primary	Commission (FEC)
blanket primary	general election
presidential primary	straight ticket
local caucus	split ticket
incumbent	first-past-the-post

SELECTED READINGS

Buchanan, Bruce. *Electing a President: The Report on the Markle Commission on the Media and the Electorate.* Austin: University of Texas Press, 1991. Analyzes the 1988 presidential election using a special set of surveys designed to measure media effects.

Diamond, Edwin, and Stephen Bates. *The Spot: The Rise of Political Advertising on Television.* Cambridge, Mass.: MIT Press, 1988. Describes the strategy, planning, creation, and execution of thirty- to sixty-second political commercials.

Kern, Montague. *30-Second Politics: Political Advertising in the Eighties.* New York: Praeger, 1989. Surveys the scene in campaign advertising and uses some original data analysis to support its contentions.

Lichtman, Allan J., and Ken DeCell. *The Thirteen Keys to the Presidency.* Lanham, Md.: Madison Books, 1990. Argues that presidents are elected or defeated on the basis of the record of the incumbent administration and that campaigns have little effect on the outcome.

Mableby, David B., and Candice J. Nelson. *The Money Chase: Congressional Campaign Finance Reform.* Washington, D.C.: Brookings Institution, 1990. Reviews problems in campaign finance and issues in reform; also provides valuable data on campaign receipts and expenditures.

Nesbit, Dorothy Davidson. *Videostyle in Senate Campaigns.* Knoxville, Tenn.: University of Tennessee Press, 1988. A study of six campaigns in three elections to the U.S. Senate in 1982 that focuses on candidates and the producers of their television advertisements.

Orren, Gary R., and Nelson W. Polsby, eds. *Media and Momentum: The New Hampshire Primary and Nomination Politics.* Chatham, N.J.: Chatham House, 1987. A series of studies of media coverage of early campaigning for the presidential nomination—mainly in New Hampshire but also in Iowa.

Runkel, David R., ed. *Campaign for President: The Managers Look at '88.* Dover, Mass.: Auburn House, 1989. A verbatim transcript of a conference of the leading managers and consultants in the 1988 presidential campaign reviewing their victories and defeats.

Salmore, Barbara G., and Stephen A. Salmore. *Candidates, Parties, and Campaigns: Electoral Politics in America,* 2d ed. Washington, D.C.: Congressional Quarterly Press, 1989. The best textbook treatment of election campaigning.

Shafer, Byron E. *Bifurcated Politics: Evolution and Reform in the National Party Convention.* Cambridge, Mass.: Harvard University Press, 1988. Explains how the conventions lost the nominating function, which now resides in the primary process. The convention is bifurcated because delegates experience one convention while television viewers see another.

Sorauf, Frank J. *Money in American Elections.* Glenview, Ill.: Scott, Foresman, 1988. Surveys receipts and expenditures in presidential and congressional campaigns, including financing by individuals, PACs, parties, and government.

10 INTEREST GROUPS

THERE ARE THINGS IN THIS life that are easier than getting a clean air bill out of the Congress. The reason is simple: So many interest groups push Congress in so many different directions. No single group can get everything that it wants, and the resulting struggle for an acceptable compromise is inevitably difficult and protracted.

In 1989, despite many recent abortive efforts (the last successful attempt had been in 1977), Congress again took up clean air legislation. The Senate succeeded in passing a bill in the spring of 1990—but not without a lot of squabbling over who would get exemptions and special privileges. One observer described the conflict over clean air as "the Super Bowl of lobbying."[1] In principle everybody is for clean air—as long as the law doesn't require them to do anything to pay for it. Power plants in North Dakota didn't want to spend the money to reduce their pollution and managed to get an exemption from the requirements of the bill. Utility plants in Florida got an exemption, too, and could save as much as $400 million in pollution-control costs. Automobile manufacturers were successful in fighting off the efforts of environmental groups to mandate an increase in gasoline mileage. Environmentalists said that improved mileage would help the fight against global warming; American car manufacturers said it would require making cars too small to suit consumer preferences. Corn farmers won a big battle when a provision was put into the bill requiring the nine smoggiest cities in the country to sell less polluting gasoline to motorists. This meant that these cities would likely have to switch to gasoline made of ethanol, a corn-distilled alcohol.

There were some big losers, too. Coal miners from West Virginia and the Midwest, who saw themselves being sacrificed on the altar of clean air, asked for financial aid because the bill would likely reduce the use of coal and thus put many miners out of work. On the floor of the Senate they lost by a single vote, 50–49. Steel manufacturers wanted less stringent standards regulating the volume of toxic emissions at their plants. They lost also. Overall, though, the Senate's version of the Clean Air Act was an amalgam of deals cut with various interest groups. One environmentalist described the process as a "special-interest feeding frenzy." He added, "It was not a pretty sight watching this happen to the bill."[2]

A clean air bill containing its own set of deals and compromises between lawmakers and interest groups was subsequently passed in the House. Many of its provisions differed from the Senate bill, but after more horse trading in a conference committee, those differences were worked out, and a clean air bill was sent to President George Bush, who signed it into law.

The history of the Clean Air Act illustrates some of the basic dynamics of interest group politics. At the heart of pluralist democracy are groups fighting for their own narrow interests. Here, various manufacturers, unions, and farm groups fought environmentalists (and sometimes each other) over different provisions in the legislation. The majoritarian interest is clean air, but clean air politics cannot simply be described as a process whereby interest groups work to weaken majority control over public policy. The American public surely does want less pollution, but it also wants cheap electricity, big cars, inexpensive gasoline, a growing economy, and low inflation. The interest groups that worked for special provisions in the Senate bill used these public preferences—sometimes quite effectively—to convince lawmakers to reduce proposed standards for clean air.

In analyzing the process by which interest groups and lobbyists come to speak on behalf of different groups, we focus on a number of questions. How do interest groups form? Who do they represent? What tactics do they use to convince policymakers that their views are best for the nation? Why has the number of interest groups grown so rapidly in recent years? And what is the impact of that growth?

Interest Groups and the American Political Tradition

An **interest group** is an organized body of individuals who share some political goals and try to influence public policy decisions.[3] Among the most prominent interest groups in the United States are the AFL-CIO (representing labor union members), the American Farm Bureau Federation (representing farmers), the Business Roundtable (representing big business), and Common Cause (representing citizens concerned with reforming government). Interest groups are also called **lobbies,** and their representatives are referred to as **lobbyists.**

Interest Groups: Good or Evil?

A recurring debate in American politics concerns the role of interest groups in a democratic society. Are interest groups a threat to the well-being of the political system, or do they contribute to its proper functioning? A favorable early evaluation of interest groups can be found in the writings of Alexis de Tocqueville, a French visitor to the United States in the early nineteenth century. During his travels, Tocqueville marveled at the array of organizations he found, and he later wrote that "Americans of all ages, all conditions, and all dispositions, constantly form associations."[4] Tocqueville was suggesting that the ease with which we form organizations reflects a strong democratic culture.

James Madison offered a different perspective. Writing in the *Federalist Papers,* he warned of the dangers of "factions," the major divisions in American society. In "Federalist No. 10," written in 1787, Madison said that it was inevitable that substantial differences would develop between factions. It was only natural that farmers would come to oppose merchants; tenants, landlords; and so on. Madison further reasoned that each faction would do what it could to prevail over other factions, that each basic interest in society would try to persuade government to adopt policies that favored it at the expense of others. He noted that the fundamental causes of faction were "sown in the nature of man."

But Madison argued against trying to suppress factions. He concluded that factions can be eliminated only by removing our freedoms: "Liberty is to faction what air is to fire." Instead, Madison suggested that "relief" from the self-interested advocacy of factions should come only through controlling the *effects* of that advocacy. This relief would be provided by

F I G U R E 10.1   *Special Interest Groups: We Just Love 'Em*

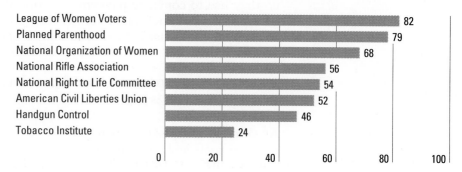

Despite some anxiety over the power of special interest groups, the results of this Gallup Poll show that Americans applaud the work of most individual lobbying organizations. Still, there is substantial variation in the approval ratings, and the low score for the Tobacco Institute indicates that some organizations are seen in a less-than-positive light. (Source: Gallup Report, *May 1989, pp. 25–27. Used by permission.)*

League of Women Voters — 82
Planned Parenthood — 79
National Organization of Women — 68
National Rifle Association — 56
National Right to Life Committee — 54
American Civil Liberties Union — 52
Handgun Control — 46
Tobacco Institute — 24

Percentage of respondents with favorable opinion

a democratic republic in which government would mediate between opposing factions. The size and diversity of the nation as well as the structure of government would also ensure that even a majority faction could never come to suppress the rights of others.[5]

How we judge interest groups—"good" or "evil"—may depend on how strongly we are committed to freedom or equality (see Chapter 1). Most Americans are generally supportive of citizen groups representing a range of ideological causes (see Figure 10.1). Giving people the freedom to organize lobbies, however, does not guarantee that they will all end up with equally powerful interest groups acting on their behalf. Judgment is also influenced by whether we believe democracy works best if it abides by majoritarian or by pluralist principles (see Chapter 2). We return to these broader questions of democratic theory after looking at the operation of interest groups more closely.

The Roles of Interest Groups

The "evil" side of interest group politics is all too apparent. Each group pushes its own selfish interests, which, despite the group's claims to the contrary, are not always in the best interest of other Americans. The "good" side of interest group advocacy may not be as clear. How do the actions of interest groups benefit our political system?[6]

Representation.   Interest groups *represent* people before their government. Just as a member of Congress represents a particular constituency, so does a lobbyist. A lobbyist for the National Association of Broadcasters, for example, speaks for the interests of radio and television broadcasters when Congress or a government agency is considering a relevant policy decision.

Whatever the political interest—the cement industry, social security, endangered species—it is helpful to have an active lobby operating in

Washington. Members of Congress represent a multitude of interests—some of them conflicting—from their own districts and states. Government administrators, too, are pulled in different directions and have their own policy preferences. Interest groups articulate their members' concerns, presenting them directly and forcefully in the political forum.

Participation.   Interest groups are also vehicles for political *participation.* They provide a means by which like-minded citizens can pool their resources and channel their energies into collective political action. People band together because they know it is much easier to get government to listen to a group than to an individual. One farmer fighting for more generous price supports probably will not get very far, but thousands of farmers united in an organization stand a much better chance of getting policymakers to consider their needs.

Education.   As part of their efforts at lobbying and increasing their membership, interest groups help *educate* their members, the public at large, and government officials. In 1987, when President Ronald Reagan nominated Judge Robert Bork for a seat on the Supreme Court, liberal and conservative citizen groups engaged in a spirited—some would say

Do I Look Like a Lobbyist to You?

Probably not, but this ad is a form of lobbying. It aims to convince people that legal abortion is an important option by arguing that it would be foolish for someone so young to raise a child. Through its use of a clean-cut, girl-next-door type, the ad also suggests that teenage pregnancy is not a problem that "happens only to other people."

"Do I look like a mother to you?"

She does if you look at the statistics.

The United States is the only industrialized nation where the teenage pregnancy rate is going up. Forty percent of all girls who are now fourteen will get pregnant before they're eighteen. One million each year.

The social consequences are enormous. Because most teenage mothers are single mothers, trapped in a cycle of poverty that costs billions extra each year. In malnutrition. Disease. Unemployment. Child abuse.

But the tragic effects of motherhood on each individual teenager can't be measured in dollars and cents. And it isn't reflected in the statistics. She's robbed of her childhood and her hope.

While we must do everything we can to help *prevent* unwanted pregnancy, we must also preserve the option of safe, legal abortion.

A teenage girl shouldn't be forced to become a mother if she's not ready.

But there's an increasingly vocal and violent minority that disagrees. They want to outlaw abortions for all women, regardless of circumstances. Even if her life or health is endangered by a pregnancy. Even if she is a victim of rape or incest. And even if she is too young to be a mother.

They're pressuring lawmakers to make abortions illegal. And that's not all. They also oppose birth control and sex education—ways of *preventing* abortion. They've already tried to slash federal funding for these and other family planning programs. And to get their way, they've resorted to threats, physical intimidation and violence.

Speak out now. Or they just might succeed. Use the coupon.

The decision is yours.

☐ I've written my representatives in Congress to tell them I support: government programs that reduce the need for abortion by preventing unwanted pregnancy; and keeping safe and legal abortion a choice for all women.

☐ Here's my tax-deductible contribution in support of all Planned Parenthood activities and programs: ☐ $25 ☐ $35 ☐ $50 ☐ $75 ☐ $150 ☐ $500 ☐ or: $_____

NAME

STREET/CITY/ZIP

Planned Parenthood® Federation of America, Inc.

810 Seventh Avenue New York, New York 10019

This ad was paid for with private contributions. © Copyright 1985

FEATURE 10.1   *Direct Mail: Your Letter Has to Grab 'Em*

People are flooded with direct mail from interest groups, politicians, and charities. Whatever the organization's cause, the letters are all trying to do the same thing: get you to part with your hard-earned cash. In this competitive environment, letters not only must be distinctive, they must pull at your emotions so that your desire to help overcomes your desire to save your money. Look at how the liberal People for the American Way Action Fund designed an appeal mailed out to thousands of prospective donors during the confirmation fight over Supreme Court nominee Robert Bork.

The first goal of a direct-mail package is to get people to open it rather than just toss it unopened into the wastebasket with other "junk mail." Consequently, envelopes often use a tease to entice readers into finding out what's in them. Here the tease is relatively straightforward: If you care about keeping Bork off the Court, you ought to open this up. The color of the envelope suggests something "official," adding to the urgency of what's inside.

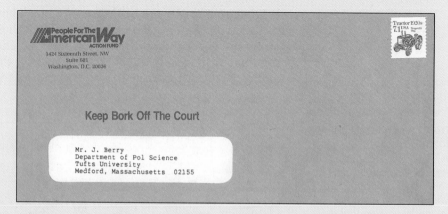

Direct-mail letters are successful if they engage the reader. The goal is to make you care about the issue discussed. This letter begins with a couple of quotations that should upset civil libertarians. Later in the letter, readers are told that Bork rejects conventional views on the right to privacy, has criticized decisions favorable to women and minorities, and holds a restrictive view of the First Amendment. Letters are typically long—this one is six single-spaced pages—and packed with specifics. By the end of the letter, the reader should be so moved that he or she pulls out the checkbook.

Groups often try to validate their appeal by including an article from an outside source that confirms the point they are trying to make. Here an editorial from the *Austin American-Statesman* is included to reinforce the message in the letter.

mean-spirited—effort to educate the American public about the nominee. Using advertisements, each side tried to show what the "real" Bork record told us about what kind of Supreme Court justice he was likely to be. (For more on how one interest group tried to sway the Bork nomination, see Feature 10.1, above.) Interest groups give only their side of the "facts," but they do bring more information out into the open to be digested and evaluated by the public.

People For The
American Way
ACTION FUND

Arthur J. Kropp
Executive Director

"Conservatives have waited over thirty years for
this. . . . [Bork's nomination] is the most exciting news for conservatives since President
Reagan's re-election."

-- Richard Viguerie, Right Wing Leader

"The Bork nomination is another part of the Reagan
Revolution . . . politically, it gives us a cause."

-- Frank Donatelli, White House Political Director

Dear Friend,

Leaders of the Far Right can scarcely hide their glee over
Robert Bork's nomination to the Supreme Court.

And it's no wonder.

Bork is their <u>best</u> <u>hope</u> to ensure that their political
agenda will live on even after Ronald Reagan leaves office.

In a sense, Robert Bork will be the Reagan Revolution's
living legacy -- for years to come. And, frankly, the Right
Wing couldn't have designed a more fitting legacy.

You see, like the Far Right, Judge Bork's views of the
Constitution and the Bill of Rights are appallingly out of step
with America -- <u>30</u> <u>years</u> <u>behind</u> <u>the</u> <u>times</u>.

Out of step with America's hard fought gains in the areas
of civil rights, individual liberty and personal privacy.

Incredibly, Robert Bork has rejected the principle of "one
man one vote" . . . Supreme Court decisions outlawing poll
taxes . . . the right of married couples to buy contraceptives.

And, even in 1963, when it was critical for all men and
women of conscience to stand up for civil rights, he <u>opposed</u>
the right of blacks to be served by white-owned businesses.

The Far Right knows, and we too can be certain:

if Robert Bork becomes the critical "swing vote" on the
Supreme Court, the extremists philosophy held by people
like Attorney General Ed Meese will dominate America's
highest court for decades to come.

<u>That</u> <u>is</u> <u>why</u> <u>PEOPLE</u> <u>FOR</u> <u>THE</u> <u>AMERICAN</u> <u>WAY</u> <u>ACTION</u> <u>FUND</u> <u>has</u>
<u>launched</u> <u>a</u> <u>$1</u> <u>million</u> <u>citizen</u> <u>mobilization</u> <u>campaign</u> <u>to</u> "KEEP
BORK OFF THE COURT."

(over, please)

1424 Sixteenth Street, N.W.   Suite 601   Washington, D.C. 20036   202 462-4777

(continued)

Agenda building. In a related role, interest groups bring new issues into the political limelight, through a process called **agenda building.** There are many problem areas in American society, but not all of them are being addressed by public officials. Interest groups make the government aware of problems through their advocacy, then try to see to it that something is done to solve them. After videocassette recorders (VCRs) became popular in the United States, competing lobbies raised a number

FEATURE 10.1   *(continued)*

Page A14   Friday   July 10, 1987

Bork's ideology demands close nomination scrutiny

Austin American-Statesman

Senate Democrats apparently will throw down the gauntlet on the nomination of Robert Bork to the Supreme Court; considering the pivotal vote he would represent on the court, a thorough confirmation process is called for and, if senators ultimately decide Bork is too radical and would push the court too far to the right, they should not hesitate to refuse confirmation and demand that President Reagan come up with a less ideological nominee.

The Democrats said this week that confirmation hearings on the nomination will not begin until Sept. 15,

point of view."

And, historically, the Senate has refused to confirm one out of five nominations submitted for its "advice and consent," beginning with the second term of the administration of George Washington.

Indeed, in 1968, Sen. Strom Thurmond (who now wants the Senate to hurry up and confirm Bork) underscored the importance of careful scrutiny by the Senate of nominee Abe Fortas:

"Therefore, it is my contention that the power of the Senate to advise and consent to this appointment

---

══ REPLY MEMORANDUM ══

Keep Bork Off The Court

TO: PEOPLE FOR THE AMERICAN WAY ACTION FUND

Robert Bork is 30 years out of step with America—we **must stop** his confirmation to the Supreme Court. Please forward the two Congressional Communications I have signed below.

Enclosed is my contribution towards the Action Fund "Keep Bork Off The Court" campaign of:

☐ $100   ☐ $50   ☐ $35   ☐ $25   ☐ Other $_____

Mr. J. Berry
Department of Pol Science
Tufts University
Medford, Massachusetts 02155

Please make check payable to PEOPLE FOR THE AMERICAN WAY ACTION FUND and return it with entire form to Post Office Box 96200, Washington, D.C. 20077-4627.

Q318

---

of questions about copyright law and royalty payments to movie studios. The Motion Picture Association of America and the Electronic Industries Association (the trade group for VCR manufacturers) brought these issues to the fore by pressing Congress for action.[7]

Program monitoring. Finally, interest groups engage in **program monitoring.** In other words, they follow government programs important to their constituents, keeping abreast of developments in Washington and in the local communities where policies are implemented. When problems emerge, interest groups push administrators to resolve them in ways that promote the group's goals. They draw attention to agency officials' transgressions and even file suit to stop actions they consider unlawful. For example, when the U.S. Department of Agriculture reduced food stamp benefits on the order of President Gerald Ford, the Food Research and Action Center acted on behalf of program recipients and took

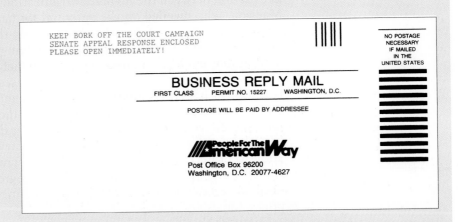

KEEP BORK OFF THE COURT CAMPAIGN
SENATE APPEAL RESPONSE ENCLOSED
PLEASE OPEN IMMEDIATELY!

NO POSTAGE
NECESSARY
IF MAILED
IN THE
UNITED STATES

BUSINESS REPLY MAIL
FIRST CLASS   PERMIT NO. 15227   WASHINGTON, D.C.

POSTAGE WILL BE PAID BY ADDRESSEE

People For The American Way

Post Office Box 96200
Washington, D.C. 20077-4627

A payment card is enclosed to ensure that donors are properly entered into the group's computerized records. The best prospects for a direct mailing are those who have given to the group before, so once a name goes on the house list, that person is solicited frequently by the organization.

The name of the recipient of this letter did not come from the house list, but from a list that People for the American Way rented from a direct-mail broker or other organization. When recruiting new members, like-minded organizations often trade or rent their members' names to each other. Note the source code "Q318" in the lower right-hand corner of the payment card. This is used to track how well the list works. If the list produces a strong response rate (usually 1 to 2 percent), it will be used again.

A return envelope rounds out the package. They want to make it easy for you. Just write a check!

Source: Reprinted with permission of People for the American Way. Reprinted with permission of the *Austin American-Statesman*, Copyright 1987.

the department to court. The court sided with the lobby, and the original benefits were reinstated.

Interest groups do, then, play some positive roles in their pursuit of self-interest. But it is too soon to assume that the positive side of interest groups neatly balances the negative. Questions remain to be answered about the overall impact of interest groups on public policymaking. Most important, are the effects of interest group advocacy being controlled, as Madison believed they should be?

How Interest Groups Form

Do some people form interest groups more easily than others? Are some factions represented while others are not? Pluralists assume that when a political issue arises, interest groups with relevant policy concerns begin to lobby. Policy conflicts are ultimately resolved through bargaining and negotiation between the involved organizations and government. Unlike Madison, who dwelled on the potential for harm by factions, pluralists believe interest groups are a good thing, that they further democracy by broadening representation within the system.

An important part of pluralism is the belief that new interest groups form as a matter of course when the need arises. David Truman outlined this idea in his classic work *The Governmental Process*.[8] He said that when individuals are threatened by change, they band together in an interest group. For example, if government threatens to regulate a particular industry, the firms comprising that industry will start a trade association to protect their financial well-being. Truman saw a direct cause-and-effect relationship in all of this: Existing groups stand in equilibrium until some type of disturbance (such as falling wages or declining farm prices) forces new groups to form.

Truman's thinking on the way interest groups form is like the "invisible hand" notion of classical economics: Self-correcting market forces will remedy imbalances in the marketplace. But in politics there is no invisible hand, no force that automatically causes interest groups to develop. Truman's disturbance theory paints an idealized portrait of interest group politics in America. In real life, people do not automatically organize when they are adversely affected by some disturbance. A good example of this "nonorganization" can be found in Herbert Gans's book *The Urban Villagers*.[9] Gans, a sociologist, moved into the West End, a low-income neighborhood in Boston, during the late 1950s. The neighborhood had been targeted for urban redevelopment; the city was planning to replace existing buildings with modern ones. This meant that the people living there—primarily poor Italian-Americans who very much liked their neighborhood—would have to move.

There Goes the Neighborhood

When the city of Boston targeted its West End for urban renewal, residents did not organize to fight the decision. Wrecking balls soon demolished the neighborhood, clearing the way for various redevelopment projects, including high-rise housing.

Being evicted is a highly traumatic experience, so the situation in the West End certainly qualified as a bona fide disturbance in Truman's scheme of interest group formation. Yet the people of the West End barely put up a fight to save their neighborhood. An organization was started but attracted little support. Residents remained unorganized; soon they were moved and buildings were demolished.

Disturbance theory clearly fails to explain what happened in Boston's West End. An adverse condition or change does not automatically mean that an interest group will form. What, then, is the missing ingredient? Political scientist Robert Salisbury says that the quality of interest group leadership may be the crucial factor.[10]

Interest Group Entrepreneurs

Salisbury likens the role of an interest group leader to that of an entrepreneur in the business world. An entrepreneur is someone who starts new enterprises, usually at considerable personal financial risk. Salisbury says that an **interest group entrepreneur** or organizer succeeds or fails for many of the same reasons a business entrepreneur succeeds or fails. The interest group entrepreneur must have something attractive to "market" in order to convince members to join.[11] Potential members must be persuaded that the benefits of joining outweigh the costs. Someone starting up a new union, for example, must convince workers that the union can win them wages high enough to offset their membership dues (see Compared with What? 10.1). The organizer of an ideological group must convince potential members that the group can effectively lobby the government to achieve their particular goals.

The development of the United Farm Workers Union shows the importance of leadership in the formation of an interest group. This union is made up of men and women who pick crops in California and other parts of the Southwest. The work is backbreaking, performed in a hot, arid climate. The pickers are predominantly poor, uneducated Mexican-Americans.

Their chronically low wages and deplorable living conditions made these farm workers prime candidates for organization into a labor union. And throughout the twentieth century, there had been efforts to organize the pickers. Yet for many reasons, including distrust of union organizers, intimidation by employers, and lack of money to pay union dues, all had failed. Then, in 1962, Cesar Chavez, a poor Mexican-American, began to crisscross the Central Valley of California, talking to workers and planting the idea of a union. Chavez had been a farm worker himself (he first worked as a picker at the age of ten), and he was well aware of the difficulties that lay ahead for his newly organized union.

After a strike against grape growers failed in 1965, Chavez changed his tactics of trying to build a stronger union merely through recruiting a larger membership. Copying the black civil rights movement, Chavez and his followers marched 250 miles to the state capitol in Sacramento to demand help from the governor. This march and other nonviolent tactics began to draw sympathy from people who had no direct involvement in farming. The Catholic clergy was a major source of support, seeing the

COMPARED WITH WHAT?   10.1

Lech Walesa: Interest Group Entrepreneur Who Organized a Nation

In an era when real political heroes seem few and far between, Polish union leader Lech Walesa stands out. Walesa came to the attention of the world when a strike broke out in 1980 at the Lenin Shipyard in Gdansk, Poland, and the workers locked themselves inside the facility. Walesa had a history of union organizing—in Salisbury's term he was an "entrepreneur"—and had actually been fired from a job in 1976 because of his organizing efforts. Unemployed when the strike at the shipyard erupted, Walesa scaled a wall to be with the workers.

The shipworkers wanted the right to form an independent union—called Solidarity—and the right to strike. These demands were utter heresy to the communist government. (In theory the workers were already represented by the Communist party, the embodiment of the "dictatorship of the proletariat" that is at the heart of Marxist-Leninist thought.) The Solidarity union movement sparked strikes across the country, threatening the government's stability.

In a historic agreement, Solidarity and the government signed an accord that allowed free and independent unions and also granted broader freedoms for the Polish press. Once unleashed, however, Solidarity pressed for more, and Walesa worked feverishly to mediate between the demands of radical elements of Solidarity and the central government. The political tumult combined with a faltering economy to plunge the country into crisis. The Soviet Union, unhappy with the new freedoms in Poland, issued a series of warnings to the Polish government to crack down on the union. Crack down they did. In December 1981, Polish troops arrested the leaders of Solidarity, including Walesa, and martial law was declared.

Walesa was held prisoner in a government-owned hunting lodge for close to a year. After his release he was harassed and followed by the government, making it impossible for him to try to re-

Lech Walesa

suscitate Solidarity. He took a job in the shipyard and basked in the glory of the Nobel Peace Prize, awarded to him in 1983.

The worsening Polish economy prompted another round of strikes in 1988, and the government, grasping for a way out of another crisis, legalized Solidarity in 1989. A few months later it held an election that was relatively free, and Solidarity, transformed from a union into a political party, participated vigorously. Much to the government's embarrassment, it swamped the Communist party, winning 99 out of 100 seats in the upper house of the legislature and all the seats it was allowed to contest in the lower house. It now is a dominant power in the new Poland, and Walesa won Poland's first direct presidential election in 1990. No matter how he performs as president, Walesa's legacy is clear: he is one of the men who toppled communism and irrevocably changed Europe.

Cesar's Soul, Bobby's Spirit
The late senator Robert F. Kennedy was a strong supporter of Cesar Chavez and the United Farm Workers. In 1988, Kennedy's widow, Ethel, renewed the family's commitment to the farm workers' cause by taking communion with Chavez after he completed a 36-day fast.

movement as a way to help poor members of the church. This support, in turn, gave the charismatic Chavez greater credibility, and his followers cast him in the role of spiritual as well as political leader. At one point, he fasted for twenty-five days to show his commitment to nonviolence. Democratic Senator Robert Kennedy of New York, one of the most popular politicians of the day, joined Chavez when he broke his fast at a mass conducted on the back of a flatbed truck in Delano, California.[12]

Chavez, now a strong, respected leader, called for a boycott. A small but significant number of Americans stopped buying grapes. The growers, who had bitterly fought the union, were finally hurt in their wallets. Under other economic pressure, they eventually agreed to recognize and bargain with the United Farm Workers Union. The union, in turn, helped its members through the wage and benefit agreements it was able to negotiate.

Who Is Being Organized?

The case of Cesar Chavez is a good example of the importance of leadership in the formation of a new interest group. Despite many years of adverse conditions, efforts to organize the farm workers had failed. The dynamic leadership of Cesar Chavez is what seems to have made the difference.

But another important element is at work in the formation of interest groups. The residents of Boston's West End and the farm workers in California were poor, uneducated or undereducated, and politically inexperienced—factors that made it extremely difficult to organize them into interest groups. If they had been well-to-do, educated, and politically experienced, they probably would have banded together immediately.

FIGURE 10.2   *Social Class and Interest Group Membership*

Membership in interest groups is clearly linked to social class. The higher their total family income, the more likely individuals will belong to at least one political interest group. The data here come from a survey of citizens in five American cities. (Source: The National Citizen Participation Development Project. Copyright, Jeffrey M. Berry, Kent E. Portney, and Ken Thomson, 1990.)

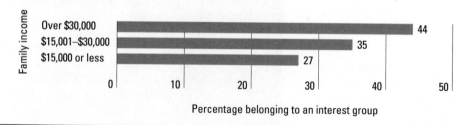

People who have money, are educated, and know how the system operates are more confident that their actions can make a difference. Together, these attributes give people more incentive to devote their time and ample resources to organizing and supporting interest groups (see Figure 10.2).

Every existing interest group has its own unique history, but the three variables just discussed help explain why groups may or may not become fully organized. First, an adverse change or disturbance can contribute to people's awareness that they need political representation. However, change alone does not ensure that an organization will form, and organizations have formed in the absence of disturbance. Second, the quality of leadership is critical in the organization of interest groups. Some interest group entrepreneurs are more skilled than others at convincing people to join their organizations. Finally, the higher the socioeconomic level of potential members, the more likely they are to know the value of interest groups and to participate in politics by joining them.

Because wealthy and better-educated Americans are more likely to form and join lobbies, they seem to have an important advantage in the political process. Nevertheless, as the United Farm Workers case shows, poor and uneducated people are also capable of forming interest groups. The question that remains, then, is not *whether* various opposing interests are represented but *how well* they are represented. Or, in terms of Madison's premise in "Federalist No. 10," are the effects of faction—in this case, the advantages of the wealthy and well educated—being controlled? Before we can answer this question, we need to turn our attention to the resources available to interest groups.

Interest Group Resources

The strengths, capabilities, and effects of an interest group depend in large part on its *resources.* A group's most significant resources are its members, lobbyists, and money, including funds that can be contributed to political candidates. The sheer quantity of a group's resources is important, and so is the wisdom with which its resources are used.

Members

One of the most valuable resources an interest group can have is a large, politically active membership. If a lobbyist is trying to convince a legislator to support a particular bill, it is tremendously helpful to have a large group of members living in the legislator's home district or state. A legislator who has not already taken a firm position on a bill might be swayed by the knowledge that voters back home are kept informed by interest groups of votes on key issues. As pointed out in Chapter 2, the National Rifle Association (NRA) is an effective interest group on Capitol Hill because its 2.6 million members care very deeply about gun control. Members of Congress know that the NRA keeps its members informed on how each senator and representative votes on proposed gun control bills, and many of those members might be influenced by that information when they go to the polls.

Members give an organization not only the political muscle to influence policy but also financial resources. The more money an organization can collect through dues and contributions, the more people it can hire to lobby government officials and monitor the policymaking process. Greater resources also allow the organization to communicate with its members more and to inform them better. And funding helps the group maintain its membership and attract new members.

Maintaining membership. To keep the members it already has, an organization must persuade them that it is doing a good job in its advocacy efforts. A major tool for shoring up support among members is a newsletter or magazine. Through publications, members are informed and reminded about the organization's activities. Executives whose corporations belong to the National Association of Manufacturers (NAM) receive *Enterprise,* a business magazine; *Briefing,* a weekly newsletter that focuses on legislative and regulatory action in Washington; and the two-page *Issue Briefs,* which summarizes current public policy disputes. Members also have access, through a toll-free number, to recordings that describe matters of immediate concern to the NAM. Most lobbies provide more modest offerings for their members, but they usually have at least a newsletter.

Business, professional, and labor associations generally have an easier time holding onto members than do **citizen groups**—groups whose basis of organization is a concern for issues that are not related to the members' jobs. In many corporations, membership in a trade group constitutes only a minor business expense. Large individual corporations have no memberships as such, but they often open up their own lobbying offices in Washington. They have the advantage of being able to utilize institutional financial resources; they do not have to rely on voluntary contributions.[13] Labor unions are helped in states where workers are required to belong to the union that is the bargaining agent with their employer. Citizen groups, on the other hand, base their appeal on members' ideological sentiments. These groups face a difficult challenge: Issues can blow hot and cold, and a particularly hot issue one year may not hold the same interest to citizens the next.

Attracting new members.   All interest groups are constantly looking for new members to expand their resources and clout. Groups that rely on ideological appeals have a special problem because the competition in most policy areas is intense. People concerned about the environment, for example, can join a seemingly infinite number of local, state, and national groups. The National Wildlife Federation, Environmental Action, the Environmental Defense Fund, the Natural Resources Defense Council, Friends of the Earth, the Wilderness Society, the Sierra Club, and the Environmental Policy Center are just a few of the national organizations that lobby on environmental issues. Groups try to distinguish themselves from competitors by concentrating on a few key issues and developing a reputation as the most involved and knowledgeable on them.[14] Still, organizations in a crowded policy area must go beyond such differentiation and aggressively market themselves to possible contributors.

One method of attracting new members that is being used more and more is **direct mail**—letters sent to a selected audience to promote the organization and appeal for contributions. The key to direct mail is a carefully targeted audience. An organization can purchase a list of people who are likely to be sympathetic to its cause or trade lists with a similar organization. A group trying to fight legalized abortion, for instance, might use a subscription list from the conservative magazine *National Review,* while a prochoice lobby might use that of the liberal *New Republic.* The main drawbacks to direct mail are its expense and low rate of return. A response rate of 2 percent of all those who receive membership or donation appeals is considered good. If the response rate falls below that level, costs usually exceed the money returned. To maximize the chances of a good return, care and thought are given to the design and content of letters (see Feature 10.1). Letters often try to play on the reader's emotions, to create the feeling that the reader should be personally involved in the struggle.[15]

The free-rider problem.   The need for aggressive marketing by interest groups suggests that it is not easy to get people who sympathize with a group's goals actually to join and support it with their contributions. Economists call this difficulty the **free-rider problem,** but we might call it, more colloquially, the "let George do it" problem.[16] The funding for public television stations illustrates this dilemma. Almost all agree that public television, which survives in large part through viewers' contributions, is of great value. But only a fraction of those who watch public television contribute on a regular basis. Why? Because people can watch the programs whether or not they contribute. The free rider has the same access to public television as the contributor.

The same problem crops up for interest groups. When a lobbying group wins benefits, those benefits are not restricted to members of the organization. For instance, if the American Business Conference wins a tax concession from Congress for capital expenditures, all businesses that fall within the provisions of the law can take advantage of the tax break. Thus many business executives might not support their firms' joining the American Business Conference, even though they might benefit from its efforts; they prefer instead to let others shoulder the financial burden.

The free-rider problem increases the difficulty of attracting paying members, but it certainly does not make the task impossible. In fact, as we discuss later in this chapter, the number of interest groups has grown significantly in recent years. Clearly, many people realize that if everyone decides to "let George do it," the job simply won't get done. Millions of Americans contribute to interest groups because they are concerned about an issue or feel a responsibility to help organizations that work on their behalf.[17] Also, many organizations offer membership benefits that have nothing to do with politics or lobbying. Business trade associations, for example, are a source of information about industry trends and effective management practices; and they organize conventions where members can learn, socialize, and occasionally find new customers or suppliers.

Lobbyists

Part of the money raised by interest groups is used to pay lobbyists, who represent the organizations before government. Lobbyists make sure that people in government know what their members want and that their organizations know what government is doing (see Features 10.2 and 10.3). For example, when an administrative agency issues new regulations, lobbyists are right there to interpret the content and implications of the regulations for rank-and-file members. The Washington representative of an oil trade association was reading the *Federal Register* (a daily compendium of all new regulations issued by the government) as part of his daily routine when he noticed that the Federal Aviation Administration was going to put out new regulations requiring detailed flight plans by noncommercial aircraft. This would make rescue efforts for noncommercial planes easier, but the lobbyist realized that it could compromise the confidentiality surrounding where company planes were going on their aerial explorations for oil and gas. These filed flight plans could be obtained by anyone. He notified the member companies, and their lobbying prevented the implementation of these regulations, precluding the possibility of competitors getting hold of this kind of secret data.[18]

Lobbyists can be full-time employees of the organization or employees of public relations or law firms who are hired on retainer. When hiring a lobbyist, an interest group looks for someone who knows his or her way around Washington. Lobbyists are valued for their experience and knowledge of how government operates. Often they are people who have served in the legislative or executive branches, where they have had firsthand experience with government. William Timmons, who heads his own lobbying firm, has attracted an impressive array of clients, among them the American Broadcasting Company, Anheuser-Busch, Chrysler, and Boeing. These companies know that Timmons's experience as a White House assistant for legislative liaison gives him a great deal of insight into the policymaking process, as well as valuable government contacts.[19]

Lobbying is a lucrative profession. One study of Washington representatives from a variety of organizations found that the average yearly salary was just over $90,000.[20] The financial rewards are such that many former members of Congress are part of the profession. As one old Washington saying has it, "They come to govern, they stay to lobby."[21] (Beginning in 1991, former members of Congress cannot lobby the House or Senate for a year after leaving office, a reform designed to prevent former members from earning large salaries lobbying on behalf of the very legislation they worked on while in Congress.)[22]

By the nature of their location, many Washington law firms are drawn into lobbying. Corporations without their own Washington offices rely heavily on law firms to lobby for them before the national government.

FEATURE 10.2   *His Client: Japan, Inc.*

When a Japanese company runs into a problem with the United States government, one person it's likely to call on for help is Stanton Anderson. Part lawyer, part troubleshooter, and part lobbyist, Anderson is very successful at all he does.

After graduating from college, Anderson became a Washington lobbyist for an aviation trade group. He also worked in Republican politics before pursuing a law degree. Later he gained invaluable experience working for the Commerce Department, where he held a high-ranking job doing congressional liaison.

In addition to being a senior partner in a law firm that he founded, Anderson is also head of Global USA, a lobbying firm. His Japanese clients include All Nippon Airways and high-tech companies like Fanuc Ltd. and Kyocera Corp. When clients like Japanese telecommunications companies are threatened with tariffs, Anderson devises strategies to convince members of Congress that a likely consequence of such a law would be retaliation by the Japanese government that would hurt American companies doing business there.

Anderson stresses that his job isn't just lobbying the United States government—he explains America to his foreign clients. Says Anderson, "I interpret things for my clients. They tend to want to solicit as much information as they can . . . I just happen to be a source."

Stanton Anderson

Sources: Clyde H. Farnsworth, "Japan's Top U.S. Lobbyist." *New York Times*, 2 June 1985, p. 6F; Kathryn Johnson, "How Foreign Powers Play for Status in Washington," *U.S. News and World Report*, 17 June 1985, pp. 35–40; and Eduardo Lachica, "Japanese Are Lobbying Hard in U.S. to Offset Big Protectionist Push," *Wall Street Journal*, 23 August 1985, p. 1.

FEATURE 10.3   *Her Client: Poor Children*

Marian Wright Edelman's constituents don't pay dues to her organization. They don't read newsletters that explain what her organization is doing for

Marian Wright Edelman

them. Indeed, precious few of this country's poor youth have ever heard of an organization called the Children's Foundation.

The Children's Foundation lobbies on behalf of a variety of health and social service issues, including family planning to prevent teenage pregnancy. Edelman knows the numbing statistics all too well: Every year 1.1 million teenage girls get pregnant. This figure includes 125,000 girls fifteen years old or younger. The poorest girls are the most likely to get pregnant.

The daughter of a small-town Baptist minister in South Carolina, Edelman went to Spellman College and Yale Law School. She worked as a civil rights lawyer for the NAACP Legal Defense Fund in Mississippi before coming to Washington. She founded the Children's Defense Fund in 1973 and has built it into a respected organization with an annual budget of $4.4 million and a staff of sixty-seven.

One focus of Edelman's lobbying is to make government officials understand that helping poor children is not only a humane thing to do but a way of saving resources in the long run. Says Edelman, "Our goal is to educate the nation about the needs of children and encourage preventive investment in children before they get sick, drop out of school, or get into trouble."

Sources: *Public Interest Profiles* (Washington, D.C.: Foundation for Public Affairs, 1986), p. 13; Lena Williams, "She Whose Constituents Are 61 Million Children," *New York Times*, 27 February 1986, p. B10; Katherine Bouton, "Marian Wright Edelman," *Ms.*, July/August 1987, pp. 98ff; and Marian Wright Edelman, "How to Prevent Teenage Pregnancy," *Ebony*, July 1987, pp. 62–66.

Over time, lawyer-lobbyists tend to develop expertise in particular policy areas.

The most common image of a lobbyist is that of an "arm twister," someone who spends most of the time trying to convince a legislator or administrator to back a certain policy. But lobbying is more subtle than that. Lobbyists' primary job is to pass on information to policymakers. Lobbyists provide government officials and their staffs with a constant flow of data that support their organizations' policy goals. Lobbyists also try to build a compelling case for their goals, showing that the "facts" dictate that a change be made. What lobbyists are really trying to do, of

Bipartisan Clout

Anne Wexler (left), a well-known Democrat, and Nancy Reynolds, a Republican, are two of the principals in a lobbying firm. The bipartisan nature of their firm is not unusual—public relations and lobbying firms want clients to believe they have access to important policymakers in both parties.

course, is to convince policymakers that their data deserve more attention and are more accurate than those presented by other lobbyists.

Political Action Committees

One of the organizational resources that can make a lobbyist's job easier is a **political action committee (PAC).** PACs pool campaign contributions from group members and donate those funds to candidates for political office. Under federal law, a PAC can give up to $5,000 for each separate election to a candidate for Congress. As Figure 10.3 shows, a change in campaign finance law in 1974 led to a rapid increase in the number of PACs. The greatest growth came from corporations, most of which had been legally prohibited from operating political action committees. There was also rapid growth in the number of **nonconnected PACs,** largely ideological groups that have no parent lobbying organiza-

FIGURE 10.3 *PAC Growth Levels Off*

After a 1974 change in election laws, the numbers of PACs grew rapidly. In recent years, however, the numbers of PACs overall and within the separate categories have remained stable. The amount of money PACs contribute has continued to grow, though at a relatively slow rate, from $140 million in 1985–1986 to $159 million in 1989–1990. (Sources: Federal Election Commission, "Decrease in Registered PACs Reported by FEC," 17 January 1990; and Federal Election Commission, "PAC Activity Falls in 1990 Election," 31 March 1991.)

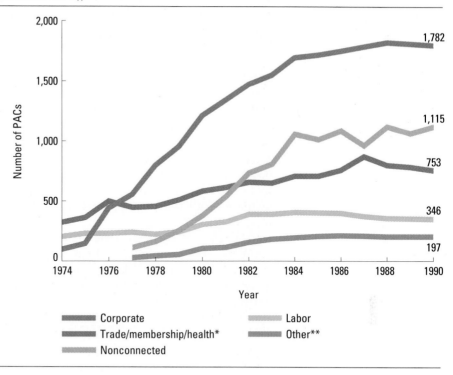

* Until 1977, this category consisted of all but labor and corporate PACs.
** Includes PACs formed by cooperatives and corporations without capital stock.

tion and are formed solely for the purpose of raising and channeling campaign funds. (So a PAC can be the campaign-wing affiliate of an existing interest group or a wholly independent, unaffiliated group.) Most PACs are rather small, and a majority of them give less than $20,000 in total contributions during a two-year election cycle.[23] Some, however are enormous. The Realtors Political Action Committee gave $3 million in the 1990 election, and the American Medical Association's PAC donated almost $2.4 million.[24]

Why do interest groups form PACs? One businessman said his company formed a PAC because "talking to politicians is fine, but with a little money they hear you better."[25] His words seem cynical, but they contain more than a kernel of truth. Lobbyists believe that campaign contributions help significantly when they are trying to gain access to a member of Congress. Members of Congress and their staffers generally are eager to meet with representatives of their constituencies, but their time is limited. However, a member of Congress or an assistant would find it difficult to turn down a request for a meeting with a lobbyist from a company, if its PAC had made a campaign contribution in the last election.

Typically, PACs, like most other interest groups, are highly pragmatic organizations; pushing a particular political philosophy takes second place to achieving immediate policy goals. Even though many corporate executives have strong beliefs in a free-market economy, for example, their company PACs tend to hold congressional candidates to a much more practical standard. As a group, corporate PACs gave 83 percent of their contributions to incumbent members of Congress—many of them liberal and moderate Democrats—during the last two-year election cycle.[26] Citizen-group PACs tend to be moved more by ideology; they give a higher proportion of their funds to challengers than do business, labor, or trade-group PACs. For most PACs donations are a means of gaining access, and that access is seen as critical to gaining influence with congressional offices.[27]

The growing role of PACs in financing congressional campaigns has become the most controversial aspect of interest group politics. Close to half of the members of the House of Representatives receive 50 percent or more of all their campaign contributions from political action committees.[28] This money may not simply bring access, but favoritism as well. Critics also charge that PAC money can lead to corruption; they point to the savings and loan scandal, which will cost taxpayers hundreds of billions of dollars, as an example. The savings and loan industry gave more than $11 million in donations to members of Congress during the 1980s.[29] Some of the influential legislators who were recipients of these funds intervened with federal regulators before the shady dealings in the industry became fully apparent and asked administrators to go easy on some S&Ls that were in financial difficulty.

It should come as no surprise that corporate PACs contribute more to congressional candidates than any other PACs. But in a democracy, influence should not be a function of money; some citizens have little to give, yet their rights need to be protected. From this perspective, the issue is political equality. In the words of Republican Senator Robert Dole, "There aren't any Poor PACs or Food Stamp PACs or Nutrition PACs or Medicare PACs."[30]

Still, strong arguments can be made for retaining PACs. They offer a means for people to participate in the political system. They allow small givers to pool their resources and to fight the feeling that one person cannot make a difference. Finally, PAC defenders also point out that prohibiting PACs would amount to a restriction on the freedom of political expression.

Lobbying Tactics

When an interest group decides to try to influence government on an issue, its staff and officers must develop a strategy, which may include a number of tactics aimed at various officials or offices. Together, these tactics should use the group's resources as effectively as possible.

Keep in mind that lobbying extends beyond the legislative branch. Groups can seek help from the courts and administrative agencies as well as from Congress. Moreover, interest groups may have to shift their focus from one branch of government to another. After a bill becomes a law, for example, a group that lobbied for the legislation will probably try to influence the administrative agency responsible for implementing the new law. Some policy decisions are left unresolved by legislation and are settled through regulations. The lobby wants to make sure regulatory decisions are as close as possible to the group's preferences.

We discuss three types of lobbying tactics here: those aimed at policymakers and implemented through interest group representatives (direct lobbying); those that involve group members (grassroots lobbying); and those directed toward the public (information campaigns). We also examine the cooperative efforts of interest groups to influence government through coalitions.

Direct Lobbying

Direct lobbying relies on personal contact with policymakers. One survey of Washington lobbyists showed that 98 percent use direct contact with government officials to express their groups' views.[31] This interaction takes place when a lobbyist meets with a member of Congress, an agency official, or a staff member (see Feature 10.4). In these meetings, lobbyists usually convey their arguments in the form of data about a specific issue. If a lobbyist from, for example, the Chamber of Commerce meets with a member of Congress about a bill the organization backs, the lobbyist does not say (or even suggest), "Vote for this bill, or our people in the district will vote against you in the next election." Instead, the lobbyist might say, "If this bill is passed, we're going to see hundreds of

FEATURE 10.4   *These Soldiers May Be Old, but They Still Know How to Fight*

The primary objective of the 1986 tax reform was to eliminate provisions and exceptions that entitled certain groups or industries to preferential treatment. By reducing such preferences (like the investment tax credit for industry), revenue would be gained and could be redistributed to taxpayers through lower tax brackets for all. Not all tax breaks and special benefits were removed though. One of the ones that remained was the tax-exempt status of veterans' disability payments.

When the Reagan administration's initial proposal (Treasury I) was released, it did in fact call for the elimination of the veterans' tax preference. Leaders of veterans' lobbies in Washington were beside themselves when they found this out, and they demanded a meeting with Assistant Secretary of the Treasury Ronald Pearlman, one of the principals overseeing the reform drive. The leaders of these groups felt that disabled veterans deserve concern and respect from the government, and that forcing veterans to pay taxes on their benefits was an insult. When the leaders confronted Pearlman in his office, he stated the philosophy behind Treasury I in rhetorical fashion: "Why should veterans' disability payments be treated differently than any other income?"

The heads of the veterans' organizations left Pearlman's office with no concessions on his part. But the battle was far from over. They requested a meeting with Pearlman's boss, Secretary of the Treasury James Baker, and came prepared with some pretty heavy ammunition. They showed Baker a full-page ad they were planning to run in the *Washington Post* and other newspapers. In the ad was a large photograph of Chad Colley, the head of the Disabled American Veterans and one of the leaders who had earlier met with Pearlman. Colley is a triple amputee (he lost both legs and an arm in Vietnam), and the photograph of him in a wheelchair made that absolutely clear. At the top of the ad, in large letters, was the question "What's So Special About Disabled Veterans?" Below, in smaller type, the ad read, "That's what a top Treasury official said to Chad Colley . . ." After the veterans left Baker's office, he called Pearlman in and told him, "I think we'll have to drop this one."

Source: Adapted from Jeffrey H. Birnbaum and Alan S. Murray, *Showdown at Gucci Gulch* (New York: Random House, 1987), pp. 79–80. Copyright © 1987 by Jeffrey Birnbaum and Alan Murray. Reprinted by permission of Random House, Inc.

new jobs created back home." The representative has no trouble at all figuring out that a vote for the bill can help in the next election.

Personal lobbying is a day-in, day-out process. It is not enough simply to meet with policymakers just before a vote or a regulatory decision. Lobbyists must maintain contact with congressional and agency staffers, constantly providing them with pertinent data. Lobbyists for the American Gas Association, for instance, keep a list of 1,200 agency personnel who are "called frequently to share informally in association intelligence." The director of the group's lobbying efforts has a shorter list of 104 key administrators with whom he has met personally and who can "be counted on to provide information on agency decisionmaking."[32]

A tactic related to direct lobbying is *testifying* at committee hearings when a bill is before Congress. This tactic allows the interest group to put its views on record and make them widely known when the hearing testimony is published. Although testifying is one of the most visible parts of lobbying, it is generally considered window dressing. Most lobbyists believe that testimony usually does little by itself to persuade members of Congress.

Another direct but somewhat different approach is *legal advocacy*. Using this tactic, a group tries to achieve its policy goals through litigation.

The National Organization for Women has had some success in suing Operation Rescue, a radical antiabortion group that has tried to block women from entering abortion clinics. Court-awarded financial judgments against Operation Rescue have played a large part in decimating the group and leaving it virtually bankrupt.[33]

Grassroots Lobbying

Grassroots lobbying involves an interest group's rank-and-file members and may also include people outside the organization who sympathize with its goals. Grassroots tactics, such as letter-writing campaigns and protests, are often used in conjunction with direct lobbying by Washington representatives. Letters, telegrams, and phone calls from a group's members to their representatives in Congress or agency administrators add to a lobbyist's credibility in talks with these officials. Policymakers are more concerned about what a lobbyist says when they know that constituents are really watching their decisions.

Group members—especially influential members (corporation presidents, local civic leaders)—occasionally go to Washington themselves to lobby. But the most common grassroots tactic is *letter writing.* "Write your representative" is not just a slogan out of a civics text. Legislators are highly sensitive to the content of their mail. Interest groups often launch letter-writing campaigns through their regular publications or special alerts. They may even provide sample letters and the names and addresses of specific policymakers. When time is of the essence, phone calls serve the same purpose as letters.

If people in government seem unresponsive to conventional lobbying tactics, a group might resort to some form of *political protest.* A protest or demonstration, such as picketing or marching, is designed to attract

Needling the Government
ACT UP, an AIDS advocacy organization, frequently uses demonstrations to bring attention to its causes. Here, members call for a needle distribution policy that would supply intravenous drug users with clean needles, reducing the shared use of needles contaminated with the HIV virus. Opponents of this policy argue that the distribution of needles condones drug use.

media attention to an issue. Protesters hope that television and newspaper coverage will help change public opinion and make policymakers more receptive to the group's demands. When three thousand farmers from the American Agriculture Movement drove tractors from their homes to Washington to show their disappointment with Carter administration farm policies, the spectacle attracted considerable publicity. Their unconventional approach increased the public's awareness of falling produce prices and stimulated the government to take some limited action.[34]

The main drawback to protest activity is that policymaking is a long-term, incremental process, whereas a demonstration is short-lived. It is difficult to sustain the anger and activism of group supporters—to keep large numbers of people involved in protest after protest—simply to keep the group's demands in the public eye. A notable exception were the civil rights demonstrations of the 1960s, which were sustained over a long period. National attention focused not only on the widespread demonstrations but also on the sometimes violent confrontations between blacks and white law enforcement officers. For example, the use of police dogs and high-power fire hoses against blacks marching in Alabama in the early 1960s angered millions of Americans who saw films of the confrontations on television programs. The protests were a major factor in public opinion, which in turn hastened the passage of the Civil Rights Act of 1964 and the Voting Rights Act of 1965.[35]

Information Campaigns

As the strategy of the civil rights movement shows, interest groups generally feel that public backing adds strength to their lobbying efforts. And because all interest groups believe they are absolutely right in their policy orientations, they believe that they will get that backing if they make the public aware of their positions and the evidence that supports them. To this end, interest groups launch **information campaigns,** organized efforts to gain public backing by bringing group views to the public's attention. The underlying assumption is that public ignorance and apathy are as much a problem as the views of competing interest groups. Various means are used to combat this apathy. Some are directed at the larger public, others at smaller audiences with long-standing interest in an issue.

Public relations is one information tactic. A public relations campaign might involve sending speakers to meetings in various parts of the country or producing pamphlets and handouts. A highly visible form of political public relations is newspaper and magazine advertising. The National Rifle Association uses advertising to try to show people that it is a responsible organization rather than a group that cares more about guns than stopping crime. It has run a series of profiles of members, such as the head of a police organization, who belie the image of irresponsibility. Newspaper and magazine advertising has one major drawback, however. It is extremely expensive. Consequently, few groups rely on it as their primary weapon.

Sponsoring *research* is another way interest groups press their cases. When a group believes that evidence has not been fully developed in a certain area, it may commission research on the subject. Groups working for the rights of the disabled have protected programs from would-be budget cutters by providing "lawmakers with abundant research findings demonstrating that it costs much more to keep people in institutions . . . than it does to utilize home and community living programs."[36]

Some groups believe that publicizing *voting records* of members of Congress is an effective means of influencing public opinion. These interest groups simply publish in their newsletters a record of how all members of Congress voted on issues of particular concern to the organization. Other groups prepare statistical indexes that compare the voting records of all members of Congress on selected key issues. Each member is graded (from 0 to 100 percent) according to how often he or she voted in agreement with the group's views. Thus the owners of small businesses who belong to the National Federation of Independent Business can assume that those lawmakers who scored well on the group's "scorecard" have usually voted in sympathy with their interests.

Coalition Building

A final aspect of lobbying strategy is **coalition building,** in which several organizations band together for the purpose of lobbying. This joint effort conserves or makes more effective use of the resources of groups with similar views. Coalitions form most often among groups that work in the same policy area and are similar in their political outlook.[37] On feminist issues, for example, the National Organization for Women, the National Women's Political Caucus, the League of Women Voters, the American Association of University Women, and the Women's Equity Action League usually work with one another.[38] Most coalitions are informal, ad hoc arrangements. Groups have limited resources and prefer not to commit those resources to long-term coalitions. Also, they do not always share an equal degree of enthusiasm for all issues; sometimes even old friends end up on different sides of an issue.

The Growth of Interest Group Politics

The growing number of active interest groups is one of the most important trends in American politics. One survey of Washington-based lobbies showed that fully 30 percent of existing groups were formed between 1960 and 1980.[39] The greatest growth occurred in three types of interest groups: PACs (which we discussed earlier), citizen groups, and business lobbies.

The Public Interest Movement

Many recently formed citizen groups are commonly known as public interest groups. A **public interest group** is generally considered to have no economic self-interest in the policies it pursues.[40] For example, the members of the environmental groups fighting for stricter pollution-control requirements in the bill described at the opening of this chapter receive no financial gain from the institution of such standards. The benefits to its members are largely ideological and aesthetic. In contrast, a corporation fighting against the same stringent standards is trying to protect its profits. A law that requires it to install expensive antipollution devices can reduce stockholders' dividends, depress salaries, and postpone expansion. Although both the environmental group and the corporation have valid reasons for their stands on the issue, their motives are different. The environmental lobby is a public interest group; the corporation is not.

Many public interest groups have become major players in national politics. Common Cause, one of the best-known "good government" groups, works for campaign finance reform, codes of ethics in government, and open congressional and administrative proceedings.[41]

The best-known public interest activist is Ralph Nader. He first came to the public's attention in 1966, when he exposed serious safety flaws in the Corvair. So damning was his indictment of the car that sales dropped significantly, and General Motors soon stopped producing the Corvair. Nader now heads a small empire of public interest groups, among them the Aviation Consumer Action Project, the Public Citizen Litigation Group, and the Health Research Group.

Nader has a reputation as a relentless, driven lobbyist for consumer protection. He mercilessly criticizes politicians who disagree with him, treating them as "enemies of the people," not as individuals who simply happen to hold different views. Nader's self-righteousness is tempered by his dedication, zeal, and ascetic lifestyle. These have made him a highly effective and credible spokesman for consumers.

Origins of the movement.   Traditionally, public interest lobbies have not been a major factor in Washington politics. Yet the upsurge of these groups that began in the late 1960s did not prove to be as short-lived a phenomenon as many had expected. At first, most new groups were on the liberal side of the political spectrum. As we will see, however, many new conservative groups have recently formed. Groups on both the Left and the Right have become more politically prominent. The public interest movement has been impressive in its collective scope and strength; many groups have been able to support themselves through the contributions of concerned citizens.

Why have so many public interest groups formed in the last two decades? The movement grew from the civil rights and anti–Vietnam War activism of the 1960s.[42] In both cases, citizens with passionate beliefs about a cause felt they had no choice but to take aggressive, even abrasive, action. Dependence on political parties and the electoral process was not producing change; collective citizen action had to be used instead.

The legacy of the civil rights and antiwar movements was the belief that individuals acting together can influence the direction of public policy. From the success of these groups, Americans learned that ordinary citizens could have an impact on government if they organized. (Most contemporary citizen groups no longer rely on the demonstrations that characterized these earlier movements. Instead, they channel the energy, resources, and outrage of their constituents into more conventional tactics, such as legislative lobbying and litigation.)

An Image That Angered a Nation

Demonstrations by blacks during the early 1960s played a critical role in pushing Congress to pass civil rights legislation. This photo of vicious police dogs attacking demonstrators in Birmingham, Alabama, is typical of the scenes that were shown in network news broadcasts and newspapers. Pictures like this helped build public support for civil rights legislation.

The late 1960s and early 1970s were also a time when Americans were becoming increasingly cynical about government. Loyalty to political parties was declining, too, as greater proportions of citizens told pollsters that they did not identify with either national party. If neither government nor political parties could be trusted to provide adequate representation in the nation's capital on such issues as preserving the environment or protecting consumers, the obvious alternative was membership in an ideological interest group.

Conservative reaction. Why conservatives were slower than liberals to mobilize is not altogether clear, but the new right-of-center groups appear in part to be a reaction to the perceived success of liberal groups. Like their liberal counterparts, conservative groups cover a wide variety of policy areas. Most stand in direct opposition to causes espoused by liberal organizations. Phyllis Schlafly's Eagle Forum, for example, fought long and hard against the Equal Rights Amendment and other positions favored by feminist groups.

But conservative groups are not merely mirror images of liberal citizen lobbies.[43] A distinctive feature of the "New Right" is the active participation of religious organizations. Groups like the Religious Roundtable and Christian Voice actively promote policies that they feel are in line with Christian teachings, such as permitting prayer in school and restricting abortions.[44] Some Americans who believe that the country is best served by a complete separation of church and state strongly criticize the lobbying of the religious Right. But the religious Right believes that its moral duty is to see that Christian principles are embodied in government policy. The conflict between liberal critics and conservative religious lobbies is more than a difference of opinion over specific policies. It is a struggle to define the fundamental values that shape our society. Although the most visible of the Christian groups, the Moral Majority, dissolved in 1989, the religious Right remains an active and important force in conservative politics.[45]

During the Reagan presidency, conservative citizen groups enjoyed substantial access to the White House, their lobbyists meeting frequently with White House aides.[46] They did not have the same degree of success with Congress, however, where many of their most cherished goals—including a constitutional amendment allowing school prayer—were not met. Conservative groups were not as initially enthusiastic about George Bush as they were toward Reagan—many groups considered him a "closet moderate." They became disenchanted because he went back on his no-new-taxes pledge, but Bush's steadfast resolve in the Persian Gulf crisis has made it more difficult for conservative groups to mount a challenge to him in the next presidential race.

Business Lobbies

The number of business lobbies in Washington has also increased. Offices of individual corporations and of business trade associations are more in evidence than ever before. A **trade association,** such as the Mortgage Bankers Association or the National Electrical Manufacturers Association, is an organization that represents companies within the same industry. At one point during the 1970s, when the boom in business lobbying began, trade associations were moving their headquarters to Washington at an average of one every week.[47] A 1981 survey of corporations revealed that more than half of the organizations with a government relations office in Washington had set up that office during the previous decade.[48] Corporations that already had offices in Washington typically upgraded them by adding staff.

The vast increase in business representation in Washington was in large part a response to the expanded scope of national government activities during the 1960s and 1970s. As the Environmental Protection Agency, the Consumer Product Safety Commission, and other regulatory agencies were created, many more companies found themselves affected by federal regulations. And those located outside of Washington often found themselves *reacting* to policies already made rather than *participating* in their making. They saw a move to Washington—where the policymakers are—as necessary if they were to obtain information on pending government actions in enough time to act on it.

Ironically, the increase in government activity and in business lobbying followed directly from the success of liberal public interest groups, strong supporters of regulation to protect the environment and consumers. By the early 1970s, many businesspeople felt that the government was reacting to an agenda set primarily by citizen groups. During that period Thomas Murphy, the CEO of General Motors said, "The truth is that we have been clobbered."[49]

The increase in business advocacy in Washington was also fueled by the competitive nature of business lobbying. The reason for this political

The Tax Lobbyist

Charls Walker is one of the most skilled business lobbyists in Washington. He holds a Ph.D. in economics and was a high-ranking official in the U.S. Treasury Department. Because of Walker's expertise and political skills, many large corporations hire him to lobby Congress on tax policy.

competition is that legislation and regulatory decisions never seem to apply uniformly to all businesses; rather, they affect one type of business or one industry more than others. Financial services is one area where growing competition and limited steps toward deregulation have transformed the lobbying scene. Insurance companies, brokerage houses, investment banks, and retail banks have all made efforts to encroach on one another's turf. So many new players have entered the picture that policymaking has become even more complex. A member of the House Banking Committee said of the change, "When I first came to Congress there were five major financial trade groups, but now there are at least five times that. Now if you're trying to satisfy all the trade groups, it's pretty hard to do."[50]

The growth of business lobbies has reinforced and possibly expanded the overrepresentation of business in national politics. As Figure 10.4 shows, approximately half of all interest groups with a Washington office are either corporations or business trade associations. If organizations with a Washington lawyer or other kind of lobbyist on retainer are added to the total, the dominance of business in the lobbying population is even greater. But the number of organizations or lobbyists is far from a perfect indicator of interest group strength. The AFL-CIO, which represents millions of union members, is more influential than a two-person corporate listening post in Washington. Still, business has an advantage in terms of Washington representation. And because business lobbies are able to draw on the institutional resources of corporations, they can fund their lobbying operations more easily than can groups that depend on the voluntary contributions of individuals.

FIGURE 10.4   *The Washington Interest Group Community*

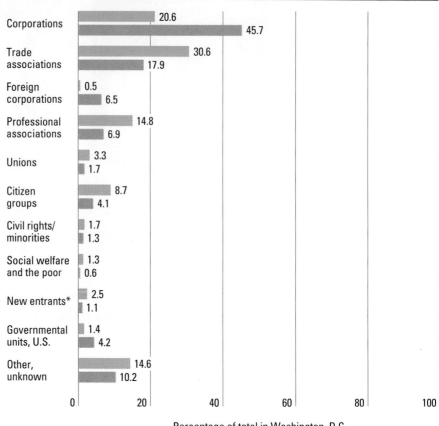

Although the interest group community is highly diverse, business organizations form the biggest part of that community. Corporations and trade associations are the most prevalent interest group actors in terms of having an office in Washington or, at the very least, employing a lobbyist there. (Source: Kay Lehman Schlozman and John T. Tierney, Organized Interests and American Democracy [New York: Harper & Row, 1986], p. 67. Copyright © 1986 by Kay Lehman Schlozman and John T. Tierney. Reprinted by permission of HarperCollins Publishers. Adapted from the Encyclopedia of Associations, ed. Denise S. Akey. Gale Research.)

Category	Office in Washington, D.C.	Retains lobbyist in Washington, D.C., or has office there.
Corporations	20.6	45.7
Trade associations	30.6	17.9
Foreign corporations	0.5	6.5
Professional associations	14.8	6.9
Unions	3.3	1.7
Citizen groups	8.7	4.1
Civil rights/ minorities	1.7	1.3
Social welfare and the poor	1.3	0.6
New entrants*	2.5	1.1
Governmental units, U.S.	1.4	4.2
Other, unknown	14.6	10.2

Percentage of total in Washington, D.C.

* Elderly, women, handicapped.

Interest Groups: An Evaluation

The pluralist scholars who wrote during the 1950s and 1960s were right on one important point, but wrong on another. They argued that interest groups are at the center of the policymaking process. Certainly, the growing number of groups in recent years seems to reflect a broad acceptance of this view by various sectors of American society. Although pluralists never predicted perfect representation of affected interests, they did assume that representation would be more balanced than it is. What we have instead is a political system increasingly centered around interest group advocacy, but one in which some interests—most notably, those of business—are much better represented than others. What are the consequences of this?

One consequence is that the large and growing number of interest groups works against a strengthening of our party system. Many activists find narrowly based interest groups more appealing than parties. The lobbies that these activists support work intensely on the few issues they care about most; parties often dilute issue stands to appeal to as broad a segment of the electorate as possible. Thus, many people who care deeply about public policy questions work to influence government through particular lobbies rather than through political parties. Interest in party reform has waned in the past few years. The satisfaction people feel with the work of their interest groups surely contributes to Americans' lack of concern for revitalizing the parties, for making them more responsive policymaking bodies.

This lack of concern is unfortunate. Interest groups can do no more than supplement the functions of parties. Most interest groups are small bodies concerned with only a few issues. Parties, however, can be instruments of majoritarian democracy. They can bring together broad coalitions of people and translate their concerns into large-scale social and economic change. Parties are particularly important because they can represent those who are not well represented by interest groups. As political scientist Walter Dean Burnham puts it, parties "can generate countervailing collective power on behalf of the many individually powerless against the relatively few who are individually—or organizationally —powerful."[51]

Most observers agree that stronger parties, which would provide a more majoritarian mechanism for influencing policy, are good. But few seem interested in reviving the parties at the cost of their own interest group's influence. If our party system is revitalized, then, it will be because of what the parties do to make themselves more appealing, not because people turn away from their interest groups.

Regulation

Interest groups contribute to democratic government by representing their supporters' interests. However, concern that individual groups have too much influence or that interest group representation is biased in favor of certain segments of society has prompted frequent calls for reform. Yet, little has been done to weaken the influence of interest groups. The problem, as Madison foresaw, is that it is difficult to limit interest group activity without limiting fundamental freedoms. The First Amendment guarantees Americans the right to petition their government, and lobbying, at its most basic level, is a form of organized petitioning.

One effort to reform lobbying was the Federal Regulation of Lobbying Act, passed in 1946. This law was intended to require all lobbyists to register and file expenditure reports with Congress. In practice, the law has been ineffective. A Supreme Court ruling held that it applies only to people or organizations whose "principal purpose" is influencing legislation.[52] This exempts many, if not most, of those who lobby. Some modest reforms have been enacted since that time, but calls for stricter regulation on interest groups have not gotten very far.[53]

Campaign Financing

Much of the debate over interest groups and political reform centers around the role PACs play in financing congressional campaigns. As the costs of political campaigning escalate sharply, politicians have to raise larger and larger sums. During the 1970s, Congress took some important steps to reform campaign-financing practices. Strong disclosure requirements now exist, so that the source of all significant contributions to candidates for national office is part of the public record. Public financing of presidential campaigns is also provided for; taxpayer money is given in equal amounts to the presidential nominees of the major parties.

Reformers have also called for public financing of congressional elections, to reduce the alleged influence of PACs in Congress. Public financing and other schemes designed to reduce the percentage of campaign funds supplied by PACs are meant to lessen the advantage of certain groups in gaining access to and sympathy from members of Congress and their staffers. But incumbents usually find it easier to raise money from PACs than their electoral challengers do, so there is a strong incentive to leave the status quo intact. Strong public criticism of current campaign financing has, however, pushed Congress to take up reform legislation. It was a contentious issue in the 1989–1990 sessions of Congress, but sharp partisan differences between Republicans and Democrats kept a reform bill from being enacted.

The debate over PACs is another manifestation of the sharp tension between the principles of freedom and equality. For many, restrictions on PACs represent restrictions on their personal freedom. Shouldn't people have the right to join others who think as they do and contribute to the candidates of their choice? For others, though, PAC contributions seem less a matter of freedom of political expression than of some people's freedom to use their wealth to further their own special interests. They believe that certain groups are buying influence on Capitol Hill, pointing to twenty-one PACs, each of which contributed over $1 million to candidates for national office during the 1990 elections.[54] And they argue that the consequence of PAC giving is to reinforce, if not expand, the inequities between rich and poor.[55]

Summary

Interest groups play many important roles in our political process. They are a means by which citizens can participate in politics, and they communicate their members' views to those in government. Interest groups differ greatly in the resources at their disposal and in the tactics they use to influence government. The number of interest groups has grown sharply in recent years.

Despite the growth and change in the nature of interest groups, the fundamental problem identified by Madison over two hundred years ago endures. In a free and open society, groups form to pursue policies that favor themselves at the expense of the broader national interest. Madison hoped that the solution to this problem would come through the diversity of the population and the structure of our government.

To a certain extent, Madison's expectations have been borne out. The natural differences between groups have prevented the tyranny of any one faction. Yet the interest group system remains unbalanced, with some segments of society (particularly business, the wealthy, the educated) considerably better organized than others. The growth of citizen groups has reduced this disparity somewhat, but there are still significant inequities in how well different interests are represented in Washington.

These inequities have led most contemporary scholars to reject two key propositions of the early pluralists: that the freedom to form lobbies produces a healthy competition among opposing groups and that the compromises emerging from that competition lead to policies that fairly represent the divisions in society. Instead, business and professional groups have an advantage because of their ability to organize more readily and their greater resources. The interest group system clearly compromises the principle of political equality as stated in the maxim "one person, one vote." Formal political equality is certainly more likely to occur outside of interest group politics, in elections between candidates from competing political parties—which better fits the majoritarian model of democracy.

Despite the inequities of the interest group system, little general effort has been made to restrict interest group activity. Madison's dictum that suppressing political freedoms must be avoided, even at the expense of permitting interest group activity that promotes the selfish interests of narrow segments of the population, has generally guided public policy. Yet, as the problem of PACs demonstrates, government has had to set some restrictions on interest groups. Permitting PACs to give unlimited contributions to political candidates would undermine confidence in the system. Where to draw the limit on PAC activity remains a thorny problem, since there is little consensus on how to balance the conflicting needs of our society.

KEY TERMS

interest group
lobby
lobbyist
agenda building
program monitoring
interest group
   entrepreneur
citizen group
direct mail
free-rider problem

political action
   committee (PAC)
nonconnected PAC
direct lobbying
grassroots lobbying
information campaign
coalition building
public interest group
trade association

SELECTED READINGS

Berry, Jeffrey M. *The Interest Group Society.* 2d ed. Glenview, Ill.: Scott, Foresman/Little, Brown, 1989. An analysis of the growth of interest group politics.

Berry, Jeffrey M. *Lobbying for the People.* Princeton, N.J.: Princeton University Press, 1977. A study of eighty-three public interest groups active in national politics.

Cigler, Allan J., and Burdett A. Loomis, eds. *Interest Group Politics.* 3d ed. Washington, D.C.: Congressional Quarterly, 1991. This reader includes eighteen separate essays on lobbying groups.

Lowi, Theodore J. *The End of Liberalism.* 2d ed. New York: Norton, 1979. A critical analysis of the role of interest groups in our society.

Olson, Mancur, Jr. *The Logic of Collective Action.* New York: Schocken, 1968. Olson, an economist, looks at the free-rider problem and the rationale for joining lobbying organizations.

Schlozman, Kay Lehman, and John T. Tierney. *Organized Interests and American Democracy.* New York: Harper & Row, 1986. A valuable and comprehensive study that draws on an original survey of Washington lobbyists.

Vogel, David. *Fluctuating Fortunes.* New York: Basic Books, 1989. The rise and fall and rise of American corporate power.

PART

FOUR

Institutions of Government

11 CONGRESS

WHEN LOUISE SLAUGHTER decided to enter the race for Congress in 1986, she was a decided underdog. Slaughter, a Democrat, ran against a sitting member of the House of Representatives, Republican Fred Eckert. It's extremely difficult to defeat sitting members *(incumbents)*, though Eckert had first won election to Congress in 1984 and was a little less secure than most incumbents. Before Eckert, another Republican had served this suburban Rochester, New York, district for twenty years.

Despite the odds, the New York state assemblywoman plunged ahead. With some early campaign contributions from labor PACs, Slaughter began to build a campaign organization. She proved effective at raising money, which gave her campaign credibility and made it easier to raise additional funds from those cautious about donating funds to the challenger of an incumbent. Eventually, hundreds of thousands of dollars from PACs would flow into Slaughter's and Eckert's campaign war chests, and overall campaign spending in this one district topped a million dollars.

During his term in Washington, Eckert was a faithful supporter of President Ronald Reagan—probably a little too faithful for his own good. Eckert ended up voting in line with President Reagan's positions 94 percent of the time, more than any other single member of Congress. His rock-ribbed conservative ideology led him to cast a number of votes that offended various constituencies back home, such as a vote to reduce social security payments, a vote against the student loan program, a vote against funding for toxic waste cleanup, and a vote against imposing sanctions on the apartheid government of South Africa. Slaughter exploited those votes with TV ads that showed an actor playing Eckert stamping a big, red "NO" on popular bills.

Slaughter did a far better job of developing a campaign organization than did Eckert. She had an energized troop of volunteers who went door-to-door in the district; Eckert recruited few people to work on his behalf. Eckert also was an erratic campaigner, while Slaughter aggressively attacked him for his unpopular votes. Despite these disadvantages, the power of incumbency almost pulled Eckert through—Slaughter won by just 3,300 votes.[1] Eckert was one of only six incumbents who lost that fall. Slaughter went on to win a second term in 1988, and in 1990 she won again easily.

The Slaughter-Eckert race illustrates one of the basic dynamics of American democracy: the conflict between local politics and national politics. Eckert went to Washington wanting to promote the ideological, conservative agenda so powerfully articulated by Ronald Reagan. If he thought he had a mandate to vote this way from his constituents, he was wrong. Different constituency groups within the district were strongly opposed to parts of the Reagan program, and when Eckert voted against the interests of senior citizens, environmentalists and so on, he was inadvertently building Slaughter's electoral base. Eckert wanted to be an instrument of majoritarian democracy; he was undone, instead, by the forces of pluralist democracy.

In this chapter and throughout Part Four of this book, we emphasize the tension between pluralist and majoritarian visions of democracy. In democracies this conflict is evident in the way legislators act as representatives of their constituencies. Thus, two central questions emerge in studying Congress. First, when members of Congress vote on policy issues, whom do they *actually* represent? And second, whom *should* they represent? We try to answer the first question here, leaving you to think about the second.

The Origin and Powers of Congress

The framers of the Constitution wanted to keep power from being concentrated in the hands of a few, but they were also concerned with creating a union strong enough to overcome the weaknesses of the government that operated under the Articles of Confederation. They argued passionately about the structure of the new government. In the end, they produced a legislative body that was as much an experiment as was the new nation's democracy.

The Great Compromise

The U.S. Congress has two separate and powerful chambers: the House of Representatives and the Senate. A bill cannot become law unless it is passed in identical form by both chambers. When the Constitution was being drafted during the summer of 1787, "the fiercest struggle for power" centered on representation in the legislature.[2] The small states wanted all states to have equal representation. The more populous states wanted representation based on population; they did not want their power diluted. The Great Compromise broke the deadlock: The small

The Capitol

The Capitol sits on a site city planner Pierre L'Enfant called "a pedestal waiting for a monument." This is what the building looked like from 1825 to 1856.

states received equal representation in the Senate, but the House, where the number of each state's representatives would be based on population, retained the sole right to originate money bills.

According to the Constitution, each state is represented by two senators, each of whom serves for six years. Terms of office are staggered, so that one-third of the Senate is elected every two years. When it was ratified, the Constitution directed that senators should be chosen by the state legislatures. However, the Seventeenth Amendment, adopted in 1913, provided for the election of senators by popular vote. From the beginning, members of the House of Representatives have been elected by the people. They serve two-year terms, and all House seats are up for election at the same time.

Because each state's representation in the House is in proportion to its population, the Constitution provides for a national census every ten years. Until the first census, the Constitution fixed the number of representatives at 65. As the nation's population grew and new states joined the Union, new seats were added to the House. (There were already 213 representatives after the census of 1820.[3]) At some point, however, a legislative body becomes too unwieldy to be efficient, and in 1929, the House decided to fix its membership at 435. Population shifts are handled by the **reapportionment** (redistribution) of representatives among the states after each census is taken. Projections from the 1990 census show that reapportionment will give California, the nation's largest state, a gain of seven seats, giving it fifty-two representatives overall. Michigan, Ohio, Illinois, and Pennsylvania will each lose two representatives, and New York will lose three.[4]

Representatives are elected from a particular congressional district within their state. The number of districts in a state is equal to the number of representatives the state sends to the House. Before a series of Supreme Court rulings in the 1960s, the states were not required to draw the boundaries of their districts in such a way that the districts had approximately equal populations. As a result, some sparsely populated rural districts had more representation in Congress than their number of residents warranted. The Court ruled that House districts, and all districts in state legislatures, had to be drawn so as to be reasonably equal in population.[5]

Duties of the House and Senate

Although the Great Compromise provided considerably different schemes of representation for the House and Senate, the Constitution gives them essentially similar legislative tasks. They share many important powers, among them the powers to declare war, raise an army and navy, borrow and coin money, regulate interstate commerce, create federal courts, establish rules for the naturalization of immigrants, and "make all Laws which shall be necessary and proper for carrying into Execution the foregoing Powers."

Of course, there are at least a few important differences in the constitutional duties of the two chambers. As noted earlier, the House alone has the right to originate revenue bills, which apparently was coveted at the Constitutional Convention. In practice, this function is of limited consequence because all bills—including revenue bills—must be approved by both the House and Senate. The House also has the power of **impeachment,** the power formally to charge the president, vice president, or other "civil Officers" of the national government with "Treason, Bribery, or other high Crimes and Misdemeanors." The Senate is empowered to act as a court to try impeachments; a two-thirds vote of the senators present is necessary for conviction. Only one president—Andrew Johnson—has ever been impeached, and in 1868 the Senate came within a single vote of finding him guilty. More recently, the House Judiciary Committee voted to impeach President Richard Nixon for his role in the Watergate scandal, but he resigned in August 1974, before the full House could vote. A small number of federal judges, however, have been impeached, convicted, and removed from the bench.

The Constitution gives the Senate the power to approve major presidential appointments (such as to federal judgeships, ambassadorships, and Cabinet posts) and treaties with foreign nations. The president is empowered to *make* treaties, but then they must be submitted to the Senate for approval by a two-thirds majority. Because of this requirement, the executive branch generally considers the Senate's sentiments when it negotiates a treaty. At times, however, a president must try to convince a doubting Senate of the worth of a particular treaty. Shortly after World War I, President Woodrow Wilson submitted to the Senate the Treaty of Versailles, which contained the charter for the proposed League of Nations. Wilson had attempted to convince the Senate that the treaty deserved its support; when the Senate refused to approve the treaty, it was a severe setback for Wilson.

Despite the long list of congressional powers in the Constitution, the question of what powers are appropriate to the Congress has generated substantial controversy. For example, although the Constitution gives Congress the sole power to declare war, many presidents have initiated military action on their own. And at times, the courts have found that congressional actions have usurped the rights of the states.

Electing the Congress

If Americans are not happy with the job Congress is doing, they can use their votes to say so. With a congressional election every two years, the voters have frequent opportunities to express themselves.

The Incumbency Effect

Congressional elections offer voters a chance to show their approval of Congress's performance by re-electing **incumbents** or "throwing the rascals out." The voters seem to do more re-electing than rascal throwing. The re-election rate is astonishingly high; in the majority of elections since 1950, more than 90 percent of all House incumbents have held

In-Your-Face Politics

Senate incumbent Jesse Helms, a Republican from North Carolina, got a spirited challenge from Democrat Harvey Gantt during the 1990 congressional elections. Fighting back, Helms's campaign emphasized the senator's firm opposition to affirmative action through some powerful television ads, designed to appeal to white voters worried about jobs. Observers felt the approach eroded support for Gantt, who is African-American. Helms won once again.

their seats (see Figure 11.1). In the 1990 congressional elections, 96.9 percent of all House incumbents running for re-election won.[6] Most House elections aren't even close; in recent elections most House incumbents have won at least 60 percent of the vote.[7]

These findings may seem surprising. Congress as a whole is not held in particularly high esteem (see Figure 11.2). Polls show that only about a third of the public expresses a good deal of confidence in the Congress.[8] People appear to distinguish between the *institution* of Congress and their own representatives and senators.* But this still does not explain why incumbents do so well within their own districts and states. (Because most research on the incumbency effect has focused on House elections, our discussion concentrates on that body.)

Redistricting.   One explanation of the incumbency effect centers on **redistricting,** the way House districts are redrawn after a census-based reapportionment. It is entirely possible for state legislatures to draw new

---

* An interesting twist to this pattern of people liking their legislators but not liking legislative institutions is that voters in three states, California, Colorado, and Oklahoma, have placed limits on the number of terms that individuals can serve in the state legislature. In other words, citizens in these states have decided to prohibit themselves from re-electing their own state representatives and state senators, no matter how popular or effective they may be, after these legislators have served a certain length of time.

FIGURE 11.1 *The Advantage of Incumbency*

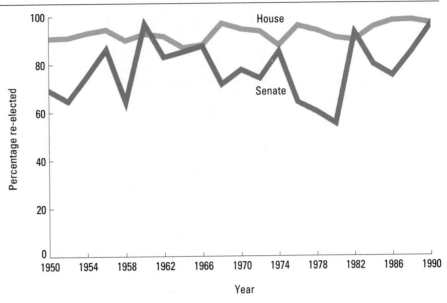

The incumbency advantage in House elections has been consistently strong in recent history. Senate elections are clearly more volatile, dipping as low as a 55.2 percent re-election rate in 1980, the year that the Reagan landslide helped to sink some liberal Democratic incumbents. (Source: Norman J. Ornstein, Thomas E. Mann, and Michael J. Malbin, Vital Statistics on Congress, 1989–1990 *[Washington, D.C.: Congressional Quarterly Inc., 1990], pp. 56–57. Used by permission.)*

districts to benefit the incumbents of one or both parties. Altering district lines for partisan advantage is commonly called **gerrymandering.**

But redistricting does not explain the incumbency effect in the House as a whole. Statistics show that after a reapportionment, redistricted and unredistricted seats end up approximately the same in terms of competitiveness.[9] Redistricting may be very helpful for an occasional incumbent, but it doesn't explain why more than 90 percent of House incumbents are routinely re-elected. Nevertheless, politicians regard gerrymandering as very important, and the political parties put considerable effort into trying to make sure that new boundaries are drawn in the most advantageous way.

Name recognition. Holding office brings with it some important advantages. First, incumbents develop significant name recognition among voters simply by being members of Congress. The name recognition advantage is helped along by congressional press secretaries' efforts to get publicity for the activities and speeches of their bosses. The primary focus of such publicity seeking is with the local media back in the district—that's where the votes are.[10] The local press, in turn, is eager to cover what their members of Congress are saying about the issues of the day. Representative Dan Glickman, a Democrat from Kansas, appears on Wichita's KAKE-TV an average of three times a week. He also is interviewed frequently on KWCH-TV's five o'clock news. And he has his own monthly television show, "Window on Washington," on KSAS-TV.[11] Members of Congress are in high demand to speak before local groups; and, thanks to generous travel allowances and easy air travel, they can make frequent trips between their districts and Washington, D.C.

FIGURE 11.2 *Vote of No Confidence*

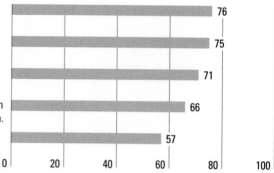

In stark contrast to voters' propensity to think highly of their incumbent representative, they tend to think that Congress as a whole is made up of rather unethical, if not downright dishonest, individuals. (Source: Survey by ABC News/Washington Post in May 1989, as shown in Everett Carll Ladd, "Public Opinion and the 'Congress Problem,'" Public Interest 100 [Summer 1990], p. 63. © 1989 The Washington Post. Reprinted with permission.)

Will tell lies if they feel the truth will hurt them politically. **76**

Care more about special interests than about people like you. **75**

Make campaign promises they have no intention of fulfilling.* **71**

Care more about keeping power than about the best interests of the nation. **66**

Make a lot of money using public office improperly. **57**

Percentage of respondents who agree with statements beginning "Most members of Congress . . ."

* This statement begins, "To win elections, most candidates for Congress. . . . "

Another resource available to members of Congress is the **franking privilege**—the right to send mail free of charge. Mailings see to it that constituents are aware of legislators' names, activities, and accomplishments. Periodic newsletters, for example, almost always highlight success at winning funds and projects for the district, such as money to construct a highway or a new federal building. Newsletters also "advertise for business," encouraging voters to phone or visit legislators' district offices if they need help with a problem. When he first ran in 1986, Maryland Democrat Tom McMillan won his House seat by a tiny margin, just 428 votes. In the next two years, he blanketed the district (about 230,000 homes) three times with mailings, spending $1 million of the taxpayers' money in the process. McMillan made himself such an overwhelming presence in the district that no credible Republican candidate came forward to challenge him when he ran for re-election.[12]

The large staff that works for a member of Congress is able to do **casework,** providing services for constituents—perhaps tracking down a social security check or directing the owner of a small business to the appropriate federal agency. Constituents who are helped in this way usually remember who assisted them (see Compared with What? 11.1). McMillan keeps ten of his twenty staffers in three district offices, to make it easier for constituents to get the help they need.[13]

In a race between an incumbent and a relatively unknown challenger, the incumbent's advantages (name recognition, staff resources, record of achievement) translate into votes. This is often enough to dissuade a potentially strong challenger from an election battle: the challenger may opt to wait for a more opportune time to run—perhaps when the incumbent retires or when his or her party seems headed for a fall.[14]

Campaign financing. It should be clear that anyone who wants to challenge an incumbent needs solid financial backing. Challengers must spend large sums of money to run a strong campaign, with an emphasis on advertising—an expensive but effective way to bring their names and records to the voters' attention. But here too, the incumbent has the advantage. It is very difficult for challengers to raise campaign funds because they have to overcome contributors' doubts about whether they can win. Political action committees (PACs) show a strong preference for incumbents (see Chapter 10). They tend not to want to risk offending an incumbent by giving money to a long-shot challenger. During the 1989–1990 election cycle, PACs contributed $116.6 million to incumbents but only slightly more than $15.8 million to challengers.[15] The attitude of the American Medical Association's PAC is fairly typical. "We have a friendly incumbent policy," says its director. "We always stick with the incumbent if we agree with both candidates."[16]

Successful challengers. Although it is very difficult for a challenger to defeat an incumbent (particularly a member of the House), it is not impossible. The opposing party and unsympathetic PACs may target incumbents (like Fred Eckert) who seem vulnerable because of age, lack of seniority, or unfavorable redistricting. The result is a flow of campaign contributions to the challenger, increasing the chance of victory. Incumbents can also be the victims of general dissatisfaction with their party. Popular disaffection with a president can translate into popular disaffection with House and Senate incumbents who belong to the president's party. In the wake of the Watergate scandal, 36 incumbent Republican representatives were unseated in the 1974 election.[17]

As Figure 11.1 shows, incumbency is less of an advantage in Senate elections than in House elections. There is no simple explanation for this, but one important factor is the greater visibility of challengers for Senate seats. These challengers usually are prominent individuals (sometimes governors or incumbent representatives), whose names and records are known to many voters. In addition, Senate challengers often are able to raise funds that House challengers cannot. And Senate races attract more public interest and press coverage than House races. All of these factors tend to reduce the identification gap between incumbent and challenger, resulting in more competitive races for the Senate.

For proponents of majoritarian democracy, the tenacious hold of House incumbents on office is disconcerting. Surveys show that voters are more likely to vote on the basis of candidates' personal characteristics or experience than on national issues.[18] The tendency toward noncompetitive House elections means that it is difficult to translate the votes cast into a meaningful policy mandate that the winning candidates should follow.[19]

Whom Do We Elect?

The people we elect (then re-elect) to Congress are not a cross-section of American society. Most members of Congress are professionals—primarily lawyers and businesspeople.[20] Although nearly a third of the American labor force works in blue-collar jobs, it is close to impossible for someone currently employed as a blue-collar worker to win a congressional nomination.

COMPARED WITH WHAT?   11.1

Manchester, New Hampshire, or Manchester, England,
There Are Constituents to Be Served

Although there are some important differences in
the structure of the U.S. Congress and the British
Parliament, there are many similarities in the way
members of both bodies do their jobs. One similarity is that U.S. representatives and members of Parliament (MPs) work extremely hard at cultivating
the grassroots. They frequently travel back to their
districts to hear what's on their constituents' minds
and to offer assistance. In both the United States
and Britain, voters believe that legislators have a
responsibility to help individuals and promote the
economic welfare of their districts. Yet there is a difference in emphasis between the two countries.
The figure on the next page charts the results of a
poll of American and British citizens who were
asked to choose which legislative role is the most
important.

In Britain, local concerns seem paramount.
Americans, on the other hand, were more likely to
cite policy concerns ("policymaking" and "over-

sight"). The weaker committee system and stronger
party system in Britain make it more difficult for
rank-and-file legislators to influence policy outcomes. The British responses to the interview questions may reflect this reality.

Legislators place such importance on their work
in the constituency because they want to be
re-elected and they believe that the help they offer
constituents wins them loyal voters. This is not
wishful thinking. Research shows that American
and British legislators who more actively promote
service to constituents are better known, more
highly rated, and more successful at the ballot box
than legislators who do not work as hard in the
constituency. It's also important to note that American representatives have large staffs—typically,
four or five full-time caseworkers—to tackle constituents' problems. British MPs have little or no
help handling casework; they have to do it the old-
fashioned way, by themselves.

The number of blacks in the House has grown modestly, but blacks are
still underrepresented in terms of their number in the general population, as are Hispanics. And women, who make up half the population of
the United States, hold only 6 percent of seats in the House and only 2
percent of seats in the Senate (see Figure 11.3). This is not to say that
Congress discriminates against minorities or women. After all, the voters elect the members of Congress. But the underrepresentation of minorities and women in Congress reflects historical patterns of opportunity—or lack of it—in American society. And the predominance of
white-collar professionals in Congress reflects the advantages of wealth
and education that make it easier for upper-middle-class people to enter
politics.

If a representative legislative body is supposed to mirror the electorate,
then Congress certainly doesn't qualify. Yet the correspondence between
the social characteristics of the population and the membership of Congress is only one way to look at the question of representation. A more
crucial measure may be how well the members of Congress represent
their constituents' views as they make policy decisions. In the next several sections, we examine the legislative process. Then we return to the
subject of representation.

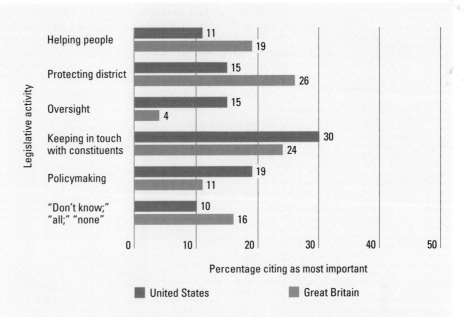

Source: Adapted by permission of the publishers from Bruce Cain, John Ferejohn, and Morris Fiorina, *The Personal Vote* (Cambridge, Mass.: Harvard University Press, 1987), especially pp. 38, 60–61, and 213. Copyright © 1987 by The President and Fellows of Harvard College.

How Issues Get on the Congressional Agenda

The formal legislative process begins when a member of Congress introduces a **bill,** a proposal for a new law. In the House, members drop new bills in the "hopper," a mahogany box near the rostrum where the Speaker presides. Senators give their bills to one of the Senate clerks or introduce them from the floor.[21] But before a bill can be introduced to solve a problem, someone must perceive that a problem exists or that an issue needs to be resolved. In other words, the problem or issue somehow must find its way onto the congressional agenda. *Agenda* actually has two meanings in the vocabulary of political scientists. The first is that of a narrow, formal agenda, such as a calendar of bills to be voted on. The second meaning refers to the broad, imprecise, and unwritten agenda that consists of all the issues an institution is considering. Here we use the term in the second, broader sense.

Many of the issues Congress is working on at any one time seem to have been around forever. Foreign aid, the national debt, and social security have come up in just about every recent session of Congress. Yet all issues begin at some point in time. For example, ten years ago members of Congress and almost all Americans outside the medical profession

FIGURE 11.3   *Congress: Still the Men's Club*

Although women have made great strides in building careers in many fields that were at one time dominated by men, national political office is not one of them. Only twenty-nine women are now serving in the House of Representatives. The number of women elected to the state legislatures has increased significantly, though. And because many congressional candidates first serve in state legislatures, there is reason to hope that as women gain experience and recognition they will win more congressional nominations and seats. (Source: "Women in Power," Ms., April 1988, p. 79.)

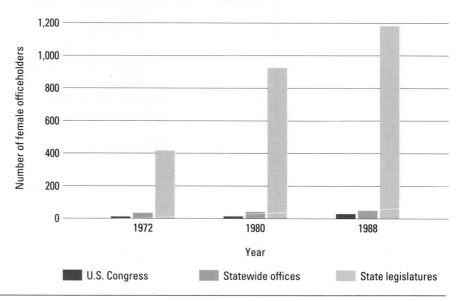

knew nothing of Alzheimer's disease. This common form of dementia strikes the elderly and causes memory loss, a decrease in cognitive ability, and personality disorders. After advances in science helped to define Alzheimer's as a particular pathology, some of those who had a family member diagnosed with Alzheimer's organized an interest group, the Alzheimer's Association. Recently, the Alzheimer's Association opened a Washington office to help with its lobbying efforts. The group's current goal is to get Congress to double the amount of federal funds devoted to Alzheimer's research.[22]

Advances in science are just one means by which new issues reach the congressional agenda. Sometimes a highly visible event focuses national attention on a problem. When an explosion in a West Virginia mine in 1968 killed seventy-eight miners, Congress promptly went to work on laws to promote miners' safety.[23] Presidential support can also move an issue onto the agenda quickly. The media attention paid to the presidency gives him enormous opportunity to draw the nation's attention to problems he believes need some form of governmental action.

Within Congress, party leaders and committee chairs have the best opportunity to influence the political agenda. National insurance for catastrophic illness is a case in point. According to surveys, only a minority of leaders (14 percent in 1977 and 33 percent in 1978) in the national health field believed that catastrophic illness insurance was a prominent issue. But when Russell Long, then chairman of the Senate Finance Committee, announced in 1979 that his committee would work up a bill on catastrophic illness insurance, the figure jumped to 92 percent. "In other words, a key congressional committee chairman single-handedly set a major portion of the policy agenda in health by his intention to move on health insurance."[24]

Although party leaders and committee chairs have the opportunity to move issues onto the agenda, they rarely act capriciously, seizing upon issues without rhyme or reason. They often bide their time, waiting for other members of Congress to learn about an issue, as they attempt to gauge the level of support. At times the efforts of an interest group spark support, or at least an awareness, of an issue. When congressional leaders—or, for that matter, rank-and-file members—sense that the time is ripe for action on a new issue, they often are spurred on by the knowledge that sponsoring an important bill can enhance their own image. In the words of one observer, "Congress exists to do things. There isn't much mileage in doing nothing."[25]

The Dance of Legislation: An Overview

The process of writing bills and getting them passed is relatively simple, in the sense that it follows a series of specific steps. What complicates the process is the many different ways legislation can be treated at each step. Here, we examine the straightforward process by which laws are made. In the next few sections, we discuss some of the complexities of that process.

After a bill is introduced in either house, it is assigned to the appropriate committee of that chamber for study (see Figure 11.4). A banking bill, for example, would be assigned to the Banking, Finance, and Urban Affairs Committee in the House or to the Banking, Housing, and Urban Affairs Committee in the Senate, depending on where it was introduced. When a committee actively considers a piece of legislation assigned to it, the bill is usually referred to a specialized subcommittee. The subcommittee may hold hearings, and legislative staffers may do research on the bill. The original bill usually is modified or revised; then, if passed in some form, it is sent back to the full committee. A bill that is approved by the full committee is *reported* (that is, sent) to the entire membership of the chamber, where it may be debated, amended, and either passed or defeated.

Bills coming out of House committees go to the Rules Committee before going before the full House membership. The Rules Committee attaches a "rule" to the bill that governs the coming floor debate, typically specifying the length of the debate and the types of amendments that can be offered. The Senate does not have a comparable committee, although restrictions on the length of floor debate can be reached through unanimous consent agreements (see page 399).

Even if a bill on the same subject is passed by both houses of Congress, the Senate and House versions are typically different from each other. In that case, a conference committee, composed of legislators from both

FIGURE 11.4 *The Legislative Process*

The process by which a bill becomes law is subject to much variation. This diagram depicts the typical process a bill might follow. It is important to remember that a bill can fail at any stage because of lack of support.

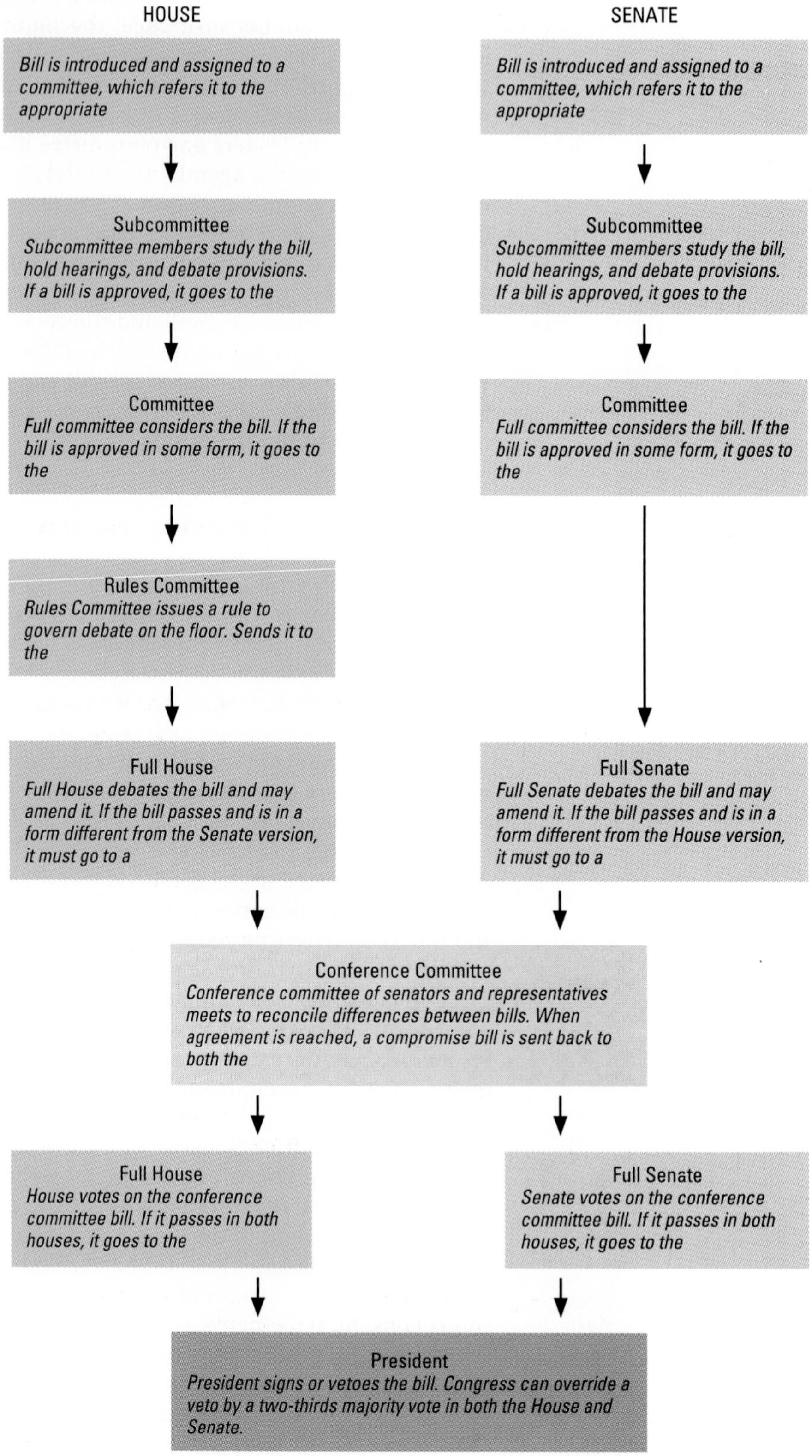

HOUSE

Bill is introduced and assigned to a committee, which refers it to the appropriate

↓

Subcommittee
Subcommittee members study the bill, hold hearings, and debate provisions. If a bill is approved, it goes to the

↓

Committee
Full committee considers the bill. If the bill is approved in some form, it goes to the

↓

Rules Committee
Rules Committee issues a rule to govern debate on the floor. Sends it to the

↓

Full House
Full House debates the bill and may amend it. If the bill passes and is in a form different from the Senate version, it must go to a

SENATE

Bill is introduced and assigned to a committee, which refers it to the appropriate

↓

Subcommittee
Subcommittee members study the bill, hold hearings, and debate provisions. If a bill is approved, it goes to the

↓

Committee
Full committee considers the bill. If the bill is approved in some form, it goes to the

↓

Full Senate
Full Senate debates the bill and may amend it. If the bill passes and is in a form different from the House version, it must go to a

↓

Conference Committee
Conference committee of senators and representatives meets to reconcile differences between bills. When agreement is reached, a compromise bill is sent back to both the

↓

Full House
House votes on the conference committee bill. If it passes in both houses, it goes to the

Full Senate
Senate votes on the conference committee bill. If it passes in both houses, it goes to the

↓

President
President signs or vetoes the bill. Congress can override a veto by a two-thirds majority vote in both the House and Senate.

houses, works out the differences and develops a compromise version. This version is sent back to both houses for another floor vote. If the bill passes in both chambers, it is then sent to the president for his signature or veto.

When the president signs a bill, it becomes law. If the president **vetoes** (disapproves) the bill, it is sent back to Congress with his reasons for rejecting it. The bill then becomes law only if Congress overrides the president's veto by a two-thirds vote of each house. If the president neither signs nor vetoes the bill within ten days (Sundays excepted) of receiving it, the bill becomes law. There is an exception here: If Congress adjourns within the ten days, the president can let the bill die through a **pocket veto,** by not signing it.

The content of a bill can be changed at any stage of the process, in either house. Lawmaking (and thus policymaking) in Congress has many access points for those who want to influence legislation. This openness tends to fit within the pluralist model of democracy. As a bill moves through the dance of legislation,[26] it is amended again and again, in a search for a consensus that will get it passed and signed into law. The process can be tortuously slow and often fruitless. Derailing legislation is much easier than enacting it. The process gives groups frequent opportunities to voice their preferences and, if necessary, to thwart their opponents. One foreign ambassador stationed in Washington aptly described the twists and turns of our legislative process: "In the Congress of the U.S., it's never over until it's over. And when it's over, it's still not over."[27]

In recent years one variation of this general process that has become very important is **omnibus legislation**. An omnibus proposal is a package of a number of different bills that are brought to the floor of the House and the Senate for consideration as a single entity. Omnibus proposals are often used for budget bills appropriating money for various functions of government. A major advantage of omnibus legislation is that it gives the Congress more leverage over the president, who is sometimes handed an omnibus appropriations bill passed at the last moment. If such a bill were vetoed, it would force much of the government to shut down for lack of funds. Omnibus appropriations bills are also advantageous to Congress because they can be brought to the floor under a rule or agreement mandating an up-or-down vote with no amendments. This way legislators can avoid having to take votes on amendments proposing to add money back to individual programs that have had their funding cut during the congressional budgetary process. Thus members can tell constituents or lobbying groups that no amendments were allowed and they were presented with a take-it-or-leave-it situation. As one analyst put it, omnibus bills "provide political cover to members."[28]

Committees: The Workhorses of Congress

Woodrow Wilson once observed that "Congress in session is Congress on public exhibition, whilst Congress in its committee-rooms is Congress at work."[29] His words are as true today as when he wrote them over one hundred years ago. A speech given on the Senate floor, for example, may convince the average citizen, but it is less likely to influence other senators. Indeed, few of them may even hear it. The real nuts and bolts of lawmaking goes on in the congressional committees.

The Division of Labor among Committees

The House and Senate are divided into committees for the same reason that other large organizations are broken into departments or divisions—to develop and use expertise in specific areas. At IBM, for example, different groups of people design computers, write software, assemble hardware, and sell the company's products. Each of these tasks requires an expertise that may have little to do with the other tasks that the company performs. Likewise, in Congress, decisions on weapons systems require a special knowledge that is of little relevance to decisions on reimbursement formulas for health insurance, for example. It makes sense for some members of Congress to spend more time examining defense issues, becoming increasingly expert as they do so, while others concentrate on health matters.

Eventually, though, all members of Congress have to vote on each bill that emerges from the committees. Those who are not on a particular committee depend on committee members to examine the issues thoroughly, to make compromises as necessary, and to bring forward a sound piece of legislation that has a good chance of being passed. Each member decides individually on the bill's merits. But once it reaches the House or Senate floor, members may get to vote on only a handful of amendments (if any at all) before they must cast their yeas and nays for the entire bill.

Standing committees. There are several different kinds of congressional committees, but the standing committee is predominant. **Standing committees** are permanent committees that specialize in a particular

Justice in the Congressional Spotlight

The Senate Judiciary Committee holds confirmation hearings for a Justice Department official, fulfilling its constitutional obligation to give "advice and consent" for top presidential appointments. Highlights on C-SPAN at 11:00.

area of legislation—for example, the House Judiciary Committee or the Senate Environment and Public Works Committee. Most of the day-to-day work of drafting legislation takes place in the sixteen standing Senate committees and twenty-two standing House committees. There are typically fifteen to twenty senators on each standing Senate committee, and thirty to forty members on each standing committee in the House. The proportions of Democrats and Republicans on a standing committee generally reflect party proportions in the full Senate or House, and each member of Congress serves on only a small number of committees.

With a few exceptions, standing committees are further broken down into subcommittees. The House Agriculture Committee, for example, has eight separate subcommittees, among them one on wheat, soybeans, and feed grains and another on livestock, dairy, and poultry. Subcommittees exist for the same reason parent committees exist: Members acquire expertise by continually working within the same fairly narrow policy area. Typically, members of the subcommittee are the dominant force in the shaping of the content of a bill.[30]

Other congressional committees. Members of Congress can also serve on joint, select, and conference committees. **Joint committees** are made up of members of both the House and the Senate. Like standing committees, the small number of joint committees are concerned with particular policy areas. The Joint Economic Committee, for instance, analyzes the country's economic policies. Joint committees operate in much the same way as standing committees, but they are almost always restricted from reporting bills to the House or Senate.

A **select committee** is a temporary committee, created for a specific purpose. Select committees are established to deal with special circumstances or with issues that either overlap or are not included in the areas of expertise of standing committees. The Senate committee that investigated the Watergate scandal was a select committee, created for that purpose only.

A **conference committee** is also a temporary committee, created to work out differences between the House and Senate versions of a specific piece of legislation. Its members are appointed from the standing committees or subcommittees that originally handled and reported the legislation to each house. Depending on the nature of the differences and the importance of the legislation, a conference committee may meet for hours or for weeks on end. A recent defense bill required House and Senate negotiators to resolve 2,003 separate issues where the two houses differed.[31] When the conference committee agrees on a compromise, the bill is reported to both houses of Congress. Each house may either approve or disapprove the compromise; they cannot amend or change it in any way. Only about 15 to 25 percent of all bills that eventually pass Congress go to a conference committee (though virtually all important or controversial bills do).[32] Differences are reconciled in other bills through informal negotiating by committee or subcommittee leaders that leads one house eventually to pass an identical version of legislation that has been passed by the other.

Pat Schroeder,
Defense Specialist

Schroeder, a Colorado Demo-crat, is a leader among House liberals on defense issues. She chairs a subcommittee of the House Armed Services Com-mittee.

Congressional Expertise and Seniority

Once appointed to a committee, a representative or senator has great incentive to remain on it and to gain increasing expertise over the years. That incentive can be translated as influence in Congress, and that influ-ence increases as a member's level of expertise grows. Influence also grows in a more formal way, with **seniority,** or years of consecutive serv-ice on a committee. In the quest for expertise and seniority, members tend to stay on the same committees. Sometimes, however, they switch places when they are offered the opportunity to move to one of the high-prestige committees (like Ways and Means or Appropriations in the House) or to a committee that handles legislation of vital importance to their constituents.

In a committee, the member of the majority party with the most sen-iority usually becomes the committee chair. (The majority party in each house controls committee leadership.) Other high-seniority members of the majority party become subcommittee chairs, while their counter-parts from the minority party gain influence as *ranking minority mem-bers*. With about 140 subcommittees in the House and 90 in the Senate, there is a great deal of power and status available to the members of Con-gress.

Unlike seniority, expertise does not follow simply from length of serv-ice. Ability and effort are critical factors too. Democratic Representative Les Aspin from Wisconsin is influential on military matters not simply because he is chairman of the House Armed Services Committee. Aspin, who has a Ph.D. from the Massachusetts Institute of Technology, is widely respected for his incisive knowledge of weapons systems and mil-itary matters. Other House members often look to him before commit-ting themselves one way or the other on important defense votes. When Aspin declared in the summer of 1990 that no more Stealth bombers ought to be built beyond the fifteen currently in production, it seriously jeopardized the future of the program.

Sam Nunn,
Defense Specialist

The cerebral Democrat from Georgia, extremely knowledge-able on defense policy, exerts a great deal of influence as the chair of the Senate Armed Services Committee.

Committee Reform

The committee system and the seniority system that determines the leadership of committees was sharply attacked during the 1970s. The push for reform came primarily from liberal and junior members of the House who "chafed under the restrictions on their participation and policy influence that the old, committee-dominated regime imposed. The committee chair, often in collaboration with the ranking minority member, dominated the panel."[33] One particularly dictatorial chair who led the Armed Services Committee as late as the 1960s normally allowed freshman members to ask only one question a year during committee hearings.[34]

A number of select committees were established to study the organiza-tion of the House and Senate. Although not all of their reforms were adopted, many significant changes were made. The power of the subcom-mittees in relation to their parent committees and their number were increased; and House Democrats (the majority party) prohibited their members from serving as chairs of more than one subcommittee. Also in the House, the seniority system was weakened by new rules that held that seniority did not have to be followed in the selection of committee chairs. In 1975, House Democrats voted out three aging, unpopular committee chairmen, serving notice to all committee chairs that autocratic rule would not be tolerated. An earlier change by House Democrats had eliminated the committee chairs' power to appoint subcommittee chairs. These changes decentralized influence in the House. Although some changes also strengthened the position of the Speaker of the House, their general thrust was to make subcommittees more autonomous and powerful.[35]

There was considerably less reform in the Senate. The smaller number of members in that body guarantees virtually all senators in the majority party at least one subcommittee chair. Moreover, the Senate's greater national visibility makes its members less dependent on their committee activities or seniority to gain recognition and influence. As one study concluded, "Committees are simply less crucial to the pursuit of personal goals in the Senate than in the House."[36]

The Lawmaking Process

The way in which committees and subcommittees are organized within Congress is ultimately significant because much public policy decision making takes place there. The first step in drafting legislation is to collect information on the issue. Committee staffers research the problem, and hearings may be held to take testimony from witnesses who have some special knowledge on the subject.

At times, committee hearings are more theatrical than informational, to draw public attention to them. When the House judiciary subcommittee on administrative law held hearings on alleged malpractice in military hospitals, it did not restrict its list of witnesses to the experts who had done relevant research. Instead, it called witnesses like Dawn Lambert, a former member of the navy, who sobbed as she told the subcommittee that she had been left sterile by a misdiagnosis and a botched operation that had left a sponge and a green marker inside her. It was an irresistible story for the network news and brought the malpractice problem to light.[37]

The meetings at which subcommittees or committees actually debate and amend legislation are called *markup sessions*. The process by which committees reach decisions varies. In many committees, there is a strong tradition of decision by consensus. The chair, the ranking minority member, and others in these committees work hard, in formal committee sessions and in informal negotiations, to find a middle ground on issues that divide committee members. In other committees, members exhibit strong ideological and partisan sentiments. Committee and subcommittee leaders prefer, however, to find ways of overcoming the inherent ideological and partisan divisions so that they can build compromise solutions that will appeal to the broader membership of their house.

Although there is considerable bargaining at markup sessions, negotiation over significant or controversial policies will precede these formal committee meetings. Sometimes these negotiations can be quite pro-

Budget Battlers Bargain

Compromise and accommodation receive less media coverage than heated debate, but they are an integral part of congressional policymaking. Here, the chairs and ranking minority members of the House and Senate budget committees (along with a staffer) try to find common ground before resuming negotiations on the annual budget with the White House.

tracted. In the late 1980s the Congress was having a difficult time reaching agreement on welfare reform legislation. Liberals and conservatives were very far apart, and the House and Senate had substantial differences in their approach to the problem. Paraphrasing Dickens, the *New York Times* said, "It was the best of bills, it was the worst of bills. It was a bill everybody wanted, it was a bill nobody wanted." The deal that was struck in the end gave each side its main priority, but also made each side accept a lot of things it was uncomfortable with. The Republicans got a "workfare" provision—which forces one parent in two-parent welfare families to work sixteen hours a week in community service. Liberal Democrats got expanded benefit coverage for Medicaid and child care for welfare families. The bill was still a tough pill to swallow because each side strongly disliked what the other side got. To build consensus behind the compromise, Daniel Moynihan, the Democratic senator from New York, lobbied each of his 99 colleagues. The chief House negotiator, Thomas Downey, also a Democrat from New York, talked individually to around 150 fellow members of the House. In the end the bill passed.[38]

Committees: The Majoritarian and Pluralist Views

It makes sense to bring as much expertise as possible to the policymaking process, and the committee system does just that. But government by committee vests a tremendous amount of power in the committees and subcommittees of Congress—especially in their leaders. This is particularly true of the House, which is more decentralized in its patterns of influence and more restrictive in the degree to which legislation can be amended on the floor. Committee members can bury a bill by not reporting it to the full House or Senate. The influence of committee members extends even further, to the floor debate. And many of them make up the conference committee that is charged with developing a compromise version of the bill.

This vesting of policy-area power in many committees and subcommittees tends to remove that power from the majority party and thus to operate against majoritarianism. At the same time, the committee system enhances the force of pluralism in American politics. Representatives and senators are elected by the voters in particular districts and states, and they tend to seek membership on the committees whose decisions are most important to their constituents. Members from farm areas, for example, want membership on the House and Senate Agriculture Committees. Westerners like to serve on the committees that deal with public lands and water rights. Urban liberals like the committees that handle social programs. As a result, the various committees are predisposed to writing legislation favorable to those who are most affected by their actions.

This is not to say that committee members care only about being re-elected and simply pass legislation that will win them votes back home. They are genuinely sympathetic to their constituents and can usually rationalize that good policy for their constituents is good policy for the nation as a whole.

A meeting of the whole House or Senate, to vote a bill up or down, may seem to be an example of majoritarianism at work. The views of the collective membership of each body may reasonably approximate the diverse mix of interests in the United States.[39] Committee decision making also anticipates what is acceptable to the entire membership. Still, by the time the broader membership begins to debate legislation on the floor, many crucial decisions have already been made in committees with a much narrower constituency in mind. Clearly, the internal structure of Congress gives small groups of members, with intense interests in particular policy areas, a disproportionate amount of influence over those areas.[40]

Leaders and Followers in Congress

Above the committee chairs is another layer of authority in the organization of the House and Senate. The Democratic and Republican leaders in each house work to maximize the influence of their own party, at the same time trying to keep their chamber functioning smoothly and efficiently. The operation of the two houses is also influenced by the rules and norms that each chamber has developed over the years.

The Leadership Task

Each of the two parties in each of the two houses elect leaders. In the House of Representatives, the majority-party leader is the **Speaker of the House,** who, gavel in hand, chairs sessions from the ornate rostrum at the front of the chamber (see Figure 11.5). The counterpart in the opposing party is the *minority leader*. The majority party chooses the Speaker at its *caucus*, a closed-door meeting of the party. The majority and mi-

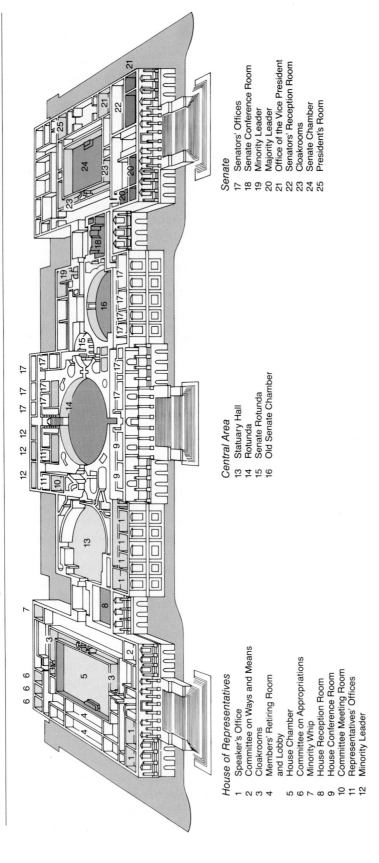

FIGURE 11.5 *The United States Capitol*

House of Representatives

1 Speaker's Office
2 Committee on Ways and Means
3 Cloakrooms
4 Members' Retiring Room and Lobby
5 House Chamber
6 Committee on Appropriations
7 Minority Whip
8 House Reception Room
9 House Conference Room
10 Committee Meeting Room
11 Representatives' Offices
12 Minority Leader

Central Area

13 Statuary Hall
14 Rotunda
15 Senate Rotunda
16 Old Senate Chamber

Senate

17 Senators' Offices
18 Senate Conference Room
19 Minority Leader
20 Majority Leader
21 Office of the Vice President
22 Senators' Reception Room
23 Cloakrooms
24 Senate Chamber
25 President's Room

Party Line

At the beginning of the 1989 session of Congress, the newly elected party leaders called the president to inform him of their selection. From left to right: Republican Bob Dole of Kansas, Senate minority leader; Democrat George Mitchell of Maine, Senate majority leader; Democrat Tom Foley of Washington, House majority leader; and Republican Bob Michel of Illinois, House minority leader. Foley later replaced Democrat Jim Wright of Texas as Speaker of the House after a financial scandal forced Wright to resign that position.

nority parties then "slate" their candidates for Speaker at the opening session of Congress. The official election follows strict party lines, affirming the majority party's caucus decision. The minority-party candidate becomes the minority leader. The Speaker is a constitutional officer, but the Constitution does not list the Speaker's duties. The minority leader is not mentioned in the Constitution, but that post has evolved into an important party position in the House.

The Constitution makes the vice president of the United States the president of the Senate. But the vice president usually does not come to the Senate chamber unless there is a possibility of a tie vote, in which case he can break the tie. The *president pro tempore* (president "for the time"), elected by the majority party, is supposed to chair the Senate in the vice president's absence, but by custom this constitutional position is entirely honorary.

The real power in the Senate resides in the **majority leader.** As in the House, the top position in the opposing party is that of *minority leader*. Technically, the majority leader does not preside (members rotate in the president pro tempore's chair); but the majority leader does schedule legislation in consultation with the minority leader. More broadly, party leaders play a critical role in getting bills through Congress. The most significant function that leaders play is steering the bargaining and negotiating over the content of legislation. When an issue divides their party, their house, the two houses, or their house and the White House, the leaders must take the initiative to work out a compromise solution.

Day in, day out, much of what leaders do is to meet with other members of their house to try to strike deals that will yield a majority on the floor. It is often a matter of finding out if one faction is willing to give up

The Johnson Treatment

When he was Senate majority leader in the 1950s, Lyndon Johnson was well known for his style of interaction with other members. In this unusual set of photographs, we see him applying the "Johnson treatment" to Democrat Theodore Francis Green of Rhode Island. Washington journalists Rowland Evans and Robert Novak offered the following description of the treatment: "Its tone could be supplication, accusation, cajolery, exuberance, scorn, tears, complaint, the hint of threat. It was all of these together. It ran the gamut of human emotions. Its velocity was breathtaking, and it was all in one direction. Interjections from the target were rare. Johnson anticipated them before they could be spoken. He moved in close, his face a scant millimeter from his target, his eyes widening and narrowing, his eyebrows rising and falling. From his pockets poured clippings, memos, statistics. Mimicry, humor, and the genius of analogy made The Treatment an almost hypnotic experience and rendered the target stunned and helpless." (Rowland Evans and Robert Novak, Lyndon B. Johnson: The Exercise of Power. *New York: New American Library, 1966. p. 104.)*

a policy preference in exchange for another concession. Beyond trying to engineer tradeoffs that will win votes, the party leaders must persuade others (often powerful committee chairs) that theirs is the best deal possible. Senator Robert Dole of Kansas aptly described himself as the "majority pleader" in his role as Senate majority leader.[41] (Dole later became the *minority* pleader when the Republicans lost control of the Senate in the 1986 elections.)

Party leaders are coalition builders, not kingmakers. Gone are the days when leaders ruled the House and the Senate with iron fists. Even as recently as the 1950s, strong leaders dominated the legislative process. When he was Senate majority leader, Lyndon Johnson made full use of his intelligence, parliamentary skills, and forceful personality to direct the Senate. When he approached individual senators for one-on-one persuasion, "no one subjected to the 'Johnson treatment' ever forgot it."[42] In today's Congress, rank-and-file representatives and senators would not stand for this kind of leadership. But there is no doubt that contemporary leaders have an impact on policy outcomes in Congress. As one expert concluded, "Although leadership contributions may be marginal, most important political choices are made at the margins."[43]

Rules of Procedure

The operation of the House and Senate is structured by both formal *rules* and informal *norms of behavior*. Rules in each chamber are mostly matters of parliamentary procedure. For example, they govern the scheduling of legislation, outlining when and how certain types of legislation can be brought to the floor. There are rules, too, that govern the introduction of floor amendments. In the House, amendments must be directly germane (relevant) to the bill at hand; in the Senate, except in certain specified instances, amendments that are not germane to the bill at hand can be added.

As noted earlier, an important difference between the two chambers is the House's use of its Rules Committee to govern floor debate. Without a similar committee to act as a "traffic cop" for legislation approaching the floor, the Senate relies on *unanimous consent agreements* to set the starting time and length of debate. If one senator objects to an agreement, it does not take effect. Senators do not routinely object to unanimous consent agreements, however, because they need them when a bill of their own awaits scheduling by the leadership.

If a senator wants to stop a bill badly enough, he or she may start a **filibuster,** trying to talk the bill to death. By historical tradition, the Senate gives its members the right of unlimited debate. During a 1947 debate, Idaho Democrat Glen Taylor "spoke for 8 1/2 hours on fishing, baptism, Wall Street, and his children." The record for holding the floor belongs to Republican Senator Strom Thurmond of South Carolina, for a twenty-four-hour, eighteen-minute marathon.[44] In the House, no member is allowed to speak for more than an hour without unanimous consent.

After a 1917 filibuster by a small group of senators killed President Wilson's bill to arm merchant ships—a bill favored by a majority of senators—the Senate finally adopted **cloture,** a means of limiting debate. A petition signed by sixteen senators initiates a cloture vote. It now takes the votes of sixty senators to invoke cloture.[45] Cloture was successfully invoked when a filibuster by southern senators threatened passage of the far-reaching Civil Rights Act of 1964. Three-quarters of senators recently surveyed professed some support for making it more difficult to filibuster, but apparently sentiment is not intense enough to propel reform forward because no changes are now being actively considered.[46]

Norms of Behavior

Both houses have codes of behavior that help keep them running. These codes are largely unwritten norms, although some have been formally adopted as rules. Members of Congress recognize that personal conflict must be eliminated (or minimized), lest Congress dissolve into bickering factions unable to work together. One of the most celebrated norms is that members show respect for their colleagues in public deliberations. During floor debate, bitter opponents still refer to one another in such terms as "my good friend, the senior senator from . . ." or "my distinguished colleague."

Members of Congress are only human, of course, and tempers occasionally flare (see Feature 11.1). For example, when Democrat Barney Frank of Massachusetts was angered by what he thought were unusually harsh charges against the Democratic party, made by Republican Robert Walker of Pennsylvania, Frank rose to ask the presiding officer if it was permissible to refer to Walker as a "crybaby." When he was informed that it was not, Frank sat down, having made his point without technically violating the House's code of behavior.[47]

Probably the most important norm of behavior in Congress is that individual members should be willing to bargain with one another. Policymaking is a process of give and take; it demands compromise. And the cost of not compromising is high. When Republican Richard Armey of Texas first came to Congress in 1985, he was a strident conservative ideologue who enjoyed trying to disrupt the Democratic-controlled House to prevent it from passing legislation that it favored. Consequently, other representatives ignored him; he was never included in the bargaining over legislation and had no real impact on the lawmaking process. By his next term in office, Armey realized that if he was going to have any influence on public policy, he had to stop thinking of the Democrats as liberal heathens and be willing to negotiate. Now, he's a "player" in the process.[48]

FEATURE 11.1   *Maybe They Ought to Make Crocodile Dundee Speaker*

We wouldn't expect a legislature with members named "Toecutter" Williams, "Dingo" Dawkins, and "Ironbar" Tuckey to be a quiet, formal, contemplative body. And the Australian Parliament is not. In fact, the Australian Parliament makes the boisterous British Parliament—after which it is modeled—seem almost subdued.

Name calling has rarely reached the heights of imagination it has in the hallowed chambers of the parliament Down Under. Cries of "harlot," "sleazebag," "mug," "boxhead," "fop," "sucker," and "thug" are hurled back and forth among members as they debate the bills before them. For the record, it's only fair to point out that the body's rules actually forbid such language. Indeed, the Senate handbook explicitly states that it's wrong to call other senators names like "arrant humbug" or "yahoo from Tasmania." But when an Australian senator gets angry, no handbook is going to stop him from calling a yahoo from Tasmania a "yahoo from Tasmania."

The Australian Parliament does have a rich sense of tradition. Legislators are called to impending votes by bells that ring for two minutes. There is no clock on the wall of the chambers; time is measured with an hourglass. And attendants who work in the chambers are dressed in wigs and gowns.

Unfortunately, one of the traditions is freely speaking one's mind. When they have something to say, Australian legislators can be quite persistent. Unlike Representative Barney Frank, who was content to sit down after a single insult, Brian Howe, an Australian representative, was only warming up when he called a colleague "something of a grub if I could put it that way." When the Speaker told Howe no, that he couldn't put it that way, Howe responded, "I will withdraw that term and substitute the term parasite." Again, the Speaker objected. Howe then substituted the phrase "this leech over there," which led the Speaker to reprimand him.

Source: Adapted from Geraldine Brooks, "In This Parliament, Decorum Often Sinks Down Under Insults," *Wall Street Journal*, 14 November 1986, p. 1. Reprinted by permission of *The Wall Street Journal*, © Dow Jones Company, Inc. 1986. All rights reserved. Worldwide.

It is important to point out that members of Congress are not expected to violate their consciences on policy issues simply to strike a deal. They are expected, however, to listen to what others have to say and to make every effort to reach a reasonable compromise. Obviously, if each of them sticks rigidly to his or her views, they will never agree on anything. Moreover, few policy matters are so clear-cut that compromise destroys one's position.

In recent years there has been an important evolution in some of these norms of behavior. Legislators have shown less patience toward the norms of apprenticeship and committee autonomy. Junior members have become much more assertive and now refuse to spend long time as apprentices gaining experience before playing a major role in the development of legislation. As one scholar notes, "The apprenticeship norm . . . has disappeared in both chambers."[49]

There is also less respect for the primacy of committees. Committees continue to be a dominant force in the Congress, but members not serving on a committee are no longer content to grant it autonomy over its policy area. Today, members not serving on committees offer more amendments on the floor to try to change the policy thrust of the committee's bill.[50]

These changing norms are fueled by the unrelenting ambition of the members of Congress. One does not get to Congress without being ambitious.[51] Once there, a new member looks for way to build his or her career. With the help of the reforms of the 1970s, these changing norms have allowed new members of Congress to be more entrepreneurial. They search out issues they can make their mark on without having to be restricted to their committees and without having to wait until they become the senior members of Congress.[52]

The Legislative Environment

After legislation emerges from committee, it is scheduled for floor debate. How do legislators make up their minds on how to vote? In this section, we examine the broader legislative environment that affects decision making in Congress. More specifically, we look at the influence of political parties, interest groups, colleagues, staff, the president, and constituents on legislators.[53]

Political Parties

The national political parties have limited influence over lawmakers. They do not control the nominations of House and Senate candidates. Candidates receive the bulk of their funds from individual contributors and political action committees, not from the national parties. The party leadership in each house, however, does try to influence the rank and file. Individual members may, for example, need their party leaders' assistance on specific legislation; members therefore have an incentive to cooperate with those leaders.

FIGURE 11.6 *Southern Democrats Come Back to the Party*

The civil rights movement of the 1960s badly divided the Democratic party in Congress. These House of Representatives party unity scores demonstrate how that division has gradually healed, spurred on by the enfranchisement of blacks after the Voting Rights Act was passed in 1965. The figures here show the percentage of House members who voted with a majority of their party on party unity votes. (Party unity votes are those in which a majority of one party votes one way and the majority of the second party votes the other way.) (Sources: Norman J. Ornstein, Thomas E. Mann, and Michael J. Malbin, Vital Statistics on Congress, 1989–1990 *[Washington, D.C.: Congressional Quarterly Inc., 1990], p. 199; "For the Record,"* Congressional Quarterly Weekly Report, *22 December 1990, p. 4212. Used by permission.)*

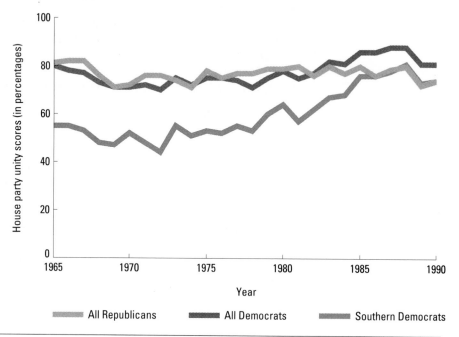

One important trend is the greater party loyalty of southern Democrats. Although they are still less likely to vote with the majority of their Democratic colleagues than are the party's northern members, their loyalty has risen significantly (see Figure 11.6). A primary reason for this increased party loyalty is that the issue of race no longer dominates southern politics or the national agenda the way it once did. Since the Voting Rights Act of 1965 was passed, blacks have registered in large numbers. They comprise a large share of the Democratic coalition in the South and act as a moderating influence on the traditionally conservative southern Democratic party.[54]

Interest Groups

As discussed in Chapter 10, lobbyists do more than tell legislators where a group stands on an issue. Their primary function is to provide lawmakers with useful and reliable information. Legislators do not need to be told that the AFL-CIO favors an increase in the minimum wage. They need reports and research analyses describing why an increase in the minimum wage would not be inflationary, why it would not reduce competitiveness in world markets, how it would raise the working poor's standard of living, and why it would reduce welfare payments.

Critics often refer to lobbies as "pressure groups." Although political scientists would choose a more neutral term, interest groups *do* try to pressure Congress. One of the most effective forms of pressure is having constituents contact their legislators with their version of the facts. Members of Congress aren't re-elected by Washington lobbyists; it's the people back home who cast the ballots. One study calls this the "Utah plant manager theory" of lobbying. A Utah senator may not want to take time out of a hectic schedule to speak with a lobbyist from an industry trade group, but if the manager of a Utah plant in this same industry comes to Washington and wants to see the senator, the senator is more likely to agree to a meeting. That senator doesn't want the manager to go back home and tell all the workers (voters) in the plant that their elected representative was too busy to hear about the industry's problems.[55]

Colleagues

Lobbyists and interest groups are a good source of information, but their facts and arguments support their own interests. For more objective information, a legislator may very well turn to a fellow representative or senator. One reason is the expertise that comes with committee specialization. It is easy for a member to find an extremely knowledgeable colleague who can offer a quick analysis of the legislative choices. A second reason is that representatives and senators form a peer group, and strong bonds of trust, friendship, and professional respect develop over time within that peer group.

Consultation with colleagues also comes through various formal groupings of legislators. Many of the state delegations in the House meet regularly to discuss issues of mutual concern. There are many other groups, or caucuses, that work together on issues that particularly concern them or their constituents. In the House, for example, there are bipartisan caucuses for steel, coal, and Irish affairs. The Hispanic caucus is another such group; it's taken an active leadership role on issues such as immigration and bilingual education.[56] Finally, there are partisan groups of legislators, like the Democratic Study Group and the Republican's Conservative Opportunity Society, both in the House.

Staff

The number of congressional staff members has risen dramatically in the last several decades, although it has now leveled off. In the mid-1950s, House members had about 2,500 personal staffers; by 1981, the figure had grown to about 7,500. Over the same period, Senate personal staffs grew from around 1,000 to about 4,000 people, which is where it is today. The number of staff members assigned to congressional committees grew significantly during this time as well.[57]

These larger staffs have helped members of Congress handle an increasing workload. (See the discussion on oversight in the next section.) Staffers reliably represent their bosses' interests during the day-to-day

Collins and Staffer

The staff in each legislator's office is responsible for a variety of tasks, including handling casework and press relations, doing research, monitoring legislation, writing speeches, and meeting with constituents and interest group representatives. Here, Democratic Representative Cardiss Collins of Illinois goes over some paperwork with one of her assistants.

negotiations over legislation.[58] Staffers are particularly helpful in involving their bosses in new issues that will increase their influence both with constituents and within Congress. More broadly, one scholar notes: "The increased use of personalized, entrepreneurial staffs has helped Congress retain its position as a key initiator of federal policy, despite the growing power of the executive branch."[59]

The President

Unlike members of Congress, who are elected by voters in individual states and districts, the president is elected by voters across the entire nation. The president has a better claim, then, to representing the nation than does any single member of Congress. But it can also be argued that Congress *as a whole* has a better claim than the president to representing the majority of voters. In fact, when Congress and the president differ, opinion surveys sometimes show that Congress's position on a given bill more closely resembles the majority view; at other times, these surveys show that the president's position accords with the majority. Nevertheless, presidents capitalize on their popular election and usually act as though they are speaking for the majority.

During the twentieth century, the public's expectations of what a president can accomplish in office have grown enormously. We now expect the president to be our chief legislator: to introduce legislation on major issues and to use his influence to push bills through Congress. This is much different from our early history, when presidents felt constrained by the constitutional doctrine of separation of powers and had to have members work confidentially for them during legislative sessions.[60]

Today the White House is openly involved not only in the writing of bills but also in their development as they wind their way through the legislative process. If the White House does not like a bill, it tries to work out a compromise with key legislators to have the legislation amended. On issues of the greatest importance, the president himself may meet with individual legislators to persuade them to vote a certain way. To monitor daily congressional activities and lobby for the broad range of administration policies, there are hundreds of legislative liaison personnel working for the executive branch.

Although members of Congress grant presidents a leadership role in proposing legislation, they jealously guard their power to debate, shape, pass, or defeat any legislation the president proposes. Congress often clashes sharply with the president when his proposals are seen as ill advised.

Constituents

Constituents are the people who live and vote in a legislator's district or state. Their opinions on an issue are a crucial factor in the legislative decision-making process. As much as members of Congress want to

Fishing for Votes

Republican Senator William Cohen of Maine talks to a voter, a lobsterman whose industry is an important part of the state's economy. Despite the emphasis on the use of electronic media by legislators, one-on-one contact with constituents is still an effective, though painstaking, way for a legislator to build a reputation as one who cares deeply about the problems of the individuals he or she serves.

please the party leadership or the president by going along with their preferences, legislators have to think about what the voters back home want. If they displease enough people by the way they vote, they might lose their seats in the next election.

In considering the influence of all these factors in the legislator's environment, it is important to keep in mind that legislators also have strong views of their own. They come to Congress deeply committed to working on some key issues and do not need to be pressured into acting on them or into voting a certain way. In fact, their strong views on certain policy questions can conflict with what their constituents want, a problem discussed in detail later in this chapter.

Of all the possible sources of influence, which are the most important? Unfortunately, there is no one way of measuring. However, in an interesting and straightforward study, political scientist John Kingdon asked a sample of House members how they made up their minds on a variety of issues. He found that colleagues and constituency were more likely to have an impact than the other factors we've talked about. Kingdon cautioned, however, that the decision-making process in Congress is complex and that no single factor "is important enough that one could conclude that congressmen vote as they do" because of its influence.[61]

Oversight: Following Through on Legislation

It is often said in Washington that "knowledge is power." For Congress to retain its influence over the programs it creates, it must be aware of how they are being administered by the agencies responsible for them. To that end, legislators and their committees engage in **oversight,** the process of reviewing agency operations to determine whether the agency is carrying out policies as Congress intended.

As the executive branch has grown and policies and programs have become increasingly complex, oversight has become more difficult. The sheer magnitude of executive-branch operations is staggering. On a typical weekday, for example, agencies issue over a hundred pages of new regulations. Even with the division of labor in the committee system, it is no easy task to determine how good a job an agency is doing in implementing a program.

Congress performs its oversight function in a number of different ways. The most visible is the hearing. Hearings may be part of a routine review or the by-product of information that reveals a major problem with a program or with an agency's administrative practices. Another way Congress keeps track of what departments and agencies are doing is to request reports on specific agency practices and operations. A good deal of congressional oversight also takes place in an informal manner. There is ongoing contact between committee and subcommittee leaders and agency administrators, and between committee staffers and top agency staffers.[62]

Congressional oversight of the executive branch has sharply increased. As Figure 11.7 demonstrates, this surge began in the early 1970s. A primary reason for this increase was that Congress gave itself the necessary

FIGURE 11.7   *More Eyes and Ears, More Oversight*

Congress long had the reputation for being rather lackadaisical about its oversight responsibilities. The addition of staff members assigned to congressional committees gave the House and Senate the resources to do more extensive oversight of the executive branch. (Source: Joel D. Aberbach, Keeping a Watchful Eye [Washington, D.C.: Brookings Institution, 1990], p. 44. Used by permission.)

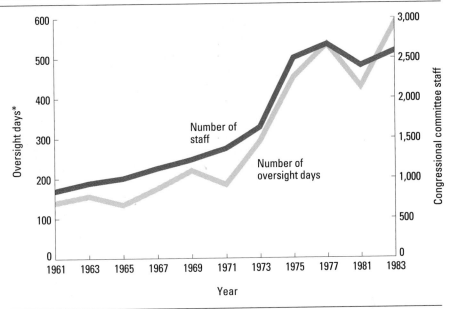

*"Oversight days" are those days that committees devote primarily to oversight activities.

staff to watch over the growing federal government. In addition to the personal and committee staffs mentioned earlier, Congress created two new specialized offices in the 1970s—the Congressional Budget Office and the Office of Technology Assessment—to do sophisticated analyses of agency operations and proposals. The longer-standing Government Accounting Office (GAO) and the Congressional Research Service of the Library of Congress also do in-depth studies for Congress. Finally, Congress was goaded into a more aggressive oversight stance by the Nixon administration's attempts to dominate the legislative branch.

Oversight is often stereotyped as a process whereby angry legislators bring some administrators before the hot lights and TV cameras at a hearing and then proceed to dress them down for some recent scandal or mistake. There is certainly some of this, but keep in mind that the pluralist nature of the Congress tends to put people on committees who are advocates of the programs they oversee. People on the agriculture committees, Democrat and Republican, want farm programs to succeed. Thus most oversight is aimed at trying to find ways of improving programs and not directed at efforts to discredit them.[63]

Congress was long criticized for doing too little oversight. Today, criticism is emerging that Congress is going too far in its efforts to keep the operation of government programs in line with its intent when it created them. Many critics charge that Congress is engaged in **micromanagement** through its constant intervention in administrative policymaking. These critics argue that Congress is violating the spirit of the separation of powers by not giving agencies the flexibility to administer programs as they see fit. For example, the veterans committees of the Congress intervene constantly in the deliberations of the Veterans Administration. Pressure from individual members of Congress has prevented the agency from taking an action that affected only ten of its 240,000 employees.[64]

Particularly interesting is the increasing aggressiveness of the Congress in the area of foreign policy, long the preserve of the presidency. In 1970 the Nixon administration refused to tell the Congress its negotiating position until just before the start of arms limitation talks with the Russians. By the 1980s, however, the Reagan administration felt compelled to allow congressional participation in its arms negotiating. When the United States was developing an arms proposal in 1983, Senators William Cohen and Sam Nunn went to the White House to hammer out a proposal with Chief of Staff James Baker.[65]

The Dilemma of Representation

When candidates for the House and Senate campaign for office, they routinely promise to work hard for their district's or state's interests. When they get to Washington, though, they all face the troubling dilemma with which we began this chapter: What their constituents want may not be what the people across the nation want.

Presidents and Shopping Bags

In doing the research for his book *Home Style*, political scientist Richard Fenno accompanied several representatives on trips back to their home districts. On one trip, he was in an airport with a congressional aide, waiting for the representative's plane from Washington to land. When the congressman arrived, he said, "I spent fifteen minutes on the telephone with the president this afternoon. He had a plaintive tone in his voice and he pleaded with me." The congressman's side of the issue had prevailed over the president's, and he was elated by the victory. When the three men reached the aide's car, the congressman saw the back seat piled high with campaign paraphernalia: shopping bags printed with the representative's name and picture. "Back to this again," he sighed.[66]

Every member of Congress lives in two worlds: the world of presidents and the world of personalized shopping bags. A typical week in the life of a representative means working in Washington, then boarding a plane and flying back to the district. There the representative spends time meeting with individual constituents and talking to civic groups, church gatherings, business associations, labor unions, and the like. A survey of House members during a nonelection year showed that each made an average of thirty-five trips back to his or her district, spending an average of 138 days there.[67]

Members of Congress are often criticized for being out of touch with the people they are supposed to represent. This charge does not seem justified. Legislators work extraordinarily hard at keeping in touch with voters, at finding out what is on their constituents' minds. The difficult problem is how to act on that knowledge.

Trustees or Delegates?

Are members of Congress bound to vote the way their constituents want them to vote, even if it means voting against their conscience? Some say no. They argue that legislators must be free to vote in line with what they think is best. This view has long been associated with the eighteenth-century English political philosopher Edmund Burke (1729–1797). Burke, who served in Parliament, told his constituents in Bristol that "you choose a member, indeed; but when you have chosen him, he is not a member of Bristol, but he is a member of *Parliament*."[68] Burke reasoned that representatives are sent by their constituents to vote as they think best. As **trustees,** representatives are obligated to consider the views of constituents, but they are not obligated to vote according to those views if they think they are misguided.

Others hold that legislators are duty bound to represent the majority view of their constituents, that they are **delegates** with instructions from the people at home on how to vote on critical issues. And delegates, unlike trustees, must be prepared to vote against their own policy preferences. When he faced a decision on how to vote on the proposed constitutional amendment to ban flag-burning, Representative Peter Hoagland knew that his constituents back in Nebraska favored the amendment. As a Democrat in a seat that has been traditionally held by the Republicans, Hoagland also knew that a vote against the flag-burning amendment

Reasoned Discourse Is the Hallmark of a Civilized Society
Members of Congress love good floor debates, but a photo opportunity may bring them more publicity back home than the carefully crafted arguments they present to their colleagues. These four members of the House are smashing a Toshiba radio to demonstrate their anger at that Japanese corporation. A Toshiba subsidiary, in conjunction with a Norwegian business consortium, had sold submarine equipment illegally to the Soviet Union.

would be used against him in the upcoming 1990 fall election. His aides strongly advised him to vote for the amendment because of the political damage a no vote would do with the generally conservative voters in his district. In the end Hoagland voted against the amendment because his conscience would not let him do otherwise.[69] (Hoagland won re-election despite the flag vote.)

Members of Congress are subject to two opposing forces, then. While the interests of the district push them toward the role of delegates, the larger national interest calls on them to be trustees. Given these conflicting role definitions, it is not surprising that Congress is not clearly a body of delegates or of trustees. Research has shown, however, that members of Congress are more apt to take the delegate role on issues that are of great concern to constituents.[70] But much of the time, what the constituency really wants is not clear. Many issues are not highly visible back home, or they cut across the constituency to affect it in different ways, or they are only partially understood. One study of House voting on the central tax and spending issues during the first year of the Reagan administration found that most members had voted with what they perceived to be the majority opinion in their districts. Yet opinion polls in those districts showed that many representatives who voted for Reaganomics came from districts that did not really favor the program. The problem was that the legislators received a great deal of mail that was strongly in favor of Reaganomics. But clearly, the sentiment of activists—those who took the time to write a letter—were not representative of the broader population in the districts.[71]

Pluralism, Majoritarianism, and Democracy

The dilemma that individual members of Congress face in adopting the role of either delegate or trustee has broad implications for the way our country is governed. If legislators tend to act as delegates, then congressional policymaking is more pluralistic, and policies reflect the bargaining that goes on among lawmakers who speak for different constituents. If, instead, legislators tend to act as trustees and vote their consciences, policymaking becomes less tied to the narrower interests of districts and states. But even here there is no guarantee that congressional decision making reflects majority interests.

We end this chapter with a short discussion of the pluralist nature of Congress. But first, to establish a frame of reference, we need to take a quick look at a more majoritarian type of legislature—the parliament.

Parliamentary Government

In our legislative system, the executive and legislative functions are divided between a president and a congress, each elected separately. Most other democracies—for example, Britain and Japan—have parliamentary governments. In a **parliamentary system,** the chief executive is the legislative leader whose party holds the most seats in the legislature after an election or whose party forms a major part of the ruling coalition. For instance, in Great Britain, voters do not cast a ballot for prime minister. They vote only for their member of Parliament, and thus must influence the choice of prime minister indirectly by voting for the party they favor in the local district election.

In a parliamentary system, government power is highly concentrated in the legislature because the leader of the majority party is also the head of government. Moreover, parliamentary legislatures are usually composed of only one house or have a second chamber that is much weaker than the other. (In the British Parliament, the House of Commons makes the decisions of government; the other chamber, the House of Lords, is largely an honorary debating club for distinguished members of society.) And parliamentary governments usually do not have a court that can invalidate acts of the parliament. Under such a system, the government is in the hands of the party that controls the parliament. With no separation of government powers, there are few checks on government action. The net effect is that parliamentary governments fit the majoritarian model of democracy to a much greater extent than do congressional governments.

Pluralism Versus Majoritarianism in the Congress

Nowadays, the U.S. Congress is often criticized for being too pluralist and not majoritarian enough. The federal budget deficit is a case in point. Americans are deeply concerned about the large deficits that have plagued our national budgets in recent years. And both Democrats and Republicans in Congress repeatedly call for reductions in those deficits. But when spending bills come before Congress, legislators' concern turns to what the bills will or will not do for their districts or states. A $604 million spending bill passed by Congress in 1988 included numerous examples of individual members winning some "pork barrel" project that benefited their district or state and added further to the deficit. Senator James McClure, a Republican, won inclusion of a $6.4 million grant to build a ski resort in Kellogg, Idaho. Democratic Representative Daniel Akaka got a $250,000 appropriation for pig and plant control at the Haleakala National Park in Hawaii. And Republican Senator Ted Stevens delivered $2.6 million to the Fisheries Promotional Fund in Alaska.[72]

Projects such as these get into the budget through bargaining among members; as you saw earlier in the chapter, congressional norms encourage it. Members of Congress try to win projects and programs that will not only benefit their constituents but will help them at election time. To win approval of something helpful to one's own constituents, a member must be willing to vote for other legislators' projects. This type of system obviously promotes pluralism.

Some feel that Congress has to be less pluralistic if it is going to attack such serious problems as the national deficit. Yet those who favor pluralism are quick to point out Congress's merits. For example, many different constituencies are well served by the spending deliberations described above. For Alaska's fishermen, an appropriation to promote new markets for their industry is not frivolous spending. It is vital to their livelihood. They pay taxes to fund the government, and they have a right to expect the government to care about their problems and try to help them.

Proponents of pluralism also argue that the makeup of Congress generally reflects that of the nation, that different members of Congress represent farm areas, oil and gas areas, low-income inner cities, industrial areas. They point out that America itself is pluralistic, with a rich diversity of economic, social, religious, and racial groups, and that even if our own representatives and senators don't represent our particular viewpoint, it's likely that someone else in Congress does.[73]

An alternative to our pluralistic legislature would operate on strictly majoritarian principles. For this kind of system to work, we would need strong parties—as described by the principles of responsible party government (see Chapter 8). That is, congressional candidates for each party would have to stand relatively united on the major issues. Then the majority party in Congress would act on a clear mandate from the voters—at least on the major issues discussed in the preceding election campaign. This would be very different from the pluralist system we now have, which furthers the influence of interest groups and local constituencies in national policymaking. But which is better?

Summary

Congress plays a central role in our government through its lawmaking function. It writes the laws of the land and attempts to oversee their implementation. It helps to educate us about new issues as they appear on the political agenda. Most important, members of Congress represent us, working to see to it that interests from home and from around the country are heard throughout the policymaking process.

We count on Congress to do so much that criticism about how well it does some things is inevitable. But certain strengths are clear. The committee system fosters expertise; representatives and senators who know the most about particular issues have the most influence over them. And the structure of our electoral system keeps legislators in close touch with their constituents.

Bargaining and compromise play important roles in the congressional policymaking process. Some find this disquieting. They want less deal making and more adherence to principle. This thinking is in line with the desire for a more majoritarian democracy. Others defend the current system, arguing that the United States is a large, complex nation and the policies that govern it should be developed through bargaining among various interests.

There is no clear-cut answer on whether a majoritarian or a pluralist legislative system provides better representation for voters. Our system is pluralistic. It serves minority interests that might otherwise be neglected or even harmed by an unthinking or uncaring majority. But there is validity to the argument that responsiveness to special interests comes at the expense of the majority of Americans.

KEY TERMS

reapportionment
impeachment
incumbent
redistricting
gerrymandering
franking privilege
casework
bill
veto
pocket veto
omnibus legislation
standing committee
joint committee

select committee
conference committee
seniority
Speaker of the House
majority leader
filibuster
cloture
constituents
oversight
micromanagement
trustee
delegate
parliamentary system

SELECTED READINGS

Aberbach, Joel D. *Keeping a Watchful Eye.* Washington, D.C.: Brookings Institution, 1990. A careful analysis of the growth of congressional oversight.

Cain, Bruce, John Ferejohn, and Morris Fiorina. *The Personal Vote.* Cambridge, Mass.: Harvard University Press, 1987. A detailed comparison of the services offered their constituents by American and British legislators.

Dodd, Lawrence C., and Bruce I. Oppenheimer. *Congress Reconsidered.* 4th ed. Washington, D.C.: Congressional Quarterly Press, 1989. This collection of essays pulls together much of the latest research on Congress.

Fenno, Richard F., Jr. *Home Style.* Boston: Little, Brown, 1978. A classic analysis of how House members interact with constituents during visits to their home districts.

Fowler, Linda L., and Robert D. McClure. *Political Ambition.* New Haven, Conn.: Yale University Press, 1989. An engaging, highly readable study of the recruitment of congressional candidates.

Loomis, Burdett. *The New American Politician.* New York: Basic Books, 1988. A study of how the ambition and entrepreneurship of legislators is changing the Congress.

12 THE PRESIDENCY

"READ MY LIPS: NO NEW TAXES." When George Bush uttered these words in his acceptance speech at the 1988 Republican convention in New Orleans, he announced to the world that he was now the keeper of his party's most precious imagery: *The GOP was against taxes.* Ronald Reagan had successfully labeled the Democrats as the party of "tax and spend," while taxes had been cut substantially during his administration. Still, Bush felt that standing for "no new taxes" wasn't enough. During the presidential campaign he proposed a cut in taxes on capital gains. (Capital gains are profits from the sale of assets like stocks and real estate.) Such a cut would be popular with people who have money to invest. A special capital gains rate is not, however, of great relevance to the majority of Americans, who live from week to week on their paycheck.

Bush almost made good on his campaign promise. In the fall of 1989, the House of Representatives passed a bill that set lower taxes for capital gains than for income earned from a salary. Such a two-tiered tax system had existed before but had been eliminated in a tax reform bill a few years earlier. There was majority support for the capital gains cut in the Senate, too, but liberal Democrats threatened a filibuster, so the Republicans threw in the towel and vowed to come back the following year with a similar proposal.

The capital gains fight reflects a traditional division in our party system. The Republicans emphasized that a capital gains cut would spur economic growth by giving people more incentive to put their money into long-term investments. Democrats claimed that it was just a tax cut for the wealthy.

Bush tried again in 1990. A major change in the equation came when the huge federal deficit and lack of cooperation between Republicans and Democrats over the budget led Bush to go back on his no new taxes pledge. He hoped, however, that in exchange for his support for some tax increases he could get some concessions, including a capital gains tax cut. Nevertheless, as the deadline for the budget approached in the fall, the Democrats stood firm against the capital gains cut. Bush conceded again, agreeing to a budget deal with congressional leaders that contained enough tax increases and budget cuts to reduce the deficit by $500 billion over five years.

The budget deal soon fell apart, however. Republicans in Congress revolted against it because it raised taxes and contained no spurs to investment (such as a capital gains cut). Democrats revolted because the tax increases hit the working class the hardest. Those making between $20,000 and $30,000 would have had their taxes raised 3.3 percent, while those making over $200,000 would have had a tax increase of only 1.7 percent.[1] Bush made a nationally televised speech asking the American people for their support, saying, "If we fail to enact this agreement, our economy will falter. Markets may tumble. And recession will follow."[2] The speech was a bomb. Americans wrote and called their congressional representatives in large numbers to tell them to vote *against* the package. One Republican representative said he got 300 phone calls in the twenty-four hours after the speech, and 98 percent of them were against

Media Moment

Before President Bush and various congressional leaders get down to business at this White House meeting, photographers are ushered in for a brief "photo opportunity." All present would like to get their faces into the newspaper or on the evening news.

the budget package.[3] The House voted down the budget bill, giving Bush a stinging defeat.

And then it got worse for the president.

Emboldened by the rejection of Bush's plea for the budget bill, the Democrats sensed that Americans were ready for some good, old-fashioned "us versus them" rhetoric. They started hammering away at the Republicans, calling them the party of the rich. They hit a responsive chord with the American public, and Bush and the Republicans were put in a defensive position. The Democrats introduced legislation that substantially raised taxes on the wealthy and reduced the amount the middle class would pay. Republicans quickly realized that higher taxes on the rich were inevitable. But if the president was going to have to give in on a big tax rise for the rich, shouldn't he get something back in return—like capital gains?

Yet it was hard to figure out what the president would settle for. After saying he would accept higher taxes in exchange for a capital gains cut, Bush changed his mind the very same day. Then he changed his mind again the next day. This indecisiveness weakened his bargaining position further. The budget bill that was finally passed contained only minor adjustments in the way capital gains are taxed. The Democrats won a clear victory. Not only did it seem like the tax increase was Bush's responsibility, the Democrats could claim that they protected the average wage earner. In contrast to the earlier budget bill, this one raised taxes on those with incomes over $200,000 by 6.4 percent. Those making between $20,000 and $30,000 got a more modest tax hike of 1.8 percent.[4]

What the Democrats had done, of course, was to play majoritarian politics. They were able to convince the American people—at least for a short while—that they were the party that cared for the middle class. It suited their interests to turn tax policy into a conflict between differing economic classes. If politics and elections can be turned into referendums on what's best for Americans with modest incomes versus what's best for the wealthy, the party aligned with the less affluent has a distinct advantage.

As we analyze the various facets of the presidency, bear in mind one recurring question: Is the presidency primarily an instrument of pluralist democracy, serving small but vocal constituencies, or does the office promote majoritarian democracy by responding primarily to public opinion? In addition to examining this question, we focus in this chapter on a number of other important aspects of the presidency. What are the powers of the presidency? How is the president's advisory system organized? How does the separation of powers between the executive and legislative branches affect public policymaking? Finally, what are the particular issues and problems that presidents face in foreign affairs?

The Constitutional Basis of Presidential Power

When the presidency was created, the colonies had just fought a war of independence; their reaction to British domination had focused on the autocratic rule of King George III. Thus the delegates to the Constitutional Convention were extremely wary of unchecked power and were determined not to create an all-powerful, dictatorial presidency.

The delegates' fear of a powerful presidency was counterbalanced by their desire for strong leadership. The Articles of Confederation—which did not provide for a single head of state—had failed to bind the states together into a unified nation (see Chapter 3). In addition, the governors of the individual states had generally proved to be inadequate leaders because they had few formal powers. The new nation was conspicuously weak; its congress had no power to compel the states to obey its legislation. With the failed confederation in mind, John Jay wrote to George Washington, asking him, "Shall we have a king?"[5]

Although the idea of establishing an American royalty was far from popular among the delegates, they knew that some type of executive office had to be created. Their task was to provide national leadership without allowing any opportunity for tyranny.

Initial Conceptions of the Presidency

Debates over the nature of the office began. Should there be one president or a presidential council or committee? Should the president be chosen by Congress and remain largely subservient to that body? Initial approval was given to a plan that called for a single executive, chosen by Congress for a seven-year term and ineligible for re-election.[6] But some of the delegates continued to argue for a strong president who would be elected independently of the legislative branch.

The final structure of the presidency reflected the "checks and balances" philosophy that shaped the entire Constitution. In the minds of the delegates, important limits were imposed on the presidency through the powers specifically delegated to the Congress and the courts. Those counterbalancing powers would act as checks, or controls, on presidents who might try to expand the office beyond its proper bounds. (The separation of the executive from the legislative branch has had an effect on the type of experience our presidential candidates have; see Compared with What? 12.1.)

The Powers of the President

The requirements for the presidency are set forth in Article II of the Constitution: A president must be a natural-born citizen, at least thirty-five years old, who has lived in the United States for a minimum of fourteen years. The responsibilities of presidents are also set forth in Article II. In view of the importance of the office, the constitutional description of the president's duties is surprisingly brief and vague. This vagueness has led to repeated conflict over the limits of presidential power.

There were undoubtedly many reasons for the lack of precision in Article II. One likely explanation was the difficulty of providing and at the same time limiting presidential power. Furthermore, the framers of the Constitution had no model—no existing presidency—on which to base their description of the office. And, ironically, their description of the presidency might have been more precise if they had had less confidence in George Washington, the obvious choice for the first president. According to one account of the Constitutional Convention, "when Dr. Franklin predicted on June 4 that 'the first man put at the helm will be a good one,' every delegate knew perfectly well who that first good man would be."[7] The delegates had great trust in Washington; they did not fear that he would try to misuse the office.

The major duties and powers that the delegates listed for Washington and his successors can be summarized as follows:

- *Serve as administrative head of the nation.* The Constitution gives little guidance on the president's administrative duties. It states merely that "the executive Power shall be vested in a President of the United States of America" and that "he shall take Care that the Laws be faithfully executed." These imprecise directives have been interpreted to mean that the president is to supervise and offer leadership to various departments, agencies, and programs created by Congress. In practice, a chief executive spends much more time making policy decisions for his Cabinet departments and agencies than trying to enforce existing policies.

- *Act as commander in chief of the military.* In essence, the Constitution names the president as the highest ranking officer in the armed forces. But it gives Congress the power to *declare* war. The framers no doubt intended Congress to control the president's military power;

COMPARED WITH WHAT?   12.1

What Kind of Experience Counts?

Candidates nominated for the presidency of the United States comprise an impressive lot in terms of their accomplishments and political experience. Nevertheless, their European counterparts are actually better seasoned in jobs providing valuable experience in government. Excellent campaign skills are critical to winning a presidential nomination in the United States. It is no small feat to conduct a lengthy campaign, putting together a winning coalition by convincing large numbers of voters that one would be a better nominee than the many other capable candidates competing in the primaries. Experience in office is hardly irrelevant in a candidate's ultimate appeal to American voters—they need to be convinced he can do the job. Still, candidates who have spent relatively modest amounts of time in governmental service and have limited ranges of experience, such as Jimmy Carter and Ronald Reagan, are able to win their party's nomination.

In European democracies, a considerably different pattern emerges. Party activists who aim for the post of prime minister in a parliamentary system must win the backing of their legislative party. As they rise in their party's hierarchy, aspiring leaders typically head major departments of state when their party is in control of the government. In Great Britain, for example, an aspiring prime minister typically has served an average of twelve years as a minister of a governmental department before he or she became a party leader in Parliament. In contrast, U.S. presidential candidates typically do not have Cabinet experience, though they may have had executive experience as a governor. As the graph indicates, American candidates are considerably less experienced in government than European political leaders.

Source: Richard Rose, "Learning to Govern or Learning to Campaign?" in *Presidential Selection*, ed. Alexander Heard and Michael Nelson (Durham, N.C.: Duke University Press, 1987), pp. 53–73. Copyright 1987, Duke University Press, Durham, N.C. Reprinted by permission of the publisher.

nevertheless, presidents have initiated military action without the approval of Congress. The entire Vietnam War was fought without a congressional declaration of war. (The Congress did pass a resolution authorizing the use of force in the Persian Gulf before the American-led coalition began its military campaign.)

- *Convene Congress.* The president can call Congress into special session on "extraordinary Occasions," though this has rarely been done. He must also periodically inform Congress of "the State of the Union."
- *Veto legislation.* The president can **veto** (disapprove) any bill or resolution passed by Congress, with the exception of joint resolutions that propose constitutional amendments. Congress can override a presidential veto with a two-thirds vote in each house.

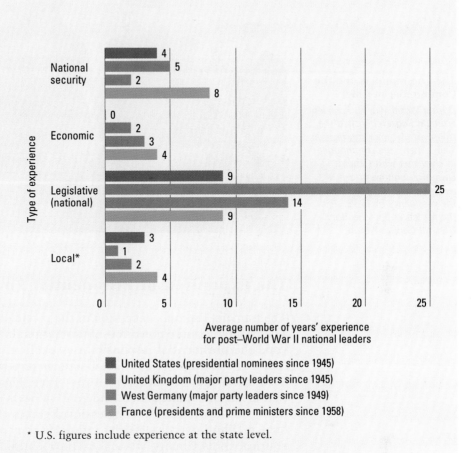

Average number of years' experience
for post–World War II national leaders

■ United States (presidential nominees since 1945)
■ United Kingdom (major party leaders since 1945)
■ West Germany (major party leaders since 1949)
■ France (presidents and prime ministers since 1958)

* U.S. figures include experience at the state level.

- *Appoint various officials.* The president has the authority to appoint federal court judges, ambassadors, Cabinet members, other key policymakers, and many lesser officials. Many appointments are subject to Senate confirmation.
- *Make treaties.* With the "advice and consent" of at least two-thirds of those senators voting at the time, the president can make treaties with foreign powers. The president is also to "receive ambassadors," a phrase that presidents have interpreted as the right to recognize other nations.
- *Grant pardons.* The president can grant pardons to individuals who have committed "Offences against the United States, except in Cases of Impeachment."

The Commanders and the Commander in Chief

During World War II, President Franklin Roosevelt visited the troops at an American base in Sicily. There, the commander in chief met with General Dwight Eisenhower (to FDR's left), who would himself win the presidency in 1952. At the far left is the legendary General George Patton.

The Expansion of Presidential Power

The framers' limited conception of the president's role has given way to a considerably more powerful interpretation. In this section, we look beyond the presidential responsibilities explicitly listed in the Constitution and examine the additional sources of power that presidents have used to expand the authority of the office. First, we look at the claims that presidents make about "inherent" powers implicit in the Constitution. Second, we turn to congressional grants of power to the executive branch. Third, we discuss the influence that comes from a president's political skills. Finally, we analyze how a president's popular support affects his political power.

The Inherent Powers

Several presidents have expanded their power by taking actions that exceeded commonly held notions of the president's proper authority. These men justified what they had done by saying that their actions fell within the **inherent powers** of the office. From this broad perspective, presidential power derives not only from those duties clearly outlined in Article II but also from inferences that may be drawn from the Constitution.

When a president claims a power that has not been considered part of the chief executive's authority, he forces the Congress and the courts to acquiesce to his claim or to restrict it. When presidents succeed in claiming a new power, they leave to their successors the legacy of a permanent expansion of presidential authority. One early use of the inherent power of the presidency occurred during George Washington's tenure in office. The British and the French were at war, and Washington was under some pressure from members of his own administration to show favoritism toward the French. Instead, he issued a proclamation of strict neutrality, angering many who harbored anti-British sentiments; the ensuing controversy provoked a constitutional debate. Washington's critics noted that the Constitution does not include a presidential power to declare neutrality. His defenders said that the president had inherent powers to conduct diplomatic relations. In the end, Washington's decision was not overturned by Congress or the courts and thus set a precedent in the area of foreign affairs.[8]

Claims of inherent powers often come at critical points in the nation's history. During the Civil War, for example, Abraham Lincoln issued a number of orders that exceeded the accepted limits of presidential authority. One of those orders increased the size of the armed forces far beyond the congressionally mandated ceiling, even though the Constitution gives only Congress the power "to raise and support armies." And because military expenditures would then have exceeded military appropriations, Lincoln clearly had also acted to usurp the taxing and spending powers constitutionally conferred on Congress. In another order, Lincoln instituted a blockade of southern ports, thereby committing acts of war against the Confederacy without the approval of Congress.

Lincoln said the urgent nature of the South's challenge to the Union forced him to act without waiting for congressional approval. His rationale was simple: "Was it possible to lose the nation and yet preserve the Constitution?"[9] In other words, Lincoln circumvented the Constitution in order to save the nation. Subsequently, Congress and the Supreme Court approved Lincoln's actions. That approval gave added legitimacy to the theory of inherent powers—a theory that over time has transformed the presidency.

Any president who lays claim to new authority runs the risk of being rebuffed by Congress or the courts and suffering political damage. After Andrew Jackson vetoed a bill reauthorizing a national bank, for example, he ordered William Duane, his secretary of the treasury, to withdraw all federal deposits and to place them in state banks. Duane refused, claiming that he was under the supervision of both Congress and the executive branch; Jackson responded by firing him. The president's action angered many members of Congress who believed that Jackson had overstepped his constitutional bounds; the Constitution does not actually state that a president may remove his Cabinet secretaries. Although that prerogative is now taken for granted, Jackson's presidency was weakened by the controversy. His censure by the Senate was a slap in the face, and he was denounced even by members of his own party. It took many years for the president's right to remove Cabinet officers to become widely accepted.[10]

Congressional Delegation of Power

Presidential power grows when presidents successfully challenge Congress, but in many instances Congress willingly delegates power to the executive branch. As the American public pressures the national government to solve various problems, Congress, through a process called **delegation of powers,** gives the executive branch more responsibility to administer programs that address those problems. One example of delegation of legislative power occurred in the 1930s, during the Great Depression, when Congress gave Franklin Roosevelt's administration wide latitude to do what it thought was necessary to solve the nation's economic ills.

When Congress concludes that the government needs flexibility in its approach to a problem, the president is often given great freedom in how or when to implement policies. Richard Nixon, for example, was given discretionary authority to impose a freeze on wages and prices in an effort to combat escalating inflation. If Congress had been forced to debate the timing of this freeze, merchants and manufacturers would surely have raised their prices in anticipation of the event. Instead, Nixon was able to act suddenly, and the freeze was imposed without warning. (Congressional delegation of authority to the executive branch is discussed in more detail in Chapter 13.)

At other times, however, Congress believes that too much power is accumulating in the executive branch, and it passes legislation reasserting congressional authority. During the 1970s, many representatives and senators agreed that Congress's role in the American political system was declining, that presidents were exercising power that rightfully belonged to the legislative branch. The most notable reaction was the passage of the War Powers Resolution (1973), which was directed toward ending the president's ability to pursue armed conflict without explicit congressional approval. More recently, Congress has demanded a much greater role in foreign policymaking and, as noted in Chapter 11, has successfully pushed the president to consult with it on arms control issues.[11]

The President's Power to Persuade

A president's influence in office comes not only from his assigned responsibilities but also from his political skills and how effectively he uses the resources of his office. A classic analysis of the use of presidential resources is offered by Richard Neustadt in his book *Presidential Power*. Neustadt develops a model of how presidents gain, lose, or maintain their influence. This initial premise is simple enough: "Presidential *power* is the power to persuade."[12] Presidents, for all their resources—a skilled staff, extensive media coverage of presidential actions, the great respect for the office—must depend on others' cooperation to get things done. Harry Truman echoed Neustadt's premise when he said, "I sit here all day trying to persuade people to do the things they ought to have sense enough to do without my persuading them. . . . That's all the powers of the President amount to."[13]

The abilities displayed in bargaining, dealing with adversaries, and choosing priorities, according to Neustadt, separate above-average presidents from mediocre ones. A president must make wise choices about which policies to push and which to put aside until more support can be found. He must decide when to accept compromises and when to stand on principles. He must know when to go public and when to work behind the scenes.

Often, a president faces a dilemma in which all the alternatives carry some risk. After Dwight Eisenhower took office in 1953, he had to decide how to deal with Joseph McCarthy, the Republican senator from Wisconsin who had been largely reponsible for creating national hysteria over alleged communists in government. McCarthy had made many wild, reckless charges, damaging a number of innocent people's careers by accusing them of communist sympathies. Many people expected Eisenhower to control McCarthy—not only because he was president but also because he was a fellow Republican. Yet Eisenhower, worrying about his own popularity, chose not to confront him. He used a "hidden hand" strategy, working behind the scenes to weaken McCarthy. Politically, Eisenhower seems to have made the right choice; McCarthy soon discredited himself.[14] Eisenhower's performance can be criticized, however, as weak moral leadership. If he had publicly denounced the senator, he might have ended the McCarthy witch-hunt sooner.

A president's political skills can be important in affecting outcomes in Congress. The chief executive cannot intervene in every legislative struggle. He must choose his battles carefully, then try to use the force of his personality and the prestige of his office to forge an agreement among differing factions. In terms of getting members to vote a certain way, presidential influence is best described as taking place "at the margins." That is, presidents don't have the power to consistently move large numbers of votes one way or the other. They can, however, affect some votes—possibly enough to affect the outcome of a closely fought piece of legislation.[15]

Neustadt stresses that a president's influence is related to his professional reputation and prestige. When a president pushes hard for a bill that Congress eventually defeats or emasculates, the president's reputation is hurt. The public perceives him as weak or showing poor judgment, and Congress becomes even less likely to cooperate with him in the future. Jimmy Carter damaged his prestige by backing bills that proposed welfare reform, hospital cost containment, and an agency for consumer protection—none of which passed. Yet the other side of this coin is that presidents cannot easily avoid controversial bills, especially if campaign promises were made. If a president backs only sure things, he will be credited with little initiative and perceived as too cautious.

The President and the Public

Neustadt's analysis suggests that a popular president is more persuasive than an unpopular one. A popular president has more power to persuade because he can use his public support as a resource in the bargaining process.[16] Members of Congress who know that the president is highly popular back home have more incentive to cooperate with the administration. If the president and his aides know that a member of Congress does not want to be seen as hostile to the president, they can apply more leverage to achieve a favorable compromise in a legislative struggle.

A familiar aspect of the modern presidency is the effort of its incumbents to mobilize public support for their programs. A president uses

Comfort and Commemoration

An unwritten part of the presidential job description is to act as a symbol of unity in times of tragedy or turmoil. Here President Reagan comforts grieving relatives of the astronauts killed in 1986 when the space shuttle Challenger *exploded shortly after takeoff.*

televised addresses and the press coverage that surrounds his speeches, remarks to reporters, and public appearances to speak directly to the American people and convince them of the wisdom of his policies. It may seem only sensible for a president to seek popular endorsement of particular bills or broad initiatives, as President Bush did with the tax proposal discussed in the chapter opening, but public appeals have not always been a part of the presidency. Our first fifteen presidents averaged fewer than ten speeches a year. It was not simply that the lack of modern communications made attempts to mobilize the public more difficult; early presidents felt constrained in the way they interacted with the public. The founders' fear that the executive office might be used to inflame popular passions led early presidents to be reserved in their communications.[17] Notice how President-elect Lincoln avoided the opportunity to galvanize support for his views on the secession unrest in the South.

> And here, fellow citizens, I may remark that in every crowd through which I have passed of late some allusion has been made to the present distracted condition of this country. It is naturally expected that I should say something upon this subject, but to touch upon it at all would involve an elaborate discussion of a great many questions and circumstances, would require more time than I can at present command, and would perhaps unnecessarily commit me upon matters which have not yet fully developed themselves.[18]

Since then, presidents have increased their direct communication with the American people. As Figure 12.1 illustrates, the number of presidential public appearances has grown sharply since World War II. Obviously, modern technology has contributed to this growth. Nonetheless, the increase in public appearances represents something more than increased visibility for the president and his views. There has also been a funda-

FIGURE 12.1 *Going Public*

These figures depict the average number of public appearances made in a year by presidents from 1929 to 1983. Only the first three years of their first terms were examined; the fourth year was not tabulated to exclude appearances arranged with an eye toward an upcoming election. Because a large portion of Gerald Ford's term was taken up by a year before an election, his time in office was excluded from analysis. (Source: Samuel Kernell, Going Public *[Washington, D.C.: CQ Press, 1986], p. 94. Used by permission.)*

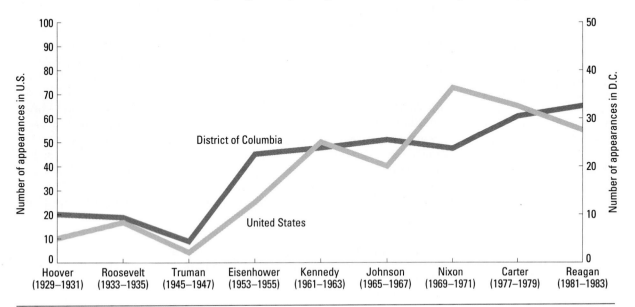

mental change in the power of the presidency. The decline of party and congressional leadership has hastened the rise of the public president; at the same time, the president's direct communication with the American people has made it more difficult for political parties and Congress to reinvigorate themselves.[19]

Presidential popularity is typically at its highest during a president's first year in office. This "honeymoon" period affords the president a particularly good opportunity to use public support to get some of his programs through Congress. During Ronald Reagan's first year in office, when he made a televised appeal for support for a legislative proposal, some congressional offices received calls and letters that ran 10 to 1 in favor of the president. At the beginning of his second term, typical congressional offices received an equal number of negative and positive responses after a Reagan appeal.[20] Perhaps the positions he advocated were less attractive, but it was also clear that Reagan had lost some of his ability to mobilize public opinion.

The rise and fall in presidential popularity can generally be explained by several factors. First, public approval of the job done by a president is affected by *economic conditions*, such as inflation and unemployment.[21] Second, a president is affected by *unanticipated events* of all types that occur during his administration. When American embassy personnel were taken hostage in Teheran by militantly anti-American Iranians,

Carter's popularity soared. This "rally 'round the flag" support for the president eventually gave way to frustration with his inability to gain the hostages' release, and Carter's popularity plummeted. The third factor that affects presidential popularity is American involvement in a *war*, which can affect public approval. Johnson, for example, suffered a loss of popularity during his escalation of the American effort in Vietnam.[22]

Politicians and journalists have a good "feel" for how well a president is doing, but objective evidence comes from a steady stream of national opinion surveys (see Chapter 5). Figure 12.2 compares the Gallup Poll's monthly measurement of the popularity of Ronald Reagan and George Bush at comparable points in their first term. The sharp decline for Reagan that began halfway through his first year was a response to the severe recession that overtook the country. Bush's popularity, which remained remarkably high after he took office in 1989, finally started to decline toward the middle of his second year as the nation's economy showed signs of deterioration. Bush's firm response to the Iraqi invasion of Kuwait gave a short-term boost to his popularity, but it fell quickly afterward. However, when the United States initiated an air war against Iraq in January 1991 and later routed its army in four days, Bush's popularity skyrocketed to record levels.

But few presidents win a war so decisively and with so few casualties. When an unpopular war, an adverse event, or a declining economy drives a president's popularity down, he is at considerable risk. The ultimate consequence of declining popularity is that a first-term president may not be able to win re-election. Both Ford and Carter, whose popularity declined sharply, were defeated for re-election. With his popularity waning, Lyndon Johnson pulled out of the 1968 Democratic primaries. Decline, however, is not inherently irreversible. When the economy recov-

It's a Matter of Priorities

During his second year in office, President Bush was confronted by an economic slowdown that deepened into a recession. Pressure to help those suffering from the effects of the recession was deflected, however, by the Iraqi invasion of Kuwait on August 2, 1990. Bush's firm commitment to liberating Kuwait became the nation's pre-eminent concern.

FIGURE 12.2 *A Very Popular President*

The monthly Gallup Poll asks, "Do you approve or disapprove of the way [the present officeholder] is handling his job as president?" These approval figures show that President Bush was remarkably popular during his first year in office. President Reagan, in comparison, dropped badly during his first year because of the recession that began in 1981. Bush's popularity began to decline in his second year, largely because of the weakening economy and poor presidential leadership on the budget. However, his approval rating skyrocketed to a remarkable 89 percent when the Iraqi army was crushed in late February 1991. (Source: Gallup Poll data compiled from various issues of Public Opinion *and* American Enterprise. *Labels added.)*

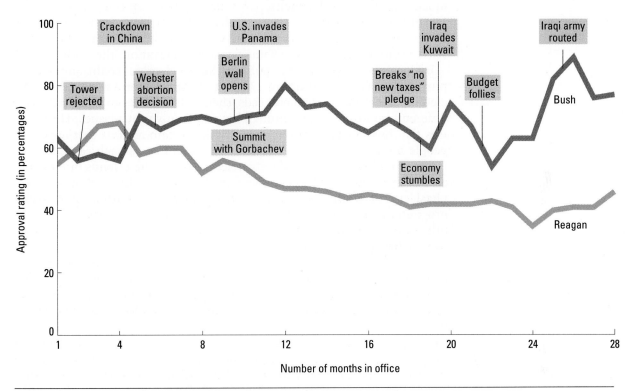

ered after the 1981–1982 recession, Reagan's popularity recovered too. After it was revealed that the Reagan administration had sold arms to Iran and used some of the profits to fund rebel forces in Nicaragua, Reagan's popularity plunged. By the end of his term, however, his popularity had moved up again.[23] Presidents who develop a strong residue of respect and approval for the basic thrust of their presidency seem more capable of recovery from adverse conditions or events.

The Electoral Connection

In his farewell address to the nation, Jimmy Carter lashed out at the interest groups that had bedeviled his presidency. Interest groups, he said, "distort our purposes because the national interest is not always the sum of all our single or special interests." Carter noted the president's singular responsibility: "The president is the only elected official charged with representing all the people."[24] Carter, like all other presidents, quickly recognized the dilemma of majoritarianism versus pluralism after he took office. The president must try to please countless separate constituencies while trying to do what is best for the whole country.

It is easy to stand on the sidelines and say that presidents should always try to follow a majoritarian path—pursuing policies that reflect the preferences of most citizens. Simply by running for office, however, candidates align themselves with particular segments of the population. As a result of their electoral strategy, their identification with activists in their party, and their own political views, candidates come into office with an interest in pleasing some constituencies more than others.

Each candidate attempts to put together an electoral coalition that will provide at least the minimum 270 (out of 538) electoral votes needed for election. As the campaign proceeds, the candidate tries to win votes from different groups of voters through his stand on various issues. He promises that once he is in office, he will take certain actions that appeal to people holding a particular view on an issue. Just as each candidate attracts voters with his stand on particular issues, he offends others who are committed to the opposite side of those issues. In 1988, Bush's emphasis on sustaining economic growth and his lack of attention to social programs helped him win the votes of many businesspeople. On the other hand, it gave those concerned about the less privileged more reason to vote for Dukakis.

Because issue stands can cut both ways—attracting some voters and driving others away—candidates may try to finesse an issue by being deliberately vague. Candidates sometimes hope that voters will put their own interpretations on ambiguous stands. If the tactic works, the candidate will attract some voters without offending others. During the 1968 campaign, Nixon said he was committed to ending the war in Vietnam but gave few details about how he would accomplish that end. He wanted to appeal not only to those who were in favor of military pressure against the North Vietnamese but also to those who wanted quick military disengagement.[25]

Candidates cannot, however, be deliberately vague about all issues. A candidate who is noncommittal on too many issues appears wishy-washy. And future presidents do not build their political careers without working strongly for and becoming associated with important issues and constituencies. As a result, presidents enter office with both a majority of voters on their side and a close identification with particular issues.

Elections and Mandates

Candidates who win the presidency inevitably claim that they have been given a **mandate**, or endorsement, by the voters to carry out the policies they campaigned on. The approval of the voters is equated with approval for the major policies they promised to pursue. Newly chosen presidents make a majoritarian interpretation of the electoral process, claiming that their selection is an expression of the direct will of the people and they are a superior embodiment of national sentiment when compared to the 535 individual members of the Congress. Members of the House and Senate are, after all, elected from much smaller constituencies, and their election often turns on local or statewide issues.

Mandates tend to be more rhetoric than reality. Although presidents claim that the vote they received at the polls is an expression of support for their policy proposals, more dispassionate observers usually find it difficult to find concrete evidence of broad public support for the range of specific policies a winning candidate wants to pursue. In the 1988 presidential race, for example, it is hard to discern a clear sense of what the public wanted. At most the presidential vote indicated that voters were comfortable with the conservative direction of Reagan and Bush and wanted to keep taxes and spending restrained. Beyond that, though, it's very difficult to figure out what specific priorities were preferred by voters. In 1980, when Ronald Reagan defeated incumbent Jimmy Carter, Republicans claimed that the voters had rejected the New Deal liberalism of the Democratic party. Yet Reagan won the three-way race with just 50.9 percent of those who voted. And those who voted comprised just over half of those who were eligible.[26]

Even a landslide at the polls does not give a president a crystal-clear mandate. Lyndon Johnson crushed his Republican opponent, Barry Goldwater, in the 1964 election, winning 61 percent of the popular vote and all but six states in the electoral college. Nevertheless, Johnson misread the public's willingness to endure a ground war in Southeast Asia, and his popularity went into a steep decline because of widespread discontent with the involvement in Vietnam. The social programs of his Great Society, which seemed so popular at the beginning of his presidency, produced a backlash by middle-class whites. Only two years after Johnson's overwhelming defeat of Goldwater, the Democrats lost forty-seven House seats in the 1966 congressional elections.

Divided Government

A major problem the president faces in translating whatever mandate he perceives into actual policies is that the separation of powers makes Congress independent of the executive branch. Not only are the branches separate, but a president has no guarantee that members of his party will be in control of the two houses of Congress. Indeed, in recent years there has been a pattern of **divided control of government**, with the Republicans controlling the White House and Democrats controlling the Congress. Between 1968 and 1988, the Republicans won five of the six presidential elections. Only for six years of that time did they control a single house of the Congress.

It might be expected that when people decide to vote for a party's presidential candidate, they will naturally vote for representatives and senators from that same party so that the president will have allies in the House and Senate who can get his program passed. However, over the course of the twentieth century, the votes for president and Congress have shown less and less of a relationship.[27] As Figure 12.3 shows, in the election of 1900, only 3 percent of all House districts were carried by a

presidential candidate of one party and a congressional candidate of another. In 1988, 34 percent of the districts had split results. Although partisan indentification remains important, American voters have become less loyal to political parties and today vote more on the basis of candidate appeal and issues.

Voters appear to use quite different criteria when choosing a president than they do when choosing congressional representatives. As one scholar has noted, "Presidential candidates are evaluated according to their views on national issues and their competence in dealing with national problems. Congressional candidates are evaluated on their personal character and experience and on their devotion to district services and local issues."[28] The Republicans have been frustrated by this; their success in presidential elections and the rise in Republican party identification would seem to suggest a growth of Republican support in the Congress, but Democratic congressional candidates have continued to be successful in identifying themselves with local concerns. The Democrats have also been more successful in fielding appealing and experienced candidates when there is an open-seat (no incumbent running) race.[29]

This congressional independence is another reason why contemporary presidents work so hard to gain public support for their policies. Without a strong base of representatives and senators who feel their election was tied to his, a president often feels that he needs to win in the court of public opinion. Favorable public opinion can help him build consensus in a highly independent legislative branch.

FIGURE 12.3 *Independent Voting, Divided Government*

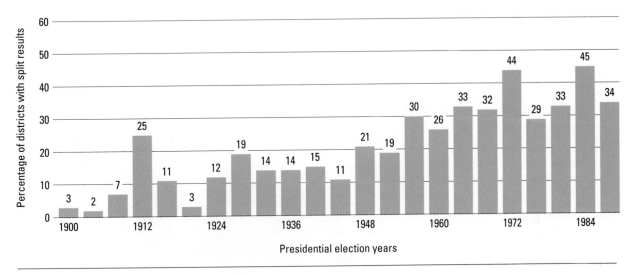

The percentage of House districts carried by a congressional candidate of one party and the presidential candidate of the other party has risen dramatically during the twentieth century. Consequently, members of Congress increasingly see their electoral fortunes as being independent of that of their presidential candidates. (Source: Norman J. Ornstein, Thomas E. Mann, and Michael J. Malbin, Vital Statistics on Congress, 1989–1990 *[Washington, D.C.: Congressional Quarterly Inc., 1990], p. 62. Used by permission. Note that data are not available for every district prior to 1952.)*

The Executive Branch Establishment

As a president tries to maintain the support of his electoral coalition for the policies he pursues, he draws on the great resources of the executive branch of government. The president has a White House staff that helps him formulate policy. The vice president is another resource; his duties within the administration vary according to his relationship with the president. The president's Cabinet secretaries—the heads of the major departments of the national government—play a number of roles, including the critical function of administering the programs that fall within their jurisdiction. Finally, within the departments and agencies, operating at a level below that of the president's appointees, are the career bureaucrats. These bureaucrats (who are discussed in Chapter 13) offer great expertise in program operations.

The White House Staff

A president depends heavily on his key aides. They advise him on crucial political choices, devise the general strategies the administration follows in pursuing congressional and public support, and control access to the president to ensure that he has enough time for his most important tasks. Consequently, he needs to trust and respect these top staffers;

many of a president's inner circle of assistants are long-time associates. (Figure 12.4 shows the location of some staffers' offices in the White House.)

Presidents typically have a chief of staff, who may be a "first among equals," or, in some administrations, the unquestioned leader of the staff. H. R. Haldeman, Richard Nixon's chief of staff, played the stronger role. He ran a highly disciplined operation, frequently prodding staff members to work harder and faster. Haldeman also felt that part of his role was to "take the heat" for the president by assuming responsibility for many of the administration's unpopular decisions: "Every president needs a son of a bitch, and I'm Nixon's."[30] Hamilton Jordan, chief of staff during the Carter administration, did not dominate the White House staff in the same way. His primary job "was to settle interagency conflict and make sure that the implementation of presidential policy was well supervised."[31]

Air Sununu

John Sununu, President Bush's chief of staff, is often described as smart, strong-willed, and abrasive. When the press revealed that Sununu had used government planes for personal travel, some observers speculated that the source of this embarrassing information had been one of Sununu's enemies in the White House.

FIGURE 12.4 *The White House*

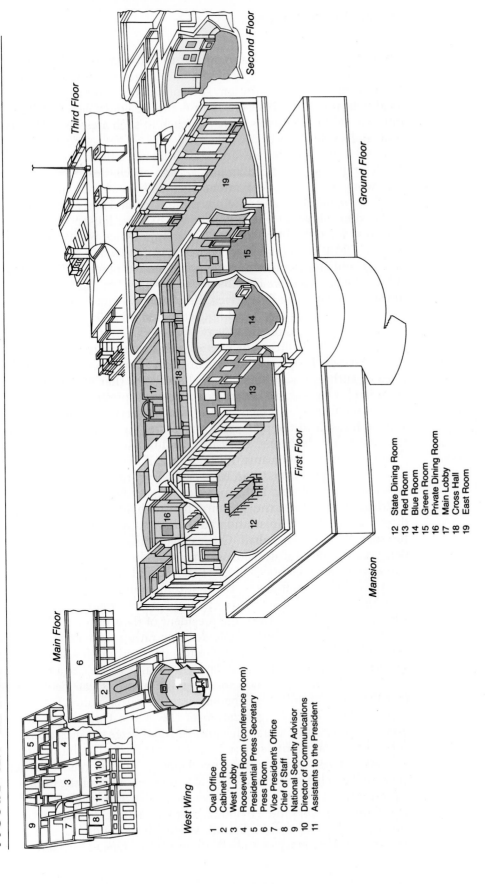

Third Floor

Second Floor

Main Floor

First Floor

Ground Floor

West Wing

Mansion

West Wing

1 Oval Office
2 Cabinet Room
3 West Lobby
4 Roosevelt Room (conference room)
5 Presidential Press Secretary
6 Press Room
7 Vice President's Office
8 Chief of Staff
9 National Security Advisor
10 Director of Communications
11 Assistants to the President

12 State Dining Room
13 Red Room
14 Blue Room
15 Green Room
16 Private Dining Room
17 Main Lobby
18 Cross Hall
19 East Room

Presidents also have a national security adviser to provide daily briefings on foreign and military affairs and longer-range analyses of issues confronting the administration. A Council of Economic Advisers is also located in the White House. Senior domestic policy advisers help determine the administration's basic approach to such areas as health, education, and social services.

Below these top aides are large staffs that serve them and the president. These staffs are organized around certain specialties. Some staff members work on "political" matters, such as liaison with interest groups, relations with ethnic and religious minorities, and party affairs. One staff deals exclusively with the press, and a legislative liaison staff lobbies the Congress for the administration. The large Office of Management and Budget (OMB) analyzes budget requests, is involved in the policymaking process, and also examines agency management practices. This extended White House executive establishment is known as the **Executive Office of the President.** The Executive Office employs around sixteen hundred individuals and has an annual budget of around $100 million.[32]

There is no agreed-on "right way" for a president to organize his White House staff. Each president creates the structure that works best for him.[33] Dwight Eisenhower, for example, a former general, wanted clear lines of authority and a hierarchical structure that mirrored a military command. One factor that influences how a president uses his senior staff is the degree to which he delegates authority to them. Carter immersed himself in the policymaking process to ensure that he made all the significant decisions. Early in his administration, he told his staff, "Unless there's a holocaust, I'll take care of everything the same day it comes in."[34] (This explains in large part why Jordan's role as chief of staff was less powerful than Haldeman's during the Nixon years.)

Ronald Reagan was the opposite: he saw his role as setting a general direction for the administration but delegated wide-ranging authority to his staff to act on his behalf. Critics charge that Reagan went too far in delegating important decisions to his staff. In his second term, his top aides even decided who his chief of staff would be. James Baker, who had been his chief of staff during the first term, and Donald Regan, who had been the secretary of the treasury, decided they wanted to switch jobs. After another aide informed the president of their desire to do this, Reagan treated it like an irreversible decision rather than a choice that was actually his to make.[35] The loose rein Reagan gave to his staff is, in fact, seen as a key cause of the Iran-Contra scandal.[36] What Reagan did do well with his staff, however, was to infuse them with clear ideolgical goals that they were to follow in shaping administration policy.[37]

Despite the formal organization of the White House staff, it suffers from the same "turf wars" that plague other large organizations. These struggles over authority stem not only from personal ambition and political differences but also from overlapping jurisdictions. Conflict frequently arises between a secretary of state (a member of the Cabinet) and a president's national security adviser; each wants primacy in shaping the administration's foreign policy. Henry Kissinger, Nixon's national security adviser, was extraordinarily shrewd in devising ways to gain advantage over Secretary of State William Rogers. One of his tactics was to create "backchannels"—information from the field would come to him secretly, bypassing the Department of State. Kissinger did this "not only to keep control of an ongoing negotiation but also to prevent his peers and subordinates from finding out what was going on."[38] Presidents, however, often find it more useful to hear competing policy views than depend to on the views of one person.

The Vice President

The vice president's primary function is to serve as standby equipment, only a heartbeat away from the presidency itself (see Feature 12.1). Traditionally, vice presidents have not been used in any important advisory capacity. Instead, presidents tend to give them political chores—campaigning, fund raising, and "stroking" the party faithful. This is often the case because vice presidential candidates are chosen for reasons that have more to do with the political campaign than with governing the nation.

Dan Quayle, President Bush's choice for vice president, illustrates this common pattern. In 1988, Quayle was a youthful second-term senator from Indiana who had served twelve years in the Congress. Although he had begun to show some legislative skills in the Senate, he was widely regarded as a "lightweight."[39] Nobody really believed that he was the best-suited person to step in as president should something happen to Bush. Bush emphasized that he chose Quayle because he wanted to reach out to younger generations. However, a firestorm of criticism erupted after Bush revealed his choice because reporters soon learned that Quayle had used family connections to get into the Indiana National Guard to avoid the draft during the Vietnam War. Thus, Quayle ended up as a liability rather than an asset to the Republican ticket.

An exception to the usual pattern was Carter's vice president, Walter Mondale. Carter was wise enough to realize that Mondale's experience in the Senate could be of great value to him, especially since Carter had never served in Congress. Although the personal chemistry between Ronald Reagan and George Bush was quite good, Bush did not seem to play as major a role as Mondale.[40] And the Bush-Quayle relationship is much more similar to Reagan and Bush than to Carter and Mondale.

The Cabinet

The president's **Cabinet** is composed of the heads of the departments in the executive branch and a small number of other key officials, such as the head of the Office of Management and Budget and the ambassador to the United Nations. The Cabinet has expanded greatly since George Washington formed his first Cabinet, which included an attorney general and the secretaries of state, treasury, and war. Clearly, the growth of the Cabinet to fourteen departments reflects the growth of government responsibility and intervention in areas such as energy, housing, and transportation.

In theory, the members of the Cabinet constitute an advisory body that meets with the president to debate major policy decisions. In practice,

FEATURE 12.1   *Who's President When the President Can't Be?*

What happens if a president dies in office? The vice president, of course, becomes the new president. But what happens if the vice president has died or left office for some reason? What happens if the president becomes senile or is disabled by illness? These are questions that the authors of the Constitution failed to resolve.

The nuclear age has made these questions more troubling. When Woodrow Wilson suffered a stroke in 1919, it meant that the country was without effective leadership for a time, but the lack of an active president during that period did not endanger the lives of all Americans. Today, with the possibility of nuclear attack, national security dictates that the nation have a commander in chief at all times. The Twenty-fifth Amendment, which was ratified in 1967, specifies a mechanism for replacing a living president in case he cannot carry out the duties of his office. A president can declare himself unable to carry on, or the vice president and the Cabinet can decide collectively that the president is incapacitated. In either case, the vice president becomes acting president and assumes all powers of the office. In 1981, when Ronald Reagan was se-

riously wounded in an assassination attempt and had to undergo emergency surgery, the Twenty-fifth Amendment was not invoked by the vice president and the Cabinet. Four years later, when Reagan underwent cancer surgery, he sent a letter to Vice President George Bush transfering the power of the office to him at the moment the president was anesthetized. Eight hours later, Reagan reclaimed his authority. Under the Twenty-fifth Amendment, if the president and the Cabinet disagree about whether he is able to resume his duties, Congress must ultimately decide.

The Twenty-fifth Amendment also provides that the president select a new vice president in the event that office becomes vacant; the president's choice must be approved by a majority of both houses of Congress. In 1973, Gerald Ford became vice president in this manner when Spiro Agnew resigned after pleading no contest to charges of income tax evasion and accepting bribes. Later, when Richard Nixon resigned and Ford became president, he chose Nelson Rockefeller as his vice president.

---

however, Cabinet meetings have been described as "vapid non-events in which there has been a deliberate non-exchange of information as part of a process of mutual nonconsultation."[41] One Carter Cabinet member called meetings "adult Show-and-Tell."[42] Why is this so? First, the Cabinet has become rather large. Counting department heads, other officials of Cabinet rank, and presidential aides, it is a body of at least twenty people—a size that many presidents find unwieldy for the give-and-take of political decision making. Second, most Cabinet members have limited areas of expertise and simply cannot contribute much to deliberations on areas they know little about. The secretary of defense, for example, would probably be a poor choice to help decide important issues of agricultural policy. Third, although Cabinet members have impressive backgrounds, they may not be personally close to the president or easy for him to work with. Cabinet choices are not necessarily made on the basis of personal relationships. The president often chooses Cabinet members because of their reputations, or he may be guided by a need to give his Cabinet some racial, ethnic, geographic, sexual, or religious balance.

Finally, modern presidents do not rely on the Cabinet to make policy because they have such large White House staffs, which offer most of the advisory support they need. In contrast to Cabinet secretaries, who may be pulled in different directions by the wishes of the president and the

Labor Costs

After an unsuccessful race for the Senate in 1990, Lynn Martin was appointed secretary of labor by President Bush. Here the former Illinois representative testifies on the Labor Department's budget before a congressional committee.

wishes of their department's clientele groups, White House staffers are likely to see themselves as responsible to the president alone. Thus, despite periodic calls for the Cabinet to be a collective decision-making body, Cabinet meetings seem doomed to be little more than academic exercises. In practice, presidents prefer the flexibility of ad hoc groups, specialized White House staffs, and the advisers and Cabinet secretaries with whom they feel most comfortable.

More broadly, presidents use their personal staffs and the large Executive Office of the President to centralize control over the entire executive branch. The vast size of the executive branch and the number and complexity of decisions that must be made each day pose a challenge for the White House. In sum, to fulfill more of their political goals and policy preferences, modern presidents have encouraged their various staffs to play increasingly important roles in executive branch decision making.[43]

The President as National Leader

With an election behind him and the resources of his office at hand, a president is ready to lead the nation. Each president enters office with a general vision of how government should approach policy issues. During his term, a president spends much of his time trying to get Congress to enact legislation that reflects his general philosophy and specific policy preferences.

From Political Values . . .

Presidents differ greatly in their views of the role of government. Lyndon Johnson had a strong liberal ideology concerning domestic affairs. He believed that government has a responsibility to help disadvantaged

Americans. Johnson described his vision of justice in his inaugral address:

> . . . justice was the promise that all who made the journey would share in the fruits of the land.
>
> In a land of wealth, families must not live in hopeless poverty. In a land rich in harvest, children just must not go hungry. In a land of healing miracles, neighbors must not suffer and die untended. In a great land of learning and scholars, young people must be taught to read and write.
>
> For more than thirty years that I have served this nation, I have believed that this injustice to our people, this waste of our resources, was our real enemy. For thirty years or more, with the resources I have had, I have vigilantly fought against it.[44]

Johnson used *justice* and *injustice* as code words for *equality* and *inequality*. They were used six times in his speech; *freedom* was used only twice. Johnson used his popularity, his skills, and the resources of his office to press for a "just" America, which he termed the "Great Society."

To achieve his Great Society, Johnson sent Congress an unprecedented package of liberal legislation. He launched such projects as the Job Corps (which created centers and camps offering vocational training and work experience to youths aged sixteen to twenty-one), Medicare (which provided medical care for the elderly), and the National Teacher Corps (which funded teachers to work in impoverished neighborhoods). Supported by huge Democratic majorities in Congress during 1965 and 1966, he had tremendous success in getting his proposals through. Liberalism was in full swing.

In 1984, exactly twenty years after Johnson's inaugural speech, Ronald Reagan took his oath of office for the second time, then addressed the nation. Reagan reasserted his conservative philosophy. He emphasized *freedom*, using the term fourteen times, and failed to mention *justice* or *equality* once. In the following excerpts, the term *freedom* is italicized for easy reference:

> By 1980, we knew it was time to renew our faith, to strive with all our strength toward the ultimate in individual *freedom* consistent with an orderly society. . . . We will not rest until every American enjoys the fullness of *freedom*, dignity, and opportunity as our birthright. . . . Americans . . . turned the tide of history away from totalitarian darkness and into the warm sunlight of human *freedom*. . . . Let history say of us, these were golden years—when the American Revolution was reborn, when *freedom* gained new life, when America reached for her best. . . . [F]reedom and incentives unleash the drive and entrepreneurial genius that are at the core of human progress. . . . From new *freedom* will spring new opportunities for growth. . . . Yet history has shown that peace does not come, nor will our *freedom* be preserved by good will alone. There are those in the world who scorn our vision of human dignity and *freedom*. . . . Human *freedom* is on the march, and nowhere more so than in our own hemisphere. *Freedom* is one of the deepest and noblest aspirations of the human spirit. . . . America must remain *freedom's* staunchest friend, for *freedom* is our best ally. . . . Every victory for human *freedom* will be a victory for world peace. . . . One people under God, dedicated to the dream of *freedom* that He has placed in the human heart.[45]

FIGURE 12.5 *The Reagan Impact on Budget Priorities*

Ronald Reagan was particularly effective in persuading Congress to shift spending priorities. Although he was not able to dismantle the welfare state, he was able to reduce funding for social programs significantly. (These figures exclude social security and Medicare from spending for human resources.) (Source: Kevin Phillips, The Politics of Rich and Poor [New York: Random House, 1990], p. 88. Copyright © 1990 by Kevin Phillips. Reprinted by permission of Random House, Inc.)

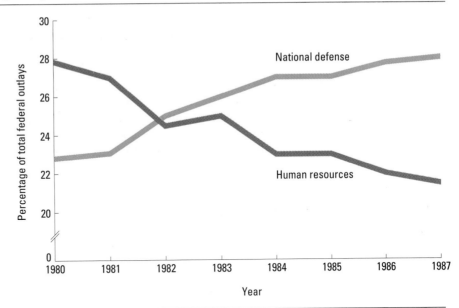

Reagan turned Johnson's philosophy on its head, declaring that "government is not the solution to our problem. Government is the problem." During his presidency, Reagan worked to undo many welfare and social service programs, and funding was reduced for programs like the Job Corps and the food stamp program. By the end of his term there had been a fundamental shift in federal spending, with sharp increases in defense spending and "decreases in federal social programs [which] served to defund Democratic interests and constituencies"[46] (see Figure 12.5).

. . . To Policy Agenda

The roots of particular policy proposals, then, can be traced to the more general political ideology of the president. A presidential candidate outlines that philosophy of government during his campaign for the White House. But when the hot rhetoric of the presidential campaign meets the cold reality of what is possible in Washington, the newly elected president must make some hard choices about what he will push for during the coming term. These choices are reflected in the bills the president submits to Congress, as well as in the degree to which he works for their passage. The president's bills, introduced by his allies in the House and Senate, always receive a good deal of initial attention. In the words of one Washington lobbyist, "When a president sends up a bill, it takes first place in the queue. All other bills take second place."[47]

The president's role in legislative leadership is largely a twentieth-century phenomenon. Not until the Budget and Accounting Act (1921) did executive branch departments and agencies have to clear their proposed budget bills with the White House. Before this, the president did not even coordinate proposals for how much the executive branch would spend on all the programs it administered. Later, Franklin Roosevelt required that *all* major legislative proposals by an agency or department be cleared by the White House. No longer could a department submit a bill without White House support.[48]

Roosevelt's impact on the relationship between the president and Congress went far beyond this new administrative arrangement. With the nation in the midst of the Great Depression, Roosevelt began his first term in 1933 with an ambitious array of legislative proposals. During the first hundred days Congress was in session, it enacted fifteen significant laws, including the Agricultural Adjustment Act, the Civilian Conservation Corps, and the National Industrial Recovery Act. Never had a president demanded—and received—so much from Congress. Roosevelt's legacy was that the president would henceforth provide aggressive leadership for Congress through his own legislative program.

A handful of presidents have entered office after a serious upheaval or a general decline of a dominant political coalition, situations that they can use to their advantage. The economic collapse that preceded Roosevelt's entry into office ended an era of conservative Republicanism that had steadfastly ruled the country for many years. Andrew Jackson and Abraham Lincoln also had fortuitous chances to redefine the terms of political debate and move the country toward a new political agenda.[49] But times of upheaval and decline merely present opportunities; presidents must be skillful enough to exploit the chances for large-scale change. And history has taught us that presidents differ greatly in their skills (see Figure 12.6).

Chief Lobbyist

When Franklin Roosevelt and Harry Truman first became heavily involved in preparing legislative packages, political scientists typically described the process as one in which "the president proposes and the Congress disposes." In other words, once the president sent his legislation to Capitol Hill, Congress decided on its own what to do with it. Over time, though, presidents have become increasingly active in all stages of the legislative process. The president is expected not only to propose legislation but also to make sure that it passes.

The president's efforts to influence Congress are reinforced by the work of his **legislative liaison staff**. All departments and major agencies have legislative specialists as well. These department and agency people work with the White House liaison staff to coordinate the administration's lobbying on major issues.

The legislative liaison staff is the communications link between the White House and Congress. As a bill slowly makes its way through Congress, liaison staffers advise the president or a Cabinet secretary on the problems that emerge. They specify what parts of a bill are in trouble and may have to be modified or dropped. They tell their boss what amendments are likely to be offered, which members of Congress need lobbying, and what the chances are for the passage of the bill with or without certain provisions. Decisions on how the administration will respond to such developments must then be reached. For example, when the Reagan

FIGURE **12.6** *Presidential Greatness*

In 1982, the Chicago Tribune *asked forty-nine leading
historians and political scholars to rate all past presidents
on a descending scale from 5
(best) to 0 (worst) in five
categories: leadership qualities, accomplishments and
crisis management, political
skills, quality of appointments,
and character and integrity.
Lincoln ranked at the top, and
Franklin Roosevelt edged out
Washington for second place.
Among more recent presi-
dents, Eisenhower, Johnson,
and Kennedy all rated far
higher than Ford, Carter, and
Nixon. Nixon's ranking suffered by his extraordinarily
low score for character and
integrity—the lowest that the
scholars gave to any president
in history. (Source: Copyrighted, 1988, Chicago Tribune
Company, all rights reserved,
used with permission.)*

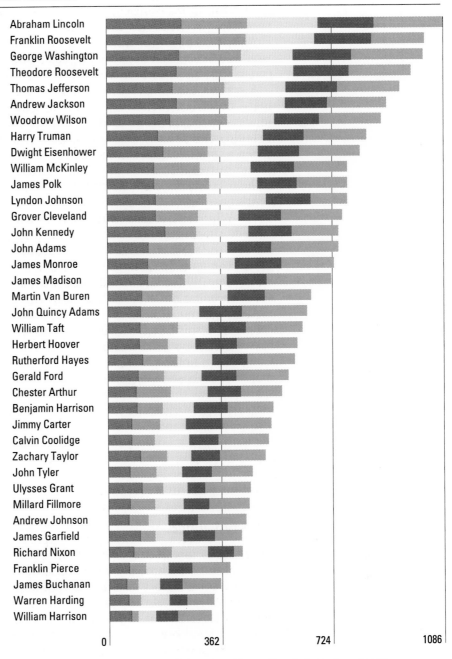

Points earned from ratings by forty-nine scholars

White House realized that it was still a few votes short of victory on a budget bill in the House, it reversed its opposition to a sugar price-support bill. This attracted the votes of representatives from Lousiana and Florida, two sugar-growing states, for the budget bill. The White House would not call what happened a "deal" but noted that "adjustments and considerations" had been made.[50]

A certain amount of the president's job is stereotypical "arm-twisting"—pushing reluctant legislators to vote a certain way. Yet most day-in, day-out interactions tend to be more subtle, as the liaison staff tries to build consensus by working cooperatively with members of Congress. When a congressional committee is working on a bill, liaison people talk to committee members individually, to see what concerns they have and to help fashion a compromise if some members differ with the president's position.

The White House also works directly with interest groups in its efforts to build support for legislation. Presidential aides hope key lobbyists will activate the most effective lobbyists of all: the voters back home. Interest groups can quickly reach the constituents who are most concerned about a bill. One White House aide said with admiration, "The Realtors can send out half a million Mailgrams within 24 hours."[51]

Although much of the liaison staff's work with Congress is done in a cooperative spirit, agreement cannot always be reached. When Congress passes a bill the president opposes, he may veto it and send it back to Congress; as noted earlier, Congress can override a veto with a two-thirds majority of those voting in each house. Presidents use their veto power sparingly, but the threat that a president will veto an unacceptable bill increases his bargaining leverage with members of Congress. We have also seen that a president's leverage with Congress is related to his standing with the American people. The ability of the president and his liaison staff to bargain with members of Congress is enhanced when he is riding high in the popularity polls and hindered when the public is critical of his performance.

Party Leader

Part of the president's job is to lead his party. This is very much an informal duty, with no prescribed tasks. In this respect, American presidents are considerably different from European prime ministers, who are the formal leaders of their party in the national legislature as well as the heads of government. Since political parties in Europe tend to have strong national organizations, there is more reason for prime ministers to lead the party organization. In the United States, national party committees play a relatively minor role in national politics, although they are active in raising money for their congressional candidates (see Chapter 8).

The simple fact is that presidents can operate effectively without the help of a national party apparatus. Lyndon Johnson, for example, was contemptuous of the Democratic National Committee. He saw to it that the committee's budget was cut and refused some advisers' request that he replace its ineffectual head. Johnson thought a weak national committee would allow him to control party affairs out of the White House. Like other modern presidents, Johnson believed he would be most effective communicating directly with the American people and did not see the need for national, state, or local party officials to be intermediaries in the process of coalition building.[52]

Work with the party may be more important for gaining the presidency than actually governing. George Bush worked tirelessly on the "rubber chicken" circuit while he was vice president and built up a hefty billfold of IOUs by campaigning for Republican candidates and appearing at their fund-raising dinners. When he and his main competitor for the 1988 Republican nomination, Senator Robert Dole, faced each other in the critical Super Tuesday primaries in 1988, Bush had enormous strength among state and local party leaders; those individuals formed the backbone of his campaign organization. Yet such party work is not absolutely essential. In 1976, Carter not only won the nomination without much of a record of party work, he campaigned as an outsider, claiming that he would be a better president without having ties to those who had long been in power.

The President as World Leader

The president's leadership responsibilities extend beyond the Congress and the nation into the international arena. Each administration tries to further what it sees as the country's best interests in its relations with allies, adversaries, and the developing countries of the world. In this role, the president must be ready to act as diplomat and crisis manager.

Foreign Relations

Since the end of World War II, presidents have been preoccupied with containing communist expansion around the globe (see Chapter 20). Truman and South Korea; Kennedy and Cuba; Johnson and Nixon and South Vietnam; and Reagan and Nicaragua are just some examples of presidents and the communist crosses they had to bear. Presidents not only used overt and covert military means to fight communism, they tried to reduce tensions through negotiations as well. President Nixon made particularly important strides in this regard, completing an important arms control agreement with the Soviet Union and beginning negotiations with the Chinese, with whom the United States had no formal diplomatic relations.

With the collapse of communism in the Soviet Union and Eastern Europe, American presidents are entering a new era in international relations. The new presidential job description places much more emphasis on managing economic relations with the rest of the world, though most importantly with Europe and Japan. Trade relations are an especially difficult problem because presidents must balance the conflicting interests of foreign countries (many of whom are our allies), the interests of particular American industries, the overall needs of the American economy, and the demands of the legislative branch. Even though they know the

Our American Friend

As a young politician, Richard Nixon was notorious for his staunch anticommunism. As president, however, he achieved a stunning reversal of U.S. policy toward the People's Republic of China. His trip there in 1972 signaled an end to the Cold War hostility between the United States and the communist regime.

virtues of free trade, presidents must often accommodate political realities at home. The steel industry, for example, beset by foreign competition, was able to convince Carter and Congress that protecting American jobs was more important than letting steel operate in a completely free American market. Import controls may have saved American jobs, but the Federal Trade Commission later calculated that the cost to the American economy was $113,600 per job.[53]

The decline of communism has not, however, enabled the president to ignore security issues. The world remains a dangerous place, and regional conflicts can still embroil the United States. When Iraq invaded and quickly conquered Kuwait in August 1990, President Bush felt he had no choice but to respond firmly to protect our economic interests and to stand beside our Arab allies in the area. Bush worked the phones hard to try to get both Western and Arab leaders to join the United States in a coordinated military buildup in the area surrounding Kuwait. He had laid the groundwork for cooperation with the heavy emphasis he placed in the early months of his administration on building personal relationships with many important heads of state. It was, said one journalist, a "dazzling performance. In roughly four days, Bush organized the world against Saddam Hussein."[54]

Bush's impressive leadership of the twenty-eight-nation coalition continued in the months that followed. The coalition remained unified even through the difficult decision to go to war in January when the air campaign began. Bush played a key role in convincing the Israelis, who were not a member of the coalition, to refrain from retaliating against Iraq after Israel came under attack from Scud missiles. (Iraq had hoped that by drawing Israel into the war, the United States' Arab allies would withdraw their support for the war because of their implacable opposition to the Jewish state.) The successful ground war against Iraqi forces was a capstone to a remarkable foreign policy achievement.

Crisis Management

Periodically the president faces a grave situation in which conflict is imminent or a small conflict threatens to explode into a larger war. Handling such episodes is a critical part of the president's job. Today, we must put enormous trust in the person who has the power to pull the nuclear trigger; voters may make the candidates' personal judgment and intelligence primary considerations in how they cast their ballots. A major reason for Barry Goldwater's crushing defeat in the 1964 election was his warlike image. Goldwater's bellicose rhetoric scared many Americans, who, fearing that he would be too quick to resort to nuclear weapons, voted for Lyndon Johnson instead.

A president must be able to exercise good judgment and remain cool in crisis situations. John Kennedy's behavior during the Cuban missile crisis of 1962 has become a model of effective crisis management. When it was discovered that the Soviet Union had placed missiles containing nuclear warheads in Cuba, U.S. government leaders saw those missiles as an unacceptable threat to this country's security. Kennedy asked a group of senior aides, including top people from the Pentagon, to advise him on possible military and diplomatic actions. An armed invasion of Cuba and air strikes against the missiles were two options considered. In the end, Kennedy decided on a less dangerous response: implementing a naval blockade of Cuba. The Soviet Union thought better of prolonging its challenge to the United States and soon agreed to remove its missiles. For a short time, though, the world held its breath over the very real possibility of a nuclear war.

Are there guidelines for what a president should do in times of crisis or at other important decision-making junctures? Drawing on a range of advisers and opinions is certainly one.[55] Not acting in unnecessary haste is another. A third is having a well-designed, formal review process that

The Handshake of Peace

One of the crowning achievements of Jimmy Carter's presidency was his role in forging a peace treaty between Egypt and Israel. Egyptian president Anwar Sadat (left) and Israeli prime minister Menachem Begin (right) came to the presidential retreat at Camp David in Maryland. For thirteen days, Carter was a mediator in the peace negotiations. After the historic accords were reached, the three flew by helicopter to the White House, where they signed the initial agreement.

promotes thorough analysis and open debate.[56] A fourth guideline is rigorously examining the chain of reasoning that has led to the chosen option, ensuring that *presumptions* have not been subconsciously equated with what is *actually known* to be true. When Kennedy decided to back a CIA plan to sponsor a rebel invasion of Cuba by expatriates hostile to Fidel Castro, he never really understood that its chances for success were based on unfounded assumptions of immediate uprisings by the Cuban population.[57]

Still, these are rather general rules and provide no assurance that mistakes will not be made. Almost by definition, each crisis is a unique event. Sometimes all the alternatives carry substantial risks. And almost always, time is of the essence. This was the situation when Cambodia captured the American merchant ship *Mayaguez* off its coast in 1975. Not wanting to wait until the Cambodian government moved the seamen inland, where there would be little chance of rescuing them, President Gerald Ford immediately sent in the marines. Unfortunately, forty-one American soldiers were killed in the fighting, "all in vain because the American captives had shortly before the attack been released and sent across the border into Thailand."[58] Even so, Ford can be defended for making the decision he did; he did not know what the Cambodians would do. World events are unpredictable, and, in the end, presidents must rely on their own judgment in crisis situations.

Presidential Character

How does the public assess which presidential candidate has the best judgment and a character suitable to the office? Americans must make a broad evaluation, considering the candidates' personalities and leadership styles. Sometimes damaging revelations suggest that a candidate's character is flawed. Senator Joseph Biden of Delaware, a candidate for the 1988 Democratic nomination for president, was forced to withdraw from the campaign because of evidence that he had plagiarized parts of his campaign speeches from stirring speeches made by other politicians and that he had lied about his record in college.

Questions about Gary Hart's character also became a major issue in the 1988 race and forced him to withdraw as well. The public was disturbed not only by the allegations of adultery that followed the Democratic candidate but also by his recklessness. As one journalist noted, "Why would any man in his right mind defy a New York *Times* reporter who asked about his alleged womanizing to 'put a tail on me,' then cancel his weekend campaign appearances and arrange a tryst at his Washington town house with a Miami party girl?"[59]

A candidate's character is clearly a valid campaign issue. A president's actions in office reflect something more than ideology and politics; they also reflect the moral, ethical, and psychological forces that comprise his character. Much of any person's character is formed in childhood, and many individual traits can be traced to early experiences. Lyndon Johnson, for example, had a troubled relationship with his father, who questioned his son's masculinity. Johnson recalled that when he ran away from home after wrecking his father's car, his father phoned him and said

A Difference in Character

The personalities of Calvin Coolidge and John F. Kennedy led to considerably different styles of presidential leadership. Coolidge's motto, "Let well enough alone," says much about his approach to the presidency. "Vigorous" was the term commonly used to describe Kennedy, and it's an apt description of his presidency as well. Historian Arthur Schlesinger, Jr., said of Kennedy, "His presidential life was instinct with action."

F E A T U R E   12.2   *Portrait of the Young President as a Complete and Utter Monster*

Few presidential biographies have so thoroughly altered our perception of a chief executive as much as Robert Caro's volumes on Lyndon Johnson. The recent publication of the second of a projected four-volume biography of Johnson has stoked the controversy over what we can learn by examining the personalities of presidents and would-be presidents. *Means of Ascent* covers the years between 1941, when Johnson lost a bid for the Senate, and 1948, when he won his second Senate race. What is remarkable—and troubling—about this book is that the young Johnson is portrayed as a entirely evil person. There are no shades of gray; Johnson is depicted as an utter monster who will stop at nothing to achieve his goals. For Lyndon Johnson, the ends always justified the means.

The "means" documented by Caro were Johnson's lying, stealing, and cowardice. As he campaigned for the Senate in 1941 he told voters that if war came he would leave that body to be "in the trenches, in the mud and blood with your boys." When war did come Johnson did his best, however, to avoid a combat assignment, even going as far as visiting the White House to ask President Roosevelt to make him an administrator of a Washington-based agency that would provide war-related training to youths. He didn't get that job, but was eventually given a position in the navy that took him to the South Pacific as an observer.

Yet when he campaigned for the Senate again in 1948, Johnson showed no shame in claiming that he was an experienced combat veteran of World

Lyndon Johnson, 1948

War II. His campaign made a consistent effort to find veterans who were amputees to introduce Johnson at campaign rallies to emphasize his status as a war veteran. Johnson never let on that

that people in town were calling Lyndon "yellow" and a coward.[60] Johnson biographer Robert Caro notes another crucial episode in young Lyndon's life—a humiliating beating he took at the hands of a dance partner's jealous boyfriend. In front of family and friends, "blood was pouring out of Lyndon's nose and mouth, running down his face and onto the crepe-de-chine shirt."[61]

Was Johnson overly concerned about his masculinity? Did this psychological problem make it difficult for him to extricate the United States from the Vietnam War? Another Johnson biographer, Doris Kearns, argues that Johnson wanted to make sure he "was not forced to see himself as a coward, running away from Vietnam."[62] Nonetheless, it is almost impossible to establish the precise roots of Johnson's behavior as president, and some might find connections between childhood humiliations he was just an observer and that his only exposure to combat was passage on a single B-26 flight that engaged the enemy for a total of thirteen minutes.

Johnson lied about other things as well. He claimed he had no role in his wife's broadcasting business, but that was not true. He accused his opponent in the 1948 race of being a communist sympathizer, but he had no evidence of that. Most revealing of Johnson's character, according to Caro, is that Johnson and his operatives stole the 1948 Senate election. Stealing votes was nothing new in Texas at that time, but Johnson's flagrant abuse of the democratic process was truly breathtaking. The campaign paid large sums of money to various political bosses to ensure that they would produce sizable pluralities on election day. When election day came and it turned out that Johnson was trailing his opponent, Coke Stevenson, Johnson's men swung into action to change the vote tallies by claiming mistakes had been made and by "discovering" votes that had supposedly not been counted. The final vote in Duval County shows just how far Johnson's vote stealing went. There were 4,679 people eligible to cast ballots on election day. Of that number, 4,662 were reported to have voted, and 4,622 (or 99.1 percent) were reported as voting for Johnson.

After days of corrections and the addition of the new votes, Johnson was still behind by a handful of votes. This led Johnson lieutenants in Jim Wells County to phone the Election Bureau to say that a mistake had been made in Precinct 13 there, and

that Johnson had actually received 965 votes rather than 765. On the tally sheet someone simply added a loop to the 7 to turn it into a 9. This put Johnson over the top, giving him victory by 87 votes out of close to a million cast by Texas voters.

Caro is quite clear in explaining why he has focused so much on Johnson's personality in the two books he has completed so far. "Lyndon Johnson's personality and character bore an unusually heavy weight" on the evolution of his administration. "To understand that history, we have to understand that personality." Caro sums up what he found about Johnson's character this way: "The pattern of pragmatism, cynicism and ruthlessness that pervaded Lyndon Johnson's entire early political career was marked by a lack of any discernible limits."

Yet there is a mystery in all of this. If Johnson was such a ruthless person, why did he do so much good as president? He compiled a remarkable record on civil rights, and his War on Poverty demonstrated an unusual commitment and compassion for the less fortunate in society. What, then, has all this psychobiography told us? If much of a president's behavior in office can be predicted by his earlier experiences, it also seems to be the case that there is much that can't be predicted.

Source: Robert A. Caro, *Means of Ascent* (New York: Alfred A. Knopf, 1990). Copyright 1990 by Alfred A. Knopf, Publisher. The first volume of the Caro biography is *The Path to Power* (New York: Alfred A. Knopf, 1982).

and presidential policy decisions rather speculative. Others, however, feel that *psychobiography*—the application of psychological analysis to historical figures—has enormous potential as an approach to studying political leaders (see Feature 12.2).

Whatever their roots, the personality characteristics of presidents clearly have an important effect on their success or failure in office. Richard Nixon had such an exaggerated fear of what his "enemies" might try to do to him that he created in the White House a climate that nurtured the Watergate break-in and cover-up. Franklin Roosevelt, on the other hand, was certainly aided in office by his relaxed manner and self-confidence.[63]

Candidates don't come neatly labeled as having healthy or unhealthy presidential characters. Although voters make their own estimations of how presidents will behave in office, there is no guarantee that those evaluations will turn out to be accurate. And a candidate's character must still be weighed along with other factors, including ideology, party affiliation, and stances on specific issues.

Summary

When the delegates to the Constitutional Convention met to design the government of this new nation, they had trouble shaping the office of the president. They struggled to find a balance between an office that was powerful enough to provide unified leadership but not so strong that presidents could use their powers to become tyrants or dictators. The initial conceptions of the presidency have slowly been transformed over time, as presidents have adapted the office to meet the nation's changing needs. The trend has been to expand presidential power. Some of this expansion has come from presidential actions under claims of inherent powers. Congress has also delegated a great deal of power to the executive branch, further expanding the role of the president.

Because the president is elected by the entire nation, he can claim to represent all citizens when proposing policy. This broad electoral base equips the presidency to be an institution of *majoritarian* democracy—compared with Congress's structural tendencies toward *pluralist* democracy. Whether the presidency actually operates in a majoritarian manner depends on several factors—the individual president's perception of public opinion on political issues, the relationship between public opinion and the president's political ideology, and the extent to which the president is committed to pursuing his values through his office.

The executive branch establishment has grown rapidly, and the White House has become a sizable bureaucracy. New responsibilities of the twentieth-century presidency are particularly noticeable in the area of legislative leadership. Now a president is expected to be a policy initiator for Congress, as well as a lobbyist who guides his bills through the legislative process.

The presidential "job description" for foreign policy has changed considerably. Post–World War II presidents had been preoccupied with containing the spread of communism, but with the collapse of communism in the Soviet Union and Eastern Europe, international economic relations now loom even larger as a priority for presidents. National security issues still remain, however, as regional conflicts can directly involve the interests of the United States.

KEY TERMS

veto
inherent powers
delegation of powers
mandate
divided control
   of government

Executive Office
   of the President
Cabinet
legislative liaison
   staff

SELECTED READINGS

Burke, John P., and Fred I. Greenstein. *How Presidents Test Reality.* New York: Russell Sage, 1989. A study of the way Eisenhower and Johnson considered intervening in Southeast Asia.

Edwards, George C. *At the Margins.* New Haven: Yale University Press, 1989. A systematic analysis of the impact of presidential leadership on congressional voting.

Jones, Charles O., ed. *The Reagan Legacy*. Chatham, N.J.: Chatham House, 1988. An excellent collection of essays that covers different aspects of the Reagan presidency.

Kernell, Samuel. *Going Public*. Washington, D.C.: Congressional Quarterly Press, 1986. A study of how modern presidents rely more and more on direct communication with the American people as a way of trying to expand their influence.

Lowi, Theodore J. *The Personal President*. Ithaca, N.Y.: Cornell University Press, 1985. In Lowi's eyes, the decline of our party system has helped give rise to a direct relationship between contemporary presidents and the people.

Neustadt, Richard E. *Presidential Power*. Rev. ed. New York: John Wiley, 1980. Neustadt's classic study examines the president's power to persuade.

Neustadt, Richard E., and Earnest R. May. *Thinking in Time*. New York: Free Press, 1986. Offers an analytical framework that presidents can use to try to minimize errors that lead to faulty decisions.

13 THE BUREAUCRACY

THE QUESTION WAS NOT whether Andres Serrano's photograph, *Piss Christ*, was art—some said it was; others said it was an obscenity. Rather the question was whether taxpayers' money should have been spent to support Serrano's work. (Serrano had been given a federal grant of $15,000 in 1987.)

The little-known Brooklyn artist had no inkling that his photograph of a thirteen-inch crucifix submerged in a small tank of his urine would ignite a firestorm of criticism and provoke a national debate over the role of the National Endowment for the Arts (NEA), a government agency that provides support for the arts. A lapsed Catholic who has explored a number of religious themes in his art, Serrano describes the picture as both a "comforting image" and as one that questions the "whole notion of what is acceptable and unacceptable."

When a Richmond, Virginia, art museum showed Serrano's photograph as part of an exhibition, a member of the American Family Association, a conservative advocacy group, sent a newspaper clipping about it to the group's head, the Reverend Donald Wildmon. Wildmon was incensed and sent a reproduction of the photo to every member of Congress. Republican Senator Alfonse D'Amato of New York indulged in some performance art of his own on the Senate floor, "ripping the Serrano catalogue, hurling it to the ground and stomping on it." Senator Jesse Helms of North Carolina, another Republican, quickly got to the heart of the matter: "He [Serrano] was trying to create indignation. That is all right for him to be a jerk, but let him be a jerk on his own time and with his own resources."

Helms struck a chord. Why was Serrano given a federal grant? Many hard-working taxpayers wondered why a portion of their federal income taxes was going to support art that satirizes the most sacred symbol of Christianity. The controversy over *Piss Christ* led to a broader examination of other grants by the NEA, such as an exhibit by photographer Robert Mapplethorpe that included pictures of men in homoerotic and sadomasochistic poses (see Chapter 15) and to performance artist Karen Finley, who as part of her act sometimes symbolically defiles her partially nude body by smearing chocolate all over it.

Inevitably, legislation was introduced to restrict NEA funding; there were even proposals to eliminate the agency. Critics charged that the NEA was out of control, that it was an all too typical case of a government bureaucracy doing whatever it wanted to do with little concern for what the public wanted.

A spirited counterattack was mounted on behalf of the NEA. Not surprisingly, much of this support came from artists, who would be most directly affected by restrictions on the NEA. They made a powerful argument that limiting NEA funding would constitute an assault on the freedom of artistic expression. The writer and humorist Garrison Keillor testified before a Senate subcommittee that "all governments have given medals to artists when they are old and saintly and successful and almost dead." What the NEA had been doing, however, was especially valuable because it encouraged "artists who are young and vital and unknown." (New artists who are at the cutting edge of their fields are likely to have

Your Tax Dollars at Work

Controversial performance artist Karen Finley has received grants from the National Endowment for the Arts in support of her work. Here she appears with her painting Holy Family on Acid.

a difficult time supporting themselves because their work can lack the commercial appeal of more established approaches.)

Congress responded to controversy as it usually does—with a compromise. Both the House and the Senate passed bills requiring artists to return their grants if they are convicted of obscenity. Congress left it to the courts, not the NEA, to determine if a work of art is obscene. Although obscenity convictions are hard to obtain, many people worry that the NEA may now be much more cautious about the kind of art it chooses to support with federal grants.[1]

The fight over the NEA illustrates the continuing tension between freedom and order in American society. Wildmon, Helms, and other critics of the NEA believed they were trying to preserve decency and religion in American life. On the other side were those who believed that what is best about America is our unswerving devotion to freedom, including freedom of expression. This episode also reflects the virtues and shortcomings of both the majoritarian and pluralist views of government. The artists who were clients of the NEA had considerable influence over its policymaking—some say too much—and the public was not well informed about this rather narrow area of federal activity. When people were aroused, it was by a few unrepresentative and sensationalistic pieces of art. Nevertheless, the opinions of ordinary citizens should not be discounted just because they have less sophisticated views of what constitutes art that is worth supporting.

Like the NEA, many government organizations are accused of being powers unto themselves, independent of democratic controls. In this chapter we try to determine who controls the bureaucracy in our government. We also analyze why people are so dissatisfied with bureaucracy and examine reforms that might make government work better.

Organization Matters

A nation's laws and policies are administered, or put into effect, by a variety of departments, agencies, bureaus, offices, and other government units, which together are known as its *bureaucracy*. **Bureaucracy** actually means any large, complex organization in which employees have very specific job responsibilities and work within a hierarchy of authority. The employees of these government units, who are quite knowledgeable within their narrow areas, have become known somewhat derisively as **bureaucrats.**

We study bureaucracies because they play a central role in the governments of postindustrial societies. Yet organizations are a crucial part of any society, no matter how elementary. A preindustral tribe, for example, is an organization. It has a clearly defined leader (a chief), senior policymakers (elders), a fixed division of labor (some hunt, some cook, some make tools), an organizational culture (religious practices, initiation rituals), and rules of behavior (what kind of property belongs to families and what belongs to the tribe). How that tribe is organized is not merely a quaint aspect of its evolution but is critical to the survival of its members.

The organization of modern governmental bureaucracies also reflects their need to survive. Preindustrial tribes often had to struggle to survive in hostile environments; the environment of modern bureaucracies, filled with conflicting polictical demands and the ever-present threat of budget cuts, can be no less hostile. The way government bureaucracies are organized also reflects the needs of their clients. The bottom line, though, is that the manner in which any bureaucracy is organized affects how well it is able to accomplish its tasks.

A recent study of America's schools vividly demonstrates the importance of organization. After studying a large number of high schools from

The Genius Was in the Logistics

The United States victory over Iraq in 1991 was not simply a military conquest; it was also a spectacular organizational achievement. The unsung heroes of the campaign were the men and women who equipped the different components of this extraordinarily complex operation and kept each supplied and functioning at all times.

around the country, two political scientists tried to determine what makes some high schools better than others. The achievement level of each school was measured by the test scores of its students. Since some high schools have students who are much better prepared than others, the authors had to base their conclusions on comparison between similar schools. In other words, schools in low-income neighborhoods with students who enter high school with average or below-average reading scores were compared to other similar schools, not to schools in wealthy suburban neigborhoods whose entering students have above-average reading scores. When similar schools were compared in terms of how much student performance improved, it was evident that the students in some schools achieved more. Why?

The authors' statistical tests led them to conclude that the difference in the performance of students attending similar schools is due to the way the schools are organized. And the largest influence on the effectiveness of a school's organization is its level of autonomy. Schools that have more control over hiring, curriculum, and discipline do better in terms of student achievement. This freedom seems to allow for strong leadership, which helps schools develop coherent goals and build staffs strongly supportive of those goals.[2]

Clearly, organization matters. The ways in which bureaucracies are structured to perform their work directly affect their ability to accomplish their tasks. Unfortunately, though, "if organization matters, it is also the case that there is no one best way of organizing."[3] Although greater autonomy may improve the performance of public schools, it may not be a good solution for improving other kinds of organizations. If a primary goal of a state social welfare agency, for example, is treating its clients equally, providing the same benefits to people with the same needs and circumstances, then giving local offices a lot of individual autonomy is not a good approach.

The Development of the Bureaucratic State

The study of bureaucracy, then, centers around finding solutions to the many different kinds of problems faced by large governmental organizations. A common complaint voiced by Americans is that the bureaucracy is too big and tries to accomplish too much. To the average citizen, the federal government may seem like an octopus—its long arms reach just about everywhere.

The Growth of American Government

American government seems to have grown without limit during this century. As one observer noted wryly, "The assistant administrator for water and hazardous materials of the Environmental Protection Agency presided over a staff larger than Washington's entire first administration."[4] Yet even during Washington's time, bureaucracies were necessary. No one argued then about the need for a postal service to deliver mail or a department of the treasury to maintain a system of currency. However, government at all levels (national, state, and local) has grown enormously in the twentieth century. There are a number of major reasons why our government has grown the way it has.

Science and technology. One reason government has grown so much is the increasing complexity of society. George Washington did not have an assistant administrator for water and hazardous materials because there was no need for one. A National Aeronautics and Space Administration (NASA) was not necessary until rockets were invented.

Even long-standing departments have had to expand the scope of their activities to keep up with technological and societal changes. Consider the changes brought about by genetic engineering, for example. The Patent Office in the U.S. Department of Commerce has had to respond to requests that new life forms be patented to protect manufacturers' interests. Under a new policy, the creators of new animals—like the geep, a species derived from the fusion of goat and sheep embryos—must receive royalties for each animal raised by a farmer.[5]

Business regulation. Another reason government has grown is that the public's attitude toward business has changed. Throughout most of the nineteenth century, there was little or no government regulation of business. Business was generally autonomous, and any government intervention in the economy that might limit that autonomy was considered inappropriate. This attitude began to change toward the end of the nineteenth century, as more Americans became aware that the end product of this laissez-faire approach was not always highly competitive markets that benefited consumers. Instead, business sometimes formed oligopolies like the infamous "sugar trust," a small group of companies that controlled virtually the entire sugar market.

Gradually, government intervention came to be accepted as necessary to protect the integrity of business markets. And if government was to police unfair business practices effectively, it needed administrative agencies. Over the course of the twentieth century, new bureaucracies were organized to regulate specific industries. Among them are the Securities and Exchange Commission (SEC), which oversees securities trading; the Food and Drug Administration (FDA), which tries to protect consumers from unsafe food, drugs, and cosmetics; and the Federal Communications Commission (FCC), which, as we discussed in Chapter 6, oversees the television, radio, and telephone industries.

Through bureaucracies like these, government has become a referee in the marketplace, developing standards of fair trade, setting rates, and licensing individual businesses for operation. As new problem areas have emerged, government has added new agencies, further expanding the scope of its activities. During the 1960s, for instance, the public became aware that certain design flaws in automobiles made them unnecessarily unsafe. For example, sharp, protruding dashboard knobs caused a car's own interior to be dangerous on impact. Congress responded to public demands for change by creating the National Highway Traffic Safety Administration in 1966.* As we discuss later in this chapter, however,

---

* It originally was called the National Safety Agency.

there has been significant movement in recent years toward lessening the government's role in the marketplace.

Social welfare. General attitudes about government's responsibilities in the area of social welfare have changed too. An enduring part of American culture has been a belief in self-reliance. People are expected to overcome adversity on their own, to succeed on the basis of their own skills and efforts. In years past, those who could not take care of themselves had to hope that their families or primitive local programs would help them.

People in this country were slow to accept government in the role of "brother's keeper." Only in the wake of the Great Depression did the national government begin to take steps to provide income security. In 1935, the Social Security Act became law, creating the social security fund that workers pay into, then collect income from during old age. A small part of that act was a provision for impoverished families, which evolved into Aid to Families with Dependent Children (AFDC), the nation's basic welfare program (see Chapter 19).

A belief in progress. A larger, stronger central government can also be traced to Americans' firm belief in the idea of progress. Another thread that runs through the fabric of American culture is faith in our ability to solve problems. No problem is too big or too complicated. This attitude was typified by President John F. Kennedy's commitment in

NASA in Good Times and Bad Times

For many years, NASA was a highly respected government agency, an embodiment of the "can do" spirit of America. The moon landing in 1969 fulfilled President John F. Kennedy's commitment to put a man on the moon before the decade was out. But in January 1986, the space shuttle Challenger *exploded, killing all seven crew members. The Rogers Commission, charged with investigating the tragedy, uncovered serious flaws in NASA's management practices, staining the agency's image.*

1961 to put a man on the moon by 1970. As difficult as the task seemed when he made the pledge, a man walked on the moon on July 20, 1969. This same spirit leads politicians to declare war on poverty or war on cancer through massive programs of coordinated, well-funded activities. Many people believe that the private sector cannot undertake large-scale programs, that government must be responsible for them. For example, when AIDS emerged as an epidemic, there was no question that it was the government's responsibility to solve the problem through its own research and the support of scientists outside of government.

Ambitious administrators.   Finally, government has grown because agency officials have expanded their organizations and staffs to take on added responsibilities. Imaginative, ambitious agency administrators look for ways to serve their clients. Each new program that is developed leads to new authority. Larger budgets and staffs, in turn, are necessary to support that authority. When, for example, the collapse of communism in the Soviet bloc threatened the budgets of the defense and security bureaucracies, the Department of Defense started to think about taking on research tasks relating to serious worldwide environmental problems.[6] The CIA, which had previously resisted efforts to join the fight against drugs, changed its mind and announced that "narcotics is a new priority."[7] Faced with the choice between smaller budgets or an expanded mission, in both cases agency administrators chose the expanded mission.

Can We Reduce the Size of Government?

When Ronald Reagan campaigned for the presidency in 1980, he promised to cut bureaucracies, which he said were wasteful, and to get government "off the back" of the American people. Reagan was preaching the traditional conservative Republican sermon: Government is too big; it's the Democrats' fault because they've started too many programs; only Republicans are committed to shrinking the government. As Figure 13.1 shows, however, Reagan expanded government (as measured by the federal work force) at a greater rate than his liberal predecessor, Jimmy Carter. Although Reagan was very successful in influencing spending priorities and reducing some agencies in scope, he actually made big government even bigger.

Presidents and members of Congress face a tough job when they try to reduce the size of the bureaucracy. Each government agency performs a service of value to some sector of society. As a group, for example, bankers favor laissez-faire capitalism, the principles of a free market, and minimal government intervention. Few bankers voiced those principles, however, when the savings and loan industry collapsed in the late 1980s. A noninterventionist government could have stood by and done nothing, but inaction would have had a disastrous effect on the U.S. financial system, and free market economics looked like a very unattractive option. Far more appealing to bankers was a rescue effort by government. To apply the medicine to the sick patient, a new bureaucracy, the Resolution Trust Corporation, was created. Big government got even bigger.

FIGURE 13.1   *Conservatives Battle Big Government, Big Government Wins*

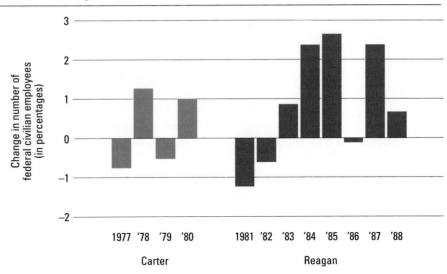

According to U.S. Census Bureau statistics, despite Ronald Reagan's vow to shrink the government, the number of bureaucrats working for the national government grew significantly during his time in office. Surprisingly, the rate of increase was greater under Reagan than under the Democratic administration that preceded him. (Source: "A Dubious Reagan Achievement," New York Times, 4 January 1990, p. A22. Copyright © 1990 by The New York Times Company. Reprinted by permission.)

Bankers are not the only group that wants to be protected by the national government. Farmers need the price supports of the U.S. Department of Agriculture. Builders profit from programs offered by the U.S. Department of Housing and Urban Development (HUD). And labor unions want a vigorous Occupational Safety and Health Administration (OSHA). Efforts to cut an agency's scope, then, are almost always resisted by interest groups that have a stake in the agency.

The American public says it wants spending restrained and government cut back. Yet when asked about specific programs or functions of government, citizens tend to be highly supportive of the activities of government. As Figure 13.2 shows, there is considerable public support for very expensive government endeavors, including guaranteeing a job for all who want one. There is no such program now, and such an effort would be a significant expansion of government's reach into the economy.

Despite their political support, agencies are not immune to change. It is rare for a department or agency to be completely abolished; however, it is not uncommon for one to undergo a major reorganization, in which programs are consolidated and the size and scope of activities are reduced.[8] Programs can lose support if they are perceived to be working poorly. And as funds are cut, bureaucratic positions are eliminated.

The tendency for big government to endure reflects the tension between majoritarianism and pluralism. Even when the public wants a smaller national government, that sentiment can be undermined by the strong preferences of different segments of society for government to perform some valuable function for them. Lobbies that represent these segments work strenuously to convince Congress and the administration that their agency's particular part of the budget is vital and that any cuts ought to come out of some other agency's hide. At the same time, that other agency is also working to protect itself and to garner support.

FIGURE **13.2** *Is Government Too Big?*

Americans are critical of government, believing that it tries to do too much, has become too powerful, and wastes a lot of money. When asked about specific programs, however, they tend to be much more supportive of what government is doing. (Source: Adapted from a November 1987 New York Times/ CBS News poll. Cited in Gary C. Jacobson, "Meager Patrimony," Looking Back on the Reagan Presidency, ed. Larry Berman [Baltimore: Johns Hopkins University Press, 1990], p. 307. Used by permission.)

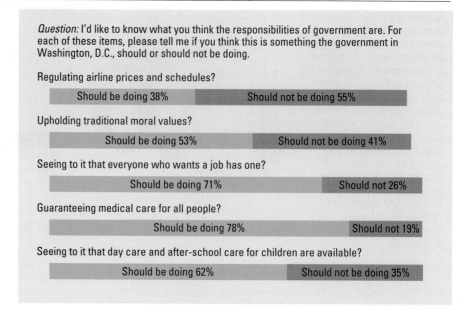

Question: I'd like to know what you think the responsibilities of government are. For each of these items, please tell me if you think this is something the government in Washington, D.C., should or should not be doing.

Regulating airline prices and schedules?
Should be doing 38% Should not be doing 55%

Upholding traditional moral values?
Should be doing 53% Should not be doing 41%

Seeing to it that everyone who wants a job has one?
Should be doing 71% Should not 26%

Guaranteeing medical care for all people?
Should be doing 78% Should not 19%

Seeing to it that day care and after-school care for children are available?
Should be doing 62% Should not be doing 35%

Bureaus and Bureaucrats

We often think of the bureaucracy as a huge monolith. In reality, the bureaucracy in Washington is a disjointed collection of departments, agencies, bureaus, offices, and commissions—each a bureaucracy in its own right.

The Organization of Government

By examining the basic types of government organizations, we can better understand how the executive branch operates. In our discussion, we pay particular attention to the relative degree of independence of these organizations and their relationship to the White House.

Departments. **Departments** are the largest units of the executive branch, covering broad areas of government responsibility. As noted in Chapter 12, the secretaries (heads) of these departments, along with a few other key officials, form the president's Cabinet. The current Cabinet departments are State, Treasury, Defense, Interior, Agriculture, Justice, Commerce, Labor, Health and Human Services, Housing and Urban Development, Transportation, Energy, Education, and Veterans Affairs. Each of these massive organizations is broken down into subsidiary agencies, bureaus, offices, and services (see Figure 13.3).

Independent agencies. Within the executive branch, there are also many **independent agencies,** agencies that are not a part of any Cabinet department. Instead, they stand alone and are controlled in varying degrees by the president. Some, among them the Central Intelligence

F I G U R E 13.3 *The U.S. Department of Health and Human Services: An Organization Chart*

The Department of Health and Human Services is made up of many agencies and offices. (Source: U.S. Department of Health and Human Services, 1986.)

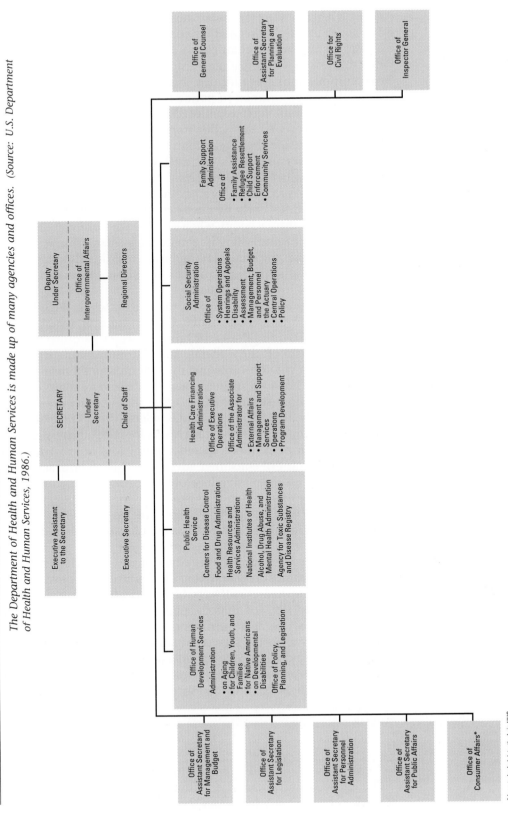

Agency (CIA), are directly under the president's control. Others, like the FCC, are structured as **regulatory commissions.** Each commission is run by a small number of commissioners (usually an odd number, which helps to prevent tie votes), appointed to fixed terms by the president. Some commissions were formed to guard against unfair business practices. Others were formed to police the side effects, or *externalities*, of business operations, such as polluted air emitted by a factory. Still others were formed to protect the public from unsafe products. Regulatory commissions are outside the direct control of the White House, so they are freer from the pressures of the political process and the partisan considerations that influence other agencies.

Still, regulatory commissions are not immune to political pressure. They are lobbied fervently by client groups and must take the demands of those groups into account when they make policy. If the Consumer Product Safety Commission is considering safety standards for chain saws, for example, the chain saw industry will do all it can to convince the agency either not to set standards or to issue them in a form the industry considers least objectionable.

The president exerts influence on these agencies through his power to appoint new commissioners when terms expire or when resignations create openings. During President Jimmy Carter's administration, his appointed chairman of the Federal Trade Commission (FTC), Michael Pertschuk, led a vigorous proconsumer commission. During the Reagan administration, however, things changed. Reagan's appointed chairman, free-market economist James Miller, gave the Reagan forces a numerical advantage on the five-member board. Under Miller's leadership, the FTC reversed its policy of industrywide checks for false advertising in favor of investigations in response to specific complaints filed with the agency. From the viewpoint of consumer advocates, this reversal meant that the FTC would be less aggressive in protecting Americans from false advertising. From the standpoint of business, it meant that the FTC would stop its "fishing expeditions."[9] Whatever the point of view, it's clear that a significant policy shift occurred as a direct result of presidential power.

Government corporations.   Finally, Congress has also created a small number of **government corporations**. The services these executive branch agencies perform theoretically could be provided by the private sector, but Congress has decided that the public would be better served if they have some link with the government. For example, the national government maintains a postal service because it feels that Americans need low-cost, door-to-door service for all kinds of mail, not just for mail on profitable routes or mail that requires special services. In some instances, there is not enough of a financial incentive for the private sector to provide an essential service. This is the case with the financially troubled Amtrak train line.[10]

The Civil Service

The national bureaucracy is staffed by around 3 million civilian employees, who account for about 2.5 percent of the U.S. work force.[11] Americans have a tendency to stereotype all government workers as face-

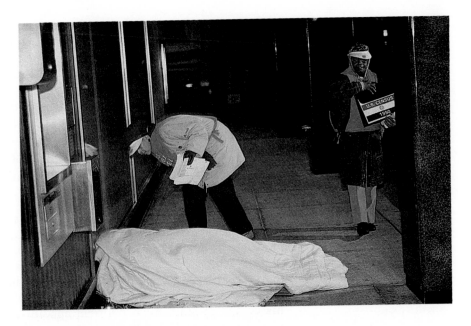

Anybody Home?

Census workers called enu-merators try to find people who did not receive a census questionnaire through the mail. During the 1990 census, big-city mayors pressured the Census Bureau to locate and count the homeless. Because the funds for many national grants-in-aid programs are based on per-capita formulas, an undercount of a city's homeless population could lessen the amount of federal aid the city receives.

less paper pushers, but the work force is actually quite diverse. Government workers include forest rangers, FBI agents, typists, foreign service officers, computer programmers, policy analysts, public relations specialists, security guards, librarians, administrators, engineers, plumbers, and people from literally hundreds of other occupations.

An important feature of the national bureaucracy is that most of its workers are hired under the requirements of the **civil service**. The civil service was created after the assassination of President James Garfield, who was killed by an unbalanced and dejected job seeker. Congress responded by passing the Pendleton Act (1883), which established the Civil Service Commission (now the Office of Personnel Management). The objective of the act was to reduce *patronage*—the practice of filling government positions with the president's political allies or cronies. The civil service fills jobs on the basis of merit and sees to it that workers are not fired for political reasons. Over the years, job qualifications and selection procedures have been developed for most government positions.

About 88 percent of the national government's workers are employed outside of Washington.[12] One reason for this decentralization is to make government offices accessible to the people they serve. The Social Security Administration, for example, has to have offices within a reasonable distance of most Americans, so that its many clients have somewhere to take their questions, problems, and paperwork. Decentralization is also a way to distribute jobs and income across the country. The government's Centers for Disease Control could easily have been located in Washington, but it is in Atlanta instead. Likewise, NASA's headquarters for space flights is located in Houston. Members of Congress, of course, are only too happy to place some of the "pork barrel" back home, so that their constituents will credit them with the jobs and money that government installations create.

Given the enormous variety of government jobs, it is no surprise that employees come from all walks of life. Studies of the social composition of the civil service as a whole indicate that it mirrors the American population on such important characteristics as father's occupation and worker's education, income, and age.[13] There is also substantial representation of minorities (27 percent) within the federal government's work force. However, at the highest-level policymaking positions, minorities are woefully underrepresented, and in recent years there has been little progress in placing more blacks, Hispanics, and other minorities into top career positions in the government.[14]

Presidential Control over the Bureaucracy

Civil service and other reforms have effectively insulated the vast majority of government workers from party politics. An incoming president can appoint fewer than 1 percent of all executive branch employees. Still, presidential appointees fill the top policymaking positions in government. Each new president, then, establishes an extensive personnel review process to find appointees who are both politically compatible and qualified in their field. Although the president selects some people from his campaign staff, most political appointees have not been campaign workers. Instead, Cabinet secretaries, assistant secretaries, agency heads, and the like tend to be drawn directly from business, universities, and government itself.

Because so few of their own people are in each department and agency, presidents often believe that they do not have enough control over the bureaucracy. Republican presidents have also worried that the civil service would be hostile to their objectives because they assumed that career bureaucrats have a liberal Democratic bias. Yet surveys of political appointees show that both Democratic and Republican appointees work well with career bureaucrats, developing a healthy respect for their ability and professionalism.[15]

Nevertheless, the White House wants greater control over the bureaucracy, and there have been repeated efforts by recent presidents to centralize power by tightening the reins over the rest of the executive branch. During his term in office, Ronald Reagan and his White House staff were very effective at gaining greater control over the bureaucracy.[16] Through a couple of key strategies, the Reagan White House was able to infuse the bureaucracy with greater ideological direction. First, the administration required that all major regulations formulated by executive branch departments and agencies be approved by the Office of Management and Budget (OMB), which is part of the White House. OMB used its authority to push the bureaucracy to develop policies more closely in line with the president's strong conservative principles.[17] (The Bush administration, which isn't as conservative on domestic policy, has placed less emphasis on OMB control of the bureaucracy and instead has tried to be more efficient and flexible in its review of proposed regulations.[18])

The Reagan administration also made a greater effort to ensure that its top appointees were steadfast in their support of the president's program. As Figure 13.4 shows, President Reagan's appointments were far more partisan in nature than either of his immediate Republican predecessors, Richard Nixon or Gerald Ford. All presidents lean strongly toward members of their own party when they choose the top officials of the various

FIGURE 13.4 *Republicans Tighten Control*

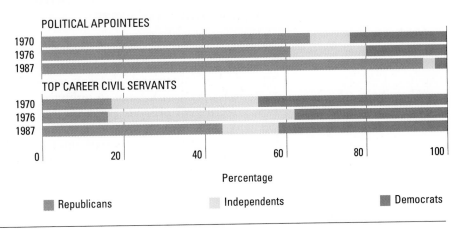

The Reagan administration proved to be much more intent on placing Republicans in control of the bureaucracy than previous Republican administrations. In addition to making its own political appointees, the administration took advantage of changes in the civil service law that gave it some choice over which civil servants to place in top positions. (Source: Joel D. Aberbach and Bert A. Rockman with Robert M. Copeland, "From Nixon's Problem to Reagan's Achievement," in Looking Back on the Reagan Presidency, ed. Larry Berman [Baltimore: Johns Hopkins University Press, 1990], p. 180. Used by permission.)

agencies and departments, but earlier presidents had been more willing to appoint people they thought were outstanding even though they weren't members of their party. The Reagan White House also made use of the 1978 Civil Service Reform Act, which gave the president more flexibility in choosing which career bureaucrats to appoint to the highest-level civil service positions in the government. As also demonstrated in Figure 13.4, these members of the Senior Executive Service were more likely to be Republicans than the top career civil servants during earlier Republican administrations.[19]

Reagan instituted these changes because he, like all presidents, felt he could not get the bureaucracy to move in the direction he wanted. All presidents would like to be able to appoint more of their own people to the bureaucracy, filling agencies and departments with people who will act quickly to institute administration policy. On the surface, it makes sense that increasing the number of political appointees in the bureaucracy would make the bureaucracy more responsive to the president. But caution is warranted here. More political appointees may actually make the bureaucracy more "bureaucratic." As one scholar noted, "The more layers, the more time it takes to forge positive relationships" between senior civil servants and presidential appointees.[20]

Those who believe that presidents should be able to make more political appointments to staff the national government argue that presidents might be able to fulfill more of their campaign promises if they had greater control over the bureaucracy. But others point out the value of a stable, experienced work force that implements policy in a consistent fashion. There is also legitimate concern about the presidency becoming too powerful. Congress might try to exert control over a stronger presidency by placing more restraints on the independence of agencies and departments.[21] And despite the frustration of recent presidents with the bureaucracy, presidents are hardly helpless, pitiful giants. They can have a substantial impact on agencies, as Reagan's appointment of James Miller to the FTC shows.

Administrative Policymaking: The Formal Processes

The sprawling diversity of the executive branch leaves many Americans with the impression that the bureaucracies of the national government are complex, impenetrable organizations. Bureaucratic actions and policies often appear irrational to ordinary citizens, who know little about how government officials reach their decisions. Many Americans wonder why agencies sometimes actually *make* policy rather than merely carry it out. Administrative agencies are, in fact, authoritative policymaking bodies, and their decisions on substantive issues are legally binding on the citizens of this country.

Administrative Discretion

What are executive agencies set up to do? First, Cabinet departments, independent agencies, and government corporations are creatures of Congress. Congress creates a new department or agency by passing a law that describes each organization's *mandate*, or mission. As part of that mandate, Congress grants to the agency the authority to make certain policy decisions. Congress long ago recognized that it has neither the time nor the expertise in highly technical areas to make all policy decisions. Ideally, it sets general guidelines for policy, and agencies are expected to act within those guidelines. The latitude that Congress gives agencies to make policy in the spirit of their legislative mandate is called **administrative discretion**.

In 1990, the Department of Education used its discretionary authority to issue a ruling that colleges could not use general operating funds for scholarship aid to minorities. Only money donated to a college for that purpose or governmental grants specifically designated for minorities could be used for such scholarships according to the new ruling. This controversial decision was made by a Bush administration political appointee who felt that it was in line with the White House's general policy views on civil rights.[22] Congress had not instructed the Department of Education to make a new policy decision on this matter. Rather, this official acted under a general grant of discretionary authority given to the department so that it can make specific decisions as it tries to implement the broader policies articulated in legislation. (Controversy over the decision prompted a promise from Lamar Alexander, the new secretary of education, to review this policy.)

Critics of bureaucracy frequently complain that agencies are granted too much discretion. In his book *The End of Liberalism*, Theodore Lowi argues that Congress commonly gives vague directives in its initial enabling legislation, instead of truly setting guidelines.[23] Agencies are charged with protecting the "public interest" but are left to determine on their own what policies best serve the public. Lowi and other critics believe that members of Congress assign too much of their responsibility for difficult policy choices to appointed administrators.

Congress *is* often vague about its intent when setting up a new agency or program. At times a problem is clear-cut, but the solution is not; yet Congress is under pressure to act. So it creates an agency or program to show that it is concerned and responsive, and leaves it to administrators to develop specific solutions. For example, the enabling legislation in 1934 that established the FCC recognized a need for regulation in the burgeoning radio industry. The growing number of stations and overlapping frequencies would soon have made it impossible to listen to the radio. But Congress avoided tackling several sticky issues by leaving the FCC with the ambiguous directive that broadcasters should "serve the public interest, convenience, and necessity."[24] In other cases, a number of "obvious" solutions to a problem may be available, but lawmakers cannot agree on which one is best. Compromise wording is thus often ambiguous, papering over differences and assuring conflict over the administrative regulations that try to settle the lingering policy disputes.

For Tomorrow's Assignment . . .

Congress is often accused of being rather lax in its oversight of the executive branch. Most bureaucrats would probably not agree. Here Secretary of Defense Richard Cheney stands next to some of the documents his department was asked to give Congress during budget preparations. Cheney hoped to indicate the need for streamlined procedures at the Pentagon.

The wide latitude Congress gives bureaucratic agencies often leads to charges that government is out of control, a power unto itself. But these claims are frequently exaggerated. Administrative discretion is not a fixed commodity. Congress does have the power to express its displeasure by reining agencies in with additional legislation. If Congress is unhappy with an agency's actions, it can pass laws invalidating specific policies. This method of control may seem cumbersome, but Congress does have periodic opportunities to amend the original legislation that created an agency or program. Over time, Congress makes increasingly detailed policy decisions, often affirming or modifying agency decisions.[25]

Informal contacts with members of Congress also influence administrators. Through these communications, legislators can clarify exactly which actions they want administrators to take. And administrators listen because they are wary of offending members of the committees and subcommittees that oversee their programs and, particularly, their budgets. In addition to getting a better idea of congressional intent, contacts with legislators allow administrators to explain the problems their agencies are facing, justify their decisions, and negotiate compromises on unresolved issues.

In general, then, the bureaucracy is not out of control. But there is one area in which Congress has chosen to limit its oversight—that of domestic and international security. Both the FBI and CIA have had a great deal of freedom from formal and informal congressional constraints because of the legitimate need for secrecy in their operations. (For an example of how security needs were met in communist East Germany, see Compared with What? 13.1.) During the years that the legendary J. Edgar

The Man with the Secrets

Even presidents were afraid of what FBI Director J. Edgar Hoover had in his files. Although the Nixon administration wasn't fond of him, Hoover let it know that if its criticism of his agency didn't stop, he would testify before Congress about some wiretapping done by a secret White House investigation unit. Hoover remained secure in his job. The White House wiretapping was later revealed as part of the Watergate scandal.

COMPARED WITH WHAT?   13.1

No Tears for the Staatsicherheit

Every society needs to maintain order, but in many countries of the world, the bureaucratic apparatus designed to maintain order is really a mechanism for ensuring the survival of an autocratic regime. Nowhere was this more vividly illustrated than in the former communist regimes in Eastern Europe. The state security agencies there were instruments of terror, enforcing control by making any kind of opposition to these governments extremely dangerous.

The East German secret police, the Staatsicherheit (or Stasi), was an enormous bureaucracy that reached into every part of that society. It had 85,000 full-time employees, including 6,000 people whose sole task was to listen in on phone conversations. Another 2,000 steamed open mail, read it, resealed the letters, and then sent them on to the intended recipients. The Stasi also employed 150,000 active informers and hundreds of thousands part-time snitches. Files were kept on an estimated 4 to 5 million people in a country that had a total population, including children, of just 17 million. And although there was a large standing army in East Germany, the Stasi kept its own arsenal of 250,000 weapons.

The Stasi infiltrated the top echelons of government, business, and universities in East Germany, placing 2,000 of its agents in positions of importance in these institutions. The Stasi's primary job was to make East Germans too scared to threaten the communist dictatorship that ran the country. Eventually, of course, the East German government did fall as a largely peaceful revolution swept through the eastern bloc countries. After a democratic transition government was installed, angry East Germans ransacked the Stasi building, piling up old uniforms that would later be sold and smashing glass and office equipment. Protestors said that they were worried that the Stasi was trying to find a role for itself in the new government.

It is understandable that East Germans were appalled at the idea of a secret police in a unified, democratic Germany. But democracies do have legitimate security needs, and these interests require that the bureaucracies in charge of security be allowed to operate largely in private. The United States has a sizable internal security establishment, including the FBI and the Secret Service. As the treatment of Martin Luther King, Jr., by the FBI demonstrates, however, the internal security bureaucracies of this country have at times acted in a highly irresponsible manner. A society's need for police powers to help it maintain order must be balanced by mechanisms of accountability. As Feature 13.1 suggests, accountability in a democracy should involve some elected representatives being fully informed of all the major activities of the state's secret police.

Sources: Steven Emerson, "Keeping Watch on the Stasi Machine," *San Francisco Chronicle*, 15 August 1990, p. Br.1; Serge Schemann, "East Berlin Faults Opposition on Raid," *New York Times*, 17 January 1990, p. A9; and Craig R. Whitney, "East Europeans Are Making Big Brother Smaller," *New York Times*, 22 January 1991, p. A1.

Hoover ran the FBI (1924–1972), it was something of a rogue elephant, independent of both Congress and presidents. Politicians were afraid of Hoover, who was not above keeping files on them and using those files to increase his power. At Hoover's direction, for example, the FBI spied on Martin Luther King, Jr., and once sent King a tape recording with embarrassing revelations gathered from bugging his hotel rooms. The anonymous letter accompanying the tape suggested that King save himself further embarrassment by committing suicide.[26]

Over the years, the CIA has also abused its need for privacy by engaging in covert operations that should never have been carried out. Congress, however, has increased its oversight over the agency and has passed legislation designed to force the administration to share more information with it. Still, members of Congress complain that they are often misled by the CIA and administration officials. Said one representative, "They treat us like mushrooms. Keep us in the dark and feed us a lot of manure" (see Feature 13.1).[27]

Rule Making

The policymaking discretion that Congress gives to agencies is exercised through formal administrative procedures, usually either *rule making* or *adjudication*. **Rule making** is the administrative process that results in regulations. **Regulations,** in turn, are rules that govern the operation of government programs. When the FCC develops policies it feels are needed to serve the public interest, it uses its broad discretionary authority to promulgate those policies in the form of regulations.

Because they are authorized by congressional statutes, regulations have the effect of law. In theory, the policy content of regulations follows from the intent of enabling legislation. As already noted, however, Congress does not always express its intent clearly. The administrative discretion available to agencies often produces political conflict when regulations are in the process of being made. A case in point is the effort of the Environmental Protection Agency (EPA) to regulate pollution from incinerators. Environmental lobbies had pushed the EPA to include in its regulations a mandatory recycling provision for incinerator operators. By recycling some of the garbage instead of incinerating it, there would be less air pollution because of a smaller volume of burning.

When agencies issue regulations, they are first published as proposals so that all interested parties have an opportunity to comment on them and to try to persuade the agency to make them final, alter them, or withdraw them. When the EPA issued its incinerator proposal in 1989, environmentalists were pleased to see that it required incinerator operators to recycle a quarter of their incoming garbage. A White House committee on competitiveness, however, disliked this component of the regulations because it placed financial burdens on the solid waste management industry. The White House forced the EPA to retreat and drop the recycling provision, though the other pollution-control provisions were finalized.[28]

The regulatory process is controversial because regulations require individuals and corporations to act in prescribed ways, often against their own self-interest. In this case both environmental groups and the waste management industry believed that they knew what was truly in the public interest. Government, however, must balance society's need for clean air with the need of industry to make a profit. When the EPA

FEATURE 13.1   *Casey's CIA: Out of Control*

In 1984, CIA Director William J. Casey decided that the United States had to do the unthinkable: assassinate Middle Eastern terrorists before they could harm Americans. Although President Reagan told Casey to clear his plan with a small group of congressional leaders, Casey set up the plan to avoid congressional oversight. He persuaded the Saudi Arabian government to fund and take operational control of the covert operations, enabling him to deny to Congress that the CIA had anything to do with any assassinations that took place.

The first covert operation was the attempted assassination of a terrorist named Sheikh Fadlallah. Fadlallah was head of Hizbollah, the Party of God, which had been connected with bombings of American facilities in Beirut. The Saudis hired an Englishman who had experience with the British Special Air Services, a commando unit, to take control of the operation. The intelligence service of the Lebanese government provided him with men to drive a car packed with explosives to Fadlallah's home in a Beirut suburb. On March 8, 1985, the car was left fifty yards from Fadlallah's residence and the explosives detonated. Fadlallah wasn't hurt by the massive explosion, but eighty innocent people were killed and two hundred others were wounded. Fadlallah's followers assumed that the bomb was sent by the CIA, but Congress had no evidence one way or the other because, as Casey's biographer noted, "Casey had flatly refused to tell the committees about this sensitive work."

Source: Adapted from Bob Woodward, *Veil* (New York: Simon & Schuster, 1987), pp. 393–397. Copyright © 1987 by Robert Woodward. Reprinted by permission of Simon & Schuster, Inc.

writes regulations that specify the details of that balance, it becomes the object of criticism from both those who would like government to do more and from those who would like it to do less. The EPA is in many ways taking the "heat" for Congress, because Congress has the ultimate responsibility for pollution policy—a responsibility it has delegated in part to the EPA.

Adjudication

Rule making is a quasi-legislative process because it develops *general* rules, just as Congress does when it passes a law. **Adjudication** is a quasi-judicial process; it is used to resolve *individual* conflicts, much as trials are used in a court of law. Adjudicatory proceedings in an agency determine whether a person or business is failing to comply with the law or with agency rules.

Congress delegates adjudicatory authority to certain agencies because it anticipates conflicts over the interpretation of laws and regulations and because it does not have the time to settle all the fine points of law when it writes statutes. The National Labor Relations Board (NLRB), which acts as a mediator in business-labor disputes, is an example of an agency that relies heavily on adjudication.

Adjudicatory decisions are made by administrative law judges, who are technically their agencies' employees. Yet they are strictly independent; they cannot be removed except for gross misconduct. Adjudicatory proceedings allow each party to present its side of the case and allow the judge to search for any information that will be helpful in reaching a decision. Somewhat less formal than a court trial, the proceedings are still adversarial in nature. In NLRB cases, the party that loses may appeal to the board, which has set up three-member panels to review decisions.[29]

Administrative Policymaking: Informal Politics

When a new regulation is being considered and the evidence and arguments on all sides have been presented, how does an administrator reach a decision? Few important policy decisions can be calculated with the efficiency of a computer solving mathematical problems. Instead, policy decisions emerge from the weighing and judging of complex problems that often have no single satisfactory solution.

The Science of Muddling Through

Administrative decisions are subject to many influences and constraints. In a classic analysis of policymaking, "The Science of Muddling Through," Charles Lindblom compared the way policy ideally should be made with the way it is formulated in the real world.[30] The ideal "rational" decision-making process, according to Lindblom, begins with an administrator tackling a problem by ranking values and objectives. After the objectives are clarified, all possible solutions to the problem are given thorough consideration. Alternative solutions are analyzed comprehensively, taking all relevant factors into account. Finally, the alternative that is seen as the most effective means of achieving the desired goal and solving the problem is chosen.

Lindblom claimed that this "rational-comprehensive" model is unrealistic. To begin with, policymakers have great difficulty defining precise values and goals. Administrators at the U.S. Department of Energy, for example, want to be sure that supplies of home heating oil are sufficient each winter. At the same time, they want to reduce dependence on foreign oil. Obviously, these two goals are not fully compatible. How do administrators decide which is more important? And how do they relate them to the other goals of the nation's energy policy?

Real-world decision making parts company with the ideal in another way: The policy selected cannot always be the most effective means to the desired end. Even if a tax at the pump is the most effective way of reducing gasoline consumption during a shortage, motorists' anger would make this theoretically "right" decision politically difficult. So the "best" policy is often the one on which most people can agree. However, political compromise may mean that the government is able to solve only part of a problem.

A final point critics of the rational-comprehensive model raise is that policymaking can never be based on truly comprehensive analysis. A secretary of energy could not possibly find the time to read a comprehensive study of all alternative energy sources and relevant policy considerations for the next two decades. A truly thorough investigation of the subject would produce thousands of pages of text. Instead, administrators usually rely on short staff memos outlining a limited range of feasible solutions for immediate problems. Time is of the essence, and problems often are too pressing to wait for a complete study.

In short, policymaking tends to be *incremental*, with policies and programs changing bit by bit, step by step. Decision makers are constrained by competing policy objectives, opposing political forces, incomplete information, and the pressures of time. They choose from a limited number of feasible options that are almost always modifications of existing policies rather than wholesale departures from those policies.

The Culture of Bureaucracy

How an organization makes decisions and performs its tasks is greatly affected by the people who work there—the bureaucrats. Americans often find that their interactions with bureaucrats are frustrating because bureaucrats are inflexible ("go by the book") or lack the authority to get things done. Top administrators can also become frustrated with the bureaucrats who work for them.

Why do people act "bureaucratically"? Individuals who work for large organizations cannot help but be affected by the "culture of bureaucracy," even in their everyday speech (see Feature 13.2). Modern bureaucracies develop explicit rules and standards in order to make operations more efficient and treat their clients fairly. But within each organization, *norms* (informal, unwritten rules of behavior) also develop and influence the way people act on the job. The Veterans Administration (VA), for example, for many years had an official rule that medical care was to be provided only to veterans in need of hospitalization; more routine treatment was to be left to private physicians. Doctors working for the VA thought this rule was irrational, and among them a norm developed whereby they would provide routine care under the guise that it was needed before hospital admission.[31]

Bureaucracies are often influenced in their selection of policy options by the prevailing customs, attitudes, and expectations of the people working within them. Departments and agencies commonly develop a

---

F E A T U R E   13.2   *Praise the Lord and Pass the Projectiles*

One rather maddening characteristic of bureaucracies is their reliance on jargon, the specialized language that people in an organization or vocation develop over time. The use of jargon is not restricted to government, but government bureaucrats seem to excel at using bizarre terminology.

Why does jargon rear its ugly head in organizations? One reason is that some people assume that jargon is a sign of professionalism and that using specialized terms reflects a command of their subject. Another reason is the decline of writing skills. It's much easier to write several long, complex, jargon-laden sentences than it is to write one that is short and crystal clear.

Although the use of jargon is ubiquitous throughout government, nowhere is it worse than in the Department of Defense. There's no close second; the military has debased the English language in ways that seem unimaginable. Some samples of Pentagonese:

Pentagonese	*English*
Frame-supported tension structure	Tent
Aerodynamic personnel decelerator	Parachute
Interlocking slide fastener	Zipper
Projectile	Bullet
Hexiform rotatable surface compressor unit	Nut
Universal obscurant	Smoke
The missile impacted with the ground prematurely.	The missile crashed.
A forcible ejection of the internal bomb components	The bomb blew up.
Ambient noncombatant personnel	Refugees
Pre-dawn vertical insertion	Invasion

Source: William Lutz, *Doublespeak* (New York: Harper and Row, 1989), as excerpted in William Lutz, "No Ordinary Nut," *Common Cause Magazine*, January/February 1990, pp. 34–35. Copyright © 1989 by William Lutz. Reprinted by permission of HarperCollins Publishers Inc.

sense of mission where a particular objective or a means for achieving it is emphasized. The Army Corps of Engineers, for example, is dominated by engineers who define the bureaucracy's objective as protecting citizens from floods by means of building dams. Certainly there could be other objectives, and certainly there are other methods of achieving this one, but the engineers promote the solutions that fit their conception of what the agency should be doing. As one study concluded, "When asked to generate policy proposals for review by their political superiors, bureaucrats are tempted to bias the search for alternatives so that their superiors wind up selecting the kind of program the agency wants to pursue."[32]

At first glance, bureaucrats seem to be completely negative sorts of creatures. They do have their positive side, however. Those agencies with a clear sense of mission are likely to have a strong *esprit de corps* that adds to the bureaucrats' motivation. Also, bureaucrats' caution and close adherence to agency rules offer a measure of consistency. It would be unsettling if government employees interpreted rules as they pleased. Simply put, bureaucrats "go by the book" because the "book" is composed of the laws and regulations of this country, as well as the internal rules and norms of a particular agency. Americans expect to be treated equally before the law, and bureaucrats work with that expectation in mind.

Problems in Implementing Policy

The development of policy in Washington is the end of one part of the policymaking cycle but the beginning of another. After policies have been developed, they must be implemented. **Implementation** is the process of putting specific policies into operation. Ultimately, bureaucrats must convert policies on paper into policies in action. It is important to study implementation because policies do not always do what they were designed to do.

One reason implementation may be difficult is that the policy to be carried out is not always clearly stated. Policy directives to bureaucrats in the field sometimes lack clarity and leave lower-level officials with too much discretion. The source of vague regulations is often vague legislation. Congress, for example, included in the Elementary and Secondary School Act (1965) a program of grants to meet the "special needs of educationally deprived children." But the act did not spell out who qualified as educationally deprived. The administering agency, the U.S. Office of Education, passed the money on to the states without specific eligibility criteria. As a result, the money was spent for a variety of purposes, not all of which were beneficial to educationally deprived children.[33]

Another reason for implementation failures is faulty coordination. Programs frequently cut across the jurisdictions of a number of agencies, and in our federal system programs must often be coordinated between national officials and state or local officials implementing the program out in the field. When William Bennett was appointed by President Bush to be head of the Office of National Drug Control Policy, he wanted to make the District of Columbia his test case for his strategy for fighting drugs. In developing his plan, however, Bennett ignored Washington, D.C., law enforcement officials. Had Bennett talked to them he would have learned that the approach he was planning to use, which relied primarily on expanded law enforcement activity, had already been unsuccessfully tried. Not surprisingly, his effort failed as well.[34]

Policymakers can create implementation difficulties by ignoring the administrative capabilities of an agency they have chosen to carry out a program. This happened in 1981 when the Reagan administration and Congress instructed the Social Security Administration to expand its review of those citizens receiving disability insurance benefits. The disability program had grown during the 1970s as eligibility requirements had been broadened to take in younger people and those with shorter-term disabilities.

The increased costs associated with these changes made the program a target of the Reagan administration's effort to cut domestic spending. The number of eligibility reviews of those currently on the program was increased dramatically as a means of assessing whether people were still disabled and merited continued payment of their benefits. State agencies, which carried out the reviews, had been doing between 20,000 to 30,000 cases a quarter. These same agencies were ordered to review 100,000 to 150,000 cases a quarter. As the number of people terminated increased, so did the legal appeals to have the terminations reversed, and the backlog of unresolved cases grew sharply. With tens of thousands of individuals believing they had been unfairly removed from the disability rolls and the administrative system inundated with more cases than it could handle, the problems with the program reached crisis proportions.

The lesson of this episode was that policymakers were so eager to cut costs that they made wholly unrealistic assumptions about the administrative capacities of the state agencies implementing the program. Since those agencies were given a huge increase in work without a significant increase in resources to hire additional people, they inevitably buckled under the expanded case load.[35]

Although obstacles to effective implementation create the impression that nothing succeeds, programs can and do work. Problems in the implementation process demonstrate why time, patience, and continual analysis are necessary ingredients of successful policymaking. To return to a term we used earlier, implementation is by its nature an *incremental* process, in which trial and error eventually lead to policies that work.

Reforming the Bureaucracy: More Control or Less?

As we saw at the outset of this chapter, organization matters. The way in which bureaucracies are designed directly affects how effective they are in accomplishing their tasks.[36] People in government constantly tinker with the structure of bureaucracies, trying to find ways of improving their performance, and many different approaches to administrative reform have been used in recent years as the criticism of government has mounted.[37] A central question that overrides much of the debate over bureaucratic reform is whether we need to establish more control over the bureaucracy or less. There is no magic bullet that will work for every type of bureaucracy: less control may be best for public schools, but the National Endowment for the Arts may need more direction by Congress if it is to retain the confidence and support of the American people.

Deregulation

Many people believe that government is too involved in **regulation,** intervention in the natural workings of business markets to promote some social goal. For example, government might regulate a market to ensure that products pose no danger to consumers. Through **deregulation** the government reduces its role and lets the natural market forces of supply and demand take over. Indeed, nothing is more central to capitalist philosophy than the belief that the free market will efficiently promote the balance of supply and demand. Some important movement toward deregulation took place in the 1970s and 1980s, notably in the airline, trucking, financial services, and telecommunications industries.[38]

In the case of the airlines, the Civil Aeronautics Board (CAB) had been determining fares and controlling access to routes. The justification for these regulatory efforts was that they would prevent overloads, both in

Fly the Unfriendly Skies
With the deregulation of the airline industry, increased traffic on many routes has tested the capacity of the Federal Aviation Administration to ensure safety in the air. Air traffic controllers form the front line of the FAA's safety efforts. The responsibility of their job and the acute concentration it requires make the controllers' work extremely stressful.

the sky and at airport facilities, and would ensure some service to all parts of the nation. But regulation had a side effect: It reduced competition among the airlines, which worked to the disadvantage of consumers. Congress responded by passing a law in 1978 mandating deregulation of fares and routes, and the airlines became more competitive. New carriers entered lucrative markets, fares dropped, and price wars broke out. In smaller cities, which major carriers no longer were required to serve, commuter airlines offered essential services. In retrospect, it is clear that government had been overregulating the airline industry. Nevertheless, in the past few years there has been a trend toward dominance of the industry by a few large and healthy carriers. Open competition has forced the mergers and bankruptcies of a number of airlines, and just what the air travel market will look like in the future is unclear. The initial phase of this era of deregulation may actually leave us with fewer airlines.

It is particularly difficult to decide on an appropriate level of deregulation of agencies dealing with health and safety issues. Companies within a particular industry may have legitimate claims that health and safety regulations are burdensome, making it difficult for them to earn sufficient profits or compete effectively with foreign manufacturers. The drug-licensing procedures used by the Food and Drug Administration illustrate the dilemma of deregulating these kinds of agencies. The thorough and lengthy process the FDA uses to evaluate drugs has as its ultimate validation the thalidomide case. The William S. Merrill Company purchased the license to market this sedative, already available in Europe, and filed an application with the FDA in 1960. The company then began a protracted fight with FDA bureaucrat Dr. Frances Kelsey, who was assigned to evaluate the thalidomide application. She demanded that the company abide by all FDA drug-testing requirements, despite the fact that the drug was already in use in other countries. She and her superiors resisted pressure from the company to bend the rules a little and expedite approval. Before Merrill had conducted all the FDA tests, news came pouring in from Europe that some women who had taken thalidomide during pregnancy were giving birth to babies without arms, legs, or ears. Strict adherence to government regulation protected Americans from the same tragic consequences.

Nevertheless, the pharmaceutical industry has been highly critical of the FDA, claiming that the licensing procedures are so complex that drugs of great benefit are kept from the marketplace for years while people suffering from a particular disease are denied access to new treatments. Manufacturers claim that there is a "drug lag," citing the fact that many more new medicines are introduced in Great Britain than in the United States. They have encouraged the FDA to adopt faster procedures to save the industry substantial research and development costs and to speed valuable drugs into the hands of seriously ill Americans. The FDA has been resistant to doing anything that would compromise what it sees as necessary precautions.

In recent years, however, the AIDS epidemic has brought about some concessions from the FDA. Although AIDS is incurable, drugs have been found to help patients deal with various symptoms and to lengthen their lives. New rules expediting the availability of experimental drugs have been issued, and, more generally, the FDA has adopted a somewhat speedier timetable for clinical tests of new drugs.[39]

Monitoring, Oversight, and Accountability

There is substantial sentiment to make government smaller by reducing government supervision of various industries and business activities. Further deregulation is championed by conservatives who see freedom in the marketplace as the best route to an efficient and growing economy. Yet making government smaller and reducing its role can entail serious risks. Nowhere are those risks more evident than in the collapse of the savings and loan industry.

Savings and loans institutions, which were primarily designed to provide mortgages for a growing housing market, were tightly regulated by the federal government. As the financial markets became much more complex and much more competitive, and the need for savings and loans to provide mortgages lessened, there was a good case for loosening the reins over the industry so that it could compete more effectively in the marketplace. Between 1980 and 1983, Congress approved a number of changes that significantly deregulated savings and loans. For example, the ceiling on the amount of interest they could pay on deposits was lifted, thus enabling them to attract deposits that were going to other types of financial institutions. Subsequently, they attracted considerably more money, but this money cost them a lot more in terms of interest and, thus, had to earn much more when lent out. Legislation also expanded the range of investments available to the S&Ls, allowing them to make loans for commercial real estate. In addition to these changes, insurance on deposits was raised from $40,000 to $100,000.

At the same time these changes were being made, the Reagan administration refused to allow the Federal Home Loan Bank Board, which then had the supervisory role over the industry, to hire the bank examiners that it felt it needed to monitor the health of the individual S&Ls. The administration was trying to shrink the size of government and didn't feel that so much money should be spent policing business practices. As the real estate market cooled off, the savings and loans got into serious trouble. So many commercial real estate developers ran into problems and couldn't repay their loans that a large number of S&Ls were plunged into insolvency. The federal bailout of the failed S&Ls will cost taxpayers hundreds of billions of dollars (see Chapter 18).

Although the savings and loan debacle is the most obvious example of the danger of removing government supervision of business markets, it is by no means an isolated case. The effort of the Reagan administration to get government "off the back" of American business and to make government less expensive led to problems at other agencies, such as the Department of Housing and Urban Development and the Farmers Home Administration. Unfortunately, one of the reasons big government exists is that it is necessary for government to expend signficant resources on monitoring the behavior of bureaucrats and those regulated by bureaucrats to ensure the integrity of both government and markets. When waste, fraud, and abuse surfaces, the public wants to know why procedures were lax. When there are demands for reform, those reforms usually involve adding new layers of bureuacracy.[40]

Thus there is a tension between the desire to make government lean, efficient, and unintrusive and the desire to protect citizens from fraud and unfair or unsafe business practices. This is in many ways a traditional dilemma between freedom and order. There is a strong case to be made for deregulated business markets, where free and unfettered competition benefits consumers and promotes productivity. The strength of capitalist economies comes from the ability of individuals and firms to compete freely in the marketplace. The regulatory state places restrictions on this freedom. But without regulation, there is nothing to ensure that marketplace participants will always act responsibly.

Summary

As the scope of government activity has grown during the twentieth century, so has the bureaucracy. The executive branch has evolved into a complex set of departments, independent agencies, and government corporations. The way in which these various bureaucracies are organized matters a great deal because the way they are structured affects their ability to carry out their tasks.

Through the administrative discretion granted them by Congress, these bodies make policy decisions through rule making and adjudication that have the force of law. In making policy choices, agency decision makers are influenced by their external environment, especially the White House, Congress, and interest groups. Decision makers are also influenced by internal norms and the need to work cooperatively with others both within and outside their agencies.

The most serious charge facing the bureaucracy is that it is out of control of the people. In fact, the White House, Congress, interest groups, and public opinion act as substantial controls on the bureaucracy. Still, to many Americans, the bureaucracy seems too big, too costly, and too intrusive. It is difficult to reduce the size and scope of bureaucratic activity because pluralism characterizes our political system. The entire executive branch may appear too large, and each of us can point to agencies that we believe should be reduced or eliminated, yet each bureaucracy has its supporters. The Department of Agriculture performs vital services for farmers. Unions care a great deal about the Department of Labor. Scholars want the National Science Foundation protected. And home builders do not want Housing and Urban Development programs cut back. Bureaucracies survive because they provide important services to groups of people, and those people—no matter how strong their commitment to less government—are not willing to sacrifice their own needs to that commitment.

There are no shortage of reform plans for making the bureaucracy work better. Proponents of deregulation believe our economy will be more productive if we free the marketplace from the heavy hand of government supervision. Opponents believe that deregulation involves considerable risk and that we ought to be very careful in determining which markets and business practices can be subjected to less government supervision. To prevent disasters like the thalidomide episode and the S&L scandal, government bureaucracies need to be able to monitor the behavior of people inside and outside of government, as well as supervise business practices in a wide range of industries.

KEY TERMS

bureaucracy
bureaucrat
department
independent agency
regulatory commission
government corporation
civil service
administrative
   discretion

rule making
regulations
adjudication
implementation
regulation
deregulation

SELECTED READINGS

Derthick, Martha. *Agency Under Stress.* Washington, D.C.: Brookings Institution, 1990. A study of how policymakers ignored the administrative capacity of the Social Security Administration when setting new goals for the agency.

Derthick, Martha, and Paul J. Quirk. *The Politics of Deregulation.* Washington, D.C.: Brookings Institution, 1985. An interesting look at why some industries have undergone deregulation while others have not.

Gormley, William T., Jr. *Taming the Bureaucracy: Muscles, Prayers, and Other Strategies.* Princeton, N.J.: Princeton University Press, 1989. An incisive look at competing strategies for reform, with particular emphasis on whether the instruments for change should be mandatory controls or informal persuasion.

Harris, Richard A., and Sidney M. Milkis. *The Politics of Regulatory Change.* New York: Oxford University Press, 1989. A study of how the new regulatory regime of the Reagan years affected policymaking at the Federal Trade Commission and the Environmental Protection Agency.

Rourke, Francis E. *Bureaucracy, Politics, and Public Policy.* 3d ed. Boston: Little, Brown, 1984. An excellent introduction to bureaucracy, with a very useful analysis of the relationship between agencies and their clients.

Wilson, James Q., ed. *Bureaucracy.* New York: Basic Books, 1989. A comprehensive look at the operations of large, complex government organizations.

14 THE COURTS

WHEN CHIEF JUSTICE FRED M. Vinson died unexpectedly on September 8, 1953, Justice Felix Frankfurter commented, "This is the first solid piece of evidence I've ever had that there really is a God."[1] Frankfurter despised Vinson as a leader and disliked him as a person. Vinson's sudden death would bring a new colleague—and perhaps new hope—to the school segregation cases known collectively as *Brown* v. *Board of Education.*

The issue of segregated schools had arrived in the Supreme Court in November 1951. Though the Court had originally scheduled argument for October 1952, the justices elected a postponement until December 1952 and merged several similar cases. When a law clerk was puzzled by the delay, Frankfurter explained that the Court was holding the case for the outcome of the national election in 1952. "I thought the Court was supposed to decide without regard to the elections," declared the clerk. "When you have a major social political issue of this magnitude," replied Frankfurter, "we do not think this is the time to decide it."[2]

The justices were bitterly divided following the December argument, with Vinson supporting racial segregation in public education. Because the justices were still not ready to reach a decision, they scheduled the cases for reargument the following year with instructions to address specific issues in the several lawsuits.

Frankfurter's caustic remark about Vinson's death reflected the critical role Vinson's replacement would play when the Court again tackled the desegregation issue. On September 30, 1953, in his first appointment to the nation's highest court, President Dwight D. Eisenhower chose California Governor Earl Warren as chief justice. The president would later regret his choice.

When the reargument of *Brown* v. *Board of Education* was heard in December 1953, the new chief justice led the Court from division to unanimity on the issue of school segregation. Unlike his predecessor, Warren began the secret conference to decide the segregation issue with a strong statement: that segregation was contrary to the Thirteenth, Fourteenth, and Fifteenth Amendments to the Constitution. "Personally," remarked the new chief justice, "I can't see how today we can justify segregation based solely on race."[3] Moreover, if the Court were to uphold segregation, he argued, it could do so only on the theory that blacks were inherently inferior to whites. As the discussion proceeded, Warren's opponents were cast in the awkward position of appearing to support racism.

Five justices were clearly on Warren's side, making six votes; two were prepared to join the majority if Warren's opinion satisfied them. With only one clear holdout, Warren set about the task of responding to his colleagues' concerns. In the months that followed, he met with them individually in their chambers, reviewing the decision and the justification that would accompany it. Finally, in April 1954, Warren approached Justice Stanley Reed, whose vote would make the opinion unanimous. "Stan," said the chief justice, "you're all by yourself in this now. You've got to decide whether it's really the best thing for the country." Ultimately Reed joined the others. On May 17, 1954, the Supreme Court unanimously ruled against racial segregation in public schools, signaling

Power Player on the Top Court

Earl Warren (1891–1974) served as the fourteenth chief justice of the United States. A true liberal, Warren led the Supreme Court by actively preferring equality to freedom and freedom to order. These decisions occasionally brought calls from Congress for Warren's impeachment. He retired in 1968 after sixteen years of championship (critics might say controversial) activity.

the end of legally created or governmentally enforced segregation of the races in the United States.[4]

Judges confront conflicting values in the cases before them, and tough cases call for fine distinctions among those values. In crafting their decisions, judges—especially Supreme Court justices—make policy. Their decisions become the precedents other judges use to rule in similar cases. One judge in one court makes public policy to the extent that he or she influences other decisions in other courts.

The power of the courts to shape policy creates a difficult problem for democratic theory. According to that theory, the power to make law resides only in the people or in their elected representatives. Yet court rulings—especially Supreme Court rulings—extend far beyond any particular case. Judges are students of the law, but they remain human beings. They have their own opinions about the values of freedom, order, and equality. And although all judges are constrained by statutes and precedents from expressing their personal beliefs in their decisions, some judges are more prone than others to interpret laws in light of those beliefs.

America's courts are deeply involved in the life of the country and its people. Some courts, like the Supreme Court, make fundamental policy decisions vital to the preservation of freedom, order, and equality. Through checks and balances, the elected branches couple the courts to democracy, and the courts hitch the elected branches to the Constitution. But does it work? Can the courts exercise political power within the pluralist model? Or are judges simply sovereigns in black robes, making decisions independent of popular control? In this chapter we try to answer these questions by exploring the role of the judiciary in American political life.

Federal Judicial Supremacy

Section 1 of Article III of the Constitution created "one supreme Court." The founders were divided on the need for other national courts, so they deferred to Congress the decision to create a national court system. Those who opposed the creation of national courts believed that the system would usurp the authority of the state courts.[5] Congress considered the issue in its first session and, in the Judiciary Act of 1789, gave life to a system of federal, or national, courts that would coexist with the courts in each state but be independent of them. Federal judges would also be independent of popular influences because the Constitution provided for their virtual lifetime appointment.

In the early years of the republic, the federal judiciary was not considered a particularly powerful branch of government. It was especially difficult to recruit and keep Supreme Court justices. They spent much of their time as individual traveling judges ("riding circuit"); disease and transportation were everyday hazards. The justices only met as the Supreme Court for a few weeks in February and August.[6] John Jay, the first chief justice, refused to resume his duties in 1801 because he concluded that the Court could not muster the "energy, weight, and dignity" to contribute to national affairs.[7] Several distinguished statesmen refused appointments to the Court, and several others, including Oliver Ellsworth, the third chief justice, resigned. But when John Marshall, an ardent Federalist, was appointed chief justice in 1801, a period of profound change began.

Judicial Review of the Other Branches

Shortly after Marshall's appointment, the Supreme Court confronted a question of fundamental importance to the future of the new republic: If a law enacted by Congress conflicts with the Constitution, which should prevail? The question arose in the case of *Marbury* v. *Madison* (1803), which involved a controversial series of last-minute political appointments.

The case began on March 2, 1801, when an obscure Federalist, William Marbury, was designated as a justice of the peace in the District of Co-

Chief Justice John Marshall

Marshall (1755–1835) clearly ranks as the "Babe Ruth" of the Supreme Court. Both Marshall and the Bambino transformed their respective games and became symbols of their institutions. Scholars now recognize both men as originators—Marshall of judicial review, and Ruth of the modern age of baseball.

lumbia. Marbury and several others were appointed to government posts created by Congress in the last days of John Adams's presidency, but these appointments were never fully finalized. The newly arrived Jefferson administration had little interest in delivering the commissions; there were qualified Jeffersonians who would welcome the jobs.

To secure their jobs, Marbury and the disgruntled appointees invoked an act of Congress to obtain the necessary papers. The act authorized the Supreme Court to issue orders against government officials. Marbury and the others sought such an order in the Supreme Court against the new secretary of state, James Madison, who held the necessary appointing documents.

In legal terms, Marbury asked the Court to exercise its "original jurisdiction." Article III of the Constitution spells out the Supreme Court's original jurisdiction, but it only covers cases involving states or foreign diplomats. Marshall observed that the act of Congress invoked by Marbury to sue in the Supreme Court conflicted with the original jurisdiction section of Article III, which did not authorize such suits. On February 24, 1803, the Court delivered its opinion.[*]

Must the Court follow the law or follow the Constitution? The High Court held, through Marshall's forceful argument, that the Constitution was "the fundamental and paramount law of the nation" and that "an act of the legislature repugnant to the constitution is void." In other words, when the Constitution—the nation's highest law—conflicts with an act of the legislature, that act is invalid. The last part of Marshall's argument vested in the judiciary the power to weigh the validity of congressional acts:

> It is emphatically the province and duty of the judicial department to say what the law is. Those who apply the rule to particular cases, must of necessity expound and interpret that rule. . . . If a law be in opposition to the constitution, if both the law and the constitution apply to a particular case, so that the court must either decide that case conformably to the law, disregarding the constitution; or conformably to the constitution, disregarding the law; the court must determine which of these conflicting rules governs the case. This is the very essence of judicial duty.[8]

The decision in *Marbury* v. *Madison* established the Supreme Court's power of **judicial review**—the power to declare congressional acts invalid if they violate the Constitution.[**] Subsequent cases extended the power to presidential acts.[9]

---

[*] Courts publish their opinions in volumes called *reporters.* Today, the United States Reports is the official reporter for the U.S. Supreme Court. For example, the Court's opinion in the case of *Brown* v. *Board of Education* is cited as 347 U.S. 483 (1954). This means that the opinion in *Brown* begins on page 483 of Volume 347 in the United States Reports. The citation also includes the year of the decision. The decision in *Brown* was made in 1954. Before 1875, the official reports of the Supreme Court were published under the names of private compilers. For example, the case of *Marbury* v. *Madison* is cited as 1 Cranch 137 (1803). This means that the case is found in Volume 1, compiled by reporter William Cranch, starting on page 137, and that it was decided in 1803.

[**] The Supreme Court had earlier *upheld* an act of Congress in *Hylton* v. *United States*, 3 Dallas 171 (1796). *Marbury* v. *Madison* stood for a component of judicial power that had never before been exercised: the power to *invalidate* an act of Congress.

Marshall expanded the potential power of the Supreme Court to equal or exceed that of the other branches of government. Should a congressional act or, by implication, a presidential act conflict with the Constitution, the Supreme Court claimed the power to declare the act void. The judiciary would be a check on the legislative and executive branches, consistent with the principle of checks and balances embedded in the Constitution. Although Congress and the president may wrestle with the constitutionality of their actions, judicial review gave the Supreme Court the final word on the meaning of the Constitution.

The exercise of judicial review—an appointed branch checking an elected branch in the name of the Constitution— appears to run counter to democratic theory. In two hundred years of practice, however, the Supreme Court has invalidated fewer than 140 provisions of federal law, and only a small number have had great significance for the political system.[10] Moreover, there are mechanisms to override judicial review (constitutional amendment) and to control the action of the justices (impeachment). In addition, the Court can respond to the continuing struggle among competing interests (a struggle that is consistent with the pluralist model) by reversing itself.

Judicial Review of State Government

The establishment of judicial review of federal laws made the Supreme Court the umpire of the national government. When acts of the national government conflict with the Constitution, the Supreme Court can declare those acts invalid. But what about state laws? If they conflict with the Constitution, federal laws, or treaties, can the Court invalidate them as well?

The Supreme Court answered in the affirmative in 1796. *Ware* v. *Hylton* involved a British creditor who was trying to collect a debt from the state of Virginia.[11] Virginia law canceled debts owed British subjects, yet the Treaty of Paris (1783), in which Britain formally acknowledged the independence of the colonies, guaranteed that creditors could collect such debts. The Court ruled that the Constitution's supremacy clause (Article VI) nullified the state law.

The states continued to resist the yoke of national supremacy. Although advocates of strong states' rights conceded that the supremacy clause obligates state judges to follow the Constitution when it conflicts with state law, they maintained that the states were bound only by their own interpretation of the Constitution. The Supreme Court said no, ruling in *Martin* v. *Hunter's Lessee* that it had the authority to review state court decisions that called for the interpretation of federal law.[12] National supremacy required the Supreme Court to impose uniformity on federal law; otherwise, the Constitution's meaning would vary from state to state. The people, not the states, had ordained the Constitution; and the people had subordinated state power in order to establish a viable national government. In time, the Supreme Court would use its judicial review power in nearly 1,200 instances to invalidate state and local laws on issues as diverse as abortion, the death penalty, rights of the accused, and reapportionment.[13]

The Exercise of Judicial Review

The decisions in *Marbury, Ware,* and *Martin* established the components of judicial review:

- The power of the courts to declare national, state, and local laws invalid if they violate the Constitution
- The supremacy of federal laws or treaties when they conflict with state and local laws
- The role of the Supreme Court as the final authority on the meaning of the Constitution

But this political might—the power to undo decisions of the representative branches of national and state governments—lay in the hands of appointed judges, people who were not accountable to the electorate. Did judicial review square with democratic government?

Alexander Hamilton had foreseen and tackled the problem in "Federalist No. 78." Writing during the ratification debates surrounding the adoption of the Constitution (see Chapter 3), Hamilton maintained that despite the power of judicial review, the judiciary would be the weakest of the three branches of government because it lacked "the strength of the sword or the purse." The judiciary, wrote Hamilton, had "neither FORCE nor WILL, but only judgment."

Although Hamilton was defending legislative supremacy, he argued that judicial review was an essential barrier to legislative oppression.[14] He recognized that the power to declare government acts void implied the superiority of the courts over the other branches. But this power, he contended, simply reflects the will of the people declared in the Constitution as compared with the will of the legislature declared in its statutes. Judicial independence, embodied in life tenure and protected salaries, minimizes the risk of judges deviating from the law established in the Constitution by freeing the judiciary from executive and legislative control.* And if judges make a mistake, the people or their elected representatives have the means to correct the error, through constitutional amendment and impeachment.

Their life tenure does free judges from the direct influence of the president and Congress. And although mechanisms to check judicial power are in place, they require extraordinary majorities and have rarely been used. When they exercise the power of judicial review, then, judges can and occasionally do operate counter to majoritarian rule by invalidating the actions of the people's elected representatives. (Compared with What? 14.1 discusses the nature of judicial review in other governments, democratic and nondemocratic.) Are the courts out of line with majority sentiment? Or are the courts simply responding to pluralist demands —the competing demands of interest groups that turn to the courts to make public policy? We return to these questions later in this chapter.

---

* Hamilton also believed that the executive, recognizing the power stemming from judicial independence, would appoint judges with the skill and intelligence to carry out their interpretive function responsibly.

COMPARED WITH WHAT?   14.1

Judicial Review

The U.S. Constitution does not explicitly give the Supreme Court the power of judicial review. In a controversial interpretation, the Court inferred this power from the text and structure of the Constitution. Other countries, trying to avoid political controversy over the power of the courts to review legislation, explicitly define that power in their constitutions. For example, Japan's constitution, inspired by the American model, went beyond it in providing that "the Supreme Court is the court of last resort with power to determine the constitutionality of any law, order, regulation, or official act."

The basic objection to the American form of judicial review is an unwillingness to place judges, who are usually appointed for life, above representatives elected by the people. The European concept of judging involves principled decision making, not "creative" interpretation of constitutions or laws. Some constitutions explicitly deny judicial review. For example, Article 28 of the Belgian constitution (1831) firmly asserts that "the authoritative interpretation of laws is solely the prerogative of the Legislative authority."

The logical basis of judicial review—that government is responsible to higher authority—can take interesting forms in other countries. In some, judges can invoke a higher authority than the constitution—God, an ideology, or a code of ethics. For example, both Iran and Pakistan provide for an Islamic review of all legislation. (Pakistan also has the American form of judicial review.)

By 1985, sixty-five countries—mostly in Western Europe, Latin America, Africa, and the Far East—had adopted some form of judicial review. Australia, Brazil, Burma, Canada, India, Japan, and Pakistan give their courts a full measure of judicial review power. All but Japan have federal governments. Australia and Canada come closest to the American model of judicial review, but the fit is never exact. And wherever courts exercise judicial review, undoing it calls for extraordinary effort. For example, in Australia, the Federal Parliament has no recourse after a law is declared unconstitutional by the High Court but to redraft the offending act in a manner prescribed by the Court. In the United States, overruling judicial review by the Supreme Court requires a constitutional amendment.

Governments with relatively consistent experience with judicial review share some common characteristics: stability, competitive political parties, distribution of power (akin to separation of powers), a tradition of judicial independence, and

The Organization of the Federal Courts Today

The American court system is complex, a function in part of our federal system of government. Each state runs its own court system and no two are identical. In addition, we have a system of courts for the national government. These federal courts coexist with the state courts (see Figure 14.1). Individuals fall under the jurisdiction of both court systems. They can sue or be sued in either system, depending mostly on what their case is about. The vast majority of cases are resolved in the state courts.

The federal courts are organized in three tiers, like a pyramid. At the bottom of the pyramid are the **U.S. district courts**, where litigation be-a high degree of political freedom. Is judicial review the cause or the consequence of these characteristics? More likely than not, judicial review contributes to stability, judicial independence, and political freedom. And separation of powers, judicial independence, and political freedom contribute to the effectiveness of judicial review.

Some constitutional courts possess extraordinary power compared with the American model. The German Constitutional Court, like the courts in the United States, has the power to strike down laws enacted by the legislature. But unlike the courts in the United States, the German Constitutional Court also has the power to invalidate the *failure* of the lawmakers to act. In 1975, for example, the German Constitutional Court nullified the legalization of abortion and declared that the government had a duty to protect unborn human life against all threats. The court concluded that the Constitution required the legislature to enact penal and nonpenal legislation to protect the unborn.

The Supreme Court of India offers an extreme example of judicial review. In 1967, the Court held that the parliament could not change the fundamental rights sections of the constitution, even by constitutional amendment! The parliament then amended the constitution to secure its power to amend the constitution. The Supreme Court upheld the amendment but declared that any amendments that attacked the "basic structure" of the constitution would be invalid. In India, the Supreme Court is truly supreme.

Switzerland also has a federal form of government. However, its Supreme Federal Court is limited by its constitution to rule on the constitutionality of cantonal laws (the Swiss equivalent of our state laws). The Supreme Federal Court lacks the power to nullify laws passed by the national assembly. The Swiss people, through a constitutional initiative or a popular referendum, exercise the sovereign right to determine the constitutionality of federal law. In Switzerland, the people are truly supreme.

Sources: Henry J. Abraham, *The Judicial Process*, 5th ed. (New York: Oxford University Press, 1986), pp. 291–330; Chester J. Antineau, *Adjudicating Constitutional Issues* (London: Oceana, 1985), pp. 1–6; Jerold L. Waltman and Kenneth M. Holland, *The Political Role of Law Courts in Modern Democracies* (New York: St. Martin's Press, 1988), pp. 46, 99–100; and Robert L. Hardgrave, Jr., and Stanley A. Kochanek, *India: Government and Politics in a Developing Nation*, 4th ed. (New York: Harcourt Brace Jovanovich, 1986), p. 93.

gins. In the middle are the **U.S. courts of appeals**. At the top is the U.S. Supreme Court. *To appeal* means to take a case to a higher court. The courts of appeals and the Supreme Court are appellate courts; with few exceptions, they review cases that have been decided in lower courts. Most federal courts hear and decide a wide array of cases; the judges in these courts are known as *generalists*.

The U.S. District Courts

There are ninety-four federal district courts in the United States. Each state has at least one district court, and no district straddles more than one state.[15] In 1990, nearly 550 full-time federal district court judges dispensed justice in various degrees in almost 267,000 criminal and civil cases.

F I G U R E   14.1   *The Federal and State Court Systems*

The federal courts have three tiers: district courts, courts of appeals, and the Supreme Court. The Supreme Court was created by the Constitution; all other federal courts were created by Congress. Most litigation occurs in state courts. The structure of state courts varies from state to state; usually there are minor trial courts for less serious cases, major trial courts for more serious cases, intermediate appellate courts, and courts of last resort. State courts were created by state constitutions. (Sources: State Court Caseload Statistics, Annual Report, 1989 [Williamsburg, Va.: National Center for State Courts, 1991]; Annual Report of the Director of the Administrative Office of the United States Courts [Washington, D.C.: Government Printing Office, 1990]; and Harold W. Stanley and Richard G. Niemi, Vital Statistics on American Politics, 2d ed. [Washington, D.C.: Congressional Quarterly, 1990]; Bureau of the Census, Statistical Abstract of the United States, 1990 [Washington, D.C.: U.S. Government Printing Office, 1990], Table 311.)

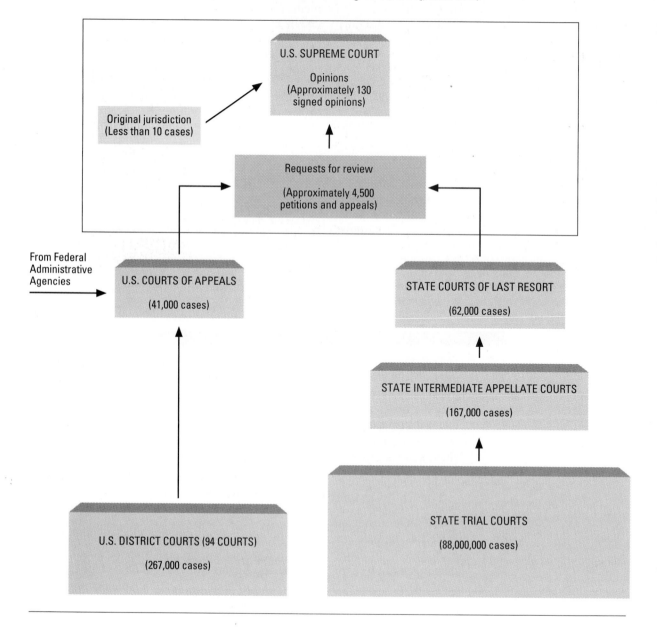

Searching for the Law

Judge Learned Hand (1872–1961) served as a federal judge for fifty-two years, a record unequaled in the twentieth century. Although many jurists regarded Hand as a leading contender for a Supreme Court seat, he never managed to get the coveted appointment. His public reputation rested on his unusual name, his eloquent style, and his physiognomy (note the bushy eyebrows and the square, strong features). Many of Hand's three thousand opinions are still cited for their lucidity and powerful reasoning. Hand was perhaps the greatest judge of his generation; his achievements stemmed from "the great way in which he dealt with a multitude of little cases."

The district courts are the entry point to the federal court system. When trials occur in the federal system, they take place in the federal district courts. Here is where witnesses testify, lawyers conduct cross-examinations, and judges and juries decide the fate of litigants. There may be more than one judge in each district court, but each case is tried by a single judge, sitting alone.

Criminal and civil cases.   Crime is a violation of a law that forbids or commands an activity. Criminal laws are defined in each state's *penal code*, as are punishments for violations. Some crimes—murder, rape, arson—are on the books of every state. Others—sodomy between consenting adults is one example—are considered crimes in certain states but not all. Because crime is a violation of public order, the government prosecutes **criminal cases**. Maintaining public order through the criminal law is largely a state and local function. Federal criminal cases represent only a fraction of all criminal cases prosecuted in the United States. The national penal code is very specialized. It does not cover ordinary crimes, just violations of federal laws, like tax fraud or possession of controlled substances banned by Congress.

The definition of crime rests with the legislative branch. And the definition is dynamic, that is, it is subject to change. For example, desktop publishing has given a big boost to the counterfeiting of stock certificates, bank checks, purchase orders, even college transcripts. As a result, government will soon make it illegal to own computers and laser printers for counterfeiting purposes.

Courts decide both criminal and civil cases. **Civil cases** stem from disputed claims to something of value. Disputes arise from accidents, contractual obligations, and divorce, for example. Often the parties disagree over tangible issues (the possession of property, the custody of children), but civil cases can involve more abstract issues too (the right to equal accommodations, damages for pain and suffering). The government can be a party to civil disputes, called on to defend or to allege wrongs.

Sources of litigation.   Today, the authority of U.S. district courts extends to

- federal criminal cases authorized by federal law (for example, robbery of a federally insured bank or interstate transportation of stolen securities).

- civil cases brought by individuals, groups, or government for alleged violation of federal law (for example, failure of a municipality to implement pollution-control regulations required by a federal agency).

- civil cases brought against the federal government (for example, enforcement of a contract between a manufacturer and a government agency).

- civil cases between citizens of different states when the amount in controversy exceeds $50,000 (for example, when a citizen of New York sues a citizen of Alabama in a United States district court in Alabama for damages stemming from an auto accident in Alabama).

Most of the cases scheduled for hearings in the U.S. district courts never are actually tried. One side may be using a lawsuit as a threat to exact a concession from the other. Often the parties settle their own dispute. Less frequently, cases end with **adjudication**, a court judgment resolving the parties' claims and ultimately enforced by the government. When district judges adjudicate cases, they usually offer written reasons to support their decisions. When the issues or circumstances of cases are novel, judges can publish **opinions**, explanations justifying their rulings.

The U.S. Courts of Appeals

All cases resolved by final judgments in the U.S. district courts and all decisions of federal administrative agencies can be appealed to one of the thirteen U.S. courts of appeals. These courts, with a corps of 158 full-time judges, handled approximately 41,000 cases in 1990. Each appeals court hears cases from a geographic area known as a *circuit*. The U.S. Court of Appeals for the Seventh Circuit, for example, is located in

Chicago; it hears appeals from the U.S. district courts in Illinois, Wisconsin, and Indiana. The United States is divided into twelve circuits.*

Appellate court proceedings. Appellate court proceedings are public, but they usually lack courtroom drama. There are no jurors, witnesses, or cross-examinations; these are features of the trial courts. Appeals are based strictly on the rulings made and procedures followed in the trial courts. Suppose, for example, that in the course of a criminal trial, a U.S. district judge allows the introduction of evidence that convicts a defendant. The defendant can appeal on the ground that the evidence was obtained in the absence of a valid search warrant and so was inadmissible. The issue on appeal is the admissibility of the evidence, not the defendant's guilt or innocence. If the appellate court agrees with the trial judge's decision to admit the evidence, then the conviction stands. If the appellate court disagrees with the trial judge and rules that the evidence is inadmissible, then the defendant must be retried without the incriminating evidence or be released.

It is common for litigants to try to settle their dispute while it is on appeal. For example, when Pennzoil won an $11 billion state court judgment against the Texaco Oil Company in 1985 (the dispute was over Texaco's questionable purchase of another company), settlement discussions began immediately. Texaco settled with Pennzoil in 1988 for $3 billion. Occasionally, litigants abandon their appeals for want of resources or resolve. Most of the time, however, appellate courts adjudicate the cases.

The courts of appeals are regional courts. They usually convene in panels of three judges to render judgments. The judges receive written arguments known as **briefs** (which are also sometimes submitted in trial courts). Often the judges hear oral arguments and question the attorneys to probe their arguments.

Precedent and decision making. Following review of the briefs and, in many appeals, oral argument, the three-judge panel will meet to reach a judgment. One of the three judges attempts to summarize the panel's views, although each judge remains free to disagree with the reasons or with the judgment. The influence of published appellate opinions can reach well beyond the immediate case. For example, a lawsuit turning on the meaning of the Constitution produces a ruling that then serves as a **precedent** for subsequent cases; that is, the decision becomes a basis for deciding similar cases in the same way. Although district court judges sometimes publish their opinions, it is the exception rather than the rule. At the appellate level, however, precedent requires that opinions be written.

Decision making according to precedent is central to the operation of our legal system, providing continuity and predictability. This bias in favor of existing decisions is captured by the Latin expression **stare decisis**,

---

* The thirteenth court, the U.S. Court of Appeals for the Federal Circuit, is not a regional court; it specializes in appeals involving patents, contract claims against the federal government, and federal employment cases.

which means "let the decision stand." But the use of precedent and the principle of stare decisis do not make lower-court judges cogs in a judicial machine. "If precedent clearly governed," remarked one federal judge, "a case would never get as far as the Court of Appeals: the parties would settle."[16]

Judges on the courts of appeals direct their energies toward correcting errors in district court proceedings and interpreting the law (in the course of writing opinions). When judges interpret the law, they often modify existing laws. In effect, they are making policy. Judges are politicians in the sense that they exercise political power, but the black robes that distinguish judges from other politicians signal constraints on their exercise of power.

Judges make policy in two different ways. Occasionally, in the absence of legislation, they employ rules from prior decisions. We call this body of rules the **common** or **judge-made law.** The roots of the common law lie in the English legal system. Contracts, property, and **torts** (an injury or wrong to the person or property of another) are common-law domains. The second area of judicial lawmaking involves the application of statutes enacted by Congress. The judicial interpretation of legislative acts is called **statutory construction**. The application of a statute is not always clear from its wording. To determine how a statute should be applied, judges first look for the legislature's intent, reading reports of committee hearings and debates in Congress. If these sources do not clarify the statute's meaning, the court does. With or without legislation to guide them, judges on the courts of appeals and district courts look to the relevant opinions of the Supreme Court for authority to decide the issues before them.

Although the Supreme Court has the final say on what a law means, its decisions often fail to address the precise issue confronting lower-court judges. This means that federal judges can sometimes exercise as much political power as the High Court justices themselves. For example, in 1955 federal judges in Alabama were called on to determine whether, in light of the Supreme Court's decision in *Brown* v. *Board of Education*, Alabama's racially segregated public transportation facilities violated the Constitution's equal protection clause. Because applicable Supreme Court precedents appeared to go in opposite directions, three federal judges from the Deep South had to decide which path to take (see Feature 14.1).

Uniformity of law.   Decisions by the courts of appeals ensure a measure of uniformity in the application of national law. For example, when similar issues are dealt with in the decisions of different district judges, their decisions may be inconsistent. The courts of appeals harmonize the decisions within their region so that laws are applied uniformly.

The regional character of the courts of appeals undermines uniformity somewhat because the courts are not bound by the decisions of other circuits. A law in one court of appeals may be interpreted differently in another. For example, the Internal Revenue Code imposes identical tax burdens on similar individuals. But thanks to the regional character of

FEATURE 14.1 *The Law and Frank Johnson*

Judge Frank Johnson issued many path-breaking decisions from the federal courthouse in Montgomery, Alabama. Appointed in 1955 by President Eisenhower, Johnson ordered the integration of public parks, interstate bus terminals, restaurants and restrooms, and libraries and museums. In 1964, Johnson applied the one-person, one-vote principle for the first time in state legislative apportionment. In 1971, he held that patients in state mental hospitals have a constitutional right to treatment. And in 1976, he ordered the reform of the Alabama prison system on the ground that the conditions of confinement violated the constitutional rights of prisoners.

In this selection from an interview with journalist Bill Moyers, Johnson recalls his participation in *Browder* v. *Gayle* (1955). The case was a direct challenge to the Supreme Court's 1896 decision in *Plessy* v. *Ferguson*, which had held that separate but equal public transportation facilities were constitutionally acceptable. The *Browder* decision desegregating the Montgomery buses was the first time (in Johnson's memory, at least) a district court had overruled a decision of the Supreme Court. It was also the first extension of the Supreme Court's decision in *Brown* v. *Board of Education* (1954). *Browder* was decided by a special three-judge district court. Participating with Judge Johnson were Judges Richard Rives and Seybourne H. Lynne.

Moyers: Anybody call you and say, "My God, Johnson, you don't know what you've done," or "Do you know what you've done?"

Johnson: Well, they didn't put it in those words.

M: How did they put it?

J: I don't think I was subjected to vilification. I don't think I was subjected to the feeling of hate comparable to that which Judge Rives was subjected. Judge Richard Rives and I are the ones that decided that case. (Judge Lynne dissented.) Judge Rives had grown up here in Montgomery. He had practiced law here in Montgomery. He was one of the most able—recognized as one of the most able—lawyers in the South. President Truman appointed him to the federal bench. He'd been on the bench about four years when I came on in '55. He helped swear me in in this courtroom. But Judge Rives's roots were here. He was one of them. He wasn't a foreigner that had been imported from the hills of North Alabama

[where Johnson was born and raised]. And it was said by several people, and probably in the newspapers—I think I recall—here in Montgomery, "Well, we didn't expect any more out of that fellow from up at North Alabama, but Richard Rives is one of our own, and we did expect more out of him, and he's forfeited the right to be buried in Confederate soil." And that's how strong it was.

M: When you were discussing that case in your private chambers, after it had been argued—

J: The junior member of the court votes first. The senior member of the court votes last. That's followed throughout the system. That's to keep the senior member from influencing the junior member in his vote.

M: And you voted first?

J: So, Judge Rives says, "Frank, what do you think about this case?" "I don't think segregation in *any* public facilities is constitutional. Violates the equal protection clause of the Fourteenth Amendment, Judge." That's all I had to say. It didn't take me long to express myself. The law was clear. And I might add this . . . the law to me was clear in practically every one of these cases that I've decided where race was involved. I had no problem with the case where we outlawed the poll tax, charging people to vote. I had no problem with the museums, the libraries, the public parks, or any public facilities. The law will not tolerate discrimination on the basis of race.

M: When you said this to Judge Rives, what did he say?

J: Well, when it came Judge Rives's time to vote, he says, "I feel the same way."

M: And that was it.

J: Absolutely. Sure. Sure. Well, well, I don't guess we deliberated over ten minutes at the outside.

M: History seems to require more dramatic moments than that.

J: There are rarely ever any dramatic moments in a judges' conference room. It's a cold, calculated, legal approach.

Source: "Bill Moyers' Journal," "Judge: The Law & Frank Johnson—Part I." Transcription, pp. 8–10. © 1980 by the Educational Broadcasting Corporation. Reprinted by permission.

FEATURE 14.2   *The Marble Palace*

The Supreme Court of the United States sits east of the Capitol in a building designed both to embrace the majesty of the law and to elevate its occupants to the status of Platonic guardians. The Corinthian-style marble building was completed in 1935 at a cost of $10 million. Until it settled in its permanent home, the Court had occupied makeshift, hand-me-down quarters in nearly a dozen places (including two taverns) since its first session in February 1790.

Each justice has a suite of offices, including space for several law clerks —top graduates from the nation's elite law schools, who serve for a year or two.

The courtroom is 82 feet by 91 feet, with a 44-foot-high ceiling and twenty-four columns of Italian marble. The room is dominated by marble panels, which were sculpted by Adolph A. Weinman. Directly above the mahogany bench, which is angled so that all the justices can see and hear one another, are two marble figures depicting Majesty of Law and Power of Government. A tableau of the Ten Commandments is between the figures.

The Court begins its official work year on the first Monday of October, known as the October Term. During its public sessions, when appeals are argued or the justices announce opinions, the court marshal (dressed in a cutaway) pounds the gavel at exactly 10:00 A.M., directs everyone in the courtroom to stand, and announces:

The honorable, the chief and the associate justices of the Supreme Court of the United States: Oyez. Oyez. Oyez. All persons having business before the honorable, the Supreme Court of the United States, are admonished to draw near and give their attention, for the Court is now sitting. God save the United States and this honorable Court.

Then the justices enter in black robes from behind a velvet curtain. In the front is the chief justice; the other justices follow in order of seniority.

Contrary to popular impression, most of the 170 cases that the Court hears annually do not involve provocative constitutional issues. The Constitution

the courts of appeals, federal tax laws may be applied differently throughout the United States. The percolation of cases up through the federal system of courts virtually guarantees that at some point two or more courts of appeals, working with a similar set of facts, are going to interpret the same law differently. However, the problem of conflicting decisions in the intermediate federal courts can be corrected by review in the Supreme Court, where policymaking, not error correcting, is the paramount goal.

The Supreme Court

Above the west portico of the Supreme Court Building are inscribed the words EQUAL JUSTICE UNDER LAW. At the opposite end of the building, above the east portico, are the words JUSTICE THE GUARDIAN OF LIBERTY (see Feature 14.2). These mottos reflect the Court's difficult

arguing a case before his brethren-to-be. One day a private practitioner completely lost the thread of his argument and began to babble incoherently. [Chief Justice Charles Evans] Hughes tried to aid him by asking simple questions about the case. Seeing that this further bewildered the lawyer, Hughes took the brief and completed the argument that counsel was unable to make. . . .

There were other occasions when the utmost restraint was necessary to maintain the dignity of the court. . . . A New York attorney argued so vehemently that his false teeth popped out of his mouth. With amazing dexterity he scooped up the errant dentures almost before they hit the counsel's table in front of him and flipped them back into his mouth, with scarcely a word interrupted. Not a smile ruffled the dignity of the bench, but the Justices' pent-up mirth broke into gales of laughter when they reached safe havens of privacy.*

* Merlo J. Pusey, *Charles Evans Hughes*, vol. 2. (New York: Macmillan, 1951), pp. 674–675.

Source: *Congressional Quarterly's Guide to the U.S. Supreme Court* (Washington: Congressional Quarterly, 1979), pp. 761, 769–772. Reprinted by permission.

provides for the Supreme Court to hear cases "arising under . . . the laws of the United States." These cases call for the interpretation of federal statutes, which may or may not be interesting to the public at large.

Oral argument is usually limited to thirty minutes for each side. Few attorneys argue appeals regularly before the Court, so the significance of the moment can overwhelm even seasoned advocates. The justices constantly question the attorneys, attempting to poke holes in every argument.

Sometimes the intensity of an argument before the court was too much for a lawyer to endure. Solicitor General Stanley Reed once fainted while

task: achieving a just balance among the values of freedom, order, and equality. Consider how these values came into conflict in two controversial issues the Court has faced in recent years.

Flag burning as a form of political protest pits the value of order—the government's interest in maintaining a peaceful society—against the value of freedom—the individual's right to vigorous and unbounded political expression. In the recent flag-burning cases (1989 and 1990), the Supreme Court affirmed constitutional protection for unbridled political expression, including the emotionally charged act of desecrating a national symbol.

School desegregation pits the value of equality—equal educational opportunities for minorities—against the value of freedom—the rights of parents to send their children to neighborhood schools. In *Brown* v. *Board of Education*, the Supreme Court carried the banner of racial equality by striking down state-mandated segregation in public schools. This decision helped launch a revolution in race relations in the United

States. The justices recognized the disorder their decision would create in a society accustomed to racial bias, but in this case equality clearly outweighed freedom. Twenty-four years later, the Court was still embroiled in controversy over equality when it ruled that race could be a factor in university admissions (to diversify the student body), in the *Bakke* case.[17] In securing the equality of blacks, the Court then had to confront the charge that it was denying the freedom of whites to compete for admission.

The Supreme Court makes national policy. Because its decisions have far-reaching impact on all of us, it is vital that we understand how it reaches those decisions. With this understanding, we can better evaluate how the Court fits within our model of democracy.

Access to the Court

There are rules of access that must be followed to bring a case to the Supreme Court. Also important is a sensitivity to the interests of the justices. The idea that anyone can take a case all the way to the Supreme Court is true only in theory, not fact.

The Supreme Court's cases come from two sources. A few (under five in 1990) arrive under the Court's **original jurisdiction,** conferred by Article III, Section 2, of the Constitution, which gives the Court the power to hear and decide "all Cases affecting Ambassadors, other public Ministers and Consuls, and those in which a State shall be a Party." Cases falling under the Court's original jurisdiction are tried and decided in the Court itself; the cases begin and end there. For example, the Court is the

F I G U R E 14.2   *Access to and Decision Making in the U.S. Supreme Court*

State and federal appeals courts churn out thousands of decisions each year. Only a small fraction end up on the Supreme Court's docket. This chart sketches the several stages leading to a decision from the High Court. (Sources: Harold W. Stanley and Richard G. Niemi, Vital Statistics on American Politics, *2d ed. [Washington, D.C.: CQ Press, 1990], Table 9-7; Bureau of the Census,* Statistical Abstract of the United States, 1990 *[Washington, D.C.: U.S. Government Printing Office, 1990], Table 311. Used by permission.)*

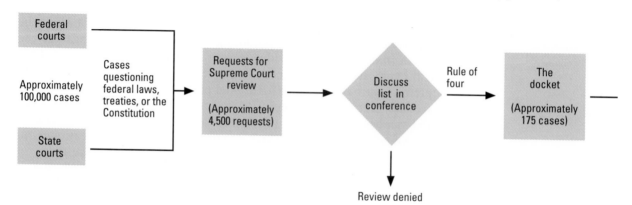

first and only forum in which legal disputes between states are resolved. The Court hears few original jurisdiction cases today, however, usually referring them to a *special master*, often a retired judge, who reviews the parties' contentions and recommends a resolution that the justices are free to accept or reject.

Most cases enter the Supreme Court from the U.S. courts of appeals or the state courts of last resort (see Figure 14.2).* This is the Court's **appellate jurisdiction.** These are cases that have been tried, decided, and reexamined as far as the law permits in other federal or state courts. The Court exercises judicial power under its appellate jurisdiction only because Congress gives it the authority to do so. Congress may change (and, perhaps, eliminate) the Court's appellate jurisdiction. This is a powerful but rarely used weapon in the congressional arsenal of checks and balances.

Litigants in state cases who invoke the Court's appellate jurisdiction must satify two conditions: First, the case must reach the end of the line in the state court system. Litigants cannot jump at will from state to federal arenas of justice. Second, the case must raise a **federal question**, an issue covered under the Constitution, federal laws, or treaties. However, even most cases that meet these conditions do not reach the High Court. Since 1925, the Court has exercised substantial (today, nearly complete) control over its **docket**, or agenda. The Court selects a handful of cases (about 170) for consideration from the 4,200 requests it receives each year. For the vast majority of the cases left unreviewed by the Court, the decision of the lower court stands. No explanations accompany cases that are denied review, so they have little or no value as court rulings.

Review is granted only when four or more justices agree that a case warrants full consideration. This unwritten rule is known as the **rule of**

---

* On rare occasions, cases can be brought to the Supreme Court after judgment in a U.S. district court but before consideration by a federal court of appeals. This happened in *United States* v. *Nixon,* 418 U.S. 683 (1974). The urgency of an authoritative decision in the Watergate tapes case short-circuited a decision in the court of appeals.

Decision-making process

| Briefs | → | Oral argument | → | Conference | → | Opinion (Approximately 130 signed opinions) |

The Supreme Court, 1990 Term: The Starting Nine

Pictured out of uniform (from left to right): John Paul Stevens, Harry Blackmun, Anthony Kennedy, Thurgood Marshall, Byron R. White, Chief Justice William H. Rehnquist, Antonin Scalia, Sandra Day O'Connor, and David Souter. In July 1991, Marshall announced his retirement, and President Bush nominated federal judge Clarence Thomas as Marshall's replacement.

four. With advance preparation by their law clerks, who screen petitions and prepare summaries, all nine justices make these judgments at conferences held twice a week. During these conferences, the justices vote on previously argued cases and consider which new cases to add to their docket. The chief justice circulates a "discuss list" of worthy petitions. Cases on this list are then subject to the rule of four. Since the retirement of Justice Brennan in 1990, no justice personally scans requests for review.[18]

The Solicitor General

Why does the Court decide to hear certain cases but not others? One theory suggests that the justices look for clues in the requests for review, for signs of an important case.[19] The most important sign is a recommendation by the solicitor general to grant or deny review.

The **solicitor general** represents the federal government before the Supreme Court. Appointed by the president, he is the third-ranking official in the U.S. Department of Justice (following the attorney general and deputy attorney general). His duties include determining whether the government should appeal lower-court decisions; reviewing and modifying, when necessary, the briefs filed in government appeals; and deciding whether the government should file an **amicus curiae brief** * in any appel-

---

*Amicus curiae is Latin for "friend of the court." Amicus briefs can be filed with permission of the Court. They allow groups and individuals who are not parties to the litigation but have an interest in it to influence the Court's thinking and, perhaps, its decision.

late court.[20] His objective is to create a cohesive program for the executive branch in the federal courts.

The solicitor general plays two different, occasionally conflicting, roles. First, he is an advocate for the president's policy preferences; second, as an officer of the Court, he traditionally defends the institutional interests of the national government. Sometimes the institutional interests prevail. For example, the Reagan administration was committed to returning power to the states. But Solicitor General Rex E. Lee argued for the exercise of federal power in his defense of a federal law setting wage requirements for a city-owned mass transit system. In a sharp blow to the administration, the Court held that the Constitution placed no specific limit on congressional power to interfere in state and local affairs.[21]

Solicitors general usually act with considerable restraint in recommending to the Court that a case be granted or denied review. By recommending only cases of general importance, they increase their credibility and their influence. Lee, who was solicitor general from 1981 to 1985, acknowledged in an unusually candid interview that he had refused to make arguments that members of the Reagan administration had urged on him: "I'm not the pamphleteer general; I'm the solicitor general. My audience is not 100 million people; my audience is nine people. . . . Credibility is the most important asset that any solicitor general has."[22]

President Bush appointed Kenneth Starr as his solicitor general in 1989. Starr reluctantly but vigorously argued that the justices should uphold an act of Congress designed to curb flag burning even though the Court struck down a similar Texas law the year before. "There was no doubt at all in my mind that the constitutionality of the statute could appropriately be defended," recalled Starr. "Once Congress passes a law, our duty is to defend it. That is perhaps the most fundamental duty of this office."[23] Starr lost; the Court struck down the prohibition.

The solicitor general is a powerful figure in the legal system. His influence in bringing cases to the Court and arguing them there has earned him the informal title of the "tenth justice."

Decision Making

Once the Court grants review, attorneys submit written arguments (briefs). Oral arguments usually follow. To conserve the justices' time and energy, these are limited to thirty minutes for each side. From October through April, the justices spend four hours a day, five or six days a month hearing arguments. The justices like crisp, concise, and conversational presentations; they disapprove of attorneys who read from a prepared text. Some justices are aggressive and relentless questioners who frequently interrupt attorneys; others are more subdued.

Court protocol prohibits justices from addressing one another directly during oral argument, but justices who are intent on debating each other anyway often pursue their match obliquely through the questions they pose to the attorneys. The justices reach no collective decision at oral argument. They reach a tentative decision only after they have met in conference.

Our knowledge of the dynamics of decision making on the Supreme Court is all secondhand (see Feature 14.3). Only the justices attend the Court's Wednesday and Friday conferences. By tradition, the justices first shake hands, a gesture of harmony. The chief justice then begins the presentation of each case with a combined discussion and vote followed in order of seniority by the discussion and vote of the other justices. Justice Antonin Scalia, who joined the Court in 1986, remarked that "not much conferencing goes on." By *conferencing*, Scalia meant efforts to persuade others to change their views by debating points of disagreement. "In fact," he said, "to call our discussion of a case a conference is really something of a misnomer. It's much more a statement of the views of each of the nine Justices, after which the totals are added and the case is assigned [for an opinion]."[24]

How do the justices decide how to vote on a case? According to some scholars, legal doctrines and past decisions explain their votes. This explanation, which is consistent with the majoritarian model, anchors the justices closely to the law and minimizes the contribution of their personal values. Other scholars contend that the value preferences and resulting ideologies of each justice provide a more powerful interpretation of their voting, and they have the evidence to boot. This explanation, which is consistent with the pluralist model, sees the justices as reflecting the public's values and acting on those value preferences.[25]

Judgment and argument.   The voting outcome is the **judgment**, the decision on who wins and who loses. Justices often disagree, not only on winners and losers but also on the reasons for their judgments. This should not be surprising, given nine independent minds and issues that can be approached in several ways. Voting in the conference does not end the work or resolve the disagreements. Votes remain tentative until the Court issues an opinion announcing its judgment.

After voting, the justices in the majority must draft an opinion setting out the reasons for their decision. The **argument** is the kernel of the opinion, its logical content separated from facts, rhetoric, and procedure. If all the justices agree with the judgment and the reasons supporting it, then the opinion is unanimous. A justice can agree with a judgment, upholding or striking down a claim, based on different reasons. This kind of agreement is called **concurrence**. Or a justice can **dissent** if she or he disagrees with a judgment. Both concurring and dissenting opinions may be drafted in addition to the majority opinion.

The opinion.   After the conference, the chief justice writes the majority opinion or assigns that responsibility to another justice in the majority. If the chief justice is not in the majority, the writing or assigning responsibility rests with the most senior associate justice in the majority. The assigning justice may consider several factors in allocating the crucial opinion-writing task: workload, expertise, public opinion, and, above all, the author's ability to hold the majority together. (Remember, at this point votes are only tentative.) If the drafting justice holds an extreme view on the issues in a case and is not able to incorporate the views of more moderate colleagues, those justices may withdraw their

FEATURE 14.3 *Name Calling in the Supreme Court: When the Justices Vent Their Spleen, Is There a Social Cost?*

The Supreme Court begins business on the first Monday in October. Refreshed and renewed, the justices shake hands in good fellowship and sit down around the conference table to begin the work of the new term. The vituperative and personal tone that marked some of the major opinions of recent terms, however, raises the question whether the justices will be able to look one another in the eye, let alone get back to work.

What do you say to someone after you have told her in public that her views are "irrational" and "cannot be taken seriously"? (Justice Antonin Scalia to Justice Sandra Day O'Connor in *Webster* v. *Reproductive Health Services,* the Missouri abortion case.) Or after you have accused someone of "an Orwellian rewriting of history"? (Justice Anthony M. Kennedy to Justice Harry A. Blackmun in *County of Allegheny* v. *American Civil Liberties Union,* the Pittsburgh case that permitted the government to display a Hanukkah menorah but barred a Nativity scene.) Or after you have dismissed someone's opinions as "a regrettably patronizing civics lecture"? (Chief Justice William H. Rehnquist to Justice William J. Brennan, Jr., in *Texas* v. *Johnson,* the flag-burning case.)

The questions go beyond the Court's mood to its credibility. Unlike the other branches, which replenish their political capital periodically when officeholders face the voters, the Court's credibility depends on the public's belief that its members are engaged in principled judging rather than personal one-upmanship.

While this is hardly the first, or even the most, stressful period in the court's history—it was Justice Oliver Wendell Holmes who described the Supreme Court half a century ago as "nine scorpions in a bottle"—the 1988 Term was the nastiest in years. Can the venom that was splattered across the pages of opinions really fade in the summer sun like so much disappearing ink?

It may not be easy to rattle Justice O'Connor. A former clerk for another Justice expressed doubt the other day that Justice O'Connor was particularly perturbed by Justice Scalia's verbal slings.

Shortly after Justice Scalia joined the Court in 1986, the ex-clerk recalled, the Justices met to discuss a pending case called *Johnson* v. *Santa Clara County,* which concerned the legality of an affirmative action program intended to benefit women. Justice Scalia treated his new colleagues to a 15-minute lecture on the evils of affirmative action, particularly affirmative action for women. When he finished, Justice O'Connor smiled and, addressing him by his nickname, said, "Why, Nino, how do you think I got my job?" Her eventual opinion supported the program; Justice Scalia attacked it in a long dissent.

Students of the Court note that even when it is running smoothly, it has not been a very collegial place in recent years. A generation has passed since Chief Justice Earl Warren cajoled his colleagues to produce the unanimous opinion that marked the end of the era of segregation. Scholars now view the unanimity of *Brown* v. *Board of Education* as an indispensable element that gave the decision its moral weight.

"The country holds an ideal of the court as a place where people sit down and reason together," Martha Minow, a Harvard law professor who clerked on the Court 10 years ago, said in a recent interview. "That's not true now even in the best of times. It's really nine separate courts. The Justices lead separate, even isolated lives. They deal with each other only in quite formalized settings. They vote the way they want to and then retreat to their own chambers."

With law clerks serving as ambassadors between the Justices' chambers, "the Justices have learned to run a Court quite well without talking to one another," another ex-clerk said.

The machinery works well enough to weather stormy periods like this one. The court can get by. Can it also inspire and lead? That is a question as important as any asked in the briefs now accumulating . . . and only the Justices have the answer.

Source: Linda Greenhouse, "At the Bar," *New York Times,* 28 July 1989, p. 21. Copyright © 1989 by The New York Times Company. Reprinted by permission.

votes. On the other hand, assigning a more moderate justice to draft an opinion could weaken the argument on which the opinion rests. Opinion-writing assignments can also be punitive. Justice Harry Blackmun once commented, "If one's in the doghouse with the Chief [former Chief Justice Warren Burger], he gets the crud."[26]

Opinion writing is the justices' most critical function. It is not surprising, then, that they spend much of their time drafting opinions. The justices usually call on their law clerks—top graduates of the nation's elite law schools—to help them prepare opinions and carry out other tasks. The commitment can be daunting. Justice Blackmun's four clerks typically work twelve hours a day, seven days a week. They write detailed memos outlining the facts and issues in each appeal, they prepare memos for each case prior to oral argument, and they prepare draft opinions that Blackmun eventually completes. According to one close Court observer, the clerks shoulder much of the writing responsibility for most of the justices.[27]

On the occasion of his eightieth birthday, after more than thirty years of service on the Court, Justice Brennan offered a rare account of the process of preparing and exchanging memoranda and drafts that leads to a final opinion: "It's startling to me every time I read these darned things to see how much I've had in the way of exchanges and how the exchanges have resulted in changes of view both of my own and of colleagues. And all of a sudden at the end of the road, we come up with an agreement on an opinion of the Court."[28]

The authoring justice distributes a draft opinion; the other justices read it, then circulate criticisms and suggestions. An opinion may have to be rewritten several times to accommodate colleagues who remain unpersuaded by the draft. Justice Felix Frankfurter was a perfectionist;

A Dynamic Playmaker . . .
Antonin Scalia, the 103d justice appointed to the Supreme Court, began his tenure in 1986 after four years as a federal appellate court judge. The confirmation hearings and subsequent Senate vote on his appointment were remarkably unanimous for this most conservative justice. Scalia has lived up to his reputation as a brilliant scholar, using his personal computer to write incisive, and occasionally scornful, opinions.

some of his opinions went through thirty or more drafts. Justices can change their votes, and perhaps alter the judgment, up until the decision is officially announced. And the justices announce their decisions only when they are ready. Often the most controversial cases pile up in a backlog as the coalitions on the Court vie for support or sharpen their criticisms. When the Court announces decisions, the authoring justices read or summarize their opinions in the courtroom. Printed and electronic copies of these opinions, known as *slip opinions*, are then distributed to interested parties and the press.

Justices in the majority frequently try to muffle or stifle dissent in order to encourage institutional cohesion. Since the mid-1940s, however, unity has been more difficult to obtain.[29] Gaining agreement from the justices today is akin to negotiating with nine separate law firms. It may be more surprising that the justices ever agree. Nevertheless, the justices must be keenly aware of the slender foundation of their authority, which rests largely on public respect. That respect is tested whenever the Court ventures into areas of controversy. Banking, slavery, and Reconstruction policies embroiled the Court in controversy in the nineteenth century. Freedom of speech and religion, racial equality, and the right of privacy have led the Court into controversy in this century.

Strategies on the Court

The Court is more than the sum of its formal processes. The justices exercise real political power. If we start with the assumption that the justices are attempting to stamp their own policy views on the cases they review, then we should expect typical political behavior from them. Cases that reach the Supreme Court's docket pose difficult choices.

. . . And a Junior Member of His Team

Supreme Court justices use recent law school graduates as short-term clerks. Here Larry Lessig, one of Scalia's four clerks, divides his time between one of the thousands of petitions for certiorari that arrive at the Court each year and the final draft of a dissent by Scalia concerning the length of time a person can be held in custody without a hearing. The Court majority established a 48-hour limit; Scalia argued that the limit should be set at 24 hours (County of Riverside v. McLaughlin, 1991).

Because the justices are grappling with conflict on a daily basis, they probably have well-defined ideologies that reflect their values. Scholars and journalists have attempted to pierce the veil of secrecy that shrouds the Court from public view and analyze these ideologies.[30]

The beliefs of most justices can be located on the two-dimensional model of political values discussed in Chapter 1 (see Figure 1.2). Liberal justices, like Thurgood Marshall and Harry Blackmun, choose freedom over order, and equality over freedom. Conservative justices—William Rehnquist and Sandra Day O'Connor, for example—choose order over freedom, and freedom over equality. These choices translate into policy preferences as the justices struggle to win votes or retain coalitions.

We know that the justices also vary in intellectual ability, advocacy skills, social graces, temperament, and the like. For example, Chief Justice Charles Evans Hughes (1930–1941) had a photographic memory and came to each conference armed with well-marked copies of Supreme Court opinions. Few justices could keep up with him in debate. Today, justices argue for the support of their colleagues, offering information in the form of drafts and memoranda to explain the advantages and disadvantages of voting for or against an issue. And we expect the justices make occasional, if not regular, use of friendship, ridicule, and patriotism to mold their colleagues' views.

A justice might adopt a long-term strategy of influencing the appointment of like-minded colleagues in order to marshal additional strength on the Court. Chief Justice (and former President) William Howard Taft (1921–1930), for example, bombarded President Warren G. Harding with recommendations and suggestions whenever a Court vacancy was announced. Taft was especially determined to block the appointment of anyone who might side with the "dangerous twosome," Justices Oliver Wendell Holmes and Louis D. Brandeis. Taft said he "must stay on the Court in order to prevent the Bolsheviki from getting control."[31]

The Chief Justice

The chief justice is only one of nine justices, but he has several important functions based on his authority. And if he does not carry them out, someone else will.[32] Apart from his role in docket control decisions and his direction of the conference, the chief justice can also be a social leader, generating solidarity within the group. Sometimes, a chief justice can embody intellectual leadership. Finally, the chief justice can provide policy leadership, directing the Court toward a general policy position. Perhaps only John Marshall could lay claim to social, intellectual, and policy leadership roles. (Docket control did not exist during Marshall's time.) Warren E. Burger, who resigned as chief justice in 1986, was a lackluster leader in all three areas.

When he presides at the conference, the chief justice can exercise control over the discussion of issues, although independent-minded justices are not likely to succumb to his views. For example, as discussed in the chapter opening, at the end of the conference on *Brown* v. *Board of Education*, Chief Justice Warren had six firm votes for his position that segregated public schools were unconstitutional. Two other justices indicated that they would join the majority if an opinion could be written to meet their concerns. In the months that followed, Warren talked frequently with his colleagues to minimize the possibility of dissenting or concurring opinions. By April 1954, only one holdout remained, and he eventually joined the others. Warren's patriotic appeals had made both the decision and the opinion unanimous.[33]

Judicial Recruitment

Neither the Constitution nor federal law imposes formal requirements for appointment to the federal courts, except for the condition that, once appointed, district court and appeals judges must reside in the district or circuit to which they are appointed.

The president appoints judges to the federal courts, and all nominees must be confirmed by the Senate. Congress sets, but cannot lower, a judge's compensation. In 1992, salaries were:

Chief justice	$166,200
Associate justices	159,000
Court of appeals judges	137,300
District court judges	129,500

State courts operate somewhat similarly to federal courts. Governors appoint judges in nearly half the states. Other states select their judges by partisan, nonpartisan, or (rarely) legislative election.[34] Nominees in

Chicago Justice

From the age of four, Bertina Lampkin accompanied her father, a criminal defense attorney, to court. Today she is an associate judge in Cook County, Illinois, assigned to Night Narcotics Court. She takes the bench at 4 P.M. "I don't think there is a better job. I love to hear the arguments. If the lawyers come prepared and give good arguments, it is the best day I can have. I'll gladly stay here until 1 A.M." (Anne Keegan, "Women on the Bench," Chicago Tribune Magazine, 12 May 1991, p. 11.)

some states must be confirmed by the state legislature. In the rest, judges are confirmed in general elections held several years after appointment. Contested elections for judgeships are unusual. In Chicago, where judges are elected, even highly publicized widespread criminal corruption in the courts failed to unseat incumbents in 1987. Most voters paid no attention whatsoever.

The Appointment of Federal Judges

The Constitution states that federal judges hold their commissions "during good Behaviour," which in practice means for life.* A president's judicial appointments, then, are likely to survive his administration, a kind of political legacy. The appointment power assumes that the president is free to identify candidates and appoint judges who favor his policies. Figure 14.3 illustrates presidential impact on the federal judiciary. President Franklin Roosevelt had appointed nearly 75 percent of the federal judges by the end of his twelve years in office. In contrast, President Ford appointed fewer than 13 percent in his three years in office. The similarity of Bush and Reagan judicial appointments suggests that their combined impact may approach, and perhaps exceed, Roosevelt's.

Judicial vacancies occur when sitting judges resign, retire, or die. Vacancies also arise when Congress creates new judgeships to handle increasing caseloads. The president then nominates a candidate, who must be confirmed by the Senate. The president has the help of the Justice Department, which screens candidates before the formal nomination, subjecting serious contenders to FBI investigation. The department and the Senate vie for control in the appointment of district court and appeals judges.

The "Advice and Consent" of the Senate.   For district court and appeals vacancies, the appointment process hinges on the nominee's acceptability to the senior senator in the president's party from the state in which the vacancy arises. The senator's influence is greatest for appointments to the district court and less for appointments to the court of appeals.

The practice of **senatorial courtesy** forces presidents to share the nomination power with members of the Senate. The Senate will not confirm a nominee who is opposed by the senior senator in the president's party in the nominee's state. The Senate doesn't actually reject the candidate. Instead, a form, called a "blue slip," is not returned by the senior senator. In the absence of the blue slip, the chair of the Senate Judiciary Committee, which reviews all judicial nominees, will not schedule a confirmation hearing, effectively killing the nomination.

Although the Justice Department is still sensitive to senatorial prerogatives, senators can no longer submit a single name to fill a vacancy. The department searches for acceptable candidates and polls the appropriate

---

* Only seven federal judges have been removed by impeachment in nearly two hundred years; nine resigned before formal impeachment charges could be lodged; and only five have ever been convicted of felonies (serious criminal conduct).

FIGURE 14.3 *Judicial Appointments by President*

The number of federal judgeships increases with every president (Ford provided the only exception). The longer a president is in office, the more appointments he can make. Roosevelt, for instance, appointed 197 judges—75 percent of the available judgeships—during his 12 years in office. Reagan currently holds the record for most judges appointed, but Bush, if he wins a second term, will likely exceed that number because he is working from a larger pool of potential judicial vacancies. (Source: Congressional Quarterly, 19 January 1991, p. 173. Used by permission.)

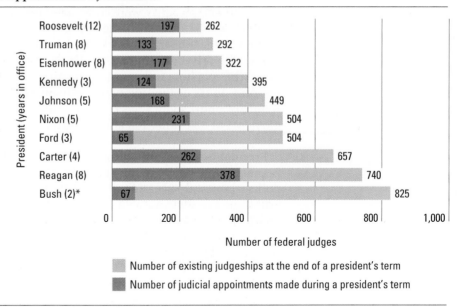

President (years in office)

Roosevelt (12) — 197 / 262
Truman (8) — 133 / 292
Eisenhower (8) — 177 / 322
Kennedy (3) — 124 / 395
Johnson (5) — 168 / 449
Nixon (5) — 231 / 504
Ford (3) — 65 / 504
Carter (4) — 262 / 657
Reagan (8) — 378 / 740
Bush (2)* — 67 / 825

Number of federal judges

0   200   400   600   800   1,000

▢ Number of existing judgeships at the end of a president's term
▮ Number of judicial appointments made during a president's term

* Data based on Bush's first two years in office.

senator for her or his reaction to them. And President Bush has asked Republican senators to seek out more qualified female and minority recommendations.[35]

The Senate Judiciary Committee conducts a hearing for each judicial nominee. The chair exercises a measure of control in the appointment process, beyond the power of senatorial courtesy. If a nominee is objectionable to the chair, he or she can delay a hearing or hold up other appointments until the president and the Justice Department consider some alternative. This kind of behavior does not win a politician much influence in the long run, however. So committee chairs are usually loathe to place obstacles in a president's path, especially when they may want presidential support for their own policies and constituencies.

The American Bar Association. The American Bar Association (ABA), the largest organization of lawyers in the United States, has been involved in screening candidates for the federal bench since 1946.[36] Its role is defined by custom, not law. At the president's behest, the ABA's Standing Committee on the Federal Judiciary routinely rates prospective appointees, using a four-value scale ranging from "exceptionally well qualified" to "not qualified."

To gather information about a candidate, the committee, in confidence, interviews lawyers and judges who know and are capable of evaluating the candidate. The committee's recommendation is supposed to address the candidate's "professional qualifications," which are defined as "competence, integrity, and judicial temperament." A candidate's politics and ideology should have no bearing on the committee's task. There used to be a loophole: "Extreme views" that affected the candidate's temperament and integrity were considered relevant to the committee's evaluation. In 1987, however, the committee's divided vote on the nomination of Judge Robert H. Bork to the Supreme Court strengthened the successful drive to stop his confirmation. The committee then eliminated the loophole following criticism of its handling of the Bork nomination.[37] In its evaluation of subsequent High Court nominees Anthony Kennedy and David Souter, the committee focused on nonideological elements of its evaluation and conferred the highest rating on both nominees.

Presidents do not always agree with the committee's judgment, in part because its objections can still mask disagreements with a candidate's political views. Occasionally, a candidate deemed "not qualified" is nominated and even appointed, but the overwhelming majority of appointees to the federal bench since 1946 have had the ABA's blessing.

Recent Presidents and the Federal Judiciary

President Jimmy Carter had two objectives in his judicial appointments. First, Carter wanted to base judicial appointments on merit, to appoint judges of higher quality than had his predecessors. Whether he succeeded is debatable—a question that only time and scholarship can answer. But he did meet his second objective, to make the judiciary more representative of the general population. Carter appointed substantially more blacks, women, and Hispanics to the federal bench than did any of his predecessors or his successors. Here his actions were consistent with the pluralist model, at least in a symbolic sense.

Early in his administration, it was clear that President Reagan did not share Carter's second objective. Although Reagan generally heeded senatorial recommendations for the district courts and, like Carter, held a firmer rein on appointments to the appeals courts, there were strong differences. By the end of his second term, only 2 percent of Reagan's appointments were blacks and only 8 percent were women; in contrast, 14 percent of Carter's appointments were blacks and 16 percent were women. Four percent of Reagan judges were Hispanics compared to 6 percent of Carter judges. Bush's record on women and minority appointments is slightly better than Reagan's, but it does not approach Carter's appointment record (see Figure 14.4). A Justice Department official maintained that Reagan's appointment record reflected demographic and political reality. "We would love to find more qualified blacks," but there was "just not even a respectable small pool" of black nominees who qualified on the basis of experience and commitment to Reagan's conservative agenda.[38]

It seems clear that political ideology, not demographics, lay at the heart of Reagan's judicial appointments. Reagan sought out nominees with particular policy preferences in order to leave his stamp on the judiciary well into the twenty-first century. Both Carter and Reagan used the nation's law schools the way major league baseball managers use farm teams. With the right statistics, a professor could move to the major leagues—in this case, one of the federal district or appellate courts. Car-

FIGURE 14.4 *Blacks, Hispanics, and Women in the Legal System*

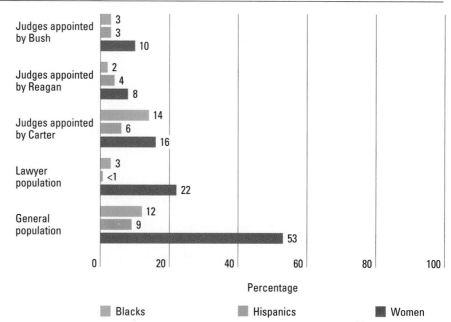

The composition of the legal profession does not mirror the composition of the general population, especially with regard to race and gender. Jimmy Carter attempted to make the federal bench more representative by appointing more blacks, Hispanics, and women. Ronald Reagan's appointments approached neither the composition of the lawyer population nor the population at large. So far, Bush's appointments are a close match to Reagan's. (Sources: "Census Shows Profound Change in Racial Makeup of the Nation," New York Times, 11 March 1991, p. A1; Congressional Quarterly, 19 January 1991, p. 172; Insight, 11 February 1991, p. 59.)

ter's liberal values led him to look for judges who were committed to equality; Reagan's conservative values led him to appoint judges who were more committed to order. Reagan surpassed Carter in reshaping the federal courts: 262 lifetime appointments for Carter compared with 378 lifetime appointments for Reagan.

Just two years into his presidency, Bush has appointed 67 people to the bench, including 18 to the courts of appeals. He has followed the example of his predecessor by nominating conservatives. In fact, Reagan's appointment of hundreds of judges in the district courts has created a judicial minor league, enabling Bush to identify and nominate appellate court judges with some confidence in their value preferences and ideology.[39]

Appointment to the Supreme Court

The announcement of a vacancy on the High Court usually causes quite a stir. Campaigns for Supreme Court seats are commonplace, although the public rarely sees them. Hopeful candidates contact friends in the administration and urge influential associates to do the same on their behalf. Some candidates never give up hope. Judge John J. Parker, whose nomination to the Court was defeated in 1930, tried in vain to rekindle interest in his appointment several times until he was well past the age—usually the early sixties—when appointments are made.[40]

The president is not shackled by senatorial courtesy when it comes to nominating a Supreme Court justice. Appointment to the High Court attracts more intense public scrutiny than do lower-level appointments.

This scrutiny limits a president's choices and focuses attention on the Senate's "Advice and Consent."

Of the 144 men and 1 woman nominated to the Court, 28—or about one in five—have failed to receive Senate confirmation. Only six such fumbles have come in this century, the last two during the Reagan administration. The most important factor in the rejection of a nominee is partisan politics. Thirteen candidates lost their bids for appointment because the presidents who nominated them were "lame ducks": The party in control of the Senate anticipated victory for its candidate in an upcoming presidential race and sought to deny the incumbent president an important political appointment.[41] The most recent nominee to be rejected, on partisan and ideological grounds, was Judge Bork.

Since 1950, eighteen of twenty-two Supreme Court nominees have had judicial experience in federal or state courts. This "promotion" from within the judiciary may be based on the idea that a judge's past opinions are good predictors of future opinions on the High Court. After all, a president is handing out a powerful lifetime appointment; it makes sense to want an individual who is sympathetic to his views. Federal or state court judges holding lifetime appointments are likely to state their views frankly in their opinions. In contrast, the policy preferences of High Court candidates who have been in legal practice or in political office must be based on the conjecture of professional associates or on the text of a speech to the local Rotary Club or on the floor of the legislature.

The resignation of Chief Justice Warren Burger in 1986 gave Reagan the chance to elevate Associate Justice William H. Rehnquist to the position of chief justice and to appoint Antonin Scalia, who was a judge in a federal court of appeals, as Rehnquist's replacement. Rehnquist faced stern questioning from liberal critics during his Senate confirmation hearings. (The testimony of Supreme Court nominees is a relatively recent phenomenon; it began in 1925 when Harlan Fiske Stone was nominated to the High Court.) But Rehnquist's opponents were unable to stop confirmation in the Republican-controlled Senate. Both Rehnquist and Scalia did not try to defend their judicial records; they argued that judicial independence meant that they could not be called to account before the Senate. Both judges also ducked discussing issues that might come to the Court for fear of compromising their impartiality.

In 1987, when Justice Lewis F. Powell, Jr., resigned, Reagan had an opportunity to shift the ideological balance on the Court toward a more conservative consensus. He nominated Judge Robert H. Bork, a conservative, to fill the vacancy. Bork advocated **judicial restraint**, which rests on the premise that legislators, not judges, should make the laws. Ironically, the legislators who opposed Bork supported the concept of **judicial activism,** which allows judges to promote desirable social goals (see Feature 14.4). Some of Bork's critics maintained that he was really an activist draped in the robes of judicial restraint. Bork's true purpose, these critics charged, was to advance his conservative ideology from the High Court.

The hearings concluded after several days of televised testimony from Judge Bork and a parade of witnesses. Liberal interest groups formed a rare coalition that included abortion rights, civil rights, feminist, labor, environmental, and senior citizen organizations. They put aside their

FEATURE 14.4   *Judicial Restraint and Judicial Activism*

The terms *judicial restraint* and *judicial activism* describe the assertiveness of judicial power. Judges are said to exercise judicial restraint when they hew closely to statutes and previous cases in reaching their decisions. Judges are said to exercise judicial activism when they are apt to interpret existing laws and rulings more loosely and to interject their own values in court decisions.

We can describe the theoretical extremes of judicial assertiveness. Judges acting according to an extreme model of judicial restraint would decide nothing at all, deferring to the superiority of other government institutions in construing the law.

Judges acting according to an extreme model of judicial activism would be an intrusive and ever-present force that dominated other government institutions. Actual judicial behavior lies somewhere between these two extremes.

In recent history, many activist judges have tended to trade freedom for equality in their decisions, which has linked the concept of judicial activism with liberalism. However, there is no necessary connection between judicial activism and liberalism. If judges interpret existing statutes and precedents more loosely to trade freedom for order, they are still activists—conservative activists.

disagreements and mounted a massive campaign to defeat the nomination, overwhelming conservative efforts to buttress Bork. At first, the public was undecided on Bork's confirmation; by the time the hearings ended, though, public opinion shifted against him. Even though his defeat was a certainty, Bork insisted that the Senate vote on his nomination, hoping for a sober discussion of his record. But the rancor never abated. Bork was defeated by a vote of 58–42, the largest margin by which the Senate has ever rejected a Supreme Court nominee.

Federal appeals court judge Douglas H. Ginsburg was nominated shortly thereafter. Ginsburg had strong conservative credentials and youth (he was forty-one when nominated) on his side. Nine days after the nomination, Ginsburg's plans went up in smoke when he confirmed allegations that he had used marijuana while he was a student and a Harvard Law School professor. This revelation was an embarrassment to the Reagan administration, which had made "Just Say No" to drugs a national campaign. Ginsburg withdrew his nomination.

Subsequently, federal appeals court judge Anthony M. Kennedy was nominated and confirmed. The Senate examined Kennedy's views in detail, and the nominee did not duck questions that assessed his stand on constitutional issues. His winning combination of wholesomeness and ideological moderation netted him a place as the 104th justice of the Supreme Court.

The rules of the game for appointment to the High Court appear to have changed in 1990 when President Bush plucked David Souter from relative obscurity to replace liberal Justice William J. Brennan, Jr., who retired because of failing health. Souter fit the model of other nominees: He had extensive judicial experience as a justice on the New Hampshire Supreme Court and had recently been appointed to the federal court of appeals. But there was one significant difference: Souter was a "Stealth" candidate. His views on provocative topics were undetectable because he had written little and spoken less on privacy, abortion, religious liberty, and equal protection. To elicit his views, some members of the Senate

Judiciary Committee tried sparing with Souter at his confirmation hearings; he successfully avoided or deflected the most controversial topics. Souter was confirmed by the Senate, 90–9. Leading legal scholars and jurists with records and views on controversial issues may now prove vulnerable, and unconfirmable, when different parties control the legislative and executive branches.

The unpredictability of a few Supreme Court justices has surprised presidents as well as professors. In recent political history, two presidents found inconsistencies between their expectations and the actual performance of their appointees. Eisenhower, a moderate conservative, called his appointment of Chief Justice Warren, a strong liberal voice, "one of the two biggest mistakes I made in my administration."[42] Harry S Truman considered his appointment of Justice Tom C. Clark the biggest mistake of his presidency. "It isn't so much that he's a *bad* man," said Truman. "It's just that he's such a dumb son of a bitch. He's about the dumbest man I think I've ever run across."[43]

The Legal Profession

As we have noted, judges bring their beliefs, values, and experiences to bear on their judicial responsibilities. We have argued that the judiciary is a vital link in the chain that connects law and politics. It follows that the legal profession is the raw material from which that link is forged. To better understand judges and the power they wield, we have to understand lawyers and the nature of their craft.[44]

Growth of the Profession

Today, the number of lawyers in the United States exceeds 755,000.[45] This translates to one lawyer for every 333 people. Thirty years ago, there was one lawyer for every 700 people. The rate at which the legal profession is growing will probably continue to outpace the rate of population growth through the end of the century.

Once a bastion of white men, the legal profession has undergone profound change in gender and, to a lesser extent, in minority composition. More than 40 percent of first-year law students today are women; and nearly 10 percent are minority group members.[46]

Why is a career in law so popular? Market forces account for some of the allure. We know that in 1988 the average salary of experienced lawyers in private practice was $110,000. If we could include in this average the salaries of all lawyers, whatever their experience, the figure would probably be much lower, certainly well below the $108,000 average salary of physicians. But lawyers' salaries are still substantially greater than those of many other professionals.[47] Salaries for newly minted lawyers heading for elite New York law firms approached $90,000 in 1990; some firms offered additional bonuses for clerkship experience in the federal courts and state supreme courts. The glamour of legal practice strengthens the attraction of its financial rewards.

What Lawyers Do

Lawyers perform four major functions.[48]

- First, lawyers counsel. This means that lawyers offer advice, even if it is advice their clients would prefer not to hear. Of course, lawyers regularly counsel clients during negotiation and litigation. And clients regularly seek lawyers' counsel prior to either negotiation or litigation.

- Second, lawyers negotiate. This means that they mediate between competing interests aiming for results that will prove advantageous to their clients and, if possible, their opponents. Since the vast majority of cases settle out of court, attorneys necessarily spend a significant portion of their time negotiating.

- Third, lawyers draft documents. This is probably their most intellectually challenging function since the objective is to compose documents (like a contract or a will) that will secure an understanding and withstand possible challenges.

- Fourth, they litigate. This is the skill most people associate with lawyers. Ironically, only a small fraction of all lawyers devote much time to courtroom activities. In fact, the majority of attorneys never venture into a courthouse except to file legal papers with a clerk.

In the endless debate over the role of lawyers in society, some scholars claim that lawyers are social architects, trained to design their vision of a better society. An alternative view proposes that we regard lawyers "not as the architects of society but as its janitors."[49] After all, lawyers spend a great deal of their time tidying up and repairing the wear-and-tear that society creates. Whether lawyers are architects or janitors, interest in the legal profession and demand for its services seem boundless. One possible explanation derives from American culture.

Materialism and individualism in American culture encourage disputes. Federalism gives us separate legal systems for each state plus the national government; thus, the structure of American government provides a number of judicial outlets. Advertising by law firms can now create demand for legal services, too, acting as tinder for disputes that might otherwise extinguish on their own. Finally, the principles of separation of powers and of checks and balances help generate lawsuits by making governing difficult and sometimes impossible. When political institutions act, they often are forced to compromise, deferring critical issues to the courts. Pluralist democracy operates when groups are able to press their interests on, and even challenge, the government. The expression of group demands in a culture that encourages lawsuits thrusts on the courts all manner of disputes and interests. Is it any wonder that America needs all the lawyers it can train?[50]

U.S. Attorneys

The Justice Department is responsible for the faithful execution of the laws under the president's authority. The main administrators of federal law enforcement are the ninety-four U.S. attorneys, who are appointed by the president with the advice and consent of the Senate. Unlike federal judges, these appointees serve at the pleasure of the president and are expected to relinquish their positions when the reins of government change hands.

There is a U.S. attorney in each federal judicial district. Their staffs of assistant attorneys vary in size with the amount of litigation in the district. U.S. attorneys have considerable discretion, which makes them powerful political figures. Their decision to prosecute or not affects the wealth, freedom, rights, and reputation of the individuals and organizations in the district. There is evidence of substantial variation in prosecution policies from district to district. In a study of seven U.S. attorney offices, investigators found that each office prosecuted certain offenses when a minimum amount of money was involved, but the amount varied a good deal from office to office for the same offense.[51]

U.S. attorneys are political appointees who often harbor political ambitions.[52] Their position commands media attention and can serve political goals. For example, Republican William F. Weld was a former U.S. attorney who ran for governor in Massachusetts in 1990. Weld earned a reputation—and valuable visibility—as a tough prosecutor, notching his briefcase with convictions against members of Boston's organized crime family and against top Democrats in Boston city government. By facing a more conservative Democratic opponent, Weld proved a moderate, enabling him to eke out a victory in a decidedly Democratic state.

The Consequences of Judicial Decisions

Lawsuits are the tip of the iceberg of disputes; most disputes never surface in the courts. Of all the lawsuits begun in the United States, the overwhelming majority end without a court judgment. Many civil cases are settled, or the parties give up, or the courts dismiss the claims because they are beyond the legitimate bounds of judicial resolution.

Most criminal cases end with a **plea bargain**, the defendant's admission of guilt in exchange for a less severe punishment. Only about 20 percent of criminal cases in the federal district courts are tried; an equally small percentage of civil cases are adjudicated. The fact that a judge sentences a criminal defendant to ten years in prison or that a court holds a company liable for $11 billion in damages does not guarantee that the defendant or the company will give up either freedom or assets. In the case of the criminal defendant, the grounds for appeal following trial and conviction are well traveled and, if nothing else, serve to delay the day when no alternative to prison remains. In civil cases, the immediate consequence of a judgment may also be an appeal, which delays the day of reckoning.

Supreme Court Rulings: Implementation and Impact

When the Supreme Court makes a decision, it relies on others to *implement* it, to translate policy into action. How a judgment is implemented rests in good measure on how it was crafted. Remember that the justices, in preparing opinions, are working to hold their majorities together, to gain greater, if not unanimous support for their arguments. This forces them to compromise in their opinions, to moderate their arguments, and creates uncertainty in many of the policies they articulate. Ambiguous opinions affect the implementation of policy. For example, when the Supreme Court issued its order in 1955 to desegregate public school facilities "with all deliberate speed,"[53] judges who opposed the Court's policy dragged their feet in implementing it. In the early 1960s, the Supreme Court struck down prayers and Bible reading in public schools. Yet state court judges and attorneys general reinterpreted the High Court's decision to mean that only *compulsory* prayer or Bible reading was unconstitutional, that state-sponsored voluntary prayer or Bible reading was acceptable.[54]

Because the Supreme Court confronts issues freighted with deeply felt social values or fundamental political beliefs, its decisions have impact beyond the immediate parties in a dispute. The Court's decision in *Roe v. Wade* legalizing abortion generated heated public reaction. The justices were barraged with thousands of angry letters. Groups opposing abortion vowed to overturn the decision; groups favoring abortion moved to protect the right they had won. Within eight months of the decision, more than two dozen constitutional amendments had been introduced in Congress, although none managed to carry the extraordinary majority required for passage. Still, the antiabortion faction achieved a modest victory with the passage of a provision forbidding the use of federal funds for abortions except when the mother's life is in jeopardy.

Opponents of abortion have also directed efforts toward state legislatures, hoping to load the abortion law with enough regulations to discourage women from terminating their pregnancies. For example, one state required that women receive detailed information about abortions, then wait at least twenty-four hours before consenting to the procedure. The information listed every imaginable danger associated with abortion and included a declaration that fathers are liable to assist in their children's support. In 1989, the Court abandoned its strong defense of abortion rights. It continued to support a woman's right to abortion but now recognized the government's power to limit the exercise of that right.

Public Opinion and the Supreme Court

Democratic theorists have a difficult time reconciling a commitment to representative democracy with a judiciary that is not accountable to the electorate yet has the power to undo legislative or executive acts. This difficulty may simply be a problem for theorists, however, because the policies coming from the Supreme Court rarely seem out of line with public opinion.[55] Surveys in several controversial areas reveal that the Court seldom departs from majority sentiment or the trend toward such sentiment.[56]

The evidence squarely supports the view that the Supreme Court holds close to public opinion at least as often as other elected institutions. In a comprehensive study matching 146 Supreme Court rulings with nationwide opinion polls from the mid-1930s through the mid-1980s, the

Court reflected public opinion majorities or pluralities in over 60 percent of its rulings. The fit is not perfect, however. The Court parted company with public opinion in a third of its rulings. For example, the Court has clearly defied the wishes of the majority for decades on the issue of school prayer. Most Americans today do not agree with the Court's position. And as long as the public continues to want prayer in schools, the controversy will continue.

There are at least three explanations for the Court's consistency with majority sentiment. First, the modern Court has shown deference toward national laws and policies, which typically echo national public opinion. Second, the Court moves closer to public opinion during periods of crisis. And, third, rulings that reflect the public view are subject to fewer changes than rulings that depart from public opinion.

Finally, the evidence also supports the view that the Court seldom influences public opinion. The Court enjoys only moderate popularity, and its decisions are not widely perceived by the public. With few exceptions, there is no evidence of shifting public opinion prior to and following its rulings.[57]

The Courts and Models of Democracy

How far should judges stray from existing statutes and precedents? Supporters of the majoritarian model would argue that the courts should adhere to the letter of the law, that judges must refrain from injecting their own values into their decisions. If the law places too much (or not enough) emphasis on equality or order, it is up to the elected legislature, not the courts, to change the law. In contrast, those who support the pluralist model maintain that the courts are a policymaking branch of government and that the individual values and interests of judges should advance the different values and interests of the population at large. To the extent that the judiciary comes to mirror group interests, it may then reflect those group preferences. Or judges may consciously attempt to advance group interests as they see fit.

The argument that our judicial system fits the pluralist model gains support from a legal procedure called **class action**. Class action is a device for assembling the claims or defenses of similarly situated individuals so that they can be tried as a single lawsuit. A class action makes it possible for people with small individual claims and limited financial resources to aggregate their claims and resources in order to make a lawsuit viable. Decisions in class action suits can have broader impact than decisions in other types of cases. Since the 1940s, class action suits have been the vehicles through which groups have asserted claims involving civil rights, legislative apportionment, and environmental problems. For example, schoolchildren have sued (through their parents) under the banner of class action to rectify claims of racial discrimination on the part of school authorities, as in *Brown* v. *Board of Education*.

Abetting the class action is the resurgence of state supreme courts in fashioning policies consistent with group preferences. Informed Americans often look to the United States Supreme Court for the protection of

Whose Deal?

The New York Court of Appeals is the highest court in the state. Although it is bound by the decisions of the U.S. Supreme Court when defining and limiting national constitutional rights, it may rely on provisions of the state constitution to extend protections to individuals beyond those granted by the Supreme Court. For example, the New York court requires police to follow stricter procedures during car searches than those implemented by the Supreme Court.

their rights and liberties. In many circumstances this observation is correct. But it is also incomplete. State courts of all levels annually resolve literally millions of decisions. They exercise substantial influence over policies that affect citizens daily, including the rights and liberties enshrined in their state constitutions, statutes, and common law.[58]

State judges need not look to the United States Supreme Court for guidance on the meaning of similar state rights and liberties (see Table 14.1). If a state court chooses to rely solely on federal law in deciding a case, then that case is reviewable by the U.S. Supreme Court. But a state court can avoid review by the U.S. Supreme Court by resting its decision solely on state law or by plainly stating that its decision rests on both state and federal law. If the U.S. Supreme Court is likely to render a restrictive view of a constitutional right, and the judges of a state court are inclined to a more expansive view, the state judges can employ the state court ground as a way of avoiding Supreme Court review. In a period when the nation's highest court is moving in a decidedly conservative direction, it should come as no surprise that some state courts have become safe havens for liberal values. And individuals and groups know where to moor their policies.

The New Jersey Supreme Court has been more aggressive than most courts of last resort in following its own liberal constitutional path. It has gone further than the U.S. Supreme Court in promoting equality at

T A B L E   14.1   *Protecting Rights and Liberties: U.S. Supreme Court Versus State Supreme Courts*

Most Americans believe that the United States Supreme Court has the last word on their constitutional rights. But state constitutions also confer rights, many of them identical to the ones enshrined in the national Bill of Rights. The states cannot provide less protection for individual rights than the U.S. Constitution, but they can provide more. State court decisions are immune from subsequent challenge in the federal courts provided the decisions rest on adequate and independent reasons in the state constitutions.

At one time, liberals spurned state courts as conservative institutions; they preferred the ideological sympathy of the Warren Court for an expansion of constitutional guarantees. Today, liberals see state courts as safer havens for expanding rights and liberties than the nation's highest court.

Issue	*U.S. Supreme Court ruling . . .*	*. . . and the state courts that have differed*
Public funding for abortion	No	Calif., Mass., N.J.
Equalized school financing	No	Ark., Calif., Conn., Ky., N.J., Texas, Wash., W. Va., Wis., Wyo.
Leafleting in shopping centers	No	Calif., Mass., N.J., Pa., Wash.
Admitting evidence seized illegally but in good faith	Yes	Conn., N.C., N.J., N.Y.

Source: *Time,* 8 October 1990, p. 76. Copyright 1990 The Time Inc. Magazine Company. Reprinted by permission.

the expense of freedom by striking down discrimination against women by private employers and by striking down the state system of public school finance. The court has also preferred freedom to order by protecting the right to terminate life-support systems and by protecting free speech against private enfringement.[59] The New Jersey judges have charted their own path despite the similarity in language between sections of the New Jersey constitution and the U.S. Constitution. The New Jersey judges have parted company with their federal "cousins" even when the constitutional provisions at issue are identical.

For example, the United States Supreme Court ruled in 1988 that warrantless searches of curbside garbage were constitutionally permissible. Both the New Jersey constitution and the federal Constitution bar unreasonable searches and seizures. Yet in a 1990 decision expanding constitutional protections, the New Jersey court ruled that police officers need a search warrant before they can rummage through a person's trash. The court claimed that the New Jersey constitution offers a greater degree of privacy than the U.S. Constitution. Since the decision rested on an interpretation of the state constitution, the presence of a similar right in the national charter had no bearing. New Jersey cannot act in a more restrictive manner than the guidelines established by the United States Supreme Court, but it can be—and is—less restrictive in its practices.[60]

When judges reach decisions, they pay attention to the views of other courts, and not just to the ones above them in the judicial hierarchy. State and federal court opinions are the legal granary from which judges regularly draw their ideas. Often the issues that affect individual lives—property, family, contracts—are grist for state courts, not federal courts. For example, when a state court faces a novel issue in a contract dispute, it will look to the way in which other state courts have dealt with the problem. (Contract disputes are not a staple of the federal courts.) And if courts in several states have addressed an issue and the direction of the opinion is largely one-sided, the weight and authority of those opinions may move the court in that direction.[61] Courts that confront new issues with cogency and clarity are likely to become leaders of legal innovation.

State courts have become renewed arenas for political conflict with litigants, individually or in groups, vying for their policies. The multiplicity of court systems with their overlapping state and federal responsibilities provides alternative points of access for individuals and groups to present and argue their claims. This description of the courts fits the pluralist model of government.

Summary

The power of judicial review, claimed by the Supreme Court in 1803, placed the judiciary on an equal footing with Congress and the president. The principle of checks and balances can restrain judicial power through several means, such as constitutional amendment and impeachment. But restrictions on that power have been infrequent, leaving the federal courts to exercise considerable influence through judicial review and statutory construction.

The federal court system has three tiers. At the bottom are the district courts, where litigation begins and most disputes end. In the middle are the courts of appeals. At the top is the Supreme Court. The ability of judges to make policy increases as one moves up the pyramid from trial courts to appellate courts.

The Supreme Court, free to draft its own agenda through the discretionary control of its docket, harmonizes conflicting interpretations of national law and articulates constitutional rights. It is helped at this crucial stage by the solicitor general, who represents the executive branch of government before the High Court. His influence with the justices affects their choice of cases to review.

Once a case is placed on the docket, the parties submit briefs and the justices hear oral arguments. A tentative vote is taken in conference. Then the real work begins: crafting an opinion that satisfies the majority without sacrificing clarity or forcefulness.

From the nation's lawyers come the nation's judges, whose political allegiance and values are usually a necessary condition of appointment by the president. The president and senators from his party share the power of appointment of federal district and appellate judges. The president has more leeway in the nomination of Supreme Court justices, although nominees must be confirmed by the Senate.

Courts inevitably fashion policy for each of the states and for the nation. They provide muliple points of access for individuals to pursue their preferences and so fit the pluralist model of democracy. Furthermore, the class action enables people with small individual claims and limited financial resources to pursue their goals in court, re-enforcing the pluralist model.

In addition to balancing freedom and order, judges must now balance freedom and equality. The impact of their decisions is much broader as well. Democratic theorists are troubled by the expansion of judicial power. But today's courts fit within the pluralist model and usually are in step with what the public wants.

As the U.S. Supreme Court heads in a more conservative direction, state supreme courts have become safe havens for less restrictive policies on civil rights and civil liberties. The state court systems have overlapping state and federal responsibilities, offering groups and individuals many access points to present and argue their claims.

In its marble palace, the Supreme Court of the United States faces and tries to resolve the dilemmas of government. Within the columned courtroom, the justices work to balance conflicting values, to ensure an orderly, peaceful society. We examine some of these conflicts in Chapters 15 and 16.

KEY TERMS

judicial review
U.S. district court
U.S. court of appeals
criminal case
civil case
adjudication
opinion
brief
precedent
stare decisis
common (judge-made) law
torts
statutory construction
original jurisdiction

appellate jurisdiction
federal question
docket
rule of four
solicitor general
amicus curiae brief
judgment
argument
concurrence
dissent
senatorial courtesy
judicial restraint
judicial activism
plea bargain
class action

SELECTED READINGS

Abraham, Henry J. *Justices and Presidents: A Political History of Appointments to the Supreme Court.* 2d ed. New York: Oxford University Press, 1985. This book examines the critical relationship between justices and presidents from the appointment of John Jay in 1789 through the appointment of Sandra Day O'Connor in 1981.

Baum, Lawrence. *American Courts: Process and Policy.* 2d ed. Boston: Houghton Mifflin, 1990. A comprehensive review of trial and appellate courts in the United States that addresses their activities, describes their procedures, and explores the processes that affect them.

Bork, Robert H. *The Tempting of America.* New York: Free Press, 1990. This nationwide best-seller offers Judge Bork's view on the current state of legal scholarship and the political agenda he claims it masks. Bork also offers his candid view of the events surrounding his unsuccessful battle for a seat on the nation's highest court.

Caplan, Lincoln. *The Tenth Justice: The Solicitor General and the Rule of Law.* New York: Knopf, 1987. An investigative study of the solicitor general's office that argues that under Reagan it was transformed from an independent office to a vehicle for ideological goals.

Coffin, Frank M. *The Ways of a Judge: Reflections from the Federal Appellate Bench.* Boston: Houghton Mifflin, 1980. A close look at the workings of a federal appellate court and the ways in which its chief judge reaches decisions.

Ely, John Hart. *Democracy and Distrust.* Cambridge, Mass.: Harvard University Press, 1980. An appraisal of judicial review that attempts to identify and justify the guidelines for the Supreme Court's application of a two-hundred-year-old constitution to conditions of modern life.

Friedman, Lawrence M. *American Law: An Introduction.* New York: Norton, 1984. A clear, highly readable introduction to the bewildering complexity of the law that explains how law is made and administered.

Jacob, Herbert. *Law and Politics in the United States.* Boston: Little, Brown, 1986. An introduction to the American legal system with an emphasis on links to the political arena.

O'Brien, David M. *Storm Center: The Supreme Court in American Politics.* 2d ed. New York: Norton, 1990. A primer on the Supreme Court, its procedures, personalities, and political impact.

Posner, Richard A. *The Federal Courts: Crisis and Reform.* Cambridge, Mass.: Harvard University Press, 1985. A provocative, comprehensive, and lucid analysis of the institutional problems besetting the federal courts. Written by a distinguished law professor, now a federal appellate judge.

Wasby, Stephen L. *The Supreme Court in the Federal Judicial System.* 3d ed. Chicago: Nelson-Hall, 1988. A thorough study of the Supreme Court's internal procedures, its role at the apex of the national and state court systems, and its place in the political system.

Wice, Paul. *Judges & Lawyers: The Human Side of Justice.* New York: HarperCollins, 1991. A thoughtful overview of the legal profession based on hundreds of interviews with lawyers and judges and on courtroom observations in fifteen cities.

PART

FIVE

Civil Liberties
and Civil Rights

15 ORDER AND CIVIL LIBERTIES

ROBERT MAPPLETHORPE'S photographs were shocking. Mapplethorpe was a critically acclaimed photographer who died in 1989. His subjects included celebrities, still lifes, nudes, children, and graphic sexual poses. The technique of the photographs was flawless. The content of some jarred and offended many viewers, who saw them as degrading, humiliating, and painful images.

A retrospective exhibition of Mapplethorpe's work traveled to several museums without incident. Then, in 1990, Cincinnati's Contemporary Arts Center and its director were charged by local officials with pandering obscenity and illegal use of a minor. At issue were seven photographs out of the 175 in the exhibit. Five photographs depicted homoerotic and sadomasochistic acts, which the city claimed were obscene. Two photographs used nude or partially nude children as subjects (one captured a toddler with her dress raised and her genitals exposed), which the city contended violated laws against child pornography. If convicted, the museum faced up to $10,000 in fines, and its director faced up to a year in jail and up to $2,000 in fines.

In Cincinnati, there are no adult bookstores, no X-rated theaters, no peep shows, no nude dancing clubs, no massage parlors. Residents cannot buy hard-core sex magazines, nor can they rent X-rated videos. Cincinnati law enforcement officials had a long history of restricting anything perceived as sexually provocative, including shows such as *Hair!* and *Oh! Calcutta*. If Cincinnati could declare such forms of expression off-limits, then surely it could punish the display of photographs that it deemed offensive.

The city used a criminal prosecution to maintain social order. The museum and its director—and countless others who came to their aid—responded with a vigorous defense of free expression. They maintained that the Mapplethorpe images were art, and the Constitution protected artistic expression from government interference and censorship. Ultimately, a court had to decide between the conflicting values of freedom and order. (The verdict is discussed later in this chapter.)

How well do the courts respond to clashes that pit freedom against order in some cases and freedom against equality in others? Are freedom, order, or equality ever unconditional? In this chapter, we explore some value conflicts that have been resolved by the judiciary. You should be able to judge from the decisions in these cases whether American government has met the challenge of democracy by finding the appropriate balance between freedom and order and between freedom and equality.

The value conflicts described in this chapter revolve around claims or entitlements that rest on law. Although we concentrate here on conflicts over constitutional issues, you should realize that the Constitution is not the only source of people's rights. Government at all levels can—and does—create rights through laws written by legislatures and regulations issued by bureaucracies.

We begin this chapter with the Bill of Rights and the freedoms it protects. Then we take a closer look at the role of the First Amendment in the original struggle—the conflict between freedom and order. Next we turn to the Fourteenth Amendment and the limits it places on the states.

No Sin in Cincinnati

Many residents of Cincinnati, Ohio, take pride in the absence of X-rated theaters and topless bars in their city; activities and forms of expression that might not raise an eyebrow in other communities are banned there. Nevertheless, not every citizen agrees with the city's self-imposed standards of conduct. Here, demonstrators show their support for the Contemporary Arts Center, which was prosecuted for exhibiting the work of photographer Robert Mapplethorpe.

Then we examine the Ninth Amendment and its relationship to issues of personal autonomy. Finally, we examine the threat to the democratic process when judges transform policy issues into constitutional issues. In Chapter 16, we look at the Fourteenth Amendment's promise of equal protection, which sets the stage for the modern dilemma of government: the struggle between freedom and equality.

The Bill of Rights

You may remember from Chapter 3 that at first the framers of the Constitution did not include a list of individual liberties—a bill of rights—in the national charter. They believed that a bill of rights was not necessary, that the extent of the national government's power was spelled out in the Constitution. But during the ratification debates, it became clear that the omission of a bill of rights was the most important obstacle to the adoption of the Constitution by the states. Eventually, twelve amendments were approved by Congress and sent to the states. In 1791, ten were ratified, and the nation had a bill of rights.

The Bill of Rights imposed limits on the national government but not on the state governments.* Over the next seventy-seven years, the Supreme Court was repeatedly pressed to extend the amendments' restraints to the states, but similar restrictions were not placed on the states until the adoption of the Fourteenth Amendment in 1868. Before then, protection from repressive state government had to come from state bills of rights.

The U.S. Constitution guarantees Americans a large constellation of liberties and rights. In this chapter we explore a number of them. We use two terms, *civil liberties* and *civil rights*, interchangeably in this context, although their meanings are different. **Civil liberties** are freedoms that are guaranteed to the individual. These guarantees take the form of negative restraints on government. For example, the First Amendment declares that "Congress shall make no law . . . abridging the freedom of speech." Civil liberties declare what the government cannot do; in contrast, civil rights declare what the government must do or provide. **Civil rights** are powers or privileges that are guaranteed to the individual and protected from arbitrary removal at the hands of the government or other individuals. The right to vote and the right to jury trial in criminal cases are civil rights. Today, civil rights have also come to include the objectives of laws that further certain values. The Civil Rights Act of 1964, for example, furthered the value of equality by establishing the right to nondiscrimination in places of public accommodations and the right to equal employment opportunity. Civil liberties are the subject of this chapter; we discuss civil rights and their ramifications in Chapter 16.

Actually, the Bill of Rights lists both civil liberties and civil rights. When we refer to the rights and liberties of the Constitution, we mean the protections enshrined in the Bill of Rights and in the first section of the Fourteenth Amendment.[1] The list includes freedom of religion, freedom of speech and the press, the right to peaceable assembly and petition, the rights of the criminally accused, the requirement of due process, and the equal protection of the laws.

Freedom of Religion

Congress shall make no law respecting an establishment of religion, or prohibiting the free exercise thereof.

Religious freedom was very important to the colonies, and later to the states. That importance is reflected in its position in the Bill of Rights: first, in the very first amendment. The amendment guarantees freedom of religion in two clauses. The first, the **establishment clause,** prohibits laws establishing religion; the second, the **free-exercise clause,** prevents

---

* Congress considered over a hundred amendments in its first session. One that was not approved would have limited the power of the states to infringe on the rights of conscience, speech, press, and jury trial in criminal cases. James Madison thought this amendment was the "most valuable" of the list, but it failed to muster a two-thirds vote in the Senate.

the government from interfering with the exercise of religion. Together they ensure that government can neither promote nor inhibit religious beliefs or practices.

The mingling of government and religion has a long history in America. At the time of the Constitutional Convention, many Americans, especially in New England, maintained that government could and should foster religion, certainly Protestantism. Many more Americans were in agreement, however, that this was an issue for state governments, that the national government had no authority to meddle in religious affairs. The religion clauses were drafted in this spirit.[2]

The Supreme Court has refused to interpret the religion clauses definitively. The effect of that refusal is an amalgam of rulings. Freedom to believe is unlimited, but freedom to practice a belief can be limited. Religion cannot benefit directly from government actions (for example, contributions to churches or synagogues), but it can benefit indirectly from those actions (for example, buying books on secular subjects for use in all schools—public, private, and parochial).

Most Americans identify with a particular religious faith, and 40 percent attend church in a typical week. The vast majority believe in God, a Judgment Day, and life after death. America is the most religious nation in the developed world.[3] Majoritarians might argue, then, that government should support religion. They would agree that the establishment clause bars government support of a single faith, but they might well maintain that government should support all faiths. This kind of support would be consistent with what the majority wants and true to the language of the Constitution. In its decisions, the Supreme Court has rejected this interpretation of the establishment clause, leaving itself

Religious Signs of the Times

Religious artifacts on public property may conflict with the First Amendment's establishment clause, which prohibits government sponsorship of religious activity. In 1989, the city of Pittsburgh attempted to bar a large menorah (a symbol of Hanukkah, the Jewish Feast of Lights) from the steps of the City-County Building. The Supreme Court ruled that the display was constitutional because it was shown in tandem with a non-religious symbol, the Christmas tree (at left).

SALUTE TO LIBERTY
DURING THIS HOLIDAY SEASON THE
CITY OF PITTSBURGH SALUTES LIBERTY.
LET THESE FESTIVE LIGHTS REMIND
US THAT WE ARE THE KEEPERS OF THE
FLAME OF LIBERTY AND OUR LEGACY
OF FREEDOM

open to charges of undermining democracy. Those charges may be true with regard to majoritarian democracy, but the freedom protected by the Court can be justified in terms of the basic values of democratic government.

The Establishment Clause

The provision that "Congress shall make no law respecting an establishment of religion" bars government sponsorship or support of religious activity. The Supreme Court has consistently held that the establishment clause requires government to maintain a position of neutrality toward religions and to maintain that position in cases that involve choices between religion and nonreligion. However, the clause has never been held to bar all assistance that incidentally aids religious institutions. In this section, we consider the application of the clause to public support for parochial education and for religion in general and to prayer in the public schools.

Government support of religion. In 1879, the Supreme Court contended, using Thomas Jefferson's words, that the establishment clause erected "a wall of separation between church and state."[4] That wall was breached somewhat in 1947, when the justices upheld a local government program that provided free transportation to parochial school students.[5] The breach seemed to widen in 1968, when the Court held constitutional a government program in which state-purchased textbooks were loaned to parochial school students.[6] The objective of the program, reasoned the majority, was to further educational opportunity. The loan was made to the students, not to the schools, and the benefits were realized by the parents, not by the church.

But in 1971, in **Lemon v. Kurtzman**, the Court struck down a state program that would have funded the salaries for teachers hired by parochial schools to give instruction in secular subjects.[7] The justices proposed a three-pronged test for constitutionality under the establishment clause:

- The law must have a secular purpose (like lending books to parochial school students).
- Its primary effect must not be to advance or inhibit religion.
- It must not entangle the government excessively with religion.

A law missing any prong would be unconstitutional.

The program in *Lemon* failed on the last ground: To be sure that they did not include religious instruction in their lessons, the state would have to constantly monitor the secular teachers. For example, the state would be required to monitor mathematics lessons to ensure that the instruction did not reinforce religious dogma. This kind of supervision would entangle the government in religious activity, violating the Constitution's prohibition.

Does the display of religious artifacts on public property violate the establishment clause? In *Lynch v. Donnelly* (1984), the Court said no, by a vote of 5–4.[8] At issue was a publicly funded Nativity scene on public property, surrounded by commercial symbols of the Christmas season (for example, Santa and his sleigh). While conceding that a crèche has religious significance, Chief Justice Warren E. Burger, writing for the majority, maintained that the display had a legitimate secular purpose: the celebration of a national holiday. Second, the display did not have the primary effect of benefiting religion; the religious benefits were "indirect, remote and incidental." And third, the display led to no excessive entanglement between religion and government. The justices hinted at a relaxation of the establishment clause by asserting their "unwillingness to be confined to any single test or criterion in this sensitive area." The upshot of *Lynch* was an "acknowledgment" of the religious heritage of the majority of Americans, even though the Christmas holiday is a vivid reminder to religious minorities and the nonreligious of their separateness from the dominant Christian culture.

The *Lynch* decision led to a proliferation of cases testing the limits of government-sponsored religious displays. In 1989, a divided Court approved the display of a menorah while rejecting the display of a crèche.[9] The menorah was displayed on the main-entrance steps of a government building alongside a Christmas tree and a sign, "Salute to Liberty." The crèche was displayed alone in a courthouse during the Christmas season. A majority found that the crèche display violated the second prong of the *Lemon* test but could not agree on the reasons validating the menorah display. In such circumstances, the justices become vulnerable to the charge that they serve as constitutional "interior designers," imposing their own value preferences on government policies when they cannot fully explain why one religious image passes muster but another one does not. Controversy seems to go with the territory. Consider the Court's policy on school prayer.

School prayer. The Supreme Court has consistently equated prayer in public schools with government support of religion. In 1962, it struck down the daily reading of this twenty-two-word nondenominational prayer in New York's public schools:

> Almighty God, we acknowledge our dependence upon Thee, and we beg Thy blessings upon us, our parents, our teachers, and our country.

Justice Hugo L. Black, writing for a 6–1 majority, held that official state approval of prayer was an unconstitutional attempt on the part of the state to establish a religion. This decision, in *Engle v. Vitale,* drew a storm of protest that has yet to ebb.[10]

The following year, the Court struck down a state law calling for daily Bible reading and recitation of the Lord's Prayer in Pennsylvania's public schools.[11] The reading and recitation were defended on the grounds that they taught literature, perpetuated traditional institutions, and inculcated moral virtues. But the Court held that the state's involvement violated the government's constitutionally imposed neutrality in matters of religion. Given the degree of religious sentiment in the United States, the burden on individual children on whose behalf these unpopular suits are brought can be overwhelming (see Feature 15.1).

FEATURE 15.1   *Schempp Family Gospel*

At one time or another, Edward and Sidney Schempp and their three children—Donna, Roger, and Ellory—have been called every pejorative name in the book. Their sleep has been disturbed by obscene late-night phone calls, and animal excrement has been sent to them through the mail and deposited at their doorstep. The Schempps have lost count of the times people have threatened to beat up their children or have prayed that they would contract deadly diseases. This harassment resulted from the Schempps' involvement in one of the most controversial cases in the history of the modern Supreme Court. The Schempps were plaintiffs in *Abington [PA] School District* v. *Schempp*, the 1963 decision that declared prayer in the public schools unconstitutional.

The Schempp Family

In 1957, a state statute required the reading of "at least 10 verses from the Holy Bible, without comment, at the opening of each public school on each school day." At Abington High School, these verses were read over the school public address system. Then the students in every classroom had to stand and recite the Lord's Prayer.

Ellory Schempp now says that "the push toward conformity at Abington had a lot to do with my decision [to protest school prayer]. It was a time of intellectual ferment for me." After discussing the matter with his parents, Ellory decided that he was going to stage a personal protest. He brought the Koran, the Islamic holy book, into school, and read it during the Bible reading. He also refused to stand during the recitation of the Lord's Prayer. Because of these infractions, Ellory's homeroom teacher sent him to the vice principal, who says Ellory "expressed enormous confusion, and saw it all as a matter of not following the rules, going against the wishes of the majority." Despite the attitudes of the school administration, Abington decided to excuse Ellory from the daily prayer for the rest of the year. In his senior year, though, the school mandated his participation.

The Schempps were not the first family to challenge school Bible reading, but previous cases were thrown out when the children involved graduated from school before the issue reached the higher courts. With a three- and five-year difference between Ellory and his younger brother and sister, the family reasoned that this obstacle would be avoided.

The Schempps' Supreme Court victory had its price. The principal at Abington High School tried unsuccessfully to pressure Tufts University into denying admission to Ellory on the ground that he was a "troublemaker." He was admitted despite the negative recommendation.

Ellory's younger sister, Donna, experienced the greatest repercussions. "Lots of kids saw me and my brother as weird, unacceptable," she said years later. "It was real traumatic. My feelings are that it was a terrible thing to do to a 12-year-old girl. It was a real isolating thing."

Not one member of the Schempp family regrets taking on the case, and even Donna says that "I think it was real important, and that it was right."

Source: Lewis Beale, "School Prayer Ban Is Still Gospel to Schempp Family," *Chicago Tribune*, 24 June 1982, sec. 3, p. 1. © Copyrighted, Chicago Tribune Company, all rights reserved, used with permission.

New challenges on the issue of school prayer continue to find their way to the Supreme Court—each a reminder of the pluralist nature of American democracy. These challenges vent widely held and strongly felt religious convictions, and the decisions are difficult. The government risks disorder when it continually frustrates strongly held majority views. The outcomes of these cases offer little immediate comfort to the majority of Americans who favor school prayer.

The Constitution bars school prayer. Does it also bar silent meditation in school? In *Wallace* v. *Jaffree* (1985), the Court struck down a series of Alabama statutes requiring elementary school teachers to observe a moment of silence for meditation or voluntary prayer at the beginning of each school day.[12] In a 6–3 decision, the Court renewed its use of the *Lemon* test and reaffirmed the principle of government neutrality between religion and nonreligion. The Court found that the purpose of the statute was to endorse religion; however, a majority of the justices hinted that a straightforward moment-of-silence statute that steered clear of religious endorsements might pass constitutional muster.

In yet another response to the school prayer controversy, Congress enacted the Equal Access Act in 1984. The act declares that no public secondary school receiving federal funds may bar after-school meetings on school property by student religious or political groups if the same privileges are allowed for other noncurriculum groups. In an 8–1 decision in 1990, the Court upheld the validity of the act, opening the door to the Bible society alongside the chess club, and making room for the witches' coven, too.[13]

The establishment clause creates a problem for government. Support for all religions at the expense of nonreligion seems to pose the least risk to social order. Tolerance of the dominant religion at the expense of other religions risks minority discontent, but support for no religion (neutrality between religion and nonreligion) risks majority discontent.

The Free-Exercise Clause

The free-exercise clause of the First Amendment states that "Congress shall make no law . . . prohibiting the free exercise [of religion]." The Supreme Court has struggled to avoid absolute interpretations of this restriction so as not to violate its complement, the establishment clause. An example: Suppose Congress grants exemptions from military service to individuals who have religious scruples against war. These exemptions could be construed as a violation of the establishment clause because they favor some religious groups over others. But if Congress forces conscientious objectors to fight—to violate their religious beliefs—the government would run afoul of the free-exercise clause. In fact, Congress has granted military exemptions to people whose religious beliefs lead them to oppose participating in war. The Supreme Court has avoided a conflict between the establishment and free-exercise clauses, however, by equating religious objection to war to any deeply held humanistic opposition to it. The continuing issue points to alternative choices: Does the free-exercise clause require government to grant exemptions from legal duties that conflict with religious obligations, or does the free-exercise clause guarantee only that religious believers will be governed by equal laws without discrimination or preference?[14]

In the free-exercise cases, the justices have distinguished religious beliefs from actions based on those beliefs. Beliefs are inviolate, beyond the reach of government control, but antisocial actions are not protected by the First Amendment. Consider the conflicting values and preferred choices in saluting the flag, working on the sabbath, and using drugs as religious sacraments.

Saluting the flag.   The values of order and religious freedom clashed in 1940, when the Court considered the first of two cases involving compulsory flag saluting in the public schools. In *Minersville School District v. Gobitis*, a group of Jehovah's Witnesses challenged the law on the ground that the action forced them to worship graven images, which their faith forbids.[15] Government order won in an 8–1 decision. The "mere possession of religious convictions," wrote Justice Felix Frankfurter, "which contradict the relevant concerns of a political society does not relieve the citizen from the discharge of political responsibilities." The reaction in Minersville and elsewhere was brutal and swift: The Gobitises were jeered on the streets; one of the children was beaten by schoolmates; and local churches led a boycott of the family business. In other communities, Witnesses were forced to swallow large amounts of castor oil when they refused to salute the flag; others were tarred, feathered, even castrated for following the dictates of their faith.[16]

Three years later, however, the Court reversed itself in *West Virginia State Board of Education v. Barnette*.[17] This time, the Court saw a larger issue: Can an individual be forced to salute the flag against his or her will? *Gobitis* was decided on the narrower issue of religious belief versus saluting the flag. In *Barnette*, the justices chose to focus instead on the broader issue of freedom of expression. In stirring language, Justice Robert H. Jackson argued in the majority opinion that no one could be compelled by the government to declare any belief.

> If there is any fixed star in our constitutional constellation, it is that no official, high or petty, can prescribe what shall be orthodox in politics, nationalism, religion, or other matters of opinion or force citizens to confess by word or act their faith therein. If there are any circumstances which permit an exception, they do not now occur to us.

Working on the sabbath.   The modern era of free-exercise thinking begins with *Sherbert v. Verner* (1963). Sherbert was a Seventh-Day Adventist. She lost her mill job because she refused to work on Saturday, which was her sabbath. She filed for unemployment compensation and was referred to a job, which she declined because it also required Saturday work. By declining the job, she was disqualified from unemployment benefits. In a 7–2 decision, the Supreme Court ruled that the disqualification imposed an impermissible burden on Sherbert's free exercise of religion. The First Amendment, declared the majority, protected *observance* as well as belief. The additional burden on religion occasioned by the government regulation could be justified only if the government could demonstrate a compelling interest in not granting an exemption.[18] And government can rarely muster enough evidence to demonstrate a "compelling" interest.

The *Sherbert* decision was an invitation to religious groups and individual believers to challenge laws that conflict with their faiths. So far, we have seen how these conflicts arise from the imposition of penalties for refusing to engage in religiously prohibited conduct. But conflicts may also arise from laws that impose penalties for engaging in religiously motivated conduct.[19]

Using drugs as sacrament. The use of illegal substances as part of a religious sacrament forces believers to violate the law. For example, the Rastafarians and members of the Ethiopian Zion Coptic Church smoke marijuana in the belief that it is the body and blood of Christ. Obviously, the freedom to practice religion taken to an extreme can be used as a license for illegal conduct. But even when that conduct stems from deeply held convictions, government resistance to it is understandable. The inevitable result is a clash between religious freedom and social order.

In 1990, the Supreme Court, by a vote of 6–3, tipped the balance in favor of social order when two members of the Native American Church sought an exemption from an Oregon law that made the possession or use of peyote a crime.[20] (Peyote is a cactus that contains the hallucinogen mescaline. It has been used for centuries in native American religious ceremonies.) Oregon did not prosecute the two church members for use or possession of peyote. Rather, the state rejected their applications for unemployment benefits after they were dismissed from their drug-counseling jobs for using peyote.

Justice Antonin Scalia, writing for the majority, examined the conflict between freedom and order through the lens of majoritarian democratic thought. He observed that the Court has never held that an individual's religious beliefs excuse him or her from compliance with an otherwise valid law prohibiting conduct that government is free to regulate. Allowing exceptions to every state law or regulation affecting religion "would open the prospect of constitutionally required exemptions from civic obligations of almost every conceivable kind." Scalia cited as examples compulsory military service, payment of taxes, vaccination requirements, and child-neglect laws.

The conflict between the commands of one's religion and the demands of one's government must reside in the political process, reasoned Scalia: "It may fairly be said that leaving accommodation to the political process will place at a relative disadvantage those religious practices that are not widely engaged in, but that unavoidable consequence of democratic government must be preferred to a system in which each conscience is a law unto itself."

Freedom of Expression

> Congress shall make no law . . . abridging the freedom of speech, or of the press; or the right of the people peaceably to assemble, and to petition the government for a redress of grievances.

The initial versions of the **speech clause** and the **press clause** of the First Amendment were introduced by James Madison in the House of Representatives on June 8, 1789. One of these early proposals provided that "the people shall not be deprived of their right to speak, to write, or to publish their sentiments, and the freedom of the press, as one of the great bulwarks of liberty, shall be inviolable." That version was rewritten several times, then merged with the religion and peaceable assembly clauses to yield the First Amendment.

The original House debates on the proposed speech and press clauses are not informative. There is no record of debate in the Senate or in the states during ratification. But careful analysis of the records of the period supports the view that the press clause prohibited only the imposition of **prior restraint**—censorship before publication. Publishers could not claim protection from punishment if works that had already been published were later deemed improper, mischievous, or illegal.

The sparse language of the First Amendment seems perfectly clear: "Congress shall make no law . . . abridging the freedom of speech, or of the press." Yet a majority of the Supreme Court has never agreed that this "most majestic guarantee" is absolutely inviolable.[21] Historians have long debated the framers' intentions regarding the **free-expression clauses.** The dominant view is that the clauses confer the right to unrestricted discussion of public affairs.[22] Other scholars, examining much the same evidence, conclude that few, if any, of the framers clearly understood the clause; moreover, they insist that prosecution for seditious statements (statements inciting insurrection) is not ruled out by the First Amendment.[23]

The passage of the Sedition Act of 1798 lends credibility to the latter claim. The act punished "false, scandalous and malicious writings against the government of the United States," seemingly in direct conflict with the free-expression clauses. President John Adams's administration used the Sedition Act to punish its political opponents for expressing contempt of the government and its officials. Thomas Jefferson and his allies attacked Adams's use of the act; they supported a broad view of the protection afforded by the First Amendment. The fines imposed on Adams's critics under the Sedition Act were later repaid by an act of Congress, and Jefferson, Adams's successor, pardoned those who had been convicted and sentenced under the law.

The license to speak freely does not move multitudes of Americans to speak out on controversial issues. Subtle restrictions are sewn into the fabric of American society. For example, the risks of criticism or ostracism by one's family, peers, or employers may confine the actual practice of free speech to individuals ready to bear the risks. As Mark Twain once remarked, "It is by the goodness of God that in our country we have three unspeakably precious things: freedom of speech, freedom of conscience, and the prudence never to practice either of them."[24]

Jefferson's libertarian view serves as the basis for the modern perspective on the First Amendment free-expression clauses. Today, the clauses are deemed to bar most forms of prior restraint (which is consistent with the initial understanding). In addition, according to the current interpretation, they also bar after-the-fact prosecution for political and other discourse.

The Supreme Court has evolved two approaches to the resolution of claims based on the free-expression clauses. First, government can regulate or punish the advocacy of ideas, but only if it can prove that the goal is to produce lawless action and that a high probability exists that such action will occur. Second, government may impose reasonable restrictions on the means for communicating ideas, which can incidentally discourage free expression.

Suppose, for example, that a political party advocates unilateral disarmament as part of its platform. (Unilateral disarmament is a policy of arms reduction or elimination without a corresponding reduction or elimination by any other nation.) Government cannot regulate or punish that party for advocating unilateral disarmament because the standards of proof—that the act be directed to inciting or producing imminent lawless action and that the act be judged likely to produce such action—do not apply. But government can impose restrictions on the way the party's candidates communicate what they are advocating. For example, government can bar them from blaring messages from loudspeakers in residential neighborhoods at 3:00 A.M. (Free expression has limits when it comes to loud music. See Feature 15.2.)

Freedom of Speech

The starting point for any modern analysis of free speech is the **clear and present danger test** formulated by Justice Oliver Wendell Holmes in the Supreme Court's unanimous decision in *Schenck v. United States* (1919).[25] Charles T. Schenck and his fellow defendants were convicted under a federal criminal statute for attempting to disrupt World War I military recruitment by distributing leaflets claiming that conscription was unconstitutional. The government believed this behavior threatened the public order. At the core of the Court's opinion, Holmes wrote:

> The character of every act depends upon the circumstances in which it is done. . . . The most stringent protection of free speech would not protect a man in falsely shouting fire in a theatre and causing a panic. . . . The question in every case is whether the words used are used in such circumstances and are of such a nature as to create a *clear and present danger* that they will bring about the substantive evils that Congress has a right to prevent. It is a question of proximity and degree. When a nation is at war many things that might be said in time of peace are such a hindrance to its effort that their utterance will not be endured so long as men fight and that no Court could regard them as protected by any constitutional right. [Emphasis added.]

Because the actions of the defendants in *Schenck* were deemed to create a clear and present danger to the United States at that time, the defendants' convictions were upheld. However, Holmes later frequently disagreed with a majority of his colleagues in applying the clear and present danger test. The test helps to distinguish the advocacy of ideas, which is protected, from incitement, which is not.

In an often-quoted dissent in *Abrams v. United States* (1919), Holmes revealed his deeply rooted resistance to the suppression of ideas.[26] The majority had upheld Jacob Abrams's criminal conviction for distributing leaflets that denounced the war and U.S. opposition to the Russian Revolution. Holmes wrote:

> When men have realized that time has upset many fighting faiths, they may come to believe even more than they believe the very foundations of their own conduct that the ultimate good desired is better reached by free trade in ideas—that the best test of truth is the power of the thought to get itself

FEATURE 15.2   *The Freedom to Be Loud*

Here's a question that will strike a resonant chord with parents, neighbors, and dorm residents: May government limit the volume of rock music? At issue before the U.S. Supreme Court in 1989 was the constitutionality of a New York City noise-control regulation requiring musical performances in Central Park to employ a city-supplied sound system and sound technician. The regulation was a response to concerns of excessive noise from nearby residents and concerns of performing musicians about the need for high-quality amplification equipment.

Rock musicians and civil libertarians blared their objections. They claimed that the city-imposed restrictions in a public forum interfered with their artistic creativity and their message. A lower court had held that government has the right to limit the sound level at concerts. However, it must use only the least restrictive means available. The court struck down the regulation, concluding that city control of sound mixing was simply too intrusive. This thunderous issue came to the Supreme Court when Big Apple officials appealed.

The justices seemed tossed between befuddlement and bemusement at a lively oral argument. Justice Anthony Kennedy wanted to know whether the sound technician responsible for the mix was as important as a conductor of a symphony. Leonard J. Koerner, who represented New York City, claimed he was just a technician. But William M. Kunstler, who represented an organization of musi-cal groups that challenged the regulation, was strongly of a different mind. "A conductor and the man that does the mix are very comparable," he declared. The substitution of the city's technician for the band's own was "as if the city said that we're going to put Georg Solti [former music director of the Chicago Symphony] in there instead of Zubin Mehta [former music director for the New York Philharmonic] because Solti plays *andante* and *dolce* and Mehta always plays loud."

Justice Antonin Scalia observed at one point that "when I was a young man occasionally I was at parties that got a little loud." Mr. Kunstler leaned forward and interjected: "Is this a confession?"

The justices handed down their ruling four months later. In a 6–3 decision, the Court upheld the regulation. Writing for the majority, Justice Kennedy said that "so long as the means chosen are not substantially broader than necessary to achieve the government's interest, the regulation will not be invalid simply because a court concludes that the government's interest could be adequately served by some less-speech-restrictive alternative." The government's hand now rests on the volume control. (Justice Scalia joined in the majority opinion.)

Sources: *New York Times,* 28 February 1989, p. 1; *New York Times,* 23 June 1989, p. 10; *Ward* v. *Rock Against Racism,* 491 U.S.___ (1989).

---

accepted in the competition of the market, and that truth is the only ground upon which their wishes safely can be carried out. That at any rate is the theory of our Constitution.

In 1925 the Court issued a landmark decision in ***Gitlow v. New York.***[27] Benjamin Gitlow was arrested for distributing copies of a "left-wing manifesto" that called for the establishment of socialism through strikes and class action of any form. Gitlow was convicted under a state criminal anarchy law; Schenck and Abrams had been convicted under a federal law. The Court held, for the first time, that the First Amendment speech and press provisions applied to the states through the due process clause of the Fourteenth Amendment. Still, a majority of the justices affirmed Gitlow's conviction. Justices Holmes and Louis D. Brandeis argued in dissent that Gitlow's ideas did not pose a clear and present danger. "Eloquence may set fire to reason," conceded the dissenters. "But whatever may be thought of the redundant discourse before us, it had no chance of starting a present conflagration."

The protection of advocacy faced yet another challenge in 1948 when eleven members of the Communist party were charged with violating the Smith Act—a federal law making the advocacy of force or violence against the United States a criminal offense. The leaders were convicted, although the government introduced no evidence that they actually urged people to commit specific violent acts. The Supreme Court mustered a majority for its decision to uphold the convictions under the act, but it could not get a majority to agree on the reasons in support of that decision. The largest bloc of four justices announced the plurality opinion in 1951, arguing that the government's interest was substantial enough to warrant criminal penalties.[28] The justices interpreted the threat to government to be the gravity of the advocated action "discounted by its improbability." In other words, a single soap-box orator advocating revolution stands a low chance of success. But a well-organized, highly disciplined political movement advocating revolution in the tinderbox of world conditions stands a greater chance of success. In broadening the meaning of clear and present danger, the Court held that the government was justified in acting preventively rather than waiting until the revolution is about to occur.

By 1969, the pendulum had swung back in the other direction: The justices began to show a stronger preference for freedom. That year, in *Brandenburg v. Ohio*, a unanimous decision extended the freedom of speech to new limits.[29] Clarence Brandenburg, the leader of the Ohio Ku Klux Klan, had been convicted under a state law for remarks he made at a Klan rally. His comments, which had been filmed by a television crew invited to cover the meeting, included threats against government officials.

The Court reversed Brandenburg's conviction because the government failed to prove that the danger was real. The Court went even further and declared that threatening speech is protected by the First Amendment unless the government can prove that such advocacy is "directed to inciting or producing imminent lawless action" and is "likely to produce such action." The ruling offered wider latitude for the expression of political ideas than ever before in the nation's history.

Symbolic expression. **Symbolic expression,** or nonverbal communication, generally receives less protection than pure speech. But the courts have upheld certain types of symbolic expression. ***Tinker v. Des Moines Independent County School District*** (1969) involved three public school students who wore black armbands to school to protest the Vietnam War.[30] Principals in their school district had prohibited the wearing of armbands on the ground that such conduct would provoke a disturbance, so the students were suspended from school. The Supreme Court overturned the suspensions. Justice Abe Fortas declared for the majority that the principals had failed to show that the forbidden conduct would substantially interfere with appropriate school discipline.

Undifferentiated fear or apprehension is not enough to overcome the right to freedom of expression. Any departure from absolute regimentation may cause trouble. Any variation from the majority's opinion may inspire fear. Any word spoken, in class, in the lunchroom, or on the campus, that deviates from the views of another person may start an argument or cause a disturbance. But our Constitution says we must take this risk.

The flag is an object of deep veneration in our society, yet its desecration is also a form of symbolic expression protected by the First Amendment. In 1989, a divided Supreme Court struck down a Texas law that barred the desecration of venerated objects. Congress then enacted the Flag Protection Act of 1989 in an attempt to overcome the constitutional flaws identified in the Texas decision. Gregory Johnson, whose 1984 flag-burning behavior in Texas led to the Court's 1989 decision, joined other protesters and burned an American flag on the steps of the Capitol on October 30, 1989, in a test of the new federal law.

The Supreme Court nullified the federal flag-burning statute in *United States v. Eichman* (1990). The Court was unpersuaded that the new law was distinguishable from its Texas cousin. By a vote of 5–4, the justices reaffirmed First Amendment protection for all expression of political ideas. The vote was identical to the Texas case, with conservative justices Scalia and Kennedy joining with the liberal wing to forge an unusual majority. The majority applied the same freedom-preferring approach used in the Texas case: "'If there is a bedrock principle underlying the First Amendment, it is that the Government may not prohibit the expression of an idea simply because society finds the idea itself offen-

sive or disagreeable.' Punishing desecration of the flag dilutes the very freedom that makes this emblem so revered, and worth revering."[31]

The Court majority relied on the substantive conception of democratic theory, which embodies the principle of freedom of speech, to justify its invalidation of the federal law. Yet a May 1990 poll revealed that most people wanted to outlaw flag burning as a means of expressing political opinions and that a clear majority favored a constitutional amendment to that end.[32] The procedural conception of democratic theory states that government should do what the people want. In the case of flag burning, then, the people are willing to abandon the freedom-of-speech principle embodied in the substantive view of democracy.

Though offensive to the vast majority of Americans, flag burning is a form of political expression. But suppose the conduct in question does not embrace a political idea. May government ever legitimately ban that conduct? Consider the recent case of three nude dancers in JR's Kitty Kat Lounge, a South Bend, Indiana, strip joint, who sought to block the enforcement of an Indiana law that includes a ban on all public nudity. If nude dancing is merely conduct, then government has the latitude to control, even ban, it. But if nude dancing is expression, then government action to prohibit it runs afoul of the First Amendment.

These positions on conduct versus expression mask underlying value conflicts. Control advocates sought to promote social order. Indiana officials argued that the statute attempted to promote public decency and morality. Expression advocates sought to promote a form of freedom. The dancers argued that they provided entertainment, communicating eroticism and sensuality. In 1991, a sharply divided Supreme Court upheld the state prohibition in the interest of "protecting order and morality" as long as the prohibition does not target the erotic message of the performance, a form of expression entitled to some protection under the First Amendment.[33]

Order versus free speech: fighting words.

Fighting words are a notable exception to the protection of free speech. In *Chaplinsky* v. *New Hampshire* (1942), a Jehovah's Witness was convicted under a state statute for calling a city marshal a "God-damned racketeer" and "a damned fascist" in a public place.[34] The Supreme Court upheld Chaplinsky's conviction on the theory that **fighting words**—words that "inflict injury or tend to incite an immediate breach of the peace"—do not convey ideas and thus are not subject to First Amendment protection.

The definition of fighting words was made much more exclusive just seven years later. Father Arthur Terminiello, a suspended Catholic priest from Alabama and a vicious anti-Semite, addressed the Christian Veterans of America, a right-wing extremist group, in a Chicago hall. The packed audience inside heard Father Terminiello call the jeering crowd of fifteen hundred angry protesters outside the hall "slimy scum," while he ranted on about the "Communistic Zionistic" Jews of America, evoking cries of "kill the Jews" and "dirty kikes" from his listeners. The crowd outside the hall heaved bottles, bricks, and rocks, while the police attempted to protect Terminiello and his listeners inside. Finally, the police arrested Terminiello for disturbing the peace.

Terminiello's speech was far more serious than Walter Chaplinsky's. Yet the Supreme Court struck down Terminiello's conviction on the ground that provocative speech, even speech that stirs people to anger, is protected by the First Amendment.[35] "Freedom of speech," wrote Justice William O. Douglas in the majority opinion, "though not absolute . . . is nevertheless protected against censorship or punishment, unless shown likely to produce a clear and present danger of serious substantive evil that rises far above public inconvenience, annoyance, or unrest."

This broad view of protection brought a stiff rebuke in Justice Jackson's dissenting opinion:

> The choice is not between order and liberty. It is between liberty with order and anarchy without either. There is danger that, if the Court does not temper its doctrinaire logic with a little practical wisdom, it will convert the constitutional Bill of Rights into a suicide pact.

The times seem to have caught up with the idealism that Jackson criticized in his colleagues. In **Cohen v. California** (1971), a nineteen-year-old department store worker expressed his opposition to the Vietnam War by wearing a jacket emblazoned with "FUCK THE DRAFT. STOP THE WAR."[36] The young man, Paul Cohen, was charged in 1968 under a California statute that prohibits "maliciously and willfully disturb[ing] the peace and quiet of any neighborhood or person [by] offensive conduct." He was found guilty and sentenced to thirty days in jail. On appeal to the U.S. Supreme Court, Cohen's conviction was reversed. The Court reasoned that the expletive he used, while provocative, was not directed toward anyone; besides, there was no evidence that people in "substantial numbers" would be provoked into some kind of physical action by the words on Cohen's jacket. In recognizing that "one man's vulgarity is another's lyric," the Supreme Court protected two elements of speech: the emotive (the expression of emotion) and the cognitive (the expression of ideas).

The latest variant of speech restrictions has arisen on university campuses. Public and private campuses have established rules barring racial or ethnic slurs because such language is seen as a form of harassment or discrimination. As we have seen, the judiciary has been wary of government power to eliminate unwelcome words or symbols from public dialogue. The "fighting words" doctrine is one exception. If such slurs generate immediate lawlessness, then banning words may be permissible. However, no government-supported restriction has withstood judicial scrutiny.

Free speech versus order: obscenity. Obscene material—words, books, magazines, films—is entirely excluded from constitutional protection. This exclusion rests on the Supreme Court's review of historical evidence surrounding freedom of expression at the time of the adoption of the Constitution. The Court observed that blasphemy, profanity, and obscenity were colonial crimes, but obscenity was not a developed area of the law at the time the Bill of Rights was adopted. Difficulties arise, however, in determining what is obscene and what is not. In *Roth* v.

United States (1957), Justice Brennan outlined a test for judging whether a work is obscene: "Whether to the average person, applying contemporary community standards, the dominant theme of the material taken as a whole appeals to prurient interest."[37] (*Prurient* means having a tendency to excite lustful thoughts.) Yet a definition of obscenity has proved elusive; no objective test seems adequate. Justice Potter Stewart will long be remembered for his solution to the problem of identifying obscene materials. He declared that he could not define it. "But," he added, "I know it when I see it."[38]

In ***Miller* v. *California*** (1973), its last major attempt to clarify constitutional standards governing obscenity, the Court declared that a work—play, film, or book—is obscene and may be regulated by government if (1) the work taken as a whole appeals to prurient interest; (2) the work portrays sexual conduct in a patently offensive way; and (3) the work taken as a whole lacks serious literary, artistic, political, or scientific value.[39] Local community standards govern application of the first and second prongs of the *Miller* test.

Recently the Court addressed the standard to be applied to the third prong. Speaking for the majority, Justice Byron White declared that the proper inquiry is not whether an "average" member of any given community would find serious value in material alleged to be obscene, but "whether a reasonable person would find such value in the material, taken as a whole."[40] The law often uses the words *reasonable person* to denote a hypothetical person in society who exercises average care, skill, and judgment in conduct. The expectation is that a reasonable person may find serious value in works alleged to be obscene whereas an average person may not. The decision here was an attempt by the Court to escape the nagging problem of reviewing state court obscenity rulings.

A Cincinnati jury applied the obscenity test in the case of the Mapplethorpe photographs discussed in the chapter opening. In less than two hours of deliberations, the mostly working-class jury of four women and four men reached a unanimous verdict of acquittal. Using the *Miller* test, they concluded that the photos appealed to prurient interest in sex and were patently offensive. However, they could not assent to the third requirement: that the photographs lacked artistic merit. In reaching the conclusion that the photographs were art, the jurors deferred to the testimony of expert witnesses. One juror's candid remarks suggested a widely shared view: "I'm not an expert. I don't understand Picasso's art. But I assume the people who call it art know what they're talking about."[41]

Feminism, free expression, and equality. Traditionally, civil liberties conflict with demands for social order. However, civil liberties may also be viewed in conflict with demands for equality. In the 1980s, city officials in Indianapolis, Indiana, influenced by feminist theorists, invoked equality principles to justify legislation restricting freedom of expression.[42]

The ordinance focused on pornography and its impact on women's status and treatment. It defined pornography as the graphic, sexually explicit subordination of women, in words or pictures, that satisfies one or more criteria, including: the presentation of women "as sexual objects who experience pleasure in being raped" and the presentation of women as "sexual objects of domination, conquest, violation, exploitation, possession, or use, or through postures or positions of servility or submission or display." The ordinance rested on three findings:

- that pornography is a form of discrimination that denies equal opportunities in society
- that pornography is central in creating and maintaining sex as a form of discrimination
- that pornography is a systematic practice of exploitation and subordination based on sex imposing differential harms on women

The ordinance then banned pornographic material according to the following argument. Government interest in equality outweighs any First Amendment interest in communication. Pornography affects thoughts; it works by socializing, by establishing the expected and permissible. Depictions of subordination tend to perpetuate subordination. And this leads to affront and to the maintenance of lower pay at work, insult and injury at home, and battery and rape in the streets. Hence, pornography conditions society to subordinate women impermissibly. An ordinance regulating expression will regulate and control the underlying unacceptable conduct.

United States District Court judge Sarah Evans Barker, in her first case as a judge, declared the ordinance unconstitutional, stating that it went beyond the categories of unprotected expression (such as child pornography) to suppress otherwise protected expression. According the the ordinance, expression treating women in the approved way—sexual encounters premised on equality—is lawful no matter how sexually explicit. And speech treating women in the disapproved way—as sexually submissive or as enjoying humiliation—is unlawful no matter how significant the literary, artistic, or political qualities of the work.

Judge Barker thus confronted the tradeoff between equality and freedom in a pluralist democracy. Interest groups using the democratic process to carve exceptions to the First Amendment benefit at the expense of everyone's rights. Although efforts to restrict behavior that leads to humiliation and degradation of women may be necessary and desirable, "free speech, rather than being the enemy, is a long-tested and worthy ally. To deny free speech in order to engineer social change in the name of accomplishing a greater good for one sector of our society erodes the freedom of all."[43]

This novel theory recasting a freedom-versus-order issue into a freedom-versus-equality framework still remains a theory. Judge Barker's tradeoff protected freedom. Her judgment was affirmed by the U.S. Court of Appeals in 1985 and affirmed without argument by the Supreme Court in 1986. An ordinance similar to the one in Indianapolis was approved by referendum in Bellingham, Washington, in 1988 but invalidated by a federal district court judge in 1989. However, in the next confrontation —and there will surely be others in a pluralist democracy—equality may prove the victor.

Freedom of the Press

The First Amendment guarantees that government "shall make no law . . . abridging the freedom . . . of the press." Although it was adopted as a restriction on the national government, the free-press guarantee has been held since 1931 to apply to state and local governments as well.

The ability to collect and report information without government interference was (and still is) thought to be at the core of a free society. The print media continue to use and defend their freedom, which was conferred on them by the framers. The electronic media, however, have had to accept government regulation that stems from the scarcity of broadcast frequencies (see Chapter 6).

Defamation of character. **Libel** is the written defamation of character.* A person who believes his or her name and character have been harmed by false statements in a publication can institute a lawsuit against the publication and seek monetary compensation for the damage. This kind of lawsuit can impose limits on freedom of expression; at the same time, false statements impinge on the rights of individuals. In a landmark decision in *New York Times v. Sullivan* (1964), the Supreme Court declared that freedom of the press takes precedence—at least when the defamed individual is a public official.[44] The Court unanimously agreed that the First Amendment protects the publication of all statements, even false ones, about the conduct of public officials except when statements are made with actual malice (with knowledge that they are false or in reckless disregard of their truth or falsity). Citing John Stuart Mill's 1859 treatise *On Liberty*, the Court declared that "even a false statement may be deemed to make a valuable contribution to public debate, since it brings about the clearer perception and livelier impression of truth, produced by its collision with error."

Three years later, the Court extended this protection to include suits brought by any public figures, whether or not they are public officials. **Public figures** are people who assume roles of prominence in the affairs of society or who thrust themselves to the forefront of public controversy—including officials, actors, writers, television personalities, and others. These people must show actual malice on the part of the publisher that prints false statements about them. Few plaintiffs prevail because the burden of proof is so great. And freedom of the press is the beneficiary.

What if the damage inflicted is not to one's reputation but to one's emotional state? Government seeks to maintain the prevailing social order, which prescribes proper modes of behavior. Does the First Amendment restrict government protection of citizens from behavior that intentionally inflicts emotional distress? This issue arose in a parody of a public figure in *Hustler* magazine. The target was the Reverend Jerry Falwell, a Baptist televangelist who founded the Moral Majority, organizing conservative Christians into a political force. The parody had Falwell—in an interview—discussing a drunken, incestuous rendezvous

---

* *Slander* is the oral defamation of character. The durability of the written word usually means that libel is a more serious accusation than slander.

**Publisher Parodies
Priggish Pastor**

The Reverend Jerry Falwell (right) claimed a tasteless parody that appeared in the soft-core porn magazine Hustler, *published by Larry Flynt, caused him emotional distress. Falwell won an initial victory in the courts, with a $200,000 judgment. When Flynt appealed to the Supreme Court, Falwell lost the case in a big way: a unanimous court decision. The First Amendment, argued the justices, protects criticism of public figures even when that criticism is outrageous and offensive.*

with his mother in an outhouse, saying, "I always get sloshed before I go out to the pulpit." Falwell won a $200,000 award for "emotional distress." The magazine appealed, and the Supreme Court confronted the issue of social order versus free speech in 1988.[45]

In a unanimous decision, the Court overturned the award. In his sweeping opinion for the Court, Chief Justice William H. Rehnquist gave a wide berth to the First Amendment's protection of free speech. He observed that "graphic depictions and satirical cartoons have played a prominent role in public and political debate throughout the nation's history" and that the First Amendment protects even "vehement, caustic, and sometimes unpleasantly sharp attacks." Free speech protects criticism of public figures even if the criticism is outrageous and offensive.

Prior restraint and the press. In the United States, freedom of the press has meant primarily immunity from prior restraint, or censorship. The Supreme Court's first encounter with a law imposing prior restraint on a newspaper was in *Near* v. *Minnesota* (1931).[46] Jay Near—an abusive, difficult man—published a scandal sheet in Minneapolis, in which he attacked local officials, charging that they were implicated with gangsters.[47] Minnesota officials obtained an injunction to prevent Near from publishing his newspaper under a state law that allowed such action against periodicals deemed "malicious, scandalous, and defamatory."

The Supreme Court struck down the law, declaring that prior restraint is a special burden on a free press. The need for a vigilant, unrestrained press was expressed forcefully by Chief Justice Charles Evans Hughes: "The fact that the liberty of the press may be abused by miscreant purveyors of scandal does not make any the less necessary the immunity of the press from previous restraint in dealing with official misconduct." The Court recognized that prior restraint may be permissible in exceptional circumstances, but it did not specify those circumstances, nor has it yet done so. Consider the following case, which occurred in a time of war, a period when the tension between government-imposed order and individual freedom is often at a peak.

In 1971, Daniel Ellsberg, a special assistant in the Pentagon's Office of International Security Affairs, delivered portions of a classified U.S. Department of Defense study to the *New York Times* and the *Washington Post*. By making the documents public, he hoped to discredit the Vietnam War and thereby end it. The highly secret study documented the history of U.S. involvement in the war. The U.S. Department of Justice sought to restrain the *Times* and the *Post* from publishing the documents, contending that publication would prolong the war and embarrass the government. The case was quickly brought before the Supreme Court, which delayed its summer adjournment to hear oral argument.

Three days later, in a 6–3 decision in **New York Times v. United States** (1971), the Court concluded that the government had not met the heavy burden of proving that immediate, inevitable, and irreparable harm would follow publication.[48] The majority's view was expressed in a brief unsigned *per curiam* (Latin for "by the court") opinion, although individual and collective concurring and dissenting views added nine opinions to the decision. Two justices maintained that the First Amendment offered absolute protection against government censorship, no matter what the situation. But the other justices left the door ajar for the imposition of prior restraint in the most extreme and compelling circumstances.

Stamp Out Secrecy!
In 1971, Daniel Ellsberg transmitted classified documents on U.S. involvement in Vietnam to the New York Times *and the* Washington Post. *The Federal Employees for Peace awarded him this "declassified" stamp. The government awarded him an indictment for theft of government property and violation of the Espionage Act. Two years later, a judge dismissed the indictment after the Watergate investigation disclosed that the government had wiretapped Ellsberg's phone and the CIA had sponsored a burglary of his former psychiatrist to obtain his files.*

The result was hardly a ringing endorsement of freedom of the press; nor was it a full affirmation of the public's right to all the information that is vital to the debate of public issues.

Freedom of expression versus maintaining order.   The courts have consistently held that freedom of the press does not override the requirements of law enforcement. A Louisville, Kentucky, reporter who had researched and written an article about drug activities was called before a grand jury to identify people he had seen in possession of marijuana or in the act of processing it. The reporter refused to testify, maintaining that freedom of the press shielded him from inquiry. In a closely divided decision, the Supreme Court in 1972 rejected this position.[49] The Court declared that no exception, even a limited one, exists to the rule that every citizen has a duty to give his or her government whatever testimony he or she is capable of giving.

A divided Supreme Court maintained again in 1978 that journalists are not protected from the demands of law enforcement when the Court upheld a lower court's warrant to search a Stanford University campus newspaper office for photographs of a violent demonstration.[50] The investigation of criminal conduct seems to be a special area—one in which the Supreme Court is not willing to provide the press with extraordinary protection of its freedom.

The Supreme Court again confronted the conflict between free expression and order in 1988.[51] The principal of a St. Louis high school deleted articles on divorce and teenage pregnancy from the school's newspaper on the ground that the articles invaded the privacy of the students and families who were the focus of the stories. Three student editors filed suit in federal court, claiming that their First Amendment rights had been violated. They argued that the principal's censorship interfered with the newspaper's function as a public forum, a role protected by the First Amendment. The principal maintained that the newspaper was just an extension of classroom instruction, that it was not protected by the First Amendment.

In a 5–3 decision, the Court upheld the principal's actions in sweeping terms. Educators may limit speech that occurs in the school curriculum and might seem to bear the approval of the school provided their actions serve "any valid educational purpose." The majority justices maintained that students in public school do not "shed their constitutional rights to freedom of expression at the schoolhouse gate," but recent Court decisions suggest that students do lose certain rights—including elements of free expression—when they pass through the public school portals.

The Right to Peaceable Assembly and Petition

The final clause of the First Amendment states that "Congress shall make no law . . . abridging . . . the right of the people peaceably to assemble, and to petition the Government for a redress of grievances." The roots of the right of petition can be traced to the Magna Carta, the charter of English political and civil liberties granted by King John at Runnymede in 1215. The right of peaceable assembly arose much later. Historically, this section of the First Amendment should read "the right of the people peaceably to assemble" *in order to* "petition the government."[52] Today, however, the right of peaceable assembly stems from the same root as free speech and free press and is held to be equally fundamental. Government cannot prohibit peaceful political meetings and cannot brand as criminals those who organize, lead, and attend such meetings.[53]

The rights of assembly and petition have merged with the guarantees of free speech and a free press under the more general freedom of expression. Having the right to assemble and to petition the government implies having the freedom to express one's thoughts and beliefs.

The clash of interests in cases involving these rights illustrates a continuing effort to define and apply fundamental principles. The concept of freedom has been tempered by the need for order and stability. And when there is a confrontation between freedom and order, the justices of the Supreme Court, who are responsible only to their consciences, strike the balance. These kinds of clashes are certain to occur again and again. Freedom and order conflict when public libraries become targets for community censors, when religious devotion interferes with military service, when individuals and groups express views or hold beliefs at odds with majority sentiment. Conflicts between freedom and order, and between minority and majority viewpoints, are part and parcel of politics and government here and abroad. How do other nations rank on the degree of civil liberties they guarantee their citizens? Is freedom increasing or declining in the world? For some answers, see Compared with What? 15.1.

Applying the Bill of Rights to the States

Remember that the major purpose of the Constitution was to structure the division of power between the national government and the state governments. Even before it was amended, the Constitution set some limits on both the nation and the states with regard to citizens' rights. Both governments were barred from passing **bills of attainder,** laws that make an individual guilty of a crime without a trial. They were also prohibited from enacting **ex post facto laws,** laws that declare an action a crime after it has been performed. And both nation and states were barred from impairing (and where necessary required to enforce) the **obligation of contracts,** the obligation of the parties in a contract to carry out its terms.

Although initially the Bill of Rights seemed to apply only to the national government, various litigants pressed the claim that its guarantees reached beyond the national government to the states. In response to one such claim, Chief Justice John Marshall affirmed what seemed plain from the Constitution's language and "the history of the day" (the events surrounding the Constitutional Convention): The provisions of the Bill of Rights served only to limit national authority. "Had the framers of these amendments intended them to be limitations on the powers of the state governments," wrote Marshall, "they would have . . . expressed that intention."[54]

Change came with the Fourteenth Amendment, which was adopted in 1868. The due process clause of that amendment is the linchpin that holds the states to the provisions of the Bill of Rights.

COMPARED WITH WHAT?   15.1

Civil Liberties Around the World

Freedom House researchers have been analyzing freedom around the world for several years. One of their objectives is to produce a comparative assessment of civil liberties. They use a 7-point scale, ranking nations from 1 (the greatest degree of freedom) to 7 (the least degree of freedom). Nations with lower ratings, then, are freer than nations with higher ratings. Of course, no nation is absolutely free or unfree.

In countries rated 1, the expression of political opinion has an outlet in the press, especially when the intent of that expression is to affect the legitimate political process. In addition, in these countries no major medium of expression serves as a simple conduit for government propaganda. The courts protect the individual; people cannot be punished for their opinions; there is respect for private rights and wants in education, occupation, religion, and residence; and law-abiding citizens do not fear for their lives because of their political activities.

Moving down the scale from 2 to 7, we see a steady loss of civil freedoms. Compared with nations rated 1, the police and courts in nations rated 2 have more authoritarian traditions or, as is the case in Greece and Portugal, a less institutionalized or secure set of liberties. Nations rated 3 or higher may have political prisoners and varying forms of censorship. Often, their security services torture prisoners. States rated 6 almost always have political prisoners. Here the legitimate media usually are completely under government supervision; there is no right to assembly; and often, narrow restrictions apply to travel, residence, and occupation. However, at level 6 there may still be relative freedom in private conversations, especially at home; illegal demonstrations can or do occur; and underground literature circulates. At 7 on the scale, there is pervasive fear; little independent expression, even in private; and almost no public expression of opposition to the government. Imprisonment and execution here are swift and sure.

A higher percentage of people live in freedom today than at any other time since the end of World War II. Much of this change results from the collapse of communism. In 1991, 39.2 percent of the world's population could be described as "free," 27.9 percent as "partly free," and 32.9 percent as "not free."

The degree of freedom within a nation varies with shifts in the political regime. The arrow symbols (↑ or ↓) indicate an increase or decline in civil liberties from 1990 to 1991. Twenty-seven countries improved their commitment to civil liberties; twelve countries weakened that commitment. For example, Czechoslovakia moved from "not free" to "free"; the Soviet Union moved from "not free" to "partly free." There was movement in the other direction, too. The United Kingdom dropped one point in the survey because of restrictions imposed on the media and revelations about forced confessions and faked evidence to obtain convictions in terrorist incidents.

Source: *Freedom Review*, vol. 22, no. 1 (1991), pp. 17–18. Reprinted from *Freedom Review* with permission of Freedom House.

Rating of Nations by Civil Liberties, 1991

1 Most Free

Australia	Costa Rica	Ireland	New Zealand	Sweden
Austria	Cyprus (G)	Italy	Norway	Switzerland
Barbados	Denmark	Japan	St. Christopher	Trinidad and
Belgium	Dominica	Luxembourg	and Nevis	Tobago
Belize	Finland	Malta	Solomon Islands	Tuvalu
Canada	Iceland	Netherlands	Spain	United States

2

Antigua and	Czechoslovakia ↑	Hungary ↑	Nauru	St. Vincent and
Barbuda ↑	France	Israel	Panama ↑	the Grenadines
Belize	The Gambia	Jamaica	Poland ↑	United Kingdom ↓
Botswana	Germany	Kiribati	Portugal	Uruguay
Chile ↑	Grenada	Mauritius	St. Lucia	Western Samoa
Cyprus (T)	Greece			

3

Argentina ↓	Ecuador	Papua New	Suriname	Venezuela
Bahamas	Honduras	Guinea ↓	Taiwan (R.O.C.)	
Bolivia	India	Paraguay	Thailand	
Brazil ↓	Korea (S)	Philippines	Tonga	
Dominican	Namibia	Senegal	Vanuatu	
Republic	Nicaragua ↑			

4

Benin ↑	Fiji	Madagascar	Nepal ↑	Tunisia ↓
Bulgaria ↑	Gabon ↑	Malaysia	Pakistan ↓	Turkey ↓
Algeria	Guatemala ↓	Mexico ↓	Peru	USSR ↑
Colombia	Guyana	Mongolia ↑	Singapore	Yugoslavia
Egypt	Ivory Coast ↑	Morocco	South Africa ↑	Zimbabwe
El Salvador	Haiti ↑			

5

Bahrain	Comoros	Kuwait ↑	Romania ↑	United Arab
Bangladesh ↓	Djibouti	Lebanon	Sao Tome and	Emirates
Bhutan	Ghana	Lesotho	Principe	Yemen
Brunei ↑	Guinea ↑	Maldives	Sierra Leone	Zambia
Burkina Faso	Guinea-Bissau ↑	Mali ↑	Sri Lanka	
Cape Verde	Indonesia	Niger ↑	Swaziland	
Central African	Iran	Nigeria	Tanzania ↑	
Republic ↑	Jordan	Qatar	Uganda ↓	

6

Albania ↑	Congo	Mozambique ↑	Saudi Arabia	Transkei
Algeria	Kenya	Oman	Seychelles	Zaire
Burundi	Malawi	Rwanda	Togo	
Cameroon	Mauritania			
Chad				

7 Least Free

Afghanistan	China (P.R.C.)	Iraq ↓	Libya	Syria
Angola	Cuba	Korea (N)	Somalia	Vietnam
Burma	Equatorial Guinea	Laos	Sudan	
Cambodia	Ethiopia	Liberia ↓		

The Fourteenth Amendment: Due Process of Law

Section 1   All persons born or naturalized in the United States, and subject to the jurisdiction thereof, are citizens of the United States and of the State wherein they reside. No State shall make or enforce any law which shall abridge the privileges or immunities of citizens of the United States; nor shall any State deprive any person of life, liberty, or property, without due process of law.

Most freedoms protected in the Bill of Rights today apply as limitations on the states. And many of the standards that limit the national government serve equally to limit state governments. These changes have been achieved through the Supreme Court's interpretation of the due process clause of the Fourteenth Amendment: "nor shall any State deprive any person of life, liberty, or property, without due process of law." Think of the due process clause as a sponge, absorbing or incorporating the specifics of the Bill of Rights and spreading or applying them to the states. Due process cases show that constitutional guarantees are often championed by unlikely litigants and that freedom is not always the victor.

The Fundamental Freedoms

In 1897, the Supreme Court declared that the states are limited by the Fifth Amendment's prohibition on taking of private property without just compensation.[55] The Court accomplished its goal by absorbing that prohibition into the due process clause of the Fourteenth Amendment, which applies to the states. Now one Bill of Rights protection—but only that one—limited both the states and the national government (see Figure 15.1).

The inclusion of other Bill of Rights guarantees within the due process clause faced a critical test in ***Palko* v. *Connecticut*** (1937).[56] Frank Palko had been charged with first-degree murder. He was convicted instead of second-degree murder and sentenced to life imprisonment. The state of Connecticut appealed and won a new trial; this time Palko was found guilty of first-degree murder and sentenced to death. Palko appealed the second conviction on the ground that it violated the protection against double jeopardy guaranteed to him by the Fifth Amendment. This protection applied to the states, he contended, because of the Fourteenth Amendment's due process clause.

The Supreme Court upheld Palko's second conviction. In his opinion for the majority, Justice Benjamin N. Cardozo formulated principles that were to direct the Court's actions for the next three decades. He noted that some Bill of Rights guarantees—such as freedom of thought and speech—are fundamental, and that these fundamental rights are absorbed by the Fourteenth Amendment's due process clause and are applicable to the states. These rights are essential, argued Cardozo, because "neither liberty nor justice would exist if they were sacrificed." Trial by jury and other rights, although valuable and important, are not essential to liberty and justice, and therefore are not absorbed by the due process clause. "Few would be so narrow or provincial," Cardozo claimed, "as to

FIGURE 15.1 *The Incorporation of the Bill of Rights*

The Supreme Court has used the due process clause of the Fourteenth Amendment as a sponge, absorbing many—but not all—of the provisions in the Bill of Rights and applying them to state and local governments. All of the provisions in the Bill of Rights apply to the national government.

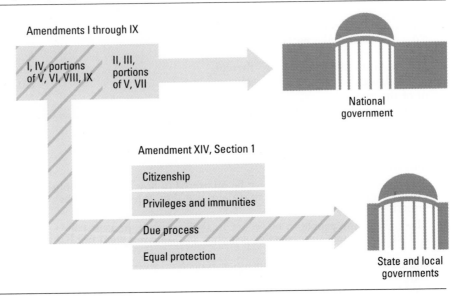

maintain that a fair and enlightened system of justice" would be impossible without these other rights. In other words, only some provisions of the Bill of Rights—the "fundamental" provisions—were absorbed into the due process clause and made applicable to the states. Because protection against double jeopardy was not one of them, Palko died in Connecticut's gas chamber in April 1938.

The next thirty years constituted a period of slow but perceptible change in the standard for determining whether or not a Bill of Rights guarantee was fundamental. The reference point was transformed from the idealized "fair and enlightened system of justice" in *Palko* to the more realistic "American scheme of justice" outlined in the decision in *Duncan* v. *Louisiana* (1968).[57] In case after case, as guarantees were tested they were found to be fundamental. By 1969, when *Palko* finally was overturned, most of the Bill of Rights guarantees had been found applicable to the states (see Table 15.1).

Criminal Procedure: The Meaning of Constitutional Guarantees

"The history of liberty," remarked Justice Frankfurter, "has largely been the history of observance of procedural safeguards."[58] The safeguards embodied in the Fourth through Eighth Amendments to the Constitution specify how government must behave in criminal proceedings. Their application to the states has reshaped American criminal justice in the last thirty years.

That application has come in two steps: The first step requires the judgment that a guarantee asserted in the Bill of Rights also applies to the states. The second step requires that the judiciary give specific meaning to the guarantee. The courts cannot allow the states to define guaran-

TABLE 15.1   *Cases Applying the Bill of Rights to the States*

Amendment	Case	Date
1. Congress shall make no law respecting an establishment of religion,	*Everson* v. *Board of Education*	1947
or prohibiting the free exercise thereof;	*Cantwell* v. *Connecticut*	1940
or abridging the freedom of speech,	*Gitlow* v. *New York*	1925
or of the press;	*Near* v. *Minnesota*	1931
or the right of the people peaceably to assemble,	*DeJonge* v. *Oregon*	1937
and to petition the Government for a redress of grievances.	*DeJonge* v. *Oregon*	1937
2. A well regulated Militia, being necessary to the security of a free State, the right of the people to keep and bear Arms, shall not be infringed.		
3. No Soldier shall, in time of peace be quartered in any house, without the consent of the Owner, nor in time of war, but in a manner to be prescribed by law.		
4. The right of the people to be secure in their persons, houses, papers, and effects, against unreasonable searches and seizures, shall not be violated,	*Wolf* v. *Colorado*	1949
and no Warrants shall issue, but upon probable cause, supported by Oath or affirmation, and particularly describing the place to be searched, and the persons or things to be seized.	*Aguilar* v. *Texas*	1964
5. No person shall be held to answer for a capital, or otherwise infamous crime, unless on a presentment or indictment of a Grand Jury,		
except in cases arising in the land or naval forces, or in the Militia, when in actual service in time of War or public danger;		
nor shall any person be subject for the same offence to be twice put in jeopardy of life or limb;	*Benton* v. *Maryland*	1969
nor shall be compelled in any criminal case to be a witness against himself,	*Malloy* v. *Hogan*	1964
nor be deprived of life, liberty, or property, without due process of law;		
nor shall private property be taken for public use, without just compensation.	*Chicago B. & Q. R.* v. *Chicago*	1897
6. In all criminal prosecutions, the accused shall enjoy the right to a speedy	*Klopfer* v. *North Carolina*	1967
and public trial	*In re Oliver*	1948
by an impartial	*Parker* v. *Gladden*	1966
jury	*Duncan* v. *Louisiana*	1968
of the State and district wherein the crime shall have been committed, which district shall have been previously ascertained by law,		
and to be informed of the nature and cause of the accusation;	*Lanzetta* v. *New Jersey*	1939
to be confronted with the witnesses against him;	*Pointer* v. *Texas*	1965
to have compulsory process for obtaining witnesses in his favor,	*Washington* v. *Texas*	1967
and to have the assistance of counsel for his defence.	*Gideon* v. *Wainwright*	1963
7. In Suits at common law, where the value of the controversy shall exceed twenty dollars, the right of trial by jury shall be preserved,		
and no fact tried by a jury, shall be otherwise re-examined in any Court of the United States than according to the rules of the common law.		
8. Excessive bail shall not be required,		
nor excess fines imposed,		
nor cruel and unusual punishments inflicted.	*Robinson* v. *California*	1962
9. The enumeration in the Constitution, in certain rights, shall not be construed to deny or disparage others retained by the people.	*Griswold* v. *Connecticut*	1965

tees themselves without risking different definitions from state to state—and differences among citizens' rights. If the rights are fundamental, their meaning cannot vary. But life is not quite so simple under the U.S. Constitution. The concept of federalism is sewn into the constitutional fabric, and the Supreme Court recognizes that there may be more than one way to prosecute the accused while heeding fundamental rights.

Consider, for example, the right to a jury trial in criminal cases, which is guaranteed by the Sixth Amendment. This right was made obligatory on the states in *Duncan* v. *Louisiana* (1968). The Supreme Court later held that the right applied to all nonpetty criminal cases—those in which the penalty for conviction was more than six months' imprisonment.[59] But the Court did not require that state juries have twelve members, the number required for federal criminal proceedings. Jury size was permitted to vary from state to state, although the minimum number was set at six. Furthermore, the federal requirement of a unanimous jury verdict was not imposed on the states. As a result, even today many states do not require unanimous verdicts for criminal convictions. Some observers question whether criminal defendants in these states enjoy the same rights as defendants in unanimous-verdict states.

In contrast, the Court left no room for variation in its definition of the fundamental right to an attorney, also guaranteed by the Sixth Amendment. Clarence Earl Gideon was a penniless vagrant accused of breaking into and robbing a pool hall. (His alleged "loot" was mainly change taken out of vending machines.) Because Gideon could not afford a lawyer, he asked the state to provide him with legal counsel for his trial. The state refused, and Gideon was subsequently convicted and sentenced to five years in the Florida State Penitentiary. From his cell, Gideon appealed to

A Pauper's Plea

Clarence Earl Gideon, penniless and without a lawyer, was convicted and sent to prison for breaking into and robbing a pool hall. At his trial, Gideon pleaded with the judge: "Your Honor, the U.S. Constitution says I am entitled to be represented by counsel." The judge was required by state law to deny Gideon's request. Undaunted, Gideon continued his quest for recognition of his Sixth Amendment right to counsel. On the basis of his penciled petition, the Supreme Court agreed to consider his case, ultimately granting Gideon the right he advocated with such conviction.

the U.S. Supreme Court, claiming that his conviction should be struck down because his Sixth Amendment right to counsel had been denied. (Gideon was also without counsel in this appeal; he filed a hand-lettered "pauper's petition" with the Court, after studying law texts in the prison library. When the Court agreed to consider his case, he was assigned a prominent Washington attorney, Abe Fortas, who later became a Supreme Court justice.)[60]

In its landmark decision in **Gideon v. Wainwright** (1963), the Court set aside Gideon's conviction and extended to the states the Sixth Amendment right to counsel.[61] Gideon was retried, but this time, with the assistance of a lawyer, he was found not guilty.

In subsequent rulings that stretched over more than a decade, the Court specified at what points a defendant was entitled to a lawyer in the course of criminal proceedings (from arrest to trial, appeal, and beyond). All states were bound by these pronouncements. In state as well as federal proceedings, legal assistance had to be furnished to those who did not have the means to hire their own attorney.

During this period the Court also came to grips with another issue involving procedural safeguards: informing suspects of their constitutional rights. Without this knowledge, safeguards are useless. Ernesto Miranda was arrested in Arizona for kidnaping and raping an eighteen-year-old woman. After the police questioned him for two hours and the woman identified him, Miranda confessed to the crime. He was convicted in an Arizona court on the basis of that confession—although he was never told he had the right to counsel and the right not to incriminate himself. Miranda appealed his conviction, which was overturned by the Supreme Court in 1966.[62]

The Court based its decision in *Miranda v. Arizona* on the Fifth Amendment privilege against self-incrimination. According to the Court, the police had forced Miranda to confess during in-custody questioning, not with physical force but with the coercion inherent in custodial interrogation. Warnings were required, the Court argued, to dispel that coercion. Warnings were not necessary if a person was only in custody or if a person was only subject to questioning without arrest. But the combination of custody and interrogation was sufficiently intimidating to require warnings before questioning. These statements are known today as the **Miranda warnings.** Among them:

- You have the right to remain silent.
- Anything you say can be used against you in court.
- You have the right to talk to a lawyer of your own choice before questioning.
- If you cannot afford to hire a lawyer, a lawyer will be provided without charge.

In each area of criminal procedure, the justices have had to grapple with the two steps in the application of constitutional guarantees to criminal defendants: the extension of a right to the states and the definition of that right. In *Duncan*, the issue was the right to jury trial, and variation was allowed from state to state. In *Gideon*, the right to counsel was applied uniformly from state to state. Finally, in *Miranda*, the Court declared that all governments—national, state, and local—have a duty to inform suspects of the full measure of their constitutional rights.

The problems of balancing freedom and order can be formidable. A primary function of government is to maintain order. What happens when individual freedom is infringed on for the sake of order? Consider the guarantee in the Fourth Amendment: "The right of the people to be secure in their persons, houses, papers, and effects, against unreasonable searches and seizures, shall not be violated." This right was made applicable to the states in *Wolf* v. *Colorado* (1949).[63] Following the reasoning in *Palko*, the Court found that the core of the amendment—security against arbitrary police intrusion—was a fundamental right, that citizens must be protected from illegal searches by state and local government. But how? The federal courts had long followed the **exclusionary rule,** which holds that evidence obtained from an illegal search and seizure cannot be used in a trial. And of course, if that evidence is critical to the prosecution, the conviction is lost. But the Court refused to apply the exclusionary rule to the states. Instead, it allowed the states to decide on their own how to handle the fruits of an illegal search. The upshot of *Wolf* was a declaration that the evidence used to convict the defendant was obtained illegally, but his conviction on the basis of that illegal evidence was affirmed.

The justices considered the exclusionary rule again twelve years later, in ***Mapp v. Ohio*** (1961).[64] Dolree Mapp had been convicted of possessing obscene materials after an admittedly illegal search of her home for a fugitive. Her conviction was affirmed by the Ohio Supreme Court, and she appealed to the U.S. Supreme Court. Mapp's attorneys argued for a reversal based on freedom of expression, contending that the confiscated materials were protected by the First Amendment. However, the Court elected to use the decision in *Mapp* to give meaning to the constitutional guarantee against unreasonable search and seizure. In a 6–3 decision, the justices declared that "all evidence obtained by searches and seizures in violation of the Constitution is, by [the Fourth Amendment], inadmissible in a state court." Mapp had been convicted illegally.

The decision was historic. It placed the exclusionary rule within the confines of the Fourth Amendment and required all levels of government to operate according to the provisions of that amendment. Failure to do so could result in the dismissal of criminal charges against otherwise guilty defendants.

Mapp launched a divided Supreme Court on a troubled course of determining how and when to apply the exclusionary rule. For example, the Court continues to struggle with police use of sophisticated electronic eavesdropping devices and the search of movable vehicles. In each case, the justices confront a rule that appears to handicap the police while it offers freedom to people whose guilt has been established by the illegal evidence. In the Court's most recent pronouncements, order has triumphed over freedom.

The struggle over the exclusionary rule took a new turn in 1984, when the Court reviewed *United States* v. *Leon.*[65] In this case, the police obtained a search warrant from a judge on the basis of a tip from an informant of unproven reliability. The judge issued a warrant without "probable cause" having been firmly established. The police, relying on the warrant, discovered large quantities of illegal drugs. The Court, by a vote of 6–3, established the **good faith exception** to the exclusionary rule. The justices held that evidence seized on the basis of a mistakenly issued search warrant *could* be introduced at trial. The exclusionary rule, argued the majority, is not a right but a remedy justified by its ability to deter illegal police conduct. The rule is costly to society. It excludes valid evidence, allowing guilty persons to go unpunished and generating disrespect for the law. These costs can be justified only if the exclusionary rule deters police misconduct. Such a deterrent effect was not a factor in *Leon:* The police acted in good faith. Hence, the Court decided, there is a need for an exception to the rule.

In 1988, the justices ruled 6–2 that police may search through garbage bags and other containers that people leave outside their houses. The case resulted from an investigation of a man who was suspected of narcotics trafficking. The police obtained his trash bags from the local garbage collector; the bags contained evidence of narcotics, which served as the basis for obtaining a search warrant for his house. That search revealed quantities of cocaine and hashish and led to criminal charges. The lower courts dismissed the drug charges on the grounds that the warrant was based on an unconstitutional search. By overturning that ruling, the Supreme Court further eroded the Fourth Amendment's protection of individual privacy[66] (see also page 526).

The exclusionary rule continues to divide the Supreme Court. In 1990, the justices again reaffirmed the rule, but by a bare 5–4 majority.[67] The retirement of William J. Brennan, Jr., and the appointment of his replacement, David Souter—who some believe will uphold conservative values, preferring order to freedom—as well as the retirement of Thurgood Marshall, suggest that the battle over the exclusionary rule is not over.

Mapp and all the cases that followed it forced the Court to confront the classic dilemma of democracy: the choice between freedom and order. If the justices tipped the scale toward freedom, guilty parties would go free, perhaps to break the law again. If they chose order, they would be giving government approval to police conduct in violation of the Constitution.

The Ninth Amendment and Personal Autonomy

> The enumeration in the Constitution, of certain rights, shall not be construed to deny or disparage others retained by the people.

The wording of the Ninth Amendment and its history remain an enigma. The evidence supports two different views. The amendment may protect rights that are not enumerated, or it may simply protect state governments against the assumption of power by the national government.[68] The meaning of the amendment was not an issue until 1965, when the Supreme Court used it to protect privacy, a right that is not enumerated in the Constitution.

Controversy: From Privacy to Abortion

In *Griswold v. Connecticut* (1965), the Court struck down, by a vote of 7–2, a seldom-used Connecticut statute that made the use of birth control devices a crime.[69] Justice Douglas, writing for the majority, asserted that the "specific guarantees in the Bill of Rights have penumbras [areas of partial illumination]" that give "life and substance" to broad, unspecified protections in the Bill of Rights. Several specific guarantees in the First, Third, Fourth, and Fifth Amendments create a zone of privacy, Douglas argued, and this zone is protected by the Ninth Amendment and is applicable to the states by the due process clause of the Fourteenth Amendment.

Three of the justices gave added emphasis to the relevance of the Ninth Amendment, which, they contended, protected fundamental rights derived from those specifically enumerated in the first eight amendments. This view was in sharp contrast to the position expressed by the two dissenters, Justices Black and Stewart. They argued that in the absence of some specific prohibition, the Bill of Rights and the Fourteenth Amendment do not license judicial annulment of state legislative policies, even if those policies are abhorrent to a judge or justice.

Griswold established the principle that the Bill of Rights as a whole creates a right to make certain intimate personal choices, including the right of married people to engage in sexual intercourse for reproduction or pleasure. This zone of personal autonomy, protected by the Constitution, gave comfort in 1973 to litigants who sought to invalidate state antiabortion laws. But rights are not absolute, and in weighing the interests of the individual against the interests of the government, the Supreme Court found itself caught in a flood of controversy that has yet to ebb.

In *Roe v. Wade* (1973), the Court in a 7–2 decision declared unconstitutional a Texas law making it a crime to obtain an abortion except for the purpose of saving the mother's life.[70] Justice Harry A. Blackmun, who authored the majority opinion, could not point to a specific constitutional guarantee to justify the Court's ruling. Instead, he based the decision on the right to privacy protected by the due process clause of the Fourteenth Amendment. The Court declared that in the first three months of pregnancy, the abortion decision must be left to the woman and her physician. In the interest of protecting the mother's health, states may restrict but not prohibit abortions in the second three months of pregnancy. Finally, in the last three months of pregnancy, states may regulate or even prohibit abortions to protect the life of the fetus except when medical judgment determines that an abortion is necessary to save the mother's life. In all, the laws of forty-six states were affected by the Court's ruling.

The dissenters—Justices White and Rehnquist—were quick to point out what critics have frequently repeated since the decision: The Court's judgment was directed by its own dislikes, not by any constitutional

The Supreme Court: Where the Twain Meets

While the justices of the Supreme Court sit inside a magisterial marble and mahogany courtroom, opposing groups of demonstrators hurl taunts across the plaza outside. Both justices and protesters have been divided over the issue of abortion. In 1989, the Court upheld state restrictions on abortion in Webster v. Reproductive Health Services; *some observers viewed this decision as an indication the Court may soon overturn* Roe v. Wade, *the 1973 decision legalizing abortion.*

compass. In the absence of guiding principles, they asserted, the majority justices simply substituted their views for the views of the state legislatures whose abortion regulations they invalidated.[71]

The composition of the Court shifted under President Ronald Reagan. His elevation of William Rehnquist to chief justice in 1986 and his appointments of Antonin Scalia in 1986 and Anthony Kennedy in 1988 raised new hope among abortion foes and old fears among abortion advocates.

A perceptible shift away from abortion rights materialized in *Webster* **v. *Reproductive Health Services*** (1989). The case was a blockbuster, attracting voluminous electronic and print media coverage. *Webster* set a record for the number of amicus briefs submitted on behalf of individuals and organizations with an interest in the outcome. (The number of briefs—78—surpassed the old record of 58 set in the landmark affirmative action case *Regents of the State of California* v. *Bakke* in 1978.)

In *Webster,* the Supreme Court upheld the constitutionality of a Missouri law that denied the use of public employees or publicly funded facilities in the performance of an abortion unless the mother's life was in danger. Furthermore, doctors were required to perform tests to determine whether fetuses twenty weeks and over could survive outside the womb. This was the first time that the Court upheld significant government restrictions on abortion.

The justices issued five opinions, but no single opinion captured a majority. Four justices (Blackmun, Brennan, Marshall, and Stevens) voted to strike down the Missouri law and hold fast to *Roe.* Four justices (Kennedy, Rehnquist, Scalia, and White) wanted to overturn *Roe* and return to the states the power to regulate abortion. The remaining justice—Sandra Day O'Connor—avoided both camps. Her position was that state abortion restrictions are permissible provided they are not "unduly burdensome." She voted with the conservative plurality to uphold the restrictive Missouri statute on the ground that it did not pose an undue burden on women's rights; but, she declined to reconsider (and overturn) *Roe.*

The Court has since moved cautiously down the road toward greater government control of abortion policy. In 1990, the justices upheld two state parental notification laws. One state required unwed teenagers to notify both parents before an abortion if the law allows minors to go to a judge instead. Another state required that a physician notify one parent of a pregnant minor of her intent to have an abortion. The Court was badly split in this case. The justices voiced widely divergent opinions, revealing the continuing division over the abortion issue.

Abortion pits freedom versus order. The decision to bear or beget children should be free from government control. Yet government has a legitimate interest in protecting and preserving life, including fetal life, as part of its responsibility to maintain an orderly society. Rather than choose between freedom and order, the majority on the Court has withdrawn the constitutional protection shrouding abortion rights and cast the politically divisive issue into the state legislative process, where elected representatives can thrash out the conflict.

Many groups defending and disparaging abortion ("prochoice" and "prolife") have now turned to state legislative politics to advance their policies. This approach will force candidates for state office to parry opponents on the abortion issue and then translate the electoral outcome into new legislation that restricts or enlarges abortion rights. If the abortion issue is deeply felt by Americans, then pluralist theory would argue that the strongest voices for or against abortion will mobilize support in the political arena.

The showdown on abortion, and on the right to privacy in general, is sure to come as the Court charts a new course between freedom and order. President Bush's 1990 appointment of David Souter to replace liberal Supreme Court justice William Brennan offers little comfort to abortion defenders. Souter may well be the vote to eliminate abortion as a fundamental constitutional right.

Personal Autonomy and Sexual Orientation

The right-to-privacy cases may have opened a Pandora's box of divisive social issues. Does the right to privacy embrace private homosexual acts between consenting adults? Consider the case of Michael Hardwick, who was arrested in 1982 in his Atlanta bedroom while having sex with a man. In a standard approach to prosecuting homosexuals, he was charged under a state criminal statute with the crime of sodomy, which means any oral or anal intercourse. The police said that they had gone to his home to arrest him for failing to pay a fine for drinking in public. Although the prosecutor dropped the charges, Hardwick sued to challenge the law's constitutionality. He won in the lower courts.

The conflict between freedom and order lies at the core of the case. "Our legal history and our social traditions have condemned this conduct uniformly for hundreds and hundreds of years," argued Georgia's

What's in a Name?

The epithet "queer"— once a degrading slur—has been adopted with pride by a generation of young homosexuals. Despite a new militancy on the part of gay and lesbian activists, the quest for national constitutional protection of homosexual rights halted with the Supreme Court's 1986 decision upholding state laws against sodomy. In response, many activists have shifted their efforts from the national level to state and local arenas.

attorney. Constitutional law, he continued, "must not become an instrument for a change in the social order." Hardwick's attorney, a noted constitutional scholar, said that government must have a more important reason than "majority morality to justify regulation of sexual intimacies in the privacy of the home." He maintained that the case involved two precious freedoms: the right to engage in private sexual relations and the right to be free from government intrusion in one's home.[72]

More than half the states have removed criminal penalties for private homosexual acts between consenting adults. The rest still outlaw homosexual sodomy, and many outlaw heterosexual sodomy as well. As a result, Hardwick's case was closely followed by homosexual rights groups and some civil liberties groups. Fundamentalist Christian groups and defenders of traditional morality expressed deep interest in the outcome, too.

In a bitterly divided ruling in 1986, the Court held in ***Bowers v. Hardwick*** that the Constitution does not protect homosexual relations between consenting adults, even in the privacy of their own homes.[73] The logic of the privacy cases in the areas of contraception and abortion seemed to compel a right to personal autonomy—to make one's own choices unconstrained by government. But the 5–4 majority maintained that only heterosexual choices—whether and whom to marry, whether to conceive a child, whether to have an abortion—fall within the zone of privacy advanced by the Court in its earlier rulings. "The judiciary necessarily takes to itself further authority to govern the country without express constitutional authority" when it expands the list of fundamental rights "not rooted in the language or design of the Constitution," wrote Justice White, the author of the majority opinion.

The arguments on both sides of the privacy issue are compelling. This makes the choice between freedom and order excruciating for ordinary citizens and Supreme Court justices alike. At the conference to decide the merits of the Hardwick case, Justice Lewis Powell cast his vote to extend privacy rights to homosexual conduct. Later he joined with his conservative colleagues, fashioning a new majority. Four years after the Hardwick decision, Powell revealed another change of mind. "I probably made a mistake," he declared, speaking of his decision to vote with the conservative majority.[74]

Powell's retirement from the Court in 1987 and the appointments of conservative associate justices Anthony Kennedy (in 1987) and David Souter (in 1990) have halted the march toward increased personal freedom. A new concern for social order—for established patterns of authority—is on the rise. And all the evidence, short of their actual participation in cases, suggests that these most recent Court appointees strongly support the new balance.

Most likely, the direction toward personal autonomy will shift to the states, where groups can continue to assert their political power. The pluralist model, then, gives us one solution to dissatisfaction with Court rulings. If state legislatures can enact laws making certain acts punishable, then they can also repeal those laws. Opponents to the Georgia statute now must mobilize support and force a change that more than half the states have already adopted. However, this kind of solution offers little comfort to Americans who believe the Constitution protects them in their most intimate decisions and actions.

Constitutionalizing Public Policies

The issues embedded in *Griswold* and *Roe* are more fundamental and disturbing for democracy than the surface issues of privacy and personal autonomy. By enveloping a policy in the protection of the Constitution, the Court removes that policy from the legislative arena, where the people's will can be expressed through the democratic process. The abortion controversy demonstrates to many critics that the courts can place under the cloak of the Constitution a host of public policies that were once debated and resolved by the democratic process. By giving a policy constitutional protection (as the Court did with abortion), judges assume responsibilities that have traditionally been left to the elected branches to resolve. If we trust appointed judges to serve as guardians of democracy, then our fears for the democratic process may be illusory. But if we believe that democratic solutions are necessary to resolve these kinds of questions, our fears may be well grounded. The controversy will continue as the Supreme Court strikes a balance between freedom and order. But in holding the balance, the justices must wrestle among themselves and with their critics over whether the Constitution authorizes them to fill the due process clause with fundamental values that cannot easily be traced to constitutional text, history, or structure.

Although the courts may be "the chief guardians of the liberties of the people," they ought not have the last word, argued the great jurist Learned Hand, because

> A society so riven that the spirit of moderation is gone, no court can save; . . . a society where that spirit flourishes, no court need save; . . . in a society

which evades its responsibilities by thrusting upon the courts the nurture of that spirit, that spirit in the end will perish.[75]

Summary

In establishing a new government, the framers were compelled to assure the states and the people, through the Bill of Rights, that their freedoms would be protected. In their interpretation of these ten amendments, the courts, especially the Supreme Court, have taken on the task of balancing freedom and order.

The First Amendment protects several freedoms: religion, speech and press, peaceable assembly and petition. The establishment clause demands government neutrality toward religions and between the religious and nonreligious. According to judicial interpretations of the free-exercise clause, religious beliefs are inviolate, but antisocial actions in the name of religion are not protected by the Constitution. Extreme interpretations of the religion clauses could bring them into conflict with each other.

Freedom of expression encompasses freedom of speech and of the press, and the right to peaceable assembly and petition. Freedom of speech and the press have never been held to be absolute, but they have been given far greater protection than other freedoms in the Bill of Rights. Exceptions to free-speech protections include some forms of symbolic expression, fighting words, and obscenity. Press freedom has had broad constitutional protection because a free society depends on the ability to collect and report information without government interference. The rights of peaceable assembly and petition stem from the same freedom protecting speech and press. Each of these freedoms is equally fundamental, but their exercise is not absolute.

The adoption of the Fourteenth Amendment in 1868 extended the guarantees of the Bill of Rights to the states. The due process clause became the vehicle for absorbing or incorporating specific provisions of the Bill of Rights, one at a time, case after case, and applying them to the states. The designation of a right as fundamental also called for a definition of that right. The Supreme Court has tolerated some variation from state to state in the meaning of certain constitutional rights. The Court has also imposed a duty on government to inform citizens of their rights so that they are able to exercise them.

As it fashioned new fundamental rights from the Constitution, the Supreme Court has become embroiled in controversy. The right to privacy served as the basis for the right of women to terminate a pregnancy, which in turn suggested a right to personal autonomy. The abortion controversy is still raging, and the justices have called a halt to the extension of personal privacy in the name of the Constitution.

In the meantime, judicial decisions raise a basic issue. By offering constitutional protection to public policies, the courts may be threatening the democratic process, the process that gives the people a say in government through their elected representatives. One thing is certain, however: The challenge of democracy requires the constant balancing of freedom and order.

KEY TERMS AND CASES

civil liberties
civil rights
establishment clause
free-exercise clause
Lemon v. *Kurtzman*
*West Virginia State
    Board of Education
    v. Barnette*
Sherbert v. *Verner*
speech clause
press clause
prior restraint
free-expression clauses
clear and present
    danger test
Gitlow v. *New York*
Brandenburg v. *Ohio*
symbolic expression
Tinker v. *Des Moines
    Independent County
    School District*
*United States
    v. Eichman*

fighting words
Cohen v. *California*
Miller v. *California*
libel
*New York Times
    v. Sullivan*
public figures
*New York Times
    v. United States*
bill of attainder
ex post facto law
obligation of contracts
Palko v. *Connecticut*
Gideon v. *Wainwright*
Miranda warnings
exclusionary rule
Mapp v. *Ohio*
good faith exception
Griswold v. *Connecticut*
Roe v. *Wade*
Webster v. *Reproductive
    Health Services*
Bowers v. *Hardwick*

SELECTED READINGS

Baker, Liva. *Miranda: Crime, Law and Politics.* New York: Atheneum, 1983. Baker uses *Miranda* as a vehicle for explaining the American legal system. She traces the case from its origin to its landmark resolution.

Barnett, Randy E., ed. *The Rights Retained by the People: The History and Meaning of the Ninth Amendment.* Fairfax, Va.: George Mason University Press, 1989. An excellent collection of writings on the Ninth Amendment, including a set of primary documents and a summary of the competing theories on this controversial area of constitutional jurisprudence.

Brigham, John. *Civil Liberties and American Democracy.* Washington, D.C.: Congressional Quarterly Press, 1984. A survey of U.S. civil rights and liberties organized around basic concepts (privacy, entitlements).

Downs, Donald Alexander. *The New Politics of Pornography.* Chicago: University of Chicago Press, 1990. An exploration of the controversial modern antipornography movement. Downs analyzes similar ordinances in Minneapolis and Indianapolis, which were rooted in the feminist thought of Catharine MacKinnon and Andrea Dworkin.

Faux, Marian. *Roe v. Wade: The Untold Story of the Landmark Supreme Court Decision That Made Abortion Legal.* New York: Macmillan, 1988. A popular account of the legal maneuvers leading to the *Roe* v. *Wade* decision in 1973. The book focuses on the two young attorneys who developed the case, Sarah Weddington and Linda Coffee.

Haiman, Franklyn C. *Speech and Law in a Free Society.* Chicago: University of Chicago Press, 1981. A thorough survey of the meaning of the First Amendment. Haiman argues that no special significance attaches to the separate speech and press clauses.

Levy, Leonard W. *The Emergence of a Free Press.* New York: Oxford University Press, 1985. This work revises Levy's original scholarship, *The Legacy of Suppression,* which caused a stir when it was published in 1960. Levy originally maintained that the generation that adopted the Constitution and the Bill of Rights did not believe in a broad view of freedom of expression, especially in the area of politics. His new position, based both on new evidence and on continued criticism of his original thesis, is that Americans were more tolerant of government criticism but that the revolutionary generation did not intend to wipe out seditious libel with the adoption of the First Amendment.

Levy, Leonard W. *The Establishment Clause: Religion and the First Amendment.* New York: Macmillan, 1986. This searching study of the establishment clause claims that the view that government can assist all religions is historically groundless. Levy argues that it is unconstitutional for government to provide aid to any religion.

Lewis, Anthony. *Gideon's Trumpet.* New York: Random House, 1964. The moving story of Clarence Earl Gideon's claim to assistance of counsel guaranteed by the Sixth Amendment.

Polenberg, Richard. *Fighting Faiths.* New York: Knopf, 1987. By focusing on the famous case of *Abrams* v. *United States,* a noted historian examines anarchism, government surveillance, freedom of speech, and the impact of the Russian Revolution on American liberals.

Tribe, Laurence H. *Abortion: The Clash of Absolutes.* New York: Norton, 1990. Tribe seeks an accommodation in the clash of absolutes in the abortion debate through a historical, political and legal analysis of the issues.

16 EQUALITY AND CIVIL RIGHTS

DIANE JOYCE AND PAUL JOHNSON worked hard patching holes, shoveling asphalt, and opening culverts for the Santa Clara County Transportation Agency. In 1980, a skilled position as road dispatcher opened up; it meant less strenuous work and higher pay. Joyce and Johnson competed along with ten other applicants for the job. At the time, all of the agency's 238 skilled positions were held by men.

Seven of the applicants—including Joyce and Johnson—passed an oral exam. Next, the agency conducted a round of interviews. Johnson tied for second with a score of 75; Joyce ranked third with a score of 73. After a second round of interviews with the top contenders, the agency gave the job to Johnson.

Joyce didn't let the matter rest. With the help of a county employee, she filed a complaint with the head of the agency, invoking the county government's affirmative action policy. **Affirmative action** is a commitment by an employer, school, or other public or private institution to expand opportunities for women, blacks, Hispanics, and members of other minority groups. Affirmative action embraces a wide range of policies from special recruitment efforts to numerical goals and quotas.

The county was trying to remedy the effects of former practices, intentional or not, that had restricted work opportunities for women, minorities, and the disabled. Its goal was the employment of individuals from these groups in upper-level jobs in proportion to their representation in the area's total work force. After reviewing its decision in light of the county's policy, the agency took the job away from Johnson and gave it to Joyce. A government-imposed equality policy thwarted Johnson's freedom to climb the ladder of success. Angered by the lost promotion, he sued.

Johnson argued that he was the victim of sex discrimination. **Discrimination** is the act of making or recognizing distinctions. When making distinctions between people, discrimination may be benign (that is, harmless) or invidious (harmful). The national government has enacted policies to prohibit invidious discrimination, which is often rooted in prejudice. Johnson invoked Title VII of the 1964 Civil Rights Act, which bars employment discrimination based on race, religion, national origin, or sex. He won the first round in a federal district court; Joyce's employer appealed and won a reversal. The final round was fought in the Supreme Court in 1987.[1] Joyce emerged the victor.

At issue in this case were the values of equality and freedom. Laws and policies that promote equality inevitably come into conflict with demands for freedom. To understand the ways government resolves this conflict, we have to understand the development of civil rights in this country.

The history of civil rights in the United States is primarily the story of the search for social and economic equality. This search has gone on for more than a century and is still going on today. It began with the civil rights of black citizens, whose subjugation roused the passions of a nation and brought about its bloodiest conflict, the Civil War. The struggle of blacks has been a beacon lighting the way for Native Americans, Hispanic-Americans, women, and the disabled. Each of these groups has confronted discrimination, sometimes subtle, sometimes overt, sometimes from other minorities. Each has achieved a measure of success by

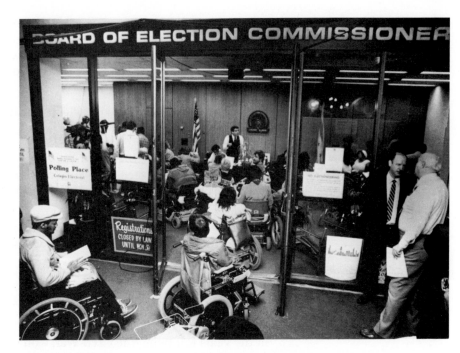

Wheel Rights

Although voting is a fundamental civil right, physical obstacles can deter some Americans from exercising it. The everyday life of many handicapped Americans is filled with barriers other people don't notice, such as revolving doors and flights of stairs. In 1986, some handicapped Chicagoans occupied the offices of the Board of Elections, claiming that 80 percent of the city's precincts were inaccessible to handicapped voters. National law requires that all polling places be accessible to the handicapped. The city responded by dispatching mobile voting units.

pressing its interests on government, even challenging government. These challenges and government's responses to them have helped shape our democracy.

Remember that **civil rights** are powers or privileges guaranteed to the individual and protected from arbitrary removal at the hands of the government or other individuals. (Rights need not be confined to humans. Some advocates claim that animals have rights, too.) In this chapter, we concentrate on the rights guaranteed by the constitutional amendments adopted after the Civil War and by laws passed to enforce those guarantees. Prominent among them is the right to equal protection of the laws. This right remained a promise rather than a reality well into the twentieth century.

The Civil War Amendments

The Civil War amendments were adopted to provide freedom and equality to black Americans. The Thirteenth Amendment, which was ratified in 1865, provided the freedom:

> Neither slavery nor involuntary servitude . . . shall exist within the United States, or any place subject to their jurisdiction.

The Fourteenth Amendment was adopted three years later. It provides first that freed slaves are citizens:

> All persons born or naturalized in the United States, and subject to the jurisdiction thereof, are citizens of the United States and of the State wherein they reside.

Next, as discussed in Chapter 15, it prohibits the states from abridging the "privileges or immunities of citizens of the United States" or depriving "any person of life, liberty, or property, without due process of law." The amendment then goes on to protect equality under the law, declaring that no state shall

> deny to any person within its jurisdiction the equal protection of the laws.

The Fifteenth Amendment, adopted in 1870, added a measure of political equality:

> The right of citizens of the United States to vote shall not be denied or abridged by the United States or by any State on account of race, color, or previous condition of servitude.

American blacks were free and politically equal—at least according to the Constitution. But it would be many years before these constitutional rights were protected.

Congress and the Supreme Court: Lawmaking Versus Law Interpreting

In the years following the Civil War, Congress went to work to protect the rights of black citizens. In 1866, lawmakers passed a civil rights act that gave the national government some authority over the treatment of blacks by state courts. This was a response to the **black codes,** laws enacted by the former slave states that restricted the freedom of blacks. For example, vagrancy and apprenticeship laws forced blacks to work and denied them a free choice of employers. One section of the 1866 act that still applies today grants all citizens—white and black—the right to make and enforce contracts, sue or be sued, give evidence, and inherit, purchase, lease, sell, hold, or convey property. Later, in the Civil Rights Act of 1875, Congress attempted to guarantee blacks equal access to public accommodations (streetcars, inns, parks, theaters).

While Congress was passing laws to protect the civil rights of black citizens, the Supreme Court seemed intent on weakening those rights. In 1873, the Court ruled that the Civil War amendments had not changed the relationship between the state and national governments. In other words, state citizenship and national citizenship remained separate and distinct; the Fourteenth Amendment did not enlarge the rights guaranteed by U.S. citizenship. In effect, the Court stripped the amendment of its power to secure the Bill of Rights guarantees for black citizens.

In the following years, the Court continued to shrink constitutional protections for blacks. In 1876, the justices crippled congressional attempts to enforce the rights of blacks.[2] A group of Louisiana whites had used violence and fraud to prevent blacks from exercising their basic constitutional rights, including the right of peaceable assembly. The justices held that the rights allegedly infringed on were not nationally protected rights and that therefore Congress was powerless to punish those who violated them. On the very same day, the Court ruled that the Fifteenth Amendment did not guarantee all citizens the right to vote; it simply listed grounds that could not be used to deny that right.[3] And in

1883, the Court struck down the public accommodations section of the Civil Rights Act of 1875.[4] The justices declared that the national government could prohibit only government action (also known as *state action*) discriminating against blacks; private acts of discrimination or acts of omission by a state were beyond the reach of the national government. For example, a state law excluding blacks from jury service was an unlawful abridgment of individual rights. However, a person who denied blacks service in a private club was outside the control of the national government because the discrimination was a private—not a government—act. The Court refused to see racial discrimination as a badge of slavery that the national government could prohibit. In case after case, the justices tolerated racial discrimination, in the process abetting **racism**, a belief that inherent differences among races determine achievement and that one's own race is superior to and has a right to rule others.

The Court's decisions gave the states ample room to maneuver around civil rights laws. In the matter of voting rights, for example, states that wanted to bar black men from the polls simply used nonracial means to do so. One popular tool was the **poll tax,** first imposed by Georgia in 1877. This was a tax of $1 or $2 on every citizen who wanted to vote. The tax was not a burden for most whites. But many blacks were tenant farmers, deeply in debt to white merchants and landowners; they just did not have any extra money for voting. Other bars to black suffrage included literacy tests, minimum education requirements, and a grandfather clause that offered voter eligibility to those who could establish that a voter's grandfather was eligible to vote before 1867 (three years before the Fifteenth Amendment declared that race could not be used to deny the right to vote).[5] Intimidation and violence were also used to keep blacks from the polls.

The Roots of Racial Segregation

Well before the Civil War, **racial segregation** was a way of life in the South: Blacks lived and worked separately from whites. After the war, southern states began to enact Jim Crow laws that *enforced* segregation. (*Jim Crow* is a derogatory term for a black person.) Once the Supreme Court nullified the Civil Rights Act of 1875, these kinds of laws proliferated. Blacks were required to live in separate and generally inferior areas; they were restricted to separate and inferior sections of hospitals, separate cemeteries, separate drinking and toilet facilities, and separate sections of streetcars, trains, schools, jails, and parks. Each day, in countless ways, they were reminded of the inferior status accorded them by white society.

In 1892, Homer Adolph Plessy—who was seven-eighths Caucasian—took a seat in a "whites only" car of a Louisiana train. He refused to move to the car reserved for blacks and was arrested. Plessy argued that Louisiana's law mandating racial segregation on its trains was an unconstitutional infringement on both the privileges and immunities and the equal protection clauses of the Fourteenth Amendment. The Supreme Court disagreed. The majority in ***Plessy v. Ferguson*** (1896) upheld state-imposed racial segregation.[6] They based their decision on the

Separate and Unequal

The Supreme Court gave constitutional protection to racial separation on the theory that states could provide "separate but equal" facilities for blacks. But racial separation meant unequal facilities, as these two water fountains dramatically illustrated. The Supreme Court struck a fatal blow against the "separate but equal" doctrine in its landmark 1954 ruling, Brown v. Board of Education.

separate-but-equal doctrine, that separate facilities for blacks and whites satisfied the Fourteenth Amendment as long as they were equal. The lone dissenter was John Marshall Harlan (the first of two distinguished justices with the same name). Harlan, who envisioned a "color-blind Constitution," wrote:

> We boast of the freedom enjoyed by our people above all other peoples. But it is difficult to reconcile that boast with a state of the law which, practically, puts the brand of servitude and degradation upon a large class of our fellow citizens—our equals before the law. The thin disguise of "equal" accommodations for passengers in railroad coaches will not mislead any one, nor atone for the wrong this day done.

Three years later, the Supreme Court extended the separate-but-equal doctrine to the schools.[7] The justices ignored the fact that black educational facilities (and most other "colored only" facilities) were far from equal to those reserved for whites.

By the end of the nineteenth century, racial segregation was firmly and legally entrenched in the American South. Although constitutional amendments and national laws to protect equality under the law were in place, the Supreme Court's interpretation of those amendments and laws limited their effectiveness. Several decades would pass before there was any discernible change.

The Dismantling of School Segregation

Denied the right to vote and be represented in government, blacks sought access to power in other parts of the political system. The National Association for the Advancement of Colored People (NAACP), founded in 1909 by W. E. B. Du Bois and others, both black and white, with the goal of ending racial discrimination and segregation, took the lead in the campaign for black civil rights. The plan was to launch legal and lobbying attacks on the separate-but-equal doctrine in two parts: first by pressing for fully equal facilities for blacks, then by proving the unconstitutionality of segregation. The process would be a slow one, but the strategies involved did not require a large organization or heavy financial backing; and, at the time, the NAACP had neither.*

Pressure for Equality . . .

By the 1920s, the separate-but-equal doctrine was so deeply ingrained in American law that no Supreme Court justice would dissent from its continued application to racial segregation. But a few Court decisions offered hope that change would come. In 1935, Lloyd Gaines graduated from Lincoln University, a black college in Missouri, and applied to the state law school. He was rejected because he was black. Missouri refused to admit blacks to its all-white law school; instead, the state's policy was to pay the costs of blacks who were admitted to out-of-state law schools. With the support of the NAACP, Gaines appealed to the courts for admission to the University of Missouri Law School. In 1938, the Supreme Court ruled that he must be admitted.[8] Under the *Plessy* doctrine, Missouri could not shift its responsibility to provide an equal education onto other states.

Two later cases helped reinforce the requirement that segregated facilities must be equal in all major respects. One was brought by Heman Sweatt, again with the help of the NAACP. Sweatt had been denied entrance to the all-white University of Texas Law School because of his race. A federal court ordered the state to provide a black law school for him; the state responded by renting a few rooms in an office building and hiring two black lawyers as teachers. Sweatt refused to attend the school and took his case to the Supreme Court.[9]

George McLaurin had been refused admission to a doctoral program in education at the all-white University of Oklahoma because he was black. There was no equivalent program for blacks in the state. McLaurin sought a federal court order for admission, but under pressure from the decision in *Gaines*, the university amended its procedures and admitted McLaurin "on a segregated basis." The sixty-eight-year-old McLaurin was restricted to hastily designated "colored-only" sections of a few rooms. He appealed this obvious lack of equal facilities to the Supreme Court under the direction of the NAACP.[10]

The Court ruled on *Sweatt* and *McLaurin* in 1950. The justices unanimously found that the facilities in each case were inadequate: The separate "law school" provided for Sweatt did not approach the quality of the white state law school; and the restrictions placed on McLaurin, through his segregation from other students within the same institution, would result in an inferior education. Both Sweatt and McLaurin had to be

---

* In 1939, the NAACP established an offshoot, the NAACP Legal Defense and Education Fund, to work on legal challenges, while the main organization concentrated on lobbying as its principal strategy.

given full student status at their respective state universities. But the Court avoided re-examination of the separate-but-equal doctrine.

. . . And Pressure for Desegregation

These decisions—especially in *McLaurin*—seemed to indicate that the time was right for an attack on segregation itself. In addition, public attitudes toward race relations were slowly changing from the predominant racism of the nineteenth and early twentieth centuries. Black troops had fought with honor—albeit in segregated military units—in World War II. Blacks and whites were working together in unions and in service and religious organizations. Social change and court decisions suggested that government-imposed segregation was assailable.

President Harry S Truman risked his political future with his strong support of black civil rights. In 1947, he established the President's Committee on Civil Rights. The committee's report, issued later that year, became the agenda for the civil rights movement over the next two decades. It called for national laws prohibiting racially motivated brutality, segregation, and poll taxes, and for guarantees of voting rights and equal employment opportunity. In 1948, Truman ordered the **desegregation** (the end of authorized racial segregation) of the armed forces.

In 1947, the U.S. Department of Justice had begun to submit briefs to the courts in support of civil rights. Perhaps the department's most important intervention was in **Brown v. Board of Education.**[11] This case was the culmination of twenty years of planning and litigation on the part of the NAACP to invalidate racial segregation in schools.

Linda Brown was a black child whose father tried to enroll her in a white public school in Topeka, Kansas. The school was close to Linda's home, and the walk to the black school required that she cross a dangerous set of railroad tracks. Brown's request was refused because of Linda's race. A federal district court found that the black public school was, in all major respects, equal in quality to the white school; therefore, by the *Plessy* doctrine, Linda was required to go to the black public school. Brown appealed the decision.

Brown v. *Board of Education* reached the Supreme Court in November 1951. The justices delayed argument on the sensitive race issue, placing it beyond the 1952 national election. The Court merged *Brown* with four similar cases brought in Delaware, South Carolina, Virginia, and the District of Columbia. Each case was brought as a class action, a device for combining the claims or defenses of similar individuals so that they can be tried in a single lawsuit (see Chapter 14). And all were supported by the NAACP and coordinated by Thurgood Marshall, who would later become the first black justice to sit on the Supreme Court.

These five cases squarely challenged the separate-but-equal doctrine. By all tangible measures (standards for teacher licensing, teacher-pupil ratios, library facilities), the two school systems in each case—one white, the other black—were equal. The issue was legal separation of the races.

The cases were argued in late 1952 but they were set for reargument at the request of the justices. The sudden death of Chief Justice Fred M. Vinson in September 1953 added further delay to the school segregation

Anger Erupts in Little Rock

In 1957, the school board in Little Rock, Arkansas, attempted to implement court-approved desegregation. The first step called for admitting nine blacks to Central High School on September 3, but the governor sent in the national guard to bar their attendance. On September 23, when the black students again attempted entry, police escorts could not control the mob that gathered at the school. Two days later, under the protection of federal troops ordered by President Eisenhower, the students were finally admitted. Although hostility and violence led the school board to seek a postponement of the desegregation plan, the Supreme Court, meeting in special session during the summer of 1958, affirmed the Brown *decision and ordered the plan to proceed.*

issue. On May 17, 1954, Chief Justice Earl Warren, who had joined the Court as Vinson's replacement, delivered a single opinion covering four of the cases. (Chapter 14 describes how he approached the cases after the reargument.) Warren spoke for a unanimous Court when he declared that "in the field of public education the doctrine of 'separate but equal' has no place. Separate educational facilities are inherently unequal, depriving the plaintiffs of the equal protection of the laws." Segregated facilities generate in black children "a feeling of inferiority . . . that may affect their hearts and minds in a way unlikely ever to be undone." In short, state-imposed public school segregation was found to violate the equal protection clause of the Fourteenth Amendment.

A companion case to *Brown* challenged the segregation of public schools in Washington, D.C.[12] Segregation here was imposed by Congress. The equal protection clause protected citizens only against *state* violations; there was no equal protection clause restraining the national government. It was unthinkable for the Constitution to impose a lesser duty on the national government than on the states. In this case, the Court unanimously decided that the racial segregation requirement was an arbitrary deprivation of liberty without due process of law, a violation of the Fifth Amendment. In short, the concept of liberty *embraced* the idea of equality.

The Court deferred implementation of the school desegregation decisions until 1955. Then, in **Brown v. Board of Education II,** it ruled that school systems must desegregate "with all deliberate speed" and placed the process of desegregation under the direction of the lower federal courts.[13]

Some states quietly implemented the *Brown* decree. Others did little to desegregate their schools. And many communities in the South defied the Court, sometimes violently. Some white business and professional people formed "white citizens councils." These councils used their economic power against blacks who asserted their rights by foreclosing on mortgages and denying blacks credit at local stores. Georgia and North Carolina resisted desegregation by paying the tuition of white students who attended private schools. Virginia and other states ordered that desegregated schools be closed.

This resistance, along with the Supreme Court's "all deliberate speed" order, placed a heavy burden on federal judges to dismantle what were by now fundamental social institutions in many communities.[14] Gradual desegregation under *Brown* was in some cases no desegregation at all. By 1969, a unanimous Supreme Court ordered that the operation of segregated school systems must stop "at once."[15]

Two years later, the Court approved several remedies to achieve integration, including busing, racial quotas, and the pairing or grouping of noncontiguous school zones. In **Swann v. Charlotte-Mecklenburg County Schools,** the Supreme Court affirmed the right of lower courts to

Dishonoring Old Glory

The struggle for racial equality in Boston in the 1970s divided the city and generated hatred and resentment among blacks and whites. Federal court orders mandating school desegregation touched off particularly violent reactions. In 1976, a white protester marching toward the federal courthouse tried to impale a black passer-by with a flagstaff. This photograph captured the ugliness of the city's conflicts more powerfully than words could.

order the busing of children to ensure school desegregation.[16] But these remedies applied only to **de jure segregation,** government-imposed segregation (for example, government assignment of whites to one school and blacks to another within the same community). Court-imposed remedies did not apply to **de facto segregation**, segregation that is not the result of government influence (for example, racial segregation resulting from residential patterns).

The busing of schoolchildren came under heavy attack in both the North and the South. Busing was seen by desegregation advocates as a possible remedy in many northern cities, where schools had become segregated as white families left the cities for the suburbs. This "white flight" left inner-city schools predominantly black and suburban schools almost all white. Public opinion strongly opposed the busing approach, and Congress sought limits on busing as a remedy. In 1974, a closely divided Court ruled in ***Milliken v. Bradley*** that lower courts could not order busing across school district boundaries to achieve racial balance unless each district had practiced racial discrimination or unless school district lines had been drawn to achieve racial segregation.[17] This ruling meant an end to extensive school desegregation in metropolitan areas.

The Civil Rights Movement

Although the NAACP concentrated on school desegregation, it also made headway in other areas. The Supreme Court responded to the NAACP's efforts of the middle to late 1940s by outlawing the whites-only primary elections that were being held in the South, declaring them to be in violation of the Fifteenth Amendment. The Court also declared segregation on interstate bus routes to be unconstitutional and desegregated restaurants and hotels in the District of Columbia. Despite these and other decisions that chipped away at existing barriers to equality, black citizens were still being denied political power, and segregation remained a fact of daily life (see Feature 16.1).

Dwight D. Eisenhower, who became president in 1953, was not as concerned about civil rights as his predecessor had been. He chose to stand above the battle between the Supreme Court and those who resisted the Court's decisions. He even refused to reveal whether he agreed with the Court's decision in *Brown* v. *Board of Education.* "It makes no difference," Eisenhower declared, because "the Constitution is as the Supreme Court interprets it."[18]

Eisenhower did enforce school desegregation when the safety of schoolchildren was involved, but he appeared unwilling to do much more to advance racial equality. That goal seemed to require the political mobilization of the people—black and white—into what is now known as the **civil rights movement**.

The black church served as the crucible of the movement. More than a place of worship, it served hundreds of extra functions, including "a bulletin board to a people who owned no organs of communication, a credit union to those without banks, and even a kind of people's court." Some of its preachers were motivated by fortune, others by saintliness. One would prove to be a modern-day Moses.[19]

FEATURE 16.1   *American Racism: An International Handicap*

In August 1955, the ambassador from India, G. L. Mehta, walked into a restaurant at the Houston International Airport, sat down, and waited to order. But Texas law required that whites and blacks be served in separate dining facilities. The dark-skinned diplomat, who had seated himself in a whites-only area, was told to move. The insult stung deeply and was not soon forgotten. From Washington, Secretary of State John Foster Dulles telegraphed his apologies for this blatant display of racism, fearing that the incident would injure relations with a nation whose allegiance the United States was seeking in the Cold War.

Such embarrassments were not uncommon in the 1950s. Burma's minister of education was denied a meal in a Columbus, Ohio, restaurant, and the finance minister of Ghana was turned away from a Howard Johnson's restaurant just outside the nation's capital. Secretary Dulles complained that segregationist practices were becoming a "major international hazard," a threat to U.S. efforts to

gain the friendship of Third World countries. Americans stood publicly condemned as a people who did not honor the ideal of equality.

Thus when the attorney general [James P. McGranery] appealed to the Supreme Court to strike down segregation in public schools, his introductory remarks [in the government's *amicus* brief] took note of the international implications. "It is in the context of the present world struggle between freedom and tyranny that the problem of racial discrimination must be viewed," he warned. The humiliation of dark-skinned diplomats in Washington D.C., "the window through which the world looks into our house," was damaging to American interests. Racism "furnished grist for the Communist propaganda mills."

Source: Mary Beth Norton, et al., *A People and a Nation: A History of the United States*, 3d ed. (Boston: Houghton Mifflin, 1990), p. 869. Copyright © 1990 by Houghton Mifflin Company. Adapted with permission.

Civil Disobedience

The call to action was first sounded by Rosa Parks, a black woman living in Montgomery, Alabama. That city's Jim Crow ordinances were tougher than those in most southern cities, where blacks were required to sit in the back of the bus and whites in the front, both races converging as the bus filled with passengers. In Montgomery, however, bus drivers were empowered to keep a floating line separating blacks and whites. Drivers would order blacks to vacate an entire row to make room for one white or order blacks to stand even when there were vacant seats. Blacks could not walk through the white section to their seats in the back; they had to leave the bus after paying the fare and then re-enter through the rear.[20] In December 1955, Parks boarded a city bus on her way home from work. Tired after the day's work, Parks took an available seat in the front of the bus; she refused to give up her seat when asked to do so by the driver and was arrested and fined $10 for violating the city ordinance.

Montgomery's black community responded to Parks's arrest with a boycott of the city's bus system. A **boycott** is a refusal to do business with a firm or individual, as an expression of disapproval or as a means of coercion. Blacks walked or car-pooled or simply did not make trips that were not absolutely necessary. As the bus company moved closer to bankruptcy and downtown merchants suffered from the loss of black business, city officials began to harass blacks, hoping to frighten them into ending the boycott. But Montgomery's black citizens now had a leader—a charismatic twenty-six-year-old Baptist minister named Martin Luther King, Jr.

King urged the people to hold out, and they did. A year after the boycott began, the federal courts ruled that segregated transportation systems violated the equal protection clause of the Constitution (see Feature 14.1, page 501). The boycott proved to be an effective weapon.

In 1957, King helped organize the Southern Christian Leadership Council (SCLC) to coordinate civil rights activities. He was totally committed to nonviolent action to bring racial issues into the light. To that end, he advocated **civil disobedience,** the willful but nonviolent violation of unjust laws.

One nonviolent tactic was the *sit-in*. On February 1, 1960, four black freshmen from North Carolina Agricultural and Technical College in Greensboro sat down at a whites-only lunch counter. They were refused service by the black waitress, who said, "Fellows like you make our race look bad." The freshmen stayed all that day and promised to return the next morning to continue what they called a "sit-down protest." Other students soon joined, rotating shifts so that no one missed classes. Within two days, 85 students flocked to the lunch counter as the "sit-in" spread. The students were abused verbally and physically. Still, they would not move. Finally, they were arrested. Soon there were similar sit-in demonstrations throughout the South and then in the North.[21] The Supreme Court upheld the actions of the demonstrators, although the unanimity that had characterized the earlier decisions of the Court was gone (in this decision, three justices argued that even bigots had the right to call on the state to protect their property interests).

The Civil Rights Act of 1964

In 1961, a new administration came to power headed by President John F. Kennedy. At first, Kennedy did not seem to be committed to civil rights. This changed as the movement gained momentum, as more and more whites became aware of the abuse being heaped on sit-in demonstrators, freedom riders (who tested unlawful segregation on interstate bus routes), and those who were trying to help blacks register to vote in southern states. Volunteers were being jailed, beaten, and killed for advocating activities that whites took for granted.

In the fall of 1962, President Kennedy ordered federal troops to ensure the safety of James Meredith, the first black to attend the University of Mississippi. In early 1963, he enforced the desegregation of the University of Alabama. In April 1963, television viewers were shocked to see marchers in Birmingham, Alabama, attacked with dogs, fire hoses, and cattle prods. (The idea of the march was to provoke confrontations with white officials in an effort to compel the federal government to intervene on behalf of blacks.) Finally, in June 1963, Kennedy asked Congress for legislation that would outlaw segregation in public accommodations.

Two months later, Martin Luther King, Jr., organized and led a march on Washington, D.C., to show support for the civil rights movement. More than 250,000 people, black and white, gathered peaceably at the Lincoln Memorial to hear King speak. "I have a dream," he told them,

FEATURE 16.2   *A Preacher's Afterthought: A Dream of Freedom from Inequality*

The Rev. Martin Luther King, Jr., gave Americans a vision of a society free from racial inequality in his famous "I Have a Dream" speech. But King's most memorable lines on the steps of the Lincoln Memorial in Washington, D.C., were not part of his prepared text. King ad-libbed.

King was the last speaker that day in Washington. He recited his prepared text until shortly near the end, when he decided not to deliver what one historian has labeled the lamest and most pretentious section. ("And so today, let us go back to our communities as members of the international association for the advancement of creative dissatisfaction.") Instead, he extemporized, urging his audience to believe that change would come "somehow" and that they could not "wallow in the valley of despair."

Voices from behind urged King on. Mahalia Jackson, the great gospel singer, added her voice: "Tell 'em about the dream, Martin." The dream device was one King had used in the past, in speeches and at the pulpit. It's not clear whether he heard Jackson's words or simply reached instinctively for a familiar and effective piece of oratory.

After the powerful "dream" sequence, King returned to a few sentences from his prepared text. But then he was off on his own again, reciting the first stanza from "My Country 'Tis of Thee," ending with "'let freedom ring.'" King continued: "And if America is to be a great nation, this must become true. So let freedom ring." King concluded with an old vision from the pulpit, born of enslavement but new to a world now riveted to his words: "And when *this* happens . . . we will be able to speed up that day when *all* God's children, black men and white men, Jews and Gentiles, Protestants and Catholics, will be able to join hands and sing in the words of the old Negro spiritual, 'Free at last! Free at last! Thank God Almighty, we are free at last!'"

Source: Taylor Branch, *Parting the Waters: America in the King Years, 1954–63* (New York: Simon and Schuster, 1988), chap. 22. Copyright © 1988 by Taylor Branch. Reprinted by permission of Simon & Schuster, Inc.

"that my little children will one day live in a nation where they will not be judged by the color of their skin but by the content of their character"[22] (see Feature 16.2).

Kennedy's public accommodations bill had not yet been passed by Congress when he was assassinated, on November 22, 1963. His successor, Lyndon B. Johnson, considered civil rights his top legislative priority. Within months, Congress passed the Civil Rights Act of 1964. It contained several parts, including a vital provision barring segregation in most public accommodations. Passage of the act was, in part, a reaction to Kennedy's death. But it was also almost surely a reaction to the brutal treatment of blacks throughout the South.

Civil rights laws had been passed by Congress in 1957 and 1960, but they dealt primarily with voting rights. The 1964 act was the most comprehensive legislative attempt ever to erase racial discrimination in the United States. It was enacted after the longest debate in Senate history, and only after the first successful use of cloture to end a civil rights filibuster.

Among its many provisions, the act

- entitled all persons to "the full and equal enjoyment" of goods, services, and privileges in places of public accommodation without discrimination on the grounds of race, color, religion, or national origin.

- established the right to equality in employment opportunities.

A Modern-Day Moses

Martin Luther King, Jr., was a Baptist minister who believed in the principles of nonviolent protest practiced by India's Mahatma Gandhi. This photograph, taken in 1963 in Baltimore, captures the crowd's affection for King, the man many thought would lead the way to a new Canaan of racial equality. King, who won the Nobel Peace Prize in 1964, was assassinated in 1968 in Memphis, Tennessee.

- strengthened voting rights legislation.
- created the Equal Employment Opportunity Commission (EEOC), charging it to hear and investigate complaints of job discrimination.*
- provided that funds could be withheld from federally assisted programs that were administered in a discriminatory manner.

The last of these provisions had a powerful impact on school desegregation when Congress passed the Elementary and Secondary Education Act in 1965. That act provided for billions of federal dollars in aid for the nation's schools; the threat of losing those funds spurred local school boards to formulate and implement new plans for desegregation.

The 1964 act faced an immediate constitutional challenge. Its opponents argued that the Constitution does not forbid acts of private discrimination—the position the Supreme Court had taken in the late nineteenth century. But this time a unanimous Supreme Court upheld the law, declaring that acts of discrimination impose substantial burdens on interstate commerce and thus *are* subject to congressional control.[23] In a companion case, Ollie McClung, the owner of a small restaurant, had refused to serve blacks.[24] McClung maintained that he had the freedom to serve whomever he wanted to in his own restaurant. The justices, however, upheld the government's prohibition of McClung's racial discrimination on the ground that a substantial portion of the food served in his restaurant had moved in interstate commerce. The Civil Rights Act of 1964 was vindicated by reason of the congressional power to regulate interstate commerce, rather than on the basis of the Fourteenth Amendment.

---

* Since 1972, the EEOC has had the power to institute legal proceedings on behalf of employees who allege that they have been victims of illegal discrimination.

Johnson's goal was a "Great Society." Soon a constitutional amendment and a series of civil rights laws were in place to help him meet his goal.

- The Twenty-fourth Amendment, ratified in 1964, banned poll taxes in primary and general elections for national office.
- The Economic Opportunity Act of 1964 focused on education and training to combat poverty.
- The Voting Rights Act of 1965 empowered the attorney general to send voter registration supervisors to areas in which fewer than half the eligible minority voters had been registered. This act has been credited with doubling black voter registration in the South in only five years.[25]
- The Fair Housing Act of 1968 banned discrimination in the rental or sale of most housing.

From Restriction to Restoration to Restriction

Civil rights on the books, however, do not ensure civil rights in action. This was the case in 1984, when the Supreme Court was called on to interpret a law that forbids sex discrimination in schools and colleges receiving financial assistance from the federal government. Must an institution comply with the regulations if it does not receive assistance?

In *Grove City College* v. *Bell*, the Court ruled that government educational grants to students implicates the institution as a recipient of government funds; therefore, it must comply with government disclosure and nondiscrimination provisions. However, only the specific department or program receiving federal funds (in Grove City's case, the financial aid program), not the whole institution, was barred from discriminating.[26] Athletic departments rarely receive federal funds, so colleges were released from the obligation to provide equal opportunity for women in their sports programs.

The decision had widespread effects since three other important civil rights laws were worded similarly. The implication was that any law barring discrimination on the basis of race, sex, age, and handicapped status would be confined to *programs* that discriminate, not to *institutions* that discriminate. So a university laboratory that received federal research grants could not discriminate, but other departments that did not receive federal money could. The effect of *Grove City* was to frustrate enforcement of civil rights laws.

Congress reacted immediately, exercising its lawmaking power to check the law-interpreting power of the judiciary. Legislators bellowed that the Court had misinterpreted the intent of the antidiscrimination laws, and they forged a bipartisan effort to make that intent crystal clear: If any part of an institution gets federal money, no part can discriminate. Their work developed into the Civil Rights Restoration Act, which became law in 1988 despite a presidential veto.

While Congress tried to restore and expand civil rights enforcement, the Supreme Court appeared to dismantle or confine it again. In a series of startling 5–4 decisions in 1989, the justices voted to limit the reach of long-standing civil rights decisions.

- The Court restricted minority contractor set-asides of state public-works funds, an arrangement it had approved in 1980. (A *set-aside* is a purchasing or contracting provision that allocates a certain percentage of business to minority-owned companies.) The five-person majority held that past societal discrimination alone cannot serve as the basis for rigid racial quotas.[27]

- The justices held that a court-approved affirmative action plan mandating race-conscious promotion decisions that favored African-Americans could be challenged years later by the affected whites who were not parties to the plan.[28]

- The Court shifted the burden of proving allegations of discrimination in hiring and promotion from the employer to the employee, making it more difficult for plaintiffs to win. This reversed a decision that had stood since 1971.[29]

- The Court held that a 1866 law, which had been used by minorities to sue for private acts of discrimination, barred discrimination only at the initial hiring stage; the law did not bar discrimination on the job.[30]

These decisions (and others) signal the ascendancy of a new conservative majority more concerned with freedom than equality. Since the issues hinged on the Court's interpretation of federal law, civil rights advocates turned to Congress to restore, and perhaps enlarge, the earlier decisions by writing them into law. The result was a new civil rights bill. In a departure from previous civil rights legislation, however, this bill was exceedingly complex and legalistic. It lacked the moral force of a law conferring rights on people. The bill passed Congress in 1990 but was vetoed by President Bush on the ground that it would force quotas in hiring and promotion. Bush's veto was sustained by a one-vote margin in the Senate.

Racial Violence and Black Nationalism

The middle and late 1960s were marked by increased violence on the part of those who demanded their civil rights and those who refused to relinquish them. Violence against civil rights workers was confined primarily to the South, where volunteers continued to work for desegregation and to register black voters. Among the atrocities that incensed even complacent whites were the bombing of dozens of black churches; the murder of three young civil rights workers in Philadelphia, Mississippi, in 1964 by a group of whites, among them deputy sheriffs; police violence against demonstrators who had started out on a peaceful march from Selma, Alabama, to Montgomery in 1965 (see page 228); and the assassination of Martin Luther King, Jr., in Memphis in 1968.

Black violence took the form of rioting in the black ghettos of northern cities. Civil rights gains had mainly been focused on the South. Northern blacks had the vote and were not subject to Jim Crow laws, yet most lived in poverty. Unemployment was high, work opportunities at skilled jobs were limited, and earnings were low. The segregation of blacks in inner-city ghettos, although not sanctioned by law, was nevertheless real; their voting power was of little moment because they constituted a small minority of the northern population. The solid gains made by southern blacks added to their frustration. Beginning in 1964, northern blacks took to the streets, burning and looting. Riots in 168 cities and towns followed King's assassination in 1968.

The lack of progress toward equality for northern blacks was an important factor in the rise of a black nationalist movement in the 1960s. The Black Muslims, led by Malcolm X until his assassination in 1965, called for separation from whites rather than integration, and for violence in return for violence. The Black Panthers denounced the values of white America. In 1966, Stokely Carmichael, then chairman of the Student Nonviolent Coordinating Committee (SNCC), called on blacks to assert "black power" in their struggle for civil rights. Organizations that previously had espoused integration and nonviolence now began to argue that blacks needed power more than they needed the friendship of whites.

The movement had several positive effects. Black nationalism promoted and instilled pride in black history and culture. By the end of the decade, colleges and universities were beginning to institute black studies programs for their students. More black citizens were voting than ever before, and their voting power was evident: Increasing numbers of blacks were being elected to public office. In 1967, Cleveland's voters elected Carl Stokes the first black mayor of a major American city. And by 1969, black representatives were able to form the Congressional Black Caucus. These achievements were incentives for other groups who also faced barriers to equality.

Civil Rights for Other Minorities

The civil rights won by black Americans apply to all Americans. Recent civil rights laws and court decisions protect members of all minority groups.

The Supreme Court underscored the breadth of this protection in an important decision in 1987.[31] The justices ruled unanimously that the Civil Rights Act of 1866 (known today as Section 1981) offered broad protection against discrimination to all minorities. Heretofore, the law could not be invoked by members of white ethnic groups in bias suits. Under the decision, members of *any* ethnic group—Italian, Iranian, Chinese, Norwegian, or Vietnamese, for example—can recover money damages if they prove they have been denied jobs, excluded from rental housing, or subjected to other forms of discrimination prohibited by the law. The 1964 Civil Rights Act offers similar protections to these ethnic groups, but the 1964 act has strict procedures for filing suits. These procedures tend to discourage litigation. Moreover, the remedies in most cases are limited. In job discrimination, for example, back pay and reinstatement are the only remedies. Section 1981 has fewer pitfalls and allows litigants to seek *punitive damages* (damages awarded by a court as additional punishment for a serious wrong). In some respects, then, the older law is a more potent weapon than the newer one in fighting discrimination.

Righting a Wrong

During World War II, Congress authorized the quarantine of Japanese residents in the western United States. More than 110,000 men, women, and children—including native-born U.S. citizens—were incarcerated simply because they were of Japanese ancestry. The Supreme Court upheld the law in 1944, the only time the Court has given constitutional protection to a legislative act promoting racial inequality. In 1988, Congress passed legislation that offered apologies and $20,000 tax-free to each surviving internee. The cost to the government: $1.25 billion.

Clearly the civil rights movement has had an impact on all minorities. In the United States, however, equality has been granted most slowly to nonwhite minorities. Here we examine the civil rights struggles of three groups—Native Americans, Hispanic-Americans, and the disabled.

Native Americans

During the eighteenth and nineteenth centuries, the U.S. government took Indian lands, isolated Native Americans on reservations, and denied them political and social rights. The government's dealings with the Indians were often marked by violence and riddled with broken promises. The agency system for administering Indian reservations kept Native Americans poor and dependent on the national government.

The national government switched policies at the turn of the century, promoting assimilation instead of separation. The government banned the use of native languages and religious rituals; it sent Indian children to boarding schools and gave them non-Indian names. In 1924, Indians were given U.S. citizenship. Until that time, they were considered members of tribal nations whose relations with government were subject to treaties made with the United States. The Native American population suffered badly during the Depression, primarily because the poorest people were affected most, but also because of the inept administration of Indian reservations. Poverty remained on the reservations well after the Depression was over, and Indian lands continued to shrink through the

1950s and into the 1960s—in spite of signed treaties and the religious significance of portions of those lands. In the 1960s, for example, a part of the Hopi Sacred Circle, which is considered the source of all life in tribal religion, was strip-mined for coal.

Anger bred of poverty, unemployment, and frustration with an uncaring government exploded into militant action in November 1969, when several American Indians seized Alcatraz Island, an abandoned island in San Francisco Bay. The group cited an 1868 Sioux treaty that entitled them to unused federal lands; they remained on the island for a year and a half. In 1973, armed members of the American Indian Movement seized eleven hostages at Wounded Knee, South Dakota—the site of a tragic battle in 1890 between the Sioux and U.S. cavalry troops. They remained there, occasionally exchanging gunfire with federal marshals, for seventy-one days.

In 1946, Congress had passed legislation establishing an Indian claims commission to compensate Native Americans for land that had been taken from them. In the 1970s, the Native American Rights Fund and other groups used that legislation to win important victories. Lands were returned to tribes in the Midwest and in the states of Oklahoma, New Mexico, and Washington. In 1980, the Supreme Court ordered the national government to pay the Sioux $117 million plus interest for the Black Hills of South Dakota, which had been stolen from them a century before. Other cases, involving land from coast to coast, are still pending.

The fight continues for survival of ancient native culture and control over lost lands. The preservation of Native American culture and the exercise of Native American rights, however, sometimes create conflict with the interests of the majority. For example, Chippewa Indians in northern Wisconsin engage in an annual battle with local fishermen on the shores of Lake Minocqua. The Indians wish to exercise their acknowledged right to spearfish for walleyed pike. Fishermen fear that the

Bury My Heart

Native American mourners gathered at Wounded Knee, South Dakota, on December 29, 1990, to remember a tragedy. On that site a hundred years earlier, two hundred Sioux—including women and children—were killed by Seventh Cavalry soldiers. Descendants of the survivors traveled by foot and horseback to mark the anniversary and honor their heritage.

Indians will deplete the stock and drive sport fishermen away. The Chippewas voluntarily limit their annual catch, but they are offended that their ancestral claims are envied as government concessions when their stake rests on legal rights.

In other instances, economic necessity may overwhelm ancient ways. One Alaskan tribe desperate for funds has been forced into unsettling choices: Sign away logging rights, permit oil drilling in a wildlife area, or allow the construction of an airfield in a vast habitat for Kodiak bears. Some tribes have allowed the use of their reservations for dumps and waste disposal only to face land and water contamination as a consequence.

Throughout American history, Native Americans have been coerced physically and pressured economically to assimilate into the mainstream of white society. The destiny of Native Americans as viable groups with separate identities depends in no small measure on curbing their dependence on the national government.[32] Litigation on behalf of Native Americans may prove to be their most effective weapon in the march toward equality.

Hispanic-Americans

Many Hispanic-Americans have a rich and deep-rooted heritage in America, but until the 1920s, that heritage was largely confined to the southwestern states and California. Then, large numbers of Mexican and Puerto Rican immigrants came to the United States in search of employment and a better life. They were welcomed by businesspeople who saw in them a source of cheap labor. Many of the Mexicans became farm workers, but both groups settled mainly in crowded, low-rent, inner-city districts: the Mexicans in the Southwest; the Puerto Ricans primarily in New York City. Both groups formed their own *barrios*, or communities, within the cities, where they maintained the customs and values of their homelands.

Like blacks who had migrated to northern cities, most of the new Hispanic immigrants found poverty and discrimination. And, like poor blacks and Native Americans, they were hit hard by the Depression. About one-third of the Mexican-American population (mainly those who had been migratory farm workers) returned to Mexico during the 1930s.

World War II gave rise to another influx of Mexicans, who this time were courted to work farms primarily in California. But by the late 1950s, most farm workers—blacks, whites, and Hispanics—were living in poverty. Those Hispanic-Americans who lived in cities fared little better. Yet millions of Mexicans continued to cross the border into the United States, both legally and illegally. The effect was to depress the value of farm labor in California and the Southwest.

In 1965, Cesar Chavez led a strike of the United Farm Workers Union against growers in California. The strike lasted several years but eventually, in combination with a boycott, resulted in somewhat better pay, working conditions, and housing for workers.

In the 1970s and 1980s, the Hispanic-American population continued to grow. The 20 million Hispanics living in the United States in the 1970s were still mainly Puerto Rican and Mexican-American, but they were joined by immigrants from the Dominican Republic, Colombia, Cuba, and Ecuador. Although civil rights legislation helped them to an extent, they were among the poorest and least-educated groups in the United States. Their problems were like those faced by other nonwhites, but, in addition, most had to overcome the further difficulty of learning and using a new language.

One of the effects of the language barrier is that voter registration and voter turnout among Hispanics are lower than among other groups. With few or no Spanish-speaking voting officials, low registration levels may be inevitable. Voter turnout, in turn, depends on effective political advertising, and Hispanics are not targeted as often as other groups with political messages that they can understand. Despite these stumbling blocks, however, Hispanics have started to exercise a measure of political power. Hispanic-Americans have been elected mayor in San Antonio, San Diego, Denver, and Miami. President Bush has appointed two Latinos to his cabinet. Cuban-Americans look with pride to the first of their number to be elected to Congress. Hispanics have also gained some access to political power through their representation in coalitions that dominate policymaking on minority-related issues.[33]

In 1990, Hispanic activists in Los Angeles won a landmark voting rights case against one of the nation's most powerful local governing bodies. A federal judge ruled that the county board of supervisors, which controls a $10.5 billion budget, had illegally diluted the power of Latinos, who make up a third of the county's population. To remedy the illegality, the board was ordered to redraw its legislative boundaries to assure Hispanic representation. Success in the judicial arena created conflict in the political arena as nine candidates (eight of them Latino) vied for the newly created slot. Ideological differences between the candidates are probably less important than the opportunity for Hispanics finally to elect one of their own.

Disabled Americans

Minority status need not be confined to race or ethnicity. After more than two decades of struggle, millions of handicapped Americans gained recognition in 1990 as an oppressed minority with the passage of the Americans with Disabilities Act.

The law extends the protections embodied in the Civil Rights Act of 1964 to people with physical or mental disabilities, including people with AIDS and recovering alcoholics and drug abusers. It guarantees access to employment, transportation, public accommodations, and communication services.

The roots of the handicapped rights movement stem from the period after World War II. Thousands of disabled veterans returned to a country and a society that were inhospitable to their needs. Institutionalization seemed the best way to care for the handicapped, but this treatment came under increasing challenge as the handicapped and their families sought care at home.

Advocates for the disabled found a ready model in the existing civil rights laws. Opponents argued that the changes mandated by the law (such as access for those confined to wheelchairs) could cost billions of dollars, but supporters replied that the costs would be offset by an equal or greater reduction in federal aid to disabled people who would rather be working.

A change in the law, no matter how welcome, does not assure a change in attitudes. Laws that end racial discrimination do not extinguish racism, and laws that ban biased treatment of the disabled will not mandate acceptance of the disabled. But attitudinal barriers toward the handicapped, like similar attitudes toward other minorities, will wither, rights advocates claim, as the disabled become full participants in a society that once held them at bay.

Gender and Equal Rights: The Women's Movement

The ballot box and the lawsuit have brought minorities in America a measure of equality. The Supreme Court—once an institution for perpetuating inequality for blacks—has expanded the array of legal weapons available to all minorities to help them achieve social equality. Women, too, have benefited from this change.

Protectionism

Until the early 1970s, laws that affected the civil rights of women were based on traditional views of the relationship between men and women. At the heart of these laws was **protectionism**—the idea that women must be sheltered from life's cruelties. Thomas Jefferson, author of the Declaration of Independence, believed that "were our state a pure democracy there would still be excluded from our deliberations women, who, to prevent deprivation of morals and ambiguity of issues, should not mix promiscuously in gatherings of men."[34] And protected they were, through laws that discriminated against them in employment and other areas. With few exceptions, women were also "protected" from voting until early in the twentieth century.

The demand for women's rights arose out of the abolitionist movement and later was based primarily on the Fourteenth Amendment's prohibition of laws that "abridge the privileges or immunities of citizens of the United States." However, the courts consistently rebuffed challenges to state protectionist laws. In 1873, the Supreme Court upheld an Illinois statute that prohibited women from practicing law. The justices maintained that the Fourteenth Amendment did not affect a state's authority to regulate admission of members to the bar.[35] In a concurring opinion, Justice Joseph P. Bradley articulated the common protectionist belief that women were unfit for certain occupations: "Man is, or should be, woman's protector and defender. The natural and proper timidity and delicacy which belongs to the female sex evidently unfits it for many of the occupations of civil life."

Protectionism reached a peak in 1908, when the Court upheld an Oregon law limiting the number of hours that women were allowed to work.[36] The decision was rife with sexist assumptions about the nature and role of women, and it gave wide latitude to laws that protected the

Free to Choose

Gloyce Qualls celebrates an important victory for women. In 1982, her employer, the Johnson Controls battery plant in Milwaukee, Wisconsin, had instituted a mandatory protection policy that placed women of child-bearing age in less hazardous (and often lower-paying) jobs. On behalf of women like Qualls, several workers challenged the fetal protection policy. In 1991, the Supreme Court unanimously declared such policy unconstitutional.

"weaker sex." It also led to protectionist legislation that barred women from working more than forty-eight hours a week and from jobs that required workers to lift more than 35 pounds. In effect, women were locked out of jobs that called for substantial overtime (and overtime pay); instead, they were shunted to jobs that men believed suited their abilities.

Protectionism can take many forms. Some employers hesitate to place women at risk in the workplace. One such policy excluded women capable of bearing children from exposure to toxic substances that could harm a developing fetus. Usually, these jobs offered more pay as a consequence of higher risk. Though they faced similar risks to their reproductivity, men were not excluded.

In 1991, the Supreme Court struck down a fetal protection policy in strong terms. The Court relied on amendments to the 1964 Civil Rights Act, which provides for very narrow exceptions to the principle that unless some workers differ from others in their ability to work, they must be treated the same as other employees. "In other words," declared the majority, "women as capable of doing their jobs as their male counterparts may not be forced to choose between having a child and having a job."[37]

Political Equality for Women

With a few exceptions, women were not allowed to vote in this country until 1920 (see page 244).*In 1869, Francis and Virginia Minor sued a

---

* The Fifteenth Amendment (as interpreted by the Supreme Court), which was passed in 1870, prohibited the use of race in denying a person the right to vote. It said nothing about gender.

St. Louis, Missouri, registrar for not allowing Virginia Minor to vote. In 1875, the Supreme Court held that the Fourteenth Amendment privileges and immunities clause did not confer the right to vote on all citizens or require that the states allow women to vote.[38]

The decision clearly slowed the movement toward women's suffrage, but it did not stop it. In 1878, Susan B. Anthony, a women's rights activist, convinced a U.S. senator from California to introduce a constitutional amendment requiring that "the right of citizens of the United States to vote shall not be denied or abridged by the United States or by any State on account of sex." The amendment was introduced and voted down a number of times over the next twenty years. However, as noted in Chapter 7, a number of states—primarily in the Midwest and West—did grant limited suffrage to women.

The movement for women's suffrage now became a political battle to amend the Constitution. In 1917, 218 women from twenty-six states were arrested when they picketed the White House demanding the right to vote. Nearly 100 went to jail—some for days, others for months. Hunger strikes and forced feedings followed. The movement culminated in the adoption in 1920 of the **Nineteenth Amendment,** which gave women the right to vote in the wording first suggested by Anthony.

Meanwhile, the Supreme Court continued to act as the benevolent protector of women. Women had entered the work force in significant numbers during World War I, and they did so again during World War II, but they received lower wages than the men they replaced. Again the justification was the "proper" role of women as mothers and homemakers. Because men were expected to be the principal providers, it followed that women's earnings were less important to the family's support. This thinking perpetuated inequalities in the workplace. Because women were expected to stay at home, they needed—and obtained—less education than men. And because they lacked education, they tended to qualify only for low-paying, low-skill jobs with little chance of advancement. Economic equality was closely tied to social attitudes.

Prohibiting Sex-Based Discrimination

The movement to provide equal rights to women advanced a step with the passage of the Equal Pay Act of 1963. That act requires equal pay for men and women doing similar work. However, state protectionist laws still had the effect of restricting women to jobs that were not usually taken by men. Where employment was stratified by sex, equal pay was an empty promise. To free them from the restrictions of protectionism, women needed equal opportunity for employment. They got it in the Civil Rights Act of 1964 and later legislation.

The objective of the Civil Rights Act of 1964 was to eliminate racial discrimination in America. In its proposed form, Title VII of the act prohibited employment discrimination based on race, color, religion, and national origin—but not gender. In an effort to scuttle this provision during House debate, Democrat Howard W. Smith of Virginia proposed an amendment barring job discrimination based on sex. Smith's intention was to make the law unacceptable; his effort to ridicule the law brought gales of laughter to the debate. But Democrat Martha W. Griffiths of Michigan used Smith's strategy against him. With her support, Smith's amendment carried, as did the act.[39] The jurisdiction of the Equal Employment Opportunity Commission was extended to cover cases of sex discrimination, or **sexism.**

Presidential authority also played a crucial role in the effort to eliminate sexism. In 1965, President Johnson issued an executive order that bound federal contractors to nondiscrimination and affirmative action in hiring and employment without regard to race, color, religion, or national origin. Three years later, he amended the order to include language that commanded nondiscrimination and affirmative action in hiring and employment without regard to sex. The result was new opportunity for women.

Subsequent women's rights legislation was motivated by the pressure for civil rights, as well as a resurgence of the women's movement, which had subsided after the adoption of the Nineteenth Amendment. One particularly important law was Title IX of the Education Amendments Act of 1972, which prohibited sex discrimination in federally aided education programs. Another boost to women came from the Revenue Act of 1972, which provided tax credits for child-care expenses. In effect, the act subsidized parents with young children so that women could enter or remain in the work force. However, the high-water mark in the effort on behalf of women's rights was the Equal Rights Amendment, which we discuss shortly.

Stereotypes Under Scrutiny

After nearly a century of broad deference to protectionism, the Supreme Court began to take a closer look at gender-based distinctions. In 1971, it struck down a state law that gave men preference over women in administering the estate of a person who died without naming an administrator.[40] The state maintained that the law reduced court workloads and avoided family battles; however, the Court dismissed those objectives because they were not important enough to sustain the use of gender distinctions. Two years later, the justices declared that the paternalism of earlier ages operated to "put women not on a pedestal, but in a cage."[41] They then proceeded to strike down several gender-based laws that either prevented or discouraged departures from "proper" sex roles. In 1976, the Court finally developed a workable standard for reviewing these kinds of laws: Gender-based distinctions are justified only if they serve some important government purpose.[42]

The objective here is to dismantle sexual stereotypes while fashioning public policies that acknowledge relevant differences between men and women. Perhaps the most controversial issue is the idea of "comparable worth," which would require employers to pay comparable wages for different jobs that are of about the same worth to an employer, even if one job might be filled predominantly by women and another mainly by men. The goal is a job standard that takes into account both the legal equality of men and women and their relevant physiological differences.[43]

The Equal Rights Amendment

Women have not enjoyed the same rights as men. Policies protecting women, based largely on sexual stereotypes, have been woven into the legal fabric of American life. That protectionism limited the freedom of women to compete with men socially and economically on an equal footing. The Supreme Court has been hesitant to extend the principles of the Fourteenth Amendment beyond issues of race. If constitutional interpretation imposes such a limit, then it can be overcome only by a constitutional amendment.

The **Equal Rights Amendment (ERA)** was first introduced in 1923 by the National Women's party, one of the few women's groups that did not disband after the Nineteenth Amendment was passed. The ERA declared that "equality of rights under the law shall not be denied or abridged by the United States or any State on account of sex." It remained bottled up in committee in every Congress until 1970, when Representative Martha Griffiths filed a discharge petition to report it to the House floor for a vote. The House passed the ERA, but the Senate scuttled it by attaching a section calling for prayer in the public schools.

A national coalition of women's rights advocates generated enough support to get the ERA through the proposal stage in 1972. Its proponents now had seven years in which to get the amendment ratified by thirty-eight state legislatures, as required by the Constitution. By 1977, they were three states short of that goal, and three states had rescinded earlier ratification. For some reason, the national coalition that had worked so effectively to move through the proposal stage seemed to lack the political strength to jump the ratification hurdle. Then, in an unprecedented action, Congress extended the ratification deadline. It didn't help. The ERA died on July 1, 1982, still three states short of adoption.

Why did the ERA fail? There are several explanations. ERA proponents mounted a national campaign to generate approval, while opponents organized state anti-ERA campaigns. After all, ratification required the approval of state lawmakers. The amendment quickly acquired opposition, including many women who had supported women's rights legislation. ERA proponents hurt their cause by inflating the amendment's impact; such claims only fueled opponents, who generated their own exaggerations. For example, the puffed-up claim that the amendment would make wife and husband equally responsible for their family's financial support caused alarm among the undecided. As the opposition grew stronger, especially from women who wanted to maintain their traditional role, state legislators began to realize that there were risks involved in supporting the amendment. Given exaggeration and counter-exaggeration, prudent lawmakers ducked. It takes an extraordinary majority to amend the Constitution, which is equivalent to saying that it takes only a committed minority to thwart the majority's will.

Despite its failure, the movement to ratify the ERA produced real benefits. It raised the consciousness of women about their social position; it spurred the formation of the National Organization for Women (NOW) and other large organizations; it contributed to women's participation in politics; and it influenced major legislation affecting women.[44]

The failure to ratify the ERA stands in stark contrast to the quick passage of many laws that now protect women's rights. But in fact there was little audible opposition to women's rights legislation. If years of racial discrimination called for government redress, then so did years of gender-based discrimination. Furthermore, laws protecting women's rights required only the amending of civil rights bills or the passage of similar bills.

In constitutional terms, the effects of an equal rights amendment are unclear. It would certainly raise gender to the same status as race in evaluating the validity of government policies. The courts have ruled that policies based on race are valid only when they are essential to achieve a compelling goal. Presumably, under an equal rights amendment, government policies based on gender classifications would be valid only when they are essential to achieve a compelling goal. Today, for example, many government policies concerning the armed services make gender distinctions. The validity of these policies would be open to question with the passage of an equal rights amendment.

For practical purposes, argue some scholars, the Supreme Court has implemented the ERA through its decisions. It has struck down distinctions based on sex and held that stereotyped generalizations of sexual differences must fall.[45] In recent rulings, the Court has held that states may require employers to guarantee job reinstatement to women returning from maternity leave and that sexual harassment in the workplace is illegal.

But Supreme Court decisions can be reversed, and statutes can be repealed. Without an equal rights amendment, argue some feminists, the Constitution will continue to bear the sexist imprint of a document written by men, for men. At the moment, said veteran feminist Betty Friedan, "We are at the mercy of a Supreme Court that will interpret equality as it sees fit."[46]

Affirmative Action: Equal Opportunity or Equal Outcome?

In his vision of the Great Society, President Johnson linked economic rights with civil rights, and equality of outcome with equality of opportunity. "Equal opportunity is essential, but not enough," he declared. "We seek not just legal equity but human ability, not just equality as a right and a theory but equality as a fact and equality as a result." This commitment led to affirmative action programs to expand opportunities for women, minorities, and the disabled.

Affirmative action aims to overcome the present effects of past discrimination. It embraces a range of public and private programs, policies, and procedures to bring about increased employment, promotion, or admission for members of designated groups. Such programs include recruitment, preferential treatment, and quotas for women, minorities, and the disabled in job training and professional education, employment, and the placement of government contracts. The goal of these programs is to move beyond equality of opportunity to equality of outcome.

Numerical goals (a specific number of places in a law school reserved for minority candidates, a government contract that specifies that 10 percent of the work must be subcontracted to minority-owned firms) are the most aggressive form of affirmative action, and they generate more debate and less agreement than any other aspect of the civil rights movement. Advocates claim that such goal setting for college admissions, training programs, employment, and contracts will move minorities, women, and the disabled out of second-class status. President Johnson explained why aggressive affirmative action was necessary:

> You do not take a person who for years has been hobbled by chains, liberate him, bring him up to the starting line of a race, and then say, "You are free to compete with all the others," and still justly believe that you have been completely fair. Thus, it is not enough just to open the gates of opportunity; all our citizens must have the ability to walk through those gates.[47]

Many arguments for affirmative action programs (from increased recruitment efforts to quotas) reduce to the following reasoning: Certain groups have historically suffered invidious discrimination, denying them educational and economic opportunities. To eliminate the lasting effects of such discrimination, the public and private sectors must take steps to provide access to good education and jobs. If the majority once used discrimination to hold groups back, it is fair to use discrimination to benefit those groups. Therefore, quotas are a legitimate means to provide a place on the ladder of success.[48]

Affirmative action opponents maintain that quotas for designated groups necessarily create invidious discrimination (in the form of *reverse discrimination*) against individuals who are themselves blameless.

Moreover, quotas lead to admission, hiring, or promotion of the less qualified at the expense of the well qualified. Such policies thwart an individual's freedom to succeed in the name of equality.

Preferential policies are seldom explicitly legislated and justified for what they are. More often, such policies are the result of administrative regulations, judicial rulings, and initiatives in the private sector as remedial responses to specific discrimination.

Government-authored preferential policies probably began in 1965 with the creation of the Office of Federal Contract Compliance. Its purpose was to ensure that all private enterprises doing business with the federal government complied with nondiscrimination guidelines. Since so many firms do business with the federal government, a large portion of the American economy became subject to these guidelines. In 1968, the guidelines required "goals and timetables for the prompt achievement of full and equal employment opportunity." By 1971, they called for employers to eliminate group "under-utilization," which meant that employers must hire minorities and women in numbers based on the government's notions of those groups' availability.[49]

Reverse Discrimination

The Supreme Court confronted an affirmative action quota program for the first time in ***Regents of the University of California v. Bakke*** (1978).[50] Allan Bakke, a thirty-five-year-old white man, had twice applied for admission to the University of California Medical School at Davis. He was rejected both times. The school had reserved sixteen places in each entering class of one hundred for "qualified" minorities, as part of the university's affirmative action program, in an effort to redress long-standing unfair minority exclusions from the medical profession. Bakke's qualifications (college grade point average and test scores) exceeded those of any of the minority students admitted in the two years his applications were rejected. Bakke contended, first in the California courts, then in the Supreme Court, that he was excluded from admission solely on the basis of race. He argued that this reverse discrimination was prohibited by the equal protection clause of the Fourteenth Amendment and by the Civil Rights Act of 1964.

The Court's decision in *Bakke* contained six opinions and spanned 154 pages. But even after careful analysis of the decision, it was difficult to discern what the Court had decided: There was no majority opinion. Four of the justices contended that any racial quota system supported by government violated the Civil Rights Act of 1964. Justice Lewis F. Powell, Jr., agreed, casting the deciding vote ordering the medical school to admit Bakke. However, in his opinion, Powell argued that the rigid use of racial quotas as employed at the school violated the equal protection clause of the Fourteenth Amendment. The remaining four justices held that the use of race as a criterion in admissions decisions in higher education was constitutionally permissible. Powell joined that opinion as well, contending that the use of race was permissible as one of several admission criteria. So, the Court managed to minimize white opposition to the goal of equality (by finding for Bakke) while extending gains for racial minorities through affirmative action.

Rights Affirmed, Dreams Fulfilled

Allan Bakke, a thirty-five-year-old engineer, was rejected twice by the Medical School of the University of California at Davis, despite having scored well above most candidates admitted through a special minority-admissions program. Bakke filed a lawsuit that eventually forced the Supreme Court to examine the constitutionality of affirmative action programs. The medical school was ordered to admit Bakke in 1978, and he received his degree in 1982. In a complicated opinion, however, the justices upheld the use of race as a permissible criterion in admissions decisions.

Although the Court sent a mixed message, *Bakke* did contribute tangible benefits. The number of minority physicians doubled in the decade after the decision. Moreover, minority physicians tended to relocate to areas where there were critical health-care shortages. They also tended to serve significantly larger proportions of poor patients regardless of race or ethnicity.[51]

Other cases followed. In 1979, the Court upheld a voluntary affirmative action plan giving preferences to blacks in an employee training program.[52] Five years later, however, the Court held that affirmative action did *not* exempt minorities (who were the last ones hired) from traditional work rules, which specify that the last hired are the first fired. Layoffs must proceed by seniority, declared the Court, unless minority employees can demonstrate that they are actual victims of discrimination.[53]

The Supreme Court seems to have greeted reverse discrimination claims with a mixture of approval and disapproval. Do preferential policies in other nations offer lessons for us? (See Compared with What 16.1.)

Victims of Discrimination

The 1984 layoff decision raised a troublesome question: Do all affirmative action programs, not just layoffs, apply solely to actual victims of past discrimination? The Supreme Court delivered a partial answer in 1986, when it struck down a school board layoff plan giving preference to members of minority groups.[54] The board layoff plan favored black teachers in an effort to redress general social discrimination and to maintain sufficient role models for black students. But the Supreme Court ruled

COMPARED WITH WHAT?   16.1

How Other Nations Struggle with Affirmative Action

Americans are not alone in their disagreements over affirmative action. Controversies—and even bloodshed—have been the order of the day in countries where certain groups receive government-sanctioned preferences over others.

India, Sri Lanka, Malaysia, Nigeria, Australia, and Canada are just some of the nations with affirmative action policies of their own. The phraseology of these policies may differ somewhat from the American model. Although Australia and Canada use the American label "affirmative action," India refers to its policy as "positive discrimination." Nigeria's preferential policy is designed to "reflect the federal character of the country." In Malaysia, the constitution recognizes the "special position" of the Malays and reserves a share of public benefits (including government jobs, educational scholarships, and land) for them.

The particular problems created by affirmative action policy in India recently claimed international attention. The untouchables, a classic pariah group, have long been the chief beneficiary of the nation's preferential policies. In 1990, the government of India decided to strengthen its policy of positive discrimination by reserving more than half of all government jobs for members of the lower castes.

Although the job quota proved popular among the lower castes, who make up well over half of India's population, it generated deep resentment among the higher castes. Students from the higher castes have traditionally viewed government jobs as a way of securing their middle-class expectations. The new ruling made government jobs much more difficult for them to obtain. Regardless of their academic success, many high-caste students will be passed over for government jobs because they are not members of the preferred group. In a singularly gruesome form of protest, scores of young upper-caste men and women have set themselves ablaze. And when the Indian courts issued a temporary injunction that halted the government's affirmative action plan, terrorists who supported the plan protested by bombing a train, killing dozens of people.

One recent study of preferential policies has aimed to generalize from the experiences of many nations. The cultures, politics, economies, and societies of nations adopting preferential policies vary enormously. The groups benefiting from these policies also vary widely; they may be locally or nationally dominant, or poor and relatively powerless politically.

Despite these variables, nations with affirmative action policies seem to share some common patterns. First, though often defined as temporary, preferential policies tend to persist and even expand to embrace more individuals and groups. Second, benefits tend to go disproportionately to the members of recipient groups who are already more fortunate. Third, antagonism among groups tends to increase following the implementation of preferential policies. The reaction of groups that do not benefit from such policies ranges from a change in voting behavior to violence, even civil war. And fourth, an increase in false claims of membership in designated beneficiary groups can be observed.

These observations have implications for majoritarian and pluralist models of democracy. All governments broker conflict in varying degrees. Under a majoritarian model, group demands could lead quickly to conflict and instability since there would be little room to compromise under a principle of majority rule. A pluralist model allows different groups to get a piece of the pie. By parceling out benefits, pluralism mitigates disorder in the short term. But in the long term, repeated demands for increased benefits can spark instability. A vigorous pluralist system should provide acceptable mechanisms (legislative, executive, bureaucratic, judicial) to vent such frustrations and yield a new allocation of benefits.

Sources: Donald L. Horowitz, *Ethnic Groups in Conflict* (Berkeley: University of California Press, 1985); *Facts on File*, 19 October 1990, pp. 784–785; Edward W. Desmond, "Fatal Fires of Protest," *Time*, 15 October 1990, p. 63; and Thomas Sowell, *Preferential Policies: An International Perspective* (New York: William Morrow and Company, 1990).

that these objectives were insufficient to force certain individuals to shoulder the severe impact of layoffs. Hiring goals impose a diffuse burden on society, argued Justice Powell for the Court. But layoffs of innocent whites, he continued, "impose the entire burden of achieving racial equality on particular individuals."

Remedies for general racial discrimination had to avoid harming innocent whites. Could remedies for repeated and outrageous forms of specific discrimination confer benefits on individuals who were not themselves the victims of that discrimination? The local chapter of a construction union in New York City practiced egregious racial discrimination for more than seventy-five years, barring most blacks and Hispanics at every turn. The list of ruses to block the entry of nonwhites seemed endless. The local required special examinations and a high school diploma for entrance; neither had any bearing on job performance. Union funds were used to provide special tutoring for members' friends and relatives who were taking the entrance exams. The local refused to keep records on the racial composition of its membership, in an attempt to avoid charges of discrimination.

In 1975, a federal court concluded that the local had violated Title VII of the Civil Rights Act of 1964, which bars employment discrimination on account of race, color, religion, sex, or national origin. The court required the local to accept equal numbers of white and nonwhite apprentices to achieve a 29 percent nonwhite membership goal, based on the percentage of nonwhites in the New York City labor pool. The decision was justified, said the court, by the local's long, persistent pattern of discrimination. But the union failed to institute employment programs that would boost minority membership, and it continued to erect new barriers as quickly as the courts struck them down.

The union took its case to the Supreme Court. It argued that the membership goal ordered by the lower courts was unlawful because it extended race-conscious preferences to individuals who were not identified victims of the local's admittedly unlawful discrimination. In ***Local 28 v. EEOC*** (1986), the Court voted 6 to 3 in support of affirmative action that would benefit individuals who were not the actual victims of discrimination.[55] The majority held that the courts may order unions to use quotas to overcome a history of egregious discrimination and that black and Hispanic applicants can benefit from affirmative action even if they themselves were not the victims of earlier bias.

Must affirmative action policies be limited to concerns over racial inequality? What about the conflict between Diane Joyce and Paul Johnson described at the beginning of this chapter? Johnson took his case all the way to the Supreme Court to argue that he was the victim of sex discrimination under Title VII of the Civil Rights Act of 1964, the provision that employers cannot "limit, segregate or classify" workers so as to deprive "any individual of employment opportunities."

The justices decided ***Johnson v. Transportation Agency, Santa Clara County*** in 1987. They ruled, 6–3, that if women and minorities are underrepresented in the workplace, employers can act to remedy the imbalance. The decision was significant for at least two reasons. First, employers with affirmative action plans do not have to admit to a history of past discrimination. And second, employees who are passed over for promo-

Headline News: Joyce Dispatches Johnson

Diane Joyce gained a promotion from laborer to road dispatcher by invoking a government affirmative action policy. Paul Johnson, who had been given the dispatcher job initially, sued; he claimed he was the victim of sex discrimination, which the Civil Rights Act of 1964 forbids. Johnson lost his case in the Supreme Court in 1987.

tions are nearly powerless to sue for reverse discrimination. The upshot of the decision is to encourage the adoption of affirmative action programs.

In hindsight, Paul Johnson's belief that he was the better-qualified candidate failed to acknowledge the full range of legitimate interests considered by employers when they make hiring and promotion decisions. After all, both Johnson and Joyce were deemed qualified for the dispatcher's position; the fact that Johnson scored a few points higher on a test hardly demonstrates clear and unequivocal superiority, as college students know all too well. Given two equally matched candidates for the job, forcing a choice on the basis of a higher exam or interview score seems excessively rigid when other factors may have a legitimate bearing on the outcome. Affirmative action was such a factor. It seems a relevant and rational way of choosing between Joyce and Johnson, according to the decision's defenders.

In a scathing dissent, Justice Antonin Scalia saw the issue in a different light. He focused on two familiar themes: values in conflict and models of democracy. Scalia declared that the majority converted "a guarantee that race or sex will *not* be the basis for employment determination, to a guarantee that it often *will*." The Court, continued Scalia, replaced the goal of a society free from discrimination with the incompatible goal of proportionate representation by race and by sex in the workplace. In simpler terms, equality trumped freedom.

Scalia then offered his observations about pluralism. The Court's decision would be pleasing to elected officials, he said, because it "provides the means of quickly accommodating the demands of organized groups to achieve concrete, numerical improvement in the economic status of particular constituencies." "The only losers in the process," he concluded, are the Paul Johnsons of the country, "predominantly unknown, unaffluent, unorganized—[who] suffer this injustice at the hands of a Court fond of thinking itself the champion of the politically impotent."

The conflict between Paul Johnson and Diane Joyce is over, but the conflict between freedom and equality continues as other individuals and groups press their demands through litigation and legislation. Americans want equality, but they disagree on the extent to which government should provide it.[56] In part, this ambivalence stems from confusion over equal opportunities and equal outcomes.

Two Conceptions of Equality

Americans want equality, at least in principle. Americans' support for the principle of equal treatment has increased dramatically from the 1940s to the 1980s. Today, more than 9 in 10 Americans espouse equal treatment for all persons in schools, public accommodations, housing, employment, and public transportation. However, Americans are far less united in their support for ways of implementing this principle.[57]

Most Americans support **equality of opportunity,** the idea that people should have an equal chance to develop their talents and that effort and ability should be rewarded. This form of equality offers all individuals the same chance to get ahead; it glorifies personal achievement through free competition and allows everyone to climb the ladder of success starting at the first rung. Special recruitment efforts aimed at identifying qualified minority or female job applicants ensure that everyone has the same chance starting out. The competition for the promotion between Joyce and Johnson illustrates equality of opportunity.

Americans are less committed to **equality of outcome,** which means greater uniformity in social, economic, and political power. Equality of outcome can occur only if we restrict the free competition that forms the basis of equality of opportunity. One restriction comes by way of a limit on personal achievement. Preferential treatment in hiring is an apt example. That treatment prevented Johnson from climbing the ladder of success.

Quota policies generate the most opposition because they deny competition. Quotas limit advancement for some individuals and ensure advancement for others. They alter positions on the ladder of success without regard to ability. Policies that benefit minorities and women at the expense of innocent white men create strong opposition because they bring individual initiative into conflict with equal outcomes. In other words, freedom clashes with equality.

 ## Summary

The Civil War amendments—the Thirteenth, Fourteenth, and Fifteenth Amendments—were adopted to provide full civil rights to black Americans. Yet, in the late nineteenth century, the Supreme Court interpreted the amendments very narrowly, declaring that they did not restrain individuals from denying civil rights to blacks and that they did not apply to powers that were reserved to the states. The Court's rulings had the effect of denying the vote to most blacks and of institutionalizing racial segregation, making racism a facet of daily life.

Through a series of court cases spanning two decades, segregation in the schools was slowly dismantled. The battle for desegregation culminated in the *Brown* cases in 1954 and 1955, in which a now-supportive Supreme Court declared segregated schools to be inherently unequal and therefore unconstitutional. The Court also ordered the desegregation of all schools and upheld the use of busing to do so.

Gains in other civil rights areas came more slowly. The motivating force was the civil rights movement, led by Martin Luther King, Jr., until his death in 1968. King believed strongly in civil disobedience and nonviolence, strategies that helped secure for blacks equality in voting rights, public accommodations, higher education, housing, and employment opportunity.

Civil rights activism and the civil rights movement worked to the benefit of all minority groups, in fact, of all Americans. Native Americans obtained some redress for past injustices. Hispanic-Americans came to recognize the importance of group action to achieve economic and political equality. Handicapped Americans won civil rights protections enjoyed by African-Americans and others. And civil rights legislation removed the protectionism that was, in effect, legalized discrimination against women in education and employment.

Despite legislative advances in the area of women's rights, the Equal Rights Amendment was not ratified. Still, the struggle for ratification produced several positive results, heightening the awareness of the role of women and mobilizing the political power of women through group activity. And legislation and judicial rulings implemented much of the amendment in practice, if not fact.

Affirmative action programs were instituted to counteract the results of past discrimination. These provide preferential treatment for women, minorities, and the handicapped in a number of areas that affect economic opportunity and well-being. In effect, such programs advocate discrimination to remedy earlier discrimination. A new conservative majority on the Supreme Court has now emerged to roll back the equality-preferring policies of a more liberal bench. Although Congress has objected to the tide of conservative policies from the Court, it has not yet reversed the trend with any legislative decisions.

Americans want equality, but they disagree on the extent to which government should provide it. At the heart of this conflict is the distinction between equal opportunities and equal outcomes. We can guarantee equal outcomes only if we restrict the free competition that is an integral part of equal opportunity. Many Americans object to this idea. They strongly oppose quotas and policies that restrict individual freedom, that arbitrarily change positions on the ladder of success. The challenge of pluralist democracy is to balance these conflicting values.

KEY TERMS AND CASES

affirmative action
discrimination
civil rights
black codes
racism
poll tax
racial segregation
Plessy v. *Ferguson*
separate-but-equal
  doctrine
desegregation
Brown v. *Board*
  of Education
Brown v. *Board*
  of Education II
Swann v. *Charlotte-*
  Mecklenburg County
  Schools
de jure segregation

de facto segregation
Milliken v. *Bradley*
civil rights movement
boycott
civil disobedience
protectionism
Nineteenth Amendment
sexism
Equal Rights
  Amendment (ERA)
Regents of the
  University of
  California v. *Bakke*
Local 28 v. *EEOC*
Johnson v. *Trans-*
  portation Agency,
  Santa Clara County
equality of opportunity
equality of outcome

SELECTED READINGS

Baer, Judith A. *Equality Under the Constitution: Reclaiming the Fourteenth Amendment.* Ithaca, N.Y.: Cornell University Press, 1983. Explores the early American concept of equality and re-examines the debates surrounding the adoption of the Fourteenth Amendment. The author points to new areas of struggle in the application of the equality principle to children, the aged, the disabled, and homosexuals.

Bass, Jack. *Unlikely Heroes.* New York: Simon & Schuster, 1981. Chronicles the efforts of four federal appellate judges in the Deep South to enforce the desegregation mandate in *Brown.*

Berger, Raoul. *Government by Judiciary: The Transformation of the Fourteenth Amendment.* Cambridge: Harvard University Press, 1977. This provocative work argues that the framers of the Fourteenth Amendment had very narrow aims and that the Supreme Court, especially since 1954, has disregarded this historical legacy in its promotion of freedom and equality.

Branch, Taylor. *Parting the Waters: America in the King Years, 1954–1963.* New York: Simon and Schuster, 1988. A riveting, Pulitzer Prize–winning narrative history and biography of the King years.

Browning, Rufus P., Dale Rogers Marshall, and David H. Tabb. *Racial Politics in American Cities.* New York: Longman, 1990. This collection of essays documents the continuing struggle for minority access to political power in cities across the United States.

Deloria, Vine, Jr., and Clifford M. Lytle. *The Nations Within.* New York: Pantheon, 1984. A thorough discussion of Native American policies from the New Deal to the present; examines the drive for Indian self-determination and self-government.

Hampton, Henry, and Steve Fayer with Sarah Flynn. *Voices of Freedom: An Oral History of the Civil Rights Movement from the 1950s Through the 1980s.* New York: Bantam, 1990. Chronologically arranged interview excerpts recorded during the production of "Eyes on the Prize," the widely acclaimed public television series.

Kessler-Harris, Alice. *Out to Work: A History of Wage-Earning Women in the United States.* New York: Oxford University Press, 1982. An informative analysis of the forces motivating women to work and the effect of work on family roles.

Kluger, Richard. *Simple Justice.* New York: Knopf, 1975. A monumentally detailed history of the desegregation cases; it examines the legal, political, and sociological events culminating in *Brown* v. *Board of Education.*

Mansbridge, Jane J. *Why We Lost the ERA.* Chicago: University of Chicago Press, 1986. A valuable case study of organizations pitted for and against the Equal Rights Amendment in Illinois.

Prucha, Francis Paul. *The Great Father: The United States Government and the American Indians.* 2 vols. Lincoln, Neb.: University of Nebraska Press, 1984. A definitive history of federal policy toward Native Americans from the beginning of the Republic to 1980.

Urofsky, Melvin I. *A Conflict of Rights: The Supreme Court and Affirmative Action.* New York: Scribner's, 1991. An absorbing case study of the events, participants, and issues surrounding the landmark affirmative action decision of *Joyce* v. *Johnson.*

Verba, Sidney, and Gary R. Orren. *Equality in America: The View from the Top.* Cambridge, Mass.: Harvard University Press, 1985. Two political scientists isolate different meanings of equality, then analyze the opinions of American leaders on the application of equality of opportunity and equality of outcome across a range of policy areas.

Williams, Juan. *Eyes on the Prize: America's Civil Rights Years, 1954–1965.* New York: Viking, 1987. A lucid account of black Americans' struggle for social and political equality; it contains vivid portraits of courageous blacks and the violence they had to endure in their fight for desegregation and the right to vote in the South.

PART

SIX

Making Public Policy

17 POLICYMAKING

EACH YEAR APPROXIMATELY 390,000 Americans die from smoking-related diseases. This statistic represents a problem for the national government because it is expected to use its resources to promote good public health. In addition, the government spends enormous sums of money for medical care, so all taxpayers share the costs of treating tobacco-related illnesses. Consequently, the government tries to discourage smoking through a variety of means. Among other things, it supports education about the hazards of smoking, requires warning labels on cigarette packages, bans advertising for tobacco products on TV, and taxes the sale of each pack of cigarettes.

There is considerable support in government for doing even more to deter smoking. In 1989, Congress banned smoking on almost all domestic flights. Proposed legislation would further restrict advertising for cigarettes, prohibit sales of cigarettes by vending machines, define tobacco as a drug (which would make it subject to regulation by the Food and Drug Administration), and require health warnings on tobacco sold in the export market.

There is one other piece of legislation that antismoking opponents would like to push through the Congress. This bill would put an end to government support of tobacco farming. Since the 1930s, the government has provided financial assistance to tobacco growers through a complicated subsidy arrangement. Proponents of the tobacco subsidy argue that this money helps struggling family farmers and widows who depend on tobacco for their income. It is not just struggling family farmers whose livelihood comes from cigarettes, though. There are more than a million people employed in the industry, and $11 billion in government revenue is gained through taxes derived from tobacco. The last time the issue of terminating the tobacco subsidy came up in the House, the antismoking forces lost by thirty votes.[1]

In short, the government has two policies on tobacco. One discourages smoking. The other encourages tobacco farming. The government is not always so contradictory in its policy positions, but each policy area (like health or farming) generates its own unique set of actors and circumstances. In the chapters on the institutions of government we looked closely at how the nature of each institution affected policymaking. In this chapter we focus on policymaking *across* institutions. First, we distinguish different types of policies based on the approach used to solve problems. Second, we tie together the processes described in earlier chapters on the different institutions of government into a general model of public policymaking. Third, we analyze how the different levels and institutions of government can produce rather fragmented approaches to solving problems (as is the case with tobacco); we also examine those forces that work toward coordination in policymaking. Fourth, we build on this discussion of fragmentation and coordination by looking at policymaking on issues where there are a very large number of actors trying to influence the outcome. This discussion of issue networks focuses on the relationships among competing interest groups working in the same policy area. Part of this analysis explores the way private organizations interact with different parts of the government that have some responsi-

The Marlboro Man in Shnzhen, China

As concern over the health hazards of smoking continues to grow in the United States, cigarette companies have begun to market their product more aggressively overseas. Cigarettes sold in foreign markets do not have to carry warning labels that inform consumers of the dangers posed by tobacco consumption.

bility for making policy on the same issue. We also examine the importance of expertise to participants in an issue network. Finally, we consider how issue networks may or may not contribute to promoting democratic policymaking. In this regard, we argue that issue networks favor pluralist instead of majoritarian democracy.

Government Purposes and Public Policies

In Chapter 1, we noted that virtually all citizens are willing to accept limitations on their personal freedom in return for various benefits of government. We defined the major purposes of government as maintaining order, providing public goods, and promoting equality. Different governments place different values on each of these broad purposes, and those differences are reflected in their public policies. A **public policy** is a general plan of action adopted by a government to solve a social problem, counter a threat, or pursue an objective. For example, our government has formulated many policies for reducing crime in cities, a serious threat to our well-being.

At times, governments choose not to adopt a new policy to deal with a troublesome situation; instead, they just "muddle through," hoping the problem will go away or diminish in importance. This, in and of itself, is a policy decision because it amounts to a choice to maintain the status quo. Sometimes government policies are carefully developed and effective. Sometimes, in contrast, they are hastily drawn and ineffective, even counterproductive. But careful planning is no predictor of success. Well-constructed policies may end up total disasters, and quick fixes may work just fine.

Whatever their form and effectiveness, however, all policies have this in common: They are the *means* by which government pursues certain *goals* within specific *situations*. People disagree over public policies because they disagree over one or more of these elements: the goals that government should have, the means it should use to meet them, and the perception of the situation.

How do policymakers attempt to achieve their goals? As a starting point, we'll divide all governmental approaches to solving problems into four broad types. We can analyze public policies according to whether they prohibit, protect, promote, or provide.

Some policies are intended to *prohibit* behaviors that endanger society. All governments outlaw murder, robbery, and rape, for example. Governments that emphasize order tend to specialize in policies of prohibition, which instruct people what they must *not* do (drink liquor, have abortions, use illegal drugs).

Government policies can also *protect* activities, business markets, or special groups of citizens. For example, taxes were once levied on colored margarine (a butter substitute) to reduce its sales and protect the dairy industry from competition. Regulations concerning the testing of new drugs are intended to protect citizens from harmful side effects; government rules about safety in the workplace are enacted to protect workers. Although governments argue that these kinds of regulations serve the public good, some people believe that most protective legislation is unwarranted government interference.

Policies can also *promote* social activities that are important to the government. One way that government promotes is by persuasion. For instance, our government has used advertising to urge people to buy bonds or to join the army. When policymakers really want to accomplish a goal they have set, they can be very generous. To promote railroad construction in the 1860s, Congress granted railroad companies huge tracts of public land along the right-of-way through western states.

The government also promotes activities through favorable treatment within the tax structure. The technical term for this form of government promotion is *tax expenditure*, because it amounts to a loss of government revenue. For example, the government encourages people to buy their own homes by allowing them to deduct from their taxable income the amount of money they pay in mortgage interest. In 1987, this tax expenditure cost the national government nearly $32 billion.[2] And of course, churches and private educational institutions typically pay no property taxes to state and local governments.

Finally, public policies can *provide* benefits directly to citizens. These benefits can be either public or private. *Public benefits* are facilities or services that all citizens share (mail service, roads, schools, street lighting, libraries, parks). *Private benefits* go to certain groups of citizens (poor people, farmers, veterans, college students). Public benefits are more difficult to deliver because they require either the construction of facilities (roads, dams, sewer systems) or the creation of organizations (transportation agencies, power companies, sanitation departments) to provide them. Private benefits are simply payments to individuals in the form of food stamps, subsidies, pensions, and loans. These payments are made because the recipients are particularly needy or politically powerful, or both.

In sum, the notion of policy is a many-splendored thing. Many different means, or approaches, can be used by government to pursue particular goals. Those means and goals, in turn, are shaped by the specific situations that surround a problem at the time. Policies aimed at specific problems are not static; means, goals, and situations all change.

The Policymaking Process

We distinguish government policies according to their approaches not simply to create an inventory of problem-solving methods, but also to emphasize the relationship between policy and process. By *process* we mean the configuration of actors involved, the procedures used for decision making, and the degree of cooperation or conflict usually present. The premise is simple: Different kinds of policies are going to affect the political process in different kinds of ways.

The Impact of Policy

One basic reason for the differences in policymaking processes is that different approaches to public policy affect people in different ways. If a policy proposal affects a well-organized constituency adversely, that constituency will fight it aggressively. Gun control bills, as noted in Chapter 2, are very difficult to pass because they adversely affect an intense and well-organized group, the National Rifle Association, that is going to struggle against any proposal to prohibit what it sees as the people's right to bear arms. The beneficiary of gun control policies, the broader public, does not feel as strongly about the issue. Thus, even though most rank-and-file citizens favor gun control, they are not as active in trying to promote their view as members of the NRA.

Other policies pit well-organized groups against each other. This can happen frequently on regulatory issues, where one part of an industry tries to gain market advantages at the expense of other businesses. Federal Communications Commission (FCC) rules on the production of television shows protect independent producers from being dominated by the large networks. Since the networks can't own the programs they show, they can't make money from syndicating the shows to independent TV stations around the country. (Syndication sales of old network shows run over $2 *billion* a year.) When the fledgling Fox network tried to gain a waiver of this rule in 1988, it set off a ferocious struggle among independent producers, Fox, and the three existing networks. It wasn't an issue the public cared about, and the FCC was left to arbitrate among the competing business lobbies. Although Fox's initial efforts to get the waiver failed, the FCC decided in 1990 to formally review the policy.[3] In this instance a single corporation was able to get consideration of its request without any sort of highly visible problem emerging that would have galvanized public opinion on the issue.

Whether a policy is intended to prohibit, protect, promote, or provide does not fully predict the level of involvement of the public, the degree of organization of affected constituencies, or the degree of competition between organizations working on the same issue. But by being aware of what kind of approach the government is proposing on an issue, we can begin to understand what kind of factors are going to influence policymaking. If there is a well-entrenched set of interest groups ready to fight a policy to prohibit, a solution emphasizing promotion might be more politically feasible. For example, as the chapter opening indicated, efforts to prohibit cigarette smoking are difficult to enact because of the tobacco lobby. Policies promoting education about the hazards of smoking are less difficult for antismoking activists to persuade government to put into place.

A government may use more than one approach to a problem not only because some alternatives engender less opposition than others but because public policy problems can be quite complex. One approach will not always solve all the manifestations of such problems. Rape is a case in point. Some men who commit rape attack women they do not know. The strict laws that prohibit and punish rape are perhaps the best approach to deterring this kind of attack. Yet a considerable number of rapes occurs during dating situations. Once date rape became more widely discussed, educational programs were designed to address the problem. This persuasion approach is strongly emphasized on college campuses.

When there are choices between the means that can be used to address a problem, consideration is going to be given to how each of those approaches will affect policymaking. Is the best approach for solving a problem one that is likely to generate a lot of conflict between opposing groups? If so, will it be possible to enact a new policy, or is the conflict likely to scuttle a new proposal and leave the status quo intact? In short, when policymakers are considering new policy options, they carefully consider the impact of each of those approaches on those most affected by them.

A Policymaking Model

Clearly, different approaches to solving policy problems affect the policymaking process, but common patterns do underlie most processes. Political scientists have produced many models of the policymaking process that distinguish among different types of policy, such as our framework of policies that prohibit, protect, promote, or provide.[4] They also distinguish different stages of the policymaking process and try to identify patterns in the way people attempt to influence decisions and in the way decisions are reached.

We can separate the policymaking process into four stages: agenda setting, policy formulation, implementation, and policy evaluation.[5] Figure

FIGURE 17.1 *The Policymaking Process*

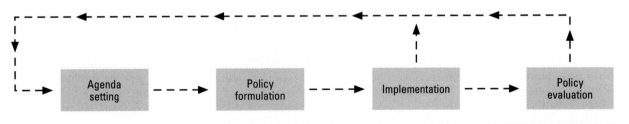

This model, one of many possible ways of depicting the policymaking process, shows four policymaking stages. Feedback on program operations and performance from the last two stages works to stimulate new cycles of the process.

17.1 shows these four stages in sequence. Notice, however, that the process does not end with policy evaluation. As you will see, policymaking is a circular process; the "end" of one phase is really the beginning of another.

Agenda setting. **Agenda setting** is the part of the process during which problems get defined as political issues. Many problems confront Americans in their daily lives, but government is not actively working to solve all of them. Today, for example, social security seems a hardy perennial of American politics, but the old age insurance program wasn't created until the New Deal (see Chapter 19). The problem of poverty among the elderly did not suddenly emerge during the 1930s—there have always been poor people of all ages—rather, that is when inadequate incomes for the elderly became *defined* as a political problem. That is, people began arguing that it was government's responsibility to create a system of income security rather than leaving old people to fend for themselves. (For a discussion of a problem now becoming defined as a political issue, see Feature 17.1.)

When the government begins looking at new issues, we say they have become part of the political agenda. Usually when we speak of *agenda* in this context, we are simply referring to the entire set of issues before all institutions of government. (There is no formal list of issues for the entire political system; the concept of an agenda for the system is merely a useful abstraction.)[6]

Why does an existing social problem become redefined as a political problem? There is no single reason; many different factors can stimulate new thinking about a problem. Sometimes highly visible events or developments push issues onto the agenda. Examples include great calamities (such as a terrible oil spill showing a need for safer tankers), technological changes (such as the development of atomic energy), or irrational human behavior (such as airline hijackings).[7]

Issues may also be placed on the agenda through the efforts of scholars and activists to get more people to pay attention to a condition that the public is generally unaware of. The problem of child abuse was long hidden in America. It's something that goes on behind closed doors, and it

FEATURE 17.1 *The Politics of Breast Cancer*

One out of every ten women will get breast cancer during her lifetime. Of those diagnosed with breast cancer, one out of every four will die from it. It's an epidemic, and it's getting worse, not better.

In the past few years, breast cancer has gone from being just a medical problem to becoming a full-fledged political issue. But why has breast cancer been placed on the nation's *political* agenda? It hardly seems like an issue that divides people. After all, who's in favor of cancer?

Breast cancer is a political problem in a number of ways. Medical research on all diseases is largely supported by the federal government. Women's groups have argued that breast cancer research is not adequately funded. By way of comparison they cite funding for AIDS research. During 1990, the government spent $1.1 billion on AIDS, a disease that killed about 23,000 Americans that year. Breast cancer, which killed about 44,000 women the same year, received $77 million. (Government officials respond that AIDS is a *contagious* disease and thus warrants urgent attention.)

Breast cancer is also a political issue because of the controversy over the responsibilities of health insurers to pay for various treatments, ranging from initial baseline mammograms for younger women to very expensive bone marrow transplant therapy for victims with advanced breast cancer. Many state governments have adopted legislation to require insurance companies to cover certain kinds of treatments.

In addition, breast cancer reflects the unfortunate differences in access to health care between those who are poor and those who are middle class. The government's Medicaid program, which pays for medical care for the poor, does not pay for mammograms in all states. At Miami's Jackson Memorial Hospital, the city's only public hospital, it takes two months for a woman to get an appointment for an evaluation. After that session, it is another two-month wait for a mammogram. If the mammogram showed a possible malignancy, it would be at least two more months before a biopsy was performed. That's at least six months simply to get to the stage where treatment might start; six months while cancer cells could be multiplying. For a middle-class woman who has a private physician, the same steps could likely be completed within a month.

Another issue is that there are no federal standards for X-ray mammography machines or licensing requirements for the technicians who conduct mammograms. Sadly, there have been many instances of incorrect evaluations of mammograms. Senator Barbara Mikulski of Maryland plans to introduce legislation that would set standards in this area.

Some see the politics of breast cancer as symptomatic of discrimination against women. One breast cancer victim whose insurance company paid for a mammogram only every *other* year, said bitterly, "If you could do a mammogram on the testes—a testegram—you'd be goddam sure that men would be having them every year and that insurance would pay." Some women's health advocates are particularly angry that large-scale studies of the effects of diet and environmental factors on the incidence of breast cancer have not been

is difficult for the victims to ask for assistance. In 1962, though, a group of pediatricians who were studying child abuse published an article in a medical journal on the "battered child syndrome." This article, in turn, stimulated popular treatments of the subject that ran in widely circulated magazines like *Time* and the *Saturday Evening Post*, articles that played a major role "in creating the sense of an urgent national problem."[8]

Policy formulation. **Policy formulation** is that stage of the policymaking process when formal policy proposals are developed and a decision is made whether to adopt one of these proposals. The most obvious kind of policy formulation is the proposal of bills by the president or the

Hoping to focus attention on the need for more breast cancer research, Marilyn and Dan Quayle participated in an event called "Race for the Cure."

disease. The National Cancer Institute recently rejected such a study as too expensive and requiring too long to complete.

Women's advocacy groups and organizations devoted to the issue of breast cancer have been a critical factor in making people understand that breast cancer is a political issue, not just a dreadful disease. Many organizations with a primary focus on breast cancer are largely staffed and supported by breast cancer victims. These advocacy groups, like the Women's Cancer Resource Center in Berkeley, the Komen Foundation for Breast Cancer in Dallas, and the Women's Community Cancer Project in Cambridge, Massachusetts, have had a great deal of success in gaining publicity for their cause. Many of the breast cancer groups have consciously imitated the aggressive tactics of AIDS groups like Act-Up, which has tried to publicly embarrass public health officials and politicians for their failure to do more for AIDS victims and AIDS research. For breast cancer activists, the same logic holds: There isn't time to be polite.

Sources: Dorothy J. Gaiter, "Although Cures Exist, Poverty Fells Many Afflicted with Cancer," *Wall Street Journal*, 1 May 1991, p. A1; Ken Schlossberg, "Equal Rights for Women's Health," *New York Times*, 23 April 1991, p. A21; Michael D. Wertheimer, "Against Minimalism in Breast Cancer Follow-up," *Journal of the American Medical Association* 265 (16 January 1991):396–397; Jane Gross, "Turning Disease into Political Cause: First AIDS, and Now Breast Cancer," *New York Times*, 7 January 1991, p. A12; Melinda Beck et al., "The Politics of Breast Cancer," *Newsweek*, 10 December 1990, pp. 62–65.

funded. American women have a much higher chance of getting breast cancer than women in many other cultures, making it important to examine the role diet and environment play in the

development of legislation by Congress. Administrative agencies also formulate policy through the regulatory process. Courts formulate policy, too, when their decisions establish new interpretations of the law. We usually think of policy formulation as a formal process in which a published document (a statute, a regulation, or a court opinion) is the final outcome. In some instances, however, policy decisions are not published or otherwise made explicit. Foreign policy is a case in point. The president and his advisers may develop a new policy on, for instance, the United States position in the debate over what to do with the Palestinians in Israel. Yet they may feel that it is best to be vague about what they are urging Israel to do. They may want some "wiggle room" to adapt their policies to events that are beyond their control. They also want the

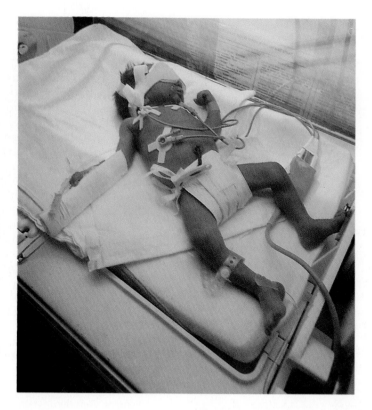

Can Government Help Them?

A relatively new item on the political agenda is the question of what the government should do about the growing number of crack babies born every year. It is a particularly difficult problem. The best solution is a most complicated one: convincing pregnant women not to use drugs. And the issue of babies damaged in utero by the willful acts of their mothers raises a troubling legal question: Does a fetus have any rights?

freedom necessary to conduct negotiations without the burden of publicly stated policies they might have to renounce if opposition to what they are advocating turns out to be too great.

Although policy formulation is depicted in Figure 17.1 as one stage, it can actually take place over a number of separate stages. For example, the Americans with Disabilities Act of 1990 was passed by Congress to protect the civil rights of those who are blind, deaf, use a wheelchair, are otherwise physically disabled, or are mentally ill. In 1991, the Architectural and Transportation Barriers Compliance Board issued administrative regulations that set some highly specific standards, including a requirement that at least 5 percent of tables in a restaurant be accessible to those with disabilities and that at least half of the drinking fountains on every floor in an office building be accessible to those in wheelchairs. The Justice Department also indicated that it might be issuing guidelines for those who wish to file suit when they see the law not being enforced.[9]

Keep in mind that policy formulation is only the development of proposals designed to solve a problem. Some issues reach the agenda and stimulate new proposals but then fail to win enactment. In the early 1980s, for example, there was a movement for a freeze on the development of nuclear weapons. Although a freeze resolution gained significant support in Congress, it could not gain passage in both houses and was never adopted. The nuclear freeze movement quickly withered and dis-

A Winning Team

The Supreme Court's power to formulate policy has never been more dramatically illustrated than when it declared in 1954 that segregation in public schools is unconstitutional. The team of litigators that won this momentous case was (left to right): George E. C. Hayes, Thurgood Marshall, and James Nabrit, Jr.

appeared from sight. (Arms control, however, remained very much an issue.) Thus, for a newly designed policy to become operative, it must win the approval of some authoritative policymaking body.

Implementation. Policies are not self-executing; **implementation** is the process by which they are carried out. When regulations are issued by agencies in Washington, some governmental bodies must then put those policies into effect. This may involve notifying the intended targets of agency actions that there have been changes in program regulations. In the case of the regulations promulgated under the 1990 Disabilities Act, the owners of an office building would probably not rebuild water fountains simply because new regulations were published in Washington. Administrative bodies at the state or local level must inform the owners that the rule exists, give them a timetable for compliance, communicate the penalties for noncompliance, be available to answer questions that emerge, and provide information back to Washington on how well the regulations are working.

As pointed out in Chapter 13, one of the biggest problems at the implementation stage of policymaking is *coordination*. After officials in Washington write a law and the subsequent regulations, people outside of Washington are typically the ones to implement the policy. These implementors may be local officials, state administrators, or federal bureaucrats headquartered in regional offices around the country.

Often state and local officials are asked to carry out policies they had no hand in writing. This is a source of conflict between them and offi-

Rolling Toward Equality

These demonstrators gathered to call for the passage of the Americans with Disabilities Act of 1990. Once the law was enacted, new regulations had to be formulated before the statute could be fully implemented.

cials in Washington, and it can be a cause of implementation failure. A case in point is the national government's efforts in 1990 to improve the quality of care provided by nursing homes. One regulation intended to accomplish this was designed to reduce the number of patients who are routinely sedated. Many nursing homes regard sedating patients as a relatively cheap way to take care of those who are not compliant. The state of California didn't like the national government's new standards. (California's nursing homes sedate 65 percent of their patients, compared with a national average of 40 percent.) The state said the care provided by its homes was excellent, and federal busybodies were simply adding unwarranted costs onto the price of nursing care. It refused to implement the new standards. Faced with this outright challenge to its authority, the national government sent its own health inspectors to California to examine nursing homes for compliance with the new regulations. Facing determined resistance and political pressure from Republican Governor Pete Wilson (an ally of the president), federal regulators backed down and promised to reconsider the regulations.[10]

Although it may seem to be a highly technical process, implementation is in fact very much a political process. It involves a great deal of bargaining and negotiation between different groups of people in and out of government. The difficulty of implementing complex policies in a federal system, which has different layers of government, and in a pluralistic system, which has so many competing interests, seems daunting. Yet there are incentives for cooperation, not the least of which is avoiding blame if the policy fails. (Later in the chapter we'll discuss coordination in more detail.)

Policy evaluation. How does government know if a policy is working? In some cases success or failure may be obvious, but in others it may take people who are highly expert in a specific field to tell government officials how well a policy is working. **Policy evaluation** is the analysis of public policy. Although there is no one method of evaluating policy, evaluation tends to draw heavily on approaches used by academics, including cost-benefit analysis, operations research, mathematical modeling, and many statistical methods.[11]

Policy evaluation tries not only to analyze which parts of a program are working and which are not, it also usually specifies alternate approaches that might improve a program's success. In the area of pollution control, for example, studies have tried to establish the optimum level of pollution. Although it might seem that the optimum level of pollution is no pollution, in the real world this is not possible. Rather, "to have a perfectly clean environment would probably bring the nation's (even the world's) economy to a standstill."[12] Thus evaluational research in this area specifies tradeoffs of various approaches to decreasing pollution. Studies use rigorous research methods to determine whether prohibiting pollution by legally restricting certain kinds of emissions or promoting pollution control with tax breaks has a more advantageous effect on the efficacy of pollution control and on economic growth.

Evaluating public policy is extremely difficult. Data may be imperfect, problematic assumptions may have to be made about future trends, and policy analysts may have biases that influence their research. In addition, there may be factors influencing the outcomes of policy that simply can't be measured. One interesting case involves initial efforts to evaluate the success of school busing. A primary objective of school integration, as discussed in Chapter 16, was to improve the quality of education provided to poor blacks isolated by residential segregation. One major policy evaluation done for the government by a prominent sociologist concluded that none of the research that had been done had demonstrated that integration had an effect on the educational achievement of students who were bused.[13] Another respected scholar, working from the very same data, concluded that "the achievement effects of 'busing' [were] more complex and positive than [previously] reported."[14] Two equally adept analysts, using the same data, had arrived at very different conclusions.

Evaluation is part of the policymaking process because the knowledge gained from it helps to identify problems and issues that arise out of current policy. Evaluation studies provide **feedback** to policymakers on program performance. (The dotted line in Figure 17.1 represents a feedback loop. Problems that emerge during the implementation stage also provide feedback to policymakers.) By drawing attention to emerging problems, policy evaluation influences the political agenda. For instance, you may recall our discussion of *oversight* in Chapter 11. When congressional committees perform oversight duties, they are evaluating policy with an eye toward identifying issues they will have to deal with in subsequent legislation. Thus, we have come full circle. The "end" of the process—evaluating whether the policy as formulated and implemented is working as envisioned—is the beginning of a new cycle of public policymaking.

A Multiplicity of Actors

Not only does the policymaking process encompass many different stages, it also encompasses many different actors at each of those stages. Here we examine some of the forces that pull the governmental structure in different directions and make problem solving less coherent than it might otherwise be. In the next section we look at some structural elements of American government that work to coordinate competing and sometimes conflicting approaches to the same problem.

Multiplicity and Fragmentation

There are many reasons why a single policy problem may be attacked in different and sometimes competing ways by government. At the heart of this **fragmentation** of policymaking is the fundamental nature of government in America. Separation of powers divides authority among the branches of the national government; federalism divides authority among the national, state, and local levels of government. These multiple centers of power are, of course, a primary element of pluralist democracy. Different groups try to influence different parts of government; there is no one entity that completely controls policymaking. Consequently, groups rebuffed by one part of government can lobby another that might be more sympathetic. And as a result, separate parts of government may make conflicting decisions in the same policy area.

Policy directed at ensuring the rights of Native Americans illustrates how the structure of government at the same time benefits a segment of the population and fails to produce a unified approach to its problems. Native Americans have had very limited success lobbying Congress. For the most part, constituents back home are not eager to cede land or special freedoms to Native Americans; this reluctance influences their members of Congress. Native Americans have, however, been more successful in convincing the courts of their property claims to various areas. Nevertheless, their legal victories have often angered people. After a court decided that members of one tribe did not have to pay local taxes, the government of Ledyard, Connecticut, prohibited the tribe from using the town library.[15]

Fragmentation exists not only because of conflict between branches or levels of government but also because of the lack of coordination *within* a branch of government. Despite the furor over the need to do more to combat drug use in America, the executive branch of the national government has been beset by chronic infighting among its different offices. There are more than 30 executive branch agencies involved in one way or another with the drug issue. In the area of drug enforcement alone, nineteen agencies share responsibility. The Customs Service and the Drug Enforcement Administration (DEA) regard each other with suspicion, even though they're ostensibly working toward the same goal. Neither wants the other to encroach on what it regards as its territory. One consequence of these attitudes is that the DEA won't give the Customs Service direct access to intelligence files it has gathered.[16]

Congress is characterized by the same diffusion of authority over drug policy. There are seventy-five separate House and Senate committees and subcommittees that claim some jurisdiction for drug legislation. These committees jealously guard their prerogatives. Even though the members of the House set up a special committee on drug policy, the Select Committee on Narcotics Abuse and Control, it has limited influence because it has no authority to write legislation.[17]

The multiplicity of institutional actors is partly the product of the complexity of public policy issues. Controlling illegal drugs is not one problem but a number of different, interrelated problems. Drug treatment questions, for example, have little in common with questions related to the smuggling of drugs into the country. Still, the responsibilities of agencies and committees do overlap. Why aren't responsibilities parceled out more precisely to clarify jurisdictions and eliminate overlap? Many actors believe such reorganizations create winners and losers, and fearing the loss of jurisdiction over an issue, they become highly protective of their "turf."

The Pursuit of Coordination

How does government overcome fragmentation so that it can make its public policies more coherent? Coordination of different elements of government is not impossible, and fragmentation often produces pressure to rethink jurisdictions.

One very common response to the problem of coordination is the formation of interagency task forces within the executive branch. The common goal of these task forces is to develop a broad policy response that all relevant agencies will endorse. Such task forces include representatives of all agencies claiming responsibility for a particular issue. They attempt to forge good policy as well as peace among competing agencies.

Sometimes the executive branch attempts to reassign jurisdictions among its agencies, even though certain players may resist the loss of their turf. Reorganization of jurisdiction is more common within rather than across agencies. A shift across agencies will likely require White House involvement. Nevertheless, the president and his aides sometimes orchestrate such restructurings, which may involve the creation of a new agency that assumes control over other existing agencies. For instance, the Bush administration, as part of a banking reform bill, has proposed a new "superregulatory" agency to watch over the financial services industry. Predictably, a big loser under this plan, the Federal Reserve Board, is fighting it.[18]

Coordination in the executive branch is also fostered by the Office of Management and Budget (OMB). The OMB does much more than review budgets and look for ways to improve management practices. It also reviews regulations before they are publicly proposed by the responsible administrative agencies. As noted in Chapter 13, the Reagan White House initiated this regulatory review role as a way of centralizing control over the executive branch. The OMB uses its power to make sure that agency policy is fully in line with the direction the White House wants to pursue. Regulations that meet with OMB disapproval are either modified or withdrawn completely.

A great virtue of OMB review is that "the presidency, of all the offices in our system of government, is the one most suited to advancing a consistent program against narrow political pressures."[19] Agencies depend on the political support of client groups and are usually less willing to antagonize their constituents by making adverse policy decisions than is the president. Thus the president uses the OMB as a counterweight to the pluralism of American politics. Many in Congress, however, are highly critical of the OMB's role because they believe it has usurped responsibilities for regulatory decisions that Congress has granted to the agencies themselves.[20]

At the same time Congress finds it difficult to eliminate overlapping jurisdictions through reorganization. Committee reorganizations are rare, and the proliferation of subcommittees has made the problem of competing jurisdictions worse. The leadership in Congress does not have the same authority to enforce coordination that the president has. Congress, however, has used the budgetary process to try to limit the independence of its committees (see Chapter 18).[21]

Finally, the fragmentation of policy created by federalism may be solved when an industry asks the national government to develop a single regulatory policy. Often the alternative is for that industry to try to accommodate various regulatory approaches used in various states. Although an industry may prefer no regulation at all, it generally prefers one master to fifty (see Feature 4.1).

The impact of pluralism on the problem of coordination is all too evident. In a decentralized, federal system of government, where there are large numbers of interest groups, fragmentation is inevitable. Beyond these structural factors is the natural tendency of people and organizations to defend their base of power. Government officials understand, however, that there must be mechanisms of coordination so that fragmentation does not overwhelm policymaking. Mechanisms of coordination like interagency task forces, reorganizations, and OMB review can bring some coherence to policymaking.

Issue Networks

So far we have emphasized how different kinds of issues can affect the policymaking process in different ways, and how government officials cope with the problems of fragmentation and coordination. We want to extend these themes by focusing more closely on interest groups. Within each issue area there are a number—often a very large number—of interest groups trying to influence policy decisions. Representatives from these organizations interact with each other and with government officials on a recurring basis. This ongoing interaction produces both conflict and cooperation.

Government by Policy Area

Earlier it was noted that policy formulation takes place across different institutions. Actors from these institutions do not patiently wait their turn as policymaking proceeds from one institution to the next. Rather, they try to influence policy at whatever stage they can. Let's suppose that Congress is considering amendments to the Clean Air Act. Since Congress does not function in a vacuum, the other parts of government that will be affected by the legislation take part in the process, too. The Environmental Protection Agency (EPA) has an interest in the outcome because it will have to administer the law. The White House is concerned about any legislation that affects such vital sectors of the economy as the steel and coal industries. As a result, officials from both the EPA and the White House work with members of Congress and the appropriate committee staffs to try to make sure that their interests are protected. At the same time, lobbyists representing corporations, trade associations, and environmental groups are doing their best to influence Congress, agency officials, and White House aides. Trade associations might hire public relations firms to sway public opinion toward industry's point of view. And outside experts from think tanks and universities might be asked to testify at hearings or to serve in an informal advisory capacity concerning the technical, economic, and social impact of the proposed amendments (see Compared with What? 17.1).

What these participants have in common is membership in an **issue network,** "a shared-knowledge group having to do with some aspect . . . of public policy."[22] The boundaries of an issue network are fuzzy, but in general terms they are made up of members of Congress, committee staffers, agency officials, lawyers, lobbyists, consultants, scholars, and public relations specialists who interact on an ongoing basis as they work to influence policies in a particular issue area. This makes for a large number of participants—the number of interest group organizations alone in a broad policy area is usually in the dozens.[23]

Not all participants in an issue network have a working relationship with all others. Indeed, some may be chronic antagonists. Others tend to be allies. Environmental groups, for example, will coalesce in trying to influence the Clean Air Act and will likely be in opposition to business groups. The common denominator that ties friends and foes together in an issue network is technical mastery of a particular policy area.

Iron Triangles

The idea of examining politics in Washington by looking at policy areas rather than at individual institutions is not new. Research by an earlier generation of political scientists and journalists described a system of *subgovernments,* tightly knit groups that dominated policymaking in an issue area. For example, journalist Douglass Cater wrote about the sugar subgovernment of the late 1950s:

Political power within the sugar subgovernment is largely vested in the Chairman of the House Agricultural Committee who works out the schedule of

COMPARED WITH WHAT?   17.1

"Go East, Young Lawyer"

The legions of lawyers, public relations experts, policy consultants, and free-lance lobbyists who provide services to clients needing access to policymakers are an integral part of Washington's issue networks. They use their specialized knowledge of issues and policymaking processes to sell their services to clients.

Washington-based law and consulting firms are especially useful to foreign governments and corporations. As the globalization of the world's economy proceeds, governments and private companies need ever more help in dealing with the political and business practices of their trading partners. As soon as the liberalization in the Soviet Union and the revolutionary changes in Eastern Europe brought the beginnings of capitalist economies to those countries, lawyers and consultants in Washington began to search for new business there. The East bloc countries are regarded as enormous commercial opportunities; their development into highly prosperous democracies is widely seen as just a matter of time. "It's like a gold rush," says one Washington consultant working with the Polish government.

A number of Washington law firms have set up offices in the East bloc countries. Sarah Carey, a Washington lawyer with Heron, Burchette, Ruckert, & Rothwell, used to spend only a small amount of her time working on trade with the Soviet Union. In the past few years it has completely taken over

her practice. She frequently travels to Moscow to the firm's small office there to tie up deals that she has helped to broker. Many firms, however, are offering their services for free to the Eastern European governments because those countries are in such difficult financial straits. Arnold & Porter and Hogan & Hartson, two prestigious Washington law firms, are working for the Polish government without charge, while at the same time trying to parlay these connections into business with private clients who want to become established there.

There is intense competition, and not all the firms trying to develop a clientele in the East bloc are going to succeed. It's too early to know which firms are going to find this eastern gold, but Washington lawyer Christopher Wall emphasizes that success will go to those who are most knowledgeable about finance, regulation, and the European community. Like any aspect of Washington law, what is most important is "expertise and experience rather than flashy marketing."

Sources: Jill Abramson, "Eager U.S. Lawyers, Lobbyists and Consultants Don't Need Any Advice to Go East, Young Man," *Wall Street Journal*, 12 January 1990, p. A14. Reprinted by permission of *Wall Street Journal*, © 1990 Dow Jones & Company, Inc. All Rights Reserved. Worldwide. W. John Moore, "*Perestroika* on the Potomac," *National Journal*, 10 February 1990, pp. 318–322. Condensed with permission from *National Journal*, Copyright 1990.

quotas. It is shared by a veteran civil servant, the director of the Sugar Division of the U.S. Department of Agriculture, who provides the necessary "expert" advice for such a complex marketing arrangement. Further advice is provided by Washington representatives of the domestic beet and cane sugar growers, the sugar refineries, and the foreign producers.[24]

According to Cater, this subgovernment had three components:

- Key members of the congressional committees and subcommittees responsible for the policy area (in this case, the chairman of the House Agriculture Committee)

- Officials from the agency or bureau that administers the policy (the director of a division of the U.S. Department of Agriculture)

- Lobbyists who represent the agency's clients (growers, refineries, and foreign producers)

These policymaking communities were called **iron triangles.** The word *iron* describes a very important property of these subgovernments: They were largely autonomous and closed; outsiders had a great deal of difficulty penetrating them. Even presidents had difficulty influencing iron triangles, which endured over time and changed little when new administrations came into power. And job changes did not usually affect them. An individual who left one component of the triangle often would move to another. Iron triangles worked because participants shared similar policy views and tried to reach a consensus that would benefit all of them.[25]

The iron triangle model was very popular with political scientists.[26] Although some used different terms (*subgovernments*, *cozy little triangles*) and some developed more sophisticated frameworks than the simplified version we've offered here, the basic ideas were the same: Typically, a small group of individuals dominated policymaking in their issue area, these policy communities were largely autonomous, and they favored those who were well organized. The model was used not only to explain how American politics operated, but also to show what was wrong with our policymaking system.[27]

The Case of Telecommunications

In recent years, it has become increasingly clear that iron triangles are not typical policymaking systems. The telecommunications industry provides a useful illustration of the changing nature of politics in Washington. Once an iron triangle, telecommunications today is a large issue network filled with conflict.

Until fairly recently, the telecommunications industry was dominated by AT&T, which, with its affiliated Bell System phone companies around the country, constituted a monopoly. Customers generally had no choice but to use the phone lines and phone equipment of "Ma Bell." It was easy for AT&T executives to defend their company's control of the industry. The United States had an impressive system with low-cost, reliable service to residential customers. Moreover, the AT&T network was a mainstay of our defense communications system. Within the telecommunications iron triangle—a policymaking community made up of some key members of Congress, the Federal Communications Commission, and AT&T—policymaking was usually consensual and uncontroversial.

At one time, AT&T was the world's largest corporation, and it seemed invulnerable. But in 1968, the FCC ruled that other companies could compete against AT&T in the "terminal" equipment market. This meant that a customer could buy a telephone (or more complex telephone equipment) from a company other than AT&T and attach it to AT&T phone lines. This jolt of competition was followed a year later by a second blow to AT&T, when the FCC ruled that MCI, a small start-up company marketing microwave technology, could sell a limited form of long-distance service to business clients.

As significant as these changes were, the greatest challenge to AT&T lay ahead. In 1974, the U.S. Department of Justice brought a lawsuit against the corporation, charging it with illegal monopolistic behavior in the telecommunications industry. The eventual outcome of the suit was an out-of-court settlement that stipulated that AT&T must divest itself of control over local operating service. The Bell System was broken up into seven regional phone companies, each independent of AT&T. AT&T was allowed to retain its long-distance service, but it would have to compete against other long-distance carriers. (AT&T did win the right to enter the computer industry, which was one of its major goals.) All in all, AT&T lost three-quarters of its assets.[28] The giant telephone company fell victim to a growing belief among academics and policymakers that government regulation was hampering the economy by restricting competition and lessening the incentives for innovation, as well as limiting the price and product choices available to consumers. Thus, telecommunications was deregulated by these changes introducing more business competition.[29]

Today, policymaking in telecommunications bears no resemblance to an iron triangle.[30] As Figure 17.2 shows, a large and varied group participates in this issue network. Although there is no single way to draw an issue network, in this representation the most important policymaking

A Phony Claim

The Consumer Federation of America and its lobbyist Gene Kimmelman are two new actors in the fractious telecommunications issue network. Kimmelman spends a lot of time pushing the regional Bell systems to provide expanded and affordable services to residential customers.

FIGURE 17.2 *The Telecommunications Issue Network*

Policymaking in telecommunications is characterized by a multitude of actors and a great deal of conflict. Among the interest group participants are AT&T, the regional phone companies, long distance carriers, equipment manufacturers, labor unions, consumer groups, and foreign corporations and trade associations. (Source: Jeffrey M. Berry, The Interest Group Society, 2d ed. [Glenview, Ill.: Scott, Foresman/Little, Brown, 1989]. Copyright © 1989. Reprinted by permission of HarperCollins Publishers.)

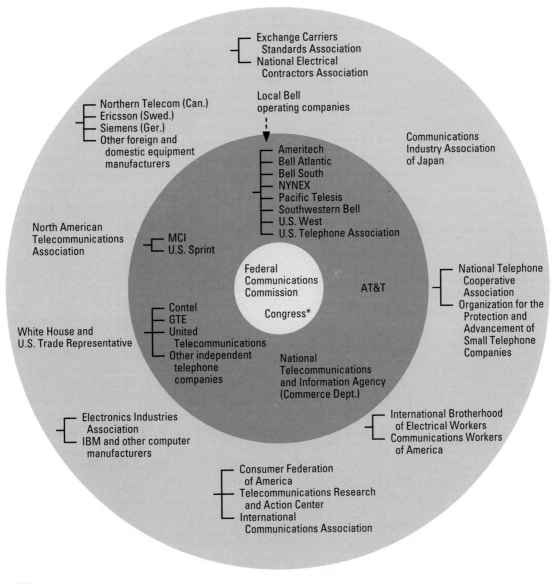

⌐ Indicates primary interest group alliance.

* Primary congressional actors are the House Committee on Energy and Commerce, Subcommittee on Telecommunications and Finance, and the Senate Committee on Commerce, Science, and Transportation, Subcommittee on Communications.

bodies lie within the inner ring. In the middle ring are the most frequent interest group participants and a secondary policymaking body in the U.S. Department of Commerce. Organizations that have a more limited focus on the telecommunications issues they work on are in the outer ring.

Conflict within the network is chronic. Alliances change rapidly as coalition partners on one issue become opponents on the next. The different lobbying organizations fight to protect their market share while trying to encroach on that of others. No one controls telecommunications policymaking, but a large array of organizations and individuals have a say in it.[31]

Not all policymaking communities in Washington have evolved into issue networks.[32] Some are still better described as iron triangles or subgovernments. For example, the Sea Grant Program, which offers grants to colleges to promote the study of marine resources, is closer to being an iron triangle than an issue network. There are just a small number of participants, and policymaking is consensual. The only ones interested in the program outside of government are the colleges, and they are all on the same side of the issue—there are no groups trying to stop the program. It is likely that this is true of many other small, uncontroversial programs that just distribute grants or benefits of some type.[33] Other types of programs where there is general agreement on goals and policies can also be characterized by routine, conflict-free operations. Again, these tend to be in smaller, less visible issue areas.

Broader policy areas, like health and agriculture, are distinguished by large numbers of participants and high degrees of conflict.[34] Why have so many iron triangles rusted through and larger, more conflicted issue networks evolved? A primary force behind this change has been the rapid growth in the number of interest groups. As more and more new groups set up shop in Washington, they demanded the attention of policymakers. These new groups brought with them new concerns, and their interests were usually at odds with at least some of the groups active in the policy area. Part of the growth of interest groups stemmed from the public interest movement. The groups that evolved from that movement were natural adversaries of business, so new conflicts emerged in many issue areas. Change also came to Congress. As indicated earlier, the number of subcommittees has expanded signficantly; this has resulted in many overlapping jurisdictions over programs.

Policy Expertise

Although contemporary issue networks may be much more open to new participants than iron triangles, there is still a significant barrier to admission. One must have the necessary expertise to enter the community of activists and politicians who influence policymaking in an issue area. Expertise has always been important, but "more than ever, policy-making is becoming an intramural activity among expert issue watchers."[35]

Oil companies, for example, are crucial to our economy, and lobbyists for the major firms have always had easy access to policymakers in government. Yet, there are lots of oil lobbyists in Washington and not all have the same influence. They compete for the attention and respect of those in government by offering solutions to problems that are technically feasible as well as politically palatable. Consider the issues addressed during a period of expanding regulation of the domestic oil industry. There was no end to seemingly obscure and complicated policy questions. How were "original costs" to be distinguished from "reproduction costs"? Was it fair for "secondary and tertiary production" to be exempted from "base-period volumes"? Did drilling that yielded "new pays" or "extensions" qualify as "new" oil or "old" oil for pricing purposes?[36]

Those in an issue network speak the same language. They can participate in the negotiation and compromise of policymaking because they can offer concrete, detailed solutions to the problems at hand. They understand the substance of policy, the way Washington works, and one another's viewpoints.[37]

One reason participants in an issue network have such a good understanding of the needs and problems of others in the network is that job switches within policy communities continue to be common. When someone wants to leave his or her current position but remain in Washington, the most obvious place to look for a new job is within the same policy field. For these **in-and-outers,** knowledge and experience remain relevant to a particular issue network, no matter which side of the fence they're on.

A common pattern of job switching—one that is the focus of much criticism—is to work in government for a number of years, build up knowledge of a policy area, then take a lobbying job (see Figure 17.3). Law firms, consulting firms, public relations firms, and trade associations generally pay much higher salaries than the government. And they pay not just for experience and know-how, but for connections with government.[38] When the Washington lobbying firm of Black, Manafort, Stone & Kelly hired James C. Healy, a former aide to the Democratic chairman of the House Ways and Means Committee, it knew that this in-and-outer would give them better access to that critical tax-writing unit. Corporations that want to influence the committee can choose among many Washington firms, but Black, Manafort, Stone & Kelly can make a convincing case to prospective clients that Healy's phone calls to the House Democratic leadership are returned.[39]

Some congressional staffers and high-ranking executive branch officials start their own firms rather than going to work for an existing firm. Despite the competition, those with valuable government experience and the respect of their peers can quickly establish themselves as the people with the right expertise and the right contacts in a particular policy field. During his seven-year stint as a high-ranking official in the Defense Department, for example, Richard Perle amassed a great deal of expertise on a variety of subjects. Among the many things he handled at the Pentagon was military assistance to Turkey. A few years after leaving the government, Perle decided to create a company, International Advisers, Inc. Before he actually established the company, he convinced the government of Turkey that he could help it in its efforts to gain military

FIGURE 17.3   *Government Service: A Useful Credential*

Individuals who have held high-level government jobs become very attractive to the private sector. This survey of political appointees to top executive branch positions shows that a little over a quarter came to those jobs directly from business or law. When they left these appointed positions, however, close to two-thirds of this group took jobs with corporations or law firms. (Source: Linda L. Fisher, "Fifty Years of Presidential Appointments," in The In-and-Outers, *ed. G. Calvin Mackenzie [Baltimore: Johns Hopkins University Press, 1987], p. 27. Used by permission.)*

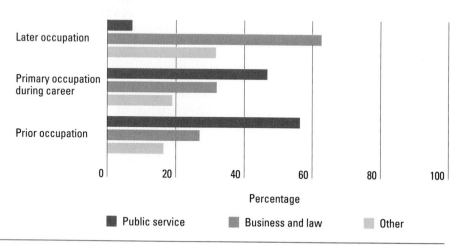

and economic assistance from Washington. The annual retainer paid to International Advisers by Turkey is $875,000 a year.[40]

In short, participation in an issue network not only gives government employees expertise, but it can also endow them with contacts that make them attractive to business clients. Personal familiarity with policymakers can be of value in and of itself, but it is of greatest utility when it is couple with the expertise that comes from extensive work on specific issues.

Although spectacular fees and salaries for those going from government to the private sector are hardly representative of what happens to in-and-outers, it is the case that for many there is a substantial financial incentive to leave government work. Indeed, it's often the case that people who *take* high-level government jobs do so at some cost to their income. One survey of political appointees to top government jobs showed that 55 percent said that it was a financial sacrifice for them to move into government. Yet even among people appointed to top government jobs, who presumably already had impressive job qualifications, roughly 50 percent indicated that government service enhanced their subsequent earning power.[41]

One constraint on in-and-outers is the Ethics in Government Act of 1978, which specifies that senior executive branch officials cannot lobby their former agency for a year after leaving the government. In 1988, the government tried to make former White House aide Lyn Nofziger the first person convicted under the lobbying restrictions of the act. Nofziger left the Reagan White House in 1982, but within less than a year he was lobbying the White House on behalf of various clients. Nofziger was found guilty at his trial, but his conviction was overturned by a federal appeals court. The court said that the law was ambiguous about whether criminal intent was required for a guilty verdict.[42]

Issue Networks and Democracy

Are issue networks making the government too fragmented? Are some issue networks beyond popular control? Has the increasing complexity of public policy given technical experts too much policymaking authority?

These questions relate to the broad issues raised in Chapter 2. For many years, political scientists have described American democracy as a system in which different constituencies work energetically to influence policies that are of concern to them. Policymaking is seen as a response to these groups rather than to majority will. This is a considerably different conception of democracy than the more traditional view, that policies reflect what most of the people want. It is a pluralist, not a majoritarian, view of American government.

When iron triangles were considered typical of the policymaking process, they were the target of much criticism. Some argued that the type of pluralism that they represented did not promote democracy through group politics but engendered closed systems that favored the status quo. The groups that were part of the iron triangles found government highly responsive, but these groups did not represent all the interests that should have been at the bargaining table. Consumer groups and environmental groups were not there to protect the public interest. Business groups that dominated the iron triangles used their position to try to stifle new competition through regulatory restrictions, as AT&T did in the telecommunications field.

In a number of ways, issue networks are an improvement over iron triangles as a model of pluralist democracy. They are open systems, populated by a much wider range of interest groups. Decision making is not centralized in the hands of a few key players; policies are formulated in a much more participatory fashion. But there is still no guarantee that all relevant interests are represented, and those with greater financial resources have an advantage. Nevertheless, issue networks come much closer to meeting the objectives of pluralist democracy than do iron triangles.[43]

For those who prefer majoritarian democracy, though, issue networks are an obstacle to the achievement of their vision of how government should operate. The technical complexity of contemporary issues makes it especially difficult for the public at large to exert control over policy outcomes. When we think of the complexity of nuclear power, toxic wastes, air pollution, poverty, drug abuse, and so on, it is easy to understand why majoritarian democracy is so difficult to achieve. The more complex the issue, the more elected officials must depend on a technocratic elite for policy guidance. And technical expertise, of course, is a chief characteristic of participants in issue networks.

At first glance, it may seem highly desirable to have technical experts play a key role in policymaking. After all, who else but the experts *should* be making decisions about toxic wastes? But a dependence on technocrats works to the advantage of interest groups, who use policy experts to maximize their influence with government. Seen in this light, issue networks become less appealing. Interest groups—at least those with which we do not personally identify—are seen as selfish. They pursue policies that favor their constituents rather than the national interest.

Although expertise is an important factor in bringing interest groups into the decision-making process, it is not the only one. Americans have a fundamental belief that government should be open and accessible to the people. If some constituency has a problem, they reason, government ought to listen to it. The practical consequence of this view is a government that is open to interest groups.

Finally, although issue networks promote pluralism, keep in mind that there are still significant majoritarian influences on policymaking. The broad contours of public opinion can be a dominant force on highly visible issues. Policymaking on civil rights, for example, has been sensitive to shifts in public opinion. Elections, too, send messages to policymakers about the most widely discussed campaign issues. What issue networks have done, however, is to facilitate pluralist politics in policy areas where majoritarian influences are weak.

Summary

Government tries to solve problems through a variety of approaches. There are public policies that prohibit, that protect, that promote, and that provide. The policymaking process can be significantly affected by the approach chosen.

Although there is much variation in the policymaking process, we can conceive of it as consisting of four stages. The first stage is agenda setting, the process by which problems become defined as political issues worthy of government attention. Once there are people in government who feel that they should be doing something about a problem, an attempt at policy formulation will follow. Policy formulation is carried out by all three branches of the national government. Once policies have been formulated and ratified, they must be implemented by administrative units of government. Finally, once policies are being carried out, they need to be evaluated. Implementation and policy evaluation influence agenda building because program shortcomings become evident during these stages. Thus, the process is really circular, with the "end" often marking the beginning of a new round of policymaking.

Our policymaking system is also characterized by forces that push it toward fragmentation and by institutional structures intended to bring some element of coordination to government. The multiplicity of actors in policymaking, the diffusion of authority within both Congress and the executive branch, the separation of powers, and federalism are chief causes of conflict and fragmentation in policymaking. The revamped budgetary process in Congress and OMB review of agency regulations are just two means government uses to foster greater coordination.

Policymaking in many areas can be viewed as an ongoing process of interaction between those in government and those outside it through issue networks. Each network is a means of communication through which information and ideas about a particular policy area are exchanged. Generally, these contemporary policy communities are more open to new participants than were the old iron triangles. Issue networks place a high premium on expertise as public policy problems grow ever more complex.

Political scientists view issue networks with some concern. There is no question that these networks facilitate the representation of many interests in the policymaking process, but they do so at a price. They allow well-organized, aggressive constituencies to prevail over the broader interests of the nation. Once again, the majoritarian and pluralist models of democracy come into conflict. It is easy to say that the majority should rule. But in the real world, the majority tends to be far less interested in issues than are the constituencies most directly affected by them. It is also easy to say that those most affected by issues should have the most influence. But experience teaches us that this kind of influence leads to policies that favor the well represented at the expense of those who should be at the bargaining table but are not.

KEY TERMS

public policy	feedback
agenda setting	fragmentation
policy formulation	issue network
implementation	iron triangles
policy evaluation	in-and-outer

SELECTED READINGS

Anderson, James E. *Public Policymaking.* Boston: Houghton Mifflin, 1990. A brief overview of the policymaking system.

Cater, Douglass. *Power in Washington.* New York: Vintage Books, 1964. One reporter's view of how policy is formulated in Washington.

Chubb, John E. *Interest Groups and the Bureaucracy.* Stanford, Calif.: Stanford University Press, 1983. An ambitious analysis of interest group–agency interaction within various energy-policy communities.

Laumann, Edward O., and David Knoke. *The Organizational State.* Madison, Wis.: University of Wisconsin Press, 1987. The authors use network theory to analyze policymaking in health and energy.

Mackenzie, G. Calvin, ed. *The In-and-Outers.* Baltimore: Johns Hopkins University Press, 1987. A collection of essays examining the problems associated with the movement of people back and forth between the private sector and the executive branch.

Portney, Kent. *Approaching Public Policy Analysis.* Englewood Cliffs, N.J.: Prentice-Hall, 1986. A sophisticated but highly readable introduction to policy evaluation.

18 ECONOMIC POLICY

THE TOWN OF VERNON, TEXAS (population 12,500), is located on the northern edge of the state, about fifteen miles south of the Oklahoma border. Like other towns its size in rural America, it had a savings and loan association. But the Vernon S&L was different from the usual small-town firm. It owned a fleet of three airplanes; three automobile dealerships in La Jolla, California (one that sold Rolls-Royces, one that sold Ferraris, and one that sold "classic cars"); a $1.8 million beach house in Del Mar, California; and a subsidiary in Switzerland.[1] The Vernon S&L had acquired all that in the six years after it was purchased by Don R. Dixon, a Dallas real estate developer in 1982. One wonders what else he would have bought with other people's money if federal bank regulators had not ousted him in 1987 and seized the S&L a few months later, with 96 percent of its loans in default. Although the S&L had no money to pay back its depositors, virtually no investors lost money because their deposits were federally insured. However, the bill to taxpayers for the Vernon S&L's losses was estimated at $1.3 *billion* dollars.[2] At the end of 1990, Don R. Dixon was the seventy-first person convicted of bank fraud in Texas in three years of investigations by a government task force.[3]

Although Texas was hardest hit by S&L failures (due to its collapsing real estate market), it did not have a monopoly on S&L fraud or mismanagement. Consider the First Network Savings Bank in Los Angeles, founded in 1983 by Carl M. Rheuban, a real estate developer with no prior experience running an S&L. Rheuban started without any tellers to collect money over the counter. Instead, he advertised high interest rates and obtained funds by mail, investing those funds in complicated and risky real estate deals. By 1988, First Network listed $517 million in assets. Rheuban, who owned 97 percent of the S&L, paid himself $11 million in dividends over six years. An amateur magician, Rheuban also spent $850,000 of the firm's money for a "museum of magic" and hired one of the world's top magicians as curator. When federal regulators took over his failed institution in 1990, they estimated its losses at $110 million. Again, the bill was passed on to taxpayers.[4]

The eventual size of the government's bailout of the S&L industry is still unknown. At the end of 1989, there were approximately 2,900 S&Ls in the United States. By mid-1990, the government's Resolution Trust Corporation (RTC), formed to salvage the industry, had taken over 330 S&Ls in thirty-nine states and had closed 93.[5] By early 1991, the RTC had spent $70 billion and asked Congress for an additional $80 billion to bail out 225 more associations. If the RTC gets its money and completes its plan for 1991, it will have closed, transferred, or sold more than 20 percent of the entire industry.[6] Unfortunately, hundreds more S&Ls are not healthy and may have to be taken over. The cost of the bailout defies comprehension. Including interest on funds that the government must borrow to finance the RTC, estimates have centered on $500 billion. That's about twice the cost of the Vietnam War and amounts to $2,000 for every person in the United States. Or think of it as $2,000 additional in taxes that *you* will have to pay to cover S&L deposits stolen by fraud or wasted by mismanagement.

Republican Representative Jim Leach of Iowa called the S&L fiasco "the single most grievous legislative error of judgment this century."[7]

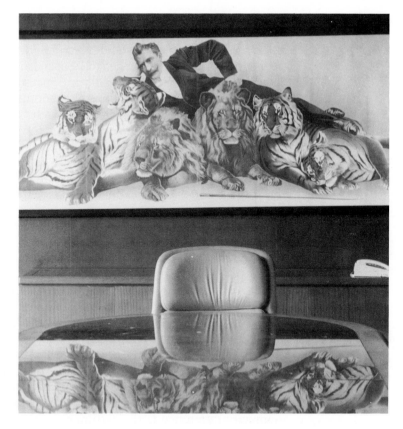

Disappearing Act
This lithograph of a magician dominated the board room of the First Network Savings Bank in Los Angeles, one of the savings and loans taken over by the government as part of the multibillion-dollar S&L bailout. Nearly $1 million of the bank's money had been spent to build a museum of magic. It was an ironically appropriate expenditure: During the 1980s, mismanagement and fraud in the S&L industry made investors' money disappear into thin air.

This "error" began, however, with the desire to save the S&L industry, which suffered from the inflation of the 1970s. Known as "thrift" institutions, S&Ls held long-term home mortgages that paid low returns, and management was limited in the rates they could pay and the loans they could make. As their depositors withdrew funds to invest in higher-yielding possibilities, Congress took three key steps to revitalize the industry. In 1980, it allowed S&Ls to pay much higher interest rates. Congress then permitted investors to open multiple accounts, each insured up to $100,000. And later it deregulated management, allowing the thrift industry to invest in virtually anything—car dealerships, tanning parlors, and other high-return but risky deals. Giving the S&L industry freedom to fly high fit perfectly with President Ronald Reagan's free-market philosophy. When he signed the deregulation act in 1982, he said, "I think we've hit the jackpot."[8]

Although S&Ls began making riskier loans, the Reagan administration denied a request by Edwin J. Gray, chairman of the Federal Home Loan Bank Board, to increase the number of bank examiners, believing the request inconsistent with administration philosophy.[9] Gray got little help from Congress in controlling the developing mess, for S&L executives were pouring money into the pockets of key members in both parties. Jim Wright, Speaker of the House, and Tony Coelho, majority whip, were both forced to resign due to contacts with S&L operators, and the "Keating Five"—Senators Alan Cranston, Dennis DeConcini, John Glenn,

John McCain, and Donald Riegle—were charged with hampering federal regulators who were trying to curtail the risky loans made by Charles Keating's Lincoln Savings and Loan. Later, the media were criticized for neglecting the developing debacle because it was a complicated and boring "numbers" story, not a titillating "people" story. So there was plenty of blame to share in this failure of economic policy.

In light of the S&L disaster, how much "free enterprise" should be allowed in financial markets and what is the proper role of government in regulating the economy? Apart from regulation, what can government do to control the economy? What effects do government taxing and spending policies have on the economy and on economic equality? We grapple with these and other questions in this chapter on the economics of public policy.

Theories of Economic Policy

Taxing and spending are the major tools with which government implements policy. How policymakers use these tools depends on their beliefs about (1) how the economy functions, and (2) the proper role of government in the economy. The American economy is so complex that no policymaker knows exactly how it works. Policymakers have to rely on economic theories to explain its functioning, and there are nearly as many theories as economists (see Feature 18.1). Unfortunately, different theories (and economists) often predict quite different outcomes. One source of difference is the assumptions that are part of every economic theory, for these differ from theory to theory. Another problem is the difference between an idealized theory and the real world. Still, despite the disagreement among economists, a knowledge of basic economics is necessary to an understanding of how government approaches public policy.

We are concerned here with economic policy in a *market economy* —one in which the prices of goods and services are determined through the interaction of sellers and buyers (that is, through supply and demand). This kind of economy is typical of the consumer-dominated societies of Western Europe and the United States. A *nonmarket economy* relies on government planners to determine both the prices of goods and the amounts that are produced. The Soviet economy was a perfect example of a nonmarket economy until President Mikhail Gorbachev's policy of *perestroika*, or economic restructuring, introduced some private elements. In a nonmarket economy, the government owns and operates the major means of production. Market economies often exhibit a mix of government and private ownership. For example, Britain has considerably more government-owned enterprises (railroads, broadcasting, and housing) than the United States.

Market economies are loosely called *capitalist economies:* They allow private individuals to own property, sell goods for profit in a free, or open, market, and accumulate wealth, called *capital.* The competing theories of market economies differ largely on how free the market should be—in other words, on the role of government in directing the economy.

FEATURE 18.1 *Economics: The Dismal Science*

Thomas Carlyle, a nineteenth-century British social critic, called economics "the dismal science." Although Carlyle was speaking in a different context, his phrase has stuck. If being a science requires agreement on fundamental propositions among practitioners, then economics is certainly a dismal science. When twenty-seven standard propositions in economic theory were put to almost a thousand economists in five Western countries, they did not agree on a single one. Consider this example: "Reducing the role of regulatory authorities (for instance, in air traffic) would improve the efficiency of the economy." About 33 percent of the economists "generally disagreed," 30 percent "generally agreed," and 34 percent "agreed with provisions." When learned economists cannot agree on basic propositions in economic theory, politicians are free to choose theories that fit their views of the proper role of government in the economy.

THE ECONOMISTS

Source: Adapted from Bruno S. Frey, et al., "Consensus and Dissension Among Economists: An Empirical Inquiry," *American Economic Review* 74 (December 1984):986–994.

Laissez-Faire Economics

We introduced the French term *laissez faire* in Chapter 1 and discussed it again in Chapter 13. It describes the absence of government control. The economic doctrine of laissez faire likens the operation of a free market to the process of natural selection. Economic competition weeds out the weak and preserves the strong. In the process, the economy prospers and everyone eventually benefits.

Advocates of laissez-faire economics are fond of quoting Adam Smith's *The Wealth of Nations*. In this 1776 treatise, Smith argued that each individual, pursuing his own selfish interests in a competitive market, was "led by an invisible hand to promote an end which was no part of his intention." Smith's "invisible hand" has been used for two centuries to justify the belief that the narrow pursuit of profits serves the broad interests of society. Strict advocates of laissez faire maintain that government interference with business tampers with the laws of nature, obstructing the workings of the free market.

Keynesian Theory

One problem with laissez-faire economics is its insistence that government should do little about **economic depressions** (periods of high unemployment and business failures) or about raging **inflation** (when price increases decrease the value of currency). Inflation is generally measured by the *Consumer Price Index (CPI)* (see Feature 18.2). Since the beginning of the Industrial Revolution, capitalist economies have suffered through many cyclical fluctuations. The United States has experienced more than fifteen of these **business cycles**—expansions and contractions

---

F E A T U R E   18.2   *The Consumer Price Index*

Inflation in the United States is usually measured in terms of the Consumer Price Index. The CPI is based on prices paid for food, clothing, shelter, transportation, medical services, and other items necessary for daily living. Data are collected from eighty-five areas across the country, from nearly 60,000 housing units and almost 20,000 businesses.

The CPI is not a perfect yardstick. One problem is that it does not differentiate between inflationary price increases and other price increases. A Ford sedan bought in 1981 is not the same as a Ford sedan bought in 1991. To some extent, the price difference reflects a change in quality as well as a change in the value of the dollar. For example, improvements in fuel economy improve the car's quality and justify a somewhat higher price. The CPI is also slow to reflect changes in purchasing habits. Wash-and-wear clothes were tumbling in the dryer for several years before the government agreed to include them as an item in the index.

These are minor issues compared with the weight given over time to the cost of housing. Until 1983, the cost of purchasing and financing a home accounted for 26 percent of the CPI. This formula neglected the facts that many people rent, rather than buy, homes and that few people buy a home every year. A better measure of the cost of shelter is the cost of renting houses similar to those that are owned. Using this method of calculating the cost of shelter dropped the weighting given to housing in the CPI from 26 percent to 14 percent. Before the correction, the CPI overstated the rate of inflation for the average citizen.

The government uses the CPI to make cost-of-living adjustments in civil service and military pension payments, social security benefits, and food stamp allowances. Moreover, many union wage contracts with private businesses are indexed (tied) to the CPI. Because the CPI almost always goes up each year, so do the payments that are tied to it. In a way, then, indexing payments to the CPI adds to both the growth of government spending and inflation itself. The United States is one of the few nations that also ties its tax brackets to a price index, which reduces revenues by eliminating the "bracket creep" of inflation.

Despite its faults, the CPI is at least a consistent measure of prices and is likely to go on being used as the basis for adjustments to wages, benefits, and payments affecting millions of people.

Source: Adapted from David S. Moore, *Statistics: Concepts and Controversies*, 2d ed. (New York: Freeman, 1985), pp. 238–241. Used by permission of W. H. Freeman. Also see Bureau of the Census, *Statistical Abstract of the United States, 1990* (Washington, D.C.: U.S. Government Printing Office, 1990), pp. 465–466.

We Make Money the Old-Fashioned Way: We Print It

The U.S. Mint stamps out coins, but paper money is produced by the Bureau of Engraving and Printing, which also prints treasury notes and other U.S. securities. Imagine how frustrating it might be to work among these sheets of money.

of business activity, the first stage accompanied by inflation and the second stage by unemployment. No one had a theory that really explained these cycles until the Great Depression of the 1930s.

That was when John Maynard Keynes, a British economist, theorized that business cycles stem from imbalances between aggregate demand and productive capacity. **Aggregate demand** is the income available to consumers, business, and government to spend on goods and services. **Productive capacity** is the value of goods and services that can be produced when the economy is working at full capacity. The value of the goods and services *actually* produced is called the **gross national product (GNP)**.

When demand exceeds productive capacity, people pay more for available goods, which leads to price inflation. When productive capacity exceeds demand, producers cut back their output of goods, which leads to unemployment. When many people are unemployed for an extended period, the economy is in a depression. Keynes theorized that government could stabilize the economy (and flatten or eliminate business cycles) by controlling the level of aggregate demand.

Keynesian theory holds that aggregate demand can be adjusted through a combination of fiscal and monetary policies. **Fiscal policies** involve changes in government spending and taxing. When demand is too low, government should either spend more itself or cut taxes, to give people more money to spend. When demand is too great, the government should either spend less or raise taxes, giving people less money to spend. **Monetary policies** involve changes in the money supply and operate less directly on the economy. Increasing the amount of money in circulation increases aggregate demand, and thus increases price inflation, assuming full employment. Decreasing the money supply decreases aggregate demand and inflationary pressures.

Keynesian theory has been widely adopted by capitalist countries. At one time or another, virtually all have used the Keynesian technique of

deficit financing—spending beyond tax revenues—to combat an economic slump. The objective of deficit financing is to inject extra money into the economy to stimulate aggregate demand. Most deficits are financed by funds borrowed through the issuing of government bonds, notes, or other securities. The theory holds that deficits can be paid off with budget surpluses after the economy recovers.

Because Keynesian theory requires government to play an active role in controlling the economy, it runs counter to laissez-faire economics. Before Keynes, no administration in Washington would undertake responsibility for maintaining a healthy economy. In 1946, the year in which Keynes died, Congress passed an employment act fixing under law "the continuing responsibility of the federal government to . . . promote maximum employment, production and purchasing power." It also created the **Council of Economic Advisers (CEA)** within the Executive Office of the President to advise the president on maintaining a stable economy. The CEA normally consists of three economists (usually university professors) appointed by the president with Senate approval. Aided by a staff of about twenty-five people (mostly economists), the CEA helps the president prepare his annual economic report, also a provision of the 1946 act. The chair of the CEA is usually a major spokesperson for the administration's economic policy. This was not the case under Reagan, however, primarily because Reagan's views on economics did not always coincide with those of the economists on the council.

The Employment Act of 1946, which reflected Keynesian theory, had a tremendous impact on government economic policy. Many people believe it was the primary source of "big government" in America. Even Richard Nixon, a conservative president, admitted that "we are all Keynesians now."

Monetary Policy

Although most economists accept Keynesian theory in its broad outlines, they disagree on its political utility. Some especially question the value of fiscal policies in controlling inflation and unemployment. They feel that government spending programs take too long to enact in Congress and to implement through the bureaucracy. As a result, jobs are created not when they are needed, but years later, when the crisis may have passed and government spending needs to be reduced.

Also, government spending is easier to start than to stop because the groups that benefit from spending programs tend to defend them even when they are no longer needed. A similar criticism applies to tax policies. Politically, it is much easier to cut taxes than to raise them. In other words, Keynesian theory requires that governments be able to begin *and* end spending quickly, and to cut *and* raise taxes quickly. But in the real world, these fiscal tools are easier to use in one way than the other. Both Ronald Reagan and George Bush made taxes such an issue that tax increases can no longer be considered a viable instrument of economic policy in contemporary politics.

Monetarists, recognizing the limitations of fiscal policies, argue that government can control the economy's performance effectively only by controlling the nation's money supply. Monetarists favor a long-range

Fed Head

As chairman of the Federal Reserve Board, Alan Greenspan heads the central banking operation of the United States. First appointed by President Reagan in 1987, Greenspan's reappointment in 1991 was rumored to be in some doubt because of the Fed's failure to act on President Bush's desire for lower interest rates. When the board eventually complied with the president's wishes, its political independence was questioned. Greenspan was reappointed to a second term.

policy of small but steady growth in the amount of money in circulation rather than frequent manipulation of monetary policies.

Major monetary policies in the United States are under the control of the **Federal Reserve System,** which acts as its central bank. Established in 1913, "the Fed" is not a single bank but a system of banks. At the top of the system is the board of governors, seven members appointed by the president for staggered terms of fourteen years. The board is directed by a chair, designated by the president, who serves a four-year term that overlaps the president's term of office. This complex arrangement was intended to make the board independent of the president and even Congress. An independent board, the reasoning went, would be able to make financial decisions for the nation without regard to political implications.

The Fed controls the money supply, which affects inflation, in three ways. It can change the *reserve requirement,* which is the amount of cash that member banks must keep on deposit in a regional Federal Reserve Bank. An increase in the reserve requirement decreases the amount of money a bank has available to lend. The Fed can also change its *discount rate,* the interest rate that member banks have to pay to borrow money from a Federal Reserve Bank. A lower rate encourages a member bank to borrow and lend more freely. Finally, the Fed can *buy and sell government securities* (such as U.S. Treasury notes and bonds) on the open market. When it buys securities, it pays out money, putting more money into circulation; when it sells securities, the process works in reverse.

The Fed's activities are essential parts of the overall economic policy, but they lie outside the direct control of the president. This can create problems in coordinating economic policy. For example, the president might want the Fed to lower interest rates to stimulate the economy, but the Fed might resist for fear of inflation. These kinds of policy clashes can pit the chair of the Federal Reserve Board directly against the president. This happened early in 1991, when President Bush publicly criticized the Fed for not taking action to lower interest rates. When the Fed finally did cut its discount rate to encourage banks to lower interest rates in the spring of 1991, some analysts felt that the cut came partly in response to Bush's criticisms.[10] Although the Fed's economic policies are not perfectly insulated from political concerns, they are sufficiently independent so that the president is not able to control monetary policy without the Fed's cooperation. This means that the president cannot be held completely responsible for the state of the economy—despite the Employment Act of 1946.

Supply-Side Economics

When Reagan came to office in 1981, he embraced a school of thought called **supply-side economics** to deal with the double-digit inflation that the nation was experiencing. Remember that Keynesian theory argues that inflation stems from an excess of aggregate demand over supply, and the standard Keynesian solution is to reduce demand (for example, by increasing taxes). Supply-siders argued that inflation could be lowered more effectively by increasing supply. (That is, they stressed the *supply side* of the economic equation.) Specifically, they favored tax cuts to stimulate investment (which, in turn, would lead to the production of more goods) and less government regulation of business (again, to increase productivity—which they held would yield more, not less, government revenue).

To support their theory, supply-side economists point to a 1964 tax cut that was initiated by President Kennedy. It stimulated investment and raised the total national income. As a result, the government took in as much tax revenue under the tax cut as it had before taxes were cut. Supply-siders also argue that the rich should receive *larger* tax cuts than the poor, because the rich have more money to invest. The benefits of increased investment then "trickle down" to working people in the form of additional jobs and income.

In a sense, supply-side economics leans toward laissez-faire economics in the form of less government regulation and less taxation. Supply-siders believe that government interferes too much with the efforts of individuals to work, save, and invest. This is what Ronald Reagan thought when he was a movie star in the 1950s, with a salary in the 91 percent tax bracket. In his 1965 autobiography, he wrote that because the government took so much of his income, he quit working for a year after he moved into that bracket.[11] Obviously, he hadn't changed his mind about taxation when he entered his first term in office. After succeeding Reagan in the presidency, George Bush demonstrated a similar opposition to taxation.

Inspired by supply-side theory, Reagan proposed (and got) massive tax cuts in the *Economic Recovery Tax Act of 1981*. Individual tax rates were reduced by 23 percent over a three-year period, and the tax rate for the highest income group was cut from 70 to 50 percent. Reagan also launched a program to deregulate business. According to the theory, these actions would generate extra government revenue, making spending cuts unnecessary. Nevertheless, Reagan also cut funding for some domestic programs, including Aid to Families with Dependent Children and the food stamp program (see Chapter 19). Contrary to supply-side theory, he also proposed major increases in military spending. This blend of tax cuts, deregulation, cuts in spending for social programs, and increases in spending for defense became known, somewhat disparagingly, as *Reaganomics.*

How well did Reaganomics work? During Reagan's administration, annual price inflation fell a whopping 11.9 percentage points—from 13.5 percent in 1980 to 1.9 percent in 1986, creeping back to 4.9 percent in 1988.[12] Although many economists credit the drop to the tight-money policies of the Federal Reserve Board, which raised interest rates, the Fed did it with Reagan's support. Higher interest rates cut back business investments, initially producing a severe recession and unemployment. However, unemployment peaked at 9.7 percent

Ticking Time Bomb

Say, buddy, do you know the deficit? If you were in New York City's Times Square on a day in May 1991, you would have seen that your family's share of the national debt was more than $53,000. And, second by second, it continues to increase.

FIGURE 18.1 *Budget Deficits over Time*

In his first inaugural address, President Reagan said, "You and I, as individuals, can, by borrowing, live beyond our means, but only for a limited period of time. Why, then, should we think that collectively, as a nation, we're not bound by that same limitation?" But borrow he did. Reagan's critics charged that the budget deficits under his adminis-tration—over $1.3 trillion—exceeded the total deficits of all previous presidents. But this charge does not take inflation into account. A billion dollars in the 1990s is worth much less than it was one hundred or even ten years ago.

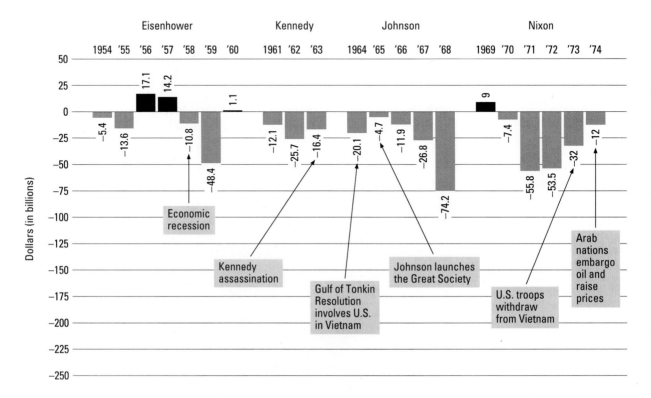

in 1982 and dropped to 5.5 percent in 1988, far below the rate when Reagan took office.[13] These were important economic accomplish-ments. Unfortunately, and in spite of supply-side theory, the tax cut was accompanied by a massive drop in tax revenues. Shortly after taking office, Reagan promised that his economic policies would balance the national budget by 1984, but lower tax revenues and higher defense spending produced the largest budget deficits ever (see Fig-ure 18.1).[14]

Public Policy and the Budget

To most people—college students included—the national budget is B-O-R-I-N-G. To national politicians, it is an exciting script for high drama. The numbers, categories, and percentages that numb normal minds cause politicians' nostrils to flare and their hearts to pound. The budget is a political battlefield, on which politicians and the programs they support wage war.

A fairer way to calculate deficits is in constant dollars—dollars whose value has been adjusted to a given year. This chart shows the actual deficits in 1982 dollars incurred under presidential administrations from Eisenhower to Bush. Even computed this way, Reagan's deficits were enormous—especially for a president who claimed to oppose government borrowing. But they pale by comparison to the huge deficit for Bush in 1991. (Source: Office of Management and Budget, Budget of the United States Government, Fiscal Year 1992 [Washington, D.C.: U.S. Government Printing Office, 1991], Part Seven, p. 17.)

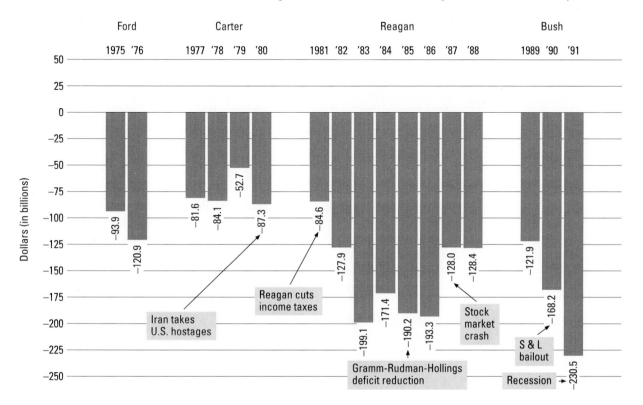

Today, the president prepares the budget and Congress approves it. This was not always the case. Before 1921, Congress prepared the budget under its constitutional authority to raise taxes and appropriate funds. The budget was formed piecemeal by enacting a series of laws that originated in the many committees involved in the highly decentralized process of raising revenue, authorizing expenditures, and appropriating funds. No one was responsible for the "big picture"—the budget as a whole. The president's role was essentially limited to approving revenue and appropriations bills, just as he approved other pieces of legislation. In fact, executive agencies even submitted their budgetary requests directly to Congress, not to the president.

Congressional budgeting (such as it was) worked well enough for a nation of farmers, but not for an industrialized nation with a growing population and a more active government. Soon after World War I, Congress realized that the budget-making process needed to be centralized. With the *Budgeting and Accounting Act of 1921*, it thrust the responsibility for preparing the budget onto the president. The act established the Bureau of the Budget to help the president write "his" budget, which had to be submitted to Congress each January. Congress retained its constitutional authority to raise and spend funds, but now Congress would begin its work with the president's budget as its starting point. And all executive agencies' budget requests had to be funneled through the Bureau of the Budget (which became the Office of Management and Budget in 1970) for review; those consistent with the president's overall economic and legislative program were incorporated into the president's budget.

The Nature of the Budget

The national budget is complex. But its basic elements are not beyond understanding. We begin with some definitions. The *Budget of the United States Government* is the annual financial plan that the president is required to submit to Congress at the start of each year. It applies to the next **fiscal year (FY)**, the period the government uses for accounting purposes. Currently, the fiscal year runs from October 1 to September 30. The budget is named for the year in which it *ends*. So, the FY 1992 budget applies to the twelve months from October 1, 1991, to September 30, 1992.

Broadly, the budget defines **budget authority** (how much government agencies are authorized to spend for programs), **budget outlays,** or expenditures (how much they are expected to spend), and **receipts** (how much is expected in taxes and other revenues). (The relationship of authority to outlays is diagrammed in Figure 18.2.) President Bush's FY 1992 budget contained authority for expenditures of $1,578 billion, but it provided for spending (outlays) of "only" $1,446 billion. The budget anticipated receipts of $1,165 billion, leaving a deficit of $281 billion—the difference between receipts and outlays.

Bush's FY 1992 budget was over fifteen hundred pages long and weighed more than five pounds, including appendixes. (The budget document contains more than numbers. It also explains individual spending programs in terms of national needs and agency objectives, and it analyzes proposed taxes and other receipts.) Although its publication was anxiously awaited by reporters, lobbyists, and political analysts eager to learn the president's plan for government spending in the coming year, the drama was lessened in 1991 because of the Budget Enforcement Act passed in the closing days of the 1990 session. This law grew out of a budget agreement between the president and Congress following months of negotiation over how to deal with the budget deficit. Because the agreement capped the amount of money that could be spent for domestic, military, and foreign assistance programs, the broad outlines of government spending were determined in advance of the president's budget. The law also made some significant changes in dealing with future deficits and in the budgeting process itself.

Preparing the President's Budget

The budget that the president submits to Congress each winter is the end product of a process that begins the previous spring under the supervision of the **Office of Management and Budget (OMB).** OMB is located

FIGURE 18.2 *Relationship of Budget Authority to Budget Outlays*

The national budget is a complicated document. One source of confusion for people studying the budget for the first time is the relationship of budget authority to budget outlay. These two figures differ because of sums that are carried over from prior years and to future years. The diagram helps explain the relationship (all amounts are in billions of dollars). Only $1,066 billion of the FY 1992 budget authority is expected to be spent in FY 1992; while $511.9 billion will be carried over for spending in future years. Similarly, $380 billion in funds authorized in prior years will be spent in FY 1992. (Source: Office of Management and Budget, Budget of the United States Government, Fiscal Year 1992 *[Washington, D.C., U.S. Government Printing Office, 1991], Part Four, p. 206.)*

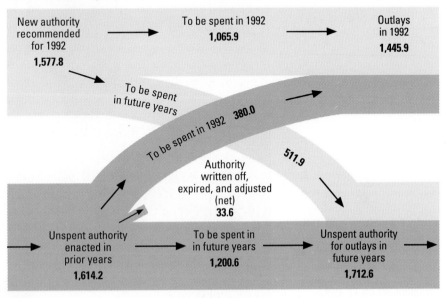

within the Executive Office of the President and is headed by a director who is appointed by the president with the approval of the Senate. The OMB, with a staff of over five hundred, is the most powerful domestic agency in the bureaucracy, and its director, who sits in the president's Cabinet, is one of the most powerful figures in government.

The OMB initiates the budget process each spring by meeting with the president to discuss the economic situation and his budgetary priorities. It then sends broad economic guidelines to every government agency and requests their initial projections of funds needed for the next fiscal year. The OMB assembles this information and makes recommendations to the president, who settles on more precise guidelines. By the summer, the agencies are asked to prepare budgets based on the new guidelines. By the fall, they submit their formal budgets to the OMB, where budget analysts scrutinize agency requests for both costs and consistency with the president's legislative program. A lot of politicking goes on at this stage, as agency heads try to go around the OMB to plead for their pet projects with presidential advisers and perhaps even the president himself. Political negotiations may extend into the early winter—often to the last possible moment before the budget goes to the printer.

The voluminous document is carefully printed and neatly bound. It looks very much like a finished product, but it is far from final. In giving

Budgetary Show and Tell

Richard G. Darman, director of the Office of Management and Budget, uses the latest in high-tech displays to explain President Bush's FY 1992 budget to reporters on the day it was officially released.

the president the responsibility for preparing the budget, Congress has provided itself with a starting point for its own work.

Passing the Congressional Budget

Congress must approve the budget. That process is a creaky conglomeration of traditional procedures overlaid with structural reforms from the 1970s, external constraints in the 1980s, and hasty changes introduced by the 1990 Budget Enforcement Act. Especially in recent years, the process has proved inadequate to the task of producing a budget according to Congress's own timetable.

The traditional procedure: the committee structure. Traditionally, the tasks of budget making were divided among a number of committees—a process that has been retained. There are three types of committees involved in budgeting:

- **Tax committees** are responsible for raising the revenues to run the government. The Ways and Means Committee in the House and the Finance Committee in the Senate consider all proposals for taxes, tariffs, and other receipts contained in the president's budget.

■ **Authorization committees** (such as the House Armed Services Committee and the Senate Banking, Housing, and Urban Affairs Committee) have jurisdiction over particular legislative subjects. The House has about twenty committees that can authorize spending, and the Senate about fifteen. Each one pores over the portions of the budget that pertain to its area of responsibility. In recent years, however, power has shifted from the authorization committees to the appropriations committees.

■ **Appropriations committees** decide which of the programs approved by the authorization committees will actually be funded (that is, given money to spend). For example, the House Armed Services Committee might decide to build a new line of tanks for the army and even get its decision enacted into law. But the tanks will never be built unless funds are appropriated for that purpose by the appropriations committees. Thirteen distinct appropriation bills are supposed to be enacted each year to fund the nation's spending.

Two major problems are inherent in a budgeting process that involves three distinct kinds of congressional committees. First, the two-step spending process (first *authorization*, then *appropriation*) is complex; it offers wonderful opportunities for interest groups to get into the budgeting act. Second, because one group of legislators in each house plans for revenues and many other groups plan for spending, no one is responsible for the budget as a whole. In the 1970s, Congress added a new committee structure that combats the pluralist politics inherent in the old procedures and allows budget choices to be made in a more majoritarian manner, by votes in both chambers.

Reforms of the 1970s: the budget committee structure. In 1921, when Congress gave the president the responsibility to prepare the budget, it surrendered considerable authority. During the next fifty years, attempts by Congress to regain control of the budgeting process failed because of jurisdictional squabbles between the revenue and appropriations committees.

Overall control of the budget is important to Congress for several reasons. First, members of Congress are politicians, and politicians want to wield power, rather than watch someone else wield it. Second, the Constitution established Congress, not the president, as the "first branch" of government and the people's representatives; this legitimated its institutional jealousy. Third, Congress as a body often disagrees with presidential spending priorities, but it has been unable to mount a serious challenge to his authority by presenting a coherent alternative budget.

After bitter spending fights with President Nixon in the late 1960s and early 1970s, Congress finally passed the Budget and Impoundment Control Act of 1974. That act fashioned a typically political solution to the problem of wounded egos and trampled jurisdictions that had frustrated previous attempts to change the budget-making procedure. All the tax and appropriations committees (and chairpersons) were retained, and new House and Senate **budget committees** were superimposed on the old committee structure. The budget committees supervised a comprehensive budget review process, aided by the **Congressional Budget Office (CBO).** The CBO, with a staff of over two hundred, acquired a budgetary expertise equal to that of the president's OMB, so it could prepare credible alternative budgets for Congress.

At the heart of the 1974 reforms was a timetable for the congressional budget process. The original timetable has since been modified several times, and its deadlines are often missed. Still, it is a useful means of guiding the process. The budget committees are supposed to propose an initial budget resolution that sets overall revenue and spending levels, broken down into twenty-one different "budget functions," among them, national defense, agriculture, and health. By April 15, both houses are supposed to have agreed on a single budget resolution to guide their work on the budget during the summer. Appropriations are supposed to be completed by June 30. Throughout, the levels of spending set by majority vote on the budget resolution are supposed to constrain pressures by special interests to increase spending in the context of pluralist politics.

This process (or one very much like it) was implemented in 1975 and worked reasonably well for the first few years. Congress was able to work on and structure the budget as a whole, rather than changing pieces of it. But the process broke down during the Reagan administration, as the president submitted annual budgets with huge deficits. Reagan kept to his economic game plan, resisting any tax increases to reduce the deficits and cutting social spending, and increased military spending. Many observers felt that Reagan actually welcomed the large deficits to pressure Congress to cut down on social spending. For its part, a Democratic Congress reversed his spending priorities where possible but refused to pro-

No Dough, No Show

In October 1990, an impasse between the president and the Congress over the national budget created a shortage of operating funds that shut down most of the government. Many museums, monuments, and agencies (including the Washington Monument and the White House) were closed to the public. The resulting publicity put pressure on both sides to settle the argument.

pose a tax increase to reduce the deficit without the president's cooperation.

At loggerheads with Reagan, Congress encountered increasing difficulty in enacting its budget resolutions according to its own timetable, and it never succeeded in passing its thirteen separate appropriation bills during any of the first seven years of the Reagan administration.[15] Instead, Congress resorted to combining appropriations for different topics in the same bill. In 1990, under Bush, Congress did pass all thirteen bills separately, but none of them cleared by the October 1 deadline and all were passed during the last eight days of the session.[16]

External constraints of the 1980s: Gramm-Rudman. Alarmed by the huge deficits in Reagan's budgets, frustrated by his refusal to raise taxes, and stymied by their own inability to eliminate the deficits, members of Congress were ready to try almost anything. Republican Senators Phil Gramm (Texas) and Warren Rudman (New Hampshire) were joined by Democrat Ernest Hollings (South Carolina) in proposing drastic action to force a balanced budget. Officially titled the *Balanced Budget and Emergency Deficit Control Act* (1985), their bill became known simply as Gramm-Rudman-Hollings, or **Gramm-Rudman** for short.

In its original form, Gramm-Rudman mandated that the budget deficit be lowered to a specified level each year until the budget was balanced in FY 1991 (see Figure 18.3). If Congress did not meet the mandated deficit level in any year, across-the-board budget cuts were to be made automatically by the comptroller general. Senator Rudman described his own bill as "a bad idea whose time has come," but congressional members' frustration with their repeated inability to cut the deficit was so great that Gramm-Rudman sailed through both houses on a wave of exasperation. The bill was not considered by congressional committees in the usual manner, nor was it subjected to formal economic, procedural, or legal analysis. No one really knew what the legislation would do—except give Congress an out in deciding which programs to cut or whose taxes to raise so as to reduce the deficit. Republican Senator Robert Packwood from Oregon confessed to the Senate, "I pray that what we are about to undertake will work."[17]

An excess in the budget deficit triggered Gramm-Rudman in 1986, the first year after it was passed. The president and Congress saw 4.3 percent sliced from every domestic and defense program (except for specific exemptions, like social security) without regard to their value for the nation, thus weakening most programs through underfunding. Thereafter, Gramm-Rudman hung like a "brooding presence" over congressional decision making and the budgetary process. Unable to make the deficit meet the law in 1987, Congress and the president changed the law to meet the deficit (see Figure 18.3). But the 1990 recession threatened a huge deficit for FY 1991 that would again trigger even the relaxed Gramm-Rudman targets, so Congress and the president agreed on a new package of reforms and deficit targets in the Budget Enforcement Act of 1990.

Reforms of 1990: the Budget Enforcement Act. This law drew distinctions in spending that drastically altered the significance of the new

FIGURE 18.3   *Timetable for Gramm-Rudman Antideficit Law*

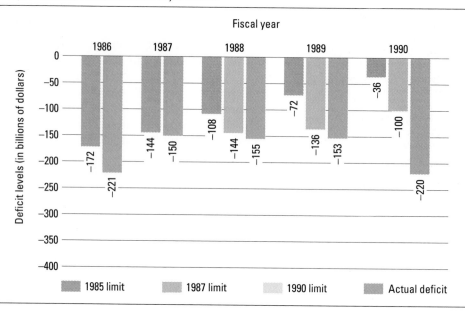

The 1985 antideficit law, known as Gramm-Rudman, aimed at reducing the national deficit by stages, resulting in a balanced budget by FY 1991—with targets depicted by the blue bars. The red bars indicate the actual budget deficits for the fiscal years since the law was passed. Realizing that the original target was too optimistic, Congress amended the antideficit law in 1987, extending the date for a balanced budget to FY 1993—with lower yearly targets (the green bars).

deficit targets. It defined **discretionary spending** as authorized expenditures from annual appropriations (such as the personnel budget for the military) and **mandatory spending** as expenditures required by previous commitments. Spending is mandatory for **entitlement** programs (such as social security and veterans' benefits) that provide benefits to individuals legally entitled to them (see Chapter 19). The law also establishes **pay-as-you-go** restrictions on mandatory spending and taxes. Under "PAYGO," any proposal to expand coverage of an entitlement program must be offset by other savings or a tax increase. Similarly, any tax cut must be offset by another tax increase or other savings.[18] The law also set limits, or "caps," on discretionary spending through 1993 in three categories—defense, domestic, and international programs—and it fixed total discretionary spending for 1994 and 1995.

By this new law, the president and Congress agreed in advance on overall expenditures across the major categories of discretionary spending. Because borrowing from one category to increase spending in another was not allowed, there was no conflict between the Republican president and the Democratic Congress over how much to spend on defense versus domestic programs in 1991. However, some Democrats chaffed at the cap on domestic spending, and it remains to be seen whether the pact struck in the Budget Enforcement Act will survive after the 1992 elections.

Significantly, the law removed most of the pressure to reduce the deficit to meet the Gramm-Rudman targets by linking them to the numbers agreed to in the caps on discretionary spending plus pay-as-you-go restrictions on mandatory spending and tax cuts. Under prior rules, any economic downturn that caused the government to spend more or to raise less revenue than expected might increase the deficit beyond the Gramm-Rudman target and trigger across-the-board cuts. But now these unexpected external events (including war and the increased costs of the

But the 1991 budget (which was supposed to have been balanced according to the original law) had a stratospheric deficit of over $300 billion. Congress again readjusted the deficit targets in 1990 (yellow bars) and made them less meaningful by not requiring automatic cuts if the targets were not reached. (Source: Congressional Quarterly Weekly Report, 9 February 1991, p. 337. Used with permission.)

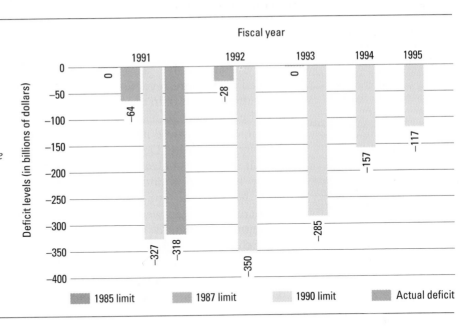

S&L bailout) are—like acts of God—regarded as "outside" the budgetary agreement, which requires only that everyone keep their part of the bargain on spending caps and pay-as-you-go restrictions.

If Congress fails to limit discretionary spending in any category to its cap in any year or violates pay-as-you-go restrictions, it will trigger a **sequestration**—an across-the-board spending cut in the overspent category or in nonexempt entitlement programs. These sequesters (cuts) would occur automatically fifteen days after Congress adjourns. Whether these new changes in the budget process will make it any more workable in the future remains to be seen. What does seem likely is that the new process will increase the power of the appropriations committees at the expense of the authorizing committees, who will have less latitude in spending, and the budget committees, who will find caps already set on overall spending in major categories.[19]

Tax Policies

So far, we have been concerned mainly with the spending side of the budget, for which appropriations must be enacted each year. The revenue side of the budget is provided by overall tax policy, which is designed to provide a continuous flow of income without annual legislation. On occasion, however, tax policy is significantly changed to accomplish one or more of several objectives:[20]

- To adjust overall revenue to meet budget outlays
- To make the tax burden more equitable for taxpayers
- To help control the economy by raising taxes (thus decreasing aggregate demand) or by lowering taxes (thus increasing demand)

The Reagan administration engineered a significant change in the nation's tax policies. In the first three years, personal income taxes were lowered by 23 percent, resulting in a total revenue loss of $500 *billion* dollars over the next five years.[21] According to supply-side economic theory, that massive tax cut should have stimulated the economy and yielded even more revenue than was lost—if not in the first year, then soon afterward. It didn't happen. Revenues lagged badly behind spending, and the deficit grew.

Still, Reagan would not agree to raise taxes, and few politicians dared mention a tax hike. Democratic presidential candidate Walter Mondale tried it in the 1984 election and was beaten badly. The Democratic leadership in Congress and many leading Republicans believed that taxes must be raised to cut the deficit, but no one was willing to propose an increase. Reagan went further. He urged Congress to enact sweeping tax reform that would (1) lower still further the rate for those in the highest income tax bracket, (2) reduce the number of tax brackets, (3) eliminate virtually all the tax loopholes through which many wealthy people avoided paying taxes, and (4) be *revenue neutral*, in the sense that it would bring in no more and no less revenue than the existing tax policy.

Tax Reform

Tax reform proposals usually are so heavily influenced by interest groups looking for special benefits that they end up working against their original purpose. However, the basic goals of Reagan's proposals were met with relatively few major changes, and in 1986 Congress passed one of the most sweeping tax reform laws in history. By eliminating many deductions, the new policy reclaimed a great deal of revenue that had been lost through tax loopholes to corporations and wealthy citizens. That revenue was supposed to pay for a general reduction in tax rates for individual citizens. By eliminating many tax brackets, the new tax policy approached the idea of a *flat tax*—one that requires everyone to pay at the same rate. A flat tax has the appeal of simplicity, but it violates the principle of **progressive taxation,** by which the rich pay proportionately higher taxes than the poor. The ability to pay has long been a standard of fair taxation, and governments can use progressive taxation to redistribute wealth and thus promote equality.

In general, the greater the number of tax brackets, the more progressive the tax can be. The old tax code included fourteen tax brackets, ranging from 11 percent to 50 percent. Under the 1986 law, there were two rates—15 and 28 percent. (Technically there were only two rates, but there was a perplexing "bubble" that set a 33 percent rate for some moderately high-income taxpayers. Few people understand how this bubble sneaked into the rate structure, and you can live without knowing.) The 1986 law did not become effective until 1988, when George Bush was campaigning for the presidency. Bush quickly allied himself with Reagan's tax policy and promised the Republican convention and the nation that he would tell Congress: "Read my lips: No new taxes." As president, however, he found that existing taxes did not produce enough revenue to

Revolt of the Yuppies

George Bush was burned by his signature issue—"no new taxes"—when the size of the national deficit forced him to recognize a need for what he called "tax revenue increases." These protesters, possibly Bush voters, had taken the president's no-taxes promise seriously.

control the deficit. By the spring of 1990, his pledge began to stick in his throat. On June 26, after fruitless budget negotiations with Congress, he admitted the need for "tax revenue increases" and reopened the issue of tax policy.

Many Republicans were furious with Bush for reneging on his promise, and key members in his party failed to support the new tax package that he negotiated with the Democratic leadership in a budget summit (see Chapter 12). When that plan failed in early October, Democratic leaders forced the president to accept their own hastily constructed deficit-reduction plan, which established a third tax rate of 31 percent for those with the highest incomes (see Figure 18.4)—and repealed the curious "bubble" in the old rate.

No one likes to pay taxes, so it is politically popular to attack taxation—which Reagan and Bush did with stunning success. But these Republican leaders may have created a problem for their party and for government. Initially, the American public was not worked up over taxes as much as Reagan was. When asked in 1984—the year Reagan won re-election over Mondale—which of five different economic problems they considered the worst, the public ranked federal income tax rates at the *bottom* of the list (only 5 percent of a national sample of registered voters chose tax rates as the worst problem). At the top of the list was the size of the national deficit (identified by 34 percent).[22] During the last decade, however, Reagan and Bush placed "high taxes" on the national agenda and worked up the electorate on the issue. By committing their party to low taxes as a first principle, these presidents have limited their options, rejecting a conservative "pay-as-you-go" philosophy in favor of a liberal "deficit spending" approach. Has the tax burden on Americans been heavy enough to justify their stand?

FIGURE 18.4   *Percent Changes in 1991 Federal Income Taxes*

President Bush backed a tax plan that came out of a 1990 budget summit with congressional negotiators. As shown here, that plan would have raised rates for everyone, but mostly for lower-income taxpayers. It was opposed by key Republicans (and many Democrats) in the House and was defeated. Then congressional Democrats passed their own plan, which cut rates for the poorest taxpayers and raised them for the wealthiest in 1991. Despite the rate changes, there is little change in the sources of government revenue between 1990 and 1991, although those with taxable incomes over $200,000 will share about 0.7 percent more of the total burden. (Source: Congressional Quarterly Weekly Report, 3 November 1990, p. 3715. Used with permission.)

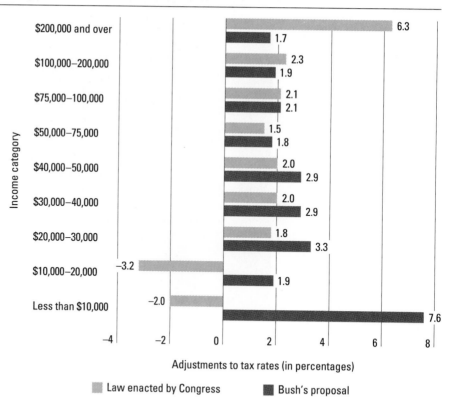

Comparing Tax Burdens

One way to compare tax burdens is to examine taxes over time in the same country; another is to compare taxes in different countries at the same time. By comparing taxes over time in the United States, we find that the tax burden of U.S. citizens has indeed been growing. For the average family, the percentage of income that goes to all federal, state, and local taxes doubled to 23 percent between 1953 and 1980. During the same period, the taxes of wealthy families increased by two-thirds, to 33 percent of their income.[23]

However, neither the federal government nor the federal income tax accounts for the bulk of that increase. First, national taxes as a percentage of the gross national product have changed very little over the last thirty years; it is the *state* and *local* tax burden that has doubled in size.[24] Second, the income tax has not been the major culprit in the increasing tax bite at the federal level; the proportion of federal budget receipts contributed by income tax has remained fairly constant since the end of World War II. The largest increases have come in social security taxes, which have risen steadily to pay for the government's largest single social welfare program, aid to the elderly (see Chapter 19).

Another way of comparing tax burdens is to examine tax rates in different countries. As you can see in Compared with What? 18.1, Ameri-

COMPARED WITH WHAT? 18.1

Tax Burdens in Twenty-Two Countries

All nations tax their citizens, but some nations impose a heavier tax burden than others. This graph compares tax burdens in 1987 as a percentage of gross domestic product (GDP), which is a country's GNP minus the value of goods produced outside the country. The percentages include national, state, and local taxes and social security contributions. By this measure, the U.S. government extracts less in taxes from its citizens than the governments of virtually all democratic nations. At the top of the list stands Sweden, well known as a social welfare state, which consumes nearly 60 percent of its gross domestic product in taxes.

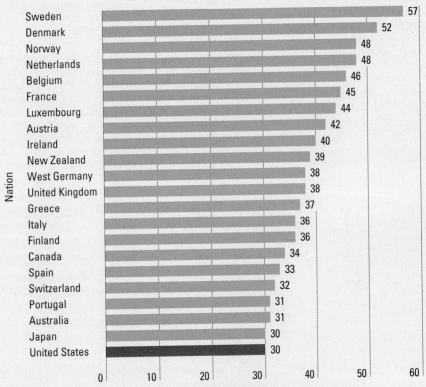

Tax revenues as percentage of GDP

Source: Bureau of the Census, *Statistical Abstract of the United States, 1990* (Washington, D.C.: U.S. Government Printing Office, 1990), p. 845.

cans' taxes are quite low compared with those in twenty-one other democratic nations: *Every* nation ranked above the United States. Despite talk about high taxes, the U.S. tax burden is not large compared with taxes in other democratic nations.

Spending Policies

The national government spends hundreds of billions of dollars every year. Where does the money go? Figure 18.5 shows the $1.4 trillion in outlays in President Bush's FY 1992 budget according to eighteen major budgetary functions. The largest amount (20 percent of the total budget) was earmarked for national defense. The social security outlay was nearly as large; the third largest was for interest on the accumulated national debt, which alone consumes nearly 15 percent of all government spending.

To understand current expenditures, it is a good idea to examine national expenditures over time (see Figure 18.6). The effect of World War II is clear: Spending for national defense rose sharply after 1940, peaked at about 90 percent of the budget in 1945, and fell to about 30 percent in peacetime. The percentage allocated to defense rose again in the early

FIGURE 18.5   *President Bush's FY 1992 Budget by Function*

Federal budget authorities and outlays are organized into twenty-one categories, three of which are mainly for bookkeeping purposes. This graph shows expected outlays for each of eighteen substantive functions in Bush's FY 1992 budget. The final budget differed somewhat from this distribution because Congress amended some of the president's spending proposals, but the proportions remained nearly the same. The pact agreed on by the president and Congress to deal with the 1991 budget deficit capped discretionary spending for domestic, defense, and international programs, so the presidential and congressional budgets were quite close in FY 1992. Note that "net interest," which is the amount paid on the national debt, is the third largest item. (Source: Congressional Quarterly Weekly Report, 9 February 1991, pp. 354–355. Used with permission.)

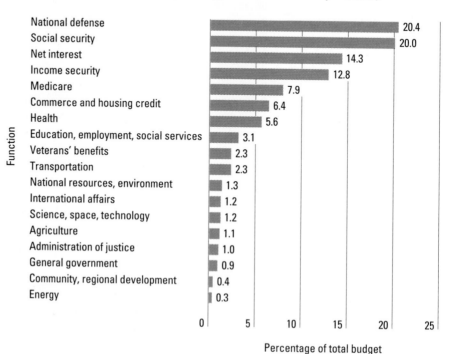

FIGURE **18.6** *National Government Outlays over Time*

This chart plots the percentages of the annual budget devoted to four major expense categories. It shows that significant changes have occurred in national spending since 1940. In the 1940s, spending for World War II consumed more than 80 percent of the national budget. Defense again accounted for most national expenditures during the Cold War of the 1950s. Since then, the military's share of expenditures has declined while payments to individuals (mostly in the form of social security benefits) have increased dramatically. Also, as the graph shows, the proportion of the budget paid in interest on the national debt has increased substantially since the 1970s. (Source: Office of Management and Budget, Budget of the United States Government, *Fiscal Year 1992 [Washington, D.C.: U.S. Government Printing Office, 1991], Part Seven, pp. 66–70.)*

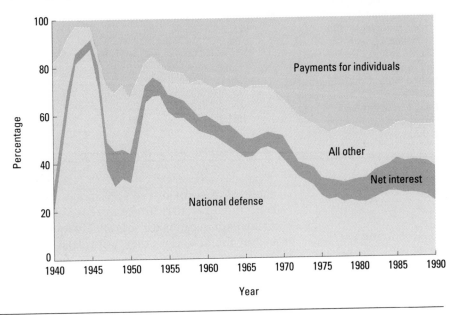

1950s, reflecting rearmament during the Cold War with the Soviet Union. Thereafter, the share of the budget devoted to defense decreased steadily (except for the bump during the Vietnam War in the late 1960s) until the trend was reversed by the Reagan administration in the 1980s. Under Bush, defense spending has turned down again.

Government payments to individuals consistently consumed less of the budget than national defense until 1971. Since then, payments to individuals have accounted for the largest portion of the national budget, and they have been increasing. Net interest payments also have increased substantially in recent years, reflecting the rapidly growing national debt. All other government outlays have been squeezed by pressure from payments for national defense, individuals, and interest on the national debt.

Because of continuing price inflation, we would expect government expenditures to increase steadily in dollar amounts. However, national spending has far outstripped inflation. Figure 18.7 graphs government receipts and outlays as a percentage of the GNP, which eliminates the effect of inflation. It shows that national spending has increased from

FIGURE 18.7 *Government Outlays and Receipts as a Percentage of the GNP*

We can see the growth of government spending—and the rising national debt—by plotting budget outlays and receipts against each other over time. In this graph, outlays and receipts are each expressed as a percentage of the GNP, to control for inflation and to demonstrate that both government spending and taxes have been taking a progressively larger share of the nation's productive output. (Source: Office of Management and Budget, Budget of the United States Government, Fiscal Year 1992 *[Washington, D.C.: U.S. Government Printing Office, 1990], Part Seven, p. 17.)*

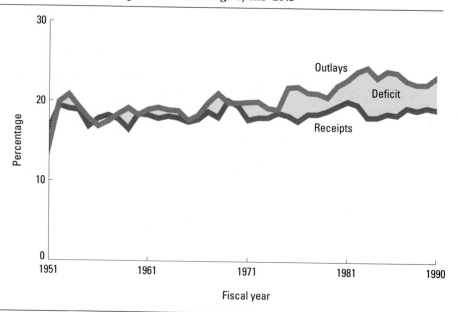

about 15 percent of the GNP soon after World War II to nearly 25 percent, most recently at the expense of the national deficit. There are two major explanations for this steady increase in government spending. One is bureaucratic; the other, political.

Incremental Budgeting . . .

The bureaucratic explanation for spending increases involves the concept of **incremental budgeting:** Bureaucrats, in compiling their budget funding requests for next year, ask for the amount they got this year plus some *increment* to fund new projects. Members of Congress pay little attention to the size of the agency's budget for the current year (the largest part of that budget), focusing instead on the extra money (the increment) requested for next year. As a result, few agencies are ever cut back, and spending continually goes up.

Incremental budgeting produces a sort of bureaucratic momentum that continually pushes up spending. Once an agency is established, it attracts a clientele that defends its existence and that supports the agency's requests for extra funds to do more year after year. However, the huge budget deficit has substantially checked the practice of incremental budgeting. For example, Bush's 1992 budget planned a cut of $15.3 billion for agriculture, and those who benefit from farm programs will do well just to reduce the size of the cut.

Caps on discretionary spending also interfere with incremental budgeting and force closer scrutiny of budgetary proposals by agencies and members of Congress alike. As a result, agencies are now more likely to engage in a form of analytical budgeting, in which existing programs are justified in terms of their effectiveness (see Chapter 13). Still, Bush will find it impossible to reduce government spending enough to balance the budget because politics has put most of the budget beyond his control.

. . . And Uncontrollable Spending

Certain spending programs are effectively immune to budget reductions because they have been (1) enacted into law, and (2) enshrined in politics. For example, social security legislation guarantees certain benefits to participants in the program when they retire from work. The same applies for other programs, among them, Medicare and veterans' benefits—which entitle citizens to certain payments. Because these payments have to be made under existing law, they represent **uncontrollable outlays.** In Bush's FY 1992 budget, about two-thirds of all budget outlays were uncontrollable or relatively uncontrollable—mainly payments to individuals under social security, Medicare, public assistance, interest on debt, and farm price supports. Most of the rest goes for defense, leaving about 15 percent in domestic discretionary spending for balancing the budget.

To be sure, Congress could change the laws to abolish entitlement payments, and it does modify them through the budget process. But politics argues against major reductions. The only major social program that escaped cutting during the Reagan administration was social security—the largest single domestic program and, according to many surveys, the most popular one. (Even Senator Gramm, coauthor of Gramm-Rudman, admitted that trying to cut spending for the elderly is "not winnable." His mother, in her eighties, told her son to "keep your mouth shut" when it came to that part of the budget.)

What spending cuts would be popular or even acceptable to the public? When voters in 1988 were asked how they felt about spending cuts in twelve different areas, a majority rejected any decrease in *any* of the domestic programs. In fact, clear majorities of both Republicans and Democrats wanted increases in spending in six areas—aid to the homeless, education, programs to fight AIDS, help for the poor, help for farmers, and cleaning up the environment.[25] A perplexed Congress, trying to reduce the budget deficit, faces a public that favors funding programs at even higher levels than those favored by most lawmakers.[26] Moreover, spending for the most expensive of these programs—social security and Medicare—is uncontrollable. Americans have grown accustomed to certain government benefits, but they do not like the idea of raising taxes to pay for them.

The largest *controllable* expenditure in the budget lies in the area of defense. Out of the twelve programs in the 1988 survey, the public proposed cuts only in defense and in the Strategic Defense Initiative (Star Wars), no doubt reflecting the easing of the Soviet threat. Bush's FY 1992 budget, which was prepared prior to the outbreak of the war with Iraq, contained the first cut in defense spending in twenty years, and the 1990 budget agreement guaranteed increases below the inflation rate through 1993.[27] Whether the war and its aftermath will alter the budget agreement and the public's support of cuts in the military remain to be seen.

Taxing, Spending, and Economic Equality

As noted in Chapter 1, the most controversial purpose of government is promoting equality, especially economic equality. Economic equality comes only at the expense of economic freedom, for it requires government action to redistribute wealth from the rich to the poor. One means of redistribution is government tax policy, especially the progressive income tax. The other instrument for reducing inequalities is government spending through welfare programs. The goal in either case is not to produce equality of outcome; it is to reduce inequalities by helping the poor.

The national government has levied an income tax every year since 1913, when the Sixteenth Amendment gave it the power to do so. From 1964 to 1981, people who reported taxable incomes of $100,000 or more paid a top tax rate of 70 percent (except during the Vietnam War), while those with lower incomes paid taxes at progressively lower rates (see Figure 18.8). About the same time, the government launched a War on Poverty through President Johnson's Great Society program. His programs and their successors are discussed at length in Chapter 19. For now, we look at the overall effect of government spending and tax policies on economic equality in America.

Government Effects on Economic Equality

We begin by asking whether government spending policies have any measurable impact on income inequality. The term **transfer payments** refers to government payments to individuals through social security, unemployment insurance, food stamps, and other programs, such as agricultural subsidies. Transfer payments need not always go to the poor. In fact, one problem with the farm program is that the wealthiest farmers have often received the largest subsidies.[28] Nevertheless, most researchers have determined that transfer payments have had a definite effect in reducing income inequality. A study of government policies from 1966 to 1985 found that families in the lowest tenth of the population in terms of income paid 33 percent of their income in federal, state, and local taxes, but they also received payments from all levels of government that almost equaled their earned income.[29] So the lowest-income group enjoyed a net benefit from government because of transfer payments. Another study for the period from 1979 to 1988 found that transfer payments nearly cut in half the percentage of families with children that were below the official poverty line.[30] In both studies, tax policies had little effect on the redistribution of income. From 1966 to 1985, ironically, families with the top 1 percent of income paid proportionately less of their income in taxes (about 28 percent).[31]

How can people in the lowest income group pay a higher percentage of their income in taxes than those in the very highest group? The answer has to do with the combination of national, state, and local tax policies. Only the national income tax is progressive, with rates rising as income rises. The national payroll tax, which funds social security and Medicare, is highly *regressive:* Its effective rate decreases as income increases beyond a certain point. Everyone pays social security at the same rate (6.2

FIGURE **18.8** *The Ups and Downs of Federal Tax Rates*

In 1913, the Sixteenth Amendment empowered the national government to collect taxes on income. Since then, the government has levied taxes on individual and corporate income and on capital gains realized by individuals and corporations from the sale of assets, such as stocks or real estate. This chart of the top tax rates shows that they have fluctuated wildly over time, from under 10 percent to over 90 percent. (They tend to be highest during periods of war.) During the Reagan administration, the maximum income tax rate fell to the lowest level since the Coolidge and Hoover administrations in the late 1920s and 1930s. The top rate increased slightly for 1991 to 31 percent as result of a law passed in 1990. (Sources: Wall Street Journal, *18 August 1986, p. 10. Reprinted by permission of the* Wall Street Journal, *© Dow Jones & Company, Inc., 1986. All rights reserved. Worldwide. Additional data from* Congressional Quarterly Weekly Report, *3 November 1990, pp. 3714–3715.)*

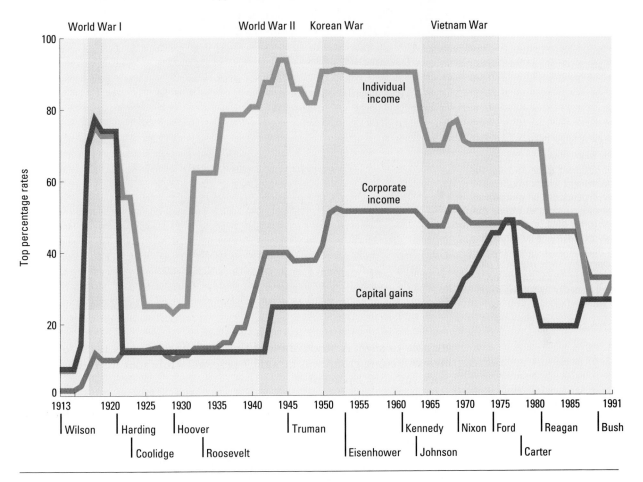

percent in 1991), but this tax is levied only up to a maximum wage ($53,400 annually in 1991). There is no tax at all on wages over that amount. So the effective rate of the social security tax is more for the lowest income group than for the very top group.

Most state and local sales taxes are equally regressive. Poor and rich usually pay the same flat rate on their purchases; but the poor spend almost everything they earn on purchases that are taxed, whereas the rich

Have a Nice Day

This unemployment office was not designed to be inviting; the government wants to discourage dependence on assistance. The office processes claims for assistance filed by people who become unemployed through no fault of their own. Under a cooperative state-national plan enacted in 1935, unemployment benefits vary from state to state.

are able to save. A study showed that the effective sales tax rate for the lowest income group was around 7 percent, while that for the top 1 percent was only 1 percent.[32]

In general, the nation's tax policies at all levels have historically favored not only the wealthy but also those who draw their income from capital rather than labor.[33] For example:

- The tax on income from the sale of real estate or stock (called *capital gains*) was typically less than the tax on income from salaries. (This was changed in the 1986 tax reform act, but, as described in Chapter 12, President Bush has pressed to restore more favorable treatment for capital gains.)

- The tax on *earned income* (salaries and wages) is withheld from paychecks by employers under national law; the tax on *unearned income* (interest and dividends) is not. Instead, the government depends on the good faith of investors to report all their unearned income.

- There is no federal tax at all on investments in certain securities, among them, municipal bonds.

Effects of Taxing and Spending Policies over Time

In 1966, at the beginning of President Johnson's Great Society programs, the poorest fifth of American families had 4.3 percent of the nation's income after taxes and transfer payments, while the richest fifth had 45.7 percent. In 1989, after many billions of dollars had been spent on social programs, the poorest fifth had only 5 percent of the nation's income, while the richest fifth had 44.1 percent (see Figure 18.9).[34] In short, there was little change in the distribution of income. (Much of the increased income of families in the lowest category came from about one-third more earners, mainly women, going to work.[35] So the extra income at the lower levels was largely earned, not redistributed from upper levels.)

The economic policies of the Reagan administration had more impact on the truly rich than on the 20 percent in the top income group, and its tax policy was key to their enjoyment. This is the conclusion of Kevin Phillips, a Republican conservative who devised the "southern strategy" that contributed to Richard Nixon's 1968 election. According to Phillips, in his book *The Politics of Rich and Poor*: "Most of the Reagan decade, to put it mildly, was a heyday for unearned income as rents, dividends,

F I G U R E   18.9 *Distribution of Family Income over Time*

During the last quarter-century, the 20 percent of U.S. families with the highest incomes received about 45 percent of all income, even after subtracting taxes and adding transfer payments. This distribution of income is one of the most unequal among Western nations. At the bottom end of the scale, the poorest 20 percent of families received 5 percent or less of total family income. Some evidence attributes the 1989 increases in the lower quintiles to additional family income from women going to work. (Sources: For the 1966 data, Joseph A. Pechman, Who Paid the Taxes, 1966–1985? *[Washington, D.C.: Brookings Institution, 1985], p. 74; for the 1989 data, Bureau of the Census, "Measuring the Effect of Benefits and Taxes on Income and Poverty: 1989,"* Current Population Reports, *Series P-60, No. 169-RD [September 1990], p. 5.)*

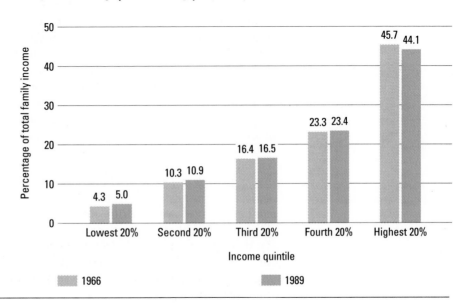

capital gains and interest gained relative to wages and salaries as a source of wealth and increasing economic inequality."[36] Phillips notes that the number of millionaires grew under the Reagan years from about 600,000 to 1.5 million. There were so many millionaires that *millionaire* no longer meant rich. The word *rich* was better suited to "decamillionaires"—those with at least $10 million—who increased from 38,000 to 100,000 by 1988. The very rich were those with $100 million, who tripled from 400 to 1,200. And the *truly* rich—the 13 billionaires in 1982—nearly quadrupled to 51 in 1988.[37] The approximately 20 percent inflation during this period could account for some of this growth, but the rich far outstripped the average family in income gains. While the average family actually *lost* about $1,500 in income between 1977 and 1988 after adjusting for inflation, the top 1 percent experienced nearly a 50 percent increase, from $270,053 to $404,566.[38] Phillips notes that these newly rich made their money in large part through deregulation of financial markets and speculative investments encouraged by the administration, and they were allowed to keep much of what they made by a large net reduction in overall federal tax rates during the period.[39]

In a capitalist system, some degree of inequality is inevitable. There may be some kind of limit to economic equality, and perhaps the United States has already reached it. If so, this would prevent government policies from equalizing income no matter what was tried. To find out, we should look to other democracies to see how much equality they have been able to sustain. A 1985 study of six other countries found that only in France is as much as 46 percent of total income received by the top fifth of the population. In Canada, Italy, West Germany, Britain, and Sweden that percentage runs from 42 down to 37 percent.[40] The comparison suggests that our society has measurably more economic inequality than others. The question is why?

Democracy and Equality

Although the United States is a democracy that prizes political equality for its citizens, its record in economic equality is not as good. In fact, its distribution of *wealth*—which includes not only income but ownership of savings, housing, automobiles, stocks, and so on—is strikingly unequal. According to the Census Bureau, the top 12 percent of American families control almost 40 percent of household wealth. Moreover, the distribution of wealth by ethnic groups is alarming. The typical white family—which has an annual income more than 1.7 times that of blacks and 1.5 times that of Hispanics—has more than ten times the accumulated wealth of black families and nearly eight times the wealth of Hispanic families.[41] If democracy means government "by the people," why are all the people not sharing more equally in the nation's wealth? If one of the purposes of government is to promote equality, why are government policies not working that way?

One scholar theorizes that interest group activity in a pluralist democracy distorts government's efforts to promote equality. His analysis of pluralism sees "corporations and organized groups with an upper-income slant as exerting political power over and above the formal one-man–

one-vote standard of democracy."[42] As you learned in Chapters 10 and 17, the pluralist model of democracy rewards those groups that are well organized and well funded.

An example: As already noted, federal income tax is withheld by law from earned income (salaries and wages), not from unearned income (interest and dividends). Early in his first term, President Reagan surprised the financial world by proposing to withhold taxes from unearned income as part of his overall economic plan, and Congress made the plan law in the summer of 1982. Financial institutions were given a year to devise procedures for withholding 10 percent of dividend and interest payments for income tax (the withholding was to begin July 1, 1983). Led by the American Bankers' Association, the banking interests urged their depositors to write legislators protesting the law; they even handed out sample letters that could be sent to members of Congress.

Some people, who apparently had never declared their bank interest as income, indignantly protested this "new" tax. Washington was flooded with mail stimulated by local banks and savings and loan associations. Congress had to hire temporary workers to answer letters from angry high-income taxpayers (who are also high-turnout voters). The president and many members of Congress were furious at the American Bankers' Association, which spent more than $300,000 in its effort to have the law repealed. Democratic Representative Thomas J. Downey of New York said that if withholding was repealed, "We send a signal that the Congress of the United States is a group of patsies to every well-organized group in America."[43] But Congress did back down, and withholding from unearned income was repealed only weeks before it was to go into effect.

What would happen if federal tax policy were determined according to principles of majoritarian rather than pluralist democracy? Perhaps not much—if public opinion is any guide. The people of the United States are not eager to redistribute wealth by increasing the only major progressive tax, the income tax. If federal taxes must be raised, Americans strongly favor a national sales tax over increased income taxes.[44] But a sales tax is a flat tax, paid by rich and poor at the same rate; it would have a regressive effect on income distribution, promoting inequality not equality. The public also prefers a weekly $10 million national lottery to an increase in the income tax.[45] Because the poor are willing to chance more of their income on winning a fortune through lotteries than are rich people, lotteries (run by twenty-six states in 1988) also contribute to income inequality through a regressive revenue system.[46]

The newest tax on the horizon is a type of national retail sales tax called the value-added tax (VAT), which is applied to the value added to a product at each stage of production and distribution. The VAT is levied by all countries in the European Economic Community, and—with the potential of a 5 percent VAT raising about $100 billion annually in revenue—it is certain to be a subject of debate in the United States.[47] But if a VAT is adopted in place of raising the income tax rate, it, like all sales taxes, will be a regressive tax.

Majoritarians might argue that most Americans fail to understand the inequities of the federal tax system. However, majoritarians *cannot* argue that the public demands "fairer" tax rates that take from richer citizens to help poorer ones. If it did, the lowest-income families might receive a greater share of the national income than they do. Instead, economic policy is determined mainly through a complex process of pluralist politics that preserves nearly half the national income in the hands of the wealthiest 20 percent of families.

Summary

Laissez-faire economics holds that the government should keep its hands off the economy. Keynesian theory holds that government should take an active role in dealing with inflation and unemployment, using fiscal and monetary policies to produce desired levels of aggregate demand. Monetarists believe fiscal policies are unreliable, opting instead to use the money supply to control aggregate demand. Supply-side economists, who had an enormous influence on economic policy during the Reagan administration, focus on controlling the supply of goods and services rather than the demand for them.

In 1921, Congress thrust the responsibility for the budget on the president. After World War II, it tried unsuccessfully to regain control of the process. Later, Congress managed to restructure the process under House and Senate Budget Committees. The new process worked well until it confronted the huge budget deficits in the 1980s.

Because so much of the budget involves military spending and uncontrollable payments to individuals, it is virtually impossible to balance the budget by reducing what remains—mainly spending for nonentitlement domestic programs. Unwilling to accept responsibility for a tax increase, Congress accepted the Gramm-Rudman antideficit law in 1985. Under that law, deficits were to be reduced in stages, through automatic across-the-board cuts, if necessary, until the budget was balanced by FY 1991. The deficit problem proved so intractable that Congress had to amend the law in 1987 to extend the deadline to 1993. Although President Bush promised "no new taxes" when he was campaigning for office, he had to admit the need for revenue increases to cut the deficit and was forced to accept the Budget Enforcement Act of 1990, which modified the budget procedure and made it easier to meet the Gramm-Rudman targets.

That act also amended the sweeping tax reform of 1986, which had eliminated tax loopholes, and drastically reduced the number of tax brackets. The new law added a third bracket at 31 percent, which was much lower than the top rate before 1986. But even with the heavily progressive tax rates of the past, the federal tax system did little to redistribute income. Government transfer payments to individuals have helped reduce income inequalities, however. Nevertheless, the distribution of income is less equal in the United States than in most major Western nations.

Pluralist democracy as practiced in the United States has allowed well-organized, well-financed interest groups to manipulate tax and spending policies to their benefit. The result is that a larger and poorer segment of society is paying the price.

KEY TERMS

economic depression
inflation
business cycle
aggregate demand
productive capacity
gross national
   product (GNP)
Keynesian theory
fiscal policies
monetary policies
deficit financing
Council of Economic
   Advisers (CEA)
monetarists
Federal Reserve System
supply-side economics
fiscal year (FY)
budget authority
budget outlays
receipts

Office of Management
   and Budget (OMB)
tax committees
authorization
   committees
appropriations
   committees
budget committees
Congressional Budget
   Office (CBO)
Gramm-Rudman
discretionary spending
mandatory spending
entitlement
pay-as-you-go
sequestration
progressive taxation
incremental budgeting
uncontrollable outlay
transfer payment

SELECTED READINGS

Levy, Frank. *Dollars and Dreams: The Changing American Income Distribution.* New York: Russell Sage Foundation, 1987. Ties government economic policies to various social and economic trends. Sees an increasingly unequal distribution of chances to purchase the middle-class dream.

Mishel, Lawrence, and David M. Frankel. *The State of Working America, 1990–91 Edition.* Washington, D.C.: Economic Policy Institute, 1990. A statistical cafeteria of information on income inequal-ity, unemployment, and poverty; also contains some useful cross-national comparisons.

Pechman, Joseph A., ed. *World Tax Reform: A Progress Report.* Washington, D.C.: Brookings Institution, 1988. A very readable account of the impact of the U.S. experience with tax reform on tax policies in other countries.

Phillips, Kevin. *The Politics of Rich and Poor: Wealth and the American Electorate in the Reagan Aftermath.* New York: Random House, 1990. A serious indictment of the economic policies of the Reagan administration from an unlikely source, a conservative Republican who outlined the victorious "southern strategy" for Richard Nixon in 1968.

Rubin, Irene S. *The Politics of Public Budgeting: Getting and Spending, Borrowing and Balancing.* Chatham, N.J.: Chatham House, 1990. Offers a comprehensive overview of budget politics and provides valuable case studies and examples that give life to the budget process.

Savage, James D. *Balanced Budgets and American Politics.* Ithaca, N.Y.: Cornell University Press, 1988. Views the concept of a balanced budget as an organizing principle or symbol in the debate over the makeup of national spending, the direction of fiscal policy, and government's role in the economy.

White, Joseph, and Aaron Wildavsky. *The Deficit and the Public Interest: Search for Responsible Budgeting in the 1980s.* Berkeley: University of California Press, 1989. Describes an elaborate "Madisonian," or pluralist, budget system, in which everyone's point of view has merit and in which the deficit has become a political weapon, paralyzing our political system.

19 DOMESTIC POLICY

TWELVE-YEAR-OLD LAFEYETTE Rivers regularly witnesses scenes of brutality. He lives in the Henry Horner Homes public housing project, a seven-block stretch of red-brick apartment buildings on Chicago's blighted West Side. During one recent summer, Henry Horner averaged one beating, shooting, or stabbing every three days. Even so, Henry Horner is far from the worst of Chicago's housing projects.

Lafeyette lives with his mother, three brothers, and two sisters in a ground-floor apartment. It has the trappings of a fortress—dirty cinder-block walls, iron grilles over the windows. The family talks about moving, but that's not a likely prospect, given the $837 a month his mother receives in public assistance.[1]

More than 5 million poor, inner-city children lead lives similar to Lafeyette's. Many youngsters routinely exposed to violence suffer nightmares, depression, and personality disorders. Some withdraw and give up hope; others become more aggressive. Safety and security have vanished from many of these inner-city communities, where crime and violence provide stark contrast to the accepted order elsewhere.

Physical safety and psychological security are the preconditions for healthy children. Good schools, accessible medical care, and lavish libraries are irrelevant to children who fear for their lives when they set foot on their own sidewalks. Somehow, in a land of promise and opportunity, countless Americans are living in an abyss of unimaginable urban violence, squalor, and decay.[2] Although America is one of the freest and richest countries in the world, Lafeyette Rivers, his peers, and his family take little comfort from its liberties and wealth. Government action helped generate this contradiction and government action aims to correct it. We call this kind of government action *public policy:* a general plan of action adopted by government to solve a social problem, counter a threat, or make use of an opportunity.

The policymaking process in general was examined in Chapter 17; in this chapter we look at specific public policies. We begin our inquiry into domestic policy by discussing policies that protect Americans from disease and policies that prohibit the sale, distribution, and use of certain drugs. Then we analyze policies that provide social insurance and public assistance. (Policies that promote disadvantaged groups through affirmative action programs were discussed in Chapter 16.) Our inquiry is guided by some key questions: What are the origins and politics of specific policies? What are the effects of those policies once they are implemented? Why do some policies succeed while others fail? Finally, do disagreements over values underlie disagreements over policy?

Public policies are as various as freight cars passing across a road: Their numbers sometimes seem endless to the person eager to get under way. With the wide range of policies worth exploring, you may be wondering why we spend much of the chapter discussing social insurance and public assistance. There are three reasons why these policies get special consideration. First, government expenditures in these areas represent nearly half of the national budget and one-tenth of our gross national product (the total market value of all the goods and services produced in this country during a year).[3] All citizens ought to know how and why their resources are allocated. Regrettably, the public has limited and distorted knowledge about national government spending. For example, only one in four Americans knows that government spending for social security rivals spending for national defense.[4] Second, one goal of social insurance and public assistance policies is to alleviate some of the consequences of economic inequality. Nevertheless, poverty remains a fixture of American life, and we must try to understand why. Third, these areas pose some vexing problems involving the conflicts between freedom and order, and freedom and equality.

We concentrate in this chapter on policies that stem in large measure from the authority of the national government to tax and spend for the general welfare, but it is important to recognize that state and local governments play a vital role in shaping and directing the policies that emanate from Washington. For example, the national government sets standards for the allocation of welfare benefits, but states may impose stricter standards for recipients—and some of them do.[5]

We begin with a discussion of two public policy areas: the protection of health and the prohibition of controlled substances. Americans disagree over public policies in these areas because they disagree over the need for government action, the goals the government should have, and the means the government should use to fulfill those goals. We will focus on some of these disagreements as a means of understanding the conflicting values that underlie them.

Policies That Protect: AIDS

Acquired Immune Deficiency Syndrome (AIDS) kills. According to national government researchers, 100,000 Americans died of AIDS between 1981 (when the disease was first officially recognized) and 1990. As many as 215,000 more will die between 1991 and 1994. AIDS is now the second leading cause of death among men between the ages of twenty-five and forty.[6] (Accidents remain the leading cause of death in this age group.) AIDS now rivals cancer as the nation's most feared disease, and many Americans believe that everyone is susceptible to it.[7] Predictably, Americans regard AIDS as the nation's "number one" health problem.[8]

Estimates vary on the spread of AIDS through the population, but one fact is certain: Most of the men, women, and children who are afflicted will die from the opportunistic infections that ravage AIDS victims. So far, most victims are either intravenous drug users or male homosexuals. There is a real possibility, however, that the disease will spread widely through the non-drug-using heterosexual population. Since the symptoms of AIDS may take seven years or more to appear, public health officials at all government levels fear that the worst is yet to come. Some of the most tragic victims of AIDS are the babies who acquire the virus from their mothers before birth. Most of these children live only a couple of years.

In 1990, the national government spent $2.9 billion on AIDS research, treatment, prevention, and income-support programs.[9] By 1992, the na-

A Moving Memorial

Each 3-by-6-foot panel of the AIDS quilt was stitched in memory of a life lost to AIDS. The entire quilt weighs 14 tons, and if the more than 12,000 panels from 22 countries were placed end to end, they would stretch four miles. Yet the quilt represents only a small fraction of those who will die of AIDS, for which there is now no cure. Organizers hope the traveling displays of portions of the quilt help raise the public's awareness of the nature and scope of the disease.

tional government plans to spend $3.5 billion on such programs. What, besides research, should the government do to stop the spread of AIDS? What public policies will be both effective and widely accepted?

Protection Through Education

Public health officials are fairly certain that HIV, the AIDS-causing virus, is spread only by the exchange of body fluids—blood or semen. In order to try to stem the spread of AIDS, the Public Health Service (the national government agency charged with public health concerns) in 1986 mounted a national campaign to educate children and young adults about the sexual practices that increase the risk of AIDS transmission. This campaign infuriated many citizens, who believed that instruction about "safe sex" infringes on a parent's freedom to guide a child's sexual education.

Some public health officials at state and local levels advocate the distribution of free condoms as a simple and relatively effective way to lessen the spread of AIDS. However, some Americans believe the distribution of free condoms and the teaching of "safe sex" in classes encourage sexual activity and undercut the moral guidance offered by parents.

Opponents of the classes-and-condoms approach maintain that schools should focus on education in the narrow sense of academic knowledge. Sex education, if unavoidable, should focus on sexual abstinence. Advocates of the educational campaign maintain that students are already sexually active and that appeals to sexual abstinence is like medicine after death: It certainly can't harm the patient, but it will surely do no good.

The evidence on the effects of sex counseling in high schools remains inconclusive. AIDS has such a long latency period that reduced rates of infection resulting from early condom use will not be known for years, if at all. A few studies report a lower incidence of teen pregnancy associated with condoms and safe-sex classes, but other studies report earlier initiation of sexual intercourse in schools where safe-sex classes are taught. (The avoidance of teen pregnancy may be viewed as a side benefit of the fight against the spread of AIDS.) The competing policies pose difficult choices: parental freedom to direct moral and personal development without government intervention, or government-imposed intervention to prevent the spread of a dreaded disease.[10]

Testing and Protection

Another way government can intervene in the lives of its citizens is to require HIV testing. A majority of Americans support this idea. Those favoring testing argue that it would assist health authorities in finding and notifying the sexual and needle-sharing partners of individuals who test positive for the virus. Since the stigma attached to the disease and the behaviors associated with it (homosexuality and intravenous drug use) reduce candor and confession, advocates of mandatory testing maintain that government has an obligation to inform persons at risk if the infected person is unlikely to do so. Almost half the states now require that physicians report the names of people who are HIV-positive to public health agencies, which may try to trace those partners who are at risk.

However, mandatory testing and name reporting may deter infected individuals from seeking care. Once their identities become known, infected persons risk discrimination from their employers, who may be unsympathetic to their plight and irrationally fearful of the spread of the disease in the workplace. Discrimination may extend to housing, where irrational fears may generate eviction notices, and to health insurance carriers, who might be unwilling to bear the high costs associated with AIDS treatment.

Public policy on AIDS generates controversy because it forces us to make difficult choices between order and freedom. Mandatory testing and reporting are adopted as means of preserving social order by curtailing the spread of the infection. But mandatory testing and reporting also invade the privacy of infected persons and may fuel discrimination against them. The freedom of AIDS victims may therefore be sacrificed for the good of the public health.

Government AIDS policy aims to protect. Let us consider government's policy against illegal drugs, which aims to prohibit traffic and trade in addictive substances.

Policies That Prohibit: Illegal Drugs

A growing number of Americans identify illegal drug use as the nation's most serious problem, outdistancing the problems of AIDS, homelessness, poverty, and the federal budget deficit. In a 1989 poll, 44 percent viewed the use of illegal drugs as the major problem facing the country—more than double the number who identified drugs as the major problem in 1988.[11]

Most Americans oppose the use of drugs such as cocaine, heroin, and marijuana. Marijuana use once had some degree of public acceptance, but that acceptance has declined sharply, from 20 percent in 1978 to only 8 percent in 1988.[12] A 1990 Gallup Poll, in fact, reported that three-quarters of young adults (ages sixteen through twenty-four) opposed the legalization of marijuana.[13]

Preliminary evidence from a variety of sources suggests that casual use of all drugs has started to decline; the number of weekly cocaine users has also dropped. By all accounts, say the experts, the drug crisis among the middle class has begun to ebb. Despite strong sanctions, however, drug abuse continues among the inner-city poor.[14] One study estimates that Americans spend between $15 and $20 billion a year on cocaine alone. A recent survey revealed that 1.5 million Americans use cocaine and crack cocaine at least once a month and that marijuana and hashish, with 12 million monthly users, are still the nation's most popular illegal "highs"[15] (see Feature 19.1). Although the government prohibits the sale and possession of these drugs, and the penalties for breaking the laws concerning drug use can be severe, the government's drug policy has been largely ineffective. Given this country's history with drug use and abuse, this ineffectiveness should not be surprising.

Historical Perspective

This is not the first time policymakers have waged war on illegal drugs.[16] In fact, this is the nation's *second* assault on the drug epidemic. Cocaine was first isolated from the coca plant in 1860 and quickly became a component of popular elixirs. American physicians were early enthusiasts, prescribing cocaine to cure Americans' widespread addiction to opiates (like morphine) and alcohol. Cocaine even became the official remedy of the American Hay Fever Assocation due to its ability to drain the sinuses and shrink irritated mucous membranes.

By 1900, cocaine addiction was becoming widespread. States adopted laws requiring a doctor's prescription for cocaine, ending the practice of over-the-counter cocaine sales, but the national government did not regulate drugs until 1906, when Congress passed the Pure Food and Drug Act. This act required manufacturers to list addictive ingredients on the labels of all patent medicines shipped in interstate commerce. Following its passage, sales of drug-laced medicines dropped by one-third. In addition, as the older, medically addicted users and their opiate- and cocaine-prescribing physicians died off, the practice of doctors prescribing cocaine for their patients declined. Cocaine consumption dropped steadily, although it never disappeared completely, especially in urban areas.

FEATURE 19.1   *American Drug Users and Abusers*

A huge number of Americans use drugs, including the legally sanctioned drugs of nicotine and alcohol.

Type of Drug	Number of Americans at a Particular Level of Involvement
cigarettes	57 million are hooked.
alcohol	18 million abuse it.
cocaine	21 million have tried it at least once.
crack	More than one million are addicted.
marijuana	7 million smoke it at least once a week.
heroin	1 million are addicted.
tranquilizers	10 million abuse them.
hallucinogens	1 million use them.

The economic cost of this drug habit is staggering. One estimate calculated the cost in health care, crime, lost productivity, forfeited education, and property destruction as more than $300 billion in 1989; it is likely to reach $1 trillion by the mid-1990s.

Source: Joseph A. Califano, "Drug War: Fool's Errand No. 3," *New York Times*, 8 December 1989, p. 31. Copyright © 1989 by The New York Times Company. Reprinted by permission.

As cocaine waned in fashion, however, other drugs arose as substitutes. Opium smoking lingered, as did alcohol addiction. Urban drug addicts switched to morphine and then to the more powerful morphine derivative, heroin. By 1910, most drug users were addicted to heroin, and most were concentrated in New York.

Many states passed narcotics control legislation. In 1914, for example, New York enacted its first law limiting the distribution of habit-forming drugs like heroin. As a result, the street price for an ounce of heroin rose from $6.50 to $100. Meanwhile, the underworld discovered that heroin was profitable—strongly addictive and easy to smuggle. Within a few years, heroin use began to spread beyond New York.

Drug policy shifted as addiction spread. Initially, government was tolerant toward addicts and their addiction. However, that approach waned with the spread of heroin and the involvement of organized crime in the distribution and sale of illegal drugs. In the 1920s, government policy switched to the attempt to eliminate the drug problem entirely. Government studies cited false or misleading information inflating the number of addicts to well over a million; in fact, the number was probably less than 300,000. This exaggeration confirmed the popular view that drug addiction was epidemic. By 1930, public revulsion to illegal drug use was widespread. Every state had comprehensive drug education programs whose aim was to impress upon young minds the evils of drug use.

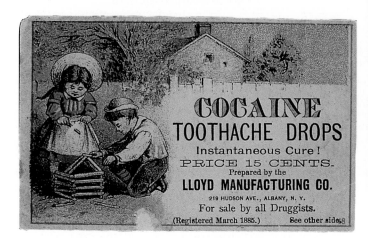

Drugs: An Old Story

Addictive substances have long been part of American life. Cocaine was once an ingredient in over-the-counter medication, as this label from 1888 indicates (left). Before the advent of antibiotics, the reduction of symptomatic pain was often the only treatment available. Later, inaccurate information helped shape public opinion about another drug. In 1938, this ad was part of a national campaign designed to convince Americans that marijuana use leads to insanity and criminal behavior (right).

The Great Depression nearly eliminated these drug education programs. At about the same time, national policymakers took the position that any discussion of drug abuse would only generate interest in drug use. For almost two generations, this government-sponsored campaign of silence contributed to the near total ignorance of illicit drugs. When government did disseminate information, it was often exaggerated. In 1937, for example, the FBI labeled marijuana the "killer weed" and the "assassin of youth." This policy of overstatement led to lurid exploitation films such as the 1938 classic *Reefer Madness*. The hyperbole backfired in the 1960s, however, as young men and women discovered that pot smoking did not lead to madness, criminality, or prostitution. The government policy of purposeful distortion tainted legitimate assertions of the harmful effects of more potent and addictive drugs, such as cocaine and heroin.

Markets and Controls

Today's market in illegal drugs, like other markets, exists because of supply and demand. In theory, the elimination of the drug supply would eliminate the market, but efforts aimed at the supply side have been notably unsuccessful. Why? One partial explanation comes from a simple observation: Drug trafficking, despite the risks, is very lucrative. It can be a short cut to wealth and, in some communities, a quick way to gain status. Penalties such as long prison terms do not act as sufficient deterrents.

The national government has also attempted to constrict or eliminate the supply and distribution network that keeps America awash in narcotics. A current plan involves trying to draw drug-producing or drug-trafficking nations into accord with U.S. drug policy. Under this plan, the president must certify whether twenty-four nations identified by Congress as major drug producers or transit points are cooperating with American drug-control efforts. If the president fails to certify a country, foreign aid and other financial assistance sent to that country are reduced substantially. The president can push for tougher sanctions, including trade embargoes, against particularly recalcitrant countries. So far, however, these sanctions have not dented the supply of illegal drugs entering the United States.

Government drug policy calls for the use of military force in addition to foreign aid. For example, in Colombia, Peru, and Bolivia, the United States has agreed to fund programs aimed at substituting crops for coca, promote more Western investment in the region, and crack down on U.S. exports (like guns and chemicals) that are essential in the drug trade. In return, the United States will send military advisers and equipment to assist in local drug-busting operations. Closer to home, the National Guard (military reserve units controlled by each state and equipped by the national government) has assisted in border patrols and customs inspections.[17]

Imposing these controls on the drug market creates costs that government must bear. In 1990, the national government spent nearly $9 billion, most of it on law enforcement. Meanwhile, the states spent at least half that amount on local antidrug efforts.[18] Despite all this money and an increased arrest rate, however, the government is not winning the drug war by stemming the supply of drugs.

Testing and Prohibition

If government policies have been unsuccessful in eliminating the supply of drugs, perhaps government should concentrate on reducing or eliminating the demand for drugs. Consider the policy of mandatory drug testing for certain national government employees begun by the Reagan administration and continued under President Bush.

The national government employs thousands of individuals in the area of drug enforcement. Proponents of drug testing for those employees argue that the government has a strong interest in ensuring that drug enforcement officials are not drug users themselves. Under the policy, if a urinalysis of an employee shows traces of an illegal drug, he or she is required to undergo counseling. Workers who refuse to be tested can be dismissed.

Polls continue to report that an overwhelming majority of Americans are willing to take drug tests. In a massive 1989 survey of college freshmen, nearly 8 in 10 favored mandatory drug testing in the workplace.[19] Opponents of mandatory drug testing argue, however, that testing would not be based on "reasonable suspicion" of drug use, that it would therefore interfere with personal liberty or privacy. Such testing, remarked one vocal opponent, would be "a comic exercise in Ty-D-Bol justice," flushing freedom in the process.[20]

Values and Policies

Currently, elected policymakers find themselves in rare agreement on how to deal with the drug issue. President Bush, his Cabinet, and the Congress aim to wage war on illegal drugs through strict prohibition, energetic enforcement, and harsher punishments against sellers and users. Will this policy of strict prohibition achieve victory in our second drug war even though it has not worked so far? A few Americans believe that it will not. They propose a policy of legalization, saying that taxing and regulating drug sales would be more successful in controlling drug use than prohibition. They assert that the money saved from futile attempts at prohibition could be more effectively spent on education, prevention, and treatment.

Legalization advocates hold to four fundamental, and sometimes controversial, views. First, they maintain that illicit drugs should be treated as a health issue, not a crime issue. As Feature 19.1 illustrated, legal drugs, like alcohol and nicotine, are as much a problem as illegal drugs. The government estimates that 8 percent of the population are frequent drinkers (twenty or more days per month), and 5 percent are heavy drinkers (five or more drinks on five or more occasions per month). More alarming still, 16 percent of the population smoke at least one pack of cigarettes a day.[21] The social and economic costs of these legal addictions

Getting High, Reaching Bottom

Crack dens like this one are facts of life in urban America. Although seizures of and arrests for cocaine and heroin are increasing, their street price is declining and their use is widespread. Despite frightening statistics, the national government has declared it is committed to the goal of a drug-free America by 1995.

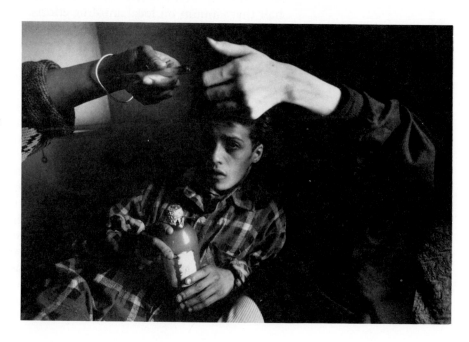

are no less serious than those resulting from illegal addictions. Addiction is the problem, and it will not be eradicated by executing drug lords and hiring more cops.

Second, advocates of legalization believe that the drug war is unwinnable. Addictive drugs are not new to American society; their existence for well over 100 years suggests that the problem is chronic. Moreover, our experiment in the 1920s with alcohol prohibition proved to be an utter failure. The same destiny awaits strict drug prohibition. Third, a policy that makes drugs illegal only creates a black market, driving prices—and drug-dealer profits—sky-high. No wonder there are so many drug entrepreneurs.

Finally, advocates of legalization maintain that legalization with strict government regulation will have little or no effect on drug use. They maintain that in areas already saturated with illegal drugs, legalization is unlikely to increase availability. And even if legalization produces a few more abusers, the cost of helping all addicts would still be far less than the cost of today's drug war.[22]

The debate over legalization sometimes erupts into a clash of moral positions. Opponents claim that legalization of hard drugs like cocaine and heroin is simply immoral. Legalizers argue that alcohol use is no different than hard drug use; tolerating one but not the other is hypocritical. The gulf between these two positions is still enormous, and legalization remains an unthinkable alternative to most Americans.[23]

The choice between drug prohibition and legalization is easy for most Americans; the majority prefers order, while few choose freedom on this issue. Most Americans continue to believe that the war on drugs will eventually end in victory, provided government supplies adequate resources and demonstrates ample resolve. Some preliminary evidence does, in fact, point to a few successes, especially among the middle class. Nevertheless, a few Americans steadfastly maintain that the current drug war is being fought against impossible odds, and legalization is inevitable.

Although most Americans agree that illicit drugs are a serious problem that warrants government action, disagreement arises when the means selected to address the problem generates value conflicts or proves ineffective. Questionable or ineffective means have stirred debates over other large domestic policy programs as well, including those designed to provide income, health, and welfare benefits to citizens.

Government Policies and Individual Welfare

The most controversial purpose of government is to promote social and economic equality among its citizens. To do so may conflict with the freedom of some citizens, for it requires government action to redistribute income from rich to poor. This choice between freedom and equality constitutes the modern dilemma of government; it has been at the center of many of the major conflicts in U.S. public policy since World War II. On one hand, most Americans believe that government should help the needy. On the other hand, they do not want to sacrifice their own standard of living to provide government handouts to those whom they may perceive as shiftless and lazy.

The Growth of the American Welfare State

At one time, governments confined their activities to the minimal protection of people and property—to ensuring security and order. Now, however, almost every modern nation may be characterized as a **welfare state,** a concept that stresses government's function as the provider and protector of individual well-being through economic and social programs. **Social welfare** encompasses government programs that are developed to provide the necessary minimum living standards for all citizens. Income for the elderly, health care, subsidized housing, and nutrition are among the concerns addressed by government social welfare programs.

The recent history of U.S. government support for social welfare policies is illustrated in Figure 19.1. In 1960, 26 cents of every dollar of national spending went to payments for individuals. In 1970, 33 cents of every dollar went to payments for individuals. And, in 1980, slightly less than half of each dollar went to individuals. By 1985, spending for individuals fell off a few percentage points, but by 1987, it had returned to the 1980 level. The government estimates that in 1991, half the national spending will go to individuals. The national government clearly remains a provider of social welfare, despite changes in administrations.

The origins of social welfare as government policy go back to the Industrial Revolution, when the mechanization of production resulted in a shift from home manufacturing to large-scale factory production. As more and more people worked for wages, many more were subjected to the dreadful consequences of a loss of employment due to sickness, injury, old age, or economic conditions. The sick, the disabled, and the

FIGURE 19.1   *Government Payments to Individuals, 1960–1991*

The national government spends a large portion of its budget on payments to individuals (for example, on social security). This spending has nearly doubled since 1960. (Source: Historical Tables, Budget of the United States Government, FY 1991, *Table 11.1.)*

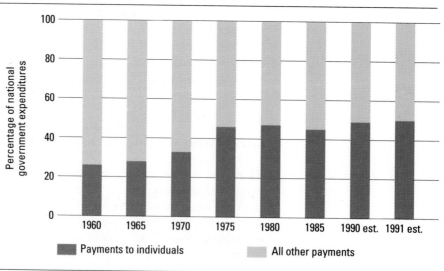

aged were tended, for the most part, by families and charities. The poor were confined to poorhouses or almshouses, which were little more than shacks that warehoused the impoverished. In the eighteenth and nineteenth centuries, poverty was viewed as a disgrace. Poor people were seen as lazy and incompetent. (Indeed, many Americans still hold this view.) The circumstances of relief were purposely made disagreeable to discourage dependence on outside assistance.

America today is far from being a welfare state in the same sense that Sweden or Great Britain is; those nations provide many more medical, educational, and unemployment benefits to their citizens. However, the United States does have several social welfare functions. To understand social welfare policies in the United States, you must first understand the significance of a major event—the Great Depression—and the two presidential plans that extended the scope of government—the New Deal and the Great Society.

The Great Depression. Throughout its history, the U.S. economy has experienced alternating good times and hard times, generally referred to as *business cycles* (see Chapter 18, page 648). The **Great Depression** was,

A Human Tragedy

The Great Depression made millions of Americans idle. By 1933, when President Herbert Hoover left office, about one-fourth of the labor force was out of work. The few available jobs attracted long lines of able-bodied workers.

by far, the longest and deepest setback that the American economy has ever experienced. It began with the stock market crash of 1929 (on October 29, a day known as Black Tuesday) and did not end until the start of World War II. By 1932, one out of every four U.S. workers was unemployed, and millions more were underemployed. No other event has had a greater effect on the thinking and the institutions of government in the twentieth century.

In the 1930s, the forces that had stemmed earlier declines were no longer operating. There were no more frontiers, no growing exports, no new technologies to boost employment. Unchecked, unemployment spread like an epidemic. And the crisis fueled itself. Workers who lost their source of income could no longer buy the food, goods, and services that kept the economy going. Thus, private industry and commercial farmers tended to produce more than could be sold profitably. Closed factories, surplus crops, and idle workers were the consequences.

The Great Depression generated powerful ironies. Producers, seeking to restore profits, trimmed costs by replacing workers with machines, which only increased unemployment. People went hungry because so much food had been produced that it could not be sold profitably; dumping it was cheaper than taking it to market.

The industrialized nations of Europe were also hit hard. The value of U.S. exports fell while the value of imports increased; this led to high tariffs, which strangled trade and fueled the Depression. From 1929 to 1932, more than 44 percent of the nation's banks failed. Farm prices fell by more than half in the same period. Marginal farmers lost their land, and tenant farmers succumbed to mechanization. The uprooted—tens of thousands of dispossessed farm families, with their possessions atop their cars and trucks—headed west in a hopeless quest for opportunity.

The New Deal. In his speech accepting the presidential nomination at the 1932 Democratic National Convention, Franklin Delano Roosevelt (then governor of New York) made a promise: "I pledge you, I pledge myself to a new deal for the American people." Although this **New Deal** was never defined, it became the label for measures advocated by the Roosevelt administration to stem the Depression. Some scholars regard these measures as the most imaginative burst of domestic policy in the nation's history. Others see them as the source of massive government growth without matching benefits.

President Roosevelt's New Deal was composed of two phases. The first, which ended in 1935, was aimed at boosting prices and lowering unemployment. The second phase, which ended in 1938, was aimed at aiding the forgotten people: the poor, the aged, unorganized working men and women, and the farmers. The Supreme Court stymied Roosevelt's first-phase reform efforts by declaring major New Deal legislation unconstitutional, beginning in 1935. A majority of the justices maintained that in its legislation, Congress had exceeded its constitutional authority to regulate interstate commerce.

The Democrats won overwhelming popular support for their efforts at relief and recovery. The voters returned Roosevelt to office in a landslide election in 1936. But the Supreme Court continued its opposition to New Deal legislation. This prompted Roosevelt to advocate an increase in the number of justices on the Court; his goal was to appoint justices sympathetic to the legislation he endorsed. However, Roosevelt's attack on the Court, coupled with increasing labor violence, alarmed conservatives and put the New Deal on the defensive. Still, within a few months of the 1936 election, the Supreme Court began to yield to a view of expanded power for the national government; in an abrupt about-face, the Court upheld the New Deal policies that comprised the second phase. (It was, said one wag, "the switch in time that saved nine.")

Roosevelt's overwhelming popularity did not translate into irresistible policy or government popularity. Public opinion polls revealed that Americans were closely divided over New Deal policies through the early 1940s. Eventually, the New Deal became the status quo, and Americans grew satisfied with it. But Americans remained wary of additional growth in the power of the national government.[24]

The New Deal programs were opportunistic; they were not guided by, or based on, a single political or economic theory. They aimed at relief for the needy, recovery for the nation, and long-range reform for the economy. Many New Deal programs were rooted in the concept of short-term relief to get people back on their feet without continuous dependence on government assistance. Administering these programs called for government growth; funding them required higher taxes. Government could no longer rely on either the decentralized political struc-

Facing the Great Depression

The despair of the Depression can be seen in the faces of this migrant mother and her children, unsuccessful in their search for work in Weslaco, Texas, in 1939. Uprooted farmers, forced from their land by foreclosure, trooped from town to town in search of jobs or food. The health, nutrition, and shelter of millions of Americans suffered as a consequence of the Depression.

ture of federalism or the market forces of laissez-faire capitalism to bring the country out of its decline. The New Deal embodied the belief that a complex economy required centralized government control.

Poverty and unemployment remained, however, despite the best efforts of the Democrats. By 1939, 17 percent of the work force (more than 9 million people) was still unemployed. Only World War II was able to provide the economic surge needed to yield lower unemployment and higher prices, the elusive goals of the New Deal. Although the actual economic value of the New Deal reforms is still undetermined, those policies did begin long-range trends toward government expansion. And another torrent of domestic policymaking burst forth three decades later.

The Great Society. John F. Kennedy's election in 1960 brought to Washington public servants sensitive to persistent poverty and the needs of minorities. But Kennedy's narrow margin of victory was far from a mandate to improve the plight of the poor and dispossessed. At first, Kennedy proposed technical and financial aid for depressed areas and programs for upgrading the skills of workers in marginal jobs. But Kennedy and influential members of his administration were motivated by politics as well as poverty; in 1962, with the economy faltering again, the Kennedy administration proposed substantial tax breaks for middle- and upper-income groups. Many low-income Americans remained untouched by the administration's programs.

Kennedy's assassination in November 1963 provided the backdrop for new policies founded on equality, proposed by his successor, Lyndon Baines Johnson. In his 1965 State of the Union address, President Johnson offered his own version of the New Deal; his vision of the **Great Society** included a broad array of programs designed to redress political, social, and economic inequality. In contrast to the New Deal, few if any of Johnson's programs aimed at short-term relief; most were targeted at chronic ills requiring long-term government commitment. Some of these programs had already been enacted, whereas others were still in the planning stage. The Civil Rights Act of 1964 was aimed at erasing racial discrimination from most areas of American life. The Voting Rights Act of 1965 had as its goal the elimination of voting restrictions that discriminated against blacks and other minorities. Both statutes prohibited conduct that was inconsistent with political and social equality (see Chapter 16).

Another part of Johnson's Great Society plan was based on the traditional American belief that social and economic equality could be attained through equality of educational opportunity. The Elementary and Secondary Education Act of 1965 provided, for the first time, direct national government aid to local school districts, based on the number of low-income families in each district. Later, the national government was able to use the threat of withholding school aid (under the 1964 Civil Rights Act) to increase the pace of school integration in the South dramatically.

Still another vital element of the Great Society was the **War on Poverty.** The major weapon in this war was the Economic Opportunity Act (1964); its proponents promised that it would eradicate poverty in ten years. The act encouraged a variety of local community programs to educate and train people for employment. Among them were college work-study programs, summer employment for high school and college students, loans to small businesses, a domestic version of the Peace Corps (called VISTA, for Volunteers in Service to America), educational enrichment for preschoolers, and legal services for the poor. It offered opportunity: a hand up, rather than a handout.

The act also established the Office for Economic Opportunity (OEO), which was the administrative center of the War on Poverty. Its basic strategy was to involve the poor themselves in administering the programs, in the hope that they would know which programs would best serve their needs. National government money was channeled directly to local community action programs to fight poverty. This approach avoided the vested interests of state and local government bureaucrats and political machines. But it also led to new local controversies by shifting the control of government funds from local politicians to other groups. (In one notorious example, the Blackstone Rangers, a Chicago street gang, received national government support to fund a job-training program.)

In 1967, the Johnson administration responded to pressure from established local politicians by requiring that poverty funds be distributed through certified state and local agencies. In addition, all sectors of the community (including business, labor, and local leaders) would now be represented, along with the poor, in administering community action programs.

The War on Poverty eventually sputtered and disappeared as funding was diverted to the Vietnam War. Although it had achieved little in the way of income redistribution, it did lead to one significant change: It made the poor aware of their political power. Candidates representing the poor ran for political office, and officeholders paid increased attention to the poor. The poor also found that they could use the legal system to their benefit. For example, with legal assistance from the OEO, low-income litigants were successful in striking down state laws requiring a minimum period of residency before people could receive public assistance.[25]

Some War on Poverty programs remain, established features of government. (Among these are the work-study program that enables many college students to finance their education.) Yet poverty also remains, and the evidence suggests that it may once again be on the rise. Public attitudes toward poverty have changed, however, since the Great Depression. When Americans were polled recently on the reasons for poverty, they cited in about equal measure circumstances beyond the control of the poor and lack of effort. Many Americans today believe that the persistence of poverty results from flawed programs that encourage dependence on government assistance.[26]

Social welfare policy is based on the premise that society has an obligation to provide for the minimum welfare of its members. In a recent national survey, the poor and nonpoor agreed that government should protect its citizens against the risks that they are powerless to combat. Americans expressed a clear conviction that money and wealth ought to be more evenly shared by a larger percentage of the population.[27] The label *welfare state* reflects this protective role of government.

By meeting minimum needs, government welfare policies attempt to promote equality. New Deal policies were aimed at meeting the needs of the poor by redistributing income: People with greater incomes paid progressively higher taxes—in effect, the wealthy paid to alleviate poverty. Today's liberals tend to follow in the New Deal path. They are willing to curtail economic freedom somewhat to promote economic equality. As a result, their policies aim at providing direct income subsidies and government jobs. Today's conservatives avoid this government-as-provider approach, preferring economic freedom to government intervention. Their policies aim at curbing inflation and reducing government spending, on the theory that the tide of a rising economy lifts all boats.

The evidence from the 1980s, however, does not bolster the conservatives' theory. Both before-tax and after-tax income inequality grew wider in the 1980s (see Chapter 18). Changes in families and household composition suggest several plausible explanations for this increased gulf between the haves and the have-nots. For one thing, the growth in the number of elderly—who have substantially lower incomes—tends to increase income inequality. The growth in the number of persons living alone (or with nonrelatives)—who typically have much lower incomes than family households—also increases income inequality. In addition, the growth in the number of female-headed households contributes to income inequality; about half of such households are in the lowest income group.[28] (We examine the subject of women and poverty in more detail later in this chapter.)

The Reduction of the Welfare State

A spirit of equality—equality of opportunity—motivated the reforms of the 1960s, many of which carried over to the 1970s. But Ronald Reagan's overwhelming election in 1980 and his landslide re-election in 1984 forced a re-examination of social welfare policy.

In a dramatic departure from his predecessors (Republicans as well as Democrats), Reagan shifted emphasis from economic equality to economic freedom. He questioned whether government alone should continue to be responsible for shouldering the economic and social well-being of less fortunate citizens. And, to the extent that government should bear this responsibility, he maintained that state and local governments could do so more efficiently than the national government. Ironically, when Reagan attempted to act on his rhetoric of limited government, his political support started to evaporate. The lesson for all post–Great Society presidents, including Reagan, is that "a powerful central government is here to stay, and its beneficiaries, many of whom approved of Reagan, want it that way."[29]

Reagan professed his support of the "truly needy" and of the preservation of a "reliable safety net of social programs," by which he meant the core programs begun in the New Deal. Nevertheless, his administration abolished a number of national social welfare programs and redirected others. Reagan proposed sharp cutbacks in housing assistance, welfare, the food stamp program, and education and training programs. Reagan and Congress also trimmed the most basic of American social welfare programs—social security—although cuts here were less severe than in other areas.[30]

Congress checked some of the president's proposed cutbacks; many Great Society programs remained in force, although at lower funding levels. Overall spending on social welfare programs (as a proportion of the gross national product) fell to about mid-1970s levels. But the dramatic growth in the promotion of social welfare that began with the New Deal ended with the Reagan administration. It remained in repose during the Bush administration. And the national budget deficit—a deficit that ballooned during the Reagan and Bush administrations—will continue to restrict future efforts to expand the government's social welfare role. The enormous government debt will force Congress to avoid new and costly social welfare programs until income and expenditures come nearer to a balance.

Policies That Provide: Social Insurance

Insurance is a device for guaranteeing an individual against loss. Since the late nineteenth century, there has been a growing tendency for governments to offer **social insurance,** which is a government-backed guarantee against loss by individuals, regardless of need (see Compared with What? 19.1). The most common forms of social insurance guard against losses due to worker sickness, injury, and disability; due to old age; and due to unemployment. The first example of social insurance in the United States was workers' compensation. Beginning early in this century, most states provided a system of insurance that compensated workers who lost income because they were injured in the workplace.

Social insurance benefits are distributed to recipients without regard to their economic status. Old-age benefits, for example, are paid to all people—rich or poor—who reach the required age. In most social insurance programs, employees and employers contribute to a fund from which later disbursements are made to recipients.*

Social insurance programs are examples of *entitlements*—benefits to which every eligible person has a legal right and which government cannot deny. National entitlement programs consume about half of every dollar of government spending; one of the largest entitlement programs is social security.

Social Security

Social security is social insurance that provides economic assistance to people faced with unemployment, disability, or old age; it is financed by

---

* Examine your next paycheck stub. It should indicate your contribution to FICA (the Federal Insurance Contribution Act). It is separated into Social Security Tax (SST) and Medicare Tax (MT). SST supports disability, survivors', and retirement benefits. In 1991, it was 6.2 percent of the first $53,400 earned. MT pays for Medicare benefits. In 1991, it was 1.45 percent of wages up to $125,000.

COMPARED WITH WHAT?   19.1

Social Insurance Programs, 1940–1988

The number of countries with some form of social insurance program has nearly tripled since 1940. The most widespread type of social security measure is the work-injury program; Americans refer to this type of insurance as "workers' compensation." Old-age and survivors programs (Americans refer to these as "social security") are nearly as common. For example, in 1988, 136 countries had a work-injury program; 134 countries had an old-age program.

Only 40 countries—most of them industrialized nations—offer some form of unemployment benefits. Growth in this area has been the slowest among all types of programs. Most programs now in place were established before World War II.

Family allowance programs provide regular cash payments to families with children, regardless of need. In some countries, these programs include grants for education and maternal and child health services. In 1988, 63 countries had such programs, including all the industrialized countries in the world, with one exception: the United States.

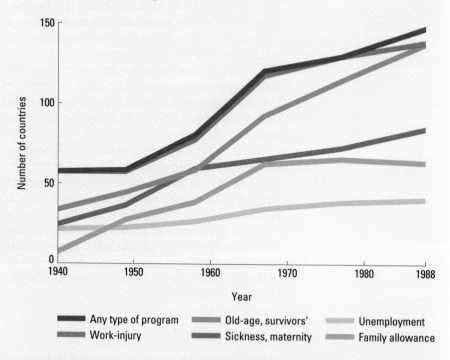

Source: *Social Insurance Programs Throughout the World—1989.* Research Report No. 62. (U.S. Department of Health and Human Services and the Social Security Administration: May 1990), pp. v–xxi.

taxes on employers and employees. Initially, social security benefits were distributed only to the aged, the unemployed, and poor people with dependent children. Today, social security also provides medical care for the elderly and income support for the disabled.

Origins of social security. The idea of social security came late to the United States. As early as 1883, Germany enacted legislation to protect workers against the hazards of industrial life. Most European nations adopted old-age insurance after World War I; many provided income support for the disabled and income protection for families after the death of the principal wage earner. In the United States, however, the needs of the elderly and the unemployed were left largely to private organizations and individuals. Although twenty-eight states had old-age assistance programs by 1934, neither private charities nor state and local governments—nor both together—could cope with the prolonged unemployment and distress that resulted from the Great Depression. It became clear that a national policy was necessary to deal with a national crisis.

The first important step came on August 14, 1935, when President Franklin Roosevelt signed the **Social Security Act;** that act is the cornerstone of the modern American welfare state. The act's framers developed three approaches to the problem of dependence. The first provided social insurance in the form of old-age and surviving-spouse benefits, and cooperative state-national unemployment assistance. A program was created to provide income to retired workers, to ensure that the elderly did not retire into poverty. This was to serve as a floor of protection against income loss for the elderly. (Most Americans associate social security with this program.) In addition, an unemployment insurance program, financed by employers, was created to provide payments for a limited time to workers who were laid off or dismissed for reasons beyond their control.

The second approach provided aid to the destitute in the form of grants-in-aid to the states. The act established the first permanent national commitment to provide financial assistance to the needy aged, needy families with dependent children, the blind, and (since the 1950s) the permanently and totally disabled.

The third approach provided health and welfare services through federal aid to the states. Included were health and family services for crippled children and orphans, and vocational rehabilitation for the disabled.

How social security works. The social security old-age benefits program is administered directly by the national government through the Social Security Administration. Old-age retirement revenue goes into its own *trust fund* (there is a separate fund for each social security program), which means that this revenue can be spent only for the old-age benefits program. Benefits, in the form of monthly payments, begin when an employee reaches retirement age, which today stands at sixty-five. (People can retire as early as age sixty-two, but with reduced benefits.) The age at which full benefits are paid will increase to sixty-seven after the year 2000.

The reason Congress doesn't touch Social Security....

GRANBO

Mike Luckovich
Times-Picayune

Many Americans believe that each person's social security contributions are set aside specifically for his or her retirement, like a savings account.[31] But social security doesn't operate quite like that. Rather, the social security revenue generated today pays benefits to those who have already reached retirement age. Thus, social security (and social insurance in general) is not a form of savings; it is a pay-as-you-go tax system. Today's workers support today's elderly.

When the social security program began, it had few beneficiaries and many contributors. The program could provide relatively large benefits with low taxes. In 1937, for example, the tax rate was 1 percent, and there were nine workers shouldering the benefits of each retiree. As the program matured and more people retired, the ratio of workers to recipients decreased. In 1989, the social security system paid benefits to 39.2 million people and collected revenues from 128 million, for a ratio of three workers for every beneficiary.[32]

At one time, federal workers, members of Congress, judges, even the president were omitted from the social security system. Today, however, there are few exceptions. Universal participation is essential for the system to operate because it is a tax program, not a savings program. If participation were not compulsory, there would not be enough revenue to provide benefits to present retirees. So government, which is the only institution that can coerce, requires that all employees and their employers contribute, thereby imposing restrictions on freedom.

Those people who currently pay into the system will receive retirement benefits financed by future participants. As with a pyramid scheme or a chain letter, success depends on the growth of the base. If the birthrate remains steady or grows, future wage earners will be able to support today's contributors when they retire. If the economy expands, there will be more jobs, more income, and a growing wage base to tax for increased benefits to retirees. But suppose the birthrate falls, or unemployment rises and the economy falters. Then contributions could decline to the point at which benefits exceed revenues. The pyramidal character of social security is its Achilles' heel (see Figure 19.2).

Who pays? Who benefits? "Who pays?" and "Who benefits?" are two important questions in government policymaking, and they continue to shape social security policy. In 1968, the Republican party platform called for automatic adjustments that would increase social security payments as the cost of living increased. The theory was simple: As the cost of living rises, so should retirement benefits; otherwise, benefits are paid in "shrinking dollars." Cost-of-living adjustments (COLAs) became a political football in 1969 as Democrats and Republicans tried to outdo each other by suggesting larger increases for retirees. The result was a significant expansion of the social security program, far in excess of the cost of living. The beneficiaries were the retired, who were beginning to flex their political muscle. Politicians knew that the alienation of this constituency could change an election.[33]

In 1972, Congress adopted automatic adjustments in benefits and in the wage base on which contributions are assessed, so that revenue would expand as benefits grew. This approach set social security on automatic pilot. When inflation exceeds 3 percent, the automatic adjustment goes into effect. (Politicians sometimes fear retribution at the polls if there is not an annual adjustment. Even though it appeared that inflation

FIGURE 19.2 *Ratio of Workers to Beneficiaries in the Social Security System*

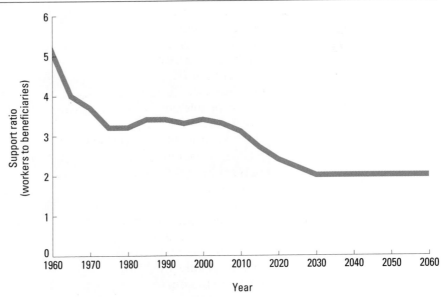

Demographers predict a steady decline in the ratio of workers to beneficiaries starting in the year 2000. By 2030, there will be two workers for every social security beneficiary. If current revenue pays current benefits, then it is a sure bet that social security taxes will increase or benefits will decrease as the worker-beneficiary ratio falls. (Source: "Federal Old-Age and Survivors Insurance and Disability Insurance Trust Funds," Social Security Administration Board of Trustees, 1985 Annual Report, *Table 29, p. 65.*)

would fall below 3 percent in 1986, Congress authorized an adjustment for that year.)

There was no assurance, however, that revenue growth would equal or exceed the growth in social security expenditures. And, in fact, when *stagflation* (high unemployment coupled with high inflation) took hold in the 1970s, the entire social security system fell into jeopardy. Stagflation gripped the social security system in an economic vise: Unemployment meant a reduction in revenue; high inflation meant growing benefits. This one-two punch drained social security trust fund reserves to critically low levels in the late 1970s and early 1980s. Other troubling factors were becoming clear. A lower birthrate meant that, in the future, fewer workers would support the pool of retirees. And the number of retirees would grow, as average life spans lengthened and the "baby-boom" generation retired. Higher taxes—an unpopular political move—loomed as one alternative. Another was to pay for social security out of general revenues, that is, income taxes. Social security would then become a public assistance program, like welfare. In 1983, shortly before existing social security benefit funds were exhausted, Congress and President Reagan agreed to a solution that called for two painful adjustments: increased taxes and reduced benefits.

The changes enacted in 1983 may have guaranteed the future of the social security system. However, future economic conditions will determine the success or failure of the system. Despite various revenue-generating plans, higher taxes or lower benefits may be the only means for ensuring the viability of social security.[34]

Today, few argue against the need for social security. But debate surrounds the extent of coverage and the level of benefits. "The [Social Se-

Life Begins at Sixty-Five

Old age and impoverishment used to go hand in hand, but not any more. Because of Social Security, people sixty-five and older are the second-richest age group in the United States. Only Americans fifty-five to sixty-four are better off. One political economist recently estimated that the government spends about $350 billion on the aged, more than on national defense. Today's elderly remain vulnerable to impoverishment in only one area: long-term nursing home care.

curity] Act is the most successful program of the modern state," declared Nobel prize laureate Paul Samuelson. Yet Milton Friedman, another Nobel laureate, labeled the act "a sacred cow that no politician can criticize." How can two renowned economists maintain such dramatically different views? Samuelson is a liberal in the Keynesian tradition; he favors equality over freedom. According to his view, social security lifted the elderly from destitution by redistributing income from workers (who have growing incomes) to the elderly (who have little or no income). Friedman is a libertarian and a monetarist; he favors freedom over equality. Because social security limits freedom to provide economic equality, Friedman would no doubt prefer that the program be scaled back or even eliminated. The political risks associated with social security cutbacks are too great, however, for most politicians to bear.

As a group, older Americans exercise enormous political power. People at or near retirement age now comprise almost 30 percent of the potential electorate, and voter turnout among older Americans is reportedly about twice that of younger people.[35] These facts may help explain the stability of social security and the creation and expansion of health care for the elderly.

Medicare

The social security system provides economic assistance conditioned on unemployment, disability, or old age. In 1962, the Senate considered extending social security benefits to provide hospitalization and medical care for the elderly. In opposing the extension, Democratic Senator Russell Long of Louisiana declared, "We are not staring at a sweet old lady in bed with her kimono and nightcap. We are looking into the eyes of the wolf that ate Red Riding Hood's grandma."[36] Long was concerned that there would be no way to limit this new push for government assistance to the elderly. Other opponents echoed the fears of the American Medical Association (AMA), which saw virtually any form of government-provided medical care as a step toward government control of medicine. Long and his compatriots won the battle that day. Three years later, however, the Social Security Act was amended to provide **Medicare**, health care for all people sixty-five and over.

Origins of Medicare. As early as 1945, public opinion clearly supported some form of national health insurance. That idea became entangled in Cold War politics, however—the growing crusade against communism in America.[37] The AMA, representing the nation's physicians, mounted and financed an all-out campaign to link national health insurance (so-called socialized medicine) with socialism; the campaign was so successful that the prospect of a national health policy vanished.

Both proponents and opponents of national health insurance tried to link their positions to deeply rooted American values: Advocates emphasized equality and fairness; opponents stressed individual freedom. In the absence of a clear public mandate on the *kind* of insurance (publicly funded or private) wanted, the AMA was able to marshal political influence to prevent any national insurance at all.[38]

By 1960, however, the terms of the debate had changed. Its focus was no longer fixed on the clash of freedom and equality. Now the issue of health insurance was cast in terms of providing assistance to the aged, and a ground swell of support forced it onto the national agenda.[39]

The Democratic victory in 1964 and the advent of President Johnson's Great Society made some form of national health policy almost inevitable. On July 30, 1965, Johnson signed a bill that provided a number of health benefits to the elderly and the poor. Fearful of the AMA's power to punish its opponents, the Democrats had confined their efforts to a compulsory hospitalization insurance plan for the elderly. (This is known today as Part A of Medicare.) In addition, the bill contained a form of an alternative Republican plan, which called for voluntary government-subsidized insurance to cover physician's fees. (This is known today as Part B of Medicare.) A third program, added a year later, is called *Medicaid*; it provides medical aid to the poor through federally assisted state health programs. Medicaid is a need-based comprehensive medical and hospitalization program for the poor. Need is the only criterion: If you are poor, you qualify. Medicaid today covers 23.5 million people at a cost in 1989 of nearly $55 billion.[40]

Medicare today. Part A of Medicare is compulsory insurance that covers certain hospital services for people sixty-five and older. Workers pay a tax; retirees pay premiums deducted from social security payments. Payments for services are made by the national government directly to participating hospitals and other qualifying facilities; they cover the reasonable costs of necessary medical services. In 1989, more than 33 million people were enrolled in Part A, and the government paid $60 billion in benefits.[41]

Part B of Medicare is a voluntary program of medical insurance for people sixty-five and older, who pay the premiums. The insurance covers the services of physicians and other qualified providers; payments for these services are based on reasonable charges or on set fees. In 1989, more than 32 million people were enrolled; the government spent more than $38 billion for Part B benefits. In 1991, the monthly premium for this insurance was $29.90.[42]

The fears that Senator Long voiced in 1962 approached reality in the 1980s: Medicare costs soared out of control. By 1986, Medicare costs exceeded $75 billion, representing a fourfold increase in ten years. For the moment, Medicare is solvent, thanks to modest payroll tax increases and low unemployment, but the program lacks the cushion presently enjoyed by the retirement trust funds. Spending reductions (through curtailed benefits) or income increases (through raised taxes) are still viable, although politically unpalatable, alternatives.[43]

With strong bipartisan support, Medicare benefits were expanded significantly in 1988 to provide the elderly with insurance against catastrophic illnesses (those that require long-term hospitalization), a ceiling on hospital and doctor bills, and much more. These benefits were designed to alleviate the worry of impoverishment by the high costs of hospitalization. Funding was to come from a small surtax on the income taxes of the wealthy elderly and $4-a-month premiums paid by the elderly who participated. Since the elderly were the chief beneficiaries, they should bear the cost. At least, that was the theory.

The idea of catastrophic health insurance was first proposed by the Reagan administration. Why would an administration committed to tax reduction and benefit curtailment make such a dramatic turnabout? Perhaps the most important reason was the political power of the elderly. In an election year, the Republicans wanted their support.

The benefit backfired for at least three reasons just one year later. First, the surtax stirred opposition from comfortable retirees, who resented paying for benefits they did not need. Second, they were not inclined to subsidize benefits for the less fortunate elderly. In other words, the fortunate elderly did not want to trade some of their economic freedom to put the less fortunate elderly on a more-or-less equal plane. And third, older Americans in massive numbers were convinced that program costs should be spread among younger Americans, in the manner of the original Medicare and social security concepts. The torrent of letters and telephone calls overwhelmed the law's defenders. Congress voted to repeal the controversial provisions in 1989.

Medicare costs continue to increase at rates well in excess of the cost of living. Consequently, government has sought to contain those costs. One attempt at cost containment makes use of economic incentives in the hospital treatment of Medicare patients. The plan seems to have had the desired economic benefits, but it raises questions about the endangerment of the health of elderly patients. Medicare payments to hospitals had been based on the length of a patient's stay; the longer the stay, the more revenue the hospitals earned. This approach encouraged longer, more expensive hospital stays, because the government, as the insurer, was paying the bill. In 1985, however, the government switched to a new payment system under which hospitals are paid a fixed, preset fee based on the patient's diagnosis. If the patient's stay costs more than the fee schedule allows, the hospital pays the difference. On the other hand, if the hospital treats a patient for less than the fixed fee, then the hospital reaps the profit. This new system provides an incentive for hospitals to discharge patients sooner, in some cases perhaps before they are completely well.

Policies That Provide: Public Assistance

Public assistance is what most people mean when they use the terms *welfare* or *welfare payments*; it is government aid to individuals who can demonstrate a need for that aid. Public assistance is directed toward those who lack the ability or the resources to provide for themselves or their families.

Public assistance programs instituted under the Social Security Act are known today as *categorical assistance programs*. They include (1) old-age assistance for the needy elderly not covered by old-age pension benefits, (2) aid to the needy blind, (3) aid to needy families with dependent children, and (4) aid to the totally and permanently disabled. Adopted initially as stopgap measures during the Depression, these programs have now become entitlements. They are administered by the states, but the bulk of the funding comes from the national government's general tax revenues. Because the states also contribute to the funding of their own public assistance programs, the benefits tend to vary from state to state.

Poverty and Public Assistance

The national government requires that national standards be used in the administration of state welfare programs. It distributes resources to each state based on the proportion of the population living in poverty in that state. That proportion is, in turn, determined on the basis of a national government **poverty level**, or poverty threshold, which is the minimum cash income that will provide for a family's basic needs. The poverty level varies by family size and is calculated as three times the cost of an economy food plan, a market basket of food that provides a minimally nutritious diet. (The threshold is computed in this way because research suggests that poor families of three or more persons spend approximately one-third of their income on food.)*

The poverty level is fairly simple to apply. It is also, of course, only a rough measure for distinguishing the poor and the nonpoor. Using it is like using a wrench as a hammer: It works, but not very well. We attach importance to the poverty level despite its inaccuracies because measuring poverty is an attempt to measure how the American promise of equality stands up against the performance of our public policies. In 1991, the government calculated that 33 to 34 million people were living in poverty in the United States.

The poverty level varies with family size, and it is adjusted each year to reflect changes in consumer prices. In 1991, the poverty threshold for a family of four was cash income below the threshold of $13,400.[44] This is income *before* taxes. If the poverty threshold were viewed as disposable income (in other words, income *after* taxes), then the proportion of the population categorized as living in poverty would increase.

Some critics believe that other factors besides income should be considered in computing the poverty level. Assets (home, cars, possessions), for example, are excluded from the poverty definition. Also, the current computation fails to take into account such noncash benefits as food stamps, health benefits (Medicaid), and subsidized housing. Presumably, the inclusion of these noncash benefits as income would decrease the proportion of individuals seen to be living below the poverty level.

Critics notwithstanding, the poverty threshold has been calculated for many years on the basis of total cash income. At the very least, that yardstick allows us to chart our progress against poverty. Figure 19.3 shows that poverty in the United States has declined since the late 1950s and early 1960s. Blacks and whites have progressed about equally. Neverthe-

---

* Although it has been the source of endless debate, today's definition of poverty retains remarkable similarity to its predecessors. As early as 1795, a group of English magistrates "decided that a minimum income should be the cost of a gallon loaf of bread, multiplied by 3, plus an allowance for each dependent." See Alvin L. Schorr, "Redefining Poverty Levels," *New York Times*, 9 May 1984, p. 27.

FIGURE 19.3 *Poverty Rate by Groups, 1965–1989*

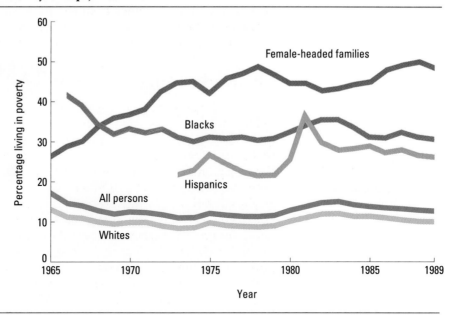

This graph shows the percentage of members of various groups who live below the poverty level. Note the marked increase in poor families that are headed by women.
(Source: Bureau of the Census, "Money and Poverty in the United States, 1989," Current Population Reports, *Series P-60, No. 168, Table 19.)*

less, in 1989 poverty was still the economic condition of one in ten whites, one in three blacks, and one in four Hispanics. Poverty retains a tight hold on the American population.

Poverty was once a condition of old age. Social security altered that picture. Today, the likelihood of poverty is still related to age, but in the opposite direction. Poverty is largely a predicament of the young; 40 percent of the poor are eighteen or younger.

And when we examine the composition of poor families, especially during the last twenty-five years, we observe a dramatic and disturbing trend. One in every two poor Americans resides in a family where a woman is the sole householder, or head of the household (see Figure 19.3). Twenty-five years ago, only one in every four poor persons resided in such a family. What accounts for this dramatic upward shift in the proportion of female-headed poor families?

This century bears witness to extraordinary changes for women. Women won the right to vote and own property. Women also gained a measure of legal and social equality (see Chapter 16). But other changes have strained women's status and roles. Increases in rates of divorce, marital separation, and adolescent pregnancy have cast more and more women in the head-of-household role. Caring for children competes with commitment to work. Affordable child care is out of reach for many single parents. In the absence of a national child-care policy, many single women who must care for their young children face limited employment opportunities and lower wages in comparison to full-time workers. These factors and others contribute to the **"feminization of poverty,"** the growing percentage of all poor Americans who are women or the dependents of women.[45]

Boxed In, Boxed Out

Most observers agree that homelessness is increasing, but there is little reliable information about the scope of the problem. Some advocates for the homeless attribute the increase to the national economy and the lack of affordable housing; others cite the deinstitutionalization of the mentally ill. With nowhere to go, the homeless are always in sight.

It is relatively easy to draw a portrait of the poor; it is much more difficult to craft policies that move them out of destitution. Critics of social welfare spending argue that antipoverty policies have made poverty more attractive by removing incentives to work. They believe these policies, which aim to provide for the poor, have actually promoted poverty.

Another explanation for the failure of government policies to reduce poverty rests on changes in racial attitudes. In the 1960s, racial barriers kept the black middle class in the same urban ghettos as the poor. The middle class's presence provided social stability, role models, and community institutions and businesses. Ironically, the decline of racial barriers prompted middle-class blacks to move out of the ghetto. As a result, the inner city became increasingly poor and increasingly dependent on welfare.[46]

Cash Assistance: AFDC

The largest public assistance program is **Aid to Families with Dependent Children (AFDC),** which was created by the 1935 Social Security Act. Each month, almost 4 million families (or roughly 11 million individuals) receive benefits through AFDC; it is the major source of government cash assistance to low-income children and their families. In 1990, the AFDC program cost $18.1 billion: $9.8 billion paid by the national government and $8.3 billion paid by the states.[47]

AFDC benefits are distributed in cash through the states. The typical AFDC family lives in a large urban area and consists of a mother under thirty and two children under eight. More than half of AFDC recipients are white; 40 percent are black. Eligibility for AFDC automatically qualifies recipients for Medicaid and other forms of public assistance. However, recipients must first go through a complicated qualifying process, because government is very wary of giving money to people who might in any way be regarded as undeserving. The process has four parts (see Figure 19.4):

1. *Family composition test.* In general, an applicant for AFDC benefits must be a single parent living with at least one child under age eighteen. In half the states, recipients can be married, but the principal wage earner must be unemployed.

2. *Assets test* (varies from state to state). Assets are savings, clothing, and furniture. The national government sets a limit on the value of the assets an AFDC family can possess (in 1991, it was $1,000). Equity in an automobile cannot exceed $1,500. States can impose stricter asset limits.

3. *Determination of need* (varies from state to state). A family is considered to be in need if its income is below a "need standard" set by each state. In Cook County, Illinois, for example, the need standard for a three-person family in 1991 was $811 a month. Only families with incomes below the need standard qualify for benefits.

4. *Benefit calculation* (varies from state to state). Each state establishes a payment standard for determining benefits. (In half the states, the payment standard is below the need standard.) For qualifying families, the difference between the payment standard and the family income is the AFDC benefit. In 1991, the typical AFDC grant for a one-parent family of three in Cook County, Illinois, was $361 a month (plus automatic Medicaid eligibility and roughly $270 in food stamps).

Inflation raises the poverty level, but eligibility for AFDC has remained stationary. In 1991, in order to qualify for AFDC (and Medicaid), a family's income could be, on average, no more than about half of the poverty level. So although many families are "poor" according to the poverty level, they are not poor enough to qualify for cash assistance or medical care.

The original purpose of AFDC was to provide assistance to fatherless families, enabling mothers to rear their children full time. But a growing chorus of critics argued that AFDC policies encouraged dependence on

FIGURE 19.4 *AFDC Qualification Process*

A family seeking AFDC benefits must complete a four-step process. Some steps vary from state to state. (Source: Tom Joe and Cheryl Rogers, By the Few, for the Few: The Reagan Welfare Legacy *[Lexington, Mass.: Lexington Books, 1985], p. 25. © 1985, Lexington Books. Reprinted by permission of the authors.)*

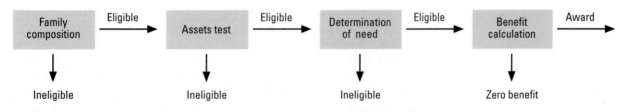

welfare. A recipient who took a job did not have to earn very much before losing all benefits. In some states, for example, full-time employment at the minimum wage meant an end to public assistance. However, researchers discovered that mandatory employment and training programs (also known as workfare) were moderately successful in ending welfare's grip on the poor. Model workfare programs in Massachusetts, Maryland, and California increased the average earnings of female participants, assured social contributions from recipients in return for public assistance, and may have discouraged dependence on welfare.[48] This evidence moved Congress to overhaul the nation's welfare system in 1988 by passing the Family Support Act.

The central provision of the Family Support Act of 1988 requires most welfare recipients whose children are over the age of three to participate in state-approved work, education, or training programs. To smooth the transition between welfare and work, the states must provide child care and health insurance during the training period and continue this assistance for as much as one year after the recipient has found a job. The reforms will cost the states and the national government more than $3.3 billion for the first five years; the effects of the new law will take years to materialize.

Unfortunately, some preliminary evidence suggests that these effects are likely to be trivial. According to the Congressional Budget Office, the reform that was supposed to "turn the welfare system upside down" will prompt only about 50,000 families (or about 1.3 percent of the current welfare case load) to leave the welfare system.[49]

The idealism inherent in the law has already run afoul of brutal budget facts. Some states, like Massachusetts and Minnesota, have found that the only way to provide mandated benefits for those on welfare is to reduce benefits for the working poor. Ironically, this will force some working poor parents to quit their jobs and return to the welfare rolls, at much greater public expense.[50]

If welfare addresses only the symptoms of poverty, what public policies will take aim at its causes? There are at least four competing approaches to the elimination of poverty, each with its promoters and detractors.

The *traditional approach* emphasizes an expansion of existing social services. This is an easy target for critics, who point to poverty's still-firm grip on one in every nine Americans. The traditionalists insist that there have been successes in reducing poverty and that jettisoning all antipoverty programs would be akin to throwing out the baby with the bath water. They claim that building on successful policies will assure an end to poverty. But success depends on identifying the winning policies, willingness to stay the course well into the future, and ability to pay the bills.

The *economic approach* maintains that inner-city poverty intensified because industrial jobs disappeared or companies moved out. The solution is jobs through improved education, job training, and economic measures aimed at full employment. Critics note that full employment has managed to elude policymakers for much of this century. Moreover, it is difficult to understand the inability of inner-city poor to capitalize on today's opportunities when many immigrant populations have managed to bootstrap their way out of similar empoverishment without additional government assistance. Thus, relying on economic policy to address poverty is akin to hiring a plumber when you need a carpenter: There is no guarantee that the right job will be done.

The *welfare-reform approach* calls for scrapping the current welfare system entirely since it perpetuates poverty by viewing unemployment as a way of life. Welfare would be replaced by guaranteed government jobs. The pay would fall just below the poverty level to encourage a shift to the private sector. Meanwhile, government would provide child care and medical insurance to ensure that willing workers would not live in poverty. And what will happen to the able-bodied persons now on welfare who shirk work under the new policy? Private charities and public shelters will be the only alternatives. Critics have a field day with this approach: It is expensive and hardhearted.

The *empowerment approach* embraces social policies that circumvent bureaucracies. Its advocates assert that the existing services for the poor are inadequate because there is no free market and, consequently, no healthy competition to promote the best quality at the lowest cost. Giving the poor real choices for schooling and housing will "empower" them to escape poverty's shackles. For example, tenant ownership in public housing will engender pride and concern, turning high-rise hovels into towering palaces. Empowerment rhetoric is a forceful tonic, critics note, but there is precious little evidence so far that empowering the poor will somehow lift them from destitution.

At the moment, there is no clear evidence or dramatic new policy initiative that gives preference to one approach over another. The status quo probably comes closest to the traditional approach without attempting to weed out failures from successes. One bona fide success in public assistance is the food stamp program.

Necessary Nutrition: Food Stamps

The national government's **food stamp program** aims to improve the diets of members of low-income households by supplementing their food-purchasing power. The nationally funded program is administered through local agencies, which distribute the stamps to needy individuals and families. The stamps are actually coupons that can be used to purchase any food meant for human consumption.

Food stamps originated in Roosevelt's New Deal years as a dual-purpose program aimed at confronting the "unsettling contradiction between unprecedented destitution and deprivation on the one hand and excessive agricultural production on the other."[51] The program accomplished its twin goals of feeding the hungry and helping the farmers, and then became dormant when the economy rebounded during World War II. But the problem of hunger remained. Later administrations either denied that there was a substantial problem of hunger in America or instituted generally ineffective programs in which surplus commodities (lard, rice, flour, butter, and cheese) were distributed to the poor in amounts too small to ensure adequate nutrition.

The revival of the food stamp program was the top legislative priority of Democratic Representative Leonor Sullivan of Missouri during the

1950s. Sullivan's dogged determination kept the idea alive through the Eisenhower and Kennedy administrations, until Congress provided a substantially expanded program in the Food Stamp Act (1964). At first, administrators were fearful that the distribution of free stamps would encourage a black market for the stamps. That is, if the stamps provided more food than recipients needed, they would be tempted to sell their excess stamps. The solution was to require recipients to purchase stamps with a portion of their incomes. In return, they would receive stamps whose value was equal to the purchase price *plus* an additional amount. As family income rose, the additional amount fell. Unfortunately, this purchase plan did not work well, because people who needed food stamps often didn't have the cash to buy them. Moreover, even the most generous food stamp allotment was not enough to ensure adequate nutrition.

Meanwhile, critics continued to point out the inadequacies of government nutrition policy. The Citizens' Crusade Against Poverty, a liberal advocacy group formed in 1965, collected evidence on the extent of hunger and malnutrition in the United States. Several other public interest groups joined the so-called "hunger lobby," and the poor also lobbied on their own behalf: More than three thousand people participated in the Poor People's March on Washington in 1968. They camped on the Mall east of the Lincoln Memorial and presented their demands to the secretary of agriculture. A CBS television documentary called "Hunger in America" focused on the problem of government ineffectiveness in combating hunger.

Some concessions were granted by the government, but they proved inadequate, and new advocates for the poor joined the lobbying effort. Finally, the Nixon administration introduced significant changes in the food stamp program. Food stamp allotments were increased to ensure a nutritionally adequate diet, and the purchase price of the stamps was reduced. Later, in 1977, the need to purchase food stamps was eliminated entirely; stamps were distributed free to eligible persons. By the end of the decade, the problem of hunger appeared on the verge of being solved. Unfortunately, some researchers now report that hunger is again on the rise.

The AFDC and food stamp programs are structured to work jointly. AFDC benefits vary from state to state, but food stamp benefits are set nationally. In states that offer lower AFDC benefits, participants receive larger food stamp allotments. In 1990, the food stamp program cost the government $15.5 billion. The 20 million participants (one in thirteen Americans) received an average of $59 a month in food stamps.[52]

The Reagan administration tried to curtail the food stamp program and had a measure of success. More than a million people lost their food stamp benefits entirely as a result of spending cuts in 1984, and benefits were reduced for many others.[53] The administration maintained that this was not as heartless as it appeared: Most of those who lost their benefits had incomes in excess of 130 percent of the poverty level. At the same time, the Reagan administration increased its distribution of surplus food to the poor. But there is no established and workable distribution system, and the food that is given away (often five-pound blocks of

The Dole Card: Don't Be Homeless Without It

The national government is experimenting with a new means of distributing welfare benefits: ATM cards. Independence Card–holders simply use their cards in machines at banks and grocery stores to obtain cash or draw against a food stamp account. Officials hope the new system will reduce administrative costs and recipient fraud; the stigma and inconvenience traditionally associated with welfare may also be reduced. But some critics view the latter result as a disadvantage, believing a sense of stigma or inconvenience serves as a useful penalty that helps keep people off welfare.

American cheese) qualifies only as a nutritional supplement, not as the basis of a nourishing diet.

Hunger remains a sordid fact in America. In a 1991 survey of low-income households, researchers defined hunger as periodic food shortages resulting from a family's limited economic resources. They estimated that there are 5.5 million hungry children under the age of twelve. The researchers readily admit that they did not establish the existence of persistent, clinical malnutrition. They did document that millions of American children go to bed hungry in a land of plenty.[54]

Benefits and Fairness

Ronald Reagan once observed, "In the war on poverty, poverty won." Americans tend to agree. About half of all Americans believe the liberal welfare policies of the 1960s made things "somewhat better" for the poor; only 10 percent maintain that those policies made the poor much better off.[55] But more than 90 percent of Americans seem convinced that poverty will remain a persistent problem, partly because, more than 70 percent believe, government doesn't know enough about how to eliminate poverty.[56]

The national government provides many Americans with benefits. There are two kinds of benefits: cash, such as a retiree's social security check, or noncash, like food stamps. Some benefits are conditional. **Means-tested benefits** impose an income test to qualify. For example, free or reduced school lunch programs and Pell college grants are available to households whose income falls below a designated threshold.

Non-means-tested benefits impose no such income test; benefits like Medicare or social security are available to all regardless of income.

Some Americans question the fairness of non-means-tested benefits. After all, benefits are subsidies, and some people need them more than others. If the size of the benefit pie remains fixed in the face of large budget deficits, then transforming some non-means-tested benefits into means-tested-benefits has real allure. For example, regardless of income all elderly now receive the same Medicare benefits. Fairness advocates maintain that the affluent elderly should shoulder a higher share of Medicare costs, shifting more benefits to low-income elderly (though, as we have seen, public outcry against such a plan forced its repeal in 1989). If the idea of shifting benefits should prove appealing sometime in the future, debate will focus on the income test below which a program will apply.

In the long run, understanding the consequences of public policy will help reduce poverty in America. For the moment, however, debates among scholars and policymakers offer no comfort to Lafeyette Rivers and children like him, who confront the daily reality of inner-city violence, hunger, and despair.

Summary

Public policies fulfill one or more purposes: protection, prohibition, provision, and promotion. Often, disagreements over public policy are disagreements over values. Choices between freedom and order are at the heart of many policies, for example, mandatory AIDS or drug testing. Choices between freedom and equality are at the heart of other policies, such as those designed to ease inner-city poverty.

Many domestic policies that provide benefits to individuals and promote economic equality were instituted during the Great Depression. Today, government plays an active role in providing benefits to the poor, the elderly, and the disabled. The object of these domestic policies is to alleviate conditions that individuals are powerless to prevent. This is the social welfare function of the modern state.

Government confers benefits to individuals through social insurance and public assistance. Social insurance does not require a demonstration of need; public assistance (welfare) hinges on proof of need. In one form of social insurance—old-age benefits—a tax on workers pays the elderly's benefits. Aid for the poor comes from government's general tax revenues.

Programs to aid the elderly and the poor have been transformed into entitlements, which are rights that accrue to eligible persons. These government programs have reduced poverty among some groups, especially among the elderly. However, poverty retains a grip on certain segments of the population. Social and demographic changes have feminized poverty, and there is little prospect of reversing that trend any time soon.

Policy planners are divided on ways to assist those in need. The traditional approach attempts to identify successful poverty policies and multiply them. The economic approach advocates full employment as the solution. The welfare-reform advocates urge scrapping the current system because it creates dependency. Finally, advocates of empowerment urge free markets and competition in areas long dominated by government monopolies.

The food stamp program is an example of a successful public assistance program. Malnutrition may be on the verge of elimination in the United States, but hunger remains a fact of life for millions of Americans.

Government provides many benefits, or subsidies, to its citizens. Some programs provide means-tested benefits wherein eligibility hinges on income. Non-means-tested benefits are available to all regardless of income. As the demand for such benefits exceeds available resources, policymakers have come to question the fairness of some programs. Subsidies for rich and poor alike are the basis for a broad national consensus. A departure from that consensus in the name of fairness may very well be the next challenge of democracy.

KEY TERMS

welfare state
social welfare
Great Depression
New Deal
Great Society
War on Poverty
social insurance
social security
Social Security Act
Medicare
public assistance
poverty level
"feminization of poverty"
Aid to Families with Dependent Children (AFDC)
food stamp program
means-tested benefits
non-means-tested benefits

SELECTED READINGS

Bennett, Linda L. M., and Stephen Earl Bennett. *Living With Leviathan: Americans Coming to Terms with Big Government.* Lawrence, Kan: University Press of Kansas, 1990. An analysis of public opinion about the powers and responsibilities of national government, from Franklin Roosevelt to Ronald Reagan.

Berry, Jeffrey M. *Feeding Hungry People: Rule-making in the Food Stamp Program.* New Brunswick, N.J.: Rutgers University Press, 1984. A thorough examination of the evolution of the food stamp program, especially the relationships among Congress, the Department of Agriculture, and interest groups.

Joe, Tom, and Cheryl Rogers. *By the Few, for the Few.* Lexington, Mass.: Lexington Books, 1985. A study of the changes in AFDC wrought by the Reagan administration, and the negative effects of those changes on incentives for welfare recipients to work.

Katz, Michael B. *The Undeserving Poor: From the War on Poverty to the War on Welfare.* New York: Pantheon, 1989. A historical overview of the ideas and assumptions that shaped policies toward the poor from the 1960s through the 1980s.

Maney, Ardith L. *Still Hungry After All These Years: Food Assistance Policy from Kennedy to Reagan.* Westport, Conn.: Greenwood Press, 1989. A carefully documented and well-reasoned analysis of one of the important legacies of the Great Society. Maney examines the motivations and consequences of food assistance policies through six presidential administrations.

Marmor, Theodore, and Jerry L. Mashaw, eds. *Social Security: Beyond the Rhetoric of Crisis.* Princeton, N.J.: Princeton University Press, 1988. This collection of essays and studies examines the future of social security in light of profound social and economic change.

Murray, Charles. *Losing Ground.* New York: Basic Books, 1985. An assessment of American social policy from 1950 to 1980. Murray argues that by attempting to remove the barriers to the good life for the poor, policymakers have created a poverty trap.

Schwartz, John E. *America's Hidden Success.* New York: Norton, 1983. A defense of the success of social policy from 1960 to 1980; it should be read in conjunction with Murray.

Starr, Paul. *The Social Transformation of American Medicine.* New York: Basic Books, 1982. The definitive work on the evolution of the American health-care system of doctors, hospitals, health plans, and government programs.

Wilson, William Julius. *The Truly Disadvantaged: The Inner City, the Underclass, and Public Policy.* Chicago: University of Chicago Press, 1987. Wilson argues that the decay of the inner city cannot be explained by racism alone and targets the class structure of ghetto neighborhoods as the most important factor in a complex web of reasons.

20 GLOBAL POLICY

IT IS HARD TO TELL WHEN the Cold War *really* ended, but its official demise occurred on November 21,1990. On that day leaders of thirty-four nations proclaimed the end of the "era of confrontation and division" that followed World War II. Adding his signature to the Charter of Paris for a New Europe, President George Bush said for the first time, "The Cold War is over."[1]

The end of the **Cold War**—an intense rivalry between the Western alliance, led by the United States, and the Eastern European nations controlled by the Soviet Union—had been signaled by earlier events. Late in 1988, Soviet President Mikhail Gorbachev, squeezed by economic troubles at home, began military cutbacks in Eastern Europe, and Soviet control over Eastern European countries began to disintegrate. One after another, the peoples of Poland, Hungary, Czechoslovakia, East Germany, and Romania ousted communist governments and proclaimed their commitment to freedom and democracy. For thirty years the menacing Berlin Wall had stood as the most prominent symbol of East-West confrontation. In late 1989, the wall began to come down. Only weeks before the Paris meeting, East and West Germany had unified.

When the leaders gathered, they signed agreements promoting human rights, democracy, the free market, and the rule of law. In addition, the twenty-two nations from the two opposing Cold War blocs accepted a far-reaching arms reduction agreement. This was cause for jubilation—the greatest threat to global peace and stability seemed to be over. Already, however, the first crisis of the post–Cold War world was brewing.

In August 1990 President Saddam Hussein of Iraq had ordered his army to invade and annex neighboring Kuwait. Most nations of the world, including the United States, quickly condemned the invasion. The United Nations Security Council backed resolutions authorizing an **embargo** (a freeze on the shipment of goods to or from a country) against Iraq. Later

The Cold War Ends

The Berlin Wall, a concrete barrier erected in 1961 by East Germany to separate East and West Berlin, symbolized the Cold War. November 9, 1989, marked the unofficial end to Cold War tensions when East Germany gave its citizens the right to travel to West Berlin. Joyous demonstrators scaled the wall, which was later dismantled. The official end to the Cold War came on November 21, 1990, when President Bush signed the Charter of Paris for a New Europe.

**The New World
Order Begins**

*Destroyed military and civilian
vehicles clog a highway near
Kuwait City in 1991. The Iraqi
invasion of Kuwait was the
first major international event
in the post–Cold War era. The
quick and decisive victory won
by the U.S.-led coalition forces
prompted President Bush to
envision a new world order,
one in which nations work
together toward the goals of
stability, prosperity, and peace.*

the Security Council permitted the use of force to make Iraq withdraw
from Kuwait. The United States sent troops to Saudi Arabia, where they
were joined by forces from twenty-seven other countries including Britain, Turkey, Syria, and Egypt.

Against this background, President Bush and other world leaders spoke
of creating a "New World Order." Although all the details of this new
international order were not spelled out, one point was clear: the decline
of Soviet power and the crisis in the Persian Gulf challenged decision
makers in the United States to reconsider American global policies. In
addition, the new international situation raised an age-old question of
American politics: "Should politics stop at the water's edge?" In other
words, is there a difference between foreign policy and other types of
public policy? Like domestic policy, *foreign policy* consists of the means
by which government pursues certain goals within specific situations.
Just as people disagree about domestic policies, they also disagree about
foreign policies because they differ about the goals government should
have, the means to reach them, and the nature of the situation. It seems
only normal, then, that America's Persian Gulf policy would immediately give rise to varying opinions.

As troops were massing in the Saudi desert, many legislators reminded
President Bush that the power to declare war rested with Congress. Congressional committees heard public testimony from some who advised
waiting longer for the embargo to work before launching a war; others
testified that delays made Saddam's conquest more secure. After several
days of open debate, both houses of Congress passed resolutions authorizing the president to use force in the Persian Gulf. The final votes
showed, however, that many lawmakers did not agree with the president
on this issue. Meanwhile, even though opinion polls showed that most
Americans supported the president, new peace groups organized to oppose the war (see Chapter 7).

Although vigorous discussion is usually thought to be a sign of vitality in a democracy, some people think it can lead to problems in foreign policy. These problems are nothing new; Alexis de Tocqueville described them in 1837:

> Foreign politics demand scarcely any of those qualities which are peculiar to a democracy; they require, on the contrary, the perfect use of almost all those in which it is deficient. . . . [A] democracy can only with great difficulty regulate the details of an important undertaking, persevere in a fixed design, and work out its execution in spite of severe obstacles. It cannot combine its measures with secrecy or await their consequences with patience.[2]

As Tocqueville predicted, sometimes the workings of foreign policy have challenged democratic government. This chapter asks whether a democracy can achieve its goals around the globe without compromising its domestic political process. Specifically, can America pursue freedom and order abroad without undermining these values at home?

In this chapter, we examine the nature of the new international order and America's role in it. Also, we focus on the foreign policymaking process and the strains it places on democratic government. We discuss America's view of the world, its foreign policy goals, and the means available to reach them. We look at the division of responsibility for foreign policy among the branches of government and the effect this division has on the policymaking process.

Americans View the World: Two Policy Paradigms

Policymakers, like everyone else, tend to interpret new occurrences in the light of lessons learned through previous experiences. During the Cold War, U.S. policymakers often relied on two historical experiences to help shape their outlooks on world politics. Each provides a distinct model (or *paradigm*) for organizing and understanding events and avoiding policy errors. The world-views of American policymakers tend to alternate between these two very different perspectives, called the Munich paradigm and the Vietnam paradigm.

The Munich Paradigm

The first view, sometimes called the **Munich paradigm**, seeks to avoid mistakes European nations made in the days leading up to World War II. At Munich in 1938, British Prime Minister Neville Chamberlain made concessions to Adolf Hitler that he believed would ensure peace in his time. He was wrong. The Germans were on a course of territorial expansion and just months after the Munich settlement, Europe went to war.

During much of the Cold War, this paradigm formed the basis of an American foreign policy consensus. For about twenty years after World War II, most Americans agreed on the need to avoid "another Munich." In their view Soviet expansionism replaced German expansionism as the central threat to peace, and the East-West split became the key division in world politics. They believed the primary goal of U.S. foreign policy should be to promote order by containing communist expansion. This meant America needed to maintain a strong military establishment.

By the late 1960s, events in Vietnam led many people to question this paradigm. A second, competing viewpoint was introduced, and America's foreign policy consensus collapsed.

The Vietnam Paradigm

This second view, the **Vietnam paradigm**, seeks to avoid mistakes America made during the Vietnam War. Throughout the 1950s and 1960s, American presidents increased (or "escalated") our military involvement in Vietnam. Influenced by the Munich paradigm, Americans tried to prevent what they saw as a Soviet-sponsored dictatorship in North Vietnam from expanding into the South. By deploying a half-million American troops and using massive bombing in both the North and South, American policymakers believed they could end the communist threat in Vietnam. As American commitment increased, casualties mounted, and antiwar protests at home began. Gradually, American public opinion turned against the conduct of the war.

The Vietnam paradigm suggested that the turmoil in Vietnam (and elsewhere in the Third World) sprang from poverty, nationalism, and anticolonialism rather than from Soviet involvement. Those who adopted this perspective saw the division between rich and poor nations as more important than the East-West split.

Adherents of the Vietnam paradigm also challenged the methods used to "win the hearts and minds" of people in other countries. They rejected military solutions and the U.S. role as world policeman. Those holding this viewpoint believed the United States should not intervene in other countries in order to avoid "another Vietnam." They feared another long-term, large-scale military commitment with no victory in sight. Instead they preferred to emphasize other tools, including "the four D's": diplomacy rather than military force, **détente** (the relaxation of tensions between East and West), disarmament and arms control, and development aid to overcome the inequalities that breed disorder and allow communist movements to thrive.

Consensus, Policy Paradigms, and the Post–Cold War World

At the end of the Vietnam War, political scientists suggested that a new foreign policy consensus might form around the Vietnam paradigm.[3] Some expected that this world-view would eventually dominate, as those clinging to the older Munich paradigm either converted or died. Today, the idea that the Vietnam experience might serve as the core of such a consensus seems highly unlikely. For one thing, members of the Vietnam generation do not really share a single world-view.[4] Not everyone agrees on what the lessons of Vietnam really were.

As the Cold War ended, no single foreign policy consensus emerged to guide policy in the new era. Instead, Americans continued to rely on the

FEATURE 20.1   *Crisis in the Gulf: Munich or Vietnam?*

As policymakers and opinion leaders tried to understand what sort of threat Saddam Hussein posed and how the United States should respond to him, they constantly compared the situation in 1990 to two previous crises—Munich and Vietnam.

Stephen Solarz (Democratic representative from New York): "Like Hitler, Saddam has an unappeasable will to power combined with a ruthless willingness to employ whatever means are necessary to achieve it. . . . If we do not stop him now, we will almost certainly be obligated to confront him later, when he will be chillingly more formidable." (*The New Republic*, 7–14 January 1991, p. 20.)

Zbigniew Brzezinski (NSC head under President Jimmy Carter): "[T]o speak of Saddam Hussein as Hitler is to trivialize Hitler and elevate Saddam." (Senate Foreign Relations Committee testimony, 5 December 1990.)

Alexander M. Haig (secretary of state under President Ronald Reagan): "Like Nazi Germany, Saddam Hussein's Iraq can only enjoy the benefits of its conquest if the international community acquiesces. Armed with the benefits of aggression, including oil, Iraq will surely be much stronger, much better able to buy and perfect the

weapons of mass destruction that its leader craves.

"In short, the appeasement of Saddam Hussein, like that of his forebears in the 1930s, would favor a greater crisis later and enlarge Iraq's capacity to prevail in such a crisis. Saudi Arabia, Jordan, the United Arab Emirates, possibly Egypt, surely Israel, would be drawn one by one into either submission or conflict." ("Gulf Analogy: Munich or Vietnam?" *New York Times*, 10 December 1990, p. A15.)

George Bush (president of the United States): "I know that there are fears about another Vietnam. . . . [T]his will not be a protracted, drawn-out war. . . . The forces arrayed are different. The opposition is different. The resupply is different. The resupply of Saddam's military would be very different. The countries united against him in the United Nations are different. The topography of Kuwait is different. And the motivation of our all-volunteer army is superb.

". . . [I]f there must be war, we will not permit our troops to have their hands tied behind their backs. And I pledge to you: There will not be any murky ending. If our American soldier has to go into battle, that soldier will have enough force behind him to win. And then get out as soon as possible, as soon as the UN objectives have been

same two paradigms to interpret events. During the Persian Gulf debates, both world-views had eloquent adherents (see Feature 20.1). Many analysts invoked the Munich analogy and portrayed Saddam Hussein as another Hitler whose aggression must be stopped. Others vowed that America's enormous military force would not get bogged down in another Vietnam. The outcome of the Persian Gulf War, in fact, reinforced the appeal of the Munich view and undermined the Vietnam paradigm. America's quick, decisive victory led President Bush to exclaim, "By God, we've kicked the Vietnam syndrome once and for all!"[5]

Disagreements over foreign policy are inevitable. Foreign policy issues require people to draw on their political orientations, values, and past experiences. These factors are complex and multidimensional, so it is not surprising that the pluralism of viewpoints found in domestic politics carries over into foreign politics as well. The essential agreement on foreign policy that existed during the period between World War II and Vietnam may have been an exception rather than the rule. Further discussion of these issues, though, requires a better understanding of modern American foreign policy in its historical context.

achieved. I will never—ever—agree to a halfway effort." (News conference, 30 November 1990; *Weekly Compilation of Presidential Documents*, vol. 26, #48 [3 December 1990], p. 1949.)

Stephen Solarz: "In Vietnam no vital American interests were at stake. The crisis in the Gulf poses a challenge not only to fundamental American interests but to essential American values. In Indochina, the cost in blood and treasure was all out of proportion to the expected gains from a successful defense of South Vietnam. In the Gulf the potential costs of the American commitment are far outweighed by the benefits of a successful effort to implement the UN resolutions calling for the withdrawal of Iraq from Kuwait. The war in Vietnam dragged on for years and ended in an American defeat. A war in the Gulf . . . is likely to end with a decisive American victory in months, if not in weeks. Sometimes you are condemned to repeat the past if you do remember it—that is, if you draw the wrong lessons from it and let the memory of the past distort your view of the present." (*The New Republic*, 7–14 January 1991, p. 20.)

Stanley Hoffman (professor of government, Harvard University): "Vietnam, alas, remains a more relevant analogy than Munich, and—

given the Americanization of the conflict both in Vietnam and in the Gulf—it cannot be exorcised so easily. Of course, the terrain is not the same, the enemy can't move and hide in the jungles, and he has no friendly suppliers abroad. . . . But he has more lethal weapons than the Vietcong and the North Vietnamese, in a more combustible part of the world. (As in the case of Vietnam, the Administration seems to minimize the possible effects of military action and to exaggerate the costs of alternative courses.) As with Vietnam, the obsession with the gulf crisis . . . strains relations with allies accused of not fully sharing a 'burden' we deem common (but whose size and direction we haven't been willing to set in common); and it concentrates on an admittedly important region resources that are needed for dealing with problems of at least equal importance in Eastern Europe or in Central America or at home. As in Vietnam, we may, if the war is not quickly over, and even if it is, but only through the annihilation of the enemy, be trapped in a quagmire of our own making." ("The Price of War," *New York Review of Books*, 17 January 1991, pp. 9–10.)

U.S. Values and Interests: The Historical Context

Above all else, the goal of American foreign policy is to preserve our national interests. The most important of these concern national security. The difficult parts of foreign policymaking come in figuring out just what "national interests" and "national security" mean in practice and then deciding exactly what to do to preserve them. During the Cold War, Americans saw their own national security tightly bound up with stopping communist expansion. In 1990, many Americans believed it was important to prevent Saddam Hussein from exercising too much power in the Middle East.

From Isolationism to Globalism

Americans have not always viewed their national security interests in global terms. For most of the nineteenth century the limits of American interests were staked out by the Monroe Doctrine of 1823. The United States rejected any European efforts to intervene in the Western hemisphere and agreed not to get involved in European politics. **Isolationism** protected Americans from Old World entanglements.

As the nineteenth century wore on, however, the United States did become increasingly involved in the affairs of non-European nations. For example, the United States expanded its power in the Pacific and intervened in Latin America. However, America's defense establishment and foreign policy commitments remained small.

World War I marked the United States' first serious foray into European politics. In 1917, the rhetoric of our entry—"to make the world safe for democracy"—showed the moralistic and idealistic tone that has often characterized America's approach to international politics. At the Versailles Peace Conference in 1919, President Woodrow Wilson championed the League of Nations as a device for preventing future wars. When the Senate refused to ratify the Versailles Treaty, and thus blocked America's entry into the League, the brief moment of American internationalism ended. For the next two decades, the United States generally maintained its traditional isolationist posture.

In 1939, America's security interests continued to be narrowly defined, and the military establishment needed to defend those interests remained small. At the outbreak of the Second World War in Europe (September 1939), the United States had no draft or compulsory military service; there were 334,473 men in the armed forces, and defense expenditures amounted to about $1.3 billion (roughly equal to 1.5 percent of

The Same in Any Language

These three World War I posters (from Germany, Italy, and the United States) were used to persuade men to join the army. Interestingly, they all employed the same psychological technique—pointing at viewers to make each individual feel the appeal personally.

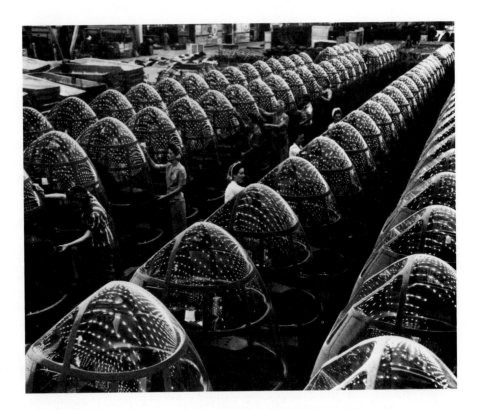

Polishing the Coneheads

War often stimulates social change. During World War II, more than 6 million women entered the labor force, many doing jobs—such as making tailgunner cones for bombers—that had previously been done by men.

the gross national product at that time).[6] No American troops were garrisoned abroad, and the country did not belong to any military alliance. The oceans were America's first line of defense.

World War II dramatically changed America's orientation toward the world. In 1949, four years after the war ended, approximately 5.5 percent of the gross national product was being spent on the armed forces.[7] That same year, the United States concluded the first of many peacetime alliances, the North Atlantic Treaty, creating the **North Atlantic Treaty Organization (NATO).** Under that treaty, America permanently committed itself to the defense of Western Europe. American troops stayed on in Europe, and the United States continued the draft to provide military manpower. In addition, U.S. attitudes toward international organizations changed after World War II. America was the driving force behind the United Nations and supported the establishment of a World Court. Americans accepted the idea that these institutions provided the basis for world order (see Feature 20.2). American isolationism seemed to have vanished, replaced by a new **globalism**. Economically, politically, and militarily, the United States had become a superpower, and its national security interests were now global in scope.

Containment and Korea

The foreign policy consensus forged at the end of the 1940s was clearly internationalist, with a strong militarist flavor. The Soviet Union, America's wartime ally, was now seen as the principal threat to order. The Soviets dominated Eastern Europe, and their ideology was spreading. They

FEATURE 20.2   *The United Nations and the New World Order*

At the end of World War II, the victorious allies established the United Nations to maintain global peace and security. As the Cold War developed, U.S.–Soviet rivalry usually paralyzed any UN effort to resolve disputes when the superpowers' interests were involved. Since the two nations had worldwide interests, the scope for UN action was quite limited. Now that Cold War tension is fading, however, both the United States and the Soviet Union have shown a new willingness to use the United Nations as a tool of foreign policy.

The structure of the United Nations makes it a large, complex, decentralized institution. Although its most attention-grabbing activities focus on security issues, it also includes many specialized agencies geared to deal with economic and social concerns.

The General Assembly. Each of the 160 member states of the United Nations has one vote in this body. The General Assembly passes nonbinding resolutions and chooses members to serve in other UN organizations (for example, the Security Council and the Economic and Social Council). The General Assembly is responsible for UN finances; it has also created a variety of organizations to deal with specific problem areas, such as UNICEF (United Nations Children's Emergency Fund) and UNEP (United Nations Environment Program).

The Security Council. This fifteen-member body has the main responsibilty for keeping the peace. Its resolutions are binding on all UN members, and it may back up its resolutions by taking enforcement measures, including deployment of blue-helmeted UN peacekeeping forces. To pass a measure, nine votes are required with no vetoes. This body is made up of five permanent members with veto power—the United States, the Soviet Union, Great Britain, France, and China—as well as ten members elected for two-year terms.

The Economic and Social Council (ECOSOC). This fifty-four-member organization is under the authority of the General Assembly. It is responsible for coordinating the economic and social programs of the UN and its numerous specialized and affiliated agencies.

The Trusteeship Council. At the end of World War II, this council administered some eleven trust territories. Today all but one of these trusts has

---

responded to NATO's establishment by setting up the Warsaw Pact, a military alliance that included the Soviet Union and its Eastern European satellites. America feared the growth of Soviet power. European conflicts had drawn the United States into war twice in twenty-five years; the Soviets, left unchecked, might well do it again.

This view (heavily shaped by the recent war with Hitler) saw the Soviets seeking to dominate the world and extend the communist system around the globe. To frustrate these designs, Americans would have to be ready to cut budgets for nondefense spending, even if this meant important domestic programs had to be delayed.[8] For the first time in peacetime, Americans were asked to give priority to defense spending over domestic spending, to guns over butter. America was not in an actual shooting war, or a "hot war," with the Soviets, but the adversarial nature of U. S.–Soviet relations was clear. The term *Cold War* was coined to describe the situation.

The Cold War required commitment and sacrifice. The American course of action, as sketched out by State Department official George Kennan, had to be "longterm, patient but firm and vigilant containment."[9] **Containment** meant holding Soviet power in check as if it were achieved independence or become part of a neighboring country. Now only the Trust Territory of the Pacific Islands (Micronesia) remains.

The International Court of Justice (ICJ).   The ICJ, or World Court, hears cases brought to it by the states involved and also, at the request of the Security Council or General Assembly, may provide advisory opinions on matters of international law. Judges from fifteen nations are elected by the Security Council and General Assembly and serve nine-year terms.

The Secretariat.   This is the executive arm of the United Nations. It administers the programs and policies set up by other UN bodies. To do this job, the Secretariat relies on a bureaucracy of some 14,000 civil servants. The head of the Secretariat is the secretary-general, who serves for five years. The secretary is recommended by the Security Council and elected by the General Assembly. In addition to coordinating the UN bureaucracy, the secretary may also play a major role in bring security threats to the Security Council and in resolving international disputes through his own diplomatic efforts.

In addition to these organizations, there are some sixteen specialized agencies connected with the UN. Among these are bodies that help promote smooth international transportation and communication (the Universal Postal Union, the International Civil Aviation Organization, the International Maritime Organization, the International Telecommunication Union), those that deal with agriculture (the Food and Agricultural Organization, the International Fund for Agricultural Development), those concerned with public health (the World Health Organization), and those concerned with supporting economic development (the International Monetary Fund, the World Bank, the United Nations Industrial Development Organization). Some agencies, such as the United Nations Educational, Scientific, and Cultural Organization and the International Labor Organization, became controversial in the United States when the Reagan administration withdrew from them, arguing they had become too "politicized."

As this list of agencies suggests, the UN does not confine itself to narrow security issues. Many people believe that instability grows out of poverty, and so, by seeking to improve the quality of life around the world, the UN promotes peace as well.

in a container. America could not return to isolationism, as President Harry S Truman explained in his 1947 speech justifying aid to Greece and Turkey. According to Truman, the spread of totalitarian systems such as communism undermined "the foundations of international peace and hence the security of the United States."[10]

Truman's foreign policy had two dimensions: one was military preparedness; the other, an economic program to thwart Soviet expansion. Secretary of State George Marshall recognized that war-weakened European nations offered good targets for Soviet opportunism. He proposed a European recovery plan, commonly known as the **Marshall Plan**, to put Europe back on its feet economically. Over four years this foreign aid program sent some $12 billion to help rebuild European countries.

While a clear American policy toward Europe was taking shape, new crises emerged in Asia. Mao Zedong (Mao Tse-tung) brought about a communist takeover in China. Since Americans thought of international politics as a **zero-sum game**—a situation in which one superpower's loss was the other's gain—America's "loss" of China to Mao and communism appeared to be a victory for the Soviets. Some policymakers resisted this idea, but their voices were soon drowned out when, on June 25,

1950, communist North Korea invaded noncommunist South Korea. The United States used the United Nations to intervene in the conflict to push the North Koreans out. The bulk of the UN force sent to Korea consisted of Americans.

The Korean War differed from the American image of what a war should be. World War II had been a "total war." America had fully committed all its economic, human, and military resources to the war effort. The goal of the Allies in the Second World War was unconditional surrender. After the fighting had begun, the time for political solutions had ended. Only military solutions were acceptable.

In contrast, U.S. economic and manpower commitments to the Korean conflict were much lower. General Douglas MacArthur, the American in command of UN forces in Korea, was not allowed to use atomic weapons or to push an offensive into China once the Chinese communists entered the fighting. Policymakers on both sides sought political solutions, trying to limit hostilities and avoid the outbreak of another world war. The conflict finally ended with an agreement that essentially restored the original north-south boundary. The United States had successfully contained communism in Korea, but the conflict opened a Pandora's box of problems that would beset the United States again in Vietnam. America's inability to translate its huge military and economic strength into consistent political success showed that its enormous power still had limits.

Cold War Commitments Under Eisenhower and Kennedy

President Dwight Eisenhower generally continued Truman's Cold War policies. But he realized that domestic political realities meant that defense spending had to have limits. He also expressed concern about the ways in which the pursuit of global interests might affect America's democratic institutions. Though a former general, Eisenhower warned against the power of the **military-industrial complex**. He worried about the "conjunction of an immense military establishment and a large arms industry," both lobbying for increased military spending. The growth of the military-industrial complex threatened pluralist democracy because it created an extremely powerful group united by two common interests—war and military spending. Eisenhower warned that its "total influence—economic, political, even spiritual—is felt in every city, every statehouse, every office of the federal government."[11] (For an example of the pervasiveness of the military-industrial complex in the 1980s, see Figure 20.1.)

During the Eisenhower years, U.S. defense policy relied chiefly on the deterrent power of nuclear weapons rather than on the strength of conventional forces. Guided by the theory of **deterrence**, American strategists believed that the Soviets would hesitate to take aggressive actions knowing they risked nuclear annihilation. In the late 1950s, however, the Russians built up their own nuclear strength, and the two superpowers approached the possibility of **mutual assured destruction (MAD)** in a nuclear conflict. Against this background, deterrence did not seem very

F I G U R E 20.1 *The Flow of Defense Dollars*

*Although the West and East Coasts receive the largest share of dollars from defense con-
tracts, every part of the nation receives income from military spending. Dollar figures are
for 1988 and represent billions of dollars. Percentages indicate proportion of total dollars
spent on defense contracts. (All figures have been rounded.) (Source: Bureau of the Census,
Statistical Abstract of the United States, 1990 [Washington, D.C.: U.S. Government Printing
Office, 1990], p. 333.)*

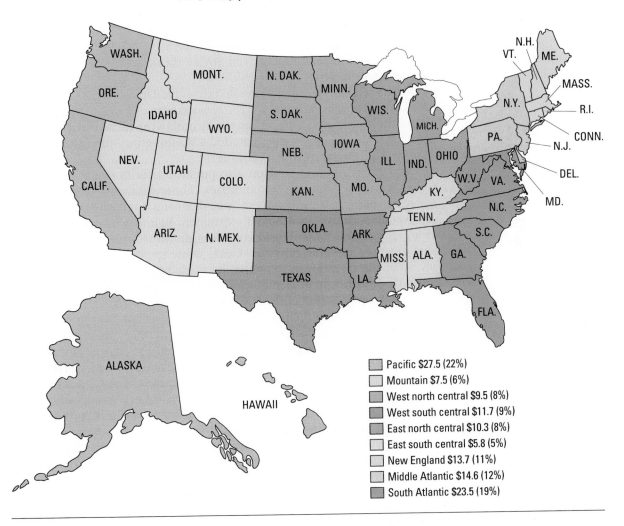

Pacific $27.5 (22%)
Mountain $7.5 (6%)
West north central $9.5 (8%)
West south central $11.7 (9%)
East north central $10.3 (8%)
East south central $5.8 (5%)
New England $13.7 (11%)
Middle Atlantic $14.6 (12%)
South Atlantic $23.5 (19%)

credible as a means of limiting Soviet expansion. It did not seem likely
that a president would risk nuclear destruction in America to stop a Soviet advance in Western Europe. To restore credibility to deterrence, analysts argued that America should develop the strategies and weapons
needed to fight a limited nuclear war.[12] They also called for America to
beef up its conventional forces, so that the country would be able to select from a range of defense options.

This last idea, called **flexible response,** became a cornerstone of defense
policy during the Kennedy administration. John F. Kennedy shared the

Cold War mindset of his two predecessors. In his inaugural address, he pledged to "pay any price, bear any burden, meet any hardship, support any friend, oppose any foe to assure the survival and success of liberty."[13] To Kennedy, the struggle against Soviet communism was paramount. The two most dramatic foreign policy incidents of his administration were the Bay of Pigs invasion and the Cuban missile crisis. The first was a debacle in which American-supported Cuban exiles failed in an attempt to invade Castro's communist Cuba. The second resulted in greater American success when a U.S. naval blockade forced the Soviets to remove missiles they had placed on the island. Both incidents were attempts to combat the perceived Soviet threat to U.S. security in the Western hemisphere.

In the wake of the Cuban missile crisis, the United States and the Soviet Union took steps to reduce the tension between them. Most notably they concluded a nuclear test ban treaty outlawing tests of nuclear weapons above ground. They also installed a Washington-Moscow communications link nicknamed the "hotline."

The Kennedy administration also pursued a series of **nation-building policies** among Third World countries. These measures were geared to shore up their economies and promote democratic reforms, making them less attractive targets for Soviet expansion. Kennedy's sensitivity to nation building in Third World countries did not outweigh his commitment to the Cold War, however. Once, while speaking about possible regimes in the Dominican Republic, he made his values clear: "There are three possibilities in descending order of preference: a decent democratic regime, a continuation of the [right-wing dictatorship under the] Trujillo [family], or a Castro regime. We ought to aim at the first but we really can't renounce the second until we are sure that we can avoid the third."[14] Threats to freedom and equality from the right seemed preferable to threats to freedom and equality from the left. The Soviets (on the left) were the real enemy; they posed the greatest threat to the American concept of order.

One of Kennedy's policies involved both nation building and resistance to a communist expansion and had a critical impact on American foreign policy. Fearing a communist takeover by forces from North Vietnam, America had been sending military aid and advisers to non-communist South Vietnam for years. Kennedy stepped up this program. At his death in 1963, sixteen thousand American military advisers were stationed in South Vietnam. During Lyndon Johnson's presidency, the price of this commitment would rise drastically in terms of both dollars and lives.

Vietnam: The Challenge to America's Foreign Policy Consensus

In November 1963, just three weeks before President Kennedy's assassination, the United States tacitly permitted a coup in South Vietnam. The instability of the regime there undermined America's efforts to contain communism in Vietnam. Its overthrow did not bring political stability, however. Over the next few years, one government succeeded another, but none proved capable of maintaining control for very long.

Meanwhile, the military situation continued to deteriorate. By early 1964, the Vietcong (South Vietnamese communists) controlled almost half of South Vietnam.

In August 1964, Congress passed the Gulf of Tonkin Resolution, which gave President Lyndon Johnson a virtual blank check for his policies in Vietnam. He ordered American bombing raids on the north, but by early 1965, the military situation had become so bad that he sent in U.S. ground troops. Eventually the United States had more than 500,000 men in Vietnam. Casualties mounted, and no end to the conflict was in sight. Opposition to the undeclared war grew, on college campuses and elsewhere. An antiwar candidate, Democratic Senator Eugene McCarthy of Minnesota, challenged Johnson in the Democratic presidential primaries. On March 31, 1968, Johnson ordered a halt to the bombing of North Vietnam. In the same speech, he bowed out of the presidential race. By that time, most Americans surveyed in a Gallup Poll said that they believed the United States had made a mistake in sending troops to Vietnam. This feeling persisted throughout the period of American involvement in the conflict.[15]

Richard Nixon, who succeeded Johnson, was well aware of public opinion on the war. He campaigned on a pledge to end the war by achieving "peace with honor." He relied on a strategy called **Vietnamization**, which meant gradually turning the fighting over to the South Vietnamese. Little by little, American forces were pulled out, casualties fell, and draft calls were cut. Americans and Vietnamese signed a peace agreement in 1973, and the remaining American troops returned home. In April 1975, the communists took South Vietnam. The economic costs of the war were high, in direct military expenditures and indirect costs (like veterans' benefits and disability payments). Other costs, however, cannot be counted so easily. Nearly fifty thousand Americans and many more Vietnamese lost their lives. The conflict deeply divided the American people and fragmented the Cold War consensus on American foreign policy.

Even while the war dragged on, President Nixon and his chief foreign policy adviser, Henry Kissinger, were making important changes in American foreign policy. They attempted to redefine America's overseas commitments through the **Nixon Doctrine**, an effort to "steer a course between the past danger of overinvolvement and the new temptation of underinvolvement."[16] In a clear contrast with Kennedy's inaugural rhetoric, Nixon stated that America would no longer "conceive all the plans, design all the programs, execute all the decisions and undertake all the defense of the free nations of the world." Instead, the United States would intervene only where "it makes a real difference and is considered in our interest."[17]

During Nixon's administration, the United States entered a period of warmer relations, or détente, with the Soviet Union. Nixon also ended the decades of U.S. hostility toward the People's Republic of China. The theory of détente emphasized the value of order—order based not only on military might but also on mutual interests among the superpowers. Kissinger believed that if the Soviets and the Chinese were treated as legitimate participants in the international system, they would then have a vested interest in supporting world order. They would have less incen-

The Costs of War

The Vietnam Veterans Memorial in Washington, D.C., is a place of national sorrow. The long chevron of black granite is etched with the names of 58,156 American soldiers who died in the nation's longest conflict. The Vietnam War cost the United States more than $3.3 trillion, divided the American people, and fragmented the Cold War foreign policy consensus.

tive to promote revolutionary challenges to international stability. Kissinger embraced **linkage**, that is, he attempted to use rewards and advantages in one area to promote Soviet compliance with U.S. policy in other areas.

Critics have noted that détente did not bring about a successful end to the Vietnam War, nor did it solve the problem of the 1973 Arab oil embargo. In fact, Kissinger's concentration on East-West politics might have made him less attentive to the increasing importance of North-South issues. Others have suggested that the brand of foreign policy promoted by Kissinger during the Nixon and Ford administrations was too cynical and paid too much attention to power and interests and not enough to basic American ideals and human rights.

Carter's Search for a New Foreign Policy

Initially, President Jimmy Carter's stance on foreign policy differed substantially from that of his predecessors. Carter tended to dismiss the

Soviet threat throughout most of his administration. He did not believe the hand of the Soviet Union was behind the revolutions in Nicaragua and Iran that occurred during his tenure in office. Instead, he interpreted these events as largely the products of internal forces. Nevertheless, he did attempt to articulate American interests—in particular, America's stake in the Persian Gulf region. By this time, détente with the Soviets had broken down. Fearing that the Soviets might see the Iranian revolution as an opportunity for them in the Middle East, he set forth the **Carter Doctrine**. This asserted that "an attempt by any outside force to gain control of the Persian Gulf region will be regarded as an assault on the vital interests of the United States of America. And such an assault will be repelled by any means necessary including military force."[18]

In contrast to the Nixon-Kissinger era, Carter was sometimes criticized as overly idealistic. He emphasized human rights, leveling criticism—and sometimes even sanctions—at both friends and enemies with poor human rights records. He usually leaned toward "open" (rather than secret) diplomacy, although his greatest foreign policy achievement, the Camp David Agreements, which brought about peace between Egypt and Israel, was the product of closed negotiations he arranged between Egyptian President Anwar Sadat and Israeli Premier Menachem Begin.

In many ways, Carter's foreign policy reflected the influence of the Vietnam paradigm, for his administration downplayed the use of military force. Many Americans were frustrated, however, by Carter's inability to develop effective responses when Iranians took American diplomats hostage or when the Soviets invaded Afghanistan.

Foreign Policy Under Reagan

Carter's successor, Ronald Reagan, came to the Oval Office with none of the doubts associated with the Vietnam paradigm. In general, Reagan accepted the Munich perspective. He believed that the Soviets were responsible for most of the evil in the world and attributed instability in Central America, Africa, and Afghanistan to Soviet meddling. He believed the best way to combat the Soviet threat was to renew and project American military strength. The Reagan years witnessed a huge increase in defense spending and a new willingness to use American military muscle, in Libya and Grenada, for example.

The administration argued that its massive military buildup was both a deterrent and a bargaining chip to use in talks with the Soviets. During much of the Reagan administration, this policy meant that the Cold War climate grew even chillier. Things changed, however, when Mikhail Gorbachev came to power in the Soviet Union. Gorbachev wished to reduce commitments abroad in order to concentrate resources needed for domestic reform (**perestroika,** or economic and political restructuring, and **glasnost,** or openness). By the end of Reagan's second term, the United States and the Soviet Union had concluded agreements outlawing intermediate-range nuclear forces (the INF Treaty) and providing for a Soviet military pullout from Afghanistan.

In addition to its tough posture toward the Soviets, the Reagan administration also took a hard line at the United Nations. Until the mid-1960s, votes in the UN General Assembly usually supported U.S.

positions. Later, however, as the UN expanded its membership to include many newly independent states, the United States and its Western European allies frequently found themselves outvoted. Under Reagan, the United States cut its financial contribution to the UN and also withdrew temporarily from membership in UN organizations (such as UNESCO) whose policies it opposed. Similarly, during this period, the United States also refused to accept the jurisdiction of the World Court when that body seemed likely to condemn U.S. actions against the government of Nicaragua.

Bush and the New World Order

When Ronald Reagan's vice president, George Bush, succeeded him as president, many people expected him to continue Reagan's foreign policy. Like his predecessor, early in his administration he showed his willingness to use military force (in Panama in December 1989). But, as noted at the beginning of this chapter, during the first two years of Bush's administration, America witnessed the end of the Cold War. For over forty years, the main goal of American foreign policy had been containing the Soviet threat. With that goal apparently achieved once and for all, how would the Bush administration redirect American foreign policy?

There were many questions. Would America continue to play a role in Europe? How? Would NATO continue? Would it emphasize political matters, now that its military value had declined? Some people predicted the development of pan-European institutions, such as the Conference on Security and Cooperation in Europe (CSCE), which included virtually all European states as well as the United States and Canada.

When the Berlin Wall came down, many Americans expected large reductions in defense spending. Though defense cuts were planned, it soon emerged that they would take place gradually, over several years. Federal budgetary problems and a recession made Washington unwilling to make bold new gestures to help underwrite Eastern Europe's development of democratic and market-oriented institutions. Instead, the United States mainly participated in assisting Eastern Europe through multilateral institutions like the World Bank.

President Bush also emphasized multilateral action and the use of international organizations like the UN in the Persian Gulf crisis. U.S. diplomats carefully built a coalition of nations, including America's Western allies, the Soviet Union, Eastern European states, many Arab states, and other Third World countries, to oppose Saddam Hussein. The United States also won UN Security Council approval for a series of motions. During the Cold War, the Security Council had usually proved ineffective in major crises, most of which pitted U.S.-backed clients against those supported by the Soviet Union. As a result, one or the other superpower could be usually counted on for a veto. However, in this first post–Cold War crisis, the two superpowers cooperated against Saddam.

Despite this emphasis on multilateral action, the Persian Gulf crisis demonstrated that the United States continues to play a leadership role in global politics. Although many nations agreed to contribute military and financial support, the United States shouldered by far the greatest share of the fighting. Despite budgetary constraints that kept the United States from undertaking other foreign policy initiatives, the Bush administration believed it critical to mount this operation and contain what it saw as an important threat to the emerging New World Order.

Conflicting Policy Paradigms and America's Foreign Policy Goals

This review of the history of U.S. foreign policy points to several goals this country has set for itself. First among these has been the preservation of American freedom and independence. For much of our history, this meant avoiding international alliances. The nation remained free to pursue the development of its own territory and to intervene in the affairs of other countries in the hemisphere. Since World War II, most policymakers have believed that protecting America's freedom and international peace meant controlling the threat of communism. In the last four decades, then, much of American foreign policy has been directed toward the goal of creating or preserving a "stable world order." As the American response to Iraq suggests, this goal remains important even when the threat to order no longer originates with the Soviet Union.

In pursuit of order, the United States has used both conflict and cooperation. On one hand, the country's search for stability led to periods of détente with China and the Soviet Union. On the other hand, America has sometimes found itself "containing communism" by opposing, undermining, and intervening against revolutionary movements in Third

The Odd Couple

When Iraq invaded and annexed the oil-rich monarchy of Kuwait, President Bush quickly promised assistance to Kuwait's head of state, the Emir Sheik Jaber al-Ahmed al-Sabah. After Kuwait was pronounced liberated on February 27, 1991, the Emir and the ruling al-Sabah family seemed less than eager to restore the country's constitution and establish democracy.

World countries. The nation has used a web of alliances to contain the expansion of communism, only to be reminded that commitments forged in the defense of freedom may also limit freedom—a lesson learned in Vietnam.

The questions of order and freedom are linked. One important U.S. goal has been spreading American-style free institutions at both the national and the international levels. America backed the establishment of international organizations, such as the United Nations and the World Court, and also supports the development of capitalist economies and liberal political systems, guaranteeing free elections and basic human rights. During the Cold War, however, policymakers were often willing to overlook violations of freedom by any regime that proclaimed itself anticommunist.

The question of order is also linked to equality. With East-West tensions reduced, some observers call for more attention to the division of the world into rich and poor nations (sometimes characterized as industrialized nations versus Third World nations, or North versus South). Supporters of this position argue that the real threat to international stability has its source in economic and political inequality. These complicated issues may require a foreign policy that relies more heavily on economic development, interdependence, redistribution of wealth, and access to the political process than on conflict and military might.

The Munich paradigm and the Vietnam paradigm generally agree on the priority of the first goal—order—but they have disagreed sharply on how best to bring about order. They also disagree on how to weight the other two goals—freedom and equality. As Tocqueville suggested, such a lack of consensus could seriously undermine the conduct of foreign policy. The dilemma becomes even greater in a system like the American system, where the power over foreign policy is split among branches of government and executive department and agencies.

Foreign Policymaking: The Constitutional Context

The Constitution clearly puts the president in charge of American foreign policy. However, the framers also included checks and balances to prevent the president from conducting foreign policy without substantial cooperation from Congress. Still, presidents have found ways to sidestep these provisions when they have felt it important to do so.

The Formal Division of Power

The Constitution gives the president four significant foreign policy-making powers:

- The president is commander in chief of the armed forces.
- The president has the power to make treaties (subject to the consent of the Senate).

Lonely at the Top

Being commander in chief of the armed forces is an awesome responsibility. Stunned by a resurgence of enemy activity during the Vietnam War in early 1968, President Lyndon Johnson decided not to seek re-election. Here, in July 1968, the president listens to a tape-recorded message from his son-in-law, who was serving in Vietnam.

- The president appoints U.S. ambassadors and the heads of executive departments (also with the advice and consent of the Senate).
- The president receives (and may refuse to receive) ambassadors from other countries.

Congress also has specific powers in the foreign policy arena:

- Congress alone may declare war.
- Congress has the legislative power.
- Congress controls the nation's pursestrings.
- Congress is charged with raising, supporting, and maintaining the army and navy.
- Congress may call out the militia to repel invasions.

The most important foreign policy power the Constitution gives to Congress is the power to declare war, a power it has used only five times.

However, Congress has become involved in foreign policy in other ways. Using its legislative power, it may create programs of international scope, such as SEED (Support for East European Democracy Act of 1989), a program to improve trade relationships with Poland and Hungary. Congress may also use its legislative power to impose legal limits on the actions of the executive branch, as it did when it restricted arms transfers under the Arms Control Export Act (1988). In addition, Congress has used its power of the purse to provide funds for activities it supports and prohibit funds to those it does not.

Finally, there are some foreign policy functions that belong to the Senate alone:

- The Senate consents to treaties.
- The Senate gives its advice and consent to the appointment of ambassadors and various other public officials.

The Senate has not been shy about using these powers. We have already mentioned its refusal to ratify the Versailles Treaty. More recently, the U.S.–Soviet SALT II treaty, an arms limitation agreement negotiated under the Carter administration, was introduced into the Senate but not brought to a vote because its supporters feared defeat.

Sidestepping the Constitution

Although the Constitution gives the executive branch enormous power in the foreign policy area, it also places limits on that power. Presidents and their advisers have often found ingenious ways around these constitutional limitations. Among the innovative devices they have used are executive agreements, discretionary funds, transfer authority and reprogramming, undeclared wars, and special envoys. Since the Vietnam War, however, Congress has attempted to assert control over the use of these presidential tools.

An **executive agreement** is a pact between the heads of two countries. Initially, such agreements were used to work out the tedious details of day-to-day international affairs. In *U.S.* v. *Curtiss-Wright* (1936), the Supreme Court ruled that executive agreements are within the inherent powers of the president and have the legal status of treaties.[19] This ruling gave the president an enormously powerful tool. Executive agreements, like treaties, have the force of law, but unlike treaties they do not require Senate approval. Until 1972, the texts of these agreements did not even have to be reported to Congress. Legislation passed that year now requires the president to send copies to the House and Senate Foreign Relations Committees.

This requirement has not seriously affected the use of executive agreements, which has escalated dramatically since World War II. In 1986, for example, executive agreements outnumbered treaties by about 24 to 1.[20] Presidents have used these agreements to make substantive foreign policy. In fact, senators have complained that the treaties now submitted for Senate approval deal with petty, unimportant matters, whereas serious issues are handled by executive agreement. Moreover, executive agreements are subject to very few limits. One observer noted that "the principal limitation on their use is political in nature–the degree to which it is wise to exclude the Senate from [its] constitutional foreign policy role."[21]

Presidents have also used several devices to circumvent congressional control over the nation's finances. For one, the chief executive is provided with **discretionary funds**—large sums of cash that may be spent on unpredicted needs to further the national interest. Kennedy used discretionary funds to run the Peace Corps in its first year; Johnson used $1.5 billion of his funds in Southeast Asia in 1965 and 1966.[22]

The president's **transfer authority,** or the **reprogramming** of funds, allows him to take money that Congress has approved for one purpose and spend it on something else. In 1989, the administration tried to shift $777 million from other defense accounts in order to avoid making personnel cuts.[23] In addition, the executive branch has control over the disposal of excess stocks including surplus or infrequently used equipment. The Central Intelligence Agency (CIA) has been an important beneficiary of **excess stock disposal**.

The Constitution makes the president commander in chief of the armed forces. In this role, he has claimed the right to involve the United States in undeclared wars by committing American troops in emergency situations. America's undeclared wars, police actions, and other interventions have outnumbered formal, congressionally declared wars by about 40 to 1. Since the last declared war ended in 1945, over 100,000 American servicemen and women have died in locations ranging from Korea and Vietnam to Grenada, Panama, and the Persian Gulf.

During the Vietnam conflict, congressional opponents of that conflict passed the **War Powers Resolution** to limit the president's ability to wage undeclared wars. Under this resolution, a president must "consult" with Congress in "every possible instance" before involving U.S. troops in hostilities. In addition, the president is required to notify Congress within forty-eight hours of committing troops to a foreign intervention. Furthermore, once troops have been deployed, he may not keep them there for more than sixty days without congressional approval (although he may take up to an additional thirty days to remove troops "safely"). President Nixon vetoed the War Powers Act as an unwarranted restriction on the president's constitutional authority, but it was passed over his veto. Some critics have charged that the legislation does *not* limit presidential power but instead gives the president a free hand to wage war for up to sixty days.* By the end of that period, Congress might find it very difficult indeed to force the president to bring the troops home. The actual impact of the War Powers Act is debatable. All of Nixon's successors in the White House have questioned its constitutionality, and no president has ever been "punished" for violating its provisions. Most recently, the congressional resolution authorizing the use of force in the Persian Gulf avoided a showdown between the branches over this thorny issue.

Although the Senate rarely rejects a presidential choice, senators have used confirmation hearings as opportunities for investigating the presi-

---

* These critics included both conservative Republican Senator Barry Goldwater of Arizona and liberal Democratic Senator Thomas Eagleton of Missouri. Eagleton's feelings were succinctly summarized in the title of his book, *War and Presidential Power: A Chronicle of Congressional Surrender* (New York: Liveright, 1974).

dent's foreign policy activities. For example, while he served as national security adviser, Henry Kissinger claimed that executive privilege protected him from being summoned to testify before congressional committees. When President Nixon nominated him to be secretary of state, however, senators were able to ask him, in the course of the confirmation process, about a variety of subjects, including his roles in the secret bombing of Cambodia and in wiretapping various news reporters and public officials. One way presidents get around the Senate's power over appointments, therefore, is to rely heavily on the White House staff, who are accountable to no one but the president, or to use **special envoys,** or "personal representatives," who may perform a wide variety of foreign policy tasks.

Foreign Policymaking: The Administrative Machinery

Although American foreign policy is developed and administered by the executive branch, it requires approval and funding by Congress and is subject to congressional oversight. When America assumed a larger role in world affairs following World War II, the old foreign policy machinery was inadequate to the demands of American superpower status. In 1947, Congress overhauled the system, passing the National Security Act, which established three new organizations with important foreign policy roles: the Department of Defense, the National Security Council, and the Central Intelligence Agency. These organizations joined the other department within the executive branch that shares major foreign policy-making power and responsibility, the Department of State.

The Department of State

The department most concerned with the overall conduct of foreign affairs is the Department of State. It helps to formulate and then executes and monitors American policy throughout the world. Its head, the secretary of state, is the highest-ranking official in the Cabinet; he is also, supposedly, the president's most important foreign policy adviser. However, different presidents have used this office in different ways. Some, like John Kennedy, preferred to act as their own secretaries of state and appointed relatively weak figures to the post. Others, such as Dwight Eisenhower, appointed stronger individuals to the post (John Foster Dulles, during Eisenhower's administration). During his first term, Richard Nixon planned to control foreign policy from the White House. He appointed William Rogers as secretary of state but took much of his advice from his national security adviser, Henry Kissinger, whose office was located in the White House.

Like other executive departments, the State Department is made up of political appointees and permanent employees selected under the civil service merit system. The former include deputy secretaries and undersecretaries of state and some—but not all—ambassadors; the latter include about 3,500 foreign service officers who alternate assignments between home and abroad. The department staffs U.S. embassies and consulates throughout the world. It has primary responsibility for representing America to the world and caring for American citizens and interests abroad. Although the foreign service is highly selective (fewer than two hundred of the fifteen thousand who take the annual examination are appointed), the State Department is often charged with a lack of initiative and creativity. Critics claim that bright young foreign service officers quickly realize that conformity is the best path to career advancement. As one observer put it: "There are old foreign service officers; and there are bold foreign service officers; but, there are no old, bold foreign service officers."[24] At times presidents have complained that the department's foreign policy machinery is too slow and unwieldy. As President Kennedy remarked, "Bundy [Kennedy's national security adviser] and I get more done in one day in the White House than they do in six months in the State Department. . . . They never have any ideas over there, never come up with anything new."[25]

Probably the most important problem facing the State Department today is the lack of a strong domestic constituency to exert pressure in support of its policies. This is in marked contrast with, say, the Department of Agriculture, which can mobilize farmers to support its activities; or the Department of Defense, which can look for help from defense industries or veterans' groups. In a pluralist democracy, the lack of a natural constituency is a serious drawback for a department.

The Department of Defense

The Department of Defense replaced two Cabinet-level departments: the War Department and the Department of the Navy. It was created to provide the modern bureaucratic structure needed to manage America's much-increased peacetime military strength and to promote greater unity and coordination among the armed forces. At the same time, in keeping with the U.S. tradition of civilian control of the military, the new department was given a civilian head—the secretary of defense—a Cabinet member with authority over the military. Successive reorganizations of the department (in 1949 and 1958) have given the secretary greater budgetary powers, control of defense research, and the authority to transfer, abolish, reassign, and consolidate functions among the military services.

The power available to defense secretaries often depends on the secretary's own vision of the job and willingness to use the tools available. Strong secretaries of defense, including Robert McNamara (under Kennedy and Johnson), Melvin Laird (under Nixon), James Schlesinger (under Nixon and Ford), and Caspar Weinberger (under Reagan), have wielded tremendous power.

Below the secretary are the civilian secretaries of the army, navy, and air force; below them are the military commanders of the individual branches of the armed forces. These military leaders make up the Joint Chiefs of Staff (JCS). In addition to their roles as heads of their respective services, the JCS meet to coordinate military policy; they are also the primary military advisers to the president, the secretary of defense, and

In the Gulf, on the Verge of War

Richard Cheney, the secretary of defense, and General Colin Powell, chairman of the Joint Chiefs of Staff, seem to feel the gravity of the moment as they visit with U.S. airmen stationed in Saudi Arabia in December 1990, one month before the air campaign against the Iraqi forces began.

the National Security Council. As advisers, the JCS have broad responsibilities for developing positions on such matters as alliances, plans for nuclear and conventional war, and arms control and disarmament.

The CIA and the Intelligence Community

Before World War II, the United States had no permanent agency specifically charged with gathering intelligence (that is, information) about the actions and intentions of foreign powers. In 1941, poor American intelligence procedures contributed to the success of the Japanese surprise attack on Pearl Harbor. After the war, America began to play a more internationalist role. In recogniton of both these factors, Congress created the Central Intelligence Agency (CIA) in 1947.

The agency's charter charges it with (1) coordinating the information and data-gathering activities of various other government departments, and (2) collecting, analyzing, evaluating, and circulating its own intelligence relating to national security matters. Most of these activities are relatively uncontroversial. By far the bulk of material obtained by the CIA comes from readily available sources: statistical abstracts, books, newspapers, and the like. The agency's Intelligence Directorate is responsible for these overt (open) information-processing activities.

The charter also empowers the CIA "to perform such other functions and duties related to intelligence affecting the national security as the

National Security Council shall direct." This vague clause has been used by the agency as its legal justification for the covert (secret) activities undertaken by its Operations Directorate. These activities have included espionage, coups, assassination plots, wiretaps, interception of mail, and infiltration of protest groups.

Critics sometimes point out that the CIA has not ended major foreign policy "surprises" for the United States. Some gaffes have been the result of faulty intelligence (as in the case of the Bay of Pigs), but others were more the result of policymakers' failure to accept or interpret analyses properly. The CIA told President Johnson that bombing North Vietnam would not bring the North Vietnamese into submission. Johnson responded to CIA interpretations by remarking, "Policymaking is like milking a fat cow. You see the milk coming out, you press more and the milk bubbles and flows and just as the bucket is full the cow with its tail whips the bucket and all is spilled. That's what the CIA does to policymaking."[26] The usual response to intelligence failures is to investigate and then propose structural changes in institutions, but at least one analyst claims that "intelligence failure is political and psychological more often than it is institutional."[27] Even the best-designed intelligence network will not prevent the United States from being caught by surprise some of the time—at most, it might minimize the frequency or intensity of such surprises.

The basic dilemma posed by the CIA and the intelligence community, though, concerns the role of covert activities. Covert operations raise both moral and legal questions for a democracy. Allen Dulles, Eisenhower's CIA director, once called these operations "an essential part of the free world's struggle against communism." Are they equally important in a post–Cold War world? Can they be reconciled with America's democratic commitment to open government, free elections, and self-determination? In practice, it also has been difficult to reconcile such activities with basic operating principles of American government, such as the principle of checks and balances. For example, though the CIA's covert activities are supposed to be approved by a National Security Council subcommittee, the president himself is not always briefed about them.

Congress has wrestled with the problem of the secrecy necessary for successful operations for many years. In 1975, it passed the Hughes-Ryan Amendment, which required all covert activities of the CIA to be reported to the appropriate congressional committees. In 1981, in the Intelligence Authorization Act, Congress required all intelligence agencies to inform appropriate committees not only of current covert operations but also of "significant anticipated operations." That act also reduced, from eight to two, the number of committees that must be informed of secret activities. In 1989, over CIA objections, Congress authorized the establishment of an independent inspector general at the agency who would make reports available to members of Congress.

The National Security Council

The **National Security Council (NSC)** is a permanent group of advisers created to help the president integrate and coordinate the details of domestic, foreign, and military affairs as they relate to national security.

Monitoring Soviet Politics

Condoleezza Rice used to be the Director for Soviet and Eastern European Affairs on the National Security Council. NSC staff members daily assemble a world intelligence briefing from thousands of reports, including satellite photos and spy and news reports. Among her responsibilities, Rice briefed air force generals on Soviet military strategy. In March 1991, Rice left the NSC to become an associate professor of political science at Stanford University.

The NSC consists of the president, the vice president, the secretaries of state and defense, and the chairman of the Joint Chiefs of Staff, as well as others appointed by the president. NSC discussions can cover a wide range of issues, such as how to deal with changes in Eastern Europe or what U.S. policy in the Middle East should be. In theory, at least, NSC discussions offer the president an opportunity to solicit advice, while allowing key participants in the foreign policymaking process to keep abreast of the policies and capabilities of other departments.

In practice, the role played by the NSC has varied considerably under different presidents. Truman and Kennedy seldom met with the NSC; Eisenhower and Nixon brought it into much greater prominence. During the Nixon administration, the NSC was critically important in making foreign policy. Much of this importance derived from the role played by Henry Kissinger, Nixon's assistant for national security affairs (the title of the head of the NSC staff). Under Nixon and Kissinger, the NSC staff ballooned to over one hundred—in effect, a little state department in the White House. Kissinger also used this staff for direct diplomacy and covert operations, as did the Reagan administration. By using the NSC, which has been almost completely exempt from outside scrutiny, staffers hoped to preserve secrecy, and, more importantly, avoid the possibility that Congress would prohibit the operations they wished to undertake.

As we have seen, Tocqueville believed that part of a democracy's weakness in foreign affairs stemmed from its inability to solve the dilemma of how to combine the secrecy necessary for foreign policy with the openness needed for democratic government. Practitioners of international relations have traditionally valued secrecy, but democratic theory requires that citizens know what their leaders are doing. This dilemma continues to cause problems for American policymakers.

The Public, the Media, and Foreign Policy

Another great difficulty Tocqueville predicted for democracies in foreign affairs stemmed from the changeable views of a mass electorate. He believed foreign relations required patience and persistence in the pursuit of long-term goals. But the public could be fickle, unwilling to set aside short-term gains for long-term security. In response to domestic pressures, leaders could be forced to act in ways that are harmful to *global* interests. Their democratic responsiveness might well be detrimental to the long-term success of their foreign policy.

The Public and the Majoritarian Model

Americans as a group know very little about politics but are still very willing to express their opinions about political issues (see Chapter 5). These findings hold for foreign affairs as well as (and perhaps even more than) domestic politics. Only about 15 percent of Americans pay attention to foreign affairs.

Americans are quick to tell policymakers what should be done, but they can rarely provide guidance on how to do it. Consider the public's response to a March 1969 poll on the Vietnam War.[28] Of those polled, 52 percent—a clear majority—believed that our involvement in Vietnam was a mistake. When asked what the United States should do next in terms of the war, 32 percent advised all-out war, 26 percent wanted American troops pulled out of Vietnam, 19 percent agreed with the present policy, and another 19 percent wanted to end the war as soon as possible.* Obviously, Americans were unhappy about the policies being pursued in Vietnam. However, they were unable to reach a consensus on what the policy should be.

The public's opinions regarding foreign policy issues are also highly volatile. The American people have historically been willing to "rally 'round the flag" and back presidential foreign policies, particularly in crisis situations. When fighting began in the Persian Gulf, for example, President Bush's approval rating soared. But past history suggests that this phenomenon lasts for only a relatively short period of time. Moreover, changes in public opinion on foreign policy can affect presidential elections. Thus, President Carter enjoyed increased public approval following the seizure of American hostages in Iran. That added support helped him win a victory over Senator Edward Kennedy of Massachusetts in the 1980 Democratic primaries. However, Carter's inability to resolve the hostage situation contributed to his defeat by Ronald Reagan a few months later.

President Reagan's commitment of troops to Lebanon dragged on for over a year, with little popular support, until a terrorist bombing incident claimed 241 American lives. Polls then showed a slight increase in support, which soon declined. As policy in Lebanon threatened to become an election issue, the president withdrew the marines. The moral to be drawn from these examples seems clear: a president had better be

---

* The remaining 4 percent made other responses.

able to produce a short-run success or expect to lose his constituency—exactly what Tocqueville would have predicted.

Those who support the majoritarian model of democracy might argue that the people are capable of evaluating the benefits and costs of a foreign policy. But this does not mean that the public can make foreign policy. Or, to put it more strongly, any idea that American foreign policy is a reflection of mass opinion is crude and simplistic, since "policy formulation does not derive from the simple preferences of an uninformed, uninterested, unstable, acquiescent and manipulable 'public voice.'"[29] In short, policymakers must look elsewhere for their cues. In foreign affairs, as in other areas of American politics, the majoritarian model does not really seem to describe American democracy.

Interest Groups and the Pluralist Model

Many people take an interest in foreign policy issues when they believe those issues affect them directly. Most auto workers and manufacturers may favor import restrictions on Japanese cars. Many Jewish citizens may pay close attention to America's relations with Israel. These individuals often join organizations that present their policy positions to policymakers.

On foreign affairs issues, two of the most prominent kinds of lobbies have included businesses and unions, often seeking trade protection, and ethnic groups looking for support for their fellows in the "old country." More recently, and in keeping with the current lobbying boom in Washington, foreign governments have begun to hire high-powered Washington lobbying firms to represent their interests (see Feature 10.2, page 354).

The impact of these groups varies with the issue. In general, lobbying seems to be more effective when it takes place behind the scenes and deals with noncrisis issues that are not considered important by the public at large. Interest groups are more effective in maintaining support for the status quo than in bringing about policy changes.[30]

As with domestic issues, there is a tendency for foreign policy interest groups to counterbalance each other. The Turkish lobby may try to offset the Greek lobby; the Arms Control Association or the Federation of American Scientists may oppose the American Legion or the Veterans of Foreign Wars on issues of defense and military spending. The result may be that "foreign policy making resembles a taffy-pull: every group attempts to pull policy in its own direction while resisting the pulls of others, with the result that policy fails to move in any discernible direction. The process encourages solutions tending toward the middle of the road and maintenance of the status quo."[31]

The Media and Foreign Policy

A potentially powerful source of influence on both public attitudes and policymakers' actions is the media—television, newspapers, magazines, and radio. Do the media shape foreign policy? Television coverage of the Vietnam War is often thought to be one reason why people turned against that war. Fearing a repetition of this, the Pentagon took special steps to limit press coverage during Operation Desert Storm in the Persian Gulf.

In general, however, the impact of the media on the public is limited. Recent events in the Persian Gulf aside, most people simply do not follow foreign affairs or care much about foreign policy.

The media themselves try to cater to their audience and generally do not devote very much space or time to foreign policy issues. When they do, their impact on the general public tends to be more indirect than direct. One observer described it as a "two-step flow."[32] The foreign policymakers and the "attentive public" obtain most of their information from the media. This information eventually filters down to the rest of the public through their communications with clergy, teachers, union officials, and other opinion leaders.

Just as they set the domestic political agenda (see Chapter 6), the media also set the foreign policy agenda. By giving play to a particular issue, policy, or crisis, the media are able to focus attention on that issue. As in domestic affairs, the media "may not tell us what to think, but they tell us what to think about."[33]

The agenda-setting role of the media can have an impact on foreign policymaking in another way. Remember that interest groups tend to be most effective in noncrisis situations that are not of general public concern. By calling attention to a particular issue, then, the media can dilute some of the effectiveness of organized special interest groups. And, in a crisis situation that calls for quick action, media attention can even work to the detriment of an interest group. On the other hand, by keeping an issue before the public, the media can increase the likelihood that it will become the focus of some interest group's lobbying efforts.[34]

The Foreign Policy Process

Now that we have looked at the historical context of American foreign policy and the cast of characters involved, we should examine the policymaking process itself. How is foreign policy made?

Sources of Information for the Executive Branch

By constitutional position and practical control of resources, the president is the lead actor in the foreign policymaking process. A president comes to the job with a world-view that helps him interpret and evaluate international events. And, as chief executive, he commands tremendous foreign policy resources, including information and personnel. The Pentagon, the State Department, and the CIA are among his main sources of information about the outside world, and they provide staffs to advise him on foreign policy and implement that policy. Often presidential advisers will present conflicting information or offer different, even contradictory, advice. Advisers may compete for a president's ear or bargain among themselves to shape administration policy.

A president's sources of foreign policy advice are not limited to executive branch officials. Members of Congress can try to pressure the White

House into a particular course of action. Foreign governments can also attempt to move an administration in a certain direction.

The president's most important task in the foreign policymaking process is figuring out whom to believe—those who agree with his policy predispositions or those who challenge them. The wrong choice can be extremely costly. Some observers argued that President Johnson's tendency to surround himself with yes-men kept him from hearing critical analyses of the Vietnam situation until quite late.

Congress and the President

Once a president has decided on a policy, he may be able to carry it out without congressional approval if he has a clear constitutional mandate (as, for example, when he recognizes a government or puts troops on alert). When his legal authority is shaky and congressional approval appears unlikely, he may use the techniques described on pages 740–742. A president's third alternative is to ask Congress for the funds or authority to carry out the policy.

The president's command of information and personnel gives him a considerable advantage over Congress. Although legislators have ample access to independent sources of information on domestic issues, their sources on foreign affairs are more limited. Members of Congress may go on fact-finding tours or get information from lobbyists, but they don't begin to have a fraction of the president's sources of information. They are forced to rely heavily on the executive branch for information.

The president may use his informational advantage to swing votes. During the congressional debate over the use of force in Iraq, CIA Director William Webster sent a letter to members of Congress providing data on the sanctions policy along with his department's conclusion that an

We're with You, George!

On March 6, 1991, President Bush addressed a joint session of Congress to announce the end of the war in the Persian Gulf. Democratic members wore flag lapel pins and yellow ribbons; Republicans waved little flags. Some Democrats, feeling outclassed, asked Republican colleagues to share their flags so they, too, could wave to the folks back home when the president paused to receive an ovation.

embargo alone would not make Saddam leave Kuwait. The White House also fed information to Congressman Les Aspin convincing him that American casualties would be very low in a military action against Iraq.

In addition, the chief executive's personnel resources give him considerable ability to influence events. Many analysts argue, for example, that the incidents that sparked the Gulf of Tonkin Resolution during the Vietnam War were pretexts that President Johnson seized on to expand American involvement.

Another potential disability of Congress in the foreign policy process is its fragmented authority over international issues. Different congressional committees have authority for the armed services, for foreign relations, for intelligence oversight, for foreign trade, and for development. There is no congressional equivalent of the National Security Council to mold a coherent approach to foreign policy. Granted, there are often disagreements within the executive branch, and these can even spill over into the congressional arena. For example, a Pentagon official might quietly appeal to friendly members of the Armed Services Committees to restore a defense cut made by the president. Disaffected officials might leak information. But, by and large, the executive is much better equipped to offer a unified approach to foreign policy.

Faced with these comparative disadvantages in terms of information, personnel, and organization, the general tendency is for Congress to accede to the president's foreign policy programs.

Lobbies and the "Lobbyist in Chief"

Lobbies participate in the foreign policymaking process in many ways. When the Bush administration floated the possibility of putting together a $21 billion arms package for Saudi Arabia during the Persian Gulf crisis, for example, lobbyists from the American Israeli Public Affairs Committee immediately began to mobilize their congressional allies; soon the administration retreated and offered only $7 billion. As the fighting began, a variety of newly organized groups geared up to express opinions on all sides of the issue. Among them were the Coalition to Stop U.S. Intervention in the Middle East, Churches for a Middle East Peace, Citizens for a Free Kuwait, and the Coalition for America at Risk.

The single most effective "lobbyist" on an issue, though, is often not really a lobbyist at all, but rather the president (see Chapter 12). Presidential lobbying was particularly effective in the vote on the use of force against Iraq. When Congress began its new session on January 3, 1991, few would have guessed that only nine days later it would, in effect, vote to authorize war. Since Republicans are in a minority in Congress, President Bush knew he had to win substantial support among Democrats for his Persian Gulf policy. He courted Representative Dante Fascell of Florida, Democratic chair of the House Foreign Affairs Committee, as well as several liberal members of Congress known for their long-standing support of Israel. He invited 100 members to the White House for breakfast to hear his side of things. In the end, presidential arm-twisting paid off in the passage of the resolution of support, 250–183 in the House and 52–47 in the Senate.

Policy Implementation

A president may decide on a course of action, and Congress may authorize it, but the policy still must be carried out. The question of who should carry out a particular policy is not always easy to answer. Although the basic functions of each department and agency are spelled out, at times they overlap. When they do, organizations may squabble over which should perform a particular mission. During the Cuban missile crisis, for example, there were disputes between the CIA and the military concerning who should fly reconnaissance flights over Cuba.

Congress, of course, is responsible for overseeing the implementation of programs. That means, among other things, monitoring the correct use of funds and evaluating the effectiveness of programs.

Foreign Policy Tools

"We have a toolbox that's full of tools and I brought them all to the party," General Colin Powell, chairman of the JCS, told reporters just before the Persian Gulf War began.[35] He was referring specifically to the variety of weapons the United States could use against Iraq. Once war broke out, the dazzling success of the American forces certainly highlighted the value of military instruments in liberating Kuwait from Iraq. But this accomplishment may have obscured the fact that President Bush also relied on other kinds of devices to help get the job done. For example, he used the United Nations Security Council to pass resolutions condemning Iraq. He also assembled and held together an unlikely coalition that included Arab states, western and eastern European states, the Soviet Union, and Israel. When necessary, he used economic measures, such as debt forgiveness for the Egyptians, to keep the coalition together. Effective as American technology, firepower, and strategy were in the Persian Gulf, foreign policy success depends on having a mix of tools available, including economic, diplomatic, and military ones. Since America faces a range of foreign policy problems, most of them not military in nature, the country needs to develop its nonmilitary capabilities.

At the beginning of this chapter, we noted that adherents to the Munich and Vietnam paradigms have very different attitudes about how and when to use the tools of American foreign policy. It oversimplifies matters to say that those influenced by the Munich paradigm see military force as the only choice, whereas those influenced by the Vietnam paradigm would never resort to force. But the two groups do differ significantly in the emphasis they place on the country's military, economic, and diplomatic resources. In this section, we will look at some tools available to foreign policymakers in the areas of defense and economics.

Defense Policy

Most people agree that in order to protect national interests, the United States needs an adequate defense. But beyond this point, agreement breaks down. Against whom are we defending ourselves? What constitutes an adequate defense? To what extent should defense spending take priority over other kinds of spending?

During the Reagan years, the United States undertook an enormous defense buildup. The main justification for this was to counter the Soviet threat. Indeed, the president maintained that the only way to gauge the adequacy of American defense was by comparing our military spending with that of the Soviet Union (see Compared with What? 20.1). As Soviet power declined, many Americans anticipated large defense cuts (the so-called "peace dividend"). Policymakers discussed how far and how fast the defense budget could be reduced, but this discussion slowed

COMPARED WITH WHAT? 20.1

Defense Expenditures, 1978–1988

President Reagan used to claim that the U.S. defense budget is set in Moscow—that is, the United States and its allies had to increase spending to keep pace with Soviet and Warsaw Pact expenditures. By 1988, Western spending on defense had pulled well ahead. In 1989, Eastern European countries began to challenge Soviet hegemony and oust their communist governments. The Warsaw Pact was dissolved. With its principal opponent gone, NATO began to search for new roles, and the Bush administration began to plan for defense cutbacks, including many military base closings.

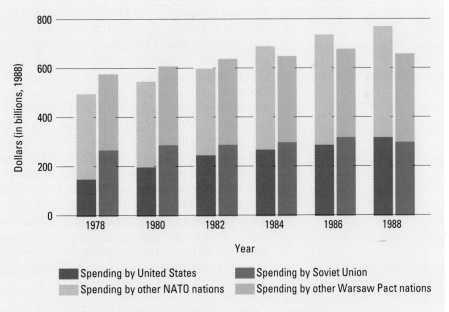

Source: U.S. Arms Control and Disarmament Agency, *World Military Expenditures and Arms Transfers, 1989* (Washington, D.C.: U.S. Government Printing Office, 1990).

with the outbreak of war in the Persian Gulf. Although U.S. allies promised to foot most of the bill, the costs of the war were still large. At the war's end, administration officials continued to discuss cutting back troop strength by as much as one-third. Nevertheless, the fact that in the post–Cold War world, the United States found itself involved in a full-scale war against a nation other than the Soviet Union raised new questions about future U.S. defense policy. In the New World Order should the United States continue high levels of defense spending to maintain its role as a global policeman?

Defense policy also requires decisions about what to buy with the defense budget. There are many important options in terms of personnel and equipment. One issue involves whether to have a volunteer military force or to require service by some or all citizens (see Feature 20.3). Others concern the kinds of weapons systems to build and the mix of nuclear and conventional forces.

The Reagan administration was particularly supportive of high-technology weapons systems, both nuclear and conventional. It also launched a large-scale American research and development effort called the **Strategic Defense Initiative (SDI)**, or "Star Wars." Its purpose was to build a system that could defend against Soviet intercontinental ballistic missiles (ICBMs). In the absence of that defense, the only protection against ICBMs is deterrence, the fear of retaliation that keeps the superpowers from using nuclear weapons. With the decline of the Soviet threat, the SDI program seemed a logical choice for cutbacks. Ironically, SDI technology debuted in combat in the Persian Gulf when U.S. Patriot missiles were used to knock down not Soviet ICBMs heading toward the United States but Iraqi Scud missiles fired at Israel and Saudi Arabia. As a result, proponents of SDI have changed their argument somewhat and now tout the usefulness of this technology against the missile capabilities of Third World nations.

Critics of defense spending worry that the United States invests too much in sophisticated military hardware and not enough on developing "human capital"—that is, preparing people to do the job. Without programs for children's nutrition and education, we may waste valuable human resources. Other critics insist that high levels of defense spending help create budget deficits that endanger the overall performance of the U.S. economy. A weak economy, in turn, could make the nation more vulnerable to outside pressures. By increasing defense outlays, then, we may actually be making the United States less secure. It is important to consider the relationship between defense policy and foreign policy. Although some believe that a strong defense is the cornerstone of foreign policy, others recognize that not every foreign policy objective can be achieved through the application of military force. Military means helped the United States push Iraq out of Kuwait, but they aren't very useful in solving the Third World debt crisis, for example.

Economic Policy

Some of the most intractable problems the United States faces around the globe are not military but economic. In fact, a recent public opinion

FEATURE 20.3   *Be All That You Can Be: The Volunteer Army as an Equal Opportunity Employer*

"The finest fighting force this nation has ever known." That's what the commander in chief called his troops when he addressed Congress at the end of the Persian Gulf War. President Bush praised his troops' motivation. And numerous commentators mentioned that the U.S. military is now better educated than ever before.

The Persian Gulf force differed from those involved in earlier large-scale American conflicts in other important ways. The 540,000 Americans who served in the Persian Gulf were all in the military voluntarily. In addition, the force was more diverse in its gender and racial composition: At least 27,000 women were stationed in the Persian Gulf; blacks comprised 20 percent of the forces, far in excess of their proportion in the general population (12 percent).

Both women and blacks face discrimination and reduced opportunities in civilian life. Some observers suggested that there is less discrimination in the military. As one soldier said, "When your life is on the line, you care that people around you know

their jobs, not that they're black or white or male or female."

But even in the military there is evidence of discrimination. Women, for example, are still legally barred from combat jobs, though legislation to change this was introduced after the war. Both women and blacks are underrepresented in the officer corps. Still, the Gulf War provided highly visible examples of blacks who had made it to the very pinnacle of the military hierarchy: Both the chairman of the joint chiefs of staff, General Colin Powell, and the deputy commander in Saudi Arabia, General Calvin Waller, are black.

The debate over the true meaning of the all-volunteer military continues. Some see the military as a road to advancement and opportunity. Others note that few children of the well-to-do ever volunteer for service. They argue that, for blacks, especially, the lack of opportunity elsewhere in society forces them into the military (the "economic draft"), causing them to bear a disproportionate share of the risks involved in war.

poll suggested that a majority of Americans consider Japanese economic power more threatening than Soviet military power.[36] America's military tools have proved very impressive; its economic tools, however, in the areas of investment, trade, and aid, seem less able to get the job done.

Although America began the 1980s as the world's leading creditor nation, it closed the decade as the number one debtor.[37] Some analysts have suggested that America's military strength and its economic weakness may be related. In their view, America has suffered from a kind of "imperial overreach" that has led it to assume too large a world military role. For example, although in 1988 the United States had a 46 percent share of the gross national product of the five most advanced industrial nations (France, Japan, West Germany, the United Kingdom, and the United States), it picked up the tab for 70 percent of their combined defense expenditures. Moreover, two-thirds of U.S. government research money goes into defense research, with only .2 percent going to discover new high tech products and processes for peaceful uses. By contrast, Japan invests 5 percent of its research money in commercial high tech research, and Germany 15 percent.[38] As historian Paul Kennedy points out in *The Rise and Fall of the Great Powers*, a similar pattern of overspending on defense combined with underspending on other areas can be found during the decline of past great powers such as Spain, the Netherlands, and Great Britain.[39]

Investment and trade. The United States invested heavily abroad well into the 1970s, prompting European concern that both profits and control of European-based firms would drain away to America. In the 1980s, however, the situation began to change. A combination of tax cuts and defense spending increases created yawning deficits in the federal budget. These gaps were largely financed by selling U.S. treasury obligations to foreigners at high rates of interest. As investors from abroad bought up American government debts, the value of the dollar soared. This made American goods very expensive on the world market and also made foreign goods relatively cheap for Americans to buy. The result was a shift in the balance of trade—the United States began to import more than it exported and continued to borrow heavily. In 1985, an agreement among the industrialized nations resulted in a devaluation of the dollar in comparison with other currencies. As the dollar fell in value, American corporations and real estate became attractive investments for foreign investors. Japanese investors bought Paramount Pictures, MCI, and Rockefeller Center. British Petroleum bought Sohio and Purina pet food, and British magnate Robert Maxwell bought the *New York Daily News* (helping to fulfill a facetious headline that appeared in a reputable business journal in 1987: "Britain Buys Back the Colonies"[40]). By 1988, foreigners held bonds totaling approximately $272 billion of the $1.7 trillion used to finance the national debt. They also owned $1.6 trillion in real property in America.[41]

Some Americans resent the penetration of the U.S. economy by foreign investors. Others complain that American trading efforts have been hampered by unfair trading practices, such as the establishment of nontariff barriers. A **nontariff barrier**, or **NTB**, is a regulation that outlines the exact specifications an imported product must meet in order to be offered for sale. The Japanese, for example, have been criticized for excessive use of NTBs. In a recent instance, American-made baby bottles could not be sold in Japan because the bottles provided level marks in ounces as well as centiliters.[42] The United States has responded by pressuring the Japanese to reduce red tape and make it easier for American firms to compete in Japan.

Although in recent years the United States has generally championed a free trade policy, the Japanese have accepted some voluntary limits on their exports. Nonetheless, American business has not been fully satisfied with these efforts. There can be strong domestic pressure to adopt import restrictions. Essentially, unions and manufacturers want to keep foreign goods from flooding the American market and driving them out of business. Lee Iacocca, president of Chrysler, wrote to President Bush in March 1991 warning that unless Japan cut its car and truck sales in the United States over the next eighteen months, Chrysler, Ford, and even General Motors could collapse.[43] The president rejected Iacocca's plea. For one thing, since the 1980s, Japanese auto companies have built factories in the United States and now increasingly compete in the American market with cars manufactured in America. Furthermore, protectionism is a double-edged sword. The countries whose products are kept out of the United States retaliate by refusing to import American goods. And protectionism complicates the foreign policymaking process enormously. It is a distinctly unfriendly move to make toward nations that may be our allies.

Still, some analysts have worried that American emphasis on free enterprise and the "magic of the marketplace" have put the United States at a disadvantage in competition with nations like Germany and Japan, who have adopted **national industrial policies**, that is, government-sponsored coordinated plans for promoting economic expansion.[44]

Foreign aid and development assistance. Inequality between rich nations and poor nations is growing. Figures show an increasing gap in income between the industrialized states of the north and the nonindustrialized states of the south.[45] This gap is a cause of concern for several reasons. Obviously, many people believe it is unjust for the developed world to enjoy great wealth while people in the **Third World** (less developed states) are deprived. Practical considerations enter in as well. Great disparities in wealth between the developed and the developing worlds may lead to political instability and disorder and thus threaten the interests of **First World** states (industrialized democracies).

The United States has many economic tools to use in support of its policies in the developing world. These include development aid, preferential trade agreements, debt forgiveness, and loans on favorable credit terms. Assistance given to developing countries often also takes the form of donation of American goods and thus directly benefits American businesses who supply the products. Still, in times of fiscal austerity, foreign aid expenditures are often easy targets for budget cutters. The United States, once the leading development aid donor, has now been surpassed by the Japanese.

Third World states have tried to reduce these inequalities by enlisting the cooperation of the developed world in a proposal for a **New International Economic Order (NIEO)**. Under the proposed NIEO, industrialized states are asked to take a variety of steps to help the Third World. These measures include providing access to markets, transferring technology, and increasing foreign development aid to .7 percent of each developed country's gross national product. On the whole, the United States has been very cool toward the NIEO. In 1988, for example, American development aid amounted to .25 percent of GNP, far short of the NIEO goal.

More recently, the countries of Eastern Europe (the **Second World**) have also begun to compete with the Third World for development dollars. The Bush administration has backed limited American aid for Eastern Europe through multilateral institutions and has also aided Poland by forgiving a considerable portion of the debt that nation owed the United States.

Sanctions and embargoes. In addition to the "rewards" offered by development aid, economic tools may also be used to punish states that do not behave as the United States would like. Sanctions, embargoes, and boycotts fall into this category. Many think the effectiveness of these tools is limited, but they are often a first resort in times of crisis. For example, when the United States wanted to force Iraq out of Kuwait, it first tried an embargo. Under the Carter administration, the United

States imposed a grain embargo against the Soviet Union—that is, the United States stopped wheat shipments to the Soviet Union—to convince the Russians to leave Afghanistan. Shortly after Castro took power in Cuba, the United States imposed a **boycott** on Cuban products—it refused to allow its citizens to import Cuban sugar, cigars, and other goods.

Neither the grain embargo nor the boycott of Cuban goods has proved particularly effective in furthering foreign policy goals. The Soviets stayed in Afghanistan to the end of Reagan's presidency, and Castro has managed to hold power in Cuba for over thirty years. The two policies did have somewhat different effects at home, which can be explained by the nature of American pluralist democracy. The Soviet grain embargo seriously hurt American grain farmers, who were left without a market for the huge amounts of wheat originally destined for the Soviet Union. They were a vocal minority, and the nation heard them. When the embargo became generally unpopular, it was lifted by President Reagan. In contrast, the boycott of Cuban sugar has helped America's domestic sugar industry. Any attempt to lift the boycott would be resisted not only by the large community of anti-Castro Cubans now living in this country but also by the sugar industry, which would suddenly have to compete with cheaper Cuban sugar. Because there is no strong pressure to remove the boycott, it remains in place. Pluralist politics triumph.

Summary

When America emerged as a superpower following World War II, the common experience of that war forged a consensus on foreign policy: Communism was a threat, and Soviet expansion had to be contained. The Vietnam War challenged that world-view and shattered the consensus. More recently, the downfall of communism in Eastern Europe seems to have ended the need for a foreign policy consensus built around the containment of communism. Today, without a consensus, some of the pluralism that characterizes other aspects of the political system also characterizes foreign policy. Those who make foreign policy disagree about appropriate ends and means. Despite the successful use of force in the Persian Gulf War, military power is not the only tool available to protect American interests; both economic and diplomatic tools have parts to play in the policymaking process.

Responsibility for foreign policy is shared by Congress, the president, and several executive departments and agencies. In the absence of a widespread consensus, foreign policy can become a political football in contests between Congress and the executive branch and among the bureaucracies. Some of these contests (like the Persian Gulf War) receive heavy media coverage and stir great public interest. Yet some observers (Tocqueville among them) have suggested that public opinion is too changeable to provide a basis for foreign policymaking.

We began this chapter by asking whether foreign policy is different from other kinds of policy. Certainly the nature of democracy—the public's right to know—at times conflicts with the planning and implementation of foreign policy. But when government officials subvert the safeguards—the system of checks and balances that protect American freedom—they risk domestic disorder in their pursuit of world order. Can Americans find a way to support freedom, order, and equality abroad while preserving them at home? This may be the ultimate challenge of democracy.

KEY TERMS

Cold War
embargo
Munich paradigm
Vietnam paradigm
détente
isolationism
North Atlantic Treaty
  Organization (NATO)
globalism
containment
Marshall Plan
zero-sum game
military-industrial
  complex
deterrence
mutual assured
  destruction (MAD)
flexible response
nation-building policy
Vietnamization
Nixon Doctrine
linkage

Carter Doctrine
perestroika
glasnost
executive agreement
discretionary funds
transfer authority
reprogramming
excess stock disposal
War Powers Resolution
special envoy
National Security
  Council (NSC)
Strategic Defense
  Initiative (SDI)
nontariff barrier (NTB)
national industrial
  policies
First, Second, and
  Third Worlds
New International Eco-
  nomic Order (NIEO)
boycott

SELECTED READINGS

Crabb, Cecil V., and Pat M. Holt. *An Invitation to Struggle*. Washington, D.C.: Congressional Quarterly Press, 1980. Describes the interplay between Congress and the executive branch on foreign policy issues.

Kennedy, Paul. *The Rise and Fall of the Great Powers*. New York: Random House, 1988. Discusses the reasons why various nations have gained and lost power in the modern world and concludes with a section entitled "The United States: The Problem of Number One in Relative Decline."

Koh, Harold. *The National Security Constitution*. New Haven: Yale University Press, 1990. Discusses how the constitutional balance of power has tipped in favor of the executive branch in matters of foreign policy.

Nathan, James, and James Oliver. *United States Foreign Policy and World Order*. 4th ed. Boston: Little, Brown, 1989. An excellent general history of American foreign policy since World War II.

Reich, Robert. *The Work of Nations*. New York: Alfred A. Knopf, 1991. Describes how national economies are giving way to a global economy and offers advice on what America should do to adapt to this change.

Spanier, John, and Eric Uslaner. *American Foreign Policy Making and the Democratic Dilemmas*. 4th ed. New York: Holt, Rinehart and Winston, 1985. A brief examination of the policy process.

APPENDICES

THE DECLARATION OF INDEPENDENCE IN CONGRESS   JULY 4, 1776

*The unanimous declaration of the thirteen
United States of America*

When, in the course of human events, it becomes
necessary for one people to dissolve the political
bands which have connected them with another, and
to assume, among the powers of the earth, the
separate and equal station to which the laws of
nature and of nature's God entitle them, a decent
respect to the opinions of mankind requires that they
should declare the causes which impel them to the
separation.

We hold these truths to be self-evident: That all
men are created equal; that they are endowed by
their Creator with certain unalienable rights; that
among these are life, liberty, and the pursuit of
happiness; that, to secure these rights, governments
are instituted among men, deriving their just powers
from the consent of the governed; that whenever any
form of government becomes destructive of these
ends, it is the right of the people to alter or to abolish
it, and to institute new government, laying its
foundation on such principles, and organizing its
power in such form, as to them shall seem most
likely to effect their safety and happiness. Prudence,
indeed, will dictate that governments long established should not be changed for light and transient
causes; and accordingly all experience hath shown
that mankind are more disposed to suffer, while evils
are sufferable, than to right themselves by abolishing
the forms to which they are accustomed. But when a
long train of abuses and usurpations, pursuing
invariably the same object, evinces a design to reduce
them under absolute despotism, it is their right, it is
their duty, to throw off such government, and to
provide new guards for their future security. Such has
been the patient sufferance of these colonies; and
such is now the necessity which constrains them to
alter their former systems of government. The
history of the present King of Great Britain is a
history of repeated injuries and usurpations, all
having in direct object the establishment of an
absolute tyranny over these states. To prove this, let
facts be submitted to a candid world.

He has refused his assent to laws, the most
wholesome and necessary for the public good.

He has forbidden his governors to pass laws of
immediate and pressing importance, unless suspended in their operation till his assent should be

A-1

obtained; and, when so suspended, he has utterly neglected to attend to them.

He has refused to pass other laws for the accommodation of large districts of people, unless those people would relinquish the right of representation in the legislature, a right inestimable to them, and formidable to tyrants only.

He has called together legislative bodies at places unusual, uncomfortable, and distant from the depository of their public records, for the sole purpose of fatiguing them into compliance with his measures.

He has dissolved representative houses repeatedly, for opposing, with manly firmness, his invasions on the rights of the people.

He has refused for a long time, after such dissolutions, to cause others to be elected; whereby the legislative powers, incapable of annihilation, have returned to the people at large for their exercise; the state remaining, in the mean time, exposed to all the dangers of invasions from without and convulsions within.

He has endeavored to prevent the population of these states; for that purpose obstructing the laws for naturalization of foreigners; refusing to pass others to encourage their migration hither, and raising the conditions of new appropriations of lands.

He has obstructed the administration of justice, by refusing his assent to laws for establishing judiciary powers.

He has made judges dependent on his will alone, for the tenure of their offices, and the amount and payment of their salaries.

He has erected a multitude of new offices, and sent hither swarms of officers to harass our people and eat out their substance.

He has kept among us, in times of peace, standing armies, without the consent of our legislatures.

He has affected to render the military independent of, and superior to, the civil power.

He has combined with others to subject us to a jurisdiction foreign to our constitution, and unacknowledged by our laws, giving his assent to their acts of pretended legislation:

For quartering large bodies of armed troops among us;

For protecting them, by a mock trial, from punishment for any murders which they should commit on the inhabitants of these states;

For cutting off our trade with all parts of the world;

For imposing taxes on us without our consent;

For depriving us, in many cases, of the benefits of trial by jury;

For transporting us beyond seas, to be tried for pretended offenses;

For abolishing the free system of English laws in a neighboring province, establishing therein an arbitrary government, and enlarging its boundaries, so as to render it at once an example and fit instrument for introducing the same absolute rule into these colonies;

For taking away our charters, abolishing our most valuable laws, and altering fundamentally the forms of our governments;

For suspending our own legislatures, and declaring themselves invested with power to legislate for us in all cases whatsoever.

He has abdicated government here, by declaring us out of his protection and waging war against us.

He has plundered our seas, ravaged our coasts, burned our towns, and destroyed the lives of our people.

He is at this time transporting large armies of foreign mercenaries to complete the works of death, desolation, and tyranny already begun with circumstances of cruelty and perfidy scarcely paralleled in the most barbarous ages, and totally unworthy the head of a civilized nation.

He has constrained our fellow-citizens, taken captive on the high seas, to bear arms against their country, to become the executioners of their friends and brethren, or to fall themselves by their hands.

He has excited domestic insurrection among us, and has endeavored to bring on the inhabitants of our frontiers the merciless Indian savages, whose known rule of warfare is an undistinguished destruction of all ages, sexes, and conditions.

In every stage of these oppressions we have petitioned for redress in the most humble terms; our repeated petitions have been answered only by repeated injury. A prince, whose character is thus marked by every act which may define a tyrant, is unfit to be the ruler of a free people.

Nor have we been wanting in our attentions to our British brethren. We have warned them, from time to time, of attempts by their legislature to extend an unwarrantable jurisdiction over us. We have reminded them of the circumstances of our emigration and settlement here. We have appealed to their native justice and magnanimity; and we have conjured them, by the ties of our common kindred, to disavow these usurpations, which would inevitably interrupt our connections and correspondence. They, too, have been deaf to the voice of justice and of consanguinity. We must, therefore, acquiesce in the necessity which denounces our separation, and hold them, as we hold the rest of mankind, enemies in war, in peace friends.

We, therefore, the representatives of the United States of America, in General Congress assembled, appealing to the Supreme Judge of the world for the rectitude of our intentions, do, in the name and by the authority of the good people of these colonies, solemnly publish and declare, that these United Colonies are, and of right ought to be, FREE AND INDEPENDENT STATES; that they are absolved from all allegiance to the British crown, and that all political connection between them and the state of Great Britain is, and ought to be, totally dissolved; and that, as free and independent states, they have full power to levy war, conclude peace, contract alliances, establish commerce, and do all other acts and things which independent states may of right do. And for the support of this declaration, with a firm reliance on the protection of Divine Providence, we mutually pledge to each other our lives, our fortunes, and our sacred honor.

JOHN HANCOCK
and fifty-five others

■

THE CONSTITUTION OF THE UNITED STATES OF AMERICA*

(Preamble: outlines goals and effect)

We the people of the United States, in order to form a more perfect union, establish justice, insure domestic tranquility, provide for the common defense, promote the general welfare, and secure the blessings of liberty to ourselves and our posterity, do ordain and establish this Constitution for the United States of America.

Article I   (The legislative branch)

(Powers vested)

Section 1 All legislative powers herein granted shall be vested in a Congress of the United States, which shall consist of a Senate and a House of Representatives.

(House of Representatives: selection, term, qualifications, apportionment of seats, census requirement, exclusive power to impeach)

Section 2 The House of Representatives shall be composed of members chosen every second year by the people of the several States, and the electors in each State shall have the qualifications requisite for electors of the most numerous branch of the State Legislature.

No person shall be a Representative who shall not have attained to the age of twenty-five years, and been seven years a citizen of the United States, and who shall not, when elected, be an inhabitant of that State in which he shall be chosen.

Representatives and direct taxes shall be apportioned among the several States which may be included within this Union, according to their respective numbers, *which shall be determined by adding to the whole number of free persons, including those bound to service for a term of years and excluding Indians not taxed, three-fifths of all other persons.* The actual enumeration shall be made within three years after the first meeting of the Congress of the United States, and within every subsequent term of ten years, in such manner as they shall by law direct. The number of Representatives shall not exceed one for every thirty thousand, but each State shall have at least one Representative; *and until such enumeration shall be made, the State of New Hampshire shall be entitled to choose three, Massachusetts eight, Rhode Island and Providence Plantations one, Connecticut five, New York six, New Jersey four, Pennsylvania eight, Delaware one, Maryland six, Virginia ten, North Carolina five, South Carolina five, and Georgia three.*

When vacancies happen in the representation from any State, the Executive authority thereof shall issue writs of election to fill such vacancies.

The House of Representatives shall choose their Speaker and other officers; and shall have the sole power of impeachment.

(Senate: selection, term, qualifications, exclusive power to try impeachments)

Section 3 The Senate of the United States shall be composed of two Senators from each State, *chosen by the legislature thereof,* for six years; and each Senator shall have one vote.

Immediately after they shall be assembled in consequence of the first election, they shall be divided as equally as may be into three classes. The seats of the Senators of the first class shall be vacated at the expiration of the second year, of the second class at the expiration of the fourth year, and of the third class at the expiration of the sixth year, so that one-third may be chosen every second year; and if vacancies happen by resignation or otherwise, during the recess of the legislature of any State, the Executive thereof may make temporary appointments until the next meeting of the legislature, which shall then fill such vacancies.

* Passages no longer in effect are printed in italic type.

No person shall be a Senator who shall not have attained to the age of thirty years, and been nine years a citizen of the United States, and who shall not, when elected, be an inhabitant of that State for which he shall be chosen.

The Vice-President of the United States shall be President of the Senate, but shall have no vote, unless they be equally divided.

The Senate shall choose their other officers, and also a President *pro tempore*, in the absence of the Vice-President, or when he shall exercise the office of President of the United States.

The Senate shall have the sole power to try all impeachments. When sitting for that purpose, they shall be on oath or affirmation. When the President of the United States is tried, the Chief Justice shall preside: and no person shall be convicted without the concurrence of two-thirds of the members present.

Judgment in cases of impeachment shall not extend further than to removal from the office, and disqualification to hold and enjoy any office of honor, trust or profit under the United States: but the party convicted shall nevertheless be liable and subject to indictment, trial, judgment and punishment, according to law.

(Elections)

Section 4 The times, places and manner of holding elections for Senators and Representatives shall be prescribed in each State by the legislature thereof; but the Congress may at any time by law make or alter such regulations, except as to the places of choosing Senators.

The Congress shall assemble at least once in every year, and such meeting *shall be on the first Monday in December, unless they shall by law appoint a different day.*

(Powers and duties of the two chambers: rules of procedure, power over members)

Section 5 Each house shall be the judge of the elections, returns and qualifications of its own members, and a majority of each shall constitute a quorum to do business; but a smaller number may adjourn from day to day, and may be authorized to compel the attendance of absent members, in such manner, and under such penalties, as each house may provide.

Each house may determine the rules of its proceedings, punish its members for disorderly behavior, and with the concurrence of two-thirds, expel a member.

Each house shall keep a journal of its proceedings, and from time to time publish the same, excepting such parts as may in their judgment require secrecy; and the yeas and nays of the members of either house on any question shall, at the desire of one-fifth of those present, be entered on the journal.

Neither house, during the session of Congress, shall, without the consent of the other, adjourn for more than three days, nor to any other place than that in which the two houses shall be sitting.

(Compensation, privilege from arrest, privilege of speech, disabilities of members)

Section 6 The Senators and Representatives shall receive a compensation for their services, to be ascertained by law and paid out of the treasury of the United States. They shall in all cases except treason, felony and breach of the peace, be privileged from arrest during their attendance at the session of their respective houses, and in going to and returning from the same; and for any speech or debate in either house, they shall not be questioned in any other place.

No Senator or Representative shall, during the time for which he was elected, be appointed to any civil office under the authority of the United States, which shall have been created, or the emoluments whereof shall have been increased, during such time; and no person holding any office under the United States shall be a member of either house during his continuance in office.

(Legislative process: revenue bills, approval or veto power of president)

Section 7 All bills for raising revenue shall originate in the House of Representatives; but the Senate may propose or concur with amendments as on other bills.

Every bill which shall have passed the House of Representatives and the Senate, shall, before it become a law, be presented to the President of the United States; if he approve he shall sign it, but if not he shall return it with objections to that house in which it originated, who shall enter the objections at large on their journal, and proceed to reconsider it. If after such reconsideration two-thirds of that house shall agree to pass the bill, it shall be sent, together with the objections, to the other house, by which it shall likewise be reconsidered, and, if approved by two-thirds of that house, it shall become a law. But in all such cases the votes of both houses shall be determined by yeas and nays, and the names of the persons voting for and against the bill shall be entered on the journal of each house respectively. If any bill shall not be returned by the President within ten days (Sundays excepted) after it shall have been presented to him, the same shall be a law, in like manner as if he had signed it, unless the Congress by their adjournment prevent its return, in which case it shall not be a law.

Every order, resolution, or vote to which the concurrence of the Senate and House of Representatives may be necessary (except on a question of adjournment) shall be presented to the President of the United States; and before the same shall take effect, shall be approved by him, or being disapproved by him, shall be repassed by two-thirds of the Senate and House of Representatives, according to the rules and limitations prescribed in the case of a bill.

(Powers of Congress enumerated)

Section 8   The Congress shall have power

To lay and collect taxes, duties, imposts, and excises, to pay the debts and provide for the common defense and general welfare of the United States; but all duties, imposts and excises shall be uniform throughout the United States;

To borrow money on the credit of the United States;

To regulate commerce with foreign nations, and among the several States, and with the Indian tribes;

To establish an uniform rule of naturalization, and uniform laws on the subject of bankruptcies throughout the United States;

To coin money, regulate the value thereof, and of foreign coin, and fix the standard of weights and measures;

To provide for the punishment of counterfeiting the securities and current coin of the United States;

To establish post offices and post roads;

To promote the progress of science and useful arts by securing for limited times to authors and inventors the exclusive right to their respective writings and discoveries;

To constitute tribunals inferior to the Supreme Court;

To define and punish piracies and felonies committed on the high seas and offenses against the law of nations;

To declare war, grant letters of marque and reprisal, and make rules concerning captures on land and water;

To raise and support armies, but no appropriation of money to that use shall be for a longer term than two years;

To provide and maintain a navy;

To make rules for the government and regulation of the land and naval forces;

To provide for calling forth the militia to execute the laws of the Union, suppress insurrections, and repel invasions;

To provide for organizing, arming, and disciplining the militia, and for governing such part of them as may be employed in the service of the United States, reserving to the States respectively the appointment of the officers, and the authority of training the militia according to the discipline prescribed by Congress;

To exercise exclusive legislation in all cases whatsoever, over such district (not exceeding ten miles square) as may, by cession of particular States, and the acceptance of Congress, become the seat of government of the United States, and to exercise like authority over all places purchased by the consent of the legislature of the State, in which the same shall be, for erection of forts, magazines, arsenals, dockyards, and other needful buildings;—and

(Elastic clause)

To make all laws which shall be necessary and proper for carrying into execution the foregoing powers, and all other powers vested by this Constitution in the government of the United States, or in any department or officer thereof.

(Powers denied Congress)

Section 9   *The migration or importation of such persons as any of the States now existing shall think proper to admit shall not be prohibited by the Congress prior to the year 1808; but a tax or duty may be imposed on such importation, not exceeding $10 for each person.*

The privilege of the writ of habeas corpus shall not be suspended, unless when in cases of rebellion or invasion the public safety may require it.

No bill of attainder or ex post facto law shall be passed.

No capitation, or other direct, tax shall be laid, unless in proportion to the census or enumeration herein before directed to be taken.

No tax or duty shall be laid on articles exported from any State.

No preference shall be given by any regulation of commerce or revenue to the ports of one State over those of another; nor shall vessels bound to, or from, one State, be obliged to enter, clear, or pay duties in another.

No money shall be drawn from the treasury, but in consequence of appropriations made by law; and a regular statement and account of the receipts and expenditures of all public money shall be published from time to time.

No title of nobility shall be granted by the United States: and no person holding any office or profit or trust under them, shall, without the consent of the

Congress, accept of any present, emolument, office, or title, of any kind whatever, from any king, prince, or foreign state.

(Powers denied the states)

Section 10 No State shall enter into any treaty, alliance, or confederation; grant letters of marque and reprisal; coin money; emit bills of credit; make anything but gold and silver coin a tender in payment of debts; pass any bill of attainder, ex post facto law, or law impairing the obligation of contracts, or grant any title of nobility.

No State shall, without the consent of Congress, lay any imposts or duties on imports or exports, except what may be absolutely necessary for executing its inspection laws: and the net produce of all duties and imposts, laid by any State on imports or exports, shall be for the use of the treasury of the United States; and all such laws shall be subject to the revision and control of the Congress.

No State shall, without the consent of Congress, lay any duty of tonnage, keep troops or ships of war in time of peace, enter into any agreement or compact with another State, or with a foreign power, or engage in war, unless actually invaded, or in such imminent danger as will not admit of delay.

Article II (The executive branch)

(The president: power vested, term, electoral college, qualifications, presidential succession, compensation, oath of office)

Section 1 The executive power shall be vested in a President of the United States of America. He shall hold his office during the term of four years, and, together with the Vice-President, chosen for the same term, be elected as follows:

Each State shall appoint, in such manner as the legislature thereof may direct, a number of electors, equal to the whole number of Senators and Representatives to which the State may be entitled in the Congress; but no Senator or Representative, or person holding an office of trust or profit under the United States, shall be appointed an elector.

The electors shall meet in their respective States, and vote by ballot for two persons, of whom one at least shall not be an inhabitant of the same State with themselves. And they shall make a list of all the persons voted for, and of the number of votes for each: which list they shall sign and certify, and transmit sealed to the seat of government of the United States, directed to the President of the

Senate. The President of the Senate shall, in the presence of the Senate and House of Representatives, open all the certificates, and the votes shall then be counted. The person having the greatest number of votes shall be the President, if such number be a majority of the whole number of electors appointed; and if there be more than one who have such majority, and have an equal number of votes, then the House of Representatives shall immediately choose by ballot one of them for President; and if no person have a majority, then from the five highest on the list said house shall in like manner choose the President. But in choosing the President the votes shall be taken by States, the representation from each State having one vote; a quorum for this purpose shall consist of a member or members from two-thirds of the States, and a majority of all the States shall be necessary to a choice. In every case, after the choice of the President, the person having the greatest number of votes of the electors shall be the Vice-President. But if there should remain two or more who have equal votes, the Senate shall choose from them by ballot the Vice-President.

The Congress may determine the time of choosing the electors and the day on which they shall give their votes; which day shall be the same throughout the United States.

No person except a natural-born citizen, *or a citizen of the United States at the time of the adoption of this Constitution,* shall be eligible to the office of President; neither shall any person be eligible to that office who shall not have attained to the age of thirty-five years, and been fourteen years a resident within the United States.

In cases of the removal of the President from office or of his death, resignation, or inability to discharge the powers and duties of the said office, the same shall devolve on the Vice-President, and the Congress may by law provide for the case of removal, death, resignation, or inability, both of the President and Vice-President, declaring what officer shall then act as President, and such officer shall act accordingly, until the disability be removed, or a President shall be elected.

The President shall, at stated times, receive for his services a compensation, which shall neither be increased nor diminished during the period for which he shall have been elected, and he shall not receive within that period any other emolument from the United States, or any of them.

Before he enter on the execution of his office, he shall take the following oath or affirmation:—"I do solemnly swear (or affirm) that I will faithfully execute the office of the President of the United States, and will to the best of my ability preserve, protect and defend the Constitution of the United States."

(Powers and duties: as commander in chief, over advisers, to pardon, to make treaties and appoint officers)

Section 2 The President shall be commander in chief of the army and navy of the United States, and of the militia of the several States, when called into the actual service of the United States; he may require the opinion, in writing, of the principal officer in each of the executive departments, upon any subject relating to the duties of their respective offices, and he shall have power to grant reprieves and pardons for offenses against the United States, except in cases of impeachment.

He shall have power, by and with the advice and consent of the Senate, to make treaties, provided two-thirds of the Senators present concur; and he shall nominate, and by and with the advice and consent of the Senate, shall appoint ambassadors, other public ministers and consuls, judges of the Supreme court, and all other officers of the United States, whose appointments are not herein otherwise provided for, and which shall be established by law: but Congress may by law vest the appointment of such inferior officers, as they think proper, in the President alone, in the courts of law, or in the heads of departments.

The President shall have power to fill up all vacancies that may happen during the recess of the Senate, by granting commissions which shall expire at the end of their next session.

(Legislative, diplomatic, and law-enforcement duties)

Section 3 He shall from time to time give to the Congress information of the state of the Union, and recommend to their consideration such measures as he shall judge necessary and expedient; he may, on extraordinary occasions, convene both houses, or either of them, and in case of disagreement between them, with respect to the time of adjournment, he may adjourn them to such time as he shall think proper; he shall receive ambassadors and other public ministers; he shall take care that the laws be faithfully executed, and shall commission all the officers of the United States.

(Impeachment)

Section 4 The President, Vice-President and all civil officers of the United States shall be removed from office on impeachment for, and on conviction of, treason, bribery, or other high crimes and misdemeanors.

Article III   (The judicial branch)

(Power vested; Supreme Court; lower courts; judges)

Section 1 The judicial power of the United States shall be vested in one Supreme Court, and in such inferior courts as the Congress may from time to time ordain and establish. The judges, both of the Supreme and inferior courts, shall hold their offices during good behavior, and shall, at stated times, receive for their services a compensation which shall not be diminished during their continuance in office.

(Jurisdiction; trial by jury)

Section 2 The judicial power shall extend to all cases, in law and equity, arising under this Constitution, the laws of the United States, and treaties made, or which shall be made, under their authority;—to all cases affecting ambassadors, other public ministers and consuls;—to all cases of admiralty and maritime jurisdiction;—to controversies to which the United States shall be a party;—to controversies between two or more States;—*between a State and citizens of another State;*—between citizens of different States;—between citizens of the same State claiming lands under grants of different States, and between a State, or the citizens thereof, and foreign states, citizens or subjects.

In all cases affecting ambassadors, other public ministers and consuls, and those in which a State shall be party, the Supreme Court shall have original jurisdiction. In all the other cases before mentioned, the Supreme Court shall have appellate jurisdiction, both as to law and fact, with such exceptions, and under such regulations, as the Congress shall make.

The trial of all crimes, except in cases of impeachment, shall be by jury; and such trial shall be held in the state where said crimes shall have been committed; but when not committed within any State, the trial shall be at such place or places as the Congress may by law have directed.

(Treason: definition, punishment)

Section 3 Treason against the United States shall consist only in levying war against them, or in adhering to their enemies, giving them aid and comfort. No person shall be convicted of treason unless on the testimony of two witnesses to the same overt act, or on confession in open court.

The Congress shall have power to declare the punishment of treason, but no attainder of treason shall work corruption of blood, or forfeiture except during the life of the person attained.

Article IV   (States' relations)

(Full faith and credit)

Section 1   Full faith and credit shall be given in each State to the public acts, records, and judicial proceedings of every other State. And the Congress may by general laws prescribe the manner in which such acts, records, and proceedings shall be proved, and the effect thereof.

(Interstate comity; rendition)

Section 2   The citizens of each State shall be entitled to all privileges and immunities of citizens in the several States.

A person charged in any State with treason, felony, or other crime, who shall flee from justice, and be found in another State, shall on demand of the executive authority of the State from which he fled, be delivered up, to be removed to the State having jurisdiction of the crime.

No person held to service or labor in one State, under the laws thereof, escaping into another, shall, in consequence of any law or regulation therein, be discharged from such service or labor, but shall be delivered up on claim of the party to whom such service or labor may be due.

(New states)

Section 3   New States may be admitted by the Congress into this Union; but no new State shall be formed or erected within the jurisdiction of any other State; nor any state be formed by the junction of two or more States, or parts of States, without the consent of the legislatures of the States concerned as well as of the Congress.

The Congress shall have power to dispose of and make all needful rules and regulations respecting the territory or other property belonging to the United States; and nothing in this Constitution shall be so construed as to prejudice any claims of the United States, or of any particular State.

(Obligations of the United States to the states)

Section 4   The United States shall guarantee to every State in this Union a republican form of government, and shall protect each of them against invasion; and on application of the legislature, or of the executive (when the legislature cannot be convened), against domestic violence.

Article V   (Mode of amendment)

The Congress, whenever two-thirds of both houses shall deem it necessary, shall propose amendments to this Constitution, or, on the application of the legislatures of two-thirds of the several States, shall call a convention for proposing amendments, which, in either case, shall be valid to all intents and purposes, as part of this Constitution, when ratified by the legislatures of three-fourths of the several States, or by conventions in three-fourths thereof, as the one or the other mode of ratification may be proposed by the Congress; provided *that no amendments which may be made prior to the year one thousand eight hundred and eight shall in any manner affect the first and fourth clauses in the ninth section of the first article;* and that no State, without its consent, shall be deprived of its equal suffrage in the Senate.

Article VI   (Prior debts; supremacy of Constitution; oaths of office)

All debts contracted and engagements entered into, before the adoption of this Constitution, shall be as valid against the United States under this Constitution, as under the Confederation.

This Constitution, and the laws of the United States which shall be made in pursuance thereof; and all treaties made, or which shall be made, under the authority of the United States, shall be the supreme law of the land; and the judges in every State shall be bound thereby, anything in the Constitution or laws of any State to the contrary notwithstanding.

The Senators and Representatives before mentioned, and the members of the several State legislatures, and all executive and judicial officers, both of the United States and of the several States, shall be bound by oath or affirmation to support this Constitution; but no religious test shall ever be required as a qualification to any office or public trust under the United States.

Article VII (Ratification)

The ratification of the conventions of nine States shall be sufficient for the establishment of this Constitution between the States so ratifying the same.

Done in Convention by the unanimous consent of the States present, the seventeenth day of September in the year of our Lord one thousand seven hundred and eighty-seven and of the Independence of the United States of America the twelfth. In witness whereof we have hereunto subscribed our names.

GEORGE WASHINGTON
and thirty-seven others

Amendments to the Constitution

(The first ten amendments—the Bill of Rights— were adopted in 1791.)

Amendment I (Freedom of religion, speech, press, assembly)

Congress shall make no law respecting an establishment of religion, or prohibiting the free exercise thereof; or abridging the freedom of speech, or of the press; or the right of the people peaceably to assemble, and to petition the government for a redress of grievances.

Amendment II (Right to bear arms)

A well-regulated militia being necessary to the security of a free State, the right of the people to keep and bear arms shall not be infringed.

Amendment III (Quartering of soldiers)

No soldier shall, in time of peace, be quartered in any house without the consent of the owner, nor in time of war, but in a manner to be prescribed by law.

Amendment IV (Searches and seizures)

The right of the people to be secure in their persons, houses, papers, and effects, against unreasonable searches and seizures, shall not be violated, and no warrants shall issue but upon probable cause, supported by oath or affirmation, and particularly describing the place to be searched, and the persons or things to be seized.

Amendment V (Rights of persons: grand juries; double jeopardy; self-incrimination; due process; eminent domain)

No person shall be held to answer for a capital, or otherwise infamous crime, unless on a presentment or indictment of a grand jury, except in cases arising in the land or naval forces, or in the militia, when in actual service in time of war or public danger; nor shall any person be subject for the same offense to be twice put in jeopardy of life or limb; nor shall be compelled in any criminal case to be a witness against himself, nor be deprived of life, liberty, or property, without due process of law; nor shall private property be taken for public use without just compensation.

Amendment VI (Rights of accused in criminal prosecutions)

In all criminal prosecutions, the accused shall enjoy the right to a speedy and public trial, by an impartial jury of the State and district wherein the crime shall have been committed, which district shall have been previously ascertained by law, and to be informed of the nature and cause of the accusation; to be confronted with the witnesses against him; to have compulsory process for obtaining witnesses in his favor, and to have the assistance of counsel for his defense.

Amendment VII (Civil trials)

In suits at common law, where the value in controversy shall exceed twenty dollars, the right of trial by jury shall be preserved, and no fact tried by a jury shall be otherwise reexamined in any court of the United States, than according to the rules of the common law.

Amendment VIII (Punishment for crime)

Excessive bail shall not be required, nor excessive fines imposed, nor cruel and unusual punishments inflicted.

Amendment IX (Rights retained by the people)

The enumeration in the Constitution, of certain rights, shall not be construed to deny or disparage others retained by the people.

Amendment X (Powers reserved to the states)

The powers not delegated to the United States by the Constitution, nor prohibited by it to the States, are reserved to the states respectively, or to the people.

Amendment XI (Suits against the states; adopted 1798)

The judicial power of the United States shall not be construed to extend to any suit in law or equity, commenced or prosecuted against one of the United States by citizens of another state, or by citizens or subjects of any foreign state.

Amendment XII (Election of the president; adopted 1804)

The electors shall meet in their respective States, and vote by ballot for President and Vice-President, one of whom, at least, shall not be an inhabitant of the same State with themselves; they shall name in their ballots the person voted for as President, and in distinct ballots the person voted for as Vice-President, and they shall make distinct lists of all persons voted for as President, and of all persons voted for as Vice-President, and of the number of votes for each, which lists they shall sign and certify, and transmit sealed to the seat of government of the United States, directed to the President of the Senate;—the President of the Senate shall, in the presence of the Senate and House of representatives, open all the certificates and the votes shall then be counted;—the person having the greatest number of votes for President shall be the President, if such number be a majority of the whole number of electors appointed; and if no person have such majority, then from the persons having the highest numbers not exceeding three on the list of those voted for as President, the House of Representatives shall choose immediately, by ballot, the President. But in choosing the President, the votes shall be taken by States, the representation from each State having one vote; a quorum for this purpose shall consist of a member or members from two-thirds of the States, and a majority of all the States shall be necessary to a

choice. And if the House of Representatives shall not choose a President whenever the right of choice shall devolve upon them, before *the fourth day of March* next following, then the Vice-President shall act as President, as in the case of the death or other constitutional disability of the President.

The person having the greatest number of votes as Vice-President shall be the Vice-President, if such number be a majority of the whole number of electors appointed; and if no person have a majority, then from the two highest numbers on the list the Senate shall choose the Vice-President; a quorum for the purpose shall consist of two-thirds of the whole number of Senators, and a majority of the whole number shall be necessary to a choice. But no person constitutionally ineligible to the office of President shall be eligible to that of Vice-President of the United States.

Amendment XIII (Abolition of slavery; adopted 1865)

Section 1 Neither slavery nor involuntary servitude, except as a punishment for crime whereof the party shall have been duly convicted, shall exist within the United States, or any place subject to their jurisdiction.

Section 2 Congress shall have power to enforce this article by appropriate legislation.

Amendment XIV (Adopted 1868)

(Citizenship rights; privileges and immunities; due process; equal protection)

Section 1 All persons born or naturalized in the United States, and subject to the jurisdiction thereof, are citizens of the United States and of the State wherein they reside. No State shall make or enforce any law which shall abridge the privileges or immunities of citizens of the United States; nor shall any State deprive any person of life, liberty, or property, without due process of law; nor deny to any person within its jurisdiction the equal protection of the laws.

(Apportionment of representation)

Section 2 Representatives shall be apportioned among the several States according to their respective numbers, counting the whole number of persons in each State, excluding Indians not taxed. But when the right to vote at any election for the choice of Electors for President and Vice-President of the

United States, Representatives in Congress, the executive and judicial officers of a State, or the members of the legislature thereof, is denied to any of the male inhabitants of such State, being twenty-one years of age and citizens of the United States, or in any way abridged, except for participation in rebellion, or other crime, the basis of representation therein shall be reduced in the proportion which the number of such male citizens shall bear to the whole number of male citizens twenty-one years of age in such State.

(Disqualification of Confederate officials)

Section 3 No person shall be a Senator or Representative in Congress, or Elector of President and Vice-President, or hold any office, civil or military, under the United States, or under any State, who, having previously taken an oath, as a member of Congress, or as an officer of the United States, or as a member of any State legislature, or as an executive or judicial officer of any State, to support the Constitution of the United States, shall have engaged in insurrection or rebellion against the same, or given aid or comfort to the enemies thereof. Congress may, by a vote of two-thirds of each house, remove such disability.

(Public debts)

Section 4 The validity of the public debt of the United States, authorized by law, including debts incurred for payment of pensions and bounties for services in suppressing insurrection or rebellion, shall not be questioned. But neither the United States nor any State shall assume or pay any debt or obligation incurred in aid of insurrection or rebellion against the United States, or any claim for the loss of emancipation of any slave; but all such debts, obligations, and claims shall be held illegal and void.

(Enforcement)

Section 5 The Congress shall have power to enforce, by appropriate legislation, the provisions of this article.

Amendment XV (Extension of right to vote; adopted 1870)

Section 1 The right of citizens of the United States to vote shall not be denied or abridged by the United States or by any State on account of race, color, or previous condition of servitude.

Section 2 The Congress shall have power to enforce this article by appropriate legislation.

Amendment XVI (Income tax; adopted 1913)

The Congress shall have power to lay and collect taxes on incomes, from whatever source derived, without apportionment among the several States, and without regard to any census or enumeration.

Amendment XVII (Popular election of senators; adopted 1913)

Section 1 The Senate of the United States shall be composed of two Senators from each State, elected by the people thereof, for six years; and each Senator shall have one vote. The electors in each State shall have the qualifications requisite for electors of [voters for] the most numerous branch of the State legislatures.

Section 2 When vacancies happen in the representation of any State in the Senate, the executive authority of such State shall issue writs of election to fill such vacancies: Provided, that the Legislature of any State may empower the executive thereof to make temporary appointments until the people fill the vacancies by election as the Legislature may direct.

Section 3 This amendment shall not be so construed as to affect the election or term of any Senator chosen before it becomes valid as part of the Constitution.

Amendment XVIII (Prohibition of intoxicating liquors; adopted 1919, repealed 1933)

Section 1 After one year from the ratification of this article the manufacture, sale or transportation of intoxicating liquors within, the importation thereof into, or the exportation thereof from the United States and all territory subject to the jurisdiction thereof, for beverage purposes, is hereby prohibited.

Section 2 The Congress and the several States shall have concurrent power to enforce this article by appropriate legislation.

Section 3 This article shall be inoperative unless it shall have been ratified as an amendment to the

Constitution by the legislatures of the several States, as provided by the Constitution, within seven years from the date of the submission thereof to the States by the Congress.

Amendment XIX (Right of women to vote; adopted 1920)

Section 1 The right of citizens of the United States to vote shall not be denied or abridged by the United States or by any State on account of sex.

Section 2 The Congress shall have power to enforce this article by appropriate legislation.

Amendment XX (Commencement of terms of office; adopted 1933)

Section 1 The terms of the President and Vice-President shall end at noon on the 20th day of January, and the terms of Senators and Representatives at noon on the 3d day of January, of the years in which such terms would have ended if this article had not been ratified; and the terms of their successors shall then begin.

Section 2 The Congress shall assemble at least once in every year, and such meetings shall begin at noon on the 3d day of January, unless they shall by law appoint a different day.

(Extension of presidential succession)

Section 3 If, at the time fixed for the beginning of the term of the President, the President-elect shall have died, the Vice-President-elect shall become President. If a President shall not have been chosen before the time fixed for the beginning of his term, or if the President-elect shall have failed to qualify, then the Vice-President-elect shall act as President until a President shall have qualified; and the Congress may by law provide for the case wherein neither a President-elect nor a Vice-President-elect shall have qualified, declaring who shall then act as President, or the manner in which one who is to act shall be selected, and such persons shall act accordingly until a President or Vice-President shall have qualified.

Section 4 The Congress may by law provide for the case of the death of any of the persons from whom the House of Representatives may choose a President whenever the right of choice shall have devolved upon them, and for the case of the death of any of the persons from whom the Senate may choose a Vice-President whenever the right of choice shall have devolved upon them.

Section 5 Sections 1 and 2 shall take effect on the 15th day of October following the ratification of this article.

Section 6 This article shall be inoperative unless it shall have been ratified as an amendment to the Constitution by the Legislatures of three-fourths of the several States within seven years from the date of its submission.

Amendment XXI (Repeal of Eighteenth Amendment; adopted 1933)

Section 1 The eighteenth article of amendment to the Constitution of the United States is hereby repealed.

Section 2 The transportation or importation into any State, Territory, or Possession of the United States for delivery or use therein of intoxicating liquors, in violation of the laws thereof, is hereby prohibited.

Section 3 This article shall be inoperative unless it shall have been ratified as an amendment to the Constitution by conventions in the several States, as provided in the Constitution, within seven years from the date of submission thereof to the States by the Congress.

Amendment XXII (Limit on presidential tenure; adopted 1951)

Section 1 No person shall be elected to the office of President more than twice, and no person who has held the office of President, or acted as President, for more than two years of a term to which some other person was elected President shall be elected to the office of President more than once. But this article shall not apply to any person holding the office of President when this article was proposed by the Congress, and shall not prevent any person who may be holding the office of President, or acting as President, during the term within which this article becomes operative from holding the office of President or acting as President during the remainder of such term.

Section 2 This article shall be inoperative unless it shall have been ratified as an amendment to the Constitution by the legislatures of three-fourths of the several States within seven years from the date of its submission to the States by the Congress.

Amendment XXIII (Presidential electors for the District of Columbia; adopted 1961)

Section 1 The District constituting the seat of Government of the United States shall appoint in such manner as the Congress may direct:

A number of electors of President and Vice-President equal to the whole number of Senators and Representatives in Congress to which the District would be entitled if it were a State, but in no event more than the least populous State; they shall be in addition to those appointed by the States, but they shall be considered for the purposes of the election of President and Vice-President, to be electors appointed by a State; and they shall meet in the District and perform such duties as provided by the twelfth article of amendment.

Section 2 The Congress shall have the power to enforce this article by appropriate legislation.

Amendment XXIV (Poll tax outlawed in national elections; adopted 1964)

Section 1 The right of citizens of the United States to vote in any primary or other election for President or Vice-President, for electors for President or Vice-President, or for Senator or Representative in Congress, shall not be denied or abridged by the United States or any State by reason of failure to pay any poll tax or other tax.

Section 2 The Congress shall have the power to enforce this article by appropriate legislation.

Amendment XXV (Presidential succession; adopted 1967)

Section 1 In case of the removal of the President from office or of his death or resignation, the Vice-President shall become President.

(Vice-presidential vacancy)

Section 2 Whenever there is a vacancy in the office of the Vice-President, the President shall nominate a Vice-President who shall take office upon confirmation by a majority vote of both Houses of Congress.

Section 3 Whenever the President transmits to the President pro tempore of the Senate and the speaker of the House of Representatives his written declaration that he is unable to discharge the powers and duties of his office, and until he transmits to them a written declaration to the contrary, such powers and duties shall be discharged by the Vice-President as Acting President.

(Presidential disability)

Section 4 Whenever the Vice-President and a majority of either the principal officers of the executive departments or of such other body as Congress may by law provide, transmit to the President pro tempore of the Senate and the Speaker of the House of Representatives their written declaration that the President is unable to discharge the powers and duties of his office, the Vice-President shall immediately assume the powers and duties of the office as Acting President.

Thereafter, when the President transmits to the President pro tempore of the Senate and the Speaker of the House of Representatives his written declaration that no inability exists, he shall resume the powers and duties of his office unless the Vice-President and a majority of either the principal officers of the executive department(s) or of such other body as Congress may by law provide, transmit within four days to the President pro tempore of the Senate and the Speaker of the House of Representatives their written declaration that the President is unable to discharge the powers and duties of his office. Thereupon Congress shall decide the issue, assembling within forty-eight hours for that purpose if not in session. If the Congress, within twenty-one days after receipt of the latter written declaration, or, if Congress is not in session, within twenty-one days after Congress is required to assemble, determines by two-thirds vote of both Houses that the President is unable to discharge the powers and duties of his office, the Vice-President shall continue to discharge the same as Acting President; otherwise, the President shall resume the powers and duties of his office.

Amendment XXVI (Right of eighteen-year-olds to vote; adopted 1971)

Section 1 The right of citizens of the United States, who are eighteen years of age or older, to vote shall not be denied or abridged by the United States or by any State on account of age.

Section 2 The Congress shall have power to enforce this article by appropriate legislation.

■

FEDERALIST NO. 10   1787

To the People of the State of New York: Among the numerous advantages promised by a well-constructed union, none deserves to be more accurately developed than its tendency to break and control the violence of faction. The friend of popular governments, never finds himself so much alarmed for their character and fate, as when he contemplates their propensity to this dangerous vice. He will not fail, therefore, to set a due value on any plan which, without violating the principles to which he is attached, provides a proper cure for it. The instability, injustice, and confusion introduced into the public councils, have, in truth, been the mortal diseases under which popular governments have everywhere perished; as they continue to be the favourite and fruitful topics from which the adversaries to liberty derive their most specious declamations. The valuable improvements made by the American constitutions on the popular models, both ancient and modern, cannot certainly be too much admired; but it would be an unwarrantable partiality, to contend that they have as effectually obviated the danger on this side, as was wished and expected. Complaints are everywhere heard from our most considerate and virtuous citizens, equally the friends of public and private faith, and of public and personal liberty, that our governments are too unstable; that the public good is disregarded in the conflicts of rival parties; and that measures are too often decided, not according to the rules of justice, and the rights of the minor party, but by the superior force of an interested and overbearing majority. However anxiously we may wish that these complaints had no foundation, the evidence of known facts will not permit us to deny that they are in some degree true. It will be found, indeed, on a candid review of our situation, that some of the distresses under which we labour have been erroneously charged on the operation of our governments; but it will be found, at the same time, that other causes will not alone account for many of our heaviest misfortunes; and, particularly, for that prevailing and increasing distrust of public engagements, and alarm for private rights, which are echoed from one end of the continent to the other. These must be chiefly, if not wholly, effects of the unsteadiness and injustice, with which a factious spirit has tainted our public administrations.

By a faction, I understand a number of citizens, whether amounting to a majority or minority of the whole, who are united and actuated by some common impulse of passion, or of interest, adverse to the rights of other citizens, or to the permanent and aggregate interests of the community.

There are two methods of curing the mischiefs of faction: The one, by removing its causes; the other, by controlling its effects.

There are again two methods of removing the causes of faction: The one, by destroying the liberty which is essential to its existence; the other, by giving to every citizen the same opinions, the same passions, and the same interests.

It could never be more truly said, than of the first remedy, that it was worse than the disease. Liberty is to faction what air is to fire, an ailment without which it instantly expires. But it could not be a less folly to abolish liberty, which is essential to political life, because it nourishes faction, than it would be to wish the annihilation of air, which is essential to animal life, because it imparts to fire its destructive agency.

The second expedient is as impracticable, as the first would be unwise. As long as the reason of man continues fallible, and he is at liberty to exercise it, different opinions will be formed. As long as the connection subsists between his reason and his self-love, his opinions and his passions will have a reciprocal influence on each other; and the former will be objects to which the latter will attach themselves. The diversity in the faculties of men, from which the rights of property originate, is not less an insuperable obstacle to an uniformity of interests. The protection of these faculties is the first object of government. From the protection of different and unequal faculties of acquiring property, the possession of different degrees and kinds of property immediately results; and from the influence of these on the sentiments and views of the respective proprietors, ensues a division of the society into different interests and parties.

The latent causes of action are thus sown in the nature of man; and we see them everywhere brought into different degrees of activity, according to the different circumstances of civil society. A zeal for different opinions concerning religion, concerning government, and many other points, as well as of speculation as of practice; an attachment to different leaders ambitiously contending for preeminence and power; or to persons of other descriptions whose fortunes have been interesting to the human passions, have, in turn, divided mankind into parties, inflamed them with mutual animosity, and rendered them much more disposed to vex and oppress each other, than to cooperate for their common good. So strong is this propensity of mankind, to fall into mutual animosities, that where no substantial occasion presents itself, the most frivolous and fanciful distinctions have been sufficient to kindle their unfriendly passions and excite their most violent conflicts. But the most common and durable source of factions, has been the various and unequal distribution of property. Those who hold, and those who are without property, have ever formed distinct interests in society. Those who are creditors, and those who are debtors, fall under alike discrimination. A landed interest, a manufacturing interest, a mercantile interest, a moneyed interest, with many lesser interests, grow up of necessity in civilized nations, and divide them into different classes, actuated by different sentiments and views. The regulation of these various and interfering interests forms the principal task of modern legislation, and involves the spirit of the party and faction in the necessary and ordinary operations of the government.

No man is allowed to be a judge in his own cause; because his interest will certainly bias his judgment, and, not improbably, corrupt his integrity. With equal, nay, with greater reason, a body of men are unfit to be both judges and parties at the same time; yet what are many of the most important acts of legislation, but so many judicial determinations, not indeed concerning the right of single persons, but concerning the rights of large bodies of citizens? And what are the different classes of legislators, but advocates and parties to the causes which they determine? Is a law proposed concerning private debts? It is a question to which the creditors are parties on one side, and the debtors on the other. Justice ought to hold the balance between them. Yet the parties are, and must be, themselves the judges; and the most numerous party, or, in other words, the most powerful faction, must be expected to prevail. Shall domestic manufactures be encouraged, and in what degree, by restrictions on foreign manufactures? are questions which would be differently decided by the landed and the manufacturing classes; and probably by neither with a sole regard to justice and the public good. The apportionment of taxes,on the various descriptions of property, is an act which seems to require the most exact impartiality; yet there is, perhaps, no legislative act, in which

greater opportunity and temptation are given to a predominant party to trample on the rules of justice. Every shilling, with which they overburden the inferior number, is a shilling saved to their own pockets.

It is in vain to say, that enlightened statesmen will be able to adjust these clashing interests, and render them all subservient to the public good. Enlightened statesmen will not always be at the helm: nor, in many cases, can such an adjustment be made at all, without taking into view indirect and remote considerations, which will rarely prevail over the immediate interest which one party may find in disregarding the rights of another, or the good of the whole.

The inference to which we are brought is, that the *causes* of faction cannot be removed; and that relief is only to be sought in the means of controlling its *effects*.

If a faction consists of less than a majority, relief is supplied by the republican principle, which enables the majority to defeat its sinister views, by regular vote. It may clog the administration, it may convulse the society; but it will be unable to execute and mask its violence under the forms of the constitution. When a majority is included in a faction, the form of popular government, on the other hand, enables it to sacrifice to its ruling passion or interest, both the public good and the rights of other citizens. To secure the public good, and private rights, against the danger of such a faction, and at the same time to preserve the spirit and the form of popular government, is then the great object to which our inquiries are directed. Let me add, that it is the great desideratum, by which alone this form of government can be rescued from the opprobrium under which it has so long laboured, and be recommended to the esteem and adoption of mankind.

By what means is this object attainable? Evidently by one of two only. Either the existence of the same passion or interest in a majority, at the same time, must be prevented; or the majority, having such coexistent passion or interest, must be rendered, by their number and local situation, unable to concert and carry into effect schemes of oppression. If the impulse and the opportunity be suffered to coincide, we well know that neither moral nor religious motives can be relied on as an adequate control. They are not found to be such on the injustice and violence of individuals, and lose their efficacy in proportion to the number combined together; that is, in proportion as their efficacy becomes needful.

From this view of the subject, it may be concluded, that a pure democracy, by which I mean a society consisting of a small number of citizens, who assemble and administer the government in person, can admit of no cure for the mischiefs of faction. A common passion or interest will, in almost every case, be felt by a majority of the whole; a communication and concert, results from the form of government itself; and there is nothing to check the inducements to sacrifice the weaker party, or an obnoxious individual. Hence, it is, that such democracies have ever been spectacles of turbulence and contention; have ever been found incompatible with personal security, or the rights of property; and have in general been as short in their lives, as they have been violent in their deaths. Theoretic politicians, who have patronized this species of government, have erroneously supposed, that by reducing mankind to a perfect equality in their political rights, they would, at the same time, be perfectly equalized and assimilated in their possessions, their opinions, and their passions.

A republic, by which I mean a government in which the scheme of representation takes place, opens a different prospect, and promises the cure for which we are seeking. Let us examine the points in which it varies from pure democracy, and we shall comprehend both the nature of the cure and the efficacy which it must derive from the union.

The two great points of difference, between a democracy and a republic, are, first, the delegation of the government, in the latter, to a small number of citizens, elected by the rest; secondly, the greatest number of citizens, and greater sphere of country, over which the latter may be extended.

The effect of the first difference is, on the one hand, to refine and enlarge the public views, by passing them through the medium of a chosen body of citizens, whose wisdom may best discern the true interest of their country, and whose patriotism and love of justice, will be least likely to sacrifice it to temporary or partial considerations. Under such a regulation, it may well happen, that the public voice, pronounced by the representatives of the people, will be more consonant to the public good, than if pronounced by the people themselves, convened for the purpose. On the other hand the effect may be inverted. Men of factious tempers, of local prejudices, or of sinister designs, may by intrigue, by corruption, or by other means, first obtain the suffrages, and then betray the interest of the people. The question resulting is, whether small or extensive republics are most favourable to the election of proper guardians of the public weal; and it is clearly decided in favour of the latter by two obvious considerations.

In the first place, it is to be remarked that, however small the republic may be, the representa-

tives must be raised to a certain number, in order to guard against the cabals of a few; and that however large it may be, they must be limited to a certain number, in order to guard against the confusion of a multitude. Hence, the number of representatives in the two cases not being in proportion to that of the constituents, and being proportionally greatest in the small republic, it follows, that if the proportion of fit characters be not less in the large than in the small republic, the former will present a greater option, and consequently a greater probability of a fit choice.

In the next place, as each representative will be chosen by a greater number of citizens in the large than in the small republic, it will be more difficult for unworthy candidates to practise with success the vicious arts, by which elections are too often carried; and the suffrages of the people being more free, will be more likely to centre in men who possess the most attractive merit, and the most diffusive and established characters.

It must be confessed, that in this, as in most other cases, there is a mean, on both sides of which inconveniences will be found to lie. By enlarging too much the number of electors, you render the representatives too little acquainted with all their local circumstances and lesser interests; as by reducing it too much, you render him unduly attached to these, and too little fit to comprehend and pursue great and national objects. The federal constitution forms a happy combination being referred to the national, the local and particular to the state legislatures.

The other point of difference is, the greater number of citizens, and extent of territory, which may be brought within the compass of republican, than of democratic government; and it is this circumstance principally which renders factious combinations less to be dreaded in the former, than in the latter. The smaller the society, the fewer probably will be the distinct parties and interests composing it; the fewer the distinct parties and interests, the more frequently will a majority be found of the same party; and the smaller the number of individuals composing a majority, and the smaller the compass within which they are placed, the more easily will they concert and execute their plans of oppression. Extend the sphere, and you take in a greater variety of parties and interests; you make it less probable that a majority of the whole will have a common motive to invade the rights of other citizens; or if such a common motive exists, it will be more difficult for all who feel it to discover their own strength, and to act in unison with each other. Besides other impediments, it may be remarked, that where there is a consciousness of unjust or dishonourable purposes, communication is always checked by distrust, in proportion to the number whose concurrence is necessary.

Hence, it clearly appears, that the same advantage, which a republic has over a democracy, in controlling the effects of faction, is enjoyed by a large over a small republic,—is enjoyed by the union over the states composing it. Does this advantage consist in the substitution of representatives, whose enlightened views and virtuous sentiments render them superior to local prejudices, and to schemes of injustice? It will not be denied that the representation of the union will be most likely to possess these requisite endowments. Does it consist in the greater security afforded by a greater variety of parties, against the event of any one party being able to outnumber and oppress the rest? In an equal degree does the increased variety of parties, comprised within the union, increase the security? Does it, in fine, consist in the greater obstacles opposed to the concert and accomplishment of the secret wishes of an unjust and interested majority? Here, again, the extent of the union gives it the most palpable advantage.

The influence of factious leaders may kindle a flame within their particular states, but will be unable to spread a general conflagration through the other states; a religious sect may degenerate into a political faction in a part of the confederacy; but the variety of sects dispersed over the entire face of it, must secure the national councils against any danger from that source: a rage for paper money, for an abolition of debts, for an equal division of property, or for any other improper or wicked project, will be less apt to pervade the whole body of the union than a particular member of it; in the same proportion as such a malady is more likely to taint a particular county or district, than an entire state.

In the extent and proper structure of the union, therefore, we behold a republican remedy for the diseases most incident to republican government. And according to the degree of pleasure and pride we feel in being republicans, ought to be our zeal in cherishing the spirit, and supporting the character of federalists.

JAMES MADISON

∎

FEDERALIST NO. 51   1788

To the People of the State of New York: To what expedient then shall we finally resort for maintaining in practice the necessary partition of power among the several departments, as laid down in the constitution? The only answer that can be given is, that as all these exterior provisions are found to be inadequate, the defect must be supplied, by so contriving the interior structure of the government, as that its several constituent parts may, by their mutual relations, be the means of keeping each other in their proper places. Without presuming to undertake a full development of this important idea, I will hazard a few general observations, which may perhaps place it in a clearer light, and enable us to form a more correct judgment of the principles and structure of the government planned by the convention.

In order to lay a due foundation for that separate and distinct exercise of the different powers of government, which to a certain extent, is admitted on all hands to be essential to the preservation of liberty, it is evident that each department should have a will of its own; and consequently should be so constituted, that the members of each should have as little agency as possible in the appointment of the members of the others. Were this principle rigorously adhered to, it would require that all the appointments for the supreme executive, legislative, and judiciary magistracies, should be drawn from the same fountain of authority, the people, through channels, having no communication whatever with one another. Perhaps such a plan of constructing the several departments would be less difficult in practice than it may in contemplation appear. Some difficulties however, and some additional expense, would attend the execution of it. Some deviations therefore from the principle must be admitted. In the constitution of the judiciary department in particular, it might be inexpedient to insist rigorously on the principle; first, because peculiar qualifications being essential in the members, the primary consideration ought to be to select that mode of choice, which best secures these qualifications; secondly, because the permanent tenure by which the appointments are held in that department, must soon destroy all sense of dependence on the authority conferring them.

It is equally evident that the members of each department should be as little dependent as possible on those of the others, for the emoluments annexed to their offices. Were the executive magistrate, or the judges, not independent of the legislature in this particular, their independence in every other would be merely nominal.

But the great security against a gradual concentration of the several powers in the same department, consists in giving to those who administer each department, the necessary constitutional means, and personal motives, to resist encroachments of the others. The provision for defense must in this, as in all other cases, be made commensurate to the danger of attack. Ambition must be made to counteract ambition. The interest of the man must be connected with the constitutional rights of the place. It may be a reflection on human nature, that such devices should be necessary to control the abuses of government. But what is government itself but the greatest of all reflections on human nature? If men were angels, no government would be necessary. If angels were to govern men, neither external nor internal controls on government would be necessary. In framing a government which is to be administered by men over men, the great difficulty lies in this: You must first enable the government to control the governed; and in the next place, oblige it to control itself. A dependence on the people is no doubt the primary control on the government; but experience has taught mankind the necessity of auxiliary precautions.

This policy of supplying by opposite and rival interests, the defect of better motives, might be traced through the whole system of human affairs, private as well as public. We see it particularly displayed in all the subordinate distributions of power; where the constant aim is to divide and arrange the several offices in such a manner as that each may be a check on the other; that the private interest of every individual, may be a sentinel over the public rights. These inventions of prudence cannot be less requisite in the distribution of the supreme powers of the state.

But it is not possible to give to each department an equal power of self defense. In republican government the legislative authority, necessarily, predominates. The remedy for this inconveniency is, to divide the legislature into different branches; and to render them by different modes of election, and different principles of action, as little connected with each other, as the nature of their common functions, and their common dependence on the society, will admit. It may even be necessary to guard against dangerous encroachments by still further precautions. As the weight of the legislative authority requires that it should be thus divided, the weakness of the executive may require, on the other hand, that it should be fortified. An absolute negative, on the legislature, appears at first view to be the natural defense with which the executive magistrate should be armed. But perhaps it would be neither altogether safe, nor alone sufficient. On ordinary occasions, it might not be exerted with the requisite firmness; and on extraordinary occasions, it might be perfidiously abused. May not this defect of an absolute negative be supplied, by some qualified connection between this weaker department, and the weaker branch of the stronger department, by which the latter may be led to support the constitutional rights of the former, without being too much detached from the rights of its own department?

If the principles on which these observations are founded be just, as I persuade myself they are, and they be applied as a criterion, to the several state constitutions, and to the federal constitution, it will be found, that if the latter does not perfectly correspond with them, the former are infinitely less able to bear such a test.

There are moreover two considerations particularly applicable to the federal system of America, which place that system in a very interesting point of view.

First. In a single republic, all the power surrendered by the people, is submitted to the administration of a single government; and usurpations are guarded against by a division of the government into distinct and separate departments. In the compound republic of America, the power surrendered by the people, is first divided between two distinct governments, and then the portion allotted to each, subdivided among distinct and separate departments. Hence a double security arises to the rights of the people. The different governments will control each other; at the same time that each will be controlled by itself.

Second. It is of great importance in a republic, not only to guard the society against the oppression of its rulers; but to guard one part of the society against the injustice of the other part. Different interests necessarily exist in different classes of citizens. If a majority be united by a common interest, the rights of the minority will be insecure. There are but two methods of providing against this evil: The one by creating a will in the community independent of the majority, that is, of the society itself; the other by comprehending in the society so many separate descriptions of citizens, as will render an unjust combination of a majority of the whole, very improbable, if not impracticable. The first method prevails in all governments possessing an hereditary or self appointed authority. This at best is but a precarious security; because a power independent of the society may as well espouse the unjust views of the major, as the rightful interests, of the minor party, and may possibly be turned against both parties. The second method will be exemplified in the federal republic of the United States. While all authority in it will be derived from and dependent on the society, the society itself will be broken into so many parts, interests and classes of citizens, that the rights of individuals or of the minority, will be in little danger from interested combinations of the majority. In a free government, the security for civil rights must be the same as for religious rights. It consists in the one case in the multiplicity of sects. The degree of security in both cases will depend on the number of interests and sects; and this may be presumed to depend on the extent of country and number of people comprehended under the same government. This view of the subject must particularly recommend a proper federal system to all the sincere and considerate friends of republican government: Since it shows that in exact proportion as the territory of the union may be formed into more circumscribed confederacies or states, oppressive combinations of a majority will be facilitated; the best security under the republican form, for the rights of every class of citizens, will be diminished; and consequently, the stability and independence of some member of the government, the only other security, must be proportionally increased. Justice is the end of government. It is the end of civil society. It ever has been, and ever will be pursued, until it be obtained, or until liberty be lost in the pursuit. In a society under the forms of which the stronger faction can readily unite and oppress the weaker, anarchy may as truly be said to reign, as in a state of nature where the weaker individual is not secured against the violence of the stronger: And as in the latter state even the stronger individuals are prompted by the uncertainty of their condition, to submit to a government which may protect the weak as well as themselves: So in the former state, will the more powerful factions or parties be gradually induced by alike motives, to wish for a government which will protect all parties, the weaker as well as the more powerful. It can be little doubted, that if the state of Rhode Island was separated from the confederacy, and left to itself, the insecurity of rights under the popular form of government within such narrow limits, would be displayed by such reiterated oppressions of factious majorities, that some power altogether independent of the people would soon be called for by the voice of the very factions whose misrule had proved the necessity of it. In the extended republic of the United States, and among the great variety of interests, parties and sects which it embraces, a coalition of a majority of the whole society could seldom take place on any other principles than those of justice and the general good; and there being thus less danger to a minor from the will of the major party, there must be less pretext also, to provide for the security of the former, by introducing into the government a will not dependent on the latter; or in other words, a will independent of the society itself. It is no less certain than it is important, notwithstanding the contrary opinions which have been entertained, that the larger the society, provided it lie within a practicable sphere, the more duly capable it will be of self government. And happily for the *republican cause,* the practicable sphere may be carried to a very great extent, by a judicious modification and mixture of the *federal principle.*

JAMES MADISON

PRESIDENTS OF THE UNITED STATES

	Party	*Term*
1. George Washington (1732–1799)	Federalist	1789–1797
2. John Adams (1735–1826)	Federalist	1797–1801
3. Thomas Jefferson (1743–1826)	Democratic-Republican	1801–1809
4. James Madison (1751–1836)	Democratic-Republican	1809–1817
5. James Monroe (1758–1831)	Democratic-Republican	1817–1825
6. John Quincy Adams (1767–1848)	Democratic-Republican	1825–1829
7. Andrew Jackson (1767–1845)	Democratic	1829–1837
8. Martin Van Buren (1782–1862)	Democratic	1837–1841
9. William Henry Harrison (1773–1841)	Whig	1841
10. John Tyler (1790–1862)	Whig	1841–1845
11. James K. Polk (1795–1849)	Democratic	1845–1849
12. Zachary Taylor (1784–1850)	Whig	1849–1850
13. Millard Fillmore (1800–1874)	Whig	1850–1853
14. Franklin Pierce (1804–1869)	Democratic	1853–1857
15. James Buchanan (1791–1868)	Democratic	1857–1861
16. Abraham Lincoln (1809–1865)	Republican	1861–1865
17. Andrew Johnson (1808–1875)	Union	1865–1869
18. Ulysses S. Grant (1822–1885)	Republican	1869–1877
19. Rutherford B. Hayes (1822–1893)	Republican	1877–1881
20. James A. Garfield (1831–1881)	Republican	1881
21. Chester A. Arthur (1830–1886)	Republican	1881–1885
22. Grover Cleveland (1837–1908)	Democratic	1885–1889
23. Benjamin Harrison (1833–1901)	Republican	1889–1893
24. Grover Cleveland (1837–1908)	Democratic	1893–1897
25. William McKinley (1843–1901)	Republican	1897–1901
26. Theodore Roosevelt (1858–1919)	Republican	1901–1909
27. William Howard Taft (1857–1930)	Republican	1909–1913
28. Woodrow Wilson (1856–1924)	Democratic	1913–1921
29. Warren G. Harding (1865–1923)	Republican	1921–1923
30. Calvin Coolidge (1871–1933)	Republican	1923–1929
31. Herbert Hoover (1874–1964)	Republican	1929–1933
32. Franklin Delano Roosevelt (1882–1945)	Democratic	1933–1945
33. Harry S Truman (1884–1972)	Democratic	1945–1953
34. Dwight D. Eisenhower (1890–1969)	Republican	1953–1961
35. John F. Kennedy (1917–1963)	Democratic	1961–1963
36. Lyndon B. Johnson (1908–1973)	Democratic	1963–1969
37. Richard M. Nixon (b. 1913)	Republican	1969–1974
38. Gerald R. Ford (b. 1913)	Republican	1974–1977
39. Jimmy Carter (b. 1924)	Democratic	1977–1981
40. Ronald Reagan (b. 1911)	Republican	1981–1989
41. George Bush (b. 1924)	Republican	1989–

TWENTIETH-CENTURY JUSTICES OF THE SUPREME COURT

Justice*	Term of Service	Years of Service	Life Span	Justice*	Term of Service	Years of Service	Life Span
Oliver W. Holmes	1902–1932	30	1841–1935	Robert H. Jackson	1941–1954	13	1892–1954
William R. Day	1903–1922	19	1849–1923	Wiley B. Rutledge	1943–1949	6	1894–1949
William H. Moody	1906–1910	3	1853–1917	Harold H. Burton	1945–1958	13	1888–1964
Horace H. Lurton	1910–1914	4	1844–1914	*Fred M. Vinson*	1946–1953	7	1890–1953
Charles E. Hughes	1910–1916	5	1862–1948	Tom C. Clark	1949–1967	18	1899–1977
Willis Van Devanter	1911–1937	26	1859–1941	Sherman Minton	1949–1956	7	1890–1965
Joseph R. Lamar	1911–1916	5	1857–1916	*Earl Warren*	1953–1969	16	1891–1974
Edward D. White	1910–1921	11	1845–1921	John Marshall Harlan	1955–1971	16	1899–1971
Mahlon Pitney	1912–1922	10	1858–1924	William J. Brennan, Jr.	1956–1990	34	1906–
James C. McReynolds	1914–1941	26	1862–1946	Charles E. Whittaker	1957–1962	5	1901–1973
Louis D. Brandeis	1916–1939	22	1856–1941	Potter Stewart	1958–1981	23	1915–1985
John H. Clarke	1916–1922	6	1857–1930	Byron R. White	1962–	—	1917–
William H. Taft	1921–1930	8	1857–1945	Arthur J. Goldberg	1962–1965	3	1908–
George Sutherland	1922–1938	15	1862–1942	Abe Fortas	1965–1969	4	1910–1982
Pierce Butler	1922–1939	16	1866–1939	Thurgood Marshall	1967–1991	24	1908–
Edward T. Sandford	1923–1930	7	1865–1930	*Warren E. Burger*	1969–1986	17	1907–
Harlan F. Stone	1925–1941	16	1872–1946	Harry A. Blackmun	1970–	—	1908–
Charles E. Hughes	1930–1941	11	1862–1948	Lewis F. Powell, Jr.	1972–1987	15	1907–
Owen J. Roberts	1930–1945	15	1875–1955	William H. Rehnquist	1972–1986	14	1924–
Benjamin N. Cardozo	1932–1938	6	1870–1938	John P. Stevens, III	1975–	—	1920–
Hugo L. Black	1937–1971	34	1886–1971	Sandra Day O'Connor	1981–	—	1930–
Stanley F. Reed	1938–1957	19	1884–1980	*William H. Rehnquist*	1986–	—	1924–
Felix Frankfurter	1939–1962	23	1882–1965	Antonin Scalia	1986–	—	1936–
William O. Douglas	1939–1975	36	1898–1980	Anthony M. Kennedy	1988–	—	1936–
Frank Murphy	1940–1949	9	1890–1949	David Souter	1990–	—	1939–
Harlan F. Stone	1941–1946	5	1872–1946	Clarence Thomas	1991–	—	1943–
James F. Byrnes	1941–1942	1	1879–1972				

* The names of chief justices are printed in italic type.

PARTY CONTROL OF THE PRESIDENCY, SENATE, AND HOUSE OF REPRESENTATIVES 1901–1993

Congress	Years	President	Senate			House		
			D	*R*	*Other**	*D*	*R*	*Other**
57th	1901–1903	McKinley T. Roosevelt	31	55	4	151	197	9
58th	1903–1905	T. Roosevelt	33	57	—	178	208	—
59th	1905–1907	T. Roosevelt	33	57	—	136	250	—
60th	1907–1909	T. Roosevelt	31	61	—	164	222	—
61st	1909–1911	Taft	32	61	—	172	219	—
62d	1911–1913	Taft	41	51	—	228	161	1
63d	1913–1915	Wilson	51	44	1	291	127	17
64th	1915–1917	Wilson	56	40	—	230	196	9
65th	1917–1919	Wilson	53	42	—	216	210	6
66th	1919–1921	Wilson	47	49	—	190	240	3
67th	1921–1923	Harding	37	59	—	131	301	1
68th	1923–1925	Coolidge	43	51	2	205	225	5
69th	1925–1927	Coolidge	39	56	1	183	247	4
70th	1927–1929	Coolidge	46	49	1	195	237	3
71st	1929–1931	Hoover	39	56	1	167	267	1
72d	1931–1933	Hoover	47	48	1	220	214	1
73d	1933–1935	F. Roosevelt	60	35	1	319	117	5
74th	1935–1937	F. Roosevelt	69	25	2	319	103	10
75th	1937–1939	F. Roosevelt	76	16	4	331	89	13
76th	1939–1941	F. Roosevelt	69	23	4	261	164	4
77th	1941–1943	F. Roosevelt	66	28	2	268	162	5
78th	1943–1945	F. Roosevelt	58	37	1	218	208	4
79th	1945–1947	Truman	56	38	1	242	190	2
80th	1947–1949	Truman	45	51	—	188	245	1
81st	1949–1951	Truman	54	42	—	263	171	1
82d	1951–1953	Truman	49	47	—	234	199	1
83d	1953–1955	Eisenhower	47	48	1	211	221	—
84th	1955–1957	Eisenhower	48	47	1	232	203	—
85th	1957–1959	Eisenhower	49	47	—	233	200	—
86th**	1959–1961	Eisenhower	65	35	—	284	153	—
87th**	1961–1963	Kennedy	65	35	—	263	174	—
88th	1963–1965	Kennedy Johnson	67	33	—	258	177	—

Sources: Department of Commerce, Bureau of the Census, *Statistical Abstract of the United States* (Washington, D.C.: U.S. Government Printing Office, 1980), p. 509, and *Members of Congress Since 1789*, 2d ed. (Washington, D.C.: Congressional Quarterly Press, 1981), pp. 176–177. Adapted from Barbara Hinckley, *Congressional Elections* (Washington, D.C.: Congressional Quarterly Press, 1981), pp. 144–145.

*Excludes vacancies at beginning of each session.

**The 437 members of the House in the 86th and 87th Congresses is attributable to the at-large representative given to both Alaska (January 3, 1959) and Hawaii (August 2, 1959) prior to redistricting in 1962.

PARTY CONTROL OF THE PRESIDENCY, SENATE, AND HOUSE OF REPRESENTATIVES 1901–1993 *(continued)*

Congress	Years	President	Senate			House		
			D	*R*	*Other**	*D*	*R*	*Other**
89th	1965–1967	Johnson	68	32	—	295	140	—
90th	1967–1969	Johnson	64	36	—	247	187	—
91st	1969–1971	Nixon	57	43	—	243	192	—
92d	1971–1973	Nixon	54	44	2	254	180	—
93d	1973–1975	Nixon Ford	56	42	2	239	192	1
94th	1975–1977	Ford	60	37	2	291	144	—
95th	1977–1979	Carter	61	38	1	292	143	—
96th	1979–1981	Carter	58	41	1	276	157	—
97th	1981–1983	Reagan	46	53	1	243	192	—
98th	1983–1985	Reagan	45	55	—	267	168	—
99th	1985–1987	Reagan	47	53	—	252	183	—
100th	1987–1989	Reagan	54	46	—	257	178	—
101st	1989–1991	Bush	55	45	—	262	173	—
102d	1991–1993	Bush	56	44	—	276	167	—

GLOSSARY

adjudication The settling of a case judicially. More specifically, formal hearings in which persons or businesses under government agency scrutiny can present their position with legal counsel present. (13, 14)

administrative discretion The latitude that Congress gives agencies to make policy in the spirit of their legislative mandate. (13)

affirmative action Programs through which businesses, schools, and other institutions expand opportunities for women and members of minority groups. (16)

agenda building The process by which new issues are brought into the political limelight. (10)

agenda setting The stage of the policymaking process during which problems get defined as political issues. (17)

aggregate demand The money available to be spent for goods and services by consumers, businesses, and government. (18)

Aid to Families with Dependent Children (AFDC) A federal public assistance program that provides cash to low-income families with children. (19)

amicus curiae brief A brief filed (with the permission of the court) by an individual or group that is not a party to a legal action but has an interest in it. (14)

anarchism A political philosophy that opposes government in any form. (1)

appellate jurisdiction The authority of a court to hear cases that have been tried, decided, or re-examined in other courts. (14)

appropriations committees Committees of Congress that decide which of the programs passed by the authorization committees will actually be funded. (18)

argument The heart of a judicial opinion; its logical content separated from facts, rhetoric, and procedure. (14)

Articles of Confederation The compact among the thirteen original states that established the first government of the United States. (3)

attentive policy elites Leaders who follow news in specific policy areas. (6)

authorization committees Committees of Congress that can authorize spending in their particular areas of responsibility. (18)

autocracy A system of government in which the power to govern is concentrated in the hands of one individual. Also called *monarchy*. (2)

bicameral Having two legislative chambers, as the Senate and House in the U.S. Congress. (3)

bill A formal proposal for a new law. (11)

bill of attainder A law that pronounces an individual guilty of a crime without a trial. (15)

Bill of Rights The first ten amendments to the Constitution. They prevent the national government from tampering with fundamental rights and civil liberties, and emphasize the limited character of national power. (3)

bimodal distribution A distribution (of opinions) that shows two responses being chosen about as frequently as each other. (5)

black codes Legislation enacted by former slave states to restrict the freedom of blacks. (16)

blanket primary A primary election in which voters receive a ballot containing both parties' potential nominees and can help nominate candidates for all offices for both parties. (9)

block grant A grant-in-aid awarded for general purposes, allowing the recipient great discretion in spending the grant money. (4)

bolter party A political party formed from a faction that has split off from one of the major parties. (8)

boycott A refusal to do business with a firm, individual, or nation as an expression of disapproval or as a means of coercion. (16, 20)

brief A written argument submitted to a judge. (14)

broadcast media Mass media that transmit information electronically. (6)

budget authority The amounts that government agencies are authorized to spend for their programs. (18)

budget committees One committee in each house of Congress that supervises a comprehensive budget review process. (18)

budget outlays The amounts that government agencies are expected to spend in the fiscal year. (18)

bureaucracy A large, complex organization in which employees have specific job responsibilities and work within a hierarchy of authority. (13)

bureaucrat An employee of a bureaucracy, usually meaning a government bureaucracy. (13)

business cycle Expansions and contractions of business activity, the first accompanied by inflation and the second by unemployment. (18)

Cabinet A group of presidential advisers; the heads of the executive departments and other key officials. (12)

capitalism The system of government that favors free enterprise (privately owned businesses operating without government regulation), based on the belief that free enterprise is necessary for free politics. (1)

Carter Doctrine A statement asserting that attempts "by any outside force to gain control of the Persian Gulf region" would be seen "as an assault on the vital interests of the United States." (20)

casework Solving problems for constituents, especially problems involving government agencies. (11)

categorical grant A grant-in-aid targeted for a specific purpose. (4)

caucus A closed meeting of the members of a political party to decide upon questions of policy and the selection of candidates for office. (8)

challenger A candidate who seeks to replace an incumbent. (9)

checks and balances A government structure that gives each branch some scrutiny and control over the other branches. (3)

citizen group An interest group whose basis of organization is a concern for issues unrelated to the members' vocations. (10)

civil case A court case that involves a private dispute arising from such matters as accidents, contractual obligations, and divorce. (14)

civil disobedience The willful but nonviolent violation of laws that are regarded as unjust. (16)

civil liberties Freedoms guaranteed to individuals. (15)

civil rights Powers or privileges guaranteed to individuals and protected from arbitrary removal at the hands of government or individuals. (15, 16)

civil rights movement Political mobilization of the people—black and white—to promote racial equality. (16)

civil service The system by which most appointments to the federal bureaucracy are made, to ensure that government jobs are filled on the basis of merit and that employees are not fired for political reasons. (13)

class-action suit A legal action brought by a person or group on behalf of a number of people with similar claims or defenses. (7, 14)

clear and present danger test A means by which the Supreme Court has distinguished between speech as the advocacy of ideas, which is protected by the First Amendment, and speech as incitement, which is not protected. (15)

closed primary A primary election in which voters must declare their party affiliation before they are given the primary ballot containing that party's potential nominees. (9)

cloture The mechanism by which a filibuster is cut off in the Senate. (11)

coalition building The banding together of several interest groups for the purpose of lobbying. (10)

Cold War In the 1950s, a period of increased tension that stopped short of outright military conflict, during which the adversarial nature of U.S.–Soviet relations was clear. Americans were called upon to give priority to defense spending over domestic spending. (20)

commerce clause The third clause of Article I, Section 8, of the Constitution, which gives Congress the power to regulate commerce among the states. (4)

common (judge-made) law Legal precedents derived from previous judicial decisions. (14)

communication The process of transmitting information from one individual or group to another. (6)

communism A political system in which, in theory, ownership of all land and productive facilities is in the hands of the people, and all goods are equally shared. The production and distribution of goods are controlled by an authoritarian government. (1)

concurrence The agreement of a judge with the court's majority decision, for a reason other than the majority reason. (14)

confederation A loose association of independent states that agree to cooperate on specified matters. (3)

conference committee A temporary committee created to work out differences between the House and Senate versions of a specific piece of legislation. (11)

Congressional Budget Office (CBO) The budgeting arm of Congress, which prepares alternative budgets to those prepared by the president's OMB. (18)

congressional campaign committee An organization maintained by a political party to raise funds to support its own candidates in congressional elections. (8)

conservatives Generally, those people whose political ideology favors a narrow scope for government. Also, those who value freedom more than equality but would restrict freedom to preserve social order. (1)

constituents People who live and vote in a government official's district or state. (11)

containment The idea that the Soviets have to be prevented from expanding further. (20)

Continental Congress A political assembly called to speak out and act collectively for the people of all the colonies. The First Continental Congress met in 1774 and adopted a statement of rights and principles; the Second Continental Congress adopted the Declaration of Independence in 1776 and the Articles of Confederation in 1777. (3)

conventional participation Relatively routine political behavior that uses institutional channels and is acceptable to the dominant culture. (7)

cooperative federalism A view that holds that the Constitution is an agreement among people who are citizens of both state and nation, so there is little distinction between state powers and national powers. (4)

Council of Economic Advisers (CEA) A group that works within the executive branch to provide advice on maintaining a stable economy. (18)

county government The government unit that administers a county. (4)

criminal case A court case involving a crime, or violation of public order. (14)

critical election An election that produces a sharp change in the existing pattern of party loyalties among groups of voters. (8)

Declaration of Independence Drafted by Thomas Jefferson, the document that proclaimed the right of the colonies to separate from Great Britain. (3)

de facto segregation Segregation that is not the result of government influence. (16)

deficit financing The Keynesian technique of spending beyond government income to combat an economic slump. Its purpose is to inject extra money into the economy to stimulate aggregate demand. (18)

de jure segregation Government-imposed segregation. (16)

delegate A legislator whose primary responsibility is to represent the majority view of his or her constituents, regardless of his or her own view. Also, to transfer authority. (11)

delegation of powers The process by which Congress gives the executive branch the additional authority needed to address new problems. (12)

democracy A system of government in which, in theory, the people rule, either directly or indirectly. (2)

democratic socialism A socialist form of government that guarantees civil liberties such as freedom of speech and religion. Citizens determine the extent of government activity through free elections and competitive political parties. (1)

department The largest unit of the executive branch, covering a broad area of government responsibility. The heads of the departments, or secretaries, form the president's Cabinet. (13)

deregulation A bureaucratic reform by which the government reduces its role as a regulator of business. (13)

desegregation The ending of authorized segregation, or separation by race. (16)

détente The reduction of tension between nations. (20)

deterrence The defense policy of American strategists during the Eisenhower administration, who believed the Soviets would not take aggressive action knowing they risked nuclear annihilation. (20)

direct action Unconventional participation that involves assembling crowds to confront businesses and local governments to demand a hearing. (7)

direct democracy A system of rule in which all members of the group meet to make decisions according to the principles of political equality and majority rule. (2)

direct lobbying Attempts to influence a legislator's vote through personal contact with the legislator. (10)

direct mail Advertising via the mails; more specifically, a method of attracting new members to an interest group by sending letters to people in a carefully targeted audience. (10)

direct primary A preliminary election, run by the state government, in which the voters choose each party's candidates for the general election. (7)

discretionary funds Sums of money that may be spent on unpredicted needs to further national interests. (20)

discretionary spending In the Budget Enforcement Act of 1990, authorized expenditures from annual appropriations. (18)

discrimination Acts of irrational suspicion or hatred, directed toward specific group of people. (16)

dissent The disagreement of a judge with a majority decision. (14)

divided control of government The situation in which one party controls the White House and the other controls the Congress. (12)

docket A court's agenda. (14)

dual federalism A view that holds the Constitution is a compact among sovereign states, so that the powers of the national government are fixed and limited. (4)

economic depression A period of high unemployment and business failures; a severe, long-lasting downturn in a business cycle. (18)

elastic clause See *necessary and proper clause.*

election A formal procedure for voting. (7)

election campaign An organized effort to persuade voters to choose one candidate over others competing for the same office. (9)

electoral college A body of electors who are chosen by voters to cast ballots for president and vice president. (3, 8)

electoral dealignment A lessening of the importance of party loyalties in voting decisions. (8)

electoral realignment The change in voting patterns that occurs after a critical election. (8)

elite theory The view that a small group of people actually makes most of the important government decisions. (2)

embargo A government freeze on the movement of goods or vessels to or from a specific country, as a means of coercion or of expressing disapproval. (20)

entitlement A benefit to which every eligible person has a legal right and that the government cannot deny. (18)

enumerated powers The powers explicitly granted to Congress by the Constitution. (3)

equality of opportunity The idea that each person is guaranteed the same chance to succeed in life. (1, 16)

equality of outcome The concept that society must ensure that people are equal, and governments must design policies to redistribute wealth and status so that economic and social equality are actually achieved. (1, 16)

equal opportunities rule Under the Federal Communications Act of 1934, the requirement that if a broadcast station gives or sells time to a candidate for any public office, it must make available an equal amount of time under the same conditions to all other candidates for that office. (6)

Equal Rights Amendment (ERA) A failed constitutional amendment first introduced by the National Women's Party in 1923, declaring that "equality of rights under the law shall not be denied or abridged by the United States or any State on account of sex." (16)

establishment clause The first clause in the First Amendment, which forbids the establishment of a national religion. (15)

excess stock disposal The selling of excess government stocks, such as surplus or infrequently used equipment. (20)

exclusionary rule The judicial rule that states that evidence obtained in an illegal search and seizure cannot be used in trial. (15)

executive agreement A pact between the heads of two countries. (20)

executive branch The law-enforcing branch of government. (3)

Executive Office of the President The president's executive aides and their staffs; the extended White House executive establishment. (12)

ex post facto law A law that declares an action to be criminal *after* it has been performed. (15)

extraordinary majorities Majorities greater than that required by majority rule, that is, greater than 50 percent plus one. (3)

fairness doctrine An FCC regulation that obligated broadcasters to discuss public issues and provide fair coverage to each side of those issues; repealed in 1987. (6)

farmer-labor party A political party that represents farmers and urban workers who believe that the working class does not get its share of society's wealth. (8)

Federal Communications Commission (FCC) An independent federal agency that regulates interstate and international communication by radio, television, telephone, telegraph, cable, and satellite. (6)

Federal Election Commission (FEC) A federal agency that oversees the financing of national election campaigns. (9)

federalism The division of power among a central government and regional governments. (3, 4)

federal question An issue covered by the Constitution, national laws, or U.S. treaties. (14)

Federal Reserve System The system of banks that acts as the central bank of the United States and controls major monetary policies. (18)

feedback Information received by policymakers about the effectiveness of public policy. (17)

"feminization of poverty" The term applied to the fact that a growing percentage of all poor Americans are women or the dependents of women. (19)

fighting words Speech that is not protected by the First Amendment because it inflicts injury or tends to incite an immediate disturbance of the peace. (15)

filibuster A delaying tactic, used in the Senate, that involves speechmaking to prevent action on a piece of legislation. (11)

first-past-the-post A British term for elections conducted in single-member districts that award victory to the candidate with the most votes. (9)

First, Second, and Third Worlds The terms applied to industrialized democracies (First World), the countries of Eastern Europe (Second World), and underdeveloped countries (Third World). (20)

fiscal policies Economic policies that involve government spending and taxing. (18)

fiscal year (FY) The twelve-month period from October 1 to September 30 used by the government for accounting purposes. A fiscal-year budget is named for the year in which it ends. (18)

flexible response The basic defense policy of the Kennedy administration, involving the ability to wage both nuclear and conventional war. (20)

food stamp program A federally funded program that increases the purchasing power of needy families by providing them with coupons they can use to purchase food. (19)

formula grant A grant-in-aid distributed according to a particular formula, which specifies who is eligible for the grants and how much each eligible applicant will receive. (4)

fragmentation In policymaking, the phenomenon of attacking a single problem in different and sometimes competing ways. (17)

franchise The right to vote. (7)

franking privilege The right of members of Congress to send mail free of charge. (11)

freedom from Immunity, as in *freedom from want*. (1)

freedom to An absence of constraints on behavior; may also be stated as *freedom of*, as in *freedom of religion*. (1)

free-exercise clause The second clause in the First Amendment, which prevents the government from interfering with the exercise of religion. (15)

free-expression clauses The press and speech clauses of the First Amendment. (15)

free-rider problem The situation in which people benefit from the activities of an organization (such as an interest group) but do not contribute to those activities. (10)

gatekeepers Media executives, news editors, and prominent reporters who direct the flow of news. (6)

general election A national election held, by law, in November of every even-numbered year. (9)

general revenue sharing Part of a federal program introduced by President Nixon that returned tax money to state and local governments to be spent largely as they wished. (4)

gerrymandering Redrawing a congressional district to intentionally benefit one political party. (11)

glasnost A domestic reform instituted by Mikhail Gorbachev in the Soviet Union: a greater openness in political affairs. (20)

globalism A policy of global, or worldwide, involvement, as is current U.S. foreign policy. (20)

good faith exception Established by the Supreme Court, an exception to the exclusionary rule maintaining that evidence seized on the basis of a mistakenly issued search warrant can be introduced at trial. (15)

government The legitimate use of force to control human behavior within territorial boundaries; also, the organization or agency authorized to exercise that force. (1)

government corporation A government agency that performs services that might be provided by the private sector, but which either involve insufficient financial incentive or are better provided when they are somehow linked with government. (13)

Gramm-Rudman   Popular name for an act passed by Congress in 1985 that, in its original form, sought to lower the national deficit to a specified level each year, culminating in a balanced budget in FY 1991. New reforms and deficit targets were agreed on in 1990. (18)

grant-in-aid   Money provided by one level of government to another, to be spent for a specific purpose. (4)

grassroots lobbying   Lobbying activities performed by rank-and-file interest group members and would-be members. (10)

Great Compromise   Submitted by the Connecticut delegation to the Constitutional Convention of 1787, and thus also known as the Connecticut Compromise, a plan calling for a bicameral legislature in which the House of Representatives would be apportioned according to population and the states would be represented equally in the Senate. (3)

Great Depression   The longest and deepest setback the American economy has ever experienced. It began with the stock market crash on October 12, 1929, and did not end until the start of World War II. (19)

Great Society   President Lyndon Johnson's broad array of programs designed to redress political, social, and economic equality. (19)

gross national product (GNP)   The total value of the goods and services produced by a country during a year or part of a year. (18)

home rule   The right to enact and enforce legislation locally. (4)

horse race journalism   Election coverage by the mass media that focuses on which candidate is ahead, rather than on national issues. (6)

impeachment   The formal charging of a government official with "treason, bribery, or other high crimes and misdemeanors." (11)

implementation   The process of putting specific policies into operation. (13, 17)

implied powers   Those powers that Congress requires in order to execute its enumerated powers. (3, 4)

in-and-outer   A participant in an issue network who has a good understanding of the needs and problems of others in the network and can easily switch jobs within the network. (17)

incremental budgeting   A method of budget making that involves adding new funds (an increment) onto the amount previously budgeted (in last year's budget). (18)

incumbent   A current officeholder. (9, 11)

independent agency   An executive agency that is not part of a cabinet department. (13)

inflation   An economic condition characterized by price increases linked to a decrease in the value of the currency. (18)

influencing behavior   Behavior that seeks to modify or reverse government policy to serve political interests. (7)

information campaign   An organized effort to gain public backing by bringing a group's views to public attention. (10)

infotainment   The practice of mixing journalism with theater, employed by some news programs. (6)

inherent powers   Authority claimed by the president that is not clearly specified in the Constitution. Typically, these powers are inferred from the Constitution. (12)

initiative   A procedure by which voters can propose an issue to be decided by the legislature or by the people in a referendum. It requires gathering a specified number of signatures and submitting a petition to a designated agency. (2, 7)

interest group   An organized group of individuals that seeks to influence public policy. Also called a *lobby*. (2, 10)

interest group entrepreneur   An interest group organizer or leader. (10)

intergovernmental relations   The interdependence and relationships among the various levels of government and government personnel. (4)

iron triangles   The members of congressional committees, federal agencies or bureaus, and lobbies who work toward policy ends in a specific area. (17)

isolationism   The policy of noninvolvement, as was the foreign policy of the United States during most of the nineteenth century. (20)

issue network   A shared-knowledge group consisting of representatives of various interests involved in some particular aspect of public policy. (17)

joint committee   A committee made up of members of both the House and the Senate. (11)

judgment   The judicial decision in a court case. (14)

judicial activism   A judicial philosophy whereby judges interpret existing laws and precedents loosely and interject their own values in court decisions. (14)

judicial branch   The branch of government that interprets laws. (3)

judicial restraint   A judicial philosophy whereby judges adhere closely to statutes and precedents in reaching their decisions. (14)

judicial review The power to declare congressional (and presidential) acts invalid because they violate the Constitution. (3, 14)

Keynesian theory A theory of the economy that states that demand can be adjusted through a combination of fiscal and monetary policies. (18)

laissez faire An economic doctrine that opposes any form of government intervention in business. (1)

legislative branch The law-making branch of government. (3)

legislative liaison staff Those people who comprise the communications link between the White House and Congress, advising the president or cabinet secretaries on the status of pending legislation. (12)

libel Written defamation of character. (15)

liberals Generally, those people whose political ideology favors a broad scope for government; those who value freedom more than order but not more than equality. (1)

libertarianism A political ideology that is opposed to all government action except as necessary to protect life and property. (1)

libertarians Those who advocate minimal government action; those who subscribe to libertarianism. (1)

linkage In international relations, the idea of using rewards and advantages in one area of negotiation to promote another country's compliance in other areas of negotiation. (20)

lobby See *interest group.*

lobbyist A representative of an interest group. (10)

local caucus A method used to select delegates to attend a party's national convention. Generally, a local meeting selects delegates for a county-level meeting, which in turn selects delegates for a higher-level meeting; the process culminates in a state convention that actually selects the national convention delegates. (9)

majoritarian model of democracy The classical theory of democracy in which government by the people is interpreted as government by the majority of the people. (2)

majority leader The head of the majority party in the Senate; the second highest ranking member of the majority party in the House. (11)

majority party A political party that regularly enjoys the support of the most voters. (8)

majority representation The system by which one office, contested by two or more candidates, is won by the single candidate who collects the most votes. (8)

majority rule The principle—basic to procedural democratic theory—that the decision of a group must reflect the preference of more than half of those participating. (2)

mandate An endorsement by voters. Presidents sometimes argue they have been given a mandate to carry out policy proposals. (12)

mandatory spending In the Budget Enforcement Act of 1990, expenditures required by previous commitments. (18)

Marshall Plan A post–World War II plan to restore European economic viability. The plan sent approximately $12 billion in aid to Europe over a four-year period. (20)

mass communication The process by which individuals or groups transmit information to large, heterogeneous, and widely dispersed audiences. (6)

mass media The means employed in mass communication, often divided into print media and broadcast media. (6)

means-tested benefits Conditional benefits provided by government to individuals whose income falls below a designated threshold. (19)

media event A situation that is so "newsworthy" that the mass media are compelled to cover it; candidates in elections often create such situations to garner media attention. (6)

Medicare A health-insurance program for all persons over the age of sixty-five. (19)

micromanagement A term applied by critics to describe Congress's constant intervention in administrative policymaking. (11)

military-industrial complex The combined interests of the military establishment and the large arms industry. The two groups are united by two common interests: war and military spending. (20)

minority party A political party that does not have the support of the most voters. (8)

minority rights The benefits of government that cannot be denied to any citizens by majority decisions. (2)

Miranda warnings Statements concerning rights that police are required to make to a person before he or she is subjected to in-custody questioning. (15)

monetarists Those who argue that government can effectively control the performance of an economy only by controlling the supply of money. (18)

monetary policies Economic policies that involve control of, and changes in, the supply of money. (18)

muckrakers Writers who practiced an early form of investigative reporting, replete with unsavory details. (6)

Munich paradigm The foreign policy view that the United States must be willing to intervene, militarily if necessary, anywhere on the globe to put down a major threat to world order and freedom. (20)

municipal government The government unit that administers a city or town. (4)

mutual assured destruction (MAD) The capability of the two great superpowers—the United States and the Soviet Union—to destroy each other, ensuring that there will be no winner of a nuclear war. (20)

national committee A committee of a political party composed of party chairpersons and party officials from every state. (8)

national convention A gathering of delegates of a single political party from across the country to choose candidates for president and vice president and to adopt a party platform. (8)

national industrial policies The government-sponsored coordinated plans adopted by some nations, including Germany and Japan, to promote economic expansion. (20)

National Security Council (NSC) A permanent group of advisers created to help the president integrate and coordinate the details of domestic, foreign, and military affairs as they relate to national security. (20)

nation-building policy A policy intended to shore up Third World countries economically and democratically, thereby making them less attractive targets for Soviet opportunism. (20)

necessary and proper clause The last clause in Section 8 of Article I of the Constitution, which gives Congress the means to execute its enumerated powers. This clause is the basis for Congress's implied powers. Also called the *elastic clause*. (3, 4)

New Deal The measures advocated by the Roosevelt administration to alleviate the Depression. (19)

"new" ethnicity A newer outlook on the people comprising America's "melting pot," with focus on race and color. (5)

New International Economic Order (NIEO) A proposal whereby industrialized states would help in the economic development of Third World countries. (20)

New Jersey Plan Submitted by the head of the New Jersey delegation to the Constitutional Convention of 1787, a set of nine resolutions that would have, in effect, preserved the Articles of Confederation by amending rather than replacing them. (3)

newsworthiness The degree to which a news story is important enough to be covered in the mass media. (6)

Nineteenth Amendment The amendment to the Constitution, adopted in 1920, that assures women of the right to vote. (16)

Nixon Doctrine An attempt to reduce America's foreign involvement by calling for U.S. intervention only where it made a "real difference" and was considered to be in our interest. (20)

nominate To designate as an official candidate of a political party. (8)

nonconnected PAC A largely ideological political action committee that has no parent lobbying organization and is formed solely for the purpose of raising and channeling campaign funds. (10)

non-means-tested benefits Benefits provided by government to all citizens, regardless of income; Medicare and social security are examples. (19)

nontariff barrier (NTB) A regulation that outlines the exact specifications an imported product must meet in order to be offered for sale. (20)

normal distribution A symmetrical bell-shaped distribution (of opinions) centered on a single *mode*, or most frequent response. (5)

North Atlantic Treaty Organization (NATO) A post–World War II international alliance, part of the U.S. commitment to defend Western Europe. (20)

nullification The declaration by a state that a particular action of the national government is not applicable to that state. (4)

obligation of contracts The obligation of the parties to a contract to carry out its terms. (15)

Office of Management and Budget (OMB) The budgeting arm of the Executive Office; prepares the president's budget. (18)

"old" ethnicity An older outlook on the people comprising America's "melting pot," with focus on religion and country of origin. (5)

oligarchy A system of government in which power is concentrated in the hands of a few people. (2)

omnibus legislation A number of different bills that are considered and passed as a single entity by Congress. (11)

open election An election that lacks an incumbent. (9)

open primary A primary election in which voters need not declare their party affiliation but must choose one party's primary ballot to take into the voting booth. (9)

opinion   An explanation written by one or more judges, justifying their ruling in a court case. (14)

opinion schema   A network of organized knowledge and beliefs that guides a person's processing of information regarding a particular subject. (5)

order   The rule of law to preserve life and protect property. Maintaining order is the oldest purpose of government. (1)

original jurisdiction   The authority of a court to hear a case before any other court does. (14)

oversight   The process of reviewing the operations of an agency to determine whether it is carrying out policies as Congress intended. (11)

parliamentary system   A system of government in which the chief executive is the leader whose party holds the most seats in the legislature after an election or whose party forms a major part of the ruling coalition. (11)

party conference   A meeting to select party leaders and decide committee assignments, held at the beginning of a session of Congress by Republicans or Democrats in each chamber. (8)

party identification   A voter's sense of psychological attachment to a party. (8)

party machine   A centralized party organization that dominates local politics by controlling elections. (8)

party of ideological protest   A political party that rejects prevailing doctrines and proposes radically different principles, often favoring more government activism. (8)

party platform   The statement of policies of a national political party. (8)

pay-as-you-go   In the Budget Enforcement Act of 1990, the requirement that any tax cut or expansion of an entitlement program must be offset by a tax increase or other savings. (18)

perestroika   A domestic reform instituted by Mikhail Gorbachev in the Soviet Union: an economic and political restructuring. (20)

picket fence federalism   A view of federalism that stresses the interactions and interrelationships among interest groups and the various levels of government. (4)

plea bargain   A defendant's admission of guilt in exchange for a less severe punishment. (14)

pluralist model of democracy   An interpretation of democracy in which government by the people is taken to mean government by people operating through competing interest groups. (2)

pocket veto   A means of killing a bill that has been passed by both houses of Congress, in which the president does not sign the bill within ten days of Congress's adjournment. (11)

police power   The authority of a government to maintain order and safeguard citizens' health, morals, safety, and welfare. (1)

policy evaluation   The analysis of public policy. (17)

policy formulation   The stage of the policymaking process during which formal proposals are developed and adopted. (17)

political action committee (PAC)   An organization that pools campaign contributions from group members and donates those funds to candidates for political office. (10)

political agenda   A list of issues that need government attention. (6)

political equality   Equality in political decision making: one vote per person, with all votes counted equally. (1, 2)

political ideology   A consistent set of values and beliefs about the proper purpose and scope of government. (1)

political participation   Actions of private citizens by which they seek to influence or support government and politics. (7)

political party   An organization that sponsors candidates for political office under the organization's name. (8)

political socialization   The complex process by which people acquire their political values. (5)

political sophistication   The depth and scope of a person's knowledge of public affairs. (5)

political system   A set of interrelated institutions that link people with government. (8)

poll tax   A tax of $1 or $2 on every citizen who wished to vote, first instituted in Georgia in 1877. Although it was no burden on white citizens, it effectively disenfranchised blacks. (16)

populists   Those people whose political ideology favors government action both to reduce inequality and to ensure social order. (1)

poverty level   The minimum cash income that will provide for a family's basic needs; calculated as three times the cost of a market basket of food that provides a minimally nutritious diet. (19)

precedent   A judicial ruling that serves as the basis for the ruling in a subsequent case. (14)

presidential primary   A special primary election used to select delegates to attend the party's national convention, which in turn nominates the presidential candidate. (9)

press clause The First Amendment guarantee of freedom of the press. (15)

primary election A preliminary election conducted within a political party to select candidates who will run for public office in a subsequent election. (9)

print media Mass media that transmits information through the publication of the written word. (6)

prior restraint Censorship before publication. (15)

procedural democratic theory A view of democracy as being embodied in a decision-making process that involves universal participation, political equality, majority rule, and responsiveness. (2)

productive capacity The total value of goods and services that can be produced when the economy works at full capacity. (18)

program monitoring Keeping track of government programs, usually by interest groups. (10)

progressive taxation A system of taxation whereby the rich pay proportionately higher taxes than the poor; used by governments to redistribute wealth and thus promote equality. (3, 18)

progressivism A philosophy of political reform based upon the goodness and wisdom of the individual citizen as opposed to special interests and political institutions. (7)

project grant A grant-in-aid awarded on the basis of competitive applications submitted by prospective recipients. (4)

proportional representation The system by which legislative seats are awarded to a party in proportion to the vote that party wins in an election. (8)

proposal The first of two stages in amending the Constitution: An amendment may be proposed, or offered, either by the Congress or by a national convention summoned by Congress. (3)

proposition An issue to be voted on in a referendum. (7)

protectionism The idea that women must be protected from life's cruelties; until the 1970s, the basis for laws affecting women's civil rights. (16)

public assistance Government aid to individuals who can demonstrate a need for that aid. (19)

public figures People who assume roles of prominence in society or thrust themselves to the forefront of public controversy. (15)

public goods Goods and services, such as parks and sanitation, that benefit all citizens but are not likely to be produced voluntarily by individuals. (1)

public interest group A citizen group that generally is considered to have no economic self-interest in the policies it pursues. (10)

public opinion The collected attitudes of citizens concerning a given issue or question. (5)

public policy A general plan of action adopted by the government to solve a social problem, counter a threat, or pursue an objective. (17)

racial segregation Separation from society because of race. (16)

racism A belief that human races have distinct characteristics such that one's own race is superior to, and has a right to rule, others. (16)

ratification The second of two stages in amending the Constitution: A proposed amendment can be ratified, or accepted, either by the legislatures of the states or by constitutional conventions held in the states. (3)

reapportionment Redistribution of representatives among the states, based on population movement. Congress is reapportioned after each census. (11)

reasonable access rule An FCC rule that requires broadcast stations to make their facilities available for the expression of conflicting views or issues by all responsible elements in the community. (6)

recall The process of removing an elected official from office. (7)

receipts For a government, the amount expected or obtained in taxes and other revenues. (18)

redistricting Redrawing congressional districts after census-based reapportionment. (11)

referendum An election on a policy issue. (2, 7)

regulation Government intervention in the workings of business to promote some socially desired goal. (13)

regulations Administrative rules that guide the operation of a government program. (13)

regulatory commission An agency of the executive branch of government that controls or directs some aspect of the economy. (13)

representative democracy See *indirect democracy*. (2)

reprogramming The use for one purpose of money that Congress has approved for some other purpose. (20)

republic A government without a monarch; a government rooted in the consent of the governed, whose power is exercised by elected representatives responsible to the governed. (3)

republicanism A form of government in which power resides in the people and is exercised by their elected representatives. (3)

responsible party government A set of principles formalizing the ideal role of parties in a majoritarian democracy. (8)

responsiveness A decision-making principle, necessitated by representative government, which implies that elected representatives should respond to public opinion—that they should do what the majority of people want. (2)

rights The benefits of government to which every citizen is entitled. (1)

rule making The administrative process that results in the issuance of regulations by government agencies. (13)

rule of four An unwritten rule that requires at least four justices to agree that a case warrants consideration before it is reviewed by the Supreme Court. (14)

school district An area for which a local government unit administers elementary and secondary school programs. (4)

select committee A temporary congressional committee created for a specific purpose and disbanded after that purpose is fulfilled. (11)

self-interest principle The implication that people choose what benefits them personally. (5)

senatorial courtesy A practice whereby the Senate will not confirm for a lower federal court judgeship a nominee who is opposed by the senior senator in the president's party in the nominee's state. (14)

seniority Years of consecutive service on a particular congressional committee. (11)

separate-but-equal doctrine The concept that providing separate but equivalent facilities for blacks and whites satisfies the equal protection clauses of the Fourteenth Amendment. (16)

separation of powers The assignment of law-making, law-enforcing, and law-interpreting functions to separate branches of government. (3)

sequestration In the Budget Enforcement Act of 1990, an automatic across-the-board spending cut in an overspent category or in nonexempt entitlement programs. (18)

sexism Sex discrimination. (16)

Shays' Rebellion A revolt led by Daniel Shays in 1786 and 1787 in Massachusetts against the foreclosure of farms resulting from high interest rates and high state taxes. The rebellion dramatized the weakness of the newly created national government. (3)

single-issue party A political party formed to promote one principle rather than a general philosophy of government. (8)

skewed distribution An asymmetrical but generally bell-shaped distribution (of opinions) whose *mode*, or most frequent response, lies off to one side. (5)

social contract theory The belief that the people agree to set up rulers for certain purposes and thus have the right to resist or remove rulers who act against those purposes. (3)

social equality Equality in wealth, education, and status. (1)

social insurance A government-backed guarantee against loss by individuals without regard to need. (19)

socialism A form of rule in which the central government plays a strong role in regulating existing private industry and directing the economy, although it does allow some private ownership of productive capacity. (1)

social security Social insurance that provides economic assistance to persons faced with unemployment, disability, or old age. It is financed by taxes on employers and employees. (19)

Social Security Act The law that provided for social security and is the basis of modern American social welfare. (19)

social welfare Government programs that provide the necessary minimum living standards for all citizens. (19)

socioeconomic status Position in society, based on a combination of education, occupational status, and income. (5)

solicitor general The third highest ranking official of the U.S. Department of Justice, and the one who represents the national government before the Supreme Court. (14)

sovereignty The power of self-rule. (3)

Speaker of the House The presiding officer of the House of Representatives. (11)

special district A government unit created to perform particular functions, especially when those functions are best performed across jurisdictional boundaries. (4)

special envoy A personal representative of the president to a foreign government. (20)

special revenue sharing Part of a federal program introduced by President Nixon that was to consolidate existing categorical grant programs. (4)

speech clause The part of the First Amendment that guarantees freedom of speech. (15)

split ticket In voting, candidates from different parties for different offices. (9)

stable distribution A distribution (of opinions) that shows little change over time. (5)

standard socioeconomic model A relationship between socioeconomic status and conventional political involvement: People with higher status and more education are more likely to participate than those with lower status. (7)

standing committee A permanent congressional committee that specializes in a particular legislative area. (11)

stare decisis Literally, "let the decision stand"; decision making according to precedent. (14)

states' rights The idea that all rights not specifically conferred on the national government by the Constitution are reserved for the states. (4)

statutory construction Judicial interpretation of legislative acts. (14)

straight ticket In voting, a single party's candidates for all the offices. (9)

Strategic Defense Initiative (SDI) A large-scale research and development effort to build a system that will defend the United States against Soviet missiles. Also called "Star Wars." (20)

substantive democratic theory The view that democracy is embodied in the substance of government policies rather than in the policymaking procedure. (2)

suffrage The right to vote. Also called the *franchise*. (7)

supply-side economics Economic policies intended to counter extreme inflation by increasing the supply of goods to match demand. (18)

supportive behavior Actions that express allegiance to government and country. (7)

supremacy clause The clause in Article VI of the Constitution that asserts that national laws take precedence over state and local laws when they conflict. (3)

symbolic expression Nonverbal communication. (15)

tax committees The two committees of Congress responsible for raising the revenue with which to run the government. (18)

torts Injuries or wrongs to the person or property of another. (14)

totalitarianism A political philosophy that advocates unlimited power for the government to enable it to control all sectors of society. (1)

trade association An organization that represents firms within a particular industry; may also represent members' interests before the government. (10)

transfer authority The president's power to use for one purpose money that Congress has approved for some other purpose. (20)

transfer payment A payment by government to an individual, mainly through social security or unemployment insurance. (18)

trustee A representative who is obligated to consider the views of constituents but is not obligated to vote according to those views if he or she believes they are misguided. (11)

two-party system A political system in which two major political parties compete for control of the government. Candidates from a third party have little chance of winning office. (8)

two-step flow of communication The process in which a few policy elites gather information and then inform their more numerous followers, mobilizing them to apply pressure to government. (6)

uncontrollable outlay A payment that government must make by law. (18)

unconventional participation Relatively uncommon political behavior that challenges or defies government channels and thus is personally stressful to participants and their opponents. (7)

unitary government A form of government in which all power is vested in a central authority. (3)

universal participation The concept that everyone in a democracy should participate in governmental decision making. (2)

U.S. court of appeals A court within the second tier of the three-tiered federal court system, to which decisions of the district courts and federal agencies may be appealed for review. (14)

U.S. district court A court within the lowest tier of the three-tiered federal court system; a court where litigation begins. (14)

veto The president's disapproval of a bill that has been passed by both houses of Congress. Congress can override a veto with a two-thirds vote in each house. (11, 12)

Vietnamization President Nixon's plan for turning over more and more of the fighting in the Vietnam

War to the South Vietnamese. This tactic finally led to the peace agreement in 1973. (20)

Vietnam paradigm The foreign policy view that not all left-wing revolutionary movements are necessarily directed from Moscow, but instead can be a product of internal nationalist forces. Proponents of this paradigm also argue that military force is not the most effective way to "win the hearts and the minds" of people in other countries. (20)

Virginia Plan A set of proposals for a new government, submitted to the Constitutional Convention of 1787; included separation of the government into three branches, division of the legislature into two houses, and proportional representation in the legislature. (3)

voting The act that individuals perform when they formally choose among alternatives in an election. (7)

War on Poverty A part of President Lyndon Johnson's Great Society program, intended to eradicate poverty within ten years. (19)

War Powers Resolution An act of Congress that limits the president's ability to wage undeclared war. (20)

welfare state A nation in which the government assumes responsibility for the welfare of its citizens, redistributing income to reduce social inequality. (1, 19)

yellow journalism The distorted, sensationalist reporting of stories that became popular toward the end of the nineteenth century. (6)

zero-sum game In international politics, a situation in which one superpower's gain is the other's loss. (20)

REFERENCES

Chapter 1 / Freedom, Order, or Equality? / pp. 3–31

1. Center for Political Studies of the Institute for Social Research, *Election Study 1988* (Ann Arbor, Mich., University of Michigan).
2. *1977 Constitution of the Union of Soviet Socialist Republics*, Article 11, in *Constitutions of Countries of the World*, ed. A. P. Blaustein and G. H. Flanz (Dobbs Ferry, N.Y.: Oceana, 1971).
3. Karl Marx and Friedrich Engels, *Critique of the Gotha Programme* (New York: International Publishers, 1938), p.10. Originally written in 1875 but published in 1891.
4. See the argument in Amy Gutman, *Liberal Equality* (Cambridge, Eng.: Cambridge University Press, 1980), pp. 9–10.
5. See John H. Schaar, "Equality of Opportunity and Beyond," in *Equality, NOMOS IX*, ed. J. Roland Pennock and John W. Chapman (New York: Atherton Press, 1967), pp. 228–249.
6. Jean Jacques Rousseau, *The Social Contract and Discourses*, trans. G.D.H. Cole (New York: Dutton, 1950), p. 5.
7. *Gallup Report*, nos. 282–283, March–April 1989, p. 8. See also Wesley G. Skogan, *Disorder and Decline: Crime and the Spiral of Decay in American Neighborhoods* (New York: The Free Press, 1990), Chap. 2.

8. *Statistical Abstract of the United States 1990* (Washington, D.C.: U.S. Government Printing Office, 1990), p. 176.
9. Jill Solowe, "The Long Hard Road to Moscow," *Time*, 12 January 1987, p. 47.
10. "State of Emergency Committee's Statement: 'A Mortal Danger Has Come,'" *New York Times*, 20 August 1991, p. A9.
11. *Chicago Tribune*, 30 July 1990, Sect. 1, p. 9.
12. Craig R. Whitney, "Moscow a Year Later: Rutted Streets and Despair," *New York Times*, 19 February 1990, p. A6.
13. Milton Friedman, *Capitalism and Freedom* (Chicago: University of Chicago Press, 1962).
14. *New York Times*, 29 July 1989, p. 6.
15. Lawrence Herson, *The Politics of Ideas: Political Theory and American Public Policy* (Homewood, Ill.: Dorsey Press, 1984), pp. 166–176.

Chapter 2 / Majoritarian or Pluralist Democracy? / pp. 33–59

1. "Five Children Killed as Gunman Attacks a California School," *New York Times*, 18 January 1989, p. A1; and Robert Reinhold, "After Shooting, Horror but Few Answers," *New York Times*, 20 January 1989, p. B6.
2. Wayne King, "Weapon Used by Deranged Man Is Easy to Buy,"

New York Times, 20 January 1989, p. B6.
3. *Gallup Report*, March–April 1989, pp. 2–5.
4. Joan Biskupic, "Anticrime Package Falters After Gun Ban Retained," *Congressional Quarterly Weekly Report*, 26 May 1990, pp. 1654–1656; Joan Biskupic, "Opponents of Gun Control Stall Crime Bill Action," *Congressional Quarterly Weekly Report*, 9 June 1990, pp. 1790–1791; Joan Biskupic, "Death Penalty, Other Hot Issues Dumped from Crime Bill, *Congressional Quarterly Weekly Report*, 27 October 1990, p. 3615.
5. Austin Ranney and Willmoore Kendall, *Democracy and the American Party System* (New York: Harcourt Brace, 1956), p. 6.
6. Kenneth Janda, "What's in a Name? Party Labels Across the World," in *The CONTA Conference: Proceedings of the Conference of Conceptual and Terminological Analysis in the Social Sciences*, ed. F. W. Riggs (Frankfurt: Indeks Verlage, 1982), pp. 46–62.
7. This distinction is elaborated in Ranney and Kendall, *Democracy*, pp. 12–13.
8. Richard F. Fenno, Jr., *The President's Cabinet* (New York: Vintage, 1959), p. 29.
9. Robert A. Dahl, *Democracy and Its Critics* (New Haven: Yale University Press, 1989), pp. 13–23.

10. Candy Frank, "New England Town Meeting Reaching End of the Road," *Today Journal*, 28 March 1986.

11. Jean Jacques Rousseau, *The Social Contract* (Harmondsworth, Eng.: Penguin, 1968), p. 141.

12. John Stuart Mill, *Considerations on Representative Democracy* (Indianapolis: Bobbs-Merrill, 1958).

13. Benjamin Barber, *Strong Democracy* (Berkeley: University of California Press, 1984).

14. See C. B. Macpherson, *The Real World of Democracy* (New York: Oxford University Press, 1975), pp. 58–59.

15. Thomas E. Cronin, *Direct Democracy* (Cambridge, Mass.: Harvard University Press, 1989), p. 47.

16. Cronin, *Direct Democracy*, p. 3.

17. Michael Oreskes, "Tax Revolt Fades as Californians Vote an Increase," *New York Times*, 7 June 1990, p. A1.

18. Clyde Haberman, "Greens Alliance Set Back in Italy," *New York Times*, 6 June 1990, p. A7.

19. Cronin, *Direct Democracy*, p. 80.

20. Richard S. Hollander, *Video Democracy: The Vote-from-Home Revolution* (Mt. Airy, Md.: Lomond, 1985); F. Christopher Arterton, *Teledemocracy: Can Technology Protect Democracy?* (Newbury Park, Calif.: Sage, 1987); and Jeffrey B. Abramson, F. Christopher Arterton, and Gary R. Orren, *The Electronic Commonwealth* (New York: Basic Books, 1988).

21. M. Margaret Conway, *Political Participation in the United States*, 2d ed. (Washington, D.C.: Congressional Quarterly, 1991), p. 44.

22. See Robert A. Dahl, *Dilemmas of Pluralist Democracy: Autonomy vs. Control* (New Haven: Yale University Press, 1982), p. 5.

23. Robert A. Dahl, *Pluralist Democracy in the United States* (Chicago: Rand McNally, 1967), p. 24.

24. Michael Useem, *The Inner Circle* (New York: Oxford University Press, 1984). On a broader level, see Charles E. Lindblom, *Politics and Markets* (New York: Basic Books, 1977).

25. Seymour Melman, *Pentagon Capitalism: The Political Economy of War* (New York: McGraw-Hill, 1970).

26. Robert A. Dahl, "A Critique of the Ruling Elite Model," *American Political Science Review* 52 (June 1958):466.

27. Thomas R. Dye, *Who's Running America? The Bush Era*, 5th ed. (Englewood Cliffs, N.J.: Prentice-Hall, 1990), p. 12.

28. The most prominent study was Robert A. Dahl's research on decision making in New Haven, Connecticut, in *Who Governs?* (New Haven: Yale University Press, 1961). G. William Domhoff criticized Dahl's study in *Who Really Rules? New Haven and Community Power Re-examined* (New Brunswick, N.J.: Transaction Books, 1978). Nelson W. Polsby supported Dahl's basic findings in *Community Power and Political Theory: A Further Look at Problems of Evidence and Inference*, 2d ed. (New Haven: Yale University Press, 1980).

29. Peter Bachrach and Morton S. Baratz, "Two Faces of Power," *American Political Science Review* 56 December 1962): 947–952; and John Gaventa, *Power and Powerlessness* (Urbana, Ill.: University of Illinois Press, 1980).

30. See Kenneth M. Dolbeare, *Democracy at Risk: The Politics of Economic Renewal* (Chatham, N.J.: Chatham House, 1984); and Edward S. Greenberg, *The American Political System: A Radical Approach* (Boston: Little, Brown, 1986).

31. See Kay Lehman Schlozman and John T. Tierney, *Organized Interests and American Democracy* (New York: Harper & Row, 1986).

32. G. Bingham Powell, Jr., *Contemporary Democracies* (Cambridge, Mass.: Harvard University Press, 1982), p. 3. Copyright 1982. Used by permission of Harvard University Press.

33. Arend Lijphart, *Democracies* (New Haven, Conn.: Yale University Press, 1984), p. 8. See also Robert Wesson, ed., *Democracy: A Worldwide Survey* (New York: Praeger, 1987), p. xi, for a similar count.

34. E. E. Schattschneider, *The Semisovereign People* (New York: Holt, Rinehart, & Winston, 1960), p. 35.

Chapter 3 / The Constitution / pp. 63–105

1. Carl Bernstein and Bob Woodward, *All the President's Men* (New York: Warner, 1975); Stanley I. Kutler, *The Wars of Watergate* (New York: Knopf, 1990).

2. Bernstein and Woodward, *All the President's Men*, p. 30.

3. Samuel Eliot Morison, *Oxford History of the American People* (New York: Oxford University Press, 1965), p. 182.

4. Richard Walsh, *Charleston's Sons of Liberty: A Study of the Artisans, 1763–1789* (1959).

5. Mary Beth Norton, *Liberty's Daughters* (Boston: Little, Brown, 1980), pp. 155–157.

6. Morison, *Oxford History*, p. 204.

7. John Plamentz, *Man and Society*, vol. 1 (New York: McGraw-Hill, 1963), pp. 162–164.

8. Extrapolated from U.S. Department of Defense, *Selected Manpower Statistics, FY 1982* (Washington, D.C.: U.S. Government Printing Office, 1983), table 2-30, p. 130; and *1985 Statistical Abstract of the United States* (Washington, D.C.: U.S. Government Printing Office, 1985), tables 1 and 2, p. 6.

9. Joseph T. Keenan, *The Constitution of the United States* (Homewood, Ill.: Dow-Jones-Irwin, 1975).

10. David P. Szatmary, *Shays' Rebellion: The Making of an Agrarian Insurrection* (Amherst, Mass.: University of Massachusetts Press, 1980), pp. 82–102.

11. Robert H. Jackson, *The Struggle for Judicial Supremacy* (New York: Knopf, 1941), p. 8.

12. Catherine Drinker Bowen, *Miracle at Philadelphia* (Boston: Little, Brown, 1966), p. 122.

13. Forrest McDonald, *Novus Ordo Seclorum: The Intellectual Origins of the Constitution* (Lawrence, Kan.: University Press of Kansas, 1985), pp. 205–209.

14. Donald S. Lutz, "The Preamble to the Constitution of the United States," *This Constitution* 1 (September 1983):23–30.

15. Richard E. Neustadt, *Presidential Power: The Politics of Leadership* (New York: Wiley, 1960), p. 33.

16. Charles A. Beard, *An Economic Interpretation of the Constitution of the United States* (New York: Macmillan, 1913).

17. Leonard W. Levy, *Constitutional Opinions* (New York: Oxford University Press, 1986), p. 101.

18. Robert E. Brow, *Charles Beard and the Constitution* (Princeton, N.J.: Princeton University Press, 1956); Levy, *Constitutional Opinions*, pp. 103–104; and Forrest McDonald, *We the People: Economic Origins of the Constitution* (Chicago: University of Chicago Press, 1958).

19. Compare Eugene D. Genovese, *The Political Economy of Slavery: Studies in the Economics and Society of the Slave South* (Middletown, Conn.: Wesleyan University Press, 1989) with Robert William Fogel, *Without Contract or Consent: The Rise and Fall of American Slavery* (New York: W. W. Norton, 1989).

20. Walter Berns, *The First Amendment and the Future of Democracy* (New York: Basic Books, 1976), p. 2.

21. Herbert J. Storing, ed., *The Complete Anti-Federalist*, 7 vols. (Chicago: University of Chicago Press, 1981).

22. Alexis de Tocqueville, *Democracy in America*, ed. J. P. Mayer and Max Lerner (New York: Harper & Row, 1966), p. 102.

23. Russell L. Caplan, *Constitutional Brinkmanship: Amending the Constitution by National Convention* (New York: Oxford University Press, 1988), p. 162.

24. *Los Angeles Times*, 17 June 1990, p. A22.

25. Jerold L. Waltman, *Political Origins of the U.S. Income Tax* (Jackson, Miss.: University Press of Mississippi, 1985), p. 10.

Chapter 4 / Federalism / pp. 107–143

1. Ronald Reagan, "National Minimum Drinking Age: Remarks on Signing HR4616 into Law (July 17, 1984)," *Weekly Compilation of Presidential Documents*, 23 July 1984, p. 1036.

2. *South Dakota* v. *Dole*, 483 U.S. 203 (1987).

3. *Budget of the United States Government, FY 1992*, Part 4, p. 863.

4. Daniel J. Elazar, "Opening the Third Century of American Federalism: Issues and Prospects," *Annals of the American Academy of Political and Social Sciences*, 509 (May 1990):14

5. William H. Stewart, *Concepts of Federalism* (Lanham, Md.: University Press of America, 1984).

6. Edward S. Corwin, "The Passing of Dual Federalism," *Virginia Law Review* 36 (February 1950), p. 4.

7. *Hammer* v. *Dagenhart*, 247 U.S. 251 (1918).

8. See Daniel J. Elazar, *The American Partnership* (Chicago: University of Chicago Press, 1962); and Morton Grodzins, *The American System* (Chicago: Rand McNally, 1966).

9. Stewart, *Concepts of Federalism*, p. 109.

10. Stewart, *Concepts of Federalism*, p. 82.

11. Stewart, *Concepts of Federalism*, p. 83.

12. Stewart, *Concepts of Federalism*, p. 174.

13. Raoul Berger, *Federalism: The Founders' Design* (Norman, Okla.: University of Oklahoma Press, 1987), pp. 61–62.

14. *Miranda* v. *Arizona*, 384 U.S. 436 (1966).

15. *Baker* v. *Carr*, 369 U.S. 186 (1962); *Wesberry* v. *Sanders*, 376 U.S. 1 (1964); and *Reynolds* v. *Sims*, 377 U.S. 533 (1964).

16. Advisory Commission on Intergovernmental Relations, *A Catalog of Federal Grant-in-Aid Programs to State and Local Government: Grants Funded in FY 1989* (Washington, D.C.: U.S. Government Printing Office, 1990).

17. *McCulloch* v. *Maryland*, 4 Wheat. 316 (1819).

18. *Dred Scott* v. *Sanford*, 19 How. 393 (1857).

19. *Gibbons* v. *Ogden*, 9 Wheat. 1 (1824).

20. James T. Patterson, *The New Deal and the States: Federalism in Transition* (Princeton, N.J.: Princeton University Press, 1969).

21. *United States* v. *Butler*, 297 U.S. 1 (1936).

22. *United States* v. *Darby*, 312 U.S. 100 (1941).

23. *Plessy* v. *Ferguson*, 163 U.S. 537 (1896).

24. *Brown* v. *Board of Education of Topeka*, 347 U.S. 483 (1954).

25. Aaron Wildavsky, "Bare Bones: Putting Flesh on the Skeleton of American Federalism," in *The Future of Federalism in the 1980s*, ed. the Advisory Commission on Intergovernmental Relations (Washington, D.C.: U.S. Government Printing Office, 1981), p. 80.

26. Advisory Commission on Intergovernmental Relations, *The Federal Role in the Federal System: The Dynamics of Growth* (Washington, D.C.: U.S. Government Printing Office, 1981), p. 101.

27. Richard M. Nixon, "Speech to National Governor's Conference, September 1, 1969," in *Congressional Quarterly Almanac* (Washington, D.C.: Congressional Quarterly Press, 1969), pp. 101A–103A.

28. Richard P. Nathan and Fred C. Doolittle, *Reagan and the States* (Princeton, N.J.: Princeton University Press, 1987), p. 65.

29. Executive Order 12612—Federalism (October 26, 1987).

30. *New York Times*, 30 December 1990, Sec. 1, p. 16.

31. Thomas R. Dye, *American Federalism: Competition Among Governments* (Lexington, Mass.: Lexington Books, 1990).

32. Morton Grodzins, "The Federal System," in *Goals for Americans* (New York: Columbia University, The American Assembly, 1960), p. 265.

33. Linda L. M. Bennett and Stephen Earl Bennett, *Living with Leviathan: Americans Coming to Terms with Big Government* (Lawrence, Kan.: University Press of Kansas, 1990).

34. Paul M. Weyrich, quoted in Neal Pierce, "Conservatives Weep as the States Make Left Turn," *National Journal*, 10 October 1987, p. 2559.

Chapter 5 / Public Opinion and Political Socialization / pp. 147–183

1. Richard G. Niemi, John Mueller, and Tom W. Smith, *Trends in Pub-*

lic Opinion: A Compendium of Survey Data (New York: Greenwood Press, 1989), p. 138. The data for 1988 are from *The Gallup Report*, No. 280 (January 1989):27.

2. *New York Times*, 3 July 1976.

3. *Furman* v. *Georgia*, 408 U.S. 238 (1972).

4. *Gregg* v. *Georgia*, 248 U.S. 153 (1976).

5. *Public Opinion* 8 (June–July 1985):39.

6. Nine national surveys taken from 1971 through 1988 found that an average of 61 percent of Americans disapproved of the ruling in *Abington School District* v. *Schempp*, 374 U.S. 203 (1963). See Niemi, Muller, and Smith, *Trends in Public Opinion*, p. 263.

7. Most of the survey findings reported here were computed from data collected by the National Opinion Research Center in 1990 as part of the General Social Surveys. Tom W. Smith, director of the GSS, kindly supplied the tabulations.

8. *Public Opinion* 5 (October–November 1982):21.

9. These questions are not ideally matched, but other survey items about private enterprise yield comparable results. See Donald J. Devine, *The Political Culture of the United States* (Boston: Little, Brown, 1972), pp. 209–214.

10. Warren E. Miller, Arthur H. Miller, and Edward J. Schneider, *American National Election Studies Sourcebook, 1952–1978* (Cambridge, Mass.: Harvard University Press, 1980), pp. 94–95. See Niemi, Muller, and Smith, *Trends in Public Opinion*, p. 19, for later years.

11. Tom W. Smith and Paul B. Sheatsley, "American Attitudes Toward Race Relations," *Public Opinion* 7 (October–November 1984):15.

12. Ibid.

13. Ibid., p. 83.

14. Steven A. Peterson, *Political Behavior: Patterns in Everyday Life* (Newbury Park, Calif.: Sage Publications, 1990), pp. 28–29.

15. Paul Allen Beck, "The Role of Agents in Political Socialization," in *Handbook of Political Socialization Theory and Research*, ed. Stanley Allen Renshon (New York: Free Press, 1977), pp. 117–118.

16. W. Russell Neuman, *The Paradox of Mass Politics: Knowledge and Opinion in the American Electorate* (Cambridge, Mass.: Harvard University Press, 1986), pp. 113–114.

17. M. Kent Jennings and Richard G. Niemi, *The Political Character of Adolescence: The Influence of Families and Schools* (Princeton, N.J.: Princeton University Press, 1974), p. 39. See also Stephen E. Frantzich, *Political Parties in the Technological Age* (New York: Longman, 1989), p. 152. Frantzich presents a table showing that more than 60 percent of children in homes where both parents have the same party preference will adopt their preference. When parents are divided, the children tend to be divided among Democrats, Republicans, and independents.

18. In a panel study of parents and high school seniors in 1965 and after graduation in 1973, Jennings and Niemi found that 57 percent of children shared their parents' party identification in 1965, but only 47 percent did by 1973. See Jennings and Niemi, *Political Character of Adolescence*, pp. 90–91. See also Robert C. Luskin, John P. McIver, and Edward G. Carmines, "Issues and the Transmission of Partisanship," *American Journal of Political Science* 33 (May 1989):440–458. They find that children are more likely to shift between partisanship and independence than to "convert" to the other party. When conversion occurs, it is more likely to be based on economic issues than on social issues.

19. Robert D. Hess and Judith V. Torney, *The Development of Political Attitudes in Children* (Chicago: Aldine, 1967). But other researchers disagree. See Jerry L. Yeric and John R. Todd, *Public Opinion: The Visible Politics* (Itasca, Ill.: F.E. Peacock, 1989), pp. 45–47, for a summary of the issues.

20. David Easton and Jack Dennis, *Children in the Political System* (New York: McGraw-Hill, 1969).

21. Jarol B. Manheim, *The Politics Within* (New York: Longman, 1982), p. 83.

22. "Government Trust: Less in West Europe than U.S.," *New York Times*, 16 February 1986. But polls in 1987 and 1990 found "a significant upswing in feelings of mistrust of political leaders." See the September 19, 1990, press release of the Times Mirror Center for the People & the Press, p. 5. See also Robin Toner, "Poll Finds Postwar Glow Dimmed by the Economy," *New York Times*, 8 March 1991, p. A11.

23. Janie S. Steckenrider and Neal E. Cutler, "Aging and Adult Political Socialization: The Importance of Roles and Transitions," in Roberta S. Sigel, *Political Learning in Adulthood: A Sourcebook of Theory and Research* (Chicago: University of Chicago Press, 1989), pp. 56–88.

24. See Robert Huckfeldt and John Sprague, "Networks in Context: The Social Flow of Information," *American Political Science Review* 81 (December 1987): 1197–1216. The authors' study of voting in neighborhoods in South Bend, Indiana, found that residents who favored the minority party were acutely aware of their minority status.

25. Theodore M. Newcomb, *Persistence and Social Change: Bennington College and Its Students After Twenty-Five Years* (New York: Wiley, 1967).

26. M. Kent Jennings and Gregory Marcus, "Yuppie Politics," *ISR Newsletter* (Ann Arbor, Mich.: Institute of Social Research, University of Michigan, August 1986).

27. See Roberta S. Sigel, ed., *Political Learning in Adulthood: A Sourcebook of Theory and Research* (Chicago: University of Chicago Press, 1989).

28. "The American Media: Who Reads, Who Watches, Who Listens, Who Cares?" (Washington, D.C.: Times Mirror Center for the People & the Press, release of July 15, 1990), p. 4.

29. This question has appeared for years in the National Opinion Research Center's *General Social Survey*. As usual, the question in

1990 had seven response categories ranging from "government should do something to reduce income differences between rich and poor" (Category 1) to "government should not concern itself with income differences" (Category 7). Categories 1 through 3 were combined to represent the "government should" response, and Categories 4 through 7 were combined to represent the "government should not" response.

30. The increasing wealth in industrialized societies may or may not be replacing class conflict with conflict over values. See the exchange between Ronald Inglehart and Scott C. Flanagan, "Value Change in Industrial Societies," *American Political Science Review* 81 (December 1987): 1289–1319.

31. For a parallel analysis, see Neuman, *Paradox of Mass Politics*, pp. 79–81.

32. For a recent review of these studies, see Robert S. Erikson, Norman R. Luttbeg, and Kent L. Tedin, *American Public Opinion*, 3d. ed. (New York: Macmillan, 1988).

33. Nathan Glazer, "The Structure of Ethnicity," *Public Opinion* 7 (October–November 1984):4.

34. Felicity Barringer, "Census Shows Profound Change in Racial Makeup of the Nation," *New York Times*, 11 March 1991, pp. 1 and 12.

35. Glazer, "Structure of Ethnicity," p. 5.

36. These figures came from the 1990 General Social Survey and were kindly provided by Tom W. Smith, director of the GSS.

37. John Robinson, "The Ups and Downs and Ins and Outs of Ideology," *Public Opinion* 7 (February–March 1984):12.

38. Angus Campbell et al., *The American Voter* (New York: Wiley, 1960), Chapter 10.

39. Neuman, *Paradox of Mass Politics*, pp. 19–20.

40. Arthur Sanders, "Ideological Symbols," *American Politics Quarterly* 17 (July 1989):235.

41. See Norman H. Nie, Sidney Verba, and John R. Petrocik. *The Changing American Voter*, 2d ed. (Cam-

bridge, Mass.: Harvard University Press, 1979).

42. Some scholars believe that the methods used for classifying respondents as ideologues was too generous. See Robert C. Luskin, "Measuring Political Sophistication," *American Journal of Political Science* 31 (November 1987):878, 887–888. For a comprehensive critique, see Eric R. A. N. Smith, *The Unchanging American Voter* (Berkeley: University of California Press, 1989), especially Chapter 1.

43. See William G. Jacoby, "Levels of Conceptualization and Reliance on the Liberal-Conservative Continuum" *Journal of Politics* 48 (May 1986):423–432.

44. *National Election Study for 1988*, pre-election survey conducted by the Center for Political Studies at the University of Michigan.

45. However, citizens can engage in ideologically consistent behavior in attitudes toward candidates and perceptions about domestic issues without thinking about politics in explicitly liberal and conservative terms. See William G. Jacoby, "The Structure of Liberal-Conservative Thinking in the American Public" (paper prepared for presentation at the 1990 Annual Meeting of the Midwest Political Science Association).

46. Milton Rokeach also proposed a two-dimensional model of political ideology grounded in the terminal values of freedom and equality. See *The Nature of Human Values* (New York: Free Press, 1973), especially Chapter 6. Rokeach found that positive and negative references to these two values permeated the writings of socialists, communists, fascists, and conservatives and clearly differentiated the four bodies of writing from one another (pp. 173–174). However, Rokeach built his two-dimensional model around only the values of freedom and equality; he did not deal with the question of freedom versus order.

47. Pamela Johnston Conover, "The Origins and Meaning of Liberal-Conservative Self-Identifications," *American Journal of Political Sci-

ence* 25 (November 1981): 621–622, 643.

48. The relationship of liberalism to political tolerance is found by John L. Sullivan et al., "The Sources of Political Tolerance: A Multivariate Analysis," *American Political Science Review* 75 (March 1981): 102. See also Robinson, "Ups and Downs," pp. 13–15.

49. Herbert Asher, *Presidential Elections and American Politics* (Homewood, Ill.: Dorsey Press, 1980), pp. 14–20. Asher also constructs a two-dimensional framework, distinguishing between "traditional New Deal" issues and "new lifestyle" issues.

50. John E. Jackson, "The Systematic Beliefs of the Mass Public: Estimating Policy Preferences with Survey Data," *Journal of Politics* 45 (November 1983):840–865, at 857.

51. The second edition of *The Challenge of Democracy*, which used the 1987 General Social Survey, reported slightly different percentages for three of the four ideological tendencies. According to the 1987 data, populists accounted for 24 percent of the sample, libertarians for 26 percent, conservatives for 28 percent, and liberals for 22 percent. The differences in percentages reflect a substantial shift in the 1990 sample of 7 percentage points away from firing a communist teacher (no doubt due to the collapse of the Soviet threat) and 6 points toward government equalizing of income. That shift is probably due to publicity about the growth of a gap between rich and poor during the Reagan administration. See Kevin Phillips, *The Politics of Rich and Poor: Wealth and the American Electorate in the Reagan Aftermath* (New York: Random House, 1990).

52. William S. Maddox and Stuart A. Lilie, *Beyond Liberal and Conservative: Reassessing the Political Spectrum* (Washington, D.C.: Cato Institute, 1984), p. 68.

53. See Neuman, *Paradox of Mass Politics*, p. 81. See also Aaron Wildavsky, "Choosing Preferences by Constructing Institutions: A Cultural Theory of Preference Forma-

tion," *American Political Science Review* 81 (March 1987):13.

54. The same conclusion was reached in a major study of British voting behavior. See Hilde T. Himmelweit et al., *How Voters Decide* (New York: Academic Press, 1981), pp. 138–141. See also Wildavsky, "Choosing Preferences," p. 13.

55. But a significant literature is developing on the limitations of self-interest in explaining political life. See Jane J. Mansbridge, ed., *Beyond Self-Interest* (Chicago: University of Chicago Press, 1990).

56. Wildavsky, "Choosing Preferences," pp. 3–21.

57. David O. Sears and Carolyn L. Funk, "Self-Interest in Americans' Political Opinions," in Mansbridge, *Beyond Self-Interest*, pp. 147–170.

58. Center for Political Studies, *1988 National Election Survey* (Ann Arbor, Mich.: Inter-University Consortium for Political and Social Research, 1989), pp. 281–291.

59. Times Mirror Center for the People & the Press, "Times Mirror News Interest Index" (July 12, 1990), p. 2.

60. Smith, *The Unchanging American Voter*, p. 5. However, Smith later argues that the information component of the definition is more important than attitude consistency or level of conceptualization (pp. 224–227). For another attempt to measure political sophistication—by using a ten-word vocabulary test—see Lawrence Bobo and Frederick C. Licari, "Education and Political Tolerance: Testing the Effects of Cognitive Sophistication and Target Group Affect," *Public Opinion Quarterly* 53 (Fall 1989):285–308.

61. Neuman, *Paradox of Mass Politics*, pp. 19–20.

62. Ibid., pp. 6–7. There is evidence that the educational system and parental practices hamper the ability of women to develop their political sophistication. See Linda L.M. Bennett and Stephen Earl Bennett, "Enduring Gender Differences in Political Interests," *American Politics Quarterly* 17 (January, 1989):105–122.

63. Ibid., p. 81.

64. Pamela Johnston Conover and Stanley Feldman, "How People Organize the Political World: A Schematic Model," *American Journal of Political Science* 28 (February 1984): 96. For an excellent review of schema structures in contemporary psychology—especially as they relate to political science—see Reid Hastie, "A Primer of Information-Processing Theory for the Political Scientist," in *Political Cognition*, ed. Richard R. Lau and David O. Sears (Hillsdale, N.J.: Erlbaum, 1986), pp. 11–39.

65. John Hurwitz and Mark Peffley, "How Are Foreign Policy Attitudes Structured? A Hierarchical Model," *American Political Science Review* 81 (December 1987):1099–1220.

66. Richard L. Allen, Michael C. Dawson, and Ronald E. Brown. "A Schema-Based Approach to Modeling an African-American Racial Belief System," *American Political Science Review* 83 (June 1989):421–441.

67. See Milton Lodge and Ruth Hamill, "A Partisan Schema for Political Information Processing," *American Political Science Review* 80 (June 1986):505–519.

68. Arthur Sanders. *Making Sense Out of Politics* (Ames, Iowa: Iowa State University Press, 1990).

69. Lee Sigelman, "Disarming the Opposition: The President, the Public, and the INF Treaty," *Public Opinion Quarterly* 54 (Spring 1990):37–47, at 46.

70. Benjamin I. Page, Robert Y. Shapiro, and Glenn R. Dempsey, "What Moves Public Opinion?" *American Political Science Review* 81 (March 1987):23–43.

71. Michael Margolis and Gary A. Mauser, *Manipulating Public Opinion: Essays on Public Opinion as a Dependent Variable* (Pacific Grove, Calif.: Brooks/Cole, 1989).

Chapter 6 / The Mass Media / pp. 185–223

1. Maureen Dowd, "Storm's Eye: Bush Decides to Go to War," *New York Times*, 17 January 1991, p. A8. See also James Warren, "Early Planning Helped CNN Register a Television Coup," *Chicago Tribune*, 18 January 1991, sec. 1, p. 9.

2. Jonathan Alter, "Ted's Global Village," *Newsweek*, 11 June 1990. See also Michael Schwelien, "CNN: Television for the Global Village," *World Press Review*, December 1990, p. 34.

3. Carroll J. Doherty, "Public Debate on Persian Gulf Poses Challenge for Members," *Congressional Quarterly Weekly Report*, 1 December 1990, p. 4004.

4. Jonathan Alter, "Clippings from the Media War," *Newsweek*, 11 March 1991, p. 52.

5. S. N. D. North, *The Newspaper and Periodical Press* (Washington, D.C.: U.S. Government Printing Office, 1884), p. 27. This source provides much of the information reported about newspapers and magazines prior to 1880.

6. Sidney Kobre, *The Yellow Press and Gilded Age Journalism* (Tallahassee, Fla.: Florida State University Press, 1964), p. 52.

7. In 1950, a total of 1,772 daily papers had a circulation of 53.8 million; in 1989, a total of 1,642 papers had a circulation of 62.7 million. Bureau of the Census, *Statistical Abstract of the United States, 1988* (Washington, D.C.: U.S. Government Printing Office, 1988), p. 528. The number of newspapers per capita was .35 in 1950 and .26 in 1987. See Harold W. Stanley and Richard G. Niemi, eds., *Vital Statistics on American Politics*, 2d ed. (Washington, D.C.: Congressional Quarterly Press, 1990), p. 48.

8. Matthew Manning, ed., *Standard Periodical Directory*, 13th ed. (New York: Oxbridge Communications, 1990).

9. Douglas Kellner, *Television and the Crisis of Democracy* (Boulder, Colo.: Westview Press, 1990), pp. 225–248.

10. Dana R. Ulloth, Peter L. Klinge, and Sandra Eells, *Mass Media: Past, Present, Future* (St. Paul, Minn.: West, 1983), p. 278.

11. Bill Keller, "In Moscow's TV Political Debates, the Unspeakable Is Now Routine," *New York Times*,

22 March 1989, p. 1; Esther B. Fein, "Gorbachev Urges Curbs on Press Freedom," *New York Times*, 17 January 1991, p. A4.

12. Steve Lohr, "European TV's Vast Growth: Cultural Effect Stirs Concern," *New York Times*, 16 March 1989, p. 1

13. Roper Organization, *Trends in Attitudes Toward Television and Other Media* (New York: Television Information Office, 1983), p. 8.

14. Bureau of the Census, *Statistical Abstract of the United States, 1982–1983* (Washington, D.C.: U.S. Government Printing Office, 1984), p. 562.

15. Doris A. Graber, *Mass Media and American Politics* (Washington, D.C.: Congressional Quarterly Press, 1984), pp. 78–79.

16. Kenneth R. Clark, "Network Audience Share at Record Low," *Chicago Tribune*, 30 November 1990, sec. 3, p. 1.

17. *Editor & Publisher International Yearbook, 1984*, pp. 435–442.

18. Christopher H. Sterling, *Electronic Media: A Guide to Trends in Broadcasting and Newer Technologies, 1920–1983* (New York: Praeger, 1984), p. 22.

19. *Broadcasting Yearbook, 1990* (Washington, D.C.: Broadcasting Publications, 1990).

20. Joseph Turow, *Media Industries: The Production of News and Entertainment* (New York: Longman, 1984), p. 18. Our discussion of government regulation draws heavily on this source.

21. Joseph R. Dominick, *The Dynamics of Mass Communication* (Reading, Mass.: Addison-Wesley, 1983), p. 331.

22. Paul Starobin, "Media-Ownership Overhaul May Divide Legislators," *Congressional Quarterly Weekly Report*, 3 June 1989, p. 1315.

23. Graber, *Mass Media*, p. 110.

24. Robert Entman, *Democracy without Citizens: Media and the Decay of American Politics* (New York: Oxford University Press, 1989), pp.103–108.

25. Michael Nelson, ed., *Guide to the Presidency* (Washington, D.C.: Congressional Quarterly Press, 1989), p. 729.

26. Nelson, *Guide to the Presidency*, p. 729.

27. Nelson, *Guide to the Presidency*, p. 735

28. Warren Weaver, "C-Span on the Hill: 10 Years of Gavel to Gavel," *New York Times*, 28 March 1989, p. 10.

29. Graber, *Mass Media*, p. 241.

30. Graber, *Mass Media*, p. 72.

31. Austin Ranney, *Channels of Power: The Impact of Television on American Politics* (New York: Basic Books, 1983), p. 46.

32. Doris A. Graber, *Mass Media and American Politics*, 3d ed. (Washington, D.C.: Congressional Quarterly Press, 1989), p. 237.

33. Harold W. Stanley and Richard G. Niemi, eds. *Vital Statistics on American Politics*, 2d ed. (Washington, D.C.: Congressional Quarterly Press, 1990), p. 57. See also Gregory Katz, "Issues Distant Second to 'Horse-Race' Stories," *USA Today*, 22 April 1988, p. 6A.

34. There was less of a difference between those who said they regularly read a newspaper and those who did so "yesterday," while *more* people (53 percent) actually listened to news on the radio the previous day than said they regularly did so (46 percent). Times Mirror Center for The People & The Press, "The American Media: Who Reads, Who Watches, Who Listens, Who Cares" (Washington, D.C.: Press release, July 15, 1990), p. 4.

35. Doris A. Graber, *Processing the News: How People Tame the Information Tide*, 2d ed. (New York: Longman, 1988), p. 101.

36. Michael J. Robinson and Andrew Kohut, "Believability and the Press," *Public Opinion Quarterly* 52 (Summer 1988):174–189.

37. Times Mirror Center for The People & The Press, "The American Media."

38. This fits with findings by Stephen Earl Bennett in "Trends in Americans' Political Information, 1967–1987," *American Politics Quarterly* 17 (October 1989): 422–435. Bennett found that race was significantly related to level of political information in a 1967 survey, but not in a 1987 survey.

39. Linda L. M. Bennett and Stephen Earl Bennett, "Enduring Gender Differences in Political Interests," *American Politics Quarterly* 17 (January 1989):105–122, at pp. 116–117.

40. Times Mirror Center for The People & The Press, "News Interest Index" (Washington, D.C.: Press release, March 1990), p. 125.

41. One seasoned journalist argues instead that the technology of minicams and satellites have set back the quality of coverage. Now a television crew can fly to the scene of a crisis and immediately televise information, without knowing much about the local politics or culture, which was not true of the old foreign correspondents. See David R. Gergen, "Diplomacy in a Television Age: The Dangers of Teledemocracy," in *The Media and Foreign Policy*, ed. Simon Serfaty (New York: St. Martin's Press, 1990), p. 51.

42. Stephen Earl Bennett, "Trends in Americans' Political Information, 1967–1987." Bennett's findings are supported by a national poll in 1990 that found only 40 percent of the sample read a newspaper "yesterday," compared with 71 percent asked the same question in 1965. Times Mirror Center for The People & The Press, "The American Media," p. 100.

43. Peter Clarke and Eric Fredin, "Newspapers, Television, and Political Reasoning," *Public Opinion Quarterly* 42 (Summer 1978): 143–160.

44. Joseph Wagner, "Media Do Make the Difference: The Differential Impact of Mass Media in the 1976 Presidential Race," *American Journal of Political Science*, 27 (August 1983):407–430, at 415–417; L. Harmon Zeigler and William Haltom, "More Bad News about the News," *Public Opinion* 12 (May–June, 1989):50–52.

45. Graber, *Processing the News*, pp. 166–169.

46. Michael J. Robinson, "American Political Legitimacy in an Era of Electronic Journalism: Reflections on the Evening News," in *Television as a Social Force*, ed. Douglass Cater (New York: Praeger, 1975), pp. 97–139.

47. Graber, *Mass Media*, pp. 66–67; and Andrew Goodman, "Television Images of the Foreign Policy Process" (Ph.D. diss., Northwestern University, 1985), chap. 11.

48. William Schneider, "Bang-Bang Television: The New Superpower," *Public Opinion* 5 (April–May 1982):13–15, at 13.

49. Benjamin I. Page, Robert Y. Shapiro, and Glenn R. Dempsey, "What Moves Public Opinion?" *American Political Science Review* 81 (March 1987):23–43, at 31.

50. Page, Shapiro, and Dempsey, "What Moves Public Opinion," p. 35.

51. Shanto Iyengar and Donald R. Kinder, *News That Matters: Television and American Opinion* (Chicago: University of Chicago Press, 1987), p. 33.

52. Iyengar and Kinder, *News That Matters*, p. 60.

53. Herbert Jacob, *The Frustration of Policy: Responses to Crime by American Cities* (Boston: Little, Brown, 1984), pp. 47–50.

54. W. Russell Neuman, "The Threshold of Public Attention," *Public Opinion Quarterly* 54 (Summer 1990):159–176.

55. David E. Harrington, "Economic News on Television: The Determinants of Coverage," *Public Opinion Quarterly* 53 (Spring 1989): 17–40.

56. Entman, *Democracy without Citizens*, p. 86.

57. Entman, *Democracy without Citizens*, pp. 47–48.

58. Richard Zoglin, "Is TV Ruining Our Children?" *Time*, 5 October 1990, p. 75. Moreover, much of what children see are advertisements. See "Study: Almost 20% of Kid TV Is Ad-Related," *Chicago Tribune*, 22 April 1991, p. 11.

59. John J. O'Connor, "Soothing Bromides? Not on TV," *New York Times*, Arts & Leisure sec., 28 October 1990, pp. 1, 35.

60. Douglas Kellner, *Television and the Crisis of Democracy* (Boulder, Colo.: Westview Press, 1990), p. 17.

61. For analysis of elections from 1964 to 1976, see S. Robert Lichter and Stanley Rothman, "Media and Business Elites," *Public Opinion* 5 (October–November 1981):42–46.

For a study of the 1980 election, see L. Brent Bozell II and Brent H. Baker, eds., *And That's the Way It Isn't* (Alexandria, Va.: Media Research Center, 1990), p. 32.

62. Bozell and Baker, *And That's the Way It Isn't*, p. 38. Similar findings were found in a larger study of 2,703 reporters and editors in 1985. See William Schneider and I. A. Lewis, "Views on the News," *Public Opinion* 8 (August–September 1985):6–11, 58–59, at 7.

63. Gregory Katz, "GOP Scrutinized More on Network Newscasts," *USA Today*, 22 April 1988, p. 6A.

64. Schneider and Lewis, "Views on the News," pp. 6–11, 58–59.

65. Stanley and Niemi, *Vital Statistics on American Politics*, p. 73.

66. Michael Robinson and Margaret Sheehan, *Over the Wire and on TV: CBS and UPI in Campaign '80* (New York: Russell Sage Foundation, 1983).

67. Michael J. Robinson, "The Media in Campaign '84: Part II; Wingless, Toothless, and Hopeless," *Public Opinion* 8 (February–March 1985):43–48, at 48.

68. Maura Clancey and Michael J. Robinson, "General Election Coverage: Part I," *Public Opinion* 7 (December–January 1985):49–54, 59, at 54.

69. Stanley Rothman and S. Robert Lichter, "Elite Ideology and Risk Perception in Nuclear Energy Policy," *American Political Science Review* 81 (June 1987):393.

70. "Television News Coverage of the Persian Gulf War," *Media Monitor* 5 (February 1991):6. See also Daniel Wattenberg, "Media Mask View of the Gulf," *Insight*, 28 January 1991, pp. 8–13; and Jonas Bernstein, "Press Showing Its Stripes," *Insight*, 28 January 1991, pp. 14–15.

71. For a historical account of efforts to determine voters' preferences before modern polling, see Tom W. Smith, "The First Straw? A Study of the Origin of Election Polls," *Public Opinion Polling* 54 (Spring 1990):21–36.

72. Michael R. Kagay, "The Use of Public Opinion Polls by *The New York Times*: Some Examples from the 1988 Presidential Election," in *Polling and Presidential Election*

Coverage, eds. Paul J. Lavrakas and Jack K. Holley (Newbury Park, Calif.: Sage Publications, 1991), p. 19.

73. Jack K. Holley, "The Press and Political Polling," in *Polling and Presidential Election Coverage*, p. 225.

74. Michael W. Traugott, "Public Attitudes about News Organizations, Campaign Coverage, and Polls," in *Polling and Presidential Election Coverage*, p. 135.

75. Schneider and Lewis, "Views on the News," p. 11.

76. Times Mirror Center for The People & The Press, "The People, the Press and the War in the Gulf," 31 January 1991, p. 1.

Chapter 7 / Participation and Voting / pp. 225–261

1. Elaine S. Povich and Steve Daley, "Bush Turns Up Heat on Gulf Vote," *Chicago Tribune*, 12 January 1991, p. 1.

2. Jason DeParle, "On the Left, Voices Amid Confusion," *New York Times*, 17 November 1990, p. 5.

3. Michael deCourcy Hinds, "Drawing on Vietnam Legacy, Antiwar Effort Buds Quickly," *New York Times*, 11 January 1991, p. 1; Anthony DePalma, "On Campuses, Coordinated Antiwar Protests," *New York Times*, 22 February 1991, p. A8.

4. Janet Cawley and Ruth Lopez, "Rallies Draw Crowds across U.S., Abroad," *Chicago Tribune*, 22 January 1991, sec. 1, p. 6; Jerry Adler, "The War Within," *Newsweek*, 4 February 1991, p. 58.

5. Jane Gross, "Anxious Nation Is Drawn Together," *New York Times*, 18 January 1991, p. A13.

6. Linda P. Campbell and Ruth Lopez, "To Illinois Protesters, War 'An Insane Move,'" *Chicago Tribune*, 20 January 1991, sec. 1, p. 8.

7. Lester W. Milbrath and M. L. Goel, *Political Participation* (Chicago: Rand McNally, 1977), p. 2.

8. *New York Times*, 4 March 1985.

9. Michael Lipsky, "Protest as a Political Resource," *American Po-*

litical Science Review 62 (December 1968):1145.

10. See Sidney Verba and Norman H. Nie, *Participation in America: Political Democracy and Social Equality* (New York: Harper & Row, 1972), p. 3.

11. Samuel H. Barnes and Max Kaase, eds., *Political Action: Mass Participation in Five Western Democracies* (Beverly Hills, Calif.: Sage, 1979).

12. Jonathan D. Casper, *Politics of Civil Liberties* (New York: Harper & Row, 1972), p. 90.

13. David C. Colby, "A Test of the Relative Efficacy of Political Tactics," *American Journal of Political Science* 26 (November 1982):741–753. See also Frances Fox Piven and Richard Cloward, *Poor People's Movements* (New York: Vintage, 1979).

14. Stephen C. Craig and Michael A. Magiotto, "Political Discontent and Political Action," *Journal of Politics* 43 (May 1981):514–522. But see Mitchell A. Seligson, "Trust Efficacy and Modes of Political Participation: A Study of Costa Rican Peasants," *British Journal of Political Science* 10 (January 1980):75–98, for a review of studies that came to different conclusions.

15. Philip H. Pollock III, "Organizations as Agents of Mobilization: How Does Group Activity Affect Political Participation?" *American Journal of Political Science* 26 (August 1982):485–503. Also see Jan E. Leighley, "Social Interaction and Contextual Influence on Political Participation," *American Politics Quarterly* 18 (October 1990):459–475.

16. Arthur H. Miller, et al., "Group Consciousness and Political Participation," *American Journal of Political Science* 25 (August 1981):495. See also Susan J. Carroll, "Gender Politics and the Socializing Impact of the Women's Movement," in *Political Learning in Adulthood: A Sourcebook of Theory and Research*, ed. Roberta S. Sigel (Chicago: University of Chicago Press, 1989), p. 307.

17. Richard D. Shingles, "Black Consciousness and Political Participation: The Missing Link," *Ameri-can Political Science Review* 75 (March 1981):76–91. See also Lawrence Bobo and Franklin D. Gilliam, Jr., "Race, Sociopolitical Participation, and Black Empowerment," *American Political Science Review* 84 (June 1990): 377–393.

18. Russell J. Dalton, *Citizen Politics in Western Democracies* (Chatham, N.J.: Chatham House, 1988), p. 65.

19. M. Kent Jennings, Jan W. van Deth, et al., *Continuities in Political Action: A Longitudinal Study of Political Orientations in Three Western Democracies* (New York: Walter de Gruyter, 1990).

20. See James L. Gibson, "The Policy Consequences of Political Intolerance: Political Repression During the Vietnam War Era," *Journal of Politics* 51 (February 1989):13–35. Gibson found that individual state legislatures reacted quite differently in response to antiwar demonstrations on college campuses, but the laws passed to discourage dissent were not related directly to public opinion within the state.

21. See Joel B. Grossman, et al., "Dimensions of Institutional Participation: Who Uses the Courts and How?" *Journal of Politics* 44 (February 1982):86–114; and Frances Kahn Zemans, "Legal Mobilization: The Neglected Role of the Law in the Political System," *American Political Science Review* 77 (September 1983):690–703.

22. See Verba and Nie, *Participation in America*, p. 69. Also see John Clayton Thomas, "Citizen-Initiated Contacts with Government Agencies: A Test of Three Theories," *American Journal of Political Science* 26 (August 1982): 504–522; and Elaine B. Sharp, "Citizen-Initiated Contacting of Government Officials and Socioeconomic Status: Determining the Relationship and Accounting for It," *American Political Science Review* 76 (March 1982):109–115.

23. Elaine B. Sharp, "Citizen Demand Making in the Urban Context," *American Journal of Political Science* 28 (November 1984):654–670, at 654, 665.

24. John R. Cranford, "Decision in Keating Five Case Settles Little for Senate," *Congresssional Quarterly Weekly Report*, 2 March 1991, p. 517.

25. Verba and Nie, *Participation in America*, p. 67; and Sharp, "Citizen Demand Making," p. 660.

26. *Brown* v. *Board of Education*, 347 U.S. 483 (1954).

27. Max Kaase and Alan Marsh, "Political Action: A Theoretical Perspective," in *Political Action*, p. 168.

28. *Smith* v. *Allwright*, 321 U.S. 649 (1944).

29. *Harper* v. *Virginia State Board of Elections*, 383 U.S. 663 (1966).

30. Everett Carll Ladd, *The American Polity* (New York: Norton, 1985), p. 392.

31. Gorton Carruth and associates, eds., *The Encyclopedia of American Facts and Dates* (New York: Crowell, 1979), p. 330.

32. Ivor Crewe, "Electoral Participation," in *Democracy at the Polls: A Comparative Study of Competitive National Elections*, ed. David Butler, Howard R. Penniman, and Austin Ranney (Washington, D.C.: American Enterprise Institute, 1981), pp. 219–223.

33. Thomas E. Cronin, *Direct Democracy: The Politics of Initiative, Referendum, and Recall* (Cambridge, Mass.: Harvard University Press, 1989), p. 127.

34. David B. Magleby, *Direct Legislation: Voting on Ballot Propositions in the United States* (Baltimore: Johns Hopkins University Press, 1984), p. 70.

35. Cronin, *Direct Democracy*, p. 197.

36. Robert Pear, "Number of Ballot Initiatives Is the Greatest Since 1932," *New York Times*, 5 November 1990, p. A11.

37. Robert Pear, "Voters Spurn Array of Plans for Protecting Environment," *New York Times*, 8 November 1990, p. A13.

38. Magleby, *Direct Legislation*, p. 59.

39. "Fears on Economy Doom Environment Issues, Tax Cuts," *Chicago Tribune*, 8 November 1990, sec. 1, p. 22.

40. Robert Reinhold, "Complicated Ballot Is Becoming Burden to California Voters," *New York Times*, 24 September 1990, p. 1.

41. Cronin, *Direct Democracy*, p. x.
42. Cronin, *Direct Democracy*, p. 251.
43. *The Book of the States 1990–91*, vol. 28 (Lexington, Ky.: Council of State Governments, 1990), p. 85.
44. *Chicago Tribune*, 10 March 1985.
45. Crewe, "Electoral Participation," p. 232.
46. Verba and Nie, *Participation in America*, p. 13.
47. Max Kaase and Alan Marsh, "Distribution of Political Action," in *Political Action*, p. 186.
48. Milbrath and Goel, *Political Participation*, pp. 95–96.
49. Verba and Nie, *Participation in America*, p. 148. For a concise summary of the effect of age on voting turnout, see Michael M. Gant and Norman R. Luttbeg, *American Electoral Behavior* (Itasca, Ill.: F. E. Peacock, 1991), pp. 103–104.
50. Richard Murray and Arnold Vedlitz, "Race, Socioeconomic Status, and Voting Participation in Large Southern Cities," *Journal of Politics* 39 (November 1977): 1064–1072; and Verba and Nie, *Participation in America*, p. 157. See also Bobo and Gilliam, "Race, Sociopolitical Participation, and Black Empowerment." Their study of 1987 national survey data with a black oversample found that African-Americans participated more than whites of comparable socioeconomic status in cities where the mayor's office was held by an African-American.
51. Carol A. Cassel, "Change in Electoral Participation in the South," *Journal of Politics* 41 (August 1979): 907–917.
52. Ronald B. Rapoport, "The Sex Gap in Political Persuading: Where the 'Structuring Principle' Works," *American Journal of Political Science* 25 (February 1981): 32–48.
53. Bruce C. Straits, "The Social Context of Voter Turnout," *Public Opinion Quarterly* 54 (Spring 1990): 64–73.
54. Stephen D. Shaffer, "A Multivariate Explanation of Decreasing Turnout in Presidential Elections, 1960–1976," *American Journal of Political Science* 25 (February 1981): 68–95; and Paul R. Abramson and John H. Aldrich, "The De-

cline of Electoral Participation in America," *American Political Science Review* 76 (September 1981): 603–620.
55. There is a sizable literature that attempts to explain the decline in voting turnout in the United States. Some authors have claimed to account for the decline with just a few variables, but their work has been criticized for being too simplistic. See Carol A. Cassel and Robert C. Luskin, "Simple Explanations of Turnout Decline," *American Political Science Review* 82 (December, 1988): 1321–1330. They contend that most of the post-1960 decline is still unexplained.
56. Abramson and Aldrich, "Decline of Electoral Participation," p. 519; and Shaffer, "Multivariate Explanation," pp. 78, 90. For a later, more complex analysis with similar conclusions, see Ruy A. Teixeira, *Why Americans Don't Vote: Turnout Decline in the United States, 1960–1984* (New York: Greenwood Press, 1987), pp. 107–108.
57. The negative effect of registration laws on voting turnout is argued in Frances Fox Piven and Richard A. Cloward, "Government Statistics and Conflicting Explanations of Nonvoting," *PS: Political Science and Politics* 22 (September 1989): 580–588. Their analysis was hotly contested in Stephen Earl Bennett, "The Uses and Abuses of Registration and Turnout Data: An Analysis of Piven and Cloward's Studies of Nonvoting in America," *PS: Political Science and Politics* 23 (June 1990): 166–171. Bennett showed that turnout declined 10 to 13 percent since 1960 despite efforts to remove or lower legal hurdles to registration. For their reply, see Frances Fox Piven and Richard L. Cloward, "A Reply to Bennett," *PS: Political Science and Politics* 23 (June 1990): 172–173. You can see that reasonable people can disagree on this matter.
58. David Glass, Peverill Squire, and Raymond Wolfinger, "Voter Turnout: An International Comparison," *Public Opinion* 6 (December–January 1984): 52.

59. G. Bingham Powell, Jr., "American Voter Turnout in Comparative Perspective," *American Political Science Review* 80 (March 1986): 25.
60. See Charles Krauthammer, "In Praise of Low Voter Turnout," *Time*, 21 May 1990, p. 88. Krauthammer says, "Low voter turnout means that people see politics as quite marginal to their lives, as neither salvation nor ruin. . . . Low voter turnout is a leading indicator of contentment."
61. Crewe, "Electoral Participation," p. 262.
62. Barnes and Kaase, *Political Action*, p. 532.
63. *1971 Congressional Quarterly Almanac* (Washington, D.C.: Congressional Quarterly Press, 1972), p. 475.
64. Benjamin Ginsberg, *The Consequences of Consent: Elections, Citizen Control and Popular Acquiescence* (Reading, Mass.: Addison-Wesley, 1982), p. 13.
65. Ginsberg, *Consequences of Consent*, pp. 13–14.
66. Ginsberg, *Consequences of Consent*, pp. 6–7.

Chapter 8 / Political Parties / pp. 263–297

1. *Congressional Quarterly Weekly Report*, 1 December 1990, p. 4002.
2. "Socialist Vows to Be Capitol Outsider," *New York Times*, 12 November 1990, p. A12.
3. *Congressional Quarterly Weekly Report*, 1 December 1990, p. 4002.
4. Center for Political Studies of the Institute for Social Research, *Election Study 1984* (Ann Arbor, Mich.: University of Michigan, 1984).
5. Alan R. Gitelson, M. Margaret Conway, and Frank B. Fiegert, *American Political Parties: Stability and Change* (Boston: Houghton Mifflin, 1984), p. 317.
6. Noble E. Cunningham, Jr., ed., *The Making of the American Party System, 1789 to 1809* (Englewood Cliffs, N.J.: Prentice-Hall, 1965), p. 123.
7. Richard B. Morris, ed., *Encyclopedia of American History* (New York: Harper & Row, 1976), p. 209.

8. See Jerome M. Clubb, William H. Flanigan, and Nancy H. Zingale, *Partisan Realignment: Voters, Parties, and Government in American History*, vol. 108 (Beverly Hills, Calif.: Sage, 1980), p. 163.

9. See Gerald M. Pomper, "Classification of Presidential Elections," *Journal of Politics* 29 (August 1967):535–566.

10. For a more extensive treatment, see Henry M. Littlefield, "The Wizard of Oz: Parable on Populism," *American Quarterly* 16 (Spring 1964):47–58.

11. Clubb, Flanigan, and Zingale, *Partisan Realignment*, p. 99.

12. "Libertarian Party Facts," distributed by the Ron Paul for President Committee, 1120 NASA Road, Houston, Texas (no date).

13. The following discussion draws heavily on Austin Ranney and Willmoore Kendall, *Democracy and the American Party System* (New York: Harcourt, Brace, 1956), chaps. 18 and 19.

14. See Steven J. Rosenstone, Roy L. Behr, and Edward H. Lazarus, *Third Parties in America: Citizen Response to Major Party Failure* (Princeton, N.J.: Princeton University Press, 1984), pp. 5–6.

15. Rosenstone, Behr, and Lazarus, *Third Parties in America*, p. 8.

16. State laws and court decisions may systematically support the major parties, but the U.S. Supreme Court seems to hold a more neutral position toward major and minor parties. See Lee Epstein and Charles D. Hadley, "On the Treatment of Political Parties in the U.S. Supreme Court, 1900–1986," *Journal of Politics* 52 (May 1990):413–432.

17. *Public Opinion* 7 (December–January 1985):26.

18. Measuring the concept of party identification has had its problems. For recent insights into the issues, see R. Michael Alvarez, "The Puzzle of Party Identification," *American Politics Quarterly* 18 (October 1990):476–491; and Donald Philip Green and Bradley Palmquist, "Of Artifacts and Partisan Instability," *American Journal of Political Science* 34 (August 1990):872–902.

19. There is some dispute over how stable party identification really is when the question is asked of the same respondents over a period of several months during an election campaign. This literature is reviewed in Brad Lockerbie, "Change in Party Identification: The Role of Prospective Economic Evaluations," *American Politics Quarterly* 17 (July 1989):291–311. Lockerbie argues that respondents change their party identification according to their expectations of whether they think that the parties will help them personally in the future. But also see Green and Palmquist, "Of Artifacts and Partisan Instability."

20. Bill Keller, "As Arms Buildup Eases, U.S. Tries to Take Stock," *New York Times*, 14 May 1985.

21. See, for example, Gerald M. Pomper, *Elections in America* (New York: Dodd, Mead, 1968); Benjamin Ginsberg, "Election and Public Policy," *American Political Science Review* 70 (March 1976):41–50; and Jeff Fishel, *Presidents and Promises* (Washington, D.C.: Congressional Quarterly Press, 1985).

22. Ian Budge and Richard I. Hofferbert, "Mandates and Policy Outputs: U.S. Party Platforms and Federal Expenditures," *American Political Science Review* 84 (March 1990):111–131.

23. Walter J. Stone, Ronald B. Rapoport, and Alan I. Abramowitz, "The Reagan Revolution and Party Polarization in the 1980s," in *The Parties Respond: Changes in the American Party System*, ed. L. Sandy Maisel (Boulder, Colo.: Westview Press, 1990), pp. 67–93.

24. Robert Harmel and Kenneth Janda, *Parties and Their Environments: Limits to Reform?* (New York: Longman, 1982), pp. 27–29.

25. Michael Nelson, ed. *Congressional Quarterly's Guide to the Presidency* (Washington, D.C.: Congressional Quarterly Press, 1989), p. 695.

26. See Ralph M. Goldman, *The National Party Chairmen and Committees: Factionalism at the Top* (Armonk, N.Y.: M.E. Sharpe, 1990). The subtitle is revealing.

27. William Crotty and John S. Jackson III, *Presidential Primaries and Nominations* (Washington, D.C.: Congressional Quarterly Press, 1985), p. 33.

28. Debra L. Dodson, "Socialization of Party Activists: National Convention Delegates, 1972–1981," *American Journal of Political Science* 34 (November 1990):1119–1141.

29. John F. Bibby, "Party Renewal in the National Republican Party," in *Party Renewal in America: Theory and Practice*, ed. Gerald M. Pomper (New York: Praeger, 1980), pp. 102–115.

30. Federal Election Commission, "Republican's [sic] Maintain 4–1 Spending Edge Despite Fundraising Decline over Prior Cycles." Press release of 1 November 1990, p. 1.

31. Tom Watson, "Machines: Something Old, Something New," *Congressional Quarterly Weekly Report*, 17 August 1985, p. 1619.

32. Advisory Commission on Intergovernmental Relations, *The Transformation of American Politics: Implications for Federalism* (Washington, D.C.: Report A–106, August 1986), pp. 112–116; see also Cornelius P. Cotter, et al., *Party Organizations in American Politics* (New York: Praeger, 1984), pp. 26–27.

33. Federal Election Commission, "Republican's [sic] Maintain 4–1 Spending Edge Despite Fundraising Decline over Prior Cycles," p. 1.

34. Cotter, *Party Organizations in American Politics*, p. 63.

35. James L. Gibson, John P. Frendreis, and Laura L. Vertz, "Party Dynamics in the 1980s: Change in County Organizational Strength, 1980–1984," *American Journal of Political Science* 33 (February 1989): 67–90. See also Paul S. Herrnson, "Reemergent National Party Organizations," in *The Parties Respond*, pp. 41–66.

36. See the evidence presented in Harmel and Janda, *Parties and Their Environments*, chap. 5.

37. David S. Broder, *The Party's Over: The Failure of Politics in America* (New York, Harper & Row, 1972); and William C. Crotty and Gary

C. Jacobson, *American Parties in Decline* (Boston : Little, Brown, 1980.

38. Barbara Sinclair, "The Congressional Party: Evolving Organizational, Agenda-Setting, and Policy Roles," in *The Parties Respond*, pp. 227–248, at 227.

39. The model is articulated most clearly in a report by the American Political Science Association, "Toward a More Responsible Two-Party System," *American Political Science Review* 44 (September 1950). See also Gerald M. Pomper, "Toward a More Responsible Party System? What, Again?" *Journal of Politics* 33 (November 1971): 916–940.

Chapter 9 / Nominations, Campaigns, and Elections / pp. 299–335

1. Stephen Engelberg, "Bush, His Disavowed Backers and a Very Potent Attack Ad," *New York Times*, 3 November, 1988, pp. 1 and 16.
2. Engelberg, "Bush."
3. See David R. Runkel, ed. *Campaign for President: The Managers Look at '88* (Dover, Mass.: Auburn House, 1989). The Willie Horton advertisement drew fifteen entries in the index to the verbatim transcript of the conference.
4. Marjorie Randon Hershey, "The Campaign and the Media," in *The Election of 1988: Reports and Interpretations*, ed. Gerald M. Pomper (Chatham, N.J.: Chatham House, 1989), p. 86.
5. Gerald M. Pomper, "The Presidential Election," in *The Election of 1988*, pp. 142–144.
6. Engelberg, "Bush."
7. Richard L. Berke, "Parties Ask Outside Groups to Stop Raising Ad Money," *New York Times*, 8 October, 1988, pp. 1 and 8.
8. Runkel, *Campaign for President*, p. 117.
9. This position is vigorously argued in Barbara G. Salmore and Stephen A. Salmore, *Candidates, Parties, and Campaigns: Electoral Politics in America*, 2d ed. (Washington, D.C.: Congressional Quarterly Press, 1989), pp. 7–9.

10. Allan J. Lichtman and Ken DeCell, *The Thirteen Keys to the Presidency* (Lanham, Md.: Madison Books, 1990), p. 6.
11. This is essentially the framework for studying campaigns that is set forth in Salmore and Salmore, *Candidates, Parties, and Campaigns*, pp. 10–11.
12. Martin P. Wattenberg, *The Rise of Candidate-Centered Politics: Presidential Elections of the 1980s* (Cambridge, Mass.: Harvard University Press, 1991).
13. Stephen E. Frantzich, *Political Parties in the Technological Age* (New York: Longman, 1989), p. 105.
14. Michael Gallagher, "Conclusion," in *Candidate Selection in Comparative Perspective: The Secret Garden of Politics*, ed. Michael Gallagher and Michael Marsh (London: Sage Publications, 1988), p. 238.
15. Kenneth Janda, *Political Parties: A Cross-National Survey* (New York: Free Press, 1980), p. 112.
16. *The Book of the States, 1990–91 Edition*, vol. 28 (Lexington, Ky.: Council of State Governments, 1990), pp. 234–235.
17. Malcolm E. Jewell and David M. Olson, *Political Parties and Elections in American States*, 3d ed. (Chicago: Dorsey Press, 1988), pp. 108–112.
18. See John G. Geer, "Assessing the Representativeness of Electorates in Presidential Elections," *American Journal of Political Science* 32 (November 1988): 929–945; and Barbara Norrander, "Ideological Representativeness of Presidential Primary Voters," *American Journal of Political Science* 33 (August 1989):570–587.
19. Byron E. Shafer, *Bifurcated Politics: Evolution and Reform in the National Party Convention* (Cambridge, Mass.: Harvard University Press, 1988), p. 8.
20. Gary R. Orren and Nelson W. Polsby, eds., *Media and Momentum: The New Hampshire Primary and Nomination Politics* (Chatham, N.J.: Chatham House, 1987), p. 23.
21. See James R. Beniger, "Winning the Presidential Nomination: National Polls and State Primary

Elections, 1936–1972," *Public Opinion Quarterly* 40 (Spring 1976):22–38.
22. Salmore and Salmore, *Candidates, Parties, and Campaigns*, p. 1.
23. "The Candidates on the Trail and in the Minds of the Voters," *New York Times*, 9 November 1988, p. 13.
24. John Theilmann and Al Wilhite, "The Determinants of Individuals' Campaign Contributions to Congressional Campaigns," *American Politics Quarterly* 17 (July 1989):312–333.
25. Quoted in E. J. Dionne, Jr., "On the Trail of Corporation Donations," *New York Times*, 6 October 1980.
26. Salmore and Salmore, *Candidates, Parties, and Campaigns*, p. 11.
27. Federal Election Commission, *The First Ten Years: 1975–1985*, April 14, 1985, p. 1.
28. Paul S. Herrnson, "Political Parties, Campaign Finance Reform, and Presidential Elections" (paper prepared for presentation at the Annual Meeting of the Midwest Political Science Association, Chicago, Illinois, April 5–7, 1990), p. 11. See also Richard L. Berke, "In Election Spending: Watch the Ceiling, Use a Loophole," *New York Times*, 3 October 1988, pp. 1 and 13.
29. Janda, *Political Parties*, p. 78.
30. Salmore and Salmore, *Candidates, Parties, and Campaigns*, p. 11.
31. David Moon, "What You Use Depends on What You Have: Information Effects on the Determinants of Electoral Choice," *American Politics Quarterly* 18 (January 1990):3–24.
32. See "The Political Pages," *Campaigns & Elections* 10 (February 1990), which contain over a hundred pages of names, addresses, and telephone numbers of people who supply "political products and services."
33. Salmore and Salmore, *Candidates, Parties, and Campaigns*, pp. 115–116.
34. Stephen Ansolabehere, Roy L. Behr, and Shanto Iyengar, "Mass Media and Elections: An Overview," *American Politics Quarterly* 19 (January 1991): 109–139.

35. James Warren, "Politicians Learn Value of Sundays—Too Well," *Chicago Tribune,* 22 October 1990, p. 1.

36. Timothy E. Cook. *Making Laws and Making News: Media Strategies in the U.S. House of Representatives* (Washington, D.C.: Brookings Institution, 1989).

37. Kiku Adatto, "The Incredible Shrinking Sound Bite," *The New Republic,* 28 May 1990, p. 20.

38. Ansolabehere, Behr, and Iyengar, "Mass Media and Elections," p. 115.

39. Montague Kern, *30-Second Politics: Political Advertising in the Eighties* (New York: Praeger, 1989), p. 57.

40. News of the National Association of Broadcasters, 13 July 1987 (Washington, D.C.). A later study of campaign spending in the 1990 House and Senate elections found similar average levels of expenditures for advertising and media consultants combined: 25 percent for House candidates and 35 percent for Senate candidates. See Sara Fritz and Dwight Morris, "Burden of TV Election Ads Exaggerated, Study Finds," *Los Angeles Times,* 18 March 1991, pp. A1 & A14. However, specialists warn that such averages, which include many uncontested elections, mask much higher levels of spending for media in contested elections. See Herbert E. Alexander and Monica Bauer, *Financing the 1988 Election* (Boulder, Colo.: Westview Press, 1991).

41. Dorothy Davidson Nesbit, *Videostyle in Senate Campaigns* (Knoxville, Tenn.: University of Tennessee Press, 1988), p. 152.

42. Darrell M. West, "Cheers and Jeers: Candidate Presentations and Audience Reactions in the 1980 Presidential Campaign," *American Politics Quarterly* 12 (January 1984):40.

43. Randall Rothenberg, "Voters Complain Negative Campaigns Are Driving Them Away," *New York Times,* 6 November 1990, p. A11.

44. *Congressional Quarterly Weekly Report,* 12 January 1991, p. 105. See also Michael Tackett, "Negative Ads Produce an Upset in Missouri," *Chicago Tribune,* 8 November 1990, sec. 1, p. 23.

45. Bureau of the Census, "Popularly Elected Officials," *Government Organization,* vol. 1 no. 2 (Washington, D.C.: 1987 Census of Governments, January 1990), p. vi.

46. Michael Nelson, ed., *Congressional Quarterly Guide to the Presidency,* (Washington, D.C.: Congressional Quarterly Press, 1989), p. 1427. You can find the other exceptions there too.

47. Harold W. Stanley and Richard G. Niemi, *Vital Statistics on American Politics,* 2d ed. (Washington, D.C.: Congressional Quarterly Press, 1990), p. 132.

48. Everett Carll Ladd, "The 1988 Elections: Continuation of the Post-New Deal System," *Political Science Quarterly* 104 (1989):1–18; and Seymour Martin Lipset, "A Reaffirming Election: 1988," *International Journal of Public Opinion Research* 1 (January 1989).

49. The 1988 National Election Study (data made available through the Inter-University Consortium for Political and Social Research).

50. Pamela Johnston Conover and Stanley Feldman, "Candidate Perception in an Ambiguous World: Campaigns, Cues, and Inference Processes," *American Journal of Political Science* 33 (November 1989):912–940.

51. Bruce Buchanan, *Electing a President: The Report on the Markle Commission on the Media and the Electorate* (Austin: University of Texas Press, 1991). These data came from Table 5.3 in excerpts from the book distributed by the Markle Commission, p. 21.

52. Buchanan, *Electing a President,* Table 5.4, p. 27.

53. Buchanan, *Electing a President,* Table 5.5, p. 32.

54. Buchanan, *Electing a President,* Table 5.7, p. 47.

55. Randall Rothenberg, "The Disarray in Dukakis's Ad Team," *New York Times,* 20 October 1988, p. 43.

56. Frantzich, *Political Parties in the Technological Age,* p. 167.

57. Michael M. Gant and Norman R. Luttbeg, *American Electoral Behavior* (Itasca, Ill.: Peacock, 1991), pp. 63–64. The literature on the joint effects of party, issues, and candidate is quite involved. See also David W. Romero, "The Changing American Voter Revisited: Candidate Evaluations in Presidential Elections, 1952–1984," *American Politics Quarterly* 17 (October 1989):409–421. Romero contends that research that finds a "new" American voter who votes according to issues is incorrectly looking at standardized rather than unstandardized regression coefficients.

58. Herbert Asher, *Presidential Elections and American Politics* (Homewood, Ill.: Dorsey Press, 1980), p. 196.

59. Conover and Feldman, "Candidate Perception in an Ambiguous World," p. 938.

60. Party identification has been assumed to be relatively resistant to short-term campaign effects, but see Dee Allsop and Herbert F. Weisberg, "Measuring Change in Party Identification in an Election Campaign," *American Journal of Political Science* 32 (November 1988):996–1017. They conclude that partisanship is more volatile than we have thought.

61. David Beiler, "The 1990 Campaign Scoreboard," *Campaigns & Elections,* 11 (December–January 1991):26–29. The number of wins and losses was computed from the table on pp. 28–29.

62. Larry J. Sabato and David Beiler, "Magic . . . or Blue Smoke and Mirrors? Reflections on New Technologies and Trends in the Political Consultant Trade" (Northwestern University: The Annenberg Washington Program in Communication Policy Studies, 1988), pp. 4–5.

63. See Michael S. Lewis-Beck, *Economics and Elections: The Major Western Democracies* (Ann Arbor: University of Michigan Press, 1988); Alan I. Abramowitz, David J. Lanoue, and Subha Ramesh, "Economic Conditions, Causal Attributions, and Political Evaluations in the 1984 Presidential Election," *Journal of Politics* 50 (November 1988):848–863; Robert S. Erikson, "Economic Conditions and the Presidential Vote," *American Political Science Review* 83

(June 1989):567–573; Robert S. Erikson, "Economic Conditions and the Congressional Vote: A Review of the Evidence," *American Journal of Political Science* 34 (May 1990):373–399; and Gary C. Jacobson, "Does the Economy Matter in Midterm Elections?" *American Journal of Political Science* 34 (May 1990):400–404.

64. Steven J. Rosenstone, *Forecasting Presidential Elections* (New Haven: Yale University Press, 1983). Rosenstone, however, thinks his model will increase the importance of campaigns, for it will help identify states where campaigns may decide the outcome.

Chapter 10 / Interest Groups / pp. 337–371

1. Jill Abramson, "Auto Makers Lobbied Hard Against Stricter Fuel Rules," *Wall Street Journal*, 4 April 1990, p. A15.
2. Michael Kranish, "Clean Air Measure Serves Some States' Special Interests," *Boston Globe*, 9 April 1990, p. 1. This account of deliberations over the Clean Air Act also draws upon Rose Gutfeld, "Senate Rejects, 50–49, Byrd Amendment to Clean Air Bill on Aid to Coal Miners," *Wall Street Journal*, 30 March 1990, p. C13; Phil Kuntz and George Hager, "Showdown on Clean-Air Bill," *Congressional Quarterly Weekly Report*, 31 March 1990, pp. 983–987; Rose Gutfeld and Barbara Rosewicz, "Battle Looms in the House as Senate Passes a Bill," *Wall Street Journal*, 4 April 1990, p. A1; John E. Yang, "Legislation Would Assist Corn Farms, Ethanol Firm," *Wall Street Journal*, 4 April 1990, p. A14; Neal Templin, "Environmentalists and Auto Makers Rev Up for Battle," *Wall Street Journal*, 4 April 1990, p. A14; Abramson, "Auto Makers Lobbied Hard"; and George Hager, "Clean Air: War About Over in Both House and Senate," *Congressional Quarterly Weekly Report*, 7 April 1990, pp. 1057–1061.
3. Jeffrey M. Berry, *The Interest Group Society*, 2d ed. (Glenview, Ill.: Scott, Foresman/Little, Brown, 1989), p. 4.
4. Alexis de Tocqueville, *Democracy in America*, ed. Richard D. Heffner (New York: Mentor Books, 1956), p. 198.
5. See Robert A. Dahl, *A Preface to Democratic Theory* (Chicago: University of Chicago Press, 1956), pp. 4–33.
6. This discussion follows from Berry, *Interest Group Society*, pp. 6–8.
7. Steven Pressman, "Lobbying 'Star Wars' Flares as Movie Industry Fights Invasion of Video Recorders," *Congressional Quarterly Weekly Report*, 4 June 1983, pp. 1099–1103.
8. David B. Truman, *The Governmental Process* (New York: Knopf, 1951).
9. Herbert Gans, *The Urban Villagers* (New York: Free Press, 1962).
10. Robert H. Salisbury, "An Exchange Theory of Interest Groups," *Midwest Journal of Political Science* 13 (February 1969):1–32.
11. See Mancur Olson, Jr., *The Logic of Collective Action* (New York: Schocken, 1968); and Terry M. Moe, *The Organization of Interests* (Chicago: University of Chicago Press, 1980).
12. Peter Matthiessen, *Sal Si Puedes* (New York: Random House, 1969); and John G. Dunne, *Delano*, rev. ed. (New York: Farrar, Straus & Giroux, 1971).
13. Robert H. Salisbury, "Interest Representation: The Dominance of Institutions," *American Political Science Review* 78 (March 1984):64–76.
14. William P. Browne, "Organized Interests and Their Issue Niches: A Search for Pluralism in a Policy Domain," *Journal of Politics* 52 (May 1990):477–509.
15. Larry J. Sabato, *The Rise of Political Consultants* (New York: Basic Books, 1981), pp. 220–263.
16. See Olson, *Logic of Collective Action*.
17. See John Mark Hansen, "The Political Economy of Group Membership," *American Political Science Review* 79 (March 1985): 79–96.
18. Edward O. Laumann and David Knoke, *The Organizational State* (Madison: University of Wisconsin Press, 1987), p. 3. Cited in Robert H. Salisbury, "The Paradox of Interest Groups in Washington— More Groups, Less Clout," in Anthony King, ed., *The New American Political System*, 2d ed. (Washington, D.C.: American Enterprise Institute, 1990), p. 226.
19. David Rogers, "A Lobbyist's Fortuitous Position," *Wall Street Journal*, 23 August 1984, p. 42.
20. Robert H. Salisbury, "Washington Lobbyists: A Collective Portrait," in *Interest Group Politics*, 2d ed., ed. Allan J. Cigler and Burdett A. Loomis (Washington, D.C.: Congressional Quarterly, 1986), p. 155.
21. Paul Taylor, "Gladiators for Hire— Part I," *Washington Post*, 31 July 1983, p. A1. See also W. John Moore, "The Alumni Lobby," *National Journal* 9 September 1989, pp. 2188–2195. Expertise gained in the executive branch can also be extremely lucrative for would-be lobbyists. See Pat Choate, *Agents of Influence* (New York: Knopf, 1990), especially pp. 49–63.
22. Carol Matlack, "Getting Around the Rules," *National Journal*, 12 May 1990, pp. 1138–1143.
23. Frank J. Sorauf, *Money in American Elections* (Glenview, Ill.: Scott, Foresman/Little, Brown, 1988), p. 82.
24. "PAC Activity Falls in 1990 Election," Federal Election Commission, 31 March 1991, p. 13.
25. Mark Green, "Political PAC-Man," *New Republic*, 13 December 1982, p. 24.
26. "PAC Activity Falls," p. 2.
27. John R. Wright, "Contributions, Lobbying, and Committee Voting in the U.S. House of Representatives," *American Political Science Review* 84 (June 1990):417–438.
28. Common Cause data cited in Berry, *Interest Group Society*, p. 122.
29. Nathaniel C. Nash, "Savings Unit Donations Criticized," *New York Times*, 29 June 1990, p. D4.
30. Elizabeth Drew, "Politics and Money—I," *The New Yorker*, 6 December 1982, p. 147.
31. Kay Lehman Schlozman and John T. Tierney, *Organized Interests and American Democracy* (New York: Harper & Row, 1986), p. 150.

32. John E. Chubb, *Interest Groups and the Bureaucracy* (Stanford, Calif.: Stanford University Press, 1983), p. 144.

33. David Shribman, "NOW's Use of RICO Against Attacks by Groups on Abortion Clinics Stirs Debate on Law's Intent," *Wall Street Journal*, 22 May 1990, p. A22.

34. Allan J. Cigler and John Mark Hansen, "Group Formation Through Protest: The American Agriculture Movement," in *Interest Group Politics*, ed. Allan J. Cigler and Burdett A. Loomis (Washington, D.C.: Congressional Quarterly, 1983), pp. 84–109.

35. David J. Garrow, *Protest at Selma* (New Haven, Conn.: Yale University Press, 1978).

36. Roger P. Kingsley, "Advocacy for the Handicapped" (paper delivered at the annual meeting of the American Political Science Association, Washington, D.C., September 1984), p. 10.

37. Robert H. Salisbury, et al., "Who Works with Whom?" *American Political Science Review* 81 (December 1987):1224–1228.

38. Anne Costain, "The Struggle for a National Women's Lobby," *Western Political Quarterly* 33 (December 1980):476–491.

39. Jack L. Walker, "The Origins and Maintenance of Interest Groups in America" (paper delivered at the annual meeting of the American Political Science Association, New York, September 1981), p. 14.

40. Jeffrey M. Berry, *Lobbying for the People* (Princeton, N.J.: Princeton University Press, 1977), pp. 6–10.

41. Andrew S. McFarland, *Common Cause* (Chatham, N.J.: Chatham House, 1984).

42. David Vogel, *Lobbying the Corporation* (New York: Basic Books, 1978), pp. 21–68.

43. On the development of the New Right, see Jerome L. Himmelstein, *To the Right: The Transformation of American Conservatism* (Berkeley: University of California Press, 1990).

44. See Allen D. Hertzke, *Representing God in Washington* (Knoxville: University of Tennessee Press, 1988).

45. Peter Steinfels, "Moral Majority to Dissolve, Says Mission Accomplished," *New York Times*, 12 June 1989, p. A14.

46. Martha Joynt Kumar and Michael Baruch Grossman, "The Presidency and Interest Groups," in *The Presidency and the Political System*, ed. Michael Nelson (Washington, D.C.: Congressional Quarterly, 1984), pp. 293–294.

47. David Vogel, "How Business Responds to Opposition" (paper delivered at the annual meeting of the American Political Science Association, Washington, D.C., December 1979.)

48. *Public Affairs Offices and Their Functions* (Boston: Boston University School of Management, 1981), p. 8.

49. David Vogel, *Fluctuating Fortunes* (New York: Basic Books, 1989), p. 194.

50. Monica Langley, "Feuding Lobbies Hinder Push to Write Comprehensive Legislation," *Wall Street Journal*, 24 March 1986.

51. Walter Dean Burnham, *Critical Elections and the Mainsprings of American Politics* (New York: Norton, 1970), p. 133.

52. *United States* v. *Harriss*, 347 U.S. 612 (1954).

53. See Matlack, "Getting Around the Rules."

54. "PAC Activity Falls," p. 13.

55. Some argue, however, that the real dynamic at work is a decline in overall interest group power. See Salisbury, "Paradox of Interest Groups in Washington"; and Paul E. Peterson, "The Rise and Fall of Special Interest Group Politics," *Political Science Quarterly* 105 (Winter 1990–1991):539–556.

Chapter 11 / Congress / pp. 375–413

1. This account of the Slaughter-Eckert race is taken from Linda L. Fowler and Robert D. McClure, *Political Ambition* (New Haven: Yale University Press, 1989), pp. 204–217.

2. Clinton Rossiter, *1787: The Grand Convention* (New York: Mentor, 1968), p. 158.

3. *Origins and Development of Congress* (Washington, D.C.: Congressional Quarterly Press, 1976), pp. 81–89.

4. "The 1990 Census: The Changing Shape of the Union," *New York Times*, 27 December 1990, p. B6.

5. *Wesberry* v. *Sanders*, 376 U.S. 1 (1964) (congressional districts within a state must be substantially equal in population); and *Reynolds* v. *Sims*, 377 U.S. 364 (1964) (state legislatures must be apportioned on the basis of population).

6. "Election Results," *The American Enterprise* 2 (January/February 1991):89.

7. Norman J. Ornstein, Thomas E. Mann, and Michael J. Malbin, *Vital Statistics on Congress, 1989–1990* (Washington, D.C.: Congressional Quarterly Press, 1990), p. 59. See also, David Mayhew, "Congressional Elections: The Case of the Vanishing Marginals," *Polity* 6 (Spring 1974):295–317; and Gary C. Jacobson, *The Politics of Congressional Elections*, 2d ed. (Boston: Little, Brown, 1987), pp. 29–36.

8. *Gallup Report*, September 1988, p. 21.

9. Norman Ornstein, "The Permanent Democratic Congress," *Public Interest* 100 (Summer 1990): 24–44; and John A. Ferejohn, "On the Decline of Competition in Congressional Elections," *American Political Science Review* 71 (March 1977):166–176.

10. Timothy E. Cook, *Making Laws and Making News* (Washington, D.C.: Brookings Institution, 1989), p. 83.

11. Bob Benenson, "Savvy 'Stars' Making Local TV a Potent Tool," *Congressional Quarterly Weekly Report*, 18 July 1987, pp. 1551–1552.

12. Brooks Jackson, "Incumbent Lawmakers Use the Perks of Office to Clobber Opponents," *Wall Street Journal*, 22 March 1988, p. 1.

13. Ibid.

14. Gary C. Jacobson and Samuel Kernell, *Strategy and Choice in Congressional Elections* (New Haven, Conn.: Yale University Press, 1983).

15. "1990 Congressional Election Spending Drops to Low Point," Federal Election Commission, 22 February 1991, p. 4; and Alan I.

Abramowitz, "Incumbency, Campaign Spending, and the Decline of Competition in U.S. House Elections," *Journal of Politics* 53 (February 1991):34–56.

16. Larry J. Sabato, *PAC Power* (New York: Norton, 1984), p. 72.

17. Ornstein, Mann, and Malbin, *Vital Statistics*, p. 52.

18. Gary C. Jacobson, "Meager Patrimony: The Reagan Era and Republican Representation in Congress," in *Looking Back on the Reagan Presidency*, ed. Larry Berman (Baltimore: Johns Hopkins University Press, 1990), pp. 311–312.

19. On the historical dimensions and consequences of this trend, see David W. Brady, *Critical Elections and Congressional Policy Making* (Stanford, Calif.: Stanford University Press, 1988).

20. Ornstein, Mann, and Malbin, *Vital Statistics*, pp. 20–31.

21. Walter J. Oleszek, *Congressional Procedures and the Policy Process*, 3d ed. (Washington, D.C.: Congressional Quarterly, 1989), p. 81.

22. Julie Kosterlitz, "Anguish and Opportunity," *National Journal*, 28 April 1990, pp. 1008–1015.

23. Roger W. Cobb and Charles D. Elder, *Participation in American Politics*, 2d ed. (Baltimore: Johns Hopkins University Press, 1983), pp. 64–65.

24. John W. Kingdon, *Agendas, Alternatives, and Public Policies* (Boston: Little, Brown, 1984), p. 37.

25. Ibid., p. 41.

26. It was Woodrow Wilson who described the legislative process as the "dance of legislation." Eric Redman used the phrase for the title of his case study of a health bill, *The Dance of Legislation* (New York: Touchstone, 1973).

27. David Shribman, "Canada's Top Envoy to Washington Cuts Unusually Wide Swath," *Wall Street Journal*, 29 July 1985, p. 79.

28. Oleszek, *Congressional Procedures*, pp. 74–76.

29. Woodrow Wilson, *Congressional Government* (Boston: Houghton Mifflin, 1885), p. 79.

30. Richard L. Hall and C. Lawrence Evans, "The Power of Subcommittees," *Journal of Politics* 52 (May 1990):342.

31. Lawrence D. Longley and Walter J. Oleszek, *Bicameral Politics* (New Haven: Yale University Press, 1989), p. 10.

32. Ibid., p. 4.

33. Leroy Rieselbach, *Congressional Reform* (Washington, D.C.: Congressional Quarterly, 1986), p. 47.

34. Brooks Jackson, *Honest Graft* (New York: Knopf, 1988), p. 35.

35. On some tentative steps toward recentralization, see Roger H. Davidson, "The New Centralization on Capitol Hill" (paper delivered at the annual meeting of the Midwest Political Science Association, Chicago, April 1988).

36. Steven S. Smith and Christopher J. Deering, *Committees in Congress* (Washington, D.C.: Congressional Quarterly Press, 1984), p. 271.

37. Philip M. Boffey, "Lawmakers Vow a Legal Recourse for Military Malpractice Victims," *New York Times*, 9 July 1985, p. A14.

38. Martin Tolchin, "Welfare Overhaul: Right Timing for a War Dance," *New York Times*, 3 October 1988, p. A18.

39. Robert Weissberg, "Collective vs. Dyadic Representation in Congress," *American Political Science Review* 72 (June 1978):535–547.

40. See Richard L. Hall, "Committee Decision Making in the Postreform Congress," in *Congress Reconsidered*, 4th ed., ed. Lawrence C. Dodd and Bruce I. Oppenheimer (Washington, D.C.: Congressional Quarterly, 1989), pp. 197–223.

41. Andy Plattner, "Dole on the Job," *Congressional Quarterly Weekly Report*, 29 June 1985, p. 1270.

42. Roger H. Davidson, "Senate Leaders: Janitors for an Untidy Chamber?" in *Congress Reconsidered*, 3d ed., ed. Lawrence C. Dodd and Bruce I. Oppenheimer (Washington, D.C.: Congressional Quarterly Press, 1985), p. 228.

43. Robert L. Peabody, *Leadership in Congress* (Boston: Little, Brown, 1976), p. 9.

44. Charles O. Jones, *The United States Congress* (Homewood, Ill.: Dorsey Press, 1982), p. 322.

45. Oleszek, *Congressional Procedures*, p. 222.

46. *Congress Speaks: A Survey of the 100th Congress* (Washington,

D.C.: Center for Responsive Politics, 1988), p. 61. See also, Janet Hook, "Dole Outburst Shows Frustration . . . Over More Than Civil Rights Bill," *Congressional Quarterly Weekly Report*, 21 July 1990, pp. 2314–2315.

47. Deborah Baldwin, "Pulling Punches," *Common Cause* (May/June 1985), p. 22.

48. Jeffrey H. Birnbaum, "Rep. Armey, Texas Firebrand, Changes Tactics and Starts Accomplishing Things in the House," *Wall Street Journal*, 2 June 1988, p. 1.

49. Steven S. Smith, *Call to Order* (Washington, D.C.: Brookings Institution, 1989), p. 138.

50. Ibid.

51. McClure and Fowler, *Political Ambition*.

52. Burdett A. Loomis, *The New American Politician* (New York: Basic Books, 1988).

53. This framework is adapted from John W. Kingdon, *Congressmen's Voting Decisions*, 2d ed. (New York: Harper & Row, 1981).

54. See David W. Rohde, "'Something's Happening Here, What It Is Ain't Exactly Clear': Southern Democrats in the House of Representatives" (paper delivered at a conference in honor of Richard Fenno, Washington, D.C., August 1986).

55. Kay Lehman Schlozman and John T. Tierney, *Organized Interests and American Democracy* (New York: Harper & Row, 1986), p. 293.

56. David Rampe, "Power Panel in Making: The Hispanic Caucus," *New York Times*, 30 September 1988, p. B5.

57. Ornstein, Mann, and Malbin, *Vital Statistics*, pp. 132–136.

58. Michael Malbin, *Unelected Representatives* (New York: Basic Books, 1980).

59. Ibid., p. 240.

60. James Sterling Young, *The Washington Community* (New York: Harcourt, Brace, 1964).

61. Kingdon, *Congressmen's Voting Decisions*, p. 242.

62. Joel D. Aberbach, *Keeping a Watchful Eye* (Washington, D.C.: Brookings Institution, 1990), pp. 84–85.

63. Ibid., pp. 162–183.

64. Jeremy Rabkin, "Micromanaging the Administrative Agencies," *Public Interest* 100 (Summer 1990):120. In the same issue see also L. Gordon Crovitz, "Micromanaging Foreign Policy," pp. 102–115; and Mackubin Thomas Owens, "Micromanaging the Defense Budget," pp. 131–146.

65. Barry M. Blechman, "The New Congressional Role in Arms Control," *A Question of Balance*, ed. Thomas E. Mann (Washington, D.C.: Brookings Institution, 1990), pp. 109–145.

66. Richard F. Fenno, Jr., *Home Style* (Boston: Little, Brown, 1978), p. xii.

67. Ibid., p. 32.

68. Louis I. Bredvold and Ralph G. Ross, eds., *The Philosophy of Edmund Burke* (Ann Arbor, Mich.: University of Michigan Press, 1960), p. 148.

69. Dirk Johnson, "Flag Vote: The People Back Home," *New York Times*, 25 June 1990, p. A12.

70. Warren E. Miller and Donald E. Stokes, "Constituency Influence in Congress," *American Political Science Review* 57 (March 1963): 45–57.

71. Darrell M. West, *Congress and Economic Policymaking* (Pittsburgh: University of Pittsburgh Press, 1987), pp. 37–64.

72. Julie Johnson, "Picking Over the Pork in the 1988 Spending Bill," *New York Times*, 5 January 1988, p. B6.

73. Weissberg, "Collective vs. Dyadic Representation."

Chapter 12 / The Presidency / pp. 415–453

1. Jeffrey H. Birnbaum and Jackie Calmes, "Bigger Tax Bite for Most Folk Imperils Democratic Support for Budget Accord," *Wall Street Journal*, 3 October 1990, p. A2.

2. David Wessel and David Rogers, "Bush Appeals to the Public in Budget Battle," *Wall Street Journal*, 3 October 1990, p. A3.

3. Jeffrey H. Birnbaum, "President's TV Plea for Public Support on Budget Backfires," *Wall Street Journal*, 5 October 1990, p. A3.

4. David E. Rosenbaum, "Leaders Reach a Tax Deal and Predict Its Approval," *New York Times*, 25 October 1990, p. A1.

5. Louis W. Koenig, *The Chief Executive*, 4th ed. (New York: Harcourt Brace Jovanovich, 1981), p. 20.

6. Clinton Rossiter, *1787: The Grand Convention* (New York: Mentor, 1968), p. 148.

7. Rossiter, *1787*, pp. 190–191.

8. Richard M. Pious, *The American Presidency* (New York: Basic Books, 1979), pp. 51–52.

9. Wilfred E. Binkley, *President and Congress*, 3d ed. (New York: Vintage, 1962), p. 155.

10. Pious, *American Presidency*, pp. 60–63.

11. Barry M. Blechman, "The New Congressional Role in Arms Control," in *A Question of Balance*, ed. Thomas E. Mann (Washington, D.C.: Brookings Institution), pp. 109–145.

12. Richard E. Neustadt, *Presidential Power* (New York: John Wiley, 1980), p. 10.

13. Neustadt, *Presidential Power*, p. 9.

14. Fred I. Greenstein, *The Hidden-Hand Presidency* (New York: Basic Books, 1982), pp. 155–227.

15. George C. Edwards III, *At the Margins* (New Haven: Yale University Press, 1989). See also Jon R. Bond and Richard Fleisher, *The President in the Legislative Arena* (Chicago: University of Chicago Press, 1990).

16. See Edwards, *At the Margins*, pp. 101–125.

17. Jeffrey K. Tulis, *The Rhetorical Presidency* (Princeton, N.J.: Princeton University Press, 1987), p. 64ff.

18. Tulis, *Rhetorical Presidency*, p. 5.

19. Theodore J. Lowi, *The Personal President* (Ithaca, N.Y.: Cornell University Press, 1985).

20. Darrell M. West, *Congress and Economic Policymaking* (Pittsburgh: University of Pittsburgh Press, 1987), p. 33.

21. Kristen Renwick Monroe, *Presidential Popularity and the Economy* (New York: Praeger, 1984).

22. Charles W. Ostrom, Jr., and Dennis M. Simon, "Promise and Performance: A Dynamic Model of Presidential Popularity," *American Political Science Review* 79 (June 1985):334–358.

23. James W. Ceaser, "The Reagan Presidency and American Public Opinion," in *The Reagan Legacy*, ed., Charles O. Jones (Chatham, N.J.: Chatham House, 1988), pp. 172–210.

24. "Prepared Text of Carter's Farewell Address," *New York Times*, 15 January 1981.

25. Benjamin I. Page, *Choices and Echoes in Presidential Elections* (Chicago: University of Chicago Press, 1978).

26. Robert A. Dahl, "Myth of the Presidential Mandate," *Political Science Quarterly* 105 (Fall 1990):355–372.

27. David W. Brady and Morris Fiorina, "The Ruptured Legacy: Presidential-Congressional Relations in Historical Perspective," in *Looking Back on the Reagan Presidency*, ed. Larry Berman (Baltimore: Johns Hopkins University Press, 1990), pp. 269–287.

28. Gary C. Jacobson, "Meager Patrimony: The Reagan Era and Republican Representation in Congress," in *Looking Back on the Reagan Presidency*, p. 300.

29. Gary C. Jacobson, *The Electoral Origins of Divided Government* (Boulder, Colo.: Westview, 1990), pp. 65–67.

30. Jeb Stuart Magruder, *An American Life* (New York: Atheneum, 1974), p. 58, quoted in Benjamin I. Page and Mark Petracca, *The American Presidency* (New York: McGraw-Hill, 1983), p. 169.

31. Page and Petracca, *American Presidency*, p. 171.

32. Gary King and Lyn Ragsdale, *The Elusive Executive* (Washington, D.C.: Congressional Quarterly Press, 1988), pp. 205–210.

33. See Burt Solomon, "In Bush's Image," *National Journal*, 7 July 1990, pp. 1642–1647.

34. Paul J. Quirk, "Presidential Competence," in *The Presidency and the Political System*, 2d ed., ed. Michael Nelson (Washington, D.C.: Congressional Quarterly Press, 1988), p. 163.

35. Jane Mayer and Doyle McManus, *Landslide* (Boston: Houghton Mifflin, 1988) pp. 22–24.

36. *The Tower Commission Report* (New York: Bantam Books, 1987).

37. Bert Rockman, "The Style and Organization of the Reagan Presidency," in *Reagan Legacy,* p. 24.

38. Seymour M. Hersh, *The Price of Power* (New York: Summit, 1983), p. 42.

39. Richard F. Fenno, Jr., *The Making of a Senator: Dan Quayle* (Washington, D.C.: Congressional Quarterly Press, 1989); and Jack W. Germond and Jules Whitcover, *Whose Broad Stripes and Bright Stars?* (New York: Warner Books, 1989), pp. 375–395.

40. Gerald F. Seib, "Bush's Role in Policy Is Difficult to Discern, Reagan Officials Say," *Wall Street Journal,* 31 March 1988, p. 1.

41. Edward Weisband and Thomas M. Franck, *Resignation in Protest* (New York: Penguin, 1975), p. 139, quoted in Thomas E. Cronin, *The State of the Presidency,* 2d ed. (Boston: Little, Brown, 1980), p. 253.

42. Griffin B. Bell with Ronald J. Ostrow, *Taking Care of the Law* (New York: Morrow, 1982), p. 45.

43. Terry M. Moe, "The Politicized Presidency," in *The New Direction in American Politics,* ed. John E. Chubb and Paul E. Peterson (Washington, D.C.: Brookings Institution, 1985), pp. 235–271.

44. *Public Papers of the President, Lyndon B. Johnson, 1965,* vol. 1 (Washington, D.C.: U.S. Government Printing Office, 1966), p. 72.

45. "Transcript of Second Inaugural Address by Reagan," *New York Times,* 22 January 1985, p. A1.

46. Kevin Phillips, *The Politics of Rich and Poor* (New York: Random House, 1990), p. 88.

47. John W. Kingdon, *Agendas, Alternatives, and Public Policies* (Boston: Little, Brown, 1984), p. 25.

48. Richard E. Neustadt, "Presidency and Legislation: The Growth of Central Clearance," *American Political Science Review* 48 (September 1954):641–671.

49. Stephen Skowronek, "Presidential Leadership in Political Time," in *Presidency and the Political System,* 2d ed., pp. 115–159.

50. Seth King, "Reagan, in Bid for Budget Votes, Reported to Yield on Sugar Prices," *New York Times,* 27 June 1981, p. A1.

51. Martha Joynt Kumar and Michael Baruch Grossman, "The Presidency and Interest Groups," in *The Presidency and the Political System,* ed. Michael Nelson (Washington, D.C.: Congressional Quarterly Press, 1984), p. 309.

52. Sidney M. Milkis, "The Presidency and Political Parties," in *Presidency and the Political System,* 2d ed., p. 337.

53. Pietro Nivola, "Trade Policy: Refereeing the Playing Field," in *Question of Balance,* p. 248.

54. Fred Barnes, "Hour of Power," *New Republic,* 3 September 1990, p. 12.

55. Alexander George, "The Case for Multiple Advocacy in Making Foreign Policy," *American Political Science Review* 66 (September 1972):751–782.

56. John P. Burke and Fred I. Greenstein, *How Presidents Test Reality* (New York: Russell Sage Foundation, 1989).

57. Richard E. Neustadt and Earnest R. May, *Thinking in Time* (New York: Free Press, 1986), p. 143.

58. Lowi, *Personal President,* p. 185.

59. Gail Sheehy, "The Road to Bimini," *Vanity Fair,* September 1987, p. 132.

60. Robert A. Caro, *The Path to Power* (New York: Alfred A. Knopf, 1982), p. 131.

61. Caro, *Path to Power,* p. 135.

62. Doris Kearns, *Lyndon Johnson and the American Dream* (New York: Signet, 1977), p. 363.

63. See, generally, James David Barber, *The Presidential Character,* 3d ed. (Englewood Cliffs, N.J.: Prentice-Hall, 1985).

Chapter 13 / The Bureaucracy / pp. 455–485

1. This account of the NEA controversy is based on Garrison Keillor, "Thanks for Attacking the N.E.A.," *New York Times,* 4 April 1990, p. A15; Richard Bernstein, "Subsidies for Artists: Is Denying a Grant Really Censorship?" *New York Times,* 18 July 1990, p. C11; Peter J. Boyer, "Mean for Jesus," *Vanity Fair,* September 1990, pp. 224ff; Bruce Selcraig, "Reverend Wildmon's War on the Arts," *New York Times Magazine,* 2 September 1990, p. 22ff; Richard L. Berke, "House Approves Compromise Bill to Continue Arts Endowment," *New York Times,* 12 October 1990, p. A1; and Martin Tolchin, "Senate Passes Compromise on Arts Endowment," *New York Times,* 25 October 1990, p. C17.

2. John E. Chubb and Terry M. Moe, *Politics, Markets, and America's Schools* (Washington, D.C.: Brookings Institution, 1990).

3. James Q. Wilson, *Bureaucracy* (New York: Basic Books, 1989), p. 25.

4. Bruce D. Porter, "Parkinson's Law Revisited: War and the Growth of American Government," *Public Interest* 60 (Summer 1980):50.

5. Keith Schneider, "Farmers to Face Patent Fees to Use Gene-Altered Animals," *New York Times,* 6 January 1988, p. A1.

6. Philip Shabecoff, "Senator Urges Military Resources Be Turned to Environmental Battle," *New York Times,* 29 June 1990, p. A1.

7. Jeff Gerth, "C.I.A. Shedding Its Reluctance to Aid in Fight Against Drugs," *New York Times,* 25 March 1990, p. A1.

8. Herbert Kaufman, *Are Government Organizations Immortal?* (Washington, D.C.: Brookings Institution, 1976).

9. "Advertisers Pleased by F.T.C. Plan," *New York Times,* 24 March 1984, p. 31; see also Michael Pertschuk, *Revolt Against Regulation* (Berkeley, Calif.: University of California Press, 1982).

10. John T. Tierney, "Government Corporations and Managing the Public's Business," *Political Science Quarterly* 99 (Spring 1984):73–92.

11. Bureau of the Census, *Statistical Abstract of the United States, 1990* (Washington, D.C.: U.S. Government Printing Office, 1990), pp. 324 and 378.

12. *Statistical Abstract, 1990,* p. 324.

13. Kenneth J. Meier, "Representative Democracy: An Empirical Assessment," *American Political Science Review* 69 (June 1975):532.

14. *Statistical Abstract, 1990,* p. 326.

15. Paul C. Light, "When Worlds Collide: The Political-Career Nexus," in *The In-and-Outers*, ed. G. Calvin MacKenzie (Baltimore: Johns Hopkins University Press, 1987), pp. 156–173.

16. See Elizabeth Sanders, "The Presidency and the Bureaucratic State," in *The Presidency and the Political System*, 3d ed., ed. Michael Nelson (Washington, D.C.: Congressional Quarterly Press, 1990), pp. 409–442.

17. Joseph Cooper and William F. West, "Presidential Power and Republican Government: The Theory and Practice of OMB Review of Agency Rules," *Journal of Politics* 50 (November 1988):864–895; and Peter M. Benda and Charles H. Levine, "Reagan and the Bureaucracy: The Bequest, the Promise, and the Legacy," in *The Reagan Legacy*, ed. Charles O. Jones (Chatham, N.J.: Chatham House, 1988).

18. David Wessel, "Administration Is Curbing Zeal Inside the OMB," *Wall Street Journal*, 24 April 1989, p. 3B.

19. Joel D. Aberbach and Bert Rockman, "From Nixon's Problem to Reagan's Achievement," in *Looking Back on the Reagan Presidency*, ed. Larry Berman (Baltimore: Johns Hopkins University Press, 1990), pp. 175–194.

20. Light, "When Worlds Collide," p. 157.

21. Joel D. Aberbach and Bert A. Rockman, "Mandates or Mandarins? Control and Discretion in the Modern Administrative State," *Public Administration Review* 48 (March/April 1988): 606–612.

22. Karen DeWitt, "Ruling Highlights a Rift Among Blacks," *New York Times*, 17 December 1990, p. B8; and Karen DeWitt, "U.S. Lets Stand Curb on College Aid Keyed to Race," *New York Times*, 19 December 1990, p. B7.

23. Theodore J. Lowi, *The End of Liberalism*, 2d ed. (New York: Norton, 1979).

24. Doris A. Graber, *Mass Media and American Politics*, 3d ed. (Washington, D.C.: Congressional Quarterly Press, 1989), p. 51.

25. Jeffrey M. Berry, *Feeding Hungry People: Rulemaking in the Food Stamp Program* (New Brunswick, N.J.: Rutgers University Press, 1984).

26. David J. Garrow, *Bearing the Cross* (New York: Morrow, 1986), pp. 373–374.

27. Gregory F. Treverton, "Intelligence: Welcome to the American Government," in *A Question of Balance*, ed. Thomas E. Mann (Washington, D.C.: Brookings Institution, 1990), p. 89.

28. "E.P.A. Drops Plan to Require Waste Incinerators to Recycle," *New York Times*, 21 December 1990, p. A33.

29. Terry M. Moe, "Control and Feedback in Economic Regulation: The Case of the NLRB," *American Political Science Review* 79 (December 1985):109–116.

30. Charles E. Lindblom, "The Science of Muddling Through," *Public Administration Review* 19 (Spring 1959):79–88.

31. Michael Lipsky, *Street-Level Bureaucracy* (New York: Russell Sage Foundation, 1980), p. 21.

32. Jonathan Bendor, Serge Taylor, and Roland Van Gaalen, "Stacking the Deck: Bureaucratic Mission and Policy Design," *American Political Science Review* 81 (Spring 1987):874.

33. George C. Edwards III, *Implementing Public Policy* (Washington, D.C.: Congressional Quarterly Press, 1980), p. 27; see also Daniel A. Mazmanian and Paul Sabatier, *Implementation and Public Policy* (Glenview, Ill.: Scott/Foresman, 1983), pp. 175–217.

34. Michael Massing, "Why Bennett Is Losing," *New York Times Magazine*, 23 September 1990, pp. 37ff.

35. Martha Derthick, *Agency Under Stress* (Washington, D.C.: Brookings Institution, 1990), pp. 33–48.

36. See generally, Terry M. Moe, "The Politics of Bureaucratic Structure," in *Can the Government Govern?*, ed. John E. Chubb and Paul E. Peterson (Washington, D.C.: Brookings Institution, 1989), pp. 267–329.

37. William T. Gormley, Jr., *Taming the Bureaucracy* (Princeton, N.J.: Princeton University Press, 1989).

38. Martha Derthick and Paul J. Quirk, *The Politics of Deregulation* (Washington, D.C.: Brookings Institution, 1985).

39. David Vogel, "AIDS and the Politics of Drug Lag," *The Public Interest* 96 (Summer 1989):73–85.

40. See James A. Morone, *The Democratic Wish* (New York: Basic Books, 1990).

Chapter 14 / The Courts / pp. 487–529

1. Philip Elman (interviewed by Norman Silber), "The Solicitor General's Office, Justice Frankfurter, and Civil Rights Litigation, 1946–1960: An Oral History," 100 *Harvard Law Review*, 817–852, 840 (1987).

2. David M. O'Brien, *Storm Center*, 2d ed. (Norton, 1990), p. 324.

3. Bernard Schwartz, *The Unpublished Opinions of the Warren Court* (New York: Oxford University Press, 1985), p. 446.

4. Ibid., pp. 445–448.

5. Felix Frankfurter and James M. Landis, *The Business of the Supreme Court* (New York: Macmillan, 1928), pp. 5–14; and Julius Goebel, Jr., *Antecedents and Beginnings to 1801*, vol. 1 of *The History of the Supreme Court of the United States* (New York: Macmillan, 1971).

6. Maeva Marcus, ed., *The Justices on Circuit, 1795–1800*, vol. 3 of *The Documentary History of the Supreme Court of the United States, 1789–1800* (New York: Columbia University Press, 1990).

7. Robert G. McCloskey, *The United States Supreme Court* (Chicago: University of Chicago Press, 1960), p. 31.

8. *Marbury* v. *Madison*, 1 Cranch 137, 177–178 (1803).

9. Interestingly, the phrase *judicial review* dates only to 1910; it was apparently unknown to Marshall and his contemporaries. Robert Lowry Clinton, *Marbury* v. *Madison and Judicial Review* (Lawrence, Kan.: University Press of Kansas, 1989), p. 7.

10. *Constitution of the United States of America: Annotated and Interpreted* (Washington, D.C.: U.S.

Government Printing Office, 1987) and 1988 *Supplement.*

11. *Ware* v. *Hylton,* 3 Dallas 199 (1976).

12. *Martin* v. *Hunter's Lessee,* 1 Wheat. 304 (1816).

13. *Constitution of the United States of America: Annotated and Interpreted.*

14. Garry Wills, *Explaining America: The Federalist* (Garden City, N.Y.: Doubleday, 1981), pp. 127–136.

15. Charles Alan Wright, *Handbook on the Law of Federal Courts,* 3d ed. (St. Paul, Minn.: West, 1976), p. 7.

16. Linda Greenhouse, "Precedent for Lower Courts: Tyrant or Teacher?" *New York Times,* 29 January 1988, p. 18.

17. *Regents of the University of California* v. *Bakke,* 438 U.S. 265 (1978).

18. "Reading Petitions Is for Clerks Only at High Court Now," *Wall Street Journal,* 11 October 1990, p. B7.

19. Joseph Tanenhaus, et al., "The Supreme Court's Certiorari Jurisdiction: Cue Thoery," in *Judicial Decision-Making,* ed. Glendon Schubert (New York: Free Press, 1963), pp. 111–132; Gregory A. Caldeira and John R. Wright, "The Discuss List: Agenda Building in the Supreme Court," *Law and Society Review* 24(3):807–836 (1990).

20. Doris M. Provine, *Case Selection in the United States Supreme Court* (Chicago: University of Chicago Press, 1980), pp. 74–102.

21. *Garcia* v. *San Antonio Metropolitan Transit Authority,* 469 U.S. 528 (1985).

22. Elder Witt, *A Different Justice: Reagan and the Supreme Court* (Washington, D.C.: Congressional Quarterly, 1986), p. 133.

23. "Solicitor General's Career Advances at Intersection of Law and Politics," *New York Times,* 1 June 1990, p. A11.

24. "Rising Fixed Opinions," *New York Times,* 22 February 1988, p. 14.

25. Jeffrey A. Segal and Albert D. Cover, "Ideological Values and the Votes of U.S. Supreme Court Justices," *American Political Science Review* 83 (2):557–565.

26. Stuart Taylor, Jr., "Lifting of Secrecy Reveals Earthy Side of Justices," *New York Times,* 22 February 1988, p. 14.

27. *Chicago Tribune,* 6 June 1990, p. 4.

28. Stuart Taylor, Jr., "Brennan: 30 Years and the Thrill Is Not Gone," *New York Times,* 16 April 1986, p. 18.

29. Thomas G. Walker, Lee Epstein, and William J. Dixon, "On the Mysterious Demise of Consensual Norms in the United States Supreme Court," *The Journal of Politics* 50 (1988): 361–389.

30. See, for example, Walter F. Murphy, *Elements of Judicial Strategy* (Chicago: University of Chicago Press, 1964); and Bob Woodward and Scott Armstrong, *The Brethren* (New York: Simon & Schuster, 1979).

31. Henry J. Abraham, *Justices and Presidents: A Political History of Appointments to the Supreme Court,* 2d ed. (New York: Oxford University Press, 1985), pp. 183–185.

32. Stephen L. Wasby, *The Supreme Court in the Federal Judicial System,* 3d ed. (Chicago: Nelson-Hall, 1988), p. 241.

33. Schwartz, *Unpublished Opinions,* pp. 446–447.

34. Lawrence Baum, *American Courts: Process and Policy,* 2d ed. (Boston: Hougton Mifflin, 1990), pp. 99–112.

35. Joan Biskupic, "Bush Boosts Bench Strength of Conservative Judges," *Congressional Quarterly,* 19 January 1991, p. 171.

36. Wasby, *Supreme Court,* pp. 107–110.

37. "Bush Appears Set to Follow Reagan by Putting Conservatives on Bench," *New York Times,* 31 May 1989, p. 12.

38. Linda Greenhouse, "Policy on Black Judicial Nominees Is Debated," *New York Times,* 3 February 1988, p. 22 (statement by Assistant Attorney General Stephen J. Markman).

39. "Bush Travels Reagan's Course in Naming Judges," *New York Times,* 10 April 1990, p. A1.

40. Peter G. Fish, "John J. Parker," in *Dictionary of American Biography,* supp. 6, 1956–1980 (New York: Scribner's, 1980), p. 494.

41. *Congressional Quarterly's Guide,* pp. 655–656.

42. Elmo Richardson, *The Presidency of Dwight D. Eisenhower* (Lawrence, Kan.: Regents Press, 1979), p. 108.

43. Merle Miller, *Plain Speaking: An Oral Biography of Harry S Truman* (New York: Berkley, 1973), pp. 225–226.

44. Paul Wice, *Judges & Lawyers: The Human Side of Justice* (New York: HarperCollins, 1991).

45. American Bar Foundation, *Lawyer Statistical Report* (1990).

46. American Bar Association, *Review of Legal Education,* 1987, pp. 66–67.

47. Bureau of Labor Statistics, *Occupational Outlook Handbook, 1986–1987* (Washington, D.C.: U.S. Government Printing Office, 1986).

48. Wice, *Judges & Lawyers,* pp. 99–109.

49. Ken Emerson, "When Legal Titans Clash," *New York Times Magazine,* April 22, 1990, p. 66 (statement attributed to Charles Fried).

50. Nicholas O. Berry, "Of Lawyers' Work, There Is No End," *New York Times,* 28 December 1985, p. 19.

51. Baum, *American Courts,* p. 185.

52. James Eisenstein, *Attorneys for the Government* (Baltimore: Johns Hopkins University Press, 1980), p. 204.

53. *Brown* v. *Board of Education II,* 349 U.S. 294 (1955).

54. Charles A. Johnson and Bradley C. Canon, *Judicial Policies: Implementation and Impact* (Washington, D.C.: Congressional Quarterly Press, 1984).

55. Alexander M. Bickel, *The Least Dangerous Branch* (Indianapolis: Bobbs-Merrill, 1962); and Robert A. Dahl, "Decision-Making in a Democracy: The Supreme Court as a National Policy-Maker," *Journal of Public Law* 6 (1962): 279–295.

56. Thomas R. Marshall, *Public Opinion and the Supreme Court* (Boston: Unwin Hyman, 1989).

57. Ibid., pp. 192–193; Gerald N. Rosenberg, *The Hollow Hope: Can Courts Bring About Social*

Change? (Chicago: University of Chicago Press, in press).

58. William J. Brennan, Jr., "State Supreme Court Judge Versus United States Supreme Court Justice: A Change in Function and Perspective," *University of Florida Law Review* 19 (1966): 225–237.

59. G. Alan Tarr and M. C. Porter, *State Supreme Courts in State and Nation* (New Haven, Conn.: Yale University Press, 1988), pp. 206–209.

60. "New Jersey Court Seen as a Leader in the Expansion of Individual Rights," *New York Times*, 19 July 1990, p. A9.

61. Baum, *American Courts*, p. 309.

Chapter 15 / Order and Civil Liberties / pp. 533–573

1. Learned Hand, *The Bill of Rights* (Boston: Atheneum, 1958), p. 1.

2. Leonard W. Levy, *The Establishment Clause: Religion and the First Amendment* (New York: Macmillan, 1986); Leo Pfeffer, *Church, State, and Freedom* (Boston: Beacon Press, 1953); and Leonard W. Levy, "The Original Meaning of the Establishment Clause of the First Amendment," in *Religion and the State*, ed. James E. Wood, Jr. (Waco. Tex.: Baylor University Press, 1985), pp. 43–83.

3. Garry Wills, *Under God: Religion and American Politics* (New York: Simon & Schuster, 1990).

4. *Reynolds* v. *United States*, 98 U.S. 145 (1879).

5. *Everson* v. *Board of Education*, 330 U.S. 236 (1947).

6. *Board of Education* v. *Allen*, 392 U.S. 236 (1968).

7. *Lemon* v. *Kurtzman*, 403 U.S. 602 (1971).

8. *Lynch* v. *Donnelly*, 465 U.S. 668 (1984).

9. *County of Allegheny* v. *ACLU Greater Pittsburgh Chapter*, 109 S. Ct. 3086 (1989).

10. *Engle* v. *Vitale*, 260 U.S. 421 (1962).

11. *Abington School District* v. *Schempp*, 364 U.S. 203 (1963).

12. *Wallace* v. *Jaffree*, 472 U.S. 38 (1985).

13. *Board of Education* v. *Mergens*, 497 U.S. __ (1990).

14. Michael W. McConnell, "The Origins and Historical Understanding of Free Exercise of Religion," *Harvard Law Review* 103 (7):1409–1517 (1990).

15. *Minersville School District* v. *Gobitis*, 310 U.S. 586 (1940).

16. David Margolick, "Pledge Dispute Evokes Bitter Memories," *New York Times*, 11 September 1988, sec. 1, p. 1.

17. *West Virginia State Board of Education* v. *Barnette*, 319 U.S. 624 (1943).

18. *Sherbert* v. *Verner*, 374 U.S. 398 (1963).

19. McConnell, "Origins and Historical Understanding of Free Exercise of Religion."

20. *Employment Division* v. *Smith*, 110 S. Ct. 1595 (1990).

21. Laurence Tribe, *Treatise on American Constitutional Law*, ad ed. (St. Paul, Minn.: West, 1988), p. 566.

22. Zechariah Chafee, *Free Speech in the United States* (Cambridge, Mass.: Harvard University Press, 1941).

23. Leonard W. Levy, *The Emergence of a Free Press* (New York: Oxford University Press, 1985).

24. Mark Twain, *Following the Equator* (Hartford, Conn.: American Publishing Co., 1897).

25. *Schenck* v. *United States*, 249 U.S. 46 (1919).

26. *Abrams* v. *United States*, 205 U.S. 616 (1919).

27. *Gitlow* v. *New York*, 268 U.S. 652 (1925).

28. *Dennis* v. *United States*, 341 U.S. 494 (1951).

29. *Brandenburg* v. *Ohio*, 395 U.S. 444 (1969).

30. *Tinker* v. *Des Moines Independent County School District*, 393 U.S 503 (1969).

31. *United States* v. *Eichman*, 110 S. Ct. 2404 (1990).

32. "Supreme Court Voids Flag Law," *New York Times*, 12 June 1990, p. A1.

33. *Barnes* v. *Glen Theatre* (no. 90-26, decided 21 June 1991).

34. *Chaplinsky* v. *New Hampshire*, 315 U.S. 568 (1942).

35. *Terminiello* v. *Chicago*, 337 U.S. 1 (1949).

36. *Cohen* v. *California*, 403 U.S. 15 (1971).

37. *Roth* v. *United States*, 354 U.S. 477 (1957).

38. *Jacobellis* v. *Ohio*, 378 U.S. 184, at 197 (concurring opinion).

39. *Miller* v. *California*, 415 U.S. 15 (1973).

40. *Pope* v. *Illinois*, 481 U.S. 497 (1987).

41. "The Cincinnati Obscenity Trial and What Makes Photos Art," *New York Times*, 18 October 1990, p. B1.

42. Donald Alexander Downs, *The New Politics of Pornography* (Chicago: University of Chicago Press, 1989).

43. *American Booksellers Ass'n* v. *Hudnut*, 598 F. Supp. 1316 (1984).

44. *New York Times* v. *Sullivan*, 376 U.S. 254 (1964).

45. *Hustler Magazine* v. *Falwell*, 485 U.S. 46 (1988).

46. *Near* v. *Minnesota*, 283 U.S. 697 (1931).

47. For a detailed account of the case and *Near*, see Fred W. Friendly, *Minnesota Rag* (New York: Random House, 1981).

48. *New York Times* v. *United States*, 403 U.S. 713 (1971).

49. *Branzburg* v. *Hayes*, 408 U.S. 665 (1972).

50. *Zurcher* v. *Stanford Daily*, 436 U.S. 547 (1978).

51. *Hazelwood School District* v. *Kuhlmeier*, 484 U.S. 280 (1988).

52. *United States* v. *Cruikshank*, 92 U.S. 542 (1876); and *Constitution of the United States of America: Annotated and Interpreted* (Washington, D.C.: U.S. Government Printing Office, 1973), p. 1031.

53. *DeJonge* v. *Oregon*, 299 U.S. 353, 364 (1937).

54. *Barron* v. *Baltimore*, 7 Pet 243 (1833).

55. *Chicago B. & O. R.* v. *Chicago*, 166 U.S. 226 (1897).

56. *Palko* v. *Connecticut*, 302 U.S. 319 (1937).

57. *Duncan* v. *Louisiana*, 391 U.S. 145 (1968).

58. *McNabb* v. *United States*, 318 U.S. 332 (1943).

59. *Baldwin* v. *New York*, 399 U.S. 66 (1970).

60. *Anthony Lewis, Gideon's Trumpet* (New York; Random House, 1964).

61. *Gideon* v. *Wainwright,* 372 U.S. 335 (1963).

62. *Miranda* v. *Arizona,* 384 U.S. 486 (1966)

63. *Wolf* v. *Colorado,* 338 U.S. 225 (1949).

64. *Mapp* v. *Ohio,* 307 U.S. 643 (1961).

65. *United States* v. *Leon,* 468 U.S. 897 (1984).

66. *California* v. *Greenwood* (slip no. 86–684) (16 May 1988).

67. *James* v. *Illinois,* 110 S. Ct. 648 (1990).

68. *Paul Brest, Processes of Constitutional Decision-making* (Boston: Little, Brown, 1975), p. 708.

69. *Griswold* v. *Connecticut,* 381 U.S. 479 (1965).

70. *Roe* v. *Wade,* 410 U.S. 113 (1973).

71. See John Hart Ely, "The Wages of Crying Wolf: A comment on *Roe* v. *Wade,*" 82 Law Journal 920 (1973).

72. *New York Times,* 1 April 1986, p. 11.

73. *Bowers* v. *Hardwick,* 106 S. Ct. 2841 (1986).

74. *New York Times,* 26 October 1990, p. A11; *New York Times,* 5 November 1990, p. A9.

75. Learned Hand, "The Contribution of an Independent Judiciary to Civilization," in *The Spirit of Liberty: Papers and Addresses of Learned Hand,* ed. Irving Dilliard, 3d ed. (New York: Knopf, 1960), p. 164.

Chapter 16 / Equality and Civil Rights / pp. 575–611

1. *Johnson* v. *Transportation Agency, Santa Clara County,* 480 U.S. 616 (1987).

2. *United States* v. *Cruikshank,* 92 U.S. 542 (1876).

3. *United States* v. *Reese,* 12 U.S. 214 (1876).

4. *Civil Rights Cases,* 109 U.S. 3 (1883).

5. Mary Beth Norton, et al., *A People and a Nation: A History of the United States,* 3d ed. (Boston: Houghton Mifflin, 1990), p. 490.

6. *Plessy* v. *Ferguson,* 163 U.S. 537 (1896).

7. *Cummings* v. *County Board of Education,* 175 U.S. 528 (1899).

8. *Missouri ex rel. Gaines* v. *Canada,* 305 U.S. 337 (1938).

9. *Sweatt* v. *Painter,* 339 U.S. 629 (1950).

10. *McLaurin* v. *Oklahoma State Regents,* 339 U.S. 637 (1950).

11. *Brown* v. *Board of Education,* 347 U.S. 487 (1954).

12. *Bolling* v. *Sharpe,* 347 U.S. 497 (1954).

13. *Brown* v. *Board of Education II,* 349 U.S. 294 (1955).

14. Jack W. Peltason, *Fifty-Eight Lonely Men,* rev. ed. (Urbana, Ill.: University of Illinois Press, 1971).

15. *Alexander* v. *Holmes County Board of Education,* 369 U.S. 19 (1969).

16. *Swann* v. *Charlotte-Mecklenberg County Schools,* 402 U.S. 1 (1971).

17. *Milliken* v. *Bradley,* 418 U.S. 717 (1974).

18. Richard Kluger, *Simple Justice* (New York: Knopf, 1976), p. 753.

19. Taylor Branch, *Parting the Waters: America in the King Years, 1955–63* (New York: Simon and Schuster, 1988), p. 3.

20. Branch, *Parting the Waters,* p. 14.

21. Branch, *Parting the Waters,* p. 271.

22. Norton, et al., *People and a Nation,* p. 943.

23. *Heart of Atlanta Motel* v. *United States,* 379 U.S. 241 (1964).

24. *Katzenbach* v. *McClung,* 379 U.S. 294 (1964).

25. But see Abigail M. Thernstrom, *Whose Vote Counts? Affirmative Action and Minority Voting Rights* (Cambridge, Mass.: Harvard University Press, 1987).

26. *Grove City College* v. *Bell,* 465 U.S. 555 (1984).

27. *City of Richmond* v. *J.A. Croson Co.,* 109 S. Ct. 706 (1989).

28. *Martin* v. *Wilks,* 109 S. Ct. 2180 (1989).

29. *Wards Cove Packing Co.* v. *Atonio,* 109 S. Ct. 2115 (1989).

30. *Patterson* v. *McLean Credit Union,* 109 S. Ct. 2363 (1989).

31. *Saint Francis College* v. *Al-Khazraji,* 481 U.S. 604 (1987).

32. Francis Paul Prucha, *The Great Father: The United States Government and the American Indian,* Vol. 2 (Lincoln, Neb.: University of Nebraska Press, 1984).

33. Rufus P. Browning, Dale Rogers Marshall, and David H. Tabb, *Protest Is Not Enough* (Berkeley, Calif.: University of California Press, 1984).

34. Cited in Martin Gruberg, *Women in American Politics* (Oshkosh, Wis.: Academia Press, 1968), p. 4.

35. *Bradwell* v. *State,* 16 Wall. 130 (1873).

36. *Muller* v. *Oregon,* 208 U.S. 412 (1908).

37. *International Union, United Automobile, Aerospace and Agricultural Implement Workers of America* v. *Johnson Controls, Inc.,* 1991 U.S. LEXIS 1715 (1991).

38. *Minor* v. *Happersett,* 21 Wall. 162 (1875).

39 John H. Aldrich, et al., *American Government: People, Institutions, and Policies* (Boston: Houghton Mifflin, 1986), p. 618.

40. *Reed* v. *Reed,* 404 U.S. 71 (1971).

41. *Frontiero* v. *Richardson,* 411 U.S. 677 (1973).

42. *Craig* v. *Borden,* 429 U.S. 190 (1976).

43. Paul Weiler, "The Wages of Sex: The Uses and Limits of Comparable Worth," *Harvard Law Review* 99 (June 1986):1728–1807.

44. Jane J. Mansbridge, *Why We Lost the ERA* (Chicago: University of Chicago Press, 1986).

45. Melvin I. Urofsky, *A March of Liberty* (New York: Knopf, 1988), p. 902.

46. *Time,* 6 July 1987, p. 91.

47. As quoted in Melvin I. Urofsky, *A Conflict of Rights: The Supreme Court and Affirmative Action* (New York: Scribner's, 1991), p. 17.

48. Urofsky, *A Conflict of Rights,* p. 29.

49. Thomas Sowell, *Preferential Policies: An International Perspective* (New York: Morrow, 1990), pp. 103–105.

50. *Regents of the University of California* v. *Bakke,* 438 U.S. 265 (1978).

51. Steven N. Keith, Robert M. Bell, and Albert P. Williams, *Assessing the Outcome of Affirmative Action in Medical Schools* (Santa Monica, Calif.: Rand, 1987).

52. *United Steelworkers of America, AFL-CIO* v. *Weber,* 443 U.S. 193 (1979).

53. *Firefighters* v. *Stotts,* 467 U.S. 561 (1984).

54. *Wygant* v. *Jackson Board of Education,* 106 S. Ct. 1842 (1986).

55. *Local 28 of the Sheet Metal Workers' International Association* v. *EEOC* 478 U.S. 421 (1986).

56. Sidney Verba and Gary R. Orren, *Equality in America: The View from the Top* (Cambridge, Mass.: Harvard University Press, 1985), especially pp. 1–51.

57. Howard Schuman, Charlotte Steeh, and Lawrence Bobo, *Racial Attitudes in America: Trends and Interpretations* (Cambridge, Mass.: Harvard University Press, 1985).

Chapter 17 / Policymaking / pp. 615–641

1. Alyson Pytte, "Tobacco's Clout Stays Strong Through Dollars, Jobs, Ads," *Congressional Quarterly Weekly Report,* 19 May 1990, pp. 1542–1548; "The Worldwide Smoking Epidemic," *Journal of the American Medical Association,* 27 June 1990, pp. 3312–3314; and Julie Rovner, "New Report Ignites Anti-Smoking Campaign," *Congressional Quarterly Weekly Report,* 21 May 1988, pp. 1401–1402.

2. Bureau of the Census, *Statistical Abstract of the United States, 1990* (Washington, D.C.: U.S. Government Printing Office, 1990), p. 423.

3. Margaret Kriz, "Fireworks on the Tube," *National Journal,* 17 February 1990, pp. 384–387.

4. For one example, see Randall B. Ripley and Grace A. Franklin, *Congress, the Bureaucracy, and Public Policy,* 5th ed. (Pacific Grove, Calif.: Brooks/Cole, 1991).

5. There are many ways to depict the policymaking process. One approach, a bit more elaborate than this, is James E. Anderson, *Public Policymaking* (Boston: Houghton Mifflin, 1990), p. 36.

6. Roger W. Cobb and Charles D. Elder, *Participation in American Politics,* 2d ed. (Baltimore: Johns Hopkins University Press, 1983), p. 14.

7. Cobb and Elder, *Participation in American Politics,* p. 84.

8. Barbara J. Nelson, *Making an Issue of Child Abuse* (Chicago: University of Chicago Press, 1984), p. 13.

9. Robert Pear, "U.S. Proposes Rules to Bar Obstacles for the Disabled," *New York Times,* 22 January 1991, p. A1.

10. "For California: A Political Fix," *New York Times,* 18 March 1991, p. A14.

11. See Kent E. Portney, *Approaching Public Policy Analysis* (Englewood Cliffs, N.J.: Prentice-Hall, 1986), pp. 2–18.

12. Portney, *Approaching Public Policy Analysis,* p. 46.

13. David J. Armor, "The Evidence on Busing," *Public Interest* 28 (Summer 1972):90–126.

14. Thomas F. Pettigrew, et al., "Busing: A Review of 'The Evidence,'" *Public Interest* 30 (Winter 1973):106. For a brief review of this controversy, see Thomas R. Dye, *Understanding Public Policy,* 5th ed. (Englewood Cliffs, N.J.: Prentice-Hall, 1984), pp. 8–13.

15. W. John Moore, "Tribal Imperatives," *National Journal,* 9 June 1990, pp. 1396–1401.

16. John E. Yang and Paul M. Barrett, "Drug Issue Triggers Washington Habit: Turf Wars in Congress, Administration," *Wall Street Journal,* 11 August 1989, p. A5.

17. Yang and Barrett, "Drug Issue Triggers Washington Habit."

18. Stephen Labaton, "Bush Plan on Finance Supervision," *New York Times,* 7 January 1991, p. D1; and David E. Rosenbaum, "Fed to Fight Part of Plan on Banks," *New York Times,* 5 March 1991, p. D1.

19. Former OMB official Christopher DeMuth, quoted in Joseph Cooper and William F. West, "Presidential Power and Republican Government," *Journal of Politics* 50 (November 1988):871.

20. Margaret Kriz, "Policing the Paperwork," *National Journal,* 31 March 1990, pp. 785–787.

21. On efforts toward recentralization in Congress, see Roger H. Davidson, "The New Centralization on Capitol Hill" (paper delivered at the annual meeting of the Midwest Political Science Association, Chicago, April 1988).

22. Hugh Heclo, "Issue Networks and the Executive Establishment," in *The New American Political System,* ed. Anthony King (Washington, D.C.: American Enterprise Institute, 1978), p. 103.

23. Robert H. Salisbury, et al., "Who Works with Whom? Interest Group Alliances and Opposition," *American Political Science Review* 81 (December 1987): 1217–1234.

24. Douglass Cater, *Power in Washington* (New York: Vintage Books, 1964), p. 18.

25. Lawrence C. Dodd and Richard L. Schott, *Congress and the Administrative State* (New York: Wiley, 1979), p. 103.

26. Although the subgovernment concept has fallen on hard times, there are some political scientists who have tried to adapt it to contemporary politics. See Daniel McCool, "Subgovernments as Determinants of Political Viability," *Political Science Quarterly* 105 (Summer 1990):269–293.

27. Jeffrey M. Berry, "Subgovernments, Issue Networks, and Political Conflict," in *Remaking American Politics,* ed. Richard A. Harris and Sidney M. Milkis (Boulder, Colo.: Westview Press, 1989), pp. 239–260.

28. This account is based on Steven Coll, *The Deal of the Century* (New York: Atheneum, 1986); and Peter Temin with Louis Galambos, *The Fall of the Bell System* (New York: Cambridge University Press, 1987).

29. Martha Derthick and Paul J. Quirk, *The Politics of Deregulation* (Washington, D.C.: Brookings Institution, 1985).

30. This discussion is drawn from Jeffrey M. Berry, *The Interest Group Society,* 2d ed. (Glenview, Ill.: Scott, Foresman/Little, Brown, 1989), pp. 189–193.

31. On recent conflicts see Mike Mills, "Baby Bells' Fate Dangling Before Congress, Courts," *Congressional Quarterly Weekly Report,* 23 February 1991, pp. 458–463; and Margaret E. Kriz, "Ganging Up on the Bells," *National Journal,* 1 September 1990, pp. 2068–2071.

32. For an alternative perspective, see James A. Thurber, "Dynamics of Policy Subsystems in American

Politics," in *Interest Group Politics*, 3d ed., ed. Allan J. Cigler and Burdett A. Loomis (Washington, D.C.: Congressional Quarterly Press, 1991), pp. 319–343.

33. Lauriston R. King and W. Wayne Shannon, "Policy Networks in the Policy Process: The Case of the National Sea Grant Program," *Polity* 19 (Winter 1986):213–231.

34. Edward O. Laumann, et al., "Organizations in Political Action" (paper presented at the annual meeting of the American Sociological Association, September 1986).

35. Heclo, "Issue Networks," p. 105.

36. John M. Blair, *The Control of Oil* (New York: Pantheon, 1976), pp. 354–370.

37. Two useful analyses of the attributes of modern issue networks are Mark A Peterson, "Institutions, Networks, and the Development of National Health Care Policy in America" (paper presented at the annual meeting of the American Political Science Association, San Francisco, August 1990); and Robert H. Salisbury, et al., "Iron Triangles: Similarities and Differences Among the Legs" (paper presented at the annual meeting of the American Political Science Association, Washington, D.C., September 1988).

38. Robert H. Salisbury and Paul Johnson, "Who You Know versus What You Know," *American Journal of Political Science* 33 (February 1989):175–195.

39. Thomas B. Edsall, "Republican Lobbyists Expanding, Advantages Seen After Landslide," *Washington Post*, 16 December 1984; p. A10a.

40. John J. Fialka, "Former Defense Official Creates Firm to Lobby in Washington for Turkey," *Wall Street Journal,* 16 February 1989, p. A16.

41. See Carl Brauer, "Tenure, Turnover, and Postgovernment Employment Trends of Presidential Appointees," in *The In-and-Outers*, ed. G. Calvin MacKenzie (Baltimore: Johns Hopkins University Press, 1987), pp. 181 and 189.

42. David Johnston, "Nofziger Given 90 Days in Jail in Ethics Case," *New York Times*, 9 April 1988, p. 9; Jill Abramson, "Bush's Ethics Commission Takes Different Tacks on Standards for Congress and Executive Branch," *Wall Street Journal*, 23 February 1989, p. A20; and Martin Tolchin, "Court Overturns Guilty Verdict in Nofziger Case," *New York Times*, 28 June 1989, p. A1.

43. Berry, "Subgovernments, Issue Networks, and Political Conflict."

Chapter 18 / Economic Policy / pp. 643–679

1. James O'Shea, "High-Rolling S&L Owner Takes Main Street for Ride," *Chicago Tribune*, 24 February 1991, sec. 7, pp. 1 and 6.

2. Thomas C. Hayes, "Texan Convicted of S&L Fraud," *New York Times*, 21 December 1990, pp. 1 and C15.

3. Hayes, "Texan Convicted of S&L Fraud."

4. Richard W. Stevenson, "How One Savings Institution Came Apart," *New York Times*, 12 June 1990, p. 1.

5. Larry Martz, "Bonfire of the S&Ls," *Newsweek*, 21 May 1990, p. 22.

6. Stephen Labaton, "Next Plea for Bailout: $80 Billion," *New York Times*, 19 January 1991, p. 21.

7. Steven Waldman and Rich Thomas, "How Did It Happen?" *Newsweek*, 21 May 1990, p. 27.

8. Waldman and Thomas, "How Did It Happen?"

9. Jeff Gerth, "A Blend of Tragedy and Farce," *New York Times*, 3 April 1990, p. C6.

10. Jonathan Rauch, "Testing the Fed," *National Journal*, 18 June 1988, p. 1612; Louis Uchitelle, "Federal Reserve Trims Loan Costs to Spur Economy," *New York Times*, 1 May 1991, p. 1.

11. Ronald Reagan with Richard G. Hubler, *Where's the Rest of Me?* (New York: Duell, Sloan and Pearce, 1965), p. 233.

12. Bureau of the Census, *Statistical Abstract of the United States, 1990* (Washington, D.C.: U.S. Government Printing Office, 1990), p. 468.

13. Bureau of the Census, *Statistical Abstract, 1990*, p. 397.

14. Jonathan Rauch, Lawrence J. Haas, and Bruce Stokes, "Payment Deferred," *National Journal*, 14 May 1988, p. 1256.

15. Lawrence J. Haas, "New Rules of the Game," *National Journal*, March 19, 1988, p. 734.

16. David S. Cloud, "Congress Cranks Out 13 Bills in Last 8 Days of Session," *Congressional Quarterly Weekly Report*, 3 November 1990, p. 3723.

17. *Congressional Quarterly Weekly Report*, 14 December 1985, p. 2605.

18. George Hager, "With Little Room to Maneuver, Bush Sets His Priorities," *Congressional Quarterly Weekly Report*, 9 February 1991, p. 336.

19. For the first point, see Lawrence J. Haas, "Unauthorized Action," *National Journal*, 2 January 1988, pp. 17–21. For the second, see George Hager, "New Rules on Taxes, Spending May Mean Budget Standoff," *Congressional Quarterly Weekly Report*, 26 January 1991, p. 237. The plight of the budget committees under the 1990 act is covered by George Hager, "Relevance of Budget Process Is Tricky Question on Hill," *Congressional Quarterly Weekly Report*, 20 April, 1991, pp. 962–968.

20. Richard A. Musgrave and Peggy B. Musgrave, *Public Finance in Theory and Practice*, 2d ed. (New York: McGraw-Hill, 1976), p. 42.

21. Kevin Phillips, *The Politics of Rich and Poor: Wealth and the American Electorate in the Reagan Aftermath* (New York: Random House, 1990), p. 78.

22. ABC/*Washington Post* Survey cited in *Public Opinion* 8 (February–March 1985):21.

23. Advisory Commission on Intergovernmental Relations, *Significant Features of Fiscal Federalism, 1981–1982* (Washington, D.C., 1983), p. 54.

24. Lawrence Mishel and David M. Frankel, *The State of Working America, 1990–91 Edition* (Washington, D.C.: Economic Policy Institute, 1990), p.62.

25. *The Polling Report*, 25 January 1988, pp. 1 and 8. For similar find-

ings in 1989, see "The People, Press & Economics," (Washington, D.C.: Times Mirror, May 1989), p. 11.

26. Fay Lomax Cook, et al., *Convergent Perspectives on Social Welfare Policy: The Views from the General Public, Members of Congress, and AFDC Recipients* (Evanston, Ill.: Northwestern University, Center for Urban Affairs and Policy Research, 1988), Table 4-1.

27. David S. Cloud, "Bush Keeps Tax Plans Modest; Democrats Split on Strategy," *Congressional Quarterly Weekly Report*, 9 February 1991, p. 340. See also Alex Mintz, "Guns versus Butter: A Disaggregated Analysis," *American Political Science Review* 83 (December, 1989):1285–1293, for evidence that military spending for weapons procurement and research and development during the Reagan years came at the expense of social programs.

28. David S. Cloud, "Farm Bloc on the Defensive as Bills Move to Floor," *Congressional Quarterly Weekly Report*, 14 July 1990, pp. 2209–2212.

29. Joseph A. Pechman, *Who Paid the Taxes, 1966–1985?* (Washington, D.C.: Brookings Institution, 1985).

30. Mishel and Frankel, *State of Working America*, pp. 178–179.

31. But the rich received only 1 percent of their income in transfer payments, suffering a net loss from government. See Pechman, *Who Paid the Taxes?*, p. 53.

32. Pechman, *Who Paid the Taxes?*, p. 80.

33. Pechman, *Who Paid the Taxes?*, p. 73.

34. Pechman, *Who Paid the Taxes?*, p. 74.

35. Mishel and Frankel, *State of Working America*, pp. 37–39. See also Gary Burtless, ed., *A Future of Lousy Jobs? The Changing Structure of U.S. Wages* (Washington, D.C.: Brookings Institution, 1990), for discussions of the rise in women's earnings and the decline in lower-paid men's earnings. Other researchers have found that women's earnings have also accounted for increases in the

"rich." See Sheldon Danziger, Peter Gottschalk, and Eugene Smolensky, "How the Rich Have Fared, 1973–87," *American Economic Association, Papers and Proceedings* 79 (May 1989): 310–314.

36.. Phillips, *Politics of Rich and Poor*, p. 11.

37. Phillips, *Politics of Rich and Poor*, p. 157.

38. Phillips, *Politics of Rich and Poor*, p. 17.

39. Phillips, *Politics of Rich and Poor*, p. 83.

40. Charles F. Andrain, *Social Policies in Western Industrial Societies* (Berkeley: University of California Press, 1985), p. 194. See also Mishel and Frankel, *State of Working America*, pp. 260–261, for a discussion of three measures of inequality in disposable income in ten democratic countries. The United States is the least equal according to all three measures.

41. "Nation Top-Heavy with Wealth," *Chicago Tribune*, 19 July 1986, p. 1; and Bureau of the Census, *Statistical Abstract of the United States, 1988* (Washington, D.C.: U.S. Government Printing Office, 1988), p. 440. See also Bureau of the Census, "Household Wealth and Asset Ownership: 1988," *Current Population Reports*, Series P-70, No. 22 (December 1990).

42. Benjamin I. Page, *Who Gets What from Government?* (Berkeley: University of California Press, 1983), p. 213.

43. *New York Times*, 13 May 1983.

44. Advisory Commission on Intergovernmental Relations, *Significant Features of Fiscal Federalism, 1984* (Washington, D.C.: U.S. Government Printing Office, 1985), p. 139.

45. *Public Opinion* 8 (February–March 1985):27.

46. "Lotteries Are Now Used in 26 States for Revenue," *New York Times National Edition*, 16 February 1988, p. 8. See also Alan J. Karcher, *Lotteries* (New Brunswick, N.J.: Transaction Books, 1989).

47. Lawrence J. Haas, "Who'll Pay the Price?" *National Journal*, 20 February 1988, pp. 444–449.

Chapter 19 / Domestic Policy / pp. 681–717

1. Alex Kotlowitz, *There Are No Children Here: The Story of Two Boys Growing Up in the Other America* (New York: Doubleday, 1991).

2. Karl Zinsmeister, "Growing Up Scared," *The Atlantic Monthly*, June 1990, p. 49.

3. *Social Security Bulletin, Annual Statistical Supplement, 1990*, Table 3.A.1, p. 100; *Budget of the United States Government, FY 1991*, Historical Table 3.1, p. A-294.

4. "The People, Press & Economics." A Times Mirror Multi-Nation Study of Attitudes Toward U.S. Economic Issues (The Gallup Organization, May 1989).

5. Thomas J. Anton, *American Federalism and Public Policy* (Philadelphia, Penn.: Temple University Press, 1989).

6. *Washington Post*, 25 January 1991, p. A10.

7. "Fear of AIDS Rivals Worry Over Cancer," *New York Times*, 12 May 1987, p. C3.

8. Rebecca Kolberg, "Americans Worried Less About AIDS, Poll Says," UPI, 15 August 1989.

9. *Budget of the United States Government, FY 1991*, p. 79.

10. Tamar Lewin, "Studies on Teen-Age Sex Cloud Condom Debate," *New York Times*, 8 February 1991, p. A10.

11. *Washington Post*, 23 August 1989, p. A22.

12. George Gallup, Jr., *The Gallup Poll, Public Opinion 1988* (Wilmington, Del.: Scholarly Resources, 1988), p. 181.

13. Karen S. Peterson, "Young Adults Are Leaning to the Right," *USA Today*, 13 December 1990, p. 1D.

14. W. John Moore, "Rethinking Drugs," *National Journal*, 2 February 1991, pp. 267–271.

15. National Institute on Drug Abuse, *1988 National Household Survey on Drug Abuse: Main Findings*, pp. 19 and 53 (1989); *Newsweek*, 14 March 1988, p. 16.

16. The history of drug abuse in America is based on David Musto, *The American Disease: The Origins of Narcotics Control*, rev. ed.

(New York: Oxford University Press, 1987); and David T. Courtwright, *Dark Paradise: Opiate Addiction in America Before 1940* (Cambridge, Mass.: Harvard University Press, 1982.)

17. *Chicago Tribune*, 11 February 1990, sec. 1, p. 1.

18. *Newsweek*, 25 December 1989, p. 47.

19. *Washington Post*, 22 January 1990, p. A20.

20. "Big John," *Time*, 2 March 1987, p. 19.

21. National Institute on Drug Abuse, *1988 National Household Survey on Drug Abuse*, pp. 85 and 99.

22. Jann S. Wenner, "Drug War: A New Vietnam?" *New York Times*, 23 June 1990, p. 23.

23. *New York Times*, 27 November 1989, p. 9; *The Gallup Report* (January 1990), pp. 2–9.

24. Linda L. M. Bennett and Stephen Earl Bennett, *Living with Leviathan: Americans Coming to Terms with Big Government* (Lawrence, Kan.: University Press of Kansas, 1990), pp. 21–24.

25. *Shapiro* v. *Thompson*, 396 U.S. 618 (1969).

26. George Gallup, Jr., *The Gallup Poll, Public Opinion 1989* (Wilmington, Del.: Scholarly Resources, 1990), pp. 183–185.

27. I. A. Lewis and William Schneider, "Hard Times: The Public on Poverty," *Public Opinion* 8 (June–July 1985):2.

28. Bureau of the Census, *Current Population Reports: Money Income and Poverty Status in the United States, 1989*, Series P-60, No. 168, pp. 5–7 (1990).

29. Bennett and Bennett, *Living with Leviathan*, p. 142.

30. D. Lee Bawden and John L. Palmer, "Social Policy: Challenging the Welfare State," in *The Reagan Record: An Assessment of America's Changing Domestic Priorities*, ed. John L. Palmer and Isabel V. Sawhill (Cambridge, Mass.: Ballinger, 1984), pp. 177–215.

31. Paul C. Light, *Artful Work: The Politics of Social Security Reform* (New York: Random House, 1985), p. 63.

32. *Social Security Bulletin, Annual Statistical Supplement, 1990*, p. 2.

33. Martha Derthick, *Policymaking for Social Security* (Washington, D.C.: Brookings Institution, 1979), pp. 346–347.

34. Julie Kosterlitz, "Who Will Pay?" *National Journal*, 8 March 1985, pp. 570–574.

35. Bureau of the Census, *Statistical Abstract of the United States, 1988* (Washington, D.C.: U.S. Government Printing Office, 1988), pp. 17, 249.

36. Derthick, *Policymaking*, p. 335.

37. Paul Starr, *The Social Transformation of American Medicine* (New York: Basic Books, 1982), pp. 279–280.

38. Starr, *Social Transformation of American Medicine*, p. 287.

39. Theodore Marmor, *The Politics of Medicare* (Chicago: Aldine, 1973).

40. *Social Security Bulletin*, p. 3.

41. *Social Security Bulletin*, p. 3.

42. *Social Security Bulletin*, Table 2.B.1, p. 62.

43. Lawrence J. Haas, "Big-Ticket Restrictions," *National Journal*, 26 September 1987, p. 2413.

44. *Social Security Bulletin*, Table 3.E.1, p. 1225; data from the Social Security Administration.

45. Barbara Ehrenreich and Frances Fox Piven, "The Feminization of Poverty," *Dissent* (Spring 1984), pp. 162–170; Harrell R. Rodgers, Jr., *Poor Women, Poor Families: The Economic Plight of America's Female-Headed Households*, 2d ed. (Armonk, N.Y.: M.E. Sharpe, 1990).

46. William Julius Wilson, *The Truly Disadvantaged: The Inner City, the Underclass, and Public Policy* (Chicago: University of Chicago Press, 1987).

47. *Social Security Bulletin*, Table 9.G.1, p. 314; data from the Department of Health and Human Services, Administration for Children and Families, Office of Family Assistance, Division of Program Evaluation.

48. *Work-Related Programs for Welfare Recipients* (Washington, D.C.: Congressional Budget Office, 1987).

49. Mickey Kaus, "Revenge of the Softheads," *New Republic*, 19 June 1989, p. 24.

50. "Pulling Families Out of Welfare Is Proving to Be an Elusive Goal,"

New York Times, 2 April 1990, p. A1.

51. Jeffrey M. Berry, *Feeding Hungry People: Rulemaking in the Food Stamp Program* (New Brunswick, N.J.: Rutgers University Press, 1984), p. 21.

52. *Social Security Bulletin, Annual Statistical Supplement, 1990*, Table 9.H.1, p. 316.

53. David E. Rosenbaum, "In Four Years, Reagan Changed Basis of the Debate on Domestic Programs," *New York Times*, 25 October 1984, p. B20.

54. "Hungry Children Put at 5.5 Million," *New York Times*, 27 March 1991, p. A18.

55. Lewis and Schneider, "Hard Times," pp. 3–7.

56. Gallup, *Gallup Poll*, pp. 183–185.

Chapter 20 / Global Policy / pp. 719–759

1. "34 Lands Proclaim a United Europe in Paris Charter," *New York Times*, 22 November 1990, p.1.

2. Alexis de Tocqueville, *Democracy in America* (Oxford, Eng.: Oxford University Press, 1946), p. 161.

3. Michael Roskin, "From Pearl Harbor to Vietnam: Shifting Generational Paradigms and Foreign Policy," *Political Science Quarterly* (Fall 1974):563–588.

4. Ole Holsti and James Rosenau, "Does Where You Stand Depend on When You Were Born? The Impact of Generation on Post-Vietnam Foreign Policy Beliefs," *Public Opinion Quarterly* (Spring 1980):1–22.

5. Quoted in Ann McDaniel, et al., "The Rewards of Leadership," *Newsweek*, 11 March 1991, p. 30.

6. U.S. Bureau of the Census, *Historical Statistics of the United States: Colonial Times to 1970* (Washington, D.C.: U.S. Government Printing Office, 1975), pp. 1140–1141.

7. U.S. Bureau of the Census, *Historical Statistics*.

8. See James A. Nathan and James K. Oliver, *United States Foreign Policy and World Order*, 2d ed. (Boston: Little, Brown, 1981), p. 108.

9. "X" [George F. Kennan], "The Sources of Soviet Conduct," *Foreign Affairs* (July 1947):575.

10. Harry S Truman, "Special Message to the Congress on Greece and Turkey (March 12, 1947)," in *Public Papers of the Presidents of the United States* (Washington, D.C.: U.S. Government Printing Office, 1963), p. 178.

11. Dwight D. Eisenhower, "Farewell Address" (18 January 1961), in *Public Papers of the Presidents of the United States* (Washington, D.C.: U.S. Government Printing Office, 1961), p. 1053.

12. Herman Kahn, *On Thermonuclear War* (Princeton, N.J.: Princeton University Press, 1961); Henry Kissinger, *Nuclear Weapons and Foreign Policy* (New York: Harper & Row, 1957).

13. John F. Kennedy, "Inaugural Address (January 20, 1961)," in *Public Papers of the Presidents of the United States* (Washington, D.C.: U.S. Government Printing Office, 1961).

14. Quoted in Arthur M. Schlesinger, Jr., *A Thousand Days* (Boston: Houghton Mifflin, 1965), pp. 704–705.

15. George Gallup Jr., *The Gallup Poll: Public Opinion, 1935–1971* (New York: Random House, 1972). See particularly polls taken in March 1968 and January 1969.

16. Richard M. Nixon, "A Redefinition of the United States' Role in the World (February 25, 1971)," in *United States Foreign Policy— 1971* (Washington, D.C.: Department of State, 1972), p. 422.

17. Richard M. Nixon, *U.S. Foreign Policy for the 1970s: A New Strategy for Peace* (Washington, D.C.: U.S. Government Printing Office, 1970), p. 2.

18. Jimmy Carter, "State of the Union (January 23, 1980)," *Public Papers of the Presidents of the United States* (Washington, D.C.: U.S. Government Printing Office, 1981), p. 197.

19. *U.S.* v. *Curtiss-Wright Export Corporation*, 299 U.S. 304 (1936).

20. *Editorial Research Reports*, 29 January 1988.

21. C. Herman Pritchett, "The President's Constitutional Position," in Rexford G. Tugwell and Thomas E. Cronin, *The Presidency Reappraised* (New York: Praeger, 1977), p. 23.

22. James A. Nathan and James K. Oliver, *Foreign Policy Making and the American Political System*, (Boston: Little, Brown, 1983), p. 125.

23. "Duels Over Dollars Shuffle," *Congressional Quarterly Weekly Report*, February 1990, p. 606.

24. James A. Nathan and James K. Oliver, *Foreign Policy Making and the American Political System*, 2d ed. (Boston: Little, Brown, 1987), p. 44.

25. Quoted in Schlesinger, *Thousand Days*, p. 406.

26. Richard K. Betts, "Analysis, War and Decision Making: Why Intelligence Failures Are Inevitable, *World Politics* (October 1978): 64–65.

27. Betts, "Analysis, War and Decision Making," p. 61.

28. Gallup, *The Gallup Poll*, p. 2189.

29. Charles W. Kegley and Eugene Wittkopf, *American Foreign Policy: Pattern and Process*, 2d ed. (New York: St. Martin's Press, 1982), p. 287.

30. Kegley and Wittkopf, *American Foreign Policy*, pp. 262–263; Lester W. Milbrath, "Interest Groups and Foreign Policy," in *Domestic Sources of Foreign Policy*, ed. James Rosenau (New York: Free Press, 1967), pp. 231–252.

31. Kegley and Wittkopf, *American Foreign Policy*, p. 267.

32. Elihu Katz, "The Two-Step Flow of Communications," *Public Opinion Quarterly* (Spring 1957): 61–78.

33. Kegley and Wittkopf, *American Foreign Policy*, p. 301.

34. Bernard C. Cohen, "The Influence of Special Interest Groups and Mass Media on Security Policy in the United States," in *Perspectives on American Foreign Policy*, ed. Charles W. Kegley and Eugene Wittkopf (New York: St. Martin's, 1983), pp. 222–241.

35. "Excerpts from Briefing at Pentagon by Cheney and Powell," *New York Times*, 24 January 1991, p. A12.

36. "U.S. Survey Rates Japan Greater Threat than U.S.S.R.," *Chicago Tribune*, 5 March 1991, sec. 3, p. 3.

37. Lester Thurow, "When the Lending Stops," *New Perspectives Quarterly* (Fall 1987):14; see also Kevin Phillips, *The Politics of Rich and Poor* (New York: Random House, 1990), chap. 5.

38. "Competitiveness: Can This War Be Won?" *Time*, 1 April 1991, p. 59.

39. Paul Kennedy, *The Rise and Decline of the Great Powers* (New York: Random House,1988); also Masahiro Sakamoto, "Pax Americana's Twin Deficits," *New Perspectives Quarterly* (Fall 1987), pp. 8–11; and Phillips, *Politics of Rich and Poor*.

40. Frank Gray, "Britain Buys Back the Colonies," *Business Month*, November 1987, p. 20.

41. Daniel S. Papp, *Contemporary International Relations* (New York: Macmillan, 1991), p. 409.

42. "Hills, in Japan, Stirs a Baby-Bottle Dispute," *New York Times*, 14 October 1989, p. 35.

43. "Chrysler Seeks Sales Curbs on Japan Autos," *New York Times*, 25 March 1991, p. C12.

44. See commentary by A. M. Rosenthal in the *New York Times*, 31 March 1989, p. 35; also Kevin Kearns, "Economic Orthodoxies Offered U.S. Students Won't Prepare Them to Work in World Markets," *The Chronicle of Higher Education*, 27 March 1991, p. B3.

45. *Papp*, Contemporary International Relations, *p. 167.*

INDEX TO REFERENCES

INDEX

Illustration Credits (continued from copyright page)

Chapter 3: **Page 62 (Opener):** Paul Conklin/Uniphoto; **65:** J. P. Laffont/Sygma; **68:** Library of Congress; **69:** Courtesy of the John Carter Brown Library at Brown University; **71:** John Trumbull, *The Declaration of Independence.* Copyright Yale University Art Gallery; **75:** The Granger Collection, New York; **78:** The Thomas Gilcrease Institute of American History and Art, Tulsa, Oklahoma; **86:** The White House; **87:** Jose Lopez/The New York Times; **90:** *Doonesbury* © 1987 G. B. Trudeau. Reprinted with permission of Universal Press Syndicate. All rights reserved; **91:** Tracy W. McGregor Library, Manuscripts Division, Special Collections Department, University of Virginia Library; **98:** National Archives.

Chapter 4: **Page 106 (Opener):** © Bob Daemmrich/The Image Works; **109:** UPI/ Bettmann Newsphotos; **112** (left): Greg Smith/Sipa Press; **112** (right): William Berry/Sygma; **113:** © Steve Liss/Gamma-Liaison; **124:** National Archives; **127:** George Tames/The New York Times; **133:** © Michael Schumann/SABA; **135** (top left): Courtesy of the City of Lakewood; **135** (top right): Courtesy of the City of Miami; **135** (bottom left): © Po-Yee McKenna; **135** (bottom right): Paul Conklin; **140:** Paul Conklin.

Chapter 5: **Page 146 (Opener):** © Walter Calahan/Folio, Inc.; **149:** © Susan May Tell/SABA; **150:** John Chiasson/Gamma Liaison; **154:** St. Louis Globe-Democrat Photo; **157:** © 1991 Bob Olson/The Picture Man; **160:** © Bob Daemmrich/Stock Boston; **166:** Andrew Holbrooke/Black Star; **170:** © Bob Riha/Gamma Liaison; **177:** © Lauren Santow; **180:** David Valdez/The White House.

Chapter 6: **Page 184 (Opener):** © Art Stein/Folio, Inc.; **190:** George B. Luks. Collection of Woody Gelman. Courtesy Life Picture Service; **191:** Steve Liss/Time Magazine; **194:** Culver Pictures; **195:** The Bettmann Archive; **197:** Wide World Photos; **204:** © 1988 Rhoda Baer; **214:** KTLA-TV/AP; **215:** Sygma.

Chapter 7: **Page 224 (Opener):** © Stone/Sygma; **227** (left): © Ralf-Finn Hestoft/ Saba; **227** (right): © Shawn Henry/Saba; **229:** Wide World Photos; **231:** UPI/Bettmann Newsphotos; **236:** David Wells/The Image Works; **237:** Bob Daemmrich/ The Image Works; **238:** Laurentzi Berman/Sygma; **243:** Library of Congress; **257:** Demann Entertainment; **258:** Wide World Photos.

Chapter 8: **Page 262 (Opener):** © Wally McNamee/Folio, Inc.; **265:** Wide World Photos; **276:** Library of Congress; **283:** © Cynthia Johnson/Gamma Liaison; **285:** Paul Szep reprinted by permission of UFS, Inc.; **290:** Paul Conklin; **291:** Paul Conklin.

Chapter 9: **Page 298 (Opener):** © Bob Daemmrich/Sygma; **301:** © Erich Hartman/ Magnum Photos; **303:** © 1988 Dennis Brack/Black Star; **311:** © Bob Daemmrich/ Uniphoto; **314:** Federal Election Commission; **315:** Insight Magazine/James Barringer; **317:** Lance Muresan/The New York Times; **319:** People Weekly © 1991 Stanley Tretick; **325:** Wide World Photos.

Chapter 10: **Page 336 (Opener):** Bob Daemmrich/The Image Works; **341:** © 1985 Planned Parenthood; **346:** Severy photograph, The Bostonian Society, Old State House; **348:** Rita Barros/Gamma Liaison; **349:** © Jim Caccavo/Picture Group; **354:** Timothy A. Murphy/U.S. News & World Report; **355:** Jose R. Lopez/The New York Times; **356:** Wide World Photos; **358:** Toles © 1990 Buffalo News. Reprinted with permission of Universal Press Syndicate. All rights reserved; **361:** Peter Marlow/Magnum; **365:** Charles Moore/Black Star; **367:** John Ficara/Woodfin Camp & Associates.

Chapter 11: **Page 374 (Opener):** Wally McNamee/Woodfin Camp & Associates; **377:** Kiplinger Washington Collection; **380:** Wide World Photos; **390:** Paul Conklin; **392** (top): © Alexandra Avakian/Woodfin Camp & Associates; **392** (bottom): Susan Steinkamp/Picture Group; **394:** Wide World Photos; **397:** Wide World Photos; **398:** George Tames/The New York Times; **404:** Paul Conklin; **405:** Courtesy Senator William S. Cohen; **409:** Glenn Stubbs/Sygma.